Please keep out of the Library.

Date Due		
5/14/27	9:30 a.m.	
5/18/27	9:30	" "

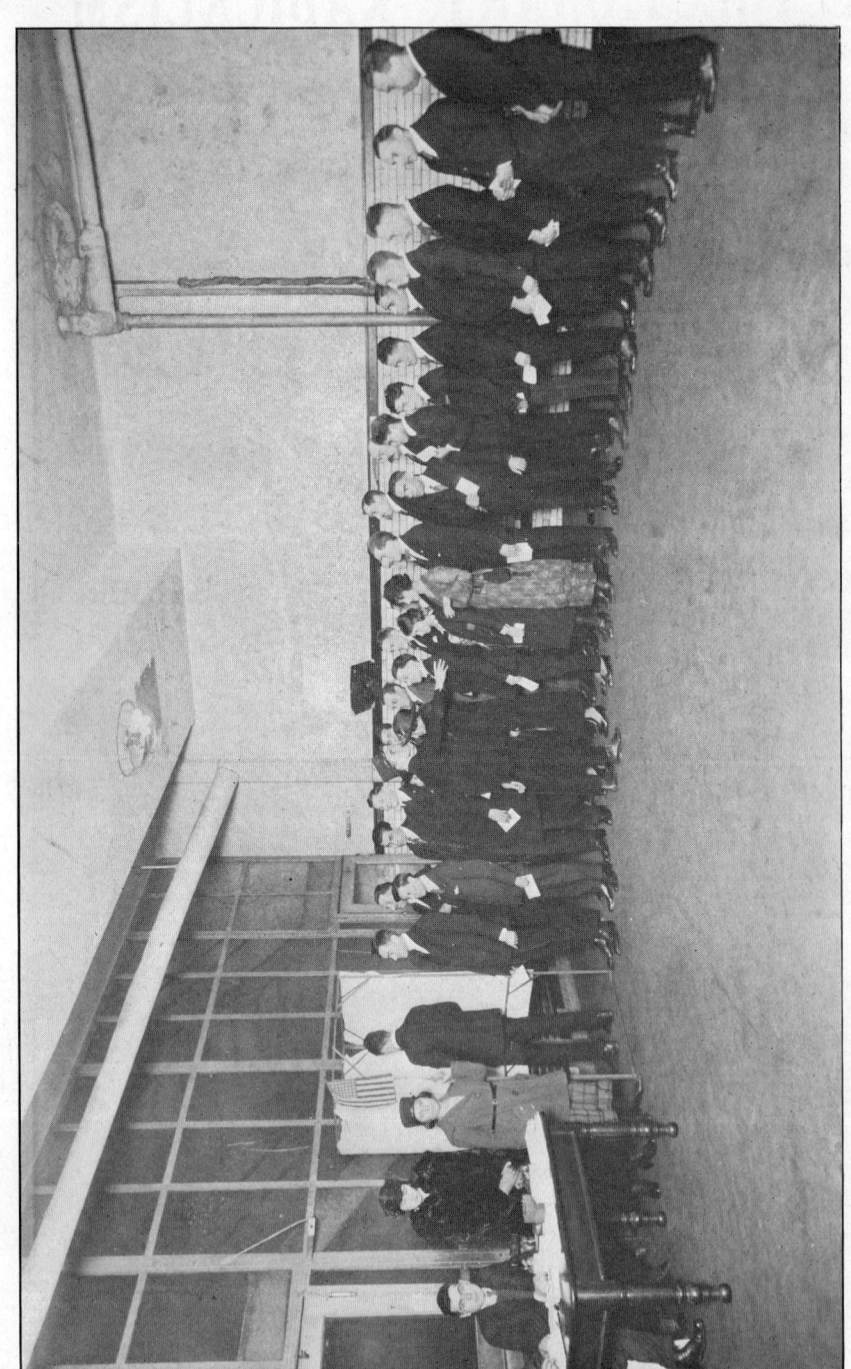

An Americanization Class in Evening School No. 27, New York City — Aliens Being Taught How to Vote.

REVOLUTIONARY RADICALISM

ITS HISTORY, PURPOSE AND TACTICS

WITH AN EXPOSITION AND DISCUSSION OF THE STEPS BEING TAKEN AND REQUIRED TO CURB IT

BEING THE

REPORT OF THE JOINT LEGISLATIVE COMMITTEE INVESTIGATING SEDITIOUS ACTIVITIES, FILED APRIL 24, 1920, IN THE SENATE OF THE STATE OF NEW YORK

PART II
CONSTRUCTIVE MOVEMENTS AND MEASURES IN AMERICA
VOLUME III

ALBANY
J. B. LYON COMPANY, PRINTERS
1920

335
N48
v.3

3888

TABLE OF CONTENTS

VOLUME III

PART II

Constructive Movements and Measures in America

SECTION I

Protective Governmental Measures

PAGE

Introduction 2013–16

CHAPTER I
Relations with Soviet Russia..................................... 2017–23

CHAPTER II
Freedom of Speech... 2024–74

CHAPTER III
Federal Action in Deportations................................. 2075–93

SECTION II

Organized Labor and Capital and Industrial Problems

Introduction 2097–2105

CHAPTER I
Trade Union Organization in the United States. The American Federation of Labor... 2106–32

CHAPTER II
Organized Labor in Politics.................................... 2133–47

CHAPTER III
Organized Labor and Socialism................................. 2148–50

CHAPTER IV
Socialism in Politics 2151–53

CHAPTER V
International Relations of American Organized Labor............ 2154–59

CHAPTER VI
The Four Railroad Brotherhoods and the "Outlaw" Strike....... 2160–65

CHAPTER VII
Organized Labor and Education................................ 2166–73

Contents

CHAPTER VIII
Employer's Views of Industrial Relations. Welfare Work. Profit Sharing 2174–79

CHAPTER IX
Industrial Democracy. Whitley Scheme. John Leitch Plan. Endicott-Johnson Plan. International Harvester Plan.............. 2180–92

CHAPTER X
Labor's Solutions. Collective Bargaining. Co-operatives.........2193–2204

CHAPTER XI
British and American Shop Committee Plans..................... 2204–15

CHAPTER XII
The Closed Shop and the Open Shop............................ 2216–25

CHAPTER XIII
Arbitration in Labor Disputes. Compulsory Arbitration.......... 2226–37

CHAPTER XIV
Guild Socialism and National Guilds........................... 2238–43

CHAPTER XV
The Plumb Plan 2244–50

CHAPTER XVI
Political Programs of the American Federation of Labor and of the Farmers 2251–73

SECTION III
Educational Training for Citizenship

RECORD OF CONSTRUCTIVE ACTIVITIES IN IMMIGRANT EDUCATION AND CITIZENSHIP TRAINING, INCLUDING STATE LAWS, EDUCATIONAL PROGRAMS AND RECOMMENDATIONS.

SUBSECTION I
General Survey of Field of Education for Citizenship

Introduction — Problems Presented 2279

CHAPTER I

Americanization Work in Progress............................. 2293
  1. State Enterprises 2293
    a. Outside New York State.............................. 2293
    b. New York State 2296
  2. Local Boards of Education............................... 2305
  3. Private Enterprises 2307
    a. Industry 2307
    b. Settlement Houses 2312
    c. Churches 2317
    d. Miscellaneous **2320**

Contents

CHAPTER II
Relative Merit of Private and Public Agencies for Americanization. 2328

CHAPTER III
Teacher Requirements and Teacher Training...................... 2335

CHAPTER IV
Curricula Recommended for Courses of Citizenship Training...... 2346

CHAPTER V
Regulated Attendance 2350

CHAPTER VI
Appropriations 2356

SUBSECTION II
Citizenship Training — The United States Government

CHAPTER I
Legislation 2361–65

CHAPTER II
Americanization Programs 2366–2410
1. Americanization Conference 2366–2406
2. United States Chamber of Commerce..................... 2406–10

SUBSECTION III
Citizenship Training in the State of New York

CHAPTER I
State Legislation 2417–38
1. Compulsion for Minors 2417–19
2. Compulsion for Minors of Employment Age............... 2419–24
3. Military and Disciplinary Training....................... 2424–30
4. Patriotism 2430
5. The Flag 2431
6. Textbooks 2431–32
7. Qualifications for Teachers............................... 2432–34
8. Special Courses for Teachers............................. 2434–35
9. Use of Schoolhouse and Grounds......................... 2435–37
10. Kindergartens and Night Schools......................... 2437
11. Registration of Institutions 2438

CHAPTER II
State Programs 2439–2563
1. Bulletin — "Immigrant Education" 2439–47
2. Report of Adult Education Committee of the Ministry of Reconstruction of England 2447–49
3. Americanization in Industry 2449–73
4. Community Organization 2473–81
5. Americanization Through Women's Organizations......... 2481–86
6. Lessons for Illiterate Foreign Women....................2486–2505
7. Methods of Teaching English to the Non-English-Speaking Foreign-Born 2506–55
8. Report from Director of the Division of Agricultural and Industrial Education 2556–63

Contents

CHAPTER III

	PAGE
State Normal Schools	2564–68
1. Brockport	2564
2. Cortland	2564
3. Fredonia	2565
4. New Paltz	2566
5. Oneonta	2566
6. Oswego	2566
7. Plattsburg	2567

CHAPTER IV

Principal Cities of the State Outside of New York City	2569–2622
1. Albany	2569
2. Amsterdam	2570
3. Auburn	2571
4. Binghamton	2573
5. Buffalo	2573
6. Cohoes	2578
7. Cortland	2578
8. Depew	2579
9. Dunkirk	2580
10. Elmira	2582
11. Fredonia	2583
12. Geneseo	2583
13. Geneva	2584
14. Glens Falls	2584
15. Gloversville	2585
16. Herkimer	2585
17. Ilion	2585
18. Ithaca	2586
19. Lancaster	2587
20. Lockport	2588
21. Malone	2590
22. Mount Vernon	2590
23. New Rochelle	2591
24. Newburgh	2593
25. Niagara Falls	2594
26. Norwich	2594
27. Ogdensburg	2594
28. Oneida	2595
29. Oneonta	2595
30. Oswego	2595
31. Peekskill	2595
32. Plattsburgh	2596
33. Port Chester	2596
34. Potsdam	2596
35. Poughkeepsie	2596
36. Rochester	2597
37. Rome	2613
38. Schenectady	2613
39. Solvay	2616
40. Syracuse	2616
41. Tonawanda	2616
42. Troy	2618
43. Utica	2618
44. Watertown	2619
45. Watervliet	2620
46. White Plains	2620
47. Yonkers	2620

CHAPTER V

Public Schools of New York City..............................2623–2700
  1. List of Evening Schools................................. 2623–31
  2. Testimony of School Officials............................ 2631–57
  3. "Unpatriotic Teaching in Public Schools"................ 2658–91
  4. Address by Arthur S. Somers — "Americanization"......... 2691–96
  5. Letters from Superintendent Ettinger to Teachers.......... 2696–97
  6. Compositions of School Boys.............................. 2698
  7. Resolutions of the Teachers' Council....................2698–2700

CHAPTER VI

Churches 2701–2947
  1. Presbyterian 2701–2882
    a. Testimony of Reverend Kenneth Miller............... 2701–02
    b. Church Publications Quoted 2702–2877
    c. Letters from Pastors 2877–81
  2. Methodist 2881–82
  3. Episcopalian 2882–2934
    a. Testimony of Dr. Thomas Burgess.................... 2882–83
    b. Conference on Christian Americanization............ 2883–85
    c. Report on Christian Americanization................2885–2909
    d. Church Publications Quoted 2909–34
  4. Baptist 2934–37
  5. Congregational 2937–41
  6. Catholic 2941–43
  7. Lutheran 2943–47
  8. Dutch Reformed 2947
  9. Religious Society of Friends............................ 2947

CHAPTER VII

Settlement Houses 2949–3017
  1. United Neighborhood Houses of New York..................2949–3001
    a. List of Officers and Members....................... 2949–50
    b. Americanization Program 2950–55
    c. Testimony Before Committee 2955–59
    d. Communications from Members 2960–3000
    e. Note — Attitude Toward Educationl Bills Proposed by
        Joint Legislative Committee 3000–01
  2. Non-Members of Association.............................. 3002–17

CHAPTER VIII

Young Men's Christian Association............................... 3018–51

CHAPTER IX

Young Women's Christian Association............................. 3052–59
  1. The Ballard School 3052–53
  2. International Institute 3053–59

CHAPTER X

Y. M. and Y. W. H. A.. 3060–78
  1. Young Men's Hebrew Association.......................... 3060–77
  2. Young Women's Hebrew Association........................ 3078

CHAPTER XI

Industries 3079–3140
  1. National Association of Corporation Schools............. 3079–87
  2. Reports from Representative Industries..................3088–3140

VOLUME IV

PART II — Continued

SECTION III — Continued

SUB-SECTION III — Continued

CHAPTER XII

	PAGE
Civic and Other Organizations — Statements from Representative Organizations	3141–3293
1. Alliance Israelite Universelle	3141–45
2. American Defense Society	3145–47
3. American Federation of Labor	3147–48
4. American Jewish Committee	3148–60
5. American Legion	3160
6. American Red Cross	3161–68
7. American Rights League	3169
8. Boy Scouts of America	3169–72
9. Bureau of Jewish Education	3172–75
10. Carnegie Foundation	3175–78
11. Chamber of Commerce of the State of New York	3178–84
12. Chinese Consolidated Benevolent Association	3185
13. Community Councils of New York City	3185–86
14. Constitutional League	3186–89
15. Cooper Union	3189
16. Federation of Galician and Bucovinian Jews of America	3189–96
17. Finnish Educational Association of Manhattan	3196–97
18. Girl Scouts	3197–99
19. Hebrew Sheltering and Immigrant Aid Society of America	3199–3202
20. Hungarian Society of New York	3202–03
21. Immigrant Publication Society	3203–29
22. Irish Emigrant Society	3229
23. Italian Bureau of Public Information	3230
24. Japanese Association, Inc.	3231
25. Japanese Christian Institute, Inc.	3231–33
26. Jewish Welfare Board	3234–38
27. Knights of Columbus	3238
28. League for the Liberation of Carpatho-Russia	3238–39
29. Maedchenheim-Verein	3239
30. National Association of Manufacturers	3239
31. National Herald	3230–40
32. National League of Women Workers	3240
33. National Liberal Immigration League	3240–49
34. National Security League	3249–68
35. New York Community Chorus	3268–69
36. New York Kindergarten Association	3269–72
37. New York State Federation of Labor	3273
38. Pan-Hellenic Union in America	3273–74
39. Patriotic Education Society	3274
40. People's Institute of New York	3275–79
41. Polish National Alliance	3279
42. Russian Collegiate Institute	3279–82

CHAPTER XII

	PAGE
Civic and Other Organizations — *Continued:*	
43. Russian Economic League	3282
44. Society for Ethical Culture	3282
45. Society for Italian Immigrants	3282–92
46. United Textile Workers of America	3292
47. Woman Suffrage Society	3292–93

CHAPTER XIII

Colleges and Universities	3294
1. Testimony of College Representatives	3294–99
a. Adelphi	3294–95
b. Columbia	3295–98
c. New York University	3298–99
2. Communications from Educators	3299–3330
a. Adelphi	3299–3300
b. Alexander Hamilton Institute	3300–02
c. Alfred University	3302
d. Barnard College	3302–03
e. Brooklyn Training School for Teachers	3303–04
f. College of the City of New York	3304–06
g. Columbia University	3306–11
h. Cornell University	3311
i. Hunter College	3311–12
j. Jewish Theological Seminary of America	3312–14
k. Keuka College	3314
l. New York School of Social Work	3314–16
m. St. Francis Xavier	3316–17
n. St. Stephen's College	3317
o. Syracuse University	3317
p. Teachers College	3317–28
q. Union College	3328–29
r. Yonkers Training School for Teachers	3329–30

CHAPTER XIV

Technical Schools	3331–34
1. Baron de Hirsch Trade School	3331
2. Bedlitz School of Languages	3331–32
3. General Society of Mechanics and Tradesmen School	3332–33
4. Hebrew Technical Institute	3333
5. Hebrew Technical School for Girls	3333–34
6. New York Trade School	3334

SUB-SECTION IV

Citizenship Training in all States Other than New York

CHAPTER I. ALABAMA

1. State Legislation — Compulsion for Minors	3346–49
2. State Legislation — Compulsion for Minors of Employment Age	3349–59
3. State Legislation — English Language	3359
4. State Legislation — Providing Facilities for Adults	3359–61
5. State Legislation — Providing Facilities for Negroes	3361–65
6. State Legislation — Regarding Teachers	3365–68
7. Special Legislation	3368–69
8. Letter from State Superintendent	3369
9. Tuskegee Institute	3369–3403

Contents

CHAPTER II. Arizona

	PAGE
1. State Legislation — Compulsion for Minors	3404
2. State Legislation — Compulsion for Minors of Employment Age	3404–06
3. State Legislation — The Flag	3406–08
4. State Legislation — Patriotic Exercises	3408
5. Letters from Superintendent of Public Instruction	3408–09
6. Letters from Superintendent of Schools, Phoenix	3409–

CHAPTER III. Arkansas

1. State Legislation — Compulsion for Minors of Employment Age	3410
2. State Legislation — Compulsion for Minors between 16 and 21	3410
3. State Legislation — English Language	3410
4. Letter from Superintendent of Public Instruction	3411

CHAPTER IV. California

1. State Legislation — Compulsion for Minors	3412–13
2. State Legislation — Patriotic Measures	3413
3. State Legislation — Flags	3413–14
4. State Legislation — English Language	3414
5. State Legislation — Teacher Requirements	3414
6. State Legislation — Teachers	3414–15
7. Illiteracy in California	3415
8. Immigrants in Los Angeles	3416–21
9. Suggestions for Speakers on Americanization	3421–25
10. Outlines for Speakers on Americanization	3425–33
11. Organization of Americanization Work for California	3433
12. Citizenship Training Through Public Schools — Civic Center Law	3433–34
13. Citizenship Training Through Industries	3435
14. Citizenship Training Through Women's Clubs	3435
15. Citizenship Training Through Visiting Teachers	3436–49
16. Letter from State Commission of Immigration and Housing	3449–51

CHAPTER V. Colorado

1. State Legislation — Compulsion for Minors	3452–53
2. State Legislation — Flags	3454–55
3. State Legislation — English Language	3455
4. Citizenship Training Program	3455–57

CHAPTER VI. Connecticut

1. State Legislation — Minors of Employment Age	3458–59
2. Population Figures	3459
3. Letter from Americanization Director	3459
4. Letter from New Britain Superintendent	3460
5. Duties of a Local Director of Americanization	3460–62
6. Americanization Work in Rural Communities	3462–64
7. Americanization Work for Religious Bodies and Through Parochial Schools	3464–66
8. Americanization in Industry	3466–67
9. Manufacturers Association of Connecticut	3468–80
10. Americanization Work for Women and Women's Organizations	3481–82

CHAPTER VII. Delaware

1. State Legislation — Compulsion for Minors	3483–86
2. State Legislation — English Language	3486
3. Letter from Commissioner of Education	3487–88
4. State Policy on Americanization	3488–3522
a. Need of Americanization	3489–94
b. Survey of the Field	3494–96
c. Census of Aliens	3496–3501

		PAGE
d.	Industrial Americanization	3501–09
e.	Training Course for Teachers	3509–13
f.	Night School Campaign	3513–14
g.	Americanization Schools	3514–16
h.	"Emergency" English Schools	3516–19
i.	Racial Cooperation	3519
j.	Proposed State Legislation	3519–22

5. Bulletin of the Service Citizens of Delaware 3523–3615
   a. Historical Introduction 3524–29
   b. Purpose of Program 3529–30
   c. Creation of Committees 3530–36
   d. Preliminary Education Work 3536–37
   e. Getting the Immigrant into the School 3538–42
   f. The Night School Experiment — Organization 3542–45
   g. Classroom Instruction 3545–52
   h. Preparation for Citizenship 3552–55
   i. Attendance 3555–62
   j. Interpretation of America 3562–68
   k. Plans for Future Work 3569–70
   l. Appendix 3570–3615

CHAPTER VIII. FLORIDA

1. State Legislation — Compulsion for Minors 3616–18
2. State Legislation — Flags 3618
3. Letter from Superintendent of Public Instruction 3618

CHAPTER IX. GEORGIA

1. State Legislation — Compulsion for Minors 3619–22
2. State Legislation — Minors of Employment Age 3622
3. Letters from Educators 3622

CHAPTER X. IDAHO

1. Letter from Commissioner of Education 3623

CHAPTER XI. ILLINOIS

1. State Legislation — Compulsion for Minors and for Minors of Employment Age 3624
2. State Legislation — Minors of Employment Age 3624–28
3. State Legislation — English Language 3628–29
4. Letter from Wilson & Company, Chicago 3629–30
5. Recommendations of Educators 3630–31

CHAPTER XII. INDIANA

1. State Legislation — Compulsion for Minors 3632–34
2. State Legislation — Flags 3634–35
3. State Legislation — Partiotic Exercises 3635
4. State Legislation — English Language 3635–37
5. Citizenship Training Through Public Schools 3637–38
6. Letter from State Superintendent of Public Instruction . 3638

CHAPTER XIII. IOWA

1. State Legislation — Compulsion for Minors 3639–40
2. State Legislation — Patriotic Measures 3640–41
3. State Legislation — Flags 3641
4. State Legislation — English Language 3641–42
5. Citizenship Training Through Public Schools 3642–44
6. Citizenship Training Through Industries 3644
7. Letter from Superintendent of Public Instruction 3644

CONTENTS

CHAPTER XIV. KANSAS

	PAGE
1. State Legislation — Compulsion for Minors	3645–46
2. State Legislation — Minors of Employment Age	3646–47
3. State Legislation — Patriotic Measures	3647
4. State Legislation — Flags	3647–49
5. State Legislation — English Language	3650–51
6. State Legislation — Facilities for Adults	3651

CHAPTER XV. KENTUCKY

1. State Legislation — Compulsion for Minors	3652
2. State Legislation — Compulsion for Minors of Employment Age	3652–53
3. Citizenship Training Through Public Schools	3653–54
4. Letter from Louisville Courier-Journal Job Printing Company	3654
5. Recommendations for Citizenship Training	3655

CHAPTER XVI. LOUISIANA

1. State Legislation — Compulsion for Minors	3656–58
2. State Legislation — Patriotic Measures	3658–61
3. State Legislation — English Language	3661
4. State Legislation — Facilities for Adults	3661
5. State Legislation — Teachers	3662
6. Letter from State Superintendent	3662

CHAPTER XVII. MAINE

1. State Legislation — Compulsion for Minors	3663–64
2. State Legislation — Minors of Employment Age	3664–65
3. State Legislation — Flags	3665
4. State Legislation — Americanization	3666
5. Proposed Legislation	3666–67
6. Letter from State Superintendent of Public Schools	3667–68

CHAPTER XVIII. MARYLAND

1. State Legislation — Compulsion for Minors and Minors of Employment Age	3669
2. State Legislation — Patriotic Measures	3670
3. Letters from Superintendent of Education	3670–71

CHAPTER XIX. MASSACHUSETTS

1. State Legislation — Compulsion for Minors and Minors of Employment Age	3672–73
2. State Legislation — Compulsion for Minors of Employment Age	3673–76
3. State Legislation — Flag	3676
4. State Legislation — English Language	3676–77
5. Citizenship Training Through Public Schools	3677
6. Citizenship Training Through Public Library	3677
7. Letter from State Supervisor of Americanization	3678
8. Americanization Letter No. 1	3679–81
9. Report of Committee on Teacher Training in Americanization	3682–86
10. Points for Workers in Americanization	3686–89
11. Letter to School Superintendents	3690
12. Plans for Education of Adult Immigrants	3690–93
13. Letter from Boston University	3693–94
14. Citizenship Training Through Industries	3694–3708
15. Letter from Y. M. C. A., New Bedford	3708–09
16. Recommendations	3709–10

CHAPTER XX. MICHIGAN

	PAGE
1. State Legislation — Compulsion for Minors and Minors of Employment Age	3711–12
2. State Legislation — Patriotic Measures	3712
3. State Legislation — Flags	3713
4. State Legislation — English Language	3713
5. Letter from Superintendent of Public Instruction	3713
6. Detroit Campaign	3714–15
7. Citizenship Training Through Industries	3715–25

CHAPTER XXI. MINNESOTA

1. State Legislation — Compulsion for Minors and Minors of Employment Age	3726–27
2. State Legislation — Flags	3727–28
3. State Legislation — English language	3728
4. Citizenship Training Through Public Schools	3728–29
5. Letter from Deputy Commissioner of Education	3729
6. St. Paul Association	3729–30
7. St. Paul Americanization Committee	3730
8. University of Minnesota	3730–57

CHAPTER XXII. MISSISSIPPI

1. State Legislation — Compulsion for Minors	3758–61
2. Letter from Assistant Superintendent of Public Education	3761
3. Citizenship Training Through Public Schools	3762–63

CHAPTER XXIII. MISSOURI

1. State Legislation — Compulsion for Minors	3764
2. State Legislation — Compulsion for Minors of Employment Age	3765–66
3. Citizenship Training Through Public Schools	3766
4. Citizenship Training Through the Y. M. C. A	3767–88

CHAPTER XXIV. MONTANA

1. State Legislation — Compulsion for Minors of Employment Age	3789–91
2. State Legislation — Flags	3791
3. Citizenship Training Through Public Schools	3792–93

CHAPTER XXV. NEBRASKA

1. State Legislation — Compulsion for Minors and Minors of Employment Age	3794–96
2. State Legislation — English Language	3796
3. Letters from State Superintendent of Public Instruction	3797

CHAPTER XXVI. NEVADA

1. State Legislation — Compulsion for Minors	3798–3805
2. State Legislation — Compulsion for Minors of Employment Age	3805–08
3. State Legislation — Flags	3808–09
4. State Legislation — Facilities for Adults	3809–10
5. State Legislation — Teacher Requirements	3811–13
6. Citizenship Training Through Public Schools	3813–14
7. Letter from Superintendent of Public Instruction	3814
8. Quotations from Nevada Education Bulletin	3814–16

CHAPTER XXVII. NEW HAMPSHIRE

1. State Legislation — Minors Between 16 and 21	3817
2. State Legislation — Adults	3817
3. State Legislation — English Language	3818
4. Citizenship Training Through Public Schools	3818–19
5. Appropriation for Citizenship Training	3819
6. Letter from Deputy Commissioner of Education	3819–22

xiv CONTENTS

PAGE

7. Tentative Course for the Teaching of English to New Americans. 3822–51
   a. Introduction 3822–24
   b. Beginners' Course 3824–35
   c. Intermediate Course 3835–43
   d. Advanced Course 3843–47
   e. Suggested List of Books.............................. 3847–51
8. Teaching of English Language in Public, Parochial and Other Private Schools, and to non-English Speaking Adults.. 3851–72
   a. Some Steps Already Taken............................ 3851
   b. Foreword 3851–52
   c. Correspondence with Bishop.......................... 3852–58
   d. Report of Conference on Evening Schools............... 3858
   e. Impression of a Going Concern........................ 3858–59
   f. Manchester's Program 3860–62
   g. Bishop's Letter to the Clergy of his Diocese........... 3862–65
   h. Editorial from New Hampshire Newspapers............ 3865–67
   i. How It Works Out.................................... 3867–68
   j. Resolutions of New Hampshire Federation of Labor...... 3868–70
   k. Resolutions of New Hampshire Manufacturers' Association 3870
   l. Resolutions of the Association Canado Americaine....... 3871
   m. Committee on Americanization — Personnel............ 3872
9. Citizenship Training Through Industries..................... 3872–73
10. Citizenship Training — Teachers 3873–74
11. Recommendation of President of Dartmouth College.......... 3874–75

CHAPTER XXVIII. NEW JERSEY

1. State Legislation — Compulsion for Minors and Minors of Employment Age 3876–79
2. State Legislation — Patriotic Measures 3879–81
   a. Service Flag 3879–80
   b. Junior Red Cross..................................... 3880
   c. Special Courses 3880–81
3. State Legislation — Flags 3881–82
4. Need of Americanization in New Jersey....................... 3882–83
5. Citizenship Training Through Public Schools................. 3883–84
6. Teacher Requirements 3885
7. Appropriation for Citizenship Training...................... 3885
8. Citizenship Training Through Industries..................... 3886–87

CHAPTER XXIX. NEW MEXICO

1. State Legislation — Facilities for Minors and Minors of Employment Age 3888–89
2. State Legislation — Flags 3890
3. State Legislation — English Language........................ 3890
4. Letter from Superintendent of Education..................... 3890
5. Citizenship Training Through Public Schools................. 3890–91
6. "Americanization Day" Bulletin — (Roosevelt Memorial)....3891–3901

CHAPTER XXX. NORTH CAROLINA

1. State Legislation — Facilities for Minors.................... 3902
2. State Legislation — Facilities for Minors and Minors of Employment Age 3902–05
3. State Legislation — Facilities for Adults.................... 3906–09
4. How to Organize and Conduct Community Schools for Adults.. 3909–12
5. Letter from State Department of Public Instruction.......... 3912
6. Citizenship Training Through Women's Clubs................ 3912–46

Contents

CHAPTER XXXI. North Dakota

	PAGE
1. State Legislation — Facilities for Minors and Minors of Employment Age	3947–48
2. State Legislation — Facilities for Adults	3949–51
3. Letter from State Superintendent of Public Instruction	3951

CHAPTER XXXII. Ohio

1. Citizenship Training in Akron........................... 3952–72
    a. Letter from Director of Americanization............... 3952
    b. Organization and Administration of Americanization School 3953–57
    c. Methods of Teaching English in Americanization Schools. 3957–62
    d. Training of Teachers and Supervision of Instruction in Americanization Schools 3962–67
    e. How Americanization Program Reaches Foreign-Born Woman and Her Home............................. 3968–72
2. Citizenship Training in Cincinnati...................... 3972–73
3. Citizenship Training in Cleveland...................... 3973–88
    a. Letter from Assistant Superintendent of Education...... 3973–74
    b. Report of Committee on Education of Chamber of Commerce 3974–88
4. Citizenship Training in Columbus........................ 3989–4016
    a. Letter from Inspector of Teacher Training............. 3989–90
    b. Letter from Ohio Institute for Public Efficiency......... 3990
    c. What Is Americanization?............................ 3990–93
    d. Practical Americanization Program................... 3993–97
    e. English Speech for Foreign Tongues.................. 3997–4007
    f. Teaching English to Immigrants..................... 4007–16
5. Report of Council of National Defense................... 4016–36
6. Americanization in Industries.......................... 4037–43
7. Americanization Through Public Library................. 4044–50

CHAPTER XXXIII. Oklahoma

1. State Legislation — Compulsion for Minors and Minors of Employment Age 4051
2. State Legislation — Patriotic Measure..................... 4051–52
3. State Legislation — Flag 4052
4. State Legislation — English Language..................... 4052–53
5. Citizenship Training Through Public Schools.............. 4053

CHAPTER XXXIV. Oregon

1. State Legislation — Compulsion for Minors and Minors of Employment Age 4054–57
2. State Legislation — Flags 4057
3. State Legislation — English Language 4058
4. Recommendation for Citizenship Training Course.......... 4058
5. State Legislation Providing Facilites for Adults............. 4058–59
6. Letter from Superintendent of Public Instruction........... 4059

CHAPTER XXXV. Pennsylvania

1. State Legislation — Compulsion for Minors and Minors of Employment Age 4060
2. State Legislation — Compulsion for Minors of Employment Age. 4061
3. State Legislation — Patriotic Measures 4062
4. State Legislation — Flags 4062
5. State Legislation Providing Facilities for Adults............. 4062–65
6. Letter from State Superintendent of Public Instruction....... 4065
7. Citizenship Training Through Industries................... 4066

Contents

CHAPTER XXXVI. Rhode Island

	PAGE
1. State Legislation — Compulsion for Minors	4067–68
2. State Legislation — Minors of Employment Age	4068–69
3. State Legislation — Patriotic Measures	4070–71
4. Act to Promote Americanization	4072–81
5. Letter from General Fire Extinguisher Company	4082

CHAPTER XXXVII. South Carolina

1. Letter from Superintendent of Education.................... 4083

CHAPTER XXXVIII. South Dakota

1. State Legislation — Compulsion for Minors and Minors of Employment Age 4084
2. State Legislation — Compulsion for Minors between 16 and 21. 4084–86
3. State Legislation — Patriotic Measures 4086–87
4. Americanization of South Dakota........................... 4087–4110
   a. South Dakota's Creed.................................. 4087–88
   b. Goal of Americanization Training...................... 4088–90
   c. Act to Promote Americanization........................ 4090–93
   d. What Americanization Is 4093–95
   e. What Americanization Is Not........................... 4095–96
   f. Reasons For Americanization Work..................... 4096–98
   g. Who Can Help In Americanization Work............. 4098–4101
   h. Justification of South Dakota Americanization Law...... 4101–02
   i. Americanization Work 4102–09
   j. Speech of Hon. Franklin K. Lane...................... 4109–10

CHAPTER XXXIX. Tennessee

1. State Legislation — Compulsion for Minors and Minors of Employment Age 4111–12
2. State Legislation — Teacher Requirements 4112

CHAPTER XL. Texas

1. State Legislation — Compulsion for Minors.................. 4113–14
2. State Legislation — Flags 4114
3. Letter from State Superintendent of Education.............. 4114

CHAPTER XLI. Utah

1. State Legislation — Compulsion for Minors and Minors of Employment Age 4115–16
2. State Legislation — Compulsion for Adults.................. 4116–18
3. Letter from Assistant Superintendent of Public Instruction.... 4119
4. Letters from Director of Americanization................... 4120

CHAPTER XLII. Vermont

1. Letter from Commissioner of Education..................... 4122–23

CHAPTER XLIII. Virginia

1. State Legislation — Compulsion for Minors.................. 4123
2. State Legislation — Flags 4124
3. State Legislation Providing Facilities for Adults.............. 4124–25
4. Letter from State Board of Education....................... 4125
5. Hampton Institute 4126–37

CONTENTS

CHAPTER XLIV. WASHINGTON

	PAGE
1. State Legislation — Directors	4138
2. State Legislation — Compulsion for Minors and Minors of Employment Age	4138–39
3. State Legislation — Patriotic Measures	4139
4. State Legislation — Flags	4139
5. State Legislation — Patriotic Exercises	4140
6. State Legislation — English Language	4140
7. State Legislation — Teacher Requirements	4140–41
8. Citizenship Training Through Industries	4141–44
9. Constitutional Government League Speeches	4145–51

CHAPTER XLV. WEST VIRGINIA

1. State Legislation — Compulsion for Minors	4152–53
2. State Legislation — Compulsion for Minors of Employment Age	4153–54
3. State Legislation — Flags	4154
4. State Legislation Providing Facilities for Adults	4155

CHAPTER XLVI. WISCONSIN

1. State Legislation — Compulsion for Minors and for Minors of Employment Age	4156–57
2. Report on Construction	4157–59
3. Letter from Superintendent of Public Instruction	4160
4. Letters from University of Wisconsin	4160–62
5. Letter from State Board of Vocational Education	4162

CHAPTER XLVII. WYOMING

1. State Legislation — Compulsion for Minors	4163
2. State Legislation — Flags	4163–64
3. Letter from Commissioner of Education	4164

SUBSECTION V
CHAPTER I

Naturalization	4169–72

APPENDIX

Naturalization Laws and Regulations	4173–4210

ADDENDUM

PART II
Constructive Measures

SECTION I
Protective Governmental Measures

NOTE ON CHAPTER I   PAGE
Trade Relations With, and Recognition of Soviet Russia.......... 4215–22

SECTION II
Organized Labor and Capital and Industrial Relations

NOTE ON CHAPTER V
International Relations of American Organized Labor............ 4225–40

NOTE ON CHAPTER XIII
The Kansas Court of Industrial Relations........................ 4241–54

SECTION III
Educational Training for Citizenship

NOTE ON SUB-SECTION II

Citizenship Training — The United States Government............ 4261
Notes on Chapters I and II..................................... 42?1

NOTES ON SUB-SECTION III
Citizenship Training in the State of New York

Note on Chapter XIII.
  1. Alfred — Alfred University 4262
  2. Brooklyn — Adelphi College 4262–63
  3. Brooklyn — Maxwell Training School for Teachers.......... 4263–69
  4. New York City 4270–76
     a. College of the City of New York..................... 4270–71
     b. Hunter College of the City of New York.............. 4271
     c. New York University 4272–74
     d. Teachers College 4274–76
  5. Rochester 4276–77
  6. Schenectady — Union College 4277

NOTES ON SUB-SECTION IV
Citizenship Training in All States Other Than New York

Note on Chaper I.   Alabama 4278
Note on Chapter IV.   California.
  1. State Activities 4278–88
  2. Sacramento 4288–89
  3. San Diego 4289–90

Contents

	PAGE
Note on Chapter **V.** Colorado	4291–92
Note on Chapter **VI.** Connecticut.	
1. State Activities	4293
2. Bridgeport	4293–98
3. Hartford	4298–99
4. Waterbury	4299–4300
Note on Chapter **VII.** Delaware	4301–39
Note on Chapter **X.** Idaho	4339
Note on Chapter **XI.** Illinois.	
1. Chicago	4339–41
Note on Chapter **XII.** Indiana.	
1. Indianapolis	4341–42
2. Evansville	4342–43
Note on Chapter **XIII.** Iowa	4343–44
Note on Chapter **XIV.** Kansas.	
1. Kansas City	4344–45
Note on Chapter **XV.** Kentucky	4345
Note on Chapter **XVI.** Louisiana.	
1. State Activities	4345
2. New Orleans	4345–46
Note on Chapter **XVII.** Maine	4346–47
Note on Chapter **XIX.** Massachusetts.	
1. State Activities	4347
2. Boston	4347–48
3. Boston University	4348–56
4. The Women's Municipal League of Boston	4356–57
5. Fall River	4357–59
6. Lawrence	4359–64
7. New Bedford	4365
Note on Chapter **XX.** Michigan.	
1. State Activities	4366
2. Grand Rapids	4366–68
Note on Chapter **XXI.** Minnesota.	
1. University of Minnesota	4369
2. Duluth	4369–71
Note on Chapter **XXIV.** Montana	4371
Note on Chapter **XXV.** Nebraska.	
1. Omaha	4371–72
Note on Chapter **XXVII.** New Hampshire	4372–73
Note on Chapter **XXVIII.** New Jersey.	
1. State Activities	4373–75
2. Newark	4375–81
3. Paterson	4381–82
Note on Chapter **XXXI.** North Dakota	4382
Note on Chapter **XXXII.** Ohio.	
1. Dayton	4382–83
2. Youngstown	4383
Note on Chapter **XXXIV.** Oregon.	
1. Portland	4384

Contents

	PAGE
Note on Chapter XXXV. Pennsylvania.	
1. State Activities	4385–93
2. Altoona	4393–94
3. Erie	4394–95
4. Pittsburgh	4395–4402
5. Reading	4403
6. Scranton	4403–18
Note on Chapter XXXVII. South Carolina	4418
Note on Chapter XL. Texas.	
1. El Paso	4418–19
2. Galveston	4419–20
3. San Antonio	4420–21
Note on Chapter XLII. Vermont.	
1. Montpelier	4421
Note on Chapter XLIII. Virginia.	
1. Richmond	4421
Note on Chapter XLIV. Washington.	
1. State Activities	4421–22
2. Seattle	4422–23
Note on Chapter XLVII. Wyoming.	
1. State Activities	4424
2. Casper	4424
Note on Immigrant Education in Canada	4425–28

LIST OF ILLUSTRATIONS

VOLUME III

	PAGE
Americanization Class in Evening School No. 27, New York City. — *Frontispiece, Vol. III*	
Illiteracy chart of New York State	2304
English class at noon hour, Mason and Seaman Taxi Co	2464
Settlement class, Rochester	2464
Alien classes in English in Auburn evening schools	2464
Night classes in Americanization, Buffalo	2592
Classes of Solvay Process Company, Syracuse	2592
Home class of Syrian women, Syracuse	2656
Home class of Jewish women, Syracuse	2656
Extension class, Atlantic Comb Works, New York	2656
Extension class, Waldorf-Astoria Hotel, New York	2656
Extension class, McAlpin Hotel, New York	2688
Mothers' class, Public School No. 4, the Bronx	2688
Church class of Italian women, Syracuse	2688
Extension class in English, Educational Alliance, New York	2688
Citizenship class in Buffalo Y. M. C. A	3072
Class at R. E. Dietz factory, Syracuse	3072
Class at Shapiro factory, Syracuse	3072
Class at Holcomb Steel Company, Syracuse	3072
Class at Nettleton Shoe Factory, Syracuse	3140

VOLUME IV

Christmas Party in Wilmington, Delaware, School, Showing Adaptation of a Typical School Room for Recreational Work. — *Frontispiece, Vol. IV*	
Home class of Delaware Americanization Committee	3488
Normal class in dressmaking	4128
The Hampton battalion	4160
Hampton students at work in the machine shops	4160
Women taking oath of allegiance before Justice Beers, New York Supreme Court	4160

[xxi]

PART II

CONSTRUCTIVE MOVEMENTS AND MEASURES IN AMERICA

SECTION I
PROTECTIVE GOVERNMENTAL MEASURES

SECTION II
ORGANIZED LABOR AND CAPITAL AND INDUSTRIAL PROBLEMS

SECTION III
EDUCATIONAL TRAINING FOR CITIZENSHIP

PART II

CONSTRUCTIVE MOVEMENTS AND MEASURES IN AMERICA

SECTION I
PROGRESSIVE GOVERNMENTAL MEASURES

SECTION II
ORGANIZED LABOR AND CAPITAL AND INDUSTRIAL PROBLEMS

SECTION III
EDUCATIONAL TRAINING FOR CITIZENSHIP

GENERAL INTRODUCTION

In the first part of this report the Committee has presented its findings with respect to the seditious and revolutionary movement in the State of New York, has traced its connections with the similar movements in other countries and in other parts of the United States; has defined the purposes and objects of the movement, the tactics and methods employed, and, in a measure, has appraised the extent to which it has spread. These findings are of so grave a character that the Committee feels it necessary that the Legislature of the State of New York take serious cognizance of the facts presented; not only with a view to constructive legislative action but with the feeling that, in session and out of session, it is everyone's duty to search for remedies to cure or at least alleviate the danger.

If the great forces which have been set in motion are not checked and the movements redirected into constructive and lawful channels, the country faces the most serious problems that it has had to meet since the establishment of this Republic.

In addition to the duty of inquiring into the nature and extent of the seditious activities, this Committee was charged with the duty of making recommendation to the Legislature, with a view to the enactment of such legislation as may be necessary to protect the government of the State and to insure the maintenance of the constitutional rights of its citizens. The problems which confront the States and Nations, however, cannot be solved by legislative enactment alone. They must be met by the loyal and courageous co-operation of the citizens of this Republic who believe that within the present structure of American society can be worked out all necessary reforms, without resorting to a new and untried scheme of social and governmental reconstruction.

In this part of the report the Committee addresses itself not only to the problems presented in the First Part, but to all the problems in the economic and social field that have forced themselves on its attention in the course of the investigation. This is the most difficult part of the problem, and, by far, the most important. The suggestions and recommendations made by the Committee do not pretend to meet adequately the situation. It aims more particularly to map out the present situation, the policies of the various economic groups, the reasons for conflicting aims and actions. It is the hope of the Committee that the problems outlined in this report will receive the earnest and careful study of the members of the Legislature and of those persons into whose hands it comes, in order that they, too, may aid in a concerted effort to bring about economic and social peace.

In dealing with these problems the Committee finds it convenient to discuss them under the following headings:

(1) Protective governmental measures.

(2) Organized labor and capital in industrial problems.

(3) Education, having particular reference to immigrant education and citizenship training.

In dealing with protective governmental measures, the Committee is impressed with the fact that there is no need for further repressive legislation in the State of New York. The adequacy of our present statute dealing with Criminal Anarchy is unquestioned. The need for its enforcement, however, is pressing, and the peculiar character of crises against the State has rendered it difficult for local district attorneys to properly prepare and render indictments against those who are guilty of violating this statute. It is for this reason that the Committee has recommended to the Legislature the establishment of a bureau under the direction of the attorney-general of the State, which is to act as a clearing house for information gathered from all parts of the State, respecting violations of this statute, and to co-operate with the various district attorneys in the preparation and prosecution of all such violations. Its purpose is not repressive but informative.

It has been proved that the subversive movements are, in large measure, inspired by the success of the Russian revolution, and although this Committee is not in a position to influence in any way the foreign policy of the United States, it considers it important to point out the consequences of recognition of Soviet Russia, and to make clear, after a thorough and exhaustive study, that it desires to go on record as firmly opposing the recognition of that regime, and urges upon those charged with the duty of conducting the foreign affairs of this nation to withhold such recognition and to deny the resumption of trade relations with that country, which, owing to the annexation of the Russian co-operatives by the government and the abolition of private trading would in itself involve the recognition of that government.

It is the belief of this Committee that should the Russian Soviet regime be destroyed and a democratic form of government be established in Russia, the menace to American institutions from radical sources would, in large measure, be dissipated.

There are other problems, however, much more fundamental, which cannot be dealt with by penal statutes nor by the enforcement of repressive legislation. The seeds of unrest which are sown by agitators are, in large measure, nourished by improper economic conditions as well as by a lack of knowledge of not only our political institutions and laws but of the simplest economic conditions and laws which exist in a large body of our population. This condition is due in a large measure to the neglect which persons of means, culture and position, leaders in finance and business and men in governmental authority have shown toward the problems of industrial relations and education. This neglect verges on the criminal when we consider its effect on public welfare.

It is, therefore, necessary that this report shall undertake to present those problems in the industrial field, which contribute to the success of the revolutionary movement, and also to discuss educational problems and deficiencies which confront the people of the State of New York.

In discussing the questions of industrial relations, it is necessary to distinguish the labor organizations which are led by conservative and constructive leaders, such as the American Federation of Labor, from the subversive labor groups, which are founded upon the principles of industrial unionism and the One Big Union idea.

No minor differences must be allowed to interfere with the co-operation of the constructive forces that must together work out the best solutions of our troubles.

It is essential to recognize one big basic fact: that we must adopt as our guides the great religious and ethical standards that have been almost by everyone thrown into the discard in any but purely personal relations. The open enmity of Bolshevism, Communism and Socialism to every form of religion and every moral standard, their open appeal to the purely material and selfish side and instincts of human nature, are merely extreme instances of a very general condition. The present industrial war is a war of egotisms. No group has any regard for the comfort, safety or rights of other groups or of the public, whenever the comfort, safety or rights stand in the way of the group's selfish demands. This fact has been brought home to all of us by the recent "outlaw" railway strike with its side-shows of minor strikes to hold up food supplies and business and disrupt all business activities.

It is time we awoke to the fact that the lack of religious and moral training which distinguishes this generation has given full swing to the baser instincts. What can be done to re-create right standard of right and wrong, of subordination of private to public good; to stimulate mutual understanding by frankness and the application of new standards of justice and mutual confidence. Knowledge of the facts is the first step in dispelling distrust. This knowledge we aim to suggest in this part of the report.

SECTION I

PROTECTIVE GOVERNMENTAL MEASURES

INTRODUCTION

Chapter I. Relations with Soviet Russia.......................... 2017
        II. Freedom of Speech................................... 2024
       III. Federal Action in Deportations....................... 2075

SECTION I

PROTECTIVE GOVERNMENTAL MEASURES

INTRODUCTION

Chapter I. Interfaces with Soviet Europe
II. Freedom of Speech
III. Central Action in Importation

CHAPTER I

Relations With Soviet Russia

The impetus given to the revolutionary activity in the United States through the success of the proletarian revolution in Russia renders it important to determine upon a firm policy towards the Russian regime. Although the foreign policy of this government cannot be influenced in any way by this Committee, we feel impelled by the circumstances to make clear our position upon this subject. There appears to be a growing sentiment on the part of many persons, including members of the Senate of the United State, to recognize Soviet Russia. Recent advices from European capitals indicate that in some of them the same tendency is being shown, France alone having taken a determined stand against such recognition.

The continued successes of the Russian arms and the apparent consolidation of the Soviet regime have stimulated the activity of those elements in our society which seek the overthrow of our government and the destruction of its institutions. The confidence thus engendered in these groups is well expressed by a cartoon which appears in the February issue of the "Liberator" — a radical magazine published in this city. It depicts the premiers of the allied countries and President Wilson seated on one side of a chess table, and Lenin on the other. The title of the cartoon is "Checkmate, Gentlemen," and it bears this legend: "There are just two moves they can make — war against Russia which will mean revolution at home; peace with Russia which will mean the spread of Soviet principles throughout the world."

The recognition of Soviet Russia by this country has been the subject of much agitation. It has been inspired and directed in large measure through the Russian Soviet Bureau in New York City under the leadership of Ludwig C. A. K. Martens, representative in the United States of the Russian Soviet regime. It has enlisted the energies of three groups in our society — first, the radical revolutionaries who seek to substitute for the government and institutions of the United States a Soviet form of government; second, the liberals who sympathize with the Russian Soviet regime; and third, certain banking and commercial interests who believe they see vast commercial possibilities in Russian trade.

It is claimed that the Russian Soviet regime stands ready to make many concessions to western democracies in order to gain their recognition. We are told that it will abandon its worldwide propaganda for the international Socialist revolution — that it stands ready to pay in part the international debt of the late Russian Empire — and in other matters to conduct itself in such a manner as to warrant its admission to the family of nations.

There can be no question that those in charge of the Russian Soviet regime will appear to make such concessions in order to gain their ends, it being vital to its continued existence that it obtain certain manufactured products and raw materials from the western countries as well as their financial aid.

It is the purpose of this Committee however, to point out that recognition of the present Russian Soviet regime would not lead to a modification of their theories or practices. On the other hand, it would give it added strength to carry on propaganda for world-wide revolution.

Ludwig C. A. K. Martens, the representative in this country of the Russian Soviet regime, in his testimony before this Committee stated that he was a member of the Russian Communist Party; that that party was in control of Soviet Russia, and that the Soviet regime is founded upon the principles of that party. These prnciples are set forth in unmistakable terms in a manifesto issued by a congress of international revolutionary Socialists held in Moscow in March, 1919. This congress was called at the instance of the leaders of the Russian Communist Party for the purpose of re-establishing the International — that is to say, for the purpose of re-creating an international body governing and controlling the revolutionary Socialist elements in all countries with the object of bringing about the international solidarity of the working classes; to guide and direct them in their respective countries in what is known as the class struggle, namely, the struggle to seize the powers of government for the working class and the establishment of proletarian rule throughout the world.

The declaration of principles and the governing rules of this International were promulgated in the form of the manifesto above referred to, which bears the signatures of Lenin, Trotzky, Rafkowsky, Zenoviev and Fritz Platten. In that document it is made plain that only those elements of the Socialist movement in other countries which had remained true to the principles of international revolutionary Socialism during the war, *i e.,* had refused support to their respective governments in the war, would be admitted to this Third International. Those branches of the Socialist movement like the majority Socialists of Germany and the majority Socialists of France were branded in this document as social patriots and traitors to the international revolutionary Socialist movement.

This manifesto which is addressed to the proletariat of all lands clearly states that the objective of the international revolutionary movement is the establishment in all lands of working-class government and advocates as a means the creation of workmen's councils. It states:

"Seizure of political power by the proletariat means destruction of the political power of the bourgeoisie. The organized power of the bourgeoisie is in the civil State, with its capitalistic army under control of bourgeoisie-junker officers, its police and gendarmes, jailers and judges, its priests, government officials, etc. Conquest of the political power means not merely a change in the personnel of ministries but annihilation of the enemy's apparatus of government."

And again:

"The Communist parties, far from conjuring up civil war artificially, rather strive to shorten its duration as much as possible — in case it has become an iron necessity — to minimize the number of its victims, and above all to secure victory for the proletariat. This makes necessary the disarming of the bourgeoisie at the proper time, the arming of the laborers, and the formation of a communist army as the protector of the rule of the proletariat and the inviolability of the social structure."

At about the same time an attempt was made by the Socialists of various countries to revive what is known as the Second International, which was organized in 1889 and endured until the outbreak of the World War. A congress was called to meet at Berne, Switzerland. The majority of this congress, however, was made up of those Socialists who had supported their respective governments during the war.

The significance of these international conventions which have been dealt with in Part I of this report, and their bearing upon the question of Soviet recognition, is disclosed by the action taken by the Socialist Party of America with respect to them. When faced with the necessity of choosing its foreign affiliations, the Socialist party rejected the proposal of joining the social democratic elements at Berne, and has recently rendered its allegiance to the Third International at Moscow.

This was the natural consequence of the position taken by the Socialist Party of America during the late war. At the very outbreak of that war the Socialist Party stated its position in a war proclamation and program in which it reaffirmed its allegiance to the principles of internationalism in the following words:

"The Socialist Party of the United States in the present grave crisis solemnly reaffirms its allegiance to the principle of internationalism and working-class solidarity the world over and proclaims its unalterable opposition to the war just declared by the government of the United States."

And in the same instrument it declared, after having called upon the workers of all countries to refuse their support to their governments including our own —

"The only struggle which would justify the workers in taking up arms is the great struggle of the working class of the world to free itself from economic exploitation and political oppression, and we particularly warn the workers against the snare and delusion of so-called defensive warfare. As against the false doctrine of national patriotism, we uphold the ideal of international working-class solidarity."

The real meaning of the official pronouncements which we have just quoted is shown by the utterances of the party leaders. A typical example is had in the following quotation from a speech made by Scott Nearing, formerly professor of economics in the University of Pennsylvania, and now an instructor in the Rand School of Social Science, delivered on November 12, 1917, at Parkview Palace, 110th street and Fifth avenue, New York City:

"So while we rejoice that the Russian revolutionists are breaking economic chains; while we send our good wishes and cheers to the German revolutionists as they throw off autocracy and set up a government of the people, let us not forget that expressions of good cheer and messages of encouragement are not the things that the Russian and German workers want from us. They want from us a workers' and soldiers' council in New York City. They want from us a workers' and soldiers' government in the United States. When we have an established government, we will have made good our claim to brotherhood and comradeship with the workers of Russia and Germany."

This statement is in complete accord with the principles which have since been enunciated in the manifesto of the Third International.

It should be noted that the term "Communism" as used in the Moscow manifesto have been adopted in place of the term "Socialism" for much the same reason that Karl Marx in his famous Communist Manifesto chose to use the word "Communist" because the word "Socialist" had been adopted by many groups which were not true to his idea of international revolutionary Socialism. This fact was made clear by the opening paragraph of the Moscow manifesto as follows:

"We Communists, representatives of the revolutionary proletariat of the different countries of Europe, America and Asia, assembled in Soviet Moscow, feel and consider ourselves followers and fulfillers of the program proclaimed seventy-two years ago."

The program proclaimed seventy-two years ago is the Communist manifesto of Marx and Engels which since its issuance has been the authorized statement of the principles and program for the Socialist movement the world over.

The Socialist Party of America today is Communist in the sense that the term is employed in the Communist manifesto of Moscow.

The program outlined by the Moscow manifesto includes the overthrow of the governments of all democratic countries, the substitution therefor of a class government controlled by and for the benefit of the so-called proletariat or propertyless class. This involves the expropriation of private property, the seizure of mills, mines, banks and all instruments of production and distribution, the repudiation of corporate and government obligations. It is this program which has won the approval of and has been adopted by the Socialist Party of America, even to the repudiation of the present war debt of the United States, although for the purpose of expediency their National Executive Committee has deleted this clause from the published platform of 1917 in order to avoid prosecution for violation of the Espionage Act.

The purpose of representing these facts here is that, although Soviet Russia, in exchange for recognition may agree to abandon its international revolutionary propaganda and may make promises of good behavior, the Russian Communist Party which created and controls that regime has established at Moscow an instrument for the continuation of that international revolutionary propaganda under the direction and control of Lenin, Trotzky and the other signers of the manifesto to which we have referred.

We must realize that recognition of the Russian Soviet regime will necessitate the receiving here of a diplomatic representative clothed with all the immunities of his office, and the establishment of consular offices in many of our cities and industrial centers, and consular agents throughout the United States, each of whom will be a member of the Russian Communist Party, bound and committed to the principles and program enunciated in the Moscow manifesto; and that these diplomatic and consular officials will find in every center where they may be located large groups of members of the Socialist Party of America, and other radical groups with whom they are allied, ready to co-operate with them in an attempt to make effective the program to which they have pledged their allegiance.

In other words, the recognition of the Russian Soviet regime amounts to inviting the setting up of an organization within our boundaries, clothed in large measure with diplomatic immunities, which is committed fundamentally to the proposition of overthrowing our government and destroying our institutions.

The red flag of world revolution would become the flag of the friendly nation and might be used on all occasions by those elements of our population who showed a desire to emulate the Russian proletariat.

It is urged by many Liberals that if Soviet Russia is not recognized, at least trade relations should be established with the Russian co-operative societies, apparently on the assumption that they are independent organizations made up of the rural peasantry of Russia. These societies, however, have been taken over and nationalized along with all other industries, and trade with them would mean trade with Soviet Russia.

The committee feels that those charged, under our form of government, with the duty of determining our international policies, should not be stampeded into the recognition of Soviet Russia by the demands of revolutionaries, or by the sentimental pleadings of their liberal sympathizers; and we feel that the business and commercial interests of this country should recognize that the prospect of temporary gain through trade with Soviet Russia is more than offset by the inevitable labor difficulties which unquestionablty will follow in this country if the Soviet regime is permitted to set up in our industrial centers an organization of diplomatic and consular representatives whose sole appeal is to the worker, urging him to organize for the purpose of seizing the power of government and, by continuous striking and demands for inordinate wage increases, to compel the surrender of business enterprises into their hands.

While the cartoon in the " Liberator " presents but two alternatives, there is a third alternative which your Committee believes should be adopted, namely, the refusal of recognition of Soviet Russia and the denial of trade relations with that regime.

The question of the recognition of Soviet Russia demands the earnest consideration of all citizens who desire the peace and prosperity of this country. The Committee feels that it is the duty of the legislature to take a definite stand in opposition to such recognition, and to call upon the officials of our government who are entrusted with the responsibility of our international relations to refuse the recognition of Soviet Russia and to prevent the resumption of trade relations therewith, so that our country may not be laid open to a period of industrial unrest brought about by the activities of Russian representatives and their allies here, which can result in nothing but embarrassment to our industries and endanger the foundation of our institutions.

CHAPTER II

Freedom of Speech

In its preliminary report to the legislature this Committee recommended that no repressive penal legislation be enacted, it being our opinion that the criminal anarchy statute of this State, which has been a law for some nineteen years is, if properly enforced, a good and sufficient statute.

That statute does not infringe upon the right of free speech, but seeks to punish only that license of speech which exists in the advocacy of the doctrine that organized government should be overthrown by force, violence or any unlawful means.

Four convictions have been had in the Supreme Court of this State under this provision of the Penal Law, the prosecutions having been instituted upon information furnished by this Committee to the prosecuting officer of New York County. In each instance the written words that were made the basis of the conviction urged the overthrow of organized government by force, violence and unlawful means, and these four convictions have been met with general public approval, in the apparent realization of the fact that in these cases the bounds of free speech had been transcended and a crime against the government committed.

During the late war there were numerous convictions under the Espionage Act, wherein the law of free speech was very clearly defined by the Supreme Court of the United States, and we will in this chapter — in order to make clear the line of demarcation which exists between free speech as defined by the Constitution of the United States and that abuse of free speech, the use of which constitutes a crime against our statutes — briefly review the law applicable thereto.

Article I, section 8 of the Constitution of the State of New York, in its first sentence, provides as follows:

> " Every citizen may freely speak, write and publish his sentiments on all subjects, *being responsible for the abuse of that right*; and no law shall be passed to restrain or abridge the liberty of speech or of the press. . . ."

The first Amendment to the Constitution of the United States reads as follows:

"Congress shall make no law respecting an establishment of religion, or prohibiting the free exercise thereof; or abridging the freedom of speech or of the press; or the right of the people peaceably to assemble, and to petition the Government for a redress of grievances."

These constitutional provisions are, of course, sacred to the American people and they safeguard rights of the most transcendent importance; but when those provisions were written into our constitutions, the framers thereof had in mind the thought that self-preservation was a primal right of nations, as of men, and that the exercise of free speech was intended for the perpetuation of a free government and not for the destruction thereof. It is these constitutional provisions that, strangely, have been invoked by those persons in the community who have attempted to pervert them and who have attempted to use these provisions as a cloak for the preaching of the doctrine that organized government should be overthrown by force and violence.

The Court of Appeals of this State, in construing the above quoted provision of our State Constitution, and defining the meaning of free speech (Judge Van writing the opinion, in the case of People *v.* Most, 171 N. Y. 423, at p. 431), used the following language:

"While the right to publish is thus sanctioned and secured, the abuse of that right is excepted from the protection of the Constitution, and authority to provide for and punish such abuse is left to the legislature. The punishment of those who publish articles which tend to corrupt morals, induce crime or destroy organized society, is essential to the security of freedom and the stability of the state. While all the agencies of government, executive, legislative and judicial, cannot abridge the freedom of the press, the Legislature may control and the courts may punish the licentiousness of the press. 'The liberty of the press,' as Chancellor Kent declared in a celebrated case, 'consists in the right to publish, with impunity, truth, with good motives, and for justifiable ends, whether it respects governments, magistracy or individuals.' (Peo. *v.* Croswell, 3 Johns. Cas. 336, 393.) Mr. Justice Story defined the phrase to mean, 'that every man shall have a right to speak, write or print his opinions upon any subject whatsoever, without any prior restraint, so always, that he does not injure any other person in his rights, person, property or reputation; and so always, that he does not thereby disturb the public peace, or attempt to subvert the Government.' (Story's Commentaries on the Const., Sec. 1874.)

"The Constitution does not protect a publisher from the consequences of a crime committed by the act of publication. It does not shield a printed attack on private character, for the same section from which the above quotation is taken expressly sanctions criminal prosecution for libel. It does not permit the advertisement of lotteries, for the next section prohibits lotteries and the sale of lottery tickets. It does not permit the publication of blasphemous or obscene articles, as the authorities uniformly hold. (People v. Ruggles, 8 Johns. 290, 297; People v. Muller, 96 N. Y. 408; In re Rapier, 143 U. S. 110.) It places no restraint upon the power of the Legislature to punish the publication of matter which is injurious to society according to the standard of the common law. It does not deprive the State of the primary right of self-preservation. It does not sanction unbridled license, nor authorize the publication of articles prompting the commission of murder or the overthrow of government by force. All courts and commentators contrast the liberty of the press with its licentiousness, and condemn as not sanctioned by the constitution of any state, appeals designed to destroy the reputation of the citizen, the peace of society or the existence of the government. (Story on Const., Chap. 1878; Cooley on Const. Lim., 518; Ordronaux on Constitutional Legislation, 237; Tiedeman on Police Powers, Chap. 81.) We think that no constitutional right of the defendant was violated by his conviction and that the judgment pronounced against him was rendered in accordance with law."

In the case of Schenck v. the United States, and Baer v. the United States, 249 U. S. 47, the Supreme Court of the United states (Mr. Justice Holmes delivering the opinion), said in part:

"But the character of every act depends upon the circumstances in which it is done. The most stringent protection of free speech would not protect a man in falsely shouting fire in a theatre and causing a panic. It does not even protect a man from an injunction against uttering words that may have all the effect of force. (Gompers v. Bucks Stove & Range Co., 221 U. S. 418, 439.) The question in every case is whether the words used are used in such circumstances and are of such a nature as to create a clear and present danger that they will bring about the substantive evils that Congress has a right to prevent. It is a question of proximity and degree. When a nation is at war, many things that might be said in time of peace are such a hindrance to its effort that their utterance will not be endured so long as men fight and that no court could regard them as protected by any constitutional right."

In the case of Berkman and Goldman, the notorious anarchists who were recently deported from the United States, the claim was advanced by the defendants that their prosecution was an infringement on the right of free speech guaranteed by the Constitution. The fact of the matter was that Berkman and Goldman counselled disobedience to the Selective Service Law and urged their hearers not to register and not to obey the provisions of the said law; and Judge Mayer, in the United States District Court, in charging the jury in the Berkman-Goldman case, used the following language:

"This is not a trial of political principles. This cannot be turned into a political or state trial in the political sense. You are not to be misled by any effort to digress your mind from the real issue, which simply is, whether these defendants are guilty or not guilty of the crime charged in the indictment.

"This is not a question of free speech. Free speech is guaranteed to us under the Constitution. No American worthy of the name believes in else than free speech; but free speech means, not license, not counseling disobedience of the law; free speech means that frank, free, full and orderly expression which every man or woman in the land, citizen or alien, may engage in, in lawful and orderly fashion; and that free speech is guaranteed to us, and no court would deny it to anyone."

On June 15, 1917, the Espionage Law was passed, with the object of reaching not only those persons who might be engaged in espionage and to protect our country and industrial resources, but also to prevent any unlawful interference with the Nation's efforts to raise an army and navy. Section 3 of that Act provided:

"Whoever when the United States is at war shall willfully cause or attempt to cause insubordination, disloyalty, munity or refusal of duty in the military or naval forces of the United States, or shall wilfully obstruct the recruiting or enlistment service of the United States to the injury of the service of the United States, shall be punished by a fine of not more than $10,000 or imprisonment for not more than twenty years, or both."

Eugene V. Debs, "our dear Gene" of the Socialist Party, and who is that party's candidate for President this year, was one of the "two thousand Socialists" who were arrested following the passage of the Espionage Act. Debs at a public meeting so couched his language that it was apparent that his purpose was to paralyze the Government of the United States in its endeavor to raise an army for the defense of the Nation. It was urged in his behalf at the time of his trial that he had committed no violation of law, that he was simply exercising the privileges of a free citizen, and that his utterances were protected under the provisions of the first Amendment to the Federal Constitution.

Mr. Justice Holmes, of the United States Supreme Court, writing the opinion in the Debs case, for a unanimous court, used the following forceful language:

"The main theme of the speech was Socialism, its growth, and a prophecy of its ultimate success. With that we have nothing to do, but if a part or the manifest intent of the more general utterances was to encourage those present to obstruct the recruiting service, and if in passages such encouragement was indirectly given, the immunity of the general theme may not be enough to protect the speech."

And then, after quoting from this speech, Mr. Justice Holmes, at another part of the opinion, said:

"The statement was not necessary to warrant the jury in finding that one purpose of the speech — whether incidental or not does not matter — was to oppose not only war in general, but this war, and that the opposition was so expressed that its natural and intended effect would be to obstruct recruiting. If that was intended, and if, in all the curcumstances, that would be its probable effect, it would not be protected by reason of its being part of a general program and expressions of a general and conscientious belief."

In the case of Patterson v. Colorado, 206 U. S. 454, at p. 462, the Supreme Court of the United States, Mr. Justice Holmes writing the opinion, used the following language:

"But even if we were to assume that freedom of speech and freedom of the press were protected from abridgment on the part not only of the United States but also of the States, still we should be far from the conclusion that the plaintiff in error would have us reach. In the first place, the main purpose of such constitutional provisions is 'To prevent all such *previous restraints* upon publications as had been practiced by other governments,' and they do not prevent the subsequent punishment of such as may be deemed contrary to the public welfare. (Commonwealth v. Blanding, 3 Pick. 304, 313, 314; Republica v. Oswald, 1 Dallas, 319, 325.) The preliminary freedom extends as well to the false as to the true; the subsequent punishment may extend as well to the true as to the false."

In the case of the People against Louis C. Fraina, 255 Federal Reporter, p. 28 et seq., the United States Circuit Court of Appeals of the Second Circuit, Judge Hough writing the opinion, used the following language:

"The mental attitude evident throughout the conduct of defense below, and argument here, is suggested rather than plainly stated by the points that it was error to permit the jury to infer guilt from the speeches, that in so doing defendants were tried for their words, and such procedure invades the right of free speech.

"We think the contention may be thus summed up: If there was a meeting of minds, it was not actually productive of any breach of peace; no one was shown to have refused physical obedience to the law; it was all words; and men cannot constitutionally and lawfully be punished for words, especially when the language relates to rights based on the moral sense, i. e., the 'idealism,' of the 'non-religious conscientious objector.'

"The matter at bottom is political, not legal. Men can be unished for words, if the legislature so decrees, within constitutional limits. Men commit crimes when they counsel or procure others to sin against the statute law, and they also commit crimes when they confederate to effect that object, and yet it is difficult to imagine any more suitable or usual method of procuring or counselling than by speech. In this inaccurate sense men have very often been punished for words by statutory enactment.

"The free speech secured federally by the first amendment means complete immunity for the publication by speech or print of whatever is not harmful in character, when tested by such standards as the law affords. For these standards we must look to the common law rules in force when the constitutional guarantees were established and in reference to which they were adopted. By legislative action the boundaries of unpunishable speech have doubtless and often been much enlarged; but the constitutional limit remains unchanged, and what the legislature has done it can undo. Legal talk-liberty never has meant, however, 'the unrestricted right to say what one pleases at all times and under all circumstances.' Warren v. United States, 183 Fed., at 721, 106 C. C. A. 156, 33 L. R. A. (N. S.) 800. Nothing said to the jury by the court below in this case went beyond the limits this stated, and there was no error.

"Complaint as to inferring guilt from speeches, or letting men be found guilty therefrom, when or if the speeches only expressed moral principles and social aspirations, is really objecting to the statutes. The statutes in question here, like most others, are of general application; they must be so unless exceptions of equal authority are also stautory. They operate alike on the religious, the atheist and the unthinking."

This is the same Louis C. Fraina who was one of the organizers of the Communist Party of America in Chicago in September, 1919.

In the case of Roger N. Baldwin, the court used the following language:

"It would be impossible for me to convey to your mind successfully the point of view which I think is entertained by the great masses of the people, and which must be entertained by the courts and by those, such as the Department of Justice, who are charged with the administration of the law.

"In all that you have said, I think that you have lost sight of one very fundamental and essential thing for the preservation of that American liberty to which, by tradition, you feel that you are genuinely devoted.

"A republic can last only so long as its laws are obeyed. The freest discussion is permitted, and should be invited, in the processes that lead up to the enactment of a statute. There should be the freest opportunity of discussion as to the method of administration of a statute by human beings, but the republic must cease to exist if disobedience to any law enacted by the orderly processes laid down by the Constitution is in the very slightest degree to be tolerated.

"That is, from my point of view, fundamental; that is essential not only from an ideal standpoint, but from a practical standpoint, and we should not be able, as I think most Americans think, to conduct what we regard as the government of the free people, if some individual, whether from good or bad motives, were able to successfully violate a statute duly, properly and constitutionally passed, because his own view of the statute might differ from that entertained by the lawmakers who had enacted the law, and the executice who has given it his approval.

"That, to my mind, is the foundation of our system; its perpetuity rests upon obedience of the law.

"It may often be that a man or woman has greater foresight than the masses of the people; and it may be that in the history of things he who seems to be wrong today may be right tomorrow, but with those possible idealistic and academic speculations a court has nothing to do."

It may be interesting to note that several of the defendants in the cases above cited which arose subsequent to the entry of this country in the Great War were Socialists, with the exception of Berkman and Goldman, who were avowed anarchists.

Roger N. Baldwin has been described as a philosophical anarchist by the Socialist, Rev. Norman M. Thomas. It is quite evident that these men and women in their written and spoken utterances were guided by the war declaration and platform of the Socialist Party of America, adopted at the St. Louis Convention in April, 1917, and which has been more fully treated elsewhere in this report, and particularly to that portion of the St. Louis Platform, which provided as follows:

". . . to continuous, active and public opposition to the war, through . . . all means within our power and to unyielding opposition to all military or industrial conscription . . . and any attempt to raise money for war expense by taxing the necessaries of life or issuing bonds which will put the burden on future generations."

The foregoing decisions clearly establish the proposition that self-defense is the primal right of a free nation — that a nation has the rught to punish either written or spoken attempts to undermine its existence, and that the constitutional provisions, both state and federal, with regard to free speech, do not protect that abuse of free speech, the object of which is the destruction or the weakening of the nation. Those misguided apologists for revolutionary radicalism who would place no curb whatever upon speech, have evidently lost sight of these fundamental principles of government. This is particularly true of such organizations as the National Civil Liberties Bureau, whose counsel, Walter Nelles, expressed the opinion that in a republic there could exist no such crime as Criminal Anarchy.

In the course of the hearing before Chief City Magistrate William McAdoo, in the case of the People of the State of New York against Benjamin Gitlow and James Larkin, Mr. Nelles, in arguing for the dismissal of the charges pending against his clients, advanced the rather anomalous argument that the use of language, the object of which was to urge the forcible and violent overthrow of organized government, did not constitute a crime, and challenged the constitutionality for that reason of the Criminal Anarchy statute of this State.

While this Committee believes that there should be the fullest freedom of speech, within constitutional limitations, we do not believe that liberty and freedom of speech under the Constitution mean the unrestrained right to do and say that which will result in the forcible and violent overthrow of our form of government.

The Circuit Court of Appeals for the Eighth Circuit, in the case of Warren *v.* The United States, 183 Fed. Rep. 718, at p. 721, very aptly said:

"Liberty and freedom of speech under the constitution do not mean the unrestrained right to do and say what one pleases at all times and under all circumstances, and certainly they do not mean that contrary to the will of Congress one may make of the post office establishment of the United States an agency for the publication of his views of the character and conduct of others, as distinguished from the carriage of the mails. The very idea of government implies some imposition of restraint in the interest of the general welfare, peace and good order. The statute under consideration is a part of a body of legislation which is being gradually enlarged, and which is designed to exclude from the mails that which tends to debauch the morals of the people, or is contrived to despoil them of their property or is an apparent, visible attack upon their good names. The competency of Congress is beyond question, and the courts have uniformly upheld the legislation and applied it in the light of its evident purposes."

The chief criticism of those persons in the community who oppose the enforcement of the criminal anarchy statute of this state is that it does not require an "overt act" for the consummation of the crime there defined, and that it is sought to punish persons for their opinions, their idea apparently being that the mere counselling of force and violence, without the actual commission of an act of violence, is not criminal. The fallacy of this argument is apparent on a moment's reflection, for really, what more overt act is needed than the urging or counselling or advising another that organized government should be overthrown by force and violence? It is in this way that riots are started — the harangue, the rousing of the hot blood of the listener, the picturing of fancied wrongs, the appeal to the mob spirit, and then the mob in action.

We have made a comparison of the statutes of many of the states of the Union dealing with the subject of criminal anarchy, syndicalism, sedition and the display of the red and black flag, which we reprint at the end of this chapter. A study of these statutes, however, leads us to the opinion expressed in our preliminary report that the criminal anarchy statute of this state is sufficiently broad and comprehensive to protect the people of our state and its institutions, provided this statute is properly enforced. The committee seeks to put no curb upon the expressions or upon the thoughts of the people of this State, other than the necessary check against that abuse of free speech that is covered by the existing criminal anarchy statute above referred to.

Many of the statutes of the other States of the Union set forth at the end of this chapter embody within them a far greater limitation upon freedom of speech and the utterances of the individual than does our own statute. The phraseology of some of them is of such a character as possibly to invite the criticism that they constitute a curb upon freedom of speech and expression, and therein lies the superiority of our statute. No person, we believe, can legitimately claim that the New York statute dealing with the subject of Criminal Anarchy constitutes a curb upon free speech, for in its essential terms it makes a crime of that only which constitutes the advocacy of the forcible, violent or unlawful overthrow of our form of government.

At the time of the writing of this report, Senate bill, Int. No. 1118, entitled "An act to amend the executive law, in relation to powers of attorney-general with respect to prosecutions for criminal anarchy, and making an appropriation therefor," and introduced in the Senate by the Chairman of this Committee, passed both the Senate and the Assembly of the State of New York, and it is now awaiting the action of the Governor thereon.

This statute confers upon the attorney-general concurrent jurisdiction with the district attorneys of the various counties of this state the power to prosecute violations of the criminal anarchy statute of this state, and places at the disposal of the attorney-general the necessary men and resources for the proper enforcement of the criminal anarchy statute.

By this statute it is not sought to usurp the functions of the district attorneys, nor to displace them, but by giving the attorney general concurrent jurisdiction in the prosecution of violators of the criminal anarchy statute, it is believed that there will be a more uniform administration of this law, and a better check kept on those who seek to violate it.

The bill follows:

STATE OF NEW YORK

No. 1272.   Int. 1118.

IN SENATE

March 17, 1920.

Introduced by Mr. LUSK — read twice and ordered printed, and when printed to be committed to the Committee on Finance.

AN ACT

To amend the executive law, in relation to powers of attorney-general with respect to prosecutions for criminal anarchy, and making an appropriation therefor.

The People of the State of New York, represented in Senate and Assembly, do enact as follows:

Section 1. Chapter twenty-three of the laws of nineteen hundred and nine, entitled "An act in relation to executive officers, constituting chapter eighteen of the consolidated laws," is hereby amended by adding thereto, at the end of article six, two new sections, to be sections sixty-nine and sixty-nine-a, to read as follows:

§ 69. **Prosecutions for criminal anarchy.** The attorney general may investigate as to violations of article fourteen of the penal law and may conduct prosecutions for violations of such article. He may conduct such prosecutions in person or by one or more of his deputies. He or his deputies may appear before any grand jury to present evidence or information for the purpose of an indictment for a violation of such article. When required by a grand jury, the attorney-general, or a deputy designated by him for the purpose, shall attend before it for the purpose of examining witnesses or giving legal advice to such jury with respect to the provisions of such article, or to acts constituting violations thereof. The attorney-general may issue subpoenas or other process for the attendance of witnesses, including subpoenas duces tecum, in connection with the exercise of any power conferred upon him by this section; but neither the attorney-general nor any of his deputies shall be present with any grand jury during the expression of their opinions or the giving of their votes upon any matter.

It shall be the duty of the district attorney of any county, in which the attorney-general believes that such violation has occurred, and of the assistants, clerks and employees in the office of such district attorney, and of all police authorities and police officers within any such county, to render to the attorney-general and his deputies and investigators, whenever requested, all aid and assistance within their power in such prosecutions and in the conduct of such cases. The jurisdiction conferred upon the attorney-general herein to prosecute for violations of such article is concurrent in each county with that of the district attorney; but whichever of such officers shall first assume jurisdiction of a particular offense shall have exclusive jurisdiction to prosecute for the same unless or until the governor shall, by written order filed with both such officers, give such jurisdiction to the other.

§ 69-a. **Organization and facilities for prosecuting violations of laws relating to anarchy.** The attorney-general shall assign or appoint one or more deputies to conduct prosecutions for violations of article fourteen of the penal law, and may employ such investigators, translators, stenographers, process servers and clerical and other assistants as may be necessary to enable him properly to exercise his powers and duties in connection with investigating such violations and crimes and in connection with prosecutions therefor. Persons so employed shall be deemed confidential agents of the attorney-general, and their appointment, promotion, demotion or removal shall not be subject to the provisions of the Civil Service Law or rules of the State Civil Service Commission. Investigators, translators and process servers so employed shall each have the powers of peace officers, as defined by law, in any part of the state. The attorney-general may from time to time purchase such equipment, books, pamphlets and other papers, and such other articles as he may deem necessary in the work of such investigations and prosecutions. He may also create a bureau of his office to have charge, subject to his supervision and control, of such investigations and prosecutions.

§ 2. The sum of one hundred thousand dollars ($100,000), or so much thereof as may be necessary, is hereby appropriated for carrying into effect the provisions of sections sixty-nine and sixty-nine-a of the executive law, as added by this act. Such moneys shall be paid out by the state treasurer on the warrant of the comptroller on the order of the attorney-general.

§ 3. This act shall take effect immediately.

TERRITORY OF ALASKA

CHAPTER 6

(H. B. 3)

AN ACT

Defining the crime of criminal syndicalism and prescribing punishment thereof.

Be it enacted by the Legislature of the Territory of Alaska:

Section 1. Criminal syndicalism is the doctrine which advocates crime, sabotage, violence, or other unlawful methods of terrorism as a means of accomplishing industrial or political reform or which advocates the overthrow, by force or violence, the government of the United States or of the Territory of Alaska. The advocacy of such doctrine, whether by word of mouth or writing, is a felony punishable as in this act otherwise provided.

§ 2. Any person who:

(1) By word of mouth or writing, advocates or teaches the duty, necessity or propriety of crime, sabotage, violence or other unlawful methods of terrorism as a means of accomplishing industrial or political reform; or

(2) Prints, publishes, edits, issues or knowingly circulates, sells, distributes, or publicly displays any book, paper, document or written matter in any form containing or advocating, advising or teaching the doctrine that industrial or political reform should be brought about by crime, sabotage, violence or other unlawful methods or terrorisms; or

(3) Openly, willfully and deliberately justifies, by word of mouth or writing, the commission or the attempt to commit crime, sabotage, violence or other unlawful methods of terrorism with intent to exemplify, spread or advocate the propriety of the doctrines of criminal syndicalism; or

(4) Knowingly and willfully organizes or helps to organize, or becomes a member of or voluntarily assembles with any society, group or assemblage of persons formed to teach or advocate the doctrines of criminal syndicalism is guilty of a felony and punishable by imprisonment in the penitentiary for not more than ten (10) years or by fine of not more than five thousand dollars ($5,000), or both.

§ 3. Whenever two or more persons assemble for the purpose of advocating or teaching the doctrines of criminal syndicalism as defined in this Act, such an assemblage is unlawful and every person wilfully, knowingly and voluntarily participating therein by his presence, aid or instigation is guilty of a felony and punishable by imprisonment in the Federal penitentiary for not more than ten (10) years or by fine of not more than five thousand dollars ($5,000), or both.

§ 4. The owner, agent, superintendent, janitor, care-taker or occupant of any place, building or room, who wilfully and knowingly permits therein any assemblage of persons prohibited by the provisions of section 3 of this act, or who, after notification by the United States Marshal or his deputy or the police authorities that the premises are so used, permits such use to be continued, is guilty of a misdemeanor and punishable by imprisonment in the Federal jail for not more than one year or by a fine of not more than five hundred dollars ($500), or both.

Approved April 18, 1919.

TERRITORY OF ALASKA

OFFICE OF THE SECRETARY

Juneau, Alaska

CHAPTER 60

(H B. 67)

AN ACT

For the preservation of Public peace and safety in time of war and for the prevention of sedition and the exciting of ill-feeling or hostility against the Government, and for the prevention of the exhibition of disrespect or contempt for the Government of the United States of America, or for the flag or for the President, or for certain officers thereof; and to provide penalties for the violation of this act, and for declaring an emergency.

Be it enacted by the Legislature of the Territory of Alaska:

Section 1. That in time of war or whenever war has been declared to exist between the United States and any other nation or country, it shall **be unlawful for any person to do** or commit, or cause to be done or committed, any seditious act or thing, or to utter, write, print or publish, or cause to be written, printed or published any seditious matter whatsoever; or to do, or cause to be done, any act or thing, or to utter, print, or publish or cause to be written, printed or published anything tending to excite discontent, trouble, ill feeling or hostility against the Government of the United States of America; or to do, or cause to be done, or to utter, write, print or publish, or cause to be written, printed or published anything which is opprobrious, insulting, disrespectful, defamatory or contemptuous of, or concerning said Government, or the President, or the flag of the United States of America, or of, or concerning any civil military or naval officer of said Government while in the lawful discharge of his duties in executing the lawful orders of the Government or any of its duly authorized officers.

Provided, however, that nothing in this act contained shall be so construed as to prohibit fair and honest criticism of the policy, orders or action of the Government or of any of said officers.

§ 2. That anyone violating the provisions of this act shall be punished by a fine of not more than one thousand dollars ($1,000), or be imprisoned in jail not more than one year, or by both fine and imprisonment; and for a second offense, by a fine of not exceeding two thousand dollars ($2,000), and imprisonment in the penitentiary not more than two years.

§ 3. That an emergency is hereby declared to exist and that this act shall take effect from and after its passage and approval.

Approved May 3, 1917.

CALIFORNIA

Assembly Bill No. 131

CHAPTER 101

AN ACT

To add a new section to the Penal Code to be numbered four hundred three-a, prohibiting the use of a red flag in aid of anarchistic or seditious activities.

(Approved May 5, 1919)

The People of the State of California do enact as follows:

Section 1. A new section is hereby added to the Penal Code to be numbered four hundred three-a, and to read as follows:

§ 403-a. Any person who displays a red flag, banner or badge or any flag, badge, banner or device of any color or form whatever in any public place or in any meeting place or public assembly, or from or on any house, building or window as a sign, symbol or emblem of opposition to organized government or as an invitation or stimulus to anarchistic action or as an aid to propaganda that is of a seditious character is guilty of a felony.

CALIFORNIA

Senate Bill No. 660

CHAPTER 188

AN ACT

Defining criminal syndicalism and sabotage, prescribing certain acts and methods in connection therewith and in pursuance thereof and providing penalties and punishments therefor.

(Approved May 5, 1919)

The People of the State of California do enact as follows:

Section 1. The term "criminal syndicalism" as used in this act is hereby defined as any doctrine or precept advocating, teaching or aiding and abetting the commission of crime, sabotage (which word is hereby defined as meaning wilful and malicious physical damage or injury to physical property), or unlawful acts of force and violence or unlawful methods of terrorism as a means of accomplishing a change in industrial ownership or control, or effecting any political change.

§ 2. Any person who:

1. By spoken or written words or personal conduct advocates, teaches or aids and abets criminal syndicalism or the duty, necessity or propriety of committing crime, sabotage, violence or any unlawful method of terrorism as a means of accomplishing a change in industrial ownership or control, or effecting any political change; or

2. Wilfully and deliberately by spoken or written words justifies or attempts to justify criminal syndicalism or the commission or attempt to commit crime, sabotage, violence or unlawful methods of terrorism with intent to approve, advocate or further the doctrine of criminal syndicalism; or

3. Prints, publishes, edits, issues or circulates or publicly displays any book, paper, pamphlet, document, poster or written or printed matter in any form, containing or carrying written or printed advocacy, teaching, or aid and abetment of, or advising, criminal syndicalism; or

4. Organizes or assists in organizing, or is or knowingly becomes a member of, any organization, society, group or assemblage of persons organized or assembled to advocate, teach or aid and abet criminal syndicalism; or

5. Wilfully by personal act or conduct, practices or commits any act advised, advocated, taught or aided and abetted by the doctrine or precept of criminal syndicalism, with intent to accomplish a change in industrial ownership or control, or effecting any political change;

Is guilty of a felony and punishable by imprisonment in the state prison not less than one nor more than fourteen years.

§ 3. If for any reason any section, clause or provision of this act shall by any court be held unconstitutional then the legislature hereby declares that, irrespective of the unconstitutionality so determined of such section, clause or provision, it would have enacted and made the law of this state all other sections, clauses and provisions of this act.

§ 4. Inasmuch as this act concerns and is necessary to the immediate preservation of the public peace and safety, for the reason that at the present time large numbers of persons are going from place to place in this state advocating, teaching and practicing criminal syndicalism, this act shall take effect upon approval by the governor.

INDIANA

CHAPTER 125

AN ACT

Making it unlawful to display or exhibit any flag, banner or emblem symbolizing and intended to symbolize a purpose to overthrow the government of the United States, the State of Indiana, or all government and making it unlawful to advocate or incite the overthrow of the government of the United States, the State of Indiana or all government and providing a penalty for its violation.

(H. 296. Approved March 14, 1919)

PREAMBLE

Whereas, While liberty within the reasonable restraints of law, and the right of free speech, are among the unalienable rights of the American citizen, and no encroachment upon either should ever be tolerated, the claim to those rights should never be allowed to cover treasonable acts or utterances, the advocacy of anarchy, the overthrow of government, or the abrogation of constitutional means for the maintenance of law and order and the protection of the lives and rights of persons, or the advocacy of or the practime of sabotage; and

Whereas, Recent occurrences in Russia and elsewhere warn us that the toleration of such unbridled license of speech and of such practices involves great danger to civilization and to organized society, **and threatens a possible lapse into barbarism;** therefore,

PROHIBITING THE DISPLAY OF CERTAIN BANNERS, EMBLEMS

Section 1. *Be it enacted by the General Assembly of the State of Indiana,* That the display or exhibition at any meeting, gathering or parade, public or private, of any flag, banner or emblem symbolizing or intended by the person or persons displaying or exhibiting the same to symbolize a purpose to overthrow, by force of violence, or by physical injury to personal property, or by the general cessation of industry, the government of the United States or (of) the State of Indiana, or all government, is hereby declared to be unlawful.

PROHIBITING THE INCITING OF VIOLENCE

§ 2. It shall be unlawful for any person to advocate or incite or to write or with intent to forward such purpose to print, publish, sell, or distribute any document, book, circular, paper, journal or other written or printed communication in or by which there is advocated or incited the overthrow by force or violence, or by physical injury to personal property, or by the general cessation of industry, of the government of the United States, of the State of Indiana, or all government.

PENALTY FOR VIOLATION

§ 3. That any person or persons convicted of violating any section of this act shall be fined not more than $5,000 or imprisoned for not more than five years, or both.

IOWA

Senate File No. 281.   Judiciary No. 1.
By EVANS.   February 22, 1919.

A BILL FOR AN ACT

Defining the crime of criminal syndicalism and prescribing punishment therefor.

Be it enacted by the General Assembly of the State of Iowa:

Section 1. Criminal syndicalism is the doctrine which advocates crime, sabotage, violence or other unlawful methods of terrorism as a means of accomplishing industrial or political reform. The advocacy of such doctrine, whether by word of mouth or writing, is a felony punishable as in this act otherwise provided.

§ 2. Any person who:

A. By word of mouth or writing, advocates or teaches the duty, necessity or propriety of crime, sabotage, violence or other unlawful methods of terrorism as a means of accomplishing industrial or political reform; or

B. Prints, publishes, edits, issues or knowingly circulates, sells, distributes or publicly displays any book, paper, document or written matter in any form, containing or advocating, advising or teaching the doctrine that industrial or political reform should be brought about by crime, sabotage, violence or other unlawful methods of terrorism; or

C. Openly, wilfully and deliberately justifies, by word of mouth or writing, the commission or the attempt to commit crime, sabotage, violence or other unlawful methods of terrorism with intent to exemplify, spread or advocate the propriety of the doctrines of criminal syndicalism; or

D. Organizes or helps to organize, or becomes a member of or voluntarily assembles with any society, group or assemblage of persons formed to teach or advocate the doctrines of criminal syndicalism, is guilty of a felony and punishable by imprisonment in the state penitentiary or reformatory for not more than ten (10) years or by a fine of not more than five thousand dollars ($5,000), or both.

§ 3. Whenever two or more persons assemble for the purpose of advocating or teaching the doctrines of criminal syndicalism as defined in this act, such an assemblage is unlawful and every person voluntarily participating therein by his aid or instigation is guilty of a felony and punishable by imprisonment in the state penitentiary or reformatory for not more than ten (10) years or by a fine of not more than five thousand dollars ($5,000), or both.

§ 4. The owner, agent, superintendent, janitor, caretaker or occupant of any place, building or room, who wilfully and knowingly permits therein any assemblage of persons prohibited by the provisions of section 3 of this act, or who, after notification by the sheriff of the county or the police authorities that the premises are so used, permits such use to be continued, is guilty of a misdemeanor and punishable by imprisonment in the county jail for not more than one year or by a fine of not more than five hundred dollars ($500), or both.

IOWA

House File No 102.   Judiciary.
By FLENNIKEN.   January 29, 1919.

A BILL FOR AN ACT

Making it a misdemeanor to display, carry or exhibit a red flag with the intent to advocate, encourage or incite anarchy or treason, and providing a penalty therefor.

Be it enacted by the General Assembly of the State of Iowa:

Section 1. Any person who displays, carries, or exhibits any red flag, or other flag, pennant, banner, ensign, or insignia, or who aids, encourages, or advises such display, carriage, or exhibition, with the intent thereby to himself, or to induce others, to advocate, encourage, or incite anarchy or treason or hostility to the Government of the United States or of the State of Iowa, or to insult or disregard the flag of the United States, shall be guilty of a misdemeanor and upon conviction shall be fined not to exceed one thousand dollars ($1,000) or be imprisoned not to exceed six (6) months or both.

§ 2. If any person so violate the provisions of section one (1) of this act, and be then and there armed with a dangerous weapon, he shall be guilty of a felony and upon conviction shall be imprisoned not to exceed five (5) years.

§ 3. In all prosecutions for violation of section one (1) of this act, the display, carriage, or exhibition of such red flag, pennant, banner, ensign, or insignia in processions, parades, meetings or assemblages, shall be presumptive evidence that the same was so displayed, carried, or exhibited with the intent thereby to advocate, teach, encourage, or incite anarchy or treason or hostility to the Government of the United States or the State of Iowa, or with intent to insult or disregard the flag of the United States.

KANSAS

House Bill No. 714.

AN ACT

Relating to the flag, standard, or banner of bolshevism, anarchy, or radical socialism; declaring any violation hereof a felony, and providing penalties therefor.

Be it enacted by the Legislature of the State of Kansas:

Section 1. That hereafter it shall be a felony for any person or persons, organization or body of persons to fly, to carry, to exhibit, or to display, or to assist in carrying, exhibiting or displaying in this state any red flag, standard or banner distinctive of bolshevism, anarchy, or radical socialism, or any flag, standard or banner of any color or design that is now or may hereafter be designated by any bolshevistic, anarchistic or radical socialistic group, body, association or society of persons as the flag, standard or banner of bolshevism, anarchism or radical socialism.

§ 2. That any person or persons who shall violate any provision of section 1 of this act shall, upon conviction of such violation, be punished by imprisonment in the State Penitentiary for a period of not less than eighteen (18) months nor more than three (3) years.

§ 3. This act shall take effect and be in force from and after its publication in the official state paper.

LOUISIANA

ACT No. 24

Senate Bill No. 7.   By Mr. Boatner.

AN ACT

Prohibiting inciting, or attempting to incite, insurrection or sedition, and providing penalties for any violation of this Act.

Penalty for inciting insurrection or sedition. Section 1. Be it enacted by the General Assembly of the State of Louisiana, That, if any person shall incite an insurrection or sedition amongst any portion or class of the population of this state, or shall attempt, by writing, speaking, or by any other means, to incite such insurrection or sedition, the person or persons so offending shall be punished by imprisonment in the State Penitentiary not exceeding twenty years and shall be fined not less than one thousand dollars nor more than ten thousand dollars, at the discretion of the court.

§ 2. Be is further enacted, etc. That any person who shall advocate, in public or private, by speech, writing, printing or by any other mode or means, the subversion and destruction by force of the Government of the United States or of the State of Louisiana, or attempt by speech, writing, printing or in any other way whatsoever to incite or abet, promote or encourage hostility or opposition to the Government of the United States or of the State of Louisiana shall be guilty of a misdemeanor and upon conviction shall be punished by imprisonment in the parish jail not less than six months nor more than one year or shall be fined not less than three hundred dollars nor more than one thousand dollars, or both, at the discretion of the court. *Penalty for encouraging hostility or opposition.*

§ 3. Be it further enacted, etc., That any person, who shall become a member of any organization, society or order organized or formed, or attend any meeting or council, or solicit others so to do, for the purpose of inciting, abetting, promoting or encouraging hostility or opposition to the Government of the United States or to the State of Louisiana, or who, in any manner, shall aid, abet or encourage any such organization, society, order or meeting in the propagation or advocacy of such a purpose, shall be guilty of a misdemeanor and upon conviction shall be imprisoned in the parish jail not less than six months nor more than one year or shall be fined not less than three hundred dollars nor more than one thousand dollars, or both, at the discretion of the court. *Penalty for joining organization, etc.*

Approved July 25, 1917.

MICHIGAN
No. 104

AN ACT

To prohibit the display of a red flag, in certain cases, in any public assembly or parade; declaring the violation to be a felony and providing penalties.

The People of the State of Michigan enact:

Unlawful to display.
Section 1. It shall be unlawful for any person or persons to display a red flag in any public assembly, parade or demonstration conducted in this State. The use of such a flag at any such assembly, parade or demonstration shall be considered as prima facie evidence of its use as an emblem of anarchy.

Penalty.
§ 2. Any person or persons violating the provisions of section one of this act shall be deemed guilty of a felony, and, upon conviction, shall be fined in a sum not exceeding one thousand dollars or by imprisonment in the State prison not exceeding the five years, or by both such fine and imprisonment in the discretion of the court.

This act is ordered to take immediate effect.

Approved April 21, 1919.

MICHIGAN
No. 255

AN ACT

Defining the crime of criminal syndicalism and prescribing punishment therefore.

The People of the State of Michigan enact:

Offense defined.
Section 1. Criminal syndicalism is hereby defined as the doctrine which advocates crime, sabotage, violence or other unlawful methods of terrorism as a means of advocacy of such doctrine, whether by word of mouth accomplishing industrial or political reform. The

or writing, is a felony punishable as in this act, otherwise provided. *Felony.*

§ 2. Any person who by word of mouth or writing, advocates or teaches the duty, necessity or propriety of crime, sabotage, violence or other unlawful methods of terrorism as a means of accomplishing industrial or political reform; or prints, publishes, edits, issues or knowingly circulates, sells, distributes or publicly displays any book, paper, document, or written matter in any form, containing or advocating, advising or teaching the doctrine that industrial or political reform should be brought about by crime, sabotage, violence or other unlawful methods of terrorism; or openly, wilfully and deliberately justifies by word of mouth or writing, the commission or the attempt to commit crime, sabotage, violence or other unlawful methods of terrorism with intent to exemplify, spread, or advocate the propriety of the doctrines of criminal syndicalism; or organizes or helps to organize, or becomes a member of or voluntarily assembles with any society, group or assemblage of persons formed to teach or advocate the doctrines of criminal syndicalism is guilty of a felony and punishable by imprisonment in the State Prison for not more than ten years or by a fine of not more than five thousand dollars, or both, at the discretion of the court. *Acts constituting guilt.* *Felony, how punished.*

Approved May 12, 1919.

MINNESOTA
Chapter 463 — H. F. No. 1270

AN ACT

Making it unlawful to interfere with or discourage the enlistment of men in the military or naval forces of the United States or of the State of Minnesota, and providing punishment therefor.

Be it enacted by the Legislature of the State of Minnesota:

Section 1. **Interfering with enlistment unlawful.** It shall be unlawful from and after the passage of this act for any person to print, publish or circulate in any manner whatsoever any book, pamphlet, or written or printed matter that advocates or attempts to advocate that men should not enlist in the military or naval forces of the United States or the state of Minnesota.

§ 2. **Speaking by word of mouth against enlistment unlawful.** It shall be unlawful for any persons in any public place, or at any meeting where more than five persons are assembled, to advocate or teach by word of mouth or otherwise that men should not enlist in the military or naval forces of the United States or the state of Minnesota.

§ 3. **Teaching or advocating by written or printed matter against enlistment unlawful.** It shall be unlawful for any person to teach or advocate by any written or printed matter whatsoever, or by oral speech, that the citizens of this state should not aid or assist the United States in prosecuting or carrying on war with the public enemies of the United States.

§ 4. **"Citizen" defined.** A citizen of this state for the purposes of this act is hereby defined to be any person within the confines of the state.

§ 5. **Violating a gross misdemeanor.** Any person violating any provisions of this act is hereby declared to be guilty of gross misdemeanor and shall be punished therefor by a fine of not less than one hundred dollars ($100), nor more than five hundred dollars ($500), or by imprisonment in the county jail for not less than three months or more than one year, or by both.

§ 6. **Officers given right to arrest.** Any police or peace officer of this state, or any regularly commissioned officer in the army or navy of the United States or of the national guard or organized militia of the state of Minnesota is hereby authorized to summarily arrest any person violating any provisions of this act.

§ 7. This act shall take effect and be in force from and after its passage.

Approved April 20, 1917.

MINNESOTA
Chapter 215 — S. F. No. 942

AN ACT

Defining criminal syndicalism, prohibiting the advocacy thereof and the advocacy of crime, sabotage, violence, or other unlawful methods of terrorism as a means of accomplishing industrial or political ends, and assemblage for the purpose of such advocacy; declaring it unlawful to permit the use of any place, building or rooms for such assemblage in certain cases; and providing penalties for violations of the provisions thereof.

Be it enacted by the Legislature of the State of Minnesota:

Section 1. Criminal syndicalism is hereby defined as the doctrine which advocates crime, sabotage (this word as used in this bill meaning malicious damage or injury to the property of an employer by an employee), violence or other unlawful methods of terrorism as a means of accomplishing industrial or political ends. The advocacy of such doctrine, whether by word of mouth or writing, is a felony punishable as in this act otherwise provided.

§ 2. Any person who by word of mouth or writing, advocates or teaches the duty, necessity or propriety of crime, sabotage, violence or other unlawful methods of terrorism as a means of accomplishing industrial or political ends, or prints, publishes, edits, issues or knowingly circulates, sells, distributes or publicly displays any book, paper, document or written matter in any form, containing or advocating, advising or teaching the doctrine that industrial or political ends should be brought about by crime, sabotage, violence or other unlawful methods of terrorism; or openly, wilfully and deliberately justifies by word of mouth or writing, the commission or the attempt to commit crime, sabotage, violence or other unlawful methods of terrorism with intent to exemplify, spread or advocate the propriety of the doctrines of criminal sydicalism, or organizes or helps to organize or becomes a member or voluntarily assembles with any society, group or assemblage of persons formed to teach or advocate the doctrine of criminal syndicalism, is guilty of a felony and punishable by imprisonment in the state prison for not more than five years or by a fine of not more than one thousand dollars or both.

§ 3. Wherever two or more persons assemble for the purpose of advocating or teaching the doctrines of criminal syndicalism defined in this act, such an assemblage is unlawful and every person voluntarily participating therein by this presence, aid or instigation is guilty of a felony and punishable by imprisonment in the county jail for not more than 10 years or by a fine of not more than $5,000 or both.

§ 4. The owner, agent, superintendent, or occupant of any place, building or rooms who wilfully and knowingly permits therein any assemblage of persons prohibited by the provisions of section 3 of this act, or who, after notification that the premises are so used, permits such use to be continued, is guilty of a gross misdemeanor and punishable by imprisonment in the county jail for not more than one year or by a fine of not more than $500 or both.

§ 5. This act shall take effect and be in force from and after the date of its passage.

Approved April 13, 1917.

NEBRASKA

SYNDICALISM STATUTE OF NEBRASKA

Chapter 261 of the Laws of 1919

Section 1 defines "criminal syndicalism" as "the doctrine which advocates crime, physical violence, arson, destruction of property or sabotage as a means of accomplishing or effecting industrial or political ends or for profit."

Sections 2 and 3 read as follows:

§ 2. Any person who, by word of mouth or writing, advocates, affirmatively suggests or teaches the duty, necessity, propriety or expediency of crime, criminal syndicalism, or sabotage, or who shall advocate, affirmatively suggest or teach the duty, necessity, propriety or expediency of doing any act of violence, the destruction of or damage to any property, the bodily injury to any person or persons, or the commission of any crime as a means of accomplishing or effecting any industrial or political ends, or for profit; or who prints, publishes, edits, issues or knowingly circulates, sells, distributes, or publicly displays any books, pamphlets papers, hand bills, posters, document or written or printed matter in any form whatsoever, containing matters advocating, advising, affirmatively suggesting or teaching crime, criminal syndicalism, sabotage, the doing of any act of physical violence, the destruction of or damage to any property, the injury to any person, or the commission of any crime as a means of accomplishing, effecting or bringing about any industrial or political ends, or for profit, or who shall openly, or at all attempt to justify by word of mouth or writing the commission or attempt to commit sabotage, any act of physical violence, the destruction of or damage to any property, the injury of any person or the commission of any crime, with the attempt to exemplify, spread or teach or affirmatively suggest criminal syndicalism, or organizes or helps to organize or becomes a member of or voluntarily assembles with any society or assemblage of persons which teaches, advocates or affirmatively suggests the doctrine of criminal syndicalism, sabotage, or the necessity or propriety or expediency of doing any act of physical violence or the commission of any crime as a means of accomplishing or effecting any industrial or political ends or for profit, shall be deemed guilty of a felony and upon conviction thereof shall be punished by imprisonment in the penitentiary for a term of not less than one year or more than ten years or by a fine of not more than one thousand dollars or both such imprisonment and fine.

§ 3. The owner, lessee, agent, superintendent or person in charge or occupation of any place, building, room or rooms or structure, who knowingly permits therein any assembly or consort of persons prohibited by the provisions of section 2 of this act, or who after notification by authorized public or peace officer that the place or premises or any part thereof is or are so used, permits such use to be continued, is guilty of a misdemeanor and punishable upon conviction thereof by imprisonment in the county jail for not less than sixty days or for not more than one year or by a fine of not less than one hundred dollars or more than five hundred dollars or both such imprisonment and fine.

NEW HAMPSHIRE
CHAPTER 155

AN ACT

To prevent the overthrow of government by force.

Be it enacted by the Senate and House of Representatives in General Court convened:

Section 1. No persons shall congregate, assemble, organize, or associate themselves together in any number, for the purpose of advocating or encouraging, or when assembled, organized or associated for any purpose shall advocate or encourage, or in any public or private place advocate or encourage by any act or in any manner, or bring into this state, prepare, produce, publish, distribute, or have in possession for distribution, any printed or written matter of any kind, including pictures, which so advocates, encourages or favors the overthrow of, or change in the form of the government of the United States or this state or any sub-division thereof, or the interference with any public or private right whatsoever, by force or any unlawful means or act of violence.

§ 2. No persons shall do, or assist in the doing of, any act or thing which advocates, or tends to urge, incite or encourage the violation of any of the laws of the United States or of this state, or any of the by-laws or ordinances of any town or city therein, now or hereafter in force.

§ 3. Any person violating any of the provisions of the preceding sections shall be guilty of a felony and be punished by a fine not exceeding five thousand dollars or by imprisonment not exceeding ten years, or both, and in addition all printed or written matter, including pictures, prohibited in section 1 shall be seized and destroyed in accordance with the provisions of chapter 258 of the Public Statutes.

§ 4. The superior court shall have jurisdiction in equity upon petition filed by the attorney general or the solicitor for any county to restrain and enjoin any person, firm or corporation from bringing into this state, preparing, producing, publishing, distributing, or having in possession for distribution any of said printed or written matter of any kind, including pictures, and said court upon like proceedings may restrain and enjoin any person, firm, society, association, organization, or corporation which is the owner, occupant or lessee of any building, structure or premises whereon or wherein any such written or printed matter is prepared, produced, published or stored, or where persons congregate or assemble for any of the purposes aforesaid, from continuing such use thereof and the violation of the provisions of any order issued by said court shall be contempt. All questions of fact arising in any proceedings had under the provisions of this act shall be tried by jury, unless the defendants file a written waiver of the right to a jury trial.

§ 5. All acts and parts of acts inconsistent with this act are hereby repealed and this act shall take effect upon its passage.

Approved March 28, 1919.

NEW JERSEY
CHAPTER 78

A Further Supplement to an act entitled "An act for the punishment of crimes (Revision of 1898)," approved June fourteenth, one thousand eight hundred and ninety-eight.

BE IT ENACTED *by the Senate and General Assembly of the State of New Jersey:*

1. Any person who shall, in public or private, display a red flag, a black flag, or any ensign or sign bearing an inscription opposed to organized government, or the flag, emblem or insignia of any organization, society or order opposed to organized government, for the purpose of inciting, promoting or encouraging hostility or opposition to or the subversion or destruction of any and all government, shall be guilty of a high misdemeanor and punished by a fine not exceeding two thousand dollars, or imprisonment at hard labor not exceeding fifteen years, or both. *Displaying red or black flag a high misdemeanor. Penalty.*

2. This act shall take effect immediately.

Approved April 10, 1919.

NEW YORK
ARTICLE 14
ANARCHY

§ 160. **Criminal anarchy defined.** Criminal anarchy is the doctrine that organized government should be overthrown by force or violence, or by assassination of the executive head or of any of the executive officials of government, or by any unlawful means. The advocacy of such doctrine either by word of mouth or writing is a felony.

§ 161. **Advocacy of criminal anarchy.** Any person who:

1. By word of mouth or writing advocates, advises or teaches the duty, necessity or propriety of overthrowing or overturning organized government by force or violence, or by the assassination of the executive head or of any of the executive officials of government, or by any unlawful means; or

2. Prints, publishes, edits issues or knowingly circulates, sells, distributes or publicly displays any book, paper, document, or written or printed matter in any form, containing or advocating, advising or teaching the doctrine that organized government should be overthrown by force, violence or any unlawful means; or,

3. Openly, wilfully and deliberately justifies by word of mouth or writing the assassination or unlawful killing or assaulting of any executive or other officer of the United States or of any State or of any civilized nation having an organized government because of his official character, or any other crime, with intent to teach, spread or advocate the propriety of the doctrines of criminal anarchy; or,

4. Organizes or helps to organize or becomes a member of or voluntarily assembles with any society, group or assembly of persons formed to teach or advocate such doctrine.

Is guilty of a felony and punishable by imprisonment for not more than ten years, or by a fine of not more than five thousand dollars, or both.

§ 162. **Assemblages of anarchists.** Whenever two or more persons assemble for the purpose of advocating or teaching the doctrine of criminal anarchy, as defined in section one hundred and sixty, such as assembly is unlawful, and every person voluntarily participating therein by his presence, aid or instigation, is guilty of a felony and punishable by imprisonment for not more than ten years, or by a fine of not more than five thousand dollars, or both.

§ 163. **Permitting premises to be used for assemblages of anarchists.** The owner, agent, superintendent, janitor, caretaker, or occupant of any place, building or room, who wilfully and knowingly permits therein any assemblage of persons prohibited by section one hundred and sixty two, or who, after notification that the premises are so used permits such use to be continued, is guilty of a misdemeanor, and punishable by imprisonment for not more than two years, or by a fine of not more than two thousand dollars, or both.

§ 164. **Liability of editors and others.** Every editor or proprietor of a book, newspaper or serial and every manager of a partnership or incorporated association by which a book, newspaper or serial is issued, is chargeable with the publication of any matter contained in such book, newspaper or serial. But in every prosecution therefor, the defendant may show in his defense that the matter complained of was published without his knowledge or fault and against his wishes, by another who had no authority from him to make the publication and whose act was disavowed by him so soon as known.

§ 165. **Leaving state with intent to elude provisions of this article.** A person who leaves the state, with intent to elude any provision of this article, or to commit any act without the state, which is prohibited by this article, or who, being a resident of this state, does any act without the state, which would be punishable by the provisions of this article if committed within the state, is guilty of the same offense and subject to the same punishment, as if the act had been committed within the state.

§ 166. **Witnesses privilege.** No person shall be excused from giving evidence upon an investigation or prosecution for any of the offenses specified in this article upon the ground that the evidence might tend to convict him of a crime. But such evidence shall not be received against him upon any criminal proceeding.

OHIO
House Bill No. 477

AN ACT

Defining the crime of criminal syndicalism and prescribing punishment therefor.

Be it enacted by the General Assembly of the State of Ohio:

Section 1. That criminal syndicalism is the doctrine which advocates crime, sabotage, which is defined as the malicious injury or destruction of the property of another, violence, or unlawful methods of terrorism as a means of accomplishing industrial or political reform. The advocacy of such doctrine, whether by word of mouth or writing, is a felony, punishable as is in this act provided.

§ 2. Any person who by word of mouth or writing, advocates or teaches the duty, necessity or propriety of crime, sabotage, violence or unlawful methods of terrorism as a means of accomplishing industrial or political reform; or prints, publishes, edits, issues or knowingly circulates, sells, distributes or publicly displays any book, paper, document, or written matter in any form, containing or advocating, advising or teaching the doctrine that industrial or political reform should be brought about by crime, sabotage, violence or unlawful methods of terrorism, or openly, wilfully, and deliberately justifies, by word of mouth or writing, the commission or the attempt to commit crime, sabotage, violence or unlawful methods of terrorism with intent to exemplify, spread or advocate the propriety of the doctrines of criminal syndicalism; or organizes or helps to organize or becomes a member of, or voluntarily assembles with any society, group or assemblage of persons formed to teach or advocate the doctrines of criminal syndicalism; is guilty of a felony and punishable by imprisonment in the state penitentiary for not more than ten years, or by a fine of not more than five thousand dollars, or both.

§ 3. Whenever two or more persons assemble for the purpose of advocating or teaching the doctrines of criminal syndicalism as defined in this act, such an assemblage is unlawful, and every person voluntarily participating therein by his presence, aid or instigation is guilty of a felony and punishable by imprisonment in the state penitentiary for not more than ten years, or by a fine of not more than five thousand dollars, or both.

§ 4. The owner, agent, superintendent, janitor, caretaker, or occupant of any place, building or room, who wilfully and knowingly permits therein any assemblage of persons prohibited by the provisions of section 3 of this act, or who, after notification that the premises are so used, knowingly permits such use to be continued, is guilty of a misdemeanor and punishable by imprisonment in the county jail for not more than one year or by a fine of not more than five hundred dollars, or both.

§ 5. This act is hereby declared to be an emergency act necessary for the immediate preservation of the public peace and safety. The emergency necessitating the enactment of this act arises out of the fact that there are persons in, and also persons threatening to enter, the state for the purpose of teaching the doctrine of criminal syndicalism as defined in this act, and advocating such doctrine and the commission of the other acts and practices declared by this act to be unlawful, the tendency of which will be to destroy our institutions and government, and put the people into condition of unrest and terror.

CARL R. KIMBALL,
Speaker of the House of Representatives.

CLARENCE J. BROWN,
President of the Senate.

Passed April 15, 1919.
Approved May 7, 1919.

JAMES M. COX,
Governor.

Filed in the office of Secretary of State, May 7, 1919.

OREGON

(Oregon Statute with reference to foreign language newspapers.)

SPECIAL SESSION LAWS 1920

CHAPTER 17

[S. B. 49]

AN ACT

Making it unlawful to print, publish, circulate, display, sell or offer for sale any newspaper and periodical in any language other than the English, unless the same contain a literal translation thereof in the English language of the same type and as conspicuously displayed and providing a penalty therefor.

Be it Enacted by the People of the State of Oregon:

Section 1. It shall be unlawful for any person, firm, corporation or association of persons to print, publish, circulate, display, sell or offer for sale any newspaper and periodical in any language other than the English, in whole or in part, unless such newspaper, periodical, pamphlet or circular shall contain a literal translation thereof in the English language of the same type and as conspicuously displayed.

§ 2. Any person, firm, corporation or association of persons violating the provisions of this act shall be deemed guilty of a misdemeanor and upon conviction thereof shall be punished by imprisonment in the county jail not exceding six months or by fine not exceding five hundred dollars ($500), or by both such imprisonment and fine.

Approved by the governor January 20, 1920.

Filed in the office of the Secretary of State January 20, 1920.

OREGON

GENERAL LAWS OF OREGON FOR 1919

CHAPTER 12
(S. B. 2)

AN ACT

Entitled an act defining criminal syndicalism, and the word "sabotage;" prohibiting the advocacy, teaching or affirmative suggestion thereof; and prohibiting the advocacy, teaching or affirmative suggestion of crime, physical violence, or the commission of any unlawful act or thing as a means to accomplish industrial or political ends, change or revolution, or for profit; and prohibiting assemblages for the purpose of such advocacy, teachings or suggestions; declaring it unlawful to permit the use of any place, building, rooms or premises for such assemblages in certain cases, and providing penalties for the violation thereof, and declaring an emergency

Be it Enacted by the People of the State of Oregon:

Section 1. Criminal syndicalism is hereby defined to be the doctrine which advocates crime, physical violence, arson, destruction of property, sabotage, or other unlawful acts or methods, as a means of accomplishing or effecting industrial or political ends, or as a means of effecting industrial or political revolution, or for profit.

§ 2. "Sabotage" is hereby defined to be malicious, felonious, intentional or unlawful damage, injury or destruction of real or personal property of any employer, or owner, by his or her employe or employes, or any employer or employers or by any person or persons, at their own instance, or at the instance, request or instigation of such employes, employers or any other person.

§ 3. Any person who, by word of mouth or writing, advocates, affirmatively suggests or teaches the duty, necessity, propriety or expediency of crime, criminal syndicalism, or sabotage, or who shall advocate, affirmatively suggest or teach the duty, necessity, propriety or expediency of doing any act of violence, the destruction of or damage to any property, the bodily injury to any person or persons, or the commission of any crime or unlawful act as a means of accomplishing or effecting any industrial or political ends, change or revolution, or for profit; or who prints, publishes, edits, issues or knowingly circulates, sells, distributes, or publicly displays any books, pamphlets, paper, handbill, poster, document or written or printed matter in any form whatsoever, containing matter advocating, advising, affirmatively suggesting or teaching crime, criminal syndicalism, sabotage, the doing of any act of physical violence, the destruction of or damage to any property, the injury to any person, or the commission of any crime, or unlawful act as a means of accomplishing, effecting or bringing about any industrial or political ends, or change, or as a means of accomplishing, effecting or bringing about any industrial or political revolution, or for profit, or who shall openly, or at all attempt to justify by word or mouth or writing, the commission or the attempt to commit sabotage, any act of physical violence, the destruction of or damage to any property, the injury of any person or the commission of any crime or unlawful act, with the intent to exemplify, spread, or teach, or affirmatively suggest criminal syndicalism, or organizes, or helps to organize or becomes a member of, or voluntarily assembles with any society or assemblage of persons which teaches, advocates or affirmatively suggests the doctrine of criminal syndicalism, sabotage, or the necessity, propriety or expediency of doing any act of physical violence or the commission of any crime or unlawful act as a means of accomplishing or effecting any industrial or political ends, change or revolution or for profits, is guilty of a felony, and upon conviction thereof shall be punished by imprisonment in the state penitentiary for a term of not less than one year nor more than ten years, or by a fine of not more than $1,000, or by both such imprisonment and fine.

§ 4. The owner, lessee, agent, superintendent or person in charge or occupation of any place, building, room or rooms, or structure, who knowingly permits therein any assembly or consort of persons prohibited by the provisions of section 3 of this act, or who after notification by authorized public or peace officer that the place or premises, or any part thereof, is or are so used, permits such use to be continued, is guilty of a misdemeanor and punishable upon conviction thereof by imprisonment in the county jail for not less than sixty days nor for not more than one year, or by a fine of not less than $100, nor more than $500, or by both such imprisonment and fine.

§ 5. It appearing that there is a very active element within this state which is determined if possible to overthrow our exist- existing political structure, destroy our industrial and economic institutions, disrupt our labor organizations, and bring ruin and chaos to our people, by organizing all lawless and dissatisfied elements which they may be able to gather here, and teach, instruct and incite crime and destroy property, this act is necessary for the immediate preservation of the public peace, health and safety; and an emergency is hereby declared to exist and this act shall take effect and be in force immediately upon its approval by the governor.

Approved by the governor February 3, 1919.

Filed in the office of the secretary of state February 3, 1919.

PENNSYLVANIA
No. 275

AN ACT

Defining sedition, and prescribing the punishment therefor.

Section 1. Be it enacted, etc., That the word " sedi- <small>Sedition.</small> tion," as used in this act, shall mean:

Any writing, publication, printing, cut, cartoon, <small>Definition.</small> utterance, or conduct, either individually or in connection or combination with any other person or persons, which tends:

(a) To make or cause to be made any outbreak or demonstration of violence against this State or against the United States.

(b) To encourage any person or persons to take any measures or engage in any conduct with a view of overthrowing or destroying or attempting to overthrow or destroy, by any force or show or threat of force, the Government of this State or of the United States.

(c) To incite or encourage any person or persons to commit any overt act with a view to bringing the

Government of this State or of the United States into hatred or contempt.

(d) To incite any person or persons to do or attempt to do personal injury or harm to any officer of this State or of the United States, or to damage or destroy any public property or the property of any public official because of his official position.

It shall also include:

(e) The actual damage to, or destruction of, any public property, or the property of any public official, perpetrated because the owner or occupant is in official position.

(f) Any writing, publication, printing, cut, cartoon, or utterance which advocates or teaches the duty, necessity, or propriety of engaging in crime, violence, or any form of terrorism, as a means of accomplishing political reform or change in government.

(g) The sale, gift, or distribution of any prints, publications, books, papers, documents, or written matter in any form, which advocates, furthers, or teaches sedition as hereinbefore defined.

(h) Organizing or helping to organize or becoming a member of an assembly, society, or group, where any of the policies or purposes thereof are seditious as hereinbefore defined.

Felony.
Penalty.

§ 2. Sedition, as defined in section one of this act, shall be a felony, and any person convicted thereof shall be sentenced to a fine of not less than one hundred dollars ($100) and not more than ten thousand dollars ($10,000), and to imprisonment not exceeding twenty years, either or both, in the discretion of the court.

Repeal.

§ 3. All acts or parts of acts inconsistent herewith be, and the same are hereby, repealed.

Approved — The 26th day of June, A. D. 1919.

WM. C. SPROUL.

The foregoing is a true and correct copy of the Act of the General Assembly No. 275.

CYRUS E. WOODS,
Secretary of the Commonwealth.

RHODE ISLAND
January Session, 1919 — Chapter 1771.
H. 947. A.

Approved April 24, 1919.

AN ACT

To protect the Government of the State of Rhode Island and the Government of the United States of America.

It is enacted by the General Assembly as follows:

Section 1. Any person who shall wilfully speak, utter, print, write or publish any language intended to incite, provoke or encourage forceful resistance to the State of Rhode Island or to the United States of America or a defiance or disregard of the Constitution or laws of the State of Rhode Island or of the United States, or shall advocate any change, alteration or modification in the form of government of the State of Rhode Island or of the United States except in the manner provided by the Constitution or the laws of the State of Rhode Island or by the Constitution or the laws of the United States or shall advocate any change in the form of government of the State of Rhode Island or of the United States by means of revolution or violence or shall advocate the assassination of persons occupying public positions or offices created by the Constitution and laws of the State of Rhode Island or of the United States, or shall advocate, incite, provoke or encourage the destruction, burning, blowing up, or damaging of any public or private property as a part or incident of a programme of force, violence or revolution, having for its purpose the overthrow of the form of government of the State of Rhode Island, or of the United States, or shall wilfully display publicly any flag or emblem, except the flag of the United States, as symbolic or emblematic of the government of the United States or of a form of government proposed by its adherents or supporters as superior or preferable to the form of government of the United States as prescribed by the Constitution of the United States shall be guilty

Penalty for inciting against the government of the state or the United States, etc.

of a felony and upon conviction be punished by a fine of not more than $10,000 or imprisonment not exceeding ten years or both.

Penalty for teaching, etc., anarchy, etc., or assault or killing of government officials, etc.

§ 2. Any person who shall wilfully teach or advocate anarchy or the overthrow by force or violence of the Government of the State of Rhode Island or of the United States, or of all forms of law, or opposition to organized government, or any person who shall wilfully become a member of or affiliated with any organization teaching and advocating disbelief in or opposition to organized government, or advocating or teaching the duty, necessity or propriety of the unlawful assaulting or killing of any officer or officers, either of specific individuals or of officers generally of the Government of the State of Rhode Island or of the United States, or of any organized government because of his or their official character, or advocating or teaching the unlawful destruction of property, shall be guilty of a felony and upon conviction shall be punishable by a fine of not more than $10,000 or imprisonment not exceeding ten years or both.

Penalty for conspiring to violate any of the provisions of this act.

§ 3. If two or more persons conspire to violate any of the provisions of sections 1 and 2 of this act and one or more of such persons does any act to effect the object of the conspiracy each of the parties to said conspiracy shall be guilty of a felony and upon conviction shall be punished by a fine of not more than $10,000 or imprisonment not exceeding ten years or both.

Certain meetings may be dispersed as unlawful assemblies.

§ 4. Any meeting at which any of the things forbidden in sections 1 and 2 of this act are advocated, taught or discussed, or any meeting called for the purpose of advocating, teaching or discussing any of the things forbidden by sections 1 and 2 of this act is hereby declared to be an unlawful assembly and may be dispersed in the manner provided for dispersing of riotous, tumultuous and treasonable assemblies in section 7 of Chapter 341 of the General Laws.

§ 5. This act shall take effect upon its passage, and all acts and parts of acts inconsistent herewith are hereby repealed.

SOUTH DAKOTA
CRIMINAL SYNDICALISM

CHAPTER 38
(S. B. 12)
RELATING TO CRIMINAL SYNDICALISM.

AN ACT

Entitled, An Act Defining Criminal Syndicalism, Prohibiting the Advocacy thereof, and of Crime, Sabotage and Violence or other Methods of Terrorism, or the Destruction of Life or Property, for the Accomplishment of Social, Economic, Industrial or Political Ends, Prohibiting Assembles for the Advocacy of Such Purposes, Making it Unlawful to Permit the Use of any Place, Building or Structure for Such Assemblies, and Fixing the Penalties for a Violation of the Provisions of this Act.

Be it enacted by the Legislature of the State of South Dakota:

1. Criminal Syndicalism is hereby defined as any doctrine or practice which teaches, practice or advocates crime, sabotage (sabotage as used in this act means willful and malicious damage or injury to the property of another), violence or other methods of terrorism, or the destruction of life or property, for the accomplishment of social, economic, industrial or political ends. The advocacy, teaching, support, practice or furtherance of any such doctrine, whether by act, speech or writing, or by any means or in any manner whatsoever, is hereby declared to be a felony and punishable as such, as in this act provided.

Any person or persons who shall, by act, or speech, or in writing, or by symbol, precept, suggestion, example or illustration, advocate, suggest or teach the duty, necessity or propriety of crime, sabotage, violence or other methods of terrorism, or the destruction of life or property for the accomplishment of social, economic, industrial or political ends, or shall print, publish, utter, sell or circulate; distribute or have in his or her possession, or display any book, paper, document, writing or article in any form which shall contain, or advocate, advise, teach or suggest, any doctrine that social economic, industrial or political ends should be brought about by crime, sabotage, violence, or other means of terrorism, with intent to suggest, exemplify, illustrate, spread or advocate any of the doctrines of criminal syndicalism, or shall organize or assist in the organization, or become a member of, or assemble with, any persons, societies, associations, groups or assemblages of persons formed for or engaged in the teaching or advocacy of any of the doctrines of criminal syndicalism, or who shall, directly or indirectly, through or by the use of any liquid, compound, chemical, or artificial or mechanical apparatus or current or other device whatsoever, in any manner destroy, or attempt to destroy, contribute to or cause the destruction of life or property of any description, or who shall have in his possession any liquid, compound, chemical or artificial or mechanical device whatsoever, with intent to destroy life or property, in the pursuance or furtherance of any of the doctrines of criminal syndicalism as defined in this act, shall upon conviction be deemed guilty of a felony and shall be punished by imprisonment in the state penitentiary for not less than one nor more than twenty-five years, or by a fine of not less than $1,000 nor more than $10,000, or by both such fine and imprisonment, in the discretion of the court.

2. Wherever two or more persons assemble for the purpose of advocating or teaching, or suggesting or illustrating, in any manner whatsoever, any doctrine of criminal syndicalism, or of any of the acts defined or referred to in section 1 of this act, such assemblage shall be unlawful, and every person participating therein by his presence or who shall aid or in any manner instigate the holding of such an assemblage, shall upon conviction be guilty of a felony and shall be punished by imprisonment in the state prison for not less than one nor more than twenty-five years, or by a fine of not less than $1,000 nor more than $10,000, or by both such fine and imprisonment, in the discretion of the court.

3. Any owner, agent, custodian, occupant, or superintendent of any place, room, structure or building, who shall permit therein any assemblage of persons for any of the purposes prohibited by the provisions of this act, or who, after notification that the said place, room, structure or building are so used, shall permit such to continue, shall be deemed guilty of a felony and shall be punished by imprisonment in the state penitentiary for not less than one year nor more than twenty-five years, or by a fine of not less than $1,000 nor more than $10,000, or by both such fine and imprisonment in the discretion of the court.

4. Whereas, There is now no law in this state defining and **prohibiting**, and providing a penalty for, the offenses described

in this act and the passage of this statute is necessary for the public safety and convenience of the people of this state and the preservation of the state government, therefore, an emergency is hereby declared to exist and this act shall take effect and be in force from and after its passage and approval.

Approved March 23, 1918.

WEST VIRGINIA
House Bill No. 104

By W. S. JOHN, of Monongalia County.

Passed February 13, 1919

Including Mr. John's statement in House of Delegates and communication addressed to the United Mine Workers of America by friends of labor in the House of Delegates.

AN ACT

To foster the ideals, institutions and government of West Virginia and of the United States, and to prohibit the teaching of doctrines and display of flags antagonistic to the form or spirit of their constitutions and laws.

Be it enacted by the Legislature of West Virginia:

Section 1. It shall be unlawful for any person to speak, print, publish or communicate, by language, sign, picture, or otherwise, any teachings, doctrines or counsels in sympathy or favor of ideals, institutions or forms of government hostile, inimical or antagonistic to those now or hereafter existing under the constitution and laws of this state or the United States, or in sympathy or favor of the propriety, duty or necessity of crime, violence or other unlawful methods of terrorism as a means of accomplishing economic or political reform, or in sympathy or favor of the overthrow of organized society, the unlawful destruction of property or the violation of law.

§ 2. It shall be unlawful for any person to have in his possession or to display any red or black flag, or to display any other flag, emblem, device or sign of any nature whatever indicating sympathy or support of ideals, institutions or forms of government, hostile, inimical or antagonistic to the form or spirit of the constitution, laws, ideals and institutions of this state or the United States.

§ 3. Any person violating any of the provisions of this act shall, for the first offense, be guilty of a misdemeanor, and, upon conviction, shall be fined not less than one hundred nor more than five hundred dollars, or imprisoned in the county jail not exceeding twelve months, or both, and, for the second offense, shall be guilty of a felony, and, upon conviction, shall be confined in the penitentiary not less than one nor more than five years.

PROCEEDINGS IN HOUSE OF DELEGATES

The following is part of the proceedings in the House of Delegates of February 14, 1919:

Mr. John rose to the right of personal privilege and stated the following, which is ordered printed in the Journal.

"In order to correct the evident misunderstanding on the part of individuals and labor unions in this state as to the purpose and meaning of House Bill No. 104, I desire, as its author, to make a statement of record. The measure has become known as the loyalty, or anti-red flag act. It forbids the teaching of doctrines hostile, inimical and antagonistic to the constitutions and ideals of our nation and state; it bars violence and terrorism; and it upholds the stars and stripes as the one flag of our freedom. It has received the unanimous votes of both branches of this legislature.

"Notwithstanding its noble purpose and unquestionable ground, the members of this legislature have received requests, nay, even demands, ostensibly in the name and on behalf of labor unions, that it be defeated. At this are we not surprised or alarmed? And must we not now again declare our judgment in its wisdom and defend its patriotism?

"On many measures we have united on the basis of honest service and fair reward, mutual rights and mutual helpfulness — the common grounds on which both industry and employees must succeed and without which both must fail. It is the purpose of this measure, as every serious thinking citizen must admit, to prevent the threatening cloud of Bolshevism from gathering over the industries which capital and labor alike must foster in order to secure prosperity, peace and orderly progress. The thwarting of that menace by this measure is the greatest blessing which this legislature has brought to all honest labor.

"Behind the red flag marches treason and disorder. No one has stepped forth from beneath the red flag to enlist in the ranks of the loyal boys who have gloriously upheld our democratic freedom upon the battle fields. The great menace of our state and nation is from those who preach the overthrow of our constitutions and laws and disregard for the flag. Freedom of speech is not the right to destroy the constitution or insult the stars and stripes. It is only the right to stand for the democracy.

"There is no common ground on which we can meet or treat with treasonable acts. There is no place in West Virginia or America for disloyalty and anarchy, with their consequent assassination and annihilation of the constitutions and ideals of our nation and state. There is no field of usefulness here, in the hours of reconstruction and Americanization, for mistaken or misguiding leadership of our men of brawn and toil. There shall be no toleration of the inflaming flag, the incendiary torch, the assassinating dagger.

"Let no man falter here. Sooner shall we die in defense of our nation's flag than recede one jot or title from the high ground we have here taken. Today and tomorrow, let us watch lest we forget, lest we forget, the undying valor of American sons, the memory of their service and lives and the honor of the fathers and mothers who gave them to the world for freedom. Our nation and state must rise in might ere their foreign born refugees or their citizens of treason shall tear down our flag and raise the bloody banner of the Bolsheviki and set the flaming torch of anarchy at the foot of our constitutions, destroying the rights and ideals which all worthy labor loyally upholds.

"We stand for one nation, with one constitution and one flag."

Mr. Starcher presented the following communication, which was read by the Clerk and ordered printed in the Journal:

"CHARLESTON, W. VA., *February* 14, 1919.

To the United Mine Workers of America in Special Convention Assembled:

"In pursuance with the request of your committee, we, the undersigned members of the House of Delegates who are card members of labor unions, submit the following in reply to the question put to us by your convention as to why we supported House Bill No. 104, known as the 'Red Flag Bill.'

"The bill was introduced in the House by Mr. John on January sixteenth (see House Journal, page fifty-six). It was referred to the Judiciary Committee, reported back with the recommendation that it do pass, and it passed the House on January thirtieth, by a vote of eighty-one for and none against the bill. (See House Journal January thirtieth, page sixteen.)

"The bill was under consideration in the House for fourteen days, during which period not a single representative of organized labor even mentioned the bill to any of us, nor did any other individual.

"It was reported to the Senate on January thirtieth, and passed that body on February tenth, by a vote of twenty-eight for and none against the bill. (See Senate Journal, page thirty-three, of that date.)

"The bill was under consideration a period of twenty-five days, and each day organized labor had its paid representatives here to watch legislation and to protest against any measure deemed unfair to our interests. We heard of no opposition to the bill from any source, and we were not approached by anyone until your special convention had been called. All of this time we were standing as a unit in striving to pass progressive legislation. Fifteen labor bills had then been introduced by the so-called labor group of the House.

"This statement of the progress of the bill is made because you are entitled to complete information. It is not made, however, as an excuse for our support of the bill. The title of the bill sets out clearly its purpose. It intends to safeguard our institutions and to protect our ideals and traditions against hostile forces within, who are unfriendly to a republican form of government and to repel foreign invasion, usurpation and invasion of evil influences from without. To this end section one of the bill makes it unlawful to use crime, violence or terrorism in an effort to change the constitution; to overthrow the established order, or to subvert the common rights.

"We do not believe that the bill abridges the right of free speech, or that it locks the lips of thought. It will protect all citizens alike, and follow the trades-union member in his support of the common good. It will only hinder the I. W. W.'s and anarchists. If any effort is made to divert its course, we rely upon the constitution of West Virginia and the United States, both with confidence and security, realizing that no act of the legislature can suspend the organic law. Further, we have endeavored to so conduct ourselves as members of the House so as to win the confidence of the courts and of the people in behalf of organized labor.

"Section two makes it unlawful to display the red flag, the black flag, or any other emblem in preference to the the flag of the Republic, or as an evidence of revolt against government and the constituted authorities. With this sentiment we are in hearty accord. As members of the legislature we took an oath to support the constitution of the United States and of the state of West Virginia, and to give full allegiance thereto.

"We look upon our form of government as the grandest in its conception; the most perfect in its organization, and the most just in its administration of any form of government in the world. 'Old Glory' is the emblem of the government. It has no peer in the realm of colors, and no equal as the champion of liberty, fraternity and equality. Its spirit of kinship with struggling peoples is broad enough to embrace world-wide democracy. Sixty thousand of your fellow craftsmen marched proudly under it with two million American soldiers during the war. Thousands of them offered the last supreme sacrifice that the 'Flag of the Free' might wave in triumph. Under its folds they struck down autocracy in the old world, dethroned a Caesar, and laid the foundation for the establishment of universal equity. It will likewise humble autocratic power in whatever form it raises its head in the new world.

"Organized labor is not afraid to trust the people. The American Federation of Labor performed a great task of patriotic duty when it set its face hard against I. W. W.-ism, Bolshevism and those forces of destruction which believe in 'sabotage' direct action and who seek to destroy the confidence of the people in the government, and would overthrow it if they had the power.

"We rejoice that the administration at Washington is deporting these advocates of terrorism from the country.

These forces are constantly working to misdirect the labor movement and the man or woman who marches under the 'red flag' is in full sympathy with their program.

"It is our deliberate judgment that we would have made a mistake if we had opposed House Bill No. 104. We would have placed organized labor in an unhappy light, and have reflected on both your loyalty and intelligence by failing to support the measure.

"All of which is submitted from your brother workmen to the calm judgment, undoubted loyalty and wise discretion of the convention.

"Fraternally yours,
G. R. BLIZZARD,
 (U. M. W. of A.)
A. F. SHOMO,
 (A. M. W. of A.)
O. W. FITCH,
 (O. A. of M.)
K. H. STOVER,
 (O. R. F. 82)
J. V. COLEMAN,
 (U. M. W. of A.)
W. E. STARCHER,
 (U. C. T.)
ORVILLE HACKNEY,
HARRY A. WEISS,
 (A. A. J. S. T. W.)
GEO. B. HENDRICKS,
J. G. O'CONNOR,
 (Vice Chairman B. of L. E. General Committee.)
J. R. MILLER,
 (Fairmont District No. 472, O. R. C.)
G. T. BANNISTER,
 (Division 594, O. R. C.)
E. J. CLEMENTS,
 (2681, Ward, W. Va.)
J. Q. MUSSER,
J. W. MOULDS,
 (O. R. T., Division 17)."

CHAPTER III
Federal Action in Deportations

One of the most effective means of dealing with aliens resident in this country who urge the violent, forcible or unlawful overthrow of the institutions of this government, or of organized government elsewhere, is deportation. The statutes dealing with this subject are broad and comprehensive, and *if properly enforced,* deportation is probably the most effective way of dealing with the alien agitator who comes to this country and, without a proper comprehension of our institutions, seeks to impress upon others the idea that our form of government should be overthrown and some other form of government, such as the type illustrated by the Soviet government of Russia, substituted in place thereof. We give at the close of this chapter those portions of the United States Immigration Laws bearing upon deportation which should be read in connection with this chapter.

There has been considerable agitation on the part of liberals, including some well-meaning, but misinformed ministers of the gospel, concerning the right of the United States to order the deportation of undesirable aliens; and though, in the case of these deportations — notably among those on what has been termed the " Soviet Ark," the Buford, every right of the deportees was safeguarded, and the provisions of law pertaining to these cases, strictly complied with — these misguided critics of the right to deportation would have it appear that the deportees in question were not accorded every right that they were entitled to.

In the Japanese Immigration case (189 U. S. 86–97), Mr. Justice Harlan, speaking of the laws providing for the deportation of aliens, said:

" The constitutionality of the legislation in question in its general aspects is no longer open to discussion in this court. That Congress may exclude aliens of a particular race from the United States, prescribe the terms and conditions upon which certain classes of aliens may come to this country, establish regulations for sending out of the country such aliens as come here in violation of the law, and commit the enforcements of such provisions, conditions and regulations *exclusively to executive officers without judicial intervention* are principles firmly established by decisions of this court."

In the case of Fong Yue Ting v. United States, 149 U. S., 711, the Supreme Court of the United States said:

"The power to exclude aliens and the power to expel them rest upon one foundation, are derived from one source, are supported by the same reasons, and are in truth but parts of one and the same power."

And in the same case:

"The order of deportation is not a banishment for crime, it is not a banishment in the sense in which that word is often applied to the expulsion of the citizen from his country by way of punishment. It is but a method of enforcing the return to his own country of the alien who has not complied with the conditions upon the performance of which the government of the nation, acting within its constitutional authority, and through the proper departments, has determined that his continuing to reside here shall depend. He has not, therefore, been deprived of life, liberty or property, without due process of law; and the provisions of the Constitution securing the right of trial by jury and prohibiting unreasonable searches and seizures and unusual punishments have no application."

Of particular interest is the case of United States ex rel. Turner v. Williams, 194 U. S. 279, in which the Supreme Court of the United States, Mr. Chief Justice Fuller writing the opinion, reviewed the laws pertaining to deportation and the theory upon which this very salutory method of ridding this country of undesirable aliens is put into effect. In the hearing before the Board of Inquiry which was had on October 24, 1903, it appeared that Turner was an Englishman who had then been in the United States but ten days. He delivered a lecture in New York City on October 23 in which he declared himself to be an anarchist, and in the course of which he urged the general strike in the following language:

"Just imagine what a universal tie-up would mean. What would it mean in New York City alone if this idea of solidarity were spread through the city? If no work was being done, if it were Sunday for a week or a fortnight, life in New York would be impossible, and the workers, gaining audacity, would refuse to recognize the authority of their employers and eventually take to themselves the handling of industries. . . . All over Europe they are preparing for a general strike, which will spread over the entire industrial world. Everywhere the employees are organizing, and to meet, at any rate, as an anarchist, as one who believes that the people should emancipate themselves, I look forward to this struggle as an opportunity for the workers to assert the power that is really theirs."

Among the papers found on Turner when he was arrested was one dealing with "The legal murder of 1887," meaning the Chicago anarchist trial, of that date, another one on "The Essentials of Anarchism," and notices of meetings, one of a mass meeting for November 9th at which "speeches will be delivered by John Turner in English, John Most in German, and several other speakers."

Excerpts from the opinion of Mr. Chief Justice Fuller in this case are here quoted:

"Whether rested on the accepted principle of international law that every sovereign nation had the power, as inherent in sovereignty and essential to self-preservation, to forbid the entrance of foreigners within its dominions or to admit them only in such cases and upon such conditions as it may see fit to prescribe; or on the power to regulate commerce with foreign nations, which includes the entrance of ships, the importation of goods, and the bringing of persons into the ports of the United States, the act before us is not open to constitutional objection. And while we held in *Wong Wing* v. *United States, supra,* a certain provision of an immigration law invalid on that ground, this act does not come within the ruling.

"In that case Mr. Justice Shiras, speaking for the court, said: 'We regard it as settled by our previous decisions that the United States can, as a matter of public policy, by congressional enactment, forbid aliens or classes of aliens from coming within their borders, and expel aliens or classes of aliens from their territory, and can, in order to make effectual such decree of exclusion or expulsion, devolve the power and duty of identifying and arresting the persons included in such decree, and causing their deportation, upon executive or subordinate officials.'

". . . The language of the act is 'Anarchists, or persons who believe in or advocate the overthrow by force or violence of the Government of the United States or of all government or of all forms of law or the assassination of public officials.' If this should be construed as defining the word 'anarchists,' by the words which follow, or as used in the popular sense above given, it would seem that when an alien arrives in this country, who avows himself to be an Anarchist, without more, he accepts the definition. And we suppose counsel does not deny that this government has the power to exclude an alien who believes in or advocates the overthrow of the government or of all governments by force or the assassination of officials. To put that question is to answer it.

"And if the judgment of the board and the secretary was that Turner came within the act as thus construed, we cannot hold as a matter of law that there was no evidence on which that conclusion could be rested. Even if Turner, though he did not so state to the board, only regarded the absence of government as a political ideal, yet when he sought to attain it by advocating, not simply for the benefit of workingmen, who are justly entitled to repel the charge of desiring the destruction of law and order, but ' at any rate, as an anarchist,' the universal strike to which he referred, and by discourses on what he called 'The Legal Murder of 1887,' *Spies* v. *People,* 122 Ill. 1, and by addressing mass meetings on that subject in association with *Most, Reg.* v. *Most,* 7 Q. B. Div., 244; *People* v. *Most,* 171 N. Y. 423, we cannot say that the inference was unjustifiable, either that he contemplated the ultimate realization of his ideal by the use of force, or that his speeches were incitements to that end.

"If the word 'anarchists' should be interpreted as including aliens whose anarchistic views are professed as those of political philosophers innocent of evil intent, it would follow that Congress was of opinion that the tendency of the general exploitation of such views is so dangerous to the public weal that aliens who hold and advocate them would be undesirable additions to our population, whether permanently or temporarily, whether many or few, and, in the light of previous decisions, the act, even in this aspect, would not be unconstitutional, or inapplicable to any alien who is opposed to all organized government.

"We are not to be understood as deprecating the vital importance of freedom of speech and of the press, or as suggesting limitations on the spirit of liberty, in itself unconquerable, but this case does not involve those considerations. The flaming brand which guards the realm where no human government is needed still bars the entrance; and as long as human governments endure they cannot be denied the power of self-preservation, as that question is presented here."

By a recent ruling of the Department of Commerce and Labor based upon an analysis of the manifesto of the Communist Party of America, very ably prepared by Mr. Assistant Attorney-General Francis P. Garvan, the members of that party are subject to deportation upon proof of membership therein. This follows a similar ruling with regard to the Union of Russian Workers. A number, both of the Union of Russian Workers, and members of the Communist Party, have recently been deported, some of whom have been turned over to the immigration authorities through the efforts of this Committee.

The Congress of the United States has been much concerned with reference to this question of deportation. In the course of a hearing held before the committee on Immigration and Naturalization of the House of Representatives on October 22, 1919, the Hon. Walter H. Newton, a representative in Congress from the State of Minnesota, in discussing a bill proposed by him used the following language:

"Gentlemen of the committee, in common with a great many other Americans I have noticed that during the late war, whereas a great bulk of our citizens of foreign birth loyally supported the Government, there were some who did not do so. Of that number a percentage of them spent their time in endeavoring to get others to avoid military service, and as the result of the efforts of those agitators, including some who were of native birth, quite a number of aliens living in this country, and who had lived in this country for some time, enjoying all of our privileges and benefits, early besought themselves to find out some way of getting out of performing the obligations and duties that they owed to a country in which they lived and enjoyed the protection of its laws and benefits and opportunities.

"My information is that something like 210,000 aliens, otherwise liable to the draft, either withdrew their citizenship papers, having declared their intention of becoming citizens, or while registering with the draft board claimed exemption from service because of the fact that they were born across the seas and were not fully naturalized citizens. . . .

"I do go on the assumption that the American people have formed a government that is the best government in the world, one that is being looked up to and has been for over a century as the place where the people can best find expression in government. I go upon the assumption and the knowledge that there are people in this world, over in Russia especially, who seek to set up an entirely different form of the government; that they are not only seeking to do it in Russia, but as the Bolshevist hearings in the Senate showed they are using their money propagandizing the Soviet idea over here in this country, and doing it with skillful men, and it has gone to the point where even employes of our Postal Service have gotten some of the ideas. In the State convention of the Minnesota Federation of Labor they introduced a resolution of sympathy with the Soviet government."

In some of the criticisms of the policies of the Federal government in ordering the deportation of so-called "philosophical anarchists" objection is made to the deportation of these individuals on the ground that they have not actually committed an overt act of violence and, therefore, should not be deported upon the fallacious theory that these men and women are being punished "for their opinions." That there is no merit to this proposition was the gist of a decision by Hon. John C. Knox, United States District Judge, in the case of Frank R. Lopez. Judge Knox said:

"The relator objects to his deportation upon the ground that since he is a 'philosophical anarchist' rather than the type which believe in assassination and other violence for the accomplishment of their ends, he does not come within the class of persons denounced by the Immigration Act of February 5, 1917.

"The opportunity is thus afforded me to enter upon an expression of my views as to the varying degrees of anarchy with which society is more or less afflicted. However, I shall refrain and content myself solely with the observation that in my judgment, the very theory of anarchy is opposed to that of organized government. The theory of anarchy and that of government must all times be in conflict, and I cannot believe that the philosophical anarchist, at least so far as his ultimate purpose is concerned, is any less dangerous than is the advocate of violence. Indeed, in a sense, the insidious character of the teachings of the one is more to be feared than are the teachings, and activities of the other. It may be that I am lacking in liberality of thought, but I am unable to divorce my mind from the idea that the doctrinnaire who spreads his doctrine that all forms of government as we know them shall be subverted to a so-called citizenry of the world is an anarchist and as such comes within both the terms and spirit of the Act of Congress upon the subject, and that such person may lawfully be excluded from the country. I find no merit in the technical objections raised. The conclusion that the relator has been found advocating and teaching anarchy is amply sustained by the record and the writ of habeas corpus will accordingly be dismissed.

"JOHN KNOX,
"December 9, 1918. U. S. D. J."

During the past two years several denaturalization proceedings have been instituted on the ground that the defendant's final citizenship papers had been secured by fraud and were, therefore, voidable under section 15 of the Act of June 29, 1906, providing a uniform rule for the naturalization of aliens. One case was that of Frederick W. Wursterbarth, a naturalized German native. The decision of Judge Haight, United States District Judge for the District of New Jersey, is, we believe, of sufficient interest to warrant quotation here in full.

The decision of Judge Haight follows:

"This is a proceeding instituted by the United States attorney for this district under section 15 of the Naturalization Act of June 29, 1906 (34 Stat. L. 596, 601, c. 3592; Comp. St. 1916, Sec. 4374), to cancel a certificate of citizenship granted to Frederick W. Wursterbarth, the respondent, by the Court of Common Pleas of the County of Passaic, in the State of New Jersey, on the ground that it was fraudulently and illegally procured. The certicate was issued on November 3, 1882; the respondent being a native of Germany and a subject of the German Emperor. The fraud alleged is that the respondent declared under oath that he absolutely and entirely renounced and abjured all allegiance and fidelity to any sovereignty, and particularly to the Emperor of Germany, whereas in fact he did not do so, but on the contrary, retained an allegiance to Germany and its ruler. The matter has come on for hearing on the issues raised by the petition of the district attorney (to which were attached affidavits supporting its allegations), and the answer of the respondent. Upon the hearing the government proved, in substance, the following facts, viz.:

"Within a few days after the outbreak of the present war between the United States and the German Empire, the respondent was approached by two ladies interested in a local chapter of the American Red Cross, in an effort to induce him to contribute money to that organization, upon which appeal the respondent became angry, and replied in substance that he would not do so, that he would do nothing to injure the country in which he had been born, brought up, and educated. Subsequently, in the month of June following another woman, who was likewise interested in the same chapter of the American Red Cross, visited him, and asked him to become a member. He angrily refused to do so, stating that he would give no money to send soldiers to the country where he was born and educated, and, in reply to some arguments which the solicitor advanced, stated that she did not know what it meant to be born in a country, and then have men go over and fight against that country. In the month of November, 1917, the respondent was approached by two gentlemen, in an effort to induce him to subscribe to the funds which the Young Men's Christian Association was then raising for war work. At that time he stated he would do nothing to help defeat Germany and in response to a question as to whether he did not want America to win the war, he replied that he did not, that he had relatives in Germany. He made the same rejoinder to the question as to whether he did not want the American soldiers in camp and cantonments to be well taken care of; and, in reply to a statement made to him that he was better off than most Americans, he replied that he only came to this country on a vacation or visit. . . .

"The question, therefore, on which the decision of this case depends, is whether it may be legitimately inferred as a fact, from his present state of mind, coupled with the circumstances to be hereinafter referred to, that he was of the same mind at the time he took the oath of allegiance and renunciation. In that aspect the case is one of first impression, so far as I am informed, or have been able to ascertain. It must be borne in mind that the respondent did not express any dissatisfaction with the aims and purposes of this country in the present war, or with the reasons which had induced Congress to declare war, but that he boldly took the position that he would do nothing to injure the country of his birth, and did not wish this country to win the present war, because of the ties which bound him to Germany. As the year succeeding his naturalization passed, coupled with the fact that he continued to dwell in our midst, associated with our citizens, receive the benefits which this nation and its institutions have conferred upon him, acquire property here, and hold public office (as the proofs show that he did), it is natural to presume that his affection and feeling of loyalty and allegiance to this country would increase, and that any ties which bound him to the country from which he came would correspondingly decrease.

"If, therefore, under such circumstances, after thirty-five years, he now recognizes an allegiance to the sovereignty of his origin, superior to his allegiance to this country, it seems to me that it is not only permissible to infer from that fact, but that the conclusion is irresistible, that at the time he took the oath of renunciation, he did so with a mental reservation as to the country of his birth, and retained towards that country an allegiance which the laws of this country required him to renounce before he could become one of its citizens. Indeed, for the reasons just stated, his allegiance to the former must at that time have been stronger than it is at present. Whatever presumption might otherwise arise in his favor from the apparent fact that during the intervening years he has lived as a good citizen of this country is of no weight when it is considered that nothing has happened during that time to call forth a manifestation of his reserved allegiance, and that as soon as something did happen, i. e., the war between this country and Germany, he immediately manifested it."

Attorney-General Gregory of the United States, in the Report of the Attorney-General for the Year 1918, referring to these proceedings, at p. 39 of said report, says:

" The department reached the conclusion, however, that in certain individual cases these utterances (disloyal utterances of naturalized citizens) were of a character which demonstrated that the naturalized citizen had never in good faith renounced his allegiance to the country of his origin. . . . The successful outcome of these early litigations, and the accompanying wide publicity, had a marked effect upon naturalized citizens of disloyal tendency throughout the country, and greatly lessened the volume of these utterances."

This Committee desires to express the opinion that the Attorney-General of the United States rendered a signal public service in rounding up the anarchists, communists, and members of the Union of Russian Workers who were recently deported on the "Buford." We believe that the misinformed or misguided persons in the community who have deprecated the efforts of the Attorney-General in connection with this matter are giving aid and comfort and encouragement to the radical agitator who would unlawfully overthrow our existing institutions.

FEDERAL STATUTES

The existing federal statutes with regard to the subject of Criminal Anarchy are not as comprehensive as the Criminal Anarchy statute of the State of New York. Aside from the provisions of the Espionage Act (Act of June 15, 1917, Chap. 30, title 1, par. 1, as amended by the Act of May 16, 1917, Chap. 75, par. 1), and the proclamation issued by the President on April 16, 1917, reciting the acts which the courts of the United States have declared to be treasonable, the only pertinent provision of the Federal Criminal Code is sec. 10170 of the United States Compiled Statutes, Criminal Code, sec. 6, which provides as follows:

Seditious conspiracy; punishment for. If two or more persons in any state or territory, or in any place subject to the jurisdiction of the United States, conspire to overthrow, put down or to destroy by force the government of the United States, or to levy war against them, or to oppose by force the authority thereof, or by force to prevent, hinder, or delay the execution of any law of the United States, or by force to seize, take, or possess any property of the United States contrary to the authority thereof, they shall each be fined not more than five thousand dollars, or imprisoned not more than six years, or both.

Sections 2 and 38 of the Act of March 3, 1903, entitled "An act to regulate the immigration of aliens into the United States," 32 Stat. 1213, c. 1012, are as follows:

Sec. 2. That the following classes of aliens shall be excluded from admission into the United States: All idiots, insane persons, epileptics, and persons who have been insane within five years previous; persons who have had two or more attacks of insanity at any time previously; paupers; persons likely to become a public charge; professional beggars; persons afflicted with a loathsome or with a dangerous contagious disease; persons who have been convicted of a felony or other crime or misdemeanor involving moral turpitude; polygamists, anarchists, or persons who believe in or advocate the overthrow by force or violence of the Government of the United States or of all governments or of all forms of law, or the assassination of public officials; prostitutes, and persons who procure or attempt to bring in prostitutes or women for the purpose of prostitution; those who have been, within one year from the date of application for admission to the United States, deported as being under offers, solicitations, promises or agreements to perform labor or service of some kind therein; and also any person whose ticket or passage is paid for with the money of another, or who is assisted by others to come, unless it is affirmatively and satisfactorily shown that such person does not belong to one of the foregoing excluded classes; but this section shall not be held to prevent persons living in the United States from sending for a relative or friend who is not of the foregoing excluded classes: Provided, That nothing in this act shall exclude persons convicted of an offense purely political, not involving moral turpitude: And provided further, That skilled labor may be imported, if labor of like kind unemployed cannot be found in this country: And provided further, That the provisions of this law applicable to contract labor shall not be held to exclude professional actors, artists, lecturers, singers, ministers of any religious denomination, professors for colleges or seminaries, persons belonging to any recognized learned profession, or persons employed strictly as personal or domestic servants.

Sec. 38. That no person who disbelieves in or who is opposed to all organized government, or who is a member of or affiliated with any organization entertaining and teaching such disbelief in or opposition to all organized government, or who advocates or teaches the duty, necessity, or propriety of the unlawful assaulting or killing of any officer or officers, either of specific individuals or of officers generally, of the government of the United States or of any other organized government, because of his or their official character, shall be permitted to enter the United States or any territory or place subject to the jurisdiction thereof. This section shall be enforced by the Secretary of the Treasury under such rules and regulations as he shall prescribe.

That any person who knowingly aids or assists any such person to enter the United States or any territory or place subject to the jurisdiction thereof, or who connives or conspires with any person or persons to allow, procure, or permit any such person to enter therein, except pursuant to such rules and regulations made by the Secretary of the Treasury, shall be fined not more than five thousand dollars, or imprisoned for not less than one nor more than five years, or both.

By the act of February 14, 1903, 32 Stat. 825, c. 552, " To establish the Department of Commerce and Labor," the jurisdiction, supervision and control possessed and exercised by the Department of the Treasury over the immigration of aliens into the United States were transferred to the Department of Commerce and Labor established by the act, to take effect and be in force the first day of July, 1903.

APPENDIX I

Excerpts from the Immigration Law, Bearing on Deportation, Together With the Amendment of 1918

Section 19. That at any time within five years after entry, any alien who at the time of entry was a member of one or more of the classes excluded by law; any alien who shall have entered or who shall be found in the United States; any alien who at any time after entry shall be found advocating or teaching the unlawful destruction of property, or advocating or teaching anarchy, or the overthrow by force or violence of the Government of the United States or of all forms of law or the assassination of public officials; any alien who within five years after entry becomes a public charge from causes not affirmatively shown to have arisen subsequent to landing; except as hereinafter provided, any alien who is hereafter sentenced to imprisonment for a term of one year or more because of conviction in this country of a crime involving moral turpitude, committed within five years after the entry of the alien to the United States, or who is hereafter, after the entry of the alien to the United States, or who is hereafter sentenced more than once to such a term of imprisonment because of conviction in this country of any crime involving moral turpitude, committed at any time after entry; . . . any alien who was convicted, or who admits the commission, prior to entry, of a felony or other crime or misdemeanor involving moral turpitude; . . . Provided further, That the provision of this section respecting the deportation of aliens convicted of a crime involving moral turpitude shall not apply to one who has been pardoned, nor shall such deportation be made or directed if the court, or the judge thereof, sentencing such alien for such crime shall, at the time of imposing or passing sentence or within thirty days thereafter, due notice having first been given to representatives of the State, make a recommendation to the Secretary of Labor that such alien shall not be deported in pursuance of this act; nor shall any alien convicted as aforesaid be deported until after the termination of his imprisonment: Provided further, That the provisions of this section, with the exceptions hereinbefore noted, shall be applicable to the classes of aliens therein mentioned irrespective of the time of their entry into the United States: Provided further, That the provisions of this section shall also apply to the cases of aliens who come to the mainland of the United States from the insular possessions thereof: Provided further, That any person who shall be arrested under the provisions of this section, on the ground that he has entered or been found in the United States in violation of any other law thereof which imposes on such person the burden of proving his right to enter or remain, and who shall fail to establish the existence of the right claimed, shall be deported to the place specified in such other law. In every case where any person is ordered deported from the United States under the provisions of this act, or of any law or treaty, the decision of the Secretary of Labor shall be final.

Section 20. That the deportation of aliens provided for in this act shall, at the option of the Secretary of Labor, be to the country whence they came or to the foreign port at which such aliens embarked for the United States; or, if such embarkation was for foreign contiguous territory, to the foreign port at which they embarked for such territory; or, if such aliens entered foreign contiguous territory from the United States and later entered the United States, or if such aliens are held by the country from which they entered the United States not to be subjects or citizens of such country, and such country refuses to permit their re-entry, or imposes any condition upon permitting re-entry, then to the country in which they resided prior to entering the country from which they entered the United States. . .

Section 28. That any person who knowingly aids or assists any anarchist or any person who believes in or advocates the overthrow by force or violence of the Government of the United States, or who disbelieves in or is opposed to organized government, or all forms of law, or who advocates the assassination of public officials, or who is a member of or affiliated with any organization entertaining or teaching disbelief in or opposition to organized government, or who advocates or teaches the duty, necessity, or propriety of the unlawful assaulting or killing of any officer or officers, either of specific individuals or of officers generally, of the Government of the United States or of any other organized government, because of his or their official character, to enter the United States, or who connives or conspires with any person or persons to allow, procure, or permit any such anarchist or person aforesaid to enter therein, shall be deemed guilty of a felony, and on conviction thereof shall be punished by a fine of not more than $5,000 or by imprisonment for not more than five years, or both.

Any person who knowingly aids or assists any alien who advocates or teaches the unlawful destruction of property to enter the United States shall be deemed guilty of a misdemeanor and on conviction shall be punished by a fine of not more than $1,000 or by imprisonment for not more than six months, or by both such fine and imprisonment.

IMMIGRATION RULES — SUBDIV. 1 — RULE 22

Subdivision 1. **Classes of warrant cases.**— All cases in which aliens may be arrested and deported are either stated in detail or mentioned in section 19. They fall into the following divisions. With respect to each of these divisions the law is retrospective or not, and the time within which deportation proceedings may be instituted is limited or not, as indicated below.

(a) Any alien who has entered the United States prior to May 1, 1917, and who at the time of entry was a member of any one of the classes excluded under any provision of the Immigration Act of February 20, 1917; limitation five years; retrospective. . . .

(i) Any alien who may be sentenced to imprisonment for a term of one year or more because of conviction in this country of a crime involving moral turpitude, unless such alien has been pardoned or the court or judge sentencing him has recommended to the department, at the time of imposing sentence or within thirty days thereafter, that he be not deported; limitation — that the crime shall have been committed within five years after entry; retrospective with respect to time of entry, but not retrospective with respect to conviction; deportation shall not occur until termination of imprisonment.

(j) Any alien who may be sentenced more than once to imprisonment for a term of one year or more because of conviction in this country of a crime involving moral turpitude, unless such alien has been pardoned or the court or judge sentencing him has recommended to the department, at the time of imposing sentence or within thirty days thereafter, that he be not deported; no limitation; retrospective with respect to time of entry, but not retrospective with respect to conviction; deportation shall not be effected until termination of imprisonment. . . .

(s) Any alien who was convicted or who admits the commission prior to entry of a felony or other crime or misdemeanor involving moral turpitude; no limitation; retrospective.

(t) Any alien who shall be found advocating or teaching the unlawful destruction of property; no limitation; retrospective.

(u) Any alien who shall be found advocating or teaching anarchy, or the overthrow by force or violence of the Government of the United States or of all forms of law or the assassination of public officials; no limitation; retrospective.

The Amendment of October, 1918, provides:

Be it enacted by the Senate and House of Representatives of the United States of America in Congress assembled, That aliens who are anarchists; aliens who believe in or advocating the overthrow by force or violence of the Government of the United States or of all forms of law; aliens who disbelieve in or are opposed to all organized government; aliens who advocate or teach the assassination of public officials; aliens who advocate or teach the unlawful destruction of property; aliens who are members of or affiliated with any organization that entertains a belief in, teaches, or advocates the overthrow by force or violence of the Government of the United States or of all forms of law, or that entertains or teaches disbelief in or opposition to all organized government, or that advocates the duty, necessity, or propriety of unlawful assaulting or killing of any officer or officers, either of specific individuals or of officers generally, of the Government of the United States or of any other organized government, because of his or their official character, or that advocates or teaches the unlawful destruction of property shall be excluded from admission into the United States.

Section 2. That any alien who, at any time after entering the United States, is found to have been at the time of entry, or to have become thereafter, a member of any one of the classes of aliens enumerated in Section 1 of this act, shall, upon the warrant of the Secretary of Labor, be taken into custody and deported in the manner provided in the Immigration Act of February fifth, nineteen hundred and seventeen. The provision of this section shall be applicable to the classes of aliens mentioned in this act irrespective of the time of their entry into the United States.

Section 3. That any alien who shall, after he has been excluded and deported or arrested and deported in pursuance of the provisions of this act, thereafter return to or enter the United States or attempt to return to or enter the United States shall be deemed guilty of a felony, and upon conviction thereof shall be punished by imprisonment for a term of not more than five years; and shall, upon the termination of such imprisonment, be taken into custody, upon the warrant of the Secretary of Labor, and deported in the manner provided in the Immigration Act of February fifth, nineteen hundred and seventeen.

CALENDAR NO. 240

SENATE
Report No. 283.

DEPORTATION OF CERTAIN UNDESIRABLE ALIENS.

October 30, 1919.— Ordered to be printed.

Mr. Dillingham, from the Committee on Immigration, submitted the following:

REPORT

(To accompany H. R. 6750.)

The Committee on Immigration, to whom was referred the bill (H. R. 6750) to deport certain undesirable aliens and to deny readmission to those deported, having considered the same, report favorably thereon with the recommendation that the bill do pass without amendment.

The bill provides for the deportation as undesirable residents of two classes, as follows:

(1) Those alien enemies at present interned as dangerous alien enemies, but not convicted of crime.

(2) Those alien enemies convicted of violation of various acts passed in connection with the war. They may be briefly described by titles as follows:

(a) The espionage act of June 15, 1917, as amended May 16, 1918.

(b) The explosive act of October 6, 1917.

(c) The act of May 22, 1918, to punish passport frauds.

(d) The act of April 20, 1918, to punish acts of injury to or destruction of war materials.

(e) The draft law, authorizing the increase of the Military Establishment, approved May 18, 1917, or any amendments thereto.

(f) The act of February 14, 1917, to punish threats against the President of the United States.

(g) The trading with the enemy act of October 6, 1917, as amended.

(h) Section 6 of the Penal Code, the "seditious conspiracy" section, which provides punishment for conspiracy against the government, the law, or the property of the United States.

(i) Section 37 of the Penal Code, which provides punishment for conspiracy to defraud the United States in any manner or for any purpose.

The necessity for the immediate passage of this measure is indicated by the following letter from the Attorney-General of the United States:

Department of Justice,
Office of the Attorney-General,
Washington, D. C., August 13, 1919.

"Hon. LeBaron B. Colt, *Chairman* Committee on Immigration, United States Senate.

"My Dear Senator Colt.—I respectfully invite your attention to the desirability of the early consideration and passage of H. R. 6750, which adds to the classes of aliens who may be deported after customary hearings and findings by the Secretary of Labor, those who have been interned as dangerous alien enemies during the war or who have been convicted since August 1, 1914, of the violation of certain specified statutes. The bill was passed by the House of Representatives on July 30, 1919, without dissenting votes.

"Four women and approximately 500 men now remain interned as dangerous alien enemies by direction of this department under authority of proclamation issued by the President pursuant to section 4067 of the Revised Statutes of the United States. These alien enemies are detained in internment camps maintained by the War Department at Fort Oglethorpe, Ga., and at Fort Douglas, Utah. Included among these internes are revolutionary radicals, convicted criminals, individuals with long police records, anti-American propagandists, and individuals known to be, or reasonably suspected of being, enemy agents. A relatively small number of these interned profess present loyalty to the United States and, because of family ties or other connections in this country, perhaps should be released when the treaty of peace is ratified. The larger portion of the interned alien enemies, however, in my opinion, should be required to show cause why they should not be returned to their native countries.

"Also there were in excess of 500 pleas of guilty and convictions under the criminal statutes specified in the bill. Some few pardons were granted and there were many commuted sentences. While not all, at least there will be a considerable number of these convicts who, not having been convicted of a crime " involving moral turpitude " whereby they would be brought within the terms of the present laws, nevertheless by reason of the nature of their crimes, in my judgment, should be required to show cause why they should not be deported.

" There is no law now on the statute books under which these persons can be excluded from the country, nor under which they can be detained in custody after the ratification of the treaty of peace. Unless H. R. 6750, or a bill similar in character, is passed, it will become necessary, on the ratification of the treaty of peace, to set free all of these dangerous individuals.

" Respectfully,
"A. MITCHELL PALMER,
"*Attorney-General.*"

SECTION II

ORGANIZED LABOR AND CAPITAL AND INDUSTRIAL PROBLEMS

INTRODUCTION

Chapter	I. Trade Union Organization in the United States, The American Federation of Labor	2106
	II. Organized Labor and Politics	2133
	III. Organized Labor and Socialism	2148
	IV. Socialism in Politics	2151
	V. International Relations of American Organized Labor	2154
	VI. The Four Railroad Brotherhoods and the "Outlaw" Strike	2160
	VII. Organized Labor and Education	2166
	VIII. Employers' Views of Industrial Relations. Welfare Work. Profit Sharing	2174
	IX. Industrial Democracy. Whitley Scheme. John Leitch Plan. Endicott-Johnson Plan. International Harvester Plan	2180
	X. Labor's Solutions. Collective Bargaining. Co-operatives	2193
	XI. British and American Shop Committee Plans	2204
	XII. The Closed Shop and the Open Shop	2216
	XIII. Arbitration in Labor Disputes. Compulsory Arbitration	2226
	XIV. Guild Socialism and National Guilds	2238
	XV. The Plumb Plan	2244
	XVI. Political Programs of the American Federation of Labor and of the Farmers	2251

SECTION II

ORGANIZED LABOR AND CAPITAL AND INDUSTRIAL PROBLEMS

INTRODUCTION

A most important part of this report is considered by the Committee to be that which relates to the constructive elements in the problems which it has been obliged to consider, and of these constructive elements those that relate to the problems of industry are the most complex as well as the most radically vital. In considering them we must view them from three angles: from the angle of organized labor; from that of organized capital of the employer; and, finally, from the point of view of the public.

There are apparently irreconcilable elements in this survey, if one takes merely the viewpoint of one of these parties to the problem.

What the Committee hopes will result from a disinterested examination of the most obvious of these problems, in their essential features, is that no such irreconcilable clash of interests exists, and that a thorough education in the character and history of these problems will help to mitigate present differences of opinion. These and cognate problems require the most careful consideration of members of the Legislature, if they are to appreciate the fields in which radical pressure is being exerted.

As a detailed study will be impossible within these limits, and as any expression of opinion in disputed questions of this sort would be inadvisable, the Committee confines itself to selecting a few central topics illustrating the present preoccupations of labor and capital and the public. But if we are to face the full problem of labor psychology we must make clear the attitude of organized labor toward practical politics, as well as its attitude toward the introduction of economic pressure and mass action. All over the world at present looms the menace to the present political order of a super-government by means of the menace and the actual use of the strike in industries vital to the public welfare. We have seen what the program and tactics of the revolutionary elements are in this field. It is necessary for a complete survey that we should show what is the attitude of the evolutionary elements, especially as represented by the American Federation of Labor.

Our survey will include a brief history of the organization and activities of the American Federation of Labor. It will give its attitude toward the important labor problems, and will publish the text of the principal documents issued by the Federation, beginning with its reconstruction program of 1918 and ending with its pronouncements in connection with the present Presidential campaign.

There are, of course, certain big questions in the relations between Labor and Capital that are a perennial source of discussion, and therefore questions that members of the Legislature should particularly familiarize themselves with. Of these we have selected for elucidation: The Open and Closed Shop; Collective Bargaining; Voluntary and Compulsory Arbitration; Shop Committees and Shop Stewards and their relation to the Unions; Industrial Democracy in its various phases, especially its evolutionary phases; Revolutionary Reconstruction as exemplified in the Guild system; Welfare and Educational Plans by the more enlightened employers, and their attempts to give various forms of representation in business to their employes.

The plan has been to present impartially the differing points of view, without passing judgment.

Back of these problems there lurk two fundamental issues. The first is the general fact recognized by an increasing number of persons as a necessity in any reconstruction program for industry, that is, the duty to give the employe some form of representation in the business in which he is engaged. The second is: To whom shall the workmen entrust the leadership of their cause? Shall it be to a big labor union of the type of the American Federation of Labor, or to a shop committee or group of shop committees? It seems quite natural to many that the workmen in any shop should feel that they are at a disadvantage in their relations with their employer unless they are at liberty to call in from the outside expert advisers, just as their employer is at liberty to call in his lawyer. In fact, workmen, being intellectually less trained and of more limited experience than the men representing the management, are thought to have reason to consider that even in ordinary business relations they should be represented by an experienced labor leader, not necessarily a member of the shop itself.

The fact upon which this report wishes to lay emphasis is the necessity of a different point of view from that which has been underlying recent industrial disputes.

In a somewhat sketchy volume by Julius H. Cohen, "An American Labor Policy," a brief survey of this very field is full of suggestiveness. He quotes from a speech of the Italian Premier Orlando in supporting the resolutions for a League of Nations, in Paris, on January 25, 1919:

> "The principle of law is not only the principle of protection and of justice against violence — it is the form guaranteed by the state of what is a vital principle to humanity — social co-operation and solidarity among men."

This idea of "social co-operation and solidarity among men" is the cornerstone for any system of right industrial policy in opposition to the revolutionary keynote of hate, distrust and class war which has ruined Russia and if applied would ruin the rest of the world. If, as Cohen does, we compare the situation in the industrial world to the situation in the political world, we find that at present we are in a state of industrial war. This is the keynote of the situation. It is a fatal keynote. What the groups in our nation should aim at, is, through "social co-operation and solidarity," to pass from the condition of industrial war to the condition of industrial solidarity. Military strategy is at the basis of the present relations.

At a hearing in 1917 before the Public Service Commission, a labor leader said:

> "I want to be fair and I will say that I do not think it is a good idea to tell the other fellow what you are going to do, and to give him thirty days, more or less, to make preparation to get ready to fight you."

The occasion for this statement was a clause in the Canadian Disputes Act, which obliged labor to give thirty days' notice before striking.

A few of the plans recently presented as offering a practical guide for carrying out the idea of co-operation and solidarity will now be quoted.

Mr. John D. Rockefeller, Jr., presented ten articles of an industrial creed to the War Emergency and Reconstruction Conference at Atlantic City, by which it was unanimously adopted. He believed that all four parties to industry could subscribe to them. These Articles are as follows:

> "(1) I believe that labor and capital are partners, not enemies; that their interests are common interests, not

opposed; and that neither can attain the fullest measure of prosperity at the expense of the other, but only in association with the other.

"(2) I believe that the community is an essential party to industry and that it should have adequate representation with the other parties.

"(3) I believe that the purpose of industry is quite as much to advance social well-being as material prosperity; that in the pursuit of that purpose the interest of the community should be carefully considered, the well-being of employees as respects living and working conditions should be fully guarded, management should be adequately recognized and capital justly compensated, and that failure in any of these particulars means loss to all four parties.

"(4) I believe that every man is entitled to an opportunity to earn a living, to fair wages, to reasonable hours of work, and proper working conditions; to a decent home, to the opportunity to play, to learn, to worship and to love, as well as to toil, and that the responsibility rests as heavily on industry as upon government or society to see that these conditions and opportunities prevail.

"(5) I believe that industry, efficiency and initiative, wherever found, should be encouraged and adequately rewarded, and that indolence, indifference and restriction of production, should be discountenanced.

"(6) I believe that the provision of adequate means for uncovering grievances and promptly adjusting them, is of fundamental importance to the successful conduct of industry.

"(7) I believe that the main measure in bringing about industrial harmony and prosperity is adequate representation of the parties in interest; that existing forms of representation should be carefully studied and availed of, in so far as they may be found to have merit and are adaptable to the peculiar conditions in various industries.

"(8) I believe that the most effective structure of representation is that which is built from the bottom up; which includes all employees, and, starting with the election of representatives and the formation of joint works committees in each industrial plant, proceeds to the formation of joint district councils and annual joint conferences of all the parties in interest in a single industrial corporation, which can be extended to include all plants in the same industry, all industries in a community, in a nation, and in various nations.

"(9) I believe that the application of right principles never fails to effect right conclusions; that the letter killeth and the spirit maketh alive; that forms are wholly secondary, while attitude and spirit are all-important, and that only as parties in industry are animated by the spirit of fair play, justice to all and brotherhood, will any plans which they may mutually work out succeed.

"(10) I believe that that man renders the greatest social service who so co-operates in the organization of industry as to afford to the largest number of men the greatest opportunity for self-development and the enjoyment of those benefits which their united efforts add to the wealth of civilization."

In order to produce the spirit that is embodied in Mr. Rockefeller's creed, the first step is greater knowledge. This applies to both groups. With the tremendous growth of large industry, the employer has grown away from his workers, and in probably the majority of cases is comparatively ignorant of the situation and conditions in his own business. On the other hand the worker, being ignorant of almost everything but his own section and his own part, is liable to misconceive entirely the general situation in his own plant. A number of employers are attempting to remedy the situation by giving educational opportunities to their employees, and by turning over the handling of men to experts.

Beside the troubles due to this increasing lack of contact between the employer and the employee, there is the increasing monotony of the work, due to the almost general introduction of machinery, which has largely killed personal interest and satisfaction in the work. To rebuild this feeling of personal interest, the modern employer has the greatest difficulties to contend with. He is attempting to do this through giving a greater amount of responsibility to the worker, a larger liberty in suggestiveness on his part. For example, the Eastman Kodak Company welcomes all suggestions for improvements of every sort from its employees, and it embodies them in an analysis sheet, the results being shown to the employee, to explain why his suggestion is or is not practicable.

The turning over to experts of the handling of the men involves study of the individual worker, in order to secure the right job for the right man. It involves an extremely important question. a question not only of technique, but also of morale.

It is the general conclusion of those who have studied the situation that the main thing is industrial justice in itself, and not the machinery for attaining it. There are no panaceas. Trade unionism is not a panacea. The open shop is not a panacea. The nearest approach to a panacea is increased production. If there is one thing which will bring about that relationship between the two groups that will lead to industrial peace, it is the joint resolution on both sides, even before permanent adjustment of disputes, to push production to the limit consistent with industrial justice.

In this connection one of the most important difficulties to be faced and met is that which might be entitled "Hiring and Firing," or "Labor and Turnover." It has been reckoned that in certain industries the labor turnover has been 400 per cent. The New York Department of Labor statistics reckoned that in one year labor turnover lost to 2,556 firms the enormous sum of $363,000,000. One of the most important fields for co-operation and co-ordination in the industrial field would, therefore, be the arrangement of all the year-round work by combining seasonal employment.

Your Committee feels that it is extremely important, in order to counteract the present popular gospel of hate and discontent, to call attention to the undoubted and constant increase in the well-being, comfort, sanitary conditions and hours of labor of the working classes; to call attention to the increasing number of employers who regard their employees as human beings like themselves and not as machines. The endless, often senseless, harping on discontent by the agitators, has brought about an unreasonable state of mind among many workers. They are often led to suspect and despise the best efforts of employers to ameliorate conditions.

The splendid and varied forms of welfare work by employers are slandered as selfish acts of self-protection, as acts of charity to be sniffed at. Certain clergymen, wandering out of their normal sphere into fields of danger of which they are ignorant, have fostered these misconceptions. There is some reason in certain cases for criticism of this sort but it is unjust to generalize from these exceptions.

In almost every industry there are slack times when labor is dismissed, and other times of tremendous increase in personnel. It has been suggested that, for example, there could be a combination effected between the concerns running the ice business and the canning business, the peaks of whose operations come at different seasons. This would be a step in the abolition of the worst features of the competitive idea, which militates against the absolutely essential idea of co-operation.

The confusion of opinion among employers in regard to the American Federation of Labor is natural, but regrettable. There can be no question that the Federation is the most valuable asset in the field of industrial production that we have. There is no assurance of safety in industrial relations unless the employer can make contracts, not with individuals, but with an association of employees that is responsible to the law and has a consequent sense of responsibility as well as a collective conscience.

It is perfectly normal and healthy that there should be conflicts of opinion. It is in the interest of the employer as well as of the public that the constructive and loyal elements that still control the A. F. of L. should be supported. It is important to note that the Federation has repeatedly declared in favor of increased production as the best means for decreasing the cost of living, is against *sabotage* and declares that the interests of the public must outweigh the selfish demands of any special class.

The most important organization of employers is, of course, the U. S. Chamber of Commerce, whose twelve basic principles, recently issued, have excited a great deal of interest.

The New York Chamber of Commerce Committee on Industrial Problems and Relations is quoted in Cohen, p. 33, as saying:

"It has been proved over and over again in industry, that, irrespective of such conditions as rate of wages paid, as cost of management, or as rates of interest or other return on capital, the condition of hearty co-operation outweighed all the others. It is a by-word of production that the cheapest and best product is compatible with the largest earnings for wage earners, the highest salaries for managers, and the largest profits for capitalists, only providing that all three elements fully co-operate. In this we find the moral factor of manufacturing, which outweighs all the physical factors."

Of the various panaceas and catchwords that have become current the most popular is "Industrial Democracy," and we shall give in detail some of the forms in which it is thought to have been embodied in recent experiments. This term and the other catch-word "The New Social Order" have been used by many inexpert persons anxious to be thought advanced thinkers.

Three definitions of Industrial Democracy, which is a most debatable title, loosely used, are given in "Industrial Management" for July, 1918, p. 68. As defined by Mr. T. W. Wallace, President, Society of Industrial Engineers, it is:

"To me, to have Industrial Democracy is to have some internal plan of government in each industrial plant, whereby the employees have a direct and an authoritative voice in the formulating of such policies as directly affect their physical, moral, social and economic welfare, as well as that of their families. This means length of hours, character of work, physical surroundings under which they work, the moral influences that concern them; the freedom of self-expression through social affairs at the plant and in community; the question of wages or some form of profit and loss sharing. All of these things vitally affect the employee and his family. Therefore, he must have a voice in their control if we are to have Industrial Democracy."

The point of view of organized labor, as represented by the American Federation of Labor, is expressed by the Secretary of the Federation, Frank Morrison, as follows:

"Industrial Democracy is no more susceptible of dogmatic definition than is political democracy. In the latter case, a man is assured according to our theory of government 'life, liberty and the pursuit of happiness,' and when they urge industrial democracy workers insist on the same principle. In a political democracy, citizens are assured a voice in the conduct of affairs in the body politic and refuse to accept any goal save 'life, liberty and happiness.' In the case of an industrial democracy, workers are asking for a voice in industry — a voice in adjusting working conditions, in the settlement of wages and in the reduction of hours.

"There is only one 'best' method of securing Industrial Democracy, and that is collective bargaining. Any other solution is democracy — only in name, for it denies workers a voice in industry through organization that they themselves control."

In an interesting recent book by John R. Commons, "Industrial Good Will," three theories of the human side of labor are put forth as embodying the principal points of view:

(1) The commodity theory;
(2) The machinery theory; and
(3) The good will theory.

Attention is called to the fact that the last of these three categories has either been overlooked or kept in the background. It should now be brought forward as the principal element in the solution of the present situation. Prof. Commons defines the commodity theory as determined solely by demand and supply, without reference to outside factors of any kind. This theory is one that is repudiated by organized labor. It attempted to get a statement embodied in the Peace Treaty in the section devoted to labor, to the effect that labor is not a commodity. Mr. Gompers was disappointed in the ultimate wording of this section, after he left Paris. It was changed to read that labor was not "merely" a commodity.

It is considered to be a fundamental principle at present that there should be a general recognition that labor should not be treated as a commodity.

The second, "Machinery," theory is that in which the value of labor is determined by the so-called law of demand and supply and in which labor is not treated as a commodity, but each laborer is regarded as a machine, the value of which is determined by the quantity of its output. This theory is that which is best exemplified by the Taylor theory of scientific management. This second theory is not acceptable to organized labor, because it is mechanistic, and takes no account of the human side of the labor problem. Both of the above theories are elements of labor that will have to be considered, but neither of them is regarded by thoughtful economists as covering the entire ground.

The human reactions against the above purely material theories come under the third theory, or the good will theory, as it is called by Mr. Commons. This is the theory which gives an opportunity for free play of individual ability, a chance for the meeting of the employer and the employee in a common effort. It has in a way been recognized by the government in the formation of the Federal Trade Commission and by the states in a number of "good will" measures enacted into legislation. It concerns itself with such questions as unemployment, the situation of the labor market, insurance against death, disability, disease and old age, with courses for instruction and with every measure to improve physical and mental conditions of the workmen.

In fact, it is of the utmost importance to organize systematically the program of industrial good will as the basis for a constructive movement.

CHAPTER I

Trade Union Organization in the United States

The History Encyclopedia Reference Book of the A. F. of L. gives an authoritative outline of the history of organized labor in the United States from which the following facts are taken:

"The growth of trade unionism in the United States had been exceedingly slow and periodical only up to 1881. For nearly a century organizations of labor had been launched, lived for a period and then died on the field of partisan politics. Politics was as fatal to labor organizations as the upas tree to the human family" (page 38).

In 1866 a National Labor Congress was called which had a second meeting under the title of National Labor Union, in Chicago, at which trade unions in both northern and southern states were represented. Annual and bi-annual conventions were held up to 1873 with an increasing drift toward political action. At this time the Knights of Labor exercised strong influence, as well as certain secret industrial societies. It was not until 1881 that a call was published by representatives of organized labor for a convention to be held in Pittsburgh, November 15th, which should eliminate politics and bring about permanent organization of labor unionism.

The call for this Convention at which the American Federation of Labor was virtually founded contains the following (p. 40):

"The time has now arrived for a more perfect combination of labor — one that will concentrate our forces so as to more successfully cope with concentrated capital. We have numberless trade unions, trade assemblies or councils, Knights of Labor and various other local, national and international labor unions, all engaged in the noble task of elevating and improving conditions of the working classes. But great as has been the work done by these bodies there is vastly more that can be done by a combination of all these organizations in a federation of trades and labor unions. In Great Britain and Ireland actual trade union congresses are held. France and other countries have similar gatherings. The work done by these assemblages of workmen speaks more in their favor than a volume of other arguments."

"There were 107 delegates at the Pittsburgh convention representing 262,000 workingmen. A permanent organization was formed and named the Federation of Organized Trades and Labor Unions of the United States and Canada. A legislative committee, now known as the Executive Council was appointed" and on it Samuel Gompers represented the International Cigar Makers' Union of New York. The assemblies of the Knights of Labor were represented as well as the trade unions, but the Knights of Labor who had been represented by fifty delegates at this convention did not attend any of the conventions of succeeding years. The opposition between them and the Federation increased and culminated in 1886.

It was in December of 1886 after several conferences, that a convention met at Columbus, Ohio, at which for the Federation of Trade and Labor Unions there was substituted the present organization of the American Federation of Labor, formed then of 25 national organizations with a membership of 316,469 workingmen, and an executive council of five members. The growth in membership after 1900 was phenomenal, especially between 1900 and 1904, when it rose from less than 350,000 to nearly 1,700,000. Again it took another spectacular rise in 1917, jumping to nearly 3,100,000.

The methods of organization as expressed in the official chart of the A. F. of L. from 1918, gives it as divided into five departments with 445 local department councils, 111 national and international unions, 45 sub-federations, 854 local trades and Federal labor unions, 782 city central bodies, and 27,755 local unions.

It is interesting to compare the attitude toward the war expressed in the official declaration of the A. F. of L. with that of the American Socialist Party in its St. Louis declaration, which has been printed in this report.

This declaration of the A. F. of L., it must be noted, was passed at a special conference of its leaders held in Washington on March 12, 1917, nearly a month before our declaration of war (April 6th). After a long statement as to the privileges and conditions that organized labor considered should be granted to it, it closes with this:

"We, the officers of the National and International Trades Unions of America, in National Conference assembled . . .

hereby pledge ourselves in peace or in war, in stress or in storm, to stand unswervingly by the standards of liberty and safety and preservation of the institutions and ideals of our Republic. . . . Despite all our endeavors and hopes should our country be drawn into the maelstrom of the European conflict, we, with these ideals of liberty and justice herein declared as the basis of national policy, offer our services to our country in every field of activity, to defend, safeguard and preserve the Republic of the United States of America against its enemies whosoever they may be, and we call upon our fellow workers and fellow citizens in the holy name of labor, justice, freedom and humanity, to devotedly and patriotically give like service."

During 1918 the A. F. of L. sent a mission to Great Britain and France. There had been held in 1918 in London an inter-allied labor and Socialist Congress at which were present representatives of Great Britain, France, Belgium, Italy, Bosnia-Herzegovina, Roumania and South Africa. It adopted a memorandum of war aims that was meant to serve as a guide to workers and to prepare the way for an international congress of similar character. The conferences held with certain labor representatives by the American delegates during April and May, 1918, in England and France, gave a much clearer idea to the A. F. of L. of the point of view held by labor in Great Britain and Europe. Then, as later, the leaders of the American organized labor were considered by their European colleagues as ultra-conservative.

Of the part played by the A. F. of L. during the war it is superfluous to speak, but it is important to give here the result of the convention held at St. Paul, June 10 to 20, 1918, to appoint a committee on reconstruction.

The St. Paul Convention of the American Federation of Labor instructed the Executive Council to appoint a committee on reconstruction. This committee was to investigate "the problem of reconstruction and to take such steps as might be found possible to safeguard the interests of the soldiers and sailors and workers during the period of reconstruction."

The committee consisted of John P. Frey, editor of the International Molders' Journal; B. M. Jewell, acting president Railroad Employees' Department; John Moore, president of the Ohio district of the United Mine Workers; G. W. Perkins, president

Cigarmakers' International Union, and Matthew Woll, president International Photo Engravers' Union.

The Executive Council received the report of the committee at its meeting in December, 1918, and transmitted it to the convention as "not only the most complete, and the most constructive proposal yet made in this country for the reconstruction period," but which "constitutes practically the only program in existence having to do with the period of rebuilding the national life on a peace basis."

The Convention at Atlantic City adopted the report as prepared by the committee. We give it at the close of this chapter.

I

DOCUMENTS

One of the outgrowths of the war in the field of organized labor was the establishment under the leadership of the American Federation of Labor of an organization called the American Alliance for Labor and Democracy, which was called into existence in May, 1917, at a conference in New York City.

The pro-German and pacifist propaganda which made itself felt throughout the United States led to a conference of the new organization in Minneapolis on September 5, 1917. Every member was asked to sign the following:

"The undersigned hereby affirms that it is the duty of all the people of the United States, without regard to call, nationality, politics or religion, faithfully and loyally to support the Government of the United States carrying on the present war for justice, freedom and democracy to a triumphant conclusion, and gives this pledge to uphold every honorable effort for the accomplishment of that purpose, and to support the American Federation of Labor, as well as the declaration of organized labor's representatives made March 12, 1917, at Washington, D. C., as 'labor's position in peace or in war,' and agrees that this pledge shall be his right to membership in this conference of the American Alliance for Labor and Democracy."

President Wilson invited, but unable to attend, sent a sympathetic message. The conference passed a resolution declaring "that the great war must be fought to a decisive result; that until autocracy has been defeated there can be no hope of an honorable peace, and that to compromise the issue is only to sow the seed for bloodier and more devastating wars in the future. . . . We strongly denounce the words and actions of these enemies of the Republic who, falsely assuming to speak in the name of labor and democracy, are now ceaselessly striving to obstruct the operations of the Government. . . . They abuse the rights of free speech, free assemblage and free press. In the name of liberty they encourage anarchy; in the name of democracy they strive to defeat the will of the majority, and in the name of humanity they render every possible aid and comfort to the brutal Prussian autocracy. If the sinister councils of these persons were followed, labor would be reduced to subjection, and democracy would be obliterated from earth. We declare that the betrayal of one's fellow-workers during a strike finds its exact counterpart in the betrayal of one's fellow citizens in time of war, and that both are offenses which deserve detestation of mankind."

The American Alliance for Labor and Democracy has continued its work since the close of the war. It has become the main propaganda organ of the American Federation of Labor distributing to the press of this country both the general daily and periodical press, and all the organized labor press of the United States, weekly bulletin sheets in which the authoritative views of leaders of organized labor are set forth and made available to the public. It is one of the most powerful agencies for the dissemination of the views of organized labor.

Report of the Convention at Atlantic City.
Reconstruction Program of the A. F. of L.

DEMOCRACY IN INDUSTRY

Two codes of rules and regulations affect the workers; the law upon the statute books, and the rules within industry.

The first determines their relationship as citizens to all other citizens and to property. The second largely determines the relationship of employer and employee, the terms of employment, the conditions of labor, and the rules and regulations affecting the workers as employees. The first is secured through the application of the methods of democracy in the enactment of legislation, and is based upon the principle that the laws which govern a free people should exist only with their consent.

The second, except where effective trade unionism exists, is established by the arbitrary or autocratic whim, desire or opinion of the employer and is based upon the principle that industry and commerce cannot be successfully conducted unless the employer exercises the unquestioned right to establish such rules, regulations and provisions affecting the employees as self-interest prompts. Both forms of law vitally affect the workers' opportunities in life and determine their standard of living. The rules, regulations and conditions within industry in many instances affect them more than legislative enactments. It is, therefore, essential that the workers should have a voice in determining the laws within industry and commerce which affect them, equivalent to the voice which they have as citizens in determining the legislative enactments which shall govern them. It is as inconceivable that the workers as free citizens should remain under autocratically made law within industry and commerce as it is that the nation could remain a democracy while certain individuals or groups exercise autocratic powers.

It is, therefore, essential that the workers everywhere should insist upon their right to organize into trade unions, and that effective legislation should be enacted which would make it a criminal offense for any employer to interfere with or hamper the exercise of this right or to interfere with the legitimate activities of trade unions.

Unemployment

Political economy of the old school, conceived by doctrinaires, was based upon unsound and false doctrines, and has since been used to blindfold, deceive and defeat the workers' demands for adequate wages, better living and working conditions, and a just share of the fruits of their labor. We hold strictly to the trade union philosophy and its developed political economy based upon demonstrated facts. Unemployment is due to underconsumption. Underconsumption is caused by low or insufficient wages. Just wages will prevent industrial stagnation and lessen periodical unemployment. Give the workers just wages and their consuming capacity is correspondingly increased. A man's ability to consume is controlled by the wages received. Just wages will create a market at home which will far surpass any market that may exist elsewhere and will lessen unemployment.

The employment of idle workmen on public work will not permanently remove the cause of unemployment. It is an expedient at best. There is no basis in fact for the claim that the so-called law of supply and demand is natural in its operations and impossible of control or regulation. The trade union movement has maintained standards, wages, hours and life in periods of industrial depression and idleness. These in themselves are a refutation of the declared immutability of the law of supply and demand. Conditions in commerce and industry, methods of production, storing of commodities, regulation of the volume of production, banking systems, the flow and direction of enterprise influenced by combinations and trusts have effectively destroyed the theory of a natural law of supply and demand as had been formulated by doctrinaire economists.

Wages

There are no means whereby the workers can obtain and maintain fair wages except through trade union effort. Therefore, economic organization is paramount to all their other activities. Organization of the workers leads to better wages, fewer working hours, improved working conditions; it develops independence, manhood and character; it fosters tolerance and real justice and makes for a constantly growing better economic, social and political life for the burden-bearing masses. In countries where wages are best, the greatest progress has been made in economic, social and political advancement, in science, art, literature, education and in the wealth of the people generally. All low wage-paying countries contrasted with America is proof for this statement.

The American standard of life must be maintained and improved. The value of wages is determined by the purchasing power of the dollar. There is no such thing as good wages when the cost of living in decency and comfort equals or exceeds the wages received. There must be no reduction in wages; in many instances wages must be increased. The workers of the nation demand a living wage for all wage-earners, skilled or unskilled — a wage which will enable the worker and his family to live in health and comfort, provide a competence for illness and old age, and afford to all the opportunity of cultivating the best that is within mankind.

Hours of Labor

Reasonable hours of labor promote the economic and social well-being of the toiling masses. Their attainment should be one of labor's principal and essential activities. The shorter work day and a short work week make for a constantly growing, higher and better standard of productivity, health, longevity morale and citizenship. The right of labor to fix its hours of work must not be abrogated, abridged or interfered with. The day's working time should be limited to not more than eight hours, with overtime prohibited, except under the most extraordinary emergencies. The week's working time should be limited to not more than five and one-half days.

WOMEN AS WAGE-EARNERS

Women should receive the same pay as men for equal work performed. Women workers must not be permitted to perform tasks disproportionate to their physical strength or which tend to impair their potential motherhood and prevent the continuation of a nation of strong, healthy, sturdy and intelligent men and women.

CHILD LABOR

The children constitute the nation's most valuable asset. The full responsibility of the Government should be recognized by such measures as will protect the health of every child at birth and during its immature years.

It must be one of the chief functions of the nation through effective legislation to put an immediate end to the exploitation of children under sixteen years by prohibiting their employment, for gain, under sixteen years of age and restricting the employment of children of less than eighteen years of age to not more than twenty hours within any one week, and with not less than twenty hours at school during the same period. Exploitation of child life for private gain must not be permitted.

PUBLIC EMPLOYEES

The fixing of wages, hours and conditions of labor for public employees by legislation hampers the necessary exercise of organization and collective bargaining. Public employees must not be denied the right of organization, free activities and collective bargaining and must not be limited in the exercise of their rights as citizens.

CO-OPERATION

To attain the greatest possible development of civilization, it is essential, among other things, that the people should never delegate to others those activities and responsibilities which they are capable of assuming for themselves. Democracy can function best with the least interference by the state compatible with due protection to the rights of all citizens.

There are many problems arising from production, transportation and distribution, which would be readily solved by applying the methods of co-operation. Unnecessary middlemen who exact a tax from the community without rendering any useful service can be eliminated.

The farmers, through co-operative dairies, canneries, packing houses, grain elevators, distributing houses, and other co-operative enterprises, can secure higher prices for their products and yet place these in the consumer's hands at lower prices than would otherwise be paid. There is an almost limitless field for the consumers in which to establish co-operative buying and selling, and in this most necessary development, the trade unionists should take an immediate and active part.

Trade unions secure fair wages. Co-operation protects the wage-earner from the profiteer. Participation in these co-operative agencies must of necessity prepare the mass of the people to participate more effectively in the solution of the industrial, commercial, social and political problems which continually arise.

The People's Final Voice in Legislation

It is manifestly evident that a people are not self-governing unless they enjoy the unquestioned power to determine the form and substance of the laws which shall govern them. Self-government cannot adequately function if there exists within the nation a superior power or authority which can finally determine what legislation enacted by the people, or their duly elected representatives, shall be placed upon the statute books and what shall be declared null and void. An insuperable obstacle of self-government in the United States exists in the power which has been gradually assumed by the Supreme Courts of the Federal and State governments to declare legislation null and void upon the ground that, in the court's opinion, it is unconstitutional.

It is essential that the people, acting directly or through Congress or state legislatures, should have final authority in determining which laws shall be enacted. Adequate steps must be taken therefore, which will provide that in the event of a Supreme Court declaring an act of Congress or of a state legislature unconstitutional and the people acting directly or through Congress or state legislature should re-enact the measure, it shall then become the law without being subject to annulment by any court.

Political Policy

In the political efforts, arising from the workers' necessity to secure legislation covering those conditions and provisions of life not subject to collective bargaining with employers, organized labor has followed two methods; one by organizing political parties, the other by the determination to place in public office representatives from their ranks; to elect those who favor and champion the legislation desired and to defeat those whose policy is opposed to labor's legislative demands, regardless of partisan politics. The disastrous experience of organized labor in America with political parties of its own amply justified the A. F. of L.'s non-partisan political policy. The results secured by labor parties in other countries never have been such as to warrant any deviation from this position. The rules and regulations of trade unionism should not be extended so that the action of a majority could force a minority to vote for or give financial support to any political candidate or party to whom they are opposed. Trade union activities cannot receive the undivided attention of members and officers if the exigencies, burdens and responsibilities of a political party are bound up with their economic and industrial organizations.

The experiences and results attained through the non-partisan political policy of the A. F. of L. cover a generation. They indicate that through its application the workers of America have secured a much larger measure of fundamental legislation, establishing their rights, safeguarding their interests, protecting their welfare and opening the doors of opportunity than have been secured by the workers of any other country. The vital legislation now required can be more readily secured through education of the public mind and the appeal to its conscience, supplemented by energetic independent political activity on the part of trade unionists, than by any other method. This is and will continue to be the political policy of the A. F. of L., if the lessons which labor has learned in the bitter but practical school of experience are to be respected and applied.

It is, therefore, most essential that the officers of the A. F. of L., the officers of the affiliated organizations, state federations and central labor bodies and the entire membership of the trade union movement should give the most vigorous application possible to the political policy of the A. F. of L. so that labor's friends and opponents may be more widely known, and the legislation most required readily secured. This phase of our movement is still in its infancy. It should be continued and developed to its logical conclusion.

Government Ownership

Public and semi-public utilities should be owned, operated or regulated by the Government in the interest of the public. Whatever final disposition shall be made of the railways of the country in ownership, management or regulation, we insist upon the right of the workers to organize for their common and mutual protection and the full exercise of the normal activities which come with organization. Any attempt at the denial by governmental authority of the rights of the workers to organize, to petition, to representation and to collective bargaining, or the denial of the exercise of their political rights, is repugnant to the fundamental principles of free citizenship in a republic and is destructive of their best interest and welfare.

The government should own and operate all wharves and docks connected with public harbors which are used for commerce or transportation.

The American merchant marine should be encouraged and developed under governmental control and so manned as to insure successful operation and protect in full the beneficent laws on the statute books for the rights and welfare of seamen. The seamen must be accorded the same rights and privileges rightfully exercised by the workers in all other employments, public and private.

Waterways and Water Power

The lack of a practical developmet of our waterways and the inadequate extension of canals have seriously handicapped water traffic and created unnecessarily high cost of transportation. In many instances it has established artificial restrictions which have worked to the serious injury of communities, owing to the schemes of those controlling a monopoly of land transportation. Our navigable rivers and our great inland lakes should be connected with the sea by an adequate system of canals, so that inland production can be more effectively fostered, the costs of transportation reduced, the private monopoly of transportation overcome and imports and exports shipped at lower costs.

The nation is possessed of enormous water power. Legislation should be enacted providing that the governments, federal and

State, should own, develop and operate all water power over which they have jurisdiction. The power thus generated should be supplied to all citizens at rates based upon cost. The water power of the nation, created by nature, must not be permitted to pass into private hands for private exploitation.

Regulation of Land Ownership

Agriculture and stock-raising are essential to national safety and well-being. The history of all countries, at all times, indicates that the conditions which create a tenant class of agriculturists work increasing injury to the tillers of the soil. While increasing the price of the product to the consumer these conditions at the same time develop a class of large land owners who contribute little, if anything, to the welfare of the community but who exact a continually increasing share of the wealth produced by the tenant. The private ownership of large tracts of usable land is not conducive to the best interests of a democratic people.

Legislation should be enacted placing a graduated tax upon all usable lands above the acreage which is cultivated by the owner. This should include provisions through which the tenant farmer, or others, may purchase land upon the lowest rate of interest and most favorable terms consistent with safety, and so safeguarded by government supervision and regulation as to give the fullest and freest opportunity for the development of land-owning agriculturists.

Special assistance should be given in the direction of allotments of lands and the establishment of homes on the public domain. Establishment of Government experimental farms, measures for stock-raising instruction, the irrigation of arid lands and reclamation of swamp and cut-over lands should be undertaken upon a larger scale under direction of the federal government.

Municipalities and States should be empowered to acquire lands for cultivation or the erection of residential buildings which they may use or dispose of under equitable terms.

Federal and State Regulation of Corporations

The creation by legislative enactment of corporations, without sufficient definition of the powers and scope of activities conferred upon them and without provisions for their adequate supervision, regulation and control by the creative body, has lead to the development of far-reaching abuses which have seriously affected commerce, industry and the masses of the people through their influence upon social, industrial, commercial and political development. Legislation is required which will so limit, define and regulate the powers, privileges and activities of corporations that their methods cannot become detrimental to the welfare of the people. It is, therefore, essential that legislation should provide for the federal licensing of all corporations organized for profit. Furthermore, federal supervision and control should include the increasing of capital stock and the incurring of bonded indebtedness with the provision that the books of all corporations shall be open at all times to federal examiners.

Freedom of Expression and Association

The very life and perpetuity of free and democratic institutions are dependent upon freedom of speech, of the press and of assemblage and association. We insist that all restrictions of freedom of speech, press, public assembly, association and travel be completely removed, individuals and groups being responsible for their utterances. These fundamental rights must be set out with clearness and must not be denied or abridged in any manner.

Workmen's Compensation

Workmen's compensation laws should be amended to provide more adequately for those incapacitated by industrial accidents or occupational diseases. To assure that the insurance fund derived from commerce and industry will be paid in full to injured workers, State insurance must supplant, and prohibit the existence of, employers' liability insurance operated for profit.

Immigration

Americanization of those coming from foreign lands, as well as our standards of education and living, are vitally affected by the volume and character of the immigration. It is essential that additional legislation regulating immigration should be enacted based upon two fundamental propositions, namely, that the flow of immigration must not at any time exceed the nation's ability to assimilate and Americanize the foreigners coming to our shores, and that at no time shall immigration be permitted when there exists an abnormal degree of unemployment. By reason of existing conditions we urge that immigration into the United States should be prohibited for a period of at least two years after peace has been declared.

TAXATION

One of the nation's most valuable assets is the initiative, the energetic, constructive and inventive genius of its people. These qualities when properly applied should be fostered and protected instead of being hampered by legislation, for they constitute an invaluable element of progress and material development. Taxation should, therefore, rest as lightly as possible upon constructive enterprise. Taxation should provide for full contribution from wealth by a tax upon profits which will not discourage industrial or commercial enterprice. There should be provided a progressive increase in taxes upon incomes, inheritances, and upon land values of such a nature as to render it unprofitable to hold land without putting it to use, to afford a transition to greater economic equality and to supply means of liquidating the national indebtedness growing out of the war.

EDUCATION

It is impossible to estimate the influence of education upon the world's civilization. Education must not stifle thought and inquiry, but must awaken the mind concerning the application of natural laws and to a conception of independence and progress.

Education must not be for a few but for all our people. While there is an advanced form of public education in many States, there still remains a lack of adequate educational facilities in several States and communities. The welfare of the republic demands that public education should be elevated to the highest degree possible. The government should exercise advisory supervision over public education and where necessary maintain adequate public education through subsidies without giving to the government power to hamper or interfere with the free development of public education by the several States. It is essential that our system of public education should offer the wage-earners' children the opportunity for the fullest possible development. To attain this end State colleges and universities should be developed.

It is also important that the industrial education which is being fostered and developed should have for its purpose not so much training for efficiency in industry as training for life in an industrial society. A full understanding must be had of those principles and activities that are the foundation of all productive efforts. Children should not only become familiar with tools and materials, but they should also receive a thorough knowledge of the principles of human control, of force and matter underlying our industrial relations and sciences. The danger that certain commercial and industrial interests may dominate the character of education must be averted by insisting that the workers shall have equal representation on all boards of education or committees having control over vocational studies and training. To elevate and advance the interest of the teaching profession and to promote popular and democratic education, the right of the teachers to organize and affiliate with the movement of the organized workers must be recognized.

Private Employment Agencies

Essentials in industry and commerce are employee and employer, labor and capital. No one questions the right of organized capital to supply capital to employers. No one should question the right of organized labor to furnish workers. Private employment agencies abridge this right of organized labor.

Where federal, State and municipal employment agencies are maintained they should operate under the supervision of joint committees of trade unionists and employers, equally represented. Private employment agencies operated for profit should not be permitted to exist.

Housing

Child life, the workers' physical condition and public health demand that the wage-earner and his family shall be given a full opportunity to live under wholesome conditions. It is not only necessary that there shall be sanitary and appropriate houses to live in, but that a sufficient number of dwellings shall be available to free the people from high rents and overcrowding.

The ownership of homes, free from the grasp of exploitative and speculative interests, will make for more efficient workers, more contented families, and better citizens. The government should, therefore, inaugurate a plan to build model homes and establish a system of credits whereby the workers may borrow money at a low rate of interest and under favorable terms to build their own homes. Credit should also be extended to voluntary non-profit making, housing and joint tenancy associations. States and municipalities should be freed from the restrictions preventing their undertaking proper housing projects and should be permitted to engage in other necessary enterprises relating thereto. The erection and maintenance of dwellings where migratory workers may find lodging and nourishing food during periods of unempolyment should be encouraged and supported by municipalties. If need should arise to expend public funds to relieve unemployment, the building of wholesome houses would best serve the public interests.

Militarism

The trade union movement is unalterably and emphatically opposed to "militarism" or a large standing army. "Militarism" is a system fostered and developed by tyrants in the hope of supporting their arbitrary authority.

It is utilized by those whose selfish ambitions for power and worldly glory lead them to invade and subdue other peoples and nations, to destroy their liberties, to acquire their wealth and to fasten the yoke of bondage upon them. The trade union movement is convinced by the experience of mankind that "militarism" brutalizes those influenced by the spirit of the institution. The finer elements of humanity are strangled. Under "militarism" a deceptive patriotism is established in the people's minds, where men believe that there is nobility of spirit and heroism in dying for the glory of a dynasty or the maintenance of institutions which are inimical to human progress and democracy. "Militarism" is the application of arbitrary and irresponsible forces as opposed to reason and justice. Resistance to injustice and tyranny is that virile quality which has given purpose and effect to ennobling causes in all countries and at all times. The free institutions of our country and the liberties won by its founders would have been impossible had they been unwilling to take arms and if necessary die in the defense of their liberties. Only a people willing to maintain their rights and defend their liberties are guaranteed free institutions.

Conditions foreign to the institutions of our country have prevented the entire abolition of organized bodies of men trained to carry arms. A voluntary citizen soldiery supplies what would otherwise take its place, a large standing army. To the latter we are unalterably opposed as tending to establish the evils of "militarism." Large standing armies threaten the existence of civil liberty. The history of every nation demonstrates that as standing armies are enlarged the rule of democracy is lessened or extinguished. Our experience has been that even this citizen soldiery, the militia of our States, has given cause at times for grave apprehension. Their ranks have not always been free from undesirable elements, particularly the tools of corporations involved in industrial disputes. During industrial disputes the militia has at times been called upon to support the authority of those who through selfish interest desire to enforce martial law while the courts were open and the civil authorities competent to maintain supremacy of civil law. We insist that the militia of our several States should be wholly organized and controlled by democratic principles so that this voluntary force of soldiery may never be diverted from its true purpose and used to jeopardize or infringe upon the rights and liberties of our people. The right to bear arms is a fundamental principle of our government, a principle accepted at all times by free people as essential to the maintenance of their liberties and institutions. We demand that this right shall remain inviolate.

Soldiers and Sailors

Soldiers and sailors, those who entered the service in the nation's defense, are entitled to the generous reward of a grateful republic. The necessities of war called upon millions of workmen to leave their positions in industry and commerce to defend, upon the battlefields, the nation's safety and its free institutions. These defenders are now returning. It is advisable that they should be discharged from military service at the earliest possible moment; that as civilians they may return to their respective homes and families and take up their peace-time pursuits. The nation stands morally obligated to assist them in securing employment.

Industry has undergone great changes due to the dislocation caused by war production and transportation. Further readjustments in industry and commerce must follow the rehabilitation of business under peaceful conditions. Many positions which our citizen soldiers and sailors filled previous to enlistment do not exist today. It would be manifestly unjust for the government after having removed the worker from his position in industry and placed him in military service to discharge him from the army or navy without having made adequate provision to assist him in procuring employment and providing sustenance until employment has been secured. The returned citizen soldier or sailor should not be forced by the bitter urgent necessity of securing food and clothing to place himself at a disadvantage when securing employment.

Upon their discharge, transportation and meals should be supplied to their places of residence. The monthly salary previously paid should be continued for a period not to exceed twelve months, if employment is not secured within that period. The federal and state employment bureaus should be directed to cooperate with trade union agencies in securing employment for discharged soldiers and sailors. In assisting the discharged soldier and sailor to secure employment, government agencies should not expect them to accept employment for less than the prevailing rate of wages being paid in the industry. Neither should any government agency request or require such discharged men to accept employment where a trade dispute exists or is threatened. Nor should the refusal on the part of any of these discharged soldiers or sailors to accept employment where trade disputes exist or are threatened or when less than the prevailing wage rate is offered, deprive them of a continuance of their monthly pay.

Legislation also should be enacted which will give the nation's defenders the opportunity for easy and ready access to the land. Favorable inducements should be provided for them to enter agriculture and husbandry. The government should assume the responsibility for the allotment of such lands, and supply the necessary capital for its development and cultivation, with such safeguards as will protect both the government and the discharged soldier and sailor.

II

BILL OF RIGHTS

(Passed by 119 unions of the Federation, December 13, 1919, in Washington.)

We speak in the name of millions who work — those who make and use tools — those who furnish the human power necessary for commerce and industry. We speak as part of the nation and of those things of which we have special knowledge. Our welfare and interest are inseparably bound up with the well-being of the nation. We are an integral part of the American people and we are organized to work out the welfare of all.

The urgent problems that sorely trouble our nation and vitally affect us as workers make necessary this special consultation.

The great victories for human freedom must not have been won in vain. They must serve as the instruments and the inspiration for a greater and nobler freedom for all mankind.

Autocratic, political and corporate industrial and financial influences in our country have sought, and are seeking, to infringe upon and limit the fundamental rights of the wage earners guaranteed by the Constitution of the United States.

Powerful forces are seeking more and more aggressively to deny to wage earners their right to cease work. We denounce these efforts as vicious and destructive of the most precious liberties of our people. The right to cease work — strike — as a final means of enforcing justice from an autocratic control of industry, must be maintained.

The autocratic and destructive action of the United States Steel Corporation and its subsidiary branches to oppress the workers by denying them the exercise of their freedom of action, freedom of association, freedom of expression, must give way to a better understanding and relation and to secure the wage earners in the exercise of their rights and liberties as free workers and citizens.

We realize fully all that is involved in the exercise of the right to strike, but only by the exercise of that right can industrial autocrats be compelled to abandon their concept of tyranny and give way to the establishment of freedom and justice in industry.

American labor sets for itself the task, gladly and proudly assumed, to preserve and perpetuate this standard of justice and measure of liberty.

We protest against the attitude and action of the majority of the representatives of the employers in the employers group who participated in the President's Industrial Conference October 6-29, 1919.

The proposals which the representatives of labor submitted at that conference were conservative, constructive and helpful. They were calculated to establish a working basis for the promotion of better relations between employers and workers — the right to organize, the right to collective bargaining through representatives of the workers' own choosing. The representatives of the public constituted as a group indorsed and voted for that principle. By a small majority the employers' group voted against it, and thus the proposals were defeated and the conference failed.

The protection of the rights and interests of the wage earners in national, state and municipal service requires for them the right of organization. Since the interests of these workers can be best promoted through legislation and administration, their right to organize and affiliate with the American Federation of Labor must at all times be fully safeguarded.

The paramount issues that concern all the people of the United States, and in particular the wage earners, are the perversion and the abuse of the writ of injunction and the necessity for full and adequate protection of the voluntary associations of wage earners organized not for profit.

Government by injunction has grown out of the perversion of the injunction process. By the misuse of that process workers have been forbidden to do those things which they have a natural and constitutional right to do.

Denounce Use of Injunction

The injunction as now used is a revolutionary measure which substitutes government by judicial discretion or bias for government by law. It substitutes a trial by one man, a judge, in his substitutes government by judicial discretion or bias for govern- discretion, for a trial by jury. This abuse of the injunctive process undermines and destroys the very foundations of our free institutions. It is subversive of the spirit of a free people working out their destiny in an orderly and rational manner.

Because we have reverence for law, because we believe that every citizen must be a guardian of the heritage given us by our fathers who fought for and established freedom and democracy, by every lawful means we must resist the establishment of a practice that would destroy the very spirit of freedom and democracy. Our protest against the abuse of the writ of injunction and its unwarranted application to labor in the exercise of labor's normal activities to realize laudable aspirations is a duty we owe to ourselves and to posterity.

Formerly injunctions issued in labor disputes were of prohibitive character. Within the recent past this abuse of the injunction writ has been enlarged to include mandatory orders whereby men have been compelled to do specific things which they have a lawful right to refrain from doing.

We declare these abuses in the exercise of the injunction writ are clearly violative of the Constitution and that this issue must be determined definitely in accordance with the guarantees of the Constitution of the United States.

Workers are free citizens, not slaves. They have the constitutional right to cease working. The strike is a protest against autocratic management. To penalize strikes or to make them unlawful is to apply an unwarranted and destructive method when a constructive one is available. To reduce the necessity for strikes the cause should be found and removed. The Government has a greater obligation in this matter than to use its coercive powers.

Legislation which proposes to make strikes unlawful or to compel the wage-earners to submit their grievances or aspirations to courts or to Government agencies, is an invasion of the rights of the wage earners, and when enforced makes for industrial serfdom or slavery.

We hold that the Government should supply information, assistance, and counsel, but that it should not attempt by the force of its own power to stifle or to destroy voluntary relations and policies of mutuality between employers and employees.

Attack the Cummins Bill

We specifically denounce the anti-strike provisions of the Cummins bill and all similar proposed legislation as un-American, as being vicious in character and establishing by legislation involuntary servitude.

The warning given by Jefferson that the danger to the people of this republic lies in the usurpation by our judiciary of unconstitutional authority, has been fully demonstrated. A judiciary unresponsive to the needs of the time, arrogating to itself powers which neither the Constitution nor the purposes of our laws have conferred upon them, demands that at least in our time Americans must insist upon safeguarding their liberties and the spirit of the sacred institutions of our republic.

We urge that the judges of our Federal courts shall be elected by the people for terms not exceeding six years.

We assert that there cannot be found in the Constitution of the United States or in the discussions of the Congress which drafted the Constitution any authority for the Federal courts of our country to declare unconstitutional any act passed by

Congress. We call upon the people of our country to demand that the Congress of the United States shall take action for the purpose of preventing the Federal courts from continuing the usurpation of such authority.

We declare that the voluntary organizations of the workers, organized not for profit, are agencies of human progress and promote justice in industry and trade. Despite legislative declarations that trade unions do not come under the provisions of anti-trust legislation courts have not understood and are not now able or willing to understand that the organizations of wage earners are not conspiracies in restraint of trade.

We submit that anti-trust legislation has not only been interpreted to serve the purpose of outlawing trade unions, robbing them of their treasures and the savings of their members, and depriving them of their legal and natural rights to the exercise of normal activities, but that it has also failed completely to protect the people against the outrageous machinations of combinations and monopolies.

Upholds Coal Miners

The United Mine Workers of America did all in their power to avert an industrial controversy in the coal industry. The autocratic attitude of the mine owners was responsible for the losses and sufferings entailed. While the miners have returned to the mines and have only now been afforded the opportunity of having their grievances and demands brought to the light of reason, it is our hope that a full measure of justice will be accorded them, even at this late date.

There is a widespread belief that wages should be fixed on a cost-of-living basis. This idea is pernicious and intolerable. It means putting progress in chains and liberty in fetters. It means fixing a standard of living and a standard of life and liberty which must remain fixed. America's workers cannot accept that proposition.

They demand a progressively advancing standard of life. They have an abiding faith in a better future for all mankind. They discard and denounce a system of fixing wages solely on the basis of family budgets and bread bills. Workers are entitled not only to a living, but modern society must provide more than what is understood by the term "a living." It must concede to all workers a fairer reward for their contribution to society, a contribution without which a progressing civilization is impossible.

No factor contributes more to industrial unrest and instability than excessive costs of necessaries of life. It is a demonstrated truth that the cost of living has advanced more rapidly than have wages. The claim that increasing wages make necessary increased prices is false. It is intended to throw upon the workers the blame for a process by which all the people have been made to suffer. Labor has been compelled to struggle desperately to keep wages in some measure up to the cost of living. The demand for higher compensation to meet new price levels has made industrial readjustment necessary.

Their Idea of High Prices

Existing high and excessive prices are due to the present inflation of money and credits, to profiteering by those who manufacture, sell and market products, and to burdens levied by middlemen and speculators. We urge:

The deflation of currency; prevention of hoarding and unfair price fixing; establishment of co-operative movements under the Rochdale system; making accessible all income tax returns and dividend declarations as a direct and truthful means of revealing excessive costs and profits.

The ideal of America should be the organization of industry for service and not for profit alone. The stigma of disgrace should attach to every person who profits unduly at the expense of his fellowmen.

Labor is fully conscious that the world needs things for use, and that standards of life can improve only as production for use and consumption increases. Labor is anxious to work out better methods for industry, and demands that it be assured that increased productivity will be used for service and not alone for profits.

Wage earners aspire to be something more than numbers on the books of an industrial plant, something more than attendants of a machine, something more than cogs in an industrial system dominated by machinery owned and operated for profit alone. The workers insist upon being masters of themselves.

Labor understands fully that powerful interests today are determined to achieve reaction in industry if possible. They seek to disband or cripple the organizations of workers. They seek to reduce wages and thus lower the standard of living. They seek to keep free from restriction their power to manipulate and fix prices. They seek to destroy the democratic impulse of the workers which is bred into their movement by the democracy of the American republic.

Labor must be, and is militant in the struggle to combat these sinister influences and tendencies. Labor will not permit a reduction in the standard of living. It will not consent to reaction toward autocratic control. In this it is performing a public service.

Only in high-wage countries is productivity in industry greatest. Only in high-wage countries do the people enjoy high standings of living. Low-wage countries present the least degree of productivity and offer to their people only low standards of living and restricted liberties. Autocracy always insists upon restricting the income and the activities of workers.

Creative power lies dormant where autocratic management prevails. No employer has a vested right to the good will of his employees. That must be earned as between men. It can be earned only when management deals with workers as human beings, and not as machines. There can not be a full release of productive energy under an autocratic control of industry. There must be a spirit of co-operation and mutuality between employers and workers. We submit that production can be enhanced through the co-operation of management with the trade-union agencies, which make for order, discipline, and productivity.

We hold that the organization of wage-earners into trade unions and the establishment of collective bargaining are the first steps toward the proper development of our industrial machinery for service.

To promote further the production of an adequate supply of the world's needs for use and higher standards of life, we urge that there be established co-operation between the scientists of industry and the representatives of organized workers.

Credit is the life blood of modern business. At present under the control of private financiers, it is administered, not primarily to serve the needs of production, but the desire of financial agencies to levy a toll upon community activity as high as "the traffic will bear."

Credit is inherently social. It should be accorded in proportion to confidence in production possibilities. Credit as now administered does not serve industry but burdens it. It increases unearned incomes at the expense of earned incomes. It is the centre of the malevolent forces that corrupt the spirit and purpose of industry.

We urge the organization and use of credit to serve production needs and not to increase the incomes and holding of financiers. Control over credit should be taken from financiers and should be vested in a public agency, able to administer this power as a public trust in the interest of the people.

Would Hold Railroads for Years

Since the Government has not worked out a constructive railroad policy, we urge for and on behalf of the railway workers and of the general public, that the railroads be retained under Government Administration for at least two years after January 1, 1920, in order that a thorough test may be made of Governmental operation under normal conditions. The common carriers of this country are the arteries of travel, commerce and industry. Transportation service and rates are intimately bound up with industrial production in all parts of the country. It is essential that a thorough test be given to all phases of railroad control and operation before a definite peace-time policy be finally concluded.

Never has the world been confronted with a more serious situation. Millions are in want, facing starvation. The children of war-stricken Europe, half-fed, under-developed, appeal for help. Only with infinite pain, unnecessary loss of life, and slowness of result can Europe rebuild her industries, restore her agriculture, and re-establish her commerce, without the help of America.

The treaty, setting forth the terms of peace, has not been ratified by the United States. Boundaries are not fixed. People are uncertain as to their allegiance. Under such conditions exchange and credit have lost voltage and in turn have paralyzed industry.

As members of an organized labor movement that has for years maintained fraternal relations with the working people of Europe, we feel that our nation cannot with honor and humanity maintain a policy of isolation and disinterestedness from the distress and suffering of the peoples of Europe. Even if the necessity of the peoples of Europe did not have a compelling appeal, the interrelated economic interests of the world would prevent our limiting our attention solely to this hemisphere.

The Peace Treaty includes provisions in an international agreement to prevent war among nations, with all its cruelties and sacrifices of human life, with its burden of indebtedness and taxations; for reduction in standing armies, the diminution of great navies, and the limitation of the production of arms and ammunition. If the Senate shall fail to ratify the Treaty of Versailles, our nation may be isolated from other countries of the world which at some time might be pitted against us. Such isolation and possibilities would make necessary the creation and maintenance of a large standing army and a greater and more effective navy in order in some degree to protect the Republic of the United States from aggression by those countries which were our allies in the great war and which were and are now our friends.

In addition, the workers of America have a deep interest and concern in the Labor Draft Convention of the Treaty, and in its purposes to raise to a higher standard the conditions of life and labor among the peoples of all countries. Its cardinal declarations and provisions are, that labor should not be regarded as a commodity; that the eight-hour day and forty-eight hour week are standard; that there shall be one day of rest, preferably Sunday, in each week; that child labor shall be abolished, and continued education for young workers assured; that men and women shall receive equal pay for equal work; that industrial betterments shall be enforced by proper inspection, in which women as well as men shall take part; that wages shall be sufficient to maintain a reasonable standard of living, as this is understood in each time and country, and that employees as well as employers have the right of association for all lawful purposes.

The United States is protected by this draft convention in two ways: (1) That the recommendations which international labor conferences under the treaty may recommend may be accepted or rejected by our Government; (2) That no recommendation that would set a lower standard for the people of the United States than already exists within our boundaries be at any time presented for consideration and action by the United States.

To give the united support of our Republic and of the allied countries to effective machinery to raise the standard of the workers' condition in backward countries, to help humanize industry for the common world weal is, we insist, a paramount duty which our republic must perform. We insist, for the reasons herein set forth, that it is the immediate duty of the Senate to ratify the Treaty of Versailles.

The American labor movement resents the attempt of reactionaries and autocrats, to classify the men and women of Labor with those groups which have nothing in common with its constructive purposes and high ideals, and with the fundamental principles of our country. Those who aim to strike a blow against the legitimate aspirations of the workers in their struggle for freedom and for a higher and a better life must be met and overcome.

We call upon all those who contribute service to society in any form to act in the furtherance of the principles and purposes and for the rectification of the grievances herein set forth. We call especial attention to the fact that there is a great community of interest between all who serve the world. All workers, whether of the city or country, mine or factory, farm or transportation, have a common path to tread and a common goal to gain.

The issues herein enumerated require the action of our people upon both the economic and political field. We urge that every practical action be taken by the American Federation of Labor, with the co-operation of all other organized bodies of workers, farmers, and sympathetic, liberty-loving citizens of the United States, to carry into effect the principles and purposes set forth in the declarations of this conference.

We call upon all to join with us in combating the forces of autocracy, industrial and political, and in the sublime task of ridding the world of the power of those who but debase its processes and corrupt its functions.

In all struggles for justice and human freedom, sacrifices have been made. Having made supreme sacrifices to crush militarism and political autocracy in Europe, America's workers will not surrender to political and industrial autocracy at home. In the struggle now before us, we will contest every effort made to fasten tyranny and injustice upon the people of our Republic. We are confident that freedom, justice and the opportunity for a better day and a higher life shall be achieved.

CHAPTER II

Organized Labor and Politics

Under the title "Forty Years of Action," the American Federation of Labor has published, in pamphlet form, a synopsis of the non-partisan political declarations that have been passed in the annual conventions since 1881, when the American Federation of Labor was substantially formed.

During this time the Federation has consistently maintained the position that it is an economic movement, and while political questions shall be discussed and the record of officeholders given wide publicity as an aid to the casting of an intelligent ballot, no attempt shall be made to question the worker's right to vote as he elects.

As far back as 1885 the convention rejected a plan to form a workmen's political party. Similar action was taken in 1889 and in 1892. In 1894 it was declared that "a political labor movement cannot and will not succeed upon the ruins of the trades-unions."

In 1896 it was stated that "our movement distinctly draws the line between political action in the interest of labor and political party action." In practically every convention the political party theory, presented in various forms, has been rejected.

The pamphlet is of value in that it shows, in concise form, that the non-partisan political policy of the American Federation of Labor is not a scheme of a few officials, but is as much a part of the trades-union movement as is every other guarantee to workers which has grown out of the experience of these workers.

We have seen in the study of the European situation that the labor parties in every country have sooner or later entered politics. This was done largely at the instigation of the so-called Social Democratic Parties, the Socialist parties, that is to say, who decided to take advantage of the parliamentary system, either with or without any intention of eventually destroying and superseding it. In doing this they necessarily felt the need of an organized party of voters, and this body had to be the workers of the country. Therefore the Socialist Party either invaded and directed the labor unions or organized to a large extent, or else created and developed, labor unions where they did not previously exist.

In the United States the policy of organized union labor has been consistently at variance with this European program. From the beginning of his career, Mr. Gompers, although coming from England, has worked against the English system. He has objected very strongly to the formation of a distinct labor party with its candidates for offices either in State or National institutions. He has induced the Federation to make specific statements of this character. The most recent statements were those at the last meeting in December at Washington, at a meeting of the Federation, a statement that is published elsewhere.

In this connection he rebukes the leaders of labor in the State of Indiana, who early in 1920 organized a special political party in the State, with their own candidates. Mr. Gompers' plan is to carry on an intensive campaign of investigation before each election, that shall lead to declarations on all questions important to labor on the part of every candidate for office in the regular parties. No matter what are the political affiliations of these candidates, those who make declarations satisfactory to labor will receive, as far as possible, the full labor vote at election. In this way labor hopes to elect a majority of men who will favor legislation to carry out the aims and purposes of organized labor, irrespective of their political affiliations.

The constitution of the American Federation, Article III, section 8, expresses this principle:

> "Party politics, whether they be Democratic, Republican, Socialistic, Populistic, Prohibition, or any other, shall have no place in the functions of the American Federation of Labor."

While local and central bodies and State federations may enter into the political field, either independently or otherwise, it is not within their province to form or become part of a national political party.

The address of President Gompers, endorsed by a meeting of the Federation, December 28, 1918, reviews the entire question, including a discussion of the part played by straight union labor in politics. There being nearly 4,000,000 organized trade unionists in the United States, it is quite clear that if the Federation were able to swing these votes to special candidates they could in most cases insure an election.

A review of the Federation's attitude in politics is given in the following letter of Mr. Gompers to the New York "Times":

"You assert, on the basis of a circular letter issued by the Executive Committee of Labor's National Non-Partisan Political Campaign, that 'the American Federation of Labor has reversed the policy which it has followed so long and has become a separate political party.' The 'Times' thinks it sees proof of this in the sentence: 'Here (in the primaries) a smashing effort can be made to nominate members of trade-unions for elective office.'

"The American Federation of Labor has not become a political party, nor has it changed its established policy. It has abandoned no principle, nor has it changed any of its principles. The American Federation of Labor is pursuing the course that has been pursued since its establishment.

" The American labor movement intends to elect its friends and defeat its enemies. If it can nominate friends and defeat its enemies in the primaries it intends to do that also. The workers always have voted in the primaries. This time it is the intention to be more vigorous in securing the nomination of men who will truly represent American manhood and womanhood. If union men can be nominated, so much the more certain will labor be of victory in the elections. Or is it the concept that the workers, as workers and citizens, have not the right to elect liberty-loving, patriotic Americans, simply because of the fact that they are workers, or is it the purpose to continue to select members of the lawyers' clubs of America of whom there are over 350 in the House of Representatives alone?

"As for the principle involved, I quote from the official announcement sent to all organized labor at the opening of the 1906 campaign:

> "We still stand by our friends and administer a stinging rebuke to men or parties who are either indifferent, negligent or hostile, and, whenever opportunity affords, to secure election of intelligent, honest, earnest trade unionists, with clear, unblemished, paid-up union cards in their possession.

"The same principle was declared in 1908 and has been reaffirmed in every succeeding campaign except when suspended during the war. Labor's concern is to see that its enemies are defeated and its friends elected. If enemies can be defeated and friends nominated in the primaries it is a step in the process of election, and one which labor does not propose to overlook. To say that such an exhibition of interest and of citizenship constitutes the formation of a political party is to resort to a distortion which I feel sure the 'Times' would not wish to permit in its more scholarly moments.

"Organization of a political party is a definite act. It requires the taking of certain steps. The American Federation of Labor, so far from taking these steps and committing this act, is definitely opposed to the formation of a separate, partisan political party, and the records leave no doubt on that point.

"The 'Times' accuses the American Federation of Labor of 'a curious forgetfulness of facts.' It is the 'Times' that forgets; the 'Times' is, however, right in saying that 'union labor candidates are to be nominated and elected if possible.' To that end labor and all those who are friendly toward labor and who have at heart the best interests of American citizenship will bend every legitimate effort. And they will bend the same effort to defeat those who have, by their records, shown themselves to be enemies of labor and foes of human progress.

"Is it not a fact that many citizens vote to support the candidates and party which, in their judgment, protect and promote their rights and interests and oppose the candidates and party which, in the judgment of the voters, are regarded as hostile to their rights and interests? Are the workers to be denied that right or criticized because they are pursuing a similar course?

"Let there be no misapprehension. This is an hour of trial, a time of testing. The despoilers of the people shall not escape unscathed. The right which the labor men and women propose to exercise is an American right. It is more; it is an American duty. If fear has crept into the hearts of the betrayers it is well. They have much to fear. The large mass of our people is aroused. It understands what its enemies are seeking. It is going to fight, and the fight will not be without its victories for human freedom.

"SAMUEL GOMPERS,
"*President American Federation of Labor.*

"New York, March 27, 1920. 'Times,' March 29, 1920."

The move to organize, in February, 1920, a State Political Labor Party was severally condemned by Mr. Gompers in the following, given out by the A. F. of L.

"HEADQUARTERS, AMERICAN FEDERATION OF LABOR,
"WASHINGTON, *February* 19, 1920.

"Mr. WILLIAM MITCHELL, Indiana State Labor Party, Indianapolis, Ind.:

"Dear Sir.— Your telegram of February 14, in which you are joined by Messrs. John Hessler, Charles W. Kern, A. A. Fessler and A. S. Kidd, received; it is as follows:

"We, the convention of the Indiana State Labor Party, is session February 14, 1920, stand opposed to the political declarations of the American Federation of Labor asking labor to elect their friends and defeat their enemies. We assert that there can be no compromise on candidates who run on a ticket whose platform is made and whose campaign is financed by big interests. We assert that the political policy of the A. F. of L. is impractical and has been absolutely unsuccessful. Therefore we stand for the labor organized by and for the workers themselves as the only consistent method of protecting labor's interests in the various political departments of our Government.

"WILLIAM MITCHELL,
"JOHN HESSLER,
"CHARLES W. KERN,
"A. A. FESSLER,
"A. S. KIDD.

"By what right do you assume to declare the work and the policy of the American Federation of Labor to be impractical? Surely the results achieved in the interests of the workers demonstrate the utter fallacy of your assumption.

"By your declaration you assert the practicability of the course you declare you will pursue. What experience have you had with your political party upon which to base so absurd a claim?

"Forsooth, some men understand not only that which is charged but the virtue which is proclaimed of political and financial honesty and dishonesty. Perhaps thorough investigation of the political and financial virtues may be a proper subject of inquiry after a political party shall have been in existence more than a day.

"Of this one thing you may rest assured — that the day of reckoning is at hand for all of those who are in antagonism to the cause of labor, and for those who are subtle and equally guilty, even though they clothe their actions in the robes of pretended friendship.

"When you shall have learned the lesson of the real struggle of labor and the cause for which our movement stands, you may become penitent for the gross injustice you have done by your pretension and your course.

"The effect of a separate political labor party can only be disastrous to the wage-earners of our country and to the interests of all forward looking people. The votes that would go to a labor party candidate would in the absence of such candidate go to the best man in the field. In no case would they go to an enemy of labor.

"There can be no hope for success of labor party candidates. The effect, therefore, of a political party will be to defeat our friends and to elect our enemies.

"Labor can look upon the formation of a political labor party only as an act detrimental to the interests of labor and exactly in line with that which is most ardently desired by those who seek to oppress labor.

"The welfare of American humanity demands, in this hour of national crisis, that there be success at the polls. This is not the time for experimenting with political theories which are proved false at the outset. The workers of America must use the tactics of success. They must have results.

"Results will not be obtained by injecting a labor party, so called, into the struggle.

"Those who are determined to be blind to the facts of the present and past will, of course, rush on to disaster and calamity. This the American labor movement will not do. It rejects and repudiates the fallacies of blind theorists, and will have nothing to do with those treacherous follies that are suited only to the purposes of labor's enemies.

"Your telegram is an affront to the labor movement and an assault upon the interests of that great body of Americans who are determined that the present campaign shall result, not in the destruction of our liberties, but in the opening of the way to national progress and the enlargement of opportunities for human welfare, safety and happiness.

"SAMUEL GOMPERS,
"President American Federation of Labor."

NATIONAL LABOR PARTY

In November, 1919, a convention met in Chicago to form a National Labor Party. Its sponsors were revolutionary Socialists, and it was opposed by the leaders of the American Federation of Labor.

The National Labor Digest for January, 1920, says:

"John Fitzpatrick, president of the Chicago Federation of Labor, and chairman of the steel strike committee, determined to keep himself in the limelight of radicalism, has turned his attention from the steel strike to the formation of a new labor party. At a recent convention in Chicago, called for that purpose, birth was given to a political organization which bears the distinct earmarks of radicalism. The call for the convention was issued by Fitzpatrick. This alone was enough to establish that the gathering would be dominated by the Left Wing element.

"In his address of welcome to the thousand or twelve hundred delegates in attendance at the convention, Fitzpatrick urged: 'the formation of a labor party, although the American Federation of Labor opposed the plan at its recent convention.'

"Socialists and extremists who dominated the convention responded to Fitzpatrick's 'battery' and immediately proceeded to elect Max Hayes, of Cleveland, Ohio, formerly member of the National Executive Committee of the Socialist Party, and, until last May a member of the party, permanent chairman of the convention. Chairman Hayes addressed the gathering and then and there outlined the principles upon which the new party was to be founded, saying: 'The National Labor Party will make demands for free speech, free press, free assemblage, and for release of all so-called political prisoners. Its platform will also favor the nationalization of railroads and mines and a public ownership plan, and it probably will adopt the Plumb Plan.'

"The convention ran true to the form prescribed by Fitzpatrick and Hayes, and included in the declaration of principles of the new labor party are the following:

"Abolition of the United States Senate.

"Election of Federal Judges by popular vote, for terms not exceeding four years.

"International solidarity of labor.

"Maximum hours of labor for men and women to be eight hours a day and forty-eight hours a week.

"Minimum wages for workers to be fixed by law.

"Old age, unemployment and sick pensions.

"Government to own and operate the banking business of the country.

"Nationalization of unused lands.

"Incomes of individuals to be limited by law.

"National initiative, referendum and recall.

"Application of the 'Home Rule' principle in state, county and city government.

"Condemnation of government by injunction.

"Repeal of the Espionage Law and all other repressive statutes passed during the war.

"Condemnation of universal military training and conscription.

"A demand for international disarmament to prevent wars.

"Immediate release of all political and industrial prisoners.

"Nationalization of all public utilities and all basic industries.

"Criminal prosecution of profiteers and exploiters of labor.

"Demand that all government work be done by day labor, instead of by contract.

"Equal pay for men and women.

"Approval of women's suffrage."

Among the motions adopted was one condemning the Peace Treaty and the League of Nations as not in the interest of the working classes; one urging the impeachment of Judge Anderson, who issued the federal injunction in the coal strike.

The headquarters of the new party were established in Chicago, and the plans were laid for a national convention in the summer of 1920, to nominate candidates for president and vice-president. In the meantime, separate organizations are being organized.

While no amalgamation with other radical organizations was planned, the platform of the party is so drafted as to enable such radical organizations as the Non-Partisan League and the Committee of Forty-Eight, as well as the co-operative societies, to work in harmony with it.

It is evident from the program, from the men who are in charge, and from the opposition of not only the Federation of Labor, and other groups of organized union labor, that this so-called labor party is much more representative of radical socialism than it is of labor.

BRITISH PROGRAM PRESENTED TO THE AMERICAN FEDERATION OF LABOR

An illuminating incident has confirmed to the mass of American workmen the report of the representatives of the A. F. of L. who went to England and realized the radical tendencies of British Labor.

Miss Margaret Bondfield, fraternal delegate from the British Trades Union Congress, addressed the Convention, bringing the greetings of the organized wage earners of Great Britain to the members of the American Federation of Labor, in session at Atlantic City.

The substance of her remarks was that the British labor movement — industrial, co-operative, and political — has united to create a new state and that its revolutionary plan to democratize industry has been formulated and is now being worked out.

She described the grouping together of the British unions into industries, the greatest combination of all being the Triple Alliance, composed of the miners, the railroad workers, and the transport workers. "So strong is this group," she said "that no government would dare ignore the direct consultation of these representatives in any question affecting their trades."

She spoke of the conference in England between the labor groups, the employers, and the Government where the British trade unionists definitely stated that the capitalist system of industrial organization had broken down and that labor was determined to challenge the whole existing order and to reorganize society on democratic lines.

Miss Bondfield emphasized the interest of the British labor movement in controlling the education of the people so that a militarist generation would not grow up; the decision of the Trade Union Congress to dissolve the General Federation of Trade Unions, which had intrigued to oppose the radicals in international affairs; and finally declared that the most revolutionary structural change in Great Britain in recent years was the addition of the third wing to the British movement. The cooperatives would bring producing genius to the already well-developed political and industrial forces of the labor movement.

A LESSON FROM BRITISH LABOR IN POLITICS

The recent developments in the political situation in England may serve as a warning to America and show us what we might expect if American labor should enter politics and at the same time be contaminated, as it is now, by industrial ideas of the "One Big Union" and by revolutionary Socialism. The recent elections in England created a large parliamentary labor party, so large that, to prevent its gaining control of the political machinery of the government, it would be neccessary for the old political parties to unite in order to prevent labor domination.

The last speech made by Lloyd George in Parliament in March, 1920, is regarded as one of the most significant political expressions of recent years. In it he threw down the glove to the Labor Party, denouncing its program as Bolshevistic, and declared that the only hope of saving England from political revolution lay in the union of the other parties to oppose it. He declared that the Independent Liberals, now led by Mr. Asquith, must choose between labor and an alliance with the present coalition government.

The danger, as Lloyd George sees it, is a danger that might happen here under similar circumstances. It is interesting to note that he considers it to have been largely a situation built up through propaganda, through soap-box orators, who have for years been given freedom to spread revolutionary doctrines. It will be remembered that the freedom given by England to such revolutionary propaganda has been urged as a reason for us to do the same.

A part of Lloyd George's speech is so important that it must be quoted:

"What is happening now? A great new party has burst into the system, and has disturbed the whole of the party. . . . It is no use making a mistake and treating this as a temporary phenomenon. It is the result of at least a generation of very hard, persistent, continuous work. How often have we crossed a common or a park on a Sunday afternoon, or watched at a street corner and seen little groups of fifty, one hundred, or sometimes three or four hundred, and a Socialist speaker expounding his doctrines, and thought nothing of it. We listened rather with amusement to their crude ideas. It was the pile driven in the mud. You thought nothing of it. Now you see the pillars above the flood, and the thing is going up and up and up. It is the result of thirty years continuous work and of thousands of meetings every Sunday. There is no other party that does that. It is not a temporary phenomenon. The people of this country move slowly, and they moved very slowly towards Socialism. They will move back slowly.

"Do not make the mistake of treating this as if it were a sort of a plague or pestilence that will pass away when the weather improves. It has come to stay. What does it mean? Have you taken the trouble to look at their program? You heard them in the House of Commons talking about high prices and putting questions about the conditions of labor here and there. That is not what they are talking about in the constituencies. The men who are here are not the exponents of the real movement. . . . 'The chief objects of the Labor Party are to procure for the producers by hand or by brain the full fruit of industry and the most equitable distribution, wherever that may be possible.' That is all right, but see what follows: 'Upon the basis of common ownership of the means of production and the best obtainable system of popular administration and control in each industry or service.' It is common ownership. In France it was known as 'Communism;' in Germany it was known as 'Socialism;' and in Russia it is known as 'Bolshevism.' It is the doctrine of common ownership.

"That is the doctrine which is put forward by a party which is second in the state, a party which, if the Liberal

Coalitionists leave the government and join the Independent Liberals, would be the break in the State, on the figures of the five elections, and, I am told, on the figures of the general elections, too. That is what you are up against. It is not a remote program. They are beginning by demanding nationalization of this industry and of the other industries. They are going on. It is not an ideal; it is a working program.

"The redress of grievances and the improvement of conditions are regarded as treason to the cause. Why? Because these strengthen the system they want to condemn. They are out for destroying this system root and branch and planting another tree with a different root.

"There are friends of mine who say, 'If you are going to coalesce, why do you not coalesce with the Socialist Party?' Would they coalesce with you? If they would, would you accept their conditions? This is the first item of their program. Can you accept it? Will they drop it? Where are you going to coalesce? How are you going to bridge the gulf? They have only just come into their big success. There may be some among them who would be willing to pigeonhole their principles and have a working understanding with this party, or another, but they are not the inspirers of this new evangel, and until repeated failure has convinced them that they cannot bring the people of the country to this doctrine they will not drop the purpose of their program, which makes it impossible to have a common understanding with them.

"Where do Liberals stand on that? This is the party which would have a majority at the elections if the Liberals and the Conservatives were to fight each other. It is not the doctrine of liberalism. The doctrine of liberalism is a doctrine which believes that private property as an incentive, as a means and a reward, is the most potent agent, not merely for the wealth but for the well being of the community. . . . It is the doctrine of the great leaders of both parties. . . . That is the doctrine that has been challenged by this new menace, and if Liberals and Conservatives fight each other that doctrine, which menaces the whole fabric of society, will triumph.

"I wonder whether my friends of the Independent Liberal

Party quite realize what the effect of the division is. That they are forced, in order to maintain their position, to criticize, to attack, to weaken the coalition government. . . . You are weakening the common front; you are undermining and sapping the bulwarks. . . . And that is why I am in favor not merely of preserving the co-operation of the two parties in the state but of strengthening it.

". . . This country is more top heavy than any country in the world; and if it begins to rock, the crash here, for that reason, will be greater than in any land. I do not want anyone to minimize what the peril is. The country is understanding it, the country is realizing it. . . .

"Somebody said the other day, 'These are political manœuvers.' Those who say that do not realize that civilization is in jeopardy in every land, and that every government in every country is trying to rally all the forces of order and liberty in order to keep down these insurgent forces that are threatening destruction. That is all I want to see done here. I want to see more co-operation, and closer co-operation, between all those who have a common purpose. Unless you do it, the forces of anarchy, the forces of subversion will inevitably triumph.

"Lord Robert Cecil said, 'What is your purpose? What are your principles?' They are quite clear. Our first purpose is to secure the adhesion of all classes, all ranks, all creeds, and all parties to a policy which will reconstruct and restore this country after the devastation of a great war. What is our second question? Peace. I may say peace is our first purpose; a real peace, not a snarling peace, not a scowling peace, but a real peace. . . . 'Peace on Earth and Good Will among Men' is not merely a great gospel, it is the soundest of political economies.

"High prices, prosperity, restoration — all depends upon your getting, not merely peace, but the spirit of peace in the world — good will among neighbors. . . .

"We mean to have a fair deal and a fair reward for individual effort. Individual enterprise should be encouraged, not destroyed and superseded. The state with all its power and resources can assist and develop, but individual enterprise must remain the supreme active power in the production of wealth and well being in the land.

. . .

"But the best protection for the present system is to improve it. A system which encourages the strong man to put forth his strength produces wealth for itself, but it is apt, if it is unchecked, to become ruthless to the weak, and even to the average. Unchecked individualism in this country is responsible for slums, sweating, prolonged hours of toil, child labor, and for starvation in periods of misfortune through ill health and unemployment; and the legislation of the last few years especially, and even of the last fifty years, has been directed to checking the abuses that strengthen that system. Every time you remove a grievance, every time you improve a system, you strengthen the system; and for that reason the greatest advocacy of this system is to improve it. That is why we are engaged at the present moment in these great measures of reform. The period following a great time of stress and strain is the time to overhaul the machine. You then see its weaknesses; you see where it goes wrong; you see where it breaks down. We are engaged in overhauling now in order to make the machine work better. That is our policy, the whole policy of liberalism. I am a Liberal because I believe in liberty. It is for that reason I fight despotism, whether it come from an autocracy in Germany or from an autocracy at home; and I do not care what the autocracy is, whether it is the despotism of an aristocracy or a trade union organization. Communism is an autocracy; Communism is a despotism; Communism means conscription. Look at Russia, with its conscription not merely of wealth but of work. As a Liberal, I am opposed to it.

"The war has taught us many lessons. It has taught us a greater sense of obligation to each other, a greater sense of responsibility to each other. One class does not feel that it has only to look after its own and not after another. No man asks 'Am I my brother's keeper?' The war taught us how dependent we were upon each other. There may be individuals who still think that all that concerns them is their part out of the needs and necessities of the day. I believe they are exceptions. The vast multitude of the people of this country take a different idea of their position, and it is because I believe in my heart that co-operation between parties is the best way of realizing that new comradeship for the purpose of restoring and enriching and making the poor our common comrade, that I stand for that co-operation and appeal to you to do so today."

ORGANIZED LABOR'S OPPOSITION TO REVOLUTIONARY SOCIALISM

Organized labor has made it extremely clear that it is absolutely opposed to revolutionary Socialism and Bolshevism. One of the most authoritative statements in that field was contained in the recent report of President Gompers to the Senate Judiciary Committee, in connection with the prohibition question. (See National Labor Digest, August, 1919.)

While Mr. Gompers was using the menace of Bolshevism and of the I. W. W. in connection with his opposition to prohibition, he has accumulated in this report a mass of evidence regarding the spread of the revolutionary movement which shows how fully he was aware of its existence and how emphatically he was working against it. He has elaborated the same attitude of opposition in a number of magazine articles and in speeches, especially in those that he has made after conferences of the National Civic Federation.

In this campaign Mr. Gompers has been ably seconded by other leaders of the A. F. of L., especially by Mr. Hugh Frayne, Mr. John Frey, and by a number of able orators, like Mr. Collins.

CHAPTER III

Organized Labor and Socialism

In the United States organized labor as represented by trade unionism and the American Federation of Labor has increasingly set itself against the ideas and inroads of Socialism. While the Federation of Labor is unable to prevent the entrance into its ranks of radicals, whose plan is to bore from within, as in the case of Mr. Foster, it has taken every occasion to express opposition to the Socialist program of revolutionary action. The Federation of Labor founds itself solidly upon the continuation of the present industrial and political system and seeks for the reforms that it works to accomplish within the scope of the present situation. This was shown very clearly at the annual meeting of the Federation in Atlantic City, at which a strong statement was made against Bolshevism.

One of the most important meetings for the expression of the conservative ideas and plans of the heads of the Federation have been for many years meetings of the National Civic Federation, at which representatives of the intellectual and employing classes met the leaders of labor for the purpose of exchanging ideas, explaining plans, and of solving questions of common interest. It was in connection with such meetings as these that the National Civic Federation sent to Europe, in 1919, a Commission to investigate the labor situation. This Commission on Foreign Inquiry published its findings in a volume entitled "The Labor Situation in Great Britain and France," which, among other subjects, treated of "Direct Action," "The Shop Steward," "Whitley Councils," "Labor in Politics," "Housing," and "Women in Industry."

Such reports are made by men representing the various elements in the Federation. In this case the members were Charles Meyer, chairman, representing shipping; Charles S. Barrett, farmer; August F. Demis, textile manufacturers; J. Grant Forbes, contracting engineers; James W. Sullivan, topographical and trade unionists; Andrew P. Nevin, attorney-at-law; and E. A. Quarles, who acted as secretary.

Such investigations as this, supplemented by the more special European trips of Mr. Gompers and other officials of the American Federation, have placed American labor in close contact with the European situation. In Europe the attitude of the American Federation of Labor is considered to be extremely conservative, more so than that of any of the European organizations. At the same time it is also felt that the organization of union labor in the United States is far more perfect and complete than in any other country, not even excepting England.

The various features of the labor situation and a discussion of the questions recently put before the Federation for decision are given under special heads, especially, the relation of labor to politics; the relation of labor to the international and national conferences on labor; the relation of labor to Socialism, and the revolutionary elements of labor; the relation to the farmers' organizations, etc.

The resolutions denouncing radicalism, at the Convention of December 13, 1913, were as follows:

Whereas, The American Federation of Labor is an American institution believing in American principles and ideas, and

Whereas, An attempt is being made to inject the spirit of Bolshevism and I. W. W. ism into the affairs of the American Federation of Labor, and

Whereas, The American Federation of Labor is opposed to Bolshevism and I. W. W. ism and to the irresponsible leadership that encourages such a policy; therefore, be it

Resolved, That this conference of representatives of trades unions affiliated with the A. F. of L. and other organizations associated with this conference repudiate and condemn the policy of Bolshevism and I. W. W. ism as being destructive to American ideals and impracticable in application; be it further

Resolved, That this conference reiterate the action of the conventions of the American Federation of Labor in the advocacy of the principles of conciliation and voluntary arbitration and collective bargaining.

The April strike of the railroad switchmen and kindred workers in the yards, tubes, wharves and so forth, called the "outlaw strike," which originated in the I. W. W. element of labor and started in Chicago, has emphasized the fight that has been working toward a combination between the conservative leaders of Union labor and certain elements both inside and outside of the organization. The signed statement issued April 9th by the chiefs of the four big transportation railroad brotherhoods is a clear statement of the situation. It reads:

"The present strike of men engaged in switching service was originated in Chicago by a new organization that has for its purpose the destruction of the Brotherhood of Railroad Trainmen and the Switchmen's Union, and its inception had nothing to do with the wage question, but was a demand for reinstatement of the leader of this opposition organization. After this strike was instituted for this purpose, the leaders of the new organization then injected the wage question for the sole purpose of deceiving the yardmen throughout the United States and to promote the 'One Big Union' idea. There can be no settlement of pending wage questions while this illegal act continues. We insist that every member of these brotherhoods do everything within their power to preserve their existing contracts, which, if abrogated, may take years to rebuild. The laws of all these organizations provide penalties for members engaging in illegal strikes, and these penalties will be enforced. E. L. Sheppard, president, Order of Railroad Conductors; W. G. Lee, President, Brotherhood of Railroad Trainmen; W. S. Stone, grand chief engineer, Brotherhood of Locomotive Engineers; W. S. Carter, president, Brotherhood of Locomotive Firemen and Trainmen."

Even before the issuing of this statement, Mr. Lee, president of the Railroad Trainmen, requested Congress to take no connizance of that strike and not to recognize the strikers in any way, declaring that the Brotherhood itself would attend to it and bring it to an end.

He says: "We will resist every effort to settle this illegal strike by mediation. There is nothing to mediate with the insurgents, and the fight now is to preserve the recognized labor organization."

This latest development is simply a continuation of the series of illegal strikes that have been especially frequent during the last year or more, aimed largely at the authority of the officials of the Federation of Labor, and which have taxed the organization to its utmost. The Federation is doing its utmost to prevent and terminate all such strikes, for two reasons: First, as a measure of self-preservation; and, second, as the best way of gaining the sympathy and support of the public for labor, a sympathy which is seriously jeopardized by any such strikes as inconvenience the public and endanger health and safety. This seems particularly necessary to the labor leaders, in view of the approaching elections.

CHAPTER IV

Socialism in Politics

An interesting experiment in what is a program of State Socialism is being carried out in North Dakota. It is based upon seven measures which have been adopted by the Legislature of the State. These measures provide for a State bank, owned by the State, to be the depository of State, county, municipal and school district funds, and to make loans, secured by property of twice their value; for an industrial commission that will arrange for the conduct of this bank and appoint its managers and also arrange for the operation of the Terminal Elevator Mill Association and the Home Building Association; for an Immigration Commission to advertise the advantages of the State and to induce settlers to come in; for a newspaper to be owned and operated by the State in every county; for making certain changes in the judicial system; for the concentration of State control over the public school system and over penal and charitable institutions; for a one-man Tax Commission. (The "Outlook," and other sources, in National Labor Digest, September, 1919.)

The campaign which resulted in the adoption of this system was headed by the famous A. C. Townley, and the organization which took charge of the propaganda work, as well as the political work, was the Non-Partisan League.

It is essentially a movement under the direction of the farmers. Farming is the one great industry in the State. The principal argument used by Townley and his lieutenants with the farmers has been to argue that they were being exploited by big business, by the Chamber of Commerce, by the railroads, by the bankers, in fact, by every other interest outside of their own farming interest. It was argued that if they had their own banks they could borrow money at a low rate of interest; that if they had their own grain elevator they could store their grain at cost.

The League program of 1919, drawn up by Townley, provided for the establishment of the Bank of North Dakota, the Mill and Elevator Association, the Home Building Association, and other radical organizations, all under the control of the Industrial Commission. The management of the bank was examined into not long ago and the bank was closed as practically bankrupt, but since then it has been reopened. The experiment will be watched with great interest, especially by neighboring states, where the Non-Partisan League has been gradually acquiring great influence, and where it is quite possible that a similar experiment will be tried.

The attitude taken toward this movement by the Socialist Party during the early part of its career is illustrated by the following resolution in 1917.

"Whereas, A new political party called the National Non-Partisan League, that according to the report made upon the same by Comrade Spargo to this convention, offers promise of speedily acquiring political power for a certain division of the industrial class of the United States, viz.: the toilers of the soil; and

"Whereas, In North Dakota and other states it appears that large numbers of comrades have affiliated with the League in the hope of speedy economic reforms through political victory under the banners of the League, and such movement being already at work in many other states with a fair promise of success in all, and it being apparent that the National Non-Partisan League presents a problem for solution that must be met and must be solved if the Socialist Party is to continue as a political or social force in such states as are invaded by the League. It being further manifest that many of the comrades in such League states propose to affiliate with the said League, merely for the reason that they mistake the mission of the Socialist Party.

"It, therefore, becomes the duty of this convention to reaffirm the principles of Socialism, and declare the positions of the party in the performance of its historic mission.

"Now, therefore, be it resolved, That the Socialist Party being the political arm of the working class in its fight for industrial freedom, and its power resting mainly in its clear cut, specific declaration of political and economic principles, rather than in the number of votes cast for party candidates, and the purpose of the Socialist movement being the emancipation of the working class from economic servitude, rather than the election to office of candidates, it is, therefore, declared to be the sense of this convention, that all state organizations facing the solution of this question be urged to remember that to fuse or to compromise is to be swallowed up and utterly destroyed; that they be urged to maintain the revolutionary position of the Socialist

Party and maintain in the utmost possible vigor the propaganda of Socialism, unadulterated by association of office seekers, to the end that the solidarity of the working class, the principles of international Socialism may continue to lay the foundations for the social revolution.

"The social revolution, not political office, is the end and aim of the Socialist Party. No compromise, no political trading." (Resolution of the Socialist Convention at St. Louis, 1917.)

CHAPTER V

International Relations of American Organized Labor

Almost from the beginning relations were opened between the American Federation of Labor and European workmen's organizations. Representatives of French workmen came to America in 1883 to open relations with the Federated Union of the central region of France. In 1885 the A. F. of L. endorsed an international law proposed by the government of Switzerland for regulating labor. In 1887 the A. F. of L. was invited to send a delegate to the International Trade Union Convention in London in 1888, but it was considered wiser to first unite the labor organizations of America before trying to unite with the workingmen of Europe.

When the International Labor Congress was held in Paris in 1889, notwithstanding the fact that the Second International was founded at that time, no steps were taken to join in the movement, nor was any encouragement found in 1890 for joining an International Labor Conference. The conservative character of the A. F. of L. prevented any co-operation with the various Socialist Congresses in Europe. An invitation to send a delegate to the International Congress of Socialists in 1895 was declined as it would imply recognition of the Socialist Party. In 1899 the President of the A. F. of L. was instructed to invite representatives of foreign trade unions to attend the A. F. of L. Convention, and the delegates sent over by the British Trade Union Congress were heartily welcomed.

It was not until 1910, however, that the A. F. of L. delegate to the International Secretariat offered a resolution recommending to the trade union centers the formation of an International Federation of Labor, and it was placed on the program for consideration in 1911. It provided that autonomy of the trade union movement of each country be guaranteed.

The misrepresentation of the A. F. of L. in Europe by representatives of Industrial Unionism came to a head in 1911 at the International Labor Convention at Budapest when a representative of the I. W. W. in the United States attempted to present himself as the sole proper representative of labor from America in opposition to the delegate from the A. F. of L. Although the I. W. W. representative — the since notorious Foster — was supported by French representatives of the Syndicalist organization of French Workmen, the Confederation Generale du Travail, the meeting expelled the I. W. W. representative, admitted the A. F. of L. representative, and repudiated the organization and ideas of the I. W. W. The program of the A. F. of L. at the International Conference is expressed in the following instructions given to him by its executive council:

"(1) We do not favor anti-patriotism or anti-militarism in the sense as proposed by representatives of the C. G. du T. of France;

"(2) We do not favor the general strike as proposed by the C. G. du T.;

"(3) We favor the organization of an International Federation of Labor, the representatives of the International Trade Union centers not to be confined to the secretaries thereof;

"(4) That every means be taken to prevent the exportation of strike breakers from one country to another, whether a strike is in actual existence or in contemplation;

"(5) For legislation in the several countries more uniform in character, governing hours of labor of women and men in dangerous trades, and for the abolition or restriction of the labor of children under the age of fourteen in any gainful occupation;

"(6) For safety appliances, sanitary conditions of labor, housing reforms and improvement of the workers;

"(7) The publication of an official monthly journal or bulletin by the International Secretariat or International Federation of Labor in several languages, in which shall be given the state of trade in each country, conditions of labor, progress and legislation and all other matters affecting the labor movement in the various countries. Also invite next conference be held in San Francisco in 1915."

In 1913 the name of the International Secretariat was changed to the International Federation of Trade Unions, and it was voted to meet in San Francisco in 1915. Twenty-two countries comprised the Federation: Great Britain, France, Belgium, The Netherlands, Denmark, Sweden, Norway, Finland, Germany, Austria, Bosnia-Herzegovina, Croatia-Slavonia, Hungary, Serbia, Roumania, Switzerland, Italy, Spain, United States, New Zealand and British South Africa.

In consequence of the war, however, the San Francisco meeting of 1915 could not be held, and the work of the International Federation was virtually suspended. In 1916 a proposed meeting of the International Federation of Trade Unions in Berne, Switzerland, was cancelled. Varied and frequent detailed correspondence between labor representatives of neutral and belligerent countries found no way of bringing about a satisfactory international meeting. When the inter-Allied labor conference was held in London, September 17, 18, 19, 1918, delegates of the A. F. of L. were present and presented resolutions which were adopted by the conference outlining the ideas of the Federation in regard to a peace settlement and what should be the main conditions of the peace treaty. The part relating to the special interest of the wage earners of all nations was expressed as follows:

"That in law and in practice the principles shall be recognized that labor of a human being is not a commodity or article of commerce. Involuntary servitude shall not exist except as punishment for crime whereof the party shall be duly convicted.

"The right of free association, free assemblage, free speech and free press shall not be abridged.

"No article or commodity shall be shipped or delivered in international commerce in the production of which children under the age of 16 years shall have been employed or permitted to work.

"It shall be declared that the basic work day in industry and commerce shall not exceed eight hours per day.

"Trial by jury should be established."

INTERNATIONAL LABOR CONFERENCE IN WASHINGTON

At the Peace Conference in Paris, a considerable part of the negotiations related to the share to be given to labor and the settlement of labor questions in connection with the political settlements. Labor organizations and Socialist organizations of the world demanded that labor should be officially recognized at the Peace Conference. We have given elsewhere the nine sections relating to labor that formed the resolution passed by the special committee on labor appointed by the representatives of the Entente and Allied power. It was decided that the First International Labor Conference resulting from the Peace Conference should take place in Washington.

Representatives from forty countries attended the meetings of the Conference in Washington October 29 to November 20, 1919. After three weeks of sessions the principles agreed upon and which were to be submitted to the Conference for adoption during the final week, were as follows:

First. The adoption of the eight-hour day and the forty-eight-hour week principles, with the exception that (a) where less than eight hours are worked on some days of the week, the hours not worked may be redistributed on other days, but with no day to exceed nine hours, and (b) that in continuous processes the limit shall not exceed fifty-six hours a week. All overtime to be paid not less than time and a quarter. This agreement cannot lower any higher standards already established by law or collective agreement.

Second. The prohibition of work in industries between 10 P. M. and 5 A. M. for all women, through the substitution of a modernized and enlarged convention for that adopted at Berne in 1906.

Third. The prohibition of the employment in industry of children under fourteen years of age, except for certain special arrangements to be made in Japan and India.

Fourth. A special commission deals with limitation of hours of work in Eastern and other special countries.

The conference issued a statement, from which the following is quoted:

"For the first time nations have agreed to submit the recommendations of an international labor measure to their legislative bodies for approval, for it should be clearly understood that until such approval is given no state is in any sense bound. The present conference, therefore, will not merely meet, adopt and pass resolutions and then adjourn, but will have the guarantee of each of the forty states represented to present its findings officially to the competent legislative authorities within one year.

"The conference is, moreover, more widely representative than any other yet held. It includes not only the highly developed industrial states of Europe and North America, but the less developed states of South America, Africa and Asia. While of course this particular representation of states with such widely varying standards makes agreement most difficult to obtain, it serves, nevertheless, on the one hand, to obtain to those states which are now becoming industrialized, the safeguards of a more liberal industrial legislation, and, on the other hand, to protect the more advanced states from the unfair competition of lower standards.

"The organization of the conference into three groups, governments, employers and workers, have also had a salutary effect. Not only has it led the employers and workers of different countries to unite on an identical program, without fear of any unfair competition from states having lower standards, but it has also assured the support of each group to any decision finally reached by the conference. Consequently, the conference's recommendation will not only have been thoroughly thrashed out by the various groups in each country called upon to endorse them, but each nation will be free of the fear of jeopardizing its interest by adopting legislation more liberal than that of its neighbors. Probably the most important outgrowth of the conference will be the constitution of the International Labor Office, which is designed to be the permanent labor office organization, associated with the League of Nations. Its function will be to act as a clearing house for information on all international labor problems, to register laws and regulations, and prepare the addenda for the annual conferences. Already many problems have been referred to it by the conference for examination."

In connection with the reference to the International Labor Office created by the conference, it may be noted that this office is already functioning in important matters and that it had in contemplation sending a delegation to Russia to investigate the present situation and the possibility of opening up industrial relations between Russia and other nations represented by the International Labor Conference. It prepared a report on Russia for the instruction of this delegation. The Soviet government, however, refused to allow it to enter Russia. This is merely part of its consistent opposition to the League of Nations.

THE AMERICAN FEDERATION OF LABOR AND THE THIRD INTERNATIONALE

In the course of a statement issued by Mr. Gompers in the *American Federationist*. in regard to the attitude of the Federation of Labor toward appeals of the International Federation of Trade Unions of Amsterdam and the British Labor Party for resistance on the part of labor to aggressive action against Soviet Russia, this official statement characterizes the appeal from Amsterdam and from London as "thoroughly revolutionary and obviously animated by the desire to use extreme measures to strengthen the Soviet hold on Russia and to enable it to extend its influence and to dominate neighboring countries."

"The American Federation of Labor is not a revolutionary body and has never had any affiliation with any revolutionary body which would require it to give serious consideration to revolutionary proposals of any kind. While recognizing the need of revolution against autocratic governments, organized labor of this country regards the American government as being essentially democratic. The American Federation of Labor is particularly and utterly opposed to anything that preaches any form of assistance to Soviets.

"There have been indications that the Italian uprising and the radical stand by Smillie in England were planned to take place at the same time as the expected fall of Warsaw and to mark the beginning of a general Bolshevik or near-Bolshevik upheaval throughout Europe.

"We are living in . . . a Republic based upon the principles of firm justice and universal suffrage. Our men and women are not likely to throw these rights and principles into the scrap heap for the dictatorship of Moscow, Lenine and Trotzky. These harangues of the Soviets in Russia will fall on deaf ears of American organized labor movements."

CHAPTER VI

The Four Railroad Brotherhoods and the "Outlaw" Strike

The four brotherhoods of railroad employees, with about a half million members, have thus far not affiliated themselves with the American Federation of Labor, although various proposals have been made to effect an amalgamation, and it has been recently stated that two of the brotherhoods have arranged to affiliate in May and the other two perhaps later. Meanwhile, a strong attempt to undermine the brotherhoods' organization, has been made during the recent unauthorized so-called "outlaw" strike of railway employees, a strike which the brotherhoods have recognized as a direct attack on their organization.

These four brotherhoods are:

(1) The Brotherhood of Locomotive Engineers, headed by W. S. Stone;

(2) The Order of Railroad Conductors, headed by A. B. Garretson;

(3) The Brotherhood of Firemen and Enginemen, headed by Timothy Shea; and

(4) The Brotherhood of Railroad Trainmen, headed by W. G. Lee.

The locomotive engineers organized in May, 1863; the conductors, in 1868; the firemen and enginemen, in 1873, and the trainmen, in 1883. These powerful brotherhoods have been recognized as conservative in character and as working harmoniously with the more conservative leaders of the American Federation of Labor. In fact, it is precisely this character of the organization that has encouraged the present disturbance. The members have felt that the organizations have not exercised strong enough pressure to secure increased wages and better hours, after a consideration of the claims of the men had been referred to the railroad commission that was to be appointed by President Wilson.

In this conservatism of the brotherhoods they have differed very strongly from the corresponding organization in Great Britain which belongs to the famous Triple Alliance, and which is a leader in the radical labor movement.

We are publishing elsewhere the description of the Plumb Plan for running the railroads of the United States, a plan which is considered to be the most radical move taken by the brotherhoods. Mr. Plumb is the attorney for the brotherhoods, and all four of the brotherhoods adopted the Plumb Plan in 1919, and it was presented to Congress in their name in the Sims bill. In the statement that was handed in at this time, signed by Stone for the locomotive engineers, by Lee for the trainmen, by Shea for the firemen and enginemen, by Sheppard for the conductors, and by Jewel for the railway employees, department of the A. F. of L., we find the following:

> "Labor faces a persistently serious situation, due to the cost of living and the impossibility of wages keeping pace with the depreciation of money. No fundamental changes are being advanced to save workers from continued defeat in the economic struggle of life. The railroad employees are in no mood to brook the return of the lines to their former control, since all the plans suggested for this settlement of the problems leave labor essentially where it has stood and where it is determined not to stand.
>
> "We realize that in the strife for wage increases we cannot win any permanent victory. It is not money, but value, which counts. The vicious circle is infinite; increased wages are over-capitalized, for inflated profits and the cost of goods mount faster than the wage level. A few grow wealthy and the multitude is impoverished.
>
> "Any basic change must begin with the railroads. . . . Our proposal is to operate the railroads democratically, applying the principles to industry for which in international affairs the nation has participated in the World War. . . . What we ask is to share the savings from economies we ourselves introduce and to share the profits from new business our efficiency makes possible. . . . In our bill the rights of the public are protected. The rate-fixing power, which is the final check upon railroad management, remains with the Interstate Commerce Commission." . . .

As we know, the Plumb Plan was not adopted, and the railroads were returned to private ownership. But the Plumb Plan still remains an ideal in the minds of the brotherhoods. In this connection, therefore, it is interesting to quote the opinion expressed at the meeting of the Chamber of Commerce of the United States, held in August, in Seattle, which characterizes the Plumb Plan as follows:

> "Demands of the railroad workers constitute a definite program for government ownership. The overwhelming

trend of sentiment through the United States is opposed to government ownership. Such ownership would increase the total debt twenty billion dollars, severely strain the credit of the nation, and depress the value of the Liberty and Victory Bonds held by millions of people. Government ownership, characterized as disastrous wherever tried, would retard development of the railroads and throw the lines into politics."

In connection with the revolt against the brotherhoods that culminated in the "outlaw" strike referred to above, which spread from Chicago to the whole country and for a time tied up, to a great extent, both freight and passenger service, it is interesting to note that the Communist Party took advantage of the situation as did also I. W. W. sympathizers and leaders to intensify the unrest and increase the power of the strike. This is exemplified in the distribution of handbills, the details of which are published as follows in the April 15th issue of the New York "Sun":

"STRIKERS BETRAYED, SAYS COMMUNIST HANDBILL

"The subjoined handbill is being distributed among the strikers. It made its appearance yesterday. The copy printed below was sent through the mails to the 'Sun' and New York 'Herald.' Agents of the Department of Justice have been unable to find the distributors.

"The popular method of getting the dodgers to the strikers is to throw small bundles of them into groups of the men. Generally it is done by someone speeding past in an automobile. They are to be found in large numbers in all the halls where the strikers meet. The handbill, with its headings and typography reproduced, reads as follows:

"DOWN WITH THE BETRAYERS OF THE WORKERS!

"PROCLAMATION TO THE STRIKING RAILWAYMEN BY THE CENTRAL EXECUTIVE COMMITTEE OF THE COMMUNIST PARTY OF AMERICA.

"You are on strike. You have been compelled to quit your jobs to enforce your demand for wages which will enable you to support your families. You are fighting to protect yourselves from the bosses.

"You did not go on strike independently until you were convinced that those who were chosen to protect your interests had betrayed you and were unworthy of your trust. Your strike is the result of the discontent of the masses of the workers with your appointed 'leaders.' It is action by the rank and file to secure wages that will enable you to live, because you are convinced that your reactionary officials cannot be trusted.

"Your strike is a part of the great class struggle of the workers against the capitalists. In this struggle there are only two sides — the workers' side and that of the capitalists. Any man, any official, who is loyal to the workers would have supported you in your strike once it was begun.

"But in place of supporting you, in place of bringing to your support all the resources of your organization and thus helping you to win the fight against the bosses, the officials of the great unions of those employed on the railroads are calling your strike 'ILLEGAL' and calling you 'OUTLAWS.'

"In their eyes it is illegal for you to demand more comforts for your families unless they approve of your demand. It is illegal for you to want to take action against the bosses without their consent. Having betrayed you by not taking up your struggle in the beginning, now that you have taken matters in your own hands, they betray you further by helping the bosses to break your strike.

"Striking railwaymen, your officials are teaching you the lesson which the workers of this country must learn before they can hope for better things for themselves.

"The reactionary heads of the Railroad Brotherhoods as well as of the American Federation of Labor, are the enemies of the masses of the workers. They betrayed the coal miners in their strike AND THEY ARE NOW BETRAYING YOU.

"The workers will never get anything for themselves so long as they follow these reactionary officials who help to uphold the bosses. These reactionary officials are the chief supporters of the whole rotten system of capitalism. The president of the Trainmen's Union W. J. Lee, has even gone so far as to endorse General Leonard Wood for the presidency — General Wood whom the capitalists are grooming for the presidency so that they can put down the strikes of the workers with bullets!

"Sweep aside the traitors to the working class in your organization! Throw them out! Make your organization the militant expression of the masses of the workers! Keep it out of the reactionary American Federation of Labor! Make it REAL fighting organization against low wages, bad working conditions, AND, MORE IMPORTANT, AGAINST THE CAPITALISTS AND THE WHOLE CAPITALIST SYSTEM!

"Stand firm in your present strike. Do not let the cry of 'illegal' and 'outlaw' frighten you. These cries are merely the means through which the reactionary betrayers of the workers maintain their power.

"The masses of the workers in other industries do not care a hang whether your strike is 'illegal' and you are 'outlaws' in the eyes of these betrayers. They know you are right in your demands. They know you are fighting against the bosses who rob and oppress you and that whatever workers fight the bosses — the workers are right.

"Other workers are joining you. The miners of Kansas are striking in spite of state laws and the 'illegality' of their strike. The Communist Party of America is in full sympathy with you and its members will give you their support.

"Stand firm! Fight it out! Force the bosses to grant your demands. You have the power to win if you stick to the finish.

"THEN REBUILD YOUR ORGANIZATION, THROW OUT THE REACTIONARY BETRAYERS OF THE WORKERS WHO HOLD FAT JOBS, LIVE IN COMFORT AND CALL YOUR DEMANDS FOR BETTER THINGS 'ILLEGAL.' MAKE IT A FIGHTING MACHINE FOR THE WORKERS, MAKE IT ONE BIG UNION OF

RAILWAYMEN, FIGHTING FOR THE WORKERS. YOU HAVE THE POWER AND CAN DO IT IF YOU STICK."

It is interesting to know that the method of distribution of these Communist hand bills both in New York and elsewhere by rapidly passing automobiles, which escaped identification, was copied from the method used by the Bolsheviki agitators under Lenin and Trotzky when they were preparing in October their revolution in Petrograd. The description of the automobile propaganda-laden brigade rushing through the streets, tossing out handbills, is common in all the descriptions that have been written of the outbreak of the Soviet movement in Russia.

CHAPTER VII

Organized Labor and Education

In the field of educational work the most vital and valuable single subject of study, if we look upon it from the point of view both from efficiency and of co-operation, is the education of the workmen in the truths and the facts of industrial economics.

One of the best examples of the way in which this can be accomplished is the system developed by Henry C. Osborn in his American Multigraph Company, at Cleveland. Its object is to counteract the purposely misleading statements of agitators in regard to the proportion that wages bear to the total cost of running any industrial plant. It is a commonplace fact that an agitator will tell the workmen that such and such a plant does a business amounting to so many millions during the year. He then foots up the wages of workmen, which amount to perhaps 10 or 15 per cent. of this total, and he peruades them that instead of this 15 per cent., they should receive the entire amount because the product is entirely their creation. Of course, such a theory, in this bald form, would not be absorbed except by extremely ignorant workers, but it is dressed up in more plausible form for practically every class of worker. Knowledge of the facts is sufficient to dispel such an illusion.

The scheme of Mr. Osborn was to show, by moving pictures, by lectures given by experts and by pamphlets and statistics illustrating the manufacturing processes, how many elements enter into the expense account. In the first place, the proper return on the capital invested in buildings, in machinery, in deterioration, in managing, in buying and selling, in the purchase of raw materials, in spoiled work, in light, in heat, taxes, insurance, and in the personnel outside of the industrial workers, such as stenographers, bookkeepers, clerks, and the supervising corps.

The American Labor World for February, 1920, gives a summary of an educational plan which is proposed on behalf of trade unionism by George Stein. It was outlined at a meeting before the teachers' training course for the continuation schools on January 24, 1920. It says:

" For many years both the American Federation of Labor and the New York State Federation of Labor conventions have appointed committees on education to study educational problems, and to define what the attitude of labor should be on this fundamental, social and civic essential, and to present to the assembled delegates a program clearly setting forth what organized labor regards as necessary to insure physically sound, intelligent, efficient and law-abiding workers. . . . Three of the twenty-seven items of labor's educational program have received legislative attention and are embodied in our state statutes. They are: the Compulsory Continuation School Law; Teachers' Salary Increase, and the Educational Program on Americanization.

"We hope that each year other items will be checked off by enactment into law, until all of them find their rightful places in an educational system assuring to future generations opportunities for merit, through physical and technical improvement that will give them a better understanding of and bring them in closer harmony with our national ideals and aspirations, by planting in the minds and hearts of those elements in our population, who give expression to feelings of bitterness and discontent, a fairer view of American institutions. . . .

"The ideal progression for a boy who has a mechanical trend is to have two years' preparation in a vocational school and then at sixteen years enter the trade for which he has prepared. After being established in his chosen vocation, if he gets the four hours' weekly tuition required under the Continuation School Law, his habits of study are not interrupted and under proper guidance he can develop into a skilled, useful artisan and is sure to become the right type of citizen. . . .

"From reliable sources we have established that there are (in the State of New York) 440,000 boys between fourteen and nineteen years. About 200,000 of these will be subject to part-time instruction. We can safely assume that every boy has one sister. We then get 400,000 children for whom instruction must be furnished. . . .

"The co-operation of the organized employer and the organized worker is necessary if the law is to be carried to anything like a satisfactory fulfilment. I believe organized labor is ready for this co-operation and I base my belief on my participation and experience in the councils of labor during the past three years. . . ."

Several unions are considering plans to bring within the scope of the law the whole of their apprentice groups. The plan proposed is as follows:

"(1) The parties to this agreement hereby pledge themselves to co-operate with the public school authorities to foster the education and vocational training of the apprentices in the .... trade to the end that each apprentice shall become a thorough mechanic, with the requisite knowledge of the science and physics of the trade; instruction in mechanical drawing and mathematics of the trade; the mechanical processes and the manipulation of tools required for full mastery of the trade. Attention shall also be given to the study of civics, history of the industry, Americanization and such other subjects as seem proper to develop the technical, moral and patriotic standards that make for good citizenship and sturdy manhood.

"(2) Apprentices must have reached the age of sixteen years and passed the eighth grade in school before entering the trade. Preference shall be given to boys who have attended trade classes in the public vocational schools. Apprenticeship to cover a period of four years.

"(3) The .... Employers' Association agrees to allow apprentices four hours off each week with pay to attend a continuation school during the school term. (Sec. 601e, Continuation School Law.)

"(4) The .... Union will withhold membership in the Union from any apprentice failing to attend such continuation school.

"(5) Attendance shall be for the full term of four years (subject to approval of the school authorities for apprentices in the eighteenth, nineteenth and twentieth years).

"(6) The parties to this agreement shall each nominate two of their members as members of an advisory board to be approved by the Board of Education. This advisory board shall counsel and advise: (a) to employ competent teachers or instructors, (b) to provide proper courses of study, (c) to purchase or acquire sites and grounds and to purchase, acquire, lease or construct and to repair suitable shops or buildings and to properly equip the same, (d) to purchase necessary machinery, tools, apparatus and supplies. (Sec. 604, Continuation School Law.)

"(7) One of each of the representatives on the advisory board of the parties to this agreement, together with a representative of the teaching staff of the continuation school, shall constitute an examining board, whose duty it shall be to pass on the fitness of apprentices to continue in the trade.

"(8) Examinations shall be held at the end of five months' period of the school term. Apprentices who do not show progress consistent with the standard set by the school and the trade can be discharged as not having the qualifications necessary for a competent mechanic. Additional attendance at an evening school can be recommended.

"(9) Apprentices completing the full four years' course shall receive a certificate signed by the presidents of the organizations, parties to this agreement and the examining board, stating that the apprentice is competent to begin work as a journeyman.

"(10) Apprentices temporarily out of regular employment shall attend school not less than twenty hours per week. (Sec. 601e, Continuation School Law.)"

The above gives a good synopsis of the recent situation in New York State and of the program which labor is trying to carry out in connection, not with the advanced workers, but in treating with the apprentice situation.

There is an interesting report on recent developments in educational work for radical labor in an article contributed by H. W. L. Dana to "Young Democracy" for October, 1919. Prof. Dana until recently was on the faculty of Columbia University and is now lecturer for the Rand School and the Boston Trade Union College. He says, after referring to the old attitude of laboring men, that they wanted their sons to have the best in education, a similar education to that of the upper classes:

"Today, however, the workers do not want to be educated out of their class, but to be educated within their class for the service of their class. They realize that our university education only reaches one one-thousandth of our population. Organized before labor had gained its present power, our colleges had failed to adapt themselves to the needs and aspirations of the working people. Since then the workers feel that they cannot rely on the universities to accomplish the tremendous task of labor education, they are busy organizing colleges of their own.

"These labor colleges, like the great Workers' Education Association in England, are gradually passing more and more into the hands of the wage earners themselves. They have been organized along three different lines: according as they have been controlled by political parties, by the co-operatives, or by the trade unions. In some cases, as in the Rand School of Social Science, the group has been along the lines of a political party, in this case the Socialist Party. In other cases, it has been the interests of workers as consumers that have formed the nucleus, and the co-operatives have carried on educational work, as in the case of the Palatine Co-operative Union in Chicago. More recently, however, it has been felt that the grouping as producers was the most logical one for education, and the different trade unions themselves have established schools.

"Sometimes a single union has established courses of education for its members, like the Workers' University, carried on by the International Ladies' Garment Workers' Union. Sometimes a group of unions have combined on an educational program, like the United Labor Education Committee, in New York. Finally, all the affiliated unions of a single state, through their central labor unions have organized colleges, like the Trade Union College, which opened last spring under the auspices of the Boston Central Labor Union. Here, instead of the business men and bankers whom we find among the trustees of most of our colleges, the committee in charge is made up of delegates from the stablemen's union, cigar factory strippers, the horseshoers, the milk wagon drivers, the stone cutters, and a number of other unions, and they are all ultimately responsible to the 60,000 members of the unions they represent. This experiment has stimulated in Washington, Seattle, and other cities, similar trade union colleges which opened this autumn. In time, as each city has its trade union college, these will naturally become affiliated in a national federation. Already the American Federation of Labor in its convention last summer recognized with enthusiasm the work begun by the Boston Trade Union College; in England, 'The Highway,' the publication of the Workers' Education Association, has cordially greeted this movement in America. Before long it is hoped to hold in the United States a national conference on labor education, and perhaps later on an international conference. What is the significance of this movement that is already on foot? . . . The young are beginning to realize that the only hope of the world lies in education and that the only hope of education lies in linking it with labor. This linking of education and labor can be brought about in two ways: by a formation of teachers' unions, affiliated with the American Federation of Labor, thus uniting the workers by hand and brain, and by the formation of these trade union colleges in which the people themselves have control."

This affiliation of teachers' unions with the A. F. of L. is now in process of being attempted or carried out in a number of cases.

Early in February, 1920, there was a conference of the United Labor Education Committee, aiming at the consolidation of trade union educational undertakings in the City of New York, with the idea, first, of establishing in New York a labor or trade union college, like those that have been opened during the last two years in Boston, Washington and Baltimore. It was proposed by Professor Crowne of the College of the City of New York that there should be in New York a Union Educational Council, composed of delegates from the Associated Teachers' Union, the Teachers' Union, Vocational Teachers' Council, and Liberal Employees' Union. There are already in New York two educational labor agencies. The United Labor Education Committee represents about forty unions, including the Amalgamated Clothing Workers, the United Hebrew Trades, Women's Trade Union League, the Jeweller's Union, Painters Brotherhood, the Metal Trade Council of Brooklyn, Central Labor Union of Brooklyn, Central Federated Union of New York. It maintains a systems of lectures, classes and musical entertainments for the members of the associated organizations, though thus far it has no permanent building.

A second and separate educational system for workers is supported by the International Ladies' Garment Workers' Union, which through its educational director arranges for classes and lectures, not only in New York but in other cities, in connection with a group organization known as Unity Centers. The more advanced classes are organized as " The Workers' University." Both of these organizations have two objects in common: first, to give cultural and educational opportunities to all working people; second, to train union members along social and economic lines from a trade union point of view. Under the latter head is included the equipment of union officials and of teachers for trade union schools, the specializing in classes of economics, history of economics and trade unionism, in parliamentary history and principles, in public speaking and writing. It is proposed to co-ordinate these two institutions in a labor college modeled after the Ruskin College at Oxford, England, which has existed for twenty years, or the similar Central Union Labor College of London, both exclusively Workingmen's universities.

The most recent large undertaking is that of the Amalgamated Clothing Workers. It cannot be too strongly stressed that these various energetic educational efforts are for almost purely propaganda purposes and not primarily for useful educational results. The whole conception is to swing labor into the revolutionary camp.

In the educational section of this report there has been a summary given of the different ways in which industrial plants have been used by employers to afford educational facilities to the employees. But nothing that is there described is on such a large scale as the institution that has been opened as this report goes to press. On April 17, 1920, at Akron, Ohio, occurred the dedication of the new Goodyear Industrial University, which is considered to be the first of its kind in existence.

This industrial university starts with a faculty of 117 teachers, with 65 classrooms and so-called recreation hall building, costing $2,500,000, built by the Goodyear Tire & Rubber Company. The enrollment of prospective students of this new university numbers 5,700 out of a total of 33,000 employees of the company. The classes are open to all employees free of charge. The subjects range from elementary Americanization work to post-graduate courses for college men and women.

FARMERS AND LABOR

During the past year, there has been intensive activity among the various organizations of farmers in the United States. The subjects that have been brought up as of the greatest importance at different conventions, have been first, the co-operative movement; second, the eight-hour day; and third, the relation to other forms of labor, especially trade unionism. A strong effort was made by the American Federation of Labor to bring about a support of its policies during the autumn of 1919. The most important farmers' organizations adopted a very conservative policy. At the Farmers' International Congress in October, at Hagerstown, Maryland, it put itself on record as opposed to all strikes, and to the methods of organized labor, adopting a resolution against the ever-increasing wages demanded by industrial labor. It stated that high wages were the allies of the profiteer in keeping up the cost of living. It favored a Federal Board of Arbitration, that would give a square deal both to capital and labor.

"We know that the forty-four hour week cannot feed the world, and we proclaim that it cannot clothe it." It said, "That those who advocate the short day in industry should not expect the farmer to work six hours before dinner and six hours after, with before breakfast and after supper chores thrown in."

The farmers at the annual session of the International Farm Congress in Atlantic City, protested against the policy of organized labor, urging greater production on the farms, while restricting the output of the factories. The resolution add:

"The farmer delegates who sound this warning to labor, know that the workmen in the factories, as a rule, are not trying to be efficient; that the output per man is greatly lessened, and that this policy is not only permitted, but encouraged by the labor organizations — even demanded, in effect, by some of them. . . . There is no moral, physiological, social or business reason why all able-bodied men should not work a reasonable number of hours each day or week; and we hold that it is an economic necessity, becoming more pronounced each year, that they do so."

The farmers' organizations are planning to form a triple alliance, which, if it goes through, will be of the greatest importance in lowering the cost of living. This triple alliance is to consist of the combined farmers' organizations, as the first element, of the public carriers, especially the railroad employees' organizations, and in particular the four brotherhoods; and third, of the industrial workers, of the trades unions. These organizations are planning to get together for some national organization during the summer of 1920.

In this connection we refer to the chapter on the co-operative movement.

CHAPTER VIII

Employers' Views of Industrial Relations

The National Association of Maunfacturers of the United States at its last annual meeting issued the following declaration of labor principles, which expresses the attitude of a large body of employers:

(1) Fair dealing is a fundamental and basic principle on which relations between employers and employees should rest.

(2) The National Association of Manufacturers is not opposed to organizations of labor as such, but it is unalterably opposed to boycotts, blacklists, and other illegal acts of interference with the personal liberty of employer or employee.

(3) No person should be refused employment or in any way discriminated against on account of membership or non-membership in any labor organization, and there should be no discriminating against or interference with any employee who is not a member of a labor organization by members of such organization.

(4) With due regard to contracts, it is the right of the employee to leave his employment whenever he sees fit, and it is the right of the employer to discharge any employee when he sees fit.

(5) Employers must be free to employ their work people at wages mutually satisfactory, without interference or dictation on the part of individuals or organizations not directly parties to such contracts.

(6) Employers must be unmolested and unhampered in the management of their business, in determining the amount and quality of their product, and in the use of any methods or systems of pay which are just and equitable.

(7) In the interest of employees and employers of the country, no limitation should be placed upon the opportunity of any person to learn any trade to which he or she may be adapted.

(8) The National Association of Manufacturers disapproves absolutely of strikes and lockouts, and favors an equitable adjustment of all differences between employers and employees, by any amicable method that will preserve the rights of both parties.

(9) Employees have the right to contract for their services in a collective capacity, but any contract that contains a stipulation that employment should be denied to men not parties to the

contract is an invasion of the constitutional rights of the American workman, is against public policy and is in violation of the conspiracy laws. This Association declares unalterable antagonism to the closed shops and insists that the doors of no industry be closed against American workmen because of their membership or non-membership in any labor organization.

(10) The National Association of Manufacturers pledges itself to oppose any and all legislation not in accord with the foregoing declaration.

WELFARE WORK

In the November, 1919, issue of "Industrial Management" Mr. Fouhry writes of "Paternal Welfare Work," and this view is criticised in the January, 1920, number of the same review by J. C. Davis. The attitude taken by the employees toward the welfare work organized by employers is on the whole adverse. For the most part it is looked upon by the workmen as a form of bribery. When it takes the form of "Dining Halls, dressing rooms, individual lockers, washing facilities and physical examinations," the workers consider that this should be done by the manufacturer, "much in the same spirit as he provides most efficient tools and machines." (January, p. 48.)

The workers do not consider such improvements as in any way a substitute for high wages or better hours. Nor do they care to have it take the form of charity, especially when it is managed by the welfare workers who are substituted for the employers themselves. "Modern welfare work is more successful when the owners of the companies are themselves welfare workers. Just as long as employers deal in substitutes, they may expect substitutes for their employees."

In other words, the employees consider that a large part of the welfare work redounds just as much to the benefit of the employer as it does to that of the employee, and, therefore, should not be considered in the nature of something for which they should be particularly grateful or in consideration of which they should forego other demands.

If this opinion is really the general consensus of workmen, it would be largely the result of propaganda, and not of a sane and disinterested judgment. It would be well worth while to conduct a careful study of the question. In this connection we refer to the official declaration of the American Federation of Labor

PROFIT-SHARING

In the case of the Goodyear Company, organized labor has voiced its determined opposition to the application of the plan of profit-sharing.

The general idea of profit-sharing has been carried out in many different ways during the last twenty-five or thirty years in not only this country but in Great Britain and France. The plan has been discontinued in a large number of cases. In England it has been frowned upon by the famous Whitley Committee. It is a general feeling in many groups of the workers that good wages are preferred to bonuses. It would seem as if there was very little future for the development of the profit-sharing plan in the United States. It is interesting, however, to study the different forms that profit-sharing has taken and some of the important and successful examples of its application. One of the plans is to pay a bonus in money. Another plan is to issue stock for the equivalent of cash. This is a combination of a profit-sharing and savings plan. In an article by P. L. Burkhard, in the July, 1919, number of "Industrial Management," several typical instances are described. The first is the fifty-fifty profit-sharing plan of the Willys-Overland Company. This plan is interesting as defining what it considers the proper interest return on capital invested. This is placed at 7½ per cent. A further 3 per cent. is charged off for depreciation, and 1 per cent, as a "rainy day fund."

It is curious that the employees showed great dissatisfaction over the scale of wages and threatened to walk out a week before the distribution of the first profits, which would have given to the employees their half of a profit of $1,150,900.

We have given elsewhere, in detail, the plan that is being carried out by the Endicott-Johnson Company, which is the second instance quoted by Mr. Burkhard.

The Eastman Kodak Company has been distributing for several years an annual wage dividend amounting to nearly a million dollars to its elder employees.

The Sears-Roebuck Company has a joint profits and savings plan that has been extremely successful. According to this, the company deposits in an employees' savings fund 5 per cent. of its net earnings before any deduction of dividends. In the same fund the employees also deposit 5 per cent. of their salaries. This fund is invested in cumulative stock of the company.

"Profits and savings may be withdrawn after ten years." Of the approximately 35,000 employees, 92 per cent. have become investors in this fund. Of course, participation is voluntary.

The Proctor & Gamble Company of Cincinati has developed a profit-sharing plan, which is open to any employee who has worked as much as eighty days for the company and it is progressive according to their time of employment in the company.

The Thrift Society, as it is called, requires the employee to save 5 per cent. of his earnings, and the company itself contributes to his credit, according to length of his employment, between 10 and 20 per cent. of his earnings. This is invested in certificates that may be converted into common stock. In connection with this plan it should be noted that the Proctor & Gamble Company have gone further than perhaps any other company in giving to the workers a voice in the management of the company. It has placed upon each of the three boards of directors of the company a representative elected by the workers themselves.

One of the objections to the profit-sharing scheme is that it has a tendency to lower the degree of efficiency to the productive ability of the weakest. It also leads to dissatisfaction among workers who are not receiving dividends during a certain period.

The United States Department of Labor, Bureau of Labor Statistics, in consequence of an investigation, gives the following causes for the discontinuance of profit-sharing schemes in twenty-six cases: in eight cases because the plan did not satisfy employees; in five cases because the men went out on strike; in five cases because the men preferred increase in pay; in 4 cases because the plan did not increase efficiency; in two cases because the plan benefited undeserving employees.

Not all profit-sharing schemes are those proposed by the employers. Several are being put forward by the employees themselves. We will select as an example the very recent plan proposed for the 2,500 employees of the Dennison Manufacturing Company, at Framingham, Mass.

The committee of the employees, called the "General Works Committee," elected by the workers, submitted in April to the directors and to the industrial partnership stockholders of the company the plan of profit-sharing worked out by the employees' committee. It is based on a provision for the distribution of profits in the form of non-voting common stock of the company, to be distributed to the employees after certain periods of service.

The Dennison Company had been reorganized in 1911. The common stock was then converted into first preferred non-voting stock, carrying a fixed cumulative dividend. The management of the company was vested in a Board of Directors which was elected by a group of principal employees, made up of the employees who had been for five years or more in the service of the company and whose positions involved managing ability and control of method of production and distribution, as well as those who had general good judgment. This group at present numbers 360 persons.

Since 1911, this group, which alone had voting power, has been entitled to the surplus profits of each year's business, which, instead of being paid in cash, have been reinvested in the business against so much dividend-bearing stock assigned in amounts in proportion to salary. Since 1911, over $2,000,000 of industrial stock has been issued to the industrial partners, with an average cash dividend of 10 per cent. The average face value of the stock distributed in 1919 to each of the principal employees was about $1,600.

The General Works Committee makes the following proposition to this group of principal employees:

It states that there are many ways in which time, money and waste can be saved, efficiency of processes and quality of product increased, and the amount of necessary supervision decreased. This will result, if the industrial partners will turn over to the employees each year one-third of the year's issue of industrial partnership stock. No voting privilege is asked for in connection with the stock, because the employees consider that the Works Committee itself gives the employees sufficient share in the management. This stock is to be non-transferrable and is to be the individual property of each person, the dividend of which is to be received by each one year by year.

The industrial partnership stock is issued in ten dollar shares, and represents the year's reinvested profits of the company. In the distribution the stock is to be divided according to terms of service. The rates run from ten points, assigned for service lasting between three and five years, up to twenty-four points, for service lasting at least twenty-five years. The amount of dividends for this non-voting stock is to be at the same rate as that of the voting industrial partnership stock.

An employee holding stock under this plan, when he leaves the employment of the company, shall surrender his partnership stock in exchange, on a par basis, for a second preferred stock, which he may sell or hold as he likes.

The plan is the result of independent thinking on the part of the employees, which is due to the company's long established plan that any employee co-operative scheme should originate with the employees, instead of with the management.

There are very few non-English speaking employees. About fifty-five are men and forty-five women. About half the men belong to seven or eight unions which are organized within the plant.

CHAPTER IX
Industrial Democracy
THE WHITLEY SCHEME

The most important scheme to settle the industrial problems that has been worked out in Great Britain, is that which goes by the name of Whitley Committee, which has become a slogan in the industrial world. In 1916, the Committee on Reconstruction set up by Mr. Asquith appointed Mr. Whitley, member of the House of Commons, and a member of a firm of Lancashire cotton spinners, chairman of a special committee, to enter into the whole question of the future relations between employer and employed. The committee consisted of twelve members, including trade union officials like J. R. Clynes, later food controller; economists like Hobson and Chapman, employers like Sir Gilbert Claughton, manager of London and Northwestern Railway. The committee was appointed:

> "To make and consider suggestions for securing a permanent improvement in the relations between employers and workmen; to recommend means for securing that industrial conditions affecting the relations between employers and workmen shall be systematically reviewed by those concerned, with a view of improving conditions in the future."

The committee recommended in March, 1917, the establishment, in all well-recognized trades, of joint standing industrial councils, representative of employers and employees. In July, a letter was addressed by the Minister of Labor to all the principal employers' associations and trade unions, asking for their views on this report. In October, a second report on joint standing industrial councils was presented, and so many favorable replies received, that the War Cabinet decided to adopt the report as part of its reconstruction policy, and instructed the Minister of Labor to assist in the formation of joint industrial councils. The machinery suggested by the Whitley reports is based on the principle of local option. The committee recommend that in addition to the national councils, representing the whole industry, there should be created joint district councils and works committees, subsidiary to the national councils. The district councils would deal with questions having a local character; the works committee would deal with all questions domestic to a particular plant. It is a feature of the scheme that the constitution of the national and district councils of the works committee, and of all sub-commitees of any of these bodies, shall be based upon the principle of equal representation of employers and employed, the chairman, as a rule, being chosen alternately from among the two groups. The exact lines on which the work committees are formed varying in different industries, are the result of agreement between the employers and the men. The Ministry of Labor supplies any national council with a representative appointed to act as liaison officer to the council, and the various government departments. Joint industrial councils were established, almost immediately, and have been rapidly popularized in almost every branch of business throughout Great Britain. Their machinery and results have been studied throughout Europe, and in the United States.

Among the important points in the scheme are, first, that it goes a long way towards securing industrial autonomy. Second, that the machinery is decentralized, and elastic, securing the settlement of local questions locally, and adapting itself easily to every form of industrial production. In the third place, the object of the councils is not merely to settle or avert disputes, but to secure co-operation in the improvement of industry; in other words, the plan is a constructive and creative plan. There is a general feeling that the Whitley reports express a practical compromise between the views of the conservative employer, who is suspicious of trades union power and activities, and those of the revolutionist, who aims at destroying the existing industrial structure. The chief practical business of the council has been the equalization of real wages throughout the country, the prevention of unemployment through better organization, arrangement for the employment of disabled soldiers and sailors, the promotion of technical training and research, the improvement of conditions of apprenticeship, and the pooling of schemes for the better conduct of the industry.

JOHN LEITCH PLAN

In the newspapers of March 19, 1920, appeared an advertisement, " Industrial Democracy is Employing Representation." " John Leitch, author of ' Man to Man,' and father of industrial democracy, has a patent organization to assist you to instal employee-representation in your plant. Many executives have proven that the Leitch Plan, properly installed, will, (1) increase quality and quantity of output; (2) decrease cost; (3) promote harmony in working relations. A description of methods and rates sent on request of executives. The John Leitch Company, 512 Fifth Avenue, New York."

This is the culmination of quite a history, which can be seen described in the "American Magazine" for December, 1919, by John Leitch himself, and by his biographer, Miss Mullett. It is a scheme which has been applied in a large number of concerns during the past two or three years. It has been described as an alleviative plan, originating more from the side of the employer than that of the employee. It has been found to work in the great majority of the cases where it has been tried.

An extremely brief synopsis of the plan is this: It is applied independently in each single plant. In other words, it is individualistic. A plant is governed by a House of Representatives, a Senate and a Cabinet. The House has one representative for every 200 to 100 workers, according to the size of the plant, the workers themselves electing their own representatives. The Senate is not elected; it includes minor executives, department heads, foremen — according to the character of the organization of the special plant. The Cabinet is composed of the executive officers of the company, with the president as chairman.

The House and the Senate pass the laws. The Cabinet has the power to veto, but this power has rarely, if ever, been exercised. Questions of wages, of piece rates, of discharges, of grievances of any kind whatsoever, as well as ways and means of reducing costs, are handled by the House. In other words, the discipline and the economic details are in the hands of the workmen. The workmen are encouraged to make suggestions of improvement in machinery, or methods, aside from those improvements that are brought forward in the form of legislation. Any suggestions that are considered useful, entitle the man who makes them to recognition of various forms, either advancement in position or wages. The House has a speaker, who is not an official of the company, but one of the workers themselves. There are various committees, the most important being the one on ways and means. Both the Senate and the House meet weekly, and these meetings are always on "company time." That is, they are held during regular working hours, for which the members are being paid. The time spent in these meetings is devoted to the interests of the business. Therefore, it should be recognized as a vital part of the work, and paid for as such. The proceedings are reported, and every man in the organization can know what is done. In a plant run on these lines of industrial democracy, an employee knows that he cannot be fired unless the House of Representatives elected by himself and his fellowworkmen, have examined his case, and approved his discharge. It is in the interest of every member that good work shall be done, so that a shiftless workman has small chance of not having his case passed on. If a plant has 15,000 employees, one representative to each twenty of them would make a House of 750 members, which is too unwieldy; so the basis in that case would be nearer one per hundred. The election of members of the House is by secret ballot, by the whole body of workers. The Cabinet does not legislate, but it can suggest legislation. The measures that it may recommend to the House and the Senate, need not be carried out any more than the recommendations of any worker. Any measure offered by both the House and the Senate that is not vetoed by the Cabinet, becomes a law.

The method of introducing this system of industrial democracy, modelled on our own government, into any business concern, has usually been to have Mr. Leitch himself come to the plant, call a meeting of the workmen, and explain to them orally, exactly what the plan is, usually in four meetings. The effect of the introduction of the scheme to bring about not only a greater degree of co-operation and understanding between the employers and the employees, but between the different branches of the workers themselves, is illustrated by a speech made by one of the men in the B. Edmund David plant:

> "Before industrial democracy was introduced among us, we were many departments, interested only in the department in which we were engaged, but through meeting together, week after week, and taking up the difficulties and straightening out the differences that have arisen, we have grasped a new thought, a broader view of our responsibilities. For we realize through education along these lines that if we do not put forth our best efforts in whatever we may do, we are not only unjust to the company, but also unjust to our fellowworkers and to ourselves."

THE INTERNATIONAL HARVESTER PLAN

A plan of industrial democracy has been carried out on a large scale by the International Harvester Company. The complete text of the industrial counsel plan proposed to its employees by the company and accepted in nineteen of the twenty plants is given in Appendix 1 to "Common Sense in Labor Management" by N. M. Clark. Mr. Meyer Bloomfield, in the "Nation," as well as in his book "Management and Men," has praised it as follows:

"On the whole, it is one of the best approaches yet made to what may be called the management sharing plan. . . . In such a scheme the men are required to give up nothing. They are recognized as factors in the management, and given an opportunity, but rarely open, as framers of labor policies. For several years the International Harvester Company has been dealing with this question intelligently, and it could do so because it took steps to prepare a large foreman body for the right organization of this work. Foremen, however, are excluded from membership in the Harvest Council. The clause reads:

'Foremen, assistant foremen, and other employees having power of employment or discharge, shall not be eligible for nomination.'

"The Harvester Industrial Council plan provides for equal representation of employees, and management in the 'consideration of all questions of policy relating to working conditions, health, safety, hours of labor, wages, recreation, education, and other similar matters of mutual interest.'

"In case of a deadlock, veto power is not lodged with a high official of the company; the procedure is the appointment of a general council which if itself becomes tied, throws the matter at issue into the hands of an arbitrator or arbitration committee, 'impartial and disinterested.'"

The son of the president of the company, Cyrus McCormick, Jr., in an address before the National Association of Employment Managers in Cleveland, some time ago, pronounced the plan an unqualified success. He says:

"Our plan, now in operation two months among thirty thousand employees, involves full representation on the part of the employee with the employer in discussing working conditions and wages. Everything that touches either interest is taken up in round table discussion at joint conferences, and at these conferences the employer does not sit on one side of the table and the employee on the other. They sit together, side by side. The workingman is given an open channel in the matter of appeal on every question that affects his interest, and there is a clause providing that there shall be no discrimination in the employment of workers. . . . Once in your employ, he is your partner. . . . We believe we have reintroduced the factor of personality in business, which belonged to it when these twenty firms (of the Harvester Company) were small, individual concerns, and which we had lost for a while. . . . The efficiency curve in the National Harvester Company is always rising.

"It has been asked whether under any plan of employee representation — where, of course, the first thing that happened was a great flood of demands for increased wages, which, en masse, had to be refused, though individual cases were granted — whether these men would accept a reduction of wages if necessary. And with every one of our hitherto-most guarded ledgers open to these men, we believed that they would see the facts as clearly as we saw them and would accept a decrease in wages, if necessary. In proof of this, I have to say that the first demand for this general increase was withdrawn by the men."

The National Labor Digest for August, 1919, considered a plan adopted by the Youngstown Tube & Sheet Company, one of the very large companies of the country, to be so important that it gives the full text of the plan, which was presented by its vice-president, Charles S. Robinson, to the National Conference of State Manufacturers' Association, at St. Louis.

THE ENDICOTT–JOHNSON PLAN

The organs of labor opinion have viewed with interest and approval the plan carried out by Messrs. Endicott and Johnson in building up their enormous leather and shoe business. The sympathy and practical understanding of the needs and legitimate aspirations of labor are shown in the following documents:

The following is a letter written by Harry L. Johnson to Henry B. Endicott, October 3, 1919, at which time Mr. Endicott was a member of the Industrial Commission in session at Washington, D. C.:

"Johnson City, N. Y., *October* 3, 1919.

"DEAR MR. ENDICOTT.— Replying to your letter, I first wish to thank you for the opportunity you give me to express my views in regard to the relations of labor and capital. I prefer not to call them theories, but to give them to you as a result of the little knowledge I have accumulated on this subject by personal contact, day in and day out, with our working partners, big and little, all over the works.

"The application of the terms 'Capital and Labor' to this subject is in itself mischievous because, in using these terms, we place the two parties in two different camps, each with their own individual, selfish interest, supposedly antagonistic, and we build up, in our minds immediately, a difference which should not exist, and which we are all working night and day to break down.

"I like the terms we use in our own business much better, namely, 'directors and workers'—capital being what we both use as a very necessary tool to success, and labor representing what we must all do if we are, with the help of capital, to produce real wealth.

"I feel strongly that lack of confidence each in the other, due to errors of the past and present, is creating all the mischief that is abroad in our country today, and is giving to the radicals their power with which to upset working conditions everywhere. If those having money to invest and seeking an adequate return would sit down one hour daily with a perfectly open mind and discuss with those who are working so hard for them the problems with which the worker has to deal, it would not take long to commence to apply the real remedy. Workers, as I have found them, are not materially different from you or me, they have the same ambitions, the same desires, they are equally as honest — up to their opportunity, just as intelligent, and just as anxious to do the right thing. Their problems are many and varied, they change hourly — they cannot be met by any rule or set of rules — certainly not by any arbitrary rules. Industry that owes so much to them, must in turn be willing to grant a great deal to them. I am not speaking of wages alone, notwithstanding they are important, but working conditions, housing conditions and cost of living with which they are surrounded, are quite as important. It may have been possible in the old days to employ a few men at some given task, to require much of them for a small return and to 'scrap' them as often as occasion seemed to warrant, but in any big industry this is absolutely impossible. The industry cannot afford either to have the workers dissatisfied, unhappy or restless, nor can it afford, having received the best a man had to give over a term of years, to ignore its obligations to him to see that he is given a chance all during his active years, and to go down to old age with something in life worth while.

" Personally, I have never found the workers unreasonable, speaking broadly. On the contrary, they have been slow to ask for many things to which they were fairly entitled without asking. If listened to with an open mind and allowed to state their case with the reasons therefor, they are usually found to be conservative, reasonable and fair. Adjustments must be made continuously and always according to the merits of the case, and never because of fear or favor.

" Employment of workers should be a fair field for all, and promotion always from the ranks, so that all the workers may understand they are to begin in the more lowly positions and may advance as they have opportunity and show the necessary ability.

" Workers should be represented in the management and in the Board of Directors, not necessarily with a man from the ranks of today, but fairly represented by someone who has their interests really at heart, and in whom they have implicit confidence. They do not ask to be heard in the Board of Directors — at least I do not believe they will ask that unless they feel that they are misrepresented and that their cause is not receiving its share of the company's attention. I think our workers are very happy to leave their representation to our directors in the hands of George F. Johnson and after him I think they would be willing that I should represent them, but they must be represented, they cannot be overlooked or ignored and their interest lost sight of.

" If I were to state in order, things to be considered by the Board of Directors, I would state first, the interest of the workers, their conditions and their wages.

" Now, to properly represent them, a man must understand them, and to understand them he must come in contact with them daily and have their interests really at heart — not because he has got to satisfy them to keep in operation, although that is true, but because it is his moral obligation, assumed when he takes over the conduct of a business, to take care of the interests of each and every worker who helps him build up the enterprise.

"I cannot speak with authority in regard to capital but my association with labor prejudices me to their point of view. Capital has been arrogant, selfish, brutal and unreasonable and altogether at fault, in many, many instances and while it may be plain and doubtless is true, that labor, badly led, has been equally as arrogant, selfish and brutal, it is a fact that capital, having within its ranks, supposedly, the broad-minded, intelligent, most successful men of affairs, labor has expected it to lead the way, and not block the way.

"Workers' Point of View"

"If Endicott-Johnson has any advantage over the average industry in its treatment of the workers, it is because we have always considered the workers' point of view, and realized something of the tremendous fight the average working man or woman has to put up to get any semblance of a 'square deal.' In thus so strongly defending the workers, I do not disguise the fact of their having been led into many errors, into shiftless ways of working and shiftless ways of living, into a desire for much pay and little work, a longing for the places of ease and the 'soft snaps,' a desire for some of the luxuries and idleness of their richer neighbors, but I do feel that they have been set a very bad example by those who, having acquired a measure of success and with it its natural penalty, money, have let up in their efforts to improve what they have and given themselves over to an insane desire to get more.

"Finally, I have come to love the working people — those who, by work, sweat and grind of toil, produce all the wealth in the world. I do not underestimate their faults, but I do say before we shall have industrial peace, the interest of the workers must be cared for, and if they are cared for, the method by which they are cared for is not important. What the industrial world needs today is contact with workers, and sympathy for their needs, and a sincere desire to provide them. Unless 'Capital,' as such, approaches the problem from that standpoint, I do not see why they will not continue to antagonize the workers instead, and, having done so, receive their antagonism as a reward. The heart of labor being right, it will respond to right treatment, and it will resent unjust and unfair treatment.

"I hope we may be able to continue to solve these problems correctly by continuous consideration of them before they become real troubles, exactly as you would treat a sick person, and not wait until they were beyond recovery.

"Very truly yours,
"(Signed HARRY L. JOHNSON,
426 Main Street, Johnson City, N. Y."

"ENDICOTT, N. Y., *April* 3, 1919.
"TO OUR WORKERS:

"Due to our mutual efforts our leather and shoe business has grown from $600,000 to $75,000,000 annually, with possibilities for future development so great that we feel the business will be strengthened and the interests of all better guaranteed under the form of a corporation than a private ownership.

"We have therefore decided to put into operation a plan which we have considered carefully, and which we feel guarantees continued growth and security after the present generation has passed away. During all these years we have tried to show our appreciation of the hearty good will and co-operation of the workers. We have considered their interests always and in this, our latest move, one of our chief considerations is to maintain and safeguard their interests, and thus avoid any possibility of interruption in the conduct of the business from any cause.

"Invested capital and management of this business is entitled to a fair return for its risks and efforts. Labor is entitled to fair wages, good working conditions, reasonable hours and fair treatment. Accordingly we announce the following plan:

"Each year, after a 7 per cent. dividend has been paid on preferred stock, and 10 per cent. set apart on the common stock, the balance of the profits, if any, shall be split 50–50 between the workers and the owners of the common stock. Every worker who has been in the employ of the company throughout the entire year will share and share alike, which means that the highest paid and lowest paid worker, and all between, receive the same amount either in common stock or cash, at the option of the directors. Divisions made once a year. Plan commences as of January 1, 1919. First division as soon as possible after January 1, 1920.

"It will be noticed in the careful study of this plan that no worker receives a share of profits in January, 1920, who was not on the payroll January 1, 1919, and this method of figuring length of serivce will apply each year thereafter.

"Any worker wishing to buy preferred stock in the new corporation paying 7 per cent. dividend, may apply before April 14, 1919, at Workers' Trust Company, Johnson City. There is no obligation on your part to buy this stock, nor will it affect your share in the profits. We consider it to your interest to purchase as much stock as you can.

"We have today the strongest and best leather and shoe business in the world. We shall continue to build and develop this business with your co-operation as rapidly as good conservative business judgment permits. We congratulate our workers that they are connected with Endicott–Johnson Corporation. We congratulate the corporation that it has such a splendid organization of loyal workers. When we have good years you will share them with us; when we have poor years you will share the disappointments also. As time goes on and you save money and wish to be larger owners of the Endicott–Johnson stock we will always give you as working partners the preference.

"This plan, the result of years of study, hard work, careful and conscientious consideration, is offered as our best conception of what industry really means. Just as long as this plan works satisfactorily to all concerned, it is our intention to continue it.

"In this announcement all our partners and the directors of the new corporation are in hearty agreement.

"During the first year of the corporation H. B. Endicott, Geo. F. Johnson, H. L. Johnson, Eliot Spalding, C. B. Lord, Geo. W. Johnson and H. W. Endicott, the former partners, will accept no salaries.

"H. B. Endicott.
"Geo. F. Johnson."

"ENDICOTT-JOHNSON WORKERS
"THE SQUARE DEAL
"JOHNSON CITY, N. Y., *March* 11, 1920.

" We feel that the keynote of whatever success we have had in our business is due to the fact that our general manager started work at the bench about twenty-five years ago, and being a worker himself, has had the interest of the workers always in mind, and has never lost their viewpoint. The business has grown from 300 workers to 13,000 workers now employed, and during all these years there has been no labor trouble.

" The men in charge of the different departments are not called ' foremen ' or ' bosses,' but are called 'directors,' thus taking the right of discharge away from them. If we find the worker not fitted for the job he is on, he is transferred to another job which he is better suited for, and only in the last extremity is a man dismissed from the company.

" The ' open door policy ' gives the worker the right to take any complaint that cannot be satisfied by the director or superintendent to the general manager, and each case is considered carefully and straightened out to the satisfaction of all concerned.

" In an effort to bring about a fair division of the profits of the industry between capital and labor, we have branched out into many activities, all of which tend to make this community a better place in which to live and work.

" In connection with our factories, we have seven or more restaurants where good, substantial meals are served three times a day for fifteen cents each.

" Our swimming pools, tennis courts and playgrounds in connection with the factories are used extensively by the workers and also by their families and the rest of the townspeople.

" We have a medical department with a staff of seventeen doctors and twenty nurses and their services are free of charge to the workers and their families, and this service is being constantly enlarged. In connection with all our factories we have a first-aid hospital where all medical and injury cases are attended to. We also have a maternity hospital with services of doctor and hospital for any of the workers and their families.

"For the sum of ten cents each week, taken from the envelopes of the workers, they are made members of the sick relief association, and in case of sickness they are paid benefits of $15 each week during a period of ninety-five days and longer, if necessary. In the case of factory accident, 100 per cent wages are paid.

"Our recreation department has charge of our swimming pools, parks and playgrounds. Musicals are given each Sunday at the libraries in the two towns and during the summer band concerts are given in different parts of the towns. At Endicott, they have a park which contains dancing pavilion, band pagoda, a merry-go-round which is operated all during the day free of charge. Also has a half-mile race track which is the scene of many horse races. Community Hall located in Johnson is the scene of many dances and social affairs given by the different departments of the factories.

"Our athletic association is in charge of all the factory ball teams and numerous athletic events which are held throughout the year, and by Spring of next year we expect to have two new clubhouses fully equipped with everything that goes to make up an athletic club house.

"We are enclosing you herewith clipping which explains our 'profit-sharing' plan which took effect March 1st of this year, of which 10,500 workers each shared $237.90. Each worker had to be in the service of the company for a year.

"We are also sending you a copy of the workers' magazine which is edited by our workers each month. This will give you an idea of what we are trying to attain.

"All of these activities are only incidental to the one big one which is that the workers who make possible the creation of the industry are entitled to a larger share of the returns from the business than they usually receive in the majority of other industries.

"We are also enclosing you herewith a little booklet which will describe what we are trying to do in the way of housing our workers. In further reference to the information contained therein, wish to say that at the present time we have about thirty houses ready for occupancy on this one tract and have built at least that many in different parts of the town.

"We are also enclosing you a pamphlet containing an article on 'Capital and Labor' which we think might interest you. "Very truly yours,

(BM.) "ENDICOTT JOHNSON."

CHAPTER X
Labor's Solutions
COLLECTIVE BARGAINING

The principle of collective bargaining is by this time universally recognized. The only difference of any importance is a difference in interpreting the term or in applying it. The National War Labor Board adopted the following policy:

"The right of workers to organize in trade unions and to bargain collectively through chosen representatives is recognized and affirmed. This right shall not be denied, abridged or interfered with by the employers in any manner whatsoever."

A similar statement was made in 1913 by the British Industrial Council:

"The desirability of maintaining the principle of collective bargaining which has been so important a constituent in the industrial life of this country cannot be called into question, and we regard it as axiomatic that nothing should be done that would lead to the abandonment of a method of adjusting relationships between employers and work people, which has proved so mutually advantageous throughout most of the trades of the country."

The other side of the question is taken by the United States Supreme Court, in connection with the right of an employer to discharge a man because he joins a union. Judge Harlan stated in the Adair case (208 U. S. 161):

"The right of a person to sell his labor upon such terms as he deems proper is, in its essence, the same as the right of the purchaser of labor to prescribe the conditions upon which he will accept such labor from the person offering to sell it. So the right of the employee to quit the service of the employer, for whatever reason, is the same as the right of the employer, for whatever reason, to dispense with the service of such employee. It was the legal right of the defendant Adair . . . to discharge Coppage because of his being a member of a labor organization, as it was the legal right of Coppage, if he saw fit to do so . . . to quit the service in which he was engaged, because the defendant employed some persons who were not members of a labor organization. In all such particulars the employer and the employee have equality of right, and any legislation that disturbs that equality is an arbitrary interference with liberty of contract which no government can legally justify in a free land."

The particular phase of collective bargaining that came to the front in connection with the steel strike of the autumn of 1919 was a difference of interpretation. In this case the question of collective bargaining was inextricably mixed with the question of the open or closed shop. Judge Gary insisted that he was perfectly willing to acknowledge the right of his employees to treat with him collectively, but that he would not recognize the right of any individual or groups of individuals who did not belong to his plant to undertake to represent the employees of his plant in presenting claims on their behalf. This was also connected with the problem elsewhere discussed as to the rights of outside influences to intimidate the workmen of a plant into joining a union. The majority of employers are perfectly willing to negotiate collectively, provided there is no interference with the right of individual workmen to negotiate individually with the company.

This question is so inextricably interwoven with that of the Open and Closed Shop that we defer further consideration of it to Ch. XII. The attitude of the American Federation of Labor is that the recognition of collective bargaining is illusory without the recognition of the union as a party to the arrangement.

CO-OPERATIVES

The co-operative movement is at last taking root in the United States. As early as 1917, the American Federation of Labor, at its annual convention, went on record as advocating Consumers' co-operation, and the subject is to come up again at the next annual meeting.

The First National Co-operative Convention of the American movement was held at Springfield, Illinois, in September, 1918, under the auspices of the Co-operative League of America. Delegates and representatives came from all parts of the United States, including many representatives of labor. The papers and discussions were largely by workingmen. There were 185 delegates from 386 co-operative societies. A single labor delegate represented 285,000 railroad men. Another delegate was the president of an organization of 250,000 workers. There was evident this union of purpose between the co-operative and the trade unionist movement, and it is becoming more and more evident that the two organizations will work in unison. At the same time, the appeal of the co-operatives is so general, that the scheme has received the support of the radical as well as the conservative elements of labor. It has been endorsed by the Socialist Party and the Communist Party, in their conventions of September, 1919.

The idea of co-operation is not a recent one in the United States, but it has until recently been a decided failure in almost every case. It remained so as long as it was in the hands of native Americans. It has shown signs of success only since it has been taken up by the different foreign elements who have made use of methods that have proved so successful in Great Britain and Europe. The principal reason for the failure up to the present in the United States has been because the movement has not taken root in the field of production, as well as distribution. Only when the greatest saving can be made on the side of production, can the plan be a success.

The history of the co-operative movement is extremely important, because it bears the closest relation to every form of the labor movement and of the Socialist movement throughout the world. The beginning of it was in England, in 1844, in the famous experiment conducted on a small scale at Rochdale, in Lancashire. The movement spread quickly throughout the north of England and Scotland, then all over Great Britain and the Continent. It is reckoned that about one-quarter of the total population of Great Britain belongs to the co-operative associations.

The British Co-operative Society owns creameries, tallow, oil and bacon factories, tea plantations, fruit farms, all over the world, and maintains buying depots in the majority of large cities. It sells practically everything of current use. It is developing its own banking and investment organizations.

It is in Russia that the co-operatives have perhaps made the most startling advances. In 1905 there were less than 2,000 locals in Russia; in 1917 there were more than 46,000. In 1914 there were 9,000,000 members. In 1917, there were 13,000,000. The present membership is more than 20,000,000.

The movement in Russia was democratic. It helped to stave off famine and disaster in Russia during the war, and has kept on doing so under the Soviet government. The question of the Russian co-operatives has become a burning one in connection with the trade relations of all nations with Russia. The Soviet government, not recognizing private property and enterprise, it seems impossible that the Russian co-operatives should have the liberty of action necessary to make them free agents in any large commercial relations with the outside world.

In fact, since this Report was first drafted the Russian Soviet government has annexed the Cooperatives and made them merely a part of government machinery, without the power to hold or acquire property or conduct any independent business.

Next to Russia and Great Britain, the most interesting group of co-operatives is in Belgium. Here, as elsewhere, the war, instead of stopping, was a stimulant to the development of the Belgian co-operatives, which became largely the intermediary between the temporary German administration and the Belgian people.

Some statistics will give an idea of the extent of co-operative operations taken largely from the American Labor Year Book. The English Co-operative Wholesale Society reported a turn-over in 1917 of $288,550,660, an increase of about $27,500,000 over that of 1916 itself. The German co-operative wholesale turnover in 1917 was $26,934,320. It must be noted that neither the British nor the German governments particularly favor the co-operative movement. The turn-over of the Finnish organization was over $18,000,000. That of the Swiss over $17,000,000, and of the Austrian over $16,000,000; of the Swedish over $16,000,000; of the Dutch over $4,000,000, and of the Norwegian, nearly $2,000,000; the French $10,500,000. The combined sales of the ten chief co-operative wholesales of the world rose from $380,000,000 in 1916, to $477,000,000 in 1917.

It is interesting to note that the International Co-operative Alliance has been created and developed as a counterpart to the International Socialist movement. There was a conference of the co-operatives of the Allied countries in Paris, in February, 1919, and the Tenth International Co-operative Congress is planned to meet in Switzerland late in 1920.

The co-operative idea is one that forms a distinct part in the program of several Socialist and labor parties, as has already been noted. It is the fundamental and essential basis for any scheme of turning over to the people the distribution of production, with the elimination as far as possible of waste, and of the profits of the middleman. It is an element in any constructive, as well as in any revolutionary, plan for the amelioration of present conditions.

There are various sections to any co-operative movement. One of the most important, of course, in the United States, as well as in Russia and Norway, is the agricultural section. There are already in the United States, more than 12,000 farmers' co-operative organizations, such as creameries and grain elevators. Groups of producers' co-operatives are being formed in other fields, beside the agricultural, to work in connection with the distributive element. There are a number of groups in the United States connected with different races. The most important of these perhaps is the Finnish group, which counts about 150 co-operative societies, where the European scheme is developed in the widest possible way. These societies have fifty grocery stores, four mills, three bakeries, 26 boarding houses, several apartment houses, three publishing houses, three daily newspapers, two monthlies, and two weeklies. They have two co-operative amusement parks, schools, libraries, meeting halls, dramatic entertainments, and concerts. They own buildings containing libraries, dormitories, billiard rooms, bowling alleys.

There is essential development of the co-operatives in Italy, under the title Società di Lavoro. The workingmen contract for their own labor, and undertake large public and private contracts such as the building of railroads and canals. The co-operatives have complete charge of the business in the great Port of Genoa. Associations of navvies, masons, bricklayers, stevedores, and other branches of workmen, are associated in these large business enterprises. It would seem that out of the different phases of the co-operative movement might spring the best solution of the present, unrest as it would certainly be the most efficient agent for the reduction of the cost of living.

It is interesting to quote the resolution of co-operative societies passed by the International Socialist Congress of Copenhagen in 1910:

> "Taking into consideration that distributive co-operative societies are not only able to secure for their members immediate material advantages, but are also capable of first increasing the influence of the proletariat by the elimination of private commercial enterprise; and secondly, by bettering the condition of the working classes, by means of productive services organized by themselves and by educating the

workers in the independent democratic management of social lines of exchange and production;

"Considering also that co-operation alone is incapable of realizing the aim of Socialism, which is the acquisition of political power for the purpose of collective ownership of the means of production;

"This Congress declares, while warning the working classes against the theory which maintains that co-operation is in itself sufficient, that the working class has the strongest interest in utilizing the weapon of co-operation in the class struggle, and urges all Socialists and all members of trade unions, to take part in the co-operative movement, in order to develop themselves in the spirit of Socialism, and keep the co-operative societies from any deviation from the path of education, and the promotion of working-class solidarity.

"The Socialist members of co-operative societies are urged to endeavor in these societies to see that the profits are not entirely returned to the members, but that part is devoted, either by the society itself, or by the Federation of Social Societies to the development of production and education and instruction, in order

"1. That the conditions of wages and work in the co-operative societies shall be regulated in accordance with trade union rules.

"2. That the organization of the conditions of employment in co-operative societies shall be the best possible, and that no purchase of goods shall be made without regard to the condition of the producers.

"It is left to the co-operative organizations of each country, to decide for themselves whether, and to what extent, they will aid from their resources the political and trade union movement.

"Furthermore, being convinced that the services which co-operation can render to the working class will be the greater in proportion as the co-operative movement is itself strong and united, the Congress declares that it is desirable that the co-operative societies of each country shall be self-constituted on this basis, and subscribe to this present resolution and form a single federation.

"It declares, besides, that the working class in its struggle against capitalism, is especially concerned with trade unions, co-operative societies and the Socialist Party, which, while preserving each its own unity and autonomy, should enter into relations more and more intimate with one another."

This resolution calls attention to the important fact in the co-operative movement, that a large part of the profits are periodically returned to the members of the associations as a sort of bonus system.

While the American Socialists until quite recently, probably on account of the failure of the co-operative movement in America, did not show the same enthusiasm as the Socialists on the other side for the movement, still, at its convention in 1912, the Socialist Party recognized the value of the co-operative movement, and expressed its support in the report adopted by the convention, in which it says:

"Just as the labor unions fight for industrial self-control for the working class, the Socialist Party for political self-control, and the labor and socialist press for intellectual self-control for the workers, so the co-operative movement fights for an increasing degree of economic self-control for the workers through the ownership and use of industrial and commercial capital by organized groups of the workers. The development and successful operation of the co-operative movement in connection with the international labor movement, is an historic fact, which cannot be disputed. While in some countries it may seem for the time being to have checked other lines of working-class activity, it must be true also that 'the economic power of a class at a given stage of development turns into political power.'"

Farmer — Labor Co-operative

The All American Farmer-Labor Co-Operative Commission was formed at a convention in Chicago, on November 21–22, 1919, called by officers of the Farmers' National Council and the National Co-operative Association. It was composed of members of the four leading farm organizations (the Grange, Farmers' Union, Society of Equity and the Gleaners), of representatives of the various railroad brotherhoods, leaders among the national and international trade unions and delegates of co-operative organizations from all parts of the United States.

The meeting elected a permanent commission of twelve which arranged for an All-American Farmer-Labor Co-operative Congress to meet in Chicago, February 12–14, 1920, with the following objects:

"1. To co-ordinate co-operative effort among the various producing and distributing groups of co-operators to the end that speculation, profiteering and all unnecessary intermediary trading and jobbing in the necessities of life should be eliminated and that there should be established, as nearly as possible, direct buying and selling between original producers and ultimate consumers.

"2. To educate the workers through their organizations and press to the almost completely neglected method of increasing the daily wage by multiplying its purchasing power through co-operative trading methods.

"3. Being both borrowers and lenders in matters of finance and outrageously exploited in transactions involving either operation by those who control the life blood of the business world, to undertake to establish among and between the workers of the mine, factory, farm and field, a financial system of their own for the permanent use of their own money and credit in co-operatively financing the means of production and distribution of life's necessities.

"4. To teach and give the widest publicity to the contrast afforded between a system of industry directed on the one hand by competition and self-interest, and, on the other, by co-operative effort; and to show that while the results in the first case have but naturally led up to the present frightful world conflagration, industrial democracy and mutuality in business are indispensable if civilization is ever to abolish industrial and military warfare and usher in a new social order."

The proposed alliance between the four big railroad brotherhoods and the farmers' organizations to further the co-operative movement, its endorsement by the American Federation of Labor, the purchase of manufacturing plants, by another railway workers' organization, the special activities of the Northwest Co-operative Association and the Pacific Coast Co-operative League, which are noted in the February issue of the National Labor Digest, led to a report on the subject by a special committee of the American Federation of Labor and to a general meeting in February at Chicago, of the National Co-operative Congress.

The new alliance proposes to establish banks throughout the country, a hundred million dollar reserve fund, and with this fund to establish factories, warehouses and other business enterprises, in order to get rid of the profiteer by eliminating the middleman and by bringing together the purchaser and the consumer. The Committee of the Federation of Labor made a favorable report on the plan and it was at the November meeting of the railroad members and the farmers in Chicago that the situation seemed promising enough to induce them to call the meeting of the Congress in February. A bulletin called the "Federal Co-operator" is the organ of the Federal Employees' Co-operative League, with headquarters in New York, which may be consulted for information in regard to the development of the movement in the United States. The two principal difficulties in the way of a successful operation of co-operative stores is, in the first place, attempting to get along with cheap and unscientific help and the second is the lack of adequate organization of the productive end.

The following short program, which has been unanimously adopted by the American Federation of Labor, was presented by the committee:

"1. That a qualified trade unionist co-operator be appointed by the president of the American Federation of Labor to serve as lecturer and advisor on the practical work of Rochdale co-operation.

"2. That this committee shall have office room in the American Federation of Labor Building in Washington, which shall be the center of information by correspondence and otherwise on the subject.

"3. That he shall visit localities in which co-operative societies are in process of formation or have already been formed, and give practical information to the officers and members of such societies, making out routes of travel for this purpose, so as to conserve his time and perform the work at a minimum of expense.

"4. That it shall be understood that central labor unions and local trade unions, as such, shall not form co-operative societies, but shall appoint committees from their membership to act in co-operation with other citizens who are in sympathy with the trade union movement in assisting in establishing and upbuilding a general co-operative movement.

"5. That every local trade union under the jurisdiction of the American Federation of Labor be requested to contribute the sum of one dollar in order to establish successfully the Federation Bureau for promoting and advancing the cause of true co-operation in the United States and Canada."

The committee excluded from consideration all forms of associated work which did not fall within the limits of the Rochdale system, the principles of which are as follows:

"1. A democratic organization.

"2. One vote for each member with equality in share ownership. No voting by proxy.

"3. Cash returns quarterly to members of the difference between the total amount they have paid for their purchases and the lesser total cost of these purchases to the co-operative society, including among the cost depreciation and a reasonable amount for a reserve fund to meet emergencies and extend the business.

"4. Rejection of the principle of profits.

"5. Current interest on loan capital.

"6. Sales where possible preferably to members only.

"7. Distributive co-operation to precede productive.

"8. A sufficient number of retail stores to be established to assure a market before a wholesale department is created.

"9. Observance of methods recommended by the International Co-operative Alliance. . . ."

The following resolution adopted by the Northwest Co-operative Convention will furnish some idea of the extensive plans of the co-operators:

"Whereas, organized labor, organized farmers, and the organized co-operative movement are united to establish and develop a united and a comprehensive co-operative program of education, organization, and finance on a national scale, and in a measure and manner worthy of commensuration with the dignity of the movement represented; now, therefore, be it

"Resolved, That we favor the organization of a comprehensive nation-wide co-operative program, unifying and centralizing the efforts of the workers to take care of their own economic interests; and

"That an effort be put forth immediately to raise the sum of at least $2,000,000, in the State of Washington, one-half of which should be raised in King County; and

"That a committee of five be appointed from this convention to serve on a reconstruction committee of fifteen, of which committee organized labor shall be requested to appoint five members and the organized farmers the other five, with the responsibility of interesting the entire working class in the supreme importance of co-operation as their next step forward."

CHAPTER XI
British and American Shop Committee Plans

We will quote from the Third Triennial Report of the Commission on Social Service of the Episcopal Church on these shop committees (p. 175):

" The shop committee proper must, at the outset, be distinguished from certain spurious forms which have given rise to widespread misconception, and have generally served to confuse the issue. Strictly speaking, the shop committee plan provides for joint meetings of employers and employees' representatives, usually, though not always, equal in number, and of varying powers: ' In most cases the management have not hesitated to agree to be bound by unanimous vote, as they are adequately protected by their own representatives.'

" This definition would rule out of consideration two other types of so-called shop committees, individual instances of which have perhaps bulked larger in the eye of the public than those of the genuine form. One of these is represented in the ' Leitch Plan,' which is simply an attempt to adopt American political machinery to industrial organization, but fails in the vital point of not providing regular joint sessions of the representatives of the two parties — management and labor.

" The second specious type includes the various other organizations ' of employees which (likewise) do not provide for any joint sessions with the management or its representatives ' — ' welfare associations, brotherhoods,' and so forth.

" What is practically the first notable American experiment in this direction — irrespective of the particular merits of the plan in question, and has a right to be classified as genuine in accordance with the foregoing definition — grew out of one of the most serious disturbances in the recent industrial history of the country — the Colorado miners' strike; and it is significant of the movement in general that it has tended to prevent strikes, particularly during the period of America's participation in the war, and in accordance with rulings and judgments of the National War Labor Board, which are responsible for many shop committees. Other plans have been voluntarily initiated, till now there are several scores of them, and more are in contemplation. In a few instances, committee plans, adopted, as at the instance of the National War Labor Board, have proved ineffective. The shop committee movement, though by no means identical with union organization, is parallel with and complementary to it. Either shop committee or local union is possible without the other, though both are founded on collective bargaining. Whereas unions originally limited themselves to, and were designed to enforce, workers' demands for higher wages, shorter hours and better conditions, it was their perception of other more fundamental matters, e. g., control and management, which prompted the committee of movement as, on one side, a development from the union. Though committees have been used in this country to prevent unionization, it must not be forgotten that the Whitley reports postulate a union organization as a *sine qua non* in the formation of shop committees. Perhaps the three or four best American shop committee plans are those of the Sprague Electric Company, Bloomfield, New Jersey (a branch of the General Electric Company), the Lynn Works of the General Electric Company, the International Harvester Company, Chicago, the Philadelphia Rapid Transit, and that advocated by the National War Labor Board. It may be pointed out at the start, however, that no one of these plans, or, in fact, any thus far instituted in this country, makes any real provision for workers' participation in the management of the enterprise, as such — this being, as already noted, the ultimate, if not the immediate, demand of British labor. The American plans, even the best of them, have to do with such matters as wages, hours, conditions, etc., but do not admit the employees, or their representatives, into the real direction of affairs."

One of the differences between the American and the British plan or organization of shop or works committees, is that in America it is made to include non-union, as well as union labor; whereas, in Great Britain, it is associated with union labor. In Great Britain such committees have been recommended by a number of plans for industrial betterment, especially by the Whitley committee; and in a number of cases they have been the outgrowth of the shop stewards scheme.

In Meyer Bloomfield's fundamental study, "Management and Men," at page 125, after referring in detail to the Whitley councils, it says:

"As big a feature of the joint government movement in British industry as the councils, are the works committees. Such committees are by no means new. They had been in operation for years before the war, but in certain industries, notably in the metal trades, the war conditions stimulated their growth to such an extent, and worked such changes in their form and activities, that works committees to-day are in many places the characteristic result of war-time necessity and better industrial relations.

"The causes that promoted the growth of the new type of works committee during the war are various, but they may be roughly traced, first, to the shop stewards, then to the dilution of the working force by a large number of unskilled workers, methods of pay, absenteeism, safeguards against overstrain, and the general sentiment looking to a closer knitting-up of the personnel.

"Most trade unions have official shop stewards, known by various names, as shop delegates, works representatives, yard committeemen, and the like. Their duties are well-known, consisting of such matters as looking after the maintenance of the agreement in force, collection of union dues, and settlement of grievances; but one effect of the war has been to enhance the position and prestige of the shop steward. Unable to strike, because of war stipulations, among which was one making the official, who called it liable to prosecution, the men naturally turned to their shop steward, who held a less conspicuous place. He was a free man. His power within the shop and, indeed, within the plant, was as wide as he chose to make it. . . .

"The most serious problem that leaders of organizing sense have to face is a strong tendency away from central control toward a larger measure of initiative locally, and within each shop. The men are impatient of delay; they want to dispose of their difficulties by short cuts . . . and the shop steward has been encouraged to take things in hand.

"The works committees, with shop stewards as the moving spirit, have been started all through the trades. . . . An automobile plant located in the north of England, and employing 6,000 men, and about 1,000 women, has a shop steward for each one of its forty departments, and the works committee is made up of these stewards. . . . There are many conferences between the management and the committee, but they are not regular, because it has been found that there is not always business to warrant it, which is settled with the foreman, and never comes before the man higher up. . . . All meetings are on employers' time, and the management has never failed to carry out a decision agreed to in conference. . . . The works committees, and, in fact, all sorts of other committees which give the men encouragement to use their heads, have succeeded in clearing away countless little obstructions and misunderstandings which in the aggregate have the result of putting up a wall between those who do their work as it should be done, need above everything, contact and frank speech.

"A factory in the north of England takes pride in the fact that it has never had a walk-out or a strike during the war. On the wall in the office of the general manager is a large framed chart, showing a fairly considerable committee system. All the committees head up in a shop steward works committee. The management and the committee keep minutes of all the meetings.

" Conferences are systematized and treated as a serious part of the executive program."

A good grouping of the shop committees is given in " Industrial Management " for July, 1918, page 79:

" The various forms of representative shop committees seem to classify into four general groups. The first, in organization, is like that of our national government. The workers elect a ' House of Representatives,' the foremen and superintendents form a ' Senate,' and the managers or directors set up a ' Cabinet.' By means of this rather complicated machinery representative action is sought in regard to problems within the shop."

This is the scheme carried out in the Leitch Plan given elsewhere in detail under " Industrial Democracy."

"A second form divides the workers into groups according to the trades or crafts and arranges for the secret election of one or more representatives from each group. These delegates from the shop committee.

"The third type divides the workers arbitrarily into approximately equal numerical groups, usually according to geographical location in the plant and without reference to trades or crafts. These elected delegates likewise form the representative committee.

"The relationship of these committees to the management differs in detail, but in general this is the simplest form of organization that has been evolved.

"A fourth plan for representative action is found in use in shipbuilding yards along the Atlantic coast, where the agreements in regard to wages, hours of labor and the like are entered into between the management and the local unions of the various trades concerned.

"The first form, which may be called the governmental type, seemed to have but limited use and has been put into effect through the activities of only a few persons. The intermediate step, where a single shop committee is set up, composed of secretly elected delegates on some basis of representation, is most common and apparently is the one spreading most rapidly; while the form of bargaining directly with the labor unions is only found in a few instances outside of the shipyard.

"If we can forecast tendencies, they seem to be toward the simple, representative shop committee plan; this is easily explained, readily understood by the working people and offers direct participation to everyone. It seems to be suited to shops of any kind and engaged in any work. Of course, details of operation vary widely in different localities and situations.

"In determining the type to be adopted in any particular plant, it is wise to keep in mind matters that are likely to come forth for determination. Mr. J. M. Larkin, in a paper presented in Cleveland last month, gave an instructive classification of 250 cases that had been determined through the representative shop committee of the Bethlehem Steel Company; 85 per cent. of these were settled in favor of the employees. The seven classifications are as follows:

	Per cent
" Employment and working conditions................	30
" Wages, hours of work, bonus, piece work and tonnage schedules	20
" Help and working sanitation........................	10
" Practice methods and economy......................	10
" Safety and prevention of accidents..................	10
" Employees' transportation	10
" Housing, domestic economics, education, living conditions, publications, pensions and relief, athletics and recreation, continuous employment and continuance of industry	8 "

On page 80 the question is raised whether the shop committee does or does not favor trade unionism:

" Mr. William M. Leiserson, in his address before the Convention of Employment Managers last month stated distinctly that the organized representative shop committee is no substitute for trade unionism and that the formation of such groups will lead inevitably to a strengthened unionism. He referred to the experience of England, and said, 'In this country the employer will find that our shop committees tend to become employers' unions, and these will develop into labor organizations independent of the employer to complete the trend toward industrial democracy.'

" Very distinctly he told the convention that the employer should know what he is about when he begins to form organizations of his employees. Mere welfare committees will not satisfy the workers. Once they begin to meet together and act collectively, they will demand the entire sweep of democratic action and control; the employer who does not realize all this is preparing trouble for himself once he helps the formation of any form of shop committee. 'If he is not ready to give up personal control of his business and wants to continue to dispense personal justice, let him beware of any employees' organization.'

" Here is the danger in the representative shop committee system, as Mr. Leiserson sees it, paving the way toward a strengthened and active trade unionism.

"But there is a decidedly opposed point of view. Trade union leaders seem to be actively against these representative shop bodies. A strike in Detroit hinged upon this very matter. After the committee system had been installed the labor union leaders called out the workers, one of the demands being the doing away with the shop committee system. A few union officials have publicly declared against the plan and its methods, holding that it is a movement that would weaken trade unionism, because a comparatively small number of workers would bargain collectively instead of joining their efforts and strength with all those represented in the larger organizations and the American Federation of Labor."

It is the opinion of a large number of observers in both the labor and the employers' fields that the shop committee would be a potent army in the hands of the revolutionary element, the One Big Union advocates, the I. W. W. and the Communist Party.

A summary called "One Year of Shop Committees" is given by W. L. Stoddard in the January, 1920, number of "Industrial Management" (p. 31). He says:

"Roughly speaking, we have had about one year of intensive growth of and experiment with shop committees, works councils, plans of employee representation, 'company unions,' or whatever term may be chosen. The three principal groups whose opinions are valuable have spoken; the public, employers and labor. It is fitting to take stock, to assess our goods and see where we are at.

"Beyond question, each of the three groups believes, as a whole, in the theory of collective bargaining made practical through some ordered process or other. I should say that the public group is not concerned so much with the details as with the general principle and with the necessity for industrial peace at an honorable price. The employers, generally speaking, incline to favor shop committee plans, which enable them to deal directly with their own employees, without interference by or reference to the trade union. Labor, again generally speaking, advocates the trade union as the best, if not the only means of carrying on collective bargaining. There are notable exceptions, . . . situations such as we find in the Lynn Works of the General Electric Company, where the trade union and the shop committee parallel each other without unnecessary waste of effort and duplication of function.

"There are employers who are utilizing the shop committee idea without reference to the union situation, as a device of intelligent and scientific management. . . .

"But, in spite of the fact that the movement is so widespread it is nevertheless very young. In less than half a dozen industries has the idea been broadened to cover national or sectional groups of employees, embracing many plants. In possibly 50 per cent of the factories where some kind of a plan is in operation the scheme is admittedly imperfect and in the experimental stages. Yet in many hundreds of factories, the idea, which after all is the vital thing, has been sown and is germinating.

"Already there is a fairly considerable literature on the subject. The most recent book is the report on 'Works Council in the United States,' made and published by the National Industrial Conference Board . . . whose report went to press last summer, at that time knew of the existence of works councils in more than 200 establishments, employing about half a million workers. By this time the number may well have been doubled; we can say with certainty that it has increased largely; the writer knows of three plants near Boston which fell into line within a few weeks early in the fall. . . . So far as organized labor speaks for American labor, organized labor is against the shop committee; the last annual convention of the A. F. of L. denounced 'company unions,' and since that time it has become apparent that other labor officials have opposed the movement. It is regarded here to show, first, what the position of labor is; and second, to show that the fact that labor has taken this position is less important than that employers, generally speaking, have taken an opposite stand.

"At this point I wish to call attention to what a dispatch from Chicago to the 'Christian Science Monitor' calls the program of organized Bolshevism in America, being the manifesto of the Communist Party, organized last autumn. . . .

"Communist Party shop committees, consisting of members of the Communist Party, shall be organized wherever possible for the purpose of Communist agitation in a particular shop or industry by the workers employed there. These committees shall be united with each other as a part of the Communist Party. . . .

"The Communist Party recognizes that the American Federation of Labor is reactionary and a bulwark of capitalism. It is actually an enemy of the workers.

"Councils of workers shall be organized in the various shops, as circumstances allow, for the purpose of carrying on the industrial struggle among the workers in these unions, uniting and mobilizing the militant elements. These councils to be unified in a central council wherever possible."

"In contrast to and by way of summing up actual fact — not propaganda — let us take the very cautious epitome of the report of the National Industrial Conference Board, a body representing associations of manufacturers: 'In view of the conflict of experience, it is as yet too early to measure definitely the permanent value of the workers councils' movement.' Three-quarters of the employers having workers' councils, from whom an expression of opinion was secured, declared themselves in favor of this form of industrial organization or that their experience had been favorable. Although further experience may lead to a revision of judgment in some cases, the results thus far obtained with workers' councils indicate that they are worthy of unprejudiced consideration on the part of American industry."

THE SHOP STEWARD MOVEMENT

It has already been noted that it was the special circumstances of the war, including the influx of non-union labor, the special regulations that forbade strikes and other special circumstances, that brought to the front a new class of subordinate authorities in industry, the shop stewards. The shop stewards were minor local officials in British industrial organizations, who occupied a position corresponding to that of foremen in our American organizations, and were shop spokesmen chosen by their fellow wage workers to face on their behalf the employer or his foreman. They had been in existence for some time, but without assuming much prominence.

With the weakening of the authority and scope of the union officials, and the large influx of workmen who did not belong to the unions, the shop stewards' authority extended over every branch of labor, including the women, who were brought in in such large numbers for the war-time work.

These men assumed a larger authority. The report of the Commission of the National Civic Federation on "The labor situation in Great Britain and France" states that (p. 105):

"Their powers and responsibilities become more and more important. Circumstances obliged them, singly or in shop committees, to 'down tools,' or to hurry up general adjustments with foremen or managers. Consequently, union stewards drifted away from the control of their executive officials at headquarters; stewards for the unorganized — new blood 'labor leaders' — became powerful men of the day. With the dilution of skilled labor came relaxed union organization, together with distrust of the higher trade union officials, because of their impotence in sudden crises. . . .

"A large proportion of the workshop people learned to look to their stewards for assistance, defence, authority, and finally, in notable cases, for political and revolutionary leadership.

"Here was an opportunity for the modern youthful agitator — energetic, unafraid, unencumbered, chafing under restraint from his elders in union positions. . . .

"It was at this stage, when stewards and committeemen had become a power to be reckoned with in British war industry, and whilst the various higher executives of the unions concerned were struggling to keep members within 'society rules,' that a deputation from the stewards of Woolwich Arsenal was assured by Winston Churchill, as Minister of Munitions, that they should be the body consulted concerning work in that important government manufactory. This understanding ignored the regular officials of the district committee, as well as the executive council of the Amalgamated Society of Engineers, sitting daily in London. Recognition of stewards over the heads of union chiefs was soon extended to Coventry, Birmingham, Manchester and other large industrial centers. Stewards in many places took command, at times ordering stoppage of work, in opposition to Executive Council decisions. Concessions were made to them by employers to obtain resumption of work, union executives being found powerless to compel obedience either to their established rules or to special adjustments.

"District committees seeing shop stewards recognized and setting aside union laws, ventured to follow suit, and in turn they were suspended by the Executive Council, this disciplinary action coming late. In many parts of the country local unofficial shop or craft spokesmen practically dominated in dealings with perplexed employers, uncertain whether agreements were to be observed. These circumstances in part explain sporadic unauthorized strikes in munitions and other works during the war.

"The outstanding effect of the labor situation in Great Britain then was that, differing from the situation in the United States, there was no authorized central executive standing for a general wage workers' organization covering all occupations in all industries for the entire country, with which these employers, singly or in bodies, might treat, or look to, for information or effective declaration of maintenance and labor principles and justice. . . .

"The British shop steward movement, mainly in its beginnings at war-time schism from regular trade unionism, and later toward nationalizing and democratizing industry, collapsed months ago. As a factor having a practical bearing on the industrial situation in Great Britain, it is today at the vanishing point."

The plan of shop stewards is one that harmonizes with the I. W. W. or One Big Union scheme, and is therefore one that has been introduced or favored sporadically in American industry, wherever there is agitation against unionism.

The famous Clyde ship-building strike had a close connection with the shop steward movement. The shop stewards of the Amalgamated Society of Engineers of the Clyde district, issued a manifesto, saying:

"The support given to the Munitions Act by the officials (of the A. S. E. and other unions) was an act of treachery to the working classes. We are out for unity and closer organization of all trades in the industry, one union being the ultimate aim. We will support the officials just so long as they rightly represent the workers, but we will act independently immediately they misrepresent them."

The philosophy of the shop stewards' movement, in their own words, is, workers' control of industry, beginning in the shop, and industrial unionism, in preference to craft unionism.

This is the opinion expressed in " British Labor and the War," by Paul U. Kellogg, and Arthur Gleason (p. 162).

They say further (p. 164) :

"As brought out on the Clyde, the shop stewards stand for something more far-reaching and constructive in its implications than the right to strike. They are asserting the right to an increased share in workshop management. They are doing it without consultation with the old-line officials of the union. (' We do not recognize them,' said Kirkwood) and they were acting through an organization of shop stewards, representing unofficially all the shops in the district."

According to this view of the situation, the shop stewards' movement, far from fading away, is likely to increase in importance as the radical element gains further control in the labor movement of Great Britain. This movement is in direct opposition to the plans for industrial reorganization, that start with the government, with employers, and with the unions.

" While . . . the government plans Whitley Committees (with the consent of the employer and the worker), and while far-seeing employers encourage them, elsewhere, the workers themselves elect their own stewards, their own committees, and set going from the bottom up the movement toward workers' control, which in its various embodiments will dominate industrial reconstruction in England.

" The shop stewards are those who have broken with tradition at the place where the fight is hardest — in their own organization, in their own workshop " (p. 167).

CHAPTER XII
The Closed Shop and the Open Shop

The conflict between many employers on the one side and organized labor on the other, in regard to the so-called closed shop and open shop systems, is an old one. The question is discussed in the Encyclopedia of the American Federation of Labor, page 304. The Federation's argument is that the term "closed shop" is a misnomer, used by opponents of organized labor to create a prejudice against the union shop, which is not closed but open to all who will join the union. The Federation declared in 1903 that the "open shop" belongs to the same category as the non-union or "scab" shop. It argues that

"The so-called open shop influences wages and the standard of life to the downward course, for it is based upon the sycophancy of the most docile, and the most immediate needs of those in direst distress, of the poorest situated among the workmen. Agreements or joint bargains of organized labor with employers depend for their success upon the good will of the union and the employers for each other. Neither should be subject to the irresponsibility or lack of intelligence of the non-unionist, or his failure to act in concert with, and bear the equal responsibility of, the unionist. Hence, the so-called open shop makes agreements and joint bargains with employers impracticable, if not impossible. The union cannot be responsible for non-unionists, whose conduct often renders the terms of the agreement ineffective and nugatory."

This question, and many others in the same field, are treated in a collection of the writings and addresses of Samuel Gompers, president of the Federation, recently published under the title "Labor and the Employer," which is one of the most interesting collections of documents for this discussion. Chapter V is entitled, "The Union Shop and the 'Open' Shop." One of the points that are made by Mr. Gompers and others is in favor of what they call the "Preferential" open shop, as a compromise arrangement, according to which members of the union would be given preference over non-union men in employment.

The renewed movement in favor of the "open shop" has changed from the old idea of the employers dealing with unorganized, individual, non-union workmen, to that of their dealing with the workmen of their own shop, organized and represented by their own shop committees, not subject to outside influences or orders. The movement has taken two entirely distinct, not to say opposite, forms. One of these is revolutionary and inimical both to the American Federation of Labor and to organized capital. It is backed by the I. W. W. and other subversive elements, and this phase can be illustrated by reference to the first part of this report. The establishment of such shop committees is urged by Lenin and the Third International as the best means for " boring in " for the purpose of destroying trade unionism.

The other influence back of the " open shop " committees is that of the workmen and employers who wish to deal with each other independently of influences outside of their particular shop or business. It will be remembered that in the Steel strike the leader of the strike movement, Fitzpatrick, acknowledged in his testimony before the Senate committee that he had never been inside a steel mill, and that he knew nothing of the different wage scales in the industry which he was attempting to disrupt. The Steel Corporation argued that men absolutely ignorant of conditions in a business should not be allowed to represent its employees and create artificial discontent. The second form of shop committee, just described, takes on various aspects according as the committees representing the shop are formed only of representative workmen dealing with their employers, or are formed of a mixture of representative both employees and employers. There are many large employers who maintain that there is no necessary conflict between the shop committee system in this form and the trade union system, if no coercion is exercised by the trade union to oblige workmen to join, and no attempt made to fasten the stigma and personal danger of " scab " to non-union men.

Seattle is experimenting with the open shop as the basis for the city's industries. All employers got together in an industry based upon the open shop, which they called the American plan. It allows no discrimination against non-union labor and insists upon the freedom of every individual to give a fair day's work for a fair day's pay.

The closed shop question which, for a time, had fallen into the background, has again become one of the burning questions.

An article entitled "The Closed Shop to the Bar," in the "Forum," of December, 1919, takes up the question from a legal point of view. It reviews the decisions of judges of the Federal courts in cases of this character that were brought before them. The first case cited is the notable, oft-quoted opinion of Justice Pitney in the Hitchman Coal & Coke Co. case in West Virginia:

"An injunction issued by District Judge Dayton to restrain union interference with contracts entered into between the Hitchman Coal & Coke Co. of West Virginia, and their employees, to conduct an open shop, was sustained by the Supreme Court in an opinion by Justice Pitney. The plaintiff sued John Mitchell, the labor leader, individually, and officers of the United Mine Workers of America, which included leaders of local districts Nos. 5 and 6 of the U. M. W. A. A long list of union officers was included in the complaint, which set forth 'that said defendants have unlawfully and maliciously agreed together, confederated, combined and formed themselves into a conspiracy, the purpose of which they are proceeding to carry out.' The complaint declared this purpose to be — to shut down the mine, to render the plants idle, and thereby to injure its contracts, 'until such time as plaintiff shall submit to the demand of the union to unionize the plant.'

"The usual demands which sustained the union policy of a closed shop were made, which practically compelled the plaintiff to employ only union labor subject to the orders of the union. The opinion of the court based its decision for a restraining order upon various definite conclusions, all of which have a direct bearing upon the present cause of strikes. . . . The fact that the U. M. W. A. was a voluntary union, unincorporated, is particularly pertinent. . . .

Judge Pitney says:

"The organization known as the United Mine Workers of America, and its branches, as conducted and managed at the time of the suit and for many years before, was a common law conspiracy in unreasonable restraint of trade, and also and especially a conspiracy against the rights of non-union miners in West Virginia.

"That the defendants, in an effort to compel the plaintiff to enter into contractual relations with the union relating to the employment of labor and the production of coal, although having knowledge of express contracts existing between plaintiff and its employees which excluded relations with the union, endeavored by unlawful means to procure a breach of these contract by the employees. . . .

"The vice-president of a sub-district of the union visited the mines, called a meeting of the miners, and addressed them in a foreign tongue, as a result of which they went on strike the next day, and the mine was shut down."

When the strike failed, the men were employed, not as members of the union, but with the understanding that the mine henceforth would be run as a non-union or open shop. The Court decided that it found proof of conspiracy, among other things, in the following statement of one of the officers of the United Mine Workers:

"When we organize West Virginia, when we organize the unorganized sections of Pennsylvania, we will organize them by strike movements. No one had made the statement that we can organize West Virginia without a strike."

The methods employed by 'strike movements' as demonstrated in this particular case, consisted of open defiance of the non-union employer. A certain employer, for instance, operating the Richland Mine, was told that if he did not recognize the union, his mine would be shut down. In almost every specific case employees of the open shop were defiantly intimidated by agents of the closed shop. Union organizers were sent into the mines to conduct a campaign of organization, although such organizers knew that contracts existed between the employer of the open shop and his employees. This interference of the union organizers with those contracts were, as the Court expressed it, " a violation of the express provisions of the agreements " in operation in the open shop.

The Court expressed the opinion that the strike movement to unionize the miners was merely a step toward unionizing the mines. He says:

"If there be any practical distinction between organizing the miners and organizing the mine, it has no application to this case. Unionizing the miners is but a step in the process of unionizing the mine, followed by the latter almost as a matter of course. Besides, the evidence shows, without any dispute, that defendants contemplated no halfway measure, but were bent on organizing the mine, the 'consent' of plaintiff to be procured through such a control of his employees as would render any further independent operation of the mine out of the question."

"The assertion that collective bargaining has its advantages to labor was dismissed by the Court in his statement that, 'Whatever may be the advantages of collective bargaining, it is not bargaining at all, in any just sense, unless it is voluntary on both sides.' . . .

"The Court said: 'What the defendants were endeavoring to do at this mine and neighboring mines cannot be treated as a bona fide effort to enlarge the membership of the union. There is no evidence to show, nor can it be inferred, that defendants intended or desired to have the men at these mines join the union, unless they could organize the mine.'

"This brief review of the salient point of the Hitchman Coal & Coke Company case in West Virginia, served to convey the impression that interference with contracts made between employer and employee is an act of conspiracy against the liberties of American citizenship, against the protection of property rights, and against the freedom of the employee to present his own case to the employer unfettered by union orders from which the employee has no escape.

"The decisions of the Courts are unanimously agreed on this point. It is on record, in innumerable cases, that wherever it appears that an outside union is endeavoring to cause the breaking by employees of their contracts of employment, that the courts can and should enjoin such union from that course of action. It has been conclusively so settled by the United States Supreme Court, by the principal state courts of appeal. A list of these cases in which such decisions were granted is available. The courts have negatived the moral right of unions to force an 'unfair list' of employers which required members of the union, who might be employees of such employers, to quit their jobs, with the purpose of preventing those employers from conducting their business. . . .

"Good will cannot thrive on coercion, and without good will no business can progress, no business can even exist. A contract is a property right, and the interference of a third party with the terms and conditions of that contract is forbidden under the laws of the Constitution. To quote the opinion of Judge Killits, on this situation, in Stephens *v.* Ohio State Telephone Co. (240 Fed. Rep. 759):

> 'If a person knowingly and intentionally interferes with the express contract rights of an employer with his employees and the purpose and intent of such interference is to injure such employer and it does result in his injury, an action will be sustained to recover damages therefor.'

"The authority of a union to decide for its members whether an employer is conducting his business in an unfair manner and shall be penalized through certain demands upon him made by that union, involving orders upon which he should run his business, is denied in court decisions. In one instance an employer was informed that union foremen must be placed on every job in his plant for over a year, that the whole shop be cleaned out of the men who worked for him previous to the trouble, it being further stipulated that each foreman should have the power to employ and discharge at will without regard to efficiency, and that the cost of the work would thus be materially increased. This penalty was imposed upon the employer, not at the instigation of the employees, who were perfectly willing to stay at work as before, but, being union members, they were called out on strike, and obeyed. The employer refused to follow the instructions given him by the union. The Court said, in this instance:

> 'Where a strike, or other action, is threatened by a labor union in violation of its contract, or of the contract of its members with their employer, the jurisdiction of a court of equity to issue an injunction is well recognized.'"

Briefly, it is a fixed principle of the Constitution as interpreted by the courts that the aid of equity is available to protect labor in their contracts of employment, as well as to protect employers in their rights under such contracts.

In the same case, the company being a public utility, the effect of strike movements upon it brings up certain special points which are covered in the following opinion of the Court:

> "The Ohio State Telephone Company is a public utility. Its first duty is to serve the public. Its work meets a vital necessity. The right of its striking employees to 'interfere by lawful means' with its business does not mean a right to cripple performance by it of its duty to the public, if it can find people willing to work for it. If labor can be had, the

company must employ and the strikers must permit it to employ and use labor to perform its public duties, and anyone willing to work for it must be allowed by everybody entire freedom to do so.

"The public, having a great need for services of this character, offered by this public utility, has an enforcible right to demand these conditions of both the company and of those associated with it. This Court is empowered to say to the company: that it must meet its public obligations. Coupled with that power of the Court is the power and duty of laying its prohibitive and punishing hand upon anyone whose wilfully unlawful conduct tends to render abortive the exercise of that power. We can no more say to the company that it must yield to the demands of its striking employees than we can say to them that they must meet the company exactions. The controversy must be carried on, on both sides, without substantial detriment to the company's public service."

"This is a decision so pregnant with the position of the courts toward any 'strike movement' that affects great public utilities that it establishes a precedent which applies vigorously to any future disorders in such industrial zones. The language of injunction orders is very specific, and, as a whole, it is obvious that the opinions of the courts do not favor 'strike movements' conspiring under the pretense that they are to increase the membership of a union or to strengthen the principle of force in labor against property rights. A general survey of this issue does not favor the procedure of unions bent upon creating a mass formation of union membership against non-union labor. The courts deny the right of interference by organized forces in the closed shop directed against the employers' right to conduct an open shop if he desires with the liberties of American citizenship to work out individually an economic salvation."

Another case in point is the recent strike on the Brooklyn Rapid Transit System. At that time the Brotherhood of New York Railway Company Employees were approached by an interfering union organization known as the Amalgamated Association of Street and Electric Railway Employees of America, for the purpose of breaking up the brotherhood and inducing its members to go on strike. District Judge Julius M. Mayer notified counsel of the Amalgamated, Mr. Louis D. Fridiger, that the Court would not countenance any interference of the sort.

The most recent, clear-cut case of the closed or open shop issue, and one that when this report was drawn up had not yet been finally decided, is that of the San Francisco metal trades war, which is fully described in the March issue of the National Labor Digest.

We read on page 13:

"Forty thousand strong they went on strike five months ago, and so far the unions engaged in the metal trades and shipbuilding plants around the Bay of San Francisco have not only failed to gain any advantage, but they are still out and have to face the loss of practically full union conditions under which they worked prior to the strike. The men went out on October 1st last and nothing indicating a settlement is in view. The loss of wages has run into millions of dollars, and the workers have been forced to exist, in most cases, on a miserably small strike benefit.

"Organized labor says it is engaged in a life and death struggle with organized industry, while the employers say they, too, are engaged in a life and death struggle, but with 'short-sighted unionists.' . . . The labor leaders of the country say that if the unions are defeated it will have a far-reaching effect on unionism status. This is also the tone of a nation-wide appeal for assistance sent out by the Bay Cities Metal Trades Council. The leaders place the importance of this strike ahead of that of the recent steel strike. . . . Every movement of the struggle has been followed by employers and organized workmen of the whole nation with keen interest and the statement has repeatedly been made that upon the outcome of this strike will be determined whether or not organized labor is to continue to remain in the metal trades industry.

"James O'Connell, president of the Metal Trades Department of the American Federation of Labor, in a recent statement said he considered the strike a crucial test of the strength of the nation-wide movement of employers to establish the so-called American plan, or open shop, and to break the control of organized labor.

"Robert W. Borden, president of the Bay Cities Metal Trades Council, has said in a report to the San Francisco Labor Council: 'If the employers can win in San Francisco, they can win any other battle they may wish to fight in any other part of the United States. The Bay Cities Metal Trades Council, composed of fifty-three unions, with a membership of 40,000 workmen, has been conceded for twenty years to be one of the strongest units of the American Federation of Labor. The strike is of vital importance to every organized worker in every industry, and we will fight it out until we win.'

"While labor claims that it was deliberately forced out as a part of the countrywide plan to break unionism, the California Metal Trade Association as emphatically asserts that union breaking did not enter into its intention, but admits the result will probably amount to that if the strike is continued 'along its present lines of violence.' "

About twenty thousand men have accepted work under the new plan, the so-called American plan of the open shop:

"We, the members of the California Metal Trades Association, hereby declare the following to be the fundamental principles to govern us hereafter in our industrial relations with each other, our employees and the public.

"We recognize the right of the employees to organize, but will not permit coercive measures to compel membership in such organizations, nor to compel employers to deal therewith.

"We are unalterably opposed to the principle of the union or non-union closed shop, as it is un-American and unfair.

"While disavowing interference with the proper functions of labor organizations, we recognize no rules nor regulations restricting production, impairing efficiency or otherwise interfering with the management of the business. No member shall be required to deal with men or groups of men not his employees, or not chosen by and from among them.

"We are strenuously opposed to strikes, sympathetic strikes, lockouts, blacklists, boycotts, and kindred evils. We will resist those selfish interests which through violence, coercion, or otherwise attempt to disrupt the relations of peace and unity existing between employer and employee.

"Since we must take the final responsibility for the work produced by our employees, we must have full discretion to designate the men — journeymen, specialists, apprentices, helpers or laborers — we consider competent to perform our work, what machines, tools and appliances shall be used and under what conditions the work shall be performed. The question of competency of the men is to be determined solely by us.

"Because it is unfair to the American boy to deny him the right to learn a trade, and in order to create mechanics in proportion to the development of industry, we will not recognize any restrictions in the employment of apprentices. It shall be the duty and obligation of all employers to instruct apprentices in all branches of the trade. The California Metal Trades Association shall actively co-operate with various technical schools in this district in an effort to raise the dignity and efficiency of the various trades.

"An employee should receive at least wages sufficient to maintain him at a proper standard of living. An employee's earning capacity should not be restricted, whether working by the day, by the piece work or by the premium system, and should be commensurate with his skill, proficiency and ability to produce.

"It is the privilege of the employee to leave our employ when he sees fit and the employer to discharge an employee when he sees fit.

"The above principles being absolutely essential to the successful conduct of our business, we cannot permit any interference therewith. In case of disagreement (concerning matters not covered by the foregoing declaration and not affecting the economic integrity of the industry) our members will meet such of their employees as are affected by such disagreement and adjust the difficulty on a fair and equitable basis.

"Since many rules, regulations and shop customs have been enforced upon employees by business agents, shop committeemen, and individual agitators resulting in constantly reduced efficiency and production, we will not tolerate rules that arbitrarily place a limit: (1) Upon the amount of work that a man can honestly perform; (2) upon the machine or machines or the kind of work upon which men may work, nor rules which permit interference by individuals with men who can and are willing to produce.

"We will not allow jurisdictional claims to enforce the use of men from several crafts on work that can easily and economically be performed by one man.

"Foremen and assistant foremen, as representatives of the management, are responsible for the efficient and economical performance of the work; therefore, all regular foremen and assistant foremen must withdraw from their unions while acting in such capacity."

CHAPTER XIII
Arbitration in Labor Disputes

In the February, 1920, number of the National Labor Digest, a full account is given of what is called a new precedent for arbitration in the adjustment of the differences between the Oakland Terminal Railway Company and its operating employees. The arbiters were Warren Olney, Jr., Associate Justice of the Supreme Court of the State of California; Ralph Merritt, Federal Food Administrator for the State of California; and E. C. Bradley, a member of President Wilson's Labor Conference Board. The official publication of the State Building Trades Council of California, Organized Labor, is confident that the decision, which speaks for itself, will be used as a guide and standard in many future arbitration proceedings.

Submission of the dispute to arbitration followed the strike which tied up transportation facilities in East Bay cities (California) from October 1 to 11. The men returned to work on the company's terms at the suggestion of the State Railroad Commission and agreed to submit all their demands to arbitration.

In awarding the employees an increase, the board laid down the following principle:

"It is our belief that regardless of the financial condition of the employing company or its ability to secure other men, or the rate of wages paid by other similar concerns, it is right that it should in any case pay what may be called a minimum living wage, meaning by that a wage which will enable a man to support himself and family in a decent and reasonable way, having in mind particularly that he shall have enough, not merely to provide his family with necessary food, clothing and housing, but also to give to his children that opportunity for education and advancement which is the birthright of every American citizen. . . .

"We have considered carefully the cost of living and in our best judgment a conservative figure at the present time would be approximately $1,600 a year for an average family. We have, therefore, determined that the forty-eight cent rate should be increased by enough to pay, on the average, approximately this amount. For this purpose an increase of six cents per hour, or $12\frac{1}{2}$ per cent., is required, making the hourly rate fifty-four cents."

The arbiters stated that they were in accord with the "general principle of an eight-hour day in industry" but the conditions are such that inauguration of the shorter work day would make it impossible to pay the men a "living wage." The eight-hour day would increase the company payroll by 45 per cent. in order to give the men the 12½ per cent. increase which the Board decided necessary to be in proportion to the cost of living. The decision of the arbiters on this point goes beyond the interests of the company and the men. It takes into consideration the public from which the company would have to draw increased revenues. In denying the shorter work day, the arbiters said:

> . . "It is out of the question for the company to pay this increase with its present revenues. Those revenues can be increased only by increasing the rates to the public, and the increase necessary would be so great as to put this likewise out of the question. The inevitable result of granting the request of the men for an eight-hour day would be disastrous to the men, the company, and the public alike. We, therefore, cannot see our way clear to grant it."

COMPULSORY ARBITRATION

Compulsory arbitration was first tried, apparently in New Zealand, where it was enacted into state law thirty years ago. It was enthusiastically described in a special work, "A Country without Strikes," by Henry D. Lloyd. The apparatus consisted of

(1) A Conciliation Board which took first cognizance, and if that failed, industrial disputes were referred to

(2) A National Arbitration Board, consisting of three members

1 elected by labor unions,
1 elected by employer's association,
1 chosen by the government from judges of courts of record.

This scheme seemed to work. For fourteen years there was not a strike in New Zealand. But it was because the third and deciding vote was that of a judge appointed by a government that favored labor, especially under Prime Minister Seddon.

There came a more conservative government, also wages had been raised as much as markets would stand. If raised higher, it was found that New Zealand could not compete in open markets.

The first strike came in the *packing industry* when the board denied the demands of the workers. The punishment for refusal to accept the board's award had been *fines*. Thus far only employers had been fined. It was found impracticable now to fine the workers. Even impounding and selling their goods and chattels failed. Then, the *coal* miners asked for increased wages. They were turned down and went on strike. This was after Parliament had strengthened the law after the packing strike had shown its weakness when applied to the workers. Fines being impossible, jail sentences were imposed without breaking the strike. This seemed to show the impossibility of forcing work by the method of compulsory arbitration, and the system became obsolete, though the law was not repealed.

But it is now being revived, especially in South Australia. Since the disastrous shipping strike of last summer in South Australia it has been decided that some legislation was necessary in order to substitute arbitration for the strike as a method for settling labor disputes. A new industrial code was drawn up and presented in the State Parliament last November, which gives far more power to the old Arbitration Court that had been functioning for the last eighteen years. This new code declares:

"Any association of employers or employees, which for the purpose of enforcing compliance with the demands of any employers and employees, orders its members to refuse to offer or accept employment, or to continue to employ or be employed, shall be deemed to do an act in the nature of a strike actually, according to the nature of the case, whether a lockout or strike actually takes place or not. The maximum penalty for lockouts or strikes is fixed at ($2,500)."

Strikes are thus pronounced illegal. The machinery or the code is elaborated in 375 clauses. A new industrial court is established called "Board of Industry." It consists of a judge of the Supreme Court, acting as president, and four commissioners, two each for the employers and the employees. This board can declare what is a living wage; can schedule and group industries under certain tribunals. It can be convoked at the request of the Minister of Industry, or of as many as twenty employers or twenty employees or an association with as many members. It can take evidence and its awards are enforceable for three years.

It is these experiments in New Zealand and South Australia where Socialism and labor have so dominant a role that we Americans can study with profit.

Of the American moves in the same direction only these have gained notoriety: the Congress railroad bills (Cummins-Esch), the Kansas Arbitration Law and the Colorado Strike Law.

The Colorado Strike Law is the least drastic. It merely provides that there must be no strike for thirty days after notice has been given. It is a mere palliative. The Kansas Arbitration Law was the work of Governor Allen. It created a court of industrial relations which has the power to fix a minimum wage and makes the state the adjudicator of labor disputes, giving it the right to inquire into industrial conditions and the right to change these conditions where it finds them unsuitable. The court consists of three judges appointed for three years by the governor at a salary of $5,000. It takes over the duties of the Public Service Commission. It has supervision of food products, clothing, mining, fuel and transportations. It is illegal to suspend manufacture or transportation of any of these necessities. In case of a labor controversy in these fields the court shall investigate, and amend or change contracts and make awards. In case either party of the dispute refuse to obey the court's award the state may take over and operate the industry. Collective bargaining is recognized but no interference with non-union labor is allowed. No employee can be discharged for appearing in the court. Striking in violation of the law is punishable by $500 fine or six months in jail or both. It is a felony to order, call or foment a strike, and this is punishable by five years in the penitentiary or a fine of $1,000 or both.

The anti-strike provisions of the Cummins railroad bill, which aroused such a storm on the part of labor are too well known to require comment.

The governmental action against strikes in public utilities in Great Britain and France that have come to the front have been done under abnormal authority that lapses in peace time. It was the Defense of Realm Act that was used by the British government: it was the right of the French government to call out every citizen of military age for military service for 35 days each year that was used to break the railway strikes.

While the experiment in New Zealand in compulsory arbitration was the earliest as well as the most drastic, it is an interesting fact that compulsory arbitration ended by spreading throughout Australia, practically along the same lines as in New Zealand. There is an interesting statement of the situation in the 1916

(November 1st) Bulletin of the United States Board of Mediation and Conciliation. In the first place, there is a law of the commonwealth of Australia establishing a Court of Conciliation and Arbitration, whose decisions have the force of a formal award. In this legislation, the initiation and the continuation of any strike or lockout is prohibited, under the penalty of £1,000 against any person or organization that is responsible for either a strike or a lock-out. In Queensland there is an industrial corps appointed by the governor, and under which are a number of local industrial boards, whose awards, if disputed, are sent up to the court. In the case of public utilities strikes and lock-outs are illegal, unless a conference held before the judge is abortive, and fourteen dissents are given after the end of the conference and secret ballot has been taken. There is a fine of £1,000 on the employer or the union, and £50 on the worker, or if a non-union man, not over £50. The charge is against wages, or against the funds of the association.

In New South Wales, there is a law similar to that of Queensland; that is, there are industrial boards for different groups of industries and callings, whose awards, if disputed, are brought before the Superior Industrial Court. Strikes and lock-outs are prohibited, and injunctions can be issued by the Industrial Court. The fine for either employer or union is £1,000, or for individuals, not over £20.

In South Australia the law is somewhat different. The judge of the Industrial Court brings the parties together, and may be assisted in his decision, if he wishes, by two assessors, representing each party to the controversy. His award is obligatory. All strikes and lock-outs are illegal. The fine under this law is £500, or three months' imprisonment. An employer who refuses to employ, or a worker who refuses to accept work, where there is an industrial agreement, or award in operation, may be fined.

In Western Australia, the law provides for a court of arbitration of three, consisting of a judge of the Supreme Court, and two representatives of the employer and the employee, as in the case of New Zealand, all of them appointed by the governor; but in this case there are no local tribunals. Here also strikes and lock-outs are illegal; but the fine is much smaller, being only £100 for either the employer or the union. It is peculiar that it is only in Australia where labor is supreme, that compulsory arbitration which, on the face of it, would be considered as detrimental to free action of labor, has been actually put in practice on a large scale.

The most recent reports from Australia and New Zealand are to the effect that compulsory arbitration has proved itself a failure in bringing about harmony and has not decreased the epidemic of strikes.

The idea, however, is gaining ground in other countries. In many countries a distinction is made between public utilities and private enterprises, and in a great many cases, strikes are prohibited in public utilities, where it would be absolutely destructive of public comfort and safety, to have service interrupted. Such prohibition is in force in Austria, in Belgium, in Italy, Portugal, Roumania, Spain, and so forth.

In Canada, both strikes and lock-outs are illegal, until after investigation by a government board, and the publication of its report. In Denmark, there is a permanent arbitration court of six. Strikes or lock-outs are prohibited, in cases where court awards or trade agreements are broken. Otherwise, they are allowable, on condition that public notice is given beforehand.

It is interesting that compulsory arbitration has been introduced into Norway, which is the most radical of the Scandinavian countries in its labor program and policy. In July, 1916, at a time of big conflicts between capital and labor, the government procured the passing of a bill, appointing obligatory arbitration boards. Every political party, with the exception of the Social Democratic Party, declared in favor of the bill. The labor unions, in accordance with the decision of the Labor Congress of two years before, declared a general strike, as a protest against the passing of the law. In spite of their protest, the law was passed, and the general strike was called off. In April, 1917, another strike against the operation of this law seemed imminent and the abdication of the King was demanded at many mass meetings.

It will be seen at once from this statement that among the Australasian countries the general tendency of legislation is to place a limitation, and with practically one exception, a prohibition upon the right to strike upon railway and practically all other classes of industrial workers. Complete machinery, however, has been provided for the settlement of controversies.

Another group of countries, on the other hand, such as Canada, the Transvaal, Spain, and Portugal, have not denied employees the right to strike, but have made the exercise of this right contingent upon certain conditions — a notification to the government of the intention to strike or after a governmental investigation and report.

In the case of other countries, as Roumania, the right of railway workers or other public utility employees to strike is absolutely prohibited, and no machinery is provided for ventilating grievances. Belgium and Holland also prohibit strikes but have devised methods for employees to take up grievances or requests with railroad managers. Strikes are not formally prohibited in Germany or Austria among railway workers, but are practically prevented by the control of the authorities over the trade-union affiliations of employees. In Germany, however, administrative machinery has been provided through which transportation workers may have a vent for their grievances. Strikes are not prohibited by formal legislative enactment on French railways, but are practically impossible, because of the policy of the government in calling employees to the colors and placing them under military orders in the event of a strike. Italy depends upon the same policy to prevent industrial conflict on her railways. In Great Britain and the United States there is no abridgement of the right to strike. Both countries have provided official machinery for the adjustment of wage and other difficulties between the railroads and their operating forces. In Great Britain the opportunities for conciliation and arbitration under the conciliation act of 1896 have also been supplemented by a general agreement between railway officials and employees which makes provision for compulsory conciliation of matters in dispute.

[1] From Monthly Review of the United States Bureau of Labor Statistics, Vol. 1, No. 6, pp. 10–12.

Documents

I. THE COLORADO COMPULSORY INDUSTRIAL DISPUTES INVESTIGATION ACT

The Legislature of Colorado at its session in 1915 enacted a law embodying provisions relative to labor disputes that differs from any other existing legislation in this country, resembling in several respects the well-known Canadian Industrial Disputes Act.

The act in question is Chapter 180, Acts of 1915, creating an industrial commission with a wide range of powers. Among the duties of the commission is that of doing all in its power to promote the voluntary adjustment of labor disputes, with a view to avoid "the necessity of resorting to strikes, lockouts, boycotts, blacklists, discriminations and legal proceedings in matters of employment." The commission may act directly, or it may appoint temporary boards of arbitration, providing also for their necessary expenses. Hearings and investigations may be conducted by the commission or a board, deputy, agent or committee, and findings, orders, awards, or decisions, when approved and confirmed by the commission, are to be deemed the conclusions of the commission. Power to enforce the attendance of witnesses, administer oaths, require the production of books, papers, etc., is conferred on the commission, or a board appointed by it, to the same extent as such power is vested in a court of record in civil cases. Parties to proceedings may be compelled to give evidence as witnesses, and evidence is not restricted to that of a strictly legal nature, but such as seems fit in equity and good conscience may be accepted.

Employers and employees must give at least thirty days' notice of any intended change affecting conditions of employment as regards wages and hours. If an investigation has been begun, and until the dispute has been finally dealt with by the commission or board, the existing status must be maintained, and the relationship of employer and employee continued "uninterrupted by the dispute or anything arising out of the dispute." Any attempt at delay in order to maintain a continuation of the status is punishable as a misdemeanor. It is also made unlawful for any employer to declare or cause a lockout, or for any employee to go on strike, on account of any dispute, prior to or during an investigation, hearing or arbitration of such dispute under the provisions of the act. Suspension or discontinuance of any industry or of work for any employer not constituting a lockout or a strike is not forbidden; nor does the cessation of operations in any industry not affected with a public interest come within the prohibition of this act. Employers may declare lockouts and employees may strike without violating the statute if they choose to do so after a dispute has been duly investigated, heard or arbitrated under the provisions of the act.

Determination by the commission or a board are binding only when the parties to a dispute have either agreed in writing prior to action that they will abide by the conclusions reached, or have accepted the action of the commission or the board after the same has been made known to them. Penalties are provided for violations of the act by employers or by employees, as well as by any person who incites, encourages or aids in any manner acts by either employers or employees in contravention of the provisions of the statute.

Awards and findings in regard to labor disputes are within the general provisions of the act as to rehearings on points objected to, and appeals to courts. Such appeals lie to procure the modification or vacation of any order or ruling made, on the ground that it is unlawful or unreasonable, and such actions take precedence in time over all civil cases of a different nature. The only grounds upon which the court can act are: that the commission acted without or in excess of its powers; that the finding, order or award was procured by fraud; that the findings of fact by the commission do not support the order or award; or that the award does not do substantial justice to the parties. If further objection is made, the matter may be brought before the Supreme Court on a writ of error for a final review of the order or judgment.

The effect of the act is, in brief, to furnish a compulsory system of investigation, requiring the continuance of the status pending such action, whether applied for or not, no act in furtherance of a dispute being permissible by either party until the matter has been gone into by an official body. (American Labor Year Book, 1917–1918, p. 150.)

II. Arbitration in Australia

The arbitration system as we have it in Australia is the outcome of the failure of the strike as a means of settlement of industrial trouble. After the failure of the great strikes of the early nineties (1890) a sentiment grew in favor of governmental intervention in the form of conciliation and arbitration, and of wage labor boards. In Victoria in 1891, and in New South Wales in 1892, acts were passed providing for the appointment of such boards to which voluntary application might be made by the contending parties. But the awards of the boards had no binding force, and were applied for but little. The first Australian state (but strange to say it became useless in its own state and had to give way to the wages board system), Western Australia, after many acts and repeals, consolidated an industrial arbitration act of 1912, while New South Wales followed suit the same year. The Federal Arbitration Act passed in 1904 applies, it should be noted, in cases only where the dispute extends beyond the limits of any one state.

After the great strike of 1890–91 it was seen that the peaceful methods of adjusting disputes were more conducive to the welfare of the community generally than the suicidal methods of strikes and lockouts. The unions, therefore, turned to legislation as an effective means of improving labor conditions. Thus a general desire was shown for arbitration — compulsory, if not voluntary. Accordingly, the industrial legislation aims at the prevention of strikes and lockouts.

Strikes have not, however, altogether ceased, even in the places where heavy penalties prohibit them. But it has been noted that, owing to arbitration, there has been a steady diminution in the number of strikes in the skilled trades. The recent strikes have been mostly among coal miners and other unions composed mainly of unskilled laborers.

But while there have been numerous strikes of the latter class of workers, the penalties have not always been enforced, unless public opinion dictated them. More than one government in Australia has lost power through enforcing penalties on strikers against the wishes of public opinion.

There is no doubt that the arbitration acts have done much in the way of abolishing sweating in factories and other places. It must be conceded that the great expansion of unionism of late years has been aided by arbitration, because of its compulsory rule that all must register in an industrial body before they can come into the court. The whole matter of preference to unionists may be said to lie at the door of industrial arbitration, since it compels the men to organize themselves in a union to secure advantages which those outside the unions cannot obtain. That is, I believe, the general opinion in Australia. But for the arbitration courts and its compulsory registration requirements, it is doubtful whether we would have now had the preference to unionists' clause. Though at times it appears that the arbitration act does not work as well as it might, we must admit generally that we have secured advantages because of it. It has helped to make us strong industrially, and though strikes are not a thing of the past in Australia yet, they are not so frequent as they were in the days when compulsory arbitration was unthought of.

Toward the end of last year we had a great coal strike involving for the first time in Australian history every miner in the commonwealth. Arbitration failed to settle that strike. The miners considered that they would not get a fair deal by arbitration, or at least they thought they would not get what they wanted, and refused to obey the mandate of the court. In the end, when the situation became desperate, the Prime Minister had to go to the aid of the court by personally ordering the coal owners to give way to the miners on every point. That proved conclusively that where a union is strong enough it can openly defy the court and get what it wishes.

There has been of late a growing desire on the part of the employers to drag every case in dispute into the arbitration court. The capitalists say that "arbitration has become an essential part of our social machinery and must be retained and assisted" simply because they have discovered that all they have to do is to flood the arbitration court with cases against the men and the court becomes congested, and the cases cannot be heard till some time in the future. There are cases now pending in the arbitration court which cannot possibly be heard within the next two years. Meanwhile the workers have to keep working under the existing awards, as any strike on their part, while a case is registered, means that they are canceled as a union and their awards are nullified, and they are again at the starting point.

To justify the arbitration system it remains now for the government to appoint subsidiary boards to hear the fast accruing cases, but whether they will do this or not remains to be seen. It would seem then that the success of arbitration largely depends on the political party in power. Another difficulty which will have to be overcome is the action of the capitalists in prolonging the arbitration cases until union funds are depleted by law expenses. This is another favorite pastime with the wealthy institutions, and unless it is remedied, it seems apparent that by bringing endless cases into the court every union can be rendered bankrupt.

Arbitration has not done all that has been expected. It has not raised the wages of every individual in the land, but on the other hand, it has not retarded industry. It has arrived at a fairly scientific living minimum wage basis. It has, of course, shortened hours and forced payment for overtime at increased rates, while on the other hand it has had a steadying influence on business and helped to bring prosperity to the employer as well as to the employee. The status of the worker is far ahead of what it was twenty years ago, thus proving that the wages awarded by arbitration have not been outpaced by the rise in the cost of living. The sweating system has been abolished, and competition in the labor market is a great deal fairer than it was years ago, inasmuch as female workers have been raised to a level which prohibits them being in direct competition to male labor, while in many industries there is equal pay for both sexes. The "preference to unionists" experiment has succeeded beyond expectation, giving to the employee an added interest in justifying his position as a skilled worker, while to the employer it has secured a continuity of labor, and the co-operation of the unions in finding additional labor as required.

But withal, with what objections there might be to the arbitration system, and I am inclined to think these are largely the result of war influences, there is not by any means a desire on the part of the Australian people to go back to the days of unrestricted competition in labor, or the period when a strike was the only method of settling a dispute.

W. FRANCIS AHEARN, *in American Labor Year Book,* 1917-1918, pp. 145-148.

CHAPTER XIV
Guild Socialism and National Guilds

A very recent solution is that proposed in Guild Socialism. Its exponents have a complete program for securing control of society, both economic and political. It is peculiar to England where the ancient guild system lasted longer than on the Continent. The plan is a radical one. It combines Syndicalism and I. W. W.ism with **Trade Unionism and State Socialism in a** progressive fusion. It is more a "high-brow" theoretical move, starting from above, than a spontaneous worker's movement. It has not yet taken a strong-hold in the United States but might do so at any moment, so that its origin and character are important questions to careful observers.

The National Guilds' League of Great Britain is conducting a strong propaganda. It has issued special pamphlets appealing to the general public, to the trade unionists, to the miners, to the railway men and on these pamphlets the following statement is largely based, the quotations being from the pamphlet addressed to the trade unionists.

The proposal of the National Guilds' League is that the trade union should recognize their mistake in adhering to the wage system; should see that only by abolishing the wage system can the selling of labor as a commodity be brought to an end; should see that in order to accomplish this Labor must assume absolute control of industry in "conjunction" with a democratized state.

In order to accomplish this the trade unions must make two fundamental changes in membership; must not be constituted merely or mainly of skilled labor but must admit on the one hand unskilled labor and on the other the brain worker.

This means the change from Craft Unionism to Industrial Unionism, with "a widening of the whole labor outlook." The end "to be achieved is freedom for the whole community, and no narrow view of industry will serve as a means. Preoccupied with the problems of the manual worker, industrial unionists have been inclined to forget that the true industrial union must include everyone who is engaged in the industry concerned, whether he work with hand or brain. Labor organization must not cease when every manual worker has been brought into the unions: clerks and foremen, works managers and managers, stationmasters and draughtsmen. designers and architects must be enrolled in their appropriate industrial unions, for they are no less essentially a part of industry than are the manual workers.

Again Industrial Unionism means solidarity not in each industry alone. It implies: the linking up of all the reorganizations of provinces in one solid body, in the interests of society as a whole. For the moment, indeed, effort must be mainly concentrated on organizing the manual workers who are still unorganized and on bringing in the lower grades of professionals whose status and rates of pay make them the natural allies of the manual workers.

But in every attempt the ideal of complete solidarity must be kept constantly in view. Only a body including every grade can undertake the full management of an industry. Out of the fighting industrial unions will come the managing and producing guilds, and Industrial Unionism is the first step towards national guilds. In a free society the organized producers must control their own life and work, and such control can only come through the development of Trade Unionism. Out of the trade unions must come the guilds — by a change in purpose and structure, and by a widening of membership.

As the workers realize that only by complete unity can capitalism and wage slavery be overthrown, reformism will give place to a more revolutionary ideal: the attempt to ameliorate will be replaced by the attempt to attain freedom through the destruction of the wage system.

The workers are ceasing to look upon mere nationalization as an ideal to be striven for. The state and the municipality as employers have turned out not to differ essentially from the private capitalist. In public employment, the worker has less freedom than under private capitalism.

The only hope for the workers lies in controlling national and municipal as well as private enterprise. Political democracy by itself would never secure more than better conditions of wage slavery. The only way in which the workers can secure freedom in their work is by fighting for control. Economic power precedes political power, and the road to freedom lies through industrial self-government.

The social and political organization planned by the guild leaders places the individual factories and workshops as producing units in relation with a central organization or national guild which secures co-ordination and exchanges. But each factory will be governed by its own local officials who will preserve its autonomy. Centralization for the getting of raw materials and the disposal of products as well as for laying down general standards and condition! The national guilds will be united in a Guild Congress which will be the supreme authority on the side of the producers as the state will be on that of the consumers.

For there will not only be a state governmental body aside from the guilds, but an entirely changed political structure, radically different from the present one, and run by the same persons as those who run the guilds but with different functions. The state and the local authorities would represent demand; the guilds would represent supply. The state would own the means of production as trustee for the community; the guilds would manage them, also as trustees for the community.

In a guild society an organization based on political grouping by locality will therefore be necessary. The political organization would, of course, be largely decentralized and a great part of its functions would be exercised locally. We would adjust financial questions between guilds, some of which would have to be maintained by levies on other guilds. A national revenue would have to be raised by levies on certain guilds. For the guilds would necessarily belong mainly to two types — civil and industrial. The public service of health and education would be in the civil category and would require subsidies.

This system would eliminate profiteering, and all profit making and all competition and artificial price making.

A very practical application of the guild idea is now being tried out in Manchester, England, and if successful it may quite revolutionize labor, at least in certain industries. Manchester is in desperate need of houses, up to 50,000 new houses Building was slow and expensive. Members of the trade union are prevented from engaging in trade in their capacity o members, but they can for other associations and enter into contracts in that new capacity. This was very recently done b workers in the various building and painting unions. The formed a building guild which offered to build 2,000 house quickly and cheaply for the city corporation, without the inter vention of private contractors or corporations. The worker supply not only the manual labor but the technical experts an business administrators. The city authorities advance the mone and take over the houses when finished. The rate of paymer by the city council is the plain cost of the labor at standard rat plus 10 per cent. The usual method of work is changed. Labor arranges to do all outside work in fair weather, and all inside work in foul weather, saving time and money and preventing laying off. The worker's status is also changed from a mere wage-earning employee to a salaried member of the guild, through what is called the full week system. Part of the 10 per cent. goes into this sytem and part of it into the purchase of necessary plant and cost of transportation. Materials, however, are bought by the city council and supplied to the guild. The guild is run by a small committee formed of representatives of each trade and of both administrative and technical experts. Men in good trade union standing are to direct the whole labor force. The guild is not required to give financial guarantees; only to pledge itself to furnish the necessary labor. The conditions of the scheme ensure efficient work on the part of the men. There are a number of towns in Lancashire ready to follow Manchester's lead and the plan is to form a Northwestern Building Guild that will do business not only with towns but with the national government.

The plan provides that disputes shall be referred to the Trade Unions Congress and the Minister of Labor, because of the guild theory that all material and assets should belong to the state which is to hold them in trust both for the community as a whole and for the guilds, the guilds having control of it.

A prominent writer on the guild system, G. Dox Cole, says of his new movement: "If the building workers can win industrial freedom and eliminate employers and private profit in this way, will they not be setting a fashion which other industries will be able to follow?"

At all events it might prove to be a good partial solution of our present tremendously difficult housing problem, especially in New York city. It would prevent such appalling situations as that when union labor recently refused to complete certain New York skyscrapers because non-union labor or material had been used in putting up the steel framework. The demand was made that the entire skeleton of these buildings should be torn down and scrapped. With the members of the unions as guildsmen in full charge such situations would not occur.

There is a big historical record back of the guild idea, a record of practical achievement and political as well as economic power during many centuries. The Romans perfected the system of guild organization. It has been part of the original scheme of division of the Roman people in the legendary days of King Numa. With the development of the bureaucratic system in the later empire the guilds, which in some cases had been considered, as they were by the Emperor Trajan, to be possible centers of sedition, were made to enter more and more into the imperial treadmill. They came to be absolutely controlled by the state. No worker could carry on his work unless he were a member of a guild. It was an absolutely closed shop. An occupation was made hereditary. The father was obliged by law to teach his son his own trade or occupation. There was no freedom of choice. Eventually, also, the worker had no choice of his place of work. He could not move from place to place, but was assigned to a certain place and could be brought back in case he should leave. The guilds, in return for the monopoly granted by the state, were obliged to give certain stated service to the state either in work or in material. The brickmakers were to furnish so many million bricks free each year; the waggoners were to furnish so many days' service for transportation; the ship owners, so many ship-trips; the stonecutters, masons, bricklayers, carpenters, painters, interior finishers and all other workers were obliged to give so many days' work free to the government. This is the explanation of the tremendous and splendid public works carried out by Roman administration throughout the civilized world. Even the Roman army became part of the building organization. It ended by the unions or guilds having their books open to government inspection, having a maximum price set on their work, having a regular rate for the purchase of all raw materials fixed by the government. This eventually brought about the ruin of art, industry and business, through the destruction of individual ambition, initiative and genius, and the rule of the bureaucracy of state control. All this developed during the third and fourth centuries of our era, between the Emperors Caracalla and Constantine. The attempt of Diocletian in about 300 A. D., a general price fixing, was a failure, owing to the riots it provoked.

With the downfall of Rome and of civilization the guilds were among the few survivals in a modest and modified form, and came to be composed of rather unskilled workmen. Still they were to form the nucleus or model of the organization of some of the earliest communities in the new Western world of the early Middle Ages. There was now no great central authority over them. They consisted of the plain people who were coming at last into their own. Gradually their members grew in skill and numbers until they became, in many cases, the backbone of the new republican communities in Italy, in Central and Northern Europe, during the twelfth and thirteenth centuries. It is interesting and suggestive to note that in such cities as Bologna in Italy the city government was run by representatives elected by the various guilds of the city from whom the city officials were chosen. The lawyers, merchants and bankers had their guilds as well as the masons, the butchers and the painters.

It is an extraordinary fact, then, that the lineal descendants of the slave guilds of Rome became the free guilds of the Middle Ages. In other Italian and Flemish cities and every German city an almost equally important role was played by the guilds in local politics. They exerted a dominant or important political role. It is a part of history that makes interesting reading for those who believe that such conditions can return in so far as such things can happen in fundamentally different civilizations.

CHAPTER XV
The Plumb Plan

In view of the nation-wide interest in the Plumb Plan for the nationalization of the railroads which was promulgated in 1919 and received the endorsement of some American Federation of Labor officials as well as that of radical leaders, we give here the text of a manifesto issued by the Plumb Plan League. Ever since the return of the railroads to private ownership the agitation for the plan has continued.

The Committee feels it necessary to point out that this plan is largely the result of radical Socialist propaganda upon more conservative elements. It is an example of the extremely dangerous tendency even among those who are not conscious opponents of our institutions to take over certain elements of the revolutionary program so modified as not to show clearly their obnoxious character.

THE A, B, C OF THE PLUMB PLAN

What is the Plumb Plan?

It is a plan for the public ownership and the democracy (*sic*) in the control of the railroads.

Who has endorsed it?

The two million organized railroad employees of America; and the American Federation of Labor, approving the principle of government ownership, has instructed its executive committee to co-operate with the officers of the railroad internationals in their efforts. It has also been endorsed by several farmers' organizations.

How does it propose to buy the roads?

By issuing government bonds with which to pay for the legitimate private interests in the railroad industry.

How does it propose to operate the roads?

By a board of fifteen directors, five named by the President, to represent the public; five elected by the operating officers; five elected by the classified employees.

Does this mean government operation?

No; it is operation by a board in which those having the responsibility have also the authority. It is superior to government operation because it prevents control by an inefficient bureaucracy; and is true democracy since it gives the men engaged in the industry a voice in its management.

What becomes of the surplus?

After operating expenses are paid, and fixed charges are met, including the interest on outstanding government securities, the surplus is divided equally between the government and the men. The employees' portion is to be divided between the managerial and classified employees, the former receiving double the rate received by the latter class. This is not a profit, since the corporation has no capital. What the men receive is a dividend on efficiency.

Is this a bonus system?

No, it is giving those who increase production a share of the results their increased effort has produced; and this share is theirs for as long as they are actually in the service, and is not forfeitable.

Why do operating officials receive the larger rate of dividend?

Because it serves as a greater stimulus to the group with the most responsibility. And since the operating officials would lose dividends if wages were increased it acts automatically to prevent collusion between land directors and the operating directors to outvote the public's directors in raising wages beyond a reasonable level. The chief argument against the plan is that the public loses control of its own property, and that the men in charge cannot be prevented from combining to pay themselves extortionate wages. This method of sharing dividends sets up a natural barrier against collusion.

Is this the only protection for the public?

No, the rate-making power remains with the Interstate Commerce Commission, and if wages were raised so high that rates had to be increased, the Commission could refuse to change them, and shippers might appeal to the courts for redress. If the operation by the directors results in a deficit Congress can revoke their charter.

Does this difference in dividends create hostility between officials and men?

No, because without harmony between them neither group can earn dividends. An official in working for his own dividend is working for the dividend of his subordinates, for one cannot gain unless all gain.

Does the plan assure a decrease in rates?

It provides that when the government's share of the surplus is 5 per cent. or more of the gross operating revenue, rates shall be reduced accordingly to absorb the amount the government receives. For instance: If the entire surplus one year is $500,000,000, and this is 10 per cent. of the gross operating revenue, the government receives $250,000,000. And because this is 5 per cent., rates are decreased 5 per cent. See what follows. Without new economies or new business the profits the next year would be only $250,000,000, and the employees and the government would receive only half the amount of the year before. But decreased rates mean more business; and also, the reduction in dividends would stimulate the employees to improve their operation by applying better methods. So the tendency is to assure constantly decreasing rates, to add to the volume of business, and to give the most efficient service human ingenuity and devotion can provide. Decreased rates mean cheaper commodities; and so, through the effectiveness of the railroads, the purchasing power of money is increased, not only for the railroad man, but for every wage earner and every purchaser.

What does the government do with its share of the surplus?

It invests in improvements and extensions, thus adding to the value of the railroads without adding to the fixed charges. It retires the outstanding bonds, thus reducing the fixed charges. Ultimately the public has its railroad service at cost.

Does the government pay for all extensions?

No, the community benefited must pay if it can; if it is able to pay all, the building of the extension is obligatory. If it only pays part, the government pays the remainder, but only makes the extension as it deems wise. And where the general public and not a local community would be benefited, the government pays the whole bill.

How are disputes between officials and men adjusted?

By the boards, to which the operating officials elect five members and the men, five members. In case of failure to reach an adjustment, the case is appealed to the directors.

Who determines the rate of wages?

The board of directors.

Who supervises the purchase of the roads?

A Purchasing Board, composed of the Interstate Commerce Commission and three directors of the new government corporation, one director from each group.

Who decides the value of the private interest in the railroads?

The courts. It is a judicial question, and is to be answered only after an examination of the charters of the existing companies, the laws under which they are created, and the manner in which the company has lived up to its charter and these laws.

Will the public have to pay for watered stock?

No. The public will probably pay less than two-thirds of what the railroads claim as their value.

Are there other savings?

Yes, the public can obtain the money to purchase the lines at 4 per cent., whereas the public is now charged rates to guarantee the roads 6½ per cent. on their money. The saving on the present capital account of the railroads would be about $400,000,000, and on an honest valuation would be nearly twice this sum. The Plumb Plan provides for a sinking fund and every year one of the fixed charges would be 1 per cent. of the outstanding indebtedness, to be used in retiring the bonds. The government also uses its profit in retiring bonds, so eventually, probably in fifty years, the people would own the roads debt-free. A further savings would be in the operation of the roads as a unified system, which permits the interchange of equipment, the end of wasteful competition, and greater economy in buying supplies. Under this plan passenger rates of one and one-half cents a mile, and a reduction of freight rates by 40 per cent. appear reasonable.

Why is it called the Plumb Plan?

Because it was conceived by Glenn E. Plumb, general counsel for the Organized Railway Employees of America.

What can you do to help its realization?

Join the Plumb Plan League (lodge membership, $10 a year; individual membership $1, payable to treasurer, Plumb Plan League, 447-453 Munsey Building, Washington), talk with your friends, and write your congressman. It is the only association to secure public ownership that has the endorsement of the organized railroad employees.

Who is eligible to the League?

Every one who believes that democracy in industry is the solution of the railroad problem.

Public and Labor Share and Share Alike

The Plumb Plan League has been formed for the purpose of uniting in a single organization the millions of American citizens who believe that the time has come when the public must take over the railroads of the country.

The organization is national in scope and non-partisan in character.

A financial panic is threatened by the demand of the railroad interests for the return of the railroads to private control on terms certain to result in disaster.

The leading financiers of Wall Street and the most prominent railway executives declare that this crisis is coming, unless their wishes are complied with. Other equally competent authorities assert that the plans of the railroad interests are certain to result in disaster if the railroads are given back on their terms.

Distinguished officials of our government — legislative, administrative and executive — agree that this danger is impending, although they disagree on the best method of averting it.

Upon but one point, apparently, is there harmony of thought, and that is in the necessity for governmental intervention to save the nation from a financial panic a few years after the closing of the World War. Such a panic would be far more serious than was the panic of 1873, which occurred within ten years after the civil war.

Over, 6,000,000 American citizens and voters, through the Organized Railway Employees of America, composed of the fourteen railroad internationals, together with the American Federation of Labor, the Non-Partisan League, various farmers' organizations and civic bodies support the Plum Plan as the only rational solution of the railroad problem.

The Plumb Plan League comes into existence, therefore, to arouse public sentiment and secure laws to accord with the determination of these millions of American citizens to make the principles of the Plumb Plan effective in the critical situation which confronts the country.

Other millions of Americans, representing all walks of life, whose interests are likewise in danger, will be appealed to and urged to join this movement on behalf of the public welfare.

The Four Corners of the Plumb Plan

Railroads are over-capitalized, hence freight and passenger rates are exorbitant, wages inadequate and service unsatisfactory.

Purchase the railroads for the actual amount invested to afford public service as determined judicially, recognizing no fictitious securities, no discounts and no improvements paid for out of earnings or by the public.

Substitute for the present Wall Street control the unhampered management of trained officials and employees — the most intelligent and efficient transportation organization in the world.

Pay capital a fair and fixed return on the dollars actually invested in railroad property and divide savings effected by economy and efficiency between the public and the operating organization — share and share alike.

Plain Facts about Railroad Financing

The income received by railroad companies is derived chiefly from the transportation of commodities and people — freight charges and passenger fares. Both of these are paid by the public. The expenditures of railroad companies include, broadly speaking, returns on securities issued, cost of upkeep and extensions, operating charges and wages to employees. Rates, which include both freight and passenger fares, must provide the income necessary to cover expenditures — otherwise bankruptcy is inevitable.

Therefore, the item of returns on securities issued or which are included in the "property investment account" is of paramount importance in rate-fixing.

This "property investment account" item is vital. It should be noted carefully. It is a bookkeeping term used to cover the billions of watered stock and billions of fictitious values upon which Wall Street demands that labor and the public shall pay tribute.

Inflated capitalizations, if officially recognized by Congress, will call for inflated earnings. These can only be produced by higher rates or reduced wages and inferior service.

Four Proposed Plans of Governmental Intervention

Four plans which have been suggested for the solution of the railroad problem are of enough importance to warrant attention. They are:

1. Return of railroads to private ownership with a governmental subsidy.

2. Return of railroads to private ownership with a rate increase.
3. Government ownership and operation of railroads.
4. The Plumb Plan, with its equitable safeguarding of all interests.

The first plan is so contrary to American thought and practice that it does not merit serious consideration.

The second plan is also objectionable and injurious, since it contemplates a general increase of commodity prices that will eventually re-establish the identical conditions that exist today.

The third plan finds favor with a very limited number of Americans, because there is a grave fear that political management will be little, if any, improvement over private management.

The Plumb Plan, alone, then, remains as meriting the attention of those who sincerely desire a correction of intolerable conditions.

It removes from discussion all talk of subsidies, higher rates and political manipulation. It offers a scientific, equable, business-like arrangement for the operation and development of the nation's transportation system on democratic principles.

Its adoption will usher in an era of industrial stability, prosperity and well-being that will influence favorably all industries and so contribute to the welfare of every citizen.

CHAPTER XVI

Political Programs of the American Federation of Labor and of the Farmers

QUESTIONS SUBMITTED BY THE ADVISORY COMMITTEE ON POLICIES AND PLATFORM, REPUBLICAN NATIONAL COMMITTEE, AND REPLIES BY PLATFORM COMMITTEE, NATIONAL NON-PARTISAN POLITICAL CAMPAIGN, AMERICAN FEDERATION OF LABOR.

WASHINGTON, D. C., *March* 29, 1920.

Mr. OGDEN L. MILLS, *Chairman*, Executive Committee, Republican National Committee, 19 West 44th Street, New York, N. Y.:

DEAR SIR:— Recently there was received at the headquarters of the American Federation of Labor copies of a questionnaire " on industrial relations and the problems of capital and labor, in the hope that the answers will define a proper governmental policy and will suggest remedies which the government and those most directly interested may profitably consider," the whole being predicated upon the thought of their possible incorporation in the platform of the National Republican Convention to be held June 20, 1920. Your questionnaire was also sent to representative labor men throughout the country and the undersigned have been communicated with regarding the same.

Believing that you should have as comprehensive answers as possible we respectfully submit your questions and our answers as follows:

1. How far is " good-will " inside the plant a valuable economic factor in production and how can it best be secured?

Good-will inside the plant not only is a valuable economic factor in production, but it is an indispensable factor if production is to be maintained at a proper rate. Good-will is not something to which the employer has an inherent right. It must be earned. It can best be earned by the establishment of just conditions in the plant and by agreements between employers and the duly authorized representatives of the worker in the industry.

2. Can the permanent interest and " good-will " of those of us who are wage-earners be developed by, and how relatively important are, any or all of the following methods?

[2251]

(a) Technical training to increase production efficiency, wages, chances of promotion, etc., without making the work less attractive.

(b) Systematic information concerning, and better understanding of the problems and point of view of business management.

(c) Training managers, foremen and superintendents in better understanding of problems and point of view of employees.

(d) Joint conferences of representatives of the management and of the workers to carry out such mutual understandings.

(e) Collective co-operation through —
(1) Trade unions.
(2) Shop committees.
(3) Combination of 1 and 2.
(4) Comprehensive organizations of both employers and employed.

(f) Welfare work — medical care, sick benefits, unemployment benefits, invalidity, retirement, old age, and the death benefits provided and administered by —
(1) Employers' organizations.
(2) Employees or trade union organizations.
(3) Joint organizations of those associated as employers and employees.

(g) Profit sharing, bonus distribution, gain sharing, parity of wages and profits, etc.

Answering this question, with its various subdivisions, a better result can be achieved by treating the question as a whole. First of all it must be said that permanent interest and good-will of the wage-earners in industry can be developed to the fullest degree only when the wage-earners are free to follow their own judgment in the matter of organization and then only when the employers confer freely and on a basis of equality with the authorized representatives of the workers so organized in the industry. There can be no question as to the manner in which American wage-earners wish to organize when left free to act in accordance with their own judgment. The American trade union movement, with more than five million members, is sufficient answer in respect to that. In modern industry shop committees and other similar devices as substitutes for trade union organization do not meet the needs of working people. The movement toward the formation of shop committees is a movement which has its inspiration and inception among employers who aim to prevent or circumvent practical organization of the workers and is in no sense the result of the study and judgment of the workers themselves. Technical training is always desirable. No movement in America has done more to secure proper technical training than the American trade union movement. Such training, however, when improperly administered or when so administered as to carry with it a spirit of antagonism toward trade union effort, defeats its own purpose and must be unreservedly opposed. Workers always manifest a deeper interest in processes over which they have complete mastery.

The training of managers, foremen and superintendents in a better understanding of the problems and viewpoints of employees is, of course, important. What is more important, however, is that the employees should at all times be free to express their viewpoints and to exercise a determining voice in the solution of shop problems and the determination of all questions affecting their relation to their employments. Joint conferences of representatives of employers and workers in the industry are indispensable.

In some American industries the employers still seek to maintain the ancient concept that the employee is not to be consulted upon any question at any time. Those who are familiar with industry understand fully that a day is near at hand when this concept will have disappeared entirely. Two things are to be gained by its complete banishment: First, it is unjust to the workers and until it disappears the workers can never manifest a proper interest in their employment and can never feel a sense of justice. Second, production can never be maintained at its highest and best. Comprehensive organization of employees along lines which they themselves deem most effective is equally desirable and must be had.

Welfare work, when administered by employers, the tendency or purpose of which is to buy the submission of the workers, is utterly out of keeping with the American spirit and has never proved worth the effort to employers who sought to utilize the idea. The points covered under the description of welfare work in the questionnaire may safely be left to the trade unions.

Establishment of proper conditions in the place of employment, the payment of a proper wage and the having of a proper regard for the well-being of the employees, while at work, will do away with the necessity of general consideration of most of these points. Proper organization of industry and the proper efficiency in management will go still further to eliminate any such need. At any rate the initiative in all such matters should rest with the organized employee.

Profit sharing, distribution of bonuses and similar schemes are usually used as a means of holding employees in subjection and preventing trade union organization. If employers can afford to pay bonuses then let them do so in the form of a higher wage and better conditions rather than in the form of gratuities. Such schemes are, at best, makeshifts and can by no means be regarded as a panacea for industrial ills.

Employers are free to pay to employees as high wages as the services performed warrant. What the trade unions insist upon is that they shall pay not less than a minimum wage which is sufficient to maintain the workers in a proper standard of living.

3. Should trade unions and organizations of employers be incorporated with right to sue and be sued?

Trade unions should not be incorporated. Trade unions are voluntary associations of working people organized not for profit but for the mutual protection and advancement of the workers. The only object in the minds of those who wish to enforce trade union incorporation is the destruction of the trade unions. They seek to bring about a condition under which trade union treasuries can be mulcted in the hope that such confiscation will destroy the organizations. This question has been fully dealt with in the "American Federationist," and the following paragraphs set forth fully and concisely the position to which American labor is committed and which it feels to be the only just position and the only position consistent with American democracy:

" The great majority of the unions are simply voluntary associations, organized for lawful and proper purposes. They have no special privilege of any kind, and claim no rights which do not, under the laws of the country, belong to all citizens.

". . . a trade union is neither a partnership, nor a corporation.

" One unionist is no more responsible, legally, for the action of another than one church member is responsible for the actions of another. The attempt to impose liabilities and burdens on unions without regard to settled principles of jurisprudence is an audacious plutocratic coup, which an independent and courageous judiciary would have checked at the first hint or suggestion.

"Our opponents charge that the labor organizations want power without responsibility, special immunities, and privileges in order to escape the legal consequences of their acts.

"This is false and nonsensical.

"The unions object to special judge-made laws directed against them. The unions do not seek to be a law unto themselves.

"Hold them responsible under the general laws, punish them for torts and crimes when they are really guilty, but do not stretch the law to establish a 'responsibility' which has never been imposed on voluntary associations.

"Labor has declined to incorporate, thus avoiding its enemies' trap. But thanks to unscrupulous lawyers and subservient, bigoted, or ignorant judges, plutocracy may be able to accomplish the same result — the seizure of union property, the crippling of labor by ruinous litigation and all sorts of legal entanglements — without incorporation."

Trade unions are not formed for the accumulation of property, nor for the making of profits. They are formed of individuals who must of necessity come together for mutual protection and advancement. Their work constitutes a great and noble contribution to the advancement of all humanity. Labor power is not a product. It is flesh and blood, brain and brawn. It is a part of the human being. Labor power is the inherent power in human beings to produce commodities for the sustenance of life. To suggest that this power and these qualities of the human race should be incorporated by law is to suggest a desperation on the part of employers which must be curbed for the very safety of society.

4. In the event of incorporation should the power of injunction be limited?

In this question the workers are asked to barter one evil for another. The workers are asked whether they prefer being struck on the left cheek. The trade union movement does not indulge in that kind of trading. It opposes all injustice. The character and integrity of the trade union movement should be better known than to permit of such an astounding suggestion.

The question of the injunction must be treated as a separate question. The trade union attitude toward the injunction is best illustrated in the declaration adopted by representatives of American labor meeting in Washington, D. C., December 13, 1919:

"The paramount issues that concern all the people of the United States, and in particular the wage-earners, are the perversion and the abuse of the writ of injunction and the necessity for full and adequate protection of the voluntary associations of wage-earners organized not for profit.

"Government by injunction has grown out of the perversion of the injunction process. By the misuse of that process workers have been forbidden to do those things which they have a natural and constitutional right to do.

"The injunction as now used is a revolutionary measure which substitutes government by judicial discretion or bias for government by law. It substitutes a trial by one man, a judge, in his discretion, for a trial by jury. This abuse of the injunctive process undermines and destroys the very foundations of our free institutions. It is subversive of the spirit of a free people working out their destiny in an orderly and rational manner.

"Because we have reverence for law, because we believe that every citizen must be a guardian of the heritage given us by our fathers who fought for an established freedom and democracy, by every lawful means, we must resist the establishment of a practice that would destroy the very spirit of freedom and democracy. Our protest against the abuse of the writ of injunction and its unwarranted application to labor in the exercise of labor's normal activities to realize laudable aspirations is a duty we owe to ourselves and to posterity.

"Formerly injunctions issued in labor disputes were of a prohibitive character. Within the recent past this abuse of the injunction writ has been enlarged to include mandatory orders whereby men have been compelled to do specific things which they have a lawful right to refrain from doing.

"We declare these abuses in the exercise of the injunction writ are clearly violative of the constitution and that this issue must be determined definitely in accordance with the guarantees of the Constitution of the United States."

5. Should such organizations come within the provision of or be specifically exempt from anti-trust laws?

Trade union organizations, as well as co-operative organizations and organizations of farmers organized not for profit but for the mutual benefit and protection of their members, should be specifically exempt from the provisions of anti-trust laws. Existing law declares that the labor of a human being is not a commodity or article of commerce. The Clayton Law lays down the guiding principle in this respect and this principle cannot, with safety, be abandoned or destroyed. It is the principle that should be followed in all states.

6. In joint conferences should the general principle be recognized that employees have the right to choose their own representatives from within or without the plant involved?

The principle should always be accepted that employees have the right to choose their own representatives from within or without the plant. Corporations, combinations of investors, dominate the field of American industry. Of necessity they operate through representatives. In selecting those who are to speak for them or negotiate for them corporations choose whom they wish. The selection is not even made by the stockholders; it is made by the directors or by an officer. There is no limitation upon the field from which selection may be made. Labor demands for itself no more than the same rights exercised by the employers. The moment it is sought to exercise any outside control over the selection of labor's representatives, at that moment a measure of democracy disappears and autocratic control begins to reclaim its lost privileges. The employer has no more right to dictate to trade unionists whom they shall select as their representatives than the employees have to dictate to the employers. In fact, representatives cannot be representative unless they are chosen freely by those who are to be represented. The right to be heard by counsel is a constitutional guarantee. That principle must not be denied, but firmly established in the industrial relations between employers and employees.

7. Do you approve of the general principles of the Kansas Court of Industrial Relations Law, and if so should it be adopted by other states and by the Federal Government as far as applicable?

The general principles in what is known as the Kansas Court of Industrial Relations Law are principles that are so anti-democratic as to he reprehensible in the extreme and repugnant to every American concept of justice, freedom and democracy. This is not the place to enter into an extended argument in relation to the Kansas law. It may be said, however, that the principles around which the law is built are the principles of compulsion and coercion constituting a negation of freedom and voluntary effort. Safety, success and justice in American industry can be achieved only through joint, constructive, voluntary effort and through the free negotiation between employers and workers in the industry.

The principle which it is sought to set up in legislation similar to that enacted in Kansas is in distinct violation of section 1 of Article XIII of the Constitution of the United States, which reads as follows:

> "Neither slavery nor involuntary servitude, except as a punishment for crime, whereof the party shall have been duly convicted, shall exist within the United States or any place subject to their jurisdiction."

8. Should lockouts and strikes be restricted by law and, if so, how?
  (a) In government employment.
  (b) In public utilities.
  (c) In private employments.

In this question there is a continuance of the discussion of compulsion and coercion. It must be understood in American industry, in practice as it has been established in law, that "the labor of a human being is not a commodity or article of commerce." Acceptance of that principle makes impossible legislation limiting the right to cease work — strike. The difference between a strike and a lockout is this: The strike is a resort to the final argument by workers seeking to establish better conditions and higher concepts in industry. A lockout is a resort to the final argument in denial of those aspirations.

The American labor movement believes that those in the employ of the government should secure redress for wrongs, through the political machinery of the nation. It is, however, equally firm in the belief that the right of such employees to cease work must be maintained. The right should be maintained, but there should never be occasion to use it.

9. What, if any, is the proper function of the secondary strike or boycott?

Definition of the proper function of what is termed in the questionnaire "secondary strike" (which, by the way, is an employer's definition) and what is the proper function of the boycott cannot well be set forth within the limitation of a proper reply to this questionnaire. It is neither possible nor desirable to set forth a dictionary definition of these terms. In its struggle to establish greater democracy in industry, a struggle which began with efforts to secure the most simple and elemental measures of justice, the measures that have been used by labor have to a large degree necessarily been determined by the conditions under which the struggle has been made. Where the boycott has been used, it has not been used out of any desire on the part of labor to do any injury to others, but it has been used because the tactics of the employers left to labor no other course to pursue. The same may be said regarding what the questionnaire terms "the secondary strike." It is not possible, nor is it desirable by law or decree to limit the freedom of action of working people who may either singly or collectively seek to improve the conditions under which they live and thus to make more valuable to the country their services and their citizenship. It would be inhuman to deny to any one group the right to go to the assistance of another group. History is largely made up of the struggles of groups of people to overcome their environment and to overcome oppression by other groups. The allied and associated nations in the World War could not have combined to overthrow German autocracy if they had permitted themselves to be bound by the principle which it is here sought to set up.

At various times and under varying conditions the struggle has taken on different forms and at times it has been attended by a roughness and even a crudeness which in the abstract might appear to be undesirable. The fact that civilization is today at such an advanced stage is due solely to this age-long struggle. No intelligent person will deny that much improvement still is necessary. Neither will any intelligent person deny that there must be a continuance of the struggle if that improvement is to be secured. Regardless of what men may write into books, the struggle will take the form, for the most part, at least, which is demanded by the conditions under which it is waged. Under any circumstances employers have no property right in the labor power of human beings nor has any one a property right in the patronage of the people.

10. Should an impartial board be established to deal with conditions of employment, and if so with what powers?

(a) In government employments.

(b) In public utilities and industries declared to be affected with a public interest.

(c) In private employments.

11. Should industrial tribunals be established as agencies for conciliation and voluntary arbitration?

12. Should the establishment of such tribunals be left to private initiative, or should provision be made by law for their establishment?

13. Should a national tribunal be established to direct the organization of industrial tribunals in regions and industries where they are desired?

14. Should the number of the regional and local industrial tribunals be specially organized for each dispute, or should they be permanent to deal with all questions?

15. Should the national, regional and local industrial tribunals be composed of representatives of employers and employees, and how should they be selected?

16. Should representatives of organized labor be chosen by the unions and the representatives of unorganized labor by those employees working under shop-representation plans?

17. Should the public be represented on any or all of the tribunals — national, regional, local?

18. How should representatives of the public be chosen?

19. Where the parties do not agree to submit their differences to the appropriate tribunal, should the tribunal have the right, through compulsory process, to investigate the matter and make public recommendations?

20. Should the decisions of the national, regional or local industrial tribunals be by a majority vote, or by a unanimous vote?

21. Should the parties maintain continuous production pending decision by the tribunals and how can this best be secured?

22. Should the continuance of production be a condition precedent to the tribunals taking jurisdiction as a board of arbitration?

23. Should there be a right of appeal where the local tribunal is unable to reach a decision?

24. If the decision is by majority vote, should there be any right of appeal to the national tribunal?

Question No. 10, and subsequent questions up to 24, inclusive, deal entirely with matters which are developed out of Question

No. 10, all having to do with the establishment of boards and tribunals for the arbitration or conciliation of industrial disputes. The answer to Question No. 10 will cover the situation. During the war organized labor was in entire accord with the establishment of the National War Labor Board and it sought generally to avail itself of the services of the board in its ardent desire that there be no interference with the processes of production while the war continued. Many institutions and many practices were made use of during the war which are not suitable to the needs of peace. The war has ended, even though Congress has not yet seen fit to make formal admission of that fact. It is clear that the thought underlying most of the proposals for so-called labor boards and tribunals of national scope for the handling of industrial disputes is that by such means the progress of labor will be retarded. There has not yet been suggested a plan for tribunals of this character which is correct in principle. The trade union movement is the normal and natural expression of labor's desire and necessity for organization. The trade union movement, in co-operation with employers, has worked out machinery for the handling of industrial disputes and for the prevention of industrial disputes. This machinery being the product of the normal and natural function of labor in its organized capacity, must stand and does stand as the proper and practical machinery for this purpose. In its creation there has been expressed the sum total of the wisdom and experience of the industries in which it is applied and it is safe to say that there is within any given industry a greater knowledge concerning the operation and the needs of that industry than can be brought to bear from any outside agency. It is a matter of record that the machinery erected by organized labor in co-operation with the employers has enabled some industries to continue without interruption, without strike or lockout, for as long as forty years. As specific examples there may be cited the glass bottle blowers, the stove molders and the newspaper printing trades. Where the machinery offered by the trade union movement is accepted and applied with intelligence, good will and earnestness, every desirable object is achieved and every fair demand is met. Where there is not intelligence, good will and earnestness, no machine will serve the purpose. The trade union movement insists that there must be a constant extension of the principles of democracy in industry, but it contends that the practical application of this principle must be worked out within the industry itself. It can not be laid down upon the history from the outside like a blanket, with anything but unfavorable and perhaps disastrous results. All of the questions in the questionnaire between and including Nos. 10 and 24, are born largely out of the realm of theory and abstraction, and have no bearing upon national political issues. The whole subject involved is a matter that is distinctly industrial in character and that must find its practical solution out of the experience and practice of the industrial field itself. The experiences of Australia and New Zealand, and even of European countries, such as Germany, and, more recently, such as England, should warn America to leave these questions to the field of which they are native and to refrain from artificial effort to transplant them to the field of politics. The nation is going through a sufficient industrial agony without adding to it by experimentation with human lives which is condemned in advance.

25. What is the proper scope of injunction in labor disputes?

The injunction has no place in labor disputes. The use of the injunction in a democratic nation to restrain the aspirations of working people for an extension of the horizon of democracy and for the enlargement of their opportunities is a strange contradiction. The injunction, like so much of the remainder of our legal structure, has come to us through a body of decrees and judge-made precedents upon precedents. The use of injunctions in labor disputes is to evade trial under law, destroy the presumption of innocence and deny the constitutional guarantee of trial by jury.

26. What abuses of injunctions in labor disputes suggest remedies or restrictions of this power?

The history of injunctions in labor disputes in the United States in the last twenty-five years is sufficient answer. A few conspicuous cases may be mentioned — the Buck Stove and Range Company case, the Hitchman Coal and Coke Company v. The United Mine Workers of America, and the recent injunction issued by Judge Anderson against the United Mine Workers of America. Attention is called to the publication by the House of Representatives of a volume containing the Hitchman Coal and Coke Company case.

27. Should sickness insurance be established in industry and, if so, how?

(a) Compulsory or voluntary.

(b) Jointly managed by employers and employees, or by either separately.

28. Should entire cost of sick benefits be borne by industry as part of cost of production or divided between employer and employees?

29. Should the government assist in the organization and development of sickness insurance?

The whole subject of health insurance is one upon which a variety of suggestions have been offered, most of which have been impractical and some of which have been vicious. Only with the greatest care and upon the best advice of the workers in their organized capacity should steps be taken toward the development of anything definite in the direction of health insurance. Schemes for health insurance usually worked out by welfare and up-lift organizations are of such a paternalistic nature as to be absolutely dangerous. The trade union movement is at the present time conducting an investigation into the whole subject of sickness insurance.

30. Would a system of local, state and federal public employment exchanges, such as is operating successfully in Great Britain today be desirable?

It was with the deepest regret that organized labor witnessed the disbanding of the system of free federal employment agencies built up during the war. Labor exerted every possible effort to prevent the disbanding of those agencies. Agencies of a similar character should be re-established. The need of the workers for employment should cease forever to offer a field for private employment agencies which are invariably oppressive and inefficient.

31. Would such a system of local, state and federal public employment exchanges be more desirable if administered by a joint commission of employers and employees rather than by government agencies?

Labor ought by all means to have a voice in the administration of public employment agencies. There is no field in which it is more proper that labor should exercise a voice commensurate with its importance. Furthermore, the voice of labor exercised in the administration of a system of free public employment agencies should be exercised in consultation with the trade union movement. Labor representation should be upon nomination by the trade union movement.

32. What is the most practical plan of bringing the worker and the job automatically together?

The intent of this question is not entirely clear. It is to be doubted whether any machinery can be erected for automatically bringing the workers and the job together. An automatic operation is an operation in which no human intelligence is required. The utmost of human intelligence would be required in the proper conduct of a system of free employment agencies.

33. Should unemployment insurance be established in industry and if so, how?

34. Is it practical to put part of the cost of unemployment benefits on the industry in the proportion of two-thirds to be paid by the employer and one-third by the employee or in any other proportion?

35. Would it be advisable to provide for invalidity, retirement, and old age benefits in the same way, as suggested above for sickness and unemployment benefits and insurance?

36. Should maternity insurance and provision for compulsory rest periods, before and after childbirth, be established as a charge upon the industry?

These four questions are so related to each other that they may be answered as one. In the first place the principle which was apparently in mind in choosing the language of these questions is a decidedly erroneous one. Two of the questions refer to "benefits." Whatever compensation ought to be awarded to those in industry by reason of unemployment, invalidity or old age, should not be by way of benefits but by way of compensation. Workers contribute their lives to industry. They give their whole lives to industry. They are entitled to get back, as the result of that contribution, sufficient to maintain them so long as life lasts. Furthermore, they are entitled to sufficient to maintain them in a standard of living fitting to our time and our country. To speak of benefits for workers who are not paid a sufficient wage to make benefits unnecessary is to emphasize the irony of industrial injustices. The industrial world must be brought to a point where it returns to the workers a sufficient amount to maintain them throughout their lives and not only that but the industrial system must be brought to a point where it affords to the workers a constantly increasing measure of life and a constantly increasing margin of safety. The terminology of benefits and charity is repugnant to the world of labor and the concept which that terminology expresses must give way and be discarded. Unemployment, invalidity, the vicissitudes of old age, when labor contribution is no longer possible, should be considered a proper charge against industry. The time has passed when industry can take from the workers the best efforts of their early years and discard them, worn out, broken down, in middle age. The point raised in question No. 36 brings out a serious and tragic reflection upon our present industrial life. It implies that it is necessary for mothers and those about to become mothers to work in gainful occupations! It seeks to find a way to make this employment tolerable, to give it a sanction and standing. If the injustices of industry do for the present make consideration of this problem necessary, and it must be admitted that they do, the principle involved must be viewed in the same light as that involved in questions 33, 34, and 35. In relation to the whole subject there can be no thought of benefits and the greatest care must be exercised so that no system of state tyranny shall be built up out of the needs of the workers.

37. How and by whom should standards for restrictive legislation for women be determined with respect to —
 (a) Limitation of hours.
 (b) Night work.
 (c) Dangerous and unhealthy occupations.

Standards for restrictive legislation and also for conditions within the industries themselves should be established in accordance with the best judgment of the trade union movement and in co-operation with the United States Department of Labor. There should be constant study and a constant development by the Department of Labor of policies and standards in the industry of the country for the safeguarding of the interests of women workers.

38. Is the principle of equal pay for equal work correct and if so, how can it be made effective?

The principle of equal pay for equal work is correct and there should be no mystery about the method of making it effective. Not only is the principle of equal pay for equal work correct, but it is also true that standards for minimum wages necessary to maintain life at a proper standard should apply to women in industry as well as men.

39. Should the standards of the Federal Child Labor Law be raised with respect to existing prohibitions?
 (a) Employment in mills, canneries, workshops, factories or manufacturing establishments prohibited for children under fourteen.

(b) Employment between fourteen and sixteen years of age not more than eight hours per day nor more than six days per week, or after 7 P. M. or before 6 A. M.

(c) Mines and quarries — employment under sixteen years of age prohibited.

It is the settled conviction of the American labor movement that the minimum age at which children should be employed in any industry is sixteen years. It is the further conviction that after this age ample provisions should be made for the continuation of education and for the proper physical development of children.

40. Should scope of Federal Child Labor Law as indicated above in question 39 be extended with respect to —

(a) Additional occupations.
(b) Agricultural labor.
(c) Mercantile establishments.
(d) Specially dangerous or morally hazardous employment.
(e) Educational and physical qualifications for employment.

Yes, and at the earliest possible moment.

41. Should higher age requirements or greater restrictions be imposed for girls than for boys?

Yes, in so far as protecting the future motherhood of the race makes such increased restrictions necessary.

42. Should one day's rest in seven be compulsory for all workers?

The duration of the work week should not exceed six days and employers should be compelled to grant at least one full day of rest in each week. The question implies that it is necessary to compel the workers to rest one day per week. The workers have struggled bitterly for decades to secure one day of rest per week. Any condition that does not allow it is solely the fault of recalcitrant and reactionary employers.

43. Is the standard eight-hour day desirable in all industries?

In no industry should the maximum work day exceed eight hours. In some industries both the health of the workers and such questions as regularity and continuity of employment may easily make a shorter work day desirable from every viewpoint. In some American industries experience has led to the conclusion that a shorter work day is desirable and to the introduction of a shorter work day.

44. Would the recognition of a standard eight-hour day with a temporary general agreement to work nine hours with one hour

overtime pay be desirable under present industrial conditions, and would such understanding serve to increase production and reduce high cost of living?

Assuming that the above question is asked seriously, permit us to say that such an understanding would be intolerable. There is no present necessity in American industry for a work day exceeding eight hours in length. Proper conduct of industry, proper organization and proper executive management can, without difficulty, obviate necessity and may be apparent for a work day exceeding eight hours in length. The excessive cost of living is not due in any degree whatever to the eight-hour work day and a work day of greater duration would have no effect in reducing the cost of living. The causes for the high cost of living lie so entirely outside the field here presented as to make the suggestion preposterous. The United States Department of Labor has recently announced that during the period which has elapsed since 1913, the average union wage has increased but 55 per cent. while the average cost of living has increased 83.1 per cent., is sufficient answer to any implication that the hours of labor or the wages of labor have had the effect of inflicting upon the American people the intolerable, shameful and unjust inflation of the cost of living. Any effort to lengthen the work day either permanently or temporarily would be a pernicious and vicious effort to throw upon the shoulders of labor a still greater burden and would not have the effect of bringing relief to any of our people.

45. Should the three shift system be compulsory in continuous industries?

There should not be less than three shifts in any continuous industry. Health, safety and welfare demand this.

46. What should be the standard number of hours in the working week?

The standard number of hours in the working week should be fixed by the employers and employees in each industry through collective agreement, but, in no case should the number of hours exceed eight per day, with one-half holiday on Saturday.

47. Should minimum wage boards be established —
  (a) For all wage-earners.
  (b) For women and minors only.
  (c) For all industries or only for specified industries.

48. Should the decisions of such boards be enforced by law as at present in the District of Columbia, Oregon and other states,

or by public opinion after publication of names of those who do not comply, as in Massachusetts law?

If employers, generally will accept the machinery offered by the trade union movement and enter into the making of trade agreements through collective bargaining, there will be no necessity for minimum wage boards. The idea of establishing such boards is in the main, an effort to defeat the purposes of organized labor and to weaken its influence, at the same time placing in the hands of political authorities, far removed from the world of industry, a power and authority which they are not qualified to exercise and which they can seldom exercise with intelligence and justice.

49. Should the principle of workmen's compensation for accidents be extended to cover occupational diseases?

Yes.

50. Should the Federal Workmen's Compensation Act, now applicable to civil employees, be extended?

(a) To railroad employees.

(b) To other employees.

(c) With respect to any other hazards of industry.

Under our dual form of government federal compensation laws should include and extend to all wage-earners not governed by state compensation laws.

51. How can thrift be encouraged among wage-earners?

Of course thrift is desirable and commendable but the encouragement of thrift among wage-earners is far from being a primary question. There can be no great enthusiasm for thrift among wage-earners until they have something with which to be thrifty. There must first be paid to the wage-earner a wage adequate to maintain the American standard of living. Too much of American industry does not yet afford such a wage. Figures show that great masses of American workers are still endeavoring to overcome the advancing costs of living and that they are still far behind in the race. Arguments for thrift can make no appeal under such circumstances. There is room for vast economy of the most fundamental and essential nature in the conduct of industry itself in the regulation of industrial processes so that there may be regular and continuous operation, in the employment of machinery to its fullest capacity and in the utilization of improved methods and processes wherever possible. Such thrift would be a true national economy. To neglect this broader and more fundamental economy while coaxing underpaid working people to be thrifty with what they do not have is typical of a great deal of present-day American statesmanship and is typical of a great deal of ignorance and misunderstanding regarding industry and its problems. Of course thrift, intelligent thrift, and thrift for patriotic purposes is commendable and has been loyally supported by the masses of the workers.

52. What form of profit sharing, if any, will promote thrift, co-operation, and a better understanding of the function of the capitalist as trustee and administrator of wealth in the interests of producers and consumers alike?

Is this question predicated upon a possible declaration of a national political party to the effect that employers are " trustees and administrators of wealth in the interests of producers and consumers alike?" Surely this is interesting. By what right have they obtained trusteeship? By Divine Right? American Labor entertains no such delusion. Trustees derive their authority from a principal who trusts them. " Producers and consumers " have, so far as the records show, never agreed upon any " trustee " of the character here suggested. The thrift section of the question should be kept distinct from the ridiculous assumption of capitalist trusteeship and is dealt with in reply to question 51.

Profit sharing is not a device for the promotion of thrift and co-operation. It is a device for the entrenchment of privilege and for the subjection of workers. It is calculated to further docility of spirit and to discourage organization among the workers. Without organization and without freedom of action among workers there can be no true and effective co-operation with employers for any of the objects which are worth while in industry. The capitalist who asks the workers to accept profit sharing has no notion that he is acting in the capacity of a trustee in the administration of the property he possesses and the implication to that effect in the question is evidently a crude and clumsy effort to give standing and circulation to a misconception. Does the question imply the resurrection of the idea of the trusteeship of wealth which was believed to have been interred with the remains of the late Geo. F. Baer?

53. What kind of " blue sky " laws or other measures will best protect small investors from worthless investments, and at the same time secure their participation and co-operation in industrial enterprises?

54. Should all issues of securities be subject to government scrutiny?

Careful study fails to remove the suspicion of inconsistency between these two questions and the question immediately preceding. The assumption that the beneficent "trustees" need to be restrained from doing violent financial injury to the small investors who have not attained to the stature of "trusteeship" is novel, at least, and on the whole interesting. The best reply to what may be the thought underlying both of these questions is found in the declaration of labor representatives (adopted in Washington, D. C., on December 13, 1919) entitled " Labor, Its Grievances, Protests and Demands." The following section from that document should be given most serious attention.

> "Credit is the life blood of modern business. At present under the control of private financiers it is administered not primarily to serve the needs of production, but the desire of financial agencies to levy a toll upon community activity as high as 'the traffic will bear.'
>
> "Credit is inherently social. It should be accorded in proportion to confidence in production possibilities. Credit as now administered does not serve industry but burdens it. It increases unearned income at the expense of earned incomes. It is the center of the malevolent forces that corrupt the spirit and purpose of industry.
>
> "We urge the organization and use of credit to serve production needs and not to increase the incomes and holdings of financiers. Control over credit should be taken from financiers and should be vested in a public agency, able to administer this power as a public trust in the interests of all the people."

55. Should the labor of prisoners be utilized for their physical and industrial training in production of goods for government uses (the state-use system) and paid for so as to provide —

(a) For the support of their dependent families.

(b) A fund to start them in an honest livelihood upon release from prison.

The American Federation of Labor has repeatedly declared that "convict labor should be employed only by the state and for state use only," and that "departure from this principle would be disastrous to the public welfare as well as to the welfare of the convicts whose confinement is primarily for reformatory purposes. We are of the opinion, however, that such labor should be performed under conditions tending to assist in the convict's reformation." It would seem not only a measure of broad national economy but a measure of fairness to make certain that released convicts be assured a fund sufficient to start them in life upon release. There is no reason why if the position of the American Federation of Labor is made effective in law, the fruits of the convict's labor, while imprisoned, should not only go at least part way towards providing for such new beginning but should also apply towards the support of dependent families during the term of imprisonment.

Very respectfully yours,
(Signed) SAMUEL GOMPERS,
MATTHEW WOLL,
FRANK MORRISON,
Platform Committee, National Non-Partisan
Campaign of the American Federation of Labor.

PROGRAM OF THE FARMERS QUESTIONNAIRE FOR CANDIDATES TO THE PRESIDENCY

The National Board of Farm Organizations, through its President, C. S. Barrett, chairman of the committee appointed for that purpose, has issued a questionnaire which was to be presented for answer to every Presidential candidate. It outlines the program which the farmers belonging to these organizations would like to have adopted as a national policy and is interesting to place by the side of the program of organized industrial labor given in the answers by the American Federation of Labor to the questionnaire of the Republican Party organization.

It was given out to the press on March 17, 1920.

Elimination of the middleman, protection of the farmer in his right to organize, appointment of an expert acceptable to organized agriculturists as Secretary of Agriculture, and representation for farmers on all boards and commissions in the membership of which various interests are recognized, are the main planks in the farmers' platform.

Other issues presented include the free and unquestioned right of collective buying, reduction of the farm tenancy evil, improvement of farm credit facilities, national conservation and the maintenance of "free speech, free press and free assembly."

There is no plan for interrogation of congressional candidates, but copies of the questionnaire will be placed in the hands of all members of the organization. Frequent reports will be made on answers received from the Presidential candidates.

The questionnaire is in the form of a letter asking the recipient to send "definite and clear replies" to twelve specific inquiries as to his views.

"Prosperity on the farm is the first condition of general prosperity," the preamble asserts. "In view of the power exercised by the President upon both the legislative and administrative branches of our government, we believe that not only the 40,000,000 people who live and work on our farms, but all Americans desire and have the right to know in advance what they may count upon a candidate to do after election." The questions follow:

Will you do your best to bring about such direct dealing between producer and consumer as will secure to the farmers a fair share of the wealth they create, reduce the cost of living to the consumer and limit or destroy the opportunity of the profiteer?

Will you do all that in you lies to secure to all farmers and consumers the full, free and unquestioned right to organize and to purchase and sell co-operatively?

Will you see that the farm people of America are represented on general boards and commissions in whose membership various interests are recognized, whether or not the work is directly concerned with agriculture?

Will you appoint a Secretary of Agriculture who knows actual farm conditions, who is satisfactory to the farm organizations of America, and who will cause to be made comprehensive studies of farm production costs at home and abroad and publish the uncensored facts?

Will you take the action necessary to ascertain and make public all obtainable facts concerning the great and growing evil of farm tenancy, so that steps may be taken to check, reduce or end it?

Will you earnestly endeavor to secure to co-operative organizations of farmers engaged in interstate commerce, service and supplies equal in all respects to those furnished private enterprises under like circumstances?

The railroads have been returned to their owners. If at the end of two years of further trial of private ownership the railroads fail to render reasonably satisfactory service to the people, will you then favor opening the railroad question?

Will you use your best efforts to secure the payment of the war debt chiefly through a highly graduated income tax or otherwise by those best able to pay?

Will you earnestly strive to uphold and enforce the national conservation policy, and especially to stop forest devastation, which already has more than doubled the price of lumber and paper to the consumer?

Will you do your best to secure and enforce effective national control over the packers and other great interstate combinations of capital engaged in the manufacture, transportation or distribution of food and other farm products and farmers' supplies?

Will you respect and earnestly strive to maintain the right of free speech, free press and free assembly?

Farmer and Labor Conference

Representatives of farmer and labor organizations with a membership of more than 3,000,000 met in Chicago, November 21, 1919, to confer on non-partisan co-operation and a joint legislative programme. Officers of the Farmers' National Council and the National Co-operative Association issued the call for the meeting.

Among the more important organizations represented at the conference in addition to those whose officers stood sponsor for it, were:

The National Non-Partisan League, Brotherhood of Locomotive Engineers, Plum Plan League, Committee for Democratic Control of Railroads, the Public Ownership League of America, State Federations of Labor of five states and granges of four Western states.

SECTION III

EDUCATIONAL TRAINING FOR CITIZENSHIP

Record of Constructive Activities in Immigrant Education and Citizenship Training, Including State Laws, Educational Programs and Recommendations.

Sub-section   I. General Survey of Field of Education for Citizenship.   2277
             II. Citizenship Training — The United States Government   2359
           III. Citizenship Training in the State of New York......   2411
           IV. Citizenship Training in All States Other Than New York State   3335
            V. Naturalization   4165

"SPECIAL NOTICE"

Statistics relating to alien population, number of illiterates and other statistical data appearing in this section of the report have been furnished by various authorities.

It will be observed that there is a marked disagreement in the statistics received from different sources bearing upon the same subject. The Committee has had no facilities for verifying these statistics and has therefore been compelled to accept them as given.

SECTION III

SUB-SECTION I

GENERAL SURVEY OF FIELD OF EDUCATION FOR CITIZENSHIP

INTRODUCTION — PROBLEMS PRESENTED

Chapter I. Americanization Work in Progress...................... 2293
    1. State Enterprises 2293
        a. Outside New York State...................... 2293
        b. New York State............................. 2296
    2. Local Boards of Education......................... 2305
    3. Private Enterprises 2307
        a. Industry 2307
        b. Settlement Houses 2312
        c. Churches 2317
        d. Miscellaneous 2320
II. Relative Merit of Private and Public Agencies for Americanization 2328
III. Teacher Requirements and Teacher Training............ 2335
IV. Curricula Recommended for Courses of Citizenship Training 2346
V. Regulated Attendance 2350
VI. Appropriations 2356

SUB-SECTION I

GENERAL SURVEY OF FIELD OF EDUCATION FOR CITIZENSHIP

INTRODUCTION

Problems Presented

In Part One of this report an effort has been made to portray the subversive influences that play upon the minds of all classes in this country. It has been shown that every cause of discontent and every injustice has been seized upon by radical groups, magnified and charged to the Government and the institutions of this country and the system under which we live. The selfishness of the individual employer, the action of an indiscreet or dishonest public official, is turned into an argument for the overthrow of this government and its institutions. It has also been shown that the propaganda of the various revolutionary and seditious groups is extremely effective in the alien population of our industrial centers.

The facts disclosed by recent investigations of the radical movement in the United States, and more particularly by the definite findings of this Committee, show that revolutionary propaganda thrives upon ignorance. There has been revealed a lamentable illiteracy and lack of appreciation of America and its institutions. "We have living in America many in whom America does not live." To give them an understanding and appreciation of our institutions and the benefits which may be derived therefrom, to keep alive in the newcomer from Europe such ideals brought over by him as may be consistent with American liberty — that is the educational problem of the immediate future.

The doors of America have always stood open. For years hordes have been pouring in from practically all nations of the earth, including thousands of refugees from political and religious persecution. Within the meager limitations prescribed by the Federal immigration laws men, women and children of all kinds and conditions have been welcome to our shores. The original need for manual labor to develop the natural resources of this country and its industrial enterprises has led to the encouragement and stimulation of immigration in overwhelming numbers, with the result that we are now confronted with a problem of Americanization far greater than the existing educational resources of the various States and of the Federal government are competent to meet.

A marked difference must be noted between the "old immigration" and the "new immigration." The old immigration was from northern and western Europe — Great Britain, Scandinavia, Germany and France. The percentage of illiteracy was small, the number of skilled workers great, and most of the older immigrants came to make America their permanent home. The new immigration comes from eastern and southeastern Europe — Italy, Russia, Poland, and the former Austro-Hungarian Empire. It represents an entirely different class. Illiteracy runs as high as 35 percent. Most of the laborers are unskilled and a large percentage of them have come with the expectation of returning to their fatherland after attaining a certain financial goal. Much of their earnings is sent abroad for the support of relatives in foreign lands. Recent records show that one-third of these immigrants not only do not become Americans but return to Europe to stay.

The old immigration for the most part came before 1890. They brought with them religious and political ideals which made their assimilation a comparatively easy matter, but the new immigration is much further removed, in its culture, from American standards, and therefore the work of assimilation is much more difficult. Among the new immigrants the prolific races from Russia, Poland and other Slavic states bring the greatest numbers and present the most serious problem of Americanization.

Not more than twenty percent of these immigrants find their way west of the Pittsburgh district. Of the other 80 percent the large majority remain in New York and its environs. Although during the years of the World War immigration almost ceased, the coming of peace has set in motion a new movement of peoples westward who seek to escape from European turmoil. It has been estimated by Federal authorities that during 1921 we may expect a million and a half immigrants, most of whom will remain in and about the City of New York.

It is for this reason that this committee is concerned with the problems of immigration. It is convinced that stringent Federal legislation should be enacted limiting immigration at least until such time as the various states can provide adequate educational facilities for properly assimilating the foreign-born as they are admitted, so that the problem will not become cumulative. The foreign-born situation is most acute in New York City, but the problems there differ from those of other industrial centers only in magnitude. There the assembling of races is without parallel in any other city in the world. Nowhere do birds of a feather flock together with such consistency and in such numbers. The average citizen who travels north and south from his home to his office passes through American streets, but if he diverges from his beaten path he will immediately lose himself in foreign cities, amid foreign tongues and exotic customs.

The alien, when he lands in this country, naturally seeks the society of his fellows. Each race has its own colony, tending to perpetuate its racial solidarity, and each colony is isolated from its neighbors by barriers of language and of custom. Every service the foreigner needs can be supplied by some fellow-countryman. A compatriot sells him foreign securities, sends his money home, procures his steamship tickets which will bring over the rest of his family, gets him a job, sells him his groceries and other necessaries (many of them made in his native land), and finally some fellow-countryman buries him.

Each colony has its own stores, theaters, dance halls, clubs, barber shops, newspapers, and its churches — the latter not too well supported.

At every turn the foreigner is met by people of his own race, speaking his own tongue, thinking his own thoughts. The ideas which he gains of American life and its institutions are often gathered from street corner gossip. At best, his viewpoint is colored by his environment. If he is ambitious he may attend evening school, but the Board of Education of the City of New York informs the committee that the great bulk of foreign-born adults, who live in districts where they hear no English, rarely go to Americanization meetings or to any American affair, rarely come into the schools, and that they are practically not touched by any educational movement in the city. This is true in spite of the fact that there are more public school buildings to the square mile in the foreign sections of the city than elsewhere.

In New York's "Little Italy" it is not uncommon to find an entire city block comprised of immigrants from one or possibly from two neighboring villages in Italy. The customs of the old country are in full swing; distinctively Italian food is the exclusive stock of the Italian provision stores. Even the colorful native costume is retained, except by the younger generation who go out into the industrial world to earn a livelihood.

It is this generation, rather than the original comer from Europe, which is subject to unwholesome influences. These children attend the public schools and become acquainted with the language of this country, to be sure, but this results in an unfortunate tendency to look down upon their parents. This attitude is aggravated when the child is in fact better educated than his parents.

One of the unfortunate conditions created by the compulsory education system for children is that it tends in large measure to divorce the children from their parents, to undermine parental authority and parental respect. Educating the children without educating the parents makes the younger generation resent parental control. This tends to disrupt the family, which is the basis of our form of society. If there is rebellion against parental authority and lack of respect for it there is likely to be the same attitude toward the government. An Italian mother wrote to a Presbyterian clergyman of New York:

"Please have my Petey locked up in some good jail until school opens. He runs the streets, he goes in swimming off the dock. We are afraid he will get killed. He does not obey us."

There is no room for recreation at home. The parks in lower New York are not adequate and the active youngster takes refuge in the streets. When he approaches his majority he becomes dissatisfied with the shabbiness of his home and finds a haven in some radical club or perhaps in the settlement houses. In the latter places, according to the Superintendent of Schools of New York City, the youth is often granted a dangerous freedom of thought and possibly encouraged in it. It is through this second generation that much of our citizenship training must be done.

A most important factor in the immigrant problem is that many aliens who settle in our great cities come from agricultural districts and from force of circumstances are compelled to enter into industrial pursuits. Living in crowded districts, in cramped quarters, and compelled to face a new type of struggle for existence, their lack of knowledge of our language and their lack of acquaintance with the laws and customs of this country have made them readily the prey of their own kind who have preceded them. The exploitation of alien labor has in very large measure been carried on by aliens who have acquired a working knowledge of American conditions and turned that knowledge to the exploitation of their fellows. The padrone system among Italians, and the sweatshops of the Russian and Polish Jews, were largely the result of this situation and have in many instances been used to prejudice the alien workers against the American industrial system.

Taking advantage of the fact that the foreigner must seek his diversion and his social life outside of the cramped limits of his own home, the subversive elements have been able to gather large audiences, to increase their membership through local organizations and to facilitate the spread of their propaganda. Balls and dances are given, musical clubs are organized and the craving for learning is satisfied through the establishment of libraries, classes of instruction in foreign languages, free lectures and social clubs also Socialist Sunday Schools and Young Peoples Socialist Leagues. This condition was well illustrated by statements made by various persons under examination by counsel for this committee, who were taken from the various headquarters of the Communist Party of America in New York City. It was obvious from their statements that many of the persons found in these headquarters were not there because they had any sympathy with or were a part of that revolutionary organization, but were attracted thither because free amusements were offered there. One man stated he went regularly to one of the headquarters because he could there join a mandolin club; another because some of the girls whom he knew and liked resorted there; others because a play was being given. It requires no emphasis to make clear that the public opinion of these alien districts can be easily controlled and directed when such tactics are employed, and the evil is particularly fruitful because of the utter ignorance of these people of the principles and ideals which form the foundation of the American government and its institutions.

Anyone who is familiar with the conditions surrounding the people living in the congested districts of our great cities can readily see the causes of the present social unrest, and it needs no profound insight to recognize the ease with which that unrest can be directed against the Government and the present social system; more particularly when, to many of these immigrants, government and governmental institutions have meant real oppression and the revolutionary spirit has been dominant in them all their lives.

It might be well to point out here that, in addition to the propaganda carried on by subversive elements, with which the first part of this report has dealt, there are still other influences which tend to retard or prevent a full sympathy with and understanding of American ideals. In each of the foreign colonies there are a number of newspapers and magazines published in the native tongue of the colony. These periodicals tend to keep the readers in close touch with the problems of the country from whence they came. In nearly every country of Europe there are at present sharp political controversies, in some verging on civil war. As a result, these differences are carried to the colony in this country, each faction being represented by its own newspapers, its own periodicals, its own organizations. Each colony is divided against itself by this means, and the attitude of these factions toward the Government of the United States depends in large measure upon the position taken by the United States Government with respect to these political controversies in European countries. As a typical example may be taken the Greek question. The Kingdom of Greece has been divided by a bitter controversy between those who remain loyal to the late King Constantine and the supporters of Venizelos. Civil war unquestionably would have developed in that country had not the allied powers intervened in support of the Venizelos faction. This controversy has torn asunder the Greek colony in this country. The respective factions are represented in New York City by two daily newspapers, the Constantine group having the "Atlantis" and the Venizelos group being represented by the "National Herald." The Great War compelled the United States Government to take part in European political controversies, and because the interests of Greece were the interests of the allied cause, the United States Government espoused the cause of Venizelos. The particular effect of such action upon the Greek colony in this country was to make loyal and law-abiding citizens and residents out of the faction supporting the Venizelos regime, and on the other hand to render discontented and potentially disloyal the elements supporting the royal faction.

Similar examples may be found in almost every colony. The attitude taken by the United States government toward the Fiume question and the disposition to be made of the littoral of the Istria will unquestionably have its reflex action upon the Italians and the Jugo-Slav elements of our population. The Great War has shown that beyond question the love of the fatherland and the influence of its customs are not wiped out in the first generation, and that the problem of Americanization cannot therefore be considered solved if one generation alone is dealt with.

The attitude of the foreign language press, the activity of agitators, the position taken by many foreign language organizations and societies upon these questions, renders the foreign colonies extremely sensitive and ready to respond to the controversies raised by the solution of European questions.

The committee does not wish to imply that the alien population is not potentially loyal to this country and that the immigrant does not constitute in the main a sturdy and progressive element of our citizenship. What we seek to emphasize is that the neglect which American citizens and the governments, not only of the states but of the United States, have shown towards the alien has permitted conditions to exist which constitute, at a moment of general worldwide unrest, a serious element of weakness in our social structure.

The conditions which we have sought to portray, when aggravated by an increasing cost of living, when stimulated by false and lying propaganda, have made the alien populations of our great industrial centers a potential menace to the government and the institutions of this country. It is with this problem that the American people must deal. Its solution requires the most careful and devoted study. It must also be borne in mind that the activities of revolutionary and seditious agitators cannot be stopped by repressive measures alone.

It is for this reason that this committee has devoted a great part of its energies to a thorough survey and analysis of the constructive forces which make for better citizenship, and lays stress not only upon the elimination of illiteracy but upon the need of inculcating a real and vital understanding of our institutions and laws in the minds of all newcomers.

The illiteracy of the foreigner is a matter of serious concern, not only because it appears to have a direct bearing upon his susceptibility to attack by radical agitators. Mr. Franklin K. Lane, while Secretary of the Interior, gave considerable prominence to the economic laws arising out of the illiteracy of the foreign born. The Department of the Interior at one time circularized 112 business concerns in regard to the percentage of turnover among their illiterate employees and found that it ranged from 20 per cent to

400 percent. These figures might be interpreted to show the relation between illiteracy and industrial unrest. The 112 concerns mentioned included some of the largest and best known in the country. Their reports also showed that 95 percent of their Roumanian employees were not American citizens, nor 92 percent of the Greeks, 95 percent of Croatians, 76 per cent of Armenians and 67 percent of Austrians. These figures take on an added significance when it is considered that 65.5 percent of Bulgarians over ten years of age are illiterate in their own country and do not read or write in any language, 57.2 percent of the Greeks over ten years of age are illiterate in Greece, and 13.7 percent of Austrians over eleven years of age are illiterate in Austria.

Illiteracy in the United States among the native-born is chiefly due to inadequate compulsory attendance laws for minors; to failure to enforce existing laws, or to inadequate educational facilities. Among other factors involved are physical and mental incompetency. In New York State it is estimated that upwards of 40,000 persons of native birth are illiterate, perhaps one-half of whom from mental incompetency cannot be expected to become literate. Most of the illiterate persons are distributed in the rural and more inaccessible districts of the State. We are informed that efforts are being made by the State Department of Education to wipe out as much of this illiteracy as possible.

Illiteracy among the foreign born in New York State and in the United States as a whole is due to three chief causes: First, lack of education in countries from which the immigrant has come (and this is particularly true of the new immigration); second, lack of educational facilities here; and third, failure to take advantage of facilities offered here for reasons warranted or unwarranted, among which may be considered fatigue after a day's work, disinclination to wash up before going to school, etc.

Foreign illiterates are scattered throughout the State, chiefly, however, in the cities and industrial districts. The statistics on illiteracy are amazing. There are 8,500,000 persons over ten years of age in the United States who cannot use the English language. This is more than the total population of Canada. There are 5,500,000 and over who cannot read one word in any language. Of this number 4,697,000 are twenty years of age and over; 57.7 percent are whites and 1,534,272 are native-born whites. Figures for the twelve-year period ending 1910 show that 26.7 percent of the total number of immigrants could neither read nor write. During the war there were 700,000 men of draft age who could not read and write English or any other language. Without special training these men would not make the best soldiers. They could not sign their names, they could not read their orders posted daily on the bulletin boards of their camps; they could not read their manual of arms; they could not read letters nor write home; they could not understand the signals or follow the Signal Corps in time of battle.

The sale of our Liberty Bonds and the war relief work was greatly hampered because immigrant peoples could not understand the appeals of lecturers nor read the notices in papers and on billboards. The conservation of food was hindered for the same reasons. Statistics of recent date concerning the number of non-English-speaking and illiterate persons in the State of New York are not available. The result of the 1920 Federal census will not be published for some time. However, the following information, taken from the 1910 census, shows the need for a far reaching program of adult immigrant education, no matter what modifications in these statistics are necessary on account of changes occurring during the intervening decade:

Total population of New York State	9,113,614
Total number of foreign-born (30.2 percent)	2,748,011
Number of illiterates, ten years of age and over	406,020
Number of illiterates, ten years of age and over (foreign-born whites, 89.1 percent)	362,025

As to the problem in specific localities, while New York City has by far the greatest immigrant problem in point of numbers, there are other communities where the problem is even more acute. Probably the most striking example that has come to the attention of this Committee is Scranton, Penn., where 52 percent of the population cannot speak English! Delaware considers herself fortunate in having a simple problem as far as Americanization is concerned. Only 8.6 percent of its population is foreign born, but the illiteracy is 8.1 percent. Although Delaware considers its problem simple, it has inaugurated one of the most comprehensive Americanization programs conducted in this country to-day, and yet there is not a single public educational facility for the adult immigrant within that State.

Alabama, Florida, Georgia, Virginia, South Carolina, Mississippi, Maryland and Louisville, Ky., report that they have comparatively few foreigners and, therefore, the problem of immigrant education is not a serious one. South Carolina, Alabama and Louisville, Ky., however, report that they make an effort to reduce illiteracy. The State of Iowa is fortunate in having only one percent of illiteracy. The problem in New Hampshire and Vermont is largely French Canadians, who are law abiding and who assimilate readily, except where they live in remote rural districts.

Arizona, on the other hand, has a very difficult problem in its Mexican population, whom they consider harder to handle than any other class of foreign-born. They find the Mexican without ambition to learn English, and the educational authorities of the State are of the opinion that compulsion will be the only successful means. The Asiatic problems of the Pacific Coast States, complicated as they are by Mexican immigration, are very different from those of the Eastern States, but are equally perplexing.

New Jersey has a total illiteracy of 5.8 percent, 9.9 percent of the negroes in the State being illiterate and only .9 percent of the native whites and 5.9 percent of foreign-born whites. New Jersey is fully awake to its problem, for during the war the surprising disclosure was made at Camp Dix that 21 percent of the first draft were illiterate, 25 percent of the second and 33⅓ percent of the third. Not all of these, of course, were from New Jersey.

Illiteracy in the State of Rhode Island is 7.7 percent; in Massachusetts 5.2 percent; New York State 4.4 percent, which is of interest in comparing the percentage of foreign-born in these states, which is shown in the following table:

Name of State	Percentage of foreign-born	Percentage of foreign-born parentage	Percentage of illiteracy
New York	30.4	33.5	5.5
Massachusetts	31.6	35.2	5.2
Rhode Island	33.4	36.6	7.7

Illiteracy is of special danger in a country which requires intelligent participation in public affairs on the part of its citizens and its residents, and yet, according to Secretary Lane, 10 percent of the adult population of our country cannot read the laws they are presumed to know and follow. Illiteracy coupled with ignorance, as it usually is, provides fertile soil for seeds of radicalism and incendiary propaganda. The strength of a nation does not rise above the intelligence of its citizenry.

Efforts to remedy some of these unfortuate and dangerous conditions in our various communities have been made for many years, chiefly by private enterprise. More recently, however, largely as a result of the recent war, consciousness of internal weakness has developed and various public agencies, national and state and local, have undertaken larger responsibilities. Much of this new effort has been labeled Americanization. Those most intimately in touch with, or responsible for, Americanization programs believe that the most effective measures of Americanization must proceed along educational lines. They are convinced that public educational agencies must function in more effective and far-reaching ways. They believe that whatever educational program is undertaken, to be of greatest value to the enormous number of immigrant peoples among us, it must square directly with fundamental American principles. Such programs must teach that there is opportunity according to capacity, that responsibility accompanies privilege, that the exercise of self-reliance and individual initiative is inseparable from progress; that justice and good government result only from enlightened and patriotic participation in public affairs.

Americanization, or training for citizenship as we prefer to call it, does not mean merely the training necessary to pass the examination of the naturalization boards, but rather involves a course of instruction which might well be taken by some who are already citizens and even by some who are native-born. Some have objected that, as the educational facilities for our own children are by no means adequate, we should not yet concern ourselves with the training of the foreign-born. Such a position, however, is untenable, in view of the large numbers of the latter and the necessity of fitting them to assume not only the privileges but the obligations and duties of citizenship.

Unquestionably the first step in the work of Americanization must be the teaching of English. It is of the utmost importance in a representative republic that every citizen shall speak the common language so that he may intelligently exercise his privilege of the franchise. Americanization, however, is not an anti-foreign-language movement. It should not be its purpose to compel the foreigner to give up his native tongue. That would be inconsistent, for it has always been considered a mark of culture here to acquire foreign languages. A foreigner may retain his own language, his religion, and even such of his social customs as are consistent with our form of society and still be a good American. He must, however, know our language and use it understandingly.

The purpose of making America a one-language country has been opposed by some on the ground that a similar policy in European countries has always defeated its own purpose, causing deep resentment and stimulating devotion to the old language. Reference is usually made, in support of this contention, to the cases of Alsace-Lorraine, Poland, and Bohemia. These instances, however, are not parallel. Conditions in these European countries are quite different. In each of the cases cited peoples remaining upon their native soil have been subjugated by alien peoples who sought to impose upon them an alien tongue. In this country the language is English. To it have come *voluntarily* the alien peoples. It is a measure for our own safety that we should impose upon them the duty of learning our own language.

At a Polish convention recently held in Detroit, Mich., reference was made to the 4,000,000 Poles in this country as the "fourth part of Poland." If this were true of our Polish residents, and all of our other foreign groups, we should have here only a physical mixture of races. The goal of Americanization is to make a chemical compound, not merely a mingling of a number of different elements, but the formation of a new compound, namely the American people with a national solidarity.

A still further object of Americanization shoud be to reconcile, adjust, and interpret the various groups of our foreigners to each other as well as to America. As our government is "we, the people of the United States," the obligation for the right spirit in Americanization rests upon the shoulders of each American citizen. Public servants in elective and appointive educational offices can be effective only so long as they have the support of an undivided public opinion with respect to Americanization.

This Committee is convinced that repressive measures taken without corresponding constructive action in dealing with radical and subversive movements must leave the situation worse than if no action were taken at all. On the other hand it must be understood that the problems cannot be solved by legislation alone It is the privilege and the duty of the legislature to enact such laws as it believes will tend to ameliorate or improve the situation as it exists. On the other hand, it is essential that the citizens as a whole shall acquaint themselves with the forces which play upon the people of less favored circumstances, to become acquainted with the facts as they are; and it is the duty of every citizen to do his part in the solution of the problems which present themselves in this community.

In order to visualize the problem confronting those charged with the duty of conducting our educational institutions in New York city, this Committee has prepared maps of the boroughs of Manhattan, Bronx and Brooklyn, showing the location and extent of racial colonies in that city. These maps accompany this report. They are intended to show graphically the great colonies of residents of alien origin which have been created in this city. The uncolored portions of the maps do not indicate purely American stock, but represent a mixture of races where no clearly defined boundary line may be drawn. The Committee has felt that in no other way could it present the immigrant problems of our industrial centers in so forceful a manner. It is a matter of regret that at the present moment the returns of the 1920 Federal census are not available, for the value of these maps would be much enhanced were reliable statistics of the alien population in New York city at hand.

It must be obvious to anyone who has studied with care Part One of this report that the conditions existing in this country to-day are extremely critical; that the great volume of propaganda issued by subversive groups is having increasing effect; that confidence in our institutions is being steadily undermined; that the greatest confusion of thought and lack of courage is manifest in the speech and writings of many political leaders; that the public press is often misled on important questions; and that at no time has there been greater need for sound thinking based upon ascertained fact. This radical trend is artificially encouraged by the groups of foreign press newspapers, apparently subsidized from unknown sources, to be the propagators of revolutionary ideas and tactics. It is, therefore, imperative that all persons in this community who believe that within the institutions of the United States may be found an opportunity for the fullest possible development of human freedom, should unite for the purpose of preserving those institutions against subtle inroads made by subversive propaganda. Every new scheme of social reform is not necessarily progressive, it is not necessarily beneficial, it is not necessarily liberal in the true sense of the word.

It is essential that the people of the United States become conservative in the sense that they shall scrutinize and weigh with the utmost care every proposition of social reform in order to ascertain whether or not its adoption will effect the purpose for which it is professedly advanced.

The problems affecting public peace and public safety which have been created by the propaganda of social unrest are in large measure the product of subversive doctrines. One of the most effective means for nullifying the effect of such teaching is, therefore, education designed to train the citizens of this State to assume the responsibilities and duties of citizenship. We do not advocate formal education as a panacea for all our social and economic unrest but the Committee is convinced that education along the general lines advocated in the succeeding chapters of this report constitutes a measure of prevention for the future. Such education must be endorsed by a sincere, sympathetic and courageous citizenry. America will not be the land of the too free so long as it is the home of the sufficiently brave.

CHAPTER I
Americanization Work in Progress

The term Americanization when properly employed is expressive of the process which the foreigner undergoes in orienting himself to American ideals and traditions, as well as to the customs and manners of this country. Unfortunately the word has been applied by some social workers to describe their activities, which have a tendency to retard rather than advance the process of Americanization.

The Committee has endeavored to make as complete a survey as possible of the Americanization work now in progress, as well as that proposed. This material is of great interest and importance to students in this field, but its chief service undoubtedly will be to bring into bold relief the necessary phases of the work which are left uncovered or inadequately dealt with.

The necessity for training teachers in the fields of immigrant and adult education to counteract revolutionary and un-American ideas, is almost wholly ignored. This is a fundamental weakness in all of the organized plans which have come to the Committee's attention. In the succeeding chapter on Teacher Requirements, we have called attention to this need and made recommendations with respect thereto.

It is the purpose of this chapter to summarize briefly the work of Americanization which is being carried on by the various states, local school boards, and private enterprises, including industries, social settlements, churches and miscellaneous agencies.

1. STATE ENTERPRISES
a. OUTSIDE NEW YORK STATE

Until recent years little aggressive effort had been made to make lasting good citizens of the school children of this country. The Great War disclosed the fact that many of the public schools had for years been instrumental in the spread of enemy propaganda through text books. Educators apparently had felt no necessity for defending the principles and institutions of this country. The law requiring the possession and display on occasions of the national flag and in some states the compulsory and routine salute to this flag at specified times, was thought all that was necessary except, possibly, singing of the national anthem. To-day, however, steps are being taken by the public school authorities with the cooperation of the legislatures of almost every state in the United States to make Americanization and citizenship training as vital and integral a part of the public school curricula as the universal teaching of the justly famed "three r's." They seem to subscribe to the belief that if we would give children in their early youth a real and sympathetic appreciation of American ideals and a respect for the institutions through which these ideals find realization, their patriotism will be deep-rooted and lasting and their loyalty to this nation so strong that it will withstand the influence of subversive propaganda.

The next step beyond the compulsory training of children, is the providing of extension facilities (in some instances accompanied by compulsory attendance) for minors of employment age. These facilities are often open to adults. In many states special facilities are provided for adults and one state, Utah, requires the attendance of adults up to the age of 45, or until they shall have attained a proficiency in the use of the English language equivalent to that required in the fifth grade of the common schools. Efforts are being made in Colorado to procure the passage of a similar law, and a bill has been introduced into the Maine legislature which differs mainly in the manner of its enforcement. The compulsory feature of it is taken care of by making employment contingent upon having attained a certain degree of proficiency in English, or upon being in attendance upon a school for this purpose. The importance of proper and adequate school facilities for teaching the adult foreign-born is touched upon in a subsequent chapter of this subsection. There are a number of states conducting programs of Americanization, chiefly educational in character, but without specific legislation provided for it, while a few are operating in accordance with special legislation providing for Americanization activities. For the most part whatever responsibility is assumed by state or local educational authorities is in conjunction with the active cooperation of other agencies. Among those doing effective work may be mentioned chambers of commerce, boards of trade, federations of labor, women's clubs, churches, fraternal orders, social welfare agencies, national and local groups of foreign-born and others. Whatever responsibility the public agencies assume, their greatest success has been achieved where their efforts have the active support of native-born and foreign-born alike and where all efforts have been coordinated by the public education authorities. Full information in regard to the Americanization activities being carried on by the several states will be found in the chapters of this report dealing with state activities. We mention here very briefly a few of the unique and outstanding methods employed.

To anyone interested in establishing or furthering Americanization work or citizenship training, the report of activities in Delaware will afford subject for study. The work is based upon a carefully taken census which shows exactly what the situation is in that state and steps have been taken to meet each phase of the problem presented. California seems to divide the honors with the State of New York in the matter of home teaching, having a Home Teacher Law and an effective program for carrying it out. California also has a Civic Center Law making all public school houses in the state available for the use of citizens in their respective communities. Ohio has thoroughly organized its work. The work there has largely grown out of measures established to meet war emergencies. That so much interest was aroused in Americanization was doubtless due to the fact that (according to the 1910 census basis) 333,985, os seven percent of the total population of the state were born in enemy countries. In Arkansas the Illiteracy Commission cooperates with the Naturalization Bureau. Colorado requires that each public school offer an Americanization course in order to fall into what is termed the "standardized class." That state emphasizes work in rural communities. There is a State Commission on Americanization, consisting of twelve members, who aim to coordinate all work. They make it a point to follow up local superintendents, principals, and teachers, who keep up their interest and enthusiasm for their task. They also foster the idea of community pageants to promote Americanism.

New Mexico and Nebraska have a "Roosevelt Americanization Day" on Colonel Roosevelt's birthday. Appropriate exercises are held in all public schools. New Mexico seems to formulate its ideas on Americanism entirely from the career and utterances of Colonel Roosevelt.

The Committee's investigation reveals the fact that in all probability New York State has one of the best, if not the best developed program of adult education, particularly for the foreign-born. It is, however, far from adequate. The following reports from the New York State educational authorities are descriptive of what is being done.

b. Americanization and Immigrant Education, New York State and City of New York*

The state program of Americanization, immigrant education, and educational extension is based upon the legislative action of the past three years.

In substance, the State legislature has conceived Americanization of the foreign-born in the State of New York to be a well-developed program of extension education, particularly of the educational service of the public evening schools and annex classes for adults.

Such legislation has placed upon the University of the State of New York and the State Department of Education the responsibility for cooperating with local public educational agencies to meet conditions and needs. Its educational program as authorized by the legislature involves in general the following:

1. The organization and conduct of public evening schools for a minimum number of nights per year, based upon the population.

2. The extending of the educational facilities now provided for adults in evening school buildings into day classes, both day and evening classes in factories, hotels, clubs, churches, settlements and homes.

3. Provisions whereby groups of twenty persons or more may successfully petition their local public school authorities for instruction in English, citizenship, history and similar themes.

4. Compulsory education of minors between sixteen and twenty-one years of age unable to read and write English, with penalties attached to the minor himself, guardians, employers or others who would seek to secure the avoidance of this law. Such minors are required to have a reading and writing knowledge of English equal to that of a child in the fifth grade.

5. Specialized training of teachers of evening schools, extension classes and all kinds of education for the foreign-born.

To carry out the intent of these laws last year, the State Board of Regents was authorized to district the state into fifteen zones,† of which Greater New York is one, for the purpose of administration. The Board of Regents was likewise instructed to perfect a

---

* Special bulletins relating to immigrant education in New York State in respect to legislation, organization, program, special features and methods of work have been issued by the Department of Education during the past year. We are informed that other bulletins are in preparation. All such material may be secured from the special Division on Immigrant Education in the above department.

† See map facing page 2286.

staff of specialists to organize and supervise the work. This has been done. A special appropriation was made to carry out the intent of the law. The State Department of Education expects to continue such activities as a regular part of the State's educational program.

A concurrent resolution now pending in the State Legislature as a proposed amendment to the Constitution of the State would require all persons, upon reaching their majority, to know how to read and write English as a requirement for voting.

The program of state effort involves the following features:

1. Effort for the opening of evening schools and extension classes where they are not now being conducted, and encouragement and assistance to those now in operation.
2. Organization and conduct of factory classes.
3. Organization and conduct of home classes.
4. Co-operative and community types of effort involving the active co-operation of immigrant groups.
5. Co-operation of naturalization authorities in training for citizenship.
6. Training of teachers.

The following table gives the most recent figures obtainable for this work in the State and New York City up to about January 1, 1920:

NUMBER OF STUDENTS REGISTERED IN AMERICANIZATION CLASS IN DECEMBER, 1919

	Evening schools	Factory classes	Home and community classes	Total registration
In New York City	14,213	725	1,825	16,763
In State outside of New York City	7,957	1,838	1,449	11,244
Total for State	22,170	2,563	3,274	28,007

NOTE.— These figures include only such classes in night schools, places of employment, home and community centers as are under the control of public school authorities. They do not include the 10,000 or more people registered in December, 1919, in " Common branch " classes in night schools, many of whom are receiving instruction in elementary English: nor do they include the minors in day continuation classes, some of whom are also being taught elementary English. No class under private control or supervision is included.

An investigation and examination of provisions now made by the schools of New York City for various forms of adult immigrant education to meet needs among the vast numbers of non-English-speaking foreign-born will show them to be wholly inadequate. Not enough evening schools and classes are conducted and requirements for the organization and conduct of such effort are not elastic enough to meet needs. There are not enough competent and trained teachers available, nor are salaries adequate to secure more of the best kind of teaching which is needed. Moreover, the evening schools are in need of more socializing features to the end that they may become more interesting and effective centers of inspiration and community effort.

It is evident to those most familiar with the situation at the present moment in New York City, where educational needs are more acute than elsewhere in the State, that public educational agencies cannot thoroughly perform their task alone. Until the State is better organized they must have the active support and interest of various industrial, civic, and welfare agencies, submitting to the supervision and direction of the State. In addition, many agencies now doing work in the general field of so-called Americanization should be encouraged to feel that they are doing splendid work but that it is largely of a pioneer nature for which ultimately the public educational system must suitably provide.

Plans and programs for extension of educational opportunities for all, irrespective of creed, condition, color, or origin are outstanding characteristics of education today. A program of immigrant education is directly in line with these tendencies. In so far as a program of so-called Americanization is one of education, the people of the State should endorse every means whereby its educational institutions, from the primary grades upward, should be made increasingly available to both native and foreign-born, according to their needs. This conception of education is the democratic ideal in education for which this Committee stands unequivocally, and in which it desires to see very material developments. Apparently every reasonable opportunity is offered for the hundreds of thousands of boys and girls in this State within the compulsory school age, who take advantage of them. In view of the fact, however, that approximately no more than twelve or fifteen percent of the children of the State enter high school and not exceeding three or four percent probably finish high school, it is readily apparent that vast numbers of young men and women are leaving the schools each year inadequately prepared for life either as workers or citizens, and thus add to the enormous number of persons in the State who, either of native or foreign birth, are not equipped educationally to cope with the problems of modern industrial and political life.

The Committee has abundant ground, as the result of its investigations, for believing that very material extensions of educational programs and facilities must be made to meet conditions and needs throughout the State. For many years some of the most progressive communities of the State have made provisions for evening schools and have conducted them with success. It is reported, however, that as late as two years ago 107 cities and school districts in the State falling within the provisions of the new evening school law had previously made no provision whatever for the organization and conduct of evening schools. As a result of the legislative effort in the State this situation is being corrected as rapidly as possible.

Where local conditions in various cities and localities of the State have seemed to warrant, evening school extension has been provided in behalf of non-English-speaking persons, and for others who desire to learn English and to fit themselves for more efficient industrial and civic life. Fortunately, moreover, the State in the past two years has passed legislation particularly emphasizing the necessity for further extension of educational facilities in the form of evening schools and otherwise, particularly designed to meet the needs of immigrants. It is reported that only 50,000 or 60,000 foreign-born persons are in the evening schools of the State. This is but two percent of the foreign-born in the State. This attendance far exceeds that of natives, however.

The extension education law referred to above definitely specifies that extension of education as required under it is provided for immigrants as such, and assumes that the foreign-born will take advantage of suitable educational opportunities when they are offered. The law is mandatory in character, and requires the organization and conduct of night schools in the common branches and additional subjects which are to be taught for a stipulated number of hours, nights, and weeks, throughout the various cities and school districts of the State. The Committee has made an investigation of similar legislation in other states, and is able to report that the following states in general within the past two or three years have developed laws pertaining to the extension of educational facilities within their borders, either general in character or specifically in application, to the needs of the foreign-born. These states are: Connecticut, Delaware, Indiana, Iowa, Kansas, Maine, Massachusetts, Minnesota, Missouri, Montana, New Hampshire, Nevada, North Dakota, Oregon and Rhode Island. Increasing responsibilities are not only being placed upon the various school districts of the several states, in the way of extending educational facilities, but responsibility is also placed in most definite ways upon the various state departments of education for promoting and extending ideas and practice in this field. All of this legislation is significant, and is indicative of a tendency in the United States to maintain educational advantages for all, irrespective of age, for the purpose of making up for lost years, to promote productive efficiency, to elevate standards of citizenship, and to promote the general welfare and well-being of the people as inidviduals, and the State at large (depending upon local conditions and circumstances) — such legislation being also accompanied by suitable appropriation for the promotion, administration and general supervision of such efforts.

This Committee unreservedly endorses every public effort that is being made in the State toward the extension of educational facilities to children and adults. It is particularly conscious of the needs for increased facilities for adults, either in evening schools or in extension classes. It believes that the public school buildings of the State should be used increasingly wherever opportunity permits, to meet the needs of communities which these buildings may respectively serve. The Committee approves efforts being made to develop public school community centers in a wholesome way, and recommends that school buildings now erected or in process of construction shall be so arranged and equipped as to provide as much as possible for adults, as well as for children of all ages.

It recommends also that wherever possible suitable changes shall be made in existing school buildings so that they will be more useful and attractive to adults, whom the schools are increasingly expected to serve. When existing educational facilities are not adequate to meet the need, the Committee strongly approves various forms of extra-mural and extension effort under the direction and supervision of public school authorities, involving the organization and conduct of classes and other educational features, particularly among illiterates and non-English-speaking persons of foreign birth, in shops, factories, homes, or public buildings if those responsible for such work believe best results may be thus obtained.

Thorough study of local conditions is recommended to educational authorities throughout the State to the end that adequate educational facilities be provided and that supervision under the direction of trained specialists shall be constant, thorough and painstaking. Furthermore, it is recommended that State educational authorities, with the cooperation of the several cities, towns and school districts of the State, shall hereafter require special detailed reports upon all such efforts and their results.

Steps are being taken towards making educational facilities in New York State more nearly adequate to changing conditions and needs in this great industrial and commercial State where illiteracy runs high and where the duties and responsibilities of citizenship are becoming increasingly complex and difficult. Extensions of educational opportunity are of the utmost importance and significance. The Committee is venturing a partial survey of the educational movement in the State to serve as a guide for present and future action. A study of the school law of the State and of the extended powers and functions of the State Department of Education is indicative of these developments.

The foundation of a thorough-going and far-reaching system of education in New York State is laid with the development of the State system of public elementary and secondary schools, and with the development of responsibilities and functions of State supervision therefor.

Aside from the detailed developments within the system of elementary and secondary education in respect to the raising of the compulsory school age, the liberalizing and enrichment of courses, the provision of recreational facilities and physical training and the encouragement of various kinds of efforts looking towards extending the period of schooling for the children of the State, marked developments may be noted in the way of extending educational privileges and opportunities in keeping with the American spirit of self-help and self-development through adult years. Some of the steps toward promoting education beyond the grammar and high school grades are as follows:

1. Permissive legislation on the part of the State and the several cities and school districts looking toward the extension of evening school service. Under these provisions many cities and school districts of the State have provided educational facilities for people above the compulsory school age.

2. The utilization of school buildings and school facilities in the State, for the purposes of community centers.

Where this privilege is granted, however, the Committee recommends that the closest scrutiny be made by the educational authorities of the activities carried on in the public school buildings. The attention of the Committee has been called from time to time to the use of public school buildings in this State, particularly in New York City, Buffalo and other large cities, by revolutionary organizations for meetings and also for lectures, which could have no other effect than to undermine the confidence of the audience in the government of this State and its institutions. Such use of public school buildings should in no case be permitted and suitable steps should be taken by the State educational authorities and by the various boards of education throughout the State to make such abuse of the public school buildings impossible.

In paragraph 455 of the Education Law of the State, as amended to July 1, 1919, will be found sections pertaining to the use of grounds and other property of the several school districts, when not in use for regular school purposes for any of the following purposes: (a) by persons assembling therein for the purpose of giving and receiving instruction in any branch of education, learning, or the arts; (b) for public library purposes; (c) for holding social, civic and recreational meetings and entertainments, and other uses pertaining to the welfare of the community, such meetings to be open to the public, except those for which fees are charged, in which case the proceeds are to be expended for educational and charitable purposes; (d) for polling places, or for use in holding primaries and elections for the registration of voters, and for holding political meetings; (e) for civic forums under proper supervision and community centers depending upon petitions of a minimum number of representative citizens residing within the district, such petitions designed for the purpose of promoting and advancing the general principles of Americanization and good citizenship.

Under this law much socialization of educational facilities may be accomplished helpfully, and the interest and co-operation and participation of adults may be promoted in a most wholesome and effective way. What is known as the Community Center School Law, is of recent date, being enacted as an amendment to the School Law by the Legislature in April, 1917.

3. Requirements for school districts to conduct evening schools. The substance of this law has been indicated in paragraphs preceding. Under this law as an amendment to the Education Law of the State, cities and school districts are required under mandatory action to provide evening school facilities.

4. Compulsory education for minors. By legislation the State now requires a speaking, reading and writing knowledge of English for every person under twenty-one years of age equal to the ability of a child of the fifth grade. This law has been referred to under that section referring to compulsory education.

5. The educational qualifications for voting. The concurrent resolution now pending in the Senate and Assembly, proposing an amendment to Section one of Article II of the State Constitution in relation to the qualification of voters, is important. In substance this amendment provides that after January 1, 1922, no person shall become entitled to vote in the State by attaining a majority, by naturalization, or otherwise, unless such person is also able, except by physical disability, to read and write English. The Legislature furthermore is empowered by suitable laws to enforce this provision. The Committee heartily endorses this amendment as being logical and urgently necessary and consistent with the highest ideals of American citizenship. The Committee furthermore suggests that it is only with the extension of educational facilities in the State among adults, particularly among the foreign-born, that the best intent of this law may be realized.

6. Extra-mural education. Efforts toward extending educational privileges outside of school buildings to meet local conditions and needs is based largely upon interpretations of the school law of the State rather than upon specific provisions. It has been found essential, particularly in providing various forms of immigrant education, to develop shop classes in factories and industries, in hotels, laundries, homes, clubs, and wherever the opportunity is presented. This work is done on the principle that extended educational privileges, particularly for adults, must be taken to them, rather than that adults should be under the handicap of going long distances at inopportune times and under unfavorable conditions to places where formal and more or less arbitrary educational facilities or provisions are made.

7. Continuation and part-time schools. Under legislation taking effect May 10, 1919, the State undertook the development of extended education for minors above the age of fourteen years and below the age of eighteen years who are not now in regular attendance upon instruction. The State Department of Education is now engaged in working out the details of this system of educaional extension, designed to wipe out much of the lost time suffered by the youth of the State in the years from fourteen to eigh-

teen, during which period they are not receiving instruction needed to equip them for vocational pursuits or for citizenship. This is one of the most far-reaching pieces of legislation the State has undertaken, and is peculiarly significant at this time when a more efficient citizenship in every respect is imperatively needed in this as well as every other commonwealth. Notwithstanding the difficulties incidental to the administration, conduct and financing of this new program of education in New York State, it is now realized that the safety and the welfare of the State depends increasingly upon such measures. During the years from fourteen to eighteen the habits of youth are largely fixed, and the ideals of most loyal citizenship are planted in the hearts of the wards of the State, thus guaranteeing not only a citizenry more enlightened, intelligent, informed and dependable, but also more loyal, patriotic and law-abiding.

8. Extension education for all adults. The Education Law, as amended July 1, 1919, in Article III, section 52, has the following clause:

> "**Extension of Educational Facilities.** The regents may extend to the people at large increased educational opportunities and facilities, stimulate interest therein, recommend methods, designate suitable teachers and lecturers, conduct examinations and grant credentials, and otherwise organize, aid and conduct such work."

It is on the basis of this law that the Committee recommends Senate bill No. 1273. The intent of this bill is to extend educational privileges to all adult citizens of the State, native and foreign-born alike, for the purpose of teaching English, citizenship, history and any other subject (as the bill indicates) needed to promote the general vocational and civic interests of the citizens of the State. It especially provides for additional competent teachers imperatively needed now to supplement present effort and to carry out faithfully the intent of the present law in respect to illiterates and non-English-speaking persons.

This proposed legislation is directly in line with the steps of educational development previously outlined. It places upon the Department of Education the responsibility for the execution of the law and also the duty of developing a body of competent trained, experienced teachers not only for the most needy non English-speaking groups, but also among all groups within the

State in need of educational advantages of which they have heretofore been deprived. It is to be noted that in many if not most of the states in which the most progressive steps have been taken in extensions of educational privileges among adults, such work is regularly organized in the division of educational extension within the several states and under the direct supervision and direction of the various state boards of education, boards of commissioners, and regularly constituted state educational authorities. This Committee is of the opinion that in order to promote, develop and conserve the general educational interests of the State, the Department of Education should take suitable steps toward extending whatever service it can, particularly among the educationally unprivileged groups of the State which are reported to be calling for educational assistance and guidance.

2. LOCAL BOARDS OF EDUCATION

In the last analysis much of the actual responsibility for the work of citizenship training and Americanization rests upon the local school board. While the survey of this Committee has shown that a great deal is being done by the various state departments of education this work is largely a matter of planning, organizing, stimulating, coordinating and sometimes financing. The local school boards in most cases are the really effective agencies in carrying on the work. We have been in direct communication with the superintendents of schools of most of the large industrial centers throughout the country.* We find that almost without exception they seek the cooperation of such local organizations as the Y. M. C. A., Chamber of Commerce, leading industries, churches, women's club, etc., to encourage attendance upon the night schools by adult foreign-born who need instruction in the English language and general training for citizenship. In many centers there is a move to encourage naturalization, but in all these local activities, as in other fields which we have investigated, there is no report of an attempt to meet radical influences directly with education.

The brunt of the problem of immigrant education rests upon New York State. New York City is the port of entry for the bulk of our immigration, and by far the largest percentage stay there. New York is therefore called upon to shoulder a responsibility which is not local and which is not altogether a State problem, but

---
* See Addendum, Part 2.

is in a great measure national. The New York City Board of Education must be credited with having evolved as efficient machinery as its funds would permit to cope with the immigrant education problem. It has, however, been seriously hampered by lack of funds and it appeals to the State for additional help. The present State appropriation is totally inadequate.

If the reader will refer to the racial maps of New York City which accompany this report he will note that the problem is general and that efforts in education cannot be concentrated geographically. Even if immigration should cease at this time and no additional burden should be added, it would be necessary to greatly increase the present appropriations if the needs of the community were to be adequately met. The City of New York has approximately thirty evening High schools, 70 evening schools and 70 annexes. In these evening schools there are 10,000* foreign-born adults, and about 1,000* additional in the extension classes of the day school. This is a mere drop in the bucket compared with the total work of immigrant education which must be done. The Department of Education of New York City estimates that they could take care of from one thousand to four thousand in each school building if they had the funds for heating and lighting and for the payment of teachers.

Inasmuch as the whole State can benefit by an intelligent Americanized citizenship in the City of New York, and inasmuch as not only the State but the nation may suffer from seditious activities arising in New York City due in large measure to the lack of Americanization efforts, this Committee urges liberality on the part of the State in the matter of appropriation of funds to New York City and other large industrial centers of the State, for immigrant education work.

Among other local school boards of New York State who are attempting Americanization work through the public schools, we mention the following: Albany, Amsterdam, Binghamton, Buffalo, Cohoes, Cortland, Depew, Dunkirk, Elmira, Geneva, Glens Falls, Gloversville, Ithaca, Lancaster, Lockport, Mt. Vernon, New Rochelle, Newburgh, Niagara Falls, Oneonta, Oswego, Peekskill, Poughkeepsie, Rochester, Schenectady, Solvay, Syracuse, Troy, Utica, Watertown, White Plains and Yonkers. Many of the school boards cooperate with local industries and other private organizations. The program of Rochester is well worth noting.

* Enrollment for the fall of 1920 shows a substantial increase.

The local board of education cooperated with the industries in its vicinity with the result that classes were established in the leading factories, many men were enrolled and many were trained for naturalization. Rochester has a Cooperative Americanization Committee to coordinate all Americanization activities. Included on the Committee are the foreign language churches and societies, foreign language press, Central Trades and Labor Council, social settlements, Monroe County Home Defense committee on aliens and on instruction, Board of Education, Naturalization Court, Federal Employment Bureau, Public Libraries, Housekeeping Center, Council of Jewish Women, several stores and hotels, and fifty industrial plants employing non-English-speaking employees.

Outside of New York State we would especially call attention to the local Americanization programs of Bridgeport, Hartford and Waterbury, Connecticut; Fall River, Boston, Lawrence and New Bedford, Massachusetts; Grand Rapids, Michigan; Newark and Paterson, New Jersey; Portland, Oregon, and Erie, Pittsburgh, Reading and Scranton, Pennsylvania.*

3. PRIVATE ENTERPRISES

a. CITIZENSHIP TRAINING THROUGH INDUSTRY

In making a survey of educational facilities throughout the country the Committee was volunteered very little information from educational sources as to work being done through factory classes. It might therefore be assumed that the Commissioners of Education with whom we corresponded did not know of activities through industries, or that they did not consider it an important feature of Americanization work. In any case, the state departments of education, except in a few cases, apparently do not cooperate with the industries to a sufficient extent to make it a prominent factor in the minds of the commissioners when discussing the subject of Americanization. Our own survey, however, leads us to believe that much important work is being done in and by the factories, sometimes at their own expense and sometimes sharing the expense with the employees and with such local and private organizations, as chambers of commerce, Y. M. C. A., etc. The Immigration Committee of the United States Chamber of Commerce in 1918 presented to chambers of commerce and industries standardized plans and suggestions for the organization of war Americanization work, which resulted in widespread

* See Addendum, Part 2.

activity among employers and commercial and trade organizations. The result was that some 150 chambers of commerce became engaged in some form of Americanization work, compared with thirty-one prior to that time. This work for the most part has been continued since the war.*

About 1913, it appeared that many industries were attempting to educate their employees along different lines and by various methods. In most instances this educational work was directed towards improving the efficiency of the employee in the particular line of work in which he was engaged. To co-ordinate their work, to encourage the exchange of ideas, and to eliminate duplication of effort in the state educational methods and processes, the National Association of Corporation Schools was formed. It would seem that the work of such an organization could be made of very great value in reaching the foreign-born workman through factory classes.

The question of who shall pay for the instruction of employees in factory classes is one that cannot well be determined by this Committee, for reports show great diversity in policy and in results. Some classes are conducted successfully entirely upon company time, with a teacher hired by the corporation and text books supplied by it. Some classes are conducted entirely on the employee's time, sometimes with a voluntary teacher from the factory, sometimes with a teacher from the Y. M. C. A. or some other private organization, and sometimes with teachers supplied by the State Board of Education or a local board. And again, classes are conducted half time at the company's expense and half time at the employee's expense, with a variety of arrangements as to the teacher. All seem to agree, however, that the instruction should be during the working day or immediately following working hours. Most educators whose opinions are based upon observation believe that the even division of expense between employer and employee has proved the most satisfactory. In this matter, however, the Committee does not venture an opinion.

In New York State the law provides for the establishment of special classes in factories, hotels, laundries, etc., and for the maintenance and conduct of such classes. This work is done on the principle that extended educational privileges, particularly for adults, must be taken to them, rather than that the adult should

---

* For additional activities carried on by labor organizations see Chapter VII, Section 2, Part 2, of this report.

be under obligation to go long distances, at inopportune times and under unfavorable conditions, to places where formal and more or less arbitrary educational facilities are provided.

In New Hampshire the State Department of Education tries to organize factory classes on the employee's time. Their slogan is "Carry the schools to the People."

In industrial plants where there is any considerable number of foreign-born employees there is no longer a question as to the value to the employer of educating them in the English language and in the duties and privileges of citizenship nor is the value to the employee less marked. One of the most immediate results of the teaching of English is the reduction of accidents, because of the ability of employees to understand verbal instructions from their foremen and from printed signs. The study, as conducted by large liability and workmen's compensation insurance has demonstrated this to be a fact. United States Director of the Bureau of Mines states that the non-English-speaking races in the anthracite regions are twice as liable to death and injury as the English-speaking workers and that this is quite true of the bituminous fields of West Virginia and Pennsylvania, and that it is approximately true wherever such labor is used in hazardous enterprises.

Another result which is usually slower in coming is that shop classes increase the loyalty of the workers to their employers. From Connecticut we receive a report that during a recent strike 53 percent of all the employees in a certain plant stayed out, but only three and one-half percent of those attending the company school were among these. The reason for this, of course, is obvious. When the employee acquires English, it is possible for his foreman to talk with him understandingly and to grasp his problem. Also, when an employee believes that his advancement in the shop is somehow connected with his advancement in his class, he takes his job more seriously.

The American Rolling Mill Company, of Middletown, Ohio, report that they have handled their foreign-born employees successfully and satisfactorily for over twenty years. This, they attribute to the fact that they have based their Americanization effort on the realization that it can be accomplished only by taking into consideration social conditions, housing conditions, and working conditions. They have never had a strike. Their employees are contented and thrifty, and ten percent of their foreign-born employees own their own homes. Twenty-five percent of the foreign-born employees are enrolled in their English and citizenship classes which are conducted entirely at the expense of the company.

A third advantage from the employer's point of view, is the decrease in labor turnover which inevitably follows the educating of his foreign-born employes. The government survey shows that the labor turnover of 112 large industrial establishments, runs from 20 to 400 percent, whereas reports from manufacturers with the shop class policy shows that they hold their help better after adopting the educational work. And these shop classes are not in the nature of "welfare". The most hard-headed business men have come to see that it is a paying investment even when they furnish the time, the text books, and the teachers, and that it is a means of attaching their workmen to the community, and thus holding them in their employ. Where facilities are offered for learning English, reports show that they are pretty generally utilized by employees. No objections on the part of employees have been recorded with this Committee except in one or two cases where the employee preferred to take advantage of doing overtime work during class hours.

Emphasis should also be laid upon the advantages in attending the class to the employee himself. He is enabled at convenient hours to acquire a working knowledge of the English language and of the institutions of this country which will enable him not only to understand his surroundings better, but offers him the opportunity of increasing his industrial efficiency, and of increasing his ability to improve his living conditions.

The State of Delaware has taken the matter of education for citizenship through industries very seriously and its Service Citizens have interested in this movement the government, the Secretary of State, the chief executives of the leading industries, leading bankers, public educational authorities, naturalization officers, and private enterprises engaged in Americanization work.

In Ohio, the Council of National Defense has enlisted the interest and support of the leading industries in training their foreign-born employees. The Associated Industries of Massachusetts have two experienced Americanization workers as secretaries who visit industrial plants contemplating conducting classes for employees, and make recommendations. This organization also furnishes speakers for foremen's meetings, and instructors for teachers of Americanization. In Wisconsin the educational work in factories is being carried on through cooperation between the public school authorities in charge of night school and other adult education. Industrial organizations are encouraged to utilize teachers provided by local school boards and the teachers are under the supervision of the official in charge of the local night schools. Arkansas, Iowa and Wyoming mention special classes conducted for mine workers. In Arkansas the Naturalization Bureau is in charge of the classes. The Packard Motor Company of Detroit in January, 1919, made employment contingent upon being a citizen of the United States or upon having filed a declaration of intention to become a citizen. To retain his position it is necessary for an employee who has only his first papers to become naturalized as soon as possible. A pre-requisite to employment is loyalty to our government and flag, and loyalty to the company itself. There are normally 12,000 employees in the Packard plant and 1750 of them have received their papers and are being assisted to obtain final naturalization papers. Employees are sent to the public schools for instruction in English and only the English language is used in official bulletins and communications of the company addressed to its employees.

The California Packing Corporation of San Francisco have a unique method of Americanization through factory kindergartens for the children of their employees. Here the children are taught the rudiments of language, citizenship and sanitation.

In reaching the foreign-born worker through his industry a very great influence may be exerted through the house organ, where one is published. The practice of Wilson & Company, in Chicago, in publishing anti-radical propaganda in their house organ is typical and can be adapted and used quite generally, provided the editors of these journals are acquainted with the subjects they must write about.

There is one phase of the problem of educating the adult immigrant which devolves upon the public school through extra-mural classes, and that is the problem of educating itinerant labor. No one reporting to the Committee has mentioned this aspect of the situation except Delaware. They mention that migratory laborers work in the canneries of the southern part of the state at certain seasons of the year, but they are not usually residents of the state. This is mentioned as a sort of relief from responsibility for their training, although, as it has been pointed out elsewhere, the Delaware program as a whole is very comprehensive. More effective means should be devised for reaching the itinerant foreign-born labor which exists, to some extent, in New York State, but to a greater extent in the West. It is from this class of labor that many of the members of the Industrial Workers of the World and similar revolutionary organizations are recruited.

Here, it seems, is another argument for the coordination of Americanization and citizenship training efforts throughout the country and for the standardization of citizenship training courses. If these courses were standardized in a manner similar to that used with such apparent success by the Berlitz School of Languages in its language courses, students could be transferred from one school to another without seriously impeding their progress.

b. Settlement Houses

Among the numerous philanthropic efforts which have grown up in recent years, the settlement house has figured prominently. These houses are to be found in congested districts of New York City and other large cities and are designed to furnish an example to the neighborhood in American ideals and modes of life. They house clubs for the girls and boys of the neighborhood, conduct classes for children and young people, as well as their parents, and from them social workers go out into the homes of the neighboring population. Unquestionably these centers have in many fields performed services of extraordinary value to the community and can still be of great use, particularly in the field of social service. In view of these facts it is a matter of extreme regret that the Committee must criticize sharply much of the work which is carried on in some settlements of New York City with respect to matters of government and political economy. The Committee wishes to take this occasion to express its conviction that a citizen may be of immense value in the fields of philanthropy and social service and at the same time constitute a serious menace when he attempts to enter the field of reconstructing the social order and the government under which we live.

In New York City out of approximately 100 settlement houses, 43 have organized in what is known as the United Neighborhood Houses of New York. The purpose of this association is described in its constitution as being

"to increase the influence and enlarge the usefulness of neighborhood houses through co-ordination and co-operation of effort, to promote the establishment of additional neighborhood houses, to act upon public matters in which neighborhood houses are inherently interested and to foster an enlightened public opinion respecting such matters; to represent affiliated neighborhood houses in applications or appeals to municipal, state or national authorities for governmental action safeguarding public health, improving public education or furthering the good order, effort or convenience of the commuity. And the Association is established for the additional purpose of speaking publicly in behalf of organizations therein affiliated through statements to the press, publications under its own direction, or its representatives before public or semi-public bodies."

In many of these neighborhood houses radical and revolutionary ideas are hospitably received. Among others, however, this Committee has found a notable exception. There are undoubtedly others. The particular one we have in mind is the Educational Alliance. Its activities are worthy of thorough commendation. Dr. Henry C. Fleischman, administrator of the Alliance in his letter to counsel for this Committee on November 17th, 1919, says: "The Educational Alliance has for its purpose the Americanization of the foreign-born and all its activities and all its efforts are bent in this direction. We stand for an unadulterated and unalloyed Americanism and we teach and preach this doctrine through every means at our disposal." An examination of the work carried on by this Alliance has convinced the Committee that the above is an accurate statement of its program.

The United Neighborhood Houses of New York appointed a committee to confer with counsel for this Committee, which resulted in that association making certain proposals and recommendations. Among these was the statement that the Neighborhood Houses would lose much of their value if they tried to present a program of Americanism from only one standpoint. They believe both sides should be given a hearing and that "truth cannot suffer in the long run from contact with fallacy." They also state that: "The Neighborhood Houses in principle oppose the repression of ideas except where change, economic or political, by force, is advocated, pernicious principles no less than worthy ones thrive on repression. The latter alone can survive free discussion."

Mr. Harold Riegelman, counsel to the United Neighborhood Houses of New York, when called to the stand testified before the Committee, in substance, as follows:

"The objects of the United Neighborhood Houses of New York have been defined. The houses themselves that are associated in the organization are not members, but are represented by members.

"Americanization work, especially in a large city like New York, carries with it a tragedy in the fact that the younger generation becomes Americanized much more quickly than the older, and here the settlement house steps in in behalf of the older generation. Also, it provides a place of recreation for the children, who on account of the progress they have made as American citizens are not satisfied with their shabby homes.

"So far as I am aware our attention has not been called to any house which is a member of the United Neighborhood Houses that has fostered consciously or unconsciously any doctrine or any conduct that is subversive of the principles and institutions of the present and existing government. I am sure that if such a complaint were received that the house in question would be rebuked, possibly expelled from the organization, and we even might go so far as to get its charter revoked.

"I believe that there should be open forums for the discussion of arguable questions that these forums should be impartial. In the case of a question of Americanism, I think the alien should be allowed to feel that in seeking further light he should be in a position to present the arguments that he had heard elsewhere and to have those arguments answered.

"By having the forums really open, you impress upon the foreigner your desire to give him a square deal. The chairman should be able to sway the meeting in case of subversive arguments being offered."

At this point the chairman of the Committee pointed out that in some of the radical literature in its possession prostitution is commended and the prostitute held up as the ideal of womanhood. Mr. Riegelman was asked if he would bring an advocate of prostitution into a forum and let everybody consider the question — if he would give the impression to the foreigners who might come to such a forum that the question was debatable. Mr. Riegelman replied:

"I certainly don't think that the subject should be emphasized. In other words, I do believe that the question impartially requires at least a strong presentation of the other side. Logically, I should say that if such a man were permitted to come into the house that I was entrusted with the guardianship of, I should take mighty good care that on the same platform, at the same time, there was a man who would completely answer the propositions that were made by the advocate of prostitution."

Mr. Riegelman further stated that if such an advocate should "transgress the laws of decency" he would get him to leave the platform!

"One of the difficulties of the settlements has been that we have not been able to get enough men to expound in clear, vigorous fashion pro-American propaganda in language which will meet the particular objections that are raised by the disloyalists, the Bolshevists, the seditionists, and whoever else is opposed to our form of government. Neither are we able to get enough of the proper sort of literature to put into the hands of these people."

When examined with respect to the settlement houses and their influence upon the people of foreign-birth or parentage, Superintendent Ettinger of the New York public schools stated at a public hearing of this Committee as follows:

"What we have to fear is the perversion of the children by influences which are very insidious. I fear that a good many of our so-called 'parlor socialists,' or philosophers, had a great deal to do with the training of some of the intellectuals among the foreign-born youth toward socialism and Bolshevism. One harmful influence is the formation of clubs at which these young people discuss questions which their immaturity of judgment will not permit them to understand with proper perspective, historical perspective; they discuss these different questions of the remedies for social ills, and they are impressed by these 'Parlor Socialists,' who are their guides and mentors, and they have not enough philosophy behind them to weigh properly the arguments pro and con, and they are led astray in that way. They have a certain glib use of language and they translate that into philosophy.

"I know several cases where I can say that the doctrines imbibed by these young men have been imbibed at the feet of some of these 'parlor socialists.' They meet them in those clubs, sometimes, I think, under the guise of settlement work. I don't know just how far that extends, but I know that a good many of these young men that I knew as youths, as boys, who afterward became, I would say, infected with these socialistic ideas, I know that they received their lessons in socialism in the clubs which they attended in the neighborhood of their particular residences, at which these questions were discussed. These youngsters discussed those questions when they were only fifteen, sixteen or seventeen years old, without guidance.

"There is a freedom of expression in the settlements and there is an encouragement to that freedom of expression without sufficient guidance. That is, I don't think that he comes in contact with the persons there who will put him straight, who will give him the other side, so to speak. I am not saying that this is characteristic of all settlements. I have no objection to boys attending these clubs. I haven't even any objection to propositions concerning socialistic theories being advanced, but have a decided objection to having it all one way; I have a decided objection to having somebody tell them, who will not guide them along right lines, but who will permit these errors to creep in. I rather think that it is not a good thing for boys or girls to come under the influence of these people without somebody being there as a check."

This Committee condemns the theory of Americanization which permits placing radical and revolutionary ideas on a parity with the ideals of American Government. It condemns the custom and conduct in many settlement houses to invite radical and revolutionary speakers to occupy their platforms for the reason that the audience is in many cases already predisposed toward radical ideas and the effect of radical or revolutionary speeches can be none other than to crystalize or confirm the radical beliefs of the hearers. That the work carried on in these centers is not effective is shown by the fact that the trend of public opinion in most o:

the congested districts served by them in the past five years has been radical in the extreme, whereas there are more Americanization centers of the settlement house type in these neighborhoods than there are radical centers. The reason for this is plain: The radical agitator or propagandist is, in most instances, animated by a real and vital conviction in the cause he serves. His attitude is militant. On the other hand the attitude of many of the social workers is apologetic and shows clearly a lack of any actual convictions with respect to the value of American ideals and institutions. When two such divergent policies come into competition, invariably the militant and aggressive will be the effective one. It is the opinion of this Committee that if the settlement houses of New York City are to become an effective force in the work of Americanization and citizenship training, a large majority of them must change their present policy and become militant and ardent advocates of American institutions and American ideals.

a. AMERICANIZATION THROUGH CHURCHES

In subsequent pages of this report will be found statements and plans relating to Americanization work from many churches and denominations. These show that the churches have been giving increasing consideration to the problems of citizenship training. This Committee, however, feels that on the whole the churches are not equipped to do effective work in this field. They can be of greater service in assisting and encouraging the public educational authorities. On the other hand, some very excellent work is being done by certain churches through parochial schools and by some Protestant organizations.

As the success of a school in Americanization depends upon the teacher, so the success of a church in this field depends upon the clergyman and his assistants. In Part One of this report the question of socialism and the churches has been dealt with. It is there pointed out that there is an ever-growing tendency toward radicalism in the clergy. Much of this attitude may be explained by the fact that they have been and are grossly underpaid, and for this reason they are unable to see economic problems in their proper perspective. On the other hand, one of the poorest paid came to the office of the Committee in answer to a letter asking information as to the Americanization activities of his church. He could not wait to write a letter, he said, he was so anxious to talk to us about what he was doing and what he would like to do in Americanization if he had the money. He was a naturalized foreigner with the twang of his mother tongue still much in evidence. His was the difficult task of keeping his fellow churchmen in church in a neighborhood where there were many agencies that worked to keep them out of it. His enthusiasm was inspiring and his sincerity is evidenced by the fact that his is one of the most successful foreign language churches in New York City.

A clergyman in an Italian Baptist Church in New York City, who has done much good work among his adherents, wrote the Committee a pathetic letter asking advice how to deal with two of his congregation who seemed to have " lost their heads on the subject of Bolshevism."

There are, of course, many other cases in which excellent work along educational lines is being conducted through the churches. Details of their activity will be found in the succeeding sections of this report, dealing with church activities. Several of the foreign language churches try to conduct classes in English, but they do not seem to be very successful on any substantial scale. This is due in most cases to lack of funds and lack of trained teachers, as well as to a lack of knowledge and experience in the educational field. There is no lack of good intention.

The church can without doubt be most effective in promoting the education of the foreign-born adult by encouraging their attendance upon the evening public schools or factory classes.

While the leading Protestant denominations have foreign language churches, it will be noted from the reports of their pastors that they number among their members only a small percentage of the foreign colonies in New York City. Therefore, at best, they could not be counted on for an appreciable amount of Americanization work, even if it were expedient for them to do it.

The Protestant Teachers' Association of New York City says that there are 860,000 children in New York City, who never attended any Sunday school or receive religious instruction in any church or synagogue. These children furnish excellent recruiting material for the Socialist Sunday Schools.*

A report from the Ohio branch of the Council of National Defense voices a situation which existed in Ohio during the war, and which we have shown in a previous chapter of this report also existed in New York City and elsewhere in New York State. The report says: " In sections where work with which we are connected met any anti-American activity, the apparent leaders,

---

* See report on Socialist Sunday Schools. Addendum, Part I.

were in many cases ministers or other religious leaders of denominations opposed to the war or composed largely of first or second generation immigrants from the enemy country." We have shown in Part One how the sentimentality of many clergymen has led them from pacifism into liberalism and thence into radicalism. This process explains the curious attitude which is found to exist in a number of New York churches.

The survey of this Committee has revealed that many churches feel the need for giving proof to the dissatisfied element of the working class, that they do not represent capitalist interests, but that they have deep concern for the interests of the less fortunate. Unfortunately in many instances this interest is manifested in lending sentimental encouragement to subversive and revolutionary groups, and also a tendency on the part of the churches to engage in scientific research and in the propounding of solutions for economic problems. We here wish to draw attention to activities such as are carried on by the Rev. Percy Stickney Grant at the Church of the Ascension in New York City, and to the activities at the Labor Temple, which is conducted under the supervision of the New York Presbytery of the Presbyterian Church. Their report says: "The institution stands as one of the most emphatic instances of what might be called the socialized church." Indeed, it would appear that it is more "socialized" than "church." It conducts open forums every Sunday evening and, according to the Director of the Temple in testimony before this Committee, most of the audience are radicals who are allowed to give voice to their theories freely. The Director further stated that in the district where it is located, "the Christian approach must be unconventional, friendly and obviously sympathetic with human problems." In trying to be "sympathetic with human problems," this church as well as some others has allowed its audience to divert it from its legitimate purpose. This is one of the instances referred to in various places in this report where actually subversive activities masquerade under the name of Americanization.*

---

* Since the preparation of this report the activities carried on at the Labor Temple have been most forcefully brought to the attention of this Committee. The program of the Labor Temple for the past year may be divided into three categories:

First, the Christian work carried on under the title of American International Church.

Second, Educational work carried on under the direct auspices of the Temple's management, and

d. Miscellaneous

In the following chapter we have discussed the advantages of concentrating the work of Americanization in the public schools or under public educational supervision. This is the judgment of the Committee after reviewing the efforts of both public and private agencies throughout the country. We feel, however, that we should give credit to some of the private enterprises at work in the following summary of their activities. For a full description of their work as given by themselves, the reader should study Sub-section III of Section III of this report.

Third, meetings held by outside organizations who rent the halls and other private rooms either for mass meetings or for private meetings of Labor organizations.

The Committee has nothing to do with the first part of this program. The second part of the program has been carried out principally by one Dr. Will Durant, who has been excluded from the public schools of New York City because of the radical doctrines he espouses. In the course of the past year he has spoken particularly upon revolutionary subjects and is announced to give a course of lectures on Lenin.

His point of view may be gathered from a letter addressed by him to Rev. Kenneth D. Miller, in which he says:

> "The purpose of the lectures on Lenin is to contrast him as a conciliatory moderate with the extremists like Zinovief and Bucharin, to show that he has realized frankly the impossibility of communism, and to use the magic of Lenin's name on the East Side as an argument for moderation. . . . Indiscriminate hostility to the Russian Revolution would be an absurd policy at Labor Temple: A discriminating support of its moderate elements as against its wilder factions is an aid to American peace."

It is unfortunate that the Committee of the New York Presbytery in charge of this work appears at the time of writing this note to approve the work of Dr. Durant in spite of his support of Lenin.

During the past year the halls of the building have been thrown open to demonstrations and mass meetings for the I. W. W. and other subversive organizations. A typical example of some of the activities that fall into the third category above mentioned may be found in a leaflet announcing meetings for the months of November and December, 1920. If the reader will consult the index of Part I of this report he will find statements relating to the subversive activities of most of the persons whose names appear in this circular. The Committee does not wish to imply that any of these lectures will violate or have violated any of the statutes in the books of this State, but the program here carried on is effective to defeat any attempt at Americanization carried on in this district. The leaflet above referred to is as follows:

The American Defense Society is committed to the upholding and promotion of the American spirit and to the defense of America from attacks from within. The Society appears to awake to the menace of radical activities in this country and has attempted to combat them through the dissemination of pamphlets which it publishes from time to time and through correspondence with public officials and leaders in the community.

The American Federation of Labor passed a resolution in June of 1919, in which they took the stand of being in favor of making English the sole language for instruction in the common schools and of providing ample facilities for teaching English to foreigners in our public schools.

The American Red Cross, through its foreign language information service, informs the alien in his own language about the government and laws of this country, what the government expects of him and what it offers to him. It clears up his misconceptions

---

SUNDAY EVENINGS — 5.00 TO 6.30 P. M.
November 14 to December 19

SIX REMARKABLE LECTURES
on
COMMUNISM
Past — Present — Future

The first Comprehensive Presentation of COMMUNISM from its beginnings; a Brilliant Analysis in an unprejudiced manner of all its aspects.

by

LINDLEY M. KEASBEY, PH.D., R. P. D.
Professor of Economics and Noted Lecturer

Nov. 14 — COMMUNISM IN THEORY and PRACTICE.
Nov. 21 — ANCIENT COMMUNISM.
　The Ideal Republic and the Relatively Best State.
Nov. 28 — MEDIAEVAL COMMUNISM.
　State and Church.
Dec. 5 — MODERN COMMUNISM.
　The Industrial Revolution.
Dec. 12 — COMMUNISM and SOCIAL DEMOCRACY.
Dec. 19 — COMMUNISM IN EUROPE and AMERICA.

LABOR TEMPLE AUDITORIUM
East 14th Street and Second Avenue

SINGLE ADMISSION 25c　　　　　　　　COURSE TICKET $1.00
　plus war tax　　　　　　　　　　　　　　plus war tax

AUSPICES — THE FINE ARTS GUILD

and adjusts his difficulties, in so far as their facilities will permit. It also attempts the equally important task of giving the native-born accurate information on the foreign-born groups and to overcome foreign prejudices and misunderstandings which stand in the way of the foreigners' assimilation. It cooperates with the American press and with the foreign language press in the gathering and distribution of news about foreign institutions and the institutions and laws of the United States.

The Boy Scouts made a good record during the war. Because of this and because of the principles on which their organization is founded, they are recognized by the American Legion and by the Director of Citizenship of the Department of Labor as being exponents of the principles of good American citizenship.

The Girl Scouts are equally sound and American.

The Chamber of Commerce of the State of New York has adopted a resolution to support Americanization bills and other educational bills designed to reduce illiteracy.

WEDNESDAY EVENINGS — 8.15 P. M.
November 17 to December 15

FIVE EXTRAORDINARY LECTURES
on
THE FIRST PRINCIPLES OF
" PSYCHOANALYSIS "

The New Science of the Unconscious Presented in a Simple, Clear and Popular Manner.

by

ANDRE TRIDON

Brilliant Lecturer and Author of " Psychoanalysis and Behavior," " Psychoanalysis; Its Theory and Practice," etc.

Nov. 17 — THE UNCONSCIOUS and ITS MYSTERIES:
or What Is Psychoanalysis?
Nov. 24 — THE INTERPRETATION OF DREAMS:
or Suppressed Desires and their Dream Gratification.
Dec. 1 — PROBLEMS OF CHILDHOOD:
or Heredity and Sexual Enlightenment.
Dec. 8 — DUAL PERSONALITIES:
or the Jekyll and Hyde case in Actual Life.
Dec. 15 — LOVE, NORMAL and ABNORMAL.

LABOR TEMPLE AUDITORIUM
East 14th Street and Second Avenue
SINGLE ADMISSION 35c . COURSE TICKET $1.25
AUSPICES — THE FINE ARTS GUILD
Four Mondays — Two Fridays
November 15 to December 20

The Constitutional League is a voluntary association of citizens who believe in the Government and Constitution of the United States. They aim to put a copy of the Constitution into every home in the United States, in the belief that people will appreciate it if they are made familiar with it.

The Immigrant Publication Society cooperates with members of the American Library Association in an effort to get into the hands of the immigrant good books describing the United States and its institutions. It publishes as many books as possible to fill some of the most urgent needs. Its Director states that there is no foreign-language history of the United States appropriate for the immigrant, the best one being written in Yiddish by a radical socialist. The Society hopes to fill this important need. It also believes that reading should be encouraged, even fiction, for in fiction the immigrant learns American customs, manners, sanitary living conditions, etc.

SIX WONDERFUL LECTURES
on
" IBSEN "
A Remarkable Analysis of the Great Playwright
In All His Moods
by
LOUIS K. ANSPACHER

One of America's Foremost Dramatists, Brilliant Lecturer and Author of " The Unchastened Woman," " Tristan and Isolde," etc.

MON., Nov. 15 — Introduction: DRAMA AS A SOCIAL FORCE IN A DEMOCRACY.
FRI., Nov. 19 — IBSEN, THE POET, Brand and Peer Gynt.
MON., Nov. 29 — IBSEN, and THE DRAMAS OF SOCIAL REVOLT. The Young Men's League. The Pillars of Society, and Enemy of the People.
MON., Dec. 6 — IBSEN and THE DRAMAS OF MORAL REVOLT. The Doll's House, Ghosts, Hedda Gabler.
FRI., Dec. 10 — IBSEN'S WOMEN.
MON., Dec. 20 — IBSEN, THE INDIVIDUALIST and IDEALIST.

LABOR TEMPLE AUDITORIUM
East 14th Street and Second Avenue

SINGLE ADMISSION 30c   COURSE TICKET $1.25
AUSPICES — THE FINE ARTS GUILD

" The course of lectures on " Ibsen " delivered before our Institute has been unusually interesting.— Brooklyn Institute of Arts and Sciences.
" In brilliancy of diction, originality of thought and dramatic power of speech, Mr. Anspacher is a remarkable lecturer."— Brooklyn Eagle.

The National Association of Manufacturers published a booklet called "Bolshevism, Self-Defined and Self-Convicted," to inform business men throughout the country of the situation in Russia. This book was of interest more from the intention animating its publication than from the actual value of its contents.

The National Liberal Immigration League advocates the careful selection, distribution, education and protection of immigrants; opposes indiscriminate restriction; studies bills introduced in Congress on immigration and kindred subjects; enlightens public sentiment as to it own views on these matters through its books, pamphlets, etc.; organizes and advises societies and individuals favoring a liberal immigration policy; and promotes the enactment of legislation of such subjects as deportation of alien criminals, Federal employment bureaus, placing industrial plants in the

---

GREGORY ZILBOORG
Eminent Author, Dramatist and Lecturer in the last two lectures of his
REMARKABLE SERIES
on
"VOICES OF SOCIAL HOPE AND DESPAIR."

TUESDAY EVENINGS, 8.15 p. m.
NOV. 9 — GUY DE MAUPASSANT: Victims of a Civilized World.
NOV. 16 — ROMAIN ROLLAND: The Voice of a Prophet.

LABOR TEMPLE AUDITORIUM
14th Street and Second Avenue
ADMISSION 30c

SEASON 1920–1921

THE FINE ARTS GUILD
is planning to present

JOHN COWPER POWYS
MAX EASTMAN
Dr. WILL DURANT
LOUIS K. ANSPACHER
BOUCK WHITE
LINCOLN STEFFENS
ANDRE TRIDON
MARGARET SANGER

LOUIS U. WILKINSON
ABRAHAM CAHAN
BENJAMIN DE CASSERES
ARTURO GIOVANNATTI
ELIZABETH G. FLYNN
GREGORY ZILBOORG
LINDLEY M. KEASBEY
OLIVER M. SAYLER

and other lecturers of merit (some of the above series are definitely determined upon; others are being arranged).

All those who are interested in receiving announcements of these lectures, kindly send your name and address to

THE FINE ARTS GUILD
21 East 14th Street   NEW YORK CITY

country or in small cities, education and protection of immigrants, and amendments to the Contract Labor Law, to exempt from its application agricultural laborers and certain skilled labor in cases where they cannot be recruited on American soil.

(It must, of course, be understood, that in mentioning these and the following organizations, the Committee does not give its full endorsement or approval to all of the views expressed or advocated by them.)

The National Security League is a non-political, non-partisan league of American men and women who are working to promote patriotic education and to spread American ideals. They furnish ideas as to methods of teaching patriotic subjects, and material for use in such course. They have also had a "flying squadron" of Americanization speakers and they have published a catechism on the Constitution of the United States in twelve lessons, which has had a wide circulation.

The New York Kindergarten Association believes that the time to make Americans of little foreigners is at the beginning. That is when they begin their kindergarten work — at the time they are most impressionable.

The Russian Collegiate Institute operates classes for children and for adults, and it is the only educational institution which has reported to the Committee on efforts to counteract Bolshevism and radicalism by direct education in this country and (through returning pupils) in Russia.

The Y. M. C. A. have two secretaries on Ellis Island, who speak a number of different languages. They meet immigrants, attempt to take care of their needs and send them to their destinations. They also have immigration secretaries throughout the country and a system whereby these various secretaries are informed of the expected arrival of immigrants in their respective towns. This allows the secretary to take care of immigrants en route and at their destinations. The Y. M. C. A. also has secretaries at the chief ports of embarkation in Europe, and on the large steamers bringing immigrants to America.

The Y. W. C. A. has established in some of the larger cities having foreign populations, International Institutes, notably in New York City, where the foreign-born girl comes in contact with American life and also learns English.

Many foreign groups have benevolent associations for taking care of unfortunates of their own nationality and for the educating of their fellow-countrymen here; for example, The Chinese Benevolent Association, the Federation of Russian and Bukovinian Jews, Finnish Educational Association of Manhattan, Hebrew Sheltering and Immigrant Aid Society of America, the Hungarian Society of New York, Irish Emigrant Society, The Japanese Association, Inc., The Japanese Christian Institute, Inc., Jewish Protectory and Aid Society, Jewish Welfare Board, Maedschenheim Verein (for German girls), Pan-Hellenic Union, Greek-American Institute, Polish National Alliance, Russian Collegiate Institute, The Society for Italian Immigrants, etc.

In all of these private enterprises radicals and intellectuals attempt to gain a footing, and in some of the instances, even among the organizations which we have cited in this chapter, they have done so to a limited extent. It is for this reason that, as previously stated, this Committee believes that the most effective work in Americanization and citizenship training can be done by the public school system.

Following are a few instances of successful work being done by private enterprise outside New York State. The summary is not comprehensive but includes the most unique and outstanding efforts.

Missouri, Kansas City

The Chamber of Commerce has an Americanization Committee which helps in the work of naturalization. They encourage attendance upon the evening schools, help the foreigners to become naturalized and once a year they arrange an Americanization celebration for the newly made citizens.

Missouri, St. Louis

The Y. M. C. A. cooperates with the leading industries in the establishment and conduct of factory classes in English. They also aid materially in the work of naturalization.

Nevada

The Y. W. C. A. has helped along the work of Americanization by making a survey of the foreign-born in the state, and they are at work on the problem of reaching the foreign-born woman in the home.

New Hampshire

In New Hampshire all forces cooperate in the matter of Americanization — state, church, schools, industry, labor, and press.

The New Hampshire State Federation of Labor passed resolutions to cooperate with the State Education Department. The Manufacturers Association of New Hampshire passed resolutions to aid in the work to the end that every employee in the state become able to read, write and speak the English language as soon as possible. The Association Canado-Americaine also passed resolutions agreeing to aid in the organization of evening schools and encouraging attendance.

Ohio

The Committee on Education of the Cleveland Chamber of Commerce cooperates in the work of Americanization, this work having grown out of its emergency work in teaching English to foreigners. The Ohio Council of National Defense publishes bulletins on methods of teaching English to foreigners.

Washington

Spokane has a Constitutional Government League. Its purposes are: to promote understanding and interest in the fundamentals of our government; to secure a higher standard of the performance of the duties of citizenship; to defend American institutions against foreign and domestic revolutionaries; to strengthen the independence of public officials and protect them against intimidation. After the murder of several ex-service men by the I. W. W. on Armistice Day of 1919, in Centralia, the League made a membership drive, in connection with which they issued some live literature. "The radicals are gaining strength," they said, "only because they have had the field all to themselves, because Americans have been too confident of the goodness of our government to realize that it needs defense." The Constitutional Government League of Spokane is one of the few agencies in the country who are working directly to counteract the radical menace. A bolt struck near home and the Constitutional Government League renewed its efforts in the defense of Americanism. If other communities would awaken to a similar responsibility, the Centralia affair could never be repeated.

CHAPTER II
Relative Merit of Private and Public Agencies for Americanization

The original design in making education a public service in this country, supported by taxation of all the people, was, and the present purpose should be, that the public schools would prepare citizens for the duties and obligations they owe to their fellows as participators in the conduct of government. This purpose must be the first function of all public teaching; never secondary or incidental. As the task of so-called Americanization is the making of good citizens, it is clear that its purpose squares with that of the principal function of the public school, and that, theoretically at least, Americanization should be the work of the public school so far as actual, formal education enters into it. It has been a general policy in respect to education in the United States to place chief responsibility upon the various states and upon the cities, towns, counties and school districts in the states. Moreover, in the field of public education, it has been the policy to relate the general education system in its administration and conduct as closely to popular control as possible. The effect of this policy has been to link public education very strongly to local educational needs. The education of minors and minors of employment age through the medium of free public schools and various part-time and extension classes is on the whole very thoroughly organized throughout the several states. The legislature of each state has the power to provide for the educational programs of that state, and although there are minor differences, the system is, generally speaking, fairly uniform in this field.

The most prevalent system provides for the annual election by the qualified electors of the state of first, a superintendent or commissioner of public education, and second, a state board of education, some of whose members are usually appointed by the governor or elected by the state legislature. To the superintendent and the state board of education are entrusted all matters pertaining to, first, the establishment and maintenance of free public schools and other public educational institutions throughout the counties and districts of the state; second, the authorization and licensing of properly qualified superintendents, principals and teachers; third, the prescription of courses of study and the standardization of text books; and fourth, the submission of the annual budget of school expenses covered by general taxation. The election of local district trustees or boards usually takes place annually.

The survey made by this Committee indicates that the public school has been the most powerful unifying force for nationalism and loyalty in this state and throughout the United States. Most Americanization agencies agree that the great responsibility for undertaking such work rests upon the public school and that the success of the work rests largely upon the teacher.

The situation in New Hampshire is not unique. There the responsibility for Americanization is put squarely on the schools. The State Deputy Commissioner of Education is the State Director of Americanization, and each city superintendent of schools is local Americanization Director. The State Deputy Commissioner arouses interest in the work, organizes it and harmonizes it. The local authorities carry the work on and report upon it. It is a policy of the State Deputy Commissioner to so organize each local Americanization committee that they will include a representative of each race and each organization in the community, so that there will be no conflict of effort and so that he is in touch with all activities.

New York State is perhaps the foremost in the field of adult immigrant education. Here, too, chief responsibility is placed upon and accepted by the public educational agencies of the Commonwealth, both local and state. Work carried on by private organizations often fails to gain the confidence of the foreign-born. It is likely to be looked upon as charity. If it is a church or a settlement house it is considered a philanthropic institution and sometimes the efforts of the workers of these organizations are resented as a form of interference. The appeal made by a public movement is likely to arouse less suspicion and immediately establishes in the foreigner's mind the idea that the government can help him, if he is given to understand that the public educational agency is a part of the government and that the teacher is a representative of the government. If a foreigner accepts the training of a public school he is likely to appreciate the fact that the government has aided him and hence to recognize his obligation to support that government.

The public library is an institution which can cooperate with the public school in its work of Americanization. As an example of what can be done through careful study of the local immigrant groups and their needs, we would refer to the work of Mrs. Eleanor Ledbetter, of the Cleveland Public Library. The public library is characteristically an American institution. Here the foreigner feels more welcome even than in the school room, where he may resent the more advanced standing of a pupil younger than himself or where he may encounter members of other nationalities who may have prejudices against him. The foreign language newspaper can do much toward Americanizing its readers if its policy is sympathetic with American principles, but in the last analysis we must look to the public schools to furnish citizenship training through education.

Chambers of commerce throughout the country have done much to support the work of local school boards, especially in the establishment and maintenance of factory classes. In this their work has been coordinated to some extent by the United States Chamber of Commerce.

We should like to acknowledge here the worthy efforts of the Young Men's Christian Association, whose workers in most cases have high ideals of loyal citizenship and Americanism. From careful and wide observation of the work of this organization in Americanization we are convinced that its first concern is the making of good citizens. In all cases coming to our attention the Young Men's Christian Association is working in accord with the public educational activities, if not in actual cooperation with them, and much of this work is designed to fill in gaps where public educational facilities have not as yet been established. The Young Men's Christian Association has recommended to this Committee that the state cooperate with private agencies and furnish them with equipment and supplies, but our investigation has revealed that most private organizations engaged in Americanization are not so efficient as the Young Men's Christian Association nor so much in accord with the aims of our public educational systems. Much of the work of other private organizations does not prove to be just what it is labelled. Much of it is theoretical and on paper only, and represents plans for what should be done rather than a report of actual operations. While much work is done by women's clubs to Americanize alien women in their homes, all reports received by the committee indicate that the most successful agency here, as in other fields of Americanization, is the public school. In small communities, however, where the foreign problem is large in proportion to the educational facilities, and where there is no provision for home teaching, women's clubs and other private enterprises can be and are of inestimable value and help if they cooperate with the public school authorities.

Just as the success of public efforts in Americanization depends upon the soundness of the teacher, so the failure of private enterprises to really Americanize, where such failure exists, is due in large measure to the incompetency of the worker and especially to his over-sentimental attitude toward the foreigner. With possibly the best intentions in the world, a large number of social workers seem to be following the principle of one of the prominent so-called Americanizers, which may be summed up in the formula, "Don't try to Americanize the foreigner; let him foreignize the Americans."

A distinct advantage to be gained by placing the work of of Americanization and citizenship training entirely in the hands of the public school authorities is that such a procedure will permit the standardizing of courses, so that a foreigner changing from one school to another in his community, or moving to another part of the state, or even to a remote part of the country, would be able to continue his studies in accordance with the same methods and without serious set-back. The Berlitz School of Languages has standarized courses so that a student may begin his study of any language in any large city of the world and at any time transfer to another large city and continue just where he left off. Such a system of standardization would seem to be the one solution of the problem of educating the itinerant laborer, who is found to some extent in New York State but more especially in the Middle and Far West. It is obvious that in the interests of economy and efficiency if for no other reasons, all efforts in Americanization should come through one source. The purpose for which our public schools are established, as well as the experience of most of our able educators, lead to the conclusion that this one source should be the public school system, headed by the state department of education. In New York State the responsibility should rest upon the state department of education. On the other hand, the committee would view with satisfaction the assumption on the part of the Federal Government of responsibility in the Americanization movement, to the extent that it should coordinate the work of the various states and aid them financially, as provided in the Kenyon bill.* This is particularly true for the reason that the

* See Section III, subdivision 2, chapter I.

admission of immigrants into this country is fixed and determined by Federal legislation, which has resulted in the past in imposing upon the State of New York an educational burden far beyond its capacity to support. The committee believes that the various States should coordinate the local Americanization work within their respective boundaries, and the local school boards should coordinate all work within their communities.

The necessity for placing the responsibility for citizenship training primarily upon the state has been forcibly brought to the attention of this Committee through its consideration of the programs of education carried on at the present time in certain radical schools.

The chapter dealing with subversive teaching in certain schools (appearing on page 1444 of this report) shows that there are in this State organized schools which have for their purpose the teaching of the doctrine that organized government should be overthrown by force, violence or the use of the general strike and industrial action. This doctrine is in violation of the criminal laws of the State of New York. These schools, therefore, are engaged in the making of criminals; and students who advocate the doctrines which are there taught them are subject to criminal prosecution by the state. The Committee is convinced that the state owes a greater duty to its citizens to protect them from criminal teachings than to punish the criminals after they have been made in this manner, with the passive approval of the state. It is more important to preserve the loyalty of citizens than to punish the disloyal after they have been subjected to subversive teaching.

Schools engaged in teaching the doctrine of criminal anarchy in one form or another entice into their courses young men and women who are potentially good citizens, who are ignorant of the consequence of the teaching they receive, and who are in many cases innocent of any desire to engage in revolutionary activities. In the interests of these students, the Committee considered what methods should be adopted for their protection.

An examination of the criminal laws of the state and of criminal procedure has convinced the Committee that they do not afford adequate protection to the citizens. If a revolutionary school is incorporated, it may be indicted, tried, and convicted for the crime of criminal anarchy and punished with a substantial fine, but during the entire process, it may continue its subversive teaching. If the officers and teachers of the school are indicted, it is the custom to admit them to bail during trial, and frequently the same is true after conviction, pending an appeal, so that they are free for a long period to continue the same activities. If the process of criminal prosecution is carried out finally to the serving of a jail sentence, other teachers will take the place of those confined. An interesting illustration of this process may be found in the Rand School of Social Science. During the war it was tried and convicted for a violation of the Espionage Act. Its conviction resulted in a fine of three thousand dollars. Its appeal was denied, and the conviction affirmed. The whole prosecution had no other effect upon the activities of the Rand School of Social Science than to deprive it of three thousand dollars, interest and costs. The teachings for which it was convicted were carried on with the same regularity in the school building as though the prosecution had not been begun. For this reason it was recognized that the criminal law was inadequate as a measure of protection to the citizens of this state.

An examination of the education laws of various states shows that a more or less rigid control of public and private educational enterprises is exerted by the state educational authorities. Most of the regulation relates to the character of education carried on in elementary schools affecting pupils of the compulsory school age. State control is also exercised over the curricula of colleges and professional schools which offer degrees. The most stringent state provision which has come to the attention of the Committee is that of the State of Alabama. The law of that state gives to the State Board of Education control of all private, denominational and parochial schools or institutions of any kind having a school in connection therewith. Such schools are required to register annually with the Department of Education, and are required to make reports to the State Department of Education in regard to the attendance of pupils within compulsory age limits, also in regard to curricula, tuition, instructors, etc. It will be seen that this statute keeps the state educational authorities in constant touch with what is being taught to the citizens of the state in both public and private educational enterprises of all sorts.

This Committee is convinced that owing to the large foreign population within our boundaries and the extreme activity of the groups which seek to subvert our institutions, it is necessary that the state shall control and supervise the curricula of all public and private educational enterprises in this state, excepting from such control only such schools as are now conducted or hereafter to be organized by recognized religious denominations or sects.

These considerations led the Committee in its preliminary report to the Legislature to propose a bill requiring all educational enterprises other than those specifically excepted from the operation of the statute to procure a license from the public educational authorities of the state; making it unlawful to conduct any school, institute, course or class without a license; and requiring applicants for license to furnish upon oath a statement of the purposes of the school, institute, course or class, the nature and extent and purpose of the instruction to be given, with a further provision that no licenses should be granted to any school, institute, course or class where it shall appear to the satisfaction of the Regents that the school, institute, course or class is being conducted in such manner as to be detrimental to public interests, or is being conducted in a fraudulent or improper manner.

This bill also provides for the revocation of licenses granted, and the means for its enforcement. The full text of the bill will be found at the close of the general introduction in Volume I of this report. It is the earnest hope of the Committee that it will become the law of this state, so that the State Department of Education may control the Americanization education of the state and may guarantee its citizens protection against the teaching of revolutionary doctrines.

CHAPTER III

Teacher Requirements and Teacher Training

In the whole scheme of citizenship training no one has the power and the opportunity to exert so much influence for good or ill as the individual teacher. The Federal Government, the State Department of Education and the local school boards may outline a faultless program of Americanization and citizenship training, but if the teacher is not capable or desirous of its effective interpretation, all other efforts will have been in vain. The efficiency of the teaching staff in the field of training the foreign-born is dependent upon, first, adequate compensation to teachers; second, discriminate selection of teachers; third, higher teacher requirements; fourth, specialized training; and fifth, a general appreciation by the public of the vital function performed by such teachers and their importance to the body politic.

With regard to teachers' salaries there is no difference of opinion. Educators all over the country report that the present inadequacy of teachers' salaries constitutes a serious obstacle to the progress of Americanization work. Teachers are underpaid and have been so for many years. The present period of high prices emphasizes a situation which has existed persistently in public and quasi-public institutions for a protracted period. This Committee believes that adequate compensation of teachers in New York State, and especially of those teachers entrusted with the important responsibility of training the foreign-born, will be a prerequisite to the solution of the acute problem of securing satisfactory teachers which is faced today. With adequate pay teaching standards may be elevated through more careful selection of teachers. Moreover, more competent persons who prefer teaching, but who are kept out of it because of low salaries, will be encouraged to offer their services. It is now the concensus of opinion that a careful selection of teachers having adequate training and ability is impossible in the face of the acute shortage occasioned by insufficient compensation. However, this Committee believes that more and more emphasis must be laid upon the selection of teachers upon the basis of character, good citizenship, background, and training. One prominent educator has wisely recommended that each teacher of the foreign-born should be required to account for his conduct during the late war.

The legislation of various states in the matter of requirements for teachers seems inadequate to insure a teaching staff able to deal with the critical situation of country-wide unrest. In more than three-fourths of the states citizenship, or even declaration of intention to become a citizen, are not prerequisites to obtaining teacher certificates. The effects of such a system, especially on those states which have a great percentage of aliens, is only too obvious. The required age of a teacher in the majority of the states is 18 years, though in Maine, Mississippi and several other states it is as low as 17, and in Texas 16. In most of the states a general provision is made that the teacher must be of good moral character, or at least a provision is made that his license shall be valid only during satisfactory conduct. Tennessee, on the other hand, goes so far as to prohibit the use of drugs, alcoholics, or cigarettes by any licensed teacher, while Kentucky prohibits gambling and profanity.

The states which require that no person shall be granted a teacher's license or certificate who is not a native or naturalized citizen of the United States or who has not already declared his intention to become one, are:

California
Montana
Nebraska
Nevada
New York
Washington

In Nevada the teacher, besides having to be a citizen, is required to take the following oath before the granting of a certificate:

"I, ..., do solemnly swear (or affirm) that I will support, protect and defend the Constitution and Government of the United States and the Constitution and Government of the State of Nevada against all enemies, whether domestic or foreign, and I will bear true faith, allegiance and loyalty to the same — any ordinance, resolution or law of any state convention or legislature to the contrary notwithstanding. And further, I will well and faithfully perform all the duties of teacher on which I am about to enter, (if an oath) so help me God; (if an affirmation) under the pains and penalties of perjury.

"Sworn and subscribed to before me, a .... of the County of ...., and State of Nevada, this .... day of ...., Anno Domini 19...."

Even in those states requiring citizenship, teachers' licenses are granted to persons who have not yet reached their majority, for in no cases is the minimum age requirement over 18 years. The following states, so far as the evidence submitted to this Committee is concerned, make no requirements for teachers with respect to character:

Delaware
Illinois
Iowa
Louisiana
Michigan
Minnesota
Oregon
South Carolina
Texas
Virginia
Wisconsin
Wyoming.

We are advised that theoretically the selection of teachers for evening schools and for extension education in New York State is based upon (1) character, personality, interest, motive and loyal citizenship; (2) experience; and (3) training. These requirements we approve and recommend their rigid enforcement.

At a Federal Americanization conference held during the war the following statement was formulated:

"We urge upon all normal schools, colleges and other agencies concerned with the training of teachers, that courses be given aiming directly at the equipment of all public school teachers, whether of children or of adults, to train citizens in the scientific knowledge and duties which will lead to a realization of the highest Americanism."

This gave impetus to the work of training Americanization workers, which is now being conducted in many of our largest universities. Much of this work is commendable, but it all shows one conspicuous lack: nothing is done to teach prospective workers in the field of Americanization how to cope with radical and revolutionary theories with which they are inevitably destined to find many foreign groups affected. The University of Minnesota* has done more than any other university from which the

* See addendum, part 2.

Committee has received a report, to train not only teachers of foreign-born adults, but also directors and organizers of Americanization work.* A six weeks' course was offered in the summer of 1919, which embraced not only immigration problems and problems concerning the foreign-born in their American environment, but also the study of Americanization movements throughout the country generally, anthropology, and the methods of teaching adults. Beginning with the season of 1919–1920 a four-year course was offered, devoted entirely to the training of teachers, organizers and directors of Americanization work. This covered the subects taught in the summer school and in addition a more intensified study of foreign and American peoples, civics and government, economics, labor problems, housing problems, socialism, social statistics, social psychology, eugenics, and other subjects which were elective. The requirements for both admission and graduation conform to those of the College of Science, Literature and the Arts. A degree of Bachelor of Science is given for the satisfactory completion of the four-year course and a Master of Arts degree may be obtained by a fifth year of post-graduate study.

The University of Minnesota believes that highly specialized workers are necessary for Americanization activities. Complex and difficult problems must be met by the worker among immigrant peoples, growing out of racial characteristics which have their origin far back of recent or modern political and economic systems and have a deeper significance and greater tenacity than those systems. It is for this reason that they include in their curriculum a course of anthropology. This course is specially planned to meet the needs of workers in the Americanization field.

California has a unique method of meeting the emergency shortage of trained Americanization workers. That state has an itinerant normal school for training teachers of the foreign-born, which may prove to be only temporary after other agencies have taken up the work permanently. It is composed of a group of speakers, each a specialist on the subject which he covers, who go about from city to city in very much the same way as the Chautauqua groups cover the rural districts in the East.

In Delaware, when an Americanization campaign was launched in 1919, an emergency institute was established to train teachers quickly, providing for 26 lectures. The enrollment was 168, mostly public school teachers. The Board of Education

---
* See reference to Boston University in addendum, part 2.

announced that it would give preference for Americanization positions to those holding certificates indicating that they had completed this course. It covered four main subjects: (1) General knowledge of the field and need for Americanization work; (2) study of racial backgrounds and conditions among foreign-born groups in America; (3) how to organize Americanization work; and (4) methods of teaching English and civics and of preparing candidates for naturalization.

Akron, Ohio, has a program of teacher training which is comparatively advanced, but which covers only European backgrounds, methods of teaching English, etc., with no instruction to meet the influence of radical propaganda upon their future students. Nor do the teacher requirements call for anything beyond moral character, even the academic requirements being only high school training or its equivalent. There is a special four-weeks' institute each fall for Americanization teachers and weekly training meetings throughout the year. Also a monthly teacher's meeting is held where matters of common interest are discussed. Every two weeks meetings are held dealing with specific methods for teaching English to foreigners, and these are in charge of the General Supervisor of Instruction. The supervisor pays each Americanization teacher a classroom visit once every two weeks, observing the good points which may be used by other teachers, as well as offering suggestions.

State superintendents of education, college presidents, and principals of normal schools have made many valuable suggestions for the training of teachers, and they have also disclosed in many instances a lack of knowledge and consideration of the problems to be met. Some of their suggestions follow:

> That each curriculum for teacher training should include actual observation and visits to successful school classes conducted for the foreign born, selecting the best in the community.
>
> That all training courses include a survey of conditions in the old country, why the immigrant leaves to come here, what his causes of discontent are here and what he needs by way of training to fit him into the complex life of America.
>
> That the prospective Americanization worker be taught the difference in backgrounds of the various groups of foreigners, so that he may be able to reconcile them not only to

America but also to reconcile the groups who have brought over the old country prejudices.

That in studying racial backgrounds special attention should be given to industrial conditions in the old country — what the leading occupations in the old country are and how that affects their choosing an occupation here.

These views are the expression of a comparatively small group of educators who have given the subject of immigration and education serious thought. But the committee found that a surprisingly large number admitted that they had given the matter no thought at all. The president of one of the best known universities in the country suggested that the teaching of adult immigrants should be in experienced(!) hands and that the teacher should have a complete high school education! We cite this instance to show the need for bringing to all in the educational field a realization of the seriousness of the matter of training and selection of teachers for the foreign-born and for enlisting the support of all educators in raising the standards and the compensation for such work. From Nevada came the recommendation that the very best teachers should be reserved for training the foreign-born instead of the least desirable, as is sometimes the case in present practice. One college president is of the opinion that in selecting teachers for the foreign-born character should be 90 per cent of the consideration. Whether the importance of character can be computed mathematically is a question, but this Committee recommends that character be given first consideration. Failing to satisfy the character requirement, which includes also loyalty to the institutions of the State and Nation, no teacher should be considered for employment of any sort, least of all in the instruction of the foreign-born, no matter what his other qualifications may be. At the present time in the State of New York the only thing that insures good character in a teacher is that the state normal schools require a certificate of good character from each student upon matriculation, but all of our teachers do not come from the state normal schools, and often in the cases of those who do the guarantee is obviously inadequate.

Another argument for the careful scrutiny of the soundness of teachers is that times have changed in the methods of teaching many subjects, especially English; whereas English was formerly taught with the use of old classics, nowadays in New York City and most of the other large centers, current events are made the subject of discussion, oral and written. The teacher is looked upon as the final judge in any discussion that arises, and hence his point of view exerts tremendous influence. It has come to the attention of the Committee that in the public schools of New York City certain teachers of English have employed current radical and liberal magazines as the guide for the discussion of current events in English classes; that discussion of complex economic problems is permitted in these classes by teachers who, through lack of training, are utterly incompetent to guide or to direct such discussions along legitimate channels. It is obvious that the qualification to teach English does not fit the teacher to determine economic questions and the discussion and determination of such questions in English classes must frequently result in fixing in the pupil's mind ideas which are entirely erroneous and destructive of the purpose of public school education.

Superintendent Ettinger of the public schools has given the matter of teacher qualifications serious consideration, for he realizes that the " proper kind of teacher means the proper kind of Americanization ". The following extract from the testimony of Mr. Ettinger voices the views of this committee:

"We have at the entrance to the educational system of New York City a Board of Examiners and to this Board of Examiners is entrusted the function of giving us teachers. All of the candidates for licenses must pass through the hands of this Board of Examiners. Of course we demand evidence of citizenship. Candidates must also take the pledge of loyalty. That is about all we can do in that respect, excepting that I think the Board of Examiners could devise probably more stringent tests in order to find out whether the applicant is 100 percent American. We could have a test as to opinions, as to convictions. I know that it looks inquisitorial and open to criticism, but, after all, the teacher is the answer to this question of citizenship training throughout this entire country. A teacher who believes in that type of socialism which calls for revolution — which calls for the destruction of existing government in order to impose something which is nebulous in his own mind, upon the ruins, is not the type of teacher to have in our schools. It does not make any difference whether he is teaching arithmetic or something else, that teacher cannot sincerely teach what we require the teacher to teach in the way of obedience to government, respect for institutions, respect for the flag, and all the other patriotic observances. We have had teachers — but very few I am proud to say — among the 23,000 in New York City who thought that it did not make any difference what they said or did in the afternoon or evening on the public platform or what they wrote in the public press, provided they did not do anything overt in the classroom between 9 and 3 o'clock. Now we have stopped that, I hope, and have established the fact that a teacher is always a teacher and that everything that teacher gives utterance to after 3 o'clock is a reflex action on that classroom just as much as if he stood in front of his class."

The educational authorities of the City of New York stand together in the view that the teacher should be considered an employee in case he proves unsatisfactory. In some cases it has been necessary to discharge teachers because the views they were impressing upon their pupils were subversive of our ideals. The teacher now has the right to counsel and the right of formal procedure under the laws of evidence. He is brought before the Board of Education and in the case of an adverse decision he may appeal to the State Commissioner. Such teachers as were brought before the Board of Education had every protection of the law and some five were dismissed and their dismissals sustained by the Commissioner of Education. The educational law of the State of New York provides that such teachers shall have a hearing, and the word "hearing" has been construed by local authorities as one requiring all the laws of evidence. The New York City authorities believe that the provision which requires the observance of all the technical rules of evidence should not be required. The teacher is not being tried for a crime, he is simply having a hearing as to his fitness to represent the State of New York in the classroom. With this latter view the Committee is in accord.

After a careful review and analysis of the present mode of selecting teachers, both as to their personal qualifications and their academic attainments in this and other states, this Committee is led to the conclusion that greater emphasis must be placed first upon the character of the prospective teacher and second upon his loyalty to the institutions of both state and nation. In its preliminary report to the State Legislature, this Committee proposed a bill which in substance required every teacher now engaged in the public school system of the State of New York, and all applicants for teacher certificates, to procure a certificate of good character and of loyalty to the State. In a representative republic such as ours, it is of transcendent importance that public school teachers should possess character above reproach and should be loyal to the institutions and laws of the government they represent. The prime purpose of the public educational system is to prepare students in the public schools to assume the obligations and duties of citizenship in this State. The public school teacher is a representative and officer of the State *as it now exists*. He is employed by that State to teach loyalty to its institutions and obedience to its laws. He is not employed to explore the controversial fields of political economy with the view of championing Utopian schemes of reform or change.

In entering the public school system the teacher assumes certain obligations and must of necessity surrender some of his intellectual freedom. If he does not approve of the present social system or the structure of our government he is at liberty to entertain those ideas, but must surrender his public office. If a change in our social system or in the structure of our government is at any time demanded by the people of this State or of the United States, the mandate must be disclosed by the verdict of the polls. The public school must not be employed as a rostrum for distinctive propaganda of any character. Its teaching staff must not be allowed to spread the gospel of discontent among the people. No person who is not eager to combat the theories of social change should be entrusted with the task of fitting the young and old of this State for the responsibilities of citizenship.

Having these considerations in mind, the Committee proposed the bill known as Senate Bill No. 1275, which appears on page 29 of this report. Although at the time of writing this report some opposition appears to have developed with respect to this bill, the Committee expresses the hope that it will become the law of this State. Opposition to a law which exacts good moral character and obedience to the Constitution and laws of this State as a necessary qualification for public school teachers indicates a lack of appreciation of the function of the public school and the power of the teacher to influence his pupils for good or evil.

As we have already indicated, no matter how splendid the school building, how sound the text books and how complete the curriculum, the object of the public school system will fail unless its program is carried out by sound and loyal teachers who in their private life may serve as moral examples to their pupils.

Those who have read the introduction to this sub-section, in which this Committee has attempted to portray the problems met in immigrant education, must recognize that the task of the teacher of the foreign-born is much more difficult and complex than that confronting the teacher in the ordinary elementary schools. Different groups of aliens must be approached in different ways. As we have pointed out, the political controversies raging in their native lands affect their attitude toward this government and its institutions. The successful teacher must know and understand the reasons for these controversies and be able to explain clearly and convincingly to his pupils the reasons for our government's attitude in these questions. The teacher must be acquainted with the prejudices of his pupils against one another and to the form of government under which we live. He must be thoroughly trained in the principles and doctrines of the various radical and revolutionary movements so that he can show how they are destructive of American ideas of liberty and so that he may convince his pupils, however justifiable such ideas may have been in the countries from whence they come, that in a land where all government is founded, guided and directed by the will of the people, as expressed periodically through the exercise of the franchise, such principles and doctrines can no longer be maintained.

Methods of teaching adults must of necessity be different from those of teaching children. These considerations have convinced this Committee that a special and thorough training is necessary to fit teachers to engage in so-called Americanization work or immigrant education. While the Committee recognizes that much has been done and is being done to raise the teaching standards in this field, it is convinced that the present methods of conducting intensive courses ranging from 10 to 30 hours is wholly inadequate to fit teachers to meet the complex and intricate problems which they must face in the class-room. It is for this reason that the Committee in its preliminary report recommended a bill providing for a special training course for all teachers employed by the State or compensated in whole or in part by the State to teach foreign-born and native adults and minors over 16 years of age, which course should continue for a period of not less than one year.

The committee's intention in proposing this bill is that the term "one year" shall consist of a full academic year's training of not less than 450 hours. This bill appears upon page 33 of this report and it is the Committee's hope that it will become the law of this state.

In addition to the usual courses of study — such as American history, political and economic; American government, federal, state, municipal, county and rural; general principles of adult education; intensive training in the teaching of English to foreigners; special courses in citizenship training and naturalization; courses in current economic questions — in addition to these this Committee urges the necessity of an intensive study of political controversies in foreign countries relating to the distribution of territory between nations, and internal questions which may have a tendency to divide the alien colonies in this country into contending groups, together with a study of the attitude of the United States Government with respect to these controversies which may have a tendency to affect the loyalty of the immigrant toward this country. In such cases where the position taken by the United States Government or its failure to take any position in respect to such controversies may tend to alienate a section of an immigrant colony in America, special study should be made of the methods of appeal and explanation of the American attitude.

The Committee further recommends, in view of the fact that large numbers of immigrants have in their own country been members of or sympathetic to some revolutionary organization, and by reason of their environment have been hostile to government, that a special study of revolutionary and radical theories as represented by the different groups of aliens must be made. This involves special courses in socialism, syndicalism, communism and anarchism, with particular reference to the methods and tactics advocated by the adherents to these theories. Such course should enable the teacher to convince his pupils that these theories of government and social order have no place in America and are destructive of American ideals of liberty.

CHAPTER IV

Curricula Recommended for Courses of Citizenship Training

If competent, properly trained teachers have been provided, the success of courses in citizenship training will depend in large measure upon their curricula. In respect to this subject this Committee believes that, so far as possible, the courses should be standardized by the Federal Government co-operating with the various state commissioners of education. The details of the curriculum for citizenship training courses must be left largely to the state departments of education, but the Committee wishes to emphasize the importance of teaching American history, principles of government, and the duties and privileges of citizenship to children and to adult immigrants alike. In the case of children this instruction should be given during the years which come within the compulsory attendance laws so that no child can leave school without an appreciation of the American government and of its ideals and a thorough understanding of what its system is, so that he will recognize that our government is not fixed and immutable but that it may be changed and modified from time to time by constitutional amendment through the exercise of the ballot, to meet changing conditions and changing requirements.

The need for a knowledge of the English language on the part of every permanent resident in the United States is so generally conceded as to require no particular emphasis in this report.

The compulsory teaching of the standard branches of study in English is required in most states in public schools, but not always in private or parochial schools. Those states requiring instruction in the English language only in all schools, public, private and parochial, are Arkansas, California, Delaware, Indiana, Iowa, Kansas, Maine, Massachusetts, New Hampshire, Nebraska, New York, Oklahoma, and Oregon. Those states making it compulsory for public schools only are Arizona, Colorado, Michigan, Minnesota, Ohio, South Dakota, and Washington. The legislature of the State of Wisconsin failed to pass a bill providing that:

> "All instruction in the common schools in common school subjects shall be in the English language."

In Louisiana, where a large portion of the population is French, the law provides that the general exercises in the public schools shall be in English, provided that "the French language may be taught in those parishes or localities where the French language predominates."

In New Mexico we find a law providing for the teaching of Spanish not only to the Spanish-speaking pupils but to those of the non-Spanish-speaking pupils who wish to learn it, but we have not found any provision requiring the instruction of common school subjects in the English language.

Owing to war prejudices many of the States passed laws prohibiting the teaching of German in the schools or the conducting of classes in the German language, but since the armistice some of these laws have been repealed.

The Director of Extension Activities of the State of New York is of the opinion that citizenship training courses should include lessons in naturalization and specific help to the foreign-born to procure his preliminary and final papers. Official help from naturalization officers would be acceptable.

New York State requires that two periods of civics per week for one year be given in the high schools. In New York City this instruction is covered in a way which, theoretically at least, is effective. In these courses it is assumed that the pupil is at all times exposed to destructive criticism of our governmental activities and that he looks upon government as a repressive rather than as a helpful agency. The object of the New York City civics courses in the high schools is to set forth what the city, state and nation are actually doing for the pupils' well-being — that from the time he arises in the morning until he goes to bed at night, this help and protection is being extended. They show that the city, cooperating with the state, makes it possible for the pupil to have a pure supply of milk; that his meat supply is made healthful by the cooperation between the city, state and nation. They take up every activity of the State of New York in the same way — the water supply brought to him by the city system; and they seek to show that there is practically nothing that he does during the day that is not made possible for him by some governmental agency. It is sought to impress upon him in a manner which will be permanently fixed in his memory that he can live a healthful, happy life only because of the operation of some governmental agency. These courses are admirable if they are taught by loyal and convincing teachers.

Wisconsin suggests that instruction be given in industrial history and in state and Federal legislation affecting the industries, and also that vocational training be required of minors up to 18 years of age with eight hours of study per week during the day.

In the teaching of English by the conversational method many subjects may be covered which will give the immigrant an understanding of American customs and manners as well as of our laws and institutions. By this method the foreign-born woman may be taught the American ways of cooking, sanitation and housekeeping and other matters of vital concern in her home life. Much of the present radicalism and adherence to revolutionary theories and practice among the foreign-born is due to ignorance and misinterpretation of the principles and policies of the American government and institutions. It is to correct this situation that the Committee emphasizes the importance of thorough-going and convincing courses of citizenship training, as among the most effective means of checking the forces of disorder in this country. Patriotic training cannot begin too early with the children. The display of the flag in the schoolroom registers upon the child's mind so that the memory of it is not easily erased. The State of New York by law requires the display of the flag, which this Committee recommends should be rigidly enforced. Such laws are quite general, as are also laws providing for patriotic exercises. We quote from the New York State law as follows:

> "In order to promote the spirit of patriotic civic service and obligation and to foster in the children of the state moral and intellectual qualities which are essential in preparing to meet the obligations of citizenship, in peace or in war, the regents of the University of the State of New York shall prescribe courses of instruction in patriotism and citizenship, to be maintained and followed in all the schools of the state. The boards of education and trustees of the several cities and school districts of the state shall require instruction to be given in such courses by the teachers employed in the schools therein. All pupils attending such schools over the age of eight years shall attend upon such instruction. Similar courses of instruction shall be prescribed and maintained in the private schools of the state and all pupils in such schools over eight years of age shall attend upon such courses."

The committee recommends that this law should be rigidly enforced.

In many States the Board of Education is required to provide a flag or several flags with appropriate equipment for its display in every public school, and in some states the law provides for patriotic exercises in connection with the flag and specifies methods of saluting it.

The State of Washington requires weekly patriotic exercises part of which is the recitation by all the pupils of the salute to the flag. The states requiring and providing flags for school buildings, in addition to New York, are as follows:

Arizona, California, Colorado, Florida, Iowa, Kansas, Maryland, Massachusetts, Michigan, Minnesota, Montana, New Jersey, New Mexico, Oklahoma, Oregon, Pennsylvania, Texas, Virginia, West Virginia and Wyoming.

In South Dakota, one hour per week in every public school throughout the state is devoted to teaching patriotism, and in Pennylvania and New Jersey it is part of the duty of the State Commissioner to provide and to have incorporated in school curricula suitable courses in patriotic citizenship and patriotic exercises.

This survey, unfortunately, is not absolutely complete as some of the state laws were not available at the time of compiling this report, but it serves to show the general tendency to reach all children with patriotic ideals.

CHAPTER V

Regulated Attendance

Having determined upon a policy that the immigrant should be educated in the English language and trained in an appreciation and understanding of our government, and having discussed the necessity of selecting and training suitable teachers for this work, the next question which presents itself in providing a completely rounded program of citizenship training is how to get the foreigner to avail himself of the facilities provided.

All sorts of policies of varying degrees of stringency have been and are now being applied in the matter of attendance, from the *laissez-faire* attitude of some of the southern states, where the immigrant does not constitute a serious problem, to the legislation of the State of Utah, where the problem is not complex but where compulsory attendance is required for adults up to the age of forty-five or until attaining a knowledge of the English language equivalent to that demanded by the fifth grade of the common schools.

Much is said on both sides of the question of compulsory attendance. Most of the objections, however, are reserved for the compulsion of adults. Compulsion for minors meets little opposition except where it seems impossible to provide the facilities for their training or to enforce any laws which might be passed covering this subject. Citizens do not attain their full civil rights until the age of twenty-one so that legislators appear willing to deny them the rights of deciding upon their schooling until that age, but several instances have been brought to the attention of this Committee of the defeat of bills which have been framed to require the attendance of adults. In fact, Utah is the only state that has succeeded in passing such a law.

In pending legislation in the Federal Congress, dealing with adult immigrant education, the compulsory features have been stricken out. When compulsion is suggested in many circles great opposition is raised on the ground that it is un-American and oppressive, and that it would create suspicion in and be repulsive to many alien adults, especially to those who have suffered from coercive laws in their native land. Of course the creation of such an attitude would not depend entirely upon legislation, but upon the circumstances of its enforcement. The attitude of the teacher and attendance officers would make or mar its success.

On the other hand many educators argue that the very people who need the influence of American schools are the ones who will not attend classes unless forced to do so. Others argue that the progress which has been made among the illiterates by radical agitators would warrant educational authorities in adopting drastic compulsory measures. Still others would make continued employment contingent upon the attainment of certain educational standards.

Where the foreigner has manifested his willingness and desire to attend school by registering, there is the problem of keeping up his attendance. Lockport and Albany, New York, charge a deposit fee of two dollars and one dollar respectively, which deposit is returned if the pupil maintains a certain attendance. In Connecticut, the State gives a rebate for each pupil who maintains satisfactory attendance, thus putting the responsibility largely upon the teacher.

Virtually all educators and legislators are in favor of making good citizens of our minors, and therefore they are willing to endorse any method to keep track of the minor until he reaches the voting age, so that he will be fully qualified as a voter. But if he once becomes a voter or reaches the voting age and has successfully avoided a reasonable amount of education, the general consensus of opinion seems to be that he should be let alone, or, at least that he has the right to say whether or not he wants to learn.

The State of Delaware seems to have a sound policy in this matter: " We decided that, without settling for all time the pros and cons of ' compulsory English ' the State of Delaware had a first responsibility in providing the facilities, and that compulsion, if it came at all, might well come later, if the facilities were not used voluntarily. Such policy provides for the improving and extending of facilities to meet the present objections of foreigners who are attending the school.

Many object, and justly so, to attending a night school after a hard day's labor. Many object to the attitude of teachers, and still others are perfectly reasonable in their dissatisfaction, where they have to sit in cramped positions on seats built for the use of children. Then there is the attitude of discouragement encountered so often when pupils are herded into a class without careful attention as to the grading. It is not an easy matter to overcome these objections.

The educational authorities are confronted with a tremendous task in the establishment of factory schools, evening classes in the schools, the raising of the qualifications of teachers; providing proper school rooms and equipment, and giving individual attention to the proper grading of each pupil. When these have been done, if the foreigner still shows reluctance to accept the advantages offered to him, then compulsory methods may be considered, but by enforcing any legislation that may be adopted to compel foreigners to attend badly organized classes, taught by incompetent or uninterested teachers, in uncomfortable school rooms at inconvenient times, the result must be to breed discontent and to defeat the purpose for which it is enacted. Instead of extending compulsory education with minimum English requirements to adults in New York City, this Committtee suggests as an alternative the extension of educational facilities of a constructive, helpful and flexible character for both native and foreign-born adults, more closely related to their needs and more effectively instrumental in promoting educational interest on a voluntary basis, with, however, as large a measure of encouragement, stimulation and incentive as employers, officials, and others may exercise.

The above suggestions apply to foreigners already in this country. What should be required of the newcomers from this time on is another matter. The literacy test for entering immigrants is a Federal matter. It has been suggested that the immigrant be allowed to enter with the understanding that he must learn English within a specified time, which varies from two to six years, or be deported.

To meet the serious conditions presented by the extraordinary amount of illiteracy in New York City, the State Legislature, in 1919 passed an amendment to the General Education Law of the state relating to attendance at schools by non-English-speaking and illiterate minors. The substance of this law, now known as Section 637 of Article XXIII of the Educational Law as amended July 1, 1919, is as follows:

> "Every minor between fifteen and twenty-one years old, unable to speak, read and write the English language as is required for the completion of the fifth grade of the public or private schools of the City or school district in which he resides, shall attend some day or evening school or school

maintained by an employer, to acquire such minimum knowledge. Failing to obey this law, the minor is subject to a fine of not exceeding five dollars. Guardians or persons in control of the minor who cause him to fail to secure such minimum education are subject to a fine of not more than twenty dollars, and whoever attempts to induce such minor to absent himself from school or employs him without providing for him the minimum education, is subject to a fine of not less than fifty dollars. Employers may satisfy the requirements of the Act by maintaining schools."

Several states have limited compulsory attendance to the ages of fourteen, fifteen or sixteen. The States of Massachusetts, New Hampshire, Oregon, Rhode Island, South Dakota, Wisconsin, Wyoming, and New York, have extended such compulsory attendance requirements in respect to a minimum knowledge of English, to persons up to twenty-one years. The States of Maine, Colorado and Ohio, are now considering the extension of compulsory attendance in like manner. Illiterate minors may be compelled to secure a minimum ability to understand, read, write, and speak the English language in these states. There is a general consensus of opinion that every person reaching the voting age in New York State at least should have the minimum ability to use our language to exercise intelligently the right of franchise. The responsibility for carrying out the intent of the Legislature in this respect has been placed upon the educational authorities. Test cases have been brought in New York State to establish the constitutionality of the law, to determine procedure and to develop ways and means by which the intent and purpose of the law shall be carried out. It must be recognized, however, that public educational authorities are already burdened with responsibility in securing conformity to the general compulsory attendance law for children in the state, and that the new educational requirements for minors places added burdens upon the public educational agencies for which adequate provisions must yet be made.

This Committee approves the compulsory attendance law for minors up to the age of 21 and urges the Department of Education and the other school authorities of the state to do their utmost to see that the intent of this law is fulfilled. This is an imperative necessity in New York State where it is estimated that possibly 400,000 persons in the state are illiterate not only in English but even in their own language.

In every state of the United States there is legislation provided for the compulsory school attendance of children between certain ages. In the majority of states all children between the ages of seven and fourteen years inclusive are required to attend, for the full term, a public or other authorized school unless entitled to some specific exemption. Children between fourteen and sixteen years of age, unless they have graduated from the grammar schools or are engaged in some regular, useful and gainful employment, are compelled to attend part-time schools or extension classes. In Virginia the age limit is particularly low, making school attendance compulsory only for children between the ages of eight and twelve years, while in several other states all children between the ages of sixteen and twenty-one years, who have not completed an education at least equivalent to the standard fifth grade of grammar school, are required to attend night school or continuation school for at least eight hours a week for the full school session. Some of the more progressive states, notably Maine, Massachusetts, and Rhode Island have not only provided for the establishment of night classes in vocational training, citizenship, Americanization, etc., but also in order to encourage extension classes, make reimbursement up to seventy-five to one hundred percent of the cost to all boards successfully operating a school of this kind.

More than half the states have compulsory attendance for minors below fourteen years of age, and compulsory part-time attendance for minors between fourteen and sixteen years of age. The states requiring such attendance are Alabama, Arkansas, Arizona, California, Colorado, Delaware, Florida, Iowa, Indiana, Kansas, Kentucky, Minnesota, Missouri, Nebraska, Nevada, New Jersey, New Mexico, Oklahoma, Pennsylvania, Tennessee, Washington, and West Virginia.

The states which require attendance of minors only up to the age of fourteen years are Georgia, Maryland, Mississippi, Montana, North Carolina, and Texas.

Virginia requires the attendance between the ages of eight and twelve years and North Dakota between eight and fifteen years. The states making attendance compulsory up to eighteen years, are Illinois, Louisiana, Oklahoma, and Nevada. A few, as previously pointed out, provide compulsory attendance for minors over sixteen years of age and up to twenty-one years. These states are Massachusetts, New Hampshire, New York, Rhode Island, Wisconsin, Wyoming.

The Assistant Director of Attendance of the New York City Public Schools stated to this Committee that it has been impossible thus far to enforce the law requiring instruction in English for minors between sixteen and twenty-one years, but he believes that it should be enforced.

Many states provide for the establishment of continuation schools upon the request of a specified number of residents or at the discretion of the local board, which are free, but not compulsory to persons above the standard school age.

Massachusetts has a comprehensive program for the education of persons over twenty-one years of age. A state commissioner has been appointed in Mississippi under a state law for the purpose of investigating illiteracy throughout the state, making recommendations and taking such measures as will in his opinion contribute to the elimination of illiteracy in the state, while Iowa shows recognition of the special needs of that state by organizing special schools for miners in the great mining camps, similar to those organized throughout New York State in factories and other industries.

CHAPTER VI

Appropriations

The universal handicaps to Americanization work, as reported to the Committee, are lack of competent teachers, and lack of sufficient funds, the former, of course, depending largely upon the latter for rectification. While the appropriation for citizenship training in New York State should be decided entirely upon the exigencies of the situation, still it is of interest to compare it with the appropriations of some of the other states. Although its funds for immigrant education exceed those in other states in actual amount, the per capita allowance for this work is still far too low even to carry on the work under present programs, to say nothing of raising the standards for teachers.

Arizona has no public funds for Americanization although private funds are contributed for some citizenship training work. A bill was presented to the Legislature calling for an appropriation for 1919, but it was defeated because of a compulsory clause which it carried. This was especially disappointing, in view of the fact that they had an appropriation of $25,000 for 1918. The State of Texas also failed to pass a bill for an appropriation, leaving the state without funds for this work.

Wyoming is doing what it can on a "small appropriation." North Dakota has $7,000 as state aid for evening schools, out of which must come whatever is spent upon adult immigrants. The New Jersey budget for 1918 shows an expenditure of $9,639.59 for citizenship training.

Delaware succeeded in getting $15,000 a year for 1919 and 1920, but it was after a struggle dating back to 1916 when Wilmington asked the local Board of Education for $1,500 to continue Americanization classes which had already been established and run on public subscription. Delaware therefore recommends that where public funds are not forthcoming for Americanization work, the enterprise should be underwritten. For, while public moneys are the logical funds for the education of the adult foreign-born, experiments can rarely be enacted into law or official policy until their wisdom is demonstrated; and therefore private funds for these experiments are often the most direct means to secure ultimately public support and public funds.

Minnesota, Ohio and Utah have an appropriation of $25,000 each, and each claims that the amount is inadequate. This is particularly unfortunate in the case of Utah where the funds were appropriated to carry out special legislation providing for the compulsory education of non-English-speaking adults up to the age of forty-five. These sums may not cover even so much work as would at first appear, if we may assume that their problems are similar to those of Connecticut. Connecticut has $25,000 a year for two years for Americanization work, but $11,000 of this amount must be expended each year for " office and departmental expenses," leaving only $14,000 for " local assistance." The evening school appropriation in Connecticut is more satisfactory, however. They have $4.00 for each pupil in average attendance for 75 sessions, as against $2.25 for last year.

It is the opinion of the Committee that local public educational authorities should have adequate resources for the establishment and development of evening schools and for such other extension education for adults as may be necessary and that local school districts should be permitted to receive such financial cooperation from local groups wishing to assist the respective boards of education in developing adequate educational facilities, as they may wish to offer. State aid should be provided where it is deemed advisable and possible with the funds placed at the disposal of the Board of Regents, especially for efforts in the field of adult education.

The President of the Board of Education of New York City believes that the machinery of the present system is adequate to handle the problem of Americanization, and that the only thing lacking is appropriation. He suggests that the State appropriate $1,000,000 for Americanization work in the City of New York. He believes that while most of the immigrants are concentrated in New York City, the training and educating of them should not be a local financial burden and that the State would thus be justified in making adequate appropriation to handle the situation properly. For 1920 the State of New York contributed $30,000 for Americanization work in New York City, which is hardly enough to take care of one assembly district. The Board of Education is spending $300,000 in Americanization work, which it knows to be inadequate.

The Committee urges the passage of such legislative appropriations as may be needed this year and in subsequent years to provide special teachers and supervisors for the field of evening school and adult education, as well as to provide for the necessary persons to train the teachers and supervisors for this work.

The Committee wishes here to express approval of the so-called Kenyon bill now pending in Congress, which seeks to allot funds to the several states on the basis of their illiterate population, said funds being made available through the Federal Bureau of Education in proportion to the efforts and expenditures of the several state departments of education and the several school districts of the various states, for the purpose of eradicating illiteracy and promoting the use of English.

SECTION III

SUB-SECTION II

CITIZENSHIP TRAINING — THE UNITED STATES GOVERNMENT

Chapter I. Legislation 2361
        II. Americanization Programs 2366
            1. Americanization Conference 2366
            2. United States Chamber of Commerce................ 2406

This section of the report gives a detailed statement of the activities of various agencies, public and private, engaged in the work of immigrant education and citizenship training throughout the United States, and particularly in the State of New York.

The data here presented is the result of a survey made by the Committee to discover what is being done by various agencies, public and private, throughout the country to counteract radical propaganda by constructive work, both directly and indirectly.

CHAPTER I
Legislation

No. 3315.

(Report No 276.)

IN THE SENATE OF THE UNITED STATES.

October 22 (calendar day, October 27), 1919.

Mr. KENYON, from the Committee on Education and Labor, reported the following bill, which was read twice and placed on the calendar.

A BILL.

To Promote Americanization by Providing for Co-operation with the Several States in the Education of Non-English-Speaking Persons and the Assimilation of Foreign-Born Residents, and for Other Purposes.

Be it Enacted by the Senate and House of Representatives of the United States of America in Congress assembled,

That the Secretary of the Interior, through the Bureau of Education, is hereby authorized and directed to co-operate with the several states in the education of illiterates or other persons unable to understand, speak, read, or write the English language and with the territories and possessions of the United States, except the Phillippine Islands, in the education of illiterates.

§ 2. That for the purpose of co-operating with the several states in the education of illiterates or other persons unable to understand, speak, read, or write the English language there is hereby appropriated, out of any money in the Treasury not otherwise appropriated, for the fiscal year ending June 30, 1920, $5,000,000, and annually thereafter until the end of the fiscal year ending June 30, 1923, the sum of $12,500,000 and an additional sum equal to the balance unexpended of the appropriation herein provided for the last preceding fiscal year.

§ 3. That of the amount appropriated by section 2 for any fiscal year, $500,000 may be deducted and used for the publication of periodicals devoted to Americanization problems; for aiding in the correlation of aims and work carried on by local bodies, private individuals, and organizations; for studies and reports through the Bureau of Education; for salaries and necessary traveling expenses of officers, assistants, and other employees in the District of Columbia, or elsewhere, as the board may deem necessary; and for all other necessary expenses connected with the administration of this Act during such fiscal year.

§ 4. That the balance of the amount appropriated by section 2 remaining after making the deduction authorized by section 3 shall, for each fiscal year, be apportioned by the Secretary of the Interior, among and allotted to the several states in the ratio which the number of resident illiterates and other persons unable to understand, speak, read or write the English language, sixteen years of age and over, bears to the number of resident illiterates and other persons unable to understand, speak, read, or write the English language, sixteen years of age and over within continental United States, exclusive of the District of Columbia, and the Territory of Alaska, according to the last published United States census;

Provided, That the total sum allotted to any state shall not be less than $5,000 for any fiscal year.

§ 5. That no money shall be paid to a state until it shall through its legislature —

(a) Accept the provisions of this Act;

(b) Designate an appropriate official to act as custodian of such money;

(c) Authorize its department of education or chief school officer to co-operate with the United States in the work herein authorized;

(d) Appropriate or make available for the purposes of this Act an amount equal to that allotted to the state by the United States;

(e) Require, under penalty, all residents who are citizens of the United States, sixteen years of age or over and under twenty-one years of age, and all residents of more than six months who are aliens, sixteen years of age or over and under forty-five years of age, who are illiterate or unable to understand, speak, read, or write the English language, to attend classes of instruction for not less than 200 hours per annum until they shall have completed a specified course approved by the Secretary of the Interior;

(f) Provided, as far as possible, subject to the approval of the Secretary of the Interior, for the education of residents who are citizens of the United States of the age of twenty-one years or more or resident aliens of the age of forty-five years or more who are illiterate or unable to understand, speak, read, or write the English language;

(g) Require the preparation and submission to the Secretary of the Interior, annually, of rules and regulations designed to enforce the provisions of such State laws and the rules and regulations of the Secretary of the Interior;

(h) Require the submission annually to the Secretary of the Interior a report which shall show (1) plan for administration and supervision, (2) courses of study, (3) methods and kind of instruction, (4) equipment, (5) qualifications of teachers, supervisors, directors of education, and other necessary administrative officers or employees, (6) plans for the preparation of teachers, supervisors, or directors of education, and (7) receipts and expenditures of money for the preceding fiscal year.

Provided, That if the governor of any state, the legislature of which does not convene before the year 1921, shall accept the provisions of this Act and cause such co-operation with the Secretary of the Interior as herein provided, such state shall be entitled to the benefits of this Act, and the Secretary of the Interior may cause to be expended in such state, until the legislature of such state convenes and has been in session sixty days, so much of the sums allotted to that state for the fiscal year as he may determine necessary for the purpose of this Act: *And further provided*: That any appropriation or donation by a county, municipality, local authority, school, corporation, partnership, society or individual available for the purposes of this Act under the direction of the state board of education or chief school officer of the state may be accepted by the Secretary of the Interior as an appropriation by the state.

§ 6. That none of the sums herein appropriated, or appropriated or made available by or in any of the states, territories or possessions to carry out the provisions of this Act shall be used for the education of persons of less than sixteen years of age, or, except as provided by section 3, for any purpose other than the payment of salaries of teachers, supervisors, or directors of education, or for the preparation of teachers, supervisors, and directors of education.

§ 7. That the Secretary of the Interior shall (a) withhold the unpaid portion of an allotment to any state whenever he determines that any portion of the sums allotted are not being applied for the purposes of this Act, or may (b) deduct from the next succeeding allotment to any state a sum equal to that portion of the previous allotment paid to the state and which he determines has not been expended for the purposes of this act: *Provided*, That no such deduction shall be made until one year after the opening of the first legislative session convened in such state after the passage of this act.

§ 8. That any portion of an allotment to any state which remains unpaid at the end of a fiscal year shall be treated as an unexpended balance of the appropriation of that year.

§ 9. That the Secretary of the Interior shall annually ascertain whether the several states are using or are prepared to use the money allotted to or received by them under this Act, and shall certify, on or before the tenth day of August of each year, to the Secretary of the Treasury (a) each state which has accepted the provisions of this act and complied therewith; (b) the amount which each state is entitled to receive.

§ 10. That the Secretary of the Treasury upon the certification of the Secretary of the Interior shall pay on the 15th of August, November, February and May of each year to the custodian of such sums in each state the money to which it is entitled under the provisions of this Act. The money so received by the state shall be paid out on the requisition of the department of education or chief school officer for services already rendered or expenditures already incurred and approved by such department or officer.

§ 11. That the Secretary of the Interior shall make such rules and regulations as may be necessary to carry out the purposes of this Act, and may co-operate with any department or agency of the government and request such agencies to co-operate with him and with the several states.

§ 12. That the Secretary of the Interior shall make a report to Congress before December 1st of each year of all operations, expenditures, and allotments under the provisions of this Act, and shall include therein the reports made by the several states on the administration of this Act and the expenditure of money alloted.

CALENDAR No. 234

66th Congress, 1st Session — **SENATE** — Report No. 276

AMERICANIZATION OF ALIENS

Mr. KENYON, from the Committee on Education and Labor, submitted the following

REPORT

(To accompany S. 3315)

The Committee on Education and Labor unanimously support S. 3315. The purpose of the bill is to consider a program of Americanizing illiterates and those unable to speak, read, or write the English language. The theory of the bill is the process of stimulating the states to adopt certain compulsory teaching of English to illiterates and to that great body of those in this country who can not speak, read, or write the English language. The money appropriated is apportioned by the Secretary of the Interior among the several states in the ratio provided by the bill but is not turned over to any state unless the state provides for the teaching of English at least 200 hours per annum to all residents who are citizens of the United States sixteen years of age or over and under twenty-one, and all residents of more than six months who are aliens sixteen years of age or over and under forty-five. When we realize that there are practically 8,000,000 people in this country above ten years of age who cannot speak our language, the seriousness of the problem is apparent. This will be the first step in correcting this situation.

Under date of April 5, 1920, Senator Kenyon wrote the Committee as follows:

"The Americanization Bill has passed the Senate and is in the House Committee on Education. It seems to be held up there."

CHAPTER II
Americanization Programs

1. AMERICANIZATION CONFERENCE

Extract from "Americanization" for June 1, 1919, published monthly by the Department of the Interior, Bureau of Education, Americanization Division:

"With a program embracing the educational, racial, industrial, and social aspects of a nation-wide Americanization movement, several hundred men and women from all sections of the country spent four days in Washington, May 12–15, comparing methods, ideas, and experiences used in their work among the foreign-born elements of the population. The gathering assembled in response to the invitation issued by the Bureau of Education, Department of the Interior, to specialists and workers in Americanization to get together and contribute their knowledge to the government toward the working out of a nation-wide program for the assimilation of this foreign-born element."

CONFERENCE SUPPLEMENT TO AMERICANIZATION
WHAT THE CONFERENCE DEVELOPED ABOUT AMERICANIZATION
WASHINGTON, D. C., *June* 1, 1919.

DIGEST OF PROGRAM ADDRESSES MADE BEFORE CONFERENCE OF AMERICANIZATION SPECIALISTS AND WORKERS HELD IN WASHINGTON MAY 12TH–15TH

Such abstracts of those papers presented to the Conference of Americanization specialists and workers held in Washington May 12–15 under the auspices of the Department of the Interior which are herewith given cannot pretend to include the full thought of the speaker. These digests were made for those who could not journey to Washington to enjoy the sessions but who may be helped by a general resume of the thought expressed at that gathering.

Purposes of the Conference
FRED C. BUTLER, *Director of Americanization*

We now find ourselves facing the future with a nation fully aroused to the importance of a real Americanization and eager to undertake the work. Calls now coming to the Americanization Division say, "We are ready for work. Just how shall we go about it?" It was to answer this question that this conference was called. No man is wise enough to lay out a program for Americanization and set forth the exact ways in which this great task can be done. We felt that this must come out of the valuable lessons you men and women have learned who have been doing this work for many years past.

The opinions crystallized here will be made the basis of our plans and subjects for special bulletins. The proceedings may possibly be issued in full and made available to you at once for such help as you can get from them.

The war has left us no greater task than that of bringing into full fellowship those among us who were born in other lands. That this must be done sympathetically and with a broad and tolerant understanding goes without saying. It is everywhere recognized that any real program of Americanization must take into consideration the shortcomings of us of native birth if we are to build a true and enduring democracy. We can succeed only if we approach our task with hearts beating in sympathy with the needs of our fellow men, with a vision unclouded by the hates and passions of war, "with charity toward all and malice toward none." Unless we are ourselves convinced that these people from other lands are desirable, potential Americans, that we need them here, that they come not with empty hands but with arts, crafts, sciences, music, and ideals which will add to the wealth of our common heritage, unless we feel that to us is given not so much a duty as a great opportunity, we shall fail. For ours is first of all a human problem.

To those who gave up their hearthstones, their homeland, the ties of love and consanguinity to begin life anew in a strange land, speaking a strange tongue, we are to interpret America.

Education in Americanization

PHILANDER P. CLAXTON, *Commissioner of Education*

Education is the fundamental thing in Americanization and of the elements comprising this fundamental, the first is instruction in the English language. This tongue is the common means of expression — the literature, the statutes, state and national constitutions, the newspapers, the very signs of instruction and warning being printed in English. Without a knowledge of the language no one can ever begin to know the American people and American ideals.

It is not a part of my duty here at this conference to indicate just how this should be done, but first it must be done for the children who come from other countries. We compel parents and guardians to send their children to school that the children may not be deprived of the opportunity offered by the state and that the state may not be cheated out of the product of good citizenship. We must require that the schools to which children are permitted to go in lieu of attendance in the public schools shall teach the things which the public schools are teaching. They shall all teach English. There is the problem of teaching the grown up man and woman who have reached the age when it is not easy for them to learn a new language.

The second element of the fundamental is giving the newcomers a knowledge of this country. The growth of the United States has been dramatic and phenomenal. This is a story worth knowing, and in some way we must get into the minds and hearts and into the ways of these people who have come from other shores that they may know what America means and that ideal of freedom for which we have been willing to fight.

These new people coming now with much the same spirit that brought our earliest settlers to America, from the great middle classes, as we are, all of us, and we have confidence in their ability and in the strength of their good right arms. In making them into Americans, we shall ourselves learn more of the spirit of America and broaden our own ideals and enrich our own material and æsthetic lives. It is in this spirit that we shall work with your co-operation on this program of education of the ten or twelve million people who need our help in this regard.

Best Technical Methods of Teaching English to the Foreign Born

CHARLES F. TOWNE, *Director of Immigrant Education, Massachusetts*

There is a natural tendency on the part of both teachers and pupils to rely on the printed pages as the instrument by which to teach language.

Experience has demonstrated that this is a fallacy. Spoken language is not learned through the eye. Consequently our teaching procedure should place oral instruction and practice in speaking ahead of instruction in reading. Pupils should first be taught the meaning of the theme through the devices of action, gesture, play of features, inflection of the voice, together with the use of objects and pictures. They should learn to voice each sentence through imitation and repetition until they are able to repeat the complete theme or that portion of the theme that serves for the lesson. The teacher should then print or write the first sentence on the board, where there should be more drill in associating the symbols with the sounds and their meanings. The remaining sentences should also be treated in this way, and only after the pupils are able to understand and speak the complete theme and to read it from the board should they be permitted to practice reading from printed page.

A comprehensive, direct method emphasizes the use of language in understanding and speaking as the features of most practical value to the foreign born. It aims to make English the language of the classroom because of its value in the training of the ear of the pupil. It holds to the sentence as the unit of thought and discounts the learning of disconnected word lists. By the arrangement of the sentences according to time sequence it assists the memory of the pupil, and by the orderly introduction of the variants it covers the field of grammar in practical fashion without resort to abstract rules and definitions. By concert work it relieves bashful pupils from embarrassment and keeps each one interested and alert. By separating the phonic drills from the reading period it maintains the continuity of the reading exercise. It can be used by any teacher with any class, and by thoroughness of organization it can be made effective in the hands of the inexperienced as well as in the hands of the well-trained and experienced. By choice of material every lesson may not only be made a lesson in English, but also a lesson in Americanization and so aid in advancing the pupil one more step along the road toward loyal American citizenship.

The Phonograph in Americanization

W. A. WILLSON, *Educational Department, Columbia Graphophone Company*

If we are to transfer our foreign communities into American communities we must create in them and around them an American atmosphere. In the accomplishment of this the influence of the phonograph is second to none. We have in the phonograph a means of spreading American ideals and standards in every home. In connection with the keeping vivid the home impressions made upon the child of foreign-born parentage at the public school, the phonograph plays a real part as the child accustomed to it at school will usually find a way to have the instrument brought into the home, where the process of making real Americans is continued.

The phonograph system of language instruction enables the student to learn the language in his home in spare moments and without the presence of a living teacher. A lesson may be reviewed a hundred times and correct pronunciation is mastered by hearing the teacher's voice repeat the sound again and again. The benefits to be conferred upon the non-English speaking population of the country through this widespread introduction of this new method of teaching cannot be overestimated. This method not only gives ability to speak and understand a language through a trained organ of hearing and mind, but also gives ability to read and write, for while the student is listening to the English record he is also reading the sentences in his textbook and becoming familiar with the general structure of the language.

Using the Stereopticon for Teaching English to the Foreign Born

H. D. RICKARD, *Putman School, Syracuse, N. Y.*

If a teacher could apply individual instruction methods to each pupil in a class of forty, all at the same time, his work is inexpensive, efficient, and practical. We try to keep all the pupils in the rooms working all the time instead of working with one individual out of a class of forty, by the use of the stereopticon slide. It has been found that three-fourths of the foreign born who begin the study of English need objective work at the start. The slides take the place of the real object, such as the table, the door, or the girl, and provide the connecting link between the written word and the object.

As a device for keeping up the interest, the stereopticon has unlimited possibilities. It affords a rest period both from the glare of the room lights and the pupils' posture. From an economic standpoint it would be cheaper to use the slide all the time the lesson is going on, for when the one bulb in the lantern is burning, the other dozen are not; and instead of being scattered, the attention of the entire class is concentrated upon the slide.

It seems to me that a very economical use of public money could be made in preparing a series of slides suitable for Americanization work and then loan them to the schools having such classes. Then, if a book could be prepared to be put in the hands of the pupils with illustrations and lessons, numbered to correspond with the lessons on the slides, the work would be put on a convenient, compact, and permanent basis for review and future reference. Civil government could be taught in this way, too.

Using Periodicals in Schools

WILLIAM MCANDREW, *Assistant Superintendent of Public Schools, New York City*

What changed thirteen colonies from British people into the American Nation? If you will look back into history you will see that the means to arouse the country was the periodical press. If this was the means effective in 1760 and in 1860, it bids fair to be the means used in 1960, and will be the channel through which ideals and ideas of Americanism are to be spread and perpetuated.

Last week, in response to an inquiry addressed to 246 school superintendents as to what they were doing to take advantage of the great awakening that has come from the war, it was learned that 226 of them are using periodical literature as a school exercise. This 91 percent, use the periodicals for one period a week. In view of the fact that they have from nineteen to twenty-five periods of other studies, five periods devoted to Latin and five periods devoted to algebra, this is a small percentage of time allotted for such work. Can you tell me any subject which, minute for minute, is more productive of thought in regard to the problems of Americanism than the study of the problems as they are presented by the weekly text-books which everybody out of school is using?

When the magazine comes in I do not hold it and prepare a lesson, but everybody takes his lesson home and spends an hour reading articles of his own selection preparatory to discussing them in class next day. The pupil is then in the position of being ready to serve those who have not read those particular articles with what knowledge he has gained and his own opinions.

Reorganization of Education Facilities for Americanization

F. V. THOMPSON, *Superintendent of Schools, Boston, Mass.*

I want to begin by emphasizing the thing which I wish to conclude with, that we need more adequate legislation and increased funds. We might just as well cease talking about the problem of Americanization unless we are disposed to face this issue. This period of stimulation, general interest and propaganda needs to be capitalized now before reaction sets in.

Education for citizenship is a public matter. It is undignified for a great nation or a great state to depend upon private enterprise for this most important matter before the nation. Knowing as I do from my experience with night schools, the limitations of the evening schools, I would like to set up an institution to be known as a daytime immigrant school. It would be a sort of holding corporation for the various devices which our recent experience has shown are proper and effective. It would have an organization to set up for full-time performance with a director and expert at the head of it. It can be the parent school for the factory-class teacher — and I am one who believes the factory class should be under the supervision of the public-school system. There would be evening classes for those who wished them, also.

In this problem of education there are three partners, the nation, the state, and the community. Each should bear the expense equally. The community has to operate the scheme, the state co-operating with it, and the nation co-operating with the state. In none of our communities where public moneys are being expended for evening school instruction — using that term as synonymous with Americanization — is the amount expended more than 1 percent of the school budget. We are spending in less than half of the communities, less than 1 percent of the public moneys for the immigrant at this moment. The education of immigrants has been thrown consequently into all sorts of private agencies, all of them well-meaning but some of them very dangerous from the standpoint of public expediency.

The Social Unit Experiment

WILBUR C. PHILLIPS, *Executive, Social Unit Organization, Cincinnati, Ohio*

The social unit experiment is being carried out in Cincinnati because that city was successful out of sixteen which competed with each other, in offering the most hearty backing and support for the idea of socializing a community. It started in a district of 15,000 people, which of several competing districts evinced the most sincere interest. About 3,200 people and 26 organizations signed the petition to the National Social Unit Organization to enter the district. An organization of 205 local people, who had banded together of their own initiative, undertook the organization extension. In each of the thirty-one blocks composing the district, a temporary committee of citizens was named with a temporary block executive having about 100 families in charge.

This year, in January, these temporary appointees were duly elected on the preferential ballot system. These block executives, who are mainly women because they have the daytime in which to become acquainted with their blocks, make up the popular chamber or the neighborhood legislature. We have a skilled chamber which is made up of representatives of the occupational groups. All occupations have not been organized, the experiments having been made with the doctors, nurses, and professional men. The thirty-one executives from the blocks have elected an executive of their own and they in turn represent thirty-one block councils. The nine skilled executives have elected an executive of their own. One of the features of this plan is the responsible executive, there being three who made a sort of commission form of government. The job of the executive is to keep in close accord with members of his committee, getting their viewpoints and opinions and after a program is once decided upon, setting to work to execute it.

Industrial Co-operation

Mrs. J. E. Owen Phillips, *Chamber of Commerce, Kalamazoo, Mich.*

Kalamazoo's plan as it is being broadened from the local industries to the whole community is purely a tentative one, an experiment in fact. We do not know whether or not it is going to succeed for we find that the great educational process of Americanization is needed for the manufacturer, for the employer, and for the citizens as a whole, as well as for the foreign-born worker. We wish to draw all of these together in a wide educational propaganda.

Some few months ago a group of manufacturers in the Chamber of Commerce at Kalamazoo decided to try to work out a plan along democratic American lines to make the people realize that in this country we are all brothers in a practical, definite way. My husband and I went up there to put into practice a plan we had thought out for such a purpose. We formed in each of the ten factories a good fellowship league, with a shop committee in each one of them. These are composed of seven persons of both sexes and were to be the point of contact between the central Good Fellowship League and the individual factories. They were elected by the workers and represented the managerial end as well as the workers' element. We are hoping to form a central industrial board in Kalamazoo and to include on it representatives of the general public, because in the industrial troubles the public is the sufferer. Efficiency talks have been given at the weekly factory meetings. We have used the auditorium in the Chamber of Commerce for activities and we have had dances, smokes, and gatherings of all kinds. We now have a shop paper, which has grown rapidly.

Co-Ordinating a Community

MRS. MARGARET LONG, *National Catholic War Council*

Can a modern American city suffering from the grave maladies, normally induced by sudden and critical industrial expansion and congestion, outgrow its growing pains and recover robust health? If co-ordination of all the forces within the command of a sick community is a remedy in one city suffering as East St. Louis has suffered, it should prove a remedy in most if not all cities.

The first field selected by the Federal Government as a demonstration project of the force of concentrated effort in the big drive for higher citizenship was East St. Louis. It was chosen because overnight it sprang from a normal city into a great industrial center with peoples pouring in from every section of this country and Europe.

The key to the co-ordination plan is the War Civics Committee. It was originally headed up in the community organization branch of the industrial section of the Ordnance Department. It is now headed in the office of Dean Keppel, Third Assistant Secretary of War, with joint responsibility to Fred C. Butler, Director of Americanization, Bureau of Education. A paid staff of workers and specialists execute the plans and the committee counts for counsel on a general committee of fifty, an executive committee of nine and subcommittees chosen from local representative men and women who give a great amount of volunteer service. The total membership of the subcommittee is about 300.

The function of the Civic Committee is to be compared with that of a central planning division in a business concern. It promotes, stimulates, develops, and co-ordinates social agencies. A fund of $184,000 was subscribed by the industries and businesses of the city to cover overhead expenses for three years.

Trained Teachers Greatest Need

W. C. SMITH, *State Supervisor of Immigrant Education for New York*

Americanization's supreme task in the field of education is the raising up of a body of trained teachers and workers who know the needs of the foreign-born students and how to meet these needs in method, technique, and measureable results. Until the state and nation places the work of properly trained teachers upon such a professional basis that it will command a sufficient financial return to induce the gifted to enter the work the results must suffer.

Any course for the training of teachers for English must furnish to the worker:

(1) A background of the histories, causes of immigration distribution in this country and effect on Americans of the foreign-born people.

(2) Actual contact with the foreign-born student or some other effective means for gaining a sympathetic attitude.

(3) Latest information concerning best methods and texts available from Americanization workers everywhere.

(4) Formation of a workable program.

(5) Comparison of texts as to various points of strength and weakness.

(6) Knowledge of the immigrants' needs in civics and citizenship.

The New York State policy of trained teachers was enacted into law in 1918 and courses embodying the points maintained in this paper were carried on in various parts of the state, training 2,700 teachers at a cost of about $20,000. About 60 percent of these courses were made up of teachers engaged in the work, and the remaining were volunteers and social workers. Thirty hours' work was required; credits and preferences were given by many cities, notably New York, Rochester, Syracuse and Buffalo.

Definite research on a wide range of subjects, from the problems of the evening school to a comparative study of the alien woman in America, was required, and an examination on the covered subjects given at the close.

Training Teachers for the Industries
C. C. DE WITT, *Ford Motor Co., Detroit, Mich.*

When industries wake up to the fact that their plants are full of potential teachers and are willing to give recognition to their talent, then our Americanization problem will practically have been solved, for it takes only a short time to teach the American language with a broad knowledge of civil government, which is one of the many by-products given with a well-outlined course. I most vigorously hold to the principle of a laid-down course and the teacher trained to follow it. There are several advantages in using the industrial teacher, because teacher and student have so many things in common. He works for the same employer the same hours, and has the same environment. Then, too, he comes in contact with his students in the shop when the class is not in session.

Once industry discovers how easy it is, every plant in the country will have its Americanization school, furnished with its own equipment and taught by leaders found under the roof of its own concern. The Ford English School uses the volunteer teacher system, and I have found that it is not necessary to have such teachers work overtime. They can be taken from their place at work at regular periods for classes, thus giving them a change and raising their prestige with the departments. These teachers are recruited from men who are natural-born leaders of other men, and they are trained in Americanization before being assigned to a class.

Training Public School Teachers for the Work
JOHN J. MAHONEY, *State Normal College, Lowell, Mass.*

About six months ago the Americanization study of the Carnegie Foundation found that only 34 per cent. of all teachers in Americanization work were trained and that 78 percent of this number were in the New England states. This does not include cities such as New York, Boston, Cleveland, and Buffalo, who did not report in the questionnaire, and 75 percent of these superintendents who replied expressed a preference for properly trained teachers.

We are barely beginning to break ground in the important task of training teachers in the Americanization work as a life vocation or the retraining of public school teachers for this work. Generally speaking, normal schools which train for all work below the high-school grades are not yet training teachers for Americanization work. The situation is improving, but considering the size of our task, our attempts to prepare for it through teacher training are as yet pitifully inadequate. There is grave danger that some of the institutions will offer courses conducted by people who never taught immigrants or had first hand contact with them. No teacher can be a first-class instructor without that knowledge. Sociology, with all its connections, should be a part of the training of Americanization teachers, for this work is a highly specialized one.

The most important thought that I can give you here is that persons trained to be Americanization teachers should have a course of lectures, reports, and discussions intended to put Americanism into Americanization. Teachers must know the social, political and industrial aspects of American democracy before they can aid others to become real Americans, and in my experience all teachers did not give evidence of knowing these things. They must understand that this is a government of the people, by the people, for the people; that this country has no aristocracy save that of worth and fineness of spirit; and that the doctrine of the economic "square deal" points the way to the enduring happiness of society as a whole.

Using the Schools at Scranton

S. E. WEBER, *Superintendent of Schools, Scranton, Pa.*

Scranton conducted a survey of its local non-English speaking industrial workers and learned that six out of every ten of these men had made no attempt to become citizens, that more than 70 per cent of this unnaturalized element had been in this country for twelve years, and that over one-half of them were wholly illiterate in any language. In view of this situation the board of education gave the superintendent of schools full authority to open as many classes as the demand warranted. Every coal operator and mine superintendent in the district was invited to co-operate and every employer of non-English-speaking labor did so. Classes were begun at once, and after the men are once enrolled, the question of holding their interest rests jointly on the school authorities and the employer. An entrance fee of $1 is charged each man, this being refunded if he attends 70 percent of the sessions.

Our teachers are carefully selected from our regular teaching force and are kept on the job as long as they demonstrate their ability to hold their students. Employers take cognizance of the efforts of their employees to study. Classes were opened for the women, and active assistance has been given by the Catholic priests.

Training Home Teachers

Miss Harriet P. Dow, *Yorkville Neighborhood Association, New York City*

Much must be made over the work that individuals can do in Americanization through volunteer service, because just now work in the homes of the foreign-born women is altogether an individual effort. Club women throughout the land who are busy making up their programs for the next winter's study can be urged to put into these programs more of the vital need of women to work with foreign women until they feel the appeal and volunteer to do it. Having recruited volunteers, how will we train them? We should train them through definite instruction. They should be taught all the materials at hand available for use in their work in the homes, and this can best be taught by people who have traveled the road before.

These instructors need to know the environment of the foreign people among whom they are to send their volunteers. They need to know more of the foreign-born woman's church, more of the practical help that the foreign-born man can give to the work. The foreign store where the woman trades is one of the greatest sources of help in knowing the real foreign situation. The doctors and nurses have the straight road to the foreign-born woman's heart. There should ever be an attitude of trying to get the foreign woman's viewpoint. We have all heard of the woman who sewed on her children's underwear in the fall and did not take them off until spring. But did we stop to think that coming from Italy, this woman did the most natural thing she could think of to protect the bodies of her children against what to her is an unusually rigorous winter? Every worker should be required to make one actual contact with a foreign-born woman before she is qualified to be a home teacher, and she should make this through her own efforts.

Using the Schoolhouses

H. H. GOLDERBERG, *Columbia University, New York City*

Only by living with Americans, by establishing a variety of contacts — social, industrial, economic and political, can the foreigner become Americanized. Such contacts may easily be established in the school. Night schools can become efficient community centers, laboratories for mixing the various elements of the citizenship.

Instead of teaching civics as it has in the past, the school may put these principles into practice by organizing democratic groups whereby the foreign-born man knows first-hand what constitutes democratic organization.

One result of the socializing of the school is the discovery through experience, rather than by the imagination of the teacher, what instruction in the English language is needed by the foreign-born pupil under his natural living conditions, outside the artificial status of the schoolroom. I wish to emphasize that all kinds of social work appeals to me not so much because of its attractiveness and advertising value, but because of the new incentive that it gives to the students to learn the language more adequately. In one New York City school, where such socializing has gone forward, the school found, after trying the idea, that the number of classes at the close of the school year for the first time in its history was larger than when the fall session had opened. So popular have these extra school activities become among the foreign-born that, I understand, participation in them is restricted to those who are enrolled in the English classes.

Promotion of Education in Industry

W. M. ROBERTS, *Assistant Superintendent of Schools, Chicago, Ill.*

If the employers representing the dominant industries in any industrial city remain indifferent as to whether the foreign-born men in their employ know the English language, it requires extraordinary effort on the part of other agencies of the community to get them started to learning English. The experiences growing out of the war have shown that the foreign-born men would like to be called American; that they would prefer to speak English in the shop and on the street, and that they have not learned largely because it was not required of them in the factory, was not necessary at home, and they could get all the news they wanted out of the foreign language newspaper. If an opportunity is given them to learn the language during the day, they usually accept it with much satisfaction, particularly the man who is too indifferent to go to evening school.

I am convinced that the vigorous community "drive" with its great publicity and reflection, is not the way to begin such a work. A better way is to have one or more industries begin quietly and quite as a matter between the management and the employees. One forceful personality or a small working committee engaged in "selling" this proposition to one establishment after another is to be preferred to a regiment of copy writers and speakers. If the quiet method does not bring results, there may be need for a drive, and much jumping on those who are blocking the game. One detail should be emphasized — there must be some one delegated by the factory management to see that all obligations assumed by the plant are always carried out, and that this person is always on the job.

Education for the Rural Foreign-Born

PETER A. SPEEK, *Slavic Section, Library of Congress*

Education for the adult foreign-born settler in the rural sections of the country should be extended through home teachers, especially trained and equipped for the work. High schools and colleges should specifically train their immigrant girl students to become teachers in the colonies of their respective nationalities so that the immigrant women might be reached.

The problem of education is acutest in the large colonies of immigrant settlers, especially in the states where the foreign-born settlers, including the un-Americanized third and fourth generations, constitute a large majority of the rural population. In many of these, entire populations of foreign-born of the same nationality elect their own local health officials, put up their own country towns, have their own bankers, newspapers, and schools. From these places came a considerable number of the American-born drafted men who could not write, speak, or even understand English.

Schools must be consolidated, school administration must be bettered, and the rural course must give the children of the farmer practical education. Rural school teachers, who show qualifications for this Americanization work, must be adequately paid throughout the calendar year. A pension for old age and health and accident insurance are calculated to win a more contented body of teachers. At the schoolhouses teacherages must be established with small experimental farms for the family of the teacher.

The school year must be changed to meet the calendar year as one means of increasing attendance at the rural school. Short vacations could be given during the special farming seasons, the work the children do for their parents at that time being considered part of their school curriculum.

Education in the Lumber Camps

FRED H. RINDGE, JR., *International Committee, Y. M. C. A., New York City*

As we Y. M. C. A. men have gone about the country from one lumber camp to another it has been increasingly evident that educational Americanization, religious and social agencies ought to greatly extend their service in co-operation with both employers and employees. During the war the Y. M. C. A. served over 200 of the 300 camps of spruce loggers who were getting out spruce for aeroplanes in Washington, Oregon and California. About 30,000 soldiers and 110,000 civilians were engaged in the spruce production division.

Any program for meeting the educational needs among loggers and lumbermen should embrace classes in English for the foreign-born and illiterates, entertainment features, physical hygiene, instruction in thrift, and opportunities for the personal human touch in character building. It is important that the students in forestry and engineering schools of the country should be reached with fundamental Americanization principles, for in their hands will largely lie the future course of such work in the camps. They should hear lectures on the human problem of the lumber camp and should be given the chance, as undergraduates, to work and serve in the lumber camps during the summer, at any rate, for their actual contact. They should be encouraged to volunteer during their college course to teach foreign-born students the English language, that they may know some of the difficulties the newcomer has with the language.

Americanization Methods in Industry Other Than Education

E. E. BACH, Americanization Bureau, Philadelphia, Pa.

(*Presented by F. H. Cody, Assistant Superintendent of Schools, Detroit, Mich.*)

Americanization in industry is an attempt to restore the old-time relationship which once existed between an employer and an employee before industrial life became so complex. Satisfactory working conditions are among the most potent factors in the building of Americans. Without word or action the employer thus shows that his workmen mean more to him than so much man power. Pure air, good light, pure drinking water, ample washing facilities, sanitary conditions, safety, first aid, hospital facilities, workmen's relief funds, and co-operative activities of whatever sort, are all available for Americanizing the foreign-born employee. When industry once fully appreciates its responsibility for providing the American standard of living as being obligatory upon it, then the workmen will be given comfortable homes, wholesome milk, sanitary conditions, ample gardens, recreation and church facilities.

Another effective method of Americanization is a protection of the workmen against exploitation. Possibly the most important industrial phase in this process of Americanization as touching the workman is the American or un-American attitude of his foreman. As the personal contact is such an important element in teaching the foreign-born those things which we value in America, this is a very vital point in industrial life. The employment manager can give the foreign-born applicant a favorable or unfavorable impression of the industry by the kind of treatment he accords him at the time of seeking a job.

Americanization Through Industrial Employment

WILLIAM LAMKIE, *Industrial Relations Service, New York City*

An Americanization standard of living cannot be maintained among foreign-born workers until a minimum wage based on the requirements of modern civilization be established. We must have health and employment insurance, old age pensions, child labor laws, and the regulation of employment to safeguard the future motherhood and to protect the rights of these mothers. Up to the present we have approached the foreign-born through his physical forces and we have neglected to appraise and utilize his spiritual faculties. After all, the employees of an establishment are its best customers and only by stimulating the desire of the foreign-born workman for the better things of life, through advertising and other means, will industry find a market for its greatest production.

To make the employment service an Americanizing force there must be a better means for distributing the alien workers who usually settle in the congested centers of ports of entry. There must be labor exchanges performing for labor the service the Federal reserve banks render the money market. The vestibule school idea developed during the war offers one of the greatest incentives for the Americanization of the foreign-born worker, as it enables him to break into the class of skilled labor. The foreign-born worker who becomes Americanized should receive a higher wage than one who has not, and the wage scale should be graduated to cover each step in the process of citizenship.

English and citizenship can best be taught the foreign-born workman by his fellow-workmen, the study following the routine of the day's work and pay.

Relation of Americanization to Safety in Industries

JOHN A. OARTEL, *Carnegie Steel Company, Pittsburgh*

I sometimes wonder if we Americans who have been accustomed to our environment all our lives can appreciate the mental attitude of the foreign-born workman in our industries. The man from any of the countries of southern Europe has been transported within a few weeks from the quiet life of a country village, where the hazard to life and limb is unknown, to the busy life of the mill or factory. Shifting locomotives, molten metal, and moving machinery confront him at every turn. Is there any wonder he sometimes becomes confused and pays the price with his life or limb?

We as Americans are becoming awakened to the fact that it is not right that 30,000 lives should be sacrificed annually and 100,000 maimed workmen should be the by-product of American industry. The words "trade risk" will no more suffice as a reason for the taking of a life. We are looking to you who are fostering this Americanism project to furnish us the means by which we can get the message of safety to our workmen. With the understanding of our language and an appreciation of our ideals, he will be led and taught to observe that personal thoughtfulness and carefulness of his own safety which we feel is the only thing lacking today.

Industrial Health

BERNARD J. NEWMAN, *Sanitarian, United States Public Health Service*

Numerous as are the losses through accidents due to ignorance of hazards and inability to understand English, they are but a minor percentage of the losses of man power in industry resulting from sickness due to preventable causes. It matters not whether the foreign-born come to these shores in search of gold or personal liberty or escape from Old World autocracies, if the grind into which they are thrown turns their days into prolonged toil and subjects them to undue exposure they will lack the leisure and strength to cultivate Americanism. Such hazards as are present in industry can be removed by the simple program of plant hygiene, personal hygiene, and the engineering and medical skill and organization that necessarily attends both. Managers of industry do not deliberately want to maintain conditions which thus bear heavily on their employees. The great difficulty has been the definite lack of knowledge of the hazards and the means to keep them under control.

Industry should study the two fields fruitful of hazards to her workers — the industrial plant and the industrial zone surrounding such a plant. It is in this latter field that more self-evident causes of diseases commonly known can be found and against which prophylactic measures may readily be adopted. In this zone the responsibility is a dual one, resting alike on the community and the plant management. No plant should be allowed to operate which does not have some form of organization for medical and surgical care. It does not follow that such organization should be uniform, as different conditions call for different forms of organization.

Industrial Recreation and Americanization

A. W. COFFIN, *War Civics Committee, East St. Louis, Ill.*

One of the greatest needs of the foreign-born industrial workers is not a plaything but a playfellow. The Human Engineer has just recently been recognized by employers as a necessary adjunct of plant organization. Too often the superintendent, the foreman, the employer, and the native-born workman miss a great opportunity to be the foreign-born workman's hero or his general or corporal instead of his taskmaster, through neglect to form a play fellowship with the newcomer.

The program of recreational activities of any plant must be the result of fostered growth, this being particularly true where the foreign-born employee is present in the majority. The director of these play times becomes at once a chemist, bringing together the best contributions from any nationalities and throwing out the slag and dross.

I would suggest that the first step toward planning the foreign employee directed recreation is to ascertain what nationalities are represented in the working personnel. If the Italians are present, buy some baccio balls and see what happens. If the Slavs enrolled, make some parallel bars, and watch who uses them most during the noon hour. If there are English, Scotchmen, or Canadians to be considered, have facilities for soccer and cricket.

For longer periods of time than the noon hour, there are the field sports, track meets and organized hikes. Music will always find an immediate response from the foreign-born man or woman as a source of recreation. Teaching domestic science and home making to the foreign-born woman and girl in industry as part of the industrial recreational program cannot be overlooked by any company. A majority of these girls will marry men of their own race in the company's employ. Properly selected food, a cheerful home, intelligent care of the children, and knowledge of thrift are fundamentals of these men's efficiency.

Securing Interest of Racial Organizations

FELIX J. STREYCKMANS, *Foreign Language Division, Liberty Loan, Chicago, Ill.*

In the Fourth Liberty Loan, the Chicago district led in the percentage of the population that subscribed. The average percentage of population subscribing in the United States was 21.9; in Chicago proper, it was over 43 percent, or double that of the country as a whole.

In local communities, where only one or two racial groups exist, they should be made a part of the community Americanization committee, and when so recognized, they will, as volunteers, do all the work that is asked of them.

The success of our organization depended upon the fact that it recognized only two classes of citizens — there were no German-Americans, or French-Americans, or Italian-Americans — there were only the loyal and disloyal. Every one strove to be in the loyal class. The place of one's birth is no guaranty of one's loyalty. No distinction was made between people who sprang from enemy, neutral or allied countries. It was found that love of country could be and was expressed in the thirty-three different tongues that were spoken by the members of the organization. The American of German descent vied with the others to show his patriotism, and some of the members of German extraction were the hardest workers.

Let us hope that the work done by the foreign-born among the foreign-born during the pendency of the war will be carried on after the dawn of peace. But in order to do this, the American-born and the foreign-born, labor and capital, the society leaders and those in the lowlier walks of life, must join hands with the same democratic spirit which they displayed while the great world's conflict was raging.

Co-Operation of Foreign Language Press

HARRY LIPSKY, *Daily Jewish Courier, Chicago*

For all purposes, the foreign language press is the one sympathetic, intelligent, and trusted medium through which the foreign-born, old and young, may be approached and through which the Americanization work can best be carried on. Official recognition of these facts by the proper governmental agency will hearten the foreign language press and give it renewed faith in our country and in its institutions, while silencing forever the attack made upon it, and secure it against the threats of annihilation.

The government should have a news service instituted for the special purpose of conveying to the foreign language press such news as may be of special interest to the foreign language press readers. This press must be given the opportunity to co-operate with the government, being invited to assist, on a basis of equality, those agencies engaged in Americanization.

The most important point of all to remember is that most foreign language communities are no longer large inarticulate masses of human beings, but are organized to carry on propaganda through press, pulpit and pamphlet. So the press cannot go at the matter of Americanization in the spirit of adventure, just hitting about blindly at what may be considered un-American attitudes or disloyal propaganda. Campaigns which tell us of the advantages of becoming citizens or of learning English or acquiring the American "social graces" can be carried on with good results to show for the amount of work necessary to be put into the thing.

Securing Co-Operation of Foreign-Born People: From Viewpoint of the Foreign-Born

ALBERT MAMATY, *Slovak League of America, Pittsburgh, Pa.*

That indifference and contempt which native Americans have evinced in the past years toward the foreign-born newcomer should be replaced by sympathy and active interest if this country is to become the great homogeneous nation we all hope it will be. This sympathy can be awakened only by a greater knowledge concerning those various races immigrating to this country, for they, too, have their glorious history, their patriotic struggles, and their great men of literature, art, science, and every line of human endeavor.

Until recently the foreign-born woman has been an almost entirely neglected factor in American civilization. Think of the millions of boys and girls these women are bringing up and who will be a part of the next generation of American citizens, and think of how these women are not given any place in the development of American communities. American-born women can do much to educate public sentiment, through their organizations, to remedy this, to influence boards of health, housing, and other municipal effort to give attention to this defect.

Workers in the Americanization movement must realize that they cannot hasten the change they wish in the foreign-born. A man or woman born in Europe cannot ever be completely transformed into just the American the native-born is found to be. But it is unnecessary to hasten the process. Natural evolution will do the work and the transformation will be complete in the second generation.

Securing Co-Operation of Foreign-Born People: From the Viewpoint of the Native Born

NATHAN PEYSER, *Educational Alliance, New York City*

If the whole-hearted and dynamic interest of the immigrant population is to be gained, our aim must be held sharply in view and a rational approach made. What should be particularly appreciated is the injurious effects upon possible co-operation liable to be made by the point of view that the foreign-born element in the United States is a menace. We cannot hope to have the loyalty and support of an individual upon whom we are continually casting animadversions and whose inner worth we are ever aspersing. The immigrant groups are an asset and a promise for the future. The new-comer is not to be looked on with distrust and suspicion as a possible criminal, but rather as our guest. He remains our guest during good behavior until he becomes a citizen and then he becomes one of us. As both guest and citizen, he is a member of the community and should be protected against unjust attacks.

The gaining of co-operation depends upon the securing of interest in the thing to be achieved. Unless this motive be developed, the active participation of the foreign-born in Americanization need not be expected. Give the foreign-born the opportunity to learn English. There are more communities without facilities for this than there are municipalities having them. Do not attack his native tongue and compel him to sacrifice his individuality or his wages to gain this knowledge. Do not keep him from contact with those who speak English. Show him the best side of citizenship. The community movement looms large as an excellent device for democratic co-operative action.

The Foreign-Born and America

HERBERT A. MILLER, *Oberlin College, Oberlin, Ohio*

The immigrant has instincts and emotions common to all mankind with limitations and prejudices such as all people have. By studying ourselves carefully we can explain many problems of the alien.

Each nationality is absolutely unique. The common language, common geographical origin, and common religion have developed characteristics that are persistent and definite. However much alike these traits may seem to an outsider, in the consciousness of each group they are most highly differentiated.

Far more than is generally appreciated, the immigrant has come here to get free from political, religious and cultural oppression. It is not without significance that practically no Roumanians or Serbs come here from Roumania or Serbia, but from

Austria-Hungary. Most of the recent immigrants have lived where the ruling power was trying to kill the national individuality of its subject peoples.

The most outstanding contribution of the immigrant to America is the object lesson in political science he presents in every industrial city of the country, an illustration of the history and results of European oppression.

Understanding of these forces is the first need of the immigrant America must reach. There will be a hold-over of psychosis until long after the European cause is removed and America must act as a physician seeking to heal the wounds for which she has no responsibility.

The peace conference is the best Americanization agency. The foreign-born will never forget the land of his birth so long as injustice prevails there; he will always be longing to help those of his racial brothers left behind.

Naturalization's Part in the Movement

RAYMOND F. CRIST, *Director of Citizenship, Department of Labor*

At the present time those of foreign birth represent 17,000,000 of our population. Approximately 4,000,000 of these 17,000,000 have come into contact with the Federal Government through the Bureau of Naturalization of the Department of Labor. With the increase in the public attention on the general subject of Americanization there has been an increase in the number of foreigners who are applying for citizenship.

In the fiscal year 1910 there were 222,264 applicants for first and second papers. In 1913 there were 276,818 applicants. In 1915 there were 354,132 applicants. In 1917 there were 571,068, while in 1918 there were 509,478. In the present fiscal year commencing July 1, 1918, 528,273 naturalization papers were filed during the first nine months, and the indications are that there will be in the neighborhood of 650,000 original applicants for first and final papers for the entire fiscal year.

There has been an average of more than one person born abroad who derives citizenship from the act of husband or father. This average has been found to be constant through years of observation, so that we may say that 1,156,546 members of the foreign-born population of the United States came forward during the first nine months of the present fiscal year and took steps necessary to have citizenship conferred upon them. With the close of the year this amount should exceed 1,250,000.

During April, May and June in 1917 more applications were filed than during any entire year with the exception of one.

Elimination of Exploitation

REGINALD HEBER SMITH, *Former Counsel in Chief, Boston Legal Aid Society*

Exploitation of the foreign-born can be prevented only through the law. This is the only democratic, American way to do it. The only way to make an American out of a foreign-born man is to treat him as an American.

Protection through the law for elimination of exploitation includes three distinct elements. The first of these is a sensitive social mechanism that will detect bad practices as rapidly as they are practiced. This may be an immigration commission or a legal aid society or a social service organization, but it must act because sharp practices have a new edge on them every day. The second thing is to have a sufficient body of well-drafted laws against exploitation. You will find 95 percent of these laws already on the statute books, the other 5 percent being those needed to be enacted to bring legislation up to current development. The law on the books is one thing, the law in action is another.

The third essential is the existence of an administration of justice which shall be accessible to all and which shall be workable by all and which will grant equal chances to all before the law. This problem on the administration of justice in the courts is the heart of the whole Americanization movement. You can work as hard as you like to teach the foreign-born resident to love American institutions, but if he doesn't get fair treatment when he comes in contact with those institutions, he will think they do not deserve his respect.

Neighborhood Work Among Foreign-Born

MRS. MARY KINGSBURY SIMKHOVITCH, *Director of Greenwich House, New York City*

To fit the foreign-born's home life and neighborhood life into American traditions and ideals we should drop the attempts to secure uniformity of customs and try to get unity of purpose. Freedom for the woman and the child is what we should be working for in Americanizing the home life of the newcomer. We do this somewhat through insisting on education for all children. We free the woman to a certain extent by opening the doors of factories, shops, and offices to her. We must more adequately free them by a social program which will protect the home against disease, against the encroachment of industry, and against congested living quarters occasioned by high rentals.

To engage the interest of the newcomer in this kind of social program is the only real way to Americanize him. He must be taken into fellowship, and he must Americanize himself. We in the settlements believe that as long as he lives apart, he will not change. We need humility, because we have given them so cold a welcome; a determination to share his life more fully and to give him the opportunity to share ours; a desire to serve him, to prove our sincerity, and an invitation to him to assume the joint responsibility of creating the new era.

The Foreign-Born in the Community

ALLEN T. BURNS, *Carnegie Corporation, New York City*

What will it profit the foreign-born if he gains the whole English language but loses the life of America? This conference marks a high-water mark as to Americanization because there has been given so large a place to the discussion of how the foreign-born and native-born Americans can enter into mutual and vital relationships. We must not slip back into the old thought that language is the foremost factor in the problem.

It seems to me that the first thing we need to realize is that foreign-born persons participate largely in American life only through their national active groupings. Whether we like it or not, we really participate in American life effectively, largely and only as we are organized. This is especially true of those who have not learned our language and they must share in American life through grouping action if they are to share at all. It is not until we find some way of making groups feel, through insistent organization of themselves, that they register somewhere in American life that we can expect to make them feel truly American.

The immigrant is going to Americanize himself and all we can do is to help him form such natural, normal, and vital group organizations. It is for us to see that these natural and normal processes remain true to type with only such adjustments as will leave base enough for the new American to develop these most essential features of Americanism — self-reliance, enterprise, self-direction, self-sufficiency, that these fundamental things may be preserved. Any process which tends to destroy these fundamentals will be a travesty upon the fair name of America itself.

America's Heritage

FRANKLIN K. LANE, *Secretary of the Interior*

The right of revolution does not exist in America. We had a revolution 140 years ago which made it unnecessary to have any other revolution in this country, because it was fundamental. One of the meanings of democracy is that it is a form of government in which the right of revolution has been lost by giving the government wholly to the people. Revolution means revolt. Against whom are we to revolt in the United States excepting the people of the United States?

If we Americans do not like officials, programs, policies, measures, systems, we can try others, but in Europe the right of self-determination as to domestic concerns has been denied and, therefore, the right of revolution has been preached.

No man can be a sound and sterling American who believes that force is necessary to effectuate the popular will. As we have taken from the duellist his pistol and compelled him to seek redress in the law, so in the larger affairs of the nation we have said, "This is your country. Make it what you will; but you must not use force, for when you came here and became a citizen, you gave over the right to resort to anything but public opinion and the methods of the law in the determination of national policies. If you are in a minority you must wait until you become a majority, and as a majority you must be content to prevail by processes which respect the rights of the minority."

Americanism does not mean that any one economic system is right, or that the United States is perfect; it does not mean that any one social philosophy must be accepted as the final expression of truth; but Americanism does mean that we have evolved for ourselves machinery by which revolution, as a method of changing our life, is outgrown and outlawed.

America, a Nation of Foreign-Born

WILLIAM C. REDFIELD, *Secretary of the Department of Commerce and Labor*

There is none of us who can afford to be so far remote from this problem in our thought as to forget our own particular relation to it, if we look far enough back. We have not far to go in this country before we run across such names as Eauclaire and Fond du Lac and La Crosse, and we must not forget what we owe to the Frenchmen who trod our land before our ancestors even knew they could walk on it. And so with the Spaniards who invaded our country in the South before a European settler ever placed his foot here.

We are in a sense, every one of us, foreigners. We are a blend, as Secretary Lane has said. In this conference we are but transmitting to our own shoulders and to the shoulders of our children the job that somebody once did for us, or else we should not have been so comfortable as we are here today. It is something that has gone on from the beginning, but I am afraid that we have, at least some of us, reached a place where we have been taking it, until lately, too much for granted. I cannot remember that anybody ever taught me very much about the value of American citizenship. I used to wonder at the pride with which a Roman was said to proclaim, "I am a Roman citizen." I did not quite understand what it meant. I rather thought it was funny for Paul to say that he was a citizen of no mean city, in his "Acts of the Apostles." What it meant I had no distinct idea, but I have it now, however. I do not know just how, but I suppose it came unconsciously to me. I have an example or two of recent months that has made me realize it. I wish we could teach those who come over here that we do not want to impose something on them, but that we want to help them to think in citizenship terms.

Making a Permanent Pentecost

JOHN H. FINLEY, *State Commissioner of Education of New York*

To make here in America a permanent Pentecost that all the people of the land may understand one another, we must begin with a common language. I know that this is not the sufficient thing, but we must begin with words, for all the good and bad that gets done in the world is done through words. I appreciate that it is not simply the method that is the important thing and I am very glad to bring you a message from my own state.

You will recall that last year at your conference the three bills which have been proposed in the New York Legislature for Americanization were submitted for your consideration. These bills were unanimously ratified by your conference and that action was responsible, I think, in a large measure, for the passage of the bills by the Legislature a week or two later. Yesterday I went to the Governor's office to ask whether or not he had signed an appropriation bill for $100,000 for carrying forward Americanization work in our state. We started a few years ago with $2,500. Last year we had $20,000 and this year we have $36,000 in our department, and then this $100,000 bill was drawn. I found that the bill had not been signed. But today, when I called at the Governor's office, I learned that the bill had been signed, and I am happy that we can make this contribution to the national program for making this land dear to all of us.

On the 12th of February I was in the Holy Land, as commissioner for the Red Cross, and I stood where Abraham is said to have been born. I was observing the birthday of Abraham Lincoln and I was very glad that Father Abraham had migrated so that the land of Abraham Lincoln was made possible.

Community Gatherings and Recreation

THOMAS WOOD STEVENS, *Carnegie Technical School, Pittsburgh, Pa.*

Granting at once the value of participation by the foreign-born in festivals common to the whole community, the question which usually arises is how to do it. The kirmess has been tried, but its limits are narrow, the sequence of dances making a monotonous show. The method to be followed in new work must be more frankly dramatic. In any case, the festival should be the work of the whole community, the foreign-born groups bearing only their proportionate share of it, and thus contributing the traditions of their history and ideals rather than conserving them apart for festivals of their own presentation.

The chief language of such a performance should be English if the audience is to be held and the occasion attain its purposes. Pantomime must be a large factor, with folk dances entering in but not dominating the whole performance. The most workable device has been found to be the herald, who is obviously of the same nationality as the group presented, to interpret the situations of the various scenes to the audience. These heralds' speeches are a vital factor in the impressiveness of the pantomime, and I have never found a foreign-born group that suggested a trifling or uninteresting subject to be presented as its contribution.

While foreign-born people take readily to festivals, the native American needs to learn more of the play spirit. The pageant and festival have done something toward making a beginning; the community drama must meet with encouragement and serious study on the part of the nation's artists.

Thrift and Protection of Savings

C. J. KEENAN, *Deputy Appraiser of the Port of New York*

To my mind there arises the grave question of whether or not the foreign-born element of our population is in greater need of this propaganda than the native-born, for I believe that the former is more likely to present an exposition of the practice of thrift in their daily living than the latter. A movement of this kind need not confine itself to any one element of the citizenship, for thrift directs itself more toward the conservation of materials than the mere saving of money.

The people of foreign countries generally look upon a bank as a government institution, which accounts for the practice so prevalent among them of patronizing private banking institutions after they come to this country. An enterprising foreign-born citizen will oftentimes, after reaching a certain stage of prosperity, open a bank with the legend, "State Bank" over the door. I will not say he deliberately misrepresents the character of his bank, but certainly he accomplishes the purpose of making the public, at least some part of it, believe it is connected with the government.

The very best plan to protect the savings of the public is to encourage one of the many forms of co-operative banking. Co-operative banking has been in operation in Europe for many years and recently it has been introduced in New York State by the Credit Union Law. This union is also designed to meet the need of the citizen who wishes to borrow and has not sufficient security with which to effect the loan, for he becomes a borrower of his own funds to the extent that he is owner of paid-up shares in the union.

Improving Housing Conditions Among the Foreign-Born

John Ihlder, *Secretary Philadelphia Housing Association*

Good management of houses leased to foreign-born tenants can be made a powerful agent for bringing the slum dwelling up to American standards. The relationship of landlord and tenant has been commercialized in this country, so far as the foreign-born resident is concerned.

We consider the American standard of housing an essential in Americanization, for there is no one thing that sets a family or group apart so surely as living in a dwelling which public opinion in the community holds in contempt. This public opinion is not based on costliness. The grapevine which adorns the Italian truck gardener's farmhouse and distinguishes it from the Anglo-Saxon's home attracts. It is the squalid, overflowing tenement which prevents the casual neighborliness between the native and the foreign-born. Until we can throw down this barrier of the repellant dwelling we shall not go far in mingling with our alien fellow townsmen. This change can be brought about first by the enforcement of laws requiring not only the proper design and construction of all dwellings, but their proper upkeep, and, secondly, by the houseowners taking American standards of l:ving into the home of the foreign-born tenant. The first change is fundamental, for by no other means can every dwelling be made to conform to American ideals. This method means sewer and water-main extension to parts of towns now neglected, the enforcement of house connections, and regular and frequent collection of garbage.

More than twenty years ago the Octavia Hill Association was formed to buy old houses in neglected sections of Philadelphia, or act as agent for owners of such property, and put such dwellings in good condition. It manages these dwellings to the best interests of the tenant, not only responding to his desire for improvement, but stimulating these desires. The rent collector takes an interest in the family problems, having information of civic and social organizations which can aid the foreign-born to become Americanized.

Co-Ordination of Americanization Agencies

C. H. PAULL, *Bureau of Vocational Guidance, Harvard University*

In Americanization work we must make every effort to avoid a tendency to monopolize from a purely selfish standpoint. No single agency is in a position to contribute all that is implied in the term "Americanization." When agencies in a community attempt to carry on this work without any mutual understanding or sympathy, the results are duplication of work, overlooking of essential work which each agency leaves for the other to do, distrust on the part of the new American of the agencies which he soon discovers are failing to work with a common motive and a loss of the enthusiasm which group action develops.

A community about to interest itself in Americanization should first make a survey or study in which both the existing facilities and the possible facilities for work are determined as accurately as possible. The next step is to bring these resources together under a single purpose with a willingness to pool their interests for the common good.

For an agency to entertain anxiety about not having enough to do is as far fetched as worrying about what we shall do when the world is wholly reformed. In both cases we can well conserve our powers for effective endeavor and leave the rest for some future generation to work out. There are a great number of functions which are in the nature of an overload to the schools and the industry which these agencies can assist materially in carrying. Regardless of the failures of the schoolman of the past, the perspective of the education is essential to Americanization work.

Y. M. C. A. in Americanization

PETER ROBERTS, *Industrial Department, International Y. M. C. A.*

Men and boys of foreign parentage are the field of the Y. M. C. A., and the work to be done there is very definitely outlined in our minds, as including basicly the teaching of English without asking that any man forget his native tongue. We emphasize the advantage of having citizenship in the United States, not asking, either, that a man forget entirely his native hearthstone. Then we provide lectures on everything pertaining to American life, the plan of the American government, and the makers of America.

We provide entertainments to bring before the American public the gifts brought to this country by the foreign-born newcomers.

Another thing we stress is recreational activity. I am sorry that more attention has not been given here in this conference to the problem of the son of foreign-born parentage. We hope to reach him through recreational activity. In our organization we have the advisory councils where the foreign-born man may go for advice to protect himself against exploitation and other evils. This advice is free. Americanization is a group of men and women enthused by the spirit of service who are interpreting the spirit of America and not a little English, a little lecture course, or an advisory council, or naturalization, but everybody working together.

The Y. W. C. A. Part in the Movement

MISS EDITH JARDINE, *International Institute, Y. W. C. A., New York City*

Realizing the need for immediate action, the Y. W. C. A. organized the International Institute as its machinery for work among foreign-born women and girls in 1912. Such work is today being extended into communities under the same designation. Now there are forty of these institutes embracing the New England states, California, New Jersey, Honolulu, Texas and New York. Over 22,000 foreign-born women have been reached through the New York center alone during the past six years.

We have been successful in reaching the hearts of the foreign-born women and girls because we have touched the women of their own respective races. We believe that we have made our best contribution to the movement of stressing the importance of using the best type of the foreign-born woman leader to help the people of her own nationality. Among the offshoots of the institute work are the mother's clubs, which are designed to reach the stay-at-home women. Parental clinics, cooking classes, food demonstrations, and English classes are taught in these clubs. The hospitality of the International Institutes are always extended to the masculine relatives of the women. We hope that our place is to act as a link and an interpreter between our foreign-born and native-born people to draw them a little nearer together in that community of spirit which constitutes real Americanization.

The Catholics in the Work

JOHN O'GRADY, *National Catholic War Council*

If you desire to regard our attitude in regard to democracy, read the reconstruction program of the National Catholic War Council. We are interested in co-operating with all agencies for the promotion of citizenship and the teaching of English. We are willing to co-operate with them provided we have a say in the plans that are formulated. We are endeavoring at the present time to interest all Catholic societies in America in the promotion of citizenship and the teaching of English. We are endeavoring particularly to interest the various racial groups. It is impossible to outline in detail in such brief time what is being done, but we are having published a textbook on civics for immigrants that will be translated into all the important languages.

This conference ought to keep in mind that the two great immediate objectives in this Americanization work before us are the teaching of English and the promotion of instruction in citizenship. We ought to get together and find out what additional machinery we need to put these great objectives into reality. We ought to have some say in any form of legislation that is proposed, for we are in closer touch with the immigrants than any other institution. We are willing to do our best for the making of a better America.

Jewish Women Aid Immigrants

MISS HELEN WINKLER, *Council of Jewish Women.*

Less than 16 percent of the girls employed in factories drawing their workers from a large foreign settlement take advantage of the night school facilities, and under one percent of the mothers attend such classes. This was learned in the industrial survey made by the Council of Jewish Women.

The reasons given by the girls of the factories for not attending night schools were mainly these: Long working hours and consequent fatigue; need for wholesome recreation which could be had at night only; natural discouragement in ungraded classes made up of aliens of both sexes and all ages; poor teaching standards. Mothers could attend daytime classes, but these are available only in very few localities.

The council has about 28,000 women representing 106 local branches in as many cities throughout this country and Canada, each organization having its immigrant aid committee, which protects the immigrant woman and girl until her destination is reached.

Civic Organization as One of the Agencies

T. A. LEVY, *Americanization League, Syracuse, N. Y.*

The Americanization committee of the chamber of commerce found the social gathering the highest type of activity for assimilating the foreign-born. After having the leaders brought together, the committee advanced to the point of having a group of native-born entertain a foreign-born group. This was followed by the foreign-born group playing host in turn to the native-born group. The University Club, the Rotary Club, and like societies have also been asked to engage in this program.

Although the chamber of commerce initiated the work of Americanization in Syracuse, in a broad-minded way, it worked itself out of a job and turned over the control of the problem to the municipality, believing that the city was less likely to incur any suspicion of a partisan basis. It thus changed its position from being the parent of the movement to that of becoming a distant relative.

The foreign-born employee spends more time in the factory, shop, or store than in any other place. His health and even his life to some extent is in the hands of the manager of the plant in which he is at work. The ethical and economical part of Americanization should not be sundered. There remains a vast field for correlation of these forces by the chamber of commerce and other civic agencies.

Using the Women's Clubs

MRS. PERCY V. PENNYPACKER, *Honorary President of General Federation of Women's Clubs*

I fully believe that there is no greater duty before this conference than to present a sane, practical, comprehensive plan of work to the organized womanhood of this country. Such a plan must be scientific without being too technical and must be presented to the club women sympathetically, dramatically, and persistently. It must be presented sympathetically, because the trained worker does not always realize the power of the volunteer force represented in an organized body of club women.

The trained worker should not expect from the volunteer worker just what she would from the person who has had all the advantages of training; but, on the other hand, she should not undervalue what the volunteer can give. She has learned lessons in the school of life that some experts have not; she has a certain practical contact with the community life about her that renders her invaluable. We have preached year in and year out that there is nothing so dangerous as ignorance at work, and we would like to make every woman's organization see this, too.

Women have proved, during the war, that they like to work under the government's direction, so if we have the government at the head of this movement it will be a tremendous incentive to women all over the land to do their best work.

Libraries: The Friend of the Foreign-Born

Prepared by JOHN FOSTER CARR; Read by MISS THERESA HITCHLER

In some respects the library has a far greater opportunity to be an aid to the foreign-born than do the schools, because being friendly and helpful its aid is oftentimes less formal and more inviting. It is open throughout the year, it makes no strenuous demands on a man after a hard day's work, and it welcomes those who think themselves too old to go to school. The library brings the immigrant in effective touch with American democracy and American ideals and helps destroy the impression of heartless commercialism that many of our immigrants continually assert is the main characteristic of our civilization.

Nearly 800 public libraries are taking part in the forward movement to aid the foreign-born. In New York City, with its forty-three branches, those branches having the largest so-called immigrant membership lead all others in circulation. The use of books in foreign language has increased so rapidly that their circulation now reaches nearly 700,000 a year. The results have been so pleasing that the supply of foreign language books have been increased 30 percent in the last two years. Once the foreign-born reader enters the library he needs personal attention to have the simple rules given him in his own language, to have the different rooms explained. He cannot use the index cards nor understand the mysteries of registration. They may be brought in by various devices, publicity and service to classrooms being handy ones.

Public Health Nurse in Americanization

MRS. BESSIE HAASIS, *Educational Secretary National Organization for Public Health Nursing*

The public health nurse enters the home of the foreign-born at a time when there is trouble. Service is needed and needed badly. Her uniform proclaims her as a worker, and to the men and women who have toiled in the workshop or field this is a passport to confidence. Those who have come from countries where ministry to the sick is the function of the church, recognize in the uniform the added sanction and beneficence of religious service. It is their thought that the priest might have sent her.

Nine times out of ten her visits bring immediate and tangible benefit. A few simple dressings for the burned hand and the father is able to return to work in three or four days. Once the gratitude of the family and its confidence is gained there is no subject on which they will not ask and accept advice. Herein lies the opportunity of the public health nurse to win the family over to such American standards and habits as are better than their own. There is no reason why the public health nurse's advice should be limited to matters of health. Her aim is to remedy not only the case of illness, but to remedy whatever is wrong with the family. The nurse can get greater results and sooner through the children. The amount of time it takes to teach one foreign-born mother how to properly care for her baby will teach a class of twenty little girls the same knowledge. The children can convince the mother, especially when the nurse works with both.

Boys' and Girls' Organizations

BURDETTE G. LEWIS, *Commissioner of Institutions, New Jersey*

We should welcome boys' gangs and function them for the purpose of Americanization. Some of the things we may do are: Select the best out of all cultures and use it as a basis of our educational work; link up our educational and recreational systems; see to it that the schools teach our boys and girls how to make a living, as well as how to read and speak English; recognize juvenile delinquency as a family affair and turn our children's court into domestic relations' courts.

We should take the finger prints of all offenders, whether they may be young or old, so that no one may make a joke of the laws of the land by falsifying about their identity. We should utilize the boys who organize the bottle-fight gangs and the girls who form peculiar cliques to bring home to their parents the benefits provided at the child welfare stations in our cities. We can use the country boy and girls' desire to associate as a great force for revivifying American rural life. We can have the boys and girls bring their parents to school to see the motion pictures which we now use in teaching history, geography, and other studies. The boys and girls can be used to renew on American soil that association of child and parent in recreational activities so characteristic of many European nations.

We can introduce these foreign-born boys and girls to their own traditional games, such as Italian dancing, Japanese kite flying and Bohemian wrestling. There are the Boy Scouts and the Camp Fire Girls to be used for instruction in personal hygiene.

Demonstration Agent's Role in Movement

MISS GERTRUDE VAN HOESEN, *Extension Work with Women, Department of Agriculture*

District organizations in the cities and community organizations in the rural sections have made it possible for the home demonstration agents of the Department of Agriculture to reach the foreign-born woman. In many places each radical group is represented on the community or district committee by intelligent leaders of that group, who are able to articulate the needs of the non-English speaking mother and housekeeper. The foreign clergy, the social workers, the visiting nurses, and the public school officials all offer opportunities for making such contracts in behalf of demonstration agents.

In many states the leaflets of the Food Administration during the war were translated in various languages. While there has been some criticism of this move, in numerous cases the very sight of the conservation receipts printed in her native tongue has been the entering wedge for developing the woman's confidence in the home demonstration agent. One of the most important things accomplished by the demonstration worker has been the closer understanding given the old American of the habits and needs of the new American, thereby inspiring enthusiasm and friendliness instead of apathy and antagonism. Social community leadership is absolutely essential to the success of any organization seeking to back up the home demonstration agent and there is a wide field for the development of the home demonstration project leader. The highest function of the home demonstration agent is to solve problems that the women may not only learn how to feed their families, but feed them accordingly.

Congress of Mothers and Parent Teacher Bodies Part in Work

Prepared by MRS. FREDERICK SCHOFF, *President of the National Associations of These Bodies.*

(Presented by MRS. JOSEPH P. MUNFORD, *Vice-President*).

There are obstacles which must be overcome in order to secure the mothers. The first one is the lack of encouragement of their husbands in regard to attending meetings. There seems to be a prejudice among foreign people against women going out or joining in club work. An important means we have found has been the placing of leaflets in schools where the fathers are learning English, showing them the necessity of having their wives learn also.

The women feel that in their own countries they have brought up children successfully and that they do not need to be told everything. By learning the good things that our foreign-born people know, and showing them that they have some things to teach us, their attitude is entirely changed. We consider this is a very important part of the success in Americanization work.

The Parent Teacher Association, because it takes in all children in our public schools, has been a splended medium for organizing foreign mothers.

The Americanization department of the Bureau of Education can do nothing better than to emphasize among the foreign men of this country the absolute necessity of keeping mothers up to the rest of the family in the knowledge of our language and our customs.

What the State and Nation Can Do to Help the Community

GEORGE H. BELL, *Former Secretary, California Immigrant and Housing Commission*

To our way of thinking, the efforts of the communities are largely wasted if they are not based on uniform standards which have been so correlated that each community is doing its share in developing a unified state and nation.

Organization is the first step that the state and nation must take to help the community. Each state must establish a central commission with the responsibility for developing and executing a state program of Americanization, properly co-ordinated with the national program. Secondly, the national government must establish a central agency charged with the full power of a broad national Americanization program carried on in co-operation with the state. I am authorized to present this plan as the suggestion of the California Immigration and Housing Commission.

One has only to point to the lack of a clear, definite authorized Americanization program during the past two years as proof of the need for one. A state commission which is to co-operate with an official central Americanization headquarters should be democratic and made up of citizens who have had actual experience with immigrants and who would represent various viewpoints in connection with the problem. The state can afford to keep experts on the various lines, even if the communities cannot do so, and make them available for survey and consultation work to these committees. The state must assume the initiative, although it is not obligatory that it maintain a large staff to do all the direct field work. The more progressive communities should aid the backward ones.

What the Churches Can Do in Americanization

REV. WORTH TIPPY, *Executive Secretary of the Commission on Church Social Service, Federal Council of the Churches of Christ in America.*

The churches have long been an important factor in Americanization. They have homes and agencies for meeting and caring for immigrants at every port in the United States, where immigrants are admitted. They have special schools and colleges for the various language groups, special seminaries for the training of ministers, and in every city where the foreign-born congregate the leading denominations spend large amounts of money and have many influential centers of activity. This work is wholly Americanization in the broadest sense of that term. In addition to the teaching of English, there is the care of the family, especially of the children, in the atmosphere of the spiritual ideals of America. All these missions and churches to the foreign-born are intensely patriotic. I can think of no better or more powerful agency for Americanization than the right kind of a church for immigrants. It should be known also that the great women's boards of home missions of the churches spend several millions of dollars in this work every year.

The Americanization problem of the church is not so much to do new work, or new kinds of work, as to do more powerfully what it has been doing for generations; and that it is preparing to do.

"Americanization" is a periodical published monthly by the Department of the Interior, Bureau of Education, Americanization Division, and sent on request to any one interested. It contains news of Americanization activities throughout the country, news of the activities of the various State Councils of Defense, proposed and new legislation bearing upon the subject of Americanization and citizenship training, and articles by leaders in the general and immigrant education field upon such pertinent subjects as "What America Means" by Franklin K. Lane (issue of February 1, 1919), "Americanization" by Franklin K. Lane (issue of February 1, 1919), etc.

Citizenship Training Through Industries

In connection with Industrial Americanization, for several months the Americanization Division has been issuing short articles and verse to house organs for publication, and many editors of these publications have written to express their approval of the material, and have used it extensively. These releases are designed to promote a better understanding between the races living in America and to harmonize them with each other and their new environment. This is reported to be of value to employers and workers alike, especially in plants that include a large number of the foreign born in their ranks.

2. United States Chamber of Commerce

The Chamber of Commerce of the United States publishes, about twice a month, a bulletin giving news of Americanization work throughout the country, especially in the industries.

SUMMARY REPORT OF THE IMMIGRATION COMMITTEE OF THE CHAMBER OF COMMERCE OF THE UNITED STATES FOR THE YEAR 1917

Our entrance into the World War about a year ago brought into sharp relief the important part played in the life of the nation by the foreign language groups resident in the United States. In this national crisis, when the united and intelligent and active participation of every able-bodied person is of such vital moment, we find a diversity of language, of citizenship, of loyalty and of concepts of freedom and democracy.

The many racial groups making up our population have been allowed to settle in groups and colonies, and no really serious national effort has been made to give them something of our national ideals, or to translate to them the true meaning of our tremendous experiment in national democracy and its fundamental belief in "the pursuit of life, liberty, and happiness."

An analysis of this situation shows how vital it has become in matters of national defense. We find, for instance:

That forty-three dialects are used in daily conversation among our foreign-born groups.

That nearly 50 per cent. of the more than 13,000,000 foreign-born persons are males of voting age, of whom only 4 percent of every 1,000 attend school to learn our language.

That one-third of our foreign-born population, or nearly 5,000,000, were born in Germany or in countries allied with Germany.

That our basic war industries depend to a considerable degree for their labor supply on foreign-born persons, most of whom do not speak or read our language, and to whom the acid tests of loyalty have heretofore not been applied.

That our foreign-born are organized in societies throughout the country, to promote their racial solidarity or the political autonomy of their native lands, and that their first interests are not always for America.

To meet these conditions, the Immigrant Committee has this year presented to chambers of commerce and industries, standards, plans and suggestions for the organization of War Americanization work which have resulted in widespread activity among employers and commercial and trade organizations. The result has been that some 150 chambers of commerce are now engaged in some form of Americanization work, compared with thirty-one chambers last year. A special pamphlet showing in detail what each chamber has undertaken or accomplished is now in preparation and will shortly be printed.

In the main, the Americanization work of chambers of commerce and industrial plants has related to:

The use of a common language for the entire nation.

The desire of all peoples in America to unite in common citizenship under one flag.

The combatting of anti-American propaganda and the stamping out of disloyalty.

The abolition of racial prejudices and discriminations and the interpretation of American ideals, traditions, standards and institutions.

The maintenance of an American standard of living and the proper housing, care, protection, and treatment of aliens.

The creation of an understanding of and love for America, and of the desire of immigrants to remain in America, to have a home here, and to support American institutions and laws.

The telling to foreign-born people why America is at war, why we must all stand together, and how they can help to win it.

These general purposes have been promoted by the Immigration Committee through practical programs of work which have included:

1. *Appointment of Americanization Committees in local chambers to deal with local conditions.*— The majority of the 150 chambers doing Americanization work have appointed special Americanization committees to act as the local clearing house for community or plant work. Others have assigned this activity to existing committees. In several cities the full time services of Americanization secretaries have been employed, either directly or in co-operation with local defense bodies, as in Detroit, Youngstown, Cleveland, Cincinnati, Syracuse, Milwaukee, and Hartford. In other cities, chairmen of committees have given freely of their time and energy, as in Rochester, Philadelphia, Boston, Providence, Jamestown, Omaha, Des Moines and Pittsburgh. In still others and in the majority of cases the chamber secretary has taken direct charge of the work.

2. *Surveys of immigration conditions in communities and industrial plants.*— Conferences on Americanization have been held with industrial leaders in some twenty-five cities and with engineers and leaders of industry and finance in New York City. Addresses on Americanization were also delivered at the national conventions of such trade organizations as the National Association of Clothing Manufacturers, National Lime Manufacturers' Association and the National Association of Cotton Manufacturers. Ten other trade organizations, such as the Rubber Association of America, the American Pulp and Paper Association, Structural Bridge Builders' Association, and the American Paint, Varnish and Oil Manufacturers' Association, circularized their firm members urging them to take a plant alien census and organize activities for Americanization.

These conferences and activities have resulted in the making of surveys of communities and plants, and the submission of detailed recommendations for the development of intensive work. So many requests have been received for information, and suggestions as to methods employed, that the Immigration Committee has prepared for publication a special pamphlet on "Americanization Forms and Methods." which contains exact copies of forms used by various agencies and which will shortly be printed for distribution to chamber members.

3. *Adult Immigration Education and Citizenship Work.*—Matters relating to the education of immigrants which involve the technical method and content of study or the creation and organization of adequate facilities, were carried on in co-operation with the United States Bureau of Education, and all naturalization problems with the United States Bureau of Naturalization. The Immigration Committee, however, distributed directly suggestions for the adjustment of working shifts to school classes, and prepared plans of campaigns to increase night school attendance which have been followed in a number of cities.

4. *Publication of Bulletins of Americanization.*— Sixteen special bulletins on Americanization have been issued by the Immigration Committee during the year and have been distributed to the entire membership of the national chamber and to some 2,500 other interested organizations and individuals. These bulletins have kept all interested organizations informed of the progress being made throughout the country and have stimulated work in many communities through social and civic, as well as industrial agencies. They have also contained detailed program of war Americanization work for chambers of commerce and for industrial plants and suggestions on how the war message can be carried to foreign-born employees. Copies of some of these issues are still available for distribution at the office of the Immigration Committee and can be secured upon request.

Wherever such practical interest in foreign-born workmen has been taken by the industrial leaders of the community, it has brought about a more wholesome fellowship and a better understanding between the native and foreign-born groups and has promoted the efficiency and earning power of the workmen in the plant. The results in Detroit and Cleveland are especially interesting.

In Detroit, the Board of Commerce reports, after its fourth city-wide campaign for the Americanization of foreign-born residents, that "practically every large employer of labor (foreign) has incorporated Americanization into his regular program of work." It says:

> "There is not a large concern in Detroit where a foreign-born person who applies for work is not requested to fill out a record which includes his citizenship status and a record of whether or not he should be a pupil in the free public evening schools. In the three years of work in Detroit we have been so successful that several of the large concerns who were conducting factory classes for their non-English-

speaking men have abandoned these classes, stating that they no longer had any trouble securing English-speaking men for their plants."

In Cleveland, the Chamber of Commerce co-operated with the Americanization Committee of the Mayor's Advisory War Committee in a city-wide effort to make Cleveland "a one-language city — its shops, one-language shops — its homes, one-language homes." Its Americanization program includes a training institute for teachers of immigrants, a campaign to enroll all non-English-speaking people in the evening schools, the establishment of plant classes, community citizenship and naturalization classes, and the development of an Americanization service to relate definitely the immigrant to the public library, the city departments and social agencies.

In submitting this brief summary of its work, the Immigration Committee desires to emphasize the fact that not only must we combat the work of alien enemies, but we must also change the ignorance and prejudice of friendly aliens through Americanization and capitalize the splendid gifts and qualities the immigrant brings to us for Americanism. We must approach our foreign language people with patience and sympathy, and deal with them in a spirit of justice, liberty and fair play, so that they may intelligently understand America and actively participate in our war for democracy.

IMMIGRATION COMMITTEE,
FRANK TRUMBULL, *Chairman,*
GEORGE A. CULLEN,
WM. FELLOWES MORGAN,
J. F. DENECHAUD,
GANO DUNN,
RICHARD H. EMONDS,
MARION E. HAY,
ALEXANDER HILTON,
W. F. HYPES,
HERBERT MYRICK,
RAYMOND B. PRICE,
JULIUS ROSENWALD,
BERNARD J. ROTHWELL,
BOLTON SMITH,
FELIX M. WARBURG,
A. C. WEISS,
WALTER F. WILCOX,
B. L. WINCHELL.

SECTION III

SUB-SECTION III. CITIZENSHIP TRAINING IN THE STATE OF NEW YORK

SECTION III.

SUB-SECTION III. CITIZENSHIP TRAINING IN THE STATE OF NEW YORK.

SECTION III

SUB-SECTION III. CITIZENSHIP TRAINING IN THE STATE OF NEW YORK

		PAGE
Chapter	I. State Legislation	2417
	1. Compulsion for Minors	2417
	2. Compulsion for Minors of Employment Age	2419
	3. Military and Disciplinary Training	2424
	4. Patriotism	2430
	5. The Flag	2431
	6. Textbooks	2431
	7. Qualifications of Teachers	2432
	8. Special Courses for Teachers	2434
	9. Use of Schoolhouse and Grounds	2435
	10. Kindergartens and Night Schools	2437
	11. Registration of Institutions	2438
II. State Programs		2439
	1. Bulletin — " Immigrant Education "	2439
	2. Report of Adult Education Committee of the Ministry of Reconstruction of England	2447
	3. Americanization in Industry	2449
	4. Community Organization	2473
	5. Americanization Through Women's Organizations	2481
	6. Lessons for Illiterate Foreign Women	2486
	7. Methods of Teaching English to the Non-English-Speaking Foreign-Born	2506
	8. Report from Director of the Division of Agricultural and Industrial Education	2556
III. State Normal Schools		2564
	1. Brockport.... 2564	5. Oneonta...... 2566
	2. Cortland...... 2564	6. Oswego....... 2566
	3. Fredonia...... 2565	7. Plattsburg.... 2567
	4. New Paltz.... 2566	
IV. Principal Cities of the State Outside of New York City		2569
	1. Albany....... 2569	13. Geneva....... 2584
	2. Amsterdam... 2570	14. Glens Falls.... 2584
	3. Auburn....... 2571	15. Gloversville... 2585
	4. Binghamton... 2573	16. Herkimer..... 2585
	5. Buffalo....... 2573	17. Ilion......... 2585
	6. Cohoes....... 2578	18. Ithaca........ 2586
	7. Cortland...... 2578	19. Lancaster..... 2587
	8. Depew....... 2579	20. Lockport..... 2588
	9. Dunkirk...... 2580	21. Malone....... 2590
	10. Elmira....... 2582	22. Mount Vernon. 2590
	11. Fredonia...... 2583	23. New Rochelle.. 2591
	12. Geneseo...... 2583	24. Newburgh.... 2593

Chapter IV. Principal Cities of State Outside of New York City—*Cont'd.* PAGE

  25. Niagara Falls.. 2594   37. Rome........ 2613
  26. Norwich...... 2594   38. Schenectady... 2613
  27. Ogdensburg... 2594   39. Solvay........ 2616
  28. Oneida....... 2595   40. Syracuse...... 2616
  29. Oneonta...... 2595   41. Tonawanda... 2616
  30. Oswego....... 2595   42. Troy.......... 2618
  31. Peekskill..... 2595   43. Utica......... 2618
  32. Plattsburgh... 2596   44. Watertown.... 2619
  33. Port Chester.. 2596   45. Watervliet.... 2620
  34. Potsdam...... 2596   46. White Plains.. 2620
  35. Poughkeepsie. 2596   47. Yonkers...... 2620
  36. Rochester..... 2597

 V. Public Schools of New York City.......................... 2623
  1. List of Evening Schools............................... 2623
  2. Testimony of School Officials......................... 2631
  3. " Unpatriotic Teaching in Public Schools ".............. 2658
  4. Address by Arthur S. Somers — " Americanization "...... 2691
  5. Letter from Superintendent Ettinger to Teachers........ 2696
  6. Compositions of School Boys........................... 2698
  7. Resolutions of the Teachers' Council................... 2698

 VI. Churches.. 2701
  1. Presbyterian... 2701
   a. Testimony of Reverend Kenneth Miller............. 2701
   b. Church Publications Quoted....................... 2702
   c. Letters from Pastors............................. 2877
  2. Methodist.. 2881
  3. Episcopalian... 2882
   a. Testimony of Dr Thomas Burgess................ 2882
   b. Conference on Christian Americanization.......... 2883
   c. Report on Christian Americanization.............. 2885
   d. Church Publications Quoted...................... 2909
  4. Baptist.. 2934
  5. Congregational....................................... 2937
  6. Catholic... 2941
  7. Lutheran... 2943
  8. Dutch Reformed....................................... 2947
  9. Religious Society of Friends.......................... 2947

 VII. Settlement Houses...................................... 2949
  1. United Neighborhood Houses of New York............... 2949
   a List of Officers and Members..................... 2949
   b. Americanization Program......................... 2950
   c. Testimony Before Committee...................... 2955
   d. Communications from Members 2960
   e. Note — Attitude Toward Educational Bills Proposed
    by Joint Legislative Committee................. 3000
  2. Non Members of Association........................... 3002

 VIII. Young Men's Christian Association....................... 3018
 IX. Young Women's Christian Association....................... 3052
  1. The Ballard School................................... 3052
  2. International Institute............................... 3053

STATE LEGISLATION 2415

	PAGE
Chapter X. Y. M. and Y. W. H. A.	3060
1. Young Men's Hebrew Association	3060
2. Young Women's Hebrew Association	3078
XI. Industries	3079
1. National Association of Corporation Schools	3079
2. Reports from Representative Industries	3088
XII. Civic and Other Organizations — Statements from Representative Organizations	3141
1. Alliance Israelite Universelle	3141
2. American Defense Society	3145
3. American Federation of Labor	3147
4. American Jewish Committee	3148
5. American Legion	3160
6. American Red Cross	3161
7. American Rights League	3169
8. Boy Scouts of America	3169
9. Bureau of Jewish Education	3172
10. Carnegie Foundation	3175
11. Chamber of Commerce of the State of New York	3178
12. Chinese Consolidated Benevolent Association	3185
13. Community Councils of New York City	3185
14. Constitutional League	3186
15. Cooper Union	3189
16. Federation of Galician and Bucovinian Jews of America	3189
17. Finnish Educational Association of Manhattan	3196
18. Girl Scouts	3197
19. Hebrew Sheltering and Immigrant Aid Society of America	3199
20. Hungarian Society of New York	3202
21. Immigrant Publication Society	3203
22. Irish Emigrant Society	3229
23. Italian Bureau of Public Information	3230
24. Japanese Association, Inc.	3231
25. Japanese Christian Institute, Inc.	3231
26. Jewish Protectory and Aid Society	3233
27. Jewish Welfare Board	3234
28. Knights of Columbus	3238
29. League for the Liberation of Carpatho-Russia	3238
30. Maedchenheim-Verein	3239
31. National Association of Manufacturers	3239
32. National Herald	3239
33. National League of Women Workers	3240
34. National Liberal Immigration League	3240
35. National Security League	3249
36. New York Community Chorus	3268
37. New York Kindergarten Association	3269
38. New York State Federation of Labor	3273
39. Pan-Hellenic Union in America	3273
40. Patriotic Education Society	3274
41. People's Institute of New York	3275
42. Polish National Alliance	3279
43. Russian Collegiate Institute	3279

Chapter XII. Civic and Other Organizations—*Continued:* PAGE

- 44. Russian Economic League........................... 3282
- 45. Society for Ethical Culture........................... 3282
- 46. Society for Italian Immigrants....................... 3282
- 47. United Textile Workers of America.................. 3292
- 48. Woman Suffrage Society........................... 3292

XIII. Colleges and Universities.................................. 3294

1. Testimony of College Representatives.................. 3294
   - a. Adelphi... 3294
   - b. Columbia....................................... 3295
   - c. New York University............................ 3298
2. Communications from Educators...................... 3299
   - a. Adelphi... 3299
   - b. Alexander Hamilton Institute..................... 3300
   - c. Alfred University................................ 3302
   - d. Barnard College................................. 3302
   - e. Brooklyn Training School for Teachers............. 3303
   - f. College of the City of New York................... 3304
   - g. Columbia University............................. 3306
   - h. Cornell University............................... 3311
   - i. Hunter College................................... 3311
   - j. Jewish Theological Seminary of America........... 3312
   - k. Keuka College................................... 3314
   - l. New York School of Social Work.................. 3314
   - m. St. Francis Xavier............................... 3316
   - n. St. Stephen's College............................ 3317
   - o. Syracuse University............................. 3317
   - p. Teachers College................................ 3317
   - q. Union College................................... 3328
   - r. Yonkers Training School for Teachers............. 3329

XIV. Technical Schools.. 3331

1. Baron de Hirsch Trade School........................ 3331
2. Berlitz School of Languages.......................... 3331
3. General Society of Mechanics and Tradesmen School..... 3332
4. Hebrew Technical Institute........................... 3333
5. Hebrew Technical School for Girls.................... 3333
6. New York Trade School.............................. 3334

CHAPTER I

State Legislation

1. COMPULSION FOR MINORS

Article 1, Section 11. Compulsory school ages. The term "child of compulsory school age" means any child between seven and sixteen years of age lawfully required to attend upon instruction.

Article 23, Section 620. Instruction required. The instruction required under this article shall be:

1. At a public school in which at least the six common school branches of reading, spelling, writing, arithmetic, English language and geography are taught in English.

2. Elsewhere than a public school upon instruction in the same subjects taught in English by a competent teacher.

§ 621. **Required attendance upon instruction.** 1. Every child within the compulsory school ages, in proper physical and mental condition to attend school, residing in a city or school district having a population of five thousand or more and employing a superintendent of schools, shall regularly attend upon instruction as follows:

a. Each child between seven and fourteen years of age shall attend the entire time during which the school attended is in session, which period shall not be less than one hundred and eighty days of actual school.

b. Each child between fourteen and sixteen years of age not regularly and lawfully engaged in any useful employment or service, and to whom an employment certificate has not been duly issued under the provisions of the Labor Law, shall so attend the entire time during which the school attended is in session. (Subdivision 1 amended by L. 1917, ch. 563, in effect May 18, 1917.)

2. Every such child, residing elsewhere than in a city or school district having a population of five thousand or more and employing a superintendent of schools, shall attend upon instruction dur-

ing the entire time that the school in the district shall be in session as follows:

    a. Each child between eight and fourteen years of age.

    b. Each child between fourteen and sixteen years of age not regularly and lawfully engaged in any useful employment or service. (Subdivision amended by L. 1913, ch. 511.)

3. The provisions of this section are intended to include all blind children, except such as may receive appointments under the provisions of article 38 of this chapter. (Section amended by L. 1911, ch. 710.)

4. A child within the prescribed ages as provided by this section shall be deemed in proper physical and mental condition to attend upon instruction unless a certificate shall have been issued by the school authorities that the child is not in proper physical and mental condition to so attend. No physical condition which is capable of correction shall avail as a defense under the provisions of this article unless it shall be made to appear that all reasonable measures for the correction of the condition and the suitable instruction of the child have been taken. (Added by L. 1919, ch. 232, in effect April 15, 1919.)

871-a. Bureau of Compulsory education, school census and child welfare. In a city having a population of one million or more there shall be a bureau of compulsory education, school census and child welfare. Said bureau shall consist of a director, an assistant director, a chief attendance officer, and such other supervisors, attendance officers, enumerators, clerks and other employees as may be necessary to carry out the provisions of articles twenty-two, twenty-three and twenty-four of the Education Law, and to perform other and related duties imposed by the provisions of any other statutes or requirements of the board of education. Attendance officers and supervising attendance officers of every grade shall be appointed from eligible lists prepared in the same manner and by the same authority as are eligible lists for teachers and subject likewise to the provisions of section eight hundred and seventy-two as to tenure of office; but an eligible list for attendance officers in existence when this act takes effect shall be exhausted before nominations are made from an eligible list subsequently established. Those persons who as the result of appointment or assignment are serving in any of the positions hereinafter described when this act goes into effect shall hold their respective positions during good behavior and efficient and competent service and shall not be removable except for cause after a hearing by a majority vote of the board of education. The director of said bureau shall have power to commit and parole truant and delinquent children in the manner provided by section six hundred and thirty-five of the Education Law but this authority may be delegated in his absence or disability as the board of education shall provide. The superintendent of schools shall have general supervision of the bureau of compulsory education, school census and child welfare. (Added by L. 1920, ch. 612, in effect May 10, 1920.)

2. COMPULSION FOR MINORS OF EMPLOYMENT AGE
Laws of 1918, Chapter 415

An act to amend the Education Law, to require the attendance at school of non-English speaking and illiterate minors.

The People of the State of New York, represented in Senate and Assembly, do enact as follows:

Section 1. Article 23 of chapter 21 of the Laws of 1909, entitled "An act relating to education, constituting chapter 16 of the consolidated laws," as amended by chapter 140 of the Laws of 1910 is hereby amended by adding thereto a new section, to read as follows:

§ 637. **Attendance of illiterate minors.** 1. Every minor, between sixteen and twenty-one years of age, who does not possess such ability to speak, read and write the English language, as is required, for the completion of the fifth grade of the public or private schools of the city or school district in which he resides, shall attend some day or evening school or some school maintained by an employer as hereinafter provided in subdivision six of this act, in the city or district in which he resides throughout the entire time such school is in session; provided that no such minor be required to attend, if the commissioner of health, or the executive officer of the board or department of health of the city, town, village or district, where such minor resides, or an officer thereof designated by such board, department or commissioner shall deem such minor physically or mentally unfit to attend.

2. Any minor subject to the provisions of this section, who wilfully violates any provisions of this section, shall be punished by a fine of not exceeding five dollars.

3. Every person having in his control any minor subject to the provisions of this section shall cause such minor to attend a school as hereby required; and if such person fails for six sessions within a period of one month to cause such minor to so attend school, unless the commissioner of health or the executive officer of the board or department of health of the city, town, village or district where such minor resides or an officer thereof designated by such board, department or commissioner shall certify that such minor's physical or mental condition is such as to render his attendance at school harmful or impracticable, such person shall, upon complaint by a truant officer and conviction thereof, be punished by a fine of not more than twenty dollars.

4. Whoever induces or attempts to induce such minor to absent himself unlawfully from school or employs such minor except as is provided by law, or harbors such who, while school is in session, is absent unlawfully therefrom shall be punished by a fine of not more than fifty dollars.

5. The employer of any minor subject to the provisions of this section shall procure from such minor and display in the place where such minor is employed the weekly record of regular attendance upon a school and it shall be unlawful for any person to employ any minor subject to the provisions of this section until and unless he procures and displays said weekly record as herein provided. It shall be the duty of the teacher or principal of the school upon which he (such minor) attends to provide each week such minor with a true record of attendance.

6. Any employer may meet the requirements of this act by conducting a class or classes for teaching English and civics to foreign-born in shop, store, plant or factory, under the supervision of the local school authorities, and any minor subject to the provisions of this act may satisfy the requirement by attendance upon such classes.

§ 2. This act shall take effect September 1, 1918.

Article 22, Section 601. Part-time or continuation schools shall be established in cities and school districts having a population of 5,000 or more inhabitants.

The board of education of each city and of each such school district in which there are twenty or more minors above the age of fourteen years and below the age of eighteen years, who are not in regular attendance upon instruction, shall establish and maintain part-time or continuation schools or classes in which such minors shall receive instruction. Such schools or classes may be established in public school buildings, in other buildings especially adapted for their operation, in manufacturing or mercantile establishments and in factories. Such schools or classes, wherever they are established or maintained, shall be under the control and management of the board of education and shall be a part of the public school system of the city or district which maintains them. Courses of study in private or parochial, part-time or continuation schools or classes which meet the requirements of the statutes and the regulations prescribed thereunder may be approved by the Commissioner of Education and, when thus approved, attendance thereon shall be accepted for that required under this article.

b. Such part-time or continuation schools or classes shall be maintained each year during the full period of time which the public schools of a city or district are in session. The sessions of such part-time or continuation schools or classes shall be on the regular schools days and for as many hours between the hours of eight o'clock forenoon and five o'clock afternoon as shall be necessary to provide the required instruction for such minors who reside in said city or district.

c. The courses of study in such part-time or continuation schools or classes shall be approved by the Commissioner of Education and shall include among other subjects instruction in American history, the rights and obligations of citizenship, industrial history, economics, the essential features of the laws relating to the industries taught, and shall also include such other subjects as will enlarge the vocational intelligence of such minors.

d. The board of education of each city and of each such school district shall make necessary arrangements to begin to operate and maintain such part-time or continuation schools or classes, on the opening of the public schools in September, 1920, and shall annually thereafter in September open and maintain additional schools and classes so that by the opening of the public schools in September, 1925, a sufficient number of such schools shall have been established as to afford the required instruction under this article to those minors who are required to attend such schools or classes.

e. Each minor under the age of eighteen years, who is not in regular attendance upon a public, private or parochial school or who is regularly and lawfully employed in some occupation or service, unless such minor has completed a four-year secondary course of instruction approved by the Regents of the University, shall attend a part-time or continuation school or class in the city or district in which such minor resides or may be employed. Such attendance shall be for not less than four hours per week and not more than eight hours per week for each week which such school or class is in session except that the school authorities may, subject to the approval of the Commissioner of Education, permit any such minor to increase the number of hours per week of required attendance and decrease the number of weeks of required attendance. Such minor who is temporarily out of regular employment or service shall attend such school not less than twenty hours per week. The attendance upon a part-time or continuation school or class shall be between the hours of eight o'clock forenoon and five o'clock afternoon.

f. The Commissioner of Education shall make a survey of each city or district to ascertain the industrial, commercial, economic and social needs of such city or district and the benefits and opportunities to be afforded through the establishment of such part-time or continuation schools or classes to the community and to those who are required to attend such schools or classes. The Industrial Commission and the Commissioner of Agriculture shall co-operate with the Commissioner of Education in making such survey.

g. The Regents of the University shall establish regulations to govern and regulate the administration of such part-time or continuation schools or classes and the attendance of minors thereon. To meet local necessities the board of education of each city or school district may establish regulations but such regulations shall not conflict with the regulations adopted by the Regents.

h. The parent, guardian or other person having the custody or control of a minor who is required under the provisions of this article to attend a part-time or continuation school or class shall cause such minor to attend such school or class. A parent, guardian or other person who refuses or fails to comply with this provision of the law shall be deemed guilty of a misdemeanor and upon conviction shall be subject to a fine of not more than one hundred dollars or by imprisonment for not more than ten days, or both such fine and imprisonment at the discretion of the court. Any minor under sixteen years of age who fails to attend upon instruction as defined by this article shall be subject to the provisions of section 635 cf the Education Law, and a minor over sixteen years of age who fails to attend upon instruction as required by this act may be punished for any such violation by a fine not exceeding ten dollars, or by imprisonment for not more than ten days, or by both such fine and imprisonment.

i. Any person, firm or corporation employing a minor between the ages of fourteen years and eighteen years shall permit the attendance of such minor upon a part-time school or class whenever such part-time school or class shall have been established in the city or district where the minor resides or may be employed, and upon the termination of employment of any such minor the employer shall return within three days the employment certificate of such minor by mail to the school authorities, and a person, firm or corporation employing a minor over fourteen years of age and less than eighteen years of age contrary to the provisions of this article shall be subject to a fine of not less than twenty-five dollars and not more than one hundred dollars for each offense or by imprisonment in the city or county jail for not less than five days and not more than ten days, or by such fine and imprisonment at the discretion of the court. A person, firm or corporation, which has in its employ a minor who fails to attend a part-time or continuation school or class as required herein, shall immediately discontinue the services of such minor upon receiving from the school authorities written notice of the failure of such minor to attend such part-time or continuation school or class, and a person, firm or corporation violating this provision of law shall be subject to a fine of fifty dollars for each offense.

j. The board of education of each city or district having a population of five thousand or more inhabitants is hereby required to enforce the provisions of this law and the Commissioner of Education is hereby charged with the duty and vested with necessary authority to supervise the enforcement and administration of this act.

k. If the authorities of such a city or school district fail or refuse to provide the necessary funds for the establishment and maintenance of such part-time or continuation schools or classes as are required under this law, the city or district shall forfeit from the funds due such city or district from the State for school purposes an amount equal to that which is estimated by the board of education as necessary to properly operate and maintain such schools or classes. The public or State funds thus forfeited by such city or district shall be apportioned by the Commissioner of Education to the board of education of such city or district for the purpose of maintaining such part-time or continuation schools or classes and the board of education of the city or district receiving such funds shall apply the same toward the maintenance of such schools or classes and in payment of the expenses incurred thereby. (Amended by L. 1919, ch. 531, in effect August 1, 1919.)

3. MILITARY AND DISCIPLINARY TRAINING (MILITARY LAW, ART. 1-A; ARTICLE ADDED BY L. 1916, CH. 568)

ARTICLE 1-A

Section 26. Military training commission, its assistants, employees and expenses.
     27. Physical and disciplinary training in schools; military training.
     28. Field training for boys.
     29. General powers and duties of the commission.
     29-b. Use of school buildings.
     29-c. Expenses of detailed officers and men.
     29-d. Definitions; article not applicable to certain schools

§ 26. Military training commission, its assistants, employees and expenses. A military training commission for the State is hereby established composed of the major-general commanding the national guard ex-officio, who shall be chairman of the commission, a member to be appointed by the Board of Regents of the University of the State and a member to be appointed by the Governor. The appointed members shall hold office for terms of four years.

The commission shall meet at such places within the State at such stated times as it determines and other meetings shall be held at the call of the chairman or of a majority of the members of the commission at a time and place stated in the call.

The commissioners shall not receive any compensation for their services as such, but they shall be paid their traveling expenses actually and necessarily incurred in the performance of their duties as commissioners.

The commission may appoint and at pleasure remove an inspector of physical training at a salary not exceeding five thousand dollars a year and other assistants and clerks and employees at salaries to be fixed by the commission.

The commission shall make an annual report to the Governor containing a summary of the business transacted with a statement in detail of its expenditures.

§ 27. **Physical and disciplinary training in schools; military training.** 1. The Military Training Commission shall advise and confer with the Board of Regents of the University of the State of New York as to the courses of instruction in physical training to be prescribed for elementary and secondary schools as provided in the Education Law.

In order to more thoroughly and comprehensively prepare the boys of the elementary and secondary schools for the duties and obligations of citizenship, it shall also be the duty of the Military Training Commission to recommend from time to time to the Board of Regents the establishment in such schools, of habits, customs and methods best adapted to develop correct physical posture and bearing, mental and physical alertness, self-control, disciplined initiative, sense of duty and the spirit of cooperation under leadership.

2. After the first day of September, 1916, all boys above the age of sixteen years and not over the age of nineteen years, except boys exempted by the commission, shall be given such military training as the commission may prescribe for periods aggregating not more than three hours in each week between September first of each year and the fifteenth day of June next ensuing. Such training periods, in the case of pupils in schools and colleges, shall be in addition to prescribed periods of other instruction therein and outside the time assigned therefor. The military training commission may in its discretion prescribe a uniform style and color of clothing and equipment which shall be the uniform and equipment worn by all persons subject to military training as provided in this section if any uniform or equipment is worn by any such person, unless such commission approves a uniform or equipment now or hereafter adopted by any school or institution subject to the provisions of this act. Such training shall be conducted under the supervision of the military training commission by such male teachers and physical instructors of schools and colleges as may be assigned by the boards of education or trustees of such schools or governing bodies of such colleges and accepted by the commission, and by officers and enlisted men of the national guard and naval militia detailed for that purpose by the major general commanding the national guard or such officer and enlisted men of the United

States army as may be available. The officers and enlisted men of the national guard and naval militia so detailed shall, while in the actual performance of the duties of the detail, receive such percentage of the pay authorized by this chapter for officers and enlisted men of the national guard and naval militia of their respective grades and length of service as may from time to time be fixed by the commission. Teachers and instructors assigned from schools and colleges shall be paid such compensation as the commission may determine out of moneys appropriated for carrying out the provisions of this article.

Such requirement as to military training, herein prescribed, may in the discretion of the commission be met in part by such vocational training or vocational training or vocational experience as will, in the opinion of the commission, specifically prepare boys of the ages named for service useful to the State, in the maintenance of defense, in the promotion of public safety, in the conservation and development of the State's resources, or in the construction and maintenance of public improvements. (Subdivision amended by L. 1919, ch. 407.)

3. The Military Training Commission shall cause to be issued to each boy above the age of sixteen years and not over the age of nineteen years, who complies with the requirements of this article, a certificate in such form and in such manner as the commission shall prescribe, stating that such boy is enrolled for military training and is meeting the requirement of the law as to such military training.

4. No boy above the age of sixteen years and not over the age of nineteen years shall be permitted to continue in attendance upon instruction in any public or private school or college within the State unless such boy is in possession of a certificate issued as hereinbefore provided, or unless such boy has been exempted by the commission for military training as provided by law and the rules and regulations of the commission. It shall be the duty of the principal or other officer or person having and exercising supervision and control over any such school or college to exclude such boys from attendance upon instruction thereat unless they possess such certificate or are exempted by the commission as herein provided. If the principal or officer in charge of a private school shall fail to comply with the provisions of this subdivision, such school may not receive any apportionment from the public school moneys or academic funds appropriated by the state legis-

lature for the aid of such schools; and if the officer or person in charge of a college shall fail to comply with the provisions of this subdivision, such college shall not be recognized as one of the colleges which may be attended by the holder of state scholarship issued under the provisions of chapter 292 of the Laws of 1913 and the acts amendatory thereof.

5. A boy above the age of sixteen years and not over the age of nineteen years who does not possess a certificate issued as herein provided, showing that he is enrolled for military training and is meeting the requirements of the Military Training Commission as to such military training, shall not be employed or continued in employment by any person, firm or corporation within this State, or by any officer, manager, superintendent or other employee acting in behalf thereof, unless such boy has been exempted by the commission under its rules and regulations. (Amended by L. 1917, ch. 49, and L. 1918, ch. 470.)

§ 28. **Field training for boys.** Within the limit of appropriations therefor, the commission shall establish and maintain State military camps of instruction for field training of boys who are physically fit and above the age of sixteen years and not over the age of nineteen years, and who are accepted therefor by the commission. In determining the persons to receive such field training, where moneys available are not sufficient to provide for all, preference shall be given in the following order unless otherwise provided by law: (1) To male pupils in attendance during the preceding school year in secondary schools; (2) pupils in attendance at State agricultural schools and State agricultural colleges during that period; (3) the other boys above specified. The camps shall be located in such places throughout the State as the commission may determine. Any society, organization or association having a fair ground and entitled to an apportionment of State moneys under sections 310 and 311 of the Agricultural Law, shall, upon the request of the commission, allow the use of its grounds, or part thereof, for any such camp, when the grounds are not needed for its own purposes, unless previously leased to other parties; and if any such society, association or organization shall refuse to allow the use of its grounds as above provided, the moneys otherwise due to it under such law shall be withheld each year in which such refusal occurs. Such field training shall be given annually, during the summer months, and shall for each detachment of boys cover a period of not less than two or more than four weeks, as the commission may determine. Such camps and the training and discipline thereat shall be under the direction and charge of the commission. The major-general commanding the National Guard shall detail for service at such camps, such number of officers and enlisted men of the National Guard and Naval Militia as may be required by the Commission. Such officers and enlisted men, during such detail shall receive pay, subsistence and transportation as authorized in this chapter and the regulations issued thereunder for officers and enlisted men of their grades and length of service on duty under orders of the major-general, commanding the National Guard. (Amended by L. 1918, ch. 470.)

§ 29. **General powers and duties of the commission.** The commission in addition to the powers elsewhere in this article conferred on it shall have power to:

1. Provide for the observation and inspection of the work and methods prescribed under the provisions of this article, or under the provisions of the Education Law relating to instruction in physical training prescribed after conference with the commission.

2. Prescribe the powers and duties of the inspection of physical training.

3. Regulate the duties of clerical and other assistants and employees of the commission.

4. Prescribe rules and regulations for compulsory attendance during the periods of military training provided in this article.

5. Regulate individual exemptions from prescribed military training.

6. Maintain, and co-operate with the colleges in the State or the federal authorities in maintaining courses of instruction for male teachers and physical instructors and others who volunteer and are accepted by the commission.

7. Make regulations and rules for fully carrying into effect the provisions of this article.

§ 29-a. **State military property, including armories, may be used.** The authorities in charge of armories shall, upon the application of the Military Training Commission, allow the use of any armory of the National Guard and Naval Militia for the conduct of military drills provided for by this article, when such armory is not then required for the use of the National Guard or Naval Militia, and shall authorize the temporary use by boys for whom military instruction is provided as prescribed in this article, for the purpose of such drills, of arms and other equipment of the National Guard and Naval Militia, belonging to the State, not then required for the use of the National Guard or Naval Militia, and of arms and other equipment which may have been rendered obsolete and unserviceable and which may be retained and issued for such purpose, under such rules and regulations as the proper military authorities may prescribe. The military authorities of the State are authorized and empowered to loan to the Military Training Commission such military property as may be necessary in the organization and maintenance of field training camps, and to carry out the provisions of this article. (Amended by L. 1918, ch. 470.)

§ 29-b. **Use of school buildings.** The school authorities throughout the State are authorized to permit the use of school buildings and school grounds for the purpose of carrying out the provisions of this article.

§ 29-c. **Expenses of detailed officers and men.** The expenditures authorized to be made by this article to officers and enlisted men of the National Guard detailed as therein authorized shall be paid from funds appropriated to carry out the provisions of this article.

§ 29-d. **Definitions; article not applicable to certain schools.** The expression "school authorities" as used in this article shall be construed to have the same meaning and effect as is given to such expression in the Education Law. "Secondary schools" means schools for "secondary education," as defined in such law, to the extent that they provide such education. None of the provisions of this article shall apply to any agricultural college in any institution in this State which receives the benefits of the act of congress of July 2, 1862, provided for instruction in agriculture, the mechanic arts, and military training, and in which instruction in military tactics is now required of pupils, nor shall it apply to pupils therein.

2. The sum of one hundred thousand dollars ($100,000), or so much thereof as may be necessary is hereby appropriated to carry out the provisions of this act, which sum shall be expended under

the direction of the Military Training Commission for its expenses, the salary of assistants, clerical hire, pay and expenses of detailed officers and enlisted men of the National Guard and Naval Militia, compensation of teachers and instructors assigned from schools and colleges for conducting military training, and the cost of maintaining training camps.

4. PATRIOTISM

ARTICLE 26-C

Instruction in Patriotism and Citizenship

Section 705. Courses of instruction in patriotism and citizenship. In order to promote a spirit of patriotic and civic service and obligation and to foster in the children of the State moral and intellectual qualities which are essential in preparing to meet the obligations of citizenship in peace or in war, the Regents of The University of the State of New York shall prescribe courses of instruction in patriotism and citizenship, to be maintained and followed in all the schools of the State. The boards of education and trustees of the several cities and school districts of the State shall require instruction to be given in such courses, by the teachers employed in the schools therein. All pupils attending such schools, over the age of eight years, shall attend upon such instruction.

Similar courses of instruction shall be prescribed and maintained in private schools in the State, and all pupils in such schools over eight years of age shall attend upon such courses. If such courses are not so established and maintained in a private school, attendance upon instruction in such school shall not be deemed substantially equivalent to instruction given to pupils of like age in the public schools of the city or district in which such pupils reside. (Added by L. 1918, ch. 241, in effect April 17, 1918.)

§ 706. **Rules prescribing courses; inspection and supervision; enforcement.** The Regents of The University of the State of New York shall determine the subjects to be included in such courses of instruction in each of the grades in such subjects. They shall adopt rules providing for attendance upon such instruction and for such other matters as are required for carrying into effect the objects and purposes of this article.

5. THE FLAG

Article 27

The flag

§ 710. Purchase and display of flag. It shall be the duty of the school authorities of every public school in the several cities and school districts of the State to purchase a United States flag, flagstaff and the necessary appliances therefor, and to display such flag upon or near the public school building during school hours, and at such other times as such school authorities may direct.

§ 711. Rules and regulations. The said school authorities shall establish rules and regulations for the proper custody, care and display of the flag, and when the weather will not permit it to be otherwise displayed, it shall be placed conspicuously in the principal room in the schoolhouse.

§ 712. Commissioner of Education shall prepare program. 1. It shall be the duty of the Commissioner of Education to prepare, for the use of the public schools of the State, a program providing for a salute to the flag and such other patriotic exercises as may be deemed by him to be expedient, under such regulations and instructions as may best meet the varied requirements of the different grades in such schools.

2. It shall also be his duty to make special provision for the observance in the public schools of Lincoln's birthday, Washington's birthday, Memorial day and Flag day, and such other legal holidays of like character as may be hereafter designated by law when the Legislature makes an appropriation therefor.

§ 713. Military drill excluded. Nothing herein contained shall be construed to authorize military instruction or drill in the public schools during school hours.

6. TEXTBOOKS

Article 25, Section 674. Textbooks containing seditious or disloyal matter. No textbook in any subject used in the public schools in this State shall contain any matter or statements of any kind which are seditious in character, disloyal to the United States or favorable to the cause of any foreign country with which the United States is now at war. A commission is hereby created, consisting of the Commissioner of Education and of two persons to be designated by the Regents of the University of the State of

New York, whose duty it shall be on complaint to examine textbooks used in the public schools of the State, in the subjects of civics, economics, English, history, language and literature, for the purpose of determining whether such textbooks contain any matter or statements of any kind which are seditious in character, disloyal to the United States or favorable to the cause of any foreign country with which the United States is now at war. Any person may present a written complaint to such commission that a textbook in any of the aforesaid subjects for use in the public schools of this State or offered for sale for use in the public schools of this State contains matter or statements in violation of this section, specifying such matter or statements in detail. If the commission determine that the textbook against which complaint is made contains any such matter or statements, it shall issue a certificate disapproving the use of such textbook in the public schools of this State, together with a statement of the reasons for its disapproval, specifying the matter found unlawful. Such certificate of disapproval of a textbook, with a detailed statement of the reasons for its disapproval, shall be duly forwarded to the boards of education or other boards or authorities having jurisdiction of the public schools of the cities, towns or school districts of this State, and after the receipt of such certificate the use of a textbook so disapproved shall be discontinued in such city, town or school district.

Any contract hereafter made by any such board of education or other school authorities for the purchase of a textbook in any of such subjects, which has been so disapproved, shall be void. Any school officer or teacher who permits a textbook in any of such subjects, which has been so disapproved, to be used in the public schools of the State, shall be guilty of a misdemeanor. (Added by L. 1918, ch. 246, in effect April 17, 1918.)

7. QUALIFICATIONS OF TEACHERS

Article 20, Section 550. Qualifications of teachers. No person shall be employed or authorized to teach in the public schools of the State who is

1. Under the age of eighteen years.
2. Not in possession of a teacher's certificate issued under the authority of this chapter or a diploma issued on the completion of a course in a State normal school of this State or in the State normal college.

3. **Not a citizen.** A person employed as a teacher on April 4, 1918, who was not a citizen, may continue in such employment provided he or she, within one year from such date, shall make application to become a citizen and within the time thereafter prescribed by law shall become a citizen. The provisions of this subdivision shall not apply to alien teachers who are citizens of countries that were allied with this country in the prosecution of the war with Germany and who were employed as teachers in this State on or prior to April 4, 1918, provided such teacher make application to become a citizen before the first day of September, 1920, and within the time thereafter prescribed by law shall become such citizen. (Amended by L. 1918, ch. 158, and L. 1919, ch. 120, in effect March 31, 1919.)

§ 551. **Minimum qualifications of teachers in primary and grammar schools.** No person shall hereafter be employed or licensed to teach in the primary and grammar schools of any city or school district authorized by law to employ a superintendent of schools who has not had successful experience in teaching for at least three years, or in lieu thereof has not completed:

1. A course in one of the State normal schools of this State or in any approved college, prescribed by the commissioner of education. (Subdivision 1 amended by L. 1920, ch. 155, in effect April 5, 1920.)

2. An examination for and received a life State certificate issued in this State by a superintendent of public instruction or the commissioner of education.

3. A course of study in a high school or academy of not less than three years approved by the commissioner of education or from some institution of learning of equal or higher rank approved by the same authority, and who subsequently to the completion of such course has not graduated from a school for the professional training of teachers having a course of not less than two years approved by the commissioner of education or its equivalent.

§ 568. **Removal of superintendents, teachers and employees for treasonable or seditious acts or utterances.** A person employed as superintendent of schools, teacher or employee in the public schools, in any city or school district of the State, shall be removed from such position for the utterance of any treasonable or seditious word or words or the doing of any treasonable or seditious act or acts while holding such position. (Added by L. 1917, ch. 416, in effect May 8, 1917.)

8. SPECIAL COURSES FOR TEACHERS

Article 4, Section 11-a. The Commissioner of Education is authorized and directed to establish and provide for the maintenance and conduct of courses of study or training in State normal institutions and in colleges and universities and other educational institutions and in connection with other educational agencies for the purpose of training teachers in principles and methods of instruction, and to give them knowledge to fit them to instruct foreign-born and native adults and minors over sixteen years of age in evening, extension, factory, home and community classes. Such courses of study shall be prescribed by the Commissioner of Education and shall continue for a period of not less than one year. No teacher employed to instruct foreign-born and native adults and minors over sixteen years of age shall be employed by the State or compensated in whole or in any part by the State, unless he shall have completed such course of study or training or shall have an equivalent thereof to be determined under the rules and regulations of the Commissioner of Education. A special certificate shall be issued to teachers who have completed such course of study or a course of instruction which is equivalent thereto, provided, however, that temporary permits may be issued by the Commissioner of Education to teachers who are qualified to give such instruction pending the completion of such a course of study or training. (Added by L. 1918, ch. 412; amended by L. 1920, ch. 851, in effect May 20, 1920. The sum of $40,000 was appropriated by the Legislature to carry out the provisions of this subdivision.)

§ 11-b. The Commissioner of Education is hereby authorized to divide the State into zones and to appoint directors thereof, teachers, and such other employees as may be necessary to promote and extend educational facilities for the education of illiterates and of non-English speaking persons. (Added by L. 1919, ch. 617, in effect May 14, 1919.)

§ 11-c. The board of estimate and apportionment of a city, the council of a city, or the common council of a city, the board of supervisors of a county, the board of trustees of an incorporated village, the town board of a town, may make appropriations to aid and promote the extension of education among the illiterates and non-English speaking persons within the jurisdiction of these respective bodies. (Added by L. 1919, ch. 617, in effect May 14, 1919. The sum of $100,000 was appropriated to the Commissioner of Education for carrying out the provisions of subdivisions 11-b and 11-c.)

§ 11-d. The Commissioner of Education may provide for the establishment of courses of instruction of study and schools in connection with factories, places of employment, or in such other places as he may deem advisable, for the purpose of giving instruction to foreign-born and native adults and minors over the age of sixteen years. Such course of instruction of study shall include instruction in English, history, civics and other subjects tending to promote good citizenship and to increase vocational efficiency. Such course of instruction and study shall be prescribed by the Regents of the University of the State of New York, and shall be in conformity with rules to be adopted by them.

The Commissioner of Education is authorized and directed to employ teachers and to fix the compensation of teachers especially trained and having certificates as provided in subdivisions 11-a of this section, and to assign such teachers to service in extension courses in factories and other places of employment, or in such other places as he may deem advisable throughout the State, established as provided by law. (Added by L. 1920, ch. 852, in effect May 20, 1920. The sum of $100,000 was appropriated by the Legislature to carry out the provisions of this subdivision.)

9. USE OF SCHOOLHOUSE AND GROUNDS

Article 16, Section 455. Use of schoolhouse and grounds out of school hours. Schoolhouses and the grounds connected therewith and all property belonging to the district shall be in the custody and under the control and supervision of the trustees or board of education of the district. The trustees or board of education may adopt reasonable regulations for the use of such schoolhouses, grounds or other property, when not in use for school purposes, for such other public purposes as are herein provided. Such regulations shall not conflict with the provisions of this chapter and shall conform to the purposes and intent of this section and shall be subject to review on appeal to the commissioner of education as provided by law. The trustees or board of education of each district may, subject to regulations adopted as above provided, permit the use of the schoolhouse and rooms therein, and the grounds and other property of the district, when not in use for school purposes, for any of the following purposes:

1. By persons assembling therein for the purpose of giving and receiving instruction in any branch of education, learning or the arts.

2. For public library purposes, subject to the provisions of this chapter, or as stations of public libraries.

3. For holding social, civic and recreational meetings and entertainments, and other uses pertaining to the welfare of the community; but such meetings, entertainment and uses shall be nonexclusive and shall be open to the general public.

4. For meetings, entertainments and occasions where admission fees are charged, when the proceeds thereof are to be expended for an educational or charitable purpose; but such use shall not be permitted if such meetings, entertainments and occasions are under the exclusive control, and the said proceeds are to be applied for the benefit of a society, association or organization of a religious sect or denomination, or of a fraternal, secret or other exclusive society or organization.

5. For polling places for holding primaries and elections and for the registration of voters, and for holding political meetings. But no such use shall be permitted unless authorized by a vote of a district meeting, held as provided by law, or, in cities, by the board of education thereof. Except in cities, it shall be the duty of the trustees or board of education to call a special meeting for such purpose upon the petition of at least ten per centum of the qualified electors of the district. Authority so granted shall continue until revoked in like manner and by the same body as granted.

6. For civic forums and community centers. Upon the petition of at least twenty-five citizens residing within the district or city, the trustees or board of education in each school district or city shall organize and conduct community centers for civic purposes, and civic forums in the several

school districts and cities, to promote and advance principles of Americanization among the residents of the State. The trustees or board of education in each school district or city, when organizing such community centers or civic forums, shall provide funds for the maintenance and support of such community centers and civic forums, and shall prescribe regulations for their conduct and supervision, provided that nothing herein contained shall prohibit the trustees of such school district or the board of education to prescribe and adopt rules and regulations to make such community centers or civic forums self-supporting as far as practicable. Such community centers and civic forums shall be at all times under the control of the trustees or board of education in each school district or city, and shall be nonexclusive and open to the general public. (Amended by L. 1913, ch. 221; L. 1917, ch. 214; and L. 1920, ch. 150, in effect April 1, 1920.)

10. KINDERGARTENS AND NIGHT SCHOOLS

Article 11, Section 311. Kindergartens; night schools. The board of education of each school district and of each city may maintain kindergartens which shall be free to resident children between the ages of four and six years.

Night schools wherein the common branches and such additional subjects as may be adapted to students applying for instruction are taught on three nights each week, for two hours each night, shall be maintained by the board of education:

1. In each city of the first class throughout the duration of the day school term.
2. In each city of the second class on at least one hundred nights.
3. In each city of the third class on at least eighty nights.
4. In each city not subject to the foregoing provisions and in each school district where twenty or more minors between the ages of sixteen and twenty-one years are required to attend school, or where twenty or more persons over the age of sixteen years make applications for instruction in a night school, for at least seventy-five nights.

All night schools shall be free to all persons residing in the districts or city. (Amended by L. 1918, ch. 409, in effect September 1, 1918.)

11. REGISTRATION OF INSTITUTIONS

Article 3, Section 50. Registrations. The Regents may register domestic and foreign institutions in terms of New York standards, and fix the value of degrees, diplomas and certificates issued by institutions of other States or countries and presented for entrance to schools, colleges and the professions in this State.

§ 51. Supervision of professions. Conformably to law the Regents may supervise the entrance regulations to and the licensing under and the practicing of the professions of medicine, dentistry, veterinary medicine, pharmacy, optometry and chiropody and also supervise the certification of nurses, public accountants, certified shorthand reporters, architects, and members of any other profession which may hereafter come under the supervision of the Board of Regents.

§ 52. Extension of educational facilities. The Regents may extend to the people at large increased educational opportunities and facilities, stimulate interest therein, recommend methods, designate suitable teachers and lecturers, conduct examinations and grant credentials, and otherwise organize, aid and conduct such work. And the Regents, and with their approval the Commissioner of Education, may buy, sell, exchange and receive by will, or other gift, or on deposit, books, pictures, statuary or other sculptural work, lantern slides, apparatus, maps, globes, and any articles or collections pertaining to or useful in and to any of the departments, divisions, schools, institutions, associations or other agencies, or work, under their supervision, or control, or encouragement, and may lend or deposit any such articles in their custody or control, when or where in their judgment compensating educational usefulness will result therefrom; and may also, from time to time, enter into contracts desirable for carrying into effect the foregoing provisions.

CHAPTER II
State Programs

1. BULLETIN — "IMMIGRANT EDUCATION"

This bulletin aims to set forth briefly the program and policy of the Education Department relative to immigrant education. It proposes to present to Americanization workers certain ideas and ideals fundamental to their work, and to indicate a definite, comprehensive program, which shall centralize all existing Americanization agencies and enlist their cooperation. The statistics concerning the number of non-English-speaking and illiterate persons in the State show the need of such a program.

Although the training of teachers for instructing immigrants in the English language and in the principles of citizenship has been the chief aim of the Department in dealing with the problem up to this time, it now proposes to extend its work by promoting the education of all illiterates, native as well as foreign-born, so that all may be united by the bonds of a common language, common standards, and common ideals. Its first duty is to help the native-born to a living realization of all that Americanism means, and its second duty is to help the foreign-born gain the vision and live it.

To show the widespread and enthusiastic approval of immigrant education by the people of the State and to indicate the scope of its program, the Department presents in this bulletin recent legislation concerning immigrant education in New York State.

A reading list, which includes sources, references, methods and texts, is also included as a guide for further study and investigation.

WILLIAM C. SMITH
*Supervisor of Immigrant Education,
New York State Department of Education*

CLARA B. SPRINGSTEED
Assistant

WHAT EVERY AMERICANIZATION WORKER SHOULD KNOW

1. The background of the life of the foreign-born.
    a. Geography of the native land.
    b. Main features in its history.
    c. Social and political life.
    d. Religious life.
    e. Education.
    f. Racial characteristics.

2. The reasons for coming to America.
    a. Economic.
    b. Social.
    c. Political.
    d. Religious.
    e. Military.
3. The means by which the foreign-born may best satisfy the longing which brought him here.
    a. Finding the work he is best fitted to do.
    b. Learning the language of America.
    c. Becoming acquainted with American laws, customs and standards of living.
    d. Becoming a citizen.
    e. Learning to know the outside agencies which can help him and enlarge his vision.
    f. Cooperating with the native American to promote and uphold real Americanism.
4. The most successful ways and means of teaching English and the principles of American citizenship to the foreign-born.
5. The value and beauty of all that the foreign-born brings us in his " gifts of mind, heart and hand."
6. The ideals of our democracy as set forth in the constitution.
    a. Political life; "A government of the people, by the people and for the people."
    b. Social life; "A man's a man for a' that."
    c. Industrial life; "A square deal."
    d. Religious life; " Freedom to worship God."
7. The ideals of our democracy as determined by the united purpose of foreign-born and native-born to create a new and better America.
8. The necessity of the foreign-born joining hands with the native-born to make these ideals of our dmocracy a living reality.

Statistics

1910 census

Total population of New York State............	9,113,614
Total number of foreign-born...................	2,748,011
Total number of illiterates, 10 years of age and over.	406,020

Foreign-born whites, 10 years of age and over, illiterates 362,025
Foreign-born whites, 10 years of age and over, unable to speak English....................... 597,012

These figures impress the vital need of an immediate carrying out of a comprehensive Americanization program in New York State.

The Americanization work of the State Department of Education has as its main objectives:

1. To eliminate illiteracy.
2. To carry the message of democracy and American ideals to non-English-speaking and illiterate residents of New York State.
3. To bring about friendly cooperation between the various foreign groups and the native-born.
4. To make America safe for democracy in every community.

Increased interest in Americanization is an outgrowth of the war with the startling revelations of the draft concerning the number of non-English-speaking and illiterate persons in our population. Americanization challenges us as members of a democracy to prove our right to the name. A real democracy must be based upon a common language, common purpose, a common ideal and an intelligent electorate. This thought was well expressed by Dr. John H. Finley when he said:

"We must recognize that thousands of aliens in this State are but waiting for an opportunity to acquire the common tongue of our social and civic life. Teaching the common language of America is incontestably the first duty of a democratic state. It is the duty of the school to teach the common language not only because it is the very cement of all social and political fabric, but because it is a possession which every man, woman and child must have to attain real citizenship. In many communities of the State, public schools and private associations are doing much to help the alien illiterates to acquire the tongue of this democracy.

"Should not the State now, seriously, vigorously, and specifically, undertake to reduce adult illiteracy as it has with such success reduced child illiteracy? Every argument for training a child into a knowledge of English and citizenship is equally good for the alien who is ignorant of our language, customs and ideals, but who wishes to become a worthy American citizen."

Since it is evident that teachers must have special training to carry on this work, the State Department of Education, in cooperation with colleges and normal schools and with local school authorities, is giving short unit courses on "principles and methods of immigrant education," in some of the larger cities of the State and in smaller districts where the number of foreign-born makes the need of this instruction imperative.

The first institutes, as they have been called, were held during July and August, 1918, in Buffalo, Rochester, Syracuse, Albany and New York City. More than 1,000 teachers and social workers took advantage of this opportunity to make themselves more capable of understanding the foreigner and of helping him.

Similar institutes have been held during the winter of 1918-19 at Hempstead, Roslyn, Babylon, Huntington, Yonkers, New York City, Albany, Utica, Syracuse, Buffalo and Watertown. The State now has about 2,500 persons trained and equipped to carry out its program. Summer sessions will be held at Syracuse University, New York State College for Teachers, Teachers College of Columbia University, and Hunter College.

Wherever institutes are held and the whole district thoroughly organized for the work, immediate results are evidenced in the starting of factory classes, the forming of new classes in night schools, and in the homes or community centers.

Outline of the Short Unit Course*

Aim. The aim of the course is to interpret the meaning of Americanization, to furnish to persons interested in Americanization a definite background for further study and practice, to develop competent teachers to give the immigrant instruction in the English language and to familiarize him with American customs, laws and standards of living.

Length of the course. The course usually consists of fifteen sessions of two hours each, which fulfils the Regents requirement for one point. Two lectures are given at each session.

Scope of the work. The subjects under discussion include: ethnological aspects of the immigrant, state and federal plans for

---

* For increased requirements and facilities, see Addendum, Part I.

Americanization, economic aspects of immigration and their interpretation, organization and supervision of English and citizenship classes, methods of teaching English to foreigners, aids in developing a good pronunciation, methods of teaching civics and preparing for naturalization, Americanization through the library, and means of cooperation by all existing agencies of Americanization.

Instructors. The instructors in these courses are all persons of intensive training and wide experience as students and teachers in this line of work. The instructors are selected from the ranks of local educational authorities and also from the following list:

 William C. Smith, Supervisor of Immigrant Education, New York State Department of Education, Albany.

 Clara B. Springsteed, Assistant in Immigrant Education, New York State Department of Education, Albany.

 Charles Towne, Supervisor of Immigrant Education, Boston, Mass.

 H. D. Rickard, Principal of Putnam School, Syracuse.

 Charles E. Finch, Director of Immigrant Education, Rochester.

 Dr. Edward Steiner, Grinnell College, Iowa.

 Dr. David Hutchinson, Professor of Civics and Government, State College for Teachers, Albany.

 Adam Walker, Professor of Sociology and Economics, State College for Teachers, Albany.

 Harriet P. Dow, Field Secretary, Yorkville Neighborhood Association, New York City.

 Elsa Alsberg, National Council of Jewish Women, New York City.

 Allen T. Burns, Director, Study of Americanization, Carnegie Corporation, New York City.

 Mrs. V. A. Simkhovitch, Director, Greenwich House, New York City.

 H. A. Miller, Secretary, Mid-European Union, Washington, D. C.

 Reginald Heber Smith, former Counsel in Chief, Boston Legal Aid Society.

 Nathan Peyser, Executive Director, Educational Alliance, New York City.

 Mrs. Nellie Michaelson, Rochester.

 John J. Mahoney, Principal, State Normal School, Lowell, Mass.

Merten A. Sturges, Chief Examiner, Bureau of Naturalization, New York City.

William McAndrew, Associate Superintendent of Schools, New York City.

E. E. Bach, Director of Americanization Bureau, Pennsylvania.

George Eisler, American House, Cincinnati, Ohio.

M. A. Ravage, Author and Publicist, New York City.

Henry H. Goldberger, Lecturer, Teachers College, New York City.

Robert T. Hill, War Camp Community Service, New York City.

John Collier, People's Institute, New York City.

Pierre Vampiere, University of Michigan, Ann Arbor, Mich.

Dr. Caroline Hedger, Social Welfare Worker in Chicago Stock Yards, Chicago, Ill.

Margery Quigley, Endicott Public Library, Endicott.

Mrs. Helen Horvath, Specialist in Work with Foreign-born Women, Cleveland, Ohio.

Dr. George E. Smith, Deputy Superintendent of Schools, Buffalo.

Henry E. Jenkins, District Superintendent of Schools, New York City.

Esther E. Lape, Section of Aliens, Council of Women's Organizations, New York City.*

Qualifications for the course. Any person who has a high school education or its equivalent, who speaks English clearly and distinctly, and who is vitally interested in the problems of Americanization is eligible to the course.

Visitors. Visitors who are unable to attend the course regularly or pursue it for credit are welcome to any or all of the lectures.

Credit. The University of the State of New York will certify the attendance and satisfactory completion of the course. School authorities will give preference to those holding this certificate when considering applicants for work with foreign-born adults.

Requirements of the course:

1. Regular attendance at 80 per cent. of the sessions of the course.

---

* The viewpoint of some of the above educators is such as to make the Committee doubt the wisdom of employing them in this work. See Index, Part I.

2. A carefully prepared notebook containing notes on all the lectures given at the institute. This notebook must be submitted for examination at the end of the course.

3. Book reviews as assigned by the local director.

4. A paper which indicates definite research and original thought.

5. A final examination which will be a real test of the main lines of thought presented at the institute.

Practical demonstrations. Wherever possible opportunities for visiting evening, factory and neighborhood classes are given to students of the course in order that they may observe various methods in operation and judge of their efficacy.

Volunteer work. The local directors of institutes organize and supervise factory, home and neighborhood classes which are taught by volunteers from the Americanization course in session.

AMERICANIZATION INSTITUTE
Topics for Study and Research — 1919

1. Organizing classes.
2. The problems of the evening school.
3. The factory class.
4. Home instruction — its difficulties and possibilities.
5. The direct method.
6. The Gouin method.
7. Method in teaching English to the foreign-born.
8. Aids in developing a good pronunciation.
9. Methods of preparing for naturalization.
10. A comparison of traits of different nationalities in America.
11. The approach to the immigrant.
12. The assimilation of the immigrant.
13. The immigrant's share in construction work on our railways.
14. Peonage.
15. The Padrone: Italian; Greek.
16. The economic effect of returned immigrants upon Italy.
17. How to become a naturalized citizen.
18. How American citizenship may be lost.
19. Naturalization treaties between the United States and foreign states.
20. The claims of foreign governments on naturalized citizens of the United States.

21. The status of aliens in the military, naval and merchant service of the United States.
22. The citizenship of women.
23. The citizenship of minor children.
24. The legal effect of a declaration of intention on women and minor children.
25. The status of the alien woman in her native land.
26. A comparative study of the alien woman in America, (*a*) The woman in industry, (*b*) The woman in the home.
27. The Americanization of the alien woman.
28. Immigration after the war.
29. The attitude of the foreign-born American to reconstruction.
30. Socializing classes for immigrants.
31. Americanizing as an after-war policy.
32. Illiteracy in New York State.
33. The district or zone system of immigrant education in New York State.
34. The immigrant's reaction to the war.

Plans for Future Americanization Work in New York State

It is proposed to divide the State into fifteen zones. These zones have been worked out on the following basis: (1) purposes of administration (local), (2) number of illiterate and non-English-speaking in each district (8 to 12,000), (3) natural geographical divisions.

It is proposed to organize under a director or supervisor a representative group of local Americanization committees, representing all the activities and forces functioning in Americanization service; for example, public schools, civic bodies, chambers of commerce, Rotary clubs, women's organizations, industries, foreign societies and leaders, social and civic forces including Y. M. C. A., Y. W. C. A., K. of C., Y. M. H. A., etc.

The function of this director will be to administer the State's activities through the local forces, to coordinate the local activities behind the public school *extension* program, to arouse and focus public attention and enlist volunteer activity upon constructive Americanization, to supervise the teachers trained in institutions through local cooperation of public school authorities, and to arrange local training centers when and where needed.

The zone plan involves the following program of immigrant education:

1. Opening of evening schools.
2. Extension and stimulation of evening school activities.
3. Promotion of factory classes.
4. Promotion of home classes.
5. Promotion of community classes.
6. Promotion of citizenship classes.
7. Promotion of history and civics instruction.
8. Participation by the foreign-born in the advantages which the State offers in agricultural lines; home demonstrations (Cornell), health education, visual instruction, vocational instruction and guidance, and civic activities.

Various phases of this program have been successfully demonstrated in whole or in part in Syracuse, Rochester, Buffalo, Watertown, Albany and New York City and also in the northern counties.

Each zone involves the following types of Americanization work: (1) educational, (2) industrial, (3) social.

Governor Smith said in his Assembly message: "Ignorance is the greatest ally of our poor citizenship. It should be our objective that no person in this State who can be brought under our influence should be without the ability to read and write, or without a clear conception of our American institutions and ideals." New York may attain this supreme educational achievement if it will.

2. REPORT OF ADULT EDUCATION COMMITTEE OF MINISTRY OF RECONSTRUCTION OF ENGLAND

In connection with immigrant education it is interesting and profitable to cite the conclusions of the Adult Education Committee of the Ministry of Reconstruction of England. In respect to the extension of educational service as a necessary function of the state, this report says:

"The Committee has based its conclusion upon the following proposition:

"1. That the main purpose of education is to fit a man for life, and therefore in a civilized community to fit him for his place as a member of that community.

"2. That the family, the school, the trade union or profession, the local town or district, are successive stages which reach their fullness and completion in the community, and that, therefore, while each part of the process of education must be related to its appropriate stage, the goal of all education must be citizenship — that is, the rights and duties of each individual as a member of the community; and the whole process must be the development of the individual in his relation to the community.

" 3. That the established democracy being not passive but active participation by all in citizenship, education in a democratic country must aim at fitting each individual progressively not only for his personal, domestic and vocational duties, but, above all, for those duties of citizenship for which these earlier stages are training grounds; that is, he must learn (a) what his nation is, and what it stands for in its past history and literature, and what is its place among the other nations of the modern world; (b) what are his duties to it, from the elementary duties of sharing in its defense and submitting to its laws up to the duty of helping to maintain and even to elevate its standards and ideals; (c) the economic, political and international conditions on which his nation's efficiency and well-being depend and the degree to which it can now or in the future enter into closer relations with other civilized nations for the just treatment of less developed races, for the furtherance of international co-operation in science, medicine, law, commerce, arts, and for the increasing establishment of world peace.

" 4. That while it is true that the great mass of a people in the modern industrial world cannot become close students of history, geography, or economics, yet it is also a truth, and a truth brought out by this war, that there is latent in the mass of our people a capacity far beyond what was recognized, a capacity to rise to the conception of great issues and to face the difficulties of fundamental problems when these can be visualized in a familiar form. They only require teachers and leaders whom they can trust; and here, as always, the successful working of democracy depends upon the people recognizing ' the natural aristocracy that is among any body of men.' It follows that while the thoughtful and studious, who will naturally lead the opinions of their fellows in mine, factory or shop, can never be more than a few thousand, yet the millions of the rank and file can certainly get the two educational essentials which will enable them to recognize those natural leaders; these two essentials being (a) the development of an open habit of mind, clear-sighted and truth-loving, proof against sophisms, shibboleths, claptrap phrases and cant; (b) the possession of certain elementary information and essential facts about such main questions as our government, the relations between capital and labor, the relations between science and production, and other such subjects.

"5. That the necessary conclusion is that adult education must not be regarded as a luxury for a few exceptional persons here and there, not as a thing which concerns only a short span of early manhood, but that adult education is a permanent national necessity, an inseparable aspect of citizenship, and therefore should be both universal and lifelong.

"6. That the opportunity for adult education should be spread uniformly and systematically over the whole community, as a primary obligation on that community in its own interest and as a chief part of its duty to its individual members, and that therefore every encouragement and assistance should be given to voluntary organizations, so that their work, now necessarily sporadic and disconnected, may be developed and find its proper place in the national educational system."

3. AMERICANIZATION IN INDUSTRY

We give here practically in toto a bulletin of the State Department of Immigrant Education.

AMERICANIZATION IN INDUSTRY

"Advancement — improvement in condition — is the order of things in a society of equals."— *Abraham Lincoln, July 1, 1854.*

From the beginning of colonial history, general education has been a chief concern of the American people. We have proudly considered our public school system the foundation of democracy and have been overweeningly confident of its power to fuse all opposing elements in our population. The disillusioning reports during the war shocked our complacency and indicated that the percentage of illiteracy given in the United States census of 1910, when tested practically, was altogether too low. According to data accumulated by the War Department, 25 per cent of the selected young men of our Nation, called together by the draft, were unable to read newspapers or write letters home. "A large proportion of this 25 per cent were as completely incapable of writing their names as the coolies of inland China."[1] This deficiency, a tremendous disadvantage to these men as individuals in times of peace, became, in the mass, in stress of war, a formidable obstacle to their efficiency as soldiers and as members of the industrial forces. In a great crisis an unfair burden was put on them and their officers to overcome this handicap.

During March, 1918, Secretary of the Interior Lane said, in letters to President Wilson and to the congressional chairmen of the committee on education: "I believe that the time has come when we should give serious consideration to the education of those in the United States who can not read or write. The war has brought facts to our attention that are almost unbelievable and that in themselves are accusatory. . . . An uninformed democracy is not a democracy." [2]

Commissioner Finley said before the New York Legislature, after he had visited a cantonment: "What a commentary upon our educational shortcomings that in the days of peace we had not taught these men, who have been here long enough to be citizens (and tens of thousands of their brothers with them) to know the language in which our history and laws are written and in which the commands of defense must now be given!"

Legislation in New York

To meet the need of the great number of illiterates in our State and of the non-English-speaking, both literate and illiterate, and to prepare them for citizenship [3] amendments to the Education Law were made, which took effect September 1, 1918. These amendments are:

1. To require night schools throughout the State.
2. To require attendance at some day or evening school or some school maintained by an employer of every minor between sixteen and twenty-one years of age " who does not possess such ability to speak, read and write the English language, as is required for the completion of the fifth grade of the public or private schools of the city or school district in which he resides. . . . Any

---

[1] The New Nationalism and Education, by Robert W. Bruere. Harpers Magazine, July, 1919.
[2] Letter quoted in the Official Bulletin, March 16, 1918.
[3] According to Census of 1910, illiterates numbered 406,020, and non-English-speaking, 597,012; aliens by state census of 1915 equaled 1,628,229.

employer may meet the requirements of this act by conducting a class or classes for teaching English and civics to foreign-born in shop, store, plant or factory under the supervision of the local school authorities."

3. To authorize the Commissioner of Education to divide the State into zones and to appoint such persons as would be necessary " to promote and extend educational facilities for the education of illiterates and of non-English speaking persons." [1]

NIGHT SCHOOLS

Most of the illiterates and non-English-speaking are above legal school age. Indeed, the large majority are over twenty-one. Night schools have never reached more than a negligible number of these who most need instruction. It is only the younger and the ambitious who enrol for an evening course, and many of these soon drop out. There are many reasons for this failure to meet a great educational need, one of the chief being that men and women, tired from a hard day's work, have not the physical strength to exert themselves for exacting mental effort. To hurry through supper, change one's clothes, and rush out again, to reach a school a long way off, seems too much of a burden. After an all day's absence they are loath to leave their families. Indeed, most of them have not the slightest desire for book-learning, for they have come from countries where, for the masses, there is no tradition of education.

Miss Sarah Elkus, who with the board of education of New York City for four years has been organizing classes in settlements, stores and factories, says:

" In considering this great problem, the query naturally is made: Why are not the evening schools sufficient to educate the foreign-born? There are several answers to this question. First of all, the worker is tired when the day's toil is over and he or she prefers amusement to instruction. Second, the foreigner who speaks no English finds the evening school uncongenial because he is at a decided disadvantage when surrounded by more advanced pupils who may thoughtlessly laugh at his mistakes.

" When I asked one man why he did not go to evening school, he said he did not like to put his boots on after he had taken them off. We have found that the only successful way to get

---

[1] Public Facilities for Educating the Aliens, F. E. Farrington. Bureau of Education Bul. 18 (1916), p. 33–35.

results with non-English-speaking foreigners is to have classes in the factories where they are employed. When given an opportunity to attend the factory classes, many workingmen and women gladly devote an hour to study, after work is over, and some of the pupils make remarkable progress in a very short time."

Night schools have been too little advertised, too meagerly financed and too inadequately planned and equipped to meet the need of adults. They have never been given the same thoughtful care as day schools. A comparison of the figures given herewith, representing the non-English-speaking and illiterate foreign-born whites in New York State and their school attendance, does not lead to complacency.

FOREIGN-BORN WHITES IN NEW YORK STATE [1]

Total number	2,729,272
Non-English-speaking	597,012
Illiterates	406,020

SCHOOL ATTENDANCE OF FOREIGN-BORN WHITES IN NEW YORK STATE

Total number attending school	187,034
10 years of age and over	131,541
15 years of age and over	43,492
21 years of age and over	9,603

CLASSES IN WORK PLACES

Since the necessity for increased facilities of education is obvious, and since night schools will inevitably reach only a small portion of those most in need of instruction, classes in work places are an essential to democracy. We must make learning accessible. This idea of taking school into industry is not new. Apprentice and corporation schools, vestibule, corridor and co-operative classes, have been widely tested. Teaching of English and civics to groups in factories is a commonplace in many cities.

These classes in English and civics will not be the cure of all troubles in a factory, but if they are intelligently and wholeheartedly conducted, they do much in bettering conditions. In advocating this instruction, the State is primarily interested in the individuals who otherwise would remain illiterate and unable to speak English. Both employers and employees, however, before

[1] Census of 1910.

giving their co-operation must be persuaded that such teaching will be advantageous to them. It is difficult to separate the specific benefits which come to the different partners in the enterprise, but what the experience in various places has been is shown by this summary:

Advantages of Factory Classes to Employers

1. Reduction of accidents to workers and machines.
    a. Fewer compensation cases.
    b. Lower insurance rate.
2. Lessened labor turnover.
3. Increased production and better quality of work.
4. Better co-operation between employed and employers.
5. Greater harmony among employees.
6. More interest in the care and cleanliness of factory.
7. Less supervision.

The worker should be made to realize that knowledge of English is primarily for his own protection. English is the language of the country and whoever is ignorant of it is at a disadvantage with fellow workmen who know it. Both inside and outside the shop he is often the victim of the unscrupulous who exploit his helplessness.

Advantages of Factory Classes to Workers

1. In general.
    a. Less risk of accidents.
    b. Greater chance to advance in wages and job.
    c. Greater self-protection from unfair deals.
    d. More intelligent workmanship.
    e. Opportunity to enter more fully into the life of the factory and community.
    f. More adequate preparation for citizenship.
2. From instruction in civics and hygiene.
    a. Understanding of functions of different departments of city, state and national governments.
    b. Knowledge of school and health laws of community.
    c. Familiarity with educational and recreational facilities of the community.

The community receives benefit, for whenever even one person demands better things, standards are raised.

Advantages of Factory Classes to the Community
1. More enlightened neighborhoods that demand better housing, sanitation, etc.
2. Greater intelligence in caring for the sick.
3. Demand for entertainment of higher grade.
4. Greater number desiring citizenship.
5. More united community.

Accidents as a Result of Ignorance of English

The most important part of factory management has to do with reducing accident rates. There is overwhelming testimony that ignorance of English is vitally concerned with this. It is impossible to give many carefully worked out investigations, for only in a few places have they been made. Nor is it wise to draw hard and fast conclusions as to the exact relation of this handicap to disaster, for the non-English-speaking foreigners are likely to be inexperienced laborers, and accident rates are admittedly highest among workers new at a job. It is the part of common sense, however, to acknowledge that the inability to understand directions increases risk in hazardous occupations. A careful study of the safety movement in the iron and steel industry from 1907 to 1917, made for the United States Department of Labor by Lucian W. Chaney and Hugh S. Hanna, supports this assumption. The period studied "embraces practically the entire history of the safety movement, not only in the manufacture of iron and steel but in the whole field of American industry. At that time, indeed (say 1907 and the years immediately preceding), there existed in American industry generally a frightful disregard of human life. Accident occurrence had reached a condition perhaps not paralleled at any other time or place. Two factors contributed to such a condition: first, an unprecedented degree of business activity; and second, a larger proportion of inexperienced immigrant labor than at any time before or since."[1]

---
[1] The Safety Movement in the Iron and Steel Industry. Bureau of Labor statistics, Bul. 234, p. 13.

Of all inexperienced workers, the man most handicapped would seem to be the one who is not only without knowledge of his task but is unable to communicate freely with those who direct him. When one large company began to study carefully their working conditions, they found it not infrequently the case that a foreman was in charge of a gang with no member of which could he communicate either directly or by an interpreter. Still more common was it to find individual men who were thus barred from communication with their immediate superior. This was at once recognized as a dangerous condition and the rule was issued that gangs should be formed in such a manner that each man should be able to communicate with his foreman directly or by interpreter.[2]

[2] Op. cit., p. 144.

In another study of accidents in machine building, the same general conclusions are reached:

> It was not possible in the plans covered to separate the employees into English and non-English speakers. For one large maching-building plant, however, separation was possible between the American-born and foreign-born. The foreign-born showed an accident rate approximately double that for the native-born. This excess rate among foreign-born is clearly attributable to the same causes which lead to a constant excess among non-English-speaking steel workers partly to their failure to understand clearly the orders given them, and partly to the fact that the recent immigrant suffers from lack of experience, and thus falls largely into the group of unskilled occupations involving exposure to inherently high accident hazards.[1]

Although few accurate studies of the relation of the inability to speak and understand English to accidents have been made, many opinions are expressed by careful writers. In "The Case Against Night Work," by Josephine Goldmark and Louis Brandeis, the statement is made: "Ignorance of the English language is the greatest obstacle to industrial advancement. It prevents the distribution of congested immigrant populations and increases injuries and occupational diseases, owing to the immigrants' inability to understand orders or hygienic regulations printed or orally given in industrial establishments."

The Commonwealth Steel Company of St. Louis reports that 80 per cent of the injuries received by their workmen are among the non-English-speaking employees "though they constitute only 34 per cent of the force."

Miss Eastman, in her study of accidents in coal mines, "Work Accidents and The Law" (The Pittsburgh Survey, 1910) says: "Ignorance covers a large share of these cases, the ignorance of young boys, of those who are 'green' at their job, of the tongue-tied alien who finds himself for the first time a part of swift and mighty processes."

Van H. Manning, director of the United States Bureau of

---

[1] Accidents and Accident Prevention in Machine Building. United States Bureau of Labor statistics Bul. 216, p. 12.

Mines, makes a strong plea for the education of these inarticulate workers:

> In the Pennsylvania anthracite mines 43 per cent of the employees are English-speaking and this number is charged with only 28.8 per cent of the fatalities, whereas the other 56 per cent (representatives of continental Europe) sustained 71 per cent of the fatalities. Likewise in the Pennsylvania bituminous mines the English-speaking employees represent 35 per cent of the total and are charged with 27 per cent of the fatalities, whereas the other 65 per cent (representatives of continental Europe) are charged with 73 per cent of the fatalities. As regards the figures for West Virginia, the English-speaking employees represent 67 per cent and notwithstanding the fact that this includes 17 per cent of colored employees, only 53 per cent of the fatalities are charged to the English-speaking employees, whereas, the other 33 per cent sustain 47 per cent of the fatalities. Almost the same ratio holds for nonfatal injuries in the three groups of mines cited.
>
> Had the fatality and injury rate for the English-speaking American been maintained throughout the three groups, there would have been a saving of 716 fatalities, and 900 very serious injuries, a strong argument for Americanization and education of the miner.[1]

Extent of Industrial Accidents in the United States

The cost of industrial accidents is appaling; a tremendous drain on the vitality and wealth of our Nation. "The probable approximate number of fatal industrial accidents among American wage-earners, including both sexes, may be conservatively estimated at 25,000 for the year 1913, and the number of injuries involving a disability of more than four weeks, at approximately 700,000."[2] In the face of the testimony that ignorance of English is a factor in this terrible waste, how can we dare to leave a stone unturned in giving workers at least an elementary vocabulary?

---

[1] Monthly Statement of Coal-mine fatalities in United States Jan. 1919, p. 11. Dept. of Interior. [Apparent errors in figures — so in original.]
[2] Industrial Accident Statistics No. 157. U. S. Dept. of Labor, Bureau of Labor Statistics, p. 6. F. L. Hoffman.

Industrial Accidents and Compensation, New York State

The following statement was furnished by the State Department of Labor:

As to the number of industrial accidents occurring in New York State, according to the latest report of the Bureau of Workmen's Compensation, there were in the year ending June 30, 1918, in round numbers, 287,000 accidents in the State, of which 53,000 were compensated under our New York State law. A rough estimate, which is all that is possible with the present available data, indicates that the cost of these accidents for compensation, medical benefits, administration of the Compensation Law, administration of the compensation insurance, and the wage and medical losses of injured employees, not covered by compensation, was in round numbers, $30,000,000. A rough estimate of the loss of production occasioned by these accidents indicates that it was in round numbers $100,000,000.

"As to what proportion of these accidents could be charged to the inability of employees to understand English, there are no data dependable enough or comprehensive enough to enable one to make an estimate. There is entirely dependable evidence, however, that that element was an important factor in the causation of these accidents. Some of the best evidence of that kind is to be found in recent bulletins concerning industrial accidents of the Federal Bureau of Labor Statistics, Washington, D. C."

An Estimate of Numbers of Non-English-Speaking Workmen Who Are Hurt in the Compensation Jurisdiction

William C. Archer, Deputy Commissioner, Bureau of Compensation, New York State Department of Labor, makes the following statement:

If I were asked to make an estimate, I think I should say that four out of ten workmen who are hurt in the compensation jurisdiction cannot speak English. If I were speaking of New York City alone I would put it at about one-half.

The Relation of Illiterates to Economic Loss

Aside from the acknowledged relation of ignorance of English to accident rates, there is an important connection between ignorance of English and illiteracy to economic loss. Secretary of the Interior Lane, in a letter to President Wilson, says:

> I beg you to consider the economic loss arising out of this condition (of illiteracy). If the production labor value of an illiterate is less only 50 cents a day than that of an educated man or woman, the country is losing $825,000,000 a year through illiteracy. This estimate is no doubt under rather than over the real loss. The Federal government and the States spend millions of dollars in trying to give information to the people in rural districts about farming and homemaking. Yet 3,700,000 or 10 percent of our country folk cannot read or write a word.[1]

Labor Turnover in Relation to Ignorance of English and to Illiteracy

Ignorance of English is a large factor in turnover. It is generally acknowledged that the non-English-speaking and illiterate workmen are the ones most easily discouraged and ready to give up the job. Misunderstandings and suspicion arise among foremen and men through inability to speak a common language. It is only recently that employers have realized the enormous expense entailed in continual replacement of their forces. The first published record of an investigation on a large scale is from a paper by Magnus W. Alexander, head of the training schools of the General Electric Company. In 1912 he made a study of twelve American factories varying in size from 300 to over 10,000 employees. He discovered that 72.8 per cent of all employees engaged during 1912 were entirely new to the factories and that most of the employers utterly failed to realize the appalling waste in continually replacing workers. The group of firms which he studied and which he considered typical "engaged about six and one-third times as many persons during the year as were necessary to account for the permanent increase in the total working force."

According to Mr. Alexander's conclusions, at least 22,031 of these changes were unnecessary. By summing up the expenses incurred in training each group, Mr. Alexander finds a total of $831,030 or an average cost of over $37 for each of the 22,031 persons apparently unnecessarily engaged.

The items considered in computing cost were (1) hiring, (2) instruction, (3) wear and tear on machinery, (4) reduced

---

[1] Letter quoted in the Official Bulletin, March 16, 1918.

production, (5) spoiled work. "This amount will be considerably greater and may reach a million dollars if the decrease of profits due to reduced production and the increase of expenses on account of an enlarged equipment investment are taken into consideration.[1]

"While one manager estimated the cost of hiring and breaking in an employee at $30 the estimate of all others ranged from $50 to $200 per employee. The great difference in these estimates is no doubt due to the diversity of the industries represented by these managers. Most estimates ranged between $50 and $100."[2]

Mr. Alexander's study was more concerned with skilled labor, men who were likely to be English-speaking and literate, and he was primarily interested in the cost of the turnover rather than in its causes. The expense of breaking in men for common labor is of course less than training them for complicated machines. Since Mr. Alexander's investigation, others have been made with varying estimates of the cost of different items. Many consider the total cost more than Mr. Alexander reckoned. Even yet there are many employers who take excellent care of their machinery and equipment, who have not learned the necessity of making a scientific study of the human element in their plants. They do not realize the paramount importance of adapting environment to workers. Men and women naturally shun a place where hazards are reported high, or where conditions are unpleasant. In general, whatever makes men and women feel that they are becoming more efficient, or whatever contributes to more complete adaptation to their surroundings, will reduce the desire of change. Where factory classes have been in operation even for a short time and on a small scale, there is testimony that they have been a stabilizing factor. In them men and women are dealt with as individuals, and they become conscious of relationships and responsibilities which before they have not felt.

Labor and Education

One of the healthful signs of the current discussion of "reconstruction," during and since the war, is the realization among increasing numbers that education has been essentially aristocratic, for the selected few and not for the mass. Organized workers are demanding that the men and women who fill our

---
[1] The Annals of the American Academy, May, 1916, p. 138–40.
[2] R. W. Kelly. Hiring the Worker, p. 198–99.

shops and factories must not for that reason be denied education. They are apprehensive of purely technical schools which train for specialized industry and not for life. The publications of the British Workers' Educational Association are illuminating. "The really great thing is that liberal education (in opposition to specialized education for undeveloped minds) should be open to all who can profit by it."[1] The platform of the Labor Party of Greater New York likewise calls for general, liberal training as a prerequisite to specialization. The educational program of the State Federation of Labor is broad and progressive.

Factory classes are only a breaking of the ground, but intelligently conducted, they atone in a slight measure for past deficiencies and prepare the way for wider training. In immediate results, they contribute to three great essentials in human relationships: sympathy, loyalty and creative impulse. With the growth of huge establishments, the direct relation between employer and man has gone. Unskilled laborers in a factory are far removed from supervision and acquaintance of the general manager, himself often an employee of some one more powerful. During the war when full production was a grim necessity, this weakness in our industrial system was recognized and we had immense mass meetings of workmen addressed by employers, who were internationally important. The effect on production of this rather artificial contact was magical. Each man, in whatever humble capacity, was made to feel that he personally had a responsibility in the nation's crisis and that he had a loyalty to show to his employer and country.

These groups of men and women, gathered for study in classes, have in a degree the old-time personal contact, for they are dealt with as individuals and not as part of a machine. The teacher is interested in their history, their country, and their family. The foremen inquire about their progress. This little leaven goes a long way in transforming the spirit of a large group.

Many thoughtful writers are discussing the creative impulse in industry and its relation to present industrial questions. Some wise employers are realizing that they cannot get intelligent whole-hearted co-operation until their employees have a more thorough knowledge of the industry than they can get by monotonous repetition of one operation. For employees handicapped

---

[1] "What Is Democratic Education?" See, too, "Labor and the Commonwealth," G. D. H. Cole.

by ignorance of English, such knowledge is very difficult. Robert Wolf, at a meeting of the Taylor Society in March, 1917, said:

> The opportunity for self-expression, which is synonymous with joy in work, is something that the workman is entitled to, and we employers who feel that management is to become a true science must begin to think less of the science of material things and think more of the science of human relationship. Our industries must become humanized, otherwise there will be no relief from the present state of unrest in the industries of the world. . . . It is beginning to be understood that when we deny to vast numbers of individuals the opportunity to do creative work, we are violating a great universal law.[1]

In the appendix is a list of cities where in one or more factories these classes for the non-English-speaking and illiterate are held. This educational experiment is not confined to one locality but is being tried throughout the country. Lists of firms in different cities are given in the appendix. The opinions of employers and organizations of the value of this work also are interesting and instructive. These are also found in the appendix.

Organization of Factory Classes

Education of adults as of children is rightly the responsibility of the community. In the organization of factory classes, public school officials and teachers in co-operation with plant officials should plan and direct the work. Other civic and educational associations well may be asked to co-operate. Three things are necessary to the success of this undertaking: (1) sympathy and active help of employers; (2) skilled teachers especially qualified for a task requiring energy, resourcefulness, tact and efficiency; (3) interest and determined effort of the men and women who need the instruction. To gain the confidence of the workers and knowledge of their needs, leaders of different national groups ought to be asked to serve on committees.

Census of the Plant

A director of educational work should be appointed. Foremen then are called together by the manager and plans carefully explained by the director. In some places, mass meetings of the employees are addressed, through interpreters, by manager and

---
[1] Bulletin of the Taylor Society, Mar. 1917.

foremen; in others, smaller groups are reached more effectively. A simple explanation of proposed classes is made carefully and emphasis laid on the point that English is necessary for the workers' protection and advancement. Their own countries, languages and cultural contributions ought to be given generous recognition and no suggestion made of a compulsory substitution of English for their native tongue. The advantages of proficiency in two languages might well be stressed.

After preliminary explanations, each employee or someone acting for him ought to fill out cards supplied by the State Department of Education giving (1) name, address, age, country of birth; (2) length of time in this country; (3) citizen or alien; (4) first papers, time since taking them; (5) amount of schooling in native country and in America; (6) ability to speak, read and write English; (7) married or single; (8) members of immediate family; (9) school attended by children; (10) length of time in the employ of firm; (11) job; (12) check number; (13) foreman; (14) hours of work; (15) desire to attend night school; (16) desire to attend factory classes.

According to information obtained in the registration, classes of different grades may be formed.

Composition of Classes

Whether employees in classes shall be separated according to nationality, age, sex, literacy, knowledge of English, etc., are matters to be decided from varying conditions in different factories. Generally speaking, in beginners' classes the best work is obtained from careful grading, based on age, nationality, literacy and understanding of English. Simple tests for grading may be obtained by sending to the State Department of Immigrant Education.

Teachers

Teachers for this work ought to be the best of the community and sufficient salaries paid to induce trained men and women to take up this highly skilled teaching. Only in exceptional instances is it advisable to have foremen or other plant employees give instruction, and then they should have an intensive course in methods. A man may be a good mechanic, a competent foreman, employment manager, or welfare worker, and still be unfitted for teaching. Public school teachers should have intensive training from some shop executive in shop vocabulary, safety directions, and history of the industry. It is easier for persons trained in pedagogy to acquire in a short time this knowledge than for shop employees to master the technic of teaching.

Financial Support of Classes

Money for factory classes should be included in the public school budget. An educational campaign may be necessary to impress upon the citizens their responsibility to illiterates and non-English-speaking adults. Experience has proved that night schools have not adequately met the emergency.

The State Federation of Labor, through its committee on education, has taken a strong stand on education and through local unions has pledged to demand public support for these continuation classes. Section 23 of its report of 1918 reads: "Acquisition of a fair knowledge of the American language by continuous shop and school instruction, supervised by state educational authorities, to be required of all employed foreign-language aliens as a condition of continued employment."

Time for Classes

Some employers, realizing that additional efficiency gained by the workers from class instruction is an asset in their business, gladly give the time for factory classes. Others give half, and the employees, half. In other plants, particularly where there is an eight-hour day, the time is entirely outside working hours. The period, forty-five minutes or thereabouts, is sometimes at the end of the day shift, sometimes in the early forenoon, or afternoon. The number of meetings a week varies in different places. Execllent results have been obtained from three a week.

Place of Meeting

Rest rooms, restaurants, recreation halls, and similar rooms are used as classrooms. If preferred, schoolhouses or libraries in the vicinity may be used. Chairs, tables, blackboards and good lighting are necessary equipment. Notebooks, pencils and textbooks entail little expense and may be provided by employees or by the public schools.

Subjects of Instruction

In the foregoing pages, the teaching of English has been stressed and it is necessarily the chief subject of instruction. That, however, is the medium of teaching other things, after once a fundamental vocabulary has been gained, as safety in shop and street, hygiene in home and factory, history of industry, citizenship, etc.

Needs of individual factories must be studied, and instruction adapted to each industry and body of workers. Closest co-operation with the safety engineer of the plant is necessary, or in a small factory with foremen who train the workers. As it is admitted that ignorance of English is certainly a factor in accidents, resulting in loss of life or disability, our first duty is to instruct efficiently in safety directions. Later, general information of the industry can be given. Whatever, in short, is of immediate use to the groups of workers in each factory should guide in choice of subjects.

Above all, it is desired that the work done in these classes — necessarily elementary and meager — will develop a " quickening of mental life" and that this instruction will be but the introduction to further study. No opportunity on the part of the teacher should be lost in using the groups to promote social life in plant and in community. A connection with the home can be formed and participation of the family in outside activities stimulated.

Regular class work may be varied by stereopticons, Victrolas, pictures, dramatization, simple talks from people representing different interests of the pupils.

Certificate of Attendance

In some cities, certificates issued by the State are given to graduates of each grade of factory classes. Some such tangible evidence of instruction is to be commended. This teaching of adults must be made dignified and matter of fact. The idea that training is only for children is a hindrance to progress. These men and women should be made to feel that school attendance is natural and every means possible ought to be taken in the factory and the community to give dignity and approbation to the work.

Cooperation

Through the war, we have learned that herculean tasks can be done if there is whole-hearted cooperation. In this great work set before us of making life fuller and better for our adult population whose childhood often, through no fault of their own, lacked opportunities for any formal mental training, cooperation is an essential.

"English Class at Noon Hour," Mason and Seaman Taxi Co.

Class of Aliens Studying English in the Auburn Public Evening School, Auburn

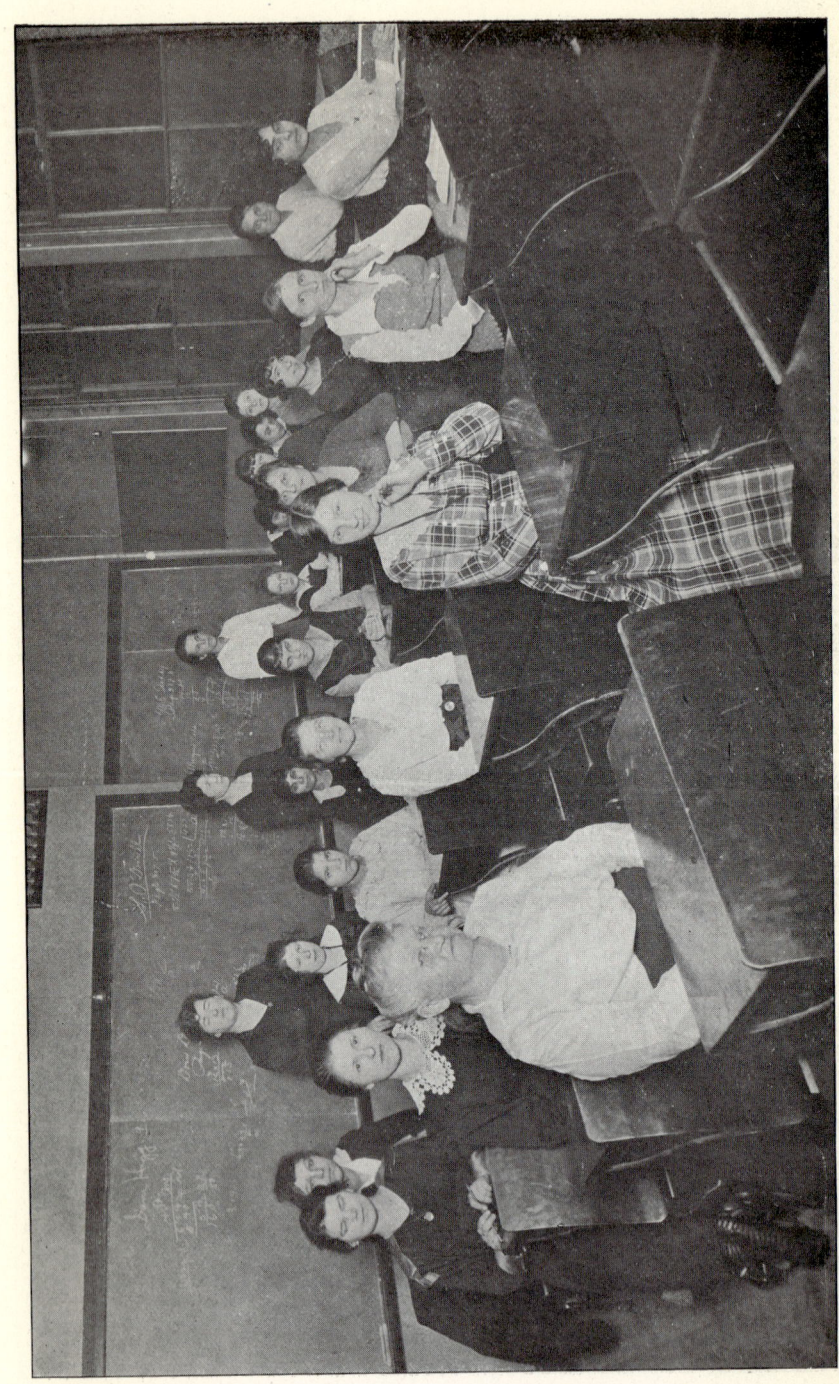

Nearly All of These Girls Come Under Compulsory

We must be free from suspicion of trying to force instruction on unwilling men and women. To this end, plans should be patiently explained through leaders of different groups. It is advisable to work with educational committees of labor unions, wherever they exist. Always there must be flexibility to adapt this work to the wishes and needs of each community and each group. A recognition of the value of old-world contributions is absolutely necessary to the full success of the undertaking.

APPENDIX
COMPOSITION OF THE POPULATION OF THE UNITED STATES IN 1910

The figures in the 1910 census are now old but they give proportions which doubtless, in general, hold true.

Total population	91,922,266
Total foreign-born	13,515,886
Total foreign-born and mixed parentage	32,480,839

OF THESE FOREIGN-BORN, ALMOST THREE MILLIONS, OR ONE IN EVERY FOUR, COULD NOT SPEAK ENGLISH

Illiterates in population of United States, ten years of age and more, according to the census of 1910:

Number	Per Cent
5,516,163	7.7

STATISTICS FOR NEW YORK STATE — 1910 CENSUS

Total population of New York State	9,113,614

More than 2,700,000 persons, or nearly 30 per cent of this number, were foreign-born whites. More than 3,000,000 persons, about 33 per cent, were of mixed parentage.

ILLITERATES IN NEW YORK STATE

Total number of illiterates 10 years of age and over:

Number		Per Cent
106,020	All classes	5.5
21,292	Native white of native parentage	0.8
15,026	Native white of foreign or mixed parentage	0.7
362,025	Foreign-born white	13.7
5,768	Negro	5.0

Illiterates of New York State in Age Groups

Number		Percentage
2,619	10 to 14 years	.03
78,845	14 to 24 years	4.4
109,836	25 to 34 years	6.7
85,578	35 to 44 years	6.4
60,305	45 to 54 years	6.5

Cities in Which Factory Classes Are Already Organized

New York, N. Y.
Cleveland, Ohio.
Chicago, Ill.
Philadelphia, Pa.
Boston, Mass.
Albany, N. Y.
Rochester, N. Y.
Buffalo, N. Y.
Middletown, Ohio.
Cincinnati, Ohio.
Lynn, Mass.
St. Louis, Mo.
St. Paul, Minn.
Milwaukee, Wis.
Detroit, Mich.
Massena, N. Y.
Deferiet, N. Y.
New Brunswick, N. J.
Akron, Ohio.
Niagara Falls, N. Y.
Waterbury, Conn.
Youngstown, Ohio.
Bridgeport, Conn.
Bayonne, N. J.
Lowell, Mass.
Pittsburgh, Pa.
Seymour, Conn.
Chester, Pa.
Elmira, N. Y.
Los Angeles, Cal.
New Britain, Conn.
Southbridge, Mass.
Kalamazoo, Mich.
Worcester, Mass.
New Bedford, Mass.
Cambridge, Mass.
Terre Haute, Ind.
West Orange, N. J.

Firms Having Factory Classes in 1919
New York City

Franklin Simon Co.
General Cigar Co.
American Tobacco Co.
A. Goodman & Sons.
National Biscuit Co.
Frank Spica Co.
L. P. Hollander.
Henri Bendel, Inc.
Hickson, Inc.
Sweets Co. of America.
American Can Co.
Atlantic Comb Works.
Kaufman & Bonday.
Cohen, Goldman & Co.
L. Greenfield's Sons.
Winter & Co.
Altro Mfg. Co.
Wm. DeMuth & Co.

Niagara Falls, N. Y.

Carborundum Co.
Acheson Graphite Co.
Union Carbide Co.
National Carbon Co.
Niagara Electric Chemical Co.
U. S. Light & Heat Co.

Buffalo, N. Y.

Contact Process Co.
Dold Packing Co.
General Chemical Co.
Aluminum Castings Co.
Lumen Bearings Co.

Rochester, N. Y.

Bausch & Lomb Co.
Michael Stern & Co.
Wollensak Optical Co.

Syracuse, N. Y.

S. Shapiro Co.
A. E. Nettleton Co.
Crouse-Hinds.
Warner Macaroni Co.
Stearns Factories.
Smith-Premier Typewriter Co.
Solvay-Process Co.
Church & Dwight Co.
Pierce, Butler & Pierce.
Brown-Lipe-Chapin.
Onondaga Pottery Co.

Opinions of Employers and Organizations on the Value of Factory Classes

In a letter to the National Americanization Committee, Charles M. Schwab said:

> It has been found repeatedly that Americanization of workers has a stabilizing effect. It shows quick results in the reduction of labor turnover and tends to create a spirit of co-operation among the workmen which is impossible when they do not speak the same language.

The board of directors of the Merchants' Association of New York City said in a recent report:

> We recommend strongly the institution of classes for manual workers and especially for illiterates, in places of employment during daylight hours, preferably with the co-operation of the public school authorities, and without loss of pay during the brief daily periods of instruction.

Mark A. Daly, general secretary of the Associated Manufacturers and Merchants of New York State, wrote to the State Department of Education in November, 1917:

> The efficiency and safety of foreigners who do not speak English and who are employed in American industry has been seriously jeopardized by the fact that they have not a sufficient knowledge of the English language to comprehend ordinary "shop English."

Miss Sarah Elkus, in charge of factory classes in New York City, says:

> As the classes progress, many employers are most enthusiastic in their approval of this innovation in factory life. They find the men become much more loyal to their country and to the company, and more efficient in their work when they have learned to read such signs as "Open at this end," "Do not tear," "Be careful to cut with scissors." A large amount of money is saved in this way, and increased pay and promotion have been given to those who learned the language.

The D. E. Sicher Company of New York City, manufacturers of women's underwear, says:

> It is worth while and most emphatically so [to have factory classes for foreign-born]. Putting it on basis of expense, I could prove to you that it is worth while. They give back in efficient labor all that it costs to instruct them, part of each working day. We do not want cheap, illiterate, irresponsible, unambitious labor, and all progressive manufacturers are coming to see that such labor does not pay.

The General Chemical Company of Bayonne, N. J., has said:

> The results have been excellent and have made it possible to promote many of the foreign-speaking employees to more important and better paying positions.

Michael Stern and Company of Rochester wrote in July, 1919

> There has unquestionably been an increase in efficiency among those who have taken advantage of the opportunity offered. The institution [factory classes] is one in which we are very much interested and which has our entire ap

proval. We hope to resume classes next season and to interest even larger number of employees if there is a possibility of so doing.

The Bausch and Lomb Optical Company of Rochester wrote in August, 1919:

> Our factory classes were established primarily to make it possible for those illiterate minors who live some distance from our factory and from an evening school to attend school, and therefore to comply with the law. We estimated that we might have twenty or twenty-five in the class; however, a careful investigation disclosed that we have but fourteen illiterate minors who found it impossible to attend one of the evening schools. Nevertheless, on January 27th, we started our first factory class with fourteen illiterate minors and two other alien adults who wanted to become Americans.
>
> Shortly after the classes opened for minors, we found a strong demand for classes in English on the part of adult males who had not been attending evening school because it was too much of a hardship for them to get out in the evening and because of their reticence in attending regular school classes. It was therefore decided to open our factory classes to alien adults in the factory. We had as a result over 100 applications of men who desired to take up the work.
>
> The school had six classes, five of the lower grade and one of the more advanced grade. These six classes were taught by four teachers furnished by the board of education. The school was in session from 5.15 to 7 o'clock Mondays, Tuesdays, Thursdays and Fridays of each week. Each class was in session for one hour. The subject matter taught was the same as in the evening schools of the city, except the advanced class was prepared for citizenship.
>
> The company co-operated in every respect to make these classes attractive and successful. It was at the suggestion of one of the members of the firm that light refreshment was served to each student after work before he started his class work.
>
> Only one pupil of the enrolment left the company's employ during school period, and as she returned a few weeks after leaving, the classes maintained an average of 99.5 percent of attendance in their departments, which showed an increase of 33 percent over an equal number who did not

attend the classes. Two men and three girls were singled out and without their knowing it, the foremen's report showed that their efficiency was increased from 25 percent to 31 percent as compared with their work prior to attending evening classes.

It is of no little satisfaction that we can make this statement that only two of the original pupils have left the company's employ since the classes were started and that those who have attended classes, have become the most loyal members of the working force in their respective departments.

The Shapiro Factory, Syracuse (employing mostly women):

We value our factory class last year very beneficial to both the factory and the employees. It raised the general intelligence of all the group, and was a socializing influence for good.

Crouse-Hinds, Syracuse:

The factory class is a great thing. The men are anxious to learn and are already asking when the school will open. Many studied from their children's books during the summer. Most of the men who could not write their names last year are now able to check up their own time. Plainly noticeable that the men respond to orders more quickly because they understand better.

Note: This factory was so well pleased with the results of the factory classes that they presented each teacher a check for $25 at the close of the term.

Smith-Premier Typewriter Co., Syracuse:

The value of the factory class to the factory is that it saves time by making it easier to give orders.

Church and Dwight, Syracuse:

The factory class experiment is still too new to draw any definite conclusions. Would not say the factory class was any marked advantage to the factory, but there is no question that it was a decided help to the employees, and any movement that benefits the people in a community has a good effect on the industry of that community. We want our factory classes again this winter, because we believe that ultimately it will prove a good investment for the factory.

Onondaga Pottery Company, Syracuse:

> We are thoroughly satisfied with the school and in a reasonable length of time it will do good. This company believes sufficiently in the value of the factory schools to be willing to give up space, light and heat and any other necessities for the class, also our time. It is the only way of teaching men.

On June 20, 1918, Seidenberg and Company, sent the following:

> We write to thank you for the keen interest you have taken in people of foreign birth, who are in the employ of our firm, and your patriotic endeavor to have them taught to read and write English. The class has made splendid progress. All are anxious to learn, are fond of their teacher, Miss Appelt, and we consider ourselves well rewarded for the time and space we have given to the class.

United States Rubber Co., New Haven, Conn.:

> Our classes are held in the various factories during working hours. The classes meet twice a week in the majority of cases, although in others they meet from three to five times each week. A day worker's time goes on in the factory, an hour's work in the Americanization school being equivalent to an hour's work in the shop. The piece workers are paid a minimum of 15 cents an hour. It is conceded by foremen generally, that the shop spirit is better, and that the number of errors in various departments, due to the lack of knowledge of English, has been reduced to a great extent by the direct method of handling these problems in classes.
>
> The teachers are obtained in almost every case from the local board of education, and paid by them. Co-operation with and supervision by the public school authorities is strongly urged. We feel that the best results are obtained only when the public character of the education is encouraged.

The Pfister and Vogel Leather Company of Milwaukee, reported, gugust 1, 1919:

> We gave six hundred of our employees a ten weeks' course in speaking, reading, writing and arithmetic in the English language, and kept away from the word "Americanization and Citizenship." We gave them full time during school

hours, which was from 8 o'clock till 12 o'clock five days a week. Classes were of one hour duration. A separate check was given the man for time put in this school, from their regular check, so that there would be no confusion.

The A. B. Kirschbaum Company of Philadelphia:

Our piece workers are allowed fifty cents per hour while in attendance and our week workers' time is not deducted while they are in attendance.

The Wisconsin Bridge and Iron Company, of Milwaukee:

Some of the manufacturers are paying the men in their employ who need instruction in English for attending these classes. The basis of payment being one hour's pay at employee's regular shop rate for every two hours spent in the class.

The Joseph & Feiss Co. of Cleveland, wrote on August 1, 1919:

It is now some years since we established classes for the teaching of English and citizenship. We have made the learning of English and attendance at classes compulsory, announcing that advancements took directly into consideration the speaking of English. At the same time, we started and have since continued a citizenship campaign. We have for the same length of time given preference in employment to those who speak English, employing no one who did not speak English well enough to pass certain tests, without a distinct understanding that his employment was conditional upon attendance at classes.

In Chicago, where there are 150 factory classes a week and a waiting list of 155 industries ready to start [1] there is enthusiastic approval of them. The superintendent of one of the International Harvester plants said:

Some of our people (in factory classes) are doubling their output.

Another Chicago manager said:

Our dream is that Americanization will banish foreign language foremen and interpreter in our employment office

---

[1] See Everybodys, July, 1919. An article by Grace Humphrey.

two great barriers between us and our men. Only think what it means when I can make an announcement to them myself.

Another said:
> It means a closer relation all along the line. Closer relation in our factory will result in better feelings, just as closer relations in our community life will result in better citizenship.

In Detroit, Mr. Ford's plant has been having successful classes for some time. They report from there:
> Accidents in this plant have decreased 54 per cent since employees have been able to read factory notices and instructions.

4. COMMUNITY ORGANIZATION

In order that the State Department of Education may carry out a definite, practical, constructive and comprehensive Americanization program, it is essential not only that the State be divided into districts for the purpose of administration, but also that every county, city, town and village be organized for the work. Accordingly, the State Department of Education recommends that all persons in each community of the State who are actively interested in Americanization and all educational, civic, industrial, religious and social organizations unite in a central body which shall act as a clearing-house, a co-ordinating and co-operating agency for the Americanization workers. The purpose of this central body shall be:

1. To co-ordinate the work of all Americanization agencies in the community.
2. To avoid duplication and overlapping of work.
3. To investigate the needs of the community.
4. To collect and classify data concerning the foreign-born.
5. To formulate and adopt a definite program of work.
6. To share the various parts of the program according to the resources and abilities of the agencies represented.
7. To supply volunteer workers.

The executive committee of this central Americanization council should have power to apportion the work to the affiliated organizations or committees according to their respective facilities.

In order that the State Department of Education may know the names of the organizations and persons in charge of the Americanization work, it is sending out through its directors, blanks to be filled in and returned to the local director of the Americanization work of the State Education Department. After making a copy of the information contained on the sheet, the local director will forward the original sheet to the office of the Supervisor of Immigrant Education, where a record of all these organizations will be kept on file.

Each central organization should work through the official agencies of Americanization activities, such as:

1. Federal agencies.
    a. Department of Interior, Bureau of Education.
    b. Department of Labor.
        (1) Bureau of Naturalization.
        (2) Bureau of Immigration.
        (3) Children's Bureau.
2. State agencies.
    a. Councils of national defense.
    b. Immigrant commissions.
    c. Industrial departments.
    d. State boards of education.
3. Municipal agencies.
    a. City boards of education.
    b. Community councils.
    c. Official municipal agencies.
4. Local agencies.
    To be filled in by the community.

Blanks for affiliated organizations or committees may be secured from the State Department through its local director. After they have been filled out by the president or chairman of the affiliated organizations or committees, they should be returned to the chairman of the central organization who will make a copy of them and send the originals to the local director of the State Education Department.

Since the state appropriation for this work is limited, it becomes necessary to depend upon volunteer workers to assist in carrying out the program. Volunteer workers should fill out cards so that the organizations will have definite records of the resources of the community. These cards may be obtained through the local director of the Americanization work of the State Department of Education, or from the Supervisor of Immigrant Education, State Education Building, Albany.

A COMMUNITY PROGRAM FOR AMERICANIZATION WORK

1. Make a community survey.

In order that every community may know its own needs and its own facilities for Americanization work and in order that the State Department of Education may be able to co-operate effectively, it is essential that a survey be made which shall disclose the attitude of the native-born toward Americanization, the illiteracy and status of citizenship of the members of the community, the attitude of the foreign-born toward Americanization, the official federal, state and local organization which would be interested in an active Americanization campaign, the unofficial agencies which would co-operate, the location of foreign groups, foreign societies, foreign churches, the names and addresses of foreign leaders, the names, place and time of meeting of foreign clubs, the plants employing foreign-born labor, and a definite estimate of what has been done and may be done in that particular community. Each community is urged to appoint a competent person or committee to make a survey at once in order that the plans for actual work may be taken up more quickly.

Cards for this community survey may be obtained from the local director of the Americanization work of the State Department of Education or by applying to the State Supervisor of Immigrant Education. After they have been filled out they should be returned to the local director who, after making copies, will forward them to the Supervisor of Immigrant Education.

2. Make a survey of the foreign-born in the community.

A survey to give the name, nationality, place of residence, degree of literacy, and status of citizenship of the foreign-born should be made by utilizing the military census, school census, and industrial plant census. The State has on file in the office of the Supervisor of Immigrant Education the name, age, address and nationality of every illiterate and non-English-speaking person between 16 and 50 years of age. This information was secured from the military census of 1917. It is filed by counties and is available through the local director of Americanization.

In many communities the board of education may be induced to take a school census which would give not only the usual information concerning children in public schools, but also the names, addresses, nationality, degree of literacy, and status of citizenship of the parents. In communities where a census has been taken, the board of education should be requested to make copies of the census returns of the foreign-born having children in the public, private and parochial schools.

Some industrial plants keep a full record not only of the names and addresses of their employees, but also of their degree of literacy and status of citizenship. Where such a record has not been kept up to this time, it is urged that it be done. Employers, superintendents and foremen working with foreign-born men and women may also give much detailed information. The names and addresses of prospective citizens may be obtained from the county clerk's office. Pastors, public health nurses, and leaders of foreign groups may also assist in making this survey.

Copies of the survey cards should be forwarded to the local director of Americanization. These cards should then be classified and arranged systematically according to wards and precincts, alphabetically by streets, and consecutively by street numbers.

Directions to Persons Making a Community Survey

a. Make out a separate card for each person over 16 years of age.

b. Give last name first.

c. Do not put explanatory remarks on the face of the card, but on back of the card.

d. Observe conditions of environment, sanitary and hygienic conditions, etc.

e. Note any complaints about housing conditions, exploitation, personal, domestic and neighborhood difficulties.

f. Offer to secure assistance in making out declaration of intention and naturalization papers.

g. Explain opportunities offered by schools, libraries, legal aid bureaus, clinics, etc.

Blank forms for making the survey may be secured from the local director of Americanization.

3. Campaign for securing attendance at classes in English and citizenship.

  a. Publicity.

    (1) Foreign press.

(2) Handbills and posters, circulated in foreign sections of community, in industrial plants, in schools, in movies, in railroad stations, in libraries, in lodging houses, in hotels, in barber shops, in employment bureaus, in elevators of public buildings, in baby welfare stations, in billiard parlors, shoe shining parlors, soft drink emporiums, etc.

Note: Experience has proved that it is better not to present the notice in more than one foreign language or in one language and the English translation, on a handbill, circular or poster.

(3) A map of the community which shows the location of free public night schools, social centers, recreational facilities and public institutions. Map should also be placed on bulletin boards in factories, libraries, baby welfare stations, etc. This map should be published in all foreign and American newspapers.

Note: Local merchants may be solicited to publish such a map as an advertisement.

(4) Notices in pay envelopes.

(5) Announcements in meetings of foreign societies, foreign churches, foreign press, groceries, meat markets, etc.

(6) Announcements on motion picture screens or on stereopticon slides.

(7) Announcements in all patriotic and mass meetings where foreign-born come together.

b. Personal calls should be made upon every member of a prospective class or group in order to secure friendly contact with the individual members and to learn what their most urgent needs are. The character of the first lesson will be determined by these calls. In case a home or neighborhood class is to be formed, the place and time of meeting may also be determined during this first call. This should be arranged according to the convenience of the majority of the prospective members.

4. Form classes.

Classes in English and civics for every illiterate and non-English-speaking person, native-born and foreign-born, should be formed in (a) day schools, (b) evening schools, (c) factories, (d) neighborhood houses, (e) club rooms, (f) libraries, (g) infant welfare stations, (h) churches, (i) parochial schools, (j) homes.

Classes should be formed wherever and whenever a reasonable number of persons will come together for instruction (3 to 25).

a. Aim of classes.

(1) To develop the ability to speak, read and write English clearly and intelligibly.

(2) To develop a knowledge of our history, laws, institutions and standards of living.

(3) To develop a love of all that is best in our American life and a desire to unite with the native-born in advancing the best.

b. Organization of classes.

The State Department of Education will appoint ten organizers of Americanization classes whose duty it will be to secure the co-operation of all educational, civic, social, industrial and religious agencies in securing members for classes in English and citizenship. As the number of these workers is limited, the State Education Department recommends that local boards of education appoint their own organizers wherever possible in order that the ten appointed by the State may be sent to communities which can not support one.

The most important step in organizing Americanization classes is the proper grouping and grading. Grouping according to sex and nationality is advisable, but the wide difference in the knowledge of English has made it impracticable to hold rigidly to this rule in the smaller cities. Grading presents a more difficult task. The following plan of grading has proved successful:

1. Beginners classes include
   a. Illiterates.
   b. Educated foreigners who speak no English.
   c. Foreigners who speak only a few words, write their names and read only simple sentences.
2. Intermediate classes including
   a. Those who have completed the beginners' work.
   b. Those who can read a simple paragraph.
   c. Those who have the ability to read fourth grade books.
3. Advanced classes including
   a. Those who can express their own opinions on topics of general or personal interest.

b. Those who have the ability to read and appreciate such books as Hale's "Man Without a Country" and Dunn's "Community and the Citizen."

c. Those who can write a short business letter or an account of some personal experience.

c. Teaching.

The State Department of Education will appoint twenty teachers of illiterate and non-English-speaking adults. They will be sent to communities where the need is very great and where the local authorities are unable to provide their own teachers. In all the other communities it is hoped that the boards of education may support their own teachers.

d. Membership of classes.

Members of these classes may be recruited from lists submitted by the organizer of Americanization classes who in turn has secured the names from the survey cards or from any agency connected with the work.

e. Requests for classes.

These requests may come from the organizer or any others interested. Requests for classes should be sent to the president of the local board of education, the superintendent of schools, or the chairman of the central organization of Americanization workers. The names and addresses of the prospective members of the class should accompany the request.

f. The first meeting.

Meeting of the class should be characterized by genuine cordiality and friendliness. The class may be taught for the first time by the local organizer or by the teacher provided by the local board of education. The lessons should not be longer than an hour. In case the local board of education is unable to supply a teacher, the central organization should send a trained volunteer teacher. It is of the utmost importance that volunteer workers have special training before taking charge of a class and that they be under the supervision of a school principal, or of a director or supervisor of classes for foreign-born adults.

All volunteer workers should present a program of work to the principal, director or supervisor in charge for his approval and should hand in at regular intervals written reports of the progress of work of the class.

It is recommended that advanced classes be organized with regular officers. The foreign-born men and women like this recognition and they may gain their first lessons in self-government in this way.

g. School equipment.

The school should be provided with suitable chairs, desks and textbooks for adults. Primers and elementary texts should not be used.

5. Make the school, the library, and the neighborhood house the center of the social and recreational life of the community. This may be done through community " sings," dances, parties where general games are played, gymnasium exercises, indoor athletic meets, outdoor entertainments, pageants.

6. Secure the interest and cooperation of employees, factory owners, managers, foremen, foreign leaders, and labor organizations in forming and maintaining factory classes by.

    a. Informing the employees, through their leaders, of the advantages of learning English and becoming American citizens.

    b. Personal interviews with factory owners, superintendents or managers, leaders among foreign groups, and representatives of labor organizations.

    c. Meeting of employees to discuss formation of classes, time and place of meeting, subjects to be taught and kind of instruction. It is important to have the management represented at this meeting to assure the employees of their approbation and cooperation.

    d. Appointment of a committee which shall be the special Americanization agent in the plant and shall keep records of the results obtained through the classes.

7. Secure the hearty support and cooperation of all foreign interpreters, bankers, clergymen, nurses, business men and lawyers.

8. Arrange for exhibits of foreign handicrafts, for folk dances, folk songs, and the use of quaint old-country musical instruments to show " the gifts of mind, heart and hand " which the foreign-born have brought to America.

9. Establish an information center. It is recommended that each community designate a certain office or building, centrally

located and easily accessible, where intelligent, sympathetic, tactful, and socially-minded men and women will be on duty at regular hours on certain days in the week to give advice on all matters that require the help of an interested American. Very often unimportant matters can be kept out of court by such helpful advice. Questions concerning noisy or disorderly neighbors, keeping animals on the premises, a misunderstanding between employer and employee, a contractual relationship between two persons might be brought to such a service station and satisfactorily adjusted.

10. Establish a legal aid bureau. Because of the serious exploitation of the foreign-born by unscrupulous lawyers, doctors and others, it is desirable that legal aid bureaus be established in communities where the need is imperative.

11. Appoint a speakers' bureau which shall arrange for mass meetings and supply speakers for community gatherings.

12. Make the clinics usable. Urge that the number of clinics be increased and their facilities enlarged so that everyone may receive just, careful, and sympathetic treatment.

13. Make the public baths usable.

14. Form mothers' clubs with English classes, for foreign-born women and lessons in homemaking as a part of the regular program.

15. Carry out a campaign against " calling names," the use of epithets commonly applied by the unthinking to our foreign-born, which anger them and arouse interracial hatred. Girl and boy scouts may carry out such a campaign.

16. Advertise all the resources and public institutions of the community.

17. Give receptions to new citizens.

18. Stimulate real, active work in all Americanization committees.

The time has come to act.
The federal census will be taken in 1920.
What will New York show?

5. AMERICANIZATION THROUGH WOMEN'S ORGANIZATIONS

The State Department of Education has been asked to present a program of work for organizations that are particularly interested in problems of foreign-born women. Illiterate and non-English-speaking women in the homes have suffered serious handicaps for they have had fewer means than their sisters in industry of becoming acquainted with our language and customs. Now, with lessons from the war fresh in our minds, all of us who believe in fair play and equal opportunity are eager to provide these home-keepers with knowledge necessary for their protection and advancement.

Unless we have a strong realization that these new Americans from other lands bring invaluable gifts to our life and culture, our desire to help them is doomed to failure. Dr. Stephen S. Wise has well said: "Our country seems destined, in the providence of God, to be the world's experimental station in brotherhood, all of us learning that other nations are not barbarians, that other races are not inferior, that other faiths are not Godless." Only in this spirit of give and take can we fulfil our hopes of real democracy. Franklin K. Lane, Secretary of the Interior, emphasized the necessity of close association in order to become a strong nation when he said: "We are trying a great experiment in the United States. Can we gather together peoples of different races, creeds, conditions and aspirations who can be merged into one? If we cannot do this, we will fail; indeed, we have already failed. If we do this, we will produce the greatest of all nations, a new race that will long hold a compelling place in the world."

New York State is one of the largest and best equipped laboratories in the country for trying out this experiment. The State Department of Education has undertaken the task and asks every organization of women for hearty co-operation.

WILLIAM C. SMITH,
Supervisor of Immigrant Education.
ELIZABETH A. WOODWARD,
Assistant, in Charge of Home Classes.

THE PROBLEM

The number of illiterate girls and women ten years of age and over in New York State, according to the census of 1910, was 218,913.

This statement means that many of these women are isolated in their homes and neighborhoods because:

1. They are unable to talk with English-speaking people.
2. They are at a disadvantage with their children, who have learned English in the public schools.

3. They cannot read or sign the reports of children in school. This encourages deception on the part of the children and causes them to lose respect for their parents.

4. They are deprived of the pleasure of reading or answering letters in English by their children away from home.

5. They are unable to read books, magazines, newspapers, notices, warnings, signs or announcements of any kind.

6. They cannot read or sign any official or legal document.

7. They are dependent upon others to transact business for them.

8. They are unable to vote intelligently.

WAYS IN WHICH THE PROBLEM MAY BE SOLVED

1. By helping every foreign-born woman to come into association with at least one American woman of ideals, sympathy and breadth of spirit.

2. By making it possible for every foreign-born woman to learn the language of this country in order:

a. That she may maintain the authority and discipline of the home.

b. That she may associate with English-speaking people outside of the home.

c. That she may vote intelligently. Aliens who have served in the army have become American citizens during the war. They have been educated in the army. Their wives have not had these advantages and, to many, citizenship has come before they are able to use our language or understand our government and its ideals.

d. That she may unite with native-born women in bringing about better conditions in the home, in politics and in industry.

3. By making every foreign-born woman appreciate all that she may contribute to our American life.

WAYS IN WHICH WOMEN'S ORGANIZATIONS MAY ASSIST IN SOLVING THE PROBLEM

General Plan

To insure co-operation and to avoid duplication it is suggested:

1. That each club or society appoint an Americanization committee.

2. That each Americanization committee send a representative to a general council of Americanization workers which shall act as a clearing house.

3. That the general council co-operate with the State Department of Education in carrying out the following program:

a. Make clear the meaning of Americanization. Dr. A. E. Jenks of the University of Minnesota says: "Our people are in three groups, so far as Americanization education is concerned: (1) the educated, old-line citizens; (2) the immigrant racial groups; (3) the illiterates, both native and foreign-born.

"For educated old-line citizens, Americanization means the purposeful continuous squaring of our private and public practices with our ideals in all fundamental relationships of life. It means not just *fair play talk, but actual fair play practice.*

"For the immigrants, Americanization means an intelligent understanding of our national ideal standards, and a definite desire to approximate, as nearly as may be, their realization by means of legal practices and authorized institutions.

"For the native-born illiterates, Americanization means, as a first step to any understanding of America, an opportunity for at least an elementary education."

b. Develop a sympathetic and appreciative attitude toward the foreign-born.

(1) Persuade your organization that race prejudice, class prejudice and religious prejudice cannot exist in a real democracy.

(2) Influence your organization to appreciate that our country is "in the making," that we need to conserve the contributions of all national groups.

(3) Lead your organization to realize that native-born women must work *with* rather than *for* foreign-born women.

c. Assist in the community survey of conditions among foreign-born women.

d. Help in a publicity campaign to explain the meaning of Americanization and to recruit members for classes in English and citizenship by making calls on foreign-born women. If such calls are made in a spirit of genuine friendliness and human interest, they may be the most effective means of understanding immigrant women and of winning their sympathy. Punctilious courtesy should be observed in entering the homes, for Europeans are notably more ceremonious than Americans.

e. Provide short unit courses or a series of lectures to train volunteers for teaching (1) English and citizenship, (2) home nursing, (3) principles of homemaking, cooking, sewing and other handiwork.

f. Supply trained volunteers for home and neighborhood classes.

g. Furnish a day nursery or play-room in a building where mothers' clubs or classes are held, so that the children may be left under proper care.

h. Secure volunteers to look after the children in these nurseries or play-rooms.

i. Help to make the classrooms attractive and suitable for the instruction of adults.

j. Persuade boards of education to send trained teachers to home and neighborhood groups.

k. Provide programs for community meetings.

l. Discover the most urgent need in a community and let the satisfaction of that need be the basis of Americanization work. With the help of the leaders among the foreign groups, provide a health center, clinic, day nursery, maternity center, milk station, kindergarten, playground, community garden or whatever seems to be most necessary.

m. Bring foreign-born women to the recreational and community centers so that all may enjoy community sings, dances, games, pageants, gymnasium exercises, athletic meets, exhibits of foreign art and handicraft.

n. Go with foreign-born mothers to see interesting parts of the city and its institutions. Arrange for picnics and outings. Parties of this kind may serve as a means of teaching English in an informal way.

o. Work with judges, with members of the Legislature, and with members of congress to bring about fair play for the foreign-born in courts. It would be of great advantage to us all if the process of becoming a citizen could be simplified and humanized.

p. Lead the foreign-born women to see that citizenship is closely related to their everyday life, to their home, children, street and neighborhood. Help them to realize that knowledge of the English language and American citizenship are necessary for their welfare and protection. They should understand that citizenship brings with it responsibilities as well as privileges.

Friendship is the keynote for all successful work with foreign-born women. They must see, in the lives of the American women whom they know, the appreciation of the worth of an individual, despite differences in race, creed or color. They must see the living realization of Burns' ideal of a democracy in his words: "A man's a man, for a' that."

"If you would win a man to your cause, first convince him that you are his friend. Therein is a drop of honey that catches his heart, which, say what you will, is the greatest highroad to his reason, and which, when once gained, you will find but little trouble in convincing his judgment of the justice of your cause, if indeed that cause be a really just one.

"On the contrary, assume to dictate to his judgment, or to command his action, or to mark him as one to be shunned or despised, and he will retreat within himself, close all the avenues to his head and heart; and although your cause be naked truth itself, transformed to the heaviest lance, harder than steel and sharper than steel can be made, and though you throw it with more than Herculean force and precision, you shall be no more able to pierce him than to penetrate the hard shell of a tortoise with a rye straw.

"Such is man, and so must he be understood by those who would lead him, even to his own interests." — *Abraham Lincoln.*

6. LESSONS FOR ILLITERATE FOREIGN WOMEN
Prepared by HARRIET P. DOW
PREFACE

The foreign women in the United States fall automatically into two classes: first, the women in industries and occupations, and second, the women in the homes. The first quickly adopt American dress and customs and naturally gain some knowledge of English. The second class keep their foreign dress, from the kerchief on their heads to their bare feet, their old-country customs, and understand and speak only their native language. For the latter group of women these lessons were first planned. They have been used successfully with groups of mothers from various countries. Immigrant women have had little or no schooling in their home land. They cannot begin to learn English by reading. They need oral and dramatic lessons. They need lessons with objects. They need lessons concerning their families, their babies, their daily surroundings and occupations. With this in mind these lessons are formulated.

FIRST SERIES
LESSONS FOR FOREIGN WOMEN
Lesson 1

Subject: The mother and her family.

Vocabulary: Woman, baby, boy, girl, man, this is (a man), I am (a woman).

Suggested Lesson Plan

If possible, seat group in a circle, mothers holding babies, small children beside them.

Woman

Point to each woman and say, slowly and distinctly, "woman," and have the group repeat it in concert each time.

Point to each woman and have her say "woman."

Baby

Present the word "baby" in the same way.

Point in turn to each woman and baby in the circle and have class name them in concert.

Point to each woman and baby and have each individual mother say "woman" and "baby" in turn.

Boy — girl

Present the word "boy" and "girl" and drill in the same way.

Show pictures of woman, baby, boy, girl and have class and individuals name them.

Man

Present the word "man" through use of picture.

Touch pictures and ask "What is this?"[1] Class and then individuals reply, "man," "woman," etc.

This is

Teach sentence form for reply "This is a man," "This is a woman," etc.

Question around circle, "What are you?"[1] Class and then individuals reply, "woman."

I am

Teach sentence form for reply, "I am a woman."

Place in a row a woman, girl, boy and baby, and have class and then individuals name them in the order seated. Change order and repeat as long as interest holds.

Questions

1. What is your name?[1]
2. Where do you live?[1]

Lesson 2

Subject: Forms of greeting.

Vocabulary: Good morning, good afternoon, good evening, goodbye, come in.

---

[1] "What is this?" "What are you?" terms used by teacher are to be sensed by group, but **not** used at this time as vocabulary. This also applies to questions 1 and 2.

Suggested Lesson Plan

Present Lesson 1 as if it were a new lesson. This is for the benefit of any new members in the group and because repetition of gestures, questions and use of pictures will help the others to remember the vocabulary.

Present Lesson 2 by play to introduce "forms of greeting." If one member of the class understands enough English to assist, send her out of the room, shut the door and have her knock for admission. If not, accompany some member, show her what you want, and leave her to knock for entrance.

Good
 afternoon
  Teacher open the door, say "Good afternoon,[1] come in."
 morning
  Have class repeat, in group and individually, "Good afternoon, come in."
 evening
  Let class take turns until each has gone out.
  Have each one who has been out "play hostess," open the door and say, "Good afternoon, come in."

Come in
Have one woman walk to meet you. When you meet say "Good morning."[2]

Goodbye
Have her repeat "Good morning." Have class repeat. Continue until the class have "played." Go to the door, open and go out saying, "Goodbye." Class repeat. Have each mother on leaving say "Goodbye" slowly and distinctly.

Questions

3. Have you a husband?
4. Have you a baby?
5. How many boys have you?
6. How many girls have you?

Indicate by use of watch the time of day for use in remaining forms of greeting and repeat play, using all three forms.

---

[1] "Good morning" or "good evening" may be taught first, according to the time of the class sessions.
[2] A market basket, hand bag or umbrella carried here will add to the interest of the class and also suggest, without words, a meeting on the street.

Cautions:

The teacher should talk as little as possible except in words of vocabulary being presented. Strange words, unless well fitted to the subject-matter and carefully enunciated, will confuse the foreign mind.

Keep vocabulary of lesson in mind. Repeat constantly.

Try learning their language as they learn English and you will understand their difficulties.

Do not force an embarrassed woman to answer. Soon interest will overcome self-consciousness.

Lesson 3

Subject: Parts of baby's body.[1]

Vocabulary: Head, eyes, nose, mouth, teeth, ears, stomach, arm, hand.

Suggested Lesson Plan:

Point first to the baby and ask, " What is this? " Have class answer, " This is a baby."

Head

Touch the baby's head and say, " head." Class repeat " head." Do this with all the babies. Ask each time, " What is this? " and class answer, " This is baby's head."

Eyes

In the same way teach the other new words of the vocabulary of lesson 3.

Nose

Mouth

Drill: 1. Say the word and see who can first touch that part of the baby's body.

Teeth

2. Touch different parts of body and see who can first call out the name. Repeat as long as interest holds.

Ears — Stomach — Arm — Hand

Review lesson 2 by playing the " hostess " game again, and using freely all the terms of greeting.

If time allows, review lesson 1 by use of large pictures of women, men and children.

---

[1] The aim of lessons 3 and 4 is to help the mother to answer questions concerning a sick baby. This has been done by request and has proved of value to nurses and doctor.

Point to picture and question, "What is this?" Have class answer in concert and then individually.

Pass pictures of family groups to the women and let each one point and tell what she sees in her picture, naming man, woman, etc., and also head, eyes, etc., using as much vocabulary, as possible.[1]

Lesson 4

Subject: Parts of mother's body.
Vocabulary: Face, fingers, body, back, leg, foot, sick, well, hot.

Suggested Lesson Plan:

Quick review of vocabulary of last lesson as follows:
Question class, "Where is your head?"
Class answer in concert, "This is my head," touching head.
Continue with eyes, nose, etc.

Face — Fingers — Body

To present new lesson, pass your hand over your face and say, "This is my face." Question class, "Where is your face?" Class answer in concert, "This is my face," passing hand over face. Question individuals, "Where is your face?" Individual answers, "This is my face," passing hand over face.

Back — Leg — Foot

Continue till new vocabulary is taught.

Drill: 1. Name parts of body in quick succession and have class touch them as named. Watch for those least confident and repeat exercise with them using over-confident women as teachers.

2. Call on various members of class to name all parts of baby's body as you touch them. She who can name all "beats."

3. Give class manikins, cut from paper, and have them find leg, foot, finger, etc., and name.

Sick

Have towel or triangular bandage. Tie up a woman's head. Have her lean back in a chair. Point to woman and say, "The woman is sick."

Well

Remove bandage. Have woman sit erect, say, "The woman is well."

---

[1] Have variety in pictures, using groups of foreign people and also colored pictures whenever possible.

Hot

Follow plan in lesson 2, teacher "play doctor" and "call at homes." Question "Is baby sick?" Touch head, say, "Is baby's head sick?" Touch stomach, say, "Is baby's stomach sick?" Touch face and hands, say, "Is baby hot?"

Caution

Always have your previous lesson fresh in your mind and ready to use as point of departure.

Lesson 5

Subject: Baby's clothes.

Vocabulary: Bonnet, blanket, coat, dress, diaper, safety pins, shirt.

Suggested Lesson Plan:

Present new lesson by a doll,[1] or a baby, if there is one properly clothed, in the group.

Bonnet

Undress it before the class. Take off the bonnet and say, "This is baby's bonnet." Hold up the bonnet and ask, "What is this?" Class reply, "This is baby's bonnet."

Blanket — Coat

Put the bonnet on desk or table.

Take off the coat and say, "This is baby's coat." Hold up coat and ask, "What is this?" Class reply, "This is baby's coat."

Dress — Diaper — Shirt — Safety-pins

Put the coat on the table and have class, then individuals, name "bonnet" and "coat."

Continue till the new words are all taught.

See who can name all articles of clothing on the table in order. Change order and name them again. Repeat many times.

Review "parts of body" using the doll. Have class touch parts as named. Have class name parts as touched.

Dress baby or doll before class, reviewing new vocabulary, that is, take up shirt and ask, "What is this?" Class answer, "This is baby's shirt."

Put the shirt on the doll and say, "Baby's shirt is on his body."

---

[1] Bring to class a baby doll, correctly dressed to illustrate clothing of baby, according to American standards.

Ask class, "Where is baby's shirt?" Class answer, "Baby's shirt is on his body."
Continue questions till the doll is fully dressed.
See if class can answer quickly, "Where is baby's bonnet?" "Where is baby's dress?", etc.

Lesson 6

Subject: Mother's clothes.

Vocabulary: Waist, skirt, apron, shoes, stockings, scarf, shawl, how many.

Suggested Lesson Plan:

Have pictures of women of various lands in native costume.[1]

Waist

Point to a picture of woman's shawl and say "shawl." Point to another shawl and ask "What is this?" Class reply, "This is a shawl."

Skirt — Apron — Shoes

Count slowly and distinctly the shawls in the pictures and say, "There are ——— shawls."[2] Question, "How many shawls?" Class reply, "There are ——— shawls."

Stockings — Scarf — Shawl — How many

Point to skirt and teach in the same way. Count the number of skirts in the pictures and say, "There are ——— skirts." Question class, "How many skirts?" Class reply, "There are ——— skirts."

Continue till all the new words have been taught.

Drill on last lesson.

Put up clothesline. Pin on line various articles of baby's clothing. Have class name clothes on line in order. Blindfold one woman. Remove bonnet from line. Unblindfold woman. See if she can name what is gone. Continue while interest lasts. Send individuals to line for various articles of clothing. Each time question, "What have you?" Individual reply, "I have a ———."

---

[1] Teach articles of women's clothing from these pictures to save embarrassing the foreign women in the class. They will apply the new names to their own clothes gradually.

[2] Counting from 1 to 6 is so easily acquired it can be introduced here without distracting the attention from the more difficult vocabulary.

Lesson 7

Subject: Health of baby.[1]

Vocabulary: How is, go, nurse, thank you, get.

Suggested Lesson Plan:

When mothers, with babies, are seated in a circle ready for the lesson, send one mother, with her baby, out of the room.

Have her close the door and knock.

Take baby doll in your arms and open the door.

Say, "Good afternoon." Wait for her to reply, "Good afternoon."

Say, "Come in." Have her come in.

Offer her a chair and say, "Sit down."

Have her sit down and say, "Thank you."

Sit down beside her and look at her baby.[2]

How is — Thank you — Nurse — Go — Get

Ask, "How is your baby?"

Have her ask, "How is your baby?"

Reply, "My baby is well, thank you."[1]

Have her say, "My baby is well, thank you."

Stand and say, "Good-by," and have her go away.

Repeat this visit with many mothers. "Play" as long as interest holds.

If a visiting nurse belongs to their town or district, show picture of woman in nurse's costume and teach "nurse."[3]

Open the door and call, "Nurse, nurse, nurse."

Have mothers call her.

Send a small child out of the room, saying, "Baby is sick, go get the nurse."

Have mothers, in turn, send for the nurse.

Lesson 8

Subject: Nurse's call.

Vocabulary: Cold,[4] water, sleep, today, night, doctor.

---

[1] Vary your answer by saying, "My baby is sick."

[2] Questions 1 to 6 of lessons 1 and 2 may be asked and answered while you are seated, visiting together.

[3] Plan, if possible, to have visiting nurse come to visit the class during the session.

[4] Have hot and cold water and give all mothers drill in saying, "This is cold water"; "This is hot water"; "I have cold water"; "I have hot water."

Suggested Lesson Plan:

Put on cap or other article of uniform to represent nurse, and say, "I am a nurse today."

Ask class, "Who am I?" Class reply, "Nurse."

Seat one woman in front of class with doll in her arms. Explain to class: "This is a good mother." "This is a sick baby."

Go out and close door. Knock.

Cold — Water — Sleep — Today — Night

Have woman with doll open the door to you.

Exchange greetings.

Have mother ask you in and give you a chair saying, "Come in," "sit down." Reply, "Thank you."

Ask, "How is your baby?" Have mother reply, "My baby is sick."

Doctor

Ask "Was the baby sick all night?"[1] Have mother reply, "Yes, my baby was sick all night."

Ask, "Did the baby sleep?"[2] Have mother reply, "No, the baby did not sleep."

Ask, "Did the baby cry all night?" Have mother reply, "Yes, the baby cried all night."

Ask, "Is the baby hot?" Take baby and feel of hands and face. Have mother reply, "Yes, the baby is hot."

Put hand on baby's stomach and ask, "Is baby's stomach sick?" Have mother reply, "Yes, baby's stomach is sick."

Say, "Your baby is very sick. Get the doctor. Give the baby cold water."

Repeat the nurse's call as long as interest holds.

Teach "doctor" from picture of doctor in hospital dispensary or office.

Lesson 9

Subject: Doctor's call.

Vocabulary: eat, bananas, milk, beer, spoon, glass, every hour, drink.

---

[1] Have at hand a watch to show "night."
[2] Have a doll that shuts its eyes to explain "sleep," or use gesture of sleeping to illustrate it.

Suggested Lesson Plan:

Eat
Bananas — Milk — Beer
Spoon
Glass
Drink — Every hour

Teach new vocabulary with objects, first.

Put on large glasses and carry small black bag to represent the doctor. Say, "I am a doctor today."

Ask class, "Who am I?" Class reply, "doctor."

Choose and explain "mother" and "sick baby" as in lesson 8.

Go out and close door. Knock.

Have "mother" with "sick baby" open the door to you.

Exchange words of greeting.

Have mother say, "Come in," "sit down." Reply, "Thank you."

Ask, "How is the baby?" Have mother reply, "My baby is sick."

Ask, "Was the baby sick all night?" Have mother reply, "Yes, my baby was sick all night."

Ask, "Did the baby sleep?" Have mother reply, "No, the baby did not sleep."

Ask, "Did the baby cry all night?" Have mother reply, "Yes, the baby cried all night."

Ask, "Is the baby's head hot?" Have mother feel of face and reply, "Yes, the baby's head is hot."

Ask, "Is baby's stomach sick?" Have mother put her hand on baby's stomach and reply, "Baby's stomach is sick."

Ask, "Did the baby eat bananas?" Have mother reply, "Yes, the baby ate bananas."

Ask, "Did the baby drink beer?" Have mother reply, "Yes, the baby drank beer."

Say, "Bananas and beer make the baby sick; give baby milk to drink; give baby cold water to drink."

"Get a glass of water." "Get a spoon."

Lesson 10

Subject: Care of sick baby.

Vocabulary: bath, tub, kettle, cloth, soap, wash, dry, bottle, pitcher, boil.

Suggested Lesson Plan:

In review

1 Meet a mother and carry on the following conversation with her concerning the baby's illness.

2 Have one mother meet another and carry on a similar conversation.

" Good morning." " Good morning."
" How do you do? " " I am well, thank you."
" How is the baby? " " My baby is well, today."
" Was your baby sick? " " My baby was very sick."
" Did you get the nurse? " " Yes, I got the nurse."
" What did the nurse say? " " Call in the doctor, the baby is very sick."
" What did the doctor say? " " The doctor said, " What did the baby eat? "
" Did the baby eat bananas? " " Yes, the baby ate bananas."
" Did the baby drink beer? " " Yes, the baby drank beer."
" What did the doctor say? " " Give the baby milk to drink; give the baby water to drink."
" Did you give the baby medicine? " " Yes, I gave the baby a spoonful every hour."
" She is a good baby." " Yes, she is a good baby."

Do this many times as long as it holds their interest.

Give a demonstration of the care of milk bottles; that is, rinse the bottle in cold water, wash in soap and hot water, fill with cold water and boil to sterilize, and cool.

Give a baby a bath, teaching new words and reviewing old words; that is, baby's clothing and parts of baby's body, hot and cold water, soap, etc.

SECOND SERIES
LESSONS FOR FOREIGN WOMEN
Lesson 11

Subject: Home.

Vocabulary: house, street, I live, church, school, park, playground.

Suggested Lesson Plan:

House — Street — I live — Church — School — Park — Playground

Show pictures of houses of the type with which the women are familiar, that is, city blocks, tenements, flats, half-houses or **bungalows.** Teach " house."

Question, "What is this?" Class reply, "This is a house."

If possible, show pictures of type of houses with which the women are familiar in the old country.

Show a picture of a near-by street.[1] Teach "street."

Question, "What is your street?"

Make a simple map that will include all the streets on which the different members of the class live. As you draw it say the names of the streets, very plainly, many times.

Question, "On what street do you live?" Ask each mother, in turn, and have her reply, "I live on —————— street."

Show picture of a house that has a number. Question, "What is your number?" "My number is 42." "What is your number and street?" Have each mother say, "I live at 42 Broad street."

Make a set of local street signs. Hold up signs and have class read the names. Put up signs in various parts of the room and send mothers to signs, that is, "Go to 44th street," "go to Beekman street," "go to 64 Main street," "go to 302 Broad street," "go to 840 East 44th street."[2]

Show picture of a church. Teach "church." On map, already drawn, draw the local churches. Question, "On what street is your church?" Have each mother say, "My church is on —————— street."[2]

Show picture of a school. Teach "school." Locate schools on near-by streets. Have class say, "A school is on —————— street."

Show picture of park. Teach "park." Locate nearest park. Have class say, "The park is on —————— street."

Show picture of playground. Teach "playground." Locate nearest playground. Have class say, "The playground is on —————— street."

Drill:

Question 1 What is your name?
          2 On what street do you live?
          3 What number is your house?
          4 On what street is your church?
          5 Where is the park?
          6 Where is the playground?

---

[1] If most of the class live on one street, a model of that street will help in making this lesson plain. It can readily be made with blocks, pictures or cuttings. Let it include stores, school, churches, etc.

[2] Many women receive an address at an employment agency and fail to find it. A knowledge of street signs is valuable in many ways.

A review of the vocabulary of lesson 6 should be introduced here; that is, "A woman wears a shawl to church." "A little girl wears a coat to school."

Lesson 12

Subject: Rooms of house and room furnishings.
Vocabulary: kitchen, bedroom, toilet, stove, table, chair, sink, bench, bed, chest, bureau, rug.

Suggested Lesson Plan:
Kitchen — Bedroom — Toilet — Stove
Table — Chair — Sink
Bench — Bed
Chest — Bureau — Rug

Review street and numbers.

If possible, take group to a kitchen and bedroom in a near-by settlement, janitor's rooms or home of class member. This should of course be prearranged. Tell street and number of house to be visited. Have each one repeat before starting out. The lesson should be taught as rooms are visited and from objects seen. If the lesson can not be given in this way, have a carefully selected group of pictures. House furnishing and furniture catalogs, as well as magazines, offer good illustrative material.

With each picture question, "What is this room?" "That is the kitchen." "What is this?" "That is the stove," etc. Continue with each room and all objects of vocabulary.

Be careful to choose simple pictures. If pictures include objects already known, as boy, girl, baby etc., use the same for review. Do not name objects which may be illustrated if they are not in the vocabulary already in use by the class.

Lesson 13

Subject: Bed and bedding.
Vocabulary: bed, mattress, sheet, pillow, pillowcase, blanket, cover, spread, that, put.

Suggested Lesson Plan:
Bed — Mattress — Sheet
Pillow — Pillowcase — Blanket
Cover — Spread — That — Put

Have a doll's bed with simple bedding at hand. Touch the bed and say, "This is a bed." Question class, pointing to bed, "What is that?" Have class reply, pointing to bed, "That is a bed."

Teach in the same way the names of all the articles of bedding. Make up the bed. Take the mattress and ask, "What is this?" Class reply, "That is a mattress."

Put in on the bed and say, "I put the mattress on the bed." Question, "What do I do?" Class reply, "You put the mattress on the bed." Continue till bed is made.

Place the doll in the bed to show the use made of two sheets.

Have the bed made many times by different members of the class, each time naming the articles of bedding.

In review ask the following questions. (*Note.* Use a game. Have one woman stand and answer till she fails to understand. Those standing longest win.)

1. What is your name?
2. On what street do you live?
3. What is your number?
4. Have you a husband?
5. How many girls have you?
6. How many boys have you?
7. Have you a baby?
8. Have you boarders?
9. On what street is your church?
10. Do you like America?

A review of the vocabularies of lessons 8, 9 and 10 should be used with this lesson; that is, make up a bed for a sick baby, and question concerning baby's illness, nurse's and doctor's calls, and care given to the child.

Lesson 14

Subject: Kitchen utensils.

Vocabulary: oil, coal, wood, paper, spoon, fork, knife, plate, pan, cover.

Suggested Lesson Plan:

Oil — Coal
Wood — Paper — Spoon — Fork — Knife — Plate — Pan — Cover

Place new objects, one at a time, on the table. Give names, that is, "This is coal." Have each woman repeat.

Place second object, giving name. Have each woman repeat. Then touch first and second objects, and have class name both. Continue till all the objects are placed in a line.

Drill:

1 Have each woman name the ten objects in order.

2 Have class close their eyes. Remove one object. Class look and see who can first shout name of object removed. The one who wins can take place of teacher and remove the object.

3 Arrange objects in row on the table. Choose two women. See who can first bring to you an object named.

4 Rearrange these objects in two rows on the table, including with them articles of bedding in lesson 13. Choose two women well matched in ability, and see which can name in quickest time all the articles in her row. Change rows and repeat.

5 Give simple directions to be obeyed, that is, " Put the spoon in the pan." " Put the blanket on the bed," etc.

Each time question, " What did you do?" and have the statement follow, that is, " I put the spoon in the pan," " I put the blanket on the bed."

Lesson 15

Subject: Cleaning.

Vocabulary: broom, sweep, she, floor, brush, dustpan, pail, mop, duster.

Suggested Lesson Plan:

Broom — Sweep
She — Floor
Brush — Dustpan
Pail — Mop — Duster

Have all the new objects at hand. Take the broom and say, " This is a broom." Question, " What is this?" Class reply, " That is a broom."

Take the broom and sweep. Say, " I sweep the room." Question, " What do I do?" Class reply, " You sweep the room."

Give a mother the following directions. " Take the broom:" " sweep the floor." Question class each time, " What does she do?" Class reply, " She takes the broom," or " A woman takes the broom."

Take the brush and say, " This is a brush." Question, " What is this?" Class reply, " That is a brush."

Take the brush and brush the dirt into a pile. Say, "I brush the dust." Question, "What do I do?" Class reply, "You brush the dust."

Use the following list of objects in the same way and develop the following statements: dustpan, pail, water, soap, mop, wipe, duster, dust. Have the action always accompany the statement and use many times.

I brush the dust on the dustpan.
She brushes the dust on the dustpan.
I take the pail.
She takes the pail.
I get hot water in the pail.
She gets hot water in the pail.
I take the soap.
She takes the soap.
I take the mop.
She takes the mop.
I wipe the floor.
She wipes the floor.
I take the duster.
She takes the duster.
I dust the room.
She dusts the room.

Let the women in the class take turns in directing one another.

As a final drill, "Mrs. ──────, please put away the broom." Have her take the broom and put it away. Question, "What did you do?" or question class, "What did Mrs. ────── do?" Continue till all the articles are put away.

At an employment agency you often hear the questions asked, "Is the woman stupid or will she understand what I say to her?" For the women who work out "by the day" cleaning, this lesson is valuable. Teach the names of the "tools" they use, not how to clean. They often excel Americans in scrubbing and scouring.

Lesson 16

Subject: Food of the family.

Vocabulary:[1] bread, meat, potatoes, milk, coffee, soup, onions, flies, screens.

---

[1] A hard and fast vocabulary for this lesson cannot be given. It should include the ten articles of food and drink most used by the group. With various nationalities it will differ greatly.

Suggested Lesson Plan:

Bread — Meat
Potatoes — Milk
Coffee — Soup — Onions — Flies — Screens

Have articles of food in the classroom. Teach the names of food from the objects. Use games suggested in lesson 14 for drill.

Borrow from some near-by dealer samples of inexpensive window screens. Show them to the class, explaining cost. Explain by illustrated posters the danger from flies.[1]

Estimate the cost of baby's sickness as compared with the cost of screens.

Drill:

Arrange in groups (1) foods suitable for a little child, (2) foods suitable for adults. Have the class name the articles of food in each group. Cover and have class name from memory.

Arrange in groups (1) food to use as substitute for meats, (2) food to use as substitute for sugar, (3) food to use as substitute for wheat flour.

Repeat game as with preceding groups.

Lesson 17

Subject: Grocery store.

Vocabulary: sugar, butter, molasses, clove, cinnamon, salt, rice, flour, beans, pound, quart, buy, cost.

Suggested Lesson Plan:

Use a table for a counter. Choose the groceries common to the small local shops. Arrange them on the "counter." Have money for change. Borrow measures and scales from a near-by store. Have paper bags at hand. These all make the "playing store" more realistic.

Sugar — Butter — Molasses — Clove — Cinnamon — Salt — Rice — Flour
Beans

Teach the vocabulary of the lesson from the objects. To teach "pound," show the one pound weight. Say, "One pound." Have class repeat. Weigh out a pound of sugar. Say, "One pound of sugar." Have class repeat, "One pound of sugar." To teach "quart," show quart measure. Fill with water, say, "One quart

---

[1] Many city boards of health furnish these posters and illustrated material on request. Coffman's "Story of the Typhoid Fly" is especially good.

of water." Have class repeat, "One quart of water." Question around the class, alternating pound and quart, "What is this?"
Pound — Quart — Buy — Cost

When class are familiar with the new vocabulary, use the following for drill.

Store game:

Be the first "clerk." Choose a "customer" who will speak freely.

Clerk	*Customer*
"Good morning."	"Good morning."
"What will you buy?"	"I will buy sugar."
"Here is good sugar."	"How much does it cost?"
"It costs 10 cents a pound."	"I will take two pounds."
"Here are two pounds."	"Here is 50 cents."
"Two pounds cost 20 cents."	
"Here is your change."	"Thirty cents. Thank you."
"Good by."	"Good by."

Let the "customer" be the second "clerk." Continue till all the class have "played."

Lesson 18

Subject: Market.

Vocabulary: Sausage, beef, pork, fish, chicken, orange, apple.

Suggested Lesson Plan:

Many advertisements have good pictures of the kinds of meat named in this lesson. Collect these and a good market picture. A picture of an open-air market in the "old country" will arrest the women's attention at once. From the illustrative material collected, teach the new vocabulary.

Review with objects the vocabulary of lesson 17.

Sausage — Beef — Pork — Ham — Fish — Chicken

Question all the class in turn, "What did you buy at the grocery store?" "What did you buy at the market?"

Orange — Apple

Drill:

Use the following game: As the class is seated, have the first woman say, "I went to market and I got fish." The second woman says, "I went to market and I got fish and apples." The third woman says, "I went to market and I got fish and apples and sausage." Continue with each woman telling the preceding purchases in order and adding a new one. Should this game prove too difficult, draw pictures on the blackboard of articles as named, so the women need to remember only the English name and not the objects in order.

Emphasize with this lesson the need of keeping meat and fish clean and away from dust and flies. Give street and number of local markets that sell food under right conditions.

An extra lesson on fruit and vegetables in common use can well be introduced here. If you fill a market basket with different kinds and "play peddler" with the class, their amused interest will easily help in acquiring the English vocabulary.

Lesson 19

Subject: Sewing materials.

Vocabulary: cloth, scissors, thread, needle, pin, measure, shears, black, white.

Suggested Lesson Plan:[1]

Cloth

Give out simple sewing; for example, dish towels to hem.

Scissors — Thread — Needle

Present the word "cloth." Have the women find in the room and touch articles made of cloth. Have statements made, "My dress is made of cloth." "The curtains are made of cloth," etc.

Pin — Measure — Shears — Black — White

Pass thread and teach name. Pass needles and teach name. Pass thimbles and teach name.

Have class sew. As sewing is being done, carry on a conversation in English. Plan this carefully so as to introduce all the new vocabulary. Give frequent directions, as, "Please give me the shears," "Take off your thimble," "Give me the black thread, please," "Mrs———, please get the measure," "Mrs ———, do you like to sew?" If class is sufficiently advanced, have simple forfeits paid by those who do not speak in English during this "sewing party."

The new interest that the mothers feel in competing with husbands and children, when once started on the difficult road of learning English, is illustrated in the case of Mrs Koics. On the day she came home from class, after learning the names of sewing

---

[1] This plan will work well with a settlement or other social group where sewing, thread, needles, etc., can be readily obtained for the class. If these supplies can not be obtained, have sample of sewing, one spool of white thread, one spool of black thread, one pair of scissors, one thimble, etc., and have different members of the class use them in turn.

"tools," she heard her eight year old son boasting, "Mother can't speak English like me." She took her sewing and sat down. Then she called, "Mike, get thimble." He said, "Naprstek! Co je to?" ("Thimble! What is it?") She replied, "And you speak the English, Mike?"

Lesson 20

Subject: Church and holidays.

Vocabulary! Sunday, Monday, Tuesday, Wednesday, Thursday, Friday, Saturday, holiday, work, flag, America.

Suggested Lesson Plan:

Sunday — Monday — Tuesday — Wednesday — Thursday — Friday — Saturday — Holiday

Teach the names of the days of the week from a large calendar. Connect with the names for the days in the women's own language.

With the following material at hand, teach "holiday," "work," "flag," and "America": Borrow from a kindergarten a set of pictures called "Occupations for the Days of the Week." These will suggest kinds of work done, but not by days, as every day is a "wash day" in most of the women's homes. Also have pictures of churches and some old world cathedrals. Pictures of festivals and parades help to explain "holidays."

Work

Use the flag, always displayed in the classroom, in connection with American holidays.

Flag — America

Drill, through question and answers, as:

1 How many days in a week?
2 Name the days in English.
3 What day do you go to church?
4 On what street is your church?
5 Name your church.
6 Name a church holiday.
7 What days does your man work?
8 What days does your boy go to school?
9 What days does your girl go to school?
10 What days do you come to school?
11 What days are the stores open?
12 What day is there no school?
13 Find our flag.
14 **Name an American holiday.**

7. METHODS OF TEACHING ENGLISH TO THE NON-ENGLISH-SPEAKING FOREIGN-BORN

This pamphlet is published to meet the persistent request throughout the State for a standard method of instruction. It was prepared by Henry H. Goldberger, Ph.D., instructor in education, Columbia University, director of Americanization institutes, New York City, and expert for Carnegie Foundation committee for investigation of methods of teaching English to the foreign-born, author of "Methods of Teaching English to Foreigners" and "English for Coming Citizens," under the direction of the Americanization Bureau of the Pennsylvania Council of National Defense, through whose courtesy we are permitted to publish it.

Teachers of English to non-English-speaking adults find the greatest difficulty with beginners. The method used in teaching advanced pupils to increase their vocabularies, to express themselves idiomatically, to understand grammatical principles, are the same methods as those employed by progressive teachers of English to English-speaking pupils. The following discussion will, therefore, present the various types of methods used with beginners, and will explain the principles underlying such methods.

Direct Methods

All methods which employ English as the medium of instruction in teaching English are called DIRECT; methods which employ a foreign language as a medium of instruction are called TRANSLATION or INDIRECT METHODS.

For practical or psychological reasons, the present tendency is to use direct methods only. It is not possible to obtain properly qualified teachers in sufficient numbers to teach English by translating it from the hundreds of different languages and dialects spoken by the three million non-English-speaking immigrants in the United States. But even if it were possible to obtain such teachers, it would be undesirable to teach English by the translation methods, for the following psychological reasons: First, a language is learned in use. To acquire the ability to speak English, one must be occupied with the process of speaking and one must hear English spoken frequently enough to have an auditory impression of what is it sounds like. Translation methods do not furnish sufficient auditory impressions nor do they give sufficient practice in speaking English to enable a learner to use English language as a medium of communication. Second, learning a new language means acquiring new associations between the objects, experiences and ideas, already familiar to the learner, and the English symbols which represent these objects, experiences or ideas. In teaching a foreigner the English word " door " we may teach him to associate the word "door" with the object "door," or we teach him to associate the word "door" with the word that stands for "door" in his own language — with "porta" in Italian or with "drzwi" in Polish. The latter — a translation method — associates, therefore, the English word with the foreign word, with the object. This is a long circuiting process. Whenever the learner wishes to recall the English word "door" he must first think of the foreign word "door" and then of the object or experience for which the word "door" stands. The direct method is a short circuiting process and requires only a single association of English word — door — with the object for which "door" stands.

Pupils who learn English by the translation method are rarely able to speak English, because they must always think in the foreign language.

It is needless to say that understanding the foreign language of the pupil is a decided help to the teacher of English to foreigners, provided he does not use the foreign language in teaching his pupils English. In the discussion which is to follow, all methods are direct.

The Gouin or Theme Method

About thirty years ago, M. Francois Gouin developed a procedure in teaching modern languages which bears his name and which has been applied very extensively to the teaching of beginning English. M. Gouin conceived the idea that a language may be learned by acquiring a number of sentences describing one central activity. These sentences make up the "theme." According to Gouin, a "theme" is a general act defined by a series of particular acts.

Thus the teacher determines the end, "to open the door." She then constructs a number of simple sentences describing the actions necessary for opening the door. In these sentences it is the verb that plays the principal part. In attaining to the end — to open the door — teacher and pupils perform the necessary action which are the means, that is, they walk, get to the door, stop, stretch out, take hold of, turn, push, etc. As each action is performed, it is accompanied by the appropriate descriptive sentence. The teacher at the same time shows her approval of intelligence and understanding. The sentences in the first themes bear to one another the relation of succession, but later they may bear such other relationships as those of cause and effect, the whole and its parts. The development of a theme is not complete until the sentences are written on the board and the verbs placed to the right for emphasis. Thus the first theme " to open the door," will appear on the board like this:

I walk to the door.....................	I walk
I get to the door.....................	I get to
I stop at the door.....................	I stop
I stretch out my hand..................	I stretch out
I turn the knob......................	I turn
I take hold of the knob................	I take hold
I push the door......................	I push
The door moves......................	moves
The door turns on its hinges............	turns
I let go the knob.....................	I let go

The following principles in constructing themes after the Gouin method must be borne in mind:

1. The teacher selects an " end " worth while to his pupils; for example: " To go to work," " to look for a job," " to visit the doctor." For a list of topics for themes, see the syllabus which follows.

2. The teacher then constructs a series of sentences each describing a certain act tending toward the accomplishment of the end sought in the theme.

3. The sentences must be short and so worded that the meaning of each and every part of each sentence may be made clear to foreigners by means of action, dramatizations, and by the use of objects or pictures.

4. The sentences must be related to one another, either in time, sequence, or by cause and effect.

5. Not more than ten sentences can profitably be used in any one theme, because of the difficulty in memorizing more than that number.

The theme method has certain special values, but it is not all of method nor can it be used for a very long time. The method is valuable because:

1. It can be used with beginners without the intermediation of a foreign langauge. To make it usable in this way, however, it is necessary that the teacher bear in mind that each sentence must be such as to be made clear by objects, actions and dramatizations. When, however, the foreigner has acquired sufficient knowledge of

English to dispense with objectifying, the method should no longer be used, but rather the simple English which the pupil knows should then be employed to give him further command of the language.

2. The method emphasizes the teaching of sentences rather than of isolated meaningless words and phrases. The fact that the sentences are coherent and related to each other, makes it easier for the pupils to understand, to learn and to recall them.

3. In the process of developing a theme, sufficient variety of drill is provided to make possible the easy retention of sentence form.

Nevertheless, the method has a number of limitations; it is not a panacea for teaching English. Moreover, it must be understood that merely cutting up a paragraph into a number of short lines and placing a word to the right will not facilitate the problem of teaching English. As soon as a foreigner understands a little English, the theme becomes a very artificial process and a distinctly schoolroom device. Its place is to serve as a bridge or a crutch as long as the pupil needs an interpreter. When used beyond that time, the formal theme is meaningless and gives the pupil a perverted notion of our language.

The Frankfort Plan

An interesting modification of the Gouin method was developed in the schools at Frankfort. The variation consists in basing sentences on "things seen" rather than on "things done," thus permitting great variety in person, number and tense. For example, the teacher steps to his desk, takes a piece of chalk and writes on the board. The pupils describe the actions of the teacher by saying, "you are going to your desk," "you are taking a piece of chalk," "you are writing on the board," "you put the chalk on the desk," "you erase the writing on the board." A pupil is then called upon to perform the actions of the teacher, while the class or another pupil says, "he is walking to the desk," etc. The pupil who performs the action speaks in the first person, while the actions are going on, other pupils speak to him and of him in the second and third persons. The tense is varied in a similar manner.

The Development Method

A method employed with pupils who can understand a little English but who express themselves imperfectly in it is to have the teacher " elicit " by means of questions, a series of answers which are written on the board to form a coherent paragraph. Thus the teacher proposes to talk about the " room." He asks such questions as the following:

> How many walls has the room?
> What color are the walls?
> What else has the room?
> What color is the ceiling?
> How many doors has the room?
> How many windows has the room?
> What are the windows made of?
> Where does the teacher stand?

The teacher accepts the best answers, corrects them as they are given and writes the sentences on the board. The pupils then read and copy the sentences into their notebooks. This procedure is less stilted than the formal theme and permits a variety of sentence structure. Moreover, the method provides for the gradual introduction of reading texts, for the immediate correction of sentences, and for their fixation in written form.

The Method of Conversation

The theme and its variations serve to build up a vocabulary in sentences. Methods thus far described fail, however, to give the foreigner the ability to use conversational English in making known his needs to English-speaking people. After all, the sentences developed in themes can not be taken out of the classroom and used in the daily life of the foreigner. As pointed out above, the theme serves as a means to bridge the gap between the teacher who does not understand the foreign language and the pupil who does not understand English. In order to give the foreigner the ability to say a few necessary things, the teacher emphasizes those sentences which the foreigner will be called upon to use in his intercourse with English speaking people and he neglects those sentences which the foreigner need not necessarily know how to say. Since teaching a person how to acquire skill in speaking is more difficult than teaching him how to understand, it becomes important to limit the number of sentences to those that are needed at once. To impart such skill, locutions must be specifically based on the probable activities in which the foreigner will engage. Unless these idiomatic expressions are taught, the foreigner will translate his own idiom and produce the tortured sentences and monstrosities frequently heard on the vaudeville stage.

For teaching these everyday expressions the method of dramatization is most successfully used. To illustrate: Two pupils are instructed to take the parts of salesman and customer. As the dialogue proceeds the teacher asks other pupils to express the same thoughts in better English, at the same time writing the correct expressions on the board. After the pupils have gone through the same exercise, the class is instructed to copy those expressions which they like best. After a ten minutes' lesson of this kind on "How to find one's way" the following conversation was carried on between a man and woman immigrant:

> Woman — I beg your pardon, can you tell me where the nearest subway entrance is?
>
> Man (removing hat as soon as spoken to) — Yes, ma'am. Walk two blocks north (pointing north), and you will see it.
>
> Woman — Thank you (bowing).
>
> Man — You're quite welcome.

Other pupils who went through the same procedure used other English expressions which they found on the board; for example, "excuse me," "would you mind telling me," "permit me to show you," "not at all." Such expressions require emphasis in the teaching process, if only to give the foreigner confidence that he is able to make himself understood. It is not intended that dramatization be the entire method, nor is it intended to supersede other methods or other exercises, which a teacher of English finds valuable. But these dramatizations provide exercises for which none others are as well adapted.

The Pictorial Methods

Situations in the classroom are usually limited to classroom activities, and do not furnish opportunity to teach English in connection with the main life contacts that the foreigner makes. To provide a wider scope for conversation, but not necessarily to employ a different procedure from any of those heretofore described, the method of teaching by means of pictures has been developed. Some publishers print elaborate pictures of various scenes, for example, a farm scene, a factory scene, a mining scene, a street scene, a family scene, etc. Teachers have, however, got excellent results by using pictures from magazines, posters and advertisements, and by throwing pictures from slides onto a screen. The teacher then points out the features of the picture and stimulates by questions such conversation as the picture demands.

Merely to point out objects in a picture — this is a house — this is a door — this is a window — catalog fashion, is no better when pictures are used than when actual objects are used. Pictures are valuable when actual objects or situations can not be introduced into the classroom or when the picture itself is the object of instruction. There is an ever-present danger that ideas got from pictures are vague as compared with ideas obtained from actual situations.

Incidental Methods of Teaching Meanings

Some words present peculiar difficulties and must be taught separately by methods which apply to special difficulties but do not apply generally. Following are some special devices for teaching the meanings of words incidentally:

1. Obeying commands; for example, " put your hands upon the desk."

The pupil performs the act and says, " I put my hands upon my desk."

This device is especially valuable for teaching the meanings of prepositions.

2. Question-answer; for example, " What is the chair made of ?" " It is made of wood."

3. Reading and acting; for example, pupil reads, " open the door " and performs the action.

4. Labeling; for example, a card with the word " chair " written on it is given to a pupil with directions to place it where it belongs.

5. Filling in context; for example, Today is.... What day was yesterday? Tomorrow will be......? It is........o'clock.

6. Pantomime or dramatization — a method valuable for giving the meaning of verbs easily illustrated by actions; for example, he sawed the board — the child stumbled — he turned and fled.

7. Reading aloud by the teacher accompanied by gesture, expression and play of features; for example, " The haughty nobleman spoke in a thin squeaky voice." By assuming an attitude of haughtiness and by using the voice, the teacher helps pupils to understand the meanings of descriptive terms.

The Textbook Method

A langauge is learned primarily through the ear, and only secondarily through the eye. Children and illiterate adults are able to speak English even though the eye has not aided them in the acquisition. Reading a text may be made a most valuable aid in teaching spoken English as well as in teaching reading, provided the text material is properly constructed, and provided further that the teacher make some use of the text to insure that the learner has understood its meaning.

Ordinarily, the tendency is very strong to ask foreigners " to read" without making sure that the reading means anything. The process of reading then consists of a series of mispronunciations punctuated by the corrections of the teacher. Each mispronunciation helps to impress itself on the pupil's mind, and the right pronunciation is acquired by accident, if it is acquired at all.

In order that the process of reading a text may be a direct help in learning English, the following principles must be understood:

1. Teaching a foreigner to read is not the same as teaching him the meaning of words. The foreigner must understand the meanings of symbols before he can interpret them in print. The teacher must, therefore, first develop the thought of the matter to be read and make clear the meanings of new words and expressions to be found in the reading matter.

2. During this process of development, the teacher pronounces words especially with which the foreigner will have difficulty before he gets a chance to mispronounce them by seeing them in print. Foreigners find no difficulty in imitating the sounds of the most difficult English words, provided they are not confused by the anomalous way in which they are spelled. Thus, such sounds as " rough," "though," " isle " present no terrors until they are to be read. The teacher prevents confusion by forestalling such difficulies in an introduction to the lesson.

3. As a test of understanding of the reading matter, the teacher must have some other means than oral reading. Modern text books are beginning to supply such tests in a series of questions based on the reading matter to insure that the pupil understands, to give him a reason for rereading, and to supply a natural method of drill. For example, in a recent text-book, the following lesson appears;

"Washing My Hands"

My hands are dirty. I turn up my sleeves. I take soap from the dish. I dip the soap into the water. I rub the soap on my hands. I wash my hands in the water. I dry my hands on a towel. My hands are clean.

Exercises

Are your hands clean or dirty?
My hands are ....
What do you turn up?
I .... my sleeves.
Where is the soap?
The soap is in the ....
Where do you dip the soap?
I .... the soap into the water.
What do you rub on your hands?
I rub the .... on my ....
With what do dry your hands?
I dry my hands with a ....

At the beginning the questions are simple and the answers suggested. Later on the questions become more difficult, and the pupil finds his answer in the text. Still later, the questions are such as to call for a reconstruction of the pupil's thought together with an answer in the pupil's own words, thus making for progress in acquiring a vocabulary and in using it for conversation purposes.

Formation of Foreign Classes in English

The best work can be done only when teachers are working with groups that are fairly homogeneous. If only enough pupils enter to form one class, a teacher may have to do individual or group teaching, especially if the members of the class are not all beginners.

Effective group teaching is accomplished by dividing the class into two or three sections on the basis of some ability, such as is used in the formation of whole classes. Each group is then taught as if it were a class by itself, while the other groups are given written work or reading to do by themselves.

The pupil's knowledge of English is the best basis for the organization of whole classes of foreigners or of groups within a single class. The following is a suggested organization for three groups or classes:

1. Beginners — to be subdivided into two groups:
 a. Those who speak no English, but who can read and write their own languages.
 b. Those who speak no English, but are illiterate in their own languages.
2. Intermediate:
Those who have completed the work of the beginners' classes — or
Those who have never gone to school before, but who can make themselves understood in English, and can read the beginning lessons in an English to foreign text.
3. Advanced:
Those who have completed the intermediate class — or
Those who can carry on a conversation in English and can read and understand a simple newspaper article.

Beginners' classes may be further subdivided on the basis of nationality, their previous education, age and sex. These subdivisions are, however, valuable only in the beginning, and should not be retained for long, because they tend to stratify groups of foreigners and to emphasize the formation of national cliques, thus counteracting Americanization forces.

General Directions for Teachers

The successful teacher of English to foreigners thinks of his pupils rather than of his subject, is interested in men and women, their needs, their problems, their desires, rather than in the prescription of a course of study. He realizes that foreigners are not innately his inferiors, that many of them have had a wide experience, and a culture obtained from grappling with life's problems.

Much initiative and energy are required to learn a second language; especially is this true of foreigners in closely settled foreign sections, where English is not spoken and where the foreigner gets along very well without knowing any English. But if they are to learn any English, they must do so by acquiring such English as will be of value to them in their daily life outside of the classroom, rather than in the classroom.

The teacher must, therefore, prepare the work very carefully, so as to determine:

1. What is the most pressing present need of the foreigner under instruction as far as his English is concerned.

2. How to develop and broaden the foreigner's further needs for more advanced instruction.

3. What content and what procedure will best satisfy the present needs of the pupils under instruction.

Such preparation, it has been found, is best when it is written, rather than when left to the inspiration of the moment.

To insure continuous growth of the foreigner's knowledge of English, it is suggested that each pupil be given a notebook in in which he keeps his written work.

Regularity and promptness of attendance depend on the worthwhileness of the instruction. It is advisable to encourage early arrival by having special exercises ready for those who come early; such as — copying from the blackboard — individual correction of papers — oral reading — personal talks with shy pupils.

Detailed Plan of Work

The following detailed plan covers six evenings of instruction each evening having two periods of forty minutes' duration together with an interval of from five to ten minutes for physical training and for recreation. It is expected that the teacher will adjust these lessons to the needs of the class, and proceed as rapidly or as slowly as the ability of the group requires. Some groups may be able to accomplish two or three times as much as other groups, but in all cases all exercises should be given.

First Evening

1. Greet pupils as they come in; show them that you are friendly. Much depends upon their first impression.

Point to yourself and say, "My name is ....

Point to a pupil and ask, "What is your name?"

If he doesn't understand, ask another pupil until you get an answer, and then go back and get the name of every pupil in the class, and make him say, "My name is ...."

Encourage pupils by using words of approval; for example "Good," "Fine," "You understand," "You're learning English," etc.

2. Develop the the sentence in theme 1

    I open the door.

    I walk into the room.

    I take my hat off.

I see the teacher.
Good evening! I sit down.
I take a piece of paper.
I take a pencil.
I write my name on the paper.
I put the pencil down.

How to develop the theme:

a. The teacher performs the act, at the same time saying the words; for example, I open the door.

b. The pupils perform the act and say the words.

c. The teacher performs the act, says the words, and writes them on the board.

d. The pupils perform the act, say the words, and read them from the board.

e. Pupils copy the sentences.

f. Review the theme by calling upon pupils to perform the various acts.

It may not be possible to go through the entire theme in one evening. Develop only so much as your class can master.

3. Divide the class into groups according to their ability while they are attempting to copy the theme from the board. Group the illiterates and let them copy their names from a model furnished by you.

While they are working walk around the room and learn to know your pupils. Help those who need your help.

Second Evening

1. Greet pupils. Try to get them to tell you their occupations, their addresses.

2. Teach "I live at .... street." Show them how to write their addresses.

3. Review the theme learned in Lesson 1 by having pupils go through the dramatization.

4. Let one pupil read the theme while another one acts it out.

5. Beginning with this evening, have a daily two-minute physical setting-up drill after the first forty minutes of instruction. Let the pupils open the windows. As you give each of the following commands, demonstrate the meaning and show the class how to perform the acts:

"Class stand."

"Face the windows."

"Breathe in" (eight times).
"Face front."
"Arms upward stretch." "Down." (Four times.)

Third Evening

1. Greet pupils; engage them in conversation about their work; teach them to say "I am a (tailor)."
2. Teach pupils to spell and write the sentence "I am a ...." (giving their own occupations).
3. Let pupils fill in blank spaces in the sentences of the theme; for example, "I .... the door," "I walk into the ...."
4. Two-minute drill, same as last evening.
5. Drill on the recognition of ten words. Select ten verbs and nouns from the theme; write them in columns on the board; drill pupils on rapid recognition of these words; for review purposes write each word on a separate card and drill the class on rapid recognition of words from the cards.

Fourth Evening

1. Greet pupils. Vary your greetings; for example, "How do you do;" "I am glad to see you."
2. Teach them how to spell from five to ten words from the theme.
3. Review the recognition of the words so far taught, and drill on the recognition of ten new words.
4. Let pupils perform the acts described in the theme and give the sentences from memory. When they forget, help them by asking, "and then?"
5. Two-minute drill. Introduce head turning.
6. Let pupils write from memory as many sentences in the theme as they can. Have them compare their work with a copy on the board.

Fifth Evening

1. Conversation with pupils. Get them to tell you the name and address of their employer. Teach them to write the name and address of their employer.
2. Recognition and spelling of ten words, either from the theme or from the short sentences written by the pupil.
3. Two-minute drill. Introduce knee-bending.
4. Counting concrete objects; for example, hands, fingers, doors windows, men, women.

5. Develop theme 2 — use the same procedure as in theme 1.
   I stand.
   I walk to the door.
   I turn the knob.
   The door moves.
   I walk out into the hall.
   I shut the door.
   I put my hat on my head.
   I walk out into the street.

Sixth Evening
1. Conversation. Hours of work; hours of rest.
2. Review theme 2 by having pupils read and dramatize.
3. Incidental reading. Have two signs on two cards, "Exit," "Entrance." Place them above doors and instruct pupils how to react to them.
4. Review the recognition and spelling of words so far taught. Let each pupil keep an individual list of words which he misspelled in his dictation or in his reproduction from memory.
5. Place on the board a summary of the conversation exercises. Leave blank spaces to be filled in by the pupils; for example, "My name is ....;" "I live at ....;" "I was born in ....;" "I am .... years old;" "My occupation is ....;" "I work for ...."

Weekly Outlines

The six daily lessons given under the heading "Detailed Plan of work" are sufficient for a period of two weeks of three lessons each. The following lessons will be outlined by weeks rather than by days and will begin with the third week of instruction. The detailed method of procedure will be given wherever a new type of exercise is introduced.

Each teacher will find it advisable to prepare a time schedule for the various exercises to be given in the course of a week. On the basis of three evenings a week of eighty minutes' instruction per lesson, the following schedule is suggested:

Reading: 35 to 50 minutes a week.
Conversation: 45 to 50 minutes a week.
Theme or topic development: 40 to 50 minutes a week.
Writing (copy, dictation or original composition): 40 to 50 minutes a week.

Language work (recognition of words, recognition of signs, mottoes, correction of errors): 20 to 30 minutes a week.
Spelling: 20 minutes a week.
Phonics: 10 minutes a week.
Two-minute drills: 6 minutes a week.

Third Week

Develop theme 3.

Getting Up in the Morning

I open my eyes.
The sun shines into my room.
I look at my watch.
It is six o'clock.
I push back the covers.
I get out of bed.
I wash myself.
I dress myself.
I eat my breakfast.

Note.— Teacher should have the following material to develop this lesson: A doll's bed, bed covers, and a clock face.

Conversation.

Review theme 2 by introducing new words, such as

Open the *book*.
Shut the book.
Open the *window*.
Walk to the window.
Put your *coat* on — *gloves* — *vest* — *tie* — *collar* — *sweater* — *rubbers*.

Writing:

Dictate four sentences from theme 3 — have pupils compare with copy on the board.

Composition:

Fill in blank space in theme 2 as follows:

I walk to the ....
I .... the knob.
The door is ....
I .... into the hall.
I .... the door.
I .... on my hat and coat.
I walk out into the ....

Reading from a text:

Most classes will be far enough advanced at this stage to make it worth while to introduce the reading of a textbook. It must be borne in mind that a foreigner, merely because he is a foreigner, is not, therefore, childish and that he resents being treated as a child. "I am a little buttercup" is not proper reading material for an ablebodied foreign laborer. The teacher must select such books as appeal to the personal interest of the pupils and stimulate the further desire to read. Books which usually begin with a vocabulary developed by the "This is a hat," "This is a chair," procedure do not make good reading material. Vocabularies are to be explained by teachers in oral lessons, as provided for in these outlines. Above all, the teacher must remember that the function of reading is to get thought from the printed page, and that in order to get this thought, the meaning of the language and the recognition of the symbols which express that language for us, must be well understood before the foreigner is asked to read. Hence, the following procedure should in all cases be followed in a reading lesson.

1. An introduction.

The function of the introduction is:

    1. To interest the class in the subject matter of a lesson by reference to a picture, a previous conversation or experience.

    2. To overcome the mechanical difficulties of understanding and of recognizing new words by means of drills on the board, introducing new words in conversation, by illustration, objectifying, but never at this early stage, by requiring definitions or by looking them up in the dictionary.

2. Oral reading by the teacher as a model of pronunciation, enunciation and expression.

3. Silent reading by the pupils to enable them to conquer one difficulty at a time and get the thought. While the pupils read silently, the teacher walks about the room helping those who need her help.

4. Testing the pupils' understanding of the reading matter by questions — by having them obey directions — by dramatizations — by summaries — by discussions.

5. Oral reading by the pupils.

Language work.

Teach the recognition of two signs; for example, "Keep to the right," "Line forms on this side."

Teach the recognition and the meaning of a motto; for example, "Never spend your money before you have it." "Look before you leap."

Introduce the motto in a story or illustration which they can understand — then write the motto on the board and have the pupils memorize it.

Phonics.

Group words beginning with "W," "Wh."

Illustrate the method of pronouncing.

NOTE.— The sound of "W" is made by pursing the lips and making a sound of "oo;" for example, "wash" is pronounced "oo-ash." The sound of "Wh" is pronounced as if it were written "hw." "When" is pronounced "Hoo-en."

Spelling.

Drill the spelling of ten words from the pupils' theme.

Two-minute drills.

Use all the exercises previously had and in addition introduce "Rising on toes."

FOURTH WEEK

Develop theme 4.

Washing Myself

I go to the sink.
I turn on the water.
The water fills the basin.
I rub soap on my hands.
I wash my hands in the water.
I dry my hands with a towel.
I empty the basin.

Conversation.

Review theme 3 and introduce in conversation the following words: Day, night, moon, stars, sun, bedroom.

Teach the telling of time from the clock face.

In connection with theme 4, teach by objectifying the following words: Hot, cold, warm, bath towel, face towel, rough, smooth.

Writing.

Fill in blank space by omitting words from theme 3.

Dictate four sentences from theme 3.

Reading from text.

Language work.

Teach the recognition of two signs; for example, "No Smoking," "Keep Out."

Have pupils memorize, after you have taught the meanings, two mottoes, for example, "Better late than never," "Do not cry over spilt milk."

Phonics.

Review words recognized as wholes; for example, walk, take. Cover with a piece of cardboard the *alk* in walk, review the pronunciation of "w."

In the same way, cover *ake* in take, and show how to pronounce "t."

In the same way, show the pronunciations of *alk* and *ake* from walk and take; now write on the board the following words: talk, chalk, sake, bake, cake, snake.

Spelling.

Drill the spelling of words misspelled by the pupils in their dictation work.

Two-minute drills.

Review the exercises so far had, and teach in addition "Arms upward, stretch."

Fifth Week

Develop theme 5.

Eating a Meal

I am hungry.
I go to the dining room.
I sit at the table.
The table is set.
On the table is a plate, a knife, a fork, and a spoon.
The waiter brings me my breakfast.
I eat my breakfast.
My appetite is good.

Note: The teacher should have a miniature table or a real table with the usual appurtenances for setting it.

Conversation.

Review theme 2 by changing it to the second person, thus:

You stand.
You walk to the door.
You turn the knob.
Etc.

Dramatize an introduction to a stranger thus:

"Mr. Brown, this is Mr. Smith." "I am glad to meet you," or "I am pleased to meet you," or "I am glad to know you."

Writing.

Let pupils copy theme 3 and vary the sentences by changing the theme to the second person, plural.

Reading from text.

Language work.

After theme 5 has been developed, introduce by variation the following terms: thirsty, parlor, bath-room, glass, napkin, table-cloth, dinner, supper.

Teach two signs; for example, " Private," " Look out for paint."

Teach two mottoes; for example, "A penny saved is a penny earned," " It is never too late to learn."

Phonics.

Group the following words in families:

    stand — and — land — band — hand — grand —
    go — so — no —
    door — floor —

Spelling.

Review the spelling of words which the pupils need in order to tell their individual addresses, their occupations, the name of the city or town in which they live.

Two-minute drills.

Teach in addition " Place your hands on your hips." " Bend your bodies to the right — to the left."

Sixth Week

Develop theme 6.

Going to Work

It is 7 o'clock.
I put on my hat and coat.
I take my lunch in a box.
I say good-bye to my family.
I go out into the street.
I walk to the corner.
I take a car.
I get off at .... (Main street).
I go into the factory.
The whistle blows.

Conversation.

Growing out of the theme, develop the names for the members of the family; for example, wife, baby, boy, girl, children, husband, married, single.

Teach counting. Count objects in the room, children, let them tell you how much money they earn, let them tell you the cost of several articles that they frequently buy.

Writing.

Let pupils write from memory one of the themes which they know very well, and have them compare it with a copy for correction.

Reading from text.

Language work.

Teach two signs; for example, " Ticket Office," " Hands Off."

Teach two mottoes; for example, " Rome was not built in one day," " Speech is silver, silence is gold."

Phonics.

Group the following words in families:

    good — wood —
    get — set — met —
    hat — cat — sat —
    out — stout — shout —
    car — far — bar.

Spelling.

Teach the spelling of words grouped in families in the phonic exercises.

Two-minute drills.

New exercises to be taught. " Hands on shoulders, place." " Arms sideways, stretch."

Seventh Week

Develop theme 7.

Going to a Doctor

  I am sick.
  My head aches.
  I have no appetite.
  I can not sleep.
  I go to the Doctor.
  The Doctor examines me.

> The Doctor gives me medicine.
> I take the medicine.
> I am well.

Conversation.
Inquiring after the health of a person, thus:
" How are you today? "
" Are you better? "
" I am very well, thank you."
" How is the baby? " (and various other members of the family taught during the lessons of last week).
Writing.
Fill in blank spaces for theme 7.
Dictate three sentences from theme 7.
Reading from text.
Language work.
Review themes 3 and 4 by having the pupil change the first person to the third person, singular, both masculine and feminine genders. Call attention to the changed form of the verb, thus:

> He opens *his* eyes.
> He looks at *his* watch.
> He pushes back the covers.

Phonics.
Group the following words in families:

> Street — sleep — sheep — feet —
> Am — examine — clam — ham —
> Well — sell — tell — bell — fell —
> Me — he — she.

Spelling.
Teach the spelling of words which pupils use in their daily greetings.
Two-minute drills.
Review all the two-minute drills thus far had.

Eighth Week

Develop theme 8.

Writing a Letter

> Today is Tuesday.
> Yesterday was Monday.
> I did not go to school yesterday.

I was not well.
I write a letter to my teacher.
I tell the teacher I was sick.
I put the letter into the envelope.
I put a stamp on the envelope.
I write the teacher's name and address on the envelope.
I drop the letter into the letter-box.

Conversation.

Teach the days of the week. Let the pupils tell you what they do on different days of the week; for example, "When do you go to church?" "On what days do you work?" "On what days do you go to school?" Inquire after the various members of the family and what they do.

Writing.

Practice pupils in addressing envelopes.

Reading from text.

Language work.

Review themes 5 and 6 by changing the first person, singular, to the first person, plural, thus:

We are hungry.
We go to the diningroom.
We sit at the table.
   Etc.

Phonics.

Group the following words in families:
Day — yesterday — Monday — Tuesday etc.
Letter — better.
Stamp — lamp — camp — damp.

Spelling.

Teach the spelling of the days of the week.

Two-minute drills.

Have the orders for the two-minute drills written on the board. Instruct the pupils to copy and then permit one pupil to give the orders, while the others execute them. Vary this procedure every evening.

Ninth Week

Develop theme 9.

Buying a Pair of Shoes

My shoes are torn.
The heels are worn down.
I go to the shoe store.
I ask the salesman for a pair of shoes.
" What size do you wear ? "
" I wear size 8."
" Here is a fine pair. Try them on, please."
" These shoes fit. How much are they ? "
" You may have them for five dollars."
" I'll take them."

Note: In developing this new kind of theme, have two pupils dramatize the situation, after they understand the original theme.
Conversation.
Based on theme 9, dramatize other situations of buying articles in stores.
Writing.
Teach pupils how to begin a letter by writing the salutation and address from copy which you place on the board.
Reading from text.
Language work.
Review themes 1, 2, 3, by having one pupil describe the actions of another in the progressive form, thus:

He is going to the sink.
He is turning on the water.
The water is filling the basin.

Phonics.
Group the following words:

worn — torn —
store — more —
pair — hair —
fit — sit — bit.

Show the effect of adding silent " e,"; for example,

bit-e; cut-cute;
can — cane;
not — note.

Spelling.
Teach ten words from theme 9.
Two-minute drills.
Vary the drills by introducing marching.

Tenth Week

Theme.

Have pupils describe a typical process in their vocations; that is, how they prepare a pattern; bake a loaf of bread; go down into a shaft, etc. Find out what vocabulary they need and develop a theme based on the process and the vocabulary used in the process.

Conversation.

Teach them how to apply for a job; for example,

"Have you a job for me?"
"I am an experienced....(tailor) (miner) (laundress)
"For whom did you work?"
"How much do you want?" Etc.

Writing.

Teach the spelling of the words which pupils need in their vocations, and have them write the themes that apply to their own vocations.

Reading from text.

Language work.

Correct typical errors which you have found your pupils making in sentence structures and in the use of words.

Phonics.

Group the following words:

ink — sink — blink — mink; turn — burn — churn.

Spelling.

Teach the spelling required for the exercises in writing of this week.

Two-minute drills.

Orders for marching, halting and double-quick to be given by pupils after the teacher's explanation and example.

SYLLABUS FOR TEACHING ENGLISH TO FOREIGNERS

First Year

The syllabus which follows is intended as a guide for the teacher in selecting the content of instruction and the method of teaching adult foreigners for the first forty weeks of three lessons a week.

The best judge of what theme to develop, what letters to write, what spelling words to teach, is the teacher in the classroom, who understands the need of his pupils. He is expected to select from the various topics which follow, such as meet the needs of the class under his instruction and after the first ten weeks, to rely on himself and to prepare his own lesson plans on the model of the detailed lessons which have preceded this syllabus. It is not intended that the teacher cover all suggested topics and exercises under the main headings, nor will any teacher find it necessary to use the exercises in the order given.

Teachers should, however, observe the following directions:

1. Follow the detailed lesson plans for the first six nights of instruction (q. v.) and the weekly plans for the first ten weeks (q. v.).

2. Prepare a daily time program as suggested in the weekly outlines.

3. Prepare a daily lesson plan in writing, using the material which follows.

For convenience sake, the subject matter for instruction has been arranged under the following heads:

1 Themes.
2 Conversation
3 Language work.
   a Correction of errors.
   b Memory gems.
4 Reading.
   a From text.
   b From newspapers.
   c Familiar signs.
5 Phonics.
6 Written work.
7 Spelling.
8 Two-minute drills.

The Theme

In the teaching of English to foreigners, the theme means a series of short related sentences on a single topic. The words " and then " are understood after each sentence so as to establish the relationship of time sequence between the ideas called forth. Furthermore, each sentence must be capable of being dramatized or illustrated graphically or mimetically. These two characteristics of the theme — sequence and possibility of dramatizing — are illustrated in the following:

Getting Up

I open my eyes at six o'clock.
I push back the covers.
I jump out of bed.
I stretch my arms.
I wash myself.
I dry myself with a towel.
I dress myself.
I eat my breakfast.

The arrangement of sentences in " theme " fashion is necessary for beginners. One sentence helps the pupil to think of the next sentence and the meaning of each sentence may be taught by other means than by translation. The theme, therefore, bridges the gap between the pupil and the teacher because they can not communicate in English. But there is nothing magical in arranging sentences as in a theme nor does beginning each sentence with "I" lessen the difficulty of teaching a foreigner English. The theme as a matter of fact is useless with pupils who speak a little English and this means should not be employed beyond the first four or five weeks and then only with beginning pupils. For advanced classes, topics may be developed in the usual paragraph form or in conversational form, but the very artificial form of the theme is not used except as indicated.

The following are the steps in the complete development of the theme:

1. The teacher performs an act, at the same time saying the words which describe the act; for example, " I open the door."
2. Pupils perform the act and say the words.
3. The teacher says the words and writes them on the board.
4. Pupils read the words and perform the act.
5. Pupils copy the theme.
6. Pupils review by going through complete dramatization description and reading.
7. Pupils write selected sentences from dictation and from memory.

From five to ten sentences are developed in one evening. Complete development of a theme usually takes three or four evenings.

Age, sex, occupation, education and many other factors in the environment determine what special vocabulary will be of greatest utilitarian value. With these determining influences, the successful teacher of English to foreigners must make himself familiar. He must overcome the reticence of his pupils by showing a personal interest in their welfare, an interest which may at times amount almost to prying into their affairs. Some activities are universal, and these form the basis of the following suggestive list of themes:

    To go to work.
    To wash myself.
    To bathe.
    To eat breakfast.
    To make the fire.
    To go to a restaurant.
    To look for work.
    To take the train.
    To go home.
    To look for rooms.
    To pay rent.
    To buy groceries.
    To go to the doctor.
    To go to school.
    To write a letter.
    To register a letter.
    To visit (the museum).
    To clean the house.
    To go to the library.
    To send money home.
    To introduce a friend.
    To telephone.
    To cook dinner.
    To deposit money.
    To draw money.
    To spend a holiday.

To prevent monotony and to introduce grammatical inflection without teaching formal grammar, the following variations of the theme are suggested:

1. Let one pupil perform the actions described in the theme and let another pupil describe the actions using the progressive form; thus:

    "You are taking off your coat."
    "You are sitting down."

2. Let one pupil recite the sentences of the theme and let another pupil perform the actions.

3. Let pupils give the sentences in a theme in the third person, singular, thus:

"He lights the gas."
"He throws the match away."

4. Let pupils change the theme to the past tense by using the adverbs of time, thus:

"Today I go to work."
"Yesterday I went to work."

Conversation

Conversation between teachers and pupils is the most natural way of teaching English and is the most valuable exercise for practical reasons. The earliest exercises are designed to furnish the teacher with necessary information about the pupils, their lives, their needs and their interests. Thus the teacher asks such questions as the following:

With whom do you board?
Where were you born?
Who is your employer?
How many hours a day do you work?
How many children have you?

A later development in the process of securing free conversation is that of questioning on the subject matter of the theme and of reading matter. Thus the pupils know the theme "Going to school."

"I put on my hat and coat. I say Goodbye.
I walk to school. I enter the building.
I come into the room."

The teacher now asks the following questions:

Mr. ——————— do you walk to school?
Does Mr. ——————— walk to school?
Walk around the room, Mr. ———————
Walk to the front of the room, Mr. ———————
Please put your hat on, etc.

For teaching these everyday expressions the method of dramatization is most successfully used. To illustrate: Two pupils are instructed to take the parts of salesman and of customer. As the dialogue proceeds, the teacher asks other pupils to express the same thoughts in better English, at the same time writing the correct expressions on the board. After other pupils have gone through the same exercise, the class is instructed to copy those expressions which they like best. After a ten minutes' lesson of this kind on " How to find one's way," the following conversation was carried on between a man and woman immigrant:

> Woman — I beg your pardon, can you tell me where the nearest subway entrance is?
> Man — (removing his hat as soon as spoken to) Yes, ma'am. Walk two blocks north (pointing north), and you will see it.
> Woman — Thank you (bowing).
> Man — You're quite welcome.

Other pupils who went through the same procedure used other English expressions which they found on the board; for example, " excuse me," " would you mind telling me " " permit me to show you," " not at all." Such expressions require emphasis in the teaching process, if only to give the foreigner confidence that he is able to make himself understood. It is not intended that dramatization be the entire method, nor is it intended to supersede other methods or other exercises which a teacher of English finds valuable. But these dramatizations provide exercises for which no others are as well adapted. The following topics suggest conversations of a practical nature from which a teacher may select those which are most needed by his pupils:

> Buying — a railroad ticket — a hat — shoes — **cigars** — suit — furniture — on the installment plan.
> Repairing — shoes — clothing — machinery — furniture.
> Renting — a flat — a room at a boarding house or hotel.
> Ordering — a meal — an expressman.
> Checking a trunk.
> Asking one's way — in street — in car — in department store — at a railroad terminal.
> Telling time.
> Applying for — position — raise in salary — day off.
> Getting a license — to peddle — to sell liquors — to marry.
> Sending money home.
> **Ordering** insurance policy — fire — life — accident.

Opening bank account.
Introducing a friend.
Seeing a friend off.
Inviting someone to call — to dinner — theatre — to visit.
Complaining to policeman — foreman.
Going to a doctor — dentist.
Taking a child to school — to be vaccinated.
Conversation on the weather.
In the witness chair.

Language Work

a — CORRECTION OF ERRORS

No list of ready-made errors to be corrected can be of great value to the teacher except in pointing out types of errors to be guarded against. The following list of typical " foreignisms " is intended as notice to the teacher to be on guard against such expressions and to give definite instruction in eradicating these errors when they are found in his classroom. The teacher will, of course, correct any other foreign or unidiomatic expressions as they occur.

Foreign Expressions for Correction

PREPOSITIONS

I was by my daughter.
He took it off me.
He stole it on me.
What's the matter of you.
I ought to of gone.
It was surrounded of mountains.
He came near to him.
I am not afraid of to work.
For reference, I can get off my teacher.
I am not sorry off it.
She was interested to the exciting story.
Subtract 7 by 12.
We bought it by a butcher.
He went on a party.
Don't be angry on me.
Why do you laught from me?
He looks different than me.

They took it off'n him.
This dress is from silk.
They enjoyed very much on a ball.

TENSE

If he would have done ————
I am here since two years.
He come home late.
He is strong like.
I had a right to go (I should have gone).
If it will continue (If it continue).
He works like he doesn't like it.

MISCELLANEOUS

Yesterday night.
My pencil is failing.
He paid for the eats.
I put myself on.
You have too much pencils.
My brother is getting 6 years old.
It stands so in the book.
He always begins with me (annoys).
He extra did it.
They made from me a captain.
We stood up late.
I got yet more money.
She goes nice dressed.
He bought for 5 cents candy.
The policeman took him arrested.
The milk is kind of sour.
A book fails me.
Leave me go.
Borrow me a nickel.
I talk so good like you.
Yours respectively.
I am interesting in the story.
The compass what I took.
I stood in the class (remain).
To my opinion.
A women.
The ship became out of motion.

Spill the mixture in the sink
They were all talking to once
I am finished
Give him eats
Mexico fighting between her own self
His stockings were with big holes through
Not every house there is in here bells
He was sick on the throat
It stands written in the book

b — MEMORY GEMS

English idioms, as expressed in pithy sayings and mottoes, are learned by foreigners with pleasure and with profit, provided the sayings have been illustrated by the teacher and are understood by the pupils. The latter should be encouraged to give further illustrations from their own experience and to use proverbs in conversation. A suggested list follows:

Haste makes waste.
A good name is better than great riches.
Never spend your money before you have it.
Speech is silver, silence is gold.
Look before you leap.
A stitch in time saves nine.
Do not cry over spilt milk.
Birds of a feather flock together.
Never find pleasure in another's misfortune.
Rome was not built in one day.
One today is worth two tomorrows.
Health is better than wealth.
Do to others as you would have others do to you.
It is never too late to learn.
Better late than never.
A penny saved is a penny earned.
Save the pennies and the dollars will take care of themselves.
Enough is better than too much.
An empty barrel makes the loudest noise
Look up and not down.
Look forward and not backward.

Always lend a helping hand.
Do not count your chickens before they are hatched.
A place for everything and everything in its place.
Never put off till tomorrow what you can do today.
Deeds are greater than words.
Well begun is half done.
When the cat's away, the mice will play.
You can not eat your cake and have it too.
Many hands make light work.
Kind words never die.
Honor thy father and thy mother.
Every little helps.
Think twice before you speak once.
It is never too late to mend.
The early bird catches the worm.
A soft answer turneth away wrath.
All things come to him who waits.
Lost time is never found again.
All that glitters is not gold.
He who can not obey can not command.
God helps those who help themselves.
Better alone than in bad company.
Live for something, do not be idle.

The United States is a government of the people, by the people, and for the people.

I pledge allegiance to my flag, and to the Republic for which it stands; one Nation indivisible with Liberty and Justice for all.

Reading

a — FROM TEXT

When a text book is read by the pupils, the teacher is cautioned to follow the procedure outlined for teaching a reading lesson. (See third week of the weekly outlines). The purpose of the steps in the method suggested is to insure that pupils will get thought and not merely be required to call words; that they will have a motive for reading and rereading a lesson and that sufficient variety in drill will be introduced to make reading a help to speaking and to understanding English.

b — FROM NEWSPAPERS

With the average first year foreign class little **or no use** can be made of the English newspaper. However, toward the close of the school year when most of the " visitors " have dropped out and the cream of the pupils are left, the newspaper may be brought in to teach pupils how to find useful information such as:

1. Arrival and departure of ships.
2. Weather conditions.
3. Help wanted ads.
4. Business troubles.
5. Advertisements.

A glance through any daily paper will enable the teacher to collect just what items would be of interest to his particular class.

Phonics

For the teacher of English to foreigners, phonic drill serves two distinct purposes, namely:

1. To correct foreign accent, enunciation and pronunciation.
2. To furnish a key for the recognition of new words.

Phonics for Word Recognition

The second aspect of the subject has been illustrated in preceding lessons.

c — FROM FAMILIAR SIGNS

The foreigner constanly sees certain signs about him with which he should be made familiar. He should be encouraged to make copies of signs he sees daily and to bring them to school. It will be surprising to one who has not tried this device to see what material will be brought to class, how beneficial this will prove and how interested the pupils will be in this kind of work.

Some teachers may be able to secure discarded car advertisement signs. Some are very simple to read and are " live " interesting material.

EXIT   ENTRANCE   THIS WAY OUT   DANGER

KEEP TO THE RIGHT   LOOK OUT FOR PAINT   LINE FORMS ON THIS SIDE

PULL   TICKET OFFICE   BOX OFFICE   PUSH

NOT RESPONSIBLE   DO NOT   NO SMOKING OR
FOR GOODS LEFT   CROSS THE   CARRYING OF
OVER 30 DAYS   TRACKS   LIGHTED CIGARS

              PASSENGERS ARE FORBIDDEN
KEEP   TO STAND ON PLATFORMS   HANDS
OUT   OF TRAINS   OFF

NOT RESPONSIBLE   OFFICE HOURS
FOR HATS AND COATS   9—12 A. M. 1—3 P. M.

STREET CLOSED   PRIVATE   SMOKING ROOM
                ROOMS
COUNT YOUR   WAITING
CHANGE   (APARTMENT, LOFT,   ROOM
              ETC.) TO LET

The following list of phonic elements will serve as a further guide. The order of teaching will depend entirely on the words which the pupils know.

An, at, ad, ab, ach, am, amp; the same final consonants with *e, i, o, u. Ess, oud, an, urn, ook, ash, ink, ing, ew, ould, ance, ack, atch, squ, ough, eigh, ove, ow.*

The following is a summary of the procedure in teaching phonic elements as a key to the recognition of new words:

  1. Pupils learn to recognize and to pronounce about 100 words in their themes. These words are recognized as wholes without any phonic analysis just as faces are recognized as wholes without analysis of the various facial parts.

  2. Troublesome words are grouped in families; for example, who, whose, whom, hands, lands, bands.

  3. Phonic elements are picked out; for example, the sound of *an, ing, squ.*

  4. New words are formed by combining with other sounds, for example, an with *t, s, f, beg.*

  5. New sounds are modified by the addition of silent *e*, for example, *can — cane; bit — bite; cut — cute.*

Caution: The new words formed must be in the vocabulary of the learner; that is, do not teach meaningless sounds or words which are meaningless sounds to foreigners.

Phonics for Correction

Judged by the results obtained it is questionable whether correcting foreign pronunciation in adult pupils deserves the time usually devoted to it. Habits are too firmly fixed to be eradicated in the short time spent by foreigners in our English to foreigners classes. The time required for this purpose may usually be more profitably spent in teaching pupils to communicate their ideas, even though perfection be not attained. Some corrective exercises, however, are desirable to prevent ambiguity and to correct certain racial characteristics which may easily be corrected. Such errors needing attention are:

1. Upward inflection in statements.
2. Sing song.
3. Guttural sounds of *R*.
4. Confusion of certain sounds:

  Long *e* and *i* — *eet* for *it*.
  Short *o* and *i* — *som* for *some*.
  t and *th* — *tank* for *thank*.
  w and *wh* — *wen* and *when*.
  v and *w* — *vay* for *way*.
  f and *v* — *fine* for *vine*.
  gs and *gz* — *eksact* for *egzact*.
  j and *ch* — *chust* for *just*.
  s and *z* — *iss* for *iz*.
  oi and *or* — *woik* for *work*.
  e and *a* — *men* for *man*.
  ing and *ink* — *kink* for *king*.
  th and *f* — *fru* for *thru*.

Phonic analysis will to some extent help in securing better enunciation and articulation. But "incidental teaching makes accidental learning," and complete success will be that teacher's only who makes enunciation and articulation focal in the consciousness of the pupil. To this end the teacher must not only serve as a model, but he must understand how consonants are formed and know how to teach the pupils to produce properly the vowels and consonants which cause trouble. Nationalities differ in the way in which they mispronounce vowels; for example, the Italians will say: *Eet* for *it, lip* for *leap, mit* for *meat, pick* for *peak,* etc. A device for teaching the proper pronunciation of the troublesome short *i* and long *e,* is to place the words in two columns; for example, *it — eat,* and ask the pupils to pronounce the word in column 1 or in column 2. The class is then called upon to decide whether the speaker called the word in column 1; if the class decided that the speaker called the word in column 2, the former is made conscious of his mispronunciation and he will then be ready to learn the distinction.

Following is a suggested list of words confused by foreigners:

hairs — has.	dip — deep.	lord — laud.
hairy — Harry.	dim — deem.	soar — saw.
Mary — marry.	bid — bead.	roar — raw.
fairy — ferry.	mill — meal.	more — mow.
chair — cheer.	lick — leak.	tore — toe.
pat — part.	pitch — peach.	sore — sow.
had — hard.	hem — ham.	bore — bow.
pack — park.	pet — pat.	shore — show.
match — march.	bed — bad.	buck — book.
badge — barge.	pen — pan.	tuck — took.
taught — tot.	shell — shall.	luck — look.
pawned — pond.	guess — gas.	sup — soap.
gnawed — nod.	thy — thou.	rub — robe.
dawn — don.	high — how.	but — boat.
caught — cot.	find — found.	must — most.
met — mate.	mice — mouse.	pull — pool.
led — laid.	signed — sound.	full — fool.
pen — pain.	pour — paw.	could — cooed.
fell — fail.	core — caw.	would — wooed.
west — waist.	fort — fought.	wood — wooed.

In order to overcome the faults of articulation the teacher must understand the placing of the mouth parts. The following chart is taken from Webster's Dictionary and names the organs used in producing the consonants:

PLACE OF ARTICULATION	ORAL Momentary surd.	sonant	Continuous surd.	sonant	NASAL Continuous sonant
Lips	p	b	—	w	m
Lips and teeth	—	—	th (in)	th (y)	—
Tongue and teeth	—	—	f	v	—
Tongue and hard palate (fwd)	t	d	s	z, r	n
Tongue and hard palate (back)	ch	j	sh	zh, r	—
Tongue, hard palate, soft palate	—	—	—	y, l	—
Tongue and soft palate	k	g	—	—	ng
Various places	h	—	—	—	—

Besides being able to instruct the pupils in the use of their organs of speech, the teacher ought to be able to suggest a number of helpful devices; for example:

Th — soft......Bite tongue between teeth and blow without sound. Prolong the sound if "*d*" is produced.

Th—hard......Same as above, but with sound. If an unvoiced sound is produced, let pupil hum while he is sounding.

W ...... Pronounce *oo* and join with the following sound; for example, —*oo*—*ait*—*wait*.

WRITING

Writing in English serves both as a means and as an end. As a means, pupils write to drill the words and sentences of use to them in oral discourse. As an end, pupils write to convey their thoughts in English. All foreign pupils require writing for drill on language forms, but they have a very limited need for communicating their thoughts in written English.

The suggestions which follow seek to meet the needs of the pupils. The order of difficulty in teaching pupils to communicate their thoughts is followed:

1. Copying pupil's name and address from copy supplied by the teacher.

2. Copying from the board into note books; not more than five sentences during one lesson.

3. Filling blank spaces to use words taught; for example:
   I sit .... a table.
   I wipe my face with a ....
   A .... is used for cutting.

4. Answering questions in writing; for example:
   What is your name?
   Where do you live?
   How old are you?
   Where do you work?
   Who is your employer?

5. Filling in application blanks for postal money orders, library cards, declaration of intention, application for license, application for workmen's compensation.

6. Dictation of easy sentences, corrected from model on the board.

7. Reproduction of themes from memory.

8. Writing short business letters after a model has been presented on the board. To prevent confusion in the minds of the pupils the following form is uniformly taught:

155 Chestnut St.,
Albany, N. Y.
Nov. 1, 1919.

Mr. John Brown,
    75 John St.,
        New York, N. Y.

Dear Sir:
....
....
....

Yours truly
HENRY SMITH.

From the following list the teacher selects such forms as will be of use to his pupils. The list is suggestive only and does not prevent the teaching of other useful letters.

Letter Forms

Letters of application
    For a position (only such trades as apply in writing).
    Increase in salary.
    License to .... (peddle, sell perishable foods).
    Membership in .... (society, club, lodge).
    A letter of recommendation.

Letter of excuse for
  Absence from school.
  A child's absence from school.
  Failure to go to work.
  Failure to do a required work.
Letters of inquiry about
  The cost of goods, board, lodging, insurance (fire, life).
  Desirable forms of insurance policies.
  Rights under various clauses of insurance policies.
  Amount due insured on his policy.
  Interpretation of — Workmen's Compensation Law.
  The work of .... in school.
Letters of request for
  Business or school catalogues, fashion books, circulars or railroad guides.
  Samples.
  Price list discounts.
  Declaration of intention.
  Rates for installing — (machinery, fire sprinkler, etc.).
  Copies of free publications.
  Repair man; for example, gas company, landlord.
Letters reporting
  Loss of parcel in street car.
  Sickness, to employer, to lodge.
  Accident — to Compensation Commission.
  Fire — to insurance company.
Letters of complaint
  To a municipal department — garbage not removed, dark halls, obstructed stairways, failure to report contagious diseases.
  To Public Service Commission — overcharge by gas company; insufficient heat in cars.
  To post-office or express company — money order lost, not paid.
  To a mercantile house — overcharge; goods not delivered; quality not satisfactory; package broken; lack of courteous treatment.
Notice
  Of removal.
  Formation of firm.
  Change of business detail (price, discount, kind of goods, etc.), new styles.
  Lodge meeting.

Sales letters
> Simple letter offering goods **for sale**.

Ordering goods
> By description; by reference to catalogues; by reference to previous transactions; duplication of orders.

Acknowledgments
> Receipt of check, money or money order; receipt of goods.

Dunning letters
> Request for salary overdue; for money loaned; for money due in business transaction. Follow-up letters.

Spelling

Pupils learn how to spell those words which they use or expect to use in writing. Words are not properly on the spelling list merely because they occur in reading or in any other subject matter. The basis of selection is usefulness in writing. Since it is fair to assume that foreigners learning English will have a very limited need for writing in English, each teacher selects for spelling words from the actual written work of the pupils.

A pupil knows how to spell when he can write words in context. Teaching a pupil how to spell involves two processes. First, focalization, or pointing out. Second, drill, reducing the spelling of words to habitual or automatic reactions.

For the first step, the following devices are usually employed:

1. Underscoring the confusing letter or syllable.
2. Contrasts; for example, *there — their*.
3. Marking the difficulty in color.
4. Keeping the words before pupils.
5. Using mnemonics; for example, for "pieces;" *ei* and *ie* after *l* and *c*.
6. Teaching simple rules; for example, The rule for doubling final consonants when a syllable is added.

Physical Training

Two-minute Drills

The purpose of these drills is to teach the vocabulary that goes with physical exercises, especially the names of the parts of the body. Instead of teaching such a vocabulary formally, "This is my hand," "This is my foot," the words are introduced in exercises valuable on their own account and repeated frequently enough to insure permanent retention. The teacher is expected to use a few of the exercises which follow during every lesson.

1. Class stand.
2. Face windows.
3. Breathe in
   through the nose
   not through the mouth.
4. Breathe out.
5. Face front.
6. Right hand upward raise (4 times).
7. Right hand down.
8. Left hand upward raise (4 times).
9. Left hand down.
10. Arms upward stretch (4 times).
11. Arms down.
12. Right arm sideways point.
13. Head turning to the right — front.
14. Head turning to the left — front.
15. Point in front of you
    back of you
    to the right of you
    to the left of you.
16. Place hands on head
    on shoulders
    on hips
    on knees.
17. Knee bending.
18. Rise on toes.
19. Forward march
    Column right
    Column left
    Double quick.
20. Halt.

Second Year

Pupils who have covered the work prescribed in the syllabus for the first year or those who can speak English well enough to make themselves understood, and who, at the same time, can read simple English are fit to undertake the work prescribed in the syllabus for the second year.

The following topics are covered in the course of study for this year:
1. Oral composition.
2. Conversation.
3. Spelling.
4. Phonics.
5. Language forms and grammar.
6. Written work.
7. Reading.
8. Memorizing.
9. Arithmetic.

1. ORAL COMPOSITION

Useful subject matter is developed by questions from the teacher and the answers written in paragraph form on the board. The class reads, asks questions and finally copies the work on the board into its notebooks. Suggestions for the topics used for development are:

Hygiene.— How to ventilate a room; keeping food clean.

Economy.— High cost of living. Planning expenditures; municipal markets; food dictators; where to put savings.

Industry.— Preparation for better position; industrial centers; wages in different trades; health consideration in occupations.

Aesthetics.— Museums; places of amusement; places to visit; public concerts.

Education.— Prevocational, vocational, technical and agricultural schools; scholarships in schools and in colleges.

History.— Brief biographies of national heroes in connection with national celebrations.

Civics.— The post-office; the library; city hospitals, dispensaries; the police department; tenement house department; municipal ordinances; for example, spitting, carrying fire arms, obstructing fire escapes, congregating, selling spoilt foods, licenses.

Examples of such topic developments are the following:

THE NEWSPAPER

The newspaper is a printed sheet of paper. It gives us an account of all the events of the day. Each newspaper has a great many reporters. It is the business of the reporters to find out what is going on. If there is a great fire in the city a reporter describes it. The next morning the paper will give an account of it.

The newspaper also tells about commerce, national and foreign affairs, music, politics and sports. The newspapers contain a great many advertisements. Each newspaper is in charge of editors and managers. Some editors write editorials upon public affairs. The newsboys sell the papers on the street.

THE HIGH COST OF LIVING

Everybody is complaining that the cost of living is going up. Everything costs more than it did a year ago. Fish, meat, bread, eggs, milk, fruit, clothes, coal, rent — all are now dearer. But wages too have been raised. The country is prosperous. Everyone is buying and selling. Almost everyone is making money and spending it.

2. CONVERSATION

Special emphasis on dramatization of actual situations requiring English conversation. Two or more pupils conduct a brief conversation, the teacher notes errors and suggests variant methods for expressing the ideas.

For suggestions as to method, see the " Introduction to Methods of Teaching English to Foreigners," and for types of subjects to be used in conversation, see the syllabus for the first year.

3. SPELLING

Words selected from the written work of the pupils.

Difficulties pointed out; words drilled orally and in written sentences.

4. PHONICS

Correction of errors in pupils' conversation and in oral reading. Review of difficult phonograms. See syllabus for first year.

5. LANGUAGE FORMS AND GRAMMAR

1. Only so much grammar is taught as will be immediately applied by foreigners in written and in spoken English; for example, plurals of nouns are taught in sentences so as to associate the correct forms of nouns and verbs.

2. The past and future tenses in sentences containing adverbs of time; for example, he went to the shop yesterday, last week, a year ago. I shall go to work tomorrow, when I feel well; later.

3. The genders of simple nouns; for example, man — woman; cock — hen; boy — girl; bachelor — maid; father — mother; bull — cow; king — queen; master—mistress; son — daughter; uncle — aunt; widower — widow; Jew — Jewess; heir — heiress; lion — lioness; actor — actress; prince — princess.

4. The use of personal pronouns to represent an antecedent; for example, This man wants a job. *He* is a good workman. *He* has a little sister. Do you know *her?* *His* father and *his* mother came to America. *They* are good people. *Your* coat is torn. *It* needs mending.

5. The use of possessive nouns and pronouns.

6. Simple and progressive forms of verbs contrasted and explained in sentences; for example

> He works every day
> He is working now, at this time

7. The use of do and have in questions.

8. The force of the conjunctions, and, or, but, not only, but also; either, or, neither, nor; both, and, and such subordinate conjunctions as the pupils require in expressing their thought.

9. Comparison of adjectives and adverbs in sentences.

6. Written Work

1. Copying paragraph developed on the blackboard.
2. Filling blank spaces; for example.
   > The .... bakes bread
   > We buy meat from the ....
   > A knife is used for ....
   > I wear a .... on my head

3. Dictation of short paragraphs or sentences having for their object (1) drill on words frequently misspelled, (2) capitalization, (3) punctuation.

4. Writing of short business letters after models have been presented. See list of suggested topics.

5. Writing original compositions on topics developed orally. Two or three compositions are written on the board and are corrected by the teacher in the presence of the class. The other compositions are corrected by the teacher and returned to the

pupils. From these compositions and from the letter the teacher selects words for spelling drill and sentence structures for correction.

6. Abbreviations: The names of states and of such common words as the pupils are likely to need: for example,

Mr.	P. O.	M. D.	amt.
Mrs.	Supt.	A. D.	etc.
Gov.	Oz.	B. C.	

7. Usual contractions; for example, I've, He doesn't, They can't, I'll go, He's, You're, I'm, It's.

8. Punctuation: The use of quotation marks, question marks, periods and commas.

9. Capitalization: The first word in a sentence, I, proper nouns and adjectives.

7. READING

For general directions, see syllabus for first year.

Subject matter and vocabulary are somewhat more difficult.

The teacher judges the reading material by the following standards: First, its interest to the class of pupils taught; second, its value to the pupils.

Excellent selections are obtained in historical and geographical readers, pamphlets and circulars freely distributed (see pamphlets of the Sons of the American Revolution). Toward the end of the term, the reading of a newspaper once a week is attempted.

8. MEMORIZING

Short sayings and mottoes. Bibical proverbs. Extracts from famous speeches. Brief verses within the comprehension of the pupils.

9. ARITHMETIC

Easy problems involving fundamental processes. The emphasis is on understanding the problems and the transactions involved rather than on securing accuracy and speed in solving. The commonly used tables, for example,

12 in. = 1 foot
36 in. = 1 yard
A city lot = 25 ft. x 100 ft.
2 pints = 1 quart
4 quarts = 1 gallon
8 quarts = 1 peck
4 pecks = 1 bushel

The writing of dollars and cents; reading and understanding familiar arithmetical signs, for example, 2 for 5 cents — 3 for a quarter — 12½ cents a yard — $3.50 a day — 3 shirts at $1.25 each.

Filling out receipts, filling out checks, deposit slips in the savings bank.

Third Year

The work prescribed in this syllabus is intended for pupils who have completed the work prescribed for the second year, or for those who speak, read and write English, but whose vocabularies are very limited and whose sentence structure is imperfect.

The following topics are covered in the course of study for this year:

1. Oral composition
2. Conversation
3. Spelling
4. Language forms and grammar
5. Written work
6. Reading
7. Memorizing
8. Arithmetic

1. Subjects for Oral Composition

Current topics — educational, economic, industrial, poetical, historical, geographic; safety-first requirements; fire prevention; the work of municipal departments; workmen's compensation.

Topics are developed and then written on the board; pupils discuss, read and copy. The sentence structure should be illustrations of the grammatical principles taught; for example, the use of capitals; quotation marks; complex sentences showing variety in the use of conjunctions, the infinitive for the noun participle to secure variety; the proper use of shall, will, in, into, between, among.

2. Conversation

1. Class discussion on topics suggested and on topics of personal interest.
2. Short stories prepared by the pupils and told in class.
3. Short debates on current topics.

3. Spelling

Words selected from the written work of the grade.

4. Language Forms and Grammar
Prefixes and Suffixes

Prefixes and suffixes are developed by deriving the meaning of the prefix or suffix from several words having the common element; thus, the prefix *un* may be derived from the following words: Untrue, unable, unwilling. Pupils may then be called upon to suggest other words containing the prefix *un* and to be on the lookout for such words in their reading material. Following is a list of prefixes to be taught.

un	dis	er—or
im	out	ish
re	a	ize
over	sub	ard
ante	ex	less
pre	ing	dom
under	ist	en
ad	ness	

Homonyms

Only such words as are frequently used:

Piece—peace	seen—scene	principle—principal
see—sea	cent—sent	air—heir
meat—meet	right—write	

How to Increase the Vocabulary

1. By learning proper use of subordinate conjunctions and of transitional words.

Likewise	so then	at the same time
wherefore	too	for all that
further	only	on the contrary
moreover	then	because of which
either	yea	on the other hand
thus	similarly	in addition
so	secondly	in consequence
whence	so that	on this account
notwithstanding	yet	in spite of this
besides	again	

2. By studying the dictionary.

Pupils arrange words beginning with the **same** letter; beginning with different letters.

Practice in finding words; in fitting meanings to context; in finding synonyms, in accenting and enunciating word.

3. By study of synonyms.

4. By varying expressions as found in reading matter — condensation of sentences into words or phrases; changing construction; for example, the **method** of beginning; the **order of** words.

5. By summarizing reading matter.

6. By writing.

7. By arousing curiosity as to the meanings of words.

8. By having pupils carry a small note book for words acquired.

Correct use of words — Choice of prepositions

Choose the proper prepositions in the following sentences:

1. (In, into). Come .... the house, and see what I have .... my desk. Who has been looking .... my desk? Throw this paper .... the fire. There is a fire .... the next room. Take this box .... the bedroom and put it .... the closet. Have you been playing .... **the** street?

2. (Between, among). There has been war .... France and Germany. .... you and me, I think the apples should have been divided .... the five boys equally. I saw .... the crowd who stood .... the tree and the house.

3. (By, with). The chair was mended .... Mr. Smith ....glue. The man struck me .... his cane. He was displeased .... my conduct. He **was** punished .... his father.

5. Written Work

Dictation

Short selections for the purpose of illustrating a rule or principle in grammar, punctuation for teaching the use of words; for testing spelling.

Written Composition

Emphasis on letter writing of a very practical nature. See list of suggested topics.

Development of written outlines after oral discussion of new subject matter.

Compositions on useful subjects from outlines developed on the board.

Variety in compositions may be secured by suggesting different ways of beginning, of ending; by changing structure, by expanding a short statement, by condensing a long one.

6. Reading

See syllabus for first year for suggestions as to method.

Newspaper and magazine articles are read at least once a week. Articles are read for their interest and because they furnish desirable information; advertisements offering positions; offering land for sale; business opportunities; important news items; simple editorials.

Textbooks like Gulick's "City and Town," Franklin's "Autobiography," Goldberger's "English for Coming Citizens" will serve the varied needs of the pupils.

7. Memorizing

Short sayings and mottoes, Biblical proverbs, short poetical and prose selections.

The Pledge of Allegiance to the Flag: "This is a government of the people, by the people, for the people;" some of Benjamin Franklin's sayings; the first and last stanzas of "America."

8. Arithmetic

Problems involving fractions; one or more processes. It is more important that the pupil understand the nature of the transaction involved than that he obtain a correct answer. Hence most of the arithmetic takes the form of language lessons on the problem with incidental solutions of the problems. No time is wasted in long problems or on problems involving arithmetical difficulty. The figures given are such as are usually found in the transactions involved.

8. REPORT FROM DIRECTOR OF DIVISION OF AGRICULTURAL AND INDUSTRIAL EDUCATION

New York State is conducting a comprehensive program of agricultural and industrial training, which is described in the following letter received from Mr. L. A. Wilson, Director of the Division of Agricultural and Industrial Education, November 1, 1919:

"At the present time we are offering a number of agricultural and industrial courses that are open to adult aliens. They are as follows:

1. Courses in agriculture. At the present time in New York State there are six special schools of agriculture located at Alfred, Canton, Cobleskill, Delhi, Farmingdale and Morrisville. A pupil may be admitted to the regular course at any of these schools who is 16 years of age and who has had eight years of elementary school training. I have no information in this office in regard to the number of foreign-born men enrolled in these agricultural courses. I doubt very much there being very many men of this type in the six special schools.

2. Evening industrial schools. Evening industrial schools are maintained at 20 centers in this State. Last year the courses offered at these schools were as follows:

I. Albany
  1. Mechanical drafting
  2. Cabinet making
  3. Printing
  4. Auto mechanics
  5. Electricity
  6. Machine shop

II. Amsterdam
  1. Mechanical drawing
  2. Cabinet making and carpentry

III. Auburn
  1. Mechanical drawing
  2. Cabinet making and carpentry

IV. Buffalo
  1. Elementary machine shop work
  2. Advanced machine shop work
  3. Drawing for machinists
  4. Mathematics for machinists
  5. Machine design
  6. Tool design

7. Tool making
8. Structural steel design
9. Drawing for machinists and pattern makers
10. Pattern making
11. Cabinet making
12. Carpentry
13. Hydroplane boat building
14. Drawing for carpenters
15. Drawing and mathematics for plumbers
16. Drawing and mathematics for sheet metal workers
17. Naval architecture
18. Sheet metal work
19. Oxy-acetylene welding
20. Steam engine theory and practice
21. Sign painting
22. Elementary electrical work
23. Advanced electrical work
24. Radio and buzzer work
25. Automobile work — cold test
26. Automobile work — carburetors
27. Automobile work — engine fitting
28. Automobile work — chassis
29. Automobile work — ignition
30. Automobile work — starting and lighting
31. Architectural drawing
32. Mechanical drawing
33. Industrial chemistry
34. Printing — hand composition
35. Printing — press work
36. Printing — monotype operating
37. Printing — linotype operating

V. Elmira
1. Machine shop practice
2. Plumbing
3. Drawing for machinists
4. Drawing for carpenters

VI. Mount Vernon
1. Machine shop work
2. Automobile repairing
3. Electrical work
4. Trade drawing

VII. Niagara Falls
1. Mathematics for machinists
2. Industrial chemistry (for carborundum, aluminum, graphite and calcium workers)
3. Electrical theory
4. Drawing for machinists
5. Drawing and estimating for carpenters
6. Automobile repairing

VIII. New York City
1. Aeroplane construction
2. Elementary machine shop construction
3. Advanced machine shop practice
4. Printing — elementary composition
5. Printing — proof reading
6. Printing — advanced composition
7. Printing — press work
8. Printing — Kelly press work
9. Printing — offset press work
10. Printing — monotype operating
11. Photo photography
12. Commercial photography
13. Plumbing (lead work)
14. Plumbing (installation)
15. Pattern making
16. Sheet metal work
17. Sheet metal theory and plan reading
18. Carpentry
19. Plan reading and estimating
20. Plumbing theory
21. Player piano mechanics
22. Municipal electrical theory
23. Machine shop theory
24. Ladies' garment design
25. Men's garment design
26. Costume design
27. Textile design
28. Poster design
29. Plastic design
30. Book illustration
31. Interior decoration
32. Jewelry design
33. Mural decoration
34. Shop drafting

35. Sheet metal design
36. Architectural drawing
37. Mechanical drawing
38. Cabinet making
39. Elementary electrical work
40. Advanced electrical work
41. Electrical theory
42. Tool making
43. Industrial chemistry
44. Blacksmithing
45. Shop mathematics
46. Steam engineering
47. Radio and buzzer work
48. Tailoring
49. Dressmaking
50. Embroidery machine operating (women only)
51. Glove machine operating (women only)
52. Garment machine operating (women only)
53. Drafting (women only)
54. Draping (women only)
55. Manicuring and shampooing (women only)
56. Novelty work
57. Straw machine operating
58. Trade millinery
59. Trade embroidery
60. Commercial retouching and commercial design

IX. Newburgh
1. Mechanical drawing
2. Layout work
3. Ship construction
4. Ship information (theory)

X. Rochester
1. Sheet metal work
2. Machine shop work
3. Electrical construction
4. Tool design
5. Industrial chemistry (metal workers and electrical workers)
6. Pattern making
7. Radio and buzzer work

XI. Schenectady
1. Mechanical drawing
2. Radio and buzzer work
3. Automobile repairing
4. Shop mathematics
5. Fuel conservation

XII. Syracuse

XIII. Troy.
1. Mechanical drawing
2. Machine shop practice
3. Automobile repairing
4. Blue print reading and estimating for carpenters
5. Electrical work
6. Shop mathematics
7. Radio and buzzer work

XIV. Yonkers
1. Architectural drawing
2. Mechanical drawing
3. Applied design
4. Sign painting
5. Shop mathematics
6. Pattern making
7. Power plant operating
8. Elementary electrical work
9. Advanced electrical work
10. Carpentry
11. Automobile construction and repairing
12. Machine shop practice

In communities of less than 25,000 inhabitants

I. Depew
1. Pattern making
2. Electrical theory
3. Electrical wiring
4. Drawing for machinists

II. Dunkirk
1. Mechanical drawing
2. Blue print reading

III. Ithaca
1. Drawing for machinists
2. Drawing for carpenters

IV. Lancaster
   1. Drawing for machinists
V. Solvay
   1. Cabinet making and carpentry
   2. Mechanical drafting.

"Any man 16 years of age who is working during the day is entitled to enter these classes if the work offered supplements in any way his daily occupation. Approximately 35,000 men and women were enrolled in these courses last year. While I have no facts in regard to the number of foreign-born students in these classes during the past year, I have facts concerning a similar group of people who were enrolled in the evening industrial schools in New York City during the year 1916.

" The distribution of these men by trades in the city of New York for the year 1915–1916 was as follows:

Electrical Trades

Native born, native parentage 103
Native born, foreign or mixed parentage 226
Foreign born 166

Total 495

Mechanical Drawing Classes

Native born, native parentage 93
Native born, foreign or mixed parentage 220
Foreign born 139

Total 452

Machine Shop Classes

Native born, native parentage 52
Native born, foreign or mixed parentage 180
Foreign born 186

Total 418

Plumbing Classes

Native born, native parentage 48
Native born, foreign or mixed parentage................ 133
Foreign born 106

Total 287

Garment Design Classes

Native born, native parentage 1
Native born, foreign or mixed parentage 26
Foreign born 184

Total 211

Automobile Classes

Native born, native parentage 49
Native born, foreign or mixed parentage............... 94
Foreign born 54

Total 197

Carpentry and Joinery

Native born, native parentage 15
Native born, foreign or mixed parentage 31
Foreign born 44

Total 90

Cabinet Making Classes

Native born, native parentage 19
Native born, foreign or mixed parentage 37
Foreign born 23

Total 79

"It is apparent from the above facts that large numbers of foreign-born men and a large number of men with mixed parentage attend evening industrial schools in this State. As a matter of fact there were more men enrolled for evening industrial work in the evening schools of New York City during the year 1915–16 who were of foreign or mixed parentage and foreign born than there were people of native parentage.

"If you desire I shall be very glad to furnish you with a complete list of all the evening industrial schools in the State together with the name of the principal in order that you may request them to send you information concerning the men in attendance in their schools this year. I am sure that all these men would be very glad to co-operate with you in making this study.

"In addition to the evening schools we have a number of very excellent unit trade schools in the State. These schools, however, are attended very largely by boys and young men under 19 years of age."

CHAPTER III
State Normal Schools

The principals of all the New York State normal schools were consulted, by mail, on the matter of requirements, training and compensation for teachers of the foreign-born. We quote verbatim from the replies.

1. Alfred C. Thomson, Principal, State Normal School, Brockport, December 26, 1919.

"As requested I am pleased to write in regard to the education and Americanization of adult foreigners.

"First, it seems to me the essentials in Americanizing a foreigner are to teach him to speak, read and write our language, and then to teach him our history, customs, traditions and ideals. A course planned to prepare teachers to do this work should include methods of teaching our language to foreigners and a study of our history, customs, traditions and ideals and methods of teaching the same to foreigners. The rest of the course for teacher training could be that which is given to the teachers of our normal schools.

"Second, in the matter of compensation, in the normal schools of our state and of the United States there is not much more than 50 percent of the pre-war enrollment. I believe a sufficient salary must be offered to induce teachers to prepare for this line of work. I presume that at least $2,000 would have to be offered as an initial salary with provisions made for advancement.

"As a city superintendent, before assuming my present position, I had experience in organizing evening schools for foreigners. If I can be of service to you in any way in the matter under consideration I shall be pleased to have you call on me."

2. Harry DeW. deGroat, Principal, State Normal and Training School, Cortland, December 22, 1919.

"At the present time I presume that it is impossible to get an adequate supply of competent teachers of Americanization work. It seems to me that every city in the state in which there are at least 500 foreigners should have a teacher to take charge of this work in the evening schools, and during such hours of the day as the Legislature might feel it advisable to prescribe. In cities of the third class this teacher might, perhaps, act as the head of the department of history in the day schools. This teacher should be a man. He should, of course, be a college man, and have had extra courses in Americanization after graduation. (I presume that nothing concerning the matter of sex could be written into the law.) Successful previous experience in teaching should be prescribed and some experience in Americanization work would be most desirable.

"It seems to me to get a man of this kind the minimum salary should start at not less than $3,000, with substantial increases after successful experience.

"I might say that this subject has been one that has had a great deal of interest for me for the more than seven years I have been in Cortland. Naturally, I have looked at it from the angle of this locality and of one preparing teachers for the elementary schools.

"I have long desired to have a man of the right type on our faculty to direct the work in history and patriotism inasmuch as about 20 or 25 percent of the children in our training schools are of foreign parentage. A man of the type I have mentioned would be a valuable asset in giving such courses in patriotism as would be required by elementary teachers. At the same time he could direct the whole Americanization program for the entire city."

3. Myron T. Dana, Principal, State Normal School, Fredonia, January 13, 1920.

"I have delayed answering your favor hoping to inform myself sufficiently on the subject of the educating and Americanizing of adult foreigners to justify an opinion. Owing to a combination of circumstances, I have not been able to do so.

"I consider it a matter the importance of which calls for the best judgment of educators and legislators. There is at present an unprecedented dearth of teachers and, even at large salaries, it would be difficult, in my opinion, to find teachers who by nature and attainments are prepared to undertake the important work which you name."

4. John C. Bliss, Principal, State Normal School, New Paltz, January 8, 1920.

"I hardly feel competent to advise what the requirements should be in choosing teachers for the work of Americanizing adult foreigners. I am sure of one thing, however, they should be adaptable. Teaching foreigners is vastly different from teaching pupils, no matter if the latter be of the older type. It seems to me that these teachers should be men, that they should have had experience in dealing with men that they may know how a man thinks and what are some of the problems that he meets. Given this understanding on the teacher's part, a pliable mind and disposition, and the ordinary professional requirements, there should be success.

"I have no experience along this line and do not feel competent to pass upon it. Those who have studied the problems are none too well prepared to take up the work. It is a hard job, but the most pressing one that we have."

5. Percy I. Bugbee, Principal, State Normal School, Oneonta, January 6, 1920.

"It seems to me that teachers for the work in question should be teachers who are duly licensed as teachers of public schools in the state, and that they should receive compensation at a rate no less than the rate which they receive as teachers in public schools."

6. James C. Riggs, Principal, State Normal and Training School, Oswego.

"The faculty of the Oswego State Normal School, conscious of the urgent need in our country of a quickening civic consciousness and of the firm establishment in the hearts of all its people, native or adopted, of a compelling patriotism and love of country, record in these resolutions its acceptance of the following:

"1. That all instruction in elementary schools be imparted in English.

"2. That adequate opportunity be given through our school system to all adult immigrants to learn the English language to enable them to more readily grasp the meaning of our institutions and to appreciate their worth.

"3. That contemporaneously with instruction in English, immigrants should be instructed in the nature and purpose of our institutions in any language which they are able to understand.

"4. That it is the duty of every teacher to be at all times fully conscious of his obligation to develop patriotism and good citizenship, and should so frame his thinking and point of view that the consciousness of this duty will be manifest in all his conduct and teaching.

"5. That state normal schools through their faculties endeavor to exert such influence through all their teachings that graduates of these institutions enter their profession with a determined purpose to contribute their part to the strengthening of real Americanism.

"6. That state normal faculties contribute their share in formulating tangible conceptions of patriotism and definite ideals of citizenship.

"With regard to the training of teachers of adult foreigners, the faculty of the Oswego State Normal School expresses the following convictions:

"1. Such teachers should be sufficiently mature to have a thorough grasp of the nature of their problem and possess that sympathy with the foreigner handicapped by a strange environment which will gain his confidence and co-operation.

"2. She should be thoroughly conversant with our social and civic institutions and American ideals.

"3. She should have a reasonable mastery of the technique of teaching and be able to adapt her efforts to the peculiar local problems which she may encounter.

"4. Compensation for the work of such teacher should be sufficient to attract the best members of the profession."

7. George K. Hawkins, Principal, State Normal School, Plattsburg, January 5, 1920.

"It is my judgment that the problem of Americanization in New York State is one that for the most part should be handled by the Education Department of the state. Co-operation of corporations and large employers of labor is, of course, necessary in any scheme.

"I know of no better service that can be enlisted than that of the trained body of high class teachers who are available in every community and would be patriotically willing for small extra compensation to engage in the work. It could probably be articulated reasonably well with their regular duties.

"A plan disassociated from the organized educational activities of the state would be not only very expensive if administered in volume, but would in my opinion be disappointing in results."

CHAPTER IV

Principal Cities of the State Outside of New York City

The following chapter of this report contains information in regard to training for citizenship in New York State outside of New York City. It does not claim to be comprehensive, but it is representative. It contains all the information obtainable from the superintendents of schools in cities having a population over 10,000, and a few others. The views of the superintendents, although more or less fragmentary, indicate the nature of their problems, the tendency of their efforts and their desire to co-operate with the State Department of Education. It may be of interest here to call attention to the fact that many educational authorities throughout the country, in response to the request of this Committee for their suggestions in regard to citizenship training and immigrant education, implied that it would be carrying coals to Newcastle to make such suggestions to New York State, where the best methods in the country are already being employed, according to their views.

1. Albany

C. Edward Jones, Superintendent of Schools.

The population of Albany is about 112,000.

The leading industries employing foreign-born labor are the railroad shops and the iron and steel foundries.

Only one factory conducts classes for its foreign-born, the average age being somewhere between thirty and forty.

Americanization work is being done by the Board of Education and by the State of New York.

The requirements for teachers of adult foreigners is the completion of the Americanization course in the State College for Teachers.

The Board of Education of the City of Albany in the fall of 1919 published a handbill announcing school courses for the season. The following paragraph from this handbill contains a unique idea:

"All courses are *free,* but a registration fee of *one dollar* will be collected for each Academic, Commercial and Vocational Course. This will be returned at the close of the course provided the student has a record of 80 percent of attendance."

There is at Albany an Americanization Council, whose aims are expressed in the Constitution as follows:

CONSTITUTION

Article I

The name of this organization shall be the Americanization Council of Albany.

Article II

Definition

"Americanization Work," as used in this constitution, is hereby defined to be the study of speaking, reading or writing the English language, the study of American history, institutions or political government, the development of patriotism, and intelligent citizenship or the interpretation of America's ideals of freedom and service.

Article III

Purpose

The object of this council shall be to promote and to act as a clearing house for organizations in the City of Albany, doing Americanization work, and to stimulate and co-ordinate all such work for better citizenship so that there shall be no duplication of plan or effort.

Article IV

Membership

Sec. 1. The membership of this council shall be composed of one representative and one alternative from any organization in the City of Albany that is actively interested in *Americanization* and which contributes annual dues. The dues shall be $2.

2. Amsterdam

Data furnished by Superintendent of Schools.

The population of Amsterdam is about 41,000.

There are about 5,000 Italians and 9,000 Poles. At least 2,000 of these foreigners attend the public schools. The average age is from five to sixteen in the day schools and over twenty-one in the evening schools.

The Americanization work in Amsterdam is supervised by the Superintendent of Schools.

We require teachers to have taken a special course for teaching adult foreigners. We pay $3 per evening to principals and $2 per evening to regular teachers. We have no bother in getting teachers.

The chief industries employing foreigners are a carpet mill and the button shops.

3. Auburn

In answer to a questionnaire, Henry D. Hervey, Superintendent of schools submitted the following:

1. What is the population of your city? 36,000
2. What is the foreign population, divided as to nationality?

Austrian	1,480
Canadian, French	126
Canadian, other	395
Cuban and other West Indian	4
Danish	7
English	1,053
Finn	1
French	18
German	745
Greek	22
Dutch	11
Hungarian	74
Irish	1,503
Italian	1,595
Norwegian	9
Roumanian	1
Russian	250
Scotch	202
Swedish	34
Swiss	21
Turkish in Asia	36
Turkish in Europe	2
Other foreigners	31

3. What are the leading industries in which foreigners are employed? International Harvester Co., Columbian Rope Co., International Harvester Co. Twine Mill and various shoe shops.

4. Do any of the industries conduct classes for teaching English, American history, civil government, etc., for their foreign-born employees? Columbian Rope Company and International Harvester Co. Twine Mill.

5. What public school facilities are open to foreign-born adults for learning English, American history, civil government, etc.? Evening school eighty nights a year, two-hour session each night.

6. How many adult students of the various nationalities attend public schools?

EVENING SCHOOL 1918–1919

Italian	104
Polish	11
Austrian	59
German	2
Irish	9
English	9
Russian	11
Greek	1
Swedish	2
Armenian	1
French	1
Canadian	1
Syrian	1
Russian Jew	3

7. Is the attendance regular? Average attendance for elementary department, 90.76.

8. What is the average age of adult alien students? Men, 15 to 44; women, 15 to 64.

9. How many hours per week do the courses cover? Six hours.

10. Is there any movement in your city to "Americanize" foreigners? By whom is it conducted? Yes, Board of Education and Chamber of Commerce.

11. What are your requirements for teachers of adult foreigners? Special training and experience for this work.

12. What salary do you think should be offered to attract teachers of competence to do this work? We secure good teachers at $2 per night.

I am giving the figures contained in the census of 1910 for the distribution of our foreign population. These figures are doubtless very much out of date, but I know of no others more reliable. The distribution of foreigners in our evening school is that for the year 1918–19. We have no figures for the current year, though I am giving the total registration in the non-English speaking department, men and women for the present year. You will note that it is somewhat less than for last year, but we are not including in our figures for this year those who are attending classes in the mills. There are probably seventy or seventy-five pupils now attending English classes not under the immediate supervision of the public schools. We are not able to give the average age of alien students, but are giving the age range. We are doing everything possible to wipe out illiteracy in our city.

4. Binghamton

Data furnished by Superintendent of Schools.

The population of Binghamton in 1910 was 53,668. It is probably 59,000 now. About one-third of the population is foreign. Shoe and cigar factories are the leading industries employing these foreigners, none of which conduct classes. In the year 1918–19 we had a registration of 130 students of foreign birth in the evening schools, with attendance about 95 percent of the registration. The average age was 22 years.

The Department of Education and the Civic Club do some Americanization work.

We require teachers of experience and natural ability. We pay them $2.50 and $3 per night. From $3 to $3.50 would be better, although we have no difficulty in securing competent help.

5. Buffalo

George E. Smith, Superintendent of Schools.

The estimated population of Buffalo is about 526,000. The foreign population is divided as follows:

Albanian		150
Bulgarian		600
Croatian		1,500
Czecho-Slovak		5,000
Greek	In Buffalo	2,600
	In Buffalo and vicinity	2,000

*Hungarian	In Buffalo	3,000
	In Buffalo	16,000
	In Buffalo and vicinity........	31,000
	In Buffalo	10,000
	In Buffalo	8,000
	In Buffalo and vicinity........	14,000
Italian...................................		60,000
*Polish		8,000 / 80,000
Negro....................................		4,500
Russian..................................		600
Ruthenian		4,000
Ukranian.................................		6,000
Serbian including Croatian...............		3,000 — 4,000
Syrian...................................		500

Some of the leading industries in the city are now conducting classes in English and plans are under way for organizing classes in about twelve more. English, American history and civil government are being taught in these classes.

About thirty evening schools are open either in the late afternoon or evening for the training of foreign-born adults. From 1,500 to 2,000 pupils are registered in these classes. The attendance is as regular as conditions admit — about 75 per cent. The average age is probably between 25 and 30 years.

There is a definite movement in progress to Americanize foreigners. It is conducted largely through the Department of Education, although some of the work is being done independently by the Knights of Columbus.

Our teachers have all had special training in Americanization methods and background and such training is required of all teachers who undertake the work. We pay them from $2 to $3 a period, and in my opinion this will be an adequate salary when the work is organized so that one teacher can cover several periods during the day. It would be desirable to effect an organization so that teachers could give their entire time to the work. In that event, they should be paid as much or more than the regular day school teacher — $1,600 and up.

---

* Various estimates given.

The above information from George E. Smith, Deputy Superintendent of Schools, was later supplemented by the following letter from him under date of November 20, 1919:

"Americanization work of whatever character naturally comes into my department. All of our night school centers, including our vocational schools, are contributing to the solution of the immigrant problem either directly or indirectly. In many of our vocational schools, foreigners are taking trade courses, not as foreigners but as members of their respective trades. We have now over seventy classes in our night schools which are studying English as a basic subject. It would be impossible at this time to give a detailed report as to the nationalities, age, etc., but the number of those in attendance runs into the thousands.

"We are at present making a canvass of the city to determine how many illiterate minors are attending and how many are not attending school, and we shall take measures at once to get into school those who are not in school."

Letter from Samuel B. Botsford, president, Buffalo Chamber of Commerce, November 3, 1919:

"By way of reply to your letter of November 4th, asking for information relative to Americanization work that we have done, or in which we have participated, I am enclosing copy of a letter covering the ground pretty thoroughly which we recently sent to Mr. George P. Sawyer of this city.

"I might state further, that at a conference held at this office this afternoon, tentative plans were outlined looking to the correlation of all Americanization work in Buffalo with a view to strengthening it where possible, and also giving widespread publicity. These plans are only in the formative stage, and it is impossible for me at this time to go into further details.

"As to compulsory education of adult foreigners, my position at this time would be against any such action."

Copy of letter to Mr. Sawyer:

"I want to thank you for the clipping from the New York 'Times' which you sent to me setting forth the plans of the Boston Chamber of Commerce, relating to Americanization of immigrants. This is a work in which the Buffalo Chamber of Commerce is interested, and it is needless to add that I also am personally, deeply interested. Long before the United States entered the war and in anticipation that its entrance was inevitable, and that steps would have to be taken toward Americanizing foreigners, the Buffalo Chamber of Commerce made exhaustive research and collated statistics and other information which afterwards proved the ground work for the establishing and carrying on of intelligent Americanization work in Buffalo.

"At the present time, we are providing offices which are used as headquarters for work of this kind, and these offices have been used in this way for upwards of three years.

"With particular reference, however, to work among immigrants, I might state that the Civic Education Association and the School Department are very active at the present time. A census of factories was started during the past few weeks and nineteen plant owners were called on by Mr. Lewis, who until last week was in charge of the organization. Of these nineteen plants, fifteen have agreed to have classes in the factories during working hours, the City School Department furnishing the trained teachers to give the instruction to foreigners in English and civics. On Monday, October 13th, four teachers of the Buffalo School Department started classes at the American Radiator Plant; two evening classes are being held at the Dold Plant and four or five teachers will go to the plant of the National Aniline & Chemical Company within the next few days.

"Dr. Smith has been conducting an institute at Hutchinson High School for the past three weeks with an attendance of approximately ninety teachers to be examined on Monday next, following which the successful candidates will be sent into factories to teach workers. The School Department has fifty-nine night school classes for men and women immigrants and fifteen afternoon classes for women only. It is expected that there will be between seventy-five and one hundred classes before Christmas.

"While the above is work being done by the School Department, the work is done in closest co-operation with the Civic Education Association of Erie County, Dr. George E. Smith of the School Department being a part of the Civic Education Association.

"Mrs. Ward J. Pierce, who is now president of the Civic Education Association and who has been very active, was instrumental in securing an appropriation a few days ago amounting to $3,500 toward the Arts and Crafts Exhibition being held at Albright Art Gallery, under the auspices of the American Federation of Arts and Crafts, which is an organization working among immigrants.

"The local organization is working in co-operation with Mr. William C. Smith, Supervisor of Immigrant Education Association, New York State Department of Education, who has an appropriation of $100,000 to cover such work in New York State. The local organization has the benefit of state assistance and direction and has the heartiest co-operation of the Buffalo School department and a number of the larger employers of labor.

"A recent law has gone into effect in New York State requiring the attendance in school of minors between the ages of sixteen and twenty-one years, who are unable to speak, read and write the English language. The Civic Education Association is co-operating in the enforcement of this law and has secured the co-operation of fifteen factories so far and the School Department.

"One reason why the Americanization work in this city and Erie County has seemed to lapse during the war was the lack of newspaper publicity and the fact that the work was done very quietly and had no spectacular features although it enjoyed a gradual and steady growth with no slipping back at any time. The work has been handicapped to some extent by loss of the services of several of the executive secretaries and other leaders, the latest man, Dr. John W. Lewis, having been connected with the bureau only one month when disqualified by our Local Civil Service Commission. They are at present looking for a new man to direct the work. Dr. George E. Smith of the Buffalo School Department has possibly the strongest hold on the work being done and has a sufficient appropriation from the city to carry on the much extended work in the schools and in the factories during the present fiscal year. He is furnishing teachers to the various industrial plants as fast as he can train them to make them competent to educate foreigners.

"Buffalo has now and has had for several years practically all of the machinery which Boston claims to be establishing for all the education of immigrants. The only criticism that might be made of the local work is that it has been somewhat slow but it has been steady and progressive, with no mistakes such as have been made in other cities.

"Again thanking you for sending me the newspaper clipping, and assuring you of my appreciation of your interest in this matter I am."

6. Cohoes

Letter from Edward Hayward, Superintendent of Schools, November 31, 1919:

"Replying to your favor of November 12th, permit me to say that the population of our city is about 26,000. As to nationalities we have practically all the nations of the earth assembled in our city. There are many Irish, French, Polish, Austrian, Italian, etc., elements.

"The leading industries are cotton and woollen goods, and in these many foreigners are employed. None of the industries conduct classes for teaching English, etc. The public schools conduct night schools and we are urging all foreigners to attend them. The attendance is fairly regular. It is impossible to judge just now as we have just opened our schools. The average age is from 18 to 40. The course covers six hours a week. Yes, there is a movement in our city to Americanize foreigners. We are taking a survey of all the foreign-born residents. To teach adult foreigners we obtain some of our best grade and high school teachers, and we pay them $2 per night for this additional work."

7. Cortland

Data furnished by F. E. Smith, Superintendent of Schools.

The estimated population is 13,000, 1,200 being Italian and 700 Russian.

The chief industries employing foreigners are the Wickwire Brothers, manufacturing steel, steel wire, wire netting and nails; Brewer Tichner Company, manufacturing drop forgings; Cortland Wall Paper Company; Cortland Silk Company and the Miller Corset factory. None of these industries conduct classes.

About thirty-five adult foreigners attend night school.

Besides the public day and evening schools, the Twentieth Century Club is doing some Americanization work.

For night school we require the same sort of teachers as for day school, and we pay them $1,000 to $1,200.

8. Depew

J. P. Sherrard, Superintendent of Schools, letter, November 20, 1919.

" In reply to your letter of November 14th, inst. it gives me great pleasure in giving you the information you desire, in order to formulate recommendations to the legislature for an increased program of education in Americanization for adult illiterate foreigners.

" I have taught school for the past 15 years, in school districts which ran from 45 to 60 per cent, foreign population. For the past ten years I have conducted evening vocational schools in these communities. In connection therewith I had classes in Americanization or Citizenship. This is, at the beginning we undertook to teach them how to read and write and answer questions whereby the courts would admit them to full citizenship. Later we spent more time in teaching them how to read and write and figure.

" Last year I conducted four classes in Americanization or Citizenship and am doing the same this year. In all my experience I find that the illiterate minor is just the one who absolutely refuses to attend these classes. It seems strange to me to hear so much said about educating the illiterate minor, for I failed to see any minor take advantage of these citizenship classes. My experience is that they always wait until they are 22, 25, 30 sometimes 40 years of age before they realize that it is necessary for them to know any English or be able to read, cipher and write. Last year I had 80 women and men registered in my foreign classes. This year I have about the same number. In this number there was no one under 22 years of age. The average age would be about 28 or 30 years. The nationalities consist of Polish, Hungarian, Austrian, Italian, Sicilian, Greek, Swedish, Spanish, and Russian. As a whole, they do not attend regularly. Once in a while we find a man or woman who will become interested and attend regularly for the entire term. Most of them come a certain period at a time and then quit, and their places are filled by others entering the class. With these older women and men I find that they work hard all day, and many of them far from their homes, and when they arrive home after their day's work they are too tired to change their clothes and walk some distance to the school building for evening school work.

"The courses that we offer them are as I stated above: Reading, writing, arithmetic, history of our country and some knowledge of our government.

"I believe that the foreign-born minor will never enter an evening school or day school unless by compulsion on the part of the state or nation. I further believe that all illiterate or non-English speaking people should be compelled by the state legislature to attend evening school or part-time day school, and the industries and corporations should be prohibited to hire non-English speaking people unless they show interest enough to attend evening school or part-time day school. Such a law would be very beneficial in stamping out propaganda which is being distributed to the non-English reading people of this country. It would help to control strikes and other seditious activities which we are now threatened with in this country.

"I would suggest that a state law be enacted requiring all non-English speaking people under 35 years of age to attend evening school or part-time school, and that all industries would be prohibited under penalty to engage such people unless they show interest and produce evidence that they are making suitable progress in the English language by attending school. Each man could be furnished with a card by the factory and have it endorsed by the school authorities.

"I shall be very glad to give you any other information on this subject that you may desire. I shall be glad to have your Committee communicate with me at any time."

9. Dunkirk

Data from F. R. Darling, Superintendent of Schools.

The population of Dunkirk is 20,000. We have some foreign population — Polish, Italian and German. The chief industries employing these foreigners are the American Locomotive Company, the Crucible Steel Company and other steel and iron industries. None of them have classes for their employees.

Public night schools are conducted in four buildings 80 nights in the year. We have about 85 foreigners in the night schools, the attendance is fairly regular, and the average age of the foreign pupils is between 30 and 40.

We employ teachers with special training in immigrant education as far as possible. We give $2.50 per session of two hours, which seems to be sufficient at present.

Letter from Mr. F. R. Darling, Superintendent of Schools and also Chairman of the Americanization Committee, November 4, 1919:

> "We have a large, active Americanization Committee which has been engaged since early last spring in furthering the work of Americanization in the city of Dunkirk. Sub-committees were formed among the various nationalities of the city, and proceeded to secure the names of every person not a citizen, to urge all such to become citizens, in case they did not respond, to find out the reason why they did not desire citizenship. As a result of this work, several hundred aliens have made application for citizenship. The committee has given assistance in every possible way to foreigners seeking naturalization.
>
> "The second task taken up by the Americanization Committee was in co-operation with the public evening schools. Here again through our sub-committees we urged non-English speaking foreigners to enroll in the night school. As a result, we have about 125 foreigners enrolled in these classes.
>
> "Our third effort was undertaken with the young women of the city for whom a club was formed, open to any young woman, which meets in the high school building each Monday evening. About 200 girls from all parts of the city are enrolled in this club and are divided into sections that give their attention to cooking, sewing, home nursing, etc., for part of each evening, the remainder of the evening being devoted to games and dancing."

10. Elmira

Data received from the Superintendent of Schools.

The population of Elmira is about 45,000. According to the 1910 census, the foreign population was as follows:

Austrian	221
Canadian, French	21
Canadian, other	194
Cuban and other West Indian	3
Danish	13
English	383
Finn	1
French	19
German	1,162
Greeks	17
Dutch	10
Hungarian	42
Irish	1,277
Italian	919
Norwegian	13
Roumanian	12
Russian	658
Scotch	94
Swedish	71
Swiss	29
Turkish in Asia	29
Turkish in Europe	9
Other foreigners	62
Total	5,259

The foundry and knitting mills are the principal industries employing these foreigners. There are no factory classes for them, but we have from fifty to 100 foreign-born students in our evening schools. The average age is 30. The attendance is regular.

For teachers of our foreign-born, we require the qualifications of a regular teacher together with a knowledge of the life and ideals of the foreigner and the best methods of creating enthusiasm for American institutions and American ideals. They receive for a school year not less than $1,000.

Americanization work is done by the Board of Education.

Letter from Mr. M. J. Duryea, managing secretary, Elmira Chamber of Commerce, January 13, 1920:

"Up to the present time we have not undertaken any definite program for Americanization in our factories. We do not have a very large foreign population in Elmira and do not have the acute situation that some cities have in this respect. However, I believe that Americanization should be one of the activities of every well-organized chamber of commerce and I hope to see the Elmira Chamber of Commerce line up soon on this work.

"We have been doing some work with the New York State League for Americanism and have had one of their speakers here to talk to our people. There is also under way through some of our organizations, a plan to emphasize the importance of naturalization papers and to make some public demonstration over the admission of some of our men to citizenship."

11. Fredonia

Data furnished by Williams B. Blaisdell, Superintendent of Schools.

The population of Fredonia is about 6,500, 2,500 of whom are Italian.

The chief industries employing our foreign-born are the Locomotive Works, Atlas Crucible Steel Works, U. S. Radiator Works, grape industry, none of which have classes for their employees.

As yet we have no night schools, but we contemplate opening such schools. Also we contemplate Americanization work, but nothing has been done as yet.

12. Geneseo

Data furnished by the Superintendent of Schools.

The population of Geneseo is about 2,500, 300 of whom are Italian.

The chief industries employing foreigners are the canning factories and salt mines.

We have about 20 foreigners in our night school and their attendance is fairly regular. They average about 25 years.

We pay our night school teachers $1.000 per year and our day school teachers $1.500.

Americanization work is being done by the State Normal School here.

13. Geneva

Data furnished by A. J. Merrill, Superintendent of Schools.

The population of Geneva is over 15,000. We have about 3,000, foreigners, mostly Italian.

The principal industries employing foreigners are the Empire Coke Company, American Can Company, U. S. Lens Company, U. S. Radiator Company, General Cutlery Company, General Preserving Company, Lehigh Valley and New York Central. None of them conduct classes for their employees as far as I know.

We have night schools, but very few foreigners attend until after the first of December. We have only one now (November 10, 1919).

We employ day school teachers and pay them $2.50 to $4 per night.

The Education Department has recently made a canvass of the city to get information in regard to the foreign-born.

Letter from J. Macques, acting secretary, Geneva Chamber of Commerce, January 20, 1920:

> "This office is in receipt of your letter of inquiry of December 22d regarding the work of Americanization in Geneva.
>
> "The work so far has been done through the Civic League which has confined to date its efforts to the following lines:
>
> "It consists mainly in classes in cooking and sewing for the women and children of the Italian settlement and in visits by their workers in the homes with a view to helping the living conditions among the foreigners. In the past the League instituted night classes for the men and, since the city opened a night school, has co-operated by securing attendance at the classes to some extent."

14. Glens Falls

Data furnished by Elbert W. Griffith, Superintendent of Schools.

The population of Glens Falls is about 18,000, with from 500 to 1,000 foreigners.

Paper and cement are the leading industries employing foreigners. They have no classes for their employees as far as I know.

We maintain night schools. We pay the teachers $3 per evening. In our union free school district are few foreigners. Such illiterate foreigners as there are, live almost entirely in District 18, a territory which is not in union school district or controlled by board of education.

In our evening school we have an interesting class of about 20 adult foreigners who attend fairly regularly, whose average age may be 25. The session is three evenings a week from 7:30 to 9:30. The teacher is superior.

15. Gloversville

Data furnished by James A. Estie, Superintendent of Schools.

The population of Gloversville is about 23,000. Italian and Jewish predominate among our foreign population.

The glove factories are the leading industries employing foreigners, but they do not conduct any classes.

We have fifty-six foreigners enrolled in our night schools, they average about 40 years of age and their attendance is fairly regular.

All societies in Gloversville are assisting in Americanization work, especially the Red Cross. We have two teachers secured from the Immigrant Education Department of the state. We also employ other teachers — normal school graduates.

16. Herkimer

Letter from George M. Elmendorf, Superintendent of Schools, October 23, 1919:

"Herewith is a reply to your questionnaire. The population of Herkimer is about 10,000 — possibly more.

"An estimate of the foreign population would be about 3,000. So far as I know none of the industries conduct classes of any kind. Three or four adult students attend our public schools. These are foreign-born men who have served in the United States army. At present there is no movement in our city to Americanize foreigners. The Superintendent of Schools is interested and a night school has been held during the winter months of certain years. One was held last year.

17. Ilion

Data furnished by Superintendent of Schools.

The population of Ilion is about 10,000, with almost no foreigners.

We have no facilities for teaching adult foreigners.

The Library Bureau does some Americanization work.

18. Ithaca

Data furnished by Superintendent of Schools.

The population of Ithaca is over 18,000, plus 6,000 students. Before the war we had about 1,000 Italians and as many more of mixed nationalities.

The industries employing foreigners are shot guns, chairs, signs, salt and cement. None of these conduct classes.

We pay our evening school teachers $2.50 per evening for a session of two hours. Our Americanization work is accomplished through our night schools with the co-operation of the State Department of Education.

The Object.—The object of the night school is to furnish instruction to men and women, young and old, whose various duties in the business of life make it impossible for them to attend the day sessions. For these there is neither age limit nor educational qualifications — *just come and we will do the rest.*

An enrollment fee of $2 is charged residents of the city, one-half of which registration fee will be refunded at the close of the session provided pupils have been perfect in attendance and have returned their text books. Otherwise 10 cents for each absence will be deducted from the amount to be returned.

Classes for Foreigners.— The English work with foreigners will be based upon (a) personal matters., e. g., articles of clothing; (b) household matters, e. g., cooking utensils, furniture, etc.; (c) civic matters, e. g., how to become a citizen, free school, police, fire and health departments; (d) state and national government.

Beginners class for those who are unable to speak or read the English language at all — first reader grade, 5 credits.

Intermediate class for those who are able to read English equal in difficulty to the first reader easily, 5 credits.

Advanced class for foreigners — same as class number one given under English courses above. Spelling and composition will also be included. Also work leading to the taking out of citizenship papers, 5 credits.

Letters from F. D. Boynton, Superintendent of Schools, October 21 and November 13, 1919.

"In addition to the night school we are conducting an extension course in the section of the city where there seems to be a large number of foreigners. We find, however, that only a few of the men can be reached, and practically not any of the women. We have made a house to house canvass, printing our literature and explaining in Italian and Hungarian languages that the night school is entirely free to foreigners.

"In my judgment we will not get the results we wish to secure until we have compulsory attendance. My whole study of this question for the Commission on Emergency in Education representing the N. E. A., goes to show that we have approximately in this state 600,000 non-English-speaking, reading and writing foreigners. Plenty of these have been in our state for a long time, and, as you probably know, do what reading they are able to do in the language of Europe, herding together so as to continue in this country the social customs, practices and traditions which they brought to this country with them, educating their children by the thousands in elementary schools where the teachers themselves are unable to read, write or speak English. My own view of the matter is that any topic, secular or religious, civic or social, which cannot be taught in the English language is an unfit subject for the consideration of decent people and should be distinctly barred from public and private schools of all grades.

"I feel that what we need is legislation which will give constituted school authorities power to (a) compel attendance of all foreigners of all ages to attend some kind of organized school which will teach them English and the principles of this government; (b) that after a definite number of years in this country every foreigner who has not learned the language must leave it; (c) that within a given period newspapers may be printed in any foreign language, but after that period in English only, *unless* printed in English and the foreign language given in parallel columns; (d) that English alone shall be the language used in all public and private elementary schools for the purpose of instruction. *Personally,* I believe that anything — religious or secular — which cannot be taught in the English language is unfit to be taught in any language, especially in America."

19. Lancaster

Letter from P. J. Zeilman, Superintendent of Schools, November 17, 1919:

"Last year we had a class for adults of foreign birth and we had enrolled three Italians, four Spaniards and one

Austrian. The Austrian attended with exceptional regularity and made good progress. The attendance of the Spaniards was poor and that of the Italians was good. One made exceptional progress. This class was conducted in connection with the evening school. This year we again offered the course, which included reading, writing and citizenship, and only three presented themselves. I advised them to attend at Depew where there are large classes organized. They took my advice and are now enrolled at Depew.

"I am of the opinion that the only way to make America safe for Americans is to make Americans of all who make this land their home. From my observation only a small percentage of those coming from Europe have any desire to become truly American, and it will, therefore, be necessary to compel attendance upon our institutions of learning or upon classes conducted in the shop. With the eight-hour day, it seems to me that no great hardship would be worked if adult illiterate foreigners were required to receive instruction in English and American ideals for at least four hours each week. It matters not whether the instruction is given in shop or school, but it must be under control of the educational authorities of the states.

"The mass of foreigners cannot be reached unless their job depends on it. This is the opinion given me by one of their number."

20. Lockport

Data furnished by Emmet Belknap, Superintendent of Schools. The population of Lockport is approximately 21,000, and the foreign part of it is estimated somewhere between 2,000 and 3,000. Steel, glass, paper, automobile parts, concrete construction are the principal industries employing foreigners. Last year some effort was made to conduct factory classes for foreigners, but it was not successful. The steel plant offered room for classes to be taught by school authorities, but we did not get them organized. The epidemic in October interfered.

We have about forty foreign-born students enrolled in evening classes, and we expect more. Their attendance is regular as far as hours of employment will permit.

We use the best qualified day school teachers that are available. Men directors receive $3.50 per night; women teachers, $2 and $2.50.

Evening classes are held three evenings per week. We are hoping to organize classes for women which may be held in the afternoon, and possibly some classes for men in the industrial plants between four and six in the afternoon. We hope for more co-operation from the industries.

Large announcements of the opening of the evening schools for season of 1919–20 appeared in the Lockport newspapers. The text of the announcement of citizenship classes appears below:

"PUBLIC EVENING SCHOOLS
"American Citizenship Classes

"will be held at West Avenue and Clinton Street schools, Monday, Wednesday and Friday evenings, beginning October 15.

"These are for attendance of men and women who wish to be able to speak, read and write the English language readily and to learn about the rights, privileges and duties of American citizens.

"Full preparation will be given to get final citizenship papers. Those who thus prepare and are certified by us do not have to take examination by the naturalization judge. All who attended last year and all others who wish to come this year are invited to come.

"Afternoon classes will be held for women if they wish.

"Emmett Belknap,
"Superintendent of Schools."

Except in the citizenship classes, an entrance deposit of $2 will be required as evidence of serious intention to attend regularly and continuously to the end of the school term or until such attendance, for good reason, becomes impossible. The deposit fee will be returned at close of term to all who have attended at least three-fourths of the evening sessions. It will be returned at any time after the first six weeks, to any who, for satisfactory reason, stated to the director, find themselves unable to further attend.

Letter from Emmet Belknap, Superintendent of Schools, October 23, 1919:

> "Please report that our projected evening school, including the vocational school, has started well with accessions still coming in; that we hope to get a larger interest and

attendance in the classes for foreign-born men and women than heretofore. Our foreign population is largely made up of men and women of mature age. The number of young men is small.

"The children of foreign-born parents in this city have for some years regularly attended public and church schools and are being universally educated. We are hoping to have also some assistance from people especially interested in this work from the city of Buffalo."

21. Malone

Data furnished by Superintendent of Schools.

The population of Malone is 7,690, the foreign part of which is the French Canadian.

The paper mill is the chief industry employing foreigners, but they have no classes.

We plan to open a night school, and we will pay the teachers $2 per hour.

22. Mount Vernon

Data furnished by W. H. Holmes, Superintendent of Schools.

The population of Mount Vernon is about 40,000, and the foreign population is as follows:

German	1,647
Irish	1,038
Italian	2,670
English	636
Russian	575
Total	6,566

The foreigners are employed chiefly by the shirtwaist factories, silversmiths, optical company, motor companies, etc. None of these industries conduct classes.

We have from 75 to 100 foreigners in our night schools, which are open four evenings each week for at least 20 weeks. The attendance is about 70 per cent. and the average age is 25 or 26.

We require teachers of foreigners to be at least normal school graduates or its equivalent. We pay from $3 to $5 an evening of two hours. Evening school teachers succeed each year in getting many foreigners to take out first papers.

Letter from C. O. Thompson, Principal, Evening Commercial School, November 19, 1919:

"We conduct an evening school at the present time in which English to foreigners is taught. There are four classes in session four evenings a week from 7:30 to 9:30 for about six months during the year, beginning in October and closing about the first of April. At present there is an attendance in these classes of between 60 and 80 with an enrollment of 94. During the year we enroll about 200. In addition to the four classes in which English is taught to foreigners, there are a number of foreigners who speak some English, attending other classes. Some are registered for machine shop, some for automobile repairing and some for drafting. Where they do not speak the language well enough to get along particularly well in the industrial arts classes, they are assigned to classes where English is taught for two evenings a week, and on two evenings a week, they receive instruction in the shops.

"We make an effort to reach just as many of the non-English speaking residences of this city as we can, and influence them to attend evening school, and those who attend are encouraged to take out their citizenship papers.

"In the elementary department we offer courses in English and civics, read some history and current events, and in the advanced classes we give a little time to arithmetic. Citizenship and Americanization are our main topics for general discussion and we recruit each year many who take out their first and some their second papers."

23. New Rochelle

Data furnished by Albert Leonard, Superintendent of Schools, November 17, 1919:

The education and Americanization of adult foreigners in the city of New Rochelle.

The population of New Rochelle is 40,000.

The foreign population is 9,000. This is divided approximately among the following nationalities:

Austrian	154
Canadian	260
French	100
British	736

German	1,240
Greek	30
Hungarian	75
Irish	1,600
Italian	3,500
Dutch and Belgian	37
Scandinavian	476
Russian and Finn	850

As New Rochelle is a surburban city within easy reach of New York City, it is virtually the home of commuters. There are few industries of any importance in New Rochelle outside of the industries needed to supply the daily life of the community. The Knickerbocker Press and Jones Speedometer are the chief industries.

The building trades of New Rochelle recruit employees from the foreign element of the population. The usual occupations in a city of this size are in the hands of the foreigners.

None of the industries in this city find it necessary to conduct classes for teaching English, American history, or civil government to their foreign-born employees.

All the public school facilities of the city are open to foreign-born adults. In addition to the regular classes in the public schools, there are evening school classes open to all the adults of the city.

The following adult students of different nationalities attend our evening schools:

American, white	17
American, colored	6
Greek	
Polish	
Irish	
West Indian	
French	
Ruthenian	
Chinese	
Spanish	
Lithuanian	
Portuguese	
Finn	

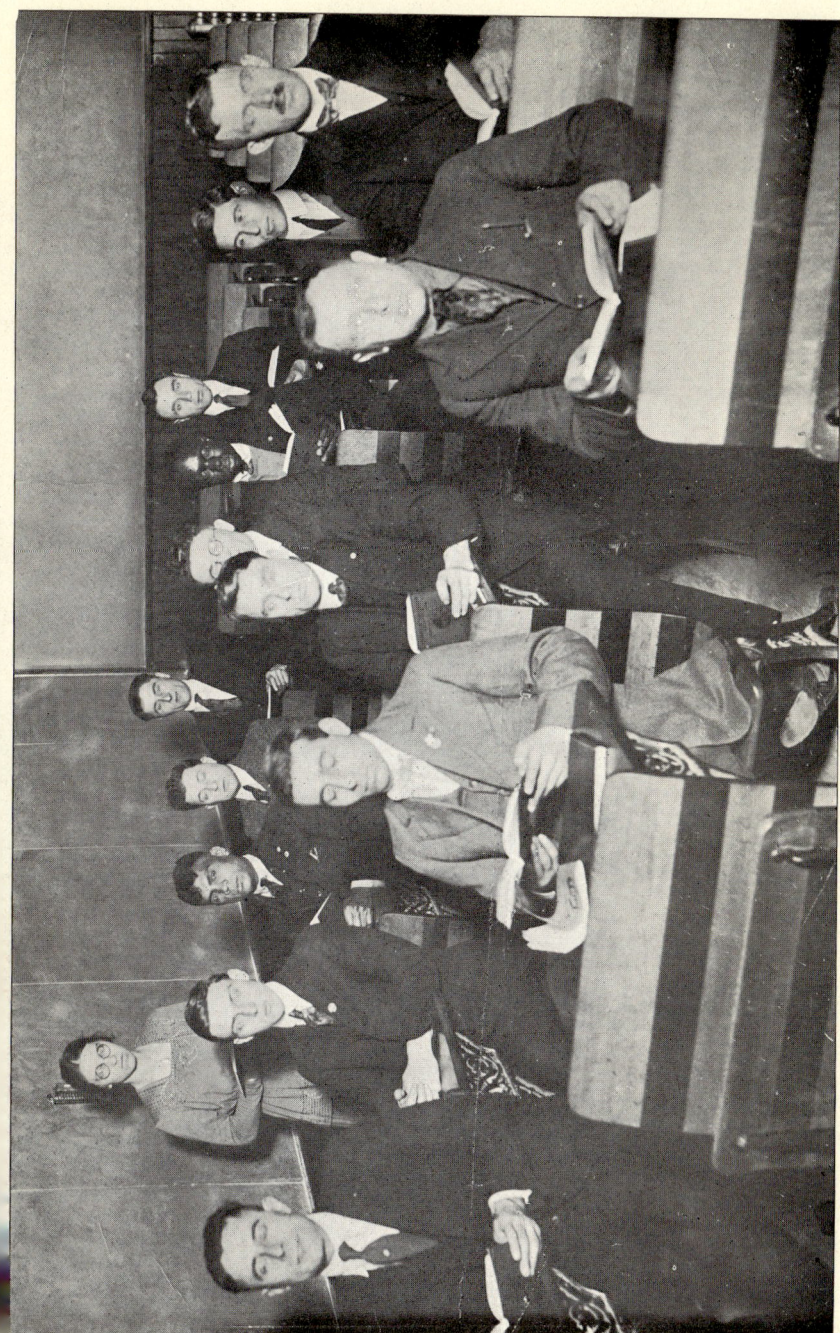

Night Class in Americanization, Buffalo

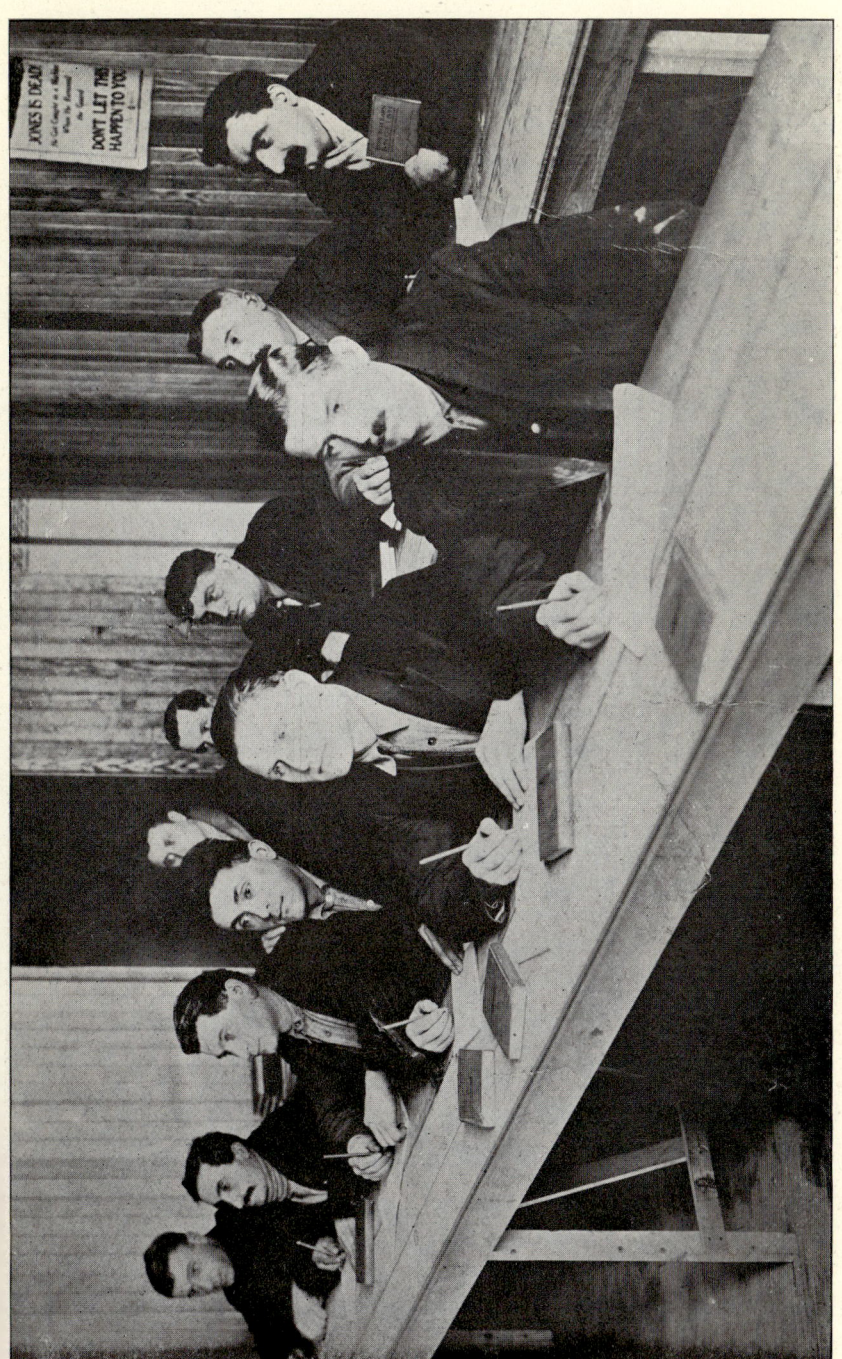

Classes of Solvay Process Company, Syracuse

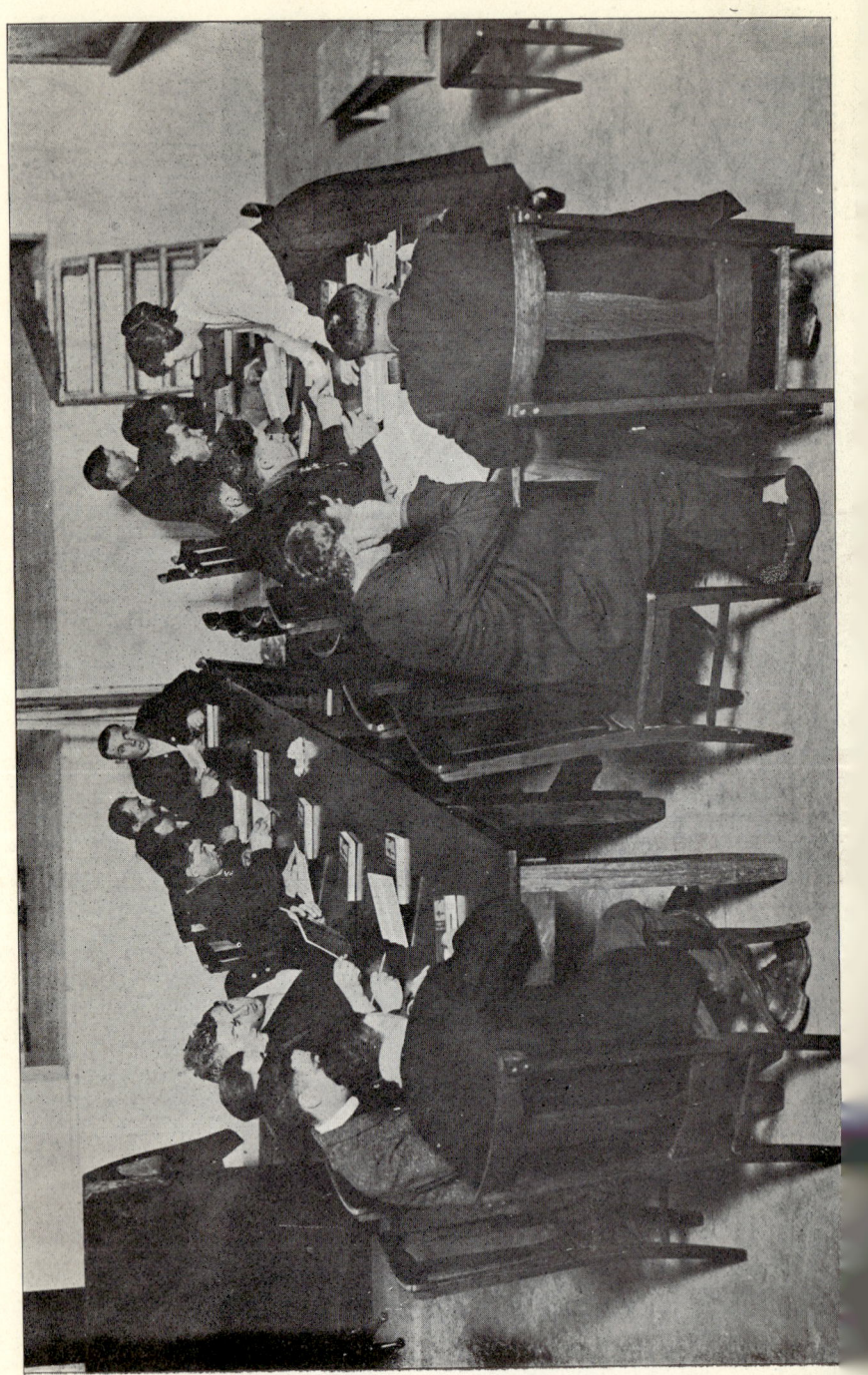

Danish 2
Italian 83
English 3
Russian 9
Hungarian 4
German 2

The attendance is fairly regular.

The average age of the adult alien student is about 25.

The courses in the evening classes cover eight hours each week.

For several years a systematic attempt has been made in this city to Americanize foreign residents who are either illiterate or are not informed on American ideals.

This Americanization work is a part of the evening school courses.

Teachers of adult foreigners must be teachers regularly licensed by the State Department of Education. As a rule, we employ in our evening schools only our best teachers of the day schools.

We are paying in this city $4 each evening for two hours' work. This seems to be a large enough remuneration to command the services of the best teachers.

24. Newburgh

Letter from George F. Hall, Superintendent of Schools, November 15, 1919:

"In reply to yours of the 14th, relative to our classes for illiterates, I beg to advise that we have not met with success. It is a subject in which I am intensely interested, but feel that we shall have to change our policies and do more field work in order to accomplish results.

"We have one class with an enrollment of ten, mostly Italians, some Poles. The line of work followed is teaching them to speak, read and write English.

"Last year we had as high as forty enrolled, but, they soon lost interest or became tired and all but a few left.

"Mr. Crawley of the State Department of Education is devoting some time to field work here and we are looking forward to putting on an Americanization program that will arouse the interest of all the industries and social and civic organizations of the city and community. Definite plans have not been laid.

"The ones who have enrolled in the classes this year are very regular in their attendance thus far."

25. Niagara Falls

Data furnished by J. B. Laidlaw, Superintendent of Schools.

According to the state census of 1915, the population of Niagara Falls was 42,257. The foreign population was 10,965. Poles and Italians predominate, but we have no detailed figures.

The Union Carbide Company, Carborundum, Hooker Electro-Chemical, Aluminum, Niagara Electro Chemical, Acheson Graphite, National Carbon are the leading industries employing foreign-born. Some factory classes are conducted by the State Board of Education.

About 270 foreigners are enrolled in night schools. Their attendance is regular as far as conditions of shift work will permit. The average age is twenty-seven.

We require that extension teachers have a special training by the Direction of Extension Work. They receive a minimum of $3.50 per night.

26. Norwich

Data furnished by Superintendent of Schools.

The population of Norwich is about 9,000, including 600 Italians.

The knitting mill is the chief industry employing these Italians, but it has no factory classes.

We did have night schools for the foreigners, but they have been discontinued. We do no Americanization work.

27. Ogdensburg

Data furnished by Francis C. Byrn, Superintendent of Schools.
The population of Ogdensburg is 13,565.

There is practically no foreign population here. A few Italians are employed by the railroads. Last year we started night school and the attendance of foreigners consisted of four Italians. We employed two teachers who had training in the Rome Custodial School for backward children. We paid $2.50 per evening. Personally I feel that a teacher who teaches in schools during the day should not teach in night school, but the only teachers available last year were the day school teachers.

28. Oneida

Data furnished by D. Keating, Superintendent of Schools.

The population of Oneida is about 10,000. It is estimated that we have 800 Germans, 1,200 Italians, and 500 other foreigners.

The canning and cement block factories are the industries employing foreigners. They conduct no classes.

We started a night school, but only four registered, so we discontinued it.

29. Oneonta

Data furnished by George J. Dann, Superintendent of Schools.

The population of Oneonta is about 12,000, of which not more than 500 are foreigners. They are principally Italians and Syrians. Most of these foreigners are employed by the railroads.

We conduct a night school. Last year we had 20 foreign students, whose attendance was regular. They average 25 years.

We require that teachers of foreigners have a regular school license, and we pay them $5 per night.

Americanization work is being done by the public schools and the D. A. R.

30. Oswego

Data furnished by C. W. Richards, Superintendent of Schools.

The population of Oswego is about 25,000.

We have no figures as to our foreign population.

We have 25 foreigners in our evening school, and they average 22 years old.

We now require that night school teachers have the same qualifications as day school teachers, but we are conducting an institute for special preparation of teachers for adult foreigners. We pay $2.50 per evening, if teachers also draw a salary as day school teacher or for any other occupation.

31. Peekskill

Data furnished by L. J. Bolemann, Superintendent of Schools.

The population of Peekskill is about 16,000, including some Italians and Hungarians. Most of these foreigners are employed by a hat factory, an oilcloth factory, or by Fleishmann's Yeast plant.

We have no classes for foreigners now. We have had night school classes for foreigners in the schools under Y. M. C. A. management. With compulsory attendance something would be accomplished, but not much without.

32. Plattsburgh

Data furnished by F. K. Watson, Superintendent of Schools.

The population of Plattsburgh is about 11,000 with no foreigners.

33. Port Chester

Data furnished by Elmer S. Redman, Superintendent of Schools.

The population of Port Chester is about 17,000, including some Italians. Most of them are employed in the bolt and nut works or in the stove works.

Men teachers would be necessary for teaching adult foreigners and they should receive $2,000 to $2,500 per year.

34. Potsdam

Data furnished by Superintendent of Schools.

The population of Potsdam is about 5,000. We have from 500 to 1,000 foreigners, mostly French Canadian, employed in the paper mills.

No Americanization work is being done.

The pay of night school teachers would depend upon the locality, but it should be equal to that of high school teachers.

35. Poughkeepsie

Data furnished by Ward C. Moon, Superintendent of Schools.

1. What is the population of your city? About 38,000.
2. What is the foreign population, divided as to nationality? Italians, Poles and others.
3. What are the leading industries? DeLaval Cream Separator Co., Dutchess Manufacturing Co., R. U. Delapenha Co., Federal Button Co., Phoenix Horseshoe Works, Smith Brothers Cough Drop Factory, Auto-Lite Co., Moline Plow Co., Federal Bearings Co., Poughkeepsie Foundry.
4. What are the leading industries in which foreigners are employed? Delapenha Separator Co., Moline Plow Co., DeLaval Separator Co., Phoenix Horsehoe Co., Federal Bearings Co., Poughkeepsie Foundry, Federal Button Co.
5. Do any of the industries conduct classes for teaching English, American history, civil government, etc., for their foreign-born employees? No.
6. What public school facilities are open to foreign-born adults for learning English, American history, civil government? Classes are conducted in English four nights a week.

7. How many adult students of the various nationalities attend public schools? Polish, 20; Swedish, 3; Italian, 20; Spanish, 2.
8. Is the attendance regular? Yes.
9. What is the average age of adult alien students? Thirty.
10. How many hours per week does the course cover? Eight.
11. Is there any movement in your city to Americanize foreigners? Yes.
12. By whom is it conducted? The Board of Education.
13. What are your requirements for teachers of adult foreigners? Special training.
14. What salary do you think should be offered to attract teachers of competence for this work? [No answer.]

36. Rochester

Letter from James A. Basker, Assistant Superintendent of Schools, November 19, 1919:

"Replying to your favor of November 14th, relative to the work which we are conducting in Americanization, I regret to say that we have no printed statement of our undertaking.

"One of the supervisors gives a large portion of his time to the organization of classes in English to foreigners; and to classes in Americanization, for those who are preparing to take out naturalization papers.

"We have twenty-nine classes, meeting three evenings per week in eight different school buildings. In addition to the evening classes we have organized classes in six factories in Rochester. These classes meet for an hour after the close of work, in rooms provided by the factory. All books, pencils, notebooks, and paraphernalia are furnished by the Board of Education.

"In order that instruction may be along the most approved lines we conduct a normal class for teachers. All teachers actively engaged in instruction have had special training. In addition to our local normal instructors we have had men from out of the city who are engaged in this work.

"We are fortunate, in Rochester, in having a very efficient Chamber of Commerce, which has a special committee on Americanization very active in participating in the work which we are formally carrying forward. Various groups of men in these committees have made a practice of visiting evening classes. We have received much encouragement and advice from this source. I believe that our work is vital and that the students (560) that enrolled last year profited greatly by the opportunity.

"Our problem of the non-English speaking members of our community, as indicated by the enclosed report from the Chamber of Commerce, is not as serious (although serious enough) as we had thought it would be.

"If you wish any more detailed statement of our work I shall be glad to secure such information, as you may indicate, from the teachers who are actively engaged in the field. Meanwhile, I will endeavor to secure the information as soon as possible."

Report Accompanying Above Letter

1. Number of factories that reported to the Chamber of Commerce, 158.
2. Number of factories having no foreign problem as indicated by the questionnaire, 86.
3. Number of factories having less than 10 per cent. who cannot read and write English, 38.
4. Total number of factories having no problem so far as illiteracy is concerned, 124.
5. Factories having between 10 and 25 who cannot read and write English, 21.
6. Factories having between 25 and 50 who cannot read and write English, 6.
7. Factories having between 50 and 100 who cannot read and write English, 3.
8. Factories having between 100 and 150 who cannot read and write English, 2.
9. Factories having over 150 who cannot read and write English, 2.
10. Total number of foreigners employed in the 158 factories reported, 4,205.
11. Total number having taken no steps toward citizenship, 1,414.
12. Data lacking, 204.
13. Total number having taken the first papers, 938.
14. Total number of aliens, 2,556.
15. Total number of citizens, 1,649.
16. Number of factories not reported, 22.

REPORT OF HERBERT S. WEET, SUPERINTENDENT OF SCHOOLS,
OCTOBER 27, 1919

1. Population of Rochester, 280,000.
2. No definite census figures available. Our largest problem according to nationalities is as follows: About one-half of our illiterates are Italians. Other nationalities having 500 or more illiterates are Russian, Austrian, Polish, and Portugese.
3. The six leading industries of Rochester are cameras and photographic supplies, optical glass and instruments, clothing, boots and shoes, precision instruments, and filing devices.
4. Foreigners are largely employed in all except the camera works.
5. Rochester either now has or has had factory classes in all of the above industries employing foreigners.
6. Eight public schools are open for this work. Two of these are open throughout the school year. Data on attendance for year 1918–19 not yet tabulated.
7. We get regular attendance to an unusual degree as compared with other communities.
8. No statistics available.
9. Six hours.
10. The Board of Education co-operating with the Chamber of Commerce.
11. All teachers in classes for foreigners must take a special course in Teacher Training for Immigrant Education and must receive a standing of at least 80 per cent. A candidate for one of these classes must have, at least, a high school education.
12. From three to four dollars a night.

REPORT OF HERBERT S. WEET, PRESIDENT OF STATE TEACHERS
ASSOCIATION (ALSO SUPERINTENDENT OF SCHOOLS),
OCTOBER 27, 1919

I. Salaries paid in Rochester:
    a. For regular evening school class, $3 per night.
    b. For factory classes and home classes, $2.50 per lesson.
II. Minimum requirements for teachers in English and citizenship.
    1. A workable knowledge of the most approved modern methods of teaching English to the foreign-born.
    2. Familiarity with the best recently published textbooks on this subject.

3. An adequate idea of grouping and grading foreign-born students so as to meet the needs of different classes of foreigners.
4. Demonstrated teaching ability.
5. Accurate knowledge of the various steps in the process of obtaining citizenship.
6. A thorough knowledge of our government, national, state, county, and local, with the ability to present the facts in the several units of government in relation to the function side of civics in the particular community where the lessons are given.
7. A sympathetic understanding of the meaning and value of American institutions.
8. Ability to select and apply significant facts in American history.
9. Some knowledge of rational backgrounds.
10. An appreciation of what Americanization realy means.

III. How shall the education of the foreign-born population in New York State be accomplished?
1. This work should be conducted under the auspices of the State Department of Education so far as the state is concerned.
2. All classes whether in factories, settlements, homes or schools, should be under the direct supervision of the educational authorities in the particular community where such classes are established.
3. Information concerning the foreign-born which is to be collected by the federal government should be made immediately available for local campaign against illiteracy.
4. Every effort should be made to assimilate the foreigners within our borders before the new tide of immigration begins.
5. Utilize all possible appeals that will create a desire on the part of the foreign-born to learn English.
6. Ascertain the objections of foreigners to learning English and try to meet them.
7. Convince the foreigner that the nation, the state, and the community are in earnest about this matter.
8. Train speakers and provide opportunities for presenting this matter in foreign lodges, in churches, in factories and in public meetings.

9. Carry on an Americanization publicity campaign in both the foreign language press and the daily papers.
10. Utilize the present zone plan of the State Department of Education by placing trained workers and organizers in all parts of the state.
11. Obtain the co-operation of all employers of foreign-born labor.
12. Get organized labor firmly behind all community efforts.

Letter from E. J. Bonner, Principal, City Normal School, October 23, 1919.

"I should say that the requirements for teachers of adults should be as follows: these teachers should have a regular normal school training, a few years' experience in the teaching of children, and a special course in the teaching of foreigners, in which citizenship and methods in teaching English should be especially emphasized.

"The compensation of such teachers should be somewhat in excess of the compensation of ordinary grade teachers inasmuch as it would require further preparation. The grade teachers of our city receive from $800 to $1,600.

"Our normal school has not considered the training of such teachers yet. Last year a series of lectures in preparation for this work was given in our school but not under our auspices. But as the training should be, in my opinion, given to experienced teachers, it does not seem that it would be very difficult to institute such work in our school."

REPORT OF AMERICANIZATION COMMITTEE OF ROCHESTER CHAMBER OF COMMERCE, 1916

CHARLES E. FINCH, *Chairman*

The Americanization Committee was one of the new committees of the year 1916, and was a result of a suggestion from the Chamber of Commerce, U. S. A., and a desire of the Board of Education for the establishment of a more vital co-operation of the business men in a mutual attempt to Americanize our foreign-born.

The first meeting was held January 27th to consider an outline of the year's work which included public meetings, conferences with employers looking toward factory co-operation, a plan for making a definite survey of foreign-born workers in our industries, the outlining of definite steps for their Americanization, and definite plans for factory co-operation.

Americanization Mass Meeting

Preparation at this meeting was begun for an "Americanization" mass meeting at Convention Hall on February 22d. Subcommittees were appointed and the members immediately went about the task of making this first meeting a great success. Through Harry H. Barnhart, chorus leader and member of the committee, the community chorus and the special choruses from the Bausch and Lomb Optical Company and the German-American Button Company, were obtained. A press committee, headed by S. Sidney B. Roby conducted a vigorous publicity compaign through newspapers, public signs, and the use of our slogan, "All and Always Americans." Many of our merchants used the slogan in their advertisements and called attention to the Americanization rally besides. As a part of this publicity campaign the committee at request outlined its ideals as follows:

1. As Americans we should place a higher value on our citizenship, we should take a deeper and more intelligent interest in the affairs of the nation, and we should seek to realize the larger meaning of the institutions which we have inherited from our forefathers.

2. The immigrants within our borders should be taught to speak and read our common tongue, they should be led to see the value of American citizenship, and encouraged to adopt American standards of living.

3. We should treat the foreigner as an asset to be developed rather than another demand upon our time, money, or sympathy. We should work with the immigrant, not for him.

4. We should realize more keenly that in a republic all the citizens must be efficient, and that it is our duty to counteract the influences of all those who would keep the immigrant in ignorance so that he might remain their prey.

5. Our program of Americanization might be defined then as an attempt to give to all those within our border a common national ideal, a point of view that is essentially American, a loyalty to America that gives the pledge of allegiance to the United States in terms of service. It should include an effort on our part to

make the English language our common tongue, to create a greater social solidarity, to raise the general level of intelligence, to protect all the children of all the people and see that they are raised and educated according to American standards, and in every possible way to emphasize the high value and real meaning of American citizenship.

A sub-committee, of which Rev. Dr. Arthur W. Grose was chairman, prepared a most excellent program. The invocation was by Rt. Rev. Thomas F. Hickey, bishop of Rochester. Hon. H. F. Atwood of Chicago, as orator, delivered a stirring, patriotic address on "Washington, Lincoln, McKinley." There were two distinctive features in the program: One, the presenting of badges to those who have served as standard bearers in the public schools, by President J. Warrant Castleman, of the Board of Education; the other, the presentation of certificates of naturalization to the citizens naturalized at the session of the Naturalization Court which preceded this meeting, by former Justice Arthur E. Sutherland.

The committee next turned its attention to the plan relating to the survey and analysis of Americanization needs in our industries. The first step in this direction was the appointment of a sub-committee to meet with the Manufacturers' Council, on May 31st. The council at the same time appointed a sub-committee to co-operate with the Americanization Committee in formulating the details of a campaign to Americanize foreign-born workers. As the night schools were closed until October it was decided to leave the details of the plans to be worked out in the fall.

Open Air Mass Meeting

On July Fourth, 107 cities throughout the country held Americanization celebrations. Rochester was not included in this list as there was no committee at that time that could give such a matter adequate attention. It was decided that Rochester this year should do its full duty towards renewing among its people the patriotic significance of Independence Day. His Honor volunteered to change plans of long standing and be present at the gathering, and promised the services of the Park Band, the splendid municipal organization conducted by Theodore Dossenbach. Exposition Park, too, was donated for the occasion.

The result was a great open-air mass meeting held at Exposition Park in the morning of July 4th. Thousands of people packed the three stands and joined in the celebration with enthusiasm. The singing, under the leadership of Harry H. Barnhart, also was an inspiration. State Tax Commissioner Ralph M. Thomas, the orator of the day, delivered a stirring patriotic address using the Declaration of Independence as his theme. Certainly, these meetings must be a yearly Rochester institution.

Questionnaire to Factories

The committee opened its fall campaign by sending a questionnaire to all factories having over 100 employees. This questionnaire asked for the following information:

1. Do you employ any foreign labor?
2. If so, about how many men?
3. If so, about how many women?
4. Would you be interested in the plans of the Americanization Committee of the Chamber of Commerce for the education of foreigners?

The replies received were gratifying and indicated a desire on the part of the manufacturers to know more about the plans.

Meeting with Manufacturers

Early in October a joint invitation from the Americanization Committee and the Manufacturers' Council was sent to the manufacturers asking them to attend a meeting to consider definite plans for the Americanization and education of foreign-born employees. The program submitted for discussion included:

1. Bringing the opportunities offered by the public evening schools to the attention of foreign-born workers.
2. Outlining plans for getting at this problem in the best way.
3. Encouraging the attendance of foreign-born employees at the evening schools.
4. Making some provision for following the educational progress of workers who attend evening school.
5. Interesting employees in becoming citizens by providing necessary information and assistance.

At this meeting, Chairman W. Roy McCanne, of the Manufacturers' Council, presided. Mortimer Adler, of the Americanization Committee, presented the attitude of manufacturers in relation to the Americanization program. The chairman of the Americanization Committee, at request, outlined the opportunities provided in the public evening schools for foreign-born workers. A spirited and interesting discussion followed and many helpful suggestions were offered. The following resolutions were passed by unanimous vote:

1. That it was the sense of the meeting that the manufacturers co-operate with the Americanization Committee in carrying out the proposed program for the education and Americanization of foreign-born workers.

2. That the Americanization Committee present a definite plan to the manufacturers of Rochester.

3. That the manufacturers then select from their organization some person to actively undertake the work of carrying out this program.

4. That another meeting be called for conference looking toward complete information and united action in carrying out the proposed program.

Practical Plan Adopted

In accordance with these resolutions the following plan was submitted to our manufacturers:

1. Appointment by you of some individual in your organization to represent you in this activity and carry on the work in your establishment.

2. A general duty of your representative in the work would be:
   a. To attend conferences.
   b. To exchange ideas as to the best methods of carrying on this work.
   c. To obtain suggestions gathered from the successful operation of the plan elsewhere.

3. Specific duties of this representative in your factory would be:
   a. To obtain the necessary data with reference to the need for this work in your particular establishment.
   b. To distribute the necessary information to your workers and answer such questions as they may raise.

At this meeting many of the manufacturers were accompanied by men who were to represent them in carrying out the Americanization program in their respective plants. As a result of this meeting the following firms appointed a representative and decided to begin work at once:

Firm	Representative
Cluett, Peabody & Co.	David Alexander.
Sherwood Shoe Co.	Gustav E. Behmer.
E. Kirstein Sons Co.	J. Bertram.
Todd Protectograph Co.	Charles E. Bradford.
New York State Railways.	L. R. Brown.
Vacuum Oil Co.	H. J. Haddleton.
Michaels, Stern & Co.	Prof. Meyer Jacobstein.
Joseph Knopf & Son.	Joseph Knopf.
James Cunningham Son & Co.	F. C. Marsluff.
Pritchard Stamping Co.	C. H. McConnell.
Yawman & Erbe.	S. D. Meech.
Bausch & Lomb.	Harry S. Moody.
Whitmore, Rauber & Vicinus.	John N. Rauber.
Rochester Stamping Co.	F. H. Swan.
Taylor Instrument Co.	R. A. Taylor.
Stromberg-Carlson Co.	R. E. Thomas.
Camera Works, Eastman Kodak Co.	C. H. Thompson.
National Car Wheel Co.	James Wilson.
Rochester Public Library	William F. Yust.
Pfaudler Co.	E. J. Bayle.

Some Results

Many men have already entered the evening school as a result of this campaign. Others who did not need the instruction in English have been induced to obtain their first papers and still others have been lead to take out their final papers.

At the request of the factory representatives. The chairman has addressed the foreman in some of the factories, presenting the opportunities and outlining the work that the committee desires to accomplish. Unboubtedly, as soon as the survey in all of the factories co-operating is completed many more employees will be induced to take advantage of the opportunities offered by the evening schools.

At the last graduation from the citizenship class at Washington Junior high evening school, at which forty-two prospective citizens received diplomas, members of the committee were present and express their appreciation of the work these classes are doing.

The press rendered valuable aid in giving liberal space to the work of this committee. The officials of the Naturalization Court and the members of the Board of Education co-operated in a most helpful manner. In public meetings, the hearty co-operation of the mayor and his official family, patriotic societies, the community chorus, the park bank, and the public in general, was fully and freely given, and contributed greatly to success achieved.

The work of the Americanization Committee has aroused an interest in our city in the Americanization movement. We hope it will continue to bear fruit until we have a common language, a single American allegiance, and American standard of living, a respect for our laws and love of our traditions among all our people.

CHARLES E. FINCH,
Chairman.

REPORT OF AMERICANIZATION COMMITTEE OF ROCHESTER CHAMBER OF COMMERCE, 1918

Americanization

One of the lessons of the World War has been the importance of Americanizing not only the immigrant, but the native-born. The Americanization Committee has realized this and has co-operated wherever possible with other organizations working on the same problems.

Washington's Birthday

On Washington's Birthday, a mass meeting attended by 4,000 persons was held at Convention Hall. Following a preliminary program of patriotic and popular songs led by Jesse B. Millham, leader of the Chamber Choir, and accompanied by the band of the Immaculate Conception Cadets, "Assembly" was sounded by Boy Scout buglers.

President Granger A. Hollister presided. Citizenship certificates were presented by Justice Robert Thompson to a class of more than 100 new citizens seated on the platform, who had been naturalized at the last previous session of the Naturalization Court. The mayor presented each with a flag, while the wives were given citizenship badges by Mrs. Henry G. Danforth, chairman of the New Citizenship Committee.

Samuel P. Orth, professor of political science at Cornell University, made a stirring address on "Our War and Washington's Legacy." The sounding of "Taps" by the buglers completed the program.

July Fourth

On July Fourth, the Chamber conducted the **annual** Independence Day exercises at Exposition Park, with the co-operation of the municipal authorities. The mayor had issued a proclamation calling upon the citizens to attend. In the parade, which opened the exercises and which was led by the park band, were 2,000 men in uniform; the Standard Bearers of the public schools, and the Women's Motor Corps. After a review by the mayor, the two speakers of the day, James W. Gerard, former United States Ambassador to Germany, and Honorable Job E. Hedges, and the officers of the Chamber of Commerce, the " Call to Colors " was sounded by buglers and the audience of 20,000 persons, said to be the largest ever gathered in Rochester, joined in pledging allegiance to the flag.

Patriotic songs were sung, led by a chorus of 1,400 trained voices, directed by Oscar Gareison, and accompanied by the Park Band. A more enthusiastic, patriotic gathering never was held in Rochester.

Flag Day

The committee obtained speakers and Boy Scout buglers for Flag Day exercises at a number of Rochester's Industrial plants.

Utilizing National Holidays to Educate in Americanism

The committee has decided that in the future, not only Washington's Birthday, Independence Day and Flag day shall be utilized here as a means of patriotic education, but that every national holiday shall serve here as a means of educating in American ideals, loyalty and patriotism, and be celebrated in the manner most suitable to its particular significance.

Co-operative Americanization Committee

The Co-operative Americanization Committee, organized in 1917 in order to co-ordinate all Americanization activities in Rochester, was continued this year under the chairmanship of Charles E. Finch, former chairman of the Chamber's Americanization Committee and Director of Immigrant Education in Rochester.

Included on this committee this year have been the foreign language churches and societies, foreign language press, Central Trades and Labor Council, social settlements, Monroe County Home Defense committees on Aliens and on Instruction, Board of

Education, Naturalization Court, Federal Employment Bureau, public libraries, Housekeeping Center, Council of Jewish Women, several stores and hotels, and about fifty industrial plants employing some non-English speaking employees.

Working in Fifty Plants

Most of these fifty industries have placed one of their executives in charge of plant Americanization, and these have in turn appointed plant Americanization committees, which work under their direction. Both the executive and the members of the committee belong to the Americanization Co-operative Committee, the meetings of which are held at the Chamber of Commerce in the evening, for the convenience of these workers.

At these meetings, Chairman Finch reports on the attendance of employees from the various factories at night school classes in English, and in citizenship. He also calls for reports from the various factories, associations, churches and other agencies represented. This interchange of experience and ideas gives those who have had difficulties an opportunity to have their problems solved, and gives those who have met with success an opportunity to be an inspiration to the others.

What Was Done in the Plants

Among the activities conducted by these plant committees during the past year, may be mentioned:

1. Arranging patriotic meetings in the factories.
2. Encouraging non-English speaking employees to join night school classes in English.
3. Getting in touch with alien employees and persuading them to take out their first papers.
4. Getting in touch with employees who have had their first papers for two years and over, and are therefore eligible for citizenship, and inducing them to take out their final papers without delay.
5. Encouraging aliens desiring to take out their final papers to join night school classes in citizenship, so that they may pass their final examination at the Naturalization Court.
6. Aiding persons desiring to take out their first or second papers in filling out the necessary blanks. In many factories, these blanks are kept on hand for this purpose. In many factories

also, the employee is permitted to go to the Naturalization Court on the employer's time. Questions are answered regarding the draft, and regarding any subject on which the non-English speaking immigrant or alien is apt to want information. Questions that cannot be answered by members of the committee, are referred to the executive; and if he cannot answer them, he in turn calls the assistant secretary assigned to the Americanization Committee.

For the benefit of these plant committees, there is now being prepared at the Chamber, a brief, concise statement of the steps to take in becoming naturalized.

Secretary Lane's Americanization Conference

Franklin K. Lane, Secretary of the Interior, called a National Americanization Conference at Washington on April 3rd and 4th, inviting governors of the states, heads of many of America's largest industries and representatives of commercial organizations. The following representatives from Rochester attended: Carl Lomb, Bausch and Lomb Optical Company; Samuel Weil, Rochester Clothiers' Exchange; William H. Gorsline, secretary, War Information Committee of the Chamber; and the chairman of the Chamber's Americanization Committee. The chairman was thereby enabled to place before the committee an outline of the national program suggested by Secretary Lane, and a summarized statement of national problems and accomplishments. The committee is working in co-operation with this nation-wide plan.

In accordance with this, it instructed its legislation subcommittee to draft a bill to be introduced in the State Legislature, requiring all elementary subjects in both public and private schools in the state to be taught in the English language only. The Chamber is also supporting the Federal Education bill now before the Senate, which creates a Federal Department of Education and appropriates federal funds to assist the states in educating immigrants and illiterates.

Employers and Board of Education

The New York State Legislature, at its last session, enacted three Americanization bills embodying the following provisions:

Illiterate minors from 16 to 21 years of age who can not speak, read and write English as required in the fifth grade, are required to attend some public day or evening school, or school maintained by the employer; the commissioner of education is authorized to establish training institutions for courses of study to train public school teachers to give instruction to illiterates over 16 years of age; first-class cities are required to maintain free night schools two hours each night for three nights a week throughout the day school term; and school districts are required to establish night schools wherever twenty or more minors between 16 and 21 are required by law to attend; or that number applies for such a school.

The committee took steps to help carry these laws into effect, holding several meetings to which the school authorities, employers and employment managers were invited. Based on an exposition of the new law made by W. C. Smith, State Supervisor of Immigrant Education, and upon a thorough discussion of its application following the exposition, the Superintendent of Schools prepared a statement setting forth the responsibility, in carrying out the provisions of the law, which would be assumed by the Board of Education; the assistance to be rendered by the Chamber's Americanization Committee; and the duty resting upon the employer. This statement was discussed at another meeting of the same group; revised after full discussion; was duplicated at the Chamber and mailed to all employers known to employ any non-English speaking workers. The committee also supplied copies of the law to employers.

Census of Non-English Speaking Aliens

In accordance with this statement, the Chamber urged all employers who had not yet done so, to place some individual in charge of plant Americanization activities in their respective organizations. These executives made a plant census from which they compiled a list of illiterate minors employed or a list of all illiterate employees, stating the age in each case, which lists they sent to the Director of Immigrant Education. In the meantime, the Chamber obtained from the Monroe County Home Defense Committee a list of the non-English speaking aliens who registered in Rochester in the State Military Census of 1917, with the nationality of each. There were 4,000 of these divided as follows:

Italians 2,237
Russians 898
Austrians 452
Polish 145
Greeks 108
Turks 79
Germans 28
Servians 23
Hungarians 16
Belgians 17
Armenians 15

and 36 others scattered among 9 different countries.

Illiterate Selective Service Men

In order that it might be equipped to co-operate with the government in getting illiterates who were in the draft to begin learning English immediately, the committee asked the general chairman of the Local Exemption Board to have registrars serving on September 12th, indicate by a cross (X) the name of each man who could not speak English. The order was given and followed, and the Chamber made a card index of the names thus checked. In this way was obtained the names of the men of military age who cannot speak English.

The Director of Immigrant Education, who is also chairman of the Co-operative Americanization Committee, has had the names of the members of night school English classes checked up against these various lists. Thus were obtained the names of several thousand adults who should be learning English, but are not attending any class in English. He is following this up by sending a representative to call on those persons who are evading the new law. It was decided later to circularize the homes of all these people, leaving them a statement in their own language, designed to inspire them with a desire to learn the language of America. This circular is now being prepared by President Rush Rhees of the University of Rochester, chairman of the Home Defense Committee on Instruction, one of the co-operating bodies.

Americanization Through Community Interest

Late in the year, the Americanization Committee adopted a plan to give an impetus to Americanization by fostering community responsibility among residents of foreign birth. A committee of four has made a tour of inspection of those sections of the city in which most of our foreign-born residents live, making notes on the characteristic features in each case. Matters of general community interest have been listed, including housing, sanitation, and disease prevention.

The committee is participating in a national crusade, advocated by the Federal Bureau of Education, against calling persons of foreign birth by nicknames.

JOSEPH R. WEBSTER, *Chairman.*

37. Rome

Data furnished by Superintendent of Schools.

The population of Rome is about 23,000, 6,000 of whom are Italians and Poles. Most of these foreigners are employed in the brass and copper industries.

The only Americanization work being done in Rome, in fact the only facilities available to adult foreigners, is by the Y. M. C. A.

38. Schenectady

Data furnished by Superintendent of Schools.

I. What is the population of your city? 100,000.

II. What is the foreign population, divided as to nationality? This information concerning the whole population is not available. Attached is the result of the school census of 1917, which may be of interest.

II. What are the leading industries? Locomotive building and manufacturing of electrical goods.

IV. What are the leading industries in which foreigners are employed? Locomotive building, manufacturing of electrical goods and railroads.

V. Do any of the industries conduct classes for teaching English, American history, civil government, etc., for their foreign-born employees? Yes. General Electric Company in co-operation with the public schools.

VI. What public school facilities are open to foreign-born adults for learning English, American history, civil government, etc.? Afternoon and evening classes in the public schools.

VII. How many students of the various nationalities attend public schools? About 450 at the present time.

VIII. Is the attendance regular? So far very good.

IX. What is the average age of adult alien students? About 28 years.

X. How many hours per week do the courses cover? From 2 hours to 6 hours.

XI. Is there any movement in your city to "Americanize" foreigners? None other than conducted by the schools.

XII. By whom is it conducted? Public schools.

XIII. What are your requirements for teachers of adult foreigners? We employ regular teachers who have attended and completed Americanization Institute courses.

XIV. What salary do you think should be offered to attract teachers? From $3 to $4 for two hours if they have had the above training.

COUNTRIES OF BIRTH OF SCHENECTADY'S 1,409 FOREIGN-BORN CHILDREN, SCHOOL CENSUS 1917

Italy	485
Russia	260
Poland	133
England	118
Austria	109
Scotland	78
Germany	58
Hungary	48
Canada	34
Ireland	17
Seventeen other countries	69
	1,409

SCHENECTADY CHILDREN 4 TO 18 YEARS OF AGE

Native-born, per cent	93
Foreign-born, per cent	7

B. H. Friss, investigator in the industrial service department of the General Electric Company submitted the following report:

GENERAL ELECTRIC COMPANY — SCHENECTADY WORKS
Employees on Factory Payroll January 1, 1920

Country of Birth	Men	Women	Total
United States	9,307	2,015	11,322
Afghanistan	1	....	1
Argentina	3	....	3
Armenia	4	....	4
Australia	3	....	3
Austria	301	50	351
Belgium	6	....	6
Bohemia	77	11	88
Brazil	6	....	6
Canada	232	27	259
Columbia	1	....	1
Chile	2	....	2
China	4	....	4
Cuba	3	....	3
Dutch Guiana	1	....	1
Denmark	82	7	89
England	419	35	454
France	35	2	37
Finland	7	....	7
Germany	573	36	609
Greece	6	....	6
Hungary	225	8	233
India	4	....	4
Italy	1,919	169	2,088
Ireland	268	35	303
Japan	7	....	7
Lithuania	18	4	22
Malta	7	....	7
Netherlands	12	1	13
New Zealand	5	1	6
Norway	24	3	27
Peru	1	....	1
Poland	1,066	221	1,287
Portugal	1	....	1
Rumania	4	1	5
Russia	182	37	219
Scotland	215	20	235
Spain	32	....	32
Sweden	83	7	90
Switzerland	47	2	49
Syria	1	....	1
Turkey	2	....	2
Uruguay	1	....	1
Wales	17	6	23
West Indies	1	1	2
Africa	4	....	4
Totals	15,219	2,699	17,918

39. Solvay

Letter from R. B. Kelley, Superintendent of Schools, November 22, 1919.

"With the co-operation of the Solvay Process Company, we are conducting factory classes five days a week at 8:15 A. M., 2:15 and 4:15 P. M., and with the Holcomb Steel Co. four days a week at 4:15 P. M. The sessions are an hour and a quarter long. Each man has two classes a week and in the Process Company's school attends an additional session on alternate weeks.

"The companies provide the schoolrooms, light, heat, books and pay the men for part of their time. The school district pays the teachers.

"The men, mainly Italian, Polish, Austrian and Spanish, ranging in ages from 20 to 45 are graded according to ability and previous education. Based upon this classification, we are conducting six classes in English for beginners, twelve for intermediate beginners and two for advanced students.

"In addition to the factory classes, we have two classes which meet three nights a week in our regular evening school from 7 to 9.

"At present, we have a total enrollment of 413, with an average daily attendance of 142. Eleven women teachers, mainly primary, are employed. This tends to remove any suspicions that might exist.

"We feel that out program is working in a most satisfactory manner."

40. Syracuse

Data furnished by Superintendent of Schools.

The population of Syracuse is about 150,000 — no figures on foreigners.

We have about 400 adult foreigners in our public schools. Their attendance is regular. The average age is about 25. We have eight night schools besides classes in several churches and factories. We pay teachers $2 per night for half hour sessions.

41. Tonawanda

Data furnished by Frank K. Sutley, Superintendent of Schools.

The population is about 10,000. We have less than 500 foreigners, mostly Hungarian. There are only 131 children of foreign parents in our schools. Most of the foreigners work in the steel plant.

We have no night schools for adult foreigners. A survey made a year or two ago showed only eleven persons in Tonawanda who might attend such a school. We have no great problem in this city.

Letter from Charles W. Ward, Secretary, Chamber of Commerce of the Tonawandas, November 25, 1919:

"Our organization has an Americanization Committee on which are also representatives of the Woman's Civic Club and the Church Federation of this city.

"After making a considerable study of the subject our committee is of the opinion that cursory and occasional Americanization work conducted by volunteer workers is of little value and may even do harm if not tactfully conducted.

"We have, therefore, confined our work largely to co-operating with and supporting the work of the School Board in the maintenance of an effective night school to which foreigners are encouraged to go. As a result of this co-operation, or at least partly attributable to it, the night school in North Tonawanda had a record attendance last year and that attendance is exceeded this year.

"As a result of the sentiment for Americanization created in this community by our committee last year, the largest factory in town, the Buffalo Bolt Co., employing about a thousand people, about 250 or 300 of whom are foreigners, chiefly Polish, and in need of Americanization work, has organized definite Americanization work and employed for the work a young woman who was particularly successful in our night school work last year. This work, we are informed, is progressing very satisfactorily indeed.

"The County Clerk is now compiling and has promised to furnish us in a few days the names and addresses of all North Tonawanda aliens who have made application for citizenship and he has promised to furnish us such lists from time to time. It is the purpose of our committee to get acquainted with all these prospective citizens, encourage them to follow out their citizenship purpose, and to encourage their friends and neighbors to become citizens.

"Our committee is just now considering lending co-operation to our Y. M. C. A. and our Y. W. C. A. to the end that each may employ an Americanization worker.

"Practically all our work is done in North Tonawanda, although our organization represents and is supported by

Tonawanda as well. It happens, however, that there are a very few foreigners in Tonawanda while there are a great many in North Tonawanda.

"We trust that we have here given a satisfactory response to your letter of the 19th inst., and we assure you that we shall be glad to lend any possible co-operation to your committee in the furtherance of this good work."

42. Troy

Data furnished by Superintendent of Schools.

The population of Troy is about 78,000 and the foreign part of it is divided as follows:

Italians	3,000
Germans	3,000
Poles	300
Others	200
Total	6,500

Most of the foreigners are employed in the collar industry. We have fifty foreigners in our night schools, but their attendance is not regular. They average about 35 years. We require that teachers take an Americanization course and we pay them the same as other teachers.

43. Utica

Data furnished by John R. DeCamp, Superintendent of Schools.

The population of Utica is about 94,000, and one-third of it is foreign. The textile, metal and building trades take most of the foreign labor. There are no factory classes. We have 225 adult foreigners in the night schools. Their attendance is regular. Their average age is 25 years.

Letter from John R. DeCamp, Superintendent of Schools, November 11, 1919:

"There has been formed here recently the Americanization Council of Utica.

"We adopted for our constitution and by-laws the constitution and by-laws of the Albany Council.

"About sixty different societies were invited to the meeting at which this council was formed. I suppose that practically all these societies will become members of the Utica Council."

44. Watertown

Letter from Frank S. Tisdale, Superintendent of Schools, October 29, 1919:

"Population of the city of Watertown is 34,000.

"Foreign population of the city is between two and three thousand, of which one-half are Italians, one-fourth Roumanians and one-fourth Polacks.

"The leading industries are New York Air Brake Company; paper manufacturing mills; Bagley & Sewall, manufacturers of paper making machinery; silk mills, etc.

"The leading industries in which foreigners are employed are railroads, New York Air Brake Co. and paper mills.

"None of the above-mentioned industries conduct classes for their foreign-born employees.

"We have four evening schools for foreign-born adults, for learning English, American history and the elementary subjects.

"We usually have an enrollment of from 60 to 100 adult foreigners who attend these evening schools.

"The attendance is reasonably regular.

"The average age of adult evening students is about twenty.

"The number of hours per week covered by the courses is six.

"There was a movement last year 'to Americanize foreigners' which was conducted by the State Department of Education.

"Teachers of adult foreigners must be possessed of a valid certificate which would entitle them to teach in the public schools of the state.

"We have paid teachers $2 for each evening's work. Another year when we commence the continuation school work it will likely be necessary to increase this rate.

"In my opinion the night schools offer the best methods of educating our foreign population. This work should be conducted under the direction of the Board of Education. In addition to this I think a course of free lectures on American history with perhaps some good moving pictures on American history would be helpful.

"When you get down to the real question of accomplishing results, the education of the foreign-born child is the most important factor. Evening classes in domestic science for women might also be helpful."

45. Watervliet

Data furnished by Hugh H. Lansing, Superintendent of Schools.

The population of Watervliet is about 16,000, including 3,500 foreigners, mostly Poles and Italians. Most of the foreigners are employed by the Malleable Iron Works, West Side Foundry and D. & H. Shops. I understand they do not conduct any factory classes.

We have no educational facilities for adult foreigners at the present time. I have urged the Board of Education for the past four years to establish such schools and hope in the near future with the assistance of the State Education Department to have such a school open where foreign-born adults may be taught English, American history, civil government and become thoroughly Americanized.

Recently the local Red Cross has aided greatly in this movement to get night schools established for adult foreigners.

46. White Plains

Data furnished by Superintendent of Schools.

The population of White Plains is about 22,000, 20 per cent. of whom are Italians. No other nationalities are prominently represented.

We have 187 foreigners in our night schools. The attendance is not regular. The average age is 24.

At present the evening school teachers are for the most part selected from the day school list and we have had no experience with special teachers for this work.

47. Yonkers

Data furnished by Charles E. Gorton, Superintendent of Schools.

The population of Yonkers is about 100,000, 33,000 of which is foreign. We have 10,000 Italians, 10,000 Slavs and Poles, and the rest are Armenians, Russians, Greeks, etc.

The sugar refineries, hat shops and carpet shops take most of the foreign labor. There are no factory classes.

We have 300 foreigners in our night schools and they attend fairly regularly. They average 25 years.

Many of our teachers have had special Americanization training under the State Department of Education. We pay them $4 per evening.

Letter from Charles E. Gorton, Superintendent of Schools, November 14, 1919:

"Many of the figures given in this report are estimates but I think they are pretty nearly accurate.

"We have made a great effort to bring foreigners into the schools where we have every facility for teaching them English, civil government and American ideas but we fail to secure anything like the attendance we ought to have. We have tried also to establish classes outside of the school but have not succeeded in getting classes large enough to justify the expense of their maintenance. The state agents are working here now and report to me weekly but so far have not accomplished much.

"As the result of many years of experience and observation, I am convinced that there is only one way to Americanize these foreigners and that is to allow them a limited time after they reach this country to learn English, secure a knowledge of our laws and institutions and secure papers of citizenship, and if they do not take these steps within the allotted time they ought to be deported."

Letter from J. J. Eaton, Director of Industrial Arts, Department of Education, November 20, 1919:

"In reply to your recent inquiry for information regarding the work of this school in the education of adult foreigners, I am pleased to state that for the last ten years we have had an evening trade school, of which the attendance is largely foreign. These foreigners are attracted to the school by the trades which are offered, particularly machine shop, plumbing, electricity, sewing, millinery, mathematics and drawing. Up until the last two years a large number came for carpentry, but owing to the depression of building trades in this section the popularity of that work has fallen off.

"In my opinion this evening school is one of the greatest socialized factors maintained by the Board of Education. We endeavor to co-operate with the general High School of the city which makes a special effort to bring the academic side of education to the notice of the foreigners, and has been, I think, quite successful.

"While we make no special effort to teach academic subjects, many have been led to appreciate their value and have taken steps to avail themselves of the opportunity offered.

by the Board of Education through the interests that have been aroused by their work in the shops in this school.

"We estimate that in most of the courses about half of the enrollment are distinctly foreigners. We find the average age is 22, and of the nationalities represented I might mention the Italian, Greek, Slav, Polish, Hungarian, and Jewish as predominating. They are for the most part earnest and interested in their work and fairly regular in their attendance. Of these of course are special cases which are notable in their progress, and in some cases these especially interested pupils have made arrangements to attend the day school part of the time. We have kept no special statistics, but as these foreigners have presented themselves for any particular work we have endeavored in every way to make our program flexible enough to permit them to secure the work that they wished."

CHAPTER V

Public Schools of New York City

1. List of Evening Schools

New York Evening High School for Men	10th Ave. & 59th St.
Harlem Evening High School	116th St. bet. Lenox & 5th Aves.
East Side Evening High School	Rivington & Forsyth.
New York Evening High School for Women	Irving Place, 16th & 17th Sts.
Harlem Evening High School for Women	114th St. bet. 7th & 8th Aves.
Seward Park Evening High School	Hester, Essex & Norfolk Sts.
Washington Heights Evening High School	145th & 146th Sts., West of Amsterdam Ave.
Morris Evening High School	166th St. & Boston Rd.
Bronx Evening High School	Prospect Ave., Jennings St. & Ritter Place.
Brooklyn Evening High School	Marcy & Putnam Aves. & Madison St.
Eastern Evening High School	Harrison Ave. & Heyward St.
Central Evening High School	Nostrand Ave. & Halsey St.
Williamsburg Evening High School	Marcy Ave., Rodney & Keap Sts.
New Lots Evening High School	Sutton Ave., Vermont & Wyona Sts.
Bay Ridge Evening High School	4th Ave., 67th & Senator Sts.
Long Island City Evening High School	Wilbur Ave. & Academy St.
Curtis Evening High School	St. Marks Place, New Brighton, S. I.

Harlem Evening Trade School.... 138th & 139th Sts., West of 5th Ave.
New York Evening School of Industrial Art .... 202–14 East 42d St.
Murray Hill Evening School...... 237 East 37th St.
Stuyvesant Evening Trade School.. 15th & 16th Sts. near 1st Ave.
Brooklyn Evening Technical and Trade School .... Seventh Ave. bet 4th & 5th Sts.
Long Island City Evening High and Trade School .... Wilbur Ave. & Academy St.
Tottenville Evening Trade School.. Academy Place, Tottenville, S. I.
Bushwick Evening Trade School... 400 Irving Ave.
Manhattan Trade School for Girls. 127 E. 22d St.
Evander Childes High School..... 2493 Valentine Ave., Bronx.

Manhattan

P. S. 2......................	116 Henry St.
4......................	203 Rivington St.
14......................	225 East 27th St.
16......................	208 West 13th St.
19......................	344 West 14th St.
25......................	330 5th St.
27......................	41st & 42d St., East of Third Ave.
29......................	Albany, Washington & Carlisle St.
32......................	357 West 35th St.
40......................	310–320 East 20th St.
42......................	Hester, Orchard & Ludlow St.
45......................	225 West 24th St.
58......................	317 West 52d St.
59......................	226 East 57th St.
67......................	120 West 46th St.
70......................	207 East 75th St.
71......................	188 7th St.
72......................	Lexington Ave., 105th St.

Manhattan — Continued

83	216 E. 110th St.
89	Lenox Ave., 134th & 135th Sts.
93	Amsterdam Ave., 93d St.
95	West Houston & Clarkson Sts., bet. Varick & Hudson Sts.
96	Ave. A. & 81st St.
103	119th St., & Madison Ave.
109	99th St. near 3d Ave.
147	Henry & Gouverneur St.
157	St. Nicholas Ave. & 127 St.
160	Rivington & Suffolk Sts.

Bronx
P. S.

3	157th St., East of Courtlandt Ave.
6	Tremont, Bryant & Vyse Aves., West Farms.
10	Eagle Ave. & 163d St.
42	Washington & Wendover Ave.
43	Brown Pl. 135th & 136th St.
45	189 W. and Hoffman Sts. and Lorillard Place.
54	Intervale Ave. & Freeman St.

Brooklyn
P. S.

5	Tillary, Bridge & Lawrence Sts.
13	Degraw St. near Hicks St.
15	Third Ave., State & Schermerhorn St.
40	15th St. near 4th Ave.
45	Lafayette near Classon Ave.
50	So. 3d St. & Driggs Ave.
64	Berriman St. Belmont & Atkins Ave.
92	Rogers Ave. & Robinson St.
112	15th Ave & 71st St.

Brooklyn — Continued

120	Barren Island
114	Remsen Ave. near Ave. F. Canarsie
123	Irving & Willoughby Ave. & Suydam St.
126	Meserole Ave. Lorimer & Guernsey St.
136	4th Ave. 40th & 41st Sts.
141	Leonard, McKibbin & Boerum St.
145	Central Ave. & Noll St.
147	Bushwick Ave. Seigel & McKibbin St.
148	Ellery & Hopkins St. near Delmonico Place.
150	Christopher Ave. & Sackman St.
164	14th Ave. 42d & 43d St.

Queens

P. S. 6	Steinway Ave. near Jamaica Ave., Long Island City.
13	Chicago Ave. & Irving Ave., Elmhurst.
20	Broadway & Whitestone Ave., Flushing.
27	13th St. & 1st Ave., College Point, L. I.
39	State St. & Roanoke Ave. Far Rockaway
47	Hillside & Union Ave., Jamaica.
58	Walker & Grafton Ave. Woodhaven.
83	Vernon Ave. bet. Pierce & Graham Ave., Long Island City.
88	Elm Ave. & Fresh Pond Rd., Ridgewood Heights
90	Napier Ave. near Jamaica Ave., Richmond Hill.

Richmond

P. S. 14	Broad & Brook St. Stapleton, S. I.
20	Heverton Ave., Port Richmond.

List of Evening School Annexes

Educational Alliance, 196 E. Broadway, New York City	E. S. 2 Man.
Hamilton House, 72 Market St., New York City	E. S. 2 Man.
Armenian Colonial Assn., 115 East 24th St., New York City	E. S. 14 Man.
Hannah Lavenberg Home, 319 E. 17th St., New York City	E. S. 40 Man.
St. Joachims Church, 26 Roosevelt St., New York City	E. S. 31 Man.
Greenwich House, 29 Barrow St., New York City	E. S. 38 Man.
Richmond Hill House, 28 McDougal St., New York City	E. S. 38 Man.
Lenox Hill Settlement, 511 E. 69th St., New York City	E. S. 70 Man.
St. Colomba Lyceum, West 25th St., bet. 8th & 9th Aves	E. S. 45 Man.
Cozani Society, 953 Second Ave., New York City	E. S. 59 Man.
Council of Jewish Women, 79 St. Mark's Place, New York City	E. S. 71 Man.
Young Women's Assn. 110th St., near 5th Ave., New York City	E. S. 83 Man.
East Side Settlement, 76th St., East River, New York City	E. S. 96 Man.
Emanuel Sisterhood, Personal Service, 318 E. 82d St., New York City	E. S. 96 Man.
Welfare of Jewish Deaf, 40–44 West 115th St., New York City	E. S. 103.
Federation Settlement, 236–240 E. 105th St., New York City	E. S. 109 Man.

Hartley House, 313 W. 46th St., New York City .... E. S. 58 Man.
Henry Street Settlement, 265 Henry St., New York City.......... E. S. 147 Man.
Syrian Community Center, 203 Clinton St., Brooklyn, N. Y.... E. S. 45 Brooklyn.
School Settlement, 120 Jackson St., Brooklyn, N. Y.............. E. S. 126 Brooklyn.
Greenpoint Neighborhood House, 185 Java St., Brooklyn, N. Y... E. S. 126 Brooklyn.
Eastern District Branch, Young Men's Christian Assn., Marcy Ave., near Broadway, Brooklyn, N. Y. .... E. S. 141 Brooklyn.
Hebrew Rd. Society, Hopkinson & Sutter Aves., Brooklyn, N. Y.... E. S. 144 Brooklyn.
Church of Our Lady of Pomposi, 225 Siegel St., Brooklyn, N. Y.. E. S. 145 Brooklyn.
Our Lady of Mt. Carmel, 627 E. 187th St. Bronx.............. E. S. 42 Bronx.
St. Philip Meri, 3076 Villa Ave., Bronx .... E. S. 42 Bronx.
Woodstock Library, 759 E. 160th St., Bronx .... E. S. 10 Bronx.
Montefiore Home & Hospital, Gun Hill Road (E. 210th St.) near Jerome Ave., Bronx........... E. S. 45 Bronx.
No. 90 Queens, Napier & Jamaica Aves., Queens .... E. S. 52 Queens.
St. Leonard's Church, Hamburg & Jefferson Sts., Brooklyn, N. Y... E. S. 145 Brooklyn.
Chelsea Neighborhood Assn., 240 W. 23d St., New York City.... E. S. 45 Man.
Young Women's Christian Assn., 575 Bedford Ave., Brooklyn, N. Y. .... E. S. 141 Brooklyn.
Our Lady of Mt. Carmel, 627 E. 187th St., Bronx............. E. S. 45 Bronx.
St. Philip Neri, 3076 Villa Ave., Bronx .... E. S. 45 Bronx.
Greenwich Settlement House, 29 Barrow St., New York City.... E. S. 95 Man.

Public Schools of New York City 2629

Hudson Guild, 426-438 West 27th St., New York City...........	E. S. 45 Man.
The Central Jewish Institute, 125 E. 85th St., New York City....	E. S. 77 Man.
Montefiore Home and Hospital, Gun Hill Road near Jerome Ave., New York City	E. S. 45 Bronx.
Training School for Nurses, Norwegian Hospital, Brooklyn, N. Y.	E. S. 136 Brooklyn.
Bush Terminal Branch Young Women's Christian Assn., 40th St. & 2d Ave., Brooklyn, N. Y...	E. S. 136 Brooklyn.
Mt. Olivet Presbyterian Church, Evergreen Ave., Cor. of Troutman St., Brooklyn, N. Y...........	E. S. 136 Brooklyn.
E. S. 64 Manhattan.............	Stuyvesant Evening Trade School.
Clara de Hirsch Home, 225 E. 63d St., New York City...........	New York Evening High School.
Wright-Aircraft Corp., Long Island City, L. I., N. Y..............	E. S. 6 Queens.
No. 150 (Brooklyn Ladies Garments Poynts, etc.).................	New Lots Evening High School.
E. E. S. 40 Manhattan...........	New York Evening High School for Women.
Wright-Aircraft Corp., Long Island City, L. I., N. Y..............	Long Island City Evening High and Trade School.
Geo. Bruce Public Library, 78 Manhattan St., New York City.....	New York Evening High School of Industrial Arts
Epiphany Branch of the New York Library (Public), 228 East 23d St., New York City...........	New York Evening High School of Industrial Arts
Madison Square Church House, 432 -436 3d Ave., Cor. of 30th St., New York City...............	E. S. 40 Man.
P. S. 64 Manhattan.............	E. S. 25 Man.

Bush Terminal Branch of the Y. W. C. A. 2d Ave. & 40th St., Brooklyn, N. Y. .... E. E. S. 136 Brooklyn.

Knights of Columbus Hut, Ft. Hamilton, Brooklyn, N. Y. ..... Bay Ridge Evening High School, Brooklyn, N. Y.

United Club, N. Y. League of Women Workers, 35 East 30th St., New York City. .... N. Y. Evening High School for Women.

Greenwich House, 27 Barrow St., New York City. .... New York Evening High School for Men.

P. S. 54, The Bronx. .... Morris Evening High School.

Naval Training Station, Pelham Bay Park, N. Y. .... Morris Evening High School.

Young Men's Hebrew Assn. of Bath Beach, Cropsey & 20th Ave., Brooklyn, N. Y. .... E. S. 136 Brooklyn.

P. S. 3 Manhattan. .... New York Evening High School for Men.

P. S. 63 Manhattan. .... East Side Evening High School for Men.

Young Men's Hebrew Assn., Bay 24th St. & Cropsey Ave., Bath Beach, Brooklyn, N. Y. .... Bay Ridge Evening High School.

P. S. 171 Manhattan. .... E. S. 83 Man.
P. S. 91 Manhattan. .... E. S. 160 Man.

Beth Israel Hospital, Monroe, Jefferson & Cherry Sts., New York City .... E. S. Evening High School for Women.

Settlement and Church of All Nations 9 2d Ave., New York City .... E. S. 25 Man.

Pallatine Sisters of Charity, 250–254 East 112th St., New York City .... E. S. 157 Man.

White Door Settlement, 211 Clinton
  St., New York City............ E. S. 4 Man.
E. S. 13 Manhattan............. E. S. 4 Man.
Building on Union Ave. near Stagg
  St., Brooklyn................. P. S. 117 Brooklyn.
E. S. 20 Richmond.............. Curtis Evening High School.
U. S. A. Debarkation No. 3, 18th
  St. & 6th Ave., New York City.. New York Evening High School for Men.
Educational Alliance............ P. S. 7 Man.
Church of Seigillum Eccl. St.
  Maria Angelorum.............. E. S. 50 Brooklyn.

2. Testimony of School Officials

On January 19, 1920, the morning session of the Committee's public hearing was devoted to five representatives of the New York City public school system, who outlined the activities of the public schools in the work of immigrant education and citizenship training. Their testimonies, in substance, follow.

Mr. WILLIAM McANDREW, *Associate Superintendent of Schools, in Charge of the Division of Extension Activities*

The division of Extension Activities includes the night schools, the vacation schools, summer playgrounds, lectures, community centers, public forums, libraries, visual instruction, stereopticons and moving picture service.

We have coming under our influence the regular school children in the vacation schools and in the athletic centers in the afternoon; the older youth who have left school in our vicinity schools; the young employed people who according to law come to us for four hours a week; foreign-born adults who are in employment who come voluntarily for such classes as we have in settlements, halls and factories; and the general public through the forums and in the lectures and through the library influence.

The bulk of the foreign-born adults who live in districts where they hear no English rarely go to an Americanization meeting, or to any American affair, or rarely come into the schoolhouse, and they are practically untouched by any educational movement in the city.

It seems to me that the Legislature of our State and other States ought to complete the original educational program of the country. I am very much impressed by the fact that the men who established America, who wrote the Constitution for, as they said, the "establishment of a more perfect union and for the general welfare," had a clear idea as to how the Americanization of succeeding generations was to be taken care of — because I find, as you will have found, that Washington and Franklin and John Adams, and notably Jefferson, specifically state in their letters and their essays and their speeches, that the only way that the American idea can be preserved is by educating all the people. And that thing comes down through Webster and Lincoln, down to our own day, as an essential part of the American scheme: that the government by the people cannot be preserved in its original purity unless all the people are educated in citizenship. And we never completed the scheme; we neglected it for years and years; it was not until along about 1880 that there was any considerable number of compulsory educational laws requiring even the young children to go to school. That is pretty generally taken care of now in all northern states. In our State, as you know, the law requires children to go to school until they are fourteen, then, unless they are lawfully employed, to go to school until they are sixteen. But it is not now from the children under fourteen, or from the children that are lawfully employed, that the danger to our institutions comes — we have taken care of that. It does seem to me as though, to make the thing logically complete, the government ought to be sure that the whole residential population is instructed in what the American Constitution is, what its advantages are, what its imperfections are and the orderly method of curing them.

In a crisis the government will insist that everybody of a designated age is instructed in military science. In a crisis the government will insist that those who are a menace to our peace here will be deported. That is to protect us largely from foreign enemies — but we now need protection from enemies within our borders who prey upon the ignorance of our large numbers of people. And the way to meet that danger, it seems to me, is by extending compulsory education to all those who are now a menace to our American institutions.

Your Committee could recommend a census by which such persons could be discovered. The experience of the draft boards has shown you how effective questionnaires are. Your Committee could suggest measures by which these people will be educated in the duties and privileges of American citizenship. In this city the Department of Education has the physical plant to take care of these people. There are school buildings enough to take care of all the foreign population, the un-American population, between five o'clock in the evening and six o'clock, every day; but there are no funds for the heating and lighting of the buildings now; there are no funds for the payment of the teachers, and at the present time there are not enough teachers skilled in educating Americans to take care of that. So the Committee's recommendations might properly cover provisions for the training of teachers to educate foreigners. But, if that were done, you could rely upon modern educational theories to see that the teaching was done with all intelligence, enthusiasm and interest that marked the educational efforts to keep up the morale of our troops abroad — a combination of interest, amusement, attractions, etc.

Our school buildings exist in the largest numbers in the very districts where they are needed. They are more numerous per square mile in the lower east side of the city than anywhere else. There are large buildings containing from thirty to fifty classrooms each. By using these buildings every evening in the week, 1,000 foreign-born could be taken care of, and in some of the larger buildings, 4,000. Even more could be accommodated if classes were held in the late afternoon from five to six as well as in the evening.

I believe that courses in citizenship training in our extension schools should include instruction in the rights and duties of the American citizen, and an interesting history of the reasons why our government is in the form that it is. There are appropriate text books for this work already in existence. There should also be included lessons on the meaning of naturalization and specific help to the foreign-born in getting their papers. Official help from naturalization officers would be acceptable. There are many complaints now that the obtaining of final citizenship papers is accompanied by negative influences that discourage many applicants who would make good citizens, and the idea of American welcome into citizenship is not very strongly pressed. Also the hours are inconvenient and the delays seem to the applicants unnecessary.

Courses of instruction are given by the City Department of Education to the foreign-born employees of such factories as will assist. I feel that there should be a specific requirement by law that would enable the state to have these Americanization classes in the factory wherever men in sufficient numbers to form a class are employed. It would be to the interest of the employer as well as to the interest of the commonwealth at large. Just now there is not a sufficient disposition on the part of employers to allow their time to be used for educational purposes. It would be desirable to have four hours a week devoted to educational work in the factory classes. I think that the employer out of his general interest in the public welfare ought to contribute that much time. He would really save the time in increased efficiency and in the reduction of the amount of waste, breakage and spoilage and the number of accidents which would follow.

Factory courses should include instruction which would give an understanding of what our government by the people is; an understanding of what its system is of working through orderly majorities; an understanding of what we call the greatness of America as a country and its advantages; and then in connection with all this such instruction in English and in vocational or industrial work as will lead the worker to take a more intelligent interest in what he is doing and to realize the advantage to himself as well as to the country in general of intelligent labor. I would show how we would die of thirst or starve to death if we did not have the service given us here by an organized government, and make it clear that the duty of every one of us as a man requires us to support orderly common welfare, which is the American government.

The men who made the American government provided for an orderly change of it. We change the national government every four years, the state government in less time, and the city government in even less time, and it is our duty in teaching the foreign-born who hear the soap box orators to show them that when they claim that this is a government of tyranny and so on they are talking nonsense, for this government is just what you and I and the rest of us in the largest part want it to be.

WILLIAM L. ETTINGER, *Superintendent of Schools*

I think that the New York City public schools have been doing all that it is possible to do along positive Americanization lines, consistent with the appropriation which they have had, and with the facilities at their command.

You know the problem of Americanization has not been considered a national problem, and it is the result of that policy that is producing these results which we are trying now to correct or avoid.

Formerly the problem of Americanization was left to the different cities through which the stream of immigration came, and of course, New York being the chief port of entry, it had to shoulder the entire problem.

One of the greatest factors in its educational budget has been the fact that a great many of these immigrants passing through this port stopped here, became residents of the city, making this city in some respects and in some regions large transplanted foreign cities, larger than any actual foreign cities of the same group and type of nationality, so that we have probably the largest Italian city in the world, the largest Russian city, and so on.

Now, the city had to take these foreigners and educate their children. Then it dawned upon the educational authorities that educating the children alone was not sufficient and the educational facilities were extended to the adults. We established classes in evening schools for adults; we established classes in the afternoon for adults who were employed in the evening; we established classes in factories wherever we could persuade the employer to give of his time, the educational authorities furnishing the teacher and the equipment or supplies. We established classes for teaching citizenship to women, foreign women, in the public schools in the neighborhood in which these foreign women reside. These women not being able to attend the evening schools on account of bringing up families, we brought them into the afternoon schools for a short time. And we established, of course, community centers throughout the city. Now, we have about 10,000 foreign-born adults in our evening school classes, and we have, I should say, about 1,000 in our day school classes. The extent to which we have been able to carry this work is evidenced by a comparison between that number and the bulk of the foreign population.

Now, when all that is done, if we are to take care of future incoming foreign population by means of education, your Americanization problem as far as education is concerned, in the final analysis, rests upon your day schools. It is the child in the day school who bears the message of Americanization to the foreign home and these people that you reach in the evening schools must be also considered in relation to the great number that you reach through the three or four hundred thousand children of foreign-born parentage who come daily to our elementary schools.

A parent comes here from the foreign shore with his own custom, with his own language, foreign ideals, he is out of tune with this environment. It is probable, very probable, that he has not met with a very cordial reception when he came here, that probably he has been exploited, sometimes by those more sophisticated of his own race, and the consequence is he looks with a little suspicion upon our institutions. His children go to school: that is a great thing for him because he realizes the lack of educational opportunities on the other side of the water. He becomes tremendously interested. He is probably not able to speak the language, but the child masters the language very readily, and in a short time — you would be surprised to know how short a time — this child, fresh from the steamer, is able to read the newspaper. He is very proud of that child. The child acts as an educational agency in the home and that country which gives those opportunities to the child is good enough country for him, the parent, and I think that instead of lecturing to these people and trying to instruct them in citizenship, in every public school where we have an auditorium we ought to have lectures for those people accompanied by their children. You would educate them against such doctrines as they hear in their daily contact with their companions of the factory, and there would be no danger of Bolshevism in those districts. We are going to start a program of that kind, if we can get the money.

The whole organization of our public schools makes for teaching children an habitual respect for the law through the discipline that is required in the schools, the discipline through the assemblies, the discipline in the high schools through what are called socialized recitations, by the assemblies at which sometimes the children carry on the program, the monitorial system where there is an election system, where elections are held by the pupils. I recall when I was a pupil in the elementary school, the children throughout the different classes elected a class president. The class president looked after all cases of discipline when the teacher was out of the class-room. The monitors in the different classes elected their chief and subchiefs for the work of discipline on the stairs, in the yards and the streets. All this, of course, makes for Americanization. The opportunities for service which have been taken advantage of by the schools during the past few years have been great factors to that end. The Liberty Loans, for example, and such a simple matter as the war chest fund. The children themselves collected about $780,000. All of these things are living lessons of respect for law and order.

In former years immigrants who have landed here have been taken in charge by people of their own race, work has been obtained for them and a sort of padrone system has been established. To a great extent that is a thing of the past, but we are still suffering from those sins of the past. Where a foreigner has been exploited by those of his own nationality on his arrival here and has some sort of grievance, the only way to cure it is gradually through contact with his fellow citizens by showing that this thing was not the fault of the government but a fault in the character of his compatriot.

There is one thing that this Committee should realize, and that is that you cannot legislate citizenship into a race of people.

We have at the entrance to the educational system a Board of Examiners and to this Board of Examiners is entrusted the function of giving us teachers. All of the candidates for license must pass through the hands of this Board of Examiners. Of course we demand evidences of citizenship. Candidates must also take a pledge of loyalty. That is about all we can do in that respect, excepting that I think the Board of Examiners could devise probably more stringent tests in order to find out whether the applicant is 100 per cent. American. We could have a test as to opinions, as to convictions. I know that it looks inquisitorial, open to criticism, but, after all, the teacher is the answer to this question of citizenship training throughout this entire country. The proper kind of teacher means the proper kind of Americanization, and you cannot be too careful in selecting your teacher. Now, that involves, of course, finding out the convictions of these teachers with respect to certain mooted problems. A teacher who believes, for instance, in that type of Socialism which calls for revolution, which calls for the destruction of existing government in order to impose something which is nebulous in his own mind upon the ruins, is not the type of teacher to have in our schools. It does not make any difference whether he is teaching arithmetic or something else, that teacher cannot sincerely teach what we require the teacher to teach in the way of obedience to government, respect for institutions, respect for the flag and all the other patriotic observances. We have had teachers, but very few, I am proud to say, among the 23,000 in New York City, who thought that it did not make any difference what they said or did in the afternoon or evening, on the public platform, or what they wrote in the public press, provided they did not do anything overt in the class-room between nine and three o'clock. Now, we have stopped that, I hope, and have established the fact that the teacher is always a teacher and that everything that teacher gives utterance to after three o'clock is a reflex action on that class-room, just as much as if he stood in front of his class.

The teacher, being the crux of the situation, I think there is one kind of legislation which would be very effective; that is, legislation which gives adequate salaries throughout the state.

As to the securing of the type of teacher which is needed in the public schools. I think a campaign of education ought to be entered upon. After all, the teachers' lot is not such a hard lot as compared with other lines of work. The trouble is that there has been no propaganda with respect to the advantages of teaching, that might be termed self-respect for one's own calling and the pleasure in one's own work. The teacher's work is so important and the fruits of teaching are so satisfactory that there is a great deal of self-satisfaction on the part of a teacher. Of course that is not all that is required. If, joined to that, you pay the teacher an adequate salary I think that you will probably attract a superior type of teacher and a greater number of teachers into the profession.

For the teaching of English to foreigners, and civics, history, etc., I should say that a good, strong, upstanding American youth or woman, with a college graduate's experience or training, with satisfactory references, and able to stand the test of Americanism, would be all that could be desired.

I would have the same standard of education as for teachers in day schools, but not the same test of knowledge; in other words we must distinguish between those two. An examination is a test of mental equipment, so to speak; it is a test of the actual knowledge of the candidate. Now, there may be some with a great deal more knowledge of a different type; there may be some with a greater range of experience along lines of knowledge, who would not be able to pass the examination that an applicant for License No. 1 would pass, because that is a particular type that we demand.

When you talk of permitting teachers to be licensed without being placed on an eligible list and undergoing an examination, you are said to interfere with the "merit system;" I think in this emergency that, provided the persons responsible, at the top, have a strong conviction of the sanctity of their work and are able to judge personality, you need not be afraid of any interference with the merit system.

I think that any contemplated State legislation should furnish a sufficient amount of money to cover a progressive educational program. Secondly, such legislation as would enable you to select your teachers without too much rigidity; and also legislation that would enable you to establish classes for the training of these teachers after you have obtained them.

I am not a pessimist in this thing at all. As I say, I think the great bulk of Americanization work being done now is being done effectively, notwithstanding statistics or anything else. You can give me the statistics about the numbers coming in, and about the numbers not being able to speak English, and the numbers of probably a few thousands of reds that have been taken in a dragnet — that does not mean the bulk of Americanization work is futile. There is the Americanization work that might be termed the remedial work; that is, we take those who come over and we try to make them new. Then there is the Americanization work that is preventive work; that is, we must Americanize not only those who are born here, but those who have been here — Americans sometimes need Americanization. The trouble is that our ideals, until the war, have been too material and the foreigner probably has got the same impression that a great many Americans have had: That this was a great big till that anybody could put his hand into and take out enough for his own needs and material advancement. That is the way they regarded this country, not as something to live in and adopt an interest in and study the institutions of and to be loyal to, but as a place where people could make money.

There is nothing to compare to the attachment of the alien, even foreign-born, who is really attached to this country, because he realizes that the institutions of this country mean so much to him and to his children.

What we have to fear is the perversion of the children by influences which are very insidious. I fear that a good many of our so-called "Parlor Socialists," or philosophers, had a great deal to do with the training of some of the intellectuals among the foreign-born youth toward Socialism and Bolshevism. One harmful influence is the formation of clubs at which these young people discuss questions which their immaturity of judgment will not permit them to understand with a proper perspective, historical perspective; they discuss these different questions of the remedies for social ills, and they are impressed by these "Parlor Socialists," who are their guides and mentors, and they have not enough philosophy behind them to weigh properly the arguments pro and con, and they are led astray in that way. They have a certain glib use of language and they translate that into philosophy.

I know several cases where I can say that the doctrines imbibed by these young men have been imbibed at the feet of some of these "Parlor Socialists." They meet them in those clubs, sometimes, I think, under the guise of settlement work. I don't know just how far that extends, but I know that a good many of these young men that I knew as youths, as boys, who afterward became, I would say, infected with these socialistic ideas, I know that they received their lessons in Socialism in the clubs which they attended in the neighborhood of their particular residences, at which these questions were discussed. These youngsters discussed those questions when they were only fifteen, sixteen or seventeen years old, without guidance.

There is a freedom of expression in the settlements and there is an encouragement to that freedom of expression without sufficient guidance. That is, I don't think that he comes in contact with the persons there who will put him straight, who will give him the other side, so to speak. I am not saying that this is characteristic of all settlements. I have no objection to boys attending these clubs. I haven't even any objection to propositions concerning Socialistic theories being advanced, but I have a decided objection to having it all one way; I have a decided objection to having somebody tell them, who will not guide them along right lines, but who will permit these errors to creep in. I rather think that it is not a good thing for boys or girls to come under the influence of these people without somebody being there as a check.

Anning S. Prall, *President of the Board of Education*

I believe the Board of Education would support all of the suggestions which have so far been made practical. I believe the main question is not one for the City of New York to meet financially. I believe with this great big educational organization, and with the men who are at its head, as superintendents, district superintendents and principals, and with its great force of teachers, that the State and the Nation has for its use in this particular question of Americanization the very finest organization in the world.

I believe that it is simply a question for the State of New York itself to solve in the matter of an appropriation sufficiently large to meet all of the conditions that need to be met.

I do not believe that the people of the City of New York should be called upon to meet this expense, inasmuch as it is not a local problem, but I do believe if your Committee would recommend to the State, and the State would appropriate a sum, say, $1,000,000 a year, that this Department of Education could, with its great organization, do more effective work than any agency anywhere else in the United States.

I believe that the law should be amended, the State Educational Law, to the extent that the Board of Education of the City of New York might treat the teacher as would the ordinary employer treat the employee. That instead of a teacher having the legal rights that he or she has at this time in the matter of discipline, in the matter of testimony when charges are made, the Board of Education should be permitted to treat its teacher as an ordinary employee in any occupation outside of state or city government positions.

That if a teacher satisfied the Board of Education by his or her actions that these actions were detrimental to the system in any way, regardless of whether the Board of Education would be justified legally in dismissing that teacher, it ought to have the right to dismiss that teacher if, in its judgment, after a hearing within the legal lines, that teacher was found to be detrimental in any way to the service, the Board of Education might have the right to dismiss or to suspend for a period.

We find at the present time that the Board of Education is restrained to some extent by the requirement of laws.

There is an appeal to the State Commissioner, and from there to the courts, for a teacher, and the board feels, and, I think, the members of bureaus and the superintendents feel, that unless they have a case that will stand the legal test, regardless of the real situation, they hesitate before bringing charges against a teacher.

We have one teacher, for instance, that gets up in a public meeting and refers to the Board of Education as a "Prussianized Board," showing the results of discontent, but not coming within the pale of the law, not coming within that point where the board feels it can legally bring that man or woman up on charges and dismiss them. We would like, from connection with this subject, a little more power to deal summarily with these people.

But I think your great problem is financial ability. There is no organization in the world equal to the educational work of this city that could handle this situation as it should be handled, except that it has not the funds to do it with, and it certainly ought to be up to the State itself to furnish the money, and charge the department of this city with that responsibility.

I would not say that the State Department of Education should have exclusive control of Americanization work, but it certainly functions with the work of all educational departments to that extent, that the State ought to expect, and might expect, and it certainly could expect, to derive more benefit through its Boards of Education or Departments of Education, throughout the State, than in any other way.

The State this year appropriated for the City of New York the sum of $30,000 to be used in Americanization work, and the City of New York to contribute one-half of that, so that it would really have cost the State $15,000. Now, $30,000 in New York City would not take care of one assembly district. The State could very well invest $1,000,000 a year for a period of ten years for the City of New York alone. A million dollars is a lot of money and you could do a lot of work with it. There is no question about it. Try it with $1,000,000 for one year, and if you find that it was a good investment, and I am sure you will find that to be true, then you might invest more.

We are now spending altogether in all forms of Americanization work about $300,000 between our evening school Americanization work and our classes and factories and settlements and afternoon classes in the schools.

I consider that the whole problem here is a matter of money. This department has the whole situation well in hand in every way, except that it cannot carry out its ideas for the reason that it is handicapped for the use of money.

JOHN L. TILDSLEY, *Associate Superintendent of Schools, In Charge of High Schools*

I believe there is a special need for an Americanization program in the high schools, because the high school is very largely the key to the whole educational system of any country. In the high school we get the more ambitious boys and girls of the city coming from the families where the parents are more ambitious and leaders. In the City of New York we have an increasingly large proportion of foreign-born boys and girls or boys and girls of the second generation from foreign countries. Whereas at one time we had 30 per cent. of children of foreigners in our high schools, we now have at least 60 per cent. of foreign-born or the second generation of foreign origin. These boys and girls are going to be leaders in city life and at the present time they come from homes where the ideas are foreign, they read the papers where the ideas are foreign to our ways of doing things and they are very largely tinged therefore with ideas not generally regarded as American. They are for the most part readers of the papers, and very largely read books and we all know the foreign population of the city is pretty largely tinged with ideas opposed to the present economic and social and political order. Now, I don't mean to say that these children share these views very largely, but are constantly exposed to them, because in the sections of the city from which they come and where the foreign-born are concentrated, we have the soap box orator, we have public meetings and we have systematic campaigns throughout the year for the inculcation of certain ideas which are subversive, I believe, of our American institutions.

Now, as I see it the danger of our American way of doing things does not come so much from ignorance, but it comes rather from the person who is partly educated. It is not the ignorant man who ultimately leads the crowd, but the man of some education. That man is the product and bound to be the product of our high schools, because he is the more ambitious man, the man of determination, the very kind that comes to the high school.

We have assumed that any system of high school education will produce a good American citizen as a by-product, but I believe that is not true, and that unless you constantly work for good citizenship in your schools you don't get it. In other words we must develop a feeling of nationality. To educate a man in the high schools does not necessarily mean to develop a man who has a right attitude toward the country's institutions and that is why I feel that in such a city as this we need an organized, constantly directed effort from the beginning of the high school course to this class, to produce thorough American boys and girls, and until recently in this State we have not had such a program.

The social and economic views of the teachers have a very far reaching influence on the student, and that point has been very generally overlooked. That is especially true in the teaching of two subjects; the teaching of English, and the teaching of history, civics and economics, these three classed as one subject, or one field. In these days in English teaching we do not rely much on books, but we take the current events, the life about us for our composition work and oral discussion, and we have come to realize that the primary aim in teaching English is to develop on the part of the student a power to express himself and not necessarily to appreciate a particular type of literature. Therefore we consider oral discussions a necessary part of the training in English and the natural thing is to discuss political, social and economic topics in the classroom. Now, if the teacher is a person who has a destructive attitude towards American institutions and the American economic order, that inevitably creeps out in the classroom. His opinions are constantly asked by the students. The students debate and in the debates they are always inclined to defer to the judgment of the teacher. Therefore it is impossible except for the strong willed teacher to refrain from impressing his views upon his students, even though he tries to refrain. It is difficult for him to do it. There is an unconscious as well as a conscious influence upon the classroom.

To avoid the subject is to avoid the most important things in life. The boy and girl who come to the school read the papers and are familiar with the subjects. They should be interested in them. A boy or girl who has not read about these subjects in the papers is not being prepared for life. It is a natural custom and it should be encouraged, and they should be encouraged to talk about them.

The very essentials of education are that you should stir up a vital interest.

The pupil will learn to express himself when he has something he wishes to say, something he is interested in. The oldfashioned English teacher would take a subject from the book and ask the boy to talk about it, and the boy would simply reproduce what he saw in the book, because he is not vitally interested. He will not prepare himself to speak and write well unless he speaks and writes of something in which he is vitally interested, and social and economic subjects give you a subject in which there is vital interest on the part of the boy and girl. But you cannot avoid temptation in this world and if the teacher is the proper kind of teacher he will develop the thinking part of the boy and it is undoubtedly a magnificent opportunity to bring to the boys and girls good fundamental ideals and notions of our institutions.

You cannot exercise restraint. You must get the right kind of teacher. You cannot lay down rules and regulations. You must leave him absolutely free to take up any subject he sees fit; but you must have a teacher with American ideals who is moderate in his point of view and not a man swept away by every tide of opinion. He ought to be a well-trained man who is a good thinker and who is steeped in American ideas. Then you can leave the boy and girl in his hands and be sure you will have a boy and girl with the right attitude toward American ideals, but if you don't have that kind of a teacher you run the danger to which you refer; but with the kind of teacher that you cannot trust and whom you must guide mostly by rules and regulations you have a teacher not worth having.

In some cases we have found it necessary to turn away a few teachers from the system because we found the views they were impressing upon their pupils were subversive of our ideals. We had a trial and under our present system the teacher has the right to counsel, the right of formal procedure with laws of evidence. He is brought before the Board of Education, and he then has appealed to the State Commission. Such teachers as were brought before the Board of Education had every protection of the law and some five were dismissed and the dismissals were sustained by the Commissioner of Education. The point is one brought up by Mr. Prall that the State Education Law states that they shall have a hearing and " hearing " has been construed by legal authorities as one requiring all the laws of evidence, and Mr. Prall stated that he felt that this should be an ordinary investigation by the Board of Education representing the citizens of the city. If in their judgment the influence of the teacher is harmful he felt that should be sufficient and that he should be dismissed, still having his right of appeal to the Commission. I believe that the provision which requires the observance of all the technical laws of evidence should not be required. The teacher is not being tried for a crime, he is simply having a hearing as to his fitness to represent the State of New York in the classroom.

We have at the present time a very deliberate program having as its end training for citizenship.

The Commissioner of Education of this State a year and a half ago announced that hereafter the equivalent of two periods a week of civics should be required for one year in the high school and we are carrying out that requirement very rigidly. We give in our schools at the present time two periods of civics for the first year and our teaching of civics has a very definite aim. We start out with the idea that the boy at all times is exposed to destructive criticism of our governmental activities. He fails perhaps to realize that government is not a repressive agency but a helping agency. The object of our work is to set forth what the city, what the State and what the nation is actually doing for his well-being and that from the time he gets up in the morning until he goes to bed at night this help is being extended. So we take up all the things the city, the State or the nation does — the milk supply, for example. We show that the city, co-operating with the State, makes it possible for him to have a pure supply of milk; that his meat supply is made healthful by the co-operation between cities, state and nation. We take up every activity of the City of New York in the same way — the water supply brought to him by the city authorities — and we show him that there is practically nothing that he does during the day that is not made possible for him by some governmental agency; our idea being to impress upon him so that he will never forget it that he can only live a healthful, happy life, because of the operation of some governmental agency, and when we get through that work we believe he will have that with him for the rest of his life and get over the idea of the old country that the government keeps him from doing something, and rather that it helps him to do the thing that he likes to do best.

The object is to promote a feeling of gratitude on the part of the pupil toward government. We believe if we change his attitude, the attitude borne in upon his parents by hardship in another country, that the policeman on the corner is not there to keep him from doing something, but is there to help him cross the street, and that the streetcleaner is not there to keep him from throwing paper around, but is there to keep the street clean and make him happy, we have done something to make him a good citizen; and we take up the whole question of who pays for this and we show him that all this must come out of taxes, therefore any waste he sees, he himself ultimately has to pay for; and the great thing we have in mind is to impress upon him when anything goes wrong in the City of New York, if the street in front of his house is not properly swept, the United States is not responsible, the Governor of the State of New York is not responsible, but the man who does the sweeping is responsible, the foreman, and over him, the Commissioner of Street Cleaning, and over him someone else, and that there is always a place to which the citizen can write an appeal and demand redress of a grievance and that no man to whom the appeal is first sent can turn the appeal to someone over him. And we think if we can impress this upon him he will not turn to revolutionary methods but to an orderly process of law to redress his grievances.

This is in the first year. Then in our senior year in high school we introduced last year the compulsory study of economics in order that the pupil may realize the significance of the right of property, may realize the importance to the community that a man shall receive the product of his labor and not have it taken away from him. We believe that he should study economics in the papers and through discussion; therefore in the school he should have impressed upon him the fundamental principles. The great trouble with the talk outside of the school room is that it is not based on an accurate knowledge of conditions and accurate reasoning, and our aim is to develop the power of accurate reasoning and the desire to find out the facts berore he applies remedies.

In addition to that, in the fourth year we have plans for systematic study of government, not only of our own country, but of other countries, from a comparative viewpoint, so that he will understand fundamental principles of government and see how they work out. In addition to that in our own city every student in our high school in the senior year must take American history and civics; it is required for graduation. Economics and civics are also required for graduation.

We also go into contemporary American history of the present day, right down to the present time. We believe that we can no longer be an isolated power, that we are a world power and that our boys and girls should understand contemporary world conditions, so we have made European history a study. We devote five periods a week for one year to a study of European history since the eighteenth century up to the conditions as they are today, because we believe a boy or girl who understands that the present is a product of a series of movements of the last century is going to absorb the idea that all progress comes slowly and that no great reform can be accomplished by a sudden overturning. All subjects are being taught with that conscious idea of developing citizenship and developing a certain attitude toward life.

Some of our graduates combat radical ideas and some favor them. You must realize that the school is only one part, that we have two diverse elements, and the school is not necessarily the stronger environment. There is the environment in the home and from the outside.

Of course, such a program as I have outlined depends primarily on having the right teachers.

The chief obstacle to the success of this program is the very great difficulty of securing properly trained teachers to teach economics in the high schools; to teach economics it requires a man with thorough training, much more thorough a training in economics than in a subject like physics, for instance, because it cannot be learned over night. He must always know much more than he teaches, he must have a pretty wide experience of life and of systems of economic thought and very few teachers at the present time have had sufficient training to teach the subject properly; so we are forced to find someone who has an interest in this subject and then we train him. So in civics, you can see if a man is going to teach about all that is done in the City of New York at the present time he ought to be thoroughly in touch with the work being done in the City of New York, and the work is enormous. In the third place, not only must the teachers have had the proper training and knowledge of contemporary events and activities, but they must have the right attitude. They must be steeped in American ideals, and it is becoming increasingly difficult to find such teachers. Men and women of the type that formerly went into our schools cannot live on the salaries paid at the present time. I think the future, therefore, of our schools in New York State is in a very desperate condition if something cannot be done. Our salaries at the present time are really only half what they were fifteen years ago. It was difficult then to obtain teachers, it is going to be impossible to obtain them, because they cannot live on the present salaries. Therefore, you will have to resort constantly to a more poorly trained lot of teachers from a poor economic order and largely from a foreign origin, so if we are not very careful, the schools, which should be the chief means of promoting good citizenship, will become a means of developing a movement opposed to Americanism.

Our intellectual tests for teachers are not too high at the present time. The great danger is, in a crisis like this, that you lower your standard. You know in any line of work, if you put your standard low enough, you can always find someone who will work for any wage, and at a time like this when we need a teacher to teach American standards, you should raise your standard instead of lowering it, and you should then raise your salaries so as to obtain the right kind of teachers, but that would cost millions of dollars, and New York must face that or face destruction of its social order.

The remedy I suggest is that New York shall compel its communities to pay large enough salaries to obtain men and women properly qualified to turn out boys and girls for citizenship. You take a person of foreign ideas and you cannot expect that the product of his teaching is going to be always the kind of citizen needed in this State.

I have one other suggestion, with regard to the qualifications of teachers. I believe that from the time the child goes to school until he finishes high school the teacher should have in mind that that child is being trained for citizenship in this State and therefore in all the teaching this idea should be prevalent, and that idea is not going to be present unless the teacher has been trained in American ideals and the simple principles of economics and civics. At the present time the teacher can enter upon the teaching field without having taken any civics and economics, and I should recommend that the State Commissioner of Education require for admission to our training schools the study of civics, economics, and that in the training school where the teachers are trained, special courses in economics, in civics and in contemporary European history should be required subjects, and that examinations should be given in those subjects as requirements for the education of the teaching force. That is not a matter involving the expenditure of a very large amount of money and undoubtedly the Commissioner would be glad to receive suggestions from such a body as this.

I would like to second a matter spoken of by the Superintendent of Schools: I believe it is impossible to do this work of Americanization of the adult class unless you can have the right kind of teacher. It is a very difficult work to do. At the present time, if I understand it, the teachers of Americanization work receive $3 a night. You can readily see that you cannot obtain the teachers that you need at such a price. They need to be specially selected for their equipment for this work. I think young business men and lawyers and other professional men might do this work as a patriotic service if invited to do it; therefore, I believe in this civic work such people should not be taken from the eligible list. I believe the work should be in the hands of the Superintendent of Schools with power to form a list of people to do this kind of work. That would require a modification of the State Law. It is almost impossible to frame a set of tests which will give you men and women of these particular characteristics, for your young lawyers and young men in politics are not going to take an examination to do this kind of work, but I believe they would accept an invitation from the President of the Board of Education to do this work for a single winter. I don't mean that it should be unpaid work, but it should be made so as to secure the right sort of teachers, free from civil service rules.

GEORGE H. CHATFIELD, *Assistant Director of Attendance of the Public Schools*

I think that the matter of compulsory education is going to be very largely a matter of opinion. Of course, in some states they have adopted compulsory measures requiring the attendance of illiterates or persons who do not speak English. One state has gone so far as to provide that up to the age of 45 they should be required to attend. It has been talked in this State and in the Education Department as to whether that should be done. There has been always raised a constitutional question as to whether or not they can do that. You may be able to do it with aliens; I don't know. With regard to the constitutionality I don't know, I have no opinion; that must come from persons especially equipped. As to desirability, that is entirely another story. The process of Americanization or teaching English or teaching about our institutions to persons beyond 21 years of age, is always a much more difficult thing to do and much harder to bring about than is the work with minors.

The Legislature a few years ago passed an act to require the attendance of all minors between 16 and 21 years of age, upon instruction in English, who did not speak, read and write English quite to the extent required for the completion of the fifth year of the school course. That is the law, although stated in an informal way. We have not been able to enforce even that law — there are a good many defects in it. One thing that I think the Committee might do properly would be to make that an effective statute.

It is very difficult to identify any person as not having that degree of ability. You can go to an ordinary home — and I am thinking of our own work as we go about from day to day with our enumerators, because we have a body in the field all the time knocking at one door and then another and asking questions: Can this person read or write English? Now, you are talking, as a rule, to a foreign mother or a foreigner of some sort. The only question you can hope to get answered in that case is Yes, he can write and read English — but how much English he can write or can read, they are not able to tell you that — in fact, that is only susceptible of determination when you bring him before a person who is qualified to answer that. There is where the legal difficulties arises. You want this person to go to an evening school, and you tell them to go, and they don't go, then what happens? I took the trouble here, when this act was first brought up, to go down to the Naturalization Bureau in the city here, and to go to the County Clerk's office and get the list of people who had applied for naturalization papers, and we visited them and tried to induce all those who could not, or appeared not to be able to, speak English, to come to the evening school, but they didn't appear. Now, the Act is compulsory, that is, we must enforce it in court; but in order to go to court and make a case against any individual, you have got to have some evidence to proceed upon. We have none. An officer can get up in court and say this person can't read or write English, but he does not know anything about it, unless he is an absolute illiterate. We have, therefore, no real means for the education of these people like we have for our own.

There are many means that have been suggested: the new continuation school law, which will become fully effective in 1925, provides that every employed person under 18 years of age shall have instruction of not less than four or more than eight hours per week. Now, all those minors between 16 and 18 who don't speak English as is required under this Act, will be normally educated because they are obliged to obtain an employment certificate, and when they apply for an employment certificate you can ascertain, as a matter of procedure at that time, how much English they do speak, read and write. You can then put a real test to them, so that you can comb all those out. But for the group above 18 years of age we have no such reuqirement; that is, those who are from 18 to 19, 19 to 20 and 20 to 21, that three-year group.

Now, it has been suggested that we might apply to that group the same plan; that is, require all those persons between 18 and 21 years of age, who work, to have either a certificate of literacy, which they might carry with them, or else to obtain an employment certificate, which will show the amount of their literacy.

There is another method which might be adopted, which has some advantages, because it could be applied to the country at large; the reason that I say it could be applied to the country at large is this: that any plans that are made in this State for instructing illiterates must take into account the fact that they move about from one locality to another and from one state to another. If there is a new demand for laborers, for instance, in Pennsylvania, the men may be gathered up in New York and shipped there, and that would take a large number of persons between 18 and 21 because they will make first-rate laborers. When they get through in Pennsylvania they may come back to New York; how are you going to know, then, when they pass back, or how are we going to notify the people in Buffalo, for instance, when they leave this section or go from New York to Buffalo? There must be some method under which it can be made effective.

Coming back to the point where I said the Federal Government might come in: Children under 16 years of age, who are admitted to residence in the United States are placed under bonds to require their attendance at school until they are 16 if, at the time when they are admitted, the immigration authorities believe there is some reason which will induce the parents or guardians not to obey the law. Here is a concrete illustration of that: this boy is sent over here to reside in a certain family, the head of which is not his father or his mother; or it may be the mother alone or the father alone or it may be an uncle or some such person. The tendency is that when that boy gets to be of an age where he can earn something he will be immediately put to work. Now, in order to prevent that, the Government imposes or exacts a bond, before he is admitted, in the sum of $500. Now, we have about 300 children of that sort in New York today whom we call "Bonded immigrant children," and we keep track of them for the Federal Government. That thing has been running along now for as long as eight years, and it works out very well; we seldom lose track of any of these children; between the immigration authorities and ourselves we keep track of them all, practically — I think in the last two years only two of them were not satisfactorily accounted for out of 300.

Now, there are of course persons coming in at Ellis Island all the time between the ages of 18 and 21. There are some coming from the English provinces down there and South America in general, and Havana, Cuba — we get a good many of those. If they are admitted knowing English, it is all right, but it does not need to be English, if they speak and read Spanish they come in.

It does seem to me that that plan of handling minors might be adopted all over the United States and that all these persons might come in and be placed under bond to attend school until they are 21 or until they reach the specified requirements. But throughout the country at large that principle should be applied. It would require action by Congress. I wrote Chairman Johnson of the Immigration Committee about it, but I don't think he was very much impressed. I think that that would be an effective way and the only effective way.

They have a new statute, as you know, under contemplation which affects immigration at the present time, which provides that every person, within certain qualifications, must pay a head tax, and that head tax is reduced year after year according as he shows facility in English — if he gets so far, his tax is so much, etc.; and then you provide a system for following them up. I don't think that you can make any statutes for them unless you have an effective follow-up system. It is perfectly practicable. With New Jersey authorities and Pennsylvania and the neighboring states about here we could have such a thing. If, for instance, a boy of school age leaves us and says he is going to live in some town in Pennsylvania, we write to such a town and find out whether he has arrived. A great many cities notify New York that a child of a certain age has left that town and is going to live in New York City; then we take the proper action and see that he goes properly to school. It is supposed to be effective throughout New York State at present, but it is not wholly so. We would have to have Federal co-operation. New York is capable of doing that. I know that New Jersey and Pennsylvania would do it, and I have no doubt that the New England States would all go into that, but I can't speak beyond them. I know conditions there pretty well.

I think that the Committee should keep in mind the fact that any statute made to affect any particular group of persons, if you make it compulsory, it must carry with it the implication of a follow-up system, if necessary, on its purely mechanical side.

I think there is only one other point in which the Committee would be interested; that is, with reference to the instruction which is carried on in private schools. As you know, a parent is free at this time to send a child — and always has been in this State — either to a public or private school or to have them instructed at home. Now, the only standards that are set up are those contained in section 620 of the Educational Law — sections 620 and 623. Section 620 defines the subjects of instruction which a child of compulsory school age must take: reading, spelling, writing, arithmetic, geography and the English language. If a child today, say of eight years of age, goes to a private school, the law requires only that he must receive instruction in those subjects, and that they must be given in English by a competent teacher; and that is as far as you get.

Section 623 says that the attendance must be for so many days per week and that throughout the year the attendance must be substantially equivalent — but practically that is all there is to it. There is no requirement that in a private school, for instance, American history must be taught, that civics or citizenship must be taught. Those sections of the Educational Law could be amended.

Also there should be some standard for instruction in secondary schools: As long as a child is of compulsory school age I think that we should say that the instruction should be given in matters of citizenship, United States history, and English, probably; and possibly there might be some penalties suggested which would make those effective.

I think there should be more definite standards for instruction than are given at the public schools; the making of this illiteracy law effective; the question of adults, whether that should be compulsory or not is a matter of training. In any event, I think there is grave doubt whether we could make it effective very far, and certainly, except for the relatively young adults, I doubt if it would serve any useful purpose unless it was voluntary.

Following is the written recommendation of Mr. Henry H. Goldberger, of the New York City public school system, co-operating with the State Department of Immigrant Education:

"I am giving you below a summary of our conversation with regard to a State program of education for immigrants.

"You will remember my argument against a compulsory education law to reach people, a law that would be more drastic than the present law, reaching immigrants up to twenty-one years of age. I feel that coercive measures in a matter of language is charged with so much danger that certainly at the present time it would be unwise to push a bill to provide for it in New York State. If such a law were passed, I think it had better come through the Federal government, so that it might be uniformly applied. Aside from its effect upon the foreigner, tending to crystallize opposition by making language the symbol for centralizing opposition to American institutions, I feel that a local compulsory education law, applying to New York State alone, would place the State at a disadvantage with other States in competition for labor. You know what happened in some of the European countries, especially in the so-called oppressed nations. In every case it was the language of the people that was used as a symbol for rousing a spirit of opposition to the dominant nation.

"Now, it is perfectly true that the position of immigrants in America is quite different from that of the suppressed nations. Our immigrants are free agents in coming to the country and can be expected to conform to any laws which they find here, since they all have the choice of refusing to come or of returning to their own countries. In many cases this would be a consummation devoutly to be wished. But, as a question of pure policy, I feel it would not be wise to put pressure on the learning of English at the present time.

"The State Education Department is working out a program for the education of immigrants which has great promise, provided the program were properly backed by the educational authorities, by employers of labor and by labor organizations. The plan includes the following:

First.— The organizing of training courses throughout the State to provide an adequate body of teachers to do the work of Americanization. Up to now these training courses have been short, so that some people could be prepared hurriedly for the work that had to be done. It is planned to make the work more intensive, and to provide optional courses to the students in the senior year of our normal school and in our colleges. A course of this kind is now being offered at Hunter College, and Columbia University is making arrangements to give such a course next summer and during the year to follow.

Second.— The encouragement of public night schools. We realize that these schools have not been as effective as we should like, but perhaps it is only fair to say that they reflect the general lack of public interest in Americanization. Boards of Education have come to regard our public night schools as step-children in the educational scheme. They have adopted no avowed policy toward adult immigrant education, and it is not to be wondered at that night schools were, therefore, poorly supervised, badly taught and meagerly attended. Where the emphasis has been on improving the service in night schools, rather than on driving people into the night schools, a marked increase in attendance has been noted.

"You will remember the experiment of changing the plan of organization in night schools that I tried two years ago, by organizing classes on the club basis rather than on a class basis — changing the organization of the school by making it a clubhouse and by providing other activities than purely class activities. That experiment has had far-reaching effects, not only in New York State, but throughout the country where it has been tried. In the forthcoming report of the Carnegie Foundation, there will appear a survey of present conditions in night schools and a series of suggestions looking to their improvement. I think the report might be studied by the Committee in estimating the work that night schools might be expected to perform.

Third.— The State is urging the organization of classes in factories, and is providing a number of paid organizers to interest employers of labor and to start the work in the shops. It seems to me that employers need a little dynamite from some authoritative source as to the need of co-operating. They are still hanging

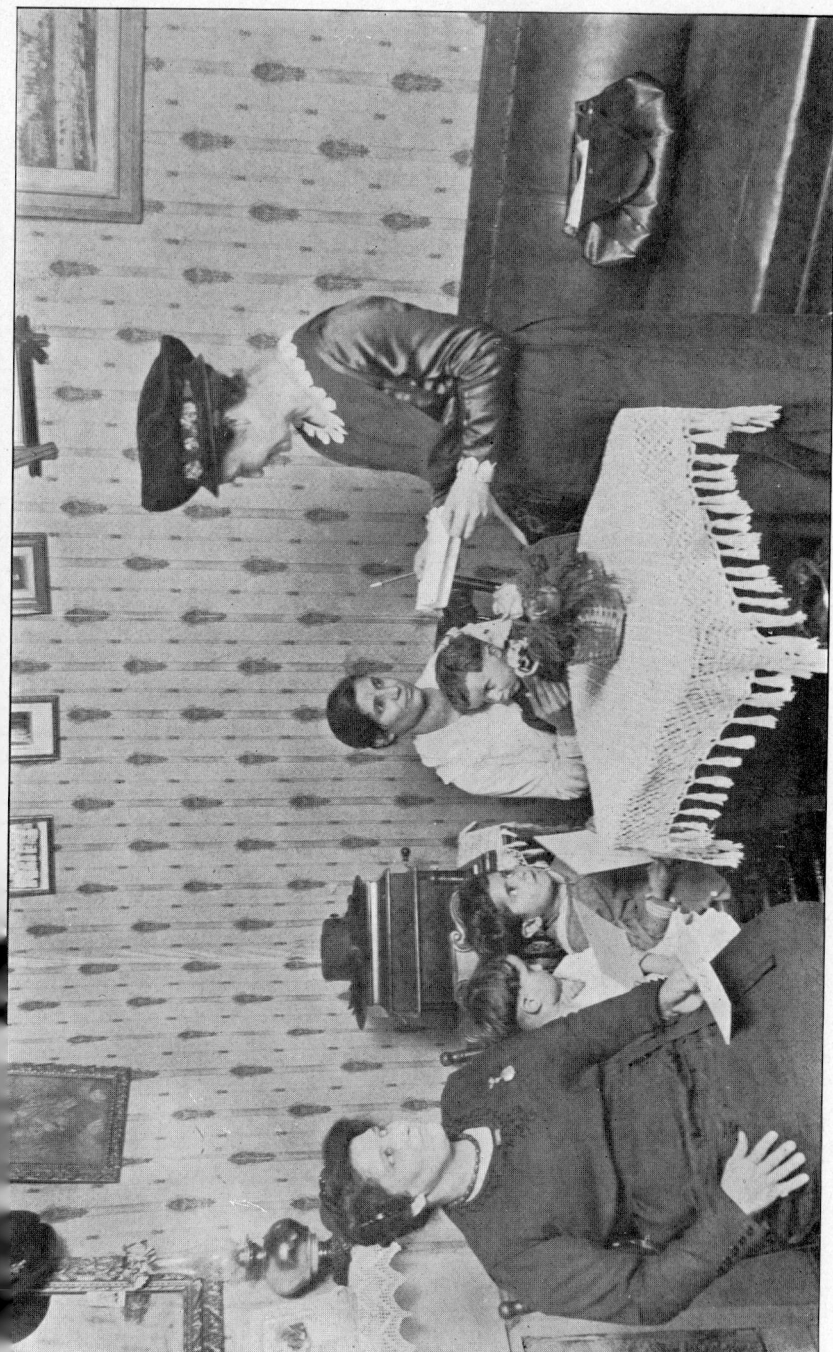

Home Class of Jewish Women, Syracuse

New York City Extension Class in Factory of Atlantic Comb Works

back, and placing the burden on the workers, thus making it difficult even where the foreigners themselves seem to be anxious for classes to be formed.

Fourth.— In Los Angeles the experiment was tried of reaching foreign mothers in the homes and organizing small groups. The workers who went into these homes were intelligent social workers, trained to do some teaching. Small groups grew into larger ones. The point of contact was not always the teaching of English — it may have begun with the cleaning of the house, with taking care of the baby, or obtaining cheaper food. As a matter of fact, it was found that the least effective point of contact was the teaching of English. In New York City the experiment is being carried on now by the International Institute of the Y. W. C. A. and by the Council of Jewish Women.

"Since July 1st of this year, the State Education Department has put a number of workers into the field to carry the message of America home to the people who will never go out into America to find out what it is like.

"Finally, through the labor organizations I feel that we have a point of contact which will reach many more than we have been able to reach in any other way and reach them more effectively. If we can secure the co-operation of the labor unions in the education of their own operatives, and if we can then provide properly trained teachers through the Boards of Education, I think we shall probably have reached most of those whom it will be worth while to reach.

"Much has been done by the New York City Board of Education to inculcate in the teachers a spirit of Americanism, and to stamp out any subversive tendencies. Mr. Tildsley, Director of High Schools, outlined his stand in the matter of teachers' loyalty in an article in the 'National Civic Federation Review' for June 30, 1919. The title is 'Freedom of Teaching in the Schools,' and the conclusion is arrived at that 'Socialists believing in the Communist manifesto have no place in the public school system.'"

What was done with three such undesirable teachers is described in a pamphlet published by the American Defense Society, the text of which follows.

3. Unpatriotic Teaching in Public Schools

THE FACTS CONCERNING THE TRANSFER AND DISMISSAL OF SOME TEACHERS OF THE DeWITT CLINTON HIGH SCHOOL

A Report Prepared by a Committee of the Schoolmasters' Association of New York and Vicinity

INTRODUCTION

A recent investigation of conditions in DeWitt Clinton High School, conducted by Dr. John L. Tildsley, Associate City Superintendent in charge of high schools, resulted in the transfer of six teachers to other schools and in the dismissal of Samuel D. Schmalhausen, Thomas Mufson, and A. Henry Schneer from the service of the Department of Education of the City of New York.

Inasmuch as many statements have been made in public speeches and in the press, both before and after the trial, that tend to cloud the issue and to create conflicting impressions in the public mind, the Schoolmasters' Association of New York and Vicinity appointed a committee to collect the data necessary to a clear understanding of the matter and to make known to the public the results of its labors.

The aim of the committee has been to obtain *facts*. The stenographic report of the testimony has been carefully studied; the exhibits cited therein have been examined; school officials and teachers have been interviewed; letters, pamphlets, reports of speeches, newspaper clippings and whatever other sources of information were available to the committee have been utilized.

The report of the committee is herewith presented with the assurance that no statement is made therein, the truth of which has not been established.

THE SCHOOLMASTERS' ASSOCIATION OF
NEW YORK AND VICINITY

THE REPORT
Preliminary Statement

(The abbreviation "Test.," followed by a numeral, refers by page to the stenographic report of the testimony, published by the defense; the abbreviation "Sum.," followed by a numeral, refers by page to a pamphlet entitled "Summary of Evidence," also published by the defense. All other references are self-explanatory.)

The committee finds that there exists in the teaching staff of the New York City schools a group of teachers who continually oppose any act or policy in educational affairs and, likewise, in municipal, state and national affairs which is not in accord with their individualistic notions with reference to that act or policy. The leaders of this group control the Teachers' Union of New York City, of which organization Henry R. Linville, of Jamaica High School, is the president. They are also active supporters of the Hillquit-Berger branch of the Socialist Party.

The first statement will be questioned by no one who knows; the second is proved by the fact that the November number of the "American Teacher," the official organ of the Teachers' Union, advocated the election of Morris Hillquit for Mayor and by the additional fact that a number of teachers from this group, among them Gabriel R. Mason, the president of the American Teacher Company, give courses of instruction in the Rand School on Socialism, 7 East 15th street, New York City. The bearing which all this has upon the case of the DeWitt Clinton teachers who were transferred and dismissed will become evident as this report proceeds.

I. THE CAUSE OF INVESTIGATION
(1) The Unpatriotic Attitude of a Certain Group of Teachers Toward the War

There is a group of teachers in the DeWitt Clinton High School which is included in the group described above, and which, in turn, includes most of the members of the Teachers' Council of that school. The attitude of this group toward the war is regarded as unpatriotic, by fellow teachers, by pupils and by the parents of pupils. The nature of this attitude is shown, in part, by the following:

A meeting of DeWitt Clinton teachers was held at the Peg Woffington Coffee House, April 21, 1917, under the auspices of this Teachers' Council, at which "many teachers expressed their opinions of the requirement that all teachers sign the loyalty pledge." (See Teachers' Council Bulletin, May 8, 1917.) There were forty-one members of the faculty present, but not all were in sympathy with the views of the group. One of the group said, "Most of the evening was spent in discussing the loyalty pledge of the Board of Education." Another is quoted as saying at the meeting, "Any teacher who signs the loyalty pledge is indecent, immoral, imbecile and idiotic." Still another said, "We decided that the pledge could be signed *as it did not bar internationalism.*" Another report is that the members expressed the opinion, "*It is best to sign the pledge; otherwise we may lose our positions and thus lose our chance to further the cause.*" The nature of the "cause" was not stated. In this connection it should be noted that the protest to the Board of Education against signing the pledge of loyalty was dated April 23d, two days after the date of this meeting, and that the three teachers who were dismissed and the six who were transferred were among those who signed the protest. It should also be noted that the name of Henry R. Linville, president of the Teachers' Union, headed the list of signers and that he was present at this meeting, although not a member of the DeWitt Clinton faculty.

An article appeared in the "New Republic," May 26, 1917, entitled "The Religion of Free Men," which takes the ground that "military participation in war is tantamount to committing murder," and asks whether "the dreamers of a true federation of mankind are to be sacrificed because they have not yet been permitted to realize their dream." This article was signed by thirteen men who call themselves "Conscientious Objectors and Their Champions." Among this number were the three teachers who were dismissed, two of the six who were transferred, four others from the DeWitt Clinton group, two others who had left DeWitt Clinton only a short time before, and Henry R. Linville, president of the Teachers' Union.

A reply to this article by Professor Lovejoy, of Baltimore, in the "New Republic," June 16, 1917, sums up the attitude of these thirteen men, as follows:

> "Their tone, throughout, is one of assured and condescending moral superiority; and the assumption of such superiority is expressly made one of the premises of the argument which is to persuade the rest of us to favor their exemption (from military service). 'You,' it is urged, 'are at all costs to be kept safe like queen bees in the hive, because you constitute an elect class of "humanists," of "visionaries," who alone are capable of the "reconstructive

task" of "recreating out of bloody chaos some new, reinspired internationalism!"' For this high duty of the future, it seems, those who serve in the war will be disqualified because 'brutalized' and 'degraded,' through that service."

These two articles should be read by every person who believes that the teachers in our schools should be 100 per cent. loyal. The magazine may be found in the reading-room of the Forty-second Street Public Library, third floor.

Other remarks and acts further reveal the attitude of this group.

When the authorities suppressed the "Masses," one of their number exclaimed, "Now we have Czar Wilson." Another, speaking of the "Wake up America" parade, said, "I should prefer to see an I. W. W. parade." Another said, when asked what he would do if the Germans were to invade America, "I think I should take to the woods. I prefer to be a live coward rather than to be a dead hero." Another posted an anti-conscription circular in the men's room of the school on the morning of the day that the president signed the Conscription Act. Another, when the blanks asking for volunteers for the State census were distributed, deliberately tore to pieces the one offered him and threw it violently on the floor.

The patience and forbearance of the school officials reached the breaking point, however, when one of the group, Samuel D. Schmalhausen, assigned as the subject of a letter to the President a topic which led a number of his pupils to make unpatriotic criticisms (Test., 20–22), and led one, Hyman Herman, to write a most disrespectful and unpatriotic letter (Test., 40) in which the President is accused of "grand wholesale murder." When this letter was shown to the principal, Dr. Paul, he said, "This thing has gone too far. It will be necessary for me to report this." (Test., 47, Paul.) He did so, and, as a result, a general investigation of the unpatriotic attitude of the teachers, not only in DeWitt Clinton, but also in other schools followed.

(2) The Charge Refuted "That the Whalen Resolutions Were the Cause"

The assertion was made at the trial (Test. 13, Smyth), by the counsel for the defense, that resolutions adopted at a meeting held under the auspices of the Teachers' Council and criticizing Mr. Whalen's action in the utterances which he made at a hearing granted to teachers and pupils on the subject of the longer school day, were "the genesis of the charges." This assertion was also repeatedly made both before and after the trial by various members of the group.

The real "genesis of the charges" has already been stated; but there is a further answer to this assertion of the defense.

The "Whalen Resolutions" were adopted after the close of school, October 24, 1917, and were published in the evening papers, October 26th. Dr. Tildsley first learned of their existence from Dr. Straubenmuller Saturday morning, October 27th. Prior to this time, the following steps had been taken in the investigation: The English assignment made by Schmaulhausen, October 19th, was handed to the principal that same day. (Test. 49, Paul.) At Dr. Paul's request, the chairman of the English department visited the class Monday, October 22d, when the topic was discussed. (Test. 31, Garrigues.) She collected the compositions and handed them to Dr. Paul the same day. (Test. 22, Garrigues.) In the afternoon Dr. Paul attended the hearing at which Mr. Whalen is alleged to have made the statements criticized in the resolutions. *Before the hearing,* Dr. Paul handed the assignment and Hyman Herman's composition to Dr. Tildsley and said, " This is a matter that I think requires your attention." Dr. Tildsley put the papers in his desk and told Dr. Paul that he would come over and look into the matter as soon as he possibly could. (Test. 61, Tildsley.) Thus the investigation was *officially* begun five days before Dr. Tildsley knew of the existence of the resolutions, two days before they were adopted and an appreciable length of time before the words which led to their adoption had even been uttered.

Owing to press of business, resulting from a strike of the high school boys (Test. 61, Tildsley), Dr. Tildsley was prevented from beginning the *actual* work of investigation until October 31st. (Ibid.) In the meantime he had heard of the "Whalen Resolutions"; and so, "on his own initiative, because it lay within the sphere of his duty," he investigated the matter of the resolutions along with the other matter. (Test. 74, Tildsley.)

From the facts at hand, the members of the committee are convinced that the "Whalen Resolutions" were in no sense the cause of the other investigation. The fact that, in general, the same teachers were involved in both investigations, does not so much prove their contention as it supports the theory that this group of teachers is a disturbing element in school as well as governmental affairs; their attitude toward national affairs has already been stated; their attitude toward school affairs will receive attention further on in this report.

(3) The Claim Refuted that These Teachers were Charged with Disloyalty

The defense claims that disloyalty was implied in the charge against the three teachers dismissed and in the action taken against the six teachers transferred. The committee was unable to find any proof that any of these teachers had even been suspected, much less accused, of disloyalty by any school official or any teacher. In fact all the evidence tends to prove the negative of this claim.

President Willcox, in addressing the Board, December 19th, said, "The main question before us is whether these teachers may be trusted to exert a positive influence in the classroom and in the schools to instill in their pupils loyal and patriotic support of the American government in the prosecution of the war, or whether they are lacking in this vital qualification for teaching in our public schools during this crisis." (New York "Tribune," December 20th.) "The issue before us is not disloyalty but qualifications for teaching." (New York "World," December 20th.)

Dr. Tildsley, in an address in the Church of the Ascension, December 9th, said, "The teachers who were tried and those who were transferred were not accused of disloyalty." In the discussion which followed he said, "I believe they are all internationalists and I doubt whether a teacher who has the spirit of internationalism has the spirit necessary to teach high school students." (New York "Times," December 20th.)

From the above, the implication seems to be, not that these teachers are pro-German and therefore disloyal, but that they are not in sympathy with this war from any standpoint and, therefore, are *unpatriotic* in their attitude toward it.

(4) The Claim Refuted That They Were Disciplined Because They Were Russian Jews

One of the dismissed teachers, Thomas Mufson, in a speech at the Star Casino, January 20th, said, "The teachers were suspended because they were Russian Jews." (See daily papers, January 21st.)

At a meeting held in DeWitt Clinton High School, December 15th, a letter from Dr. Charles A. Beard, formerly of Columbia University, was read by the chairman in which Dr. Beard makes this charge.

The Committee was unable to find any evidence of any statement, real or implied, which even intimated such prejudice on the part of Dr. Straubenmuller who directed the charges to be preferred, of any member of the committee on high schools which presented a unanimous report in favor of their dismissal, or of any one of the twenty-five, twenty-six and thirty members of the Board of Education who voted respectively for the dismissal of Schmalhausen, Mufson and Schneer from the service of the Department of Education.

The testimony at the trial shows that Dr. Tildsley, while principal of DeWitt Clinton, had never entertained any such prejudice against any of them. (For Schmalhausen, see Test. 102; for Mufson, Ibid. 165; for Schneer, Ibid. 234.) This testimony was brought out by the lawyer for the defense.

In a circular published by the defense, there is one article in which Isidore Montefiore Levy, member of the Board of Education for six years, severely criticized the methods employed by Dr. Tildsley in the investigation. Yet, in the same article, he says, "It is unfortunate that there is a feeling about that Dr. Tildsley has prejudices of a religious character. This came to my attention at the time that Dr. Tildsley was nominated for Associate City Superintendent. On making inquiries, I was glad to learn that this was an injustice to Dr. Tildsley."

In the light of the above evidence, the members of the Committee believe that the charge made by Dr. Beard and Mr. Mufson has absolutely no foundation in fact.

(5) The Charge Refuted that Suppression of Democracy was the Motive

In a pamphlet issued by the defense the statement is made that "the object of the inquisition at DeWitt Clinton High School was to trap the so-called leaders of the widely growing agitation for more democracy in the school system." Again, "Some drastic action, some show of authority was necessary wherewith to intimidate the liberal-minded teachers."

After going through the testimony and the exhibits in the case of the three defendants, the members of the committee are convinced that the kind of democracy and the kind of liberal-mindedness advocated and exemplified by these men should not be tolerated in any school system. When the testimony and exhibits are reached further along in this report, the reader will realize how valid this conclusion is.

HENRY R. LINVILLE

At the meeting held in DeWitt Clinton, December 15th, Henry R. Linville said that the charges against the three teachers was the culmination of a "long history of official oppression in the name of discipline, it is the most cruel of all similar acts, as well as the most dangerous."

As Mr. Linville is the acknowledged leader of the group that is rallying to the support of these teachers, his attitude toward matters of public concern should be known to the public. The Committee will now endeavor to make known to the reader this attitude as revealed by his public acts and utterances. As the Committee obtained much of its information from the columns of the "American Teacher," the reader will please remember that this magazine is the official organ of the Teachers' Union, of which Mr. Linville is president; that it is the official organ of the American Federation of Teachers of which Mr. Linville is one of the trustees; that he was one of its founders; that he is, and has been from the first, one of its owners; and that from the first he has been a member of the editorial staff. Consequently, the Committee is justified in assuming that the policy of the magazine and any anonymous or unsigned utterances given place therein meet with his approval.

The Committee finds that Mr. Linville's first public attack upon what he designates as "official oppression" was made about twelve years ago, when he filed a list of charges against his principal, Mr. John T. Buchanan, a man who was idolized by every boy in DeWitt Clinton High School who really knew him. The authorities, after giving Mr. Linville full opportunity to prove his charges, did not sustain a single charge. Soon after, he was transferred to the Jamaica High School; but this transfer was not a case of "official oppression," for, under the by-laws at that time, such transfer was impossible without his consent.

THE "AMERICAN TEACHER" MAGAZINE

Failing in his attack, he, with the help of others, founded the magazine now known as the "American Teacher." The keynote of its policy, as stated on the front cover is "Democracy in Education. Education for Democracy"; but the tone of its editorials throughout is one of assured and condescending mental and moral superiority. (Adapted from words of Professor Lovejoy, previously quoted.) Perhaps its appeal for subscriptions will sufficiently illustrate the point. (See inside page of front cover of November, 1917, number.)

"Will the Teachers Ever Grow Up?

"In the name of uncommon sense, do realize that the destiny of Teachers-in-Ordinary has been newly oriented.

"Not so many moons ago, we were timid underlings, office boys and serving girls in the personal employ of self-perpetuating bureaucrats.

"To-day, we are grow-up men and women, nobly self-conscious, aggressive, disillusioned, wise.

"To-day, we know ourselves as our official superiors do not know themselves!

"We are group-conscious, united, politically canny, evolving into a powerful force for good.

"Let not foolish modesty tie our enlightened tongues.

"We are on the threshold of great realizations.

"Let us take our destiny seriously (and ourselves philosophically) and we shall soon astound the Manipulators who sit and dawdle in the seats of the Mighty.

"The Teachers' Union is Ours to do with as suits our developing purposes.

"The 'American Teacher' (the most critical Magazine in the School World) is Ours to do with as our illuminating intelligences direct.

"The Board of Education is Ours (or will soon be) to do with as befits our deeper insight.

"The very ideals of our nascent social democracy are ours to do with as our dynamic philosophy of social amelioration guides and inspires us to do.

"We are on the eve of tremendous happenings.

"To achieve greatly we must be greatly informed.

"One indispensable Organ of Enlightened Opinion among Teacher-Educators is our own — your own — The American Teacher.

"Subscribe — Subscribe Now!"

If the reader thinks that the above, since it is an advertising appeal, is not to be taken too seriously, let him read the following quotations concerning the seriousness of which there can be no question. These quotations are taken from the article, already cited, which appeared in the "New Republic," May 26, 1917; an article signed by thirteen "conscientious objectors" among whom are, Henry R. Linville, Franklin J. Keller and Samuel D. Schmalhausen, from the editorial staff of the "American Teacher;" and Gabriel R. Mason, the president of the American Teacher Company:

"In the evolution of the human mind we discover a gradually widening hiatus between physical competence and intellectual moral competence. So deeply imbedded in our life values is this distinction that we feel rather ashamed of being too expert physically. The man of blood and iron does not appeal to our finer perceptions as a being altogether worthy of our worshipful attention.

"Then consider this: Sooner or later war will cease. The tremendous enterprise of recreating out of bloody chaos some new, reinspired internationalism will be the order of the day. Who is better fitted for that reconstructive task than those humanists now in imminent danger of being bullied out of existence because their visions and their faiths extend beyond the time of bloody chaos? . . .

"Hasn't our evolving democracy any use for the student, the reflective man, the lonely thinker, the gentle philosopher, the Socialist, the disciple of Jesus, the vision-haunted educator, the pity-racked lover of the human kind? . . .

"We desire to contribute our intellectual and moral energies to the creation of that humaner world in which conscience and tolerance and personality and philosophy will count as mightily as do their fierce negations now."

Because of this attitude of mental and moral superiority, Mr. Linville and his followers feel under no obligation to respect the opinion of their superior officers; and they view any official act as "autocratic," and out of harmony with the spirit of "democracy," unless it meets with their "complete intellectual approval." In several instances this lack of respect has found expression in anonymous articles, published in their magazine, in which scurrilous attacks have been made upon school officials; not by name, but through some clue, such as age of school building, number of pupils, or some similar clue, so that the school official and his friends can readily see who is meant.

These attacks have even descended to vulgar personalities in which physical appearance and dress are held up to ridicule. For example, bald head; big, round head; gigantic mustache; thick, umbrageous mustache; flamboyant necktie; unspeakable smirk; dignified pugilist; janitor, and bartender. These are some of the terms employed in the "American Teacher" to further its alleged policy of "Democracy in Education; Education for Democracy." Presumably, therefore, such attacks and the use of such personalities meet with the "complete intellectual (and moral) approval" of Mr. Linville and the others of our school system who are in sympathy with him and his methods.

Socialism

The statement has already been made that the leaders of the group of which the "American Teacher" is the official organ, are active supporters of the Hillquit-Berger branch of the Socialist Party. This reveals some further inconsistencies on the part of Mr. Linville and his followers; among whom are the three dismissed and the six transferred teachers.

The January number of the "American Teacher" gives the number of officers and editors as ten. Nine of these, including Mr. Linville, protested against signing the loyalty pledge of the Board of Education. Yet they, through the November number of their magazine, advocate support of a party which requires its members to sign a pledge agreeing to be guided by the constitution and platform of that party in all their political actions. (See Article II, section 5, National Constitution of Socialist Party, 1917.) Just what this pledge means in time of war will be stated later on.

Mr. Linville and his followers ask that their views on military service be respected. Yet they, through their magazine, advocate support of a party which expels from that party any members, elected to an office, who shall in any way appropriate moneys for military or naval purposes, or war. (See Art. II, Sec. 6, Ibid.)

Mr. Linville and his followers insist upon "democracy" in the schools. Yet they, through their magazine, advocate support of a party no member of which shall, under any circumstances, vote in any political election for any candidate other than Socialist Party members nominated, endorsed or recommended as candidates by the Socialist Party, or advocate voting for them. To do so will constitute party treason and result in expulsion from the party. (See Art. X, Sec. 3 (b), Ibid.)

Mr. Linville and his followers believe in promotion for fitness. Yet they, through their magazine, advocate support of party no member of which shall accept or hold any appointive public office, honorary or remunerative (civil service positions excepted), without the consent of the state organization; and no member of which shall be a candidate for public office without the consent of the city, county or state organizations, according to the nature of the office. (See Art. II, Sec. 2, Ibid.)

Mr. Linville and his followers object to the manner in which the recent investigation and trial were conducted. Yet they, through their magazine, advocate support of a party which expelled from membership Charles Edward Russell without a hearing, without affording him opportunity either to be present or represented by counsel, and without even communicating to him the fact that charges were pending against him. (See letter of J. G. Phelps Stokes in New York " Call," July 10, 1917.)

Mr. Linville and his followers (or at least some of them) have " instinctive respect for conscientious objectors." (See " New Republic " article cited above.) Yet they, through their magazine, advocate support of a party whose representatives in the Assembly at Albany, February 11th, refused to vote for resolution of tribute to Abraham Lincoln, carrying an expression of appreciation to the men of America who are on the firing line in France. (New York " Times," February 12th.)

In the light of the above evidence, the members of the Committee are unanimous in the belief that the unprofessional and unpatriotic attitude of Henry R. Linville and the group of agitators of which he is the acknowledged leader, marks them as unfit to instill into their pupils respect for authority and love of country. The members of the Committee are also unanimous in the belief that, if these agitators continue their pernicious activities for their so-called " democracy," they should feel the weight of " official oppression in the name of discipline " to the fullest extent of the law.

This concludes a review of the facts bearing upon the " cause of the investigation " which led to the dismissal of three and the transfer of six teachers in DeWitt Clinton High School. From these facts the members of the Committee are convinced that the cause of the investigation was " The unpatriotic attitude of a certain group of teachers toward the war," and that none of the claims to the contrary, advanced by the members of the Teachers' Union and their supporters, is established by the evidence.

II. THE TRIAL

(1) The Hearing was a Fair One

The statement was made by Samuel D. Schmalhausen in an address at Terrace Garden, November 21st, that he and the other two defendants would be tried before a " packed jury." (New York " Call," November 22d.) After the trial an editorial stated, " They did not get a fair trial; it was a lynching." (New York " Call," December 21st.)

The evidence shows that the specific charges were placed in the hands of the defendants at 9:30 P. M., November 19th. (Test. 4.) The hearing was set for the 22d, at 3 P. M. On that date the High School Committee met with seven members present out of a total of nine. The defendants asked for a postponement. This was granted without any serious opposition; in fact, four out of the seven members spoke in favor of it. (Test. 6-7.) The date which was finally agreed upon for the hearing, December 3d, was suggested by Mr. Schmalhausen himself (Test. 9); also, the date fixed for filing the answers, November 28th, was acceptable to the defendant's counsel. (Test. 10.)

At the hearing on December 3d, the defendants were represented by counsel, although it is a question whether under the new educational law, they were entitled to this privilege. (Test. 8.) Also, at the suggestion of Chairman Whalen, reporters were permitted to be present. (Test. 17.) No attempt was made to hasten the examination of witnesses, while, on the other hand, opportunity was offered counsel to sum up the evidence if they so desired. (Test. 143, 186, 261.)

These facts alone should brand as unfounded the charge that the Committee was " packed " and that the trial was unfair. When, however, one reflects upon the character and high standing of the persons who sat as jurors — John Whalen, Fred W. Atkinson, Olivia Leventritt, Franklin H. Giddings, Egerton L. Winthrop, Jr., John Green, William Harkness, Arthur S. Somers — one feels that the charge should be branded, not merely as unfounded, but as absurd.

(2) The Charges Made Were Established

The general charge in all three cases was, "conduct unbecoming a teacher." The specific charges in each case together with the testimony bearing on each charge are summarized below:

A. The Case of Samuel D. Schmalhausen

(a) He considers it not to be his duty to develop in the student under his control instinctive respect for the President of the United States, as such; Governor of the State of New York, as such; and other federal, state and municipal officers, as such.

TESTIMONY

He believes in absolute freedom of expression in classroom. (Test. 38, Paul; 65, Tildsley; 92, Anthony; 123, Schmalhausen.)

He thought it proper (Test. 38, Paul) for Hyman Herman to express the sentiments found in his letter (Test. 40), and thought they were perfectly proper sentiments for boys to express. (Test. 92, Anthony.)

He thought reading of such a letter would not endanger other boys in the class. (Test. 66, Tildsley.)

He would rely upon criticisms of class to correct offensive statements. (Test. 115, Schmalhausen.)

He would criticize only organization or form of English. (Test. 38, Paul.)

In speaking of the attitude of boys toward discussing the President he said that he was loyal to the truth rather than to persons. (Test. 35, Garrigues.)

(b) He failed to make such written criticisms of the contents of the letter written by Hyman Herman as would lead the pupil to perceive the gross disloyalty involved in his point of view, as expressed in the said letter.

TESTIMONY

From letter, "In short, you are ready to slaughter us all." Comment, "Is there any sanity in this assertion?" (Test. 44.)

From letter, "Surely, then, your purpose is to get supreme domination and to crush Germany for no reason it seems except a mad desire for murder, meanwhile making us the goats." Comment, "For a thoughtful student this statement sounds irrational." (Test. 47.)

From letter, "But, my Most Venerable Lord, I fear I am tiring you, and I shudder to think that as a result you may be delayed in your grand wholesale murder." Comment, "For a thoughtful student this statement sounds irrational. Sorry to find this unintelligent comment in your work." (Test. 47.)

The reader will please note that these criticisms deal only with the intellectual phase, not with the moral and patriotic phase.

Dr. Tildsley's opinion of the criticisms, "There is not a single sign of moral abhorrence on the part of the teacher who criticized that paper, nor is there any indication to the boy that he had done anything essentially wrong. . . . In my judgment a letter of that kind should not have been criticized at all. . . . The teacher should have simply written on it a general criticism that this letter shows an absolutely wrong attitude on the part of the boy, that it is essentially seditious and immoral, and then he should have called the boy into his presence and explained that to him and convinced him of that fact." (Test. 71.)

(c) He would consider it proper to allow the said pupil to write and to read aloud to his classmates similar seditious letters addressed to the President of the United States. (Note.—Several unpatriotic letters were read in class, but this particular pupil was not called upon, to read his letter. Test. 20-23 Garrigues.)

TESTIMONY

He thought that if this boy brought in another letter showing the same sentiment at the end of the week, it would be proper for him to have it read; also, if same type of letter was brought in a third time in succession. (Test. 39, Paul; 65, Tildsley; 92, Anthony.)

In explanation of his attitude he took the ground that free expression should be permitted as "the school was not a doll's house." (Test. 39, Paul; 65, Tildsley.)

(d) As evidenced by newspaper articles printed over his signature, he has a concept of his function as teacher that renders him unfit to be an instructor of high school students.

EXHIBITS

Exhibit 9. Article in American Teacher, December, 1915
The Logic of Free Speech (Extracts)

" ' Silence is golden ' was spoken by a tactful, timid fool. The business of courageous is to enthrone unfettered freedom of utterance as the one imperishable safeguard of everyone's unique contribution to ' morality's melting pot.' "

" The logic of freest speech is the perception that expression with all its abuses is more productive of general human welfare than repression with all its so-called virtues."

" Is it not wiser and infinitely fairer to permit and encourage the freest speech as the genuine honesty of mind?"

" Speech unfettered, unchained, socially censured but never throttled or vindictively punished is the genuine freedom."

How Mr. Schmalhausen applies the above philosophy is seen in his conduct regarding assignments in English and his failure to correct in a proper manner the unpatriotic letters resulting from the assignments.

Exhibit 7. Article in American Teacher, May, 1914
The Ethics of Wrong Doing (Extracts)

(Note by Committee.— This article was written shortly after a number of pupils in DeWitt Clinton High School had been found guilty of stealing lunch checks and selling them at reduced rates to other boys who knew they were stolen property. It was proven that at least one boy secured a position as waiter simply to steal lunch checks and that he supplied four or five others with the stolen property at the reduced rates. As this lunch room is under the management of the General Organization of the school, these boys were indirectly stealing from their fellow pupils.)

" Pray, let me know why are we so flustered over the fact that a few of our boys are caught stealing lunch checks and that many others are caught lying now and then. Does any one seriously believe that these offenses are important in a school when 90 per cent. of the students never steal with wicked purpose nor lie because they have premeditated wrong doing? When the motive is not serious, then the act is not serious. To forgive and forget is the only common sense feeling. Mere detection is sufficient pain and punishment for most human beings."

"We must be kind and lenient, not in order to save the wrong-doer from the consequences of his offense, but primarily to save ourselves from those twin corruptions that lie eternally awake in the human breast, self-righteousness and persecution."

"To me all systems of morality are deeply immoral because they intensify the egotism and vanity of the self-appointed few who feel it their duty to stand aloof as judge of their bungling fellow-men. A deep allegiance to any kind of austere morality corrupt the mind, making one either a charlatan or a prosecutor."

Mr. Schmalhausen would not punish the 90 per cent. because their motive is not serious; and he would not punish the remaining 10 per cent. for fear he would become corrupted by self-righteousness and persecution.

Exhibit 8. Article in New York "Call," October 28, 1917
The Tragedy of Mal-Education (Extracts)

"Though the majority of my pupils will be pressed at an early age into competitive profit-grinding industries, I haven't the courage or the intelligence to tell them the ignoble truth about competition's swinish regime. My sole mission seems to be to keep the young in a demoralizing ignorance of life so that they may fall easy prey to industrial bandits who anxiously look to the feeble public schools to sacrifice to the money theistic God little needy children, our spineless men and women in future bondage gripped tight.

"When I think these things, I grow so dependent *I am in a mood for revolutions.* I realize my insignificance. I realize the tragedy of my tactful cowardice, the guilt of my cowardly evasions. I realize that to be a teacher, is to be a craven, a blind fool, an apologist, anything, great God, but a truth-teller. . . ."

"Our school education is a colossal pretence."

"Is there anything more distressingly patent than the stupidity of the human race, embalmed in books, resurrected in experience, glorified in institutions like the church, the family and the school? Every youth must have 'his fling' to relearn the tragedy of sensuality. Every adult must indulge his inordinate conceit to relearn the futility of unbridled egotism."

"School education is a sham."

The Committee believes that the above exhibit, in itself, establishes the charge that the defendant has a concept of his function as teacher that renders him unfit to be an instructor of high school students.

B. The Case of Thomas Mufson

(a) He fails to live up to his duty as teacher, inasmuch as he conceives it proper to maintain before his (English) classes an attitude of strict neutrality in class discussions dealings with

(1) The relative merits of anarchism as compared with the present government of the United States.

(2) The duty of everyone to support the government of the United States in all measures taken by the Federal government to insure the proper conduct of the present war.

TESTIMONY

He would maintain a neutral attitude in case of a class discussion on either of the above topics. (Test. 157, 158, Tildsley; 169, 170, Paul.)

He stated that he believed in free discussion, that any mistakes the students might make would be corrected by the other boys in the class. (Test., 169, Paul.)

He offered a letter (Test., 178) written by himself, which appeared in the New York "Globe," April 5, 1917, as evidence of his antipathy toward the German government.

(The Committee was unable to find in this letter, however, any evidence of his love for the American government.)

The following extract from the cross-examination of Mr. Mufson by Mr. McIntyre is also of interest on the question of his attitude toward the American government and the present war: (Test. 183, 184.)

"Q. Do you believe that you do labor under an obligation to inculcate respect for the President of the United States in the minds of your pupils? A. *I decline to answer the question.*

"Q. Are you in sympathy with the United States in this war against the German government? A. *I decline to answer the question.*

"Mr. Smyth (his counsel).— On what ground? You are getting yourself in a position you do not appreciate.

"Mr. McIntyre.— One moment —

"Mr. Smyth.— Wait a moment. I think the witness is so entirely strange to the witness chair that he does not appreciate where he is placing himself.

"The Witness.— I appreciate fully just what I am saying. I am not irresponsible. I know what I am saying.

"Mr. Smyth.— The question is, do you feel it your duty to inculcate respect for the President of the United States?

"The Witness.— I decline to answer that question.

"Mr. Smyth.— Because it is not in the charges?

"The Witness.— Because it is not in the charges.

"Mr. Smyth.— All right, let us see; let us waive that for a moment, because after all they are entitled to know that.

"The Witness.— I do not think so.

"Mr. Smyth.— Yes, oh, yes; I think you had better answer that. It is a very simple question.

"The Witness.— I decline to answer.

"Mr. McIntyre.— Do you believe it is your duty to urge the pupils in your class to give active support to the United States in this war against the German government?

"The Witness.— Will you show that I have not done so in the class room?

"Q. Will you answer my question or not? A. *No, I will not.*"

The Committee believes that a person who is unwilling to give an affirmative answer to the above questions is unfit to teach in our American schools.

C. The Case of A. Henry Schneer

(a) He stated that patriotism should not be discussed in the DeWitt Clinton High School.

TESTIMONY

Does not believe in teaching patriotism in the schools. (Test. 200, Tildsley; 215, Paul.)

(b) He stated that persons wearing the uniform of a soldier of the United States should not be permitted to address the student body in the assemblies of the DeWitt Clinton High School.

TESTIMONY

He would not allow a person in a khaki uniform to appear on the platform of the DeWitt Clinton High School and speak to the students. (Test. 200, Tildsley; 215, Paul; 221, Anthony.)

Later on, he said that if a person wearing the khaki uniform was allowed to speak, he would insist that a person who would present the opposite side be allowed to speak at the same time. (Test. 201, Tildsley; 215, Paul; 221, Anthony.)

(c) He stated that the Board of Education has no right to institute military training in the schools.

TESTIMONY

He does not believe that the Board of Education has any right to have military training in the schools. (Test. 201, Tildsley; 215, Paul.)

(d) He wrote, in or about the year 1917, a bibliography of contemporary literature, copies of which he caused to be placed on sale in the store of the DeWitt Clinton High School, which contained references to works which should not have been called to the attention of the students of that school.

(Note.— The list of books contains sub-titles, originated by the defendant, characterizing the underlying theme of the books referred to. (Sum. 20.)

TESTIMONY

As the booklet was received in evidence as Exhibit 5, a partial list is herewith submitted that the reader may judge whether or not they are suitable books for boys to read; also whether or not boys should have access to them in the reading room of the Public Library. A list of some sub-titles is also submitted.

LIST OF BOOKS

Sons and Lovers, D. H. Lawrence.
The Genius, Theodore Dreiser.
The Song of Songs, Hermann Sudermann.
Sanine, Michael Artzibasheff.
Kreutzer Sonata, Leo Tolstoi.
The Coming of Love, Carpenter.
Anarchism, Eltzbacher.
Psychology of Sex, Vol. 1, H. Ellis.
" The Masses " (a magazine now suppressed by the government) was also recommended.

SUB-TITLES

The Tremulous Poesy of Passion.
Violets of Tenderness.
Fragrant Kisses of Youth.
Shadowed Strains of Love.
Arias of a Vibrant Soul.
The Wilder Fires of Sex.
The Clouded Crystals of Love.
The Cold Grays of Lovelight.
Warm with Struggling Manhood.
The Hidden Springs of Sex and Desire.
Clicking Castanets of Passion.
Heart-throbs of the Midnight Hour.

TESTIMONY OF DEFENDANT

The G. O. store (school store) is under faculty supervision, and they passed on it and inserted the advertisement in the Magpie (school paper) and admitted it in the G. O. store. (Test. 203, Schneer.)

Booklet put on sale at suggestion of one of the English teachers. He said it might be good for the boys, and I tried to put ten or so on sale. (Test. 228.)

The librarian, when presented with a copy, asked me to place it on sale. (Test. 230.)

Dr. Paul saw the booklet three months before it was put on sale. (Test. 228.)

On sale to anybody of the teachers and pupils who wished to buy it. (Test. 203.)

All are standard works, and are to be had at the usual branches of the Public Library. (Test. 230.)

All are accessible to boys at the reading room of the 42d Street Public Library, including Havelock Ellis's "Psychology of Sex," Vol. 1. (Test. 251, 252.)

Dr. Tildsley and Dr. Paul objected to the booklet on the basis of the same sub-title, namely, that regarding Theodore Dreiser's "The Genius." (Test. 228.)

ANSWER

Although Dr. Paul received a complimentary copy several months before the question of its removal came up (Test. 220, Paul) yet his attention was first called to the book as on sale by Miss Garrigues, head of the English Department. (Test. 219, Paul.)

At her request the book was removed from store on the ground that it was an improper book. (Test. 219, Paul.)

On June 22, 1917, Dr. Paul received a letter from defendant asking him to investigate the hasty removal of his booklet. (Test., 219.)

If the book was placed on sale with official sanction, how is it that the principal did not know it was on sale and that the head of the English department requested its removal on the ground that it was an improper book?

The Committee believes that all four charges were established.

This concludes the statement of the charges made, and the summary of the testimony bearing upon each specific charge. In each of the three cases the testimony of the school officials (together with the exhibits), in the opinion of the Committee, establishes the charges made. Their statements are simple, straightforward and positive. The testimony of one official is corroborated by that of the others. On the other hand, the testimony of the defendants consists of quibbling, hair-splitting distinctions and evasive answers. Taken as a whole, it lacks the ring of sincerity. The testimony of Mr. Mufson consisted, in great part, of refusals to answer the questions put to him.

The seven members of the High School Committee who were present at the trial, held a second meeting, December 10th, at which the testimony was again carefully considered. These members were unanimous in their decision to sustain the charges and to recommend dismissal.

On December 12th, when the question of the adoption of the report in the cases came up before the Board of Education, the point was made that the members had been unable to familiarize themselves with the evidence, as there were only three copies of the testimony for the use of forty-three members. Accordingly, the consideration of the report was postponed until a special meeting to be held December 19th. Within a day or two a printed copy of the testimony was placed in the hands of each member by the Defense Committee of the Teachers' Union. Presumably, therefore, the members were familiar with all the facts when they voted upon the question of dismissal. If they were not, it was certainly not because " they had no opportunity to read the testimony before reaching the decision in the case," as is claimed by the defense. The result of the vote has already been stated, a result which the Committee feels was reached by a fair trial and based upon charges made and established.

III. SOME FACTS NOT IN THE RECORD OF THE TRIAL; REFUTATION OF MANY OF THE CLAIMS OF THE DEFENDANTS AND MUCH OF THEIR TESTIMONY GIVEN UNDER OATH

(1) Regarding the "Whalen Resolutions"

The defense has repeatedly claimed that 105 members of the faculty were present at the meeting when the resolutions were adopted, and that only two or three voted against them and that all the others voted for them.

Linville.— One hundred and two out of 105 *signed* the protest. (New York "Globe," November 21st.)

"American Teacher."— *Signed* by 102 of those present. (December number, page 160.)

Schmalhausen (under oath).— Approved by 103 out of 105 who were present. (Test., 107.)

Schneer (under oath).— Voted for by 102 out of 105. (Test., 226). Schneer was asked (Test., 261) to send in the names of the 105. In reply he sent in a list of names, 105 in number, headed by this statement: "Teachers of the DeWitt Clinton High School who were present at the meeting called by the Teachers' Council on Wednesday, October 24, 1917." Then followed the list of 105 names with two (not three) names underlined. At the end he says, "All voted for the Whalen Resolutions except those underlined above. This list comprises all those present as far as our knowledge goes."

(Signed)   A. HENRY SCHNEER,
Secretary Teachers' Council, DeWitt Clinton High School.
New York, December 10, 1917.

Dr. Tildsley (under oath).— I found that no report had been kept of the attendance during the meeting. (Test., 77.)

The Committee canvassed 30 of those whom Mr. Schneer claimed voted for the resolutions and learned the following facts:

Five voted for the resolutions as claimed by Mr. Schneer.

Mrs. Brady was absent from school that day.

Mr. Salzano arrived after the vote was taken.

Messrs. Benjamin, Donnelly, McTiernan and Michaels were present only a few minutes; left before vote was taken.

Miss Watson and Messrs. Horton, Hourihan, Kroll, Luria and Tietz were present but did not vote.

Miss Van Vliet and Messrs. Clark, Delaney, Grow, Guernsey, Kelley, Long, Moyer, O'Connor, Volckhausen and Yokel did not attend the meeting.

Mr. Schwarzenbach voted against the resolutions; also Mr. Thomas.

While there is no question that the resolutions were adopted, the above certainly raises the serious doubt as to the accuracy of the testimony given by Mr. Schmalhausen and Mr. Schneer, both concerning the number present and the number voting for the resolutions. Mr. Linville was still further in error, as a yea and nay vote was taken; consequently *no one signed a protest.*

(2) Regarding the Claim of the Defendants That Their Attitude is Patriotic

All three are "conscientious objectors" and believe that "military participation in war is tantamount to committing murder." (See article in "New Republic," before cited.)

According to the New York "Call" of November 28, 1917, all three are Socialists. If so, they believe in "resistance to military training and to conscription of life and labor;" also, "repudiation of war debts." (See Socialist Party platform adopted by national referendum, July 24, 1917. For platform, see American Labor Year Book, 1917–18, page 377, under "Immediate Demands," sections 6 and 7.)

On April 18, 1917, Mr. Mufson wrote to his principal as follows: "I shall not be able to take part in the (Wake Up America) parade tomorrow, because I sincerely want peace and not war."

As before stated, Mr. Schmalhausen's class was visited by Miss Garrigues on the day (October 22d) that several unpatriotic compositions were read. (Test., 20–23.) In her written report to the principal on this visit she says, "After each paper, chance for criticism was given the class. There was little or no comment from the teacher except when serious mistakes in English were made. The chairman asked Mr. Schmalhausen to meet her. She asked him if he thought so worded an assignment was wise, and he said 'Yes.' She told him that she and the boys felt that the reading and the atmosphere of the class indicated that the unfavorable criticism of the administration would be welcomed. He denied this and said, but for the action of the chairman (in taking up the papers) the discussion would have adjusted itself in the class-room. The chairman suggested that the teacher was not loyal to institutions and he replied that he was loyal only to truth."

Mr. Schmalhausen does not believe it to be his duty to develop in his pupils *instinctive* respect for the President of the United States and other federal, state and municipal officers, as such. He would develop *reflective* respect. He distinguishes between the two as follows: "I assume instinctive respect to mean doglike fealty, a blind mechanical attitude which people are capable of, young people are capable of. By reflective, I simply had in mind the constant corollary between the dignity of the high office and the dignity of the man who occupies the office." (Test., 121.)

As "conscientious objectors," he and the other two defendants say (see "New Republic," May 26, 1917), "It is good for us to remind ourselves of our *instinctive* respect for *conscientious objectors*." (The italics are ours.) They have instinctive respect for *themselves and their kind,* but not for the *President of the United States.*

(3) Regarding Mr. Schneer's Bibliography

Schneer claims that his booklet was approved by the principal. (See petition for reinstatement, New York "Globe," February 2, 1918.) Dr. Paul says that it was presented to him simply as a complimentary copy and that nothing was said about placing it on sale; he never expressed approval of the booklet.

Schneer claims that the booklet was approved by the faculty. (See ibid.; also Test., 203, Schneer.) The faculty never passed upon the booklet; it has no authority in the matter.

Schneer stated under oath (Test., 230) that the librarian of the school, when presented with a copy, asked him to place it on sale. Miss Arden, the librarian, says that the booklet was presented to her simply as a complimentary copy and that nothing was said about placing it on sale in the school store.

Mr. Horton, the faculty member who is in charge of the student salesmen in the store, says that he did not know that the booklet was in the store until the time when objection was made to it and its removal was ordered.

Schneer stated under oath that only ten copies were sold; nine to teachers and one to a boy. (Test., 228.) Paul McNulty, a student salesman in the store, says that thirteen copies were sold;

that he sold at least five, all to boys. John Austin, another student salesman in the store, says that he also sold at least five, all to boys.

The defense claims that the same books or a number of the same books found in his list are also found in a list given in the DeWitt Clinton Red Book, a list approved by those in authority. The defense also claims that the difference between the two lists consists solely in the fact that Mr. Schneer's list contains sub-titles. (Sum. 20.)

These statements are not true. Mr. Schneer's list contains over 200 titles; the list in the Red Book contains 100 titles. Only ten titles are found in both lists and none of the books objected to in Mr. Schneer's list is found among these ten. The ten are as follows:

The Call of the Wild, London.
Up From Slavery, Washington.
Silas Lapham, Howells.
The Crock of Gold, Stephens.
Half Hours, Barrie.
Justice, Galesworthy.
Cyrano de Bergerac, Rostand.
The Weavers, Hauptmann.
Play Boy of the Western World, Synge.
The Hour Glass, Yeats.

Schneer stated under oath that all the books in his list are to be had at the usual branches of the Public Library. (Test., 231.) Miss E. F. Cragin, chief of catalogue office, circulation department, says that the following books in his list are in no branch of the circulation department:

The Genius, Dreiser.
The Song of Songs, Sudermann.
Sanine, Artzibasheff.
Kreutzer Sonata, Tolstoi.
The Coming of Love, Carpenter.
Anarchism, Eltzbacher.
Psychology of Sex, Vol. 1, Ellis.

Schneer stated under oath that all the books in his list can be found in the reading room of the 42d Street Public Library and that they are *accessible to boys*. (Test. 251–252.) At the request of the Committee, Mr. H. M. Lydenberg, chief of the reference library, went over the list. He then summoned Mr. F. A. Waite, chief of the information division, who went over the list, title by title. Both these gentlemen said that the following books are *not* accessible to boys:

The Genius, Dreiser.
Madame Bovary, Flaubert.
The Song of Songs, Sudermann.
Sanine, Artzibasheff.
Kreutzer Sonata, Tolstoi.
The Coming of Love, Carpenter.
Psychology of Sex, Vol. 1, Ellis.

The book "Sanine" is thus reviewed in the Book Review Digest, March, 1915: "Sanine is a superman who looks forward to a Golden Age when nothing shall stand between man and his happiness. . . Every character in the book is obsessed with the idea of sex, and while those who are cowardly in the matter of giving themselves to all attainable enjoyments are made to suffer, Sanine moves triumphantly onward to meet the sun."

There are only four copies of this book in the Public Library, and none of these is printed in English.

A rule of the Library forbids even adults to read certain books out in the reading room. These books must be read behind the counter under the eye of the attendant. Two of the books in this class are, "The Genius" and "The Song of Songs."

Schneer stated under oath, in answer to a specific question by Mr. Greene, that "Psychology of Sex, Vol. 1," is accessible to boys at the reading room of the Public Library (Test., 252.) Mr. Waite, chief of the information division, said that this book was not given out even to adults unless the person was known to be a physician, lawyer or clergyman; or, unless the person could satisfy them that he wanted it for some legitimate purpose, such as advanced scientific study.

The book is thus listed in the Publishers' Trade List Annual: "Sold by subscription and only to physicians, lawyers, clergymen, advanced teachers and advanced scientists." A prominent book-seller said that the book cannot be purchased at any reputable book-store except by a person belonging to one of the above-named classes. An officer of the Comstock Society gave his opinion to the effect that any book-seller who sold this book indiscriminately would render himself liable to arrest under section 1141 of the Penal Code.

In view of these facts, it would seem that Mr. Schneer's defenders either are ignorant of the character of these books or else they are lost to all sense of shame. In the opinion of the Committee this charge alone, proven as it has been, brands Mr. Schneer as unfit for any school position whatsoever.

(4) Regarding Claim of Defense That Most of the Testimony Does Not Bear Upon the Charges

The defense claims that there was not one act done by any of the teachers in the classroom or in his capacity as a teacher which was in any way either the subject of the charges or of criticism. (Sum. 21.)

The testimony at the trial speaks for itself. (See II, 2 of this Report.) Moreover, the Committee does not believe that a teacher's influence over his pupils is limited to his "acts done in the classroom or in his capacity as a teacher; nor does it believe that his responsibility for his influence should be determined by these limitations." Bertrand Russell, whose opinions are highly valued by the group to which the defendants belong, says, "The genuine beliefs, though not usually the professed precepts, of parents and teachers, are almost unconsciously acquired by children."

The general attitude of the teacher, a significant look, a toss of the head, a shrug of the shoulders, an impatient gesture, an unfinished remark — all these are means by which a teacher may insidiously influence the minds of his pupils without openly expressing an opinion or committing an overt act. In support of this contention is a remark made to Dr. Tildsley by a pupil of DeWitt Clinton High School: "The boys all knew pretty well who were going to be transferred and who were going to be dismissed before they (the orders) went into effect." When asked how they knew it, he replied, "I suppose because of the attitude of the teachers in the classroom the boys would know it. One boy would repeat to another boy and in that way it got around the school."

Also, acts committed by a teacher, although not in his capacity as a teacher, have their influence upon his pupils. The article in the "New Republic," signed by several teachers in DeWitt Clinton High School, was easily accessible to the pupils of that school and was doubtless read by very many of them. Much more is this true of the article entitled, "The Tragedy of Mal-Education," written by Mr. Schmalhausen and printed in the New York "Call," October 28, 1917; for this newspaper is widely read among the pupils of the school as a large number of them are Socialists. (Note.— In a straw vote for mayor, Hillquit polled more votes among the pupils than all the other candidates taken together.) The teacher, therefore, through such means may influence his pupils for weal or woe, just as surely as by acts done as a teacher. Moreover, he exerts his influence much more widely, for, in this way, he reaches a far greater number of pupils than he reaches in the classroom.

The claim of the defense that acts done in the classroom or in the capacity of a teacher are the only things that can properly be considered under the charges of "conduct unbecoming a teacher," is a claim so manifestly opposed to the true conception of a teacher's duty that, in the opinion of the Committee, those who make it stand self-condemned. The teacher in the public schools is employed by the state to develop American children into intelligent and patriotic American citizens. It becomes his duty, then, so to regulate his conduct *at all times* and *under all circumstances* as will enable him best to attain that end. If he does not do this, the state is justified in discharging him for "conduct unbecoming a teacher." It is also well to remember that there are sins of omission as well as of commission, and that a teacher who maintains a neutral attitude toward questions of a vital importance to the state is conducting himself in such a way that he does not exert an active and positive influence over his pupils toward the end for which he is employed. A refusal to take sides is in itself an *act*. Consequently, if a teacher maintains a neutral attitude such as was described above, the state is justified in discharging him for "conduct unbecoming a teacher."

The committee, therefore, is unanimous in the belief that, in so far as the three defendants showed, either by neutral attitude or overt act, an unwillingness to be actively and positively patriotic in their support of the government at all times and under all circumstances, the Board of Education was amply justified in sustaining the charge against them of "conduct unbecoming a teacher," and in dismissing them from the service of the Department of Education of the City of New York.

IV. THE RELATION BETWEEN THIS CASE AND THE SOCIALIST PARTY

1. The Claim Made by The New York " Call "

It has already been stated (see Preliminary Statement) that the dismissed teachers and the group to which they belong are active supporters of the Hillquit-Berger branch of the Socialist Party. The " Call " points to this fact as a probable cause of the recent investigation.

" It is the belief of a number of teachers that a drive is being made against Socialistic school teachers. In support of this belief is the fact that every one of the suspended and transferred teachers is a Socialist." (New York " Call," November 28, 1917.)

" Discharged as these teachers have been by the boss of DeWitt Clinton High School on framed-up charges for socialistic activities." (New York " Call," January 22, 1918.)

As every one knows, Socialist teachers have taught undisturbed in our schools for years and many are still doing so. There are many Socialists who, in matters pertaining to the present war, are placing loyalty to the government ahead of fealty to their party. As soon as war was declared they bowed to the inevitable and promptly arrayed themselves with those who are fighting to " make the world safe for democracy." Against Socialist teachers of this class no " drive " has been made for the simple reason that their attitude toward the present war is not "unpatriotic." If any " drive " is being made against Socialist teachers, it is not being made against them as a class, but simply against those who, because of their active support of the most radical branch of the Socialist Party, are maintaining an " unpatriotic attitude toward the war." In this connection it is of interest to know some of the principles to which a member of the Hillquit-Berger branch of the Socialist Party pledges his support. Some pertinent examples are given below.

2. The Attitude of the Hillquit-Berger Branch of the Socialist Party Toward the War

From National Constitution of Socialist Party, 1917, Article II, section 5: " In all my political actions while a member of the Socialist Party I agree to be guided by the constitution and platform of that party." The reader will please keep this pledge in mind while reading the following extracts:

From National Constitution of Socialist Party, 1917, Article II, section 6: "Any member of the Socialist Party, elected to an office, who shall in any way vote to appropriate moneys for military or naval purposes, or war, shall be expelled from the party."

From National Platform of 1917: The following are measures which we believe of immediate practical importance and for which we wage an especially energetic campaign — Political Demands: (For Platform, see American Labor Year Book, 1917–18, pages 376–78.)

6. Resistance to compulsory military training and to conscription of life and labor.

7. Repudiation of war debts.

From Report of Committee on War and Militarism adopted by referendum vote, July, 1917, and therefore binding upon the members of the party. (Ibid., pages 50–53.)

"The Socialist Party of the United States . . . proclaims its unalterable opposition to the war just declared by the government of the United States. . . .

"As against the false doctrine of national patriotism we uphold the ideal of international working-class solidarity. In support of capitalism, we will not willingly give a single life or a single dollar; in support of the struggle of the workers for freedom we pledge our all. . . .

"The war of the United States against Germany cannot be justified even on the plea that it is a war in defense of American rights or American 'honor.' Ruthless as the unrestricted submarine policy of the German government was and is, it is not an invasion of the rights of the American people, as such, but only an interference with the opportunity of certain groups of American capitalists to coin cold profits out of the blood and sufferings of our fellow-men in the warring countries of Europe. . . .

"We brand the declaration of war by our government as a crime against the people of the United States and against the nations of the world.

"In all modern history there has been no war more unjustifiable than the war in which we are about to engage. . . .

"Should such (military or industrial) conscription be forced upon the people, we pledge ourselves to continuous efforts for the

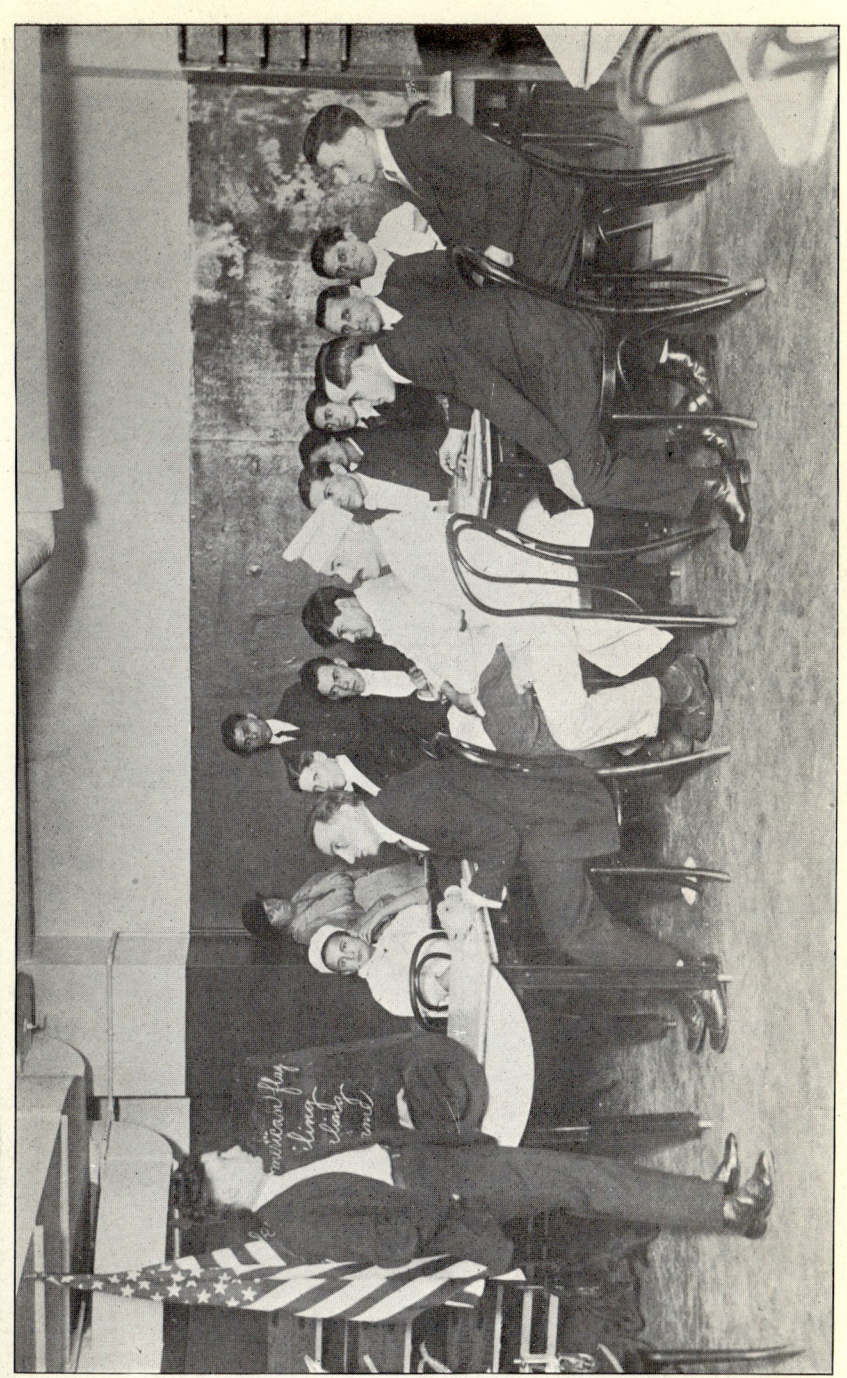

New York City Extension Class in English for Employees of the McAlpin Hotel

Church Class of Italian Women, Syracuse

repeal of such laws and to the support of all mass movements in oposition to conscription. We pledge ourselves to oppose with all our strength any attempt to raise money for payment of war expense by taxing the necessaries of life or issuing bonds which will put the burden upon future generations. We demand that the capitalist class, which is responsible for the war, pay its cost. Let those who kindled the fire, furnish the fuel."

If by " Socialist teacher," the " Call " means Socialist teachers who subscribe to the principles set forth above, the Committee is unanimous in the belief that, because they advocate and support such principles, they should be dismissed from service in the public schools.

3. The Attitude Toward These Principles of the Group to Which the Defendants Belong

In view of the above stated principles of the Hillquit-Berger branch of the Socialist Party the following editorial declaration of the "American Teacher" is of the utmost significance: (November, 1917.)

(Note.— Morris Hillquit was temporary chairman of the National Convention of the Socialist Party, 1917, at which the above platform and report were adopted. He was also a member of the Committee on War and Militarism and, in the convention, read the majority report from which the above extracts are taken. (Am. Labor Year Book, 1917–18, pages 373, 375.)

" If you want a city run for the human beings, you are asked to vote for Hillquit. . . . In the midst of the hysteria and hatred, in the midst of suspicions and jealousies, in the midst of corruption and bunglings, we find no sign of clear thinking, we find no evidence of constructive programs, except in the Socialist movement."

The attitude of the defenders of the dismissed teachers as well as of the dismissed teachers themselves in the present national crisis is perfectly clear. One further quotation from the organ of the Teachers' Union drives the nail to the head. In May, 1917, the "American Teacher" pays its respects to the teachers' loyalty pledge.

The Board of Education had asked the teachers in the public schools to sign the following pledge:

" We, the undersigned teachers in the public schools of the City of New York, declare our unqualified allegiance to the government of the United States of America and pledge ourselves by word and example to teach and impress upon our pupils the duty of loyal obedience and patriotic service as the highest ideal of American citizenship."

No normal American could hesitate a moment in indorsing such a pledge. The "American Teacher," however, comments upon it as follows:

" The pledge *as proposed* has some points of interest, albeit *narrow* and *primitive* in its idealism."

The mental attitude here displayed is plainly lacking in the quality of loyalty. But the whole attitude both mental and moral becomes unmistakable and undeniable by the next statement:

"But it may be well not to be over-anxious about yielding or teaching 'loyal obedience' yet awhile."

Here, then, is a positive and unvarnished statement. This group of teachers hesitates either to *yield* or *teach* "loyal obedience" to the govrnment.

In the opinion of the Committee, no teacher who hesitates to teach "loyal obedience" to the government should be permitted to teach in any school. But in the case of a public school teacher who receives pay out of public funds, to hesitate to yield "loyal obedience" and to teach "loyal obedience" presents a situation where the proper solution is dismissal from service.

SUMMARY

Your Committee finds unanimously that Messrs. Schmalhausen, Mufson and Schneer were justly dismissed from the service of the Board of Education of the City of New York; that such other teachers in the service as express like views should be dismissed; and that the plea of the dismissed teachers to the State Commissioner of Education for reinstatment should be denied.

Signed: FREDERICK H. PAINE, *Chairman, Eastern District High School,*

EUGENE C. ADLER, *Adelphi Academy,*
I. N. BEARD, *Cathedral Choir School,*
A. I. DOTEY, *DeWitt Clinton High School,*
FRANK S. HACKETT, *Riverdale Country School,*
ADAM LEROY JONES, *Columbia University,*
WILLIAM T. MORREY, *Bushwick High School.*

Constructive efforts to instill a spirit of Americanism in the public school teachers have been made by the President of the Board of Education and by the Superintendent of Schools, whose suggestions follow.

4. Address by Arthur S. Somers, President of the Board of Education, to the Teachers of New York City

AMERICANIZATION

My purpose in addressing this meeting tonight is twofold. In the first place, it gives me an opportunity of saying in this larger atmosphere how deeply the Board of Education appreciates the generous response made by the teachers of this city to every appeal for service that meant sacrifice in more ways than one. You have a right to feel proud, because there is so much to be proud of, and the fine thing about it is that all that has been done since America fired the first shot in this conflict has been done without ostentation and without any loud acclaim for credit. You have worked quietly but effectively. You have demonstrated the bigness of your view and the greatness of your power.

My second purpose is to point out in my humble way the paths that lead to the fields of the future where you and your successors will be asked to toil unceasingly in order that the seed already sown shall take hold and blossom, and that the principle for which we are fighting shall be so firmly established, that never more will its security be threatened by invasion.

The question might be asked why, since our teachers have demonstrated by past performance their dependability, their willingness, their almost frantic eagerness to aid by every means in their power in the defense of our national honor and in the dethronement of a power that seeks to crush and stifle individual opportunity, they should be asked to dedicate themselves for further service. My answer is that, notwithstanding all that we may do, there is more to be done. Notwithstanding the unmistakable evidence that we present, there is always needed a manifestation of a desire to do more.

I want to discuss tonight in the few moments at my disposal one very great problem with which we will have to deal and which is born of this conflict. I refer to the problem of how best to Americanize our people, not only those of foreign birth who come to our shores seeking wider fields of opportunity for the exercise of the diverse abilities with which they are endowed, but those, as well, who are native born, many of whom, we regret to say, have a false conception of the ideals and purposes of our American form of government.

There are two ways of considering the problem of Americanization; one is didactic, the other personal. The first conceives the question from the standpoint of our own opinion. It lays down procedures and fixes methods.

Some there are who rather glory in the fact that the immigrant is an alien animal, to be relaundered from the outside, looking, as a final achievement, to the period when he dons a white shirt and the store clothes of the older residents. The other view is concerned with the immigrant's own attitude, the manner in which he meets the experiences in the new land. Such a view demands that we think of the process in his terms as well as our own. Let us suppose a type. A new arrival disembarks, after leaving a country where he suffered from want, military or social oppression. He has certain fixed habits, intellectual and physical. He brings his own handicaps; sometimes illiteracy, sometimes prejudice; sometimes ignorance; and these handicaps are part of the accumulated experience of his own life and of those of centuries of his forefathers. Yet, not everything he brings is a handicap. He has something to give, whether it be his labor or other things, as well. The disposition to immigrate is, itself, an evidence of initiative. The law requires that he be healthy and in some degree removed from the danger of social dependence. These are assets. Then, too, he may bring his folk-songs, his fiestas, his home-crafts — something of the poetry of his land, and every land gives some. More and more am I convinced that we can do little towards Americanization until we approach the immigrant from some angle other than a mere feeling of patronage or philanthropy; until we are prepared to consider not only what we propose to give to him, but, as well, what he can bring to us. For some contribution he does bring, just as millions of immigrants have brought theirs in the past. Look back through the years of an ordinary lifetime and see everywhere wherein his labor has helped. Cutting the path through the forest, leveling giant mountains, bridging the impassable stream, bringing close to each other peoples widely separated.

His music, his painting, his sculpture, may ofttimes be crude but they appeal to our finer sense and awaken our dormant appreciation of human achievements.

Out attitude, then, must be sympathetic, but never sentimental. What we do is less for the immigrant, less for ourselves, than for the benefit and glory of our country.

Hitherto, if I may except the teaching in the schools and, more lately, some beneficient activities of our federal government, it is fair to say that the Americanization process has been left to chance. If the immigrant has been exploited, sometimes by industry, sometimes by party politics, sometimes, alas, by members of his own race or country, our easy-going assurance of our ability somehow to assimilate any number of immigrants has permitted us to indulge in pleasant slumbers. At times, we have been rudely awakened by some sinister outbreak — disorder, disloyalty, or defiance,— but, on the whole, we have slept soundly. This comfortable faith is less a testimony to our patriotism than to our indifference.

This great war has made us think. For Americans, the flag has come to mean much more than our personal fortune or family comfort. We have learned that democracy is a privilege, not a word whose mere pronouncement is a panacea. Democracy is that which yields its gifts only as our attention and our own effort are given to preserve it. Never again, let us hope, shall we make the painful discovery that there are American citizens who are in doubt as to their sympathies when the country has entered upon the greatest struggle in history for its own preservation.

If, then, we remember to look at both sides of the problem, our next work is to organize and to continue conscientiously those agencies which affect most directly the development of Americanization in an immigrant population. The first of these is education; the second is legislation; and the third, and greatest, is intelligent social realization that all of us must have a share in this national effort.

I shall not, at this time, dwell at length on the work of the schools of our country, but surely they have spoken with a voice so resonant that even its faintest whisper is heard round the world. We have a fashion, we Americans, of criticising our institutions, not for the solid things they do, but for the things they have failed to do. We take the 90 or 95 per cent. for granted, but we grumble at the non-accomplishment of the 10 or 5 per cent. That, however, is at bottom something of a pose. I do not suppose there is any real American who does not feel with me the debt we owe to the teachers of America, the fruitage of whose work is our army of 5,000,000 men, many of whom, either of foreign-born parents or themselves foreign-born, learned their duty to their country in our schoolhouses. We have builded better than we knew. How proud we all felt the day the United States marine obeyed the command "Forward March!" And have we yet had cause to blush for the morale of the lads in khaki? What has sustained these boys?

Yet, the schools cannot work without support. What we call taxation is merely the evidence of that support. The real support must lie in the minds and hearts of citizens. When they realize keenly how essential to our country is the work that must be done in the schools in the teaching of English and the fundamental organization of the Republic, then adequate financial resources will be forthcoming. Our business therefore is not to educate the foreigner alone, but the citizen as well.

But it is not through taxation alone that this public spirit can be evidenced. Legislation, as well, is needed.

I have said the greatest factor in Americanization is the realization by society of its own relation to the immigrant, not as a vague, abstract term, but as a relation to these foreign men and women whom we meet in factories, in offices, and in homes. It is true that these peoples, largely through ignorance of our language, and scarcely less through our lack of effort, tend to segregate themselves; so that, as a people, they are too long with us, but not of us. Even favorable legislation and the influence of education do not suffice. A clear understanding by Americans generally of their own duties is part of the work of Americanization. If I may put it paradoxically, we must Americanize Americans. Organizations of a civic nature must include Americanization in their program; not as a general topic, but with direct reference to the needs and conditions in their own locality. The Community Councils of National Defense, that is, the Neighborhood Councils which the President has requested to be made up of local residents, should make this work part of their permanent program. Every community should seek to invite the activity of alien residents, not because they are aliens, but because they are fellow residents.

However important the functions of the school, however significant the value of legislation, it still remains true that the process of induction by which men and women may become Americans cannot be rapidly accomplished. Socially, it consists in sharing in social and civic activities precisely as other people share in them. And that means that the opportunity and invitation to do so must be afforded these newcomers, not in a spirit of patronage but in that fellowship for which America stands.

One final work on naturalization. The United States of America, now, as heretofore, extends the right of citizenship to every person who fulfills the conditions laid down by law. No greater mistake could be made, however, than to create the index that citizenship is a gift to be forced. Rather it is a privilege. If there be those among us who have not in the past realized that citizenship is the greatest privilege that can be conferred in a democracy, the realization of its magnificence must have come to them with a thrill in the face of the magnificent response that the nation has made during this Great War. In no vogue sense are we to be proud that we are Americans. To be a citizen of this country is for each of us the right to serve his country; to labor for its interest; to keep pure its institutions and to save it from ignorance and evil, with a merciless ostracism of those who are guilty of disloyalty to it. And by disloyalty I do not mean the open attack on our government or the conspiracy to injure its soldiers or destroy its resources. With these we can deal easily enough. There is a more dangerous disloyalty of which the loudest patriot may be guilty. I refer to the disloyalty of indolence, the negligence of government and the imperfect performance of its agents. If we must remind ourselves of these duties, how necessary is it that we should require an understanding of them, a profound responsibility for them, from those who have come from other lands. Therefore let the immigrant approach the ceremony of naturalization as the devotee approached the altar, profoundly impressed with the great privilege that is to be conferred upon him.

Citizenship is a thing to be won, and in demanding from others this grave acceptance of its distinction, let our demands react upon ourselves, and awaken in ourselves that proper appreciation of what the alien is, what is his inheritance, what is the best he brings to us, that we may capitalize his assets, and from them develop a citizen imbued with the spirit of

American liberty, with vision broadened, with hope enkindled, speaking, reading, and thinking in our language in preference to all others, and fired with a determination to make life, liberty, and the pursuit of happiness the right of all men and the foundation upon which will rest the government of the Nations of all the earth. Toward this fulfillment, I believe the teachers of America solemnly dedicate themselves. So, too, may we, month by month and year by year, learn more clearly, more truly, that to be an American, is to have not rights alone, but duties — duties whose discharge must receive from us whatever is finest of our hands, our thoughts, our hearts."

5. Letter from Superintendent Ettinger to Teachers

February 22, 1919.

Fellow Teachers: I conceive it my duty to urge upon all supervisors to insist that the instruction given in our elementary, high, and training schools be of such a character as to be the enduring basis of loyal Americanism.

Every member of the teaching and supervising staff is bound, as a matter of contractual and moral obligation, to carry into effect by example and precept, those ideals of patriotism and civic responsibility, of which our school system, as expressed in its State law, by-laws, and organization, is the concrete embodiment.

Our system has no place for any teacher whose personal convictions make it impossible for him to be a sympathetic expounder of the cherished ideals and institutions of our national life, which although subject to modification, should be to our children institutions worthy of reverence and respect, to be modified, not by chaotic and destructive revolutions such as we find exemplified in the Bolshevistic movement in Europe, but by the gradual and orderly changes that have always been characteristic of the development of the Anglo-Saxon institutions. Teachers who cannot assent to this general point of view are, in my opinion, ineligible, as a matter of law, and undesirable as a matter of self-respect, to contract with the Board of Education to carry out the ideals to which the State law and by-laws give expression.

Neither by act nor omission should any teacher fail to fulfill the high obligation incurred when, on entrance to the service, he took the following oath of office:

"I do solemnly swear that I will support the Constitution of the United States, and the Constitution of the State of New York, and that I will faithfully discharge the duties of the office of teacher in the Department of Education of the City of New York, according to the best of my ability."

In this connection, let me quote the recent decision rendered by the Acting State Commissioner of Education:

"There is also no difference of opinion among the patriotic people of this State or Nation as to the obligation of every person who assumes the office of teacher of boys in a public school of the State, to support the Government, to teach respect and love for our democratic institutions, and for the President, as such, of this Republic. The standard by which teachers are to be judged in this respect was well stated by Dr. John H. Finley, Commissioner of Education, in an address before the teachers of the State, at the annual meeting of their association at Syracuse in November, 1917. His words upon this subject are as follows:

"As to ourselves, the teachers, representing, as we do, the State which has entrusted to us her most precious possession, there is just one answer: We must do with our mind and daily speech what the soldier does with his body and in his daily training or fighting; that is, support our country in the cause to which it is committed in its own defense and that of human freedom. The same degree of loyalty is asked of a teacher as of a soldier. If a teacher cannot give that unquestioning support to the country that makes his own individual freedom in time of peace possible, his place is not in the school. I will not say where it is, but of all places in the world, he should not be in the school, as the representative of his country."

Please make this subject a matter of conference and also a matter of instruction and direction to the teachers under your supervision. Assure them that, while I sincerely deprecate any supervision involving espionage or oppression, it is the duty of every supervising official to make certain that no teacher with a warped conception of his sacred duty takes advantage of the privacy of the classroom and the immaturity of his auditors, to express views which are in conflict with the solemn obligation that rests upon him as a teacher and a public servant.

Cordially yours,
WILLIAM L. ETTINGER,
Superintendent of Schools.

6. Compositions of School Boys

To indicate the results of the citizenship training, on her own initiative, of one teacher, herself of foreign parentage, we quote from two compositions written by boys in Grade 6 B 4 of Public School No. 103 on the upper East Side on "What I do to Uphold the Constitution." Both compositions are typical of the work of an entire class. The first was written by Abraham Fleischman, a Russian boy, who had been in the United States only one year. Soon afterward Abraham died from influenza contracted in discharging his duties as monitor of his class, by keeping order among the younger boys after a snow storm when snow-ball fights were the order of the day.

A. "What would become of our country if the Constitution was lost? In order to keep the Constitution we must obey it ourselves and teach others to obey. We must obey the laws and love our flag and our country. We must convince our good American citizens that they should not listen to radical talk that might lead their thoughts astray.

"We must teach the foreigners our language and our history and show them how to be good citizens and love our flag and our country. We must teach everybody to obey the laws and show the people that no one has a right to interfere with somebody's business and show them that no country can exist without laws."

B. "While my father and my cousin were talking about the Bolsheviks my cousin said that they were smart and I interrupted and said: 'If Bolsheviks were smart they would not make so many strikes. They want to be rich without working. They want to sit on a rocking chair and smoke a cigar like Rodman Wanamaker. If you want to be rich you got to work for it. They want to work shorter hours and get more pay. I think they ought to work longer hours and get more pay and then the United States would be the leading country in the world,' and then I went downstairs after doing a good hour's work."

7. Resolutions of the Teachers' Council

In connection with the question of the loyalty of teachers, the action taken by the teachers themselves in the Teachers' Council, May 16, 1919, is of interest. The following resolution was adopted:

Whereas the Socialist Party of the United States, by referendum vote in 1917 after the United States had declared war, adopted in its platform: The following are measures which we believe of immediate practical importance, and for which we wage an especially energetic campaign: . . .

6. Resistance to compulsory military training and to the conscription of life and labor.

7. Repudiation of war debts. And

Whereas the Socialist Party in 1917, after the United States entered the war, adopted by referendum vote the majority St. Louis Report on War, declaring: . . .

The Socialist Party . . . proclaims its unalterable opposition to the war just declared . . . . As against the *false doctrine of national patriotism* we uphold the ideal of international working class solidarity. In support of capitalism we will not willingly give a single life or a single dollar; in support of the struggle of the workers for freedom we pledge our all. . . . We pledge ourselves . . . to the support of all *mass movements* in opposition to conscription. And

Whereas the phrase "mass movement" meant the use of violence. It has never meant anything else in Socialist writings.

(New York "Call," May 13, 1917.) And

Whereas every person becoming a member of the party, according to their constitution, signs a pledge that . . . "In all my political actions while a member of the Socialist Party I agree to be guided by the constitution and platform of that party." (See Const., Art. II, Sec. 5.) And

Whereas Debs, Berger, and other leaders are in jail or under sentence for expressing their Socialist sentiments.

Whereas the preceding principles were adopted by overwhelming majorities of the votes cast; those supporting the patriotic attitude were expelled or maligned; and the attempts to modify the attitude of the party on the war met on May 7, 1918, the following request: "The National Executive Committee requests the party locals not to attempt to initiate any referendums on the subject of war, as the Committee cannot submit such motions to the membership." (See the "National Office Review," Vol. I, No. 8, May, 1918, page 4.)

Now, therefore, *be it resolved* that the Teachers' Council is of the opinion that membership in the Socialist Party, while it upholds such views, and membership in the teaching body of our public schools are incompatible.

Be it further resolved that, in the opinion of the Teachers' Council, it is "conduct unbecoming a teacher" in our public schools to accept public money and at the same time to engage in propaganda for the Socialist Party of America, to run for public office on the Socialist ticket, or to teach in a school, whose bulletin for 1917–18, states, that for "eleven years .... has served the revolutionary Socialist movement."

CHAPTER VI
Churches

1. PRESBYTERIAN
a. Testimony of Reverend Kenneth D. Miller

Rev. Kenneth D. Miller, Associate Director of the City Immigration Work Department of the Presbyterian Board of Home Missions, in a public hearing before the Committee, said, in substance, the following:

One thing which I have tried in my own work to emphasize and have tried to get the churches to emphasize is to bring out and preserve the best there is in the traditions and ideals and backgrounds of these people that come here to this country and to tie that up with the best that America has to give.

We have a great many centers, some in New York City and others throughout the country where we deal with various racial groups. Here in New York we have, for instance, a Bohemian Colony, where we are trying to establish a place which in its architecture and in its general atmosphere will preserve the artistic surroundings that have come down through the traditions of the Czecho-Slovak people. Here, under the leadership of the highest type of Americans we can get, we are trying to teach these people real Americanism and also give them a chance to exhibit their folk music and folk dancing.

We conduct English classes here for both men and women and our experience with the women of this group is especially interesting. Most of them are cigar makers and work all day. We find that even though they have been here twenty or twenty-five years, they do not speak English, for they work in a Bohemian factory where no English is necessary. But as their children grow up, they find they have no control over them and they take up English to break down the barrier between themselves and the second generation. It is a slow process for them, and they do not learn English perfectly at this age.

Every Sunday night we have an open forum at Labor Temple at 14th Street and Second Avenue, which is in a great polyglot community. This used to be a church and now it is a center for Christianizing influences. I spoke down there recently on Bolshevism and got into the biggest bunch of radicals I have met in a long while. It is gratifying work because they are all people of radical tendencies, and you can give them something really constructive. The audience is very fair about seeing the other person's point of view. There are a number of labor unions that meet in Labor Temple. Some of their members are Socialists and some are inclined to radicalism, but not all.

The following figures give an idea of the immigrant work done by 106 of our Presbyterian churches or missions aided by the Home Board:

45 Polyglot	Members	440
	Sunday School	1748
27 Bohemian	Members	1397
	Sunday School	1995
20 Italian	Members	1380
	Sunday School	1815
4 Magyar	Members	832
	Sunday School	323
5 Slavic	Members	152
	Sunday School	281
5 Other Churches	Members	172
	Sunday School	178
Total	Members	4373
	Sunday School	6340

Following is a list of Foreign Language Presbyterian churches in New York City:

Bethlehem Memorial Church of the Gospel, 5–7 King Street.
Chinese Presbyterian Church, 225 East 31st Street.
Bohemian Brotherhood Church.
American Parish, 324 Pleasant Avenue.
Church of the Sea and Land, 61 Henry Street.
French Evangelical Church, 126 West 16th Street.
Jan Hus Bohemian Church, 347 East 74th Street.
Spring Street Presbyterian Church, 244 Spring Street.

b. Church Publications Quoted

The Presbyterian Board publish considerable literature from which we quote to describe their activities with the foreign-born in New York City.

" There were attempts for non-English speaking people which deserve mention.

" First, there were the German churches which at various times had connection with our denomination and received aid from one source or another. All of them today have either been dissolved or united with other churches and denominations.

" It is important to notice, however, that the character of the German immigrants, their Protestant traditions, their literacy and rapid economic success in America, made the problem of Christian work among them far different from that among the newer immigrants.

" Other instances of work in foreign languages were the French Evangelical Church and the Jan Hus Bohemian Church. The French Evangelical Church was received by the Fourth Presbytery of New York in 1866. Its history as a church goes back to 1853, when it was organized out of the French Mission. Its present membership is 616.

" A third enterprise, which shows the reflex action of foreign missions, was the formation in the year 1898 of a Chinese Mission under the care of a Special Committee of Presbytery. This mission was organized into a church in 1910 and on April 1, 1916, it had a membership of 85.

" The work of the Home Missions Committee falls into two general classes.

" a. *Co-operation with well-established churches in carrying on work in a foreign language.* At Sea and Land, at Spring Street, and at Calvary Church on Staten Island, Italian missionaries are maintained by the Committee, to work with these churches under the direction of their pastors and sessions. A similar service was rendered to the John Hall Chapel of the Fifth Avenue Church until the success of the Italian work led the Fifth Avenue Church to take over and enlarge the enterprise. The work on Staten Island has grown to a point where the Italian congregation, under the leadership of Mr. De Rogatis, is to have its own church, for which it is giving generously in addition to the appropriation of the Church Extension Committee and the aid of Calvary Church. Calvary Church now pays part of Mr. De Rogatis' salary. Mr. Villelli at the Church of the Sea and Land, and Mr. Sibilio at Spring Street are rendering fine service.

"b. *Churches directly under the care of the Home Missions Committee.* This class is divided into three main groups: the Labor Temple and the Parish House at Second avenue and 14th street; Jan Hus Church and Neighborhood House on East 74th street, with which work in other Bohemian centers is associated for purposes of administration; and the American Parish, a federation of four churches, the Neighborhood House and the Magyar House on the upper East Side. Dr. Day, of Labor Temple, Mr. Miller, of Jan Hus House, and Mr. Thomas, of the American Parish, meet regularly with the committee, which is thus kept in direct contact with the field.

5. *Principles and Policy of the Committee*

"The plan of the committee's work involves the following:

" a. *Careful study of the field.* In a problem so complex and difficult as ours no work is more important than the attempt to understand our problem and to proceed on well-thought-out lines rather than at haphazard.

" b. The widest possible Christian service to the community, combined with an earnest ministry to each individual soul in the spirit of Christ. The committee is convinced that immigrant and industrial work requires well-organized and well-directed efforts rather than a multitude of feeble missions, which may enjoy a certain temporary mushroom growth, but do not minister to the community in adequate fashion.

" c. Co-operation with all possible agencies making for social righteousness and personal salvation.

" d. The fearless presentation to our immigrant and industrial communities of a positive uncontroversial Christian message as we understand it. We are concerned not with bitter attacks upon Judaism or Romanism, but with constructive Christian work. As a matter of fact, as the chapters on special enterprises make clear, in many of our immigrant districts the choice is between violent atheism on one hand and peculiarly superstitious and ecclesiastical, rather than spiritual, form of Catholicism on the other. Between the two is a great mass of religious indifference. Surely we have not only a right but a duty to show constructively what we have found to be the more excellent way of enlightened Christian faith and love.

" e. The combination of foreign and American born leadership. Both types are necessary. One reason for the death of many German churches formerly connected with us has been the loss of the second generation. To guard against this, it is the settled policy of the Committee to associate with the pastors of immigrant churches leaders of American birth and training to work among the young people.

"f. Adaptation of method to particular fields. This is illustrated in the chapters that follow. The principles remain the same, but it is one of the interesting features of life in New York that methods which prove most successful on the lower East Side are not necessarily so successful elsewhere. Differences in environment and in the character of the people make it impossible to follow rigidly any one plan. For example, it is a question whether the work of the Labor Temple would be possible in any other location. It is in the very heart of the congested, polyglot East Side, throbbing with life, burning with intellectual curiosity, intensely conscious of economic problems, the home of strong labor unions and of social radicalism. The Jewish element, with its intellectual power and its marvelous combination of materialism with idealism, is very strong. In such a district the Christian approach must be unconventional, friendly, obviously sympathetic with human problems. The church, which is so often charged with undue alliance with capitalism, has had here a rare opportunity to show her sympathy with the working class and the Labor Temple's wise and discriminating hospitality to labor unions, especially when on strike, has been of infinite value in affording a decent meeting place for these men and women, restraining them from violence of despair, and showing a spirit of fairness on the part of Church.

"The Jan Hus field is almost exclusively Bohemian and has had a strong church in it for many years. It has been possible, therefore, to do a remarkable successful piece of work in showing how the valuable heritage of one immigrant group can be built into the structure of our American life.

"In the American Parish we face the problem of the well-rounded development of imperfectly equipped missions in poor and difficult immigrant colonies. It has been necessary to devise a scheme of co-operation and efficient and economical administration. Conditions were not and are not favorable for the type of work done at Jan Hus, nor has the district as yet that intellectual thirst or zeal for discussion so characteristic of the Labor Temple.

"The problems of our work in all these fields have shown the pressing necessity for properly trained workers. We need men and women with vision and knowledge of social and economic forces and of the language and history of immigrant races. In large part, of course, this is the problem of our seminaries, but there is an increasing need of lay workers, both men and women, and that need is by no means confined to work in New York. What we venture to hope is a long step toward meeting it was taken this fall when sixteen picked graduates of our women's colleges began work in connection with the Graduate Training Course offered under the auspices of the Home Missions Committee. The initiative came from members of the Committee and some of its workers, and the Course has its hearty approval. It is actually managed by a separate committee which includes many men and women not immediately concerned in the work of the Home Missions Committee. The students give half of their time to the practical work in various organized churches in New York in return for their room and board; the other half they give to their studies. The success of the first year's experiment has led to a two years' course in co-operation with Teachers College.

Labor Temple *

"Labor Temple, is an institution carried on under the supervision of New York Presbytery, on one of the most unique fields of the world. It began under the Board of Home Missions of the Presbyterian Church, in the spring of 1910. Charles Stelzle had charge of it for the first two years. Jonathan C. Day succeeded him as superintendent in 1912, and has since that time supervised the work. (Dr. Day has been replaced by Dr. Shriver.)

"Labor Temple was transferred from the care of the Board of Home Missions to New York Presbytery by action of the General Assembly at Atlanta in 1913. Since that time it has been under the care of the New York Presbytery, directed by the Home Missions Committee of the Presbytery.

The Field

"A survey of the cities of America shows that the section of New York City, in Manhattan, south of 14th street and east of Third avenue and the Bowery, is one of the most cosmopolitan fields to be found anywhere. The population is approximately

---

* See index for other references.

500,000, and the races living together in this district are extremely varied.

"Churches have moved out of the locality until there are less than 50 Protestant and Catholic churches in the whole district. Pittsburgh, with a similar population, has 100 Presbyterian churches, besides all the other Protestant and Catholic churches, which minister to its population.

"In addition to the many races there are the peculiar classes of the community, with whom the Church as an institution has largely lost contact. In this section, largely made up of the laboring class, labor union people live in great numbers.

"The dance hall, the saloon, the low motion picture place, the vaudeville, and the burlesque of the worst order to be found in New York, abound. In fact, every institution that lives at the expense of the moral welfare of the community has its activity in this field.

"The purpose of Labor Temple is to establish such contact with the people living in the community as to make it possible to render a service worth while, which will, at the same time, compete in some measure with the institutions which appeal to the people with no good motive in mind.

Particular Problems of the Field

"What gives unique significance to the work of Labor Temple, however, is not the fact that it is in such a congested district, but that it is in a neighborhood which raises so acutely many of the problems which the Church everywhere has to face. The lower East Side is intellectually hungry. There is a tremendous ferment of life. In one generation, old immigrant customs are giving way to ultra-modern ideas. The children of the cities of the Russian Pole, of Ruthenian, Galician, and Hungarian villages are becoming a part of the tremendously complex life of our greatest American city. It is small wonder that problems emerge in an acute form.

"1. *The Jewish question.* Here are thousands upon thousands of Jews who are still intensely conscious of race, whose bitter memories of centuries of persecution in the name of Christ have given them a hatred for the organized Church not easily to be forgotten. In what spirit shall the Church of Christ approach them? The younger generation is too often without real and vital faith of any sort, but it is not for that reason ready to turn easily to the church of the persecutors of its fathers.

"2. *Labor questions are peculiarly acute in the district.* Social injustice takes its toil in the well-being of the people and not uncommonly they turn with great zest to all sorts of theories of social radicalism. They are suspicious of the Church as an ally of capitalism. Indeed, they have never known the Church in its most Christian form, but think of it in terms of the state churches of Europe, or of those Protestant churches which belong to Americans who seem alien to them in race and social class, and unsympathetic toward their problems and their social needs. How can the Church promote a better understanding and a truer vision of Christ? How can she show her love of social justice free from the bitterness and materialism of much radical thought? The answer to these questions must be found in the Church's relation to the Jews, to the second generation of all immigrant races, and to the problems of labor.

"The Labor Temple is trying to unite the religious activities of a Christian church with a wider social work, thoroughly imbued with the spirit of Christ, for a non-Christian community. It believes that its own life is to be found not in being ministered unto, but in ministering to those neighbors whose burdens are so heavy. The Labor Temple has not thought it wise to begin a direct proselyting work among the Jews, but it has opened its doors to all who would come, and has preached the Gospel fearlessly to Jew and Gentile. It has been a source of great gratification that in this way it has been able to put the truths of the Gospel before so many of our Hebrew brethern.

"The Labor Temple has not espoused any particular theory of social reconstruction, but in its forums it has given an opportunity for all honest men to state their views, and so it has promoted that common understanding, without which none of our problems can be solved.

"The following sections will describe in detail some of its methods and accomplishments.

Methods of Work

"1. *Equipment.* The equipment in this field is not adequate. It does, however, illustrate what can be done if proper use is made of buildings, even when not constructed with the purpose of meeting the problem of the community.

"The old church has an auditorium with a seating capacity of about 700; it has a lecture room, with entrance on 14th street which will seat about 300; and a smaller room which will seat about 150. In addition to these, there are three small rooms for office space, which give place also for club meetings in the evenings. With schedules covering every afternoon and evening of the week and sometimes the forenoons as well, over 250,000 people were accommodated in the various meetings held in the building during the last year.

"Two years ago a generous friend gave through the Church Extension Committee a much needed Neighborhood House. It is equipped with a kitchen, social rooms for girls and women, game and social rooms for men and boys, and a number of rooms for clubs and classes of various kinds, and is much more adequate than the old church building for its purpose. Over 105,000 people in the aggregate used the House during the past year.

"2. *Approach to the community.* The method of approach to the community is one of the most interesting features of the work of Labor Temple. It may be called 'The Unconventional Method of Approach.'

"The doors of the institution have been thrown open to the people for meetings, such as forums, lectures, discussions, preaching services. The people have been invited to take part. They have not only heard addresses and sermons, but have had a chance in questions and discussions to express their own views. The people have been encouraged to speak frankly their own thoughts. In this way we have been able to find what the people of the community consider their fundamental problems. They have talked freely on religion, politics, economics, and education — in fact, on every topic connected with their living. We have learned how to speak to them in their own tongue because we first learned their own tongue.

"The children of the community have offered one of the greatest avenues of approach to the homes of the community. Instead of first visiting in homes and trying to find out how many children there are and what religious and social affiliations they have, we have opened the institution to the children of the whole community, regardless of race or religion. This has been done through play-grounds, motion pictures, song hours, story hours, clubs, sewing classes, cooking classes, and other gatherings. Gradually this contact with the children has developed until more than 2,000 children in the community belong to the various activities of Labor Temple and are regularly enrolled. A record of attendance has been kept. Over 1,000 of these children belong to the Labor Temple Bible School. An average attendance of over 600 at the sessions of this school was attained during the past year.

"The large number of immigrant peoples in this section of New York has offered a great opportunity for instruction in English and preparation for citizenship. Labor Temple has specialized along both these lines. The institution has made a serious attempt to give the fundamentals of English and history and civics to large numbers of immigrants from practically every European nation. During the summer of 1916 English classes were conducted two evenings each week — Tuesdays and Thursdays. The people wanted the classes every evening. That, however, we found impossible, on account of other meetings and the limited number of teachers available. Over 500 were registered in these classes. Many of those who registered had never had any instruction in English. Persons registered who had lived in New York for fifteen years and who had spoken nothing during that time except the language of the country from which they came. In addition to the instruction in English, Labor Temple helped many of these people to get their citizenship papers.

"Columbia University became so much interested in the work of teaching English and civics to immigrants through their extension department that they have put on two courses for the fall and winter of 1916-17, at Labor Temple. One of these is in history and civics, given by Professor Muzzey of Columbia, and the other in economics and sociology, given by Professor Robinson of Columbia. The membership of these classes came largely from those who have been in our summer courses in English and citizenship. Columbia furnishes all printed matter. Labor Temple furnishes the rooms, and the classes themselves paid the instructors.

"Two special courses of lectures were given during the past year, for forty consecutive weeks. One debt with biological evolution, including twelve lectures on the great evolutionists such as Darwin and Haeckel. An average attendance of 175 for the entire course, was the record of this class. The lecture was paid by the offerings which the class made. His remuneration was $10 an evening. The offering more than paid for the lecture. The second course was on Sunday afternoons, followin the adult Bible class, for forty consecutive Sundays, lectures being given on modern prophets. The average attendance at these lectures, for forty weeks, was 475. The lecturer was paid $10 for each meeting at which he spoke. The collection from those who attended paid for the speaker and other incidental expenses connected with the meeting. By having one person give the entire course of lectures, with a series of related topics, the courses proved to be constructive and satisfactory, so much so, in fact, that those who attended the lectures during 1915 and 1916 requested Labor Temple to offer them similar courses for 1916 and 1917.

"3. *Dealing with the problem of labor.* A very large opportunity is offered in connection with the labor unions — particularly those affiliated with the American Federation of Labor. There are always many unions, representing large numbers of workers in their membership, looking for suitable places to hold their meetings, both temporary and regular weekly and monthly business meetings.

"The Church, as an institution, has been rather slow to see the opportunity here offered, which the saloons have recognized only too quickly. The superintendent of Labor Temple, because of his relation to the unions of Greater New York, as the fraternal delegate from the Presbytery, has made it know to union members that Labor Temple desires to co-operate in any effective way in bettering the conditions of the workers. On account of the small number of rooms at Labor Temple available for union meetings, it has not been possible to accommodate all unions which have asked for places in which to meet. There are now represented in the unions which hold regular meetings at Labor Temple some 10,000 members. Many times this number could be fraternally related if the proper meeting places were available.

"In case of strikes, which appeared to us abundantly justified by intolerable conditions and which have been waged without resort to violence, we have found it possible to aid the workers by giving them places free from evil surroundings in which to meet. Rental for meeting places is one of the big items to be considered always in cases of strike. Relief funds are limited and big rentals for halls soon eat up these resources and strikers have been compelled again and again to yield, not because of the injustice of their demand, but because of their financial inability to hold out. Some outstanding instances of the co-operation of the Church, through Labor Temple, with the workers, are the white goods strike of the winter of 1913, the Garment Makers' strike of the summer of 1916, and that of the Leather Goods Workers of the summer of 1916.

"During the White Goods strike a little while ago in New York, there were many girl strikers who had their headquarters at Labor Temple. The strike lasted six weeks. There were many other places of meeting in Greater New York, in small halls, etc. The leaders of the girls during the strike appealed to the Mayor and the Police Commissioner more than once for protection against white slavers and persons of kindred occupations. At Labor Temple we found it possible to protect the girls effectively without the assistance of the police. We became suspicious first, on finding dozens of young men in Labor Temple who could furnish no adequate reason for being there. We cleared these out and put our guards at the door. On a single day the superintendent of Labor Temple, through the guards at the door, turned away over 500 men, nearly all of them very young men who could give no bona fide evidence that they were entitled to entrance. It was the testimony of the strike leaders that our work of protecting the girls at the time that they were out of employment and out of money and, in many instances, without a home, except that afforded by the result of relief money, was one of the finest pieces of service ever rendered in their experience in similar situations.

"In these ways the Church has shown the workingman that she is not his enemy, no matter how much misunderstanding there has been on both sides, and because of this policy, Labor Temple was peculiarly fit to deal with the radical outbreak led by the I. W. W. It will be remembered that in the winter of 1913–14, when there were great numbers of unemployed in New York City, the leaders of the I. W. W. started demonstrations against churches. The fact that the Presbyterian Church had an unconventional institution like Labor Temple made it possible for it to meet the syndicalists upon their own grounds at once. They started their propaganda with the idea that the Church was opposed to them, that the Church was not interested in unemployed men. They found, however, in their very first visit to Labor Temple that the Church was not only interested but had been doing some constructive things, of which the I. W. W. was unaware. The raids on the Church turned out to be an opportunity for the I. W. W. to find out some things the Church was interested in doing, and it gave the Church at the same time an opportunity to find out some things that the I. W. W. was thinking about as needed reforms in society. This new acquaintance, made possible because the Church was ready with the proper kind of institution, was mutually profitable.

"A second service to laboring men has been rendered through the employment bureau, which secures positions for men, women, boys, and girls. Just at the present time there are not large numbers of unemployed, but during the past three years the need of a good and efficient employment department was felt very keenly by those at Labor Temple. During the winter of 1914-15 there were about 500,000 unemployed in New York. For the last two years the employment conditions have been improving. Still, Labor Temple has been placing 150 people a month, on an average, for the last three years. The time is rapidly coming when employment work can be dispensed with at Labor Temple and other such institutions, because it is being gradually taken over by the City and State and Federal bureaus.

"*The American International Church*

"Of course, the thing that finally tells in any activity is whether fruits have been produced that are worth while. Just to have so many meetings, so many open forums, so many motion pictures shows, or so many preaching services, is not enough. Has the Church, by this new approach and through these new avenues of contact, found results that are at all encouraging?

Direct results in the growth of the church. In the first years of the life of Labor Temple the problem of the organization of a church caused serious concern. Would such an organization awaken prejudice and check the growing good-will felt by the neighbors toward Christianity? Would it make it harder to carry on some of these social and educational activities which have been so successful? Would it be possible, on the other hand, for a church to live in that atmosphere? On both sides of this question there were many fears and doubts, but after much planning, thought, and prayer a church organization has been completed which is in reality a cosmopolitan institution. Preaching, Bible study, and Services of Worship are conducted at Labor Temple every week in Russian, Ruthenian, Hungarian, Italian, and English. The church organization is called 'The American

International Presbyterian Church.' The elders and deacons are elected by the whole congregation, representing the various groups and tongues in its membership. There is a preacher who is the leader in each of these languages and intimately associated with the superintendent of Labor Temple, who is the pastor of the church and the moderator of the Session. There are an Italian elder and deacon; a Russian elder and deacon; a Ruthenian elder and deacon; a Hungarian elder and deacon; two English-speaking elders and deacons. Two communion services are held each year, in which the whole congregation joins. The various groups conduct such services more frequently in their own languages, if they so desire. The church has been organized less than two years. There are now on the church roll 585 members. The American International Church reported to Presbytery last April 180 accessions for the year, 6 by letter and 174 by examination. There is a very large number of children in the communicant classes, to be received into the membership within the near future. Each Friday evening is given up to Bible study and services of worship. An average of 300, during the past year, attended these services on Friday evening. An average of over 400 attended the English-speaking preaching servies on Sunday.

"Encouraging interest has been shown on the part of the people in real Bible study. The adult club that meets on Sunday for Bible study has over 300 enrolled. The average attendance at meetings, for forty consecutive weeks, was 165. There are various other organizations, including the women's club, the brotherhood, the mothers' club. The women's club includes the women who belong to the church and other women of the community who have become interested in Labor Temple because of their children attending other meetings. There is an enrollment of over 100 in the women's club; an average attendance at their weekly meetings for the year of 85. Labor Temple Brotherhood, which is affiliated with the Presbyterian Brotherhood of New York, has a membership of 125, with an average weekly attendance of 50. There are 500 children in various clubs at Labor Temple, with an average weekly attendance of 350.

"Through the church, Bible School, Employment Bureau, People's Forum, children's meetings, mothers' clubs, sewing classes, English classes, and citizenship clubs, Labor Temple is serving the community. The institution stands as one of the most emphatic instances of what might be called the 'Socialized Church.'

"*Indirect results in contact with individuals.* In the matter of pastoral work in connection with an unconventional institution like Labor Temple, a word ought to be said. We are in contact with hundreds of people who are not definitely interested in institutionalized religion, but who are, nevertheless, earnestly religious — if not devoutly so. It has been the experience of the superintendent of Labor Temple in his five years that opportunity for personal and pastoral work of an effective kind in this parish is multiplied many fold, as compared with that of the conventional church and conventional parish. The calls that come from homes and individuals who are in any kind of distress are very many. The opportunities for personal touch and conversation on religious topics abound always. The serious interest that many non-churched people take in Bible study is also striking testimony to the opportunity for personal and pastoral work. There is no limit, except time, to the opportunity for pastoral work in the homes of the people who have either become members or are in some way affiliated with Labor Temple."

Work with the Bohemians
The Bohemians of New York

On the upper East Side of New York City, between 67th street and 80th street, there is a community of 30,000 Bohemians. An intelligent, progressive, and fairly prosperous people, they are among the best of all the foreigners in our country. Their love of cleanliness and their kindly hearts relieve life among them of many of the distressing conditions so sadly prevalent in many of our foreign communities. But one thing is lacking to make them the peers of any foreign people in this country, namely, the embodiment in their individual and community life of the joyous idealism and consecrated spirituality of the Gospel of Christ.

The Jan Hus Church

The only distinctively Bohemian Protestant Christian work carried on among these 30,000 people is that of the Jan Hus Bohemian Presbyterian Church, 347 East 74th street. This church is housed in a dignified edifice erected twenty-six years ago at a cost of $50,000. The Jan Hus Church has been the scene of the long and faithful ministry of the Rev. Vincent

Pisek, D. D., who has been the pastor of the church since its organization, and who by his interest in and care over the people, not only of his own congregation but of the whole Bohemian community, has so endeared himself to them, that today he wields an influence in the community second to none. Witness to Dr. Pisek's efforts are the active congregation of 350 members, and the flourishing Sunday school of over 1,000 members. This church is one of the very few self-supporting foreign churches in our country.

The Presbytery of New York, seeing the extent of the church's influence upon the community, and recognizing the impossibility of carrying on a modern church work with the limited equipment at hand, decided through its Church Extension and Home Mission Committees, to co-operate with Dr. Pisek and his congregation to take advantage of what seemed an unparalleled opportunity to minister to 30,000 Bohemians in the name of the Christian America and her Lord.

The Jan Hus Neighborhood House

Through the generosity of an American friend of the work a lot adjoining the church was secured, and $5,000 towards the erection upon it of a parish house. Sixty-five hundred dollars additional was secured through the efforts of the loyal congregation and the gifts of generous American friends. The Church Extension Committee of New York Presbytery, with its liberal appropriation in 1914 of $28,500, made possible the erection upon this lot of a handsome six-story building, which was opened January 1, 1915. This building provides ample facilities for all the clubs, classes, and meetings necessary for a faithful ministry to the needs of the congregation and of the community. Furthermore, the house has living quarters for ten people according to the settlement plan, and the purpose is to create the atmosphere of a Christian home, which will make its influence felt upon all who come within its doors. The Rev. Kenneth D. Miller, who has spent sixteen months in Bohemia, as an Immigrant Fellow under the Board of Home Missions in preparation for this work, is in charge of the House and its social and educational work, laboring in full and sympathetic co-operation with Dr. Pisek.

Already the amount of money, thought, and Christian consecration devoted to the work at this center is beginning to bear fruit in the community. The year just past has been a difficult one, inasmuch as the enlargement of the work necessitated new methods and policies and many readjustments; but the ideals and aims of the workers gradually became crystallized, and are meeting with an ever increasing response on the part of the people. The aim of the Jan Hus Church and Neighborhood House is to bring and preserve what is best in the Czechs and other Slavonic peoples — particularly their arts, music, and historic religious ideals — for the betterment of the people themselves and the enrichment of this land of ours which they so dearly love.

A Christian Community Work

Neither workers nor people are permitted to lose sight of the fact that the primary and central purpose of the work is to promote the religion of Christ among the people of the community. The response to this distinctively religious appeal has been gratifying. The active membership of the church is, as has been said, 350, and most loyal and zealous members they are. In addition to this there is a host of others who, while not bona fide members of the church, still count themselves as such, and support the work by their attendance from time to time, and by their influence. That their influence is considerable is shown by the fact that in no city in the United States is the influence of Protestantism among the Bohemians greater than it is in New York, the very place where anarchy, socialism, and free thought have the strongest hold upon the Bohemian people. For this fact we have Dr. Pisek and his co-workers in the Jan Hus Church to thank. During the past summer tent meetings were held for six weeks under the auspices of the Evangelistic Committee, and as a result twenty new members were received into the church on the first Sunday in October.

The Second Generation

The young people's services held on Sunday evenings in English are doing much to increase the hold of the church upon the second generation. It is interesting to notice that of the active members of the congregation 45 per cent. are of the second generation. This percentage will undoubtedly increase from year to year, as the work among the young people is strengthened.

The Sunday school was crowded to capacity as usual (1,050 children being on roll during the winter season). The school has made considerable progress during the past year in its organization, in the training of teachers, and the hold of the school upon those over fourteen years of age. We are aiming to have this year seventy-five teachers in the school recruited from our own young people. The Daily Vacation Bible school held last summer, notwithstanding the epidemic of infantile paralysis, was remarkably successful and effective. Each year the school at Jan Hus has made a great name for itself, and its value and importance as a factor in religious education cannot be exaggerated. During the coming year it is planned to utilize the Daily Vacation Bible School idea in a Saturday morning craft school, thus making a beginning at week-day religious instruction.

Slavonic Art and Music

In the social and educational work in the Neighborhood House emphasis has been placed upon the development of the arts and music of the Bohemian people. The furnishing and decoration of some of our rooms in true Slavonic style, the cultivation of Slavonic embroidery and handpainted china lends a Slavonic atmosphere to the House, which makes the Bohemians feel more at home there, and at the same time gives to it a distinction and charm which never fails to arouse the enthusiasm of American visitors, and to increase their regard for the Bohemian people.

Along musical lines the season just past has been a notable one. The Jan Hus Choral Union, an organization composed of some seventy children and young people, gave at Aeolian Hall last year two performances of an operetta "An Evening with the Czechs." The audiences were large and highly enthusiastic, and musical critics termed it "one of the most unique refreshing and delightful performances of the season." So this work not only proved of great value to the young people, but gained for our work and the Bohemian people a host of new friends among the Americans. Such public appearances as these do much to create a sympathetic attitude toward the foreigner on the part of the Americans. Inasmuch as American provincialism and racial prejudice are large contributing factors in our so-called immigration problems, we are glad to do all we can to substitute for this prejudice a kindly sympathetic interest an respect. Dr. Pisek, who arranges for these entertainments, and Mr. Atherton, who directed the music, are deserving of credit for a splendid piece of work.

Besides this Choral Union, the following activities have been carried on regularly in the Church and Neighborhood House:

Junior choir; music school; Bohemian school; classes in sewing, English, cooking, millinery, dramatics, dressmaking, and Slavonic embroidery; kindergarten; story hour; Mothers' club; weekly socials and entertainments; meetings of societies which would otherwise have to meet in a saloon; gymnastic classes for boys and girls of all ages; boys' and girls' clubs; fresh air work; relief work; co-operation with the C. O. S. in housing the Yorkville Dental Clinic. This list of activities is certainly an indication that the year has been a busy one. For the coming year we will do more intensive work than extensive work. The church and Neighborhood House reaches in all about 750 families, and we feel that we can do intensive religious work with such a group of people as that, and that we shall not have labored in vain.

Affiliated Work

The Bohemian Brethren Church in the Bronx, although an independent organization, has sustained very close relationship to the Jan Hus Church, through the supervision exercised over its work by Mr. Miller. We are very glad to welcome to this field a new student worker, Mr. Jan A. Valis. The work in The Bronx and Astoria will be strengthened this year by the addition of a church visitor on full time.

The work among the 4,500 Bohemians in Astoria, Queens Borough, although within the bounds of Nassau Presbytery, is so intimately connected with the Bohemian work in New York, that it cannot be considered apart from it. This year two lots have been purchased for the erection of a chapel in Astoria, and before the year is out it is hoped that a portable church will be erected there, which will be called Jeronym Chapel in memory of the Bohemian martyr Jeronym of Prague, who died 500 years ago. The Synodical Committee has assumed the financial responsibility for this work, but has placed the direction of it in the hands of Mr. Miller.

Work in the American Parish

In the beginning of the year 1911, the Home Missions Committee of New York Presbytery found itself in charge of four missionary churches on the upper East Side. They were: the Church of the Ascension, then worshiping in a store on the corner of First avenue and 106th street; East Harlem Church, with an English and an Italian department; the First Magyar Church, which shared the building of the East Harlem Church at 233 East 116th street; and the Church of the Holy Trinity, for which a building was authorized but not completed, at 253 East 153d street.

The Parish Plan

These missions for immigrants were in various degrees successful, but all more or less isolated from the thought and life of the great body of the Church, and all of them were in crowded immigrant districts. It occurred to Mr. Shriver that if these churches were federated into one parish, much might be gained in spirit and administrative efficiency. The plan was adopted by the Home Missions Committee and so the American Parish was formed.

Each church under the new arrangement kept its ecclesiastical independence, and had its own pastor, or technically speaking, stated supply. Mr. Thomas became pastor of the English-speaking church at East Harlem (made up of many racial stocks) and chairman of the Board of Pastors and Workers of the Parish. As such he is responsible to the Home Missions Committee for reporting the needs of the churches and for preparing budgets after consultation with the pastors. His approval is necessary for the payment of bills. Beyond his definite official task as administrative agent of the Home Missions Committee within this particular territory, lay the important work of becoming the personal friend of pastors, visitors, and people in each center; of getting from them their point of view, which it is essential that our older American churches should understand, and helping to give them in turn something of the best ideals of the Presbyterian Church in America.

Advantages of the American Parish Plan

Now, after five years, it is possible to speak of the plan as no longer an experiment in church administration. Without doubt it has promoted a better understanding between the Home Missions Committee and the churches, a matter of vital importance in administration. Within the parish itself a new and bigger spirit of brotherhood and loyalty to the Church has been created, and the bane of racial prejudice has been partially removed, despite the coming of the war which concerns our people so intimately and so tragically. The thanksgiving service, for example, at the East Harlem Church, where four or sometimes five different languages have been employed, has been an impressive demonstration of the spirit of unity that grows stronger year by year. One of the pleasantest illustrations by this spirit is to be seen in the English-speaking congregation at East Harlem. Owing to the character of the district, it is not likely for many years that this congregation will be very strong numerically; and those who are at all acquainted with conditions of life in neighborhoods into which new immigration is rapidly coming know how hard it is for the older stock to adapt itself to the new conditions and welcome those of strange race and language. It is, therefore, a peculiar joy to see the developing missionary spirit in the English-speaking congregation which, in many practical ways as well as in spirit, has watched over, promoted, and rejoiced in the growth of the foreign-speaking work, not merely in this one church but throughout the parish.

It is these things of the spirit which count for most in justifying the plan of the American Parish, but there are certain practical benefits which by no means can be overlooked. Any one of these churches would be rather lonesome in its great task, but when all unite they create a fund of common experience which not only cheers the spirit but proves very suggestive to each of the workers, pastors, boys' club leaders, and others. They can compare notes. An intra-parish athletic schedule proves helpful with the boys' clubs. Parish boys' and girls' conferences have been most successful. It is easier under a system of parish organization to get the work fairly well done with a limited number of workers than it would be if we were dealing with isolated churches. For instance, few of our workers have served only in one church and many of our Sunday school teachers are able to teach in more than one Sunday school because they meet at different hours.

Finally, it has been possible in certain very important ways to deal with the needs of the churches. The "American Parish," a monthly paper published by the workers of the parish, gives news, instruction, and inspiration in both Italian and English. No one church could maintain such a paper, invaluable though it is for old members and for winning strangers.

The summer camp at Oak Ridge, New Jersey, on land generously given by Mr. William S. Coffin, has proved absolutely indispensable in the social and religious work of the parish, and of course such a camp is possible only because these churches are united in administration. Under splendid leadership, it has become perhaps our chief unifying and character building agency.

Another impressive illustration was found in facing the appalling problem of unemployment during the winter of 1915. The Parish Organization commanded the confidence of some who gave generously. Part of this money was spent in putting our unemployed at work to make repairs in our own churches. Much of it went for the building up of workrooms in co-operation with Union Settlement, and we were so fortunate as to get aid from the Mayor's Committee and the Inter-Church Committee. In this way each church was enabled to get through the winter with some sense of having provided for its own people in a time of desperate need. It would have been impossible for the individual churches alone to have faced the problem so well.

All this is said with full consciousness of how much is yet to be done in perfecting the organization of the parish in matters of spirit and method. In providing for the bodily needs of the poor and still more in meeting their hunger for spiritual food, we are very far from perfect; but we are making progress. The accompanying statistical tables give evidence of our satisfactory numerical growth. A more definite picture of the work can be given by a few words concerning the different churches.

Something About Our Churches

First.— The Church of the Ascension, 340 East 106th street. This is, we believe, the largest Italian Protestant Church in the country and the largest church in the parish. It is a beautiful church and was built by the generosity of the Church Extension Committee and dedicated in 1913. Mr. Pirazzini is the pastor and he is a leader of rare power. The Sunday school and the social work of the church already overtax the room at our disposal, and a church-house is a necessity if we are to carry on the work we ought to do in the community. East 106th street is in the heart of the enormous uptown Italian colony. Across the street from the church is the room of the notorious "Bresci Circle," named in honor of the anarchist who shot King Humbert of Italy. It is composed of some misguided but sincere radicals whose attitude is a reaction against the injustice of present conditions, and of many men of criminal tendencies who desire license for their own evil ends. The members themselves testify that the Church of the Ascension has been a bulwark against the spread of their "circle" within the Italian colony. It is interesting to know that the leading deacon of the Church of the Ascension was himself a leader of a group of anarchists. Perhaps even more serious in this district is the problem of criminal gangs, which hold the neighborhood in terror. More than police work is necessary in dealing with the conditions that foster gang life. The Church must do her part and in this the Church of the Ascension has not failed.

Second.— The East Harlem Church. Services are held here in four languages each Sunday. The Italian department of the Church is now under the leadership of Rev. F. J. Panetta, who began his work October 1st. Its members are included with the English congregation in the East Harlem Church organization, and are the more numerous body. There is a steady growth in the English church and that day in 1911 when only twelve people had the curiosity to see who the new pastor might be — so few and discouraged were the members of the English congregation — seems very remote. In generosity and in spirit they hold a unique place in the Parish.

Third.— The First Magyar Church, which shares the East Harlem Building, is also doing good work. In addition to the use of the church, the Home Missions Committee has rented for the past two years the Magyar House at 454 East 116th street, which the Magyars have run themselves as a Neighborhood House. The Magyars are a very interesting people, whose needs have never been properly met. A large proportion of them have been Protestants since the Reformation. In New York they are not so definitely colonized as other races, but they are even more tenacious of their language and customs. They have excellent benefit societies, but these are too largely under dominance of the saloons in whose halls they meet. This makes it the more necessary to provide for them some proper place. Unfortunately the Hungarian government subsidizes the so-called National Reformed Church. This is a political rather than a religious agency, and it is evident that its main principle is to hold the loyalty of the people to Hungary. Its ethical and religious standards are low and formalistic and from this Church comes a continual attack upon our American churches which try to do any work at all among the Magyar people. To meet this difficult social and religious situation adequately requires a different equipment and larger budget than heretofore provided. A great step forward was taken when we secured the co-operation of the Dutch Reformed Church. Now (December, 1916) there is a joint committee of Presbytery and Classes under whose direction the Rev. Harvey E. Holt, formerly Immigrant Fellow of the Home Board in Hungary, is to come to work with Mr. Harsanyi, especially among the young people, and to survey the whole field with a view to a larger ministry. Mr. Harsanyi, the devoted pastor of the church, is doing splendid work under many difficulties. Here is a situation requiring more than our current glib phrases of "Americanism" for its solution. It is a challenge to our Christianity even more truly than to our patriotism.

Fourth.— The East Harlem Building is also used by a Swedish Sunday school which is connected with the Swedish Congregational Church on the West Side, and which ministers with a fine Christian spirit to the few Swedish families who are left in the neighborhood.

Fifth.— The Neighborhood House, at 324 Pleasant avenue, has been a valuable adjunct to the work of the whole parish, but especially to that in the East Harlem field. It is used as a residence for workers, and for religious, athletic, social, and educational classes. Around it is an admirable playground which also affords a fine place for outdoor religious meetings in the summer. There have been this past winter 34 classes and clubs in the House and we regard ourselves as particularly fortunate in having reached certain gangs of boys, some of whom were already successful criminals and many of whom were headed in that direction. Miss Murray, girls' worker of the Parish, has been remarkably successful in gathering together clubs of working girls of Italian parentage and we are very proud of these clubs. This is a notable achievement because many of the parents have the old notions about keeping the girls strictly at home in the evenings, with small liberty for recreation or for choice of husbands! Such ideals of peasant villages too often prove a dangerous anachronism in the ultra-modern industrial and social life of the city. It is therefore necessary to get the girls into clubs which have the approval of the parents and to guide them in many new world conditions.

The House has also enabled us to render service to the Slovak people, who are beginning to come into the neighborhood, as well as the other nationalities which have been mentioned. The clubs of the House are open to the neighborhood without any requirement of creed, church attendance, or race, but it is understood to be a definitely Christian agency. We are concerned rather with making Christians than Protestants and we recognize that the two terms are not exact equivalents. In the circumstances of the district with its religious indifference we have a wide field, and for most of our people membership in the Protestant Church is the natural result of their new love of Christ. The House is ridiculously inadequate for the work which has been put upon it and inasmuch as the East Harlem Church was never built to meet the needs of the district, it is of the utmost importance that we should have an adequate Neighborhood House. This is the outstanding need of the whole parish, all parts of which will be benefited by such a house.

Sixth.— Church of the Holy Trinity. This Church is in a densely populated Italian colony in the Bronx, which is from a religious and social standpoint as much neglected as anything in Manhattan. Various difficulties, external and internal, have hampered the work, but under the present pastor, Rev. Rino Venturini, encouraging and substantial progress is being made. Mr. Venturini has done admirable work with his night school for the Italian men.

Pastors and workers in all our churches hold no narrow view of the functions of the Church. Sometimes their tasks are astonishing in variety, and a day with one of these workers gives a strange but vivid picture of life with its humor, its tragedies, its problems, its baseness, its nobility, above all its hopefulness when guided by the Spirit of Christ.

The Church of the Ascension and the Church of the Holy Trinity have sessions composed of elders from American churches, who are glad to serve in brotherly capacity in these new churches. They elect their own deacons. This plan provides for gradual training in self-government.

A special word should be said concerning the rapid growth of the English-speaking congregations among the young people. Already the Church of the Ascension and the Church of the Holy Trinity, as well as East Harlem, have an English church service which takes the place of the rather aimless "opening exercises" of most Sunday schools. For their use we have prepared a little book of worship. The vital point of all our work is in the Sunday schools and the crying need is for more trained and devoted teachers. With them we could not only greatly increase the attendance but multiply results in character building. So impossible is it to get enough teachers at the Church of the Holy Trinity that Mr. Deary, the boys' worker, is giving religious training to the boys after their clubs on week days so that on Sunday they meet chiefly for worship.

Thanks for the Past — Hopes for the Future

Thanks are due to the Women's Home Missionary Society of New York Presbytery, which supports missionary visitors in the Church of the Ascension, and the First Magyar Church; to the Church Extension Committee which has erected two admirable buildings; to the many generous individuals who have supported our camp and relief work, and above all to the Home Missions Committee.

But one who sees our tremendous needs in the parish and the problems before us can hardly wait even to express gratitude, but must instead try to burn upon the conscience of the Church a new sense of responsibility. Hundreds and thousands of our neighbors are practically atheistic, many of them boast of their lack of faith; too many others are in the grip of Roman Catholicism, which is not of the fine type so often found in America, but rather that of Southern Europe, with its bigotry, superstition, and low ethics. If any one doubts this, let him witness that amazing sight, the Feast of Our Lady of Mt. Carmel in July, and ask himself how far such a spectacle accords with the mind of Christ. Therefore, a great appeal is for men and women to give themselves as teachers in the Sunday school and as leaders in our clubs. The work of a volunteer is not easy. It requires initiative, perseverance, ideas, and above all, deep devotion to Christ and the desire to make Him known to His brethren and ours. Who will come to our aid?

And finally our need is for money. Our financial statement shows how economically our work is done. That economy is too often at the price of efficiency and its results are seen in the starved lives of boys and girls and older people whom we might enrich in the spirit of Christ. The budget for our work does not include anything for relief, and it is out of the question to turn over our own poor to outside agencies in their time of need.

Furthermore, the maintenance of our summer camp, which is one of the most important features of our work, has to be met by money raised outside of the budget. A situation like this is of concern not merely to the workers of the parish or to the Home Missions Committee, but to the whole church, and calls for sacrificial giving. The parish must go forward! New buildings are imperatively needed and increasing work demands an increasing budget. This is a plain statement of the case to the church, which surely cannot shirk its responsibility or fail to show gratitude for the success already won. We must press forward through the door which God, Himself, has opened, looking to Him for strength to do His will.

Reports as of April 1, 1916

Church of the Ascension

Received on confession		221
Received by letter		4
Net gain (deducting losses)		164
Sunday school membership, 1916	525	
Sunday school membership, 1911	267	
Gain in Sunday school attendance		258
Church membership, 1916	654	
Church membership, 1911	234	
Gain in church attendance		420
Average church attendance		350
Average Sunday school attendance		375

East Harlem Church

Received on confession		77
Received by letter		7
Net gain (deducting losses)		67
Sunday school membership, 1916	266	
Sunday school membership, 1911	122	
Gain in Sunday school attendance		144
Church membership, 1916	341	
Church membership, 1911	73	
Gain in church attendance		268
Average church attendance		150
Average Sunday school attendance		136

Reports as of April 1, 1916 — (Continued)

Holy Trinity
Received on confession		67
Received by letter		....
Net gain (deducting losses)		62
Sunday school membership, 1916	199	
Sunday school membership, 1911	75	
Gain in Sunday school attendance		124
Church membership, 1916	147	
Church membership, 1911	102	
Gain in church attendance		45
Average church attendance (two services)		169
Average Sunday school attendance		118

First Magyar
Received on confession		6
Received by letter		134
Net gain (deducting losses)		114
Sunday school membership, 1916	154	
Sunday school membership, 1911	75	
Net gain in Sunday school attendance		79
Church membership, 1916	440	
Church membership, 1911	78	
Net gain in church attendance		362

American Parish
Church membership, 1916	1,582	
Church membership, 1911	487	
Gain		1,095
Sunday school membership, 1916	1,114	
Sunday school membership, 1911	539	
Gain		675

Reports as of April 1, 1916 — (*Concluded*)
Camp, 1916 (number at camp)
Boys	101
Girls (average length of stay, 2 weeks)	100
Adults	15
Special Labor Day party	48

Superintendents, Mr. and Mrs. A. S. Lovett, Jr.

Our Duty for the Future

In the enterprises of the Labor Temple, the Bohemian work, and the American Parish, New York Presbyterians are engaged in a work of great significance for the whole country. The widespread attention and interest aroused by the Labor Temple are matters of common knowledge. Mr. Miller has been enabled to be of real service to Bohemian work throughout the United States by a visit he paid to our Bohemian Presbyteries in the Middle West, and the American Parish has been the forerunner of an increasing number of parishes in mining and industrial communities throughout the country where the idea has been modified to suit local conditions. It may fairly be said that the eyes of home mission workers throughout the country are upon us. We have reached a place in our work where it is unthinkable to go backward, and to stand still means virtually to retreat. We must press on with new vigor. What does this involve?

1. *Co-operation*

It is perfectly clear from the history already given that an uncoordinated and opportunistic attack up the problem of New York is doomed to failure. We have made progress in evolving order, system, and purpose out of the haphazard situation in our own Presbytery. This cannot be allowed to stop. All committees and agencies of the Presbytery, which are in any way touching the problem of home missions in its widest sense, must work together with common purpose and plan. We have made fine beginnings in co-operation between the Church Extension Committee and the Home Missions Committee, but now that the distinction between the two classes of work is so hard to draw and the need of unity and plan so great, we feel that the time is drawing near when there should be one strong committee of control and direction in this whole field, or, if this is not immediately advisable, that we should take steps toward the preparation of a joint budget carefully worked out, with a view to relative values and a unified appeal to the Church for support.

In any co-ordination of our own denominational forces, the work of the Women's Societies must also be considered as a most vital factor. In their excellent service in the American Parish they have made a beginning along genuinely co-operative lines.

There must also be a full and frank conference between Presbytery's Committee and those individual churches which are doing work in immigrant and industrial centers. Much may be gained by an exchange of ideas and a sharing of experiences, and those who are doing this type of work ought to confer frequently, regardless of the particular auspices under which they are engaged. Especially is it necessary that individual churches should not start new enterprises in new districts without such consultation and common planning as characterized the action of the West Park Church in taking over from the Church Extension Committee the development of the work at Fort Washington.

But the work of co-operation cannot stop with this coordination of our own denominational activities. Protestantism deserves to die if it cannot at least unite its forces in missionary service. One of the encouraging signs of the times is the existence of the City Mission Council of which we have spoken elsewhere.

Another really notable advance has been the co-operation of the Dutch Reformed Church with us in Magyar work, to which reference has already been made. We shall be disloyal to the spirit of Christ and undeserving of God's blessing if we fail to see how small and petty are the things which have divided us in the face of the loneliness, the sorrow, the sin, and the misery of New York, which are a standing challenge, not to one denomination, but to Christianity.

2. *Support*

The work of the Church which tries to meet the needs of New York costs and will cost increasingly. We cannot depend on legacies and endowments, however valuable they may be, but must look to the living for generous and even sacrificial giving. In other chapters the needs of particular parts of our work have been strongly emphasized. The whole task of Church Extension and Home Missions requires increasing support, and victory cannot come to our churches unless men give for the prosecution of the wars of Christ with something of the same unselfishness which has led men in Europe cheerfully to submit to the appalling taxation demanded by the wars of nationalism. The principle of the "Every Member" plan of giving ought to mean that every Presbyterian is giving directly to the work of winning New York for Christ through the agencies of our Presbytery.

3. *Service*

We are not asking alone for money. Our missionary work is a summons to individual dedication of Christians for actual service. The Sunday schools need teachers, clubs and classes of all sorts need leaders, and various committees of management need new and interested members; the work of the Church in relieving poverty and misery in its own membership has been sadly neglected and the newly formed Deacons' Association needs those who will give themselves in the spirit of service and brotherhood. Many a group in our immigrant communities would answer to the appeal of music if leaders could be found. This list is only partial. Officers of Committees of Presbytery will be glad to give fuller information. Who will come to our aid?

4. *The Spirit of Our Work*

Necessarily the emphasis of this pamphlet has been on the importance of organization and method, but deeper and more vital than these things is the question of spirit. More than mechanical efficiency the Church needs the power of God and the passion for brotherhood. The deepest concern of the Church is the Christian message, and the Christian life. A man cannot be a Christian in his church relation and be guided in his social, civic, and economic life by the principles of self-interest only, and we cannot have strong Christian churches in a fundamentally unChristian society. Marvelous as are the things that have been done in the churches themselves, conditions of bitter poverty and excessive luxury in the world necessarily affect the inner life of our churches and set very definite limits to the realization of the ideals of Christian brotherhood. For the sake of her own life as well as for the sake of the Kingdom of God, the Church must face the problem of social regeneration and individual salvation. Indeed, neither can be perfect without the other. If, therefore, organization tends to quench the spirit, or if our desire to keep our churches and their ameliorative agencies going makes us cautious about fearlessly preaching the whole truth to rich and poor alike, then our usefulness will have departed. The Church of the living God will have become the church of the elaborate machinery. But no such fate is necessary. Not organization and efficiency, but indifference and selfishness are the foes of the spirit of Christ within the Church. The Church with a prophetic message of love and justice, thoroughly loyal to Christ, will not fail to declare that message with power from its pulpit and to incarnate it in the lives of its members and in the efficient organization of its activities. God, who has given us some vision of the task, will give us strength to perform it if we work with Him for His children.

IMMIGRANTS — WHO THEY ARE AND WHAT THEY HAVE DONE FOR US

By DAVIS W. LUSK, Board of Home Missions of Presbyterian Church of the U. S. A., 156 Fifth Avenue, New York

We generally call them immigrants. Webster says that an immigrant is "one who comes to a country for the purpose of permanent residence." Let us ask some questions.

I. WHO ARE THEY?

Abraham came out of Ur of Chaldea — he was the first immigrant.

Jacob went down in the land of the Pharaohs, seventy strong. Later they came back, 3,000,000 strong. They were immigrants.

Aryans from Central Asia, following the paths of the wild goats, settled in Greece and became the Greek nation. They were immigrants.

The Apostle Paul, sitting at the feet of Gamaliel, afterward the herald of salvation to Europe and Asia, America and all the world, was an immigrant.

Our forefathers for the sake of religious liberty crossed the stormy Atlantic and amid untold hardships established themselves on this western wild. Those people in the Mayflower were immigrants!

So the immigrant is an historic character; since the days of creation his restless feet have been making new paths across the earth. His desire for a new land is born of a craving for more liberty and a better wage. He looks to the United States with a heart-beat quickened by a new-born hope. And now the brilliant work of our boys at the front has inflamed the imagination of the oppressed everywhere, and the immigrant will possibly be more in evidence than ever before. The flood tide will return.

II. WHAT IS THEIR NUMBER?

The year before the Great War began 1,218,480 people came to America. This excels all other years except 1907 which brought 1,285,349. The ten years before the war brought nearly 10,000,000 — equal to the population of all New England, New Jersey and Delaware combined. They came at a rate that would have depopulated Mexico in ten years, Ireland and Scotland in six years, and Switzerland in one year.

In the ten years before the Great War we received over 2,000,000 Italians. Somebody has put them in line like this:

Start at the Grand Central Depot, New York, with an Italian. Place another beside him close enough for them to join hands. Line them up to Albany, then across New York State to Buffalo, then out to Chicago, then down to St. Louis, then across Missouri, and the line would reach about 100 miles into Kansas before we came to the last dark-faced son of far and beautiful Italy!

Over 32,000,000 people from many nations have come to the United States since the year 1820 — the year the government began to count. There is no sure way of knowing how many came before that. This is equal to the population of all Canada multiplied by three and room for several cities as big as Trenton besides.

There are more Irish in the United States than there are in Ireland, and fifteen times as many Jews in New York as in all Palestine. One-half of the Jews in the United States are in New York. It is said there are over 15,000,000 Jews in the world — 11,000,000 of these are in Europe. It is from Europe that we get our Jews.

Germany has sent us 6,000,000 of her people and Great Britain over 8,000,000 of hers.

There are enough Italians in the United States to make five cities like Rome; enough Greeks to make two cities like Athens.

There are more Poles than there were in Warsaw before the war, and more Scandinavians than there are in Stockholm.

Besides, we have the Ruthenian (Ukrainian), Bohemian, Bulgarian, Dalmatian, Mexican (1,500,000), Lithuanian, Korean,

East Indian, Roumanian, etc., etc. America is said to have sixty-five nationalities and seventy-seven languages and dialects.

In 1910 the American Bible Society is reported to have sold on the Pacific Coast portions of the Scriptures in forty-seven languages and six dialects.

When the census was taken in the Newark public schools a few years ago, it was found that there were present that day the representatives of forty-four nationalities. One school of about 1,500 pupils are all Italians save two — one a Hebrew and the other a Norwegian. That school now numbers 2,000, nearly all Italians.

In 1910 there were in the United States about 13,500,000 foreign-born people, equal to six cities like Chicago or, excluding New York and Chicago, equal to forty-eight of the largest cities in the United States. This is according to the last government census — write out the list and see what it means.

But this is not all. The proper way to count is by families. So the 13,500,000 becomes 30,000,000 — the foreign-born and their children, well on toward one-third of the population of the United States. This does not count the one-third of the whole number who have returned to their native lands. Of course a portion of these are from northern Europe and Canada and came here speaking our language.

III. How are They Distributed?

Not much over 20 percent get west of the Pittsburgh district. The bulk stop in New York, New Jersey and Pennsylvania, and eastward in Connecticut, Massachusetts and Rhode Island.

Go up to the top of the Metropolitan Tower in New York, cast your eye around the circle, and you look over a territory containing over 7,000,000 people, or one-fifteenth of the population of the United States. The greater number of these are foreign-born with their children.

It means a new frontier. Formerly we sent our missionaries west. Now we must send them east as well. The firing line is now on the banks of the Hudson, the Passaic, the Delaware, the Susquehanna and the Ohio, as well as in the woods of Oregon and on the plains of Texas.

Thus the question of the immigrant comes pressing in upon the synods and presbyteries of the east and middle west and bulks large in their home mission task. The Home Board spends every year approximately $100,000 in working among immigrants. Three-fifths is for work in congested city centers, for there the recent immigrants colonize in racial groups, Italians, Poles, Jews, or in polyglot communities where a score of languages are spoken.

But the immigrant is not restricted to the city. The coal and iron mining communities present the same conditions and where ordinarily there are more intolerable conditions of housing and sanitation. Attracted by the higher wages of our mills, mines and shops the peasant workers of Europe distribute themselves over the great industrial zone of America and live in relative isolation until economic progress and the second generation pushes them up and out into our larger community life. The immigrant has come to stay. The America of tomorrow is largely in his hands.

IV. WHAT ARE THEIR ANTECEDENTS?

There are two periods of immigration called the old and the new. In the old period they came mostly from northern Europe; in the new period they have come mostly from southern and eastern Europe. The new period began about forty years ago.

Four things can be said of the immigrant of the new period:

He has come from a country
1. Where the government was monarchial;
2. Where education was for the few;
3. Where economically he lived on the margin;
4. Where the religion was non-Protestant.

Consequently three things result:

1. He knows little about political democracy; he has had no opportunity for practice. Is it much wonder that in the process of advance he may in some places have to pass through upheavals as in some parts of Europe today?

2. There is a large percentage of illiteracy — among the old immigrants about 3 per cent. and among the new immigrants from 20 to 70 per cent., according to the place from which they emigrate.

3. Multitudes have no Bible. The old immigrant brought his Bible with him — to large numbers of the new immigrants it is a sealed or unknown book.

The old and new immigrant are alike in that both came from village or country life, but they are unlike in that many of the old immigrants went to the country and most of the new immigrants go to the city. This makes the stress on both the individual and society. They come to conditions for which they are wholly unprepared.

V. What is Their Religious Condition?

Multitudes come from Roman Catholic countries. But in the adjustments to new conditions the Church is pushed out. However, there are degrees of loyalty to the old Church about as follows:

A. The Irish are the most loyal of all. The Irishman is the backbone of the Roman Catholic Church.

B. The Poles are fairly loyal. Alas! There was no Poland even before the war. The powers came together and sliced up Poland as you would divide a pie, each taking a piece. The Pole has lived in the hope that some day there would be a Poland again. The old Church has not been averse to that anticipation, so the Pole has adhered fairly well to the Church.

C. The Ruthenians (they call themselves Ukrainians) have broken away in part. Up in Canada they have about thirty Presbyterian churches and stations. In Newark, N. J., is the Mother Presbyterian Church called the First Ruthenian Presbyterian Church of St. Peter and St. Paul, organized December 13, 1908, the oldest Ruthenian Presbyterian Church in the world.

D. The Italians have fallen away in large numbers. The majority of Italian men care little for the Pope or the Bishop or the ecclesiastical machinery. This feeling has been intensified since the war began. The Italian has felt that the Pope sympathized with Austria, so the breach has been widened. The great majority of Italian men no longer go to confession. Their broken relation to the Church does not help in morals. The young Italian is in danger of going to the bad.

E. The Bohemians have not only broken with the old Church, but great masses of them have broken with religious faith itself. Their numerous social societies take the place of the Church. But the intelligence of the people may some day lead them back to the faith of their great apostle, John Hus, for among the Bohemians there is less illiteracy than among any other of the new peoples who come to us.

The Jews

As to the Jews, it is well known that they are neglecting the Synagogue, the young Jew especially. A considerable number on the East Side of New York are trying to live without the Church and so without God. This has been tried before and brings but one result. No Church means no God, and no God means gunmen! The Jew of orthodox faith is a safe citizen. The agnostic makes the problem.

Trotzky, who rules Russia, saw the tenement houses and sweat shops of New York. On the other hand, he saw unparalleled wealth. These to him were American democracy. With this education America gave Trotzky back to Russia. This was our contribution toward the solution of the human problem in Europe!

The Protestant Teachers' Association of New York gives out some figures that rather startle. There are 860,000 children in New York that never attend Sunday school. This means that there are more than twice as many adults who never darken a church door.

Newark with its nearly half a million people has at least 150,000 churchless and many thousands more whose attachment to the Church is very loose. Jersey City, Paterson and many other cities are not very different.

VI. What Do They Do For Us?

A. *They suffer for us.* They have a monopoly of the dangerous and extra-hazardous trades. They are the structural iron workers and mine workers. They go up the highest; they go down the lowest. They toil in rolling mills and factories. They dig ditches. They build bridges. They are injured for life and are killed by the thousand every year. It is estimated that there are 30,000 killed each year. Secretary of the Interior Lane reported for 1917 that there were 2,695 men killed in coal mines.

Some people think of them as "Wops" and say "Never mind!" or "Well, they are tough and don't mind it!" The fact is that our civilization is built on the rockbed of human suffering. We have our comforts because somebody is willing to suffer for them.

B. *They produce the things we need.* Haskin, in his book "The Immigrant, an Asset and a Liability," represents the immigrant as saying:

"I am an immigrant;
"I contribute 85 per cent. of all the labor in the slaughtering and meat-packing industries;
"I do seven-tenths of the bituminous coal mining;
"I do seven-eighths of all the work in the woolen mills;
"I contribute nine-tenths of all the labor in the cotton mills;
"I make nineteen-twentieths of all the clothing;
"I manufacture more than half the shoes;
"I build four-fifths of all the furniture;
"I make half of the collars, cuffs, and shirts;
"I turn out four-fifths of all the leather;
"I make half the gloves;
"I refine nearly nineteen-twentieths of the sugar;
"I make half the tobacco and cigars;
"No wonder I am a problem! What would you do without me?"

C. *They and their people have handed down to us untold benefits.* Who discovered this land? An Italian name Columbus. Who gave it a name? Another Italian named Americus Vespucius. Where do we get our conception of law? From these same people, the Romans. What names stand in the front rank as artists? Raphael and Michaelangelo, Italians. Who made popular true astronomy and invented the microscope and the thermometer and the proportional compass? Galileo, an Italian. Who stands among the immortals in literature? Dante, an Italian. Who discovered dynamic electricity? Galvani, an Italian — and from him we get the word "galvanic." Who gave us the word "volt?" An Italian named Volta. Who gave us wireless telegraphy? Marconi, an Italian. The Italian has made the world debtor to his genius. These countrymen of Caesar and Virgil are now our neighbors. When we studied Caesar and Virgil in college it never occurred to us that we would live to see the day when some of their people would be living next door to us. It has come to pass. Last year the writer lived in an apartment house owned by an Italian.

We are indebted to the Slav also. Who gave us the true theory of the heavens? Copernicus, a Slav. It was a Slav named

Comenius who gave us advanced views on education and was the forerunner of Froebel and Mann. A Slav named John Huss anticipated Martin Luther by a century in the announcement of the principles of the Reformation — sealing these principles in his martyr blood. It was a Slav named Sobieski who in 1688 defeated the Turkish army and prevented Europe from becoming Mohammedan. It was a Slav named Kosciusko who planned the fortifications at Saratoga and was chief engineer in constructing the fortifications at West Point. It was a Slav named Pulaski who, by the authority of Congress, organized Pulaski's Legion, and in the siege of Savannah gave his life in order to make democracy safe in America. Another Slav, soon after the landing of the Pilgrims, settled in New Jersey and founded the large and well-known Zabriski family. One member of this family was chancellor of New Jersey; another was dean of Harvard College; and it is said that their blood runs in the veins of such distinguished families as that of Gouverneur Morris, the Bayards, the Jays, and the Astors. The Slav has made a distinguished contribution to American life.

The Jew comes to us in numbers about equal to the Slav. This is his New Jerusalem and about the only New Jerusalem some of his people care for. He is called one of the "undesirables." No doubt he gives some occasion for this. His doctrine of seclusion breeds opposition. It is a law of life that we get back what we give. Practice seclusion and be secluded. But notwithstanding this the Jew has a great record. The world owes the Hebrew race a debt it can never pay. Who taught the world the idea of one God? The Jew. Who gave the world the idea of democracy? The Jew. Who gave the world the Savior, Christ? The Jew. Who gave the world the revelation of God? The Jew. Who gave the world the Christian faith? The Jew.

The greatest names of history are those of Jews: Abraham, Joseph, Moses, David, Isaiah, Elijah, Daniel, Matthew, Mark, John, Peter, Paul, and, greatest of all, Jesus, the Son of Mary. How poor this world would be without these! Our debt to the Jew is greater than to any other people who ever lived or will live.

The Jew was one of the great sufferers in the present Great War. This has been called "his third exil," with sorrow and suffering equal to some of the past. He has been fighting in all armies and playing a distinguished role. He has held chief positions in all the warring nations. Lord Chief Justice Reading of

England is a Jew. The first man taken as a hostage in Antwerp was a Jew named Rothchild. Several Jews held important positions in the French Cabinet. The Cabinet Minister of Italy, M. Salvatore Barzillai, was a Jew. The transportation of all the German troops was under the direction of Albert Ballein, a Jew, and the only man who dared defy the Kaiser in the Reichstag and vote openly against the German War Loan was a Jew, Herr Liebknecht, who in the streets of Berlin has recently given his life for his principles. And now the man who reigns in Russia is a Jew — Leon Trotzky!

In America a Jew has been exalted to the high position of a Justice of the Supreme Court, and New Jersey has honored a Jew with a position in her higher court. The immigrant peoples have made us great contributions.

D. *He brings wealth.* What makes a nation great? Not silver and gold, not land, not cities, not railroads; none of these things in themselves make a nation great. A nation is great as its citizens are great.

It is a slow and expensive thing to produce citizens. We can raise a pig in six months or a year — a pretty good pig. But it requires more than twenty years to grow a man. It requires the care and attention of one or more persons who will make sacrifices. It costs money to house and feed and clothe and educate. It is an expensive thing to grow men and women. But the immigrant comes to us full grown. He has cost not a penny for housing or feeding or clothing or education. Probably he is not what we would have made him, but here he is, and Europe has paid all the bills. We get him gratis, and, besides, he hands us on landing $25. What if he does send back some of the money that he earns? He can't send back the Hudson River Tunnel that he built, nor the East River Bridge that he constructed, nor the coal that he mined, nor the buildings that he helped to erect. He is a contributor to our wealth.

Now, What Is Our Part?

The answer might be given in one sentence: We must either get him or he will get us! He is already a power in politics. The Italian takes to politics as the duck takes to water. The Jew inclines to education and newspapers and moving pictures. Already he has a big influence among the educators and in the near future his activities will be still greater. The Slav is beginning to come to himself, and before long through his new citizenship he will reveal his power. The Greek has monopolized some branches of trade.

Two things we must do:

1. *Give him a decent environment.* He does not have it now. He lives in the worst part of every city. One colony of Italians in Newark, of over 30,000 people, has nearly 100 saloons. How can these people be properly Americanized or evangelized in the presence of such a menace? Who put these saloons there? The Italians did not bring them from Italy. The answer must be that American commercialism put them there. Thank God this day is about over. But when the saloon is gone the terrible housing problem remains. The immigrant must have a better environment and better working conditions.

2. *Give him a Gospel with two sides — the spiritual and the social.* He has never had either properly. He has had a partial Gospel — a dead Christ. He has had too much Cross and not enough life. Robert E. Speer, in his book on South America, tells us that in that land everywhere you look you see the representation of the dead Christ. The trouble with Mexico and South America is that they have a dead Christ. Hosts of immigrants have a dead Christ.

We must give the immigrants the Gospel of the living Christ and show them how that Gospel has to do with real life. What is the great problem in America? Not political democracy, for that has been worked out or is in the process of being worked out. Neither is the problem how to make men good — we know about that — we have the only recipe we will ever have. But the great problem is how to make men who are good, or in the process of being made good, live together so as to make good society — the Kingdom of Heaven on Earth. The problem is not how to get men to heaven, but how to get heaven into men, so as to make good society. This comes through regenerated individuals. The regenerating and socializing power of the Gospel is the need of the hour. Real democracy includes industry and economics. To be permanent it must be based on spiritual religion.

Men and women of the Church, are we equal to the task? It is the greatest opportunity and the greatest responsibility that has ever come to the American Church. There is no doubt about results. The children of these foreigners are more responsive than are the children of the old line native Americans. We must not expect to make Scotch-Irish Presbyterians out of Slavs and Italians, but we can make Christians. Scratch the ground, sow the seed, and a harvest will spring up. Hundreds and thousands of dollars are needed for this work. We have been giving liberally for the saving of democracy. No sacrifice was too great! Why can't we give for the saving of the people and human society?

We are living in a new age. Nations are being born in a day. The Jew and Gentile in lands where they never had a chance before are trying their hands at the new democracy. All the world is in motion. Shall the Church sit still and take no part in the movements of humanity? Appealing hands are everywhere lifted toward better things. Shall we take advantage of this human awakening and respond to the call with MEN AND MONEY?

Rural Immigrant Communities

The recent immigration from Europe is slowly infiltrating on the land. The Poles are largely engaged in market-gardening on Long Island and are acquiring the abandoned farms of New England. The Italians have made a number of rural settlements in New Jersey, California and the southwest. The Finns are clearing land in the northwest. But as yet there is nothing comparable to the early settlement of Scandinavians and Germans in the northwest, or the Bohemian farming communities in the west and in Texas. Among these latter the two Bohemian presbyteries have been established. Both are largely home mission presbyteries, the Board aiding twenty-one fields at an annual outlay of $7,000. Dr. W. E. Finley, of the Board's staff, made a tour of these presbyteries in the early spring and bears eloquent testimony to the loyalty of these Bohemian Presbyterians to Church and Nation. Their work is of outstanding significance in the new community life of these agricultural states. Both English and Bohemian are employed in the services.

Summary

During the past year the Board aided 106 churches and missions in immigrant communities, as follows:

45 Polyglot	20 Italian
27 Bohemian	4 Magyar
5 Other Slavic	5 Others

These churches and missions enrolled a total membership of 4,373, with 6,340 in the Sunday-school.

CHRISTIAN AMERICANIZATION; OUR NATIONAL IDEALS AND MISSION

I. Introduction and Explanations

The Melting Pot

Does it Melt?

America should be a great Christian brotherhood. She was founded as a home of religion, and has received contributions of rich ethical and religious meaning. She is a part of the world named by the Master in his great commission, "And teach all nations" ("teach" here in America, as well as elsewhere).

Yet, not all are taught; not all are religious; not all are kindly disposed toward their fellows.

America has land, and minerals, and farms, and herds, and factories, and stores, and banks. She possesses marvelous wealth.

More than 1,000,000,000 people dwell within her borders. Great cities have arisen. Comforts and luxuries have multiplied. Concentrated material and social power are here.

America's government is a great venture in applying the Christian principles of fraternity and equity. Democracy aims at exemplifying the Golden Rule. In theory it incorporates in government the second great commandment, "Thou shalt love thy neighbor as thyself," giving him the same powers, privileges and treatment as we enjoy. And yet the theory fails of full expression in practice.

Hither have come multitudes from all lands, desiring liberty, seeking wealth, making homes. The melting pot has not always melted; the fires have not continuously burned; the divergent elements have not altogether fused.

Some Compensations of War

Offsetting the awful cost of war already some compensating gains appear.

We know each other better: We have made acquaintance with people the world over, their lands, their rivers and cities, their rulers, their laws and customs. We know our neighbors here better. Barriers between races, between churches, between classes, have broken down. The rich and the poor meet together.

In Liberty Loan drives, in Red Cross campaigns, in great surging movements of generosity toward every form of war service and war relief, we have mingled work and workers and gifts. We are a better blended brotherhood than ever before.

Together we have volunteered for war, and together we have faced the national draft. Our boys are side by side on land and on sea, under the one flag. We are dropping the hyphen. We have become Americans as never before. In closer combination and co-operation we realize our common citizenship.

We are consecrating all our toil to common national ends, the preservation of democracy, for service to the world, recognizing that those who build ships, and those who make munitions, and those who raise crops, and those who use sparingly the wheat and meat — that others may be fed — are all serving the common weal as worthily as those who wear the blue and the khaki. Daily drudgery derives a dignity of patriotism when devoted to national needs.

Conventionalities are less rigid. Deep feeling disregards form. Hearts speak to hearts, in loyal devotion, in strong determination, in great surrenders of self for sacrifice, in pain and suffering, when men die and the places at home become vacant. Losses of life level inequalities. The language of pain is universal. There can be no misunderstanding when men unite in paying the great price. A National Calvary makes many an atonement.

The Church, Her Spirit

It is not a time for the Christian Church to concern herself with phrases and forms. The spirit of Christ in a new evangel is taking the hidden things of life and almost without words is transfusing them amongst the people. One hears of "The Religion of the Inarticulate." There is an inarticulate brotherhood, created in the fear of God, based upon altruistic self-surrender, and dedicated to a living confidence in immortality.

The men who face death deliberately, understandingly, with the conscious purpose of giving all for the sake of others, lay hold upon some realities, which must be recognized, whether or not suitable words be spoken.

The Church herself is becoming more simple, more hearty and whole-souled, more genuinely devoted to all classes and conditions of men. Her interests are becoming wider. She is beginning to recognize the hosts of her allies, social, economical, industrial, educational, which in service to men have caught much of the Master's spirit.

The Church does not abandon her distinctive mission, but she entertains a wider sympathy, she engages in a broader activity, she is more comprehensive, more inclusive; hallowed by a deeper consecration, she is more sacrificial.

The Pastor — His Opportunity

It is a glorious time for the office of the Christian ministry, a time of great privilege and opportunity. The ranks are not over-crowded; indeed the ranks are depleted, and those who now minister in holy things must serve with a fuller, richer service. The message from an honest mind and a pure heart, receives a more attentive hearing than has been usual. The place and power of the pulpit are assured, if there be the message; and the homes and hearts of men have been opened for the sayings of a friend in the solace and the assurances of the Gospel. But mere words and the phrases of long ago seem out of place. A new interpretation of Christ in terms understandable today seems necessary. The present puts a new challenge in the command of old, " Go . . . teach."

The Message and the Method

The time was when definitions and intellectual creeds occupied the chief place. They need not be ignored now, but there is a language of life more compelling than definition and dogma. May a man be a Christian and not call himself a Christian, perhaps not know what the word " Christian " means? In Palestine none of those who followed the Master, in those early days, knew this name or confessed it. They were " called Christians first in Antioch." Yet they were followers of Jesus before names and definitions were used.

Jesus came to found the Kingdom of God amongst men. He pronounced no set phrases nor formulae. He established a new social order, based upon great principles of love and fellowship.

The spirit of Jesus needs interpretation — re-interpretation today by preaching and by living — in all departments of life.

Less important is it to create new organizations and found new missions than it is to infuse into the whole Church, and into the agencies now existing, the spirit of Jesus.

We Americans over-organize; we do not often over-energize. Now we need to energize — energize — not organize.

A National Acknowledgment of the Need of Ministry

In the Conscription Act, which was enacted by Congress, and has been accepted with surprising willingness and unanimity by the nation, ministers and theological students are exempted from the draft. Why is this? On what good ground of national economy does the exemption rest? Many have debated the point? Dr. Shailer Mathews of the University of Chicago, former president of the Federal Council of Churches, declared that clerical exemption is either " an insult or a challenge." In the " Biblical World," which he edits, he says, " it is an insult, if such exemption implies that ministers are not as ready to serve their country as any other citizens, that they are slackers, or that they are so effeminate that they would not make good soldiers." On the other hand, he points out, " it is a challenge, if it means that ministers are engaged in a work so important that the government is not warranted in calling them from it even for the defense of the nation. The interpretation to be put upon this exemption will be determined by ministers themselves." And Dr. Mathews put it squarely up to them:

" If in the present crisis they go about their work with no increase of labor or the spirit of sacrifice, making an excuse out of a holy calling, they accept the exemption as an insult to their calling.

" No minister has a right to be a religious slacker.

"A Church in a time of war should show a sacrificial loyalty to man and God as great as does a nation in war. For a church member to economize on the Church is to brand himself not only a disloyal Christian, but a disloyal citizen. By the very action of the government itself, in exempting the Church's leaders, the Church in the time of war is called upon to render special service to its community.

"And what is the special service?

" Incidentally, of course, a Church can assist in the conservation campaigns, Red Cross service at home and abroad, the protection of the boys in camp from evil surroundings, maintenance of Christian work in the camps and on the battle-field. It can contribute to the increasing needs of those families who will have suffered the death of some member. Any minister who does not attempt to further this mobilization of the nation's resources is unworthy of his calling.

" But there is still a greater service which the Church can

render, a service peculiarly its own. It is spiritual. We shall know sad days when the casualty lists are cabled across the sea. We shall need religion then.

"We may see our sense of national mission and our indignation against the brutalities of our enemy developing into hatred of individuals. We shall need religion then.

"We shall have moments of hesitation, doubt, it may be despair, as we think of our sons and brothers trained to kill other people, and see them actually engaged in the work. We shall need religion then.

"We may have moments when we wonder whether God is really at work in his world, and whether the forces of evil have not got the better hand of him. We shall need religion then.

"There will come a time when the world will have to be readjusted and peace be reestablished — a time when our social problems will come to us in unaccustomed struggles and the giving of social justice demand unaccustomed sacrifices. We shall need religion then.

"And we need religion now, when our new epoch and our new trials and testings are beginning to shape themselves."

Has the ministry any message for today and tomorrow? He asks, questioning if our ministers are "to be leaders or mere markers of time";

"If the latter, it were a thousand times better that every able-bodied man of them should be drafted and sent to the front in defence of ideals which demand a spiritual basis and enthusiasm to which they have refused to devote themselves.

"It may be urged that such a call to increased labor and sacrifice will lead ministers to work too hard, endanger their health, induce nervous prostration.

"Very well. So be it.

"Only a coward refuses to face tasks that involve death.

"Exemption from military service means a draft into spiritual service, and a real man will be as ready to die from overwork as from an enemy's bullet."

NOTE.—To indicate how widely Dr. Matthews' words have been quoted, it may be said that the epitome here used is taken from the "Baptist Missionary Review," published at Udayagiri, India, which took it from the "Literary Digest," published in New York.

Home Mission Week

For several years the Home Missions Council, which includes in its membership thirty-five different homes, mission bodies, representing twenty-three denominations, and the council of women for Home Missions including in its membership, as constituent and corresponding boards, seventeen home mission organizations of women, have designated a week in November, known as Home Mission Week, and have issued various kinds of helps for its observance. This year the week falls between November 17th and 24th, including two Sundays. The theme of the week particularly fits the year: "Christian Americanization; our National Ideals and Mission."

Home Mission Week is a time of uniting thought, sympathy, speech and prayer upon the task of the Christian Church in America of making America Christian. Nearly all denominations join, indeed all, save a few which, because of the church calendar, or special conditions, cannot use exactly the same days.

The Theme

The theme is not new; but it does fit the new conditions. It relates to the unifying of the American people under Christian standards. It seeks to quicken the Church and all her members in revitalizing the spirit of Jesus amongst men, with special reference to the strangers who have come amongst us, and have been but partially assimilated in our American life, or have been left altogether untouched by the Christian spirit, which is at the foundation of our democracy.

This war is a war of ideals, even more than it is a war of armies and of material resources. Our Christian ideals must be kept regnant, they must spread among the people. We are recognizing that we must be homogenous in spirit, however, unlike we may be in race, and attainments, and occupation.

The Fusion of Native and Foreign-Born

A careful investigation of agencies already at work in the field of Americanization is now being made under the direction of a committee, supported by the Carnegie Corporation. The statement of this committee indicates the variety of ways in which the commingling of races is taking place.

Our country has suddenly realized the need for uniting all her people in common aims and efforts for the general welfare. Various agencies have arisen in the past twenty-five years, and other and older influences and experiences are potent in fusing the foreign with the native-born into national solidarity. Many of these have done useful work; it may be possible that others need to be added. In any case, the present time seems fitted for an examination of these various agencies and processes, their operation, their success and their aims and usefulness for the future.

For these reasons the Carnegie Corporation of New York has undertaken to furnish the money for a study of the existing methods by which Americanization is being fostered. The conduct of the inquiry is under the supervision of Mr. Allen T. Burns, who has associated with him a number of specialists in various fields.

Theodore Roosevelt of New York, John M. Glenn, director of the Russell Sage Foundation, John Graham Brooks of Cambridge, and John A. Voll, president, National Glass Bottle Blowers' Association, have consented to serve on an advisory council to Mr. Burns in the conduct and oversight of this study.

The study has been divided into ten divisions, for each of which a chief has been appointed who is a specialist of national influence in his field. He will have the assistance of field workers, who will gather material under his direction in different communities. The reports, in their final form, will be the work of the specialists, who will be, individually, the responsible authors.

The following are the divisions of the study, with the chief for each:

Schooling of the Immigrant

    Frank V. Thompson, Assistant Superintendent of Schools, Boston, Mass.

Press and Theater

    Robert E. Park, Professor of Sociology, University of Chicago.

Adjustment of Homes and Family Life

    S. P. Breckinridge, Assistant Professor of Household Administration, University of Chicago.

Legal Protection and Correction
    Grace Abbott, Director of Child Labor Division, United States Department of Labor.

Health Standards and Care
    Michael M. Davis, Jr., Director, Boston Dispensary.

Naturalization and Political Life
    John P. Gavit, Editorial Staff, Harper and Brothers.

Industrial and Economic Amalgamation
    William M. Leiserson, Professor of Political Science, Toledo University.
    Grace Abbott, Associate Chief for Women in Industry.

Treatment of Immigrant Heritages
    Herbert A. Miller, Professor of Sociology, Oberlin College.

Neighborhood Agencies
    Rowland Haynes, Director, War Camp Community Service, New York City.

Rural Developments
    P. A. Speek, Head of Russian Section, Library of Congress.

As an auxiliary to all these divisions, a division of information, statistical and bibliographical, has been organized under the direction of C. C. Williamson, statistician, formerly Librarian of the Municipal Reference Library of New York.

NOTE.— Information respecting these investigations may be obtained from Allen T. Burns, Director, 576 Fifth Avenue, New York City.

Caution in the Midst of Cross-Currents

Several points of view are involved in definitions of Americanization. The Woman's Board of Domestic Missions of the Reformed Church in America sounds this warning:

> "We face another momentous issue as yet shadowy, keeping itself from the clear light of open statement of intention, growing in the darkness in hidden places like a fungus, in mines and lumber camps, passed along to farm laborers and wherever great industries mass together those who labor with their hands; it has possibilities affecting the whole social structure of the world and thus must rightly be taken account of in any outlook on America's needs.

"We refer to the insidious well-defined undercurrent of class consciousness among large bodies of laborers who claim a pernicious type of internationalism and whose religion is a pseudo-socialistic formula of brotherhood, but a brotherhood which fails to include in equal and proportionate consideration members of the so-called higher classes. That a new and fairer basis for all human living must be found quickly we all gladly concede and desire to work for. But in view of the awful power for destruction and disintegration of established order and institutions, including the Christian Church, inherent in this movement, and in view of the great masses of ignorant negroes and foreigners in this country, inflammable and open to propaganda approach, the Home Mission enterprise becomes of tremendous national and world significance and enlists the most earnest, enthusiastic, devoted adherence and service of every follower of Christ in this country — it challenges the Church's best *efforts.*"

The secretary of the Board of Domestic Missions of the Reformed Church in America, Mr. William T. Demarest, sets the same caution forward in these terms:

"There has never been a more crucial time in the history of our country than the present. All about us are forces antagonistic to Christ and His Church; forces that appeal to the ignorant in terms of brotherhood, but which ignore the fact that the real brotherhood of man has its foundation in the Fatherhood of God. Advantage is taken of the stress of war times to push a propaganda that can lead nowhere save to confusion and sin. The Church should make itself heard with no uncertain voice in order to combat false leadership and mistaken doctrine. It should teach insistently that individual and social regeneration are possible only when Jesus Christ is accepted as the Saviour of mankind; when men constantly and consistently live in accordance with His precepts and by His example. The churches will themselves lay aside internal dissension if they truly follow their Divine Leader, and every congregation of Christians will unitedly strive for the growth of the Kingdom of God here in America."

The Leavening of Christian Missions

One of our boards says this to its churches, which we may repeat to all:

"Too much cannot be said of the urgency and the strategic value of quickly permeating groups of foreign-tongued people with the leavening of Christian missions. Oneness in ideals, conception of duty and love of God and country is terribly needed in America today. Certain national government agencies are urging all organizations doing any type of civic or philanthropic work among foreigners to take up Americanization efforts among them — Americanization not meaning merely a selfish attempt to force all people into a national mold, but Americanization which means releasing certain spiritual forces and uplifting ideals of human relationships, doing away with segregation and race consciousness, adopting the use of the common language of the country, thus making a medium for free intercourse and exchange of thought and opinions both spoken and written. Of great significance along this line is the fact that 1,500,000 persons in the United States of draft age cannot read or write in English, 3,000,000 aliens of military age are unnaturalized, and that at one army camp alone 1,600 men cannot read or write English."

The Definition of Investigators

The committee, acting under the auspices of the Carnegie Corporation, furnishes the following definition:

"Americanization is the uniting of new with native born Americans in fuller common understanding and appreciation to secure by means of self-government the highest welfare of all. Such Americanization should produce no unchangeable political, domestic, and economic regime delivered once for all to the fathers, but a growing and broadening national life, inclusive of the best wherever found. With all our rich heritages, Americanism will develop best through a mutual giving and taking of contributions from both newer and older Americans in the interest of the common weal."

Here a process of mutual giving and taking is recognized.

The War Challenge

That which should have been done before must now be done quickly. The war is urgent. The Church must perform her part. If she does not respond, as every organization about her, and as every person in an individual way is doing, how can she retain the respect of any one and her own self-respect? But it is more than a question of reputation; it is a matter of fidelity and of intrinsic worth. She must sacrificially serve, because it is the spirit of the Master. His spirit must be hers, else she is none of His.

Two critical conditions require the home missionary ministrations of the Christian Church now, immediately, as never before:

1. The crowding multitudes in the new war industry communities, where munitions are manufactured and ships are built, and mills and foundries and shops are speeded up, must be cared for by the Church and be taught the meaning of American brotherhood in the Christian sense.

2. The rural people, to whom the Church has access, such as no other agency has, bear now the responsibility of supplying many of the raw materials, and most of the foodstuffs upon which all the world depends; and among them are men of alien blood and often of alien speech, who need to hear, as America has never spoken to them before, the voice of the American conscience and the language of Christian brotherhood.

Winning the War

The startling statement has been made that the war cannot be won without the aid of the foreign-born population of America. Here are some of the reasons:

1. *Soldiers.* In the first draft 1,275,902 foreign-born men were registered. A large percentage of these are now in the service. Several thousand more are in the army and navy through voluntary enlistment.

2. *Ships.* The labor that constructed the great ship yards was 80 per cent. foreign. Seventy per cent. of the workers in iron and steel are either foreign-born or native-born of foreign parents. About two-thirds of the work of mining and smelting the ore for the steel and copper plates was done by immigrant employees.

3. *Food.* We depend upon our immigrant friends for nineteen-twentieths of the sugar refining, for 85 per cent. of the labor

in the slaughtering and meat-packing industries; practically all the market gardening; and a considerable amount of farming.

4. *Clothing.* The foreigner does 78 per cent. of the work in the woolen mills, nine-tenths of all labor in the cotton mills. He turns out four-fifths of all the leather; half the gloves; more than half the shoes; half the collars, cuffs and shirts; and more than half the silk goods.

5. *Transportation.* The railroads would be helpless without the Italian, the Mexican, the Japanese and the Hindoo to lay the tracks and keep them in repair.

6. *Lumber.* Airplanes will win the war. This is a common saying. But airplanes require spruce and the lumber jacks are now mostly of foreign birth. Wooden ships demand the output of the immigrant laborer in lumber camp and saw mill.

Our Alien Fellow Citizen

The "Survey" of May 25, 1918, reprints the following statement concerning the great contribution made by the immigrant to our national welfare:

"The Immigrant Contribution

"I am the immigrant.

"Since the dawn of creation my restless feet have beaten new paths across the earth.

"My uneasy bark has tossed on all seas.

"My wanderlust was born of the craving for more liberty and a better wage for the sweat of my face.

"I looked towards the United States with eager eyes kindled by the fire of ambition and heart quickened with new-born hope.

"I approached its gates with great expectation.

"I entered in with fine hope.

"I have shouldered my burden as the American man-of-all-work.

"I contribute 85 per cent. of all the labor in the slaughtering and meat packing industries.

"I do seven-tenths of the bituminous coal mining.

"I do seven-eighths of all the work in the woolen mills.

"I contribute nine-tenths of all the labor in the cotton mills.

"I make nineteen-twentieths of all the clothing.

"I manufacture more than half the shoes.
"I build four-fifths of all the furniture.
"I make half of the collars, cuffs and shirts.
"I turn out four-fifths of all the leather.
"I make half the gloves.
"I refine nearly nineteen-twentieths of the sugar.
"I make half of the tobacco and cigars.
"And yet I am the great American Problem.

"When I pour out my blood on your altar of labor, and lay down my life as a sacrifice to your God of Toil, men make no more comment than at the fall of a sparrow.

"My children shall be your children, and your land shall be my land because my sweat and my blood will cement the foundations of the America of Tomorrow.

"If I can be fused into the body politic, the melting pot will have stood the supreme test."

The Proper Observance of Home Mission Week

Here are specific recommendations for the week:

1. Preach on the subject at least on one of the Sundays. Why not on both? The subject is of sufficient importance.

2. Devote the Sunday evening and the mid-week prayer meeting to the subject. It is worthy of meditation and prayer. In some churches it should be an occasion of deep contrition and confession, perhaps of conversion.

3. Be sure that your Sunday school follows the program. Children at school and in play meet the foreign-descendent children. They should mingle in the right spirit. The Sunday school opportunity must not be lost.

4. Help your Young People's Society with its observance. There is a fine program for them. Perhaps they will reach out into the community and enlist the foreigners in a pageant, or in other exercises.

5. "Help those women," also. The women have exercises. Do not let your church and community fail of the rich blessing which will come through the women. Among the foreigners often the women are most accessible; and sometimes, when they are hardest to reach, they are the most needy. Usually the women of the home are the key to the whole situation.

6. Utilize the press of your community with some kindly message of sympathy and brotherliness, suited to the occasion.

7. With the educational, or commercial, or social, or philanthropic agencies of your community plan some new means of bringing men together in mutual enterprises for the common good.

Helpful Literature

A supply of helpful literature has been specially prepared for Home Mission Week. Use it.

1. Here is this bulletin for you.
2. A very attractive Sunday school exercise, in red, white and blue colors, entitled "They Come Bringing Gifts," is all ready, accompanied by a separate pamphlet of nine fascinating stories of children from other lands told for children in our land.
3. A striking poster showing the immigrant and his American home speaks its message. In the border small vignettes show the influences affecting the foreigner and the activities in which he is engaged. Accompanying this poster are programs and topics appropriate to the meetings of young peoples' societies.
4. An attractive pamphlet is furnished particularly for the women's societies. It includes a definite program for women's missionary societies, a program for the Interdenominational Day of Prayer, which comes in this week, a program for young women's or young college women's societies, a series of suggested plans for other programs and events during Americanization week, a series of suggestions for definite practical services in Americanization work, and a list of literature on Americanization.

All of this literature can be procured of your Home Mission Board, or of the Home Missions Council, 156 Fifth Avenue, New York City.

Channels of Publicity

The pulpit, the platform, the press.

Pathways of Publicity

The poster, the pageant, and the parade.

A great Procession of P's for the Pungent Preacher and the Practical Pastor to Push!

Some Slogans

A slogan, well chosen and seen at a glance to be appropriate, serves many purposes:

1. It arrests and holds attention.
2. Through the eye-and-the-ear-gate it easily reaches the judgment and secures consent.

3. It epitomizes, compacts and enforces thought.
4. It is easily expressed and passed on to others.
5. It is often remembered when other things are forgotten.

Our slogan is:
Christian America, the Lasting Liberty Bond.
A slogan set forth last Fourth of July was:
One Nation, One God, One Ideal.

Under the heading of this slogan the Centenary Bulletin of the Methodist Episcopal Church said:

"What could be more fitting for Independence Day this year than the celebration shared by all the various races which are being merged in the making of America? One newspaper called it 'a great public demonstration by the foreign-born of their loyalty to the United States.' More than this, it was a demonstration of what America has begun to do for these people, as well as of what they propose to do for her.

"In New York City fifty different races had part in a pageant depicting the contributions which their homelands have made to the cause of freedom. These representatives of other peoples came with their ideals to unite with the common ideal of America. The Fourth of July has strengthened America, as it strengthened the component parts by welding them together. A stronger nation it will be, as the once alien people are brought into closer fellowship.

"Is not this the ideal of the Centenary? It means nothing if not the blending of the ideals of many races which are found in the parish of Methodism today. It is worth no second thought if it have not as its deep purpose such ministrations as will build the foreign-born into the life of the nation and the life of the Church. The Centenary does mean this, and it will do this. In city and country the program has place for the men and women of other races to show them that a Church cares and a nation cares, as it shows them that a God cares.

"The Centenary program of the Board of Home Missions is of deepest significance in the emphasis which it places upon the Americanization of the strangers who are among us; the Centenary program in its entirety means most in its stress upon the redemptive message of Christian democracy to all the races of the world."

In some churches it may be well to devote a little time to the making of slogans. Perhaps this can best be done in a part of one of the young people's meetings. It is a stimulating exercise.

Here are some samples:

Fellowship and Brotherhood for the Foreign Born;
Bridge all Chasms with Brotherhood;
Fuse Fine Feeling in Fellowship;
United in Sympathy and Service;
Liberty and Loyalty from Many Lands.

Follow-up Plans

The most important part of Home Mission Week will be what follows after. Shall it all end in fine feeling?

May there not remain an abiding spirit of prayer for the foreigner?

A continuing expectancy that he will enter into our charitable fellowship, and in friendly relations really become " one of us?"

Permanent plans for prosecution in the church and in the community?

A church in America possessing more "the mind of Christ toward all men?"

II. SIGNIFICANT FACTS FROM FAR AND NEAR

A Cross-Section of American Life

Dr. Charles L. White, in his book "The Churches at Work," describes the mixed relations into which an American enters in ordinary every-day contact with people:

"On Monday morning a Roumanian ash-man cleaned his cellar and a Pole whitewashed its walls. A Hollander pruned his vines; a German plumber came to stop a leak in his bathroom and this man's helper was a Dane. He remembered that his cook was a Swede and the waitress was a Norwegian. As he left his home for his office a seamstress entered to help his wife. She was a Belgian, and the man who was painting his front fence was from Switzerland. He left his laundry with a Chinaman. Later he visited his Russian tailor, ordered groceries of a Welshman, meat of a Scotchman, and purchased his fish dinner for the next day at a Frenchman's store. As he waited for an electric car an Italian vegetable man passed, while he was talking with an Irish policeman. The next day he bought some hardware from an Armenian and learned that his milkman was a Lapp, and his cobbler was a Hungarian. That evening a Philippine bell-boy showed him to a room in a hotel and he learned that among its waiters were Slovaks, Greeks, and Servians.

" The next day he lunched in a Turkish restaurant, engaged a Syrian to mend his rugs and purchased two more of an Armenian. In the afternoon he met by accident a college classmate, a Bulgarian, who introduced him to a Montenegrin. That evening he learned that the Austrian consul of the city had rented the house opposite. The following Sunday he met a Cuban Protestant at church and found a Mexican, a Brazilian, a Lithuanian, a Peruvian, and a Haitian in a popular Sunday school class of one hundred men. That evening a Japanese merchant and his family attended service and the next day, as chairman of the committee that looked after the repairs of the church, he learned that the Portuguese sexton had died, and he selected a Canadian in his place. The following day the man who washed his office windows proved to be a Spaniard, and a Jew wished him a Merry Christmas. Soon after this, in an early train, he counted twenty-eight passengers in the car. Four were reading German papers, twelve Jewish, six Italian, and he concluded that the only American-born man in the car besides himself was a negro!"

Russians in Idaho Make Good Congregational Americans

In the vicinity of American Falls and Kimana, Idaho, there are eight churches whose members without exception came from Russia. A hundred years ago their ancestors sought freedom from Prussian misrule, and emigrated to the wheat raising districts around Odessa. Within the last quarter of a century these people have again sought freedom in Idaho, Kansas and other wheat raising states in large numbers, and many have sought religious freedom in the Congregational Church. During the century in Russia, they retained their German languages, still speak the same, and have maintained the German conferences.

Recently they organized an English Congregational Conference. A constitution was adopted, and officers elected regardless of nationality. Nearly every man present wore a flag, Red Cross, Liberty Loan or Service Star badge.

The members of this church, and all the other German churches, are clearing up the land which was raw sage-brush desert six years ago. Practically all are home-steaders under the desert claim law. They had a crop failure last year, and have a like prospect this year, yet the church at Kimana, which was asked for $50 for the Red Cross, paid $250 which makes them 100 per cent. perfect, as every man and every family made some payment.

Italian Work in Grantwood, N. J.

Outside of our social and religious work, the pastor has been and is doing some work for the government, being a "Four Minute Man," meeting many people who have never heard of an Italian Protestant preacher before. Through the local Red Cross, we have been in touch with many new families; and also through the draft, many new boys have attended our meetings. The following are a few helps given in American brotherhood:

Speeches made in behalf of the government.............	10
Boys helped in the questionnaire of the draft...........	75
Compensation cases settled through our mediation........	3
Letters for people received in our office................	91
Hospital calls made.................................	4
Work provided for people of our mission	11
People recruited for the Public Service Reserve..........	60
Families helped to get allotment from the government for boys in the army	9

Besides all this, the pastor is an agent for the selling of War Savings Stamps. Eleven of our boys are serving Uncle Sam for the cause of democracy.— *Congregationalist.*

German Congregationalists

The church of fifty-six members has a Service Flag with eight stars, and more have been called out. The pastor has preached for the Liberty Loan and been active in securing subscriptions. Considering the means of his people, the church has made a good record. *Billings, Montana.*

Patriotic Women

Our Auxiliary took part in the Red Cross campaign, and also the men from our church helped the women to canvass for the money. We collected over $400 in our district, and were much pleased with our success, as our district had only about 15 per cent. business men, the rest being laboring men who had given through their shops. Our auxiliary took part in the great parade. Just about one-half could march — eight — yet they received great applause from the people standing by. They carried a banner with the sign, "Slovak Congregational Church Auxiliary," which was the only banner except Italians indicating foreign element. Although there were many Slavic people who took part in the parade, they went under names of some American clubs.— *Slovak Congregational Church, Pittsburgh, Pa.*

The ladies of the church (Congregational) are devoting much of their time to the Red Cross work. Sixteen of our boys are in military service. Some are in France, and some in the camps at home.— *Mankato and Kasota, Minn.*

The Various Ministries of the Protestant Episcopal Church

The work among Oriental races chiefly limited to the Pacific Coast, may be described in the following brief paragraphs:

Japanese

Sacramento.— Resident deaconess; native priest serving at intervals.

San Francisco.— Thriving mission in charge of an American woman. Large kindergarten superintended by a Japanese Christian. Church services every Sunday.

Los Angeles.— Work in charge of a native priest, with church building, and parish house. Average congregation, sixty-four. Sixty-six in the Sunday school. Sewing class. Cooking class. English night school. Kindergarten.

Seattle.— Work in charge of Japanese deacon and a Japanese Bible-woman, with several American helpers. Thirty-two communicants. Forty children in Sunday school. Steady progress reported here, as well as in Taylor and Tacoma. These are all centers of wide-spread influence, as the converts move to other places.

Odgen, Utah.— One priest and one deacon have charge of a mission among the Japanese. This promises aggressive development.

Honolulu.— A very large amount of work, largely of an educational and evangelical nature is being done in the Islands under Bishop Restarick. This work is of far-reaching importance owing to the constant emigration of the Japanese and Chinese converts.

Chinese

San Francisco and Oakland.— Native priest and two women helpers. Afternoon, evening, and night schools. Class for organ instruction. Large and growing Sunday schools.

Honolulu.— See above.

Other work among the Chinese is scattered.

Italians

Work is being carried on in many dioceses, but it is scattered, and statistics are difficult to obtain. There are four very successful missions in New York City; one in Chicago; one in Gary, Ind.; one in Philadelphia. In other centers a valuable work is being done, but it is less well organized. The services of the Church appeal to the mystical and emotional side of the Italian temperament; the Sunday schools, kindergartens, and Bible classes provide the necessary balance. Social gatherings and other agencies are used to familarize the people with American ways and customs. The Episcopal Church makes no attempt to proselytize from the Roman Church, but seeks to offer an ecclesiastical home to the many Italians who have drifted away from their own Church.

Swedes

Strong centers of work in Providence, R. I.; New York, N. Y.; Boston, Mass.; Chicago, Ill.; Minneapolis, Minn.; Duluth, Wis. These represent communicant lists of 200 to 500 each. Services are conducted in both Swedish and English. Parish-halls, homes for the aged and infirm and good Sunday schools are among the usual activities. The agricultural and mechanical proclivities of the Swedes tend to make of them either a shifting population or country communities. Among the latter, temporary chapels are used for services, and the work is furthered by the free distribution of bibles, prayer-books, tracts, etc. The Sunday school in country communities is found to be a most efficient agency.

Greeks and Syrians

Attitude of Episcopal Church toward the Greek and Syrian churches must be one of sympathetic understanding and co-operation. These people are as a rule loyal to their own churches. Natural sympathy is rapidly growing between them and the Episcopal Church, through the constant opportunities offered to the latter to afford places of worship with familiar surroundings to communities of Greeks and Syrians who have no such place of their own. Very little, if any, " missionary " work is attempted or deemed advisable.

Other Races

Before the war there were a number of German Episcopal churches in the United States. It is impossible to get statistics at present.

French Episcopal churches exist in Philadelphia and New York.

Hungarians are organized into Episcopal congregations in New Jersey and Indiana.

Some work is done among the Armenians, chiefly along the line of ecclesiastical hospitality.

In Pennsylvania, and possibly elsewhere, there is active work among the Poles.

Along the New England coast sporadic attempts have been made to reach the unchurched Portuguese.

In the case of all races of immigrants, the Episcopal Church relies largely upon the distribution of bibles in the language of the immigrant, and upon the Book of Common Prayer which is now procurable in the languages of most of the immigrant races.

The Methodist Episcopal Church and the Immigrant

The Methodist Episcopal Church has been a strong factor in the Americanization of those coming from foreign shores. It is significant that the celebration of one hundred years of Methodist Missions is coincident with the close of the first century of immigration as recorded by the immigration authorities. The Methodist Episcopal Church placed its first missionary among the French at New Orleans in 1819. Since then its task has involved the greeting of the changing groups of newcomers as they have arrived, teaching them the way of evangelical Christianity and guiding them to acceptance of the highest ideals of American democracy.

While for administrative purposes there have been foreign-speaking conferences, the tendency has been for these people to become a part of English-speaking churches as rapidly as possible. The foreign tongue has been used because it has been the best means of approach. There are still German, Swedish, Norwegian and Danish, Japanese and Chinese conferences in the Methodist Episcopal Church. But the Italian conference has been dissolved, the last meeting of the Italian preachers being conducted entirely in English. There is a strong movement on foot to have the other non-English speaking conferences merged with English-speaking conferences in the near future.

The process by which the Methodist Episcopal Church has performed its ministry of leading alien folks up the pathway of Christian democracy has varied. The Jefferson Park Italian Methodist Episcopal Church, New York, instils the dreams of the new land through clubs. Of these there are boy and girl scouts, glee club, school of music, orchestra, cooking class, night school for English-Italian and Italian-English, mothers' meetings, choral class, bugle-drum corps, athletic club and typesetting and printing club. During these days the women meet to make garments for their men " over there."

The Plaza Community Church at Los Angeles, Cal., is now in process of erection for a ministry to Latin-Americans. In addition to the church proper there is a six-story building and roof garden. Here will be carried on every phase of industry, recreation, and religious training needed. The program of this church is modeled largely after the work of the Morgan Memorial Church, Boston, which, in addition to its regular evangelistic, industrial, children's and rescue work, has now a fine Church of All Nations.

The Church of All Nations at 9 Second avenue, New York, carries on an Americanization Christianizing work among several nationalities. Among the most significant of its present activities is its labors among the Russians. It has become the Russian center of New York. Here at the forum conducted weekly are discussed all the problems of Russia and the United States. Many of the men who have figured prominently in recent Russian affairs have spoken from this platform. A Russian periodical is also published, which extends the influence of this ministry throughout the United States and Canada.

The Old Broadway Methodist Episcopal Church, Cleveland, Ohio, is in the center of the Bohemian population of that city.

Apart from services conducted for adults in Bohemian, all of its services are in English. Through its Sunday school it has for years been reaching and influencing thousands of the youth of the Bohemian immigrant, many of whom are now officials of the church and leaders in the affairs of the community. A $300,000 building adequate for the needs of this ministry is now being built through the aid of the Board of Home Missions and Church Extensions. All of the churches mentioned receive help from this source.

These are but types of the work that is being done. Throughout the denomination local English speaking churches are assimilating the foreign-born and the children of foreign-born without any ado about it. They come into the membership of the church as a part of its regular ministry. They share all other community blessings, why not this blessing, which is greatest of all?

At the present time the Board of Home Missions and Church Extension of the Methodist Episcopal Church carries on work in the United States among the following people: Armenians, Bohemians, Chinese, Danish, Finnish, Italians, Welsh, Greeks, Japanese, Koreans, Norwegians, Portuguese, Slavs, Mexican and other Latin-Americans, Syrians, Germans, Swedes, etc. A bureau of foreign work has supervision of these varied enterprises.

Baptists Mobilized for War Service

The following significant action has been taken by the Board of Managers of the American Baptist Home Mission Society on the recommendation of the Headquarters Council:

Entrusted with the interests of the American Baptist Home Mission Society, which has a large share in Christianizing America, and through America the world, whose watchword is "North America for Christ," and whose work in each generation is to pass to future generations the primary gifts to Christianity and its by-products, the board of managers desires to announce to the world its attitude and position in this present world crisis.

Immediately following the declaration of war with Germany, an official communication was addressed to our foreign-speaking missionaries, requesting from each a formal statement concerning his loyalty to the United States, his adherence to the principles of democracy, and insisting that each missionary must be loyal to the government under whose protection he lives, whether a citizen or not. He was also asked to give written assurance that his own personal service, and the use of his meeting house, if it were needed, shall be placed at the disposal of the Red Cross and other allied activities.

We encouraged the organization of the War Commission of the Northern Baptist Convention, and have advanced considerable amounts that it might have sufficient funds with which to carry on its helpful work, pending contributions from our constituency, co-operating therein with the American Baptist Publication Society and the American Baptist Foreign Mission Society. We have encouraged service to be rendered by our missionary pastors in the camps and cantonments, giving also the labors of various servants of the society, notably that of the Superintendent of Evangelism, whose salaries and expenses have been paid as a part of the society's contribution toward spiritualizing the forces engaged in winning the war and in safeguarding democracy for the world.

We have also encouraged our foreign-speaking missionaries to become army chaplains, releasing them from their present positions to engage in this important work, and have granted them indefinite absence from service, to labor under the Young Men's Christian Association, or to enter military service in the American, French and Italian armies.

Rural Service Among Presbyterian Patriots

At Batesville, Mississippi, the Presbyterian pastor, Rev. R. A. N. Wilson, toured the county with a committee made up of bankers and business men, in the recent drive for Liberty Bonds and Red Cross. The county went "over the top" in its subscriptions. Mr. Wilson exerted a great influence also through the negro ministers of the county, who came to him for direction and advice. Their people have been large subscribers in this county to the Red Cross. One old colored man came to a banker seeking a confidential interview. He brought out $2,000 in crumpled and moldy bills which had not been unfolded for years. He had been accustomed to keep a deposit account of $200 in the bank and the banker supposed that was all he had. The $2,000 was his first investment in any securities. In many towns and counties of Mississippi the negroes contributed the quota to the Red Cross subscriptions and the white folks put them "over the top." The State was asked for $123,000 and subscribed $1,000,000.

In the southern mountains, the remoteness of many people from newspapers and from contact with business life has made them slow to appreciate the meaning of the war; but the churches, especially the leading northern and southern churches, in the mountains, have been centers of Americanism to these lonesome people. Rev. Victor C. Detty of Huntsville, Tennessee, has led in War Savings Day in Huntsville and in Helenwood and his people have exceeded the amount asked of them.

Rev. Dr. W. E. Finley of Hot Springs, North Carolina, led his people in subscriptions which exceeded those of any part of Madison County and brought the county up to its quota. Hot Springs is the center of an immense camp of interned enemy aliens.

At Kingston, Arkansas, an old confederate soldier, who had become known for his advocacy of food conservation, sought the pastor of the Presbyterian church, Rev. Elmer J. Bouher. The old soldier introduced himself as a resident of a hamlet "back in the sticks" about twenty miles, and said that he had heard the government was to take all the corn. He brought with him a statement of the quantity of corn in their settlement and offered it on behalf of his neighbors and himself. He presented a request that those of them who had mules and cows be permitted to keep feed enough for one mule and one heifer.

This touching devotion represents the spirit of many country people. In previous wars, we have had peace parties and sometimes a reactionary pacifist group; but the country ministers have been a big factor in keeping the isolated, rural people informed as to the war.

At Wilder, Tennessee, is a great lumber camp owned by Germans. The minister, Rev. Dr. A. B. Buchanan, is a stalwart and loyal supporter of the war. He has appealed to the patriotism of the mountain men gathered in lumber camps up the various branches of the creek, and for a time suffered the displeasure of the owners who felt that his patriotic statements were extreme.

A riot developed in July against one of the two owners because of pro-German remarks he made in a prayer. A committee of workers forced him to withdraw from public connection with the church work. The pastor, Dr. Buchanan, has been a great influence for peace in the neighborhood, and for patriotism and loyalty.

The Presbyterian Board of Home Missions has been maintaining community organizers in every section of the country, one being appointed in each Presbytery. Their business is to organize conferences in remote places unreached by the influences that are promoting the war. In these conferences the various forms of war service, which country people should render, are described. Many are enlisted in Bond subscriptions, War Savings societies, Red Cross auxiliaries and in subscriptions for the Young Men's Christian Association. This work is under the guidance of Rev. Hermann N. Morse. Many ministers have had an opportunity, by this means, of great service.

The following are extracts from letters received from Presbyterian pastors who are working under the National Service Commission and the Board of Home Missions in the holding of War Service Conferences:

"We had a very profitable meeting at Albany, Illinois, on Thursday evening. The people were quite responsive to the appeal to co-operate with all war measures, and in the preparing of the church for responsibilities and opportunities after the war. This church has not been very aggressive in meeting the war time demands, but gave assurance of a quickening endeavor along this line."

"A popular meeting was held at White Hall at which an extended war address was made by the organizer and those present were urged to co-operate with the government in its conservation programs and with the Red Cross and the Y. M. C. A. The work of these organizations was described in detail and those present were much interested and seemed greatly instructed. There are two Red Cross branches within the bounds of this parish in which the members of the congregation are largely engaged."

"On April fourth we had a fine meeting in Aberdeen. An afternoon conference of workers was held, lasting from 2:30 to 5:00. A number of Red Cross workers were present and the wife of a Y. M. C. A. camp secretary, and a very animated and profitable discussion was engaged in an entirely informal way, with many questions and answers. Co-operation with the National Service Commission was gladly pledged and a local secretary appointed to send details and keep in touch with the commission."

"I have held two more National Service meetings. I found the Red Cross doing good work at both places. At Providence they were doing practically nothing in the way of food conservation. I organized them for this. They had bought a good many Liberty Bonds, but they were doing nothing with the War Savings Stamps. I started them on this work."

Glimpses from a Community House (Disciples)

The status of the foreign-born woman, especially of the peasant class, is very different from that of the American woman. For instance, we expected to have the Children's Day program at seven o'clock in the evening. One girl spoke up and said she was so glad, then her mother could come, because at that time she would have given out the supper and her father would not be home yet. She added, "My father don't leaves my mother go no place."

Sadder still is the abuse to which the women are subjected. The godfather of two of the children, and some of his friends, called at the home on a Sunday afternoon. The men were drinking freely. The mother was the only woman present. They offered some to her, but she refused, saying that she did not care for it. The godfather was angered by her refusal, and picked up a glass of beer and dashed it into her face.

One Russian man said: "We drink when we meet together, because that is the only form of amusement we know."

If this be true, how needful that we provide wholesome recreation, and an enlargement of interests, for the poor, uneducated Russian peasant, who comes to our big cosmopolitan cities?

The Russian spends his increased earnings for his two luxuries, meat and beer. In their native land, they are an out-of-door people, living simply. Here they have new and different food, without being told how to prepare it. One man said: "I was two months learning to eat tomatoes."

Yet those tomatoes were prepared in such a way that we would not have liked them.

In one home it was through a baby that an opportunity was given for Christian Americanization. The husband and wife were converted, and became very earnest Christians. They were expecting a little one, and its arrival was so happily anticipated, because they had had a little girl which died when it was nine months old. The wife, scarcely able to speak a word of English, came to the Mother's Club to learn English and how to sew, so she could make some pretty clothes for the baby. She was able to attend only two meetings. Then I asked one of our Sunday school classes of young ladies to make a layette for the baby. They spent several enjoyable evenings doing it. When the baby was two days old, I called. It was a boy and the father and mother were so proud of it, but felt so hurt that no one had been to see it. The custom is to have something to drink and for people to come in and drink to the health of the baby. The father said that when the girl was born, so many people were in, and he was so drunk all the time that he did not know what his wife said to him. Now it was a boy, but they were Christians and no one came to see it. On Sunday I told the young ladies' class that was making the layette about it, and six of them called and brought the little clothes. The parents were so happy about it, and said: "Oh, you care."

Some of the ladies called frequently, and when they moved to a different part of the city the mother begged that I would tell Christian American women to call on her.

This is the so-called era of the child, yet as the foreign child has expressed it, "someone is always hollering on me." Many feel that the soul of the new-born babe will be lost if it dies before it is christened.

The third day after the baby was born one mother tried to get up and get the house cleaned up for the christening, but she could not do it. She waited a week, but still she did not have the strength. In her great distress, she sent her little girl to call me. I tried to comfort and reassure her and told her that Jesus had said, "Suffer little children to come unto me and forbid them not, for of such is the Kingdom of God."

Through the children I gained entrance into the home, and then, sooner or later, an opportunity comes to definitely link up the whole family with the work through rendering Christian service in case of an emergency, sickness or death.

To them it is magic, perhaps miraculous, not science, when one can regulate a clock, and have it keep good time or put hot poultices on a festered finger and relieve the pain.

One nine-year old girl had been observing me for a long time and one day asked me, in an awesome sort of way, "if I was God, then some relation to Him?" To her it seemed that I was above physical danger or harm, and so different.

Miss BERTHA MERRILL
Disciples Church, Chicago.

The Influence of the Gospel on Community Life

Bennington, Neb., is a town almost as old as Omaha. Yet until about fifteen years ago, no church of any denomination had been planted there. A church was not wanted, in fact all attempts to begin religious work there were blocked by the people. When this condition of affairs was reported to the German Lutheran synod of the state, it was arranged to send a missionary there. A young man was selected who was told to ask nothing of the people for himself. No house in the village would open to him; no one would rent him a room in which to live. Finally a saloon keeper in a spirit of banter offered to rent him an attic-room over his saloon. Into that room the pastor with his wife and babe moved. Services were begun in the schoolhouse; and the children invited into a Sunday school. After a year's service there the Board of Church Extension offered $500 aid to build a small church in the place. With this offer the pastor went to all in the community and succeeded in getting $900 more together, and a church building costing $1,500 was erected. When that building was dedicated the community in general turned out to hear. After the service an influential man in the community called some of the men together and said: "Men, I felt ashamed today. This little preacher has come here and gathered our children together, and given them instruction; and we have treated him like a dog and allowed him to live in a place like that. If you men will stand with me, I favor building him a parsonage at once." They agreed to the proposition and a house was built and the preacher moved into it. Soon after a congregation was organized, and the word of God regularly preached. The railroad agent gave this testimony to me a few years after: "I have lived in a number of towns, but never in one quite as tough as this. I have come down to this office on Monday morning and found young men and sometimes young women drunk on the streets after dancing all Sunday night. I am not a church member and would never have believed that the preaching of the Gospel would make such a change in any community. The dance hall has been torn down and hauled to the country for corn cribs, and it is seldom that a man intoxicated is seen on our streets. We have a new town and a respected one now."

H. L. YARGER, D.D., *General Superintendent of the General Synod of the Evangelical Lutheran Church in the United States.*

By Elocution, Also

One of my greatest interests this month has been the watching of two Polish-Jewish girls of eighteen or twenty years, develop. The first step was when they were ready to come to our church for their lessons. Then they joined the elocution class we hold each Saturday night. Two weeks ago our teacher asked us all to prepare a talk on the war. I helped the girls and it was one of the most delicate situations I ever had a chance to handle. I found them very pronouncedly socialistic and pacifistic, and still harboring the hatred they felt for treatment they had received in Russia, because Jews. I suggested speech after speech which they promptly rejected, but at last we really did work out some beautiful ones, in which they told of the blessings America brings and the reason why we ought to wish to save and pass on these blessings. And to my delight by the time they saw what a fine effect their speeches would have, one of them said, "Oh, I want to put another sentence on the end of mine" — it was the only sentence she wrote of it all — "I want to say 'My best wishes for liberty and democracy.'" And the other one promptly said, "And I will put one on the end of mine too. I will say, 'I hope Germany also will become a Democracy.'" Their little speeches took very well, and that made them happier than ever, and the next time they came for their lessons, they must needs talk about the war, and two more patriotic advocates one would not wish to see. They are teaching me to read Yiddish characters in the newspapers too, with a zeal that knows no bounds, and certainly isn't proportioned to the progress I am making in that literature. I have been giving them some verses from the Old Testament to read, and the fact that they wondered how I got hold of them gave me a chance to tell them how closely their Scriptures and ours are related, and we had a very interesting time one night comparing methods of Bible reading.

Incident sent by Miss Bertha W. Clark, who has charge of the work of teaching English to foreigners in New York City, under the Woman's American Baptist Home Mission Society.

Bulgarians in Toledo are Learning to be American Citizens.
The Leaven of Loyalty.

As you know all foreigners were called to take part in the celebration of the Fourth of July. I am the one responsible for the participation of the Bulgarians in this city. The War

Educational Committee had me attend all of their meetings discussing and instructing about preparations. I called a number of meetings for my people and organized our division and line for the parade. At first the people were disinterested. The socialistic element has been quite active trying to discourage our men, but in spite of all odds we had a very good turn out and well organized and drilled men, of over 160, that marched under the Stars and Stripes on that day. But the most interesting part were the meetings to which hundreds came and took part with quite a bit of enthusiasm. One evening I called all the business men and other leaders to a meeting. They responded to the last one and at the mass meetings hundreds came out. On the very first meeting I suggested that we shall need some money to meet some of the expenses in connection with the parade preparations. Some $40 came in a very few minutes. At these meetings I urged that we organize an educational society for instruction, literary work and good influence. Everyone realized the need of such society and pledged to help.

Rev. P. D. Vassileff,
Toledo, Ohio.

The Church Must Help

The Armenians began to come to the United States, not from purely economic and commercial motives, but fundamentally to escape the oppression and injustice of the unspeakable Turk. They came like the Pilgrim Fathers, seeking a land of liberty, where they might find shelter and home and enjoy security of life and property.

Rev. Mihran T. Kalaidjian,
Troy, N. Y.

Will You Touch Him?

If the alien is to be saved for God and man, he must be touched. The church, the pastor, and the church member must come in touch with him. Not by proxy (as it has been well put), but by proximity; not by purse, but in person. This was the way of Jesus, and no better way has been discovered. There is no such thing as salvation by wholesale. Society is uplifted only by uplifting the individual, and no individual can rise far except as another individual comes into immediate touch with him.

Rev. M. G. Papazian,
New York City.

Shall They Rise, Or We Sink?

No greater work can be done by a philanthropic or religious society than to stretch out the helping hand to the men and women who come here to this country to become citizens, and the parents of citizens, and therefore to do their part in making up for weal or for woe the future of our land. If we do not take care of them, if we do not try to uplift them, then as sure as fate our own children will pay the penalty. If we do not see that the immigrant and the children of the immigrant are raised up, most assuredly the result will be that our children and our children's children are pulled down. Either they will rise or we shall sink.

THEODORE ROOSEVELT.

Will Your Church Assimilate?

The church and the schoolhouse which shaped New England character are just as good for every immigrant from every land across the sea — the Pacific as truly as the Atlantic. From the time that Jesus took the penitent by the hand and lifted him up, or Andrew found Simon, till today, the love of God in Jesus Christ has been the triumphant motive of every disciple. The alien must find a welcome in the English church because the love of God compels the welcome. That the alien should be unwelcome in any church of Jesus Christ is abhorrent to the thought.

JOEL S. IVES,
Secretary and Treasurer of the Missionary Society of Connecticut.

III. SERMONIC HINTS AND PRAYER MEETING TOPICS

Working Over Against Your Own House
(Nehemiah 3:28.)

Near tasks are usually the most urgent, and usually the most profitable in results. Many work at arm's length, but work at a disadvantage. The foreigner near us offers the largest opportunities for Christian service.

Three agencies for reaching him must be employed together: the Home Missionary Society, the Special Mission, and the Individual Church; but the most effective agency for the evangelization of our migrant brethren is the local church, equipped with its present plant and workers, and adapting its methods to the needs of the field in which it is placed.

Three Preliminary Considerations

1. Delegated effort, through an equipped mission and hired workers, is not going "straight up." It is indirect and roundabout. But personal participation in Christian service is the only method of really imparting the Christian spirit.

2. A mere romantic regard for the picturesque immigrant is evanescent; but neighborliness, which shares the house of worship and serves in mutual accord, becomes intensely real and human, grows heroic and beautiful, and leads to honor and love.

3. This work must not become a religious fad. It must be patient and persistent, putting up with many an annoyance, and grappling earnestly with one of the stubbornest and most perplexing problems that the evangelical churches ever faced.

We Have the Plant

Our elegant churches, closed a large part of the time, should be more continuously utilized. It is sinful folly to house mission work in barrack-like halls. A closed church is the easy victim of stagnation and dry-rot. If our church edifices have been created simply for our luxurious comfort, then they are not tools for the Kingdom.

We Have the Workers

Teaching and visiting—the whole ministering grace of Christian friendship, which is the gist of this service—can be done only by the old American for the new American. We must break down artificial barriers. We must drop from our vocabulary all contemptible terms applied to foreigners. There is power enough and grace enough within us, if we will but behold the people of our immediate environment.

We Have the Methods

The problem is the evangelization of these people, the majority of whom have no true conception of the nature of the new life which is established through faith in Christ. The Apostolic message must be conveyed in the Apostolic manner, by personal contact, by personal service, by personal love. We must know one another and love one another; and when all is for Christ's sake, we have the method which is necessary for this new business.

The New Work and the Old

There is no need of crippling old activities. Every society in the church can be maintained, and the new work can also be done. Indeed, the old activities will renew their strength under the gracious reflex influences of the new endeavors. Experience of the past proves that the ministry of the church, through its accustomed channels, is deepened and enriched, rather than impoverished, by a new mission in the fuller realization of Christian brotherhood.

Rev. Ozora S. Davis, D. D.,
President Chicago Theological Seminary,
Chicago, Ill.

Christian Americanization — Our National Ideals and Mission

The greatness of a nation is not based upon its material resources, but upon its conception of moral and spiritual values in government. These moral and spiritual values depend largely upon the conception of deity held by the people. A nation never rises above its gods.

The American nation was founded by men who were humble followers of a god who was essentially moral above all else. They carried their conceptions of Him into their government. It was a wise policy. We have proved the truth of Psalm 33:12. "Blessed is the nation whose God is the Lord."

We should never forget that our colonization was markedly Christian. This fact may explain much of our success.

I. *We must not, as a people, forget that our God is the Lord.*

a. The Great Moral Governor of the Universe must constantly be in our consciousness.

b. The revelation of that God is best seen in his Son.

II. *We must also never forget that as a people we are chosen for a great task in the world.*

a. In a peculiar way we are physically and historically equipped for world leadership.

b. This leadership must be along the lines of our historical development (namely in moral and humanitarian paths).

III. *We must see to it that these very qualities are made prominent in our school systems — immigration work — and in all work which has as its object, the making of " Good Americans."*

Conclusion.— The Church has a great field here, and she has the equipment as no other organization has it.

Rev. George F. Finnie,
Pastor of United Baptist Church, Lewiston, Maine.

The Cross on the Crucible
(Isaiah 55:5)

Introduction — Legend.— In past ages the Cross was marked on crucibles to exorcise evil spirits.

Fact.— Effectively applied, Christianity safeguards the process of assimilation of the peoples of our country.

I. The Crucible — U. S. A.

Israel Zangwill's phrase, " The Melting Pot," sticks as a burning figure of the truth.

1. Form of government — democracy.— The individual has a voice in law-making, in law-enforcement, in selection of officers. He may hold office. He exercises influence through freedom of personal opinion.

2. Social structure.— Schools, public, private — Industry — System of Ownership — The Wage System, trades unions, etc.— Growing industrial democracy — Business, corporations, the credit system — Religion, elective.

All presupposes the development of the individual citizen.

II. Ingredient — The People of the United States.

1. Original stock — the pilgrim, the cavalier, and the like. " God sifted a whole nation, that he might send choice seed grain over into this wilderness." Descendants of original stock most useful, most useless, most dangerous. (Outline the characteristics of descendants of original stock.)

2. Earlier immigration — from the North and West of Europe, Britain, Ireland, Holland, Germany, France, Portugal, Sweden, etc.— These fused easily with original stock.

3. Later immigration, since 1883. Increasing from the South and East of Europe — Italians, Hebrews, Slavic peoples, also Asiatics, Mexicans, South Americans, etc.— Census 1910 cited 47 distinct nationalities, 13,500,000 foreign born, 19,000,000 children foreign born. Last census decade 3 9/10 per cent. decrease in peoples of the north and west of Europe, 175 per cent. increase in peoples from the South and East of Europe, meaning rapid increase of Catholic population and illiterate population — peoples of superstitious faith, hatred of the church, hatred of the government, low idea of women and of children — subnormal living conditions, lack of family life, tenement congestion, construction camps, city slums — the nation is renewed

from the lower strata — the immigrant is not the problem, but the adjustment of the immigrant with his neighbors is the problem.

Majority from the middle class peasants, physically strong, hard workers, uneducated from lack of opportunity, come to better economical condition — Secret of America's economic development.— In addition, 10,000,000 negroes, race problem — Recent influx of million Mexicans, ignorant, disloyal — the Jew is right, " The real American has not yet arrived, he is only in the crucible."

Evident importance of process calculated to Americanize and to Christianize heterogeneous peoples.

III. The Cross — Meaning the Christianity of the United States.

1. Its functions — to regenerate individuals — " to fuse a score of racestocks, with a half dozen colors of skin, speaking forty languages and inheriting the most diverse social and religious traditions into a single, homogeneous, democratic and righteous nation "; fusibility of various peoples — Irish, Teutonic, Hebrew, Slavic, Asiatic, Ethiopian, first versus second generation.

2. Its forces — 40,000,000 nominal Christians; denominational divisions — could God trust a united Church in America — increase of co-operative movements — organized Christian forces at present.

3. Its challenge — to this church, for personal service, for an adequate church program (emphasize Americanization) — what is our church doing in Christian Americanization? What more could we do, for the support of local work, for the support of denominational agencies (give facts concerning the work and needs of your denomination); Protestants employ approximately 5,000 paid workers in foreign tongues in America at a cost of about $2,000,000 annually (give denominational figures).

Conclusion.— Unify the argument for Christian Americanization by a comprehensive review of the points above and close with emphasis on the privilege of having part in this fundamental work.

REV. C. E. BURTON, D. D.,
General Secretary, Congregational Home Missionary Society, New York City.

Who is Our Neighbor?
(Luke 10:29)

In answer to this question Jesus told an inimitable story. The gist of his answer is that whoever has need of help that we can give, is neighbor to us.

This breaks down all limits built on birth or circumstance. We may be grateful that we are Americans born, but we may not be supercilious, much less indifferent, to those born in other lands.

Just because these foreign-born have been reared in a non-American atmosphere they need us.

1. Thy need our help to acquire our language. Naturally, they form little colonies, where their mother-tongue is spoken. While the children in our schools and on the streets learn English speedily, the parents, especially the mothers, have no such opportunity. American women have an open door of opportunity just here.

2. They need our help that they may become familiar with our national institutions and the principles that underlie them. An unassimilated population is an element of danger. Most of the foreign-born come to us with the crudest ideas of liberty and democracy. Our safety lies in helping them to intelligent citizenship.

3. They need our help that they may learn what Christianity is, and may find Christ for themselves. They need to be set face to face with Jesus Christ; to cast out fear of the priest and dependence upon forms. This cannot be done save by personal contact. It cannot be done except as we seek them out.

The Samaritan was a friend to the wounded man. Just that we must be to the ignorant peoples who have come to make their homes among us. As lovers of our country and as lovers of Christ we should be neighborly; not to a chosen few but to all.

Rev. L. A. CRANDALL, D. D.,
Trinity Baptist Church, Minneapolis, Minn.

Contribution of the Nations to the Religious Life of America
(Romans 1:17)

"Justification by faith" is the life-giving water of all Christian ages. But many lands gave it color. Dashing down the Alps like the "arrowy Rhone;" broadening past German hills, like the Rhine, slower and yet broader on the flats of Holland, like the Maas, and springing like unexpected fountains in a hundred flowering fields of England, the doctrines of Luther stirred the hope of the world like rivers in the desert to weary travelers.

And these varying streams of the same essential Truth, in varying volume, color and speed, swept from European shores of American, a veritable Arethusa amid the brackish waters of a world's despair. And on these new shores it left the deposit of the lands whence it came.

The cosmopolitan character of our national building is conspicuous; both strength and beauty are in the varieties of our spiritual architecture; we are richer and more secure because into our great building, the cynosure now of the eyes of the world, elements which seemed conflicting in their origin in our clearer atmosphere appear rounded and symmetrical and mutually sustaining.

Spain in her early contributions gave us piety and zeal. The French Huguenots brought us buoyance and cheerfulness and lightness, with a love of the beautiful. Anglo-Saxon migrations brought to these shores a code of strict personal ethics, and an ideal of sturdy individualism, insisting upon liberty. The Dutch, thrifty and tolerant, emphasized social equity. The Quakers, disciples of an inner light, with unflinching insistence on absolute freedom of opinion, touched us all with mysticism and sympathy. The Scotch-Irish, adventurous colonizers, endured hardness in a new social sense; deep religiousness characterized every experience and toned every action. The Germans, exponents of careful industrialism, early showed an appreciation of federation. The Moravians were our foremost missionary people. And the Jews, consistent home-makers, hard working, with marked organizing capacity, have testified to the ideals of social solidarity.

These contributions are prophetic of the value of wider diversities. Herbert Spencer tells us the interaction of dissimilar elements secures the strongest life.

If taught and encouraged by our early experiment in nation-making, we shall dare to accept elements we had disregarded or perhaps antagonized, perhaps by their inclusion, our final national building will rest more securely on a broader basis and so be knit into final beauty and strength. If once Teuton and Frank and Anglo-Saxon combine their expressions of Reformation Truth to build the free Christian constitution of the western republic, may not Latin and Greek and Oriental have some contribution to make to the ultimate temple of humanity, with foundations laid indeed in America, but with a dome comprehending the world?

With such hopes in this dark year of grace we may get some lessons of encouragement from the past and some new courage to face a stormy present and be able in quiet confidence to look on to the future.

Rev. CHARLES L. THOMPSON, D. D.,
President, Home Missions Council, New York City.

The Home Relation to the World Problem
(Mark 16:15)

1. The cosmopolitan conditions in America bring the world to our very door and the Christianizing of America means in a peculiar way the Christianizing of the world. The nations of the earth have come to our very door and have come to live upon our shores. The study of the composite of America is a study of the nations of the world. The problem of our great cities is complex and international in scope. Civilizing influence without Christian power cannot solve the problem. We must preach the gospel to every nation among us.

2. Only the preaching of the gospel can save our nation for her highest usefulness and extending obligations. All forms of social service fail in succeeding generations where Christian principles have not been preached and taught and Christian character developed. The American problem is fast becoming the foreign problem at home and the methods of Christianizing communities used in foreign fields must be used in our own country.

3. America's world-wide and self-sacrificing spirit as revealed in her war issues and war arrangements compel the nations of the earth to consider and study the spirit of Godwillness and righteousness back of such attitude and principle. We may conclude by relating the word and work of Jesus Christ to our own day in the principles and methods of his organization, simple, strong, personal, but comprehensive, far-reaching and infinite, as a gospel preached and presented to individuals as a very expanding, comprehensive means of self-perpetuation.

Rev. JOHN TIMOTHY STONE, D. D.,
Fourth Presbyterian Church, Chicago, Ill.

Of One Blood All Nations of Men
(Acts 17:21-31)

Paul's sense of the universality of religion was keen. His experience with many races and many faiths enabled him to know that men " feel after " God.

He based the universal brotherhood upon (1) a common Creator (God " hath made "); (2) a common physical nature (" of one blood "); (3) common, though diversified, habitations. (" to dwell on all of the face of the earth "); (4) common providential dealings (" hath determined the times before appointed, and the bounds of their habitation "); (5) common religious nature and aspirations (" seek the Lord," " feel after " and " find him "); (6) common spiritual privileges (" though he be not far from every one of us "); (7) common daily dependence upon God (" in him we live, and move, and have our being "); and (8) common filial relationship (" for we are also His offspring ").

A. W. A.

Thy Neighbor As Thyself
(Matt. 22:34-40; Luke 10:25-37)

Usually men are concerned in a theoretical way in discussing who is "neighbor." But the more important matter is, to be sure of the way in which to treat him. In the second great commandment of Jesus the manner of treatment of a neighbor is based upon the same considerations which justify a proper treatment of self — " love thy neighbor as thyself."

The right philosophy of treating another, which is the right philosophy of treating self, involves these fair dealings:

(1) No careless indifference, " Laissez faire " has been exploded, most of all where human souls are involved.

(2) No contemptous scorn. Every soul is precious. The one lost sheep on the mountain side must be recovered. As a man individualizes and sets value upon himself so must he individualize and appreciate every other man.

(3) No supercilious condescension. Class distinctions, the mouthings of conceit, and the assumptions of pride are out of place.

(4) Grant him the right of being what he is as freely as you claim the right to be what you are, even though he be black, while you are white, or he be foolish, while you are wise, or he be aged and infirm, while you are young and strong.

(5) See that he has justice, exactly as you claim justice for yourself.

(6) Keep the door of opportunity open before him and his children, just as you want that door never closed before your face, and the faces of your children.

(7) Give him companionship, and fellowship and friendship. You cannot live alone. Nor can he.

(8) Are there divine privileges and special favors either here, or hereafter, which you hope to enjoy? Then the obligation is upon you to share them all, the greatest and the best, with him.

A. W. A.

Paul's Solvent Indebtedness
(Rom. 1:9–17)

Paul uses commercial terms in commenting upon his sense of obligations to Romans, Greeks, and Barbarians, to all men of all conditions.

His assets are "as much as in me is," conjoined with divine grace and strength which those who live "by faith" may freely attain.

"I am debtor," he says. It is as though he wrote this note:

On demand, for value received through the power of God unto salvation, which I by faith in Jesus Christ have received, I promise to pay to every man whom I can reach, be he Jew, Greek, Roman, or any nationality whatsoever, the very best I have of pity, sympathy, light, leading, time, talents, home, possessions and service, all I have.

In witness whereof, not by my profession, but by my living testimony of ministry and sacrifice, I pledge myself in the name of Jesus, my Master, whose slave I am.

PAUL.

That note did not go to protest. Paul's missionary career shows that his credit was kept good.

Who will write a note like that?

The recognition of social and Christian obligation is a great need to-day. The payment of social indebtedness should be demanded. If all holy vows for human welfare could now be cashed in, how this great world would leap forward into the prosperity of the Kingdom and the riches of mercy in Christ Jesus!

A. W. A.

The Symbolism of Ideal Completeness
(Rev. 21:10–22:5)

It is somewhat remarkable that the story of redemption, which begins with a garden in which is a single pair, man and woman, should close with the vision of a city, vast, inclusive, assessible, self-sustaining; " and the nations of them which are saved shall walk in the light of it; and the Kings of the earth do bring their glory and honor into it!"

The story passes through all the gradations of isolated individualism, and the multitudinous intricacies of social relations up to an ideal purified social order.

A. W. A.

Parables of the Kingdom's Power and Penetration
(Matt. 13:1–52)

The Kingdom, which Jesus established among men, has many characteristics, all of which relate to the assimilation and transformation of men. In this group of parables these are prominent:

1. The Kingdom is of slow growth.
2. The Kingdom receives many of varied kinds and talents.
3. The Kingdom takes possession of its subjects in varying degrees.
4. The Kingdom patiently puts up with imperfection.
5. The Kingdom is worth more than any other possession of man.
6. The Kingdom cannot be buried and defeated; it permeates and transforms that which contains it.
7. The Kingdom, waxing great, gives shelter and rest to mankind.

The seed of this Kingdom is for every manner of soil and every manner of soul.

A. W. A.

The Mark of Cain
(Gen. 4:1–16)

A Cain among nations stands in the fields of the world, bloody-handed, disclaiming responsibility for the life and welfare of other nations.

The philosophy of might is false, proven false in the history of men, and shown to be false by the revelations of God.

Kindness and good will are the attributes of God toward men.

Our fellowmen are our brothers. We cannot shake off our responsibility and be guiltless. Already we have suffered as a nation, because we have failed so largely in caring for the strangers who have come to our shores.

A large part of crime, particularly that part which is due to drink, springs out of the loneliness and isolation.

Lawlessness in many cases arises solely from failure to understand our laws and customs, and that, because we have been lacking in neighborliness and good will.

The menace of the alien during the war has been at times threatening, because we have done so little in making him feel at home, and become a loyal part of our institutions.

The mark of Cain may not yet be upon us, but his fate impends, if we, like Cain, disclaim responsibility for our brothers in the great family of God.

We are our brother's keepers.

A. W. A.

Love to Strangers in Olden Times
(Deut. 10:12-22)

If our history be traced back far enough, we would all be found to be immigrants. Through great migrations in times past the providences of God have been revealed, and his purposes worked out.

A foreigner is only some one away from home. Pity is needed, not contempt and scorn. God is near to all, as near to one as to another. He is not a "respecter of persons."

The children of Israel had been strangers in a strange land; they had been slaves down in Egypt.

The Israelites were taught that God was impartial toward all; that he loved the stranger and furnished him food and raiment. On two reasons the exhortation rested, to love the stranger:

1. Because of past experiences; and
2. Because of God's love for, and treatment of, the stranger.

A. W. A.

IV. Bibliography
Americanization

In this section are included books on community organization and community drama, undertakings which are vital to the development of national ideals. Americanization means much more than teaching English and promoting nationalism.

STEINER, EDWARD A. "Introducing the American Spirit."
    New York, Fleming H. Revell, 1915, 274 pp. An admirable and timely book making a definite contribution to self criticism on the part of Americans.

MACKAYE, PERCY W. "New Citizenship."
    New York, MacMillan Company, 1915, 92 pp. A civic ritual for the use of candidates for American citizenship.

ROBERTS, PETER. "Civics for Coming Americans."
    New York, Association Press, 1917. 118 pp. A civics catechism. Simple in form and matter.

FOERSTER, N., and PIERSON, W. W. (editors). "American Ideals."
    Boston and New York, Houghton, Mifflin & Co., 1917. 326 pp.

TALBOT, WINTHROP (editor). "Americanization."
    New York, H. W. Wilson Co., 1917. 320 pp. These two books are compilations from many sources interpreting the American spirit and formulating American ideals. The latter has an extensive bibliography.

WARD, EDWARD J. "The Social Center."
    New York, D. Appleton & Company, 1913. 359 pp. A record of experience in one of the most significant of modern undertakings looking toward the development of community ideals; contains a bibliography.

JACKSON, HENRY E. "A Community Center."
    New York, MacMillan Company, 1918. 159 pp. $1.00. An official publication, issued by the United States Bureau of Education.

MACKAYE, PERCY W. "A Substitute for War."
    New York, MacMillan Company, 1918. 55 pp. A valuable little book urging civic organization and enterprise as a psychological equivalent for warfare.

    "The Pageant and Masque of St. Louis." St Louis Pageant and Drama Association, 1914. The word book of the Great St. Louis Pageant.

BEEGLE, M. P., and CRAWFORD, J. R. "Community Drama and Pageantry."
    Yale University Press, 1916. 370 pp.

THOMPSON, CHARLES L. "The Religious Foundations of America."
   A study in National Origins. New York, Fleming H. Revell, 1917. 307 pp. An appreciation of the contributions made by different nationalities in the founding and settlement of America.

MCCLURE, ARCHIBALD. "Leadership of the New America."
   New York, Doran, 1916.

PAULL, C. H. "Americanization."
   The Solvay Process Co., 1918. A report submitted to the company.

There are certain books of rare human interest, which might belong under "Immigration," which have distinct value for Americanization work:
   ANTIN, MARY. "The Promised Land," Houghton, 1912.
   STERN, E. G. "My Mother and I," MacMillan, 1917.
   STEINER, E. A. "From Alien to Citizen," Revell, 1914.

Note.— This bibliography is prepared by Rev. F. Ernest Johnson, pastor Duane Methodist Episcopal Church, New York City, for the Commission on Church and Social Service of the Federal Council.

RELIGIOUS WORK AMONG ITALIANS IN AMERICA
A SURVEY FOR THE HOME MISSIONS COUNCIL
By ANTONIO MANGANO

Published for the Immigrant Work Committee of the Home Missions Council Missionary Education Movement of the United States and Canada

NEW YORK

1917

FOREWORD

In the years 1916–1917 the Immigrant Work Committee of the Home Missions Council, representing the interests of thirteen evangelical denominations, engaged in a survey of the Italian communities of this country, with particular reference to their religious needs and the work of the churches. A similar survey of "Religious Work among the Poles in America" has been made by Rev. Joel B. Hayden. (Missionary Education Movement, New York, 15 cents, prepaid.) A survey of conditions among the Bohemians in America is now being completed by Rev. Kenneth D. Miller. For the survey of the Italians, Rev. Antonio Mangano, of the Italian Department of Colgate Theological Seminary, Brooklyn, volunteered his services. His expense was met by the Home Missions Council. Mr. Mangano visited many city and industrial communities in the East, Middle West, and South. He was at the same time engaged in writing "Sons of Italy" for the Missionary Education Movement, a mission study book syndicated by the various denominational home mission societies. This pamphlet presents material collateral to this book and of particular interest to denominations and other agencies engaged in work with the Italians, and to leaders in home mission work. For the general point of view, the mode of presentation, and the recommendations, Mr. Mangano holds himself responsible. In the Appendix statements are furnished by denominational and other agencies.

In so broad a field with such rapid changes in population and in the work of the churches, a publication of this sort is soon out of date and subject to correction. The Immigrant Work Committee of the Home Missions Council, however, submits this study as the first effort at a comprehensive survey of religious work among the Italians of America from the standpoint of the Protestant Church. It makes greatful acknowledgment of the painstaking service of Professor Mangano. Added information, corrections, criticism, and constructive suggestion will be heartily welcomed.

NEW YORK, *July* 1, 1917.

RELIGIOUS WORK AMONG ITALIANS IN AMERICA

I. POPULATION

It is impossible to state accurately the total number of Italians now resident in the United States, for these reasons: (1) No statistics are available to show the total number of Italian deaths; (2) it is impossible to tell how many have returned to Italy permanently; many, especially single men, make the voyage back and forth several times; (3) the war has recalled thousands to fight under the banner of Savoy.

In 1914 a total of 294,689 Italians entered the country, and 97,073 departed, making a net gain of 197,616 in the Italian population; while in 1915 the Bureau of Immigration records show that a total of 51,655 were admitted and 116,985 departed, making a loss of 65,330.

We may perhaps get a fair idea of our Italian population by approximating it as follows:

A careful study of one of the Brooklyn colonies in 1910 showed the children born of Italian parents just about equal in number to the adult population of the colony. If then, as is indicated by the Bureau of Immigration statistics, 3,000,000 Italians have come here during the past thirty years, allowing 1,000,000 for deaths and permanent departures, that would leave us 2,000,000 of native-born Italians with 2,000,000 children born in this country. But it must be remembered that in many parts of the country there are construction and labor camps made up of men without families; also many thousands have departed for war service. To be wholly fair, we can take off 500,000 more, and then safely say that the Italian population in the United States is at least 3,500,000.

There is not a single state in the Union that does not have Italians within its borders, but they are most numerous in New York, Pennsylvania, New Jersey, Massachusetts, Connecticut, and Rhode Island. In recent years they have made their way westward, and large colonies are now found in West Virginia, Ohio, and Illinois. A large group of northern Italians have settled at Asti, California, and are engaged in vine culture. It is estimated that there are 91,000 in the state. The recent industrial development of the Southern states has drawn a large number to Alabama, Georgia, Florida, Louisiana, and North Carolina. It is estimated that no less than 100,000 Italians are employed on the sugar plantations in the Southern states.

The chief centers are New York City with its 600,000, the second largest Italian city in the world; Philadelphia, 200,000; Boston, 60,000; Chicago, 74,000; New Haven, 30,000; Providence, 40,000; San Francisco, 30,000; Newark, 36,000; and Bridgeport, 25,000. The State of New York has the largest Italian population of all the states of the Union, nearly 1,000,000, forming over one-eighth of the population of the state.

II. Economic Conditions
A. Occupations

As Italians are to be found in every state in the Union, and even in Alaska, Hawaii, and the Philippine Islands, so it may justly be said that they are engaged in all the occupations which are common to the life of the American people. The Department of Commerce and Labor Report for 1914 shows that out of a total of 294,689 Italians admitted to the United States in that year, there were 73,335 classed with no occupation, this number including women and children; 193,284 were classed as agents, bankers, teamsters, farm laborers, manufacturers, merchants, and servants; 28,679 were classed as skilled workmen, as barbers, carpenters, gardeners, jewelers, mechanics, painters, stone-workers, engineers, tailors, shoe-makers, etc., while 1,116 were counted under the professions — actors, architects, clergymen, editors, professional engineers, lawyers, scientists, musicians, physicians, sculptors, and artists. While many of these do not secure employment in their own trade or profession, because of the handicap of language, still in our Northern states Italians are engaged in fifty-one different occupations and in twenty-four trades in the South. New York City alone has over 200 registered Italian physicians, 250 sculptors, and a goodly number of teachers in public schools and colleges. One Italian, Mr. Tanzola, has recently been appointed to teach mathematics at the Naval Academy at Annapolis.

B. Wages

The deft fingers of Italian women and children make $3,000,000 worth of artificial flowers annually. An expert colorist can make $50 a week. By rapid and constant work, early and late, women can make from $4 to $5 a week in their homes. Glove-making is another home trade, practiced especially in Gloversville, New York, and the surrounding home towns. Also in New York City a woman by constant work can sew a dozen pairs daily, for which she receives $1.20.

Musical instruments, banners, and badges, dolci (sweet cakes), and caramels, wood-working, furniture, and decorating are industries employing hundreds of Italians, while silk-weaving and hat-making occupy thousands more. Fifty per cent. of the weavers in the factories at Astoria, New York; Paterson, New Jersey; and West Hoboken, New Jersey, are Italians from Piedmont and Lombardy. They average about $23 a week as do also the bookbinders and hatmakers of Orange, New Jersey. It may be worthly of note, in passing, that, contrary to public opinion, it is these nothern Italian weavers in Paterson and stone cutters in Barre, Vermont, who are the most fiery and irreconcilable anarchists, and strikes are frequent among these justice-loving workers.

The great bulk of Italian immigrants fall into the ranks of unskilled laborers and are employed in the construction camps of railroads and subways, in cutting sewers, gas and water mains, and in road-making. In Barre, Vermont, the Italian stone cutters are indispensable in the granite sheds. In West Virginia they share with the Slav the task of mining soft coal. In Birmingham, Alabama, and Pittsburgh, Pennsylvania, they work in iron foundries; in Ohio the glass industry claims them. Massachusetts has thousands of Italians at work in her cotton mills and shoe factories. In New York and Brooklyn they throng the small tailor, cloak, cap, paper box, and candy factories, which are usually owned by Jews.

The Italians almost monopolize the barber trade. Hundreds are waiters at the large hotels. The Greeks are now rivaling the Italians as street venders of small fruits and are also crowding them up and out of the shoe-shining business. The wholesale fruit trade in our large cities is almost entirely in the hands of Italians, and they have their own chambers of commerce in such centers as New York, New Orleans, and San Francisco. There are 3,000 fruit stores owned by Italians in Greater New York. Their merchants import $3,000,000 worth of lemons and oranges, besides $5,000,000 worth of oil and wine annually, not to mention macaroni, cheeses, and dried fruits.

It is greatly to the credit of Italian self-respect that, in spite of low wages, less than one-half of one per cent. of the Italian population seeks charitable help. The report from our public almshouses and charitable institutions made for 1910 shows:

Foreign-born White Paupers in Almshouses

1,048.5 per 100,000 Irish.
  410.9 per 100,000 Swiss.
  390.7 per 100,000 French.
  313.0 per 100,000 Scotch.
  304.7 per 100,000 English and Welsh.
  300.0 per 100,000 German.
   75.0 per 100,000 Austro-Hungarian.
   43.7 per 100,000 Russian.
   31.8 per 100,000 Italian.

Taken as a whole, the Italians are distinguished not only as to their high quality of industry but in their love of saving and ambition to rise in the world. A well-known senator was having his shoes blacked late one afternoon and noticed an open book on the stool the bootblack had just left. "What are you reading?" he asked. "Livy," replied the youth. "Livy"? "Yes, I attend City College."

C. Housing

Unmarried men find the housing problem easier to solve than the men with their families. They either board with the family of some paesano (compatriot) in the cities, or live in the dilapidated box cars furnished by the railroads for the section gangs or in the patched tin and tar paper shacks of road construction groups. It is very unusual if in any of these places they find any privacy or comfort. If they board, they must share the room with several others. Miss Dunwiddie found during her investigation in Philadelphia that seven persons ate, cooked, washed and slept in one room. Sometimes in the larger cities, in quarters where rents are exceedingly high, there are day and night shifts occupying the same beds, and even sweatshop work may be carried on at the windows during the day by women and children, while the beds are occupied by night workers. In the slums of our cities the small dark rooms are a serious menace to health as well as to morals, and tuberculosis, a disease formerly unknown among Italians in their native land, is claiming thousands yearly in such tenements.

D. Property Owners

It is the earlier Italian settlers who own most of the property within the limits of the Italian colonies, both dwellings and property used for business. In 1915, $100,000,000 worth of real estate in Greater New York was listed under Italian ownership. Italians usually take property that has little or no value, and in the course of a few years improve it greatly. In Rochester, N. Y., property in the Italian colony has increased 200 per cent. since the Italians became owners of it. In Canastota, N. Y., they bought for a song large tracts of muck land and planted it with celery and onions. Today that land is worth from $400 to $800 an acre. The Italians went to South Jersey and took up the sandy land about Vineland and Hammonton, and they have made it blossom like a rose. One man who ten years ago had nothing but strong arms and a stout heart sold his crop of peaches in 1916 for $15,000. He owns a fine farm and a comfortable home.

III. Religious Situation

A. General Situation

It is a common belief among Americans that all Italians are Roman Catholics, and there seems to be good reason for this impression. Out of Italy's population of 36,000,000 60,000 are Protestants, but there are unnumbered thousands, yes, tens of thousands of anti-clerics and even atheists. Ninety-nine per cent. of the Italians landing on our shores would give the Roman Catholic as their religious belief, but if questioned a large number would add that they were not faithful to its celebrations nor its services, except perhaps at times of births, deaths, and marriages. A questionnaire sent to all Baptist, Presbyterian, Methodist, and Congregational Italian pastors on the question, " What per cent. of Italians in your colony are loyal to the Roman Church?" evoked an amazingly unanimous reply, "About one-third." One or two reported one-fourth; and one reported one-half.

In one city of Massachusetts out of a population of 1,700 Italians, only 60 attend the Roman Church; and in another city there is a colony of 6,000 Italians, of whom only 300 attend that church. There is a colony of 35,000 Italians in Brooklyn which has only one Italian church, seating at the utmost 400 persons. It conducts three masses on Sunday, and, granting it were filled to its capacity each time, it could only administer to 1,200 persons, less than 4 per cent. of the population. Out of the 600,000 Italian population of Greater New York, the Roman Church, by its own figures, so far as I could obtain them, lays claim to only 180,000, including children, as members of Roman Catholic Italian churches — less than one-third of the total Italian population.

There is need for the widest publicity of these facts in order to refute the common charge of proselyting, which all evangelical mission work among the Italian meets, and also because officials of city governments, health, probation, juvenile court and charity organizations and even school teachers commonly assume that all Italians, adults or children, are Catholics and insist on treating them as such.

Religiously, then, Italians, both in Italy and America, may be divided into four general groups: (1) All who are loyal to the Roman Church; (2) a larger group who are indifferent to religion, because they are disgusted with the priests and have ceased to believe what they teach; (3) the atheistic, anarchistic, and socialist group, which is actively hostile to religion of whatever name. To this latter class belong the great throng of younger men who have lost faith in Roman Catholicism and who firmly believe that all religions are only worn-out superstitions, imposed upon ignorant people to keep them in subjection. They have rebelled against the soul tyranny of the Roman Church, and, mistaking liberty for license, they acknowledge no authority except their own wish and individual advantage. They have an organized propaganda aided by public debates, street meetings, clubs, and socialist papers, all seeking to enlighten and free their fellow Italians from the yoke of superstition and their consequent condition of slavery for the benefit of the rich and the powerful. "You are taught," they say, "that it is wrong to steal and commit violence, so you will not injure the property of your oppressors, and they are flinging you a mere pittance, robbing you of a just share in the profit of your labor. You are taught that to limit your families is an awful sin, because industry must have a steady stream of workers, and if they are numerous your oppressors need pay them little. Men and women, control the size of your families. Do not raise up sons and daughters to be the slaves of the privileged classes." These newcomers, seeing for the most part only the under side of American life, and treated often, it must be admitted, unfairly, and with discrimination, ought not to be allowed to blunder in their conceptions of liberty. If they continue to come, a million or more a year, they will soon rule America through the ballot-box. How will they rule? By what standards? According to what ideals? It is for us to determine while yet there is time.

Among the better educated this revolt against the traditions and infallible authority of the Roman Church is called modernism, or perhaps it is better to say that modernism is an attempt to correct and modify the teaching and the practices of the ancient church and bring them into harmonious relations with modern thought and knowledge.

The fourth group is made up of what may be called "the faithful remnant"—men and women who have seen a new truth and have been willing to endure the bitterest criticism and unite themselves with the "insignificant" and "feeble" evangelical groups. As in the case of Israel, it was the few that held up true ideas about Jehovah, so it is only the few among the Italians who are holding up the vital and life-giving principles of Christianity before the eyes of their nationality.

B. Activities of the Roman Church

For a number of years the Roman Church paid little attention to the Italians in America. Consequently the work of Italian evangelization was much easier fifteen years ago than at the present time. The common report among Protestants throughout the length and breadth of our land is: "When we opened our mission the Catholics were doing nothing for Italians; now they have built a church, are building a parochial school, and are copying our various social activities." Realizing that the majority of the Italian priests were unable to hold the people, as early as ten or more years ago, young American seminarians, mainly of Irish descent, were sent to Rome to learn the Italian language and to become familiar with Italian thought and feeling. They are now taking part in this new aggressive campaign. In Lawrence, Mass., where the evangelical work of the Rev. Ariel Ballondi has created considerable comment, a new Catholic church has just been reared and seven nuns have been brought into town to visit the homes and so overcome the "devilish influence of the Protestants." In Providence there is a large, prosperous and influential Italian colony of 40,000. Two years ago in one section of the city there was built the beautiful church of Saint Anna. It is a copy of the church of St. John and St. Paul in Venice, and an Italian bell tower stands beside it. Padre Bove, who seems to be an energetic wide-awake priest, is now completing an equally well-equipped parochial school building. The plant is estimated to cost $50,000. This school will contain an auditorium which will be used as a theatre and for concerts, rooms for an orchestra, and a day nursery with forty beds for babies. There are to be also eight good-sized classrooms where the religion of the fatherland will be taught and l'Italianita, which means "Italian feeling," and which can hardly be conducive to Americanization.

In other localities the Catholic Church conducts sewing schools, music classes, gymnasiums, athletic activities, classes for the study of English, kindergartens, day schools for the boys and girls, and boy scout troops. In a New York Catholic settlement, vocal, piano and organ lessons are given free to the people. A large number of fresh air homes have been established, and there is a long list of homes and protectorates for foundlings, orphans, and wayward boys and girls. These children are committed through the courts, the city paying for their maintenance. These helpful ministries are the direct result of the example of Protestant work. Indeed, the Pope considered the apathy of the Italian clergy of such importance that he not long ago sent a special encyclical letter urging them to stop abuses in Italian parishes and do all in their power to hold the Italian people to the Church. In August, 1915, an appeal was sent out to all the Catholic clergy to support and distribute a weekly Italian Catholic paper which it is proposed to publish. It will be ably edited, and will make an up-to-date, valuable magazine for Italians in their own language.

Italian priests are both good and bad, but the doctrine the Church has taught her children for generations, and still teaches them, that the value of the priest's ministry, his authority and power are independent of his character and private life, is the cause of much moral looseness in priestly life. "When the priest stands before the altar, he represents God, he stands in the place of God, and he is the only channel for the flow of divine grace."

Some priests take their office most seriously, and with the authority that such a doctrine confers, there is great opportunity for limitless good under wise leadership. Father Bandini is such a priest. He headed a little colony and founded Tontitown, Arkansas, in 1898. His courage and faith held them together in spite of a cyclone and frost which killed a first harvest. For more than twenty years he has been the veritable Moses of his flock. He has established good schools, taught his people to appreciate the best in American life, and has become the moral force of the community. I shall long remember my visit to the colony, to his home, to his church. He knew that I was of a different faith, yet we talked in a natural and friendly manner, even about things upon which we did not agree. It would be well for Italians, yes, and for America, if there were many more of his type. This splendid man has but recently died.

C. Organizations Outside the Church Working for the Italians

While the churches and religious bodies were the first to move in behalf of the social and general welfare of Italians in this country, there have been other organizations that have lent a helping hand. The public schools in many of the large cities have established night schools for the study of English, while New York, Pittsburgh, Chicago, and other large cities have a special lecture department of the public school system to give free illustrated lectures in the Italian language on subjects of interest, such as " The Beauties of America; " " The Lives of Great Americans;" " The Value of the Public School System," etc. In Greater New York, the Board of Health has an Italian department which provides special lecturers to churches and social institutions who give in illustrated lectures information of how to avoid various diseases, especially tuberculosis which is becoming a great menace among Italians here. In addition to this the organization known as the University Extension furnishes doctors, both men and women, to speak before mothers' meeting on such subjects as " The Home," Ventilation," " The Care and Feeding of Children," and other important topics. The Y. M. C. A. has had a special branch for Italians in upper New York, the only institution of the kind in the United States, and the work which the Y. M. C. A. is doing for the foreigner in general has touched in a most helpful way the life of the Italian.

The one effort on a large scale to reach the foreigner with the English language and American influences is that which has been put forth in Detroit. The Board of Education and the Chamber of Commerce undertook jointly the task of getting the adult immigrant to study English as the first step in Americanization. The result was the organization of the entire industrial, educational, social, and religious force of the city into one whole, to carry on a campaign for the purpose of getting the foreigner under American influences. The public libraries, the City Recreation Committee, the Health Committee, all social agencies, the Y. M. C. A., Y. W. C. A., babies' milk funds, Children's Home Society, the Salvation Army, Associated Charities, employment bureaus, Boy Scouts, women's clubs, and the great power of the foreign language pres were all enlisted in the campaign. The campaign is only a year old and there was an increase in the registration at night schools of 153 per cent, a 25 per cent. increase of young mechanics in the high schools, and a greatly increased feeling of responsibility on the part of employers and community in general for their foreign population.

The National Americanization Committee is also occupying itself with the task of Americanizing the foreigner. It makes this fourfold suggestion to the American people:

1. Americanize one immigrant woman.
2. Get one immigrant to become a citizen.
3. Teach one foreign-born mother English.
4. Put one immigrant family on your calling list.

One of the most helpful signs in connection with the development of the life of the foreigner is the interest which the Americanized foreigner takes in his own people. A splendid example of this is the activity of the Italian Medical Association of New York City which publishes a bi-weekly magazine called "The Word of the Doctor," which furnishes information of a most valuable sort regarding all questions of hygiene and health. One of the chief objects of this propaganda is to eliminate the quack doctor, both American and Italian, who is so prone to become a parasite upon the life of the ignorant foreigner.

No right-minded person can fail to appreciate the value of the service which these different organizations are rendering in connection with the Americanization of the foreigner. And yet it must in all fairness be said that, with the single exception of Detroit, so far as the adult immigrant is concerned, the great Americanization influence throughout the entire country has not been the public school nor the social settlement, but the evangelical churches. Throughout the entire country our missionaries are everywhere teaching English, showing the people what is best in American life, in American history, and in our present political institutions. One of the finest examples of this kind of work is to be found in Fairmont, West Virginia, where a consecrated woman, with a real love in her heart for the foreigner, has reached through her English classes over 250 young Italians. But no one receives English lessons from this woman, without receiving something that is infinitely better, the appreciation of the value of an upright, moral, and straightforward Christian life. In a word they learn English but also learn Christ. The biggest educational factor in the life of the adult is the evangelical church. Many a man who did not know how to read and write has been impelled to make every effort to learn how to read and write because he wanted to sing the hymns of the church. Even poor peasant women have been inspired by the church atmosphere with the desire to read. Young men who speak nothing but a dialect have been led to study through the inspiration of the church to learn their native tongue as well as the English language.

Another factor in the educational process of the church is the Daily Vacation Bible School. Everywhere, especially in the South and the West, are to be found these schools in connection with our foreign churches and missions throughout the summer months. These provide a helpful influence for the thousands of children who would otherwise play in the hot streets, and bring to them the impressive Bible stories, the beautiful hymns of our Christian faith, and various lines of industrial activities, such as sewing, weaving, hammock-making, etc.

IV. PROTESTANT WORK AMONG ITALIANS

A. Early Stages

During the early years of Italian immigration, the evangelical churches of America assumed the same attitude toward Italians they had previously taken toward the Irish in the early fifties. The Italians were regarded as the natural property of the Roman Church. But, as we have already indicated, the Roman Church did not interest itself in attempting to reach this nationality, and this was due in part to a natural hostility on the part of the Irish toward the Italian. As they increased in numbers, and Mulberry Bend grew famous for the violent crimes committed there, American people were roused to a sense of obligation towards these aliens. They believed that these people were in need of having the gospel preached to them since they were so largely outside of all religious influences.

The first mission for Italians in America was established thirty-seven years ago by that dean of Italian work in the United States, the Rev. Antonio Arrighi, under the auspices of the New York City Mission Society. This church has had a wonderful history and at the present time it is keeping up its record by the aggressive work that it is doing. The work is housed in the old Broome Street Tabernacle, and according to its last report, it has a membership of 300, an average attendance in the Sunday school for the past year of 453, while during the church's thirty-seven years of existence no less than thirty-two men have been sent out to preach the gospel to the Italians in the various parts of our country. The church has also sent out eight women workers. The bond of fellowship that is created within the church circle is so strong that no matter where the members live, in the Bronx, in Brooklyn, or even in the towns of New Jersey, they feel drawn back to their home church for communion service.

B. Denominational Survey and Comment

A good deal of the work of the Italians during the first few years was necessarily in the nature of an experiment, feeling the way, as a good friend of mine used to say, "merely tentative;" but as time went on, it became apparent that Italians were responsive to the gospel appeal, and the various denominations began to plan for a permanent work and equipment.

1. Presbyterian Church in the U. S. A.

The first to enter the field of Italian evangelization in this country were the Presbyterians, and as they were the leaders in the enterprise, so today, it must in fairness be stated, that they are setting the standards for all other denominations. They are doing most thorough and aggressive work with the most far-reaching plans for future development. The immigrant work office of the Board of Home Missions is busy making thorough surveys of Italian colonies in many states. They aim to build up a system of parishes which shall lead and minister to the entire community life.

From the beginning the Presbyterians have been in close touch with the Waldensians, "The Israel of the Alps," the Protestant Church of Italy which dates back to three centuries before the Reformation, and surviving many cruel and bloody persecutions, has come down to the present day. Needless to say, the Presbyterians' work has gained much from its associations with these old Italian Protestants, and the Waldensian Church has furnished a goodly number of excellent ministers and missionaries for the Presbyterian work. Among this number none was more highly respected nor more valuable than the Rev. Alberto Clot, who has recently died. A cultured, Christian gentleman, born in the Waldensian valleys, speaking and writing French, Italian and English with equal ease and polish, he had a remarkable grasp of all plans of Italian work both here and in Italy. He left in manuscript a just complete history of the Waldensian colony in Valdese, North Carolina, which we may all hope to see in print. This Waldensian element has been a valuable asset to the work of this denomination in laying a broad and firmly reliable foundation for future work.

The Presbyterians have in a special manner caught a vision of the possibilities of the future, and are spending large sums of money in every department of their work, without putting too great emphasis upon immediate results. They are cultivating the community in a sensible and scientific manner. Twenty-five years from now they will reap an abundant harvest for the kingdom of God. They are endeavoring to minister to the foreigner not only through his spiritual nature, but to touch his life at as many points as possible; recreation, amusements, education, music, genuine friendship. The next generation of Italians in these centers will understand American ideals and will appreciate the significance of religion and the effect which it ought to have upon human life.

2. *Methodist Episcopal*

The beginning of religious work for the Italians by the Methodist Episcopal Church is well described in a report of their City Mission Society under the date of March 31, 1889. It contains the following statements: " There came to this country in May last, in company with Dr. Vernon and Dr. Gay a local preacher of our Italy Conference, by the name of Vita Calabrese. He offered himself for work among his countrymen of whom there are more than 30,000 in New York. . . . The Rev. O. R. Bouton opened his chapel at the Five Points to us free of charge. (Then in the very heart of the Italian quarter.) In October, Dr. Vernon, returning from fourteen years of work in Italy, visited this humble mission at Five Points, and told me that in the line of gathering a congregation willing to hear the gospel more had been accomplished there in four months than could be accomplished at any point in Italy in four years."

During the past thirty years, Methodists, under inspiration of the splendid work which the denomination has been carrying on in Italy, have made great strides in the task of Italian evangelization. They depended almost entirely for missionaries on men trained in Italy, in their own Methodist Theological School. Some splendid work has been done by these men. Some of the leaders of the denomination, however, have felt for some time the need of workers who have been educated in this country under influence of American Christianity. It has too often happened that a man who has received all his training in Italy, however excellent that may have been, has not been able to do effective work in America. The reason for this is that a man prepared in Italy under a social order where the priestly idea in religion is dominant cannot very well adapt himself to the requirements of the work in this country. Usually, the dominating idea of the ministry in Italy is that the only function of the minister is to preach the gospel, and they do not easily adapt themselves to the variety of social activities which we feel in this country are essential if we are to present to the foreigner the true meaning of religion and establish a point of contact with him, so that we may lead him to the knowledge of Jesus Christ.

For this reason arrangements were nearly completed for the establishment of an Italian department in connection with Drew Theological Seminary, where young men might be trained under the best American influences and ideals. But this idea has been dropped for the present.

For a number of years the Italian work of the Methodist Church has been under the direction of a bishop and superintendent, Rev. Dr. William Burt, and Rev. Dr. Frederick H. Wright. The so-called "Italian Mission" of the Methodist Church has for the past seven years had an independent existence, meeting each year in an annual session, where the reports of the superintendent and of the various committees of the mission were presented and discussed. At these annual sessions also each missionary gave a report of his own work and the examinations on studies pursued and books read were held.

During 1916 a change has taken place in the policy of the Methodist Church, regarding its Italian Mission. Indeed the "Mission" as an independent institution has been abolished. Hence there is no bishop or superintendent for Italian work as such. Each Italian mission and worker is now under the care of the respective local conference and the resident bishop. Other denominations will watch the experiment with interest.

The Home Mission Society of the Methodist Church during the past year has appropriated for the Italian work $50,000. This item, however, does not even represent one-half of the sum that is spent in connection with the work that the Methodist Church is doing to reach the Italians of America.

3. Protestant Episcopal.

The Episcopal Church was one of the early comers in the field of Italian evangelization, and during the time it has been at work, has made considerable progress, owing to its farsighted policy of fine equipment in buildings and a large number of trained, characterful American women. Arch-deacon Nelson of the Diocese of New York City is the source of the information concerning the beginnings of their denominational work. The Rev. Mr. Stouder undertook to minister to the Italians almost forty years ago. He began in a rented store, later transferring his activities to the old Grace Chapel, opposite the Academy of Music. They had the use of the building for a service Sunday afternoon and a communion service in the early morning. Later, the old St. Philip's Church, Mulberry street, was bought by Mrs. Wolf and presented to the Italian Mission. Sixteen years ago the city preempted the property and the Mission was transferred to a rented store once again, till the new beautiful building on Broome street was erected at a cost of $100,000. This building is thoroughly Italian in its external as well as internal construction.

The largest work of the Episcopal Church is housed in Grace Chapel, 14th street and First avenue, and Grace Neighborhood House, 98 Fourth avenue, New York City, supported by the contributions of the historic Grace Church. The Neighborhood House serves as an effective point of contact with the people through its various activities, while the strictly religious services are held in the beautiful chapel on 14th street.

This Mission to Italians was begun in 1905 by the late William R. Huntington, D. D., then rector of Grace Church, and was in charge of the Rev. Melville K. Bailey, who had loved and learned the Italian language so that he was able to preach to the newcomers.

Mr. Bailey was assisted from the beginning by a young Italian, the Rev. Francesco G. Urbano, at that time a candidate for orders, and since 1911 the minster in charge of this work. Mr. Urbano has a comprehensive grasp of the conditions under which his people live, and by his thorough American training is peculiarly fitted to be a leader in his community.

Today Grace Chapel numbers over 600 communicants and has an average attendance at its services of 250 throughout the year. A confirmation class of 108 persons was received last April. There has been a steadily increasing growth from year to year. The broad, firm foundations of friendship and trust were laid by years of many-sided social ministry under the guidance of Deaconess Gardner. The various workers that co-operate in the several branches of the church activity unite in working together for a regular attendance upon the church services. The deaconesses are in constant touch with the different families of the church and are in a position to understand the problems of the people. There is such an attachment to this church that it is rare to lose any that have been received as members, and families that have moved to other quarters come back again and again to visit their loved church home.

The Episcopal Church has eight missions in New York City with fourteen paid workers. Other important missions of this church are in Philadelphia and Boston.

4. Lutheran

While the Lutheran Church is classed as one of the largest denominations in this country, it has done little mission work outside of the nationalities it would most naturally be interested in, as for example, Germans, Swedes and Slavs of various nationalities. About ten years ago St. Peter's Church in Philadelphia found itself surrounded by Italians. Its own communicants were rapidly withdrawing to other parts of the city. The call of God to minister to these new neighbors came clearly one Sabbath day, when, drawn by the music, a black-eyed little child strolled wandering up the aisle, and the church was not disobedient to the heavenly vision. Today an Italian congregation meets for worship in St. Peter's Church, while around the corner stands the Martin Luther House, equipped for various kinds of modern social and religious ministery to its needy neighbors. There is a daily kindergarten, a sewing school for girls, classes in English, industrial and recreational clubs for boys and girls, etc. This is the only mission work the Lutherans are conducting for Italians, and it largely owes its existence to the faith and courage of one woman, Mrs. Cassidy. "After five years of kindergarten and three years of church services, the results are a confirmed membership of thirty-three, a Sunday school of sixty, a kindergarten of eighty, and an evening class of English of fifteen." There is every reason to hope that the example set in Philadelphia may be imitated in other parts of our country where the Lutherans are strongly entrenched and where because of their financial ability they could render a worthy and effective service.

5. Reformed Church in the U. S. A.

The Dutch Reformed Church is not so widely distributed outside of New York City, hence one cannot expect to find a very extensive work for the foreigners under their auspices. What they are doing for the Italians is well done. Eight years ago they realized their responsibility toward the Italians of Newburg, New York, and commenced a work for them. It has grown so rapidly, that they are now planning to build a church which, judging from the plans, will be the most churchly in appearance and the most artistic building used exclusively for Italian work in this country.

For the past three years, the Knox Memorial Church of New York City has in its own building carried on a mission for Italians. Now the Waldensian Church of New York City meets in their auditorium every Sunday. During the past years there has also been opened a work for Italians in Hackensack, New Jersey.

It is to be hoped that this old historic church, in addition to its many noble activities in behalf of the kingdom of God, will take more strongly to heart this cause of evangelizing the Italians.

6. *Baptist*

The Baptist denomination was one of the pioneers in attempting to give the gospel to the Italians. The first Italian Baptist Church in the United States was established by Rev. Ariel B. Bellondi, in Buffalo, New York, in 1893, while he was still a student at Colgate Theological Seminary, and later at Rochester Theological Seminary. The history of the initiation and founding of this mission is unique in that it was the Baptist Young People's Union of Buffalo that made its existence possible. The Union not only studied the question of the necessity of Italian evangelizing, but took an active and leading part in the actual work. It was this wide-awake organization, under the wise and efficient leadership of Dr. E. E. Chivers, of blessed memory, that raised the money, built the building and induced Mr. Bellondi to do the preaching. This church has never become a strong organization numerically, as it was established in a small but select suburban colony on the outskirts of Buffalo; but it has always been a very effective institution. Some of its members are among the well-known business men of that community. Two years ago they contributed in money and work something like $2,000 for the improvement of their own property. But even prior to the establishment of the Church in Buffalo, Baptists at different points had attempted to reach the Italian. English-speaking workers started Sunday schools and meetings for

Italian children in Newark, New Jersey; Stamford, Connecticut; Mount Vernon, New York, and Mariner's Temple, Chatham Square, New York City, as early as 1889. The early attempts of an Italian evangelization were left for a number of years in the hands of the American Baptist Home Mission Society. This organization was greatly handicapped in the prosecution of the work because of the lack of properly trained and tried men. They had to employ such material as was available and in some cases with disastrous results. The need was realized by the Baptist Education Society of New York State, and in 1907, the Italian Department of Colgate Theological Seminary was opened in Brooklyn with two students selected from eight applicants. Of the sixty applicants during the nine years of the department's existence, twenty-one have been graduated, while eleven are at present enrolled. The others were counseled to seek other lines of employment.

The course of three years prescribed by the faculty of Colgate Theological Seminary includes a systematic study of the whole Bible, courses in church history, English and Italian languages, New Testament, Greek, theology, homiletics with weekly exercises in preaching, and a considerable experience on various mission fields. Provisions are also made for the most efficient students, after finishing the department's three years' course, to take a special course of two years in Colgate University at Hamilton, New York.

It is worthy of note that during the past seventeen years the Italian Baptist workers have met in their annual convention in connection with one of the Italian churches, there to discuss problems affecting the development of the work entrusted to them. The last convention was held in Lawrence, Massachusetts, with forty-five missionaries and pastors present.

V. GENERAL RECOMMENDATONS
1. *Attitude*

A change of attitude is necessary before we can Americanize the great mass of the Italian immigrants. Outside of pastors and settlement or lay workers, who come in close contact with Italians and both respect and love them, the ordinary American dislikes, distrusts, fears and shuns Italians, noticing only their external dirt, the smell of garlic, and the picturesque violent crimes committed by their black sheep. Too often we study the

Italian objectively, and it is unfair for anyone to pass unfavorable judgment upon a race group merely on hearsay. To deal fairly with any nationality we must enter into sympathetic and intimate relations with a number of these people at least, so that we may know them. Those who know the Italian at first hand all give testimony to the responsive attitude of the Italian and to his willingness to accept the best which America has to give. But with what Americans worthy of emulation does he come in contact? In his limited world he knows his boss, who in many cases lords it over him; he knows the political ward leader, who is usually an Irish-American; he comes into occasional contact with the police authority of the city; in a word, virtually everybody that has to do with him preys upon him. What conception can he have of America? He frankly says, "With money you can do anything in America." It remains with Christian Americans to give the Italian a different conception of American standards of life, but they must do it through the medium of personal contact.

2. A More Comprehensive Attack

In the course of our Italian work we have passed through two distinct stages. The first was the experimental stage; various denominations attempted something here and there; missions were opened in many places just to try out Italian evangelization. This stage, generally speaking, lasted from the beginning up to about fifteen years ago. Then came the stage of permanent work; buildings were erected and definite policies were adopted; workers commenced study and training for Italian work. We are now entering upon the third stage, which we might call the intensive stage. There are still places where missions, as in the past, should be established, but the great work to be done during the next period of ten or fifteen years is to put upon more solid foundations the existing works. We must now select some of our greatest centers, and the most promising fields in these centers which are inadequately manned and equipped and bring them up to the highest state of efficiency. It is self-evident that, given a large community where we already have a work but which does not meet the needs of the colony, every extra thousand dollars which we put into such a field will place the entire work upon a more effective basis than if that sum were spread about at various points where there might be little or no support for the work beyond the meager salary of the missionary.

But there are certain strategic points which ought to have new and better equipments and more workers, in order to make the money now expended at those points tell for the most. In Providence, Rhode Island, for example, which has, outside of California, the finest and most highly developed Italian conony in the United States, the one colony known as Federal Hill, has a population of over 30,000. They own millions of dollars worth of property, the houses they live in are modern, well built, and occupied by one or two families. There is no crowding, no dirty streets, no slums there. On Broadway, which up to within very recent years was considered one of the most select highways in the city, one-third of that splendid boulevard property is owned by Italians. Everything about the entire community has a prosperous air; people are well dressed, stores are neatly and attractively kept, the streets are well lighted and scrupulously clean, and I am told that it is as well behaved a community as can well be found in any part of the city.

One of the striking features of the colony is that the Italians have succeeded in working together for common ends. This is rather unusual for an Italian colony. The impossible has happened in Providence. The Italians have elected by their own votes five members of the State legislature, two aldermen, one councilman, a member of the Board of Education, and an assistant district attorney. One-half of the male population is naturalized. They have twenty-two doctors, twelve lawyers, and many other men in the higher walks of life, especially prominent business men.

In this exceptional colony the Roman Catholics have reared a fine and imposing church building for those who are disposed to attend it, but as Protestants we have three tiny missions carried on by three different denominations, Baptists, Methodists and United Presbyterians. The total property value is $18,500, while the sum of $5,140 is expended yearly upon these three fields, mainly for workers, and the total membership for these missions does not reach the 200 mark.

It is unreasonable, given the love of Italians for churchly buildings, to expect that these prosperous, intelligent Italians who are in no wise interested in religion are going to be drawn to these little, insignificant, unchurchly mission buildings. The wise thing to do in such a case is to face the situation squarely and determine to put up a church plant with facilities for social work in the very best spot obtainable on Federal Hill, a building which would command the attention and the respect of the people. Then place a group of trained and devoted men and women in this place and back them up in their efforts to possess the land for God. There should be no tentative spirit in the matter. We have passed the experimental stage, we know now what we must do and what we may logically expect. This, of course, would mean the expenditure of possibly $10,000 a year, a little less than twice the sum now spent upon the three fields, but it does not require a prophet to see that the fruits of such an enterprise would be more than double what they now are.

Now I realize that it might be impossible for any one of the denominations now engaged upon the field to undertake such a task single-handed. Then it is rash for me to hazard the suggestion that in order to obtain the end desired, one denomination should assume the responsibility for the work of that field, while the other denominations co-operate in the support and in the actual work with every means at their disposal? A splendid example of this principle has recently been furnished us in Middletown, New York, where the work was taken under the care of the Presbyterian denomination, while all the Protestant denominations of the town co-operated in gifts of money and helpers. Even in the matter of securing a building for the work, while the Presbyterian Church took the initiative, the Protestant people of every name contributed almost $5,000.

3. *Concerning Self-Support*

There are 326 Protestant churches and missions in the United States, with something over 15,000 members who contributed during the past year a total of $50,000, at the rate of $3.25 per member toward their own support, while over $400,000 is annually spent by home and city mission boards and individual churches for the support of this work. The question is often raised as to how long it will be necessary to expend this large sum of money. When will Italian churches be able to care for their own work? In investigating causes for the present conditions certain facts appeared:

A. One of the main reasons for the alienation of Italians from the Roman Church is the fact that the priests have extorted money from the people in every way open to them. The people have felt the injustice of the system whereby those with plenty of money could get the services of the church while the poor must do without.

B. To offset the belief that religion can be bought and paid for, the missionaries have emphasized the fact that the gospel of Christ is free to all. In church and on the public streets the missionaries have done all in their power to make the people understand that everything is free to all alike, no special privilege, no paying for a dispensation. The people have accepted these statements and are acting upon them. It is a matter of concern to many of the leaders in Italian work to lead the people toward self-support. This **must** be done, but wisdom and tact must be used.

C. While the Roman Catholic Church manages to secure money from the people, she does not do it by the direct method of voluntary gifts. She receives it in indirect ways for which the people suppose they receive some valuable equivalent, such as masses for the dead, special feasts in honor of saints, sale of objects of indulgence, as medals, scapulars, printed prayers, beads and candles. Large sums of money are received also for the yearly masses, which societies pay for in honor of their favorite saints. The fee for baptisms, funerals and weddings are taken as a matter of course. It is difficult to train our church-members in direct, voluntary, regular giving, although it must be said that the converts to Jesus Christ who do give systematically through the envelope and pledge system give more than they ever gave to the Roman Catholic Church, in their regular collection.

D. The matter of regular contribution rests wholly with the Italian pastor. Some men secure a fine response from a small congregation. If he has taken special pains to educate his people as to the necessity and value of regular giving, he gets results.

According to a study made of the Italian churches in Greater New York, the following facts are brought out: One Italian Presbyterian Church of 654 members raised in one year $1,360, while six other missions and churches of the same denomination with a total membership of 628 gave only $405. Eight Episcopal churches, with a total membership of 1,190 gave $1,037 during the same year. Forty-six Methodist churches and missions in various parts of the country, with a total membership of 3,952, contributed for all purposes $8,745, while a total of forty-five Presbyterian churches, with 4,290 members, gave $14,353. Forty-five Baptist churches, with a membership of 2,000, gave $7,000 during the same **year.**

A study of the detailed reports of each individual church shows that not always do churches upon which the most money is spent show the largest increase of membership. This is because considerable sums of money are spent in social and educational work, such as day kindergartens, clinics, Boy Scouts, gymnasiums, etc. This work is very expensive and does not bring immediate results in church members, but if this work is adequately followed up by careful visiting in the homes and personal work with individuals, keeping in close, friendly contact with all that the various activities bring under the influence of the church, it is laying the foundation for large future ingathering.

4. *Workers*

It is one of the axioms of Christian work that the personal life of the worker is far more potent in the long run than what he or she may say. No man or woman should be entrusted with the important work of leadership in our Italian missions until they have given full proof of the necessary qualifications in character. There is too much at stake to run any risk in connection with this matter. Many a man has been alienated from the church and even from God because of the questionable and immoral life of religious workers. As I visited Italian missions in many cities from Massachusetts to Texas during the last summer, one of the expressions which I heard most often from Italians as well as from Americans was this: " We had a good work here some years ago, but then the Board sent us a man who ought never to have been authorized to preach. He destroyed not only what we had already accomplished, but he has made it impossible for us to continue our work with any success for a number of years to come. We must live down the bad example of that man." Such experiences not only turn the foreigner against the evangelical propaganda, but they are too effective in making our American friends who support the work lose their interest in our project.

One of the most essential things in a worker, aside from personal character, is the knowledge of the life, the customs, the views, the prejudices, the ideals, and the ordinary problems of life that the foreigner has to meet. There are too many people who have theories of their own regarding what should be done for the foreigner and how it should be done, but the theories are not based upon either knowledge or experience. All workers should study the national characteristics and dispositions of the people they are attempting to reach.

5. Women Workers

The part which the woman missionary can have in our great task of foreign evangelization is beyond our power to estimate. But it must be understood that it is not so much what she does in public meetings or in her departments in the Sunday school and the sewing school that makes her work important, but it is her personal influence with the young people, especially the girls of the mission church. These young folk are exceedingly anxious to acquire American ways, they are ready to imitate everything their leader does. What a great responsibility this lays upon the worker! We need the best educated, most refined, and truly cultured persons to advise and lead these responsive, loyal, idealistic young people. Too often we have had well-meaning, devotedly Christian, but light-weight women of scant education who were in culture and refinement little above the young people they were trying to lead. Their work for little children is in many cases excellent, but they cannot cope with the growing intelligence of the high school boys and girls. The worker must by her mere presence inspire to noble thinking, noble feeling, and noble acting. The worker must not feel above those she is seeking to reach, but she must be above them if they are to be drawn to a higher level.

The work of women missionaries should be planned in connection with the entire activity of the mission church. It is disastrous to separate the work too much into independent departments. All need the unified influence of regular conference to plan their work. Many little frictions that lead to serious disturbances between workers might be eliminated through this regular weekly or monthly conference.

6. Associative Spirit

The Italian minister has in the past held himself too much aloof from social, political, and other organizations composed of Italians. It is becoming more and more the conviction of those that have had considerable experience that it would of great advantage if the Italian missionary would associate himself with various orders and would enter as fully as possible into the life of the community in which he works. One of the most powerful organizations recently formed among Italians is " I Figlia D'Italia," or " Sons of Italy." This is a strictly democratic organization where the Protestant missionary would be cordially welcomed. Already a number of our Italian pastors have seen their opportunity and thrown themselves into the task of giving direction and ideals to this rapidly growing order. This is one of the rare openings for the exertion of wholesome Christian influence upon an institution that is destined to mould to a great extent the spirit and attitude of the Italian people in the great centers of population.

7. *The Message*

Our Italian missionaries should be taught as far as possible to refrain from railing at the Roman Catholic Church. Preaching should be constructive and practical. It is necessary in many cases for the sermon to have an apologetic note. One of the common questions which even intelligent Italians ask is, " What is the difference between the Protestant religion and the Catholic religion? " It is very evident that to meet the state of the Italian mind with a religious message one must be familiar with Roman Catholic views, doctrines and practises. In presenting the message to a non-Protestant audience, it is essential that a man shall draw comparisons between the two systems, but such comparison should be made in a conciliatory manner. Ex-priests who enter as workers in our missionary fields are usually the bitterest denunciators of the Roman Catholic Church and of its priests. I shall never forget an expression used by an ex-priest Protestant missionary in speaking about his antagonism toward the class from which he came, before a public audience: " If I had the hearts of all the priests in my hand, I would throw them to the dogs." It is unnecessary to say that this kind of preaching does not make indifferent Catholics favorable to the Protestant position. When the message of Christ is presented in all its simplicity and power and the moral side of religion is given emphasis and prominence, the Italian, whether a zealous Catholic or not, says: " Yes, you are right, that is true," and in many cases he is willing to confess, even though he is still attached to the Roman Church, that Protestant teaching is better than Roman Catholic teaching, and that Protestant ethics are better than Roman Catholic.

8. *Literature and Publications*

The four denominational Italian papers that are published weekly are of great value in the prosecution of our evangelical propaganda. But we need now, as we have needed in the past, tracts that may be freely distributed to the Italian people everywhere. The ready disposition on the part of the Italian to receive and read virtually anything that is placed in his hands gives us a rare opportunity. The old tract literature has served its purposes well, but we are now face to face with the problem of meeting certain well defined and strongly entrenched views on the part of the people that we seek to reach. There is an imperative need for a new literature in order to present our fundamental ideas and conceptions of the religion of Jesus Christ to the Italian. This literature must be apologetic as well as evangelistic. Our motives as Christians and our methods of worship are now assailed, and so many false statements are spread broadcast by the Roman Church that we must prepare short tracts that in a clear and simple manner will state the Protestant point of view. This literature might very well be prepared in such a way as to be used by all the denominations, because the problems are the same for all. It would be an extravagance for each denomination to do its own work in the matter of preparing tracts to meet the same needs.

The importance of the press in all sorts of propaganda cannot be over-estimated. The Christian church knows well its power. There are at the present time four denominational papers printed in the Italian language: "L'Era Nuova," Presbyterian; "La Fiaccola," Methodist; "Il Cristiano," Baptist, and "L'Ape Evangelico," United Presbyterian. While the denominational spirit is quite strong among Italians, it is a most interesting fact that, with only three exceptions, of the seventy-five or more missionaries whom I have interviewed, all approved of a plan to merge all the papers into one, having a board of editors drawn from the different denominations. This would have three great advantages: First, the financial burden, which now has to be borne for the conduct of four papers, would be greatly reduced; the conviction on the part of some is that such a paper could be made to pay for itself; second, we Protestants should be able to present a united front before the bewildered Italians who are used to one church wherever they go; third, we should without question be able to produce a much better paper than any one of the four can now be. Such a paper would include not only strictly religious articles, but a discussion of the leading topics of the day from the Christian point of view, an Italian "Outlook." It should also include a generous English department for young people and children.

9. *Work for Women and Young People*

Work for other women and girls is primarily woman's work. It is not enough to reach the fathers and develop them through the civic clubs and English classes nor yet enough to get the children into kindergartens or Sunday schools. Unless the mother is reached, the children are invariably lost at confirmation age. This fact was soon discovered in our foreign fields, and specially trained Bible women are now sent into the homes to teach the heathen mothers the gospel.

All women who do missionary work among the Italians should learn the Italian language in order to converse directly with the mother about the care of her home, the health of her family, as well as about the religious training of her children. The life of the Italian mother in this country is very barren indeed. She slaves from morning till night and very seldom has she a moment's time for anything pleasurable and inspiring. A visit from the church missionary who knows her language and can speak to her about matters that are of vital concern to her can be very effective in influencing the mother along the lines of social and religious thinking. In some places classes in English for foreign mothers have been successfully conducted, but since unexpected duties or a sick child may make the mother's attendance irregular, it is better to have the woman teacher of English go regularly into the Italian homes, gathering in several of the neighbors who would be glad to listen to the lesson. The true missionary is able to give a religious message with every English lesson. But the mothers are in need every now and then of a little entertainment. A social gathering where there is singing and instrumental music, and light refreshments are served, offers them some diversion in the midst of their life of drudgery and perplexities. The church must be to them not only a place where they shall come to hear sermons, but where they shall receive a social ministry, as well that may open up their lives to the legitimate pleasures of this world.

We need to do more effective work for our young people. In many mission churches we are facing a situation which will react very favorably upon our work in the future. All missionaries agree they have no great difficulty in getting plenty of little children into the Sunday school, sewing school, play hour, and kindergarten. The difficulty comes when they leave school and go to work, to hold them until they establish Christian homes of their own. In our search for a solution of the problems, we have considered the activities for young people of many settlements and churches, campfires, groups, dress-making classes, gymnastics, Boy Scouts, athletic associations, and musical and dramatic societies. These serve to attract and hold large numbers, though in some places there are many comers and goers and often those who become prominent in an organization are quite alien to the ideals of the church. There are notable exceptions, but to my mind the reason for this is the inefficiency of workers entrusted with the young people's work in our missions. The emphasis has been placed on the value of the child for so long that women missionaries pay most of their attention to the children. They fail to realize that adolescence is the period in which ideals are formed, personal problems arise, and the standards by which later life is ruled become fixed. Our duty by our young people is not done by having a few clubs or entertainments, excellent as they are, but by heart to heart talks about life's problems and ideals, by persons whom they cannot help respecting.

10. *Americanization*

The term Americanization is on the lips of many people in these days, and in many cases it is doubtful as to whether those who use it could give any definite idea about its meaning. To superficial people it means simply that a foreign-born individual must turn his back upon everything that has any association with the land of his birth, that he shall have no contact with people from his native land, that he shall even forget his language, and take on external American customs. But surely a person may do this and still not be an American. We must be on our guard against zeal for quick Americanization of these people, by many of our well-meaning but short-sighted workers. They urge the young men and women to throw off their race customs and adopt the American ones. But this is exceedingly dangerous until moral character and the ideals of this country are understood. True Americanization comes from a culture of the heart and mind and when that is accomplished, external manners and customs will take care of themselves. Let those of us who are working with Italians value the best of everything connected with the land of their birth, their great men, their artists, their martyrs, their statesmen and writers, their wonderful history, and the present progressive state of their country. When we have made them see the best in their own land, we shall be in a far better position to make them see the best in American life.

11. *A Day and Boarding School*

So much of the work in our Sunday schools, clubs, and classes is continuously counteracted by bad home influences and unwholesome effects of our city street life, that if we wish really to develop a strong leadership in an adequate fashion among the Italians, we should imitate the example of our foreign missionaries in India and China, where they have established missionary schools. The results of this work are discernible in the numbers of influential Christian men in the public life of China and India today. In a missionary school the best home influences and Christian ideals constantly surround the young people, systematic Bible study is a part of the regular curriculum, and home-making duties are carefully taught. I will venture to say that if we could have such boarding and day schools for Italians, in fifteen or twenty years their graduates would be leaders of thought in our Italian communities. The Roman Church realizes the value of environment and is busy establishing parochial schools to hold the Italian children to the church. One priest acknowledged to me that the leaders of the church " are crazy to get the Italian children; they are going to make a place for themselves in this country." We have our opportunity now. One hundred thousand dollars invested in a modern, well-equipped school along the lines that have proved so successful on the foreign field would yield rich returns in Christian Americanized Italian leaders for the next generation.

12. *Local Supervision and Care*

It is still too often the practise to appoint a missionary, provide him with a meager salary, and place him upon a field with a very inadequate equipment, and with no backing of the English-speaking people of the community, and then tell him to go ahead and evangelize Italians. What has happened in so many cases will continue to happen unless we adopt a different policy, a policy which indeed has proved very successful in a score of places where it has been put to the test. My own impression would be that wherever it is impossible to secure the cordial and general co-operation of the local church or churches for the Italian mission it would be better not to undertake the work at all. And a number of mission fields could be enumerated where after years of service, home missions and state organizations having put into the work many thousands of dollars, the missions had to be closed because they were accomplishing nothing. And this failure was due to the lack of hearty co-operation on the part of the local church.

On the other hand the most successful missions and churches are those which have the care and sympathetic and active co-operation of the local church, or at least of far-visioned individuals connected with the local church. For example, the success of the work in the Presbyterian Mission in Newark, N. J.; the Baptist Mission in Orange, N. J.; the Methodist Church in Fall River, Mass.; the Congregational Church in New Haven, Conn.; and the Dutch Reformed Church in Newburg, N. Y.; the work of Grace Chapel in New York City, and a host of others that might be mentioned have succeeded because of local whole-hearted co-operation.

13. *Denominational Changes*

There are certain men who have gone the rounds of the various denominations. In some cases, these men have not left a record which redounds to the glory of God or the success of the evangelical propaganda. Has the time not come, when for mutual protection, we should stiffen our attitude toward the men who have to change periodically their denominational affiliation? If they have not succeeded under the care of one church they will in all probability not succeed in any church.

My conviction is that the leaders in our foreign work should discourage this changing of denominations. If a man, already in the care of any denomination, desires to make a change to some other, the reasons should be carefully determined through counseling with those who have been responsible for his work. And here, perfect frankness and veracity cannot be too much insisted upon. There have been cases where an inefficient man or even one who did not enjoy the fullest confidence has been recommended to another body, to get rid of him. This is not fair, for it hurts the cause of Christ.

However much any denomination may be in need of workers, it is not just that it shall endeavor to meet its own needs by reaching out and taking that which belongs to another. We need in every way to create and sustain an attitude of loyalty toward one's denomination. While, on the other hand, we must endeavor to inculcate a spirit of fraternity and real co-operation among the workers of different names, we must at the same time see to it that nothing is done to loosen that bond of fidelity to the body to which a man is attached. Hence, every suggestion to leave one denomination and take up work with another because a little more remuneration may be offered, or because the man may be *persona non grata* where he is, should be strictly avoided. The only way to secure and maintain a stable corps of workers that can be depended upon, is for each denomination to create its own ministry. We must not attempt to fill our own ranks by depleting the ranks of others, because this method not only does harm to the worker in that it tears down in him the fine sense of loyalty, but such men as are not inspired with conviction of the value of their denominational ideals can never give themselves unreservedly to the ends and aims of the bodies under whose auspices they work.

14. *Types of Organization*

(See "Sons of Italy," Chapter VI, for more detailed statement, Missionary Education Movement, New York, 60 cents, prepaid.)

There are usually two types of churches and missions among Italians. The one is the branch church, where the converts are taken into the membership of some American church. In some cases the work of these branches is carried on in a room of the American church, while in others the Italian congregation meets in a separate building used exclusively for Italian work. The common experience is that the best results can be obtained in separate buildings, where the people feel free to come and go and the place is used every day in the week if need be; whereas, when the work is conducted in an American church, the mission can only have the use of the building for a couple of hours on Sunday, and once or twice during the week. Besides, the Italian is somewhat timid when he meets with Americans in the church building who are usually not over-cordial to the foreigner.

The ideal is, wherever it is possible, to have a separate building and as soon as possible to effect a complete church organization having its regular officers and privileged to administer in their own place the rites of baptism and of the Lord's Supper.

A distinction should be made here, between a church that is organized for the conduct of its own work and an independent church, strictly so-called. When such a church is organized it should be made very clear to the members of it that no church can be actually independent until it is able to provide for its own expenses. There is no objection if the members of the organized church are considered members of some American church, if that serves the purpose of developing interest on the part of the American in behalf of the Italian work. But the converts must be given a sense of responsibility for the conduct of their own work. If they are ever to reach the point of self-support, they must now be given considerable freedom of action, under wise direction, in order that they may feel their obligation for reaching the people of their community. The ideal that the work carried on for Italians is not an enterprise that devolves upon the Americans, but that the Italians themselves are to look upon it as their task and that they are to make every effort possible to maintain it financially, must be ever held before them. This can be done only when they feel that they are the masters of their work. Too often Americans have so completely dictated and controlled the work that the Italians have said, whenever an appeal was made to them for the maintenance of the work, "This is the Americans' business, let them do it," and, unfortunately, this has been the attitude even on the part of some of our missionaries. It is true that the Italians, unused to democracy in church life, if given large freedom, will doubtless make many mistakes. Every precaution should be taken to avoid serious blunders, but we must also recognize that by mistakes they will learn better to conduct their own affairs.

15. *Co-operation of American Christians*

In view of the many difficulties that have arisen in cases where the semi-independent mission churches have been left to govern themselves, an experiment has been attempted which has worked very satisfactorily. The following organization has been devised: The local church nearest to the mission or the one most vitally interested appoints a committee of three or four consecrated men from its own members, men who are sympathetic to the foreigner, and who are willing to give some attention to study the people that they are going to try to assist, to meet at regular intervals and counsel with the official body of the Italian congregation. This group combined with the workers at the mission discuss together all problems that may arise and also all plans for any departures from the ordinary lines of activity. Reports of the work done by the staff are presented also to this body.

Two ends are effectively served by such an organization: First, it is a protection against ill-advised or rash actions on the part of the Italian congregation; and, second, it enables the American people better to understand and sympathize with the Italian temperament and point of view. Both sides would learn to respect, love, and help each other more as they thus become acquainted.

16. Large Opportunity to Reach the Foreigner

When the real attitude of the Italian toward the faith of his fathers is understood, a great field is opened up before the evangelical churches and consecrated individuals. It would be a splendid thing if every church all over this whole land in country or city, wherever there are foreigners, should have a standing missionary committee, not simply to arrange for a missionary meeting once a month, but which would act and go out and make a careful survey of the foreign peoples in the vicinity or community, gathering information about their economic, social, and religious conditions; and then seek through English classes, sewing schools, civic clubs, and friendly visitations, to establish a point of contact with the stranger. This would serve as the first step in the problem of leadership. If those undertaking the task cannot speak the tongue of the people, they can, with some effect, find some well-disposed man or woman who would willingly serve as interpreter for them.

VI. A Model Program of Work for Italians
Schedule — Good Will Center, Brooklyn

Day	Hour	Activity
Monday	4–5	Girls.
	5–7	Jolly Club (Polish girls).
	7–9	Good Will Club (girls).
Tuesday	4–5:30	Happy Girls' Club.
	5:30–7	Bannerman Boys' Club.
	7–9	Anita Garibaldi Club (girls).
	7–9	Good Will Athletic Club.
	8	Mothers' Meeting (monthly).
Wednesday	4–5:30	Small Boys' Club.
	6–8	Young Citizens.
	8–9	Prayer Meeting.
	9–10	Men's Citizenship Class.
	8	**Neighborhood Mothers' Meeting (monthly).**

Day	Hour	Activity
Thursday	2–3	Mothers' Meeting.
	2–3	Children in Gym.
	4–5:30	Sunshine Club (girls).
	8	Edmondo de Amicis Circolo.
Friday	3:30–5	Sewing School.
	5–7	Boys' Club.
	8	Choir Practice.
	8	Boy Scouts.
Saturday	4	Children's Meeting and Motion Pictures.
	8	Popular Entertainment and Lectures.
	8	Boys' Neighborhood Club.
Sunday	3–4	Sunday School.
	4:15	Italian Church Service.
Others, unlisted		Girls' Protective League (monthly).
		Kindergarten (daily).
		Day Nursery (daily).
		Italian and English Classes.
		Cookery and Basketry.
		Columbus Club (monthly).

APPENDIX

A. THE POLICY OF THE BAPTIST CHURCHES AND MISSIONARY SOCIETIES IN THE EVANGELIZATION OF THE ITALIAN PEOPLE

By Rev. CHARLES A. BROOKS, *Superintendent City and Foreign-Speaking Work, American Baptist Home Mission Society*

It is difficult to define our policy, because Baptists have no centralized ecclesiastical or missionary authority. Notwithstanding this there is a fairly uniform policy among our churches and societies.

First, a general word as to a fundamental principle which we recognize in all our missionary work among the various races in America.

1. Each race represents not only peculiar racial problems, but an important and distinctive contribution to the enrichment of the life of America and the Kingdom of God.

2. While we expect and desire the Americanization of these groups, we do not desire the obliteration or destruction of their unique racial heritage, but invite them to share these gifts with us, as we seek to make our contribution to them.

It is important that we keep these two principles in even balance.

3. We believe that Christianity is a spirit of life with infinite variety of expression, and that our American conception of God and His kingdom needs enriching by communion of all saints. Hence, we believe in the freedom of religious life according to racial type. An Italian Protestant church will have and should have distinctive characteristics, distinguishing it from an American Protestant church. This means the enrichment of the Protestant conception of God, and of social life.

There is no Italian gospel, but there is a gospel for the Italian, which is the secret of his highest and best development, and the rebirth of Italian character according to the mind of Christ. Italians will be won for the Kingdom of God only as the gospel is interpreted to them in the terms of their own thinking. This is recognized as a fundamental truth on the foreign field, in China, and India. It is no less true in America among the Italian, Poles, and Russians.

It is important that we keep this in mind, because some of our earnest people are alarmed if our foreign-speaking groups develop a distinctive and aggressive religious life of their own. Their idea and measure of success is the rapid merging and consequent loss of identity of the new converts in the life of the American church. But this means the loss of their distinctive influence in winning their fellow countryman for Christ. The use of the Italian language in worship and service is not primarily a matter of privilege, but of responsibility for winning the Italian people for Christ.

While no two of our missions have had the same history, the work has usually developed in one of two ways which have been determined by local conditions, such as the distribution of population and the location of the American church. Beginnings have been made more frequently through the local American church, as a part of its ministry to the community or "parish" which includes Italian families. This has usually been through clubs, classes, or the Sunday school, which have included Italians, but have not excluded others. The ministry of the church to some needy individual Italian or a family has demonstrated the friendliness of the American church and opened the door of access to the Italian heart.

Where a colony of Italians is segregated and separated by distance from an American church, a separate mission at the first has been largely to the children through clubs, classes, kindergartens, or day nurseries, with Sunday schools and classes in English. Workers have usually come from one fostering American church, or from various churches where a federated movement has promoted the work.

The conversion of one or more Italians has demonstrated the possibility of reaching these people in a larger way than through the English language, and has usually been the determining factor in the employment of an Italian missionary, who usually becomes a member of the staff of an English church. The same type of work, as we have already described, has been continued, but the Italian pastor or missionary supplements this with the preaching of the gospel and the proclamation of a distinctively evangelical message.

The spiritual and disciplinary oversight of this work is usually in the hands of a local American church. But the general missionary policy is usually under the direction of a local city or state missionary organization, with the co-operation of the national societies, both general and women's, who co-operate in the financial support of the work.

The Italian members of the mission usually become members of the American church and are received upon the recommendation of their Italian fellow Christians. We have been slow to encourage the organization of separate churches until mature Christian character and experience has been developed and a good deal of autonomy has been exercised for some time. We encourage such autonomy, and strive to develop a spirit of self-reliance and self-support.

We are developing a fine body of missionaries, trained in our American school. The Italian department of Colgate Theological Seminary, of which Prof. Mangano is dean, is training a splendid type of Americanized Italian missionary.

We are encouraging, and have succeeded in developing, excellent material equipment, separate chapels, and church edifices which are set apart for distinctively Italian work, and which the Italians may feel are their own. These are being built upon modern lines, making provision for social and educational work, as well as preaching and public worship.

We are emphasizing the fundamental importance and necessity of an adequately trained and trustworthy ministry, and an adequate interpretation of the gospel. Our disappointments and our failures have been due almost always to unwise and unworthy leadership. We have been constantly and firmly eliminating unfit men from our missionary staff, and are insisting upon as high a standard of Christian character for our Italian ministry as for our general ministry. By an adequate interpretation of the gospel we mean the warm, loving, intelligible presentation of the good news of God's saving grace, not in a controversial or polemic spirit, but in the characteristic spirit of Jesus; the training and development of Christian character by a thoroughgoing program of Christian education; and the interpretation of social relationships and responsibilities in the terms of human brotherhood and the Kingdom of God.

B. ITALIAN CONGREGATIONALISTS

By PHILIP M. ROSE, *Supervisor of Italian Congregational Churches in Connecticut*

Congregationalists have no country-wide or denomination-wide work for Italian immigrants. Without a doubt the widest observation of their efforts would fail to discover any systematic policy with respect to Italian evangelization. Yet, just as Congregational influence has gone far beyond its own limited constituency to permeate the life of America, so its efforts in this particular line command a keen and intelligent interest out of proportion to their size and number.

The denomination is awake to its duty where this race enters its field. Where Congregational churches are springing up and growing strong in the miscellaneous life of the cities or suburban towns, they are taking note of the Italians in their midst. Witness the missions in South Brooklyn, in Grantwood, New Jersey; in Portland, Maine; in San Francisco. Occasionally a church in the mining regions has found Italians to whom to reach out a helping hand, as in Spring Valley, Illinois. In Maine, where Italians are invading various century-old Congregational parishes, a group of small missions is springing up. And in general in those portions of New England and New Jersey, adjacent to the great ports of entry, where Congregationalism is at all strongly entrenched, we find the most serious attempts to minister to the incoming Italian life. For instance, the fifteen Congregational churches of New Haven do not and cannot forget the fact of the 50,000 Italians in their midst, one-third of the population of that city so historically Congregational.

The only policy discoverable that our churches have had toward the Italian work has been the policy of experiment. There have been some notable and varied experiments. According to the genius of the order, these have been on account of the local churches. At most, some state organization has been responsible. Moreover, Congregationalists have not been at all careful that all efforts should bear the Congregational name — enough for them that the work was being done. Denominational lines have bothered them but little more than they have bothered the rank and file of Italian pastors and communicants who grow impatient with the incomprehensible divisions with which their Catholic kinsmen reproach them. Congregationalists have therefore supported generously union missions in which often the missionary in charge was of another communion. They have been strong supporters of the Waldensian aid societies, casting their bread on the waters of over-sea Italian life whence in increasing frequency it comes back to them after many days. They have thrown their strength largely behind social settlement and independent boys' clubs. They have been slow to believe ill of the Italian Roman Catholic Church, and they still insist that all enlightened effort and sincere faith in that body be respected and be met halfway. Nevertheless, they are saying to the Roman Church: "If you are feeding our Italian neighbors husks, if you refuse to give them real spiritual life, and thus fail to hold them, they are for us a legitimate field of effort." In a time when social effort has been popularly secularized, they are stoutly supporting Firman House in Chicago, Good-Will Centre in Brooklyn, Davenport House in New Haven as religious settlements, with religious ideals, Christian workers and church services held paramount. Withal the ideal is not proselytism but Christian character.

Many pastors of smaller towns are pondering on the "little Italys" of gardners, quarrymen, or operatives in some neglected corner of their parish; a few have succeeded in drawing one or more Italian families into their church, and a larger number of Italian children into their Sunday schools; one or two have had the joy of sending away a bright boy or girl to the American International College at Springfield, Massachusetts, or to the Bible Teachers' Training School. For oh, how great is the need for more and superior leaders for the race till now in ideals and faith so indifferently led.

The variety of the actual mission work is striking. Here is a mission in a New Jersey town with an isolated Italian colony to which the American pastor has deeply devoted and greatly endeared himself. His sympathy, the employment of an Italian worker at the right time, and the introduction of religious social effort has done wonders to evangelize and assimilate the stranger. Another mission, developed by its Italian pastor, who was a prince alike among Americans and Italians for his friendly qualities, contentedly shares the building and joins in the Sunday school and Lord's Supper of the American church. Still another becomes increasingly attached to its American woman missionary, although she speaks but little Italian. A member of this mission recently sent his personal check for $50 to the missionary society in recognition of his debt to it. The church at Waterbury, largest of all Congregational Italian churches, has been built up around and through music. Its pastor, unique as a music master, has sung and played the gospel into Italian hearts during many years, until his choir and orchestra are the pride of the city, and he can produce Italian young women Sunday school teachers, trained by his own hand. The Hartford church makes a specialty of outdoor preaching during the summer. The Bridgeport church, housed in its own building, has a flourishing mutual aid society. The New Haven church, integral part of Davenport Settlement and ministered to by the residents as well as by its pastor and missionary, has, to serve it, perhaps the most beautiful church building, finest organ and plant of any Italian work in the country — a real cathedral. By all of which it may be seen that variety is prized in Connecticut.

But the boldest experiment of Connecticut Italian Congregationalism is yet to be told. It is almost unique of its kind in Italian work, and entirely unique in its thoroughness. Believing that the Italian churches and missions could be more efficiently directed, and their leaders inspired through his interpretation of Italians to Americans and of Americans to Italians, the proper authorities took a young man of thorough collegiate and theological training, and sent him to Italy for two years' training in the Italian language and character. He returned with this equipment, and assumed the full pastorate of the church at New Haven. He was received by Italian colleagues with great satisfaction, and is gradually assuming his intended work of interpretation and superintendence.

To conclude, briefly, Congregational experience suggests the following lines of attachment in Italian evangelization:

1. While showing all tolerance for and willingness to co-operate with the Italian Roman Catholic Church, we must recognize that the majority of our Italian-Americans are, spiritually, unchurched, and hence our legitimate field.

2. The first move in establishing an Italian Protestant mission or nucleus is personal sympathy and service on the part of American church-members toward the Italians, and especially of friendship between American and Italian women.

3. There is a loud cry for an itinerant missionary or colporteur, who can do the work of pastor for scattered and small Italian colonies.

4. Afterwards there should be employed in the larger colonies a man or woman missionary, better both.

5. Social and musical work and house-visiting are fundamental.

6. The careful, sympathetic superintendence by an American of a group of Italian missions is highly desirable.

7. We must urge our best Italian youth to prepare themselves to be the intellectual and spiritual leaders of their own race.

C. Italian Methodism in America

By Frederick H. Wright, D.D., *Formerly Superintendent of the Italian Mission*

The Methodist Episcopal Church was perhaps the first Protestant church to do any specific work for Italians in America. This, as a matter of record, is interesting, and for historical purposes is worthy of note. In 1858 a young Italian vender of plaster models, Antonio Arrighi by name, was converted in a Methodist church in Des Moines, Iowa. After his conversion he attended the Iowa Wesleyan College, and while there delivered his first speech in Italian, on the invitation of President Charles Elliott, who was afterwards mainly instrumental in inaugurating Methodist missionary work in the Eternal City. This young man aided the pastor of the Mount Pleasant church in the camp-meeting just outside the city. In 1860 he met Abraham Lincoln in Bloomington, Illinois, who told him that " Italy will never be great again unless united and one, but united upon the terms of Mazzini, ' a free church in a free state.' " About this time young Arrighi met Peter Cartwright, who later on furnished him with a letter of recommendation as follows:

"JACKSONVILLE, ILL., *July* 23, 1860.

"I very cordially and earnestly would recommend to all the friends of humanity the bearer, Antonio Arrighi, a poor young Italian lately converted from popery, who is striving for an education to qualify himself to return and preach the gospel to his benighted nation.

"(Signed) PETER CARTWRIGHT."

When the war broke out, he volunteered and served during the whole of the war. Then he studied at Ohio Wesleyan University and Dickinson College, and in 1865 went to Boston Theological Seminary. In 1871 he started for Rome and labored with the Methodists and the Free Italian Church until 1880, being ordained to the gospel ministry by Bishop Matthew Simpson, probably the first Protestant minister ordained in the city of Rome. He then returned to America, and on June 21, 1881, preached his first sermon at the Five Points Mission in New York City. Still living, the erstwhile galley slave of Italy, a victim of papal intolerance, and a veteran missionary of the cross, has seen Protestant missions among Italians established by all churches throughout the land. It was a small beginning, but it meant great things for Italy and America, and at the time of the last report in 1916 of the organized Italian Mission of the Methodist Episcopal Church, which covered a territory extending from the Atlantic Ocean to the Mississippi River, there were fifty-two preaching places with forty-six ministers. From the Mississippi River westward other missions were established at New Orleans and San Francisco and at Des Moines, Iowa; Denver, and Pueblo, Colorado; and Butte, Montana.

In the first years of the organized work very little was done toward self-support, but the report of 1916 shows that the amount of $8,749 was raised for self-support and the benevolent enterprises of the church.

Methodism has shown its faith in the future of this work by investing in church edifices and other buildings a sum approximately $480,000; while the Board of Home Missions and Church Extension expends in round figures $50,000 a year. If the sums raised locally by the city missionary societies were added, it would be revealed that close to twice that amount is invested for Italian evangelization, though there were no exact figures available on this point.

The effort is made to emphasize the church as a social center, in direct opposition to the Roman idea, which places the stress upon the church edifice being simply and solely a place of devotion. Care is taken, however, to eliminate as far as possible any criticism, by keeping the church proper sacred for public and private worship, but in the other parts of the building every effort is made to attract the people, so as to make it a community center, thus accentuating the social power of Christianity. This is an entirely new idea to the Italians, and as they enter into it, they soon appreciate its value. This social life is encouraged by (1) the organization of evening classes for the purpose of teaching the Italian the English language. A large percentage of the Italian immigrants are illiterates, and they must be taught their own language first before they can be interested in the English language; at least, that is the experience of our Italian missionaries. These Italian workers use these schools as feeders to our church services. There is no attempt to hide our identity. They know that we are Protestants, and by means of the disinterested spirit manifested by our Italian and American workers, confidence is won, and unreasoning prejudice is overcome.

(2) The classes for instruction in American citizenship are another powerful means of developing the social life of the Italian church. Hundreds of Italians have been aided in securing their citizen's papers. Our missionaries are continually in demand for services which are purely social in their character, and yet have a tremendous impact for evangelical faith.

(3) The organization of kindergarten schools, together with classes for instruction in cooking and domestic economy. In some centers, such as Five Points Mission and the Church of All Nations in New York City, day schools have been opened for the community, where 90 per cent. and even more of the pupils are Italians. Then on Sunday large Sunday schools, averaging an attendance of from 500 to 800, composed chiefly of Italians, flourish, and the lessons of the Bible, in the English language, are taught. There is no reason for segregating the Italian children from other American children, for they are Americans in fact.

(4) Classes for physical exercises for both girls and boys, with baths and reading rooms, have done much to make the church a social center, and are being encouraged.

Added to all this, of course, is the preaching of the gospel in the Italian tongue. There is no wish to perpetuate this feature of the work, but only two things will lead to its discontinuance: (1) Cessation of immigration, and (2) absorption of the young and rising generation into our American Sunday schools and churches. As to the first, it is absolutely essential to have Italian services for the adult immigrant. He must go where he can understand and be understood; and as to the latter, this absorption will be gauged by the friendly attitude of the Protestant Christians. It ought not to be necessary to have Italian Sunday schools for children; they sit side by side with American boys and girls in the public schools; they prefer to speak English, and if we are to save them from being hyphenated Americans, we must give them the glad hand to our churches and Sunday schools. This is the ideal of Methodism, despite all difficulties, and we shall win out only as we strive after this ideal.

The Methodist Episcopal Church is doing constructive work for Italian evangelization, and the future will witness great growth in interest and results. Under the reorganization of the Board of Home Missions and Church Extension last year, the Italian Mission as a separate organization was discontinued, and each mission is placed under the direction of the local district superintendent, in the hope that greater efficiency and interest will be developed. This Board, through its Bureau of Foreign Work, at a conference of district and city society superintendents having oversight of Italian work, has outlined its present policy as follows:

I. Program of Work for the Local Italian Church

1. Approach to the family as a whole.

(a) Home visitor, a woman speaking Italian, with the American training and American spirit. Such a one, bilingual, could work with little children in English, and conduct older classes possibly in Italian. The problem is one of young women as well as mothers. The future objective is to have young Italian women thoroughly trained.

(b) Family gathering for everybody in the church parlors or church house. Music, games, pictures, etc. Recognize the family unit.

(c) Meetings in the homes. The coming of the stranger draws all the neighbors in so that a program may be used. Special attention to home meetings for girls.

2. Approach in Italian for adult Italian groups.

(a) Religious services of worship in Italian. (b) Bilingual staff members, a lawyer, physician, employment agent, and a printer, whose services may be used for help among Italians in the community. (c) Mothers' club in Italian. (d) Men's clubs for learning English and citizenship (civic questions, citizenship papers, etc.). (e) Use of Italian literature. (f) Religious instruction in Italian. (g) Illustrated lectures. (h) Italian patriotism as point of contact (Italian days, the 20th of September, etc.). (i) Make use of musical interest.

3. Approach in English to children and young people.

(a) Attendance at English church services. (b) Religious instruction (Sunday school). (c) Related week-day club activities, emphasis on expressional work, such as recreational clubs, gymnasium clubs, choral societies, dramatic clubs, Boy Scouts, Knights of King Arthur, Camp Fire Girls, Girl Scouts, sewing, painting, drawing, and sculpture. (d) Illustrated lectures and moving pictures. (e) Daily vacation Bible school. (f) Flower mission. (g) Fresh air work. (h) Camps.

II. *Program of Training for non-English-speaking Leadership by the Board of Home Missions and Church Extension of the Methodist Episcopal Church.*

1. The Board of Home Missions and Church Extension of the Methodist Episcopal Church, in co-operation with the Board of Education of the Methodist Episcopal Church is to begin immediately the task of (a) training American ministers for work among Italians in this country, these men to have a college and theological seminary training and, in addition, while studying at the theological seminary, to be in attendance upon a training center in connection with some Italian church where they may receive lectures in Italian and Italian culture, and be guided in clinic work in different Italian parishes; (b) training Italian ministers for work among Italians in this country, these men to have college and theological training and, in addition, while studying at the theological seminary, to be in attendance upon a training center in connection with some Italian church where they may receive lectures in Italian and Italian culture, and be guided in clinic work in different Italian parishes.

2. Training institutes for Italian ministers in service are to be held in different parts of the country as the Board of Home Missions and Church Extension may be able to plan.

3. The Board of Home Missions and Church Extension of the Methodist Episcopal Church is to be made a clearing-house for information concerning Italian parishes and Italian workers; district and city society superintendents and pastors to report to the Board concerning their work twice a year.

D. AT WORK WITH THE ITALIANS — THE PRESBYTERIAN CHURCH IN THE U. S. A.

By WILLIAM P. SHRIVER, *Director of City and Immigrant Work, Board of Home Missions*

In the spring of 1916 the Presbyterian Church in the U. S. A. had 107 churches and missions using the Italian language, with 4,800 members and more than 8,000 enrolled in the Sunday schools. In the last year over 1,100 were received upon confession of their faith in sixty-one churches and missions alone. Sixty Italian-speaking pastors are employed; twenty-three lay workers, thirty-two visitors, and over 350 American volunteers are regularly engaged in the work of sixty-seven churches and missions reporting. Large funds have been invested in the permanent equipment of this work ($350,000 in twenty-eight churches and missions). The progress of these Presbyterian Italian churches and missions in the matter of self-support is highly encouraging; forty-seven churches and missions reported over $14,000 contributed for all purposes in the last year. Over $75,000 annually is being contributed toward this work by Presbyterian churches and home mission agencies, not including funds made available by the Presbyterian Board of Education, funds contributed for colportage and publication, nor funds contributed for the maintenance of the Italian Department in the Bloomfield Theological Seminary, New Jersey, and for schools and seminaries in other parts of the country. At least $100,000 annually is being contributed by the Presbyterian Church in the U. S. A. for this work of evangelization among Italians, over and above the amounts contributed by its Italian-speaking constituency.

Auspices and Administration

The Presbyterian Church in the U. S. A. has at this time no unified approach to this field of evangelization nor central administrative agency. Work among Italians is largely carried out under the auspices of the presbyteries or local churches, and in two cases is directly administered by synods (state-wide organizations). Over twenty Presbyterian Italian churches and missions are directly under the auspices of a local church, and this type of work is increasing in favor.

The Board of Home Missions, through its Immigrant Work office, with headquarters in New York, endeavors to survey the whole field and to keep in touch with all Presbyterian work among Italians. It maintains in this office a card catalogue of all such enterprises in which are collated the annual statistics of churches and missions. The Board, however, has no administrative responsibility, excepting as hereafter mentioned under its individual parish plan, and employs no field representative whose time is exclusively devoted to Italian evangelization. In the fiscal year ending March 31, 1916, the Board of Home Missions disbursed approximately $32,000 for Italian evangelization, or 38.5 per cent. of its total appropriation for immigrant work.

Permanent Conference on Italian Evangelization

In the spring of 1916, at a Conference on Italian Evangelization held at Princeton, New Jersey, which included both Italian speaking pastors and workers, and representatives from presbyteries and home mission agencies concerned, steps were taken looking to the setting up of a Permanent Conference on Italian Evangelization. It was proposed that delegates to this conference include all pastors and missionaries of the Presbyterian Church in the U. S. A. who are regularly and definitely engaged in work with Italians, together with representatives of presbyteries and synods concerned, the boards of the church, and other agencies. For the present, biennial conferences will be held. Standing committees will be elected as follows:

1. Survey of the field.
2. Literature and publications.
3. Education.
4. Fraternal relations.
5. Community service and evangelism.
6. Program and arrangements.

The General Assembly of the Presbyterian Church in the U. S. A. has given its approval to this plan, which will bring about a greater unity in Presbyterian work among Italians. The method is original in that it proposes a conference not of Italian-speaking pastors and workers alone, but of all those who are definitely interested in Presbyterian work with Italians. By this method, it is felt, the various points of view will be harmonized and a better understanding brought about.

Types and Conduct of Work

Among seventy-four churches and missions for which data is available, it is of interest to note that seventeen are conducted as organized churches, thirty-six as missions, and twenty-one as departments of established American churches. This latter, or departmental work, in many cases is most encouraging in its efficiency. Where Italian communities have grown up about well-established American churches, an Italian-speaking pastor has been added to the staff and departmental work has been begun. Frequently, as in the case of John Hall Memorial Chapel, the Church of the Sea and Land, and Spring Street Church in New York City, and Olivet Institute in Chicago, the facilities of well-equipped institutional churches have been placed at the service of the Italian community. Presbyterian work among Italians has now happily outgrown the primitive mission stage. Among seventy-six churches and missions, only ten are housed in a hall or store. Thirty-four have separate church buildings or chapels, and thirty-two share the equipment of older American churches. In a number of city and suburban communities, new and beautiful buildings have been erected for Italian communities. The First Italian Church, Philadelphia, the Italian churches in Germantown, the Presbyterian Italian Mission at Bernardsville, several churches in Newark, Holy Trinity Church and the Church of the Ascension in New York, are all illustrative of excellent new buildings erected for Italian evangelization.

The Board of Church Erection has shared in the building of a number of churches and chapels employed for Italian evangelization. While new buildings are seeking to provide facilities for educational and social work, full recognition is being made of the Italian's interest in a reverent place for worship. Nearly all Presbyterian Italian churches and missions engage in educational or social work. Forty-two report English classes for men. Twenty have English classes for women. Twenty-two have civic clubs. English in nearly all cases is used in the Sunday school.

Parish Methods

While Presbyterian work among immigrants recognizes the importance of a sympathetic approach to the various racial groups, and that Presbyterian churches and missions employing a foreign language are indispensable, it also recognizes the increasing implications of community life and interests. Its objective is not only a work of evangelization projected from such churches and missions, and in a foreign language, but the establishing of a Christian community life. This latter aim necessarily calls for the co-ordination of many forces and a larger and more comprehensive undertaking. Under the leadership of the Immigrant Work office of the Board of Home Missions, industrial communities are being ministered to through the so-called parish plan, which federates all Presbyterian churches or agencies in a given community and supplies additional leadership and increased facilities which may be used in common by the churches or missions at work in the field. Thus in the Range Parish, in an iron ore producing region in Minnesota, where there is a population of from 6,000 to 10,000 Italians, a staff of five parish workers is employed in addition to the regular pastors of Presbyterian churches on the Range. This staff includes two Italian speaking pastors whose work is sustained and strengthened in this larger fellowship. The American Parish in New York, under the direction of Rev. Norman M. Thomas, includes two Italian communities with a population exceeding 100,000, with four centers of Presbyterian Italian work, two being fully organized Presbyterian Italian churches, the third an Italian department, and the fourth, a settlement or neighborhood work with an Italian constituency.

Training Schools

The Bloomfield Theological Seminary at Bloomfield, New Jersey, with an academic and collegiate department, has a department especially for the training of an Italian speaking ministry. Italian speaking students, however, are enrolled in Dubuque, Auburn, Princeton and McCormick theological seminaries and other schools. The Home Missions Committee of the Presbytery of New York has established a graduate training course for lay workers, and is offering to a group of college women courses in " Immigrant Backgrounds," including the Italians, with instruction in the Italian language. In 1917 this training course will be carried on under the auspices of Teachers' College, Columbia University, and will be open to all who fulfill the conditions of matriculation.

Publications

The Board of Publications and Sabbath School Work of the Presbyterian Church in the U. S. A. publishes an Italian religious weekly, "L'Era Nuova," Rev. Francis J. Panetta, editor, 114 East 116th street, New York City. The Board also issues Sunday school cards and has other religious features in the Italian language.

E. MISSION WORK AMONG ITALIANS IN CANADA

By REV. F. C. STEPHENSON, *Secretary of Young People's Forward Movement, Missionary Society, Methodist Church, Canada*

The Methodist and Presbyterian churches are the only Protestant denominations which have organized mission work among the Italians in Canada. The Presbyterians have missions among this race in Montreal, Sault Sainte Marie and Winnipeg. The Methodists carry on work among them in Sidney, B. C., Montreal, Toronto, Hamilton, Niagara Falls, Welland, Thirold, North Bay and Copper Cliff. In all of these places, regularly appointed, and for the most part, ordained, Italian missionaries are in charge of the work. In other places, throughout the Dominion, mission work is being conducted among European foreigners, among whom are many Italians.

In Toronto the work is carried on in three centers, and may be classified under three heads, namely, educational, institutional, and evangelistic, and is typical of what is being done in a modified form in other places. The educational work includes kindergarten classes in each center, a primary class at Elm Street Church, and night classes for adults in all branches. The institutional work consists of clubs for boys and girls, sewing classes, athletic and gymnastic exercises, mothers' meetings, also citizen and musical associations for the young men. The evangelistic effort consists of regular Sunday preaching services, Sunday schools, private conferences, tract distribution, and open air services.

The Italians in Toronto, and for the most part throughout Canada, came from Sicily and Calabria, though there are quite a number who claim northern Italy as their birthplace. They are an industrial people and most of them engage in heavy labor, or work in fruit or small grocery stores. Others pursue the same varieties of occupation as our own English people. The majority are illiterate, but very bright and ambitious. They have artistic temperaments, are naturally very religious, and, though born Roman Catholics, have little love for the Church of Rome, and are in danger of becoming atheists unless early brought under the influence of some church that will inspire their confidence.

Housing conditions among them are not satisfactory. They live in the most congested areas in the city and in the poorest houses, which are usually overcrowded with the children of the family and men boarders. One result of our work among the Italians in Toronto has been the movement from the separate Catholic schools to the public schools. Many scores of families are sending their children to the public schools, to which they now pay their taxes. There is no assimilator like the public school, and we hope this movement will continue. In many other respects our work among the Italians is producing most gratifying results.

There is no class of European immigrants among whom missionary work is so successful as among the Italians. A large number have been converted and are leading upright Christian lives. Their migratory habits disorganize our work somewhat at certain seasons of the year, but wherever the Christian Italians go they carry the leaven of the gospel with them. From the construction camps of the north, from the cities of the far West, from the trenches in Flanders, and from the army in the homeland, come cheering words testifying to the permanent blessings received by thousands who have come under the influence of the gospel in Canada.

F. Work Among the Italians by the American Bible Society

By Rev. W. I. Haven, D.D., *Secretary*

In 1834 the Board of Managers of the American Bible Society became perplexed with the problem of immigration from Europe into the United States, and decided that these strangers could not be left without the Bible, of which many of them knew nothing whatever.

Accordingly the secretaries were ordered to obtain from the British and Foreign Bible Society Scriptures in Polish, Swedish, Dutch, Portuguese and Italian. The report of 1837 shows that thirty-one Italian Bibles and Testaments were put in circulation in the United States. The growth of this work can be more quickly understood by noting the number of Italian Scriptures issued in each tenth year since that date. In 1837 it was 31; 1847, 289; 1857, 753; 1867, 1,494; 1877, 4,499; 1887, 6,786. This seems to have been the real commencement of a large influx of Italians, for in 1897 the number of Italian Scriptures put in circulation was 20,427. In 1907 the number was 38,282. There has been a steady increase until the beginning of the war. The last year before the war broke out the number was 101,779 volumes. The figures for the report of 1917, eighty years since the work began, are not yet available, but the report of 1916 shows issues in Italian in the United States of 95,581 volumes. The falling off is probably due to the fact that a considerable number of Italians returned to their native land to go into the army.

These figures show one thing which is repeated again and again by the agents of the society. Rev. Dr. Eckard, secretary of the Atlantic agency, writes from Philadelphia: "In general there has been more success with Italians than with any other nationality of Europeans who come to the United States." The same statement is expressed in other words by Rev. Dr. Kirkbride, secretary of the Northwestern agency, who says: "No class of foreigners is more accessible to the gospel and give quicker and fuller response to the gospel teachings, than the Italians."

Our reports of the work among Italians for the year 1916 have come from the secretaries of the nine agencies of the American Bible Society, and the fields from which they report work among Italians are as follows: Rev. Dr. Eckard at Philadelphia; Pennsylvania and New Jersey. Rev. Mr. Porter, Richmond, Va.; Virginia, West Virginia, Georgia and Florida, the most important work for Italians in this field being in Florida. Rev. Dr. Broome, secretary at Cincinnati, Ohio, reports work for Italians in Ohio and at Birmingham, Ala. Rev. Dr. Kirkbride, the secretary at Chicago has carried on work among Italians, especially in Illinois, Minnesota, Wisconsin, and adjacent regions. Dr. Ragatz, secretary of the agency at Denver, Col., reports good work in St. Louis, Kansas City, Denver, and some of the mining regions of Colorado, besides the states of Montana, Idaho and Utah. The Rev. J. J. Morgan, secretary at Dallas, Texas, reports several correspondents and a number of voluntary workers in Louisiana, Texas, Arkansas and Oklahoma. The number of Italians in these four last-named states is estimated at 95,000. Rev. Mr. Mell, secretary of the agency at San Francisco, reports that there were no Italian colporteurs at work this year, but the coast cities have been carefully canvassed in the three years previous. The work among the Italians this year has been conducted by two colporteurs and eight other workers who were engaged in general Bible distribution. These sold about 3,000 volumes in Italian. Mr. Mell adds that 100,000 Italians scattered along the Pacific Coast have been carefully served to the extent of the ability of the agency during five years past. Rev. H. J. Scudder, secretary of the Eastern agency, having headquarters in Brooklyn, has the assistance of several Italian ministers who make a point of giving a certain amount of time to Bible distribution among their compatriots. In this way Scriptures were circulated in Harlem, in different parts of Westchester County, and on Long Island, during 1916, amounting to 673 Bibles, 2,770 Testaments, and 13,121 Gospels, a total of 16,564 volumes.

As we said above full returns for the year 1916 are not yet available, so that a general view of the circulation in the whole of the United States is not possible. The work of these agencies among Italians is carried on by Italians so far as Italian colporteurs can be found to do the work. It has been increasingly difficult to find men suited for this work in recent years because of the number of missions and evangelical churches which need the assistance of every thoroughly converted Italian they can find for their local work. It is the experience of the secretaries, howver, that to attempt to circulate Scriptures among Italians through people of another race is very disappointing. Where a thoroughly converted Italian could persuade and convince a number of men and women in every place and induce them to buy Testaments or at least portions of Gospels, requests from a man of another race, even speaking a little Italian, would be immediately rejected. In many parts of the United States the Bible Society agents have partly avoided this difficulty by making arrangements with wide-awake Italian pastors to give a certain amount of their time to Bible distribution. The Bible Society supplies them with Scriptures without charge and gives them a liberal discount on Bibles which they buy for their people, and they make it a point to take the books to the outlying districts and let them go for less than cost, if necessary, provided there is a serious willingness to read them. In this way the pastors increase their circle of acquaintance, and the people gradually become accustomed to reading the Word of Life.

Work among the Italians is not without obstruction, and sometimes violent opposition. During the past year Mr. Morgan reports that at Bryan, Texas, some priests came in, gathered up all the Bibles and Testaments in town, and made a grand bonfire. The spirit of the Italian pastor at this place, as well as of the people who lost their Scriptures, is seen from the fact that he immediately sent to Mr. Morgan, ordering a second shipment of Scriptures to take the place of those which had been burned.

At Denver, Colorado, one Sunday morning, a mob of Italians surrounded the evangelical church with the purpose of killing the pastor. It seemed for a time that he could not escape. A dozen policemen, however, made a valiant fight and succeeded in saving his life. Such disturbances are not frequent.

It is pleasant to know that the work of Bible distribution has rapidly sown the seed of permanent growth. In Denver the evangelical Italian church is said to be the largest such church connected with the Methodist Episcopal denomination throughout the world, and this church was built up by the co-operation of home missionaries with the Bible Society's colporteurs. Mr. Sibilio, now the pastor of the Spring Street Church in New York City, was a colporteur of the American Bible Society in Denver. As little by little a group of Bible readers collected about him, his work was followed up by mission workers, with the result which has been mentioned. In Cincinnati and in Cleveland, Ohio, there are strong and influential Italian churches which have grown in the same way from the small groups of Bible readers, brought together by the colporteurs of the Bible Society. Dr. Kirkbride of Chicago, writing about his work in 1916 among the Italians, mentions Mr. Frank Malta, who was working at Kensington, Illinois, as a colporteur at the American Bible Society. The Reformed Church asked the Bible Society agent to allow Mr. Malta to give part of his time to work in their mission. From this labor sprang the Italian church at Kensington, Illinois, connected with the Reformed Church in the U. S. A., and making rapid growth.

Another case of the same character is the Italian Presbyterian Church at Hibbing, Minn., which grew out of the work of a colporteur of the American Bible Society, the Presbyterian Home Mission Board undertaking the work and following it up energetically. Another of the Bible Society's Italian colporteurs, Mr. Lizzi, is working at Virginia, Minn., with the prospect of a church of Italians being organized there very soon.

This hasty glance at the work of the American Bible Society for Italians in the United States suggests that the field is most comprehensive and encouraging, that a certain amount of progress has already been made in evangelizing these interesting people, and finally, that the greater the co-operation between home missionaries and the Bible School Society laborers, the more thorough and permanent are the results of sowing the seed.

G. The American Tract Society and the Italians
By Judson Swift, D.D., *General Secretary*

The American Tract Society is carrying in stock about 250 titles in the Italian language. The Italian hymnal, both word and music editions, has had a large circulation, totaling 48,000 copies. "Pilgrim's Progress" in Italian has had a circulation of 5,000 in the past few years. The total circulation of books, tracts and hymnals in the Italian language reaches a grand total of 1,250,000 copies. During the past four years seven colporteurs have been working among our Italian population, and over 30,000 copies of books and tracts have been distributed.

From our records, going back as far as twenty years, we learn that upwards of 350,000 volumes have been circulated in Italian, and the colporteurs working among the Italians during the past four years have made in round numbers 75,000 family visits, and held about 500 meetings. It is understood, of course, that the holding of meetings is the most limited part of their work, as their principal and almost sole duty is to go from house to house, and also address themselves to individuals wherever they meet them. The Tract Society has no colporteur mission or churches

H. The Y. M. C. A. and Immigrants
By Peter Roberts, Ph. D.

The Y. M. C. A. will next summer complete a decade of special service to immigrants coming to North America. It owes an answer to the Christian church and to the nation of what service it has rendered immigrants during this time. This article aims to do this.

In the fall of 1907 a special secretary was put in charge of work for immigrants. By conferences with European and Canadian representatives of the Y. M. C. A., secretaries were stationed at twelve European ports, six Atlantic, and two Pacific. The work of these men was so co-ordinated that a man leaving Liverpool, or Naples, or Libau, met representatives of the Y. M. C. A. at many points en route, and found himself at destination with a card of introduction to the secretary of the local branch or a corresponding member. A Pole who knew not a word of English remembered the letters, Y. M. C. A., and meeting them at Fiume, New York, and Chicago, placed confidence in the men who wore caps with the letters on them, and found guidance, help, and direction when in difficulty. The three men on Ellis Island serving the Y. M. C. A. have command of twenty-three different tongues or dialects. The organization has conducted twelve experiments on board ships crossing the Atlantic by placing men to work among immigrants. The service is worth while, and we hope a way to finance such a work will be found when the tide of immigration becomes normal. One of the many by-products of the present war is the complete disorganization of the port work in Europe and Canada conducted by the Y. M. C. A.

The second step in the program of service is the manning of points of distribution, such as Philadelphia, Pittsburgh, Buffalo, St. Louis, Detroit, Chicago, San Francisco, etc. Immigrants coming to these centers by main railroad routes from ports of landing are dumped by the government and left to their own wits. At these points vultures watch for prey. The depot secretaries protect the newcomer, they co-operate with the police, in some instances are clothed with police power, and are in alliance with trustworthy car conductors and expressmen, and in every way try to defeat the cunning devices of men who rob and cheat the immigrant. When immigration is normal, fifty such men could well be stationed and render valuable service to immigrants at points of distribution.

The third and greatest part of the program is the intensive work done in immigrant colonies in North America. This part of the program has four distinct aims —

1. To teach the foreign-speaking men the English language. A special course of instruction has been prepared for this work, issued by the Association Press. Thousands of men have learned to talk, read and write our language in these classes, and at present no fewer than 30,000 people of forty-two different nationalities or dialects, are being taught. Students in colleges, clerks and foremen — men of all classes — are enlisted to teach, most

of whom give their services free of charge. It is missionary work of the first importance.

2. The advanced course in English comprises civics, by which the alien is prepared to take out his naturalization papers. Thousands have been and are still being helped to pass the examination conducted by the court, and on several occasions, both east and west, the judges on the bench have spoken most enthusiastically of the effort, not only as help to aliens, but also as reacting upon their work, making it more agreeable and pleasing.

3. The alien should know something about the history of America, the men and women who have made the nation, the form of government, the customs and institutions, of the country, the standards which obtain on the continent, and the opportunities awaiting them and their children in the "land of opportunity." This information is imparted to the newcomers by slide and reel, in halls and parks, in schools and on highways. Last year the work was done by 110 associations, and an estimate of the people reached in these gatherings was 500,000.

The foreign speaking people bring with them to North America much that deserves conservation. The Association tries to open an avenue of self-expression to these people. Hence branches of the Y. M. C. A. all over the land plan and carry out concerts, entertainments, and socials to which come representatives of as many as twenty-five distinct peoples, most of whom witness friends taking part in the entertainment. Peoples of various groups are given the chance to meet each other and meet native-born men who believe in democracy and the kingdom of God. These cosmopolitan meetings have brought together representatives of nations, now at war, and they have broken bread together, joined their voices in singing our songs, and joined hands and hearts in pledging allegiance to the Stars and Stripes.

From these services, meeting the needs of immigrants, as well as rendering service to the state and nation, many spiritual experiences have come. The centers established in foreign-speaking colonies have been rallying places for the best among the group to come together; many of them have sought higher spiritual realities; many have been led to closer affiliation with the church of their fathers; some Bible classes have grown out of them; and in a hundred ways the secretaries in charge of the work have had, through personal interview, opportunities to render the highest possible service man can give his brother.

I. DISTRIBUTION OF ITALIANS (FOREIGN BORN AND NATIVE BORN OF FOREIGN OR MIXED PARENTAGE) BY STATES ACCORDING TO CENSUS OF 1910

State	Population	State	Population
Maine	4,588	West Virginia	21,183
New Hampshire	2,942	North Carolina	770
Vermont	6,617	South Carolina	548
Massachusetts	130,577	Georgia	972
Rhode Island	42,864	Florida	7,413
Connecticut	80,773	Kentucky	2,545
New York	739,059	Arizona	2,189
New Jersey	191,849	Utah	4,228
Pennsylvania	298,554	Nevada	4,012
Ohio	62,332	Washington	16,576
Indiana	9,140	Oregon	6,819
Illinois	116,685	California	102,618
Michigan	24,753	Tennessee	3,758
Wisconsin	13,240	Alabama	4,767
Minnesota	13,007	Mississippi	3,859
Iowa	7,560	Arkansas	2,652
Missouri	21,118	Louisiana	42,911
North Dakota	1,365	Oklahoma	4,069
South Dakota	1,603	Texas	14,013
Nebraska	4,840	Montana	8,001
Kansas	5,630	Idaho	2,627
Delaware	4,529	Wyoming	2,489
Maryland	11,169	Colorado	14,190
Virginia	4,069	New Mexico	22,826

J. ITALIAN POPULATION OF LEADING CITIES AND THE PERCENTAGE OF THE TOTAL POPULATION ACCORDING TO CENSUS OF 1910

City	Italian Population	Percentage
Albany	3,278	3
Baltimore	8,473	2
Boston	49,753	7
Buffalo	19,123	5
Bridgeport	*25,000	24
Chicago	74,943	3
Cincinnati	3,924	1
Cleveland	16,989	3

City	Italian Population	Percentage
Detroit	9,092	2
Jersey City	20,691	7
Los Angeles	6,461	2
Milwaukee	4,788	1
Newark	35,861	10
New Haven	*30,000	22
New Orleans	18,581	5
New York	544,449	11
Philadelphia	76,734	5
Pittsburg	22,258	4
Providence	*30,000	13
St. Louis	12,002	2
San Francisco	29,081	7
Washington	4,553	1

* Estimated 1917.

K. Location of Italian Agricultural Colonies in the United States

ASTI, CALIFORNIA. A colony of northern Italians, engaged in vine culture, produces 13,240,000 gallons of table wine a year. Six small towns in the vicinity are inhabited mainly by Italians, owning 5,000 acres of land, and working 10,000 more. These Italians are from Tuscany and Piedmont. They acquired land at $50 an acre, and it is now worth $200.

ALEXANDRIA, TENNESSEE. Is in the cotton belt. Fifty families from northern Italy are working plantations there.

BRYAN, TEXAS. There are from 300 to 350 Italian families, 25,000 souls. This colony was founded twenty-five years ago by railroad laborers who sent for their families and friends as they earned the passage money. More than one-half of the families own their own farms of from 30 to 160 acres on which they raise corn and some cotton. The entire colony owns a district covering eighteen square miles.

BOOMER, WEST VIRGINIA. Contains over 500 Italian families, mostly Calabrians and Sicilians. The people live in cheap company houses, almost entirely isolated from outside influences. A quick workman earns $5 a day in the soft coal mines, but the work is dangerous. Twenty-four men were recently killed by an explosion. The Italians here feel keenly the lack of proper school advantages for their children. It is estimated that there are between 8,000 and 10,000 in the soft coal regions of West Virginia, lacking all Americanizing influences.

CANASTOTA, NEW YORK. About 15,000 Southern Italians are raising onions and celery on what was previously waste land and are making it pay very well.

AUSTIN, GULFPORT, NATCHEZ AND VICKSBURG, MISSISSIPPI. There are several groups of families from Bologna and vicinity that are successfully raising cotton.

DAPHNE AND LAMBERT, ALABAMA. There are small colonies in which every family possesses from ten to twenty-five acres of land, and raises sugar and cotton.

DICKINSON, TEXAS. This is a community of 500 Sicilians who are doing market gardening. Their prosperity is swelling the numbers in the colony.

HAMMONTON, NEW JERSEY. Has a population of nearly 4,000 Italians profitably engaged in raising berries, peaches and vegetables. One Italian made $15,000 from his peach crop the past year.

INDEPENDENCE, LOUISIANA. The Italian colony here has a good location on an island in the Mississippi river, sixty-five miles north of New Orleans. There are about 200 Sicilian families from the province of Palermo, who raise strawberries. Eighty own their farms of from twenty to eighty acres. They cleared the land themselves and it now yields them incomes of $75 to $100 per acre.

Of the success of the Italian immigration, some idea may be gained by the following letter from C. L. Bush, of Independence (Lord, Trenor, and Barrows, " The Italian in America," page 72): " Twenty years ago land could be bought in and around the town for $1 to $5 per acre that is now selling readily at $25 to $100 per acre. One tract here of 1,500 acres sold twenty-five years ago for $1,600. Two hundred acres of it was sold a few weeks ago for $10,400. One will ask what was the principal cause of the development. The answer must be the Italian immigration, which has come here and improved the conditions in respect to production. The majority of farmers have done away with negro labor. Why? Because the negroes generally are shiftless, whereas the Italian laborer is a success. The question of his desirability as a citizen is often asked. I can say that thus far, in our twelve or fifteen years' experience with them, they have given no trouble to any one. They are prompt to pay their debts at the stores, meet their paper at the banks when due, and often before. I do not think there is a case on record in this parish where the state has had to prosecute them for a crime or misdemeanor, and that is saying a good deal, when we consider that there are 150 to 200 families living here and every berry season probably 500 more come to assist in harvesting the crop."

KNOBVIEW, MISSOURI. Contains fifty families who left Sunnyside, Arkansas, after malaria broke out there. Twenty of the Italian families have joined them. All have good homes, and have paid for their land, which is worth $50 an acre. The men divide their time between working their fields and on the railroads. This colony was founded under the auspices of the Roman Catholic church.

MARSHFIELD, MISSOURI. Contains another agricultural Italian colony, composed of Tyrolese, men accustomed to mountain life, who find this region of the Ozark mountains particularly congenial to them. They raise cereals and live-stock.

SOUTHEASTERN TEXAS. There is a number of small colony groups of Italians working in the rice fields and lumber camps. Round about the cities of Galveston, Houston, Austin, San Antonio and others, are to be found settlements of Italians who devote themselves to market gardening.

SUNNYSIDE, ARKANSAS. This colony was founded by Austin Corbin and Prince Ruspoli, but great misfortunes due to climate and location, where strict sanitary precautions should be observed, have driven large numbers of Italians from the locality. There are still 100 families, tenants of the estate, who remain because of the large profits in growing cotton. One man, after working a number of years, returned to Italy with $8,000 in his pocket. Many others are not so fortunate, but spend a large part of their profits in trying to keep in good health. The company that runs the colony has charged the Italians exorbitant prices for land, tools, and farm animals, even as high at the very beginning at $160 per acre, this sum payable after twenty years, if so desired.

TONTITOWN, ARKANSAS. Father Bandini took a group of Italian fugitives from Sunnyside twenty years ago to this region in the Ozark mountains which he had previously carefully examined. The land was a wilderness of scrub pines. The Italians cleared the land and are now, after two decades, successfully raising apples, peaches, grapes, and all kinds of vegetables. Each of the eighty families owns its own land and house. Each family possesses from 20 to 160 acres. The community life centers about

Father Bandini, the church and the parish school he has built there. In strong contrast with Sunnyside, there is here good air, good water, and a climate similar to that in Italy.

ST. ELENA, NORTH CAROLINA. This is another agricultural colony of fifteen Venetian families induced to come to this region by the North Carolina Trust and Development Company. Each family was sold ten acres at an average price of $30 an acre, a sum far above the land's value at that time.

VALDESE, NORTH CAROLINA. A colony of 400 Italians from the Waldensian valley in Italy, who went there to found a religious colony. Uncleared pine land was sold the pioneers by a land improvement company. The Italians made the best of the situation, cleared the land, and now raise corn, grapes, vegetables, and cow peas for fodder. About sixty families are there at present, most of them owning their land. Shortly after the establishment of the colony, a cotton mill was built which now employs 500 young men and women, a good many Americans among them, who prefer the factory to the farm. Consequently the farms are not so well tilled as formerly. The Waldensian Church, which was built by the Italians themselves (the only work done by an outsider was that of a certain section of the roof), is the center of the community life.

VINELAND, NEW JERSEY. This region has forty square miles of territory occupied by 7,000 Italians, each family holding from 10 to 160 acres. This colony is one of the oldest in the country, having been established by Calvaliere Secchi De Casale, an Italian patriot, in 1873. The sandy soil is adapted to grape culture, garden truck and fruit. The farmers find their markets in New York and Philadelphia. The Italian houses are well built, furnished with carpets, American furniture and pianos. These homes are worth from $1,000 to $7,000.

There are also innumerable groups of ten to fifteen and even thirty families scattered through the South and West. Near San Francisco these groups are engaged in market gardening, and the women and children work in the fruit canneries. About Salt Lake City, Utah, are also to be found small groups of Italians engaged in market gardening. In Louisiana there are ten small towns near New Orleans containing from ten to one hundred families engaged in market gardening and cultivation of sugar cane and cotton, while in the regions of Tampa and Pensacola, Florida, there are numerous small Italian settlements devoted to peach-growing or making of cigars.

L. DIRECTORY OF PROTESTANT ITALIAN MISSION STATIONS OR FIELDS IN UNITED STATES

I. Baptist

Massachusetts
1. Boston (First).
2. Boston (Second).
3. East Boston.
4. Framingham.
5. Franklin.
6. Haverhill.
7. Hyde Park.
8. Lawrence.
9. Lynn.
10. Mansfield.
11. Milford.
12. Monson.
13. Springfield.
14. Wakefield.
15. Worcester.

Connecticut
16. Ansonia.
17. Bridgeport.
18. Bristol.
19. Hartford.
20. Southington.
21. Meriden.
22. Norwich.
23. New Haven (First).
24. New Haven (Second).
25. Shelton.
26. Waterbury.
27. Wallingford.
28. Winsted.

Rhode Island
29. Providence (First).
30. Providence (Second).
31. Natick.

New York
32. Batavia.
33. Brooklyn (First).
34. Brooklyn (Strong Place).
35. Buffalo (First).
36. Buffalo (Second).
37. Buffalo (Cedar Street).
38. Gloversville.
39. Mount Vernon.
40. New York (First).
41. New York (Second Ave.).
42. New York (Judson Memorial).
43. New York (Bronx).
44. Ossining.
45. Port Chester.
46. Rochester.
47. Syracuse.
48. Utica.
49. White Plains.

New Jersey
50. Camden.
51. Hoboken.
52. Millburn.
53. Newark.
54. Orange.
55. Passaic.
56. Silver Lake.
57. Trenton.

Pennsylvania
58. Jeanette.
59. Pittsburgh.
60. Philadelphia.
61. Philadelphia (Settlement).
62. Scottdale.
63. Uniontown.

I. Baptist — Continued

Vermont
64. Barre.

Michigan
65. Detroit.

West Virginia
66. Boomer.
67. Longacre.

Ohio
68. Youngstown.
69. East Youngstown.
70. Cleveland.

Florida
71. West Tampa.

Louisiana
72. Amite.
73. Independence.

Texas
74. Beaumont.
75. Dickinson.
76. Galveston.
77. Houston.

Wisconsin
78. Racine.

California
79. Los Angeles.
80. Fresno.

Oregon
81. Portland.

District of Columbia
82. Washington.

II. Congregational

California
1. San Francisco* (Greene Street).

Connecticut
2. Branford.
3. Bridgeport.*
4. Hartford.*
5. Kensington.
6. New Britain.
7. New Haven.*
8. Saugatuck.
9. Stony Creek.
10. Torrington.
11. Waterbury.*
12. Winsted.

Illinois
13. Chicago* (Ewing Street).
14. La Salle.*
15. Oglesby.
16. Spring Valley.*

Maine†
17. Biddeford.
18. Hallowell.
19. Livermore Falls.
20. Lewiston.
21. Mexico.
22. Millinocket.
23. Millinocket (East).
24. North Jay.
   Portland.‡
25. Rockland.
26. Riley.
27. Rumford.*
28. Smith's Crossing.
29. Stonington.
30. Virginia.
31. Westbrook.

*A regularly constituted church.
† Missions in Maine are branches of American churches without Italian workers.
‡ A union enterprise.

II. Congregational — Continued

Massachusetts
32. North Plymouth.*
33. Pittsfield.*

New Jersey
34. Cliffside.
35. Grantwood.*
36. Jersey City.
37. Northvale.*

New York
38. Brooklyn.
39. Buffalo.

Rhode Island
40. Providence (Silver Lake Region).
41. House of Good Will, Boston, Mass.§
42. Endicott House, Worcester, Mass.§
43. Emerson House, Chicago, Ill.§
44. Bethlehem Institute, Los Angeles, Cal.§

III. Evangelical Association

Illinois
1. Chicago.

Wisconsin
2. Milwaukee.
3. Racine and Kenosha.

IV. Lutheran
1. Philadelphia, Pa.

V. Methodist Episcopal and Methodist Episcopal, South

New York
1. Albany.
2. Astoria.
3. Buffalo.
4. Dobb's Ferry.
5. Elmira.
6. Frankfort.
7. Jamestown.
8. New York (East Side Parish).
9. New York (Five Points).
10. New York (Corona).
11. New York (Jamaica).
12. New York (Jefferson Pk.).
13. New York (People's Home).
14. New York (Bronx).
15. New York (Washington Square).
16. Rochester.
17. Schenectady.
18. Syracuse.
19. Troy.
20. Utica.
21. Yonkers.

Pennsylvania
22. Altoona.
23. Clearfield.
24. Hillsville.
25. New Castle.
26. Oakmont.
27. Philadelphia.
28. Pittsburgh.
29. Reading.
30. Scranton.
31. Wilkesbarre.

§ Settlements under Congregationalist auspices without attached missions, yet serving Italian groups with religious purpose.

V. Methodist Episcopal and Methodist Episcopal, South—Cont'd.

New Jersey
32. Jersey City.
33. Newark.
34. Paterson.
35. Rahway.

Connecticut
36. Middletown.
37. New Haven.

Massachusetts
38. Boston.
39. Fall River.

Ohio
40. Youngstown.
41. Columbus.

Illinois
42. Chicago.
43. Joliet.

Maryland
44. Baltimore.
45. Cumberland.

Indiana
46. Indianapolis.

Maine
47. Portland.

Rhode Island
48. Providence.

Delaware
49. Wilmington.

Florida
50. Tampa.

Louisiana
51. New Orleans.

Colorado
52. Pueblo.
53. Butte.

Montana
54. Butte.

California
55. San Francisco.

Alabama
56. Birmingham.

Missouri
57. Kansas City.
58. St. Louis.

Texas
59. Thurber.

West Virginia
60. Welch.

VI. Presbyterian (U. S. A.)

New York
1. Auburn.
2. Binghamton.
3. Brooklyn (Gregg Chapel).
4. Brooklyn (Elton Street).
5. Brooklyn (Central).
6. Endicott.
7. Middletown.
8. Mount Kisco.
9. New Rochelle.
10. New York (Labor Temple).
11. New York (East Harlem).
12. New York (Holy Trinity).
13. New York (Ascension).
14. New York (Calvary).

VI. Presbyterian (U. S. A.) — Continued

15. New York (Sea and Land).
16. New York (Spring Street).
17. New York (Madison Square).
18. New York (Covenant).
19. New York (John Hall Memorial).
20. New York (Bethlehem Chapel).
21. New York (Church of the Gospel).
22. Nyack.
23. Pleasantville.
24. Port Chester.
25. Rochester.
26. Rome.
27. Schenectady.
28. Solvay.
29. White Plains.

Pennsylvania

30. Berwick.
31. Bristol.
32. Chester.
33. Clairton.
34. Dunmore.
35. Easton.
36. Edge Hill.
37. Germantown.
38. Greensburg.
39. Hazelton.
40. Johnstown.
41. McKeesport.
42. Midland.
43. Norristown.
44. Old Forge.
45. Philadelphia (First).
46. Philadelphia (Second).
47. **Philadelphia (Tioga).**

48. Pittsburgh.
49. Pittston.
50. Roseto.
51. Salemville.
52. Scranton.
53. Windber.
54. New Alexandria.

New Jersey

55. Asbury Park.
56. Bernardsville.
57. Beverly.
58. Burlington.
59. East Orange.
60. Elizabeth.
61. Garfield.
62. Hammonton.
63. Jersey City.
64. Montclair.
65. Newark (East Side).
66. Newark (Olivet Chapel).
67. Newark (Friendly Center 4).
68. Newark (Friendly Center 5).
69. Paterson.
70. Plainfield.
71. Princeton.
72. Red Bank.
73. Riverside.
74. Trenton.
75. Vineland.

Minnesota

76. Chisholm.
77. Virginia.
78. Eveleth.
79. Gilbert.
80. Hibbing.
81. Keewatin.
82. Mountain Iron.

VI. Presbyterian (U. S. A.) — Continued

Illinois
83. Chicago (Olivet Institute).
84. Chicago (Italian Christian Institute).
85. Chicago (First).
86. Chicago (Church of Our Saviour).
87. Chicago (Samaritan House).
88. Chicago (Centre Mission).
89. Chicago (Burr Mission).

Ohio
90. Cincinnati.
91. Cleveland (West Side).
92. Cleveland (Beckwith Memorial).
93. Bellaire.
94. Steubenville.

Indiana
95. Clinton.
96. Gary.

Massachusetts
97. Quincy.
98. Somerville.

Michigan
99. Calumet.
100. Detroit.

West Virginia
101. Clarksburg.
102. Follansbee.

California
103. San José.

Colorado
104. Trinidad.

Delaware
105. Wilmington.

Maryland
106. Baltimore.

Wisconsin
107. Hurley.

VII. Protestant Episcopal

Massachusetts
1. Boston.
2. East Boston.

Connecticut
3. Hartford.
4. New Haven.

New York
5. New York (San Salvadore).
6. New York (Saint Ambrogio).
7. New York (Saint Mark's).
8. New York (Ellis Island).
9. New York (Calvary).
10. New York (Grace).
11. New York (Bronx).
12. New York (Saint John's Cathedral).
13. New York (East 111th Street).
14. New York (Staten Island).
15. New York (Brooklyn).
16. Oyster Bay.

VII. Protestant Episcopal — Continued

Pennsylvania
17. Easton (First).
18. Easton (Second).
19. Philadelphia (First).
20. Philadelphia (Second).
21. Philadelphia (Third).

Maryland
22. Baltimore.

Michigan
23. ....

Illinois
24. Chicago.

VIII. Reformed in U. S. A.

New York
1. Newburg.
2. Union Hill.

New Jersey
3. Hackensack.

IX. United Presbyterian

Pennsylvania
1. Mount Pleasant.
2. New Kensington.
3. Pittsburgh (First).
4. Pittsburgh (Second).
5. Wilmerding.

Rhode Island
6. Providence.

California
7. Los Angeles.

Washington
8. Tacoma.

M. Statistics of Italian Work by Several Denominations in the United States *

Baptist (Northern Convention)	82	2,750	....	......	60	$9,000	$69,030
Congregational	44	983	....	1,000	19	961	13,279
Evangelical Association†	3	......	....	....	....	......	......
Methodist Episcopal and Methodist Episcopal, South†	60	‡5,241	42	4,927	52	$7,357	45,000
Presbyterian in U. S. A	107	4,800	....	8,000	70	14,263	100,000
Protestant Episcopal†	24	......	....	......	....	......	......
Reformed in U. S. A†	3	......	....	......	....	......	......
United Presbyterian†	8	......	....	......	....	......	......
	326	13,774	42	13,927	201	$31,571	$227,309

* Table does not include many fields cultivated, and large sums of money expended by local churches are not reported.
† Statistics not included, except for the number of churches or missions.
‡ Of this number, 1,839 are probationers.
§ This sum reported by 46 churches.
First column represents: Number of churches or missions doing Italian work.
Second column represents: Number of Italian church members.
Third column represents: Number of church schools with Italian pupils.
Fourth column represents: Number of Italian church school pupils.
Fifth column represents: Salaried Italian workers engaged in Italian work.
Sixth column represents: Total contributions of Italian members for all purposes.
Seventh column represents: Total expenditure of the denomination for Italian work.

At Work With the Italians

By William P. Shriver, *Director of City and Immigrant Work, Board of Home Missions of the Presbyterian Church in the U. S. A.*

The various denominational home mission societies are conducting a propaganda throughout the churches of America in behalf of a friendly and neighborly interest in the 3,000,000 Italians who are so important a factor in our new community life. The wide circulation of Prof. Mangano's book, "Sons of Italy," and other literature which has been specially prepared for this Italian year, will in many quarters provoke the question, "What can we do for the Italians in our community?" This manual is designed to help answer that question. It gathers together much fruitful suggestion embodied in Mr. Mangano's book along with experience gained by many others. It is needless to point out that unless this widespread propaganda does lead to this practical expression of our interest in the Italians, it will have shot far of the mark.

Literature

The approach to any immigrant group ought to be preceded by a careful study of their social and religious background and of their racial heritage. We Americans know too little of the countries from which our recent immigrants are coming, and this lack of knowledge is the occasion of a good deal of blundering in our effort to serve the immigrant. A thoughful study of "Sons of Italy," by Antonio Mangano, should be made. Where a group is brought together for the study of this book, "Suggestions for Leaders" will be found helpful.

"Religious Work among Italians in America," by Antonio Mangano, is a pamphlet which enters with more detail into religious conditions among Italians than was possible in "Sons of Italy." It also has statements from the various denominations concerning their policy and work among Italians, and a complete list of all Protestant Italian churches and missions in this country. This pamphlet will be of the greatest aid to the church contemplating work with Italians.

A recent book throwing much light on the problems of the immigrant is "The Immigrant and the Community," by Grace Abbott. The author, a former resident of Hull House, served as director of the Immigrants' Protective League of Chicago, and from such first-hand experience writes suggestively concerning the journey of the immigrant, the immigrant in the courts, the immigrant and the public health, and the education of the immigrant. "Immigrant Forces," by William P. Shriver, may also be consulted. "Leadership of the New America," by Archibald McClure, is an excellent brief introduction to the immigrant groups, presenting particularly the immigrant's point of view. Withal, nothing will be so fruitful as first-hand contact with the Italians themselves.

A Point Of View

At the outset, it is essential that we get a wholesome and sympathetic point of view. While many of the Italians who have come to this country have suffered many handicaps because of conditions beyond their control, they are a self-respecting people. They do not want to be patronized. In the last fifteen years, furthermore, the Italians have made rapid progress in this country. In every community there are Italians of ability in business and the professions. They should be our allies for community betterment. What the Italians ask is not our charity nor commiseration, but a fair chance to share with us in rearing that community life in which every individual may come into his own best heritage. Our aim should be not to do something *for* the Italian, but to work *with* him. Sympathy, comradeship, co-operation, are the keywords of Christian democracy.

Getting Together

As we aim to line up Americans and Italians in this co-operative spirit we may consider

1. The Italian colony or community.
2. The Italian household or family.
3. The Italian as an individual.
4. The Italian in his religious need and aspiration.

On the other side, we have to reckon with

1. The American community, organized for community service through the local government, or in unofficial and voluntary groups.
2. The American family, as a friendly neighbor to the Italian.
3. The American as an individual, a new comrade to the Italian.

4. The American evangelical church, with its discovery of a "mission field" in its own city, town, or community.

The crossing of these interests, Italian and American, marks out a number of fields for co-operative service. A diagram may make this clearer.

Fields for Co-operative Service
The * indicates outstanding opportunities for service.

	The Italian colony	The Italian household	The Italian as an individual	The Italian in his religious life
The American community..	*	*	*	....
The American family......	....	*	*	*
The individual American...	....	*	*	*
The American evangelical church	*	*	*	*

Here are at least thirteen opportunities for getting together in mutually helpful co-operation.

The American community has a very definite responsibility for conditions in the Italian colony and in assuring equal opportunity for the local Italian population. Its concern may also sympathetically reach into the Italian household. It may have frequent occasion to protect and aid the individual Italian. By the community is meant the city or town organized in the local government with its various departments of health, education, public safety, etc.; or, the people of the community organized in voluntary groups, such as the Town Improvement Club, the Woman's Club, or the Parent-Teacher Association. Where any church establishes a parochial school, the community should see to it and insist that the same standards are maintained as in the public schools. Beyond this the organized community will not, under existing conditions, concern itself with the religious situation other than to see that fullest protection is given any group of Italians to worship according to the mode of their own choice without being molested.

While the American family may feel impotent to move in the larger matters of community betterment, alone and of itself, in the Italian family it may find a field for friendly co-operation. The American home in its warmth and welcome may be tellingly effective for the young Italian.

The individual American who wants to extend a friendly hand to the Italian will not have to wait for a community-wide movement. He may get acquainted with an Italian family.

There are opportunities on every hand to cultivate some young Italian as a friend.

To the American evangelical church the whole field is open. It may set up a program of community betterment which may at length gain the adherence of all elements in the community; it may relate itself to the Italian home, it will find many opportunities to co-operate with the individual Italian; and the religious life of the Italian will be its normal concern.

From these standpoints, then, the following pages will consider with greater detail the opportunities of working *with* the Italian.

Making A Survey

Preparatory to a program of service, either on the part of the American community or the church, it is desirable to make a survey, which is nothing more nor less than a careful and orderly study of existing conditions. Where possible, it would be better to make a survey of the entire town or community, up-town and down-town, or at least of a certain area or ward, rather than a survey of the Italians. No group of people particularly relishes being "studied," and often the process serves to emphasize divisions rather than to obliterate them. It would be helpful to enlist the co-operation of some of the representative Italians. This may save misunderstanding, facilitate the work, and lay the basis for co-operation. In a New Jersey town a community survey was made. When completed an exhibit was displayed in a vacant store on a main street down-town. A group of Italians visited this exhibit. One of the men was outraged to find on a screen designed to illustrate home conditions in the Italian colony a photograph of his wife. The Italians tore down the picture and a small tempest was stirred in the Italian colony.

Where a comprehensive survey of a city or town is contemplated from a municipal or community standpoint, the effort should be made to enlist in preliminary conference, and thereafter in the committee to carry forward the survey, a wide and representative group of men and women, not overlooking the industrial workers and the immigrant population. The ground is thus prepared for co-operative action in carrying out the recommendations of the survey. A community engaging in such a thorough-going survey should correspond with the Department of Surveys and Exhibits, Russell Sage Foundation, New York.

Where the churches undertake such a community survey, assistance may be had from denominational home mission headquarters. The Board of Home Missions of the Methodist Episcopal Church (Philadelphia) maintains a Bureau of Social Service and Surveys; the Immigrant and City Work Office of the Presbyterian Board of Home Missions (U. S. A.) and the Department of City and Foreign Speaking Work of the American Baptist Home Mission Society, New York, will co-operate in planning community surveys.

Where volunteer service must be used, a pamphlet, "What Social Workers Should Know about Their Own Communities," by Margaret F. Byington (Charity Organization Department, Russell Sage Foundation, New York, 15 cents), will be most helpful. It outlines questions bearing on community problems under such headings as Housing, Health, Recreation, Industrial Problems, the Immigrant, Children; and also suggests a line of inquiry concerning agencies for relief and for the improvement of social conditions.

"A Survey Blank for an Immigrant Community," by William P. Shriver (5 cents), will be suggestive. It outlines a brief inquiry under such heads as Housing, Industrial Conditions, Home Life and Health, Recreation and Amusements, Social Agencies and Schools.

The camera is a valuable ally in bringing home community conditions to the public. From small kodak negatives enlargements may be made, about 10 x 13 inches; mounted on cards 22 x 28 inches, there will be room for two pictures with brief inscriptions. Lantern slides may be made directly from negatives $3\frac{1}{4}$ x $4\frac{1}{4}$ inches at a cost of about 25 cents each.

Graphs or charts may also be made setting forth statistical information on cards 22 x 28 inches. It is desirable to present a single fact in as simple, clear, and convincing a way as possible. Line cuts for publication may also be made from these larger exhibit cards.

A survey of conditions having been made, the way is opened for a program of service.

I. *The American Community and the Italian Colony.*

1. *Housing and Neighborhood Sanitation.* Where a survey reveals, as is so often the case, bad conditions in housing and neighborhood sanitation, pressure should be brought to bear on

the local government. But mere laws will be ineffective unless there are means of regular inspection and enforcement. As Miss Byington points out, "With our foreign colonies, ignorant of American standards and legal rights, and not knowing where and how to make complaint, it is not enough for the Board of Health to act on complaint; it should make regular inspections." This principle of calling upon and utilizing the facilities of the local government should be stressed. But the co-operation of the Italians should be enlisted. Because they may not readily understand English and are not acquainted with local ordinances bearing on health, housing, sanitation, and public order, a community that will take the pains to print a pamphlet (English and Italian in parallel pages) explaining some of the more important ordinances, will have taken a first step in securing such co-operation. The public school may also be an agency for instruction and in securing the co-operation of parents and pupils.

2. *Protection and Justice for the Italian.* The Italian suffers from many exploiters. His dealings with the unscrupulous banker, the land shark masquerading as a real estate agent, and the unregulated employment agency are disastrous. Many of the offenses of the immigrant are, furthermore, due to ignorance. Such information as is suggested in the preceding paragraph concerning local ordinances will lessen the number of arrests. It is unfortunately true that in many communities the immigrant gets scant justice at the hand of the courts. There is a convincing and suggestive discussion of "The Immigrant in the Courts" in Miss Abbott's book, "The Immigrant and the Community."

Lack of competent court interpreters often prevents the immigrant from securing justice. Mr. Mangano writes in "Sons of Italy:" "Before the Italian or any other foreigner can have proper regard for our political institutions, America must see to it that they are free from graft and that protection and justice are assured to rich and poor alike. This matter of court interpreters, for example, is calling for instant action. There is no standard of qualifications for the position. Many of them speak Italian poorly, and as far as education goes, are not fit for the place. These positions are given to particular friends of the politicians. They wield great power, the fate of an accused man often depending upon a truthful and exact translation of what is said. Only men of high character and unquestioned integrity should have such a responsibility."

3. *Juvenile Delinquency.* " Does a city's court still consider the delinquent child a criminal to be punished, or is he now looked upon as a wayward child who must be protected and helped or a defective child needing special care and treatment? In all stages of its proceedings, one attitude or the other must be evident." This field of co-operative service is opened up in Miss Byington's "What Social Workers Should Know About Their Own Communities" (page 28). Loss of parental control is one of the tragedies of immigrant life in America and a source of juvenile delinquency. Mr. Mangano finds the solution in the reunion of the family life. We must teach the boys and girls to respect and honor their parents and to speak their native tongue as well as English. Imagine the helplessness of a mother who knows no English and whose children feel that Italian is to be despised and cast aside. The children talk English in the home and even plan to disobey her before her eyes when she has no idea what they are saying. What becomes of Italian boys in your community when arrested? In a New Jersey community which prides itself on its community spirit, two boys, one colored and one Italian, were committed to the county jail for trial. It was later discovered that the county sheriff had placed them in a room with adult prisoners. When this undesirable situation was discovered, the judge directed that they be detained in separate quarters. This is the sort of thing worth being informed about.

4. *Education.* The public school is first and foremost in its contact with the immigrant and in its opportunity for heplful and co-operative service. Study your local schools in their relation to the Italian or other immigrant population. " Schools of Tomorrow," by John Dewey, is a prophetic book. It describes schools throughout the country that are pioneering for the new democracy. But the public school is not limiting its facilities to the children of the community. It is being made a community center. Consult "A Wider Use of the School Plant," by Clarence Arthur Perry. It is suggestive, also, of a wider use of the church plant.

The education of the adult immigrant has not begun to receive the consideration in this country it deserves. Many communities feel that they have discharged their responsibility for the foreigner when they offer in the public school a class in English for foreigners, four nights a week, often in a school remote from the immigrant community and taught by a day-school teacher already tired by the day's work. When in the autumn of 1917, roused by the war, the Mayor's Committee on National Defense set afoot a campaign for the Americanization of aliens living in New York, it was stated: "The brunt, of course, has so far fallen on the schools. The new campaign will extend far outside the schoolroom. The facilities, organization, leadership and resourcefulness of social agencies are to be used in every possible way." The public schools, libraries, settlements, clubs, churches, synagogues, employers' associations, and city departments were enlisted. Some of the most successful instruction of adult immigrant women — the most difficult group to reach we know of — was carried on by a highly intelligent young American woman who formed her classes in the homes, the objects of the home suggesting the vocabulary to be used.

But the older Italian men and women who will never learn English should be considered. In her practical discussion of the education of the immigrant Miss Abbott writes, "We should long ago have recognized that much of the opportunity for education which is offered the adult immigrants should be in their native language. Many of the older men and women will never learn English, and with others it will be many years before they will understand it easily. Most of them have lived in the country and are having their first contact with the problem of city life in the United States. They need at once a knowledge of the city's water and milk supply; of its sanitary regulations; of the labor laws designed for their protection; of the naturalization requirements; something of the history of the United States; and more of the problems of municipal government with whose right solution they, as much as any one else, are concerned. The public libraries are beginning to meet the cultural needs of the immigrant, but books with concrete information along these lines are not available for the educated and would not be used by those of little education or by the illiterate. These people must be reached by moving pictures explained by lecturers who speak their language."

5. *Recreation.* "We live in a boarding house, where we have to drink beer. It is served at every meal, and they would put us out if we didn't drink it. I have no place to go in the evening; I can't stay shut up in my rooms. So I walk the streets or go to moving pictures or the pool-room." Here is the problem of recreation from the standpoint of a young Italian in Barre, Vermont. He voiced the need of thousands of young Italians

throughout this country. " In this city," reports Mr. Mangano in " Sons of Italy," " the socialists have built a big hall where there are dances and meetings, but the serious minded Italian, and there are many, would like a place where they could go, read the papers, study English, and indulge in gymnastics for recreation. In less than six weeks' time two years ago, it was possible to gather a group of twenty-two fine young men, all away from home ties and influences, into a club for the study of English." The dramatic instinct is highly latent in the Italian. Getting up a play, staging and performing it before a group of neighbors, has furnished interest and expression for many groups of young Italians.

Supervised playgrounds are increasingly being featured in programs of community welfare. The Playground and Recreation Association of America, New York, will be glad to correspond with any community interested. The association furnishes stereopticon lectures showing the need of playgrounds and playground equipment.

6. *Co-operating Agencies.* It is impossible in the brief compass of this manual to take up in detail the varied forms of community service being successfully carried on among Italians. It is hoped that a point of view has been gained. A number of concrete suggestions have been made. Attention has been directed to books replete with further suggestion. As an addendum to this manual there is a list of organizations which hold themselves in readiness to advise communities or groups along the line of their specific interest.

II. The American Community and the Italian Family

The problems of health, of child welfare, and of education are frequently best met through a sympathetic relation with the family. The visiting or school nurse is a connecting link between the Italian household and the community. In California, state legislation has been enacted providing for " home teachers." The duty of the home teachers is to visit her entire district in order to discover the homes that need care, and then to teach English to the foreign mother in her home, as well as sanitation, household tasks, purchase of supplies, clothing, and concerning our American system of government.

The Italian should be protected from medical quacks and nostrums. Mr. Mangano states, " The Italian quacks to whom many

Italians go because of language are unscrupulous, and the quacks of all races who advertise in Italian free advice and sure cures for all manner of trouble, take thousands of hard-earned dollars. Realizing the injury to the Italian people and the disgrace upon the profession, some of the finest Italian physicians in New York recently banded together and are publishing a health culture journal in Italian, called ' La Parola del Medico ' (' The Word of the Doctor '). The aim is to teach personal hygiene to the Italians and expose fraudulent quacks. The constructive articles deal with such subjects as ' Fruit Diet,' ' Examples of Good Living,' 'Wheat, Cereals, and Legumes,' ' The Work of the Italian Hospital.' The recent epidemic of infantile paralysis was discussed, and part of the blame for its spread laid squarely upon the bad housing conditions among Italians."

The fight against tuberculosis and the saving of the lives of babies are causes in which the community should seek the cooperation of the Italian home. In order to meet the constantly increasing demand for a simple educational card or pamphlet on tuberculosis, which can be supplied in quantity at a reasonable price and in several different languages, the National Association for the Study and Prevention of Tuberculosis (New York) has arranged that a simple card or folder be printed in large quantities, thus giving local bodies the advantage of the reduced cost. Arrangements have been made whereby this card may be secured in Italian and eighteen other languages for $2.50 per thousand, and $2.20 per thousand in English.

The " Save the Seventh Baby " campaign carried on by the " Delineator " and similar movements will furnish concrete suggestion for helpfulness in the Italian family. The Italian mothers and their new-born babies often suffer irreparable injury at the hands of unskilled midwives. The Italians should be made acquainted with physicians of competence and character.

Those interested in a thoroughgoing study of family rehabilitation should consult " Social Diagnosis," by Mary E. Richmond, especially Chapter XXI on " The Immigrant Family." There is an extended questionnaire bearing on the family.

III. The American Family and the Italian Home

" What can any Christian American do to reach the foreigner ? " asks Mr. Mangano. " Let him play the host to the stranger. We too often blame the stranger within our gates for his un-American standards of living. How is he ever to attain the true American standard if he never crosses the threshold of an American home? Not long ago a well-educated foreign worker startled his audience by telling them that he had been laboring in their city for over six years and had never been invited to an American home. People are honestly seeking how to reach Italians, but they do not use the most potent means at their disposal to establish a point of contact — their homes."

Much that has been written in the preceding paragraphs will be suggestive in this connection. The National Americanization Committee has prepared a fine program of activities for mothers' organizations, which includes this standard for individual women:

1. Americanize one immigrant woman.
2. Teach English to one foreign-born mother.
3. Put one immigrant family on your calling list.

It would be impossible to estimate the enormous transformation that could be wrought if every Christian woman would earnestly set herself to the task, taking the foreign-born woman who lives nearest her as her particular work and care. The relation of an American family or visitor to the Italian home, while friendly and sympathetic, should be guarded against an ill-considered charity or patronage.

IV. The American Individual and the Italian

To know one Italian or a single Italian family intimately; to have entered with sympathy into his or her life story, ambitions and progress; in the real spirit of comradeship to give oneself heartily as to a new friend — here is an opportunity for every American. Multiply these comradeships a hundred thousand times and forces will be set at work that will mean more to the Italians of this country than scores of settlements or social agencies.

V. The American Evangelical Church

1. *Community Work.* With the sympathy and service of Jesus as its burning passion in inspiration, it would be expected that the Christian church will be first and foremost in its solicitude and care for the immigrant, as he makes his adventure in the new world so full of vexing problems. As a local church presses its program of missionary education, it should include a first-hand

study of the conditions of life in the Italian or other immigrant community nearest at hand. This near-by need should be kept before the congregation and the church school in some graphic and appealing way. It should be accompanied by some definite program of service.

The local church should put its forces back of all well-accredited community movements making for the common welfare. The church furnishes a large share of workers actively engaged in social betterment. Their outlook and experience should be capitalized in the church's missionary or social service committee. When in any city or town there is outstanding need in the Italian or other immigrant colony, and efforts to arouse the American constituency have failed, a church or group of churches may well take the matter in hand and work confidently in the faith that the enterprise, when demonstrated, will be taken over by the city or community. A kindergarten in the immigrant section of Gary conducted by the Women's Missionary Societies of Indiana was the pioneer kindergarten in that great industrial center now noted throughout the country for its progressive public schools. Where such a community service is undertaken by a local church, it must not expect immediate returns in the terms common to its evangelistic propaganda. The service rendered must be reckoned worth while in itself. All the preceding sections bearing on community and welfare work will be suggestive to churches.

2. *The Evangelical Church and the Religious Needs of the Italians.* (a) Why carry on religious work for Italians? Any specific religious work undertaken by a church or group of churches must be based on a clear and unmistakable conviction that the Italians of the community have social and religious needs which are not being met by the Roman or any other churches. In a statement concerning the work of the Congregational Church, Philip M. Rose, supervisor of Italian Congregational churches in Connecticut, writes: "While showing all tolerance for and willingness to co-operate with the Italian Roman Catholic Church, we must recognize that the majority of our Italian-Americans are, spiritually, unchurched, and hence are our legitimate field." In the pamphlet, "Religious Work Among Italians," Mr. Mangano frankly estimates the loyalty of the Italian to his traditional faith: "It is a common belief among Americans that all Italians are Roman Catholics, and there seems to be good reason for this impression. Out of Italy's population of 36,000,000 there are

not more than 60,000 Protestants, but there are unnumbered thousands, yes, tens of thousands of anti-clerics and even atheists. Ninety-nine per cent. of the Italians landing on our shores would give the Roman Catholic as their religious belief, but if questioned a large number would add that they were not faithful to its celebrations nor its services, except perhaps at times of births, deaths, and marriages." A questionnaire sent to all Baptist, Presbyterian, Methodist, and Congregational Italian pastors on the question "What per cent. of Italians in your colony are loyal to the Roman Church?" evoked an amazingly unanimous reply, "About one-third." One or two reported, one-fourth; and one reported, one-half.

In one city of Massachusetts, out of a population of 1,700 Italians, of whom only sixty attend the Roman Church; and in another city there is a colony of 6,000 Italians, of whom only 300 attend that church. There is a colony of 35,000 Italians in Brooklyn which has only one Italian church, seating at the utmost 400 persons. It conducts three masses on Sunday, and granting it were filled to its capacity each time, it could only minister to 1,200 persons, less than 4 per cent. of the population. Out of 600,000 Italian population of Greater New York, the Roman Church, by its own figures, so far as I could obtain them, lays claim to only 180,000, including children, as members of the Roman Catholic Italian churches — less than one-third of the total Italian population.

There is need for the widest publicity of these facts in order to refute the common charge of proselyting, which all evangelical mission work among the Italians meets, and also because officials of city departments, health, probation, juvenile court, and charity organizations, and even school teachers, commonly assume that all Italians, adults or children, are Catholics, and insist on treating them as such.

Religiously then, Italians both in Italy and America may be divided into four general groups: (1) All who are loyal to the Roman Church; (2) a larger group who are indifferent to religion; (3) the atheistic, anarchistic group, which is actively hostile to religion of whatever name; to this latter class belong the great throng of younger men who have lost faith in Roman Catholicism and who firmly believe that all religions are only worn-out superstitions, imposed upon ignorant people to keep them in subjection; (4) the membership of the evangelical churches.

(b) An objective. Religious work among Italians is no longer an experiment. The statistical table in the Appendix of "Religious Work Among Italians" indicates over 325 Protestant churches and missions employing the Italian language, with 14,000 members and over 15,000 in church or Sunday schools. The figures, moreover, do not in any adequate degree convey the influence which these 325 churches and missions are exerting in Italian communities. In the beginning of Italian work in this country many missions were started under serious limitations. Stores were rented and meagerly equipped; budgets were small and not always assured; leadership available was frequently poorly trained and as poorly paid. While many such enterprises have since developed into strong churches, it is the conviction of a number of leading denominational agencies that a bolder faith and larger enterprise ought now to characterize our work with Italians. When a new work is contemplated, the church or committee concerned ought to "count the cost." When the field has been carefully surveyed and the need demonstrated, a program should be drawn up forecasting the equipment required; provision should be made for a staff of thoroughly trained and competent workers; an ample budget should be assured. Unless it is the purpose of those concerned to carry the work through to some worthy conclusion, it were better and fairer to the Italians not to begin. The initial years of pioneering in this new home mission field have established a more or less definite form for an organized religious work among Italians. The Bureau of Foreign Work of the Board of Home Missions and Church Extension of the Methodist Episcopal Church has set up the following program of work for the local Italian church:

1. Approach to the family as a whole.

(a) Home visitor, a woman speaking Italian, with the American training and American spirit. Such a one, bilingual, could work with little children in English, and conduct older classes possibly in Italian. The problem is one of young women as well as mothers. The future objective is to be young Italian women thoroughly trained.

(b) Family gathering for everybody in the church parlors or church house. Music, games, pictures, etc. Recognize the family unit.

(c) Meetings in the home. The coming of the stranger draws all the neighbors in so that a program may be used. Special attention to home meetings for girls.

2. Approach in Italian for adult Italian groups.

(a) Religious services of worship in Italian. (Members of the staff should speak both English and Italian.)

(b) Volunteer workers: A lawyer, a physician, an employment agent, and a printer, whose services may be used for help among the Italians in the community.

(c) Mothers' clubs in Italian.

(d) Men's clubs for learning English and citizenship (civic questions, citizenship papers, etc.).

(e) Use of Italian literature.

(f) Religious instruction in Italian.

(g) Illustrated lectures.

(h) Italian patriotism as point of contact (Italian days, the 20th of September, Columbus Day, etc.).

(i) Make use of musical interest.

3. Approach in English to children and young people.

(a) Attendance at English church services.

(b) Religious instruction (Sunday school).

(c) Related week-day club activities, emphasis on expressional work, such as recreational clubs, gymnasium clubs, choral societies, dramatic clubs, Boy Scouts, Knights of King Arthur, Camp Fire Girls, Girl Scouts, sewing, painting, drawing, and sculpture.

(d) Illustrated lectures and moving pictures.

(e) Daily Vacation Bible school.

(f) Flower Mission.

(g) Fresh air work.

(h) Camps.

The conduct of religious work with Italians is discussed in a practical way by Mr. Mangano in "Sons of Italy," Chapter VI. Out of a wide range of experience and observation, recommendations are also made in "Religious Work Among Italians" concerning a more comprehensive attack, a plea for a better considered, adequately equipped, and worthily supported work for Italian communities. The question of workers, the message, literature, and publications are also discussed.

(c) *Leadership. The family* should be the unit of our interest. The adult members are seldom accessible except through the ministration of an Italian-speaking pastor or missionary. The trained and diligent Italian pastor knows his people and can best interpret the Christian message to them. Language is a strong bond. Where a new work may not warrant nor afford the undivided time of a pastor, occasional addresses or services, with home visitation by the nearest neighboring Italian-speaking pastor will help make the unselfish purpose of the work understood.

When an Italian pastor is to be engaged, a man of thorough training should be sought. He should speak both Italian and English and be resourceful in modes of educational and community work. In the beginning of the church's work with Italians in this country and when missionaries were difficult to obtain, many young Italians with a sincere Christian experience, but with limited training, were enlisted. Their work in many instances has been signally blessed. But with the steady growth of Italian evangelization and with opportunities now offered for training, the Italian ministry itself is urging that young men enlisting for this service should submit themselves to the most thorough preparation and that there should not be two standards of ministerial education, one for Americans and a lower standard for Italians.

On the part of the American church, it should sustain the Italian-speaking minister and his family with an adequate salary.

(d) *Equipment.* Where a church has become surrounded or is near an Italian community, it will cheerfully extend its facilities for Italian meetings and group activities. Its hospitality should be unmistakable and unstinted. A church that offers its basement or lecture room for Italian work, but is hesitant about the church auditorium, had better reconsider its motive. If it is necessary at the outset to begin work in a rented building or hall, see that the equipment is fresh and new. Do not send the old and tuneless piano or organ, or the discarded hymn books. If possible, let the room devoted to worship be maintained exclusively for such purposes. The Italian sense of reverence cannot associate the place of worship with an ice cream party.

Where a new building is to be erected, however small, the best architectural consideration should be given to its design. A building in the simple yet pleasing style of the early Tuscan architecture carried out in brick will be thoroughly acceptable. Great interest should be given to the place of worship. It should be set apart from the rooms designed for educational and social purposes.

(e) *Departmental Work.* Where a church is near an Italian community it may find a number of opportunities for distinctive work with Italians. The following are among methods which have been successfully employed:

Home visitation.
English classes.
Civic clubs.
Week-day craft school.
Visiting nurse.
Mothers' clubs.
Daily Vacation Bible school.
Boys' clubs or Boy Scouts.
Stereopticon lectures.

If the occasional services of an Italian-speaking minister may be secured, through visitation and a series of lectures or evangelistic meetings, the purpose of the work may be made clearer to the Italian community.

Work thus begun may lead to the employment of an Italian-speaking visitor or minister. Such a worker should be recognized as a member of the church staff. While a church wholly given over to an Italian congregation, with its own pastor and official boards, may be an ideal arrangement, there are a number of illustrations of English-speaking churches which are maintaining with great encouragement a departmental work in Italian. In most cases services of worship are maintained in Italian, while all children attend the same Sunday school. A work of this sort calls for a generous spirit of accommodation.

(f) *Literature and Bibles.* Four weekly papers are published by denominational societies in the Italian language. The tendency is to print the Sunday school lesson and other articles of interest to the young people in English. These papers will be pleased to furnish terms concerning club rates or sample packages for distribution.

"Il Cristiano." American Baptist Publication Society, 18 Jackson street, Brooklyn, N. Y.; C. Buffa, editor. Subscription price, $1 a year.

"La Fiaccola." (The Italian Christian Advocate.) Methodist Book Concern, 150 Fifth avenue, New York City; Piero M. Petacci, editor. Subscription price, $1 a year.

"L'Era Nuova." Presbyterian Board of Publication and Sabbath School Work, 114 East 116th street, New York City; F. J. Panetta, editor. Subscription price, $1 a year.

"Il Vessillo." Board of Home Missions, United Presbyterian Church, 7716 Tioga street, Pittsburg, Pa.; Michael Renzetti, editor. Subscription price, $1 a year.

The distribution of tract literature should be carried on with discrimination. The following, published by the American Tract Society, 101 Park avenue, New York, have been recommended:

Envelope Series (In Italian)
(Price, 1,000 pages for $1 and postage 12 cents extra)

No.		Pages
1.	"Good News for You"	4
6.	"How a Garibaldian Soldier Became a Soldier of Christ"	8
9.	"Turn the Key" (Temperance)	12
10.	"Jesus Christ for Everybody"	8
13.	"Why Should I Read the Bible?"	8
14.	"You, Me, or Anybody Else"	8
15.	"The Dying Drummer Boy"	12
16.	"Looking Unto Jesus"	4

Hymn Books

"Il Nuovo Innario Evangelico." Rev. Stefano L. Testa and Rev. Agide Pirazzini, editors. With tunes, cloth 8vo., 50 cents. Words only, 25 cents. (Half price for mission purposes.)

The Bibliography of "Sons of Italy," and the list of leaflets, pamphlets, periodicals, lectures, etc., given in the "Suggestions to Leaders" on "Sons of Italy" give very complete and valuable information on literature.

The American Bible Society, Bible House, New York (or nearest depository: Atlanta, Chicago, Richmond, Denver, San Francisco, Dallas, Brooklyn, Cincinnati, Philadelphia), publishes Bibles, New Testaments, and single Gospels in the Italian language. The following numbers will prove acceptable:

Italian No. 4. Italian Bible (Diodati). Roan, burnished red edge. With references, family record, and maps. Small pica type. Size, quarto. 8 x 10 inches. (Family Bible.) Price, $2.25 each.

Italian No. 8. Italian Bible (Diodati). Cloth, red edge. Brevier type. Size, 12 mo. 5 x 7¾ inches. Price, 63 cents each.

Italian No. 12. Italian Bible (Diodati). Cloth, red edge. With references and maps. Minion type. Size, 16 mo. 4¾ x 6¾ inches. Price, 28 cents each.

Italian No. 26. Italian and English New Testament. Parallel columns. Brevier type. Size, 12 mo. 4¾ x 7 inches. Price, 42 cents each.

Italian No. 28. Italian New Testament and Psalms. Pica type. Size, 8vo. 5¾ x 8¼ inches. Price, 50 cents each.

Italian No. 32. Italian New Testament and Psalms. Long primer type. Size, 12mo. 5 x 7 inches. Price, 25 cents each.

Italian No. 45. Italian and English St. Matthew. Parallel columns. Brevier type. Size, 12mo. 4¼ x 6¾ inches. Cloth, cut flush, red edge. Price, 14 cents each.

Italian Nos. 46–49. Single Gospels. Cloth, cut finish, flexible, round corners, plain edge. Brevier type. Size, 2¾ x 4¾ inches. Price, 3 cents.

(g) *The Church and Social Justice for the Italian.* It will be frankly recognized that many of the modes of service suggested in this pamphlet are after all but efforts to alleviate conditions which have no place in a Christian social order. They do not go to the root of the matter. The Italian immigrant is the marginal worker. He is the last man in. His needs are urgent. His wages are small. He must frequently attempt to sustain a family on an annual income of $600. Here follows a whole chain of untoward circumstances. To secure social justice for the Italian immigrant and his fellow immigrant workers is a field of service in which all churches must engage.

Correspondence

Information concerning any of the books referred to in this pamphlet may be had by addressing your denominational home mission quarters; or the Missionary Education Movement, 156 Fifth avenue, New York, will forward your request, together with any other inquiries you may make, to the proper headquarters, if you will mention the name of your church or denomination.

Co-operating Agencies

The following agencies will furnish literature and suggestions bearing on community service. In writing, state with all possible definiteness the problem you are confronting.

Federal Council of the Churches of Christ in America. Constituted by thirty Protestant denominations. Rev. Charles S. MacFarland, general secretary; 105 E. 22d street, New York. Commission on the Church and Social Service. Rev. Worth M. Tippy, executive secretary. Campaign for the Conservation of Human Life; and "Strengthen America" campaign in the interest of nation-wide prohibition. Charles Stelzle, secretary.

Russell Sage Foundation. For the improvement of living conditions. John M. Glenn, director, 130 E. 22d street, New York.

Department of Surveys and Exhibits. Shelby M. Harrison, director; E. G. Routzahn, associate director.

Library: open free to public; one of the best working collections in the United States on sociology and social work; Frederick Warren Jenkins, librarian.

Playground and Recreation Association of America. Howard Braucher, secretary, 1 Madison avenue, New York.

Playground activities, equipment, and administration; community centers; field work in communities; rural recreation; physical efficiency tests for boys and girls. Pamphlet A 105, "Athletic Badge Test for Boys" (5 cents), and A 121, "Athletic Badge Test for Girls" (5 cents), specially recommended. Send for list of publications. National Kindergarten Association, 250 Madison avenue, New York. Object: To have the kindergarten established in every public school. Furnishes bulletins, exhibits, lecturers, advice, and information.

National Consumers' League. Mrs. Florence Kelley, general secretary, 289 Fourth avenue, New York. 87 branch leagues. 15,000 members. War program: To help our industrial army by promoting clinics for treatment of new diseases (incident to munitions work and to fatigue and strain); reasonable working hours; safe and sanitary working conditions; decent standards of living; safeguards for women taking men's places in industry; protection for children. Minimum membership, $2.

National League of Women Workers. Jean Hamilton, organization secretary, 35 E. 30th street, New York. Evening clubs for girls; recreation and instruction in self-governing and supporting groups for girls over working age.

National Association for the Study and Prevention of Tuberculosis. 105 E. 22d street, New York. Organization of tuberculosis compaigns; tuberculosis hospitals, clinics, nurses, etc.; open air schools; Red Cross seals, educational methods, etc.

National Child Labor Committee. Owen R. Lovejoy, secretary, 105 E. 22d street, New York. Thirty-five state branches. Industrial and agricultural investigations; legislation; enforcement; education; mothers' pensions; juvenile delinquency; health; recreation.

National Child Welfare Exhibit Association, Inc. 70 Fifth avenue, New York. Educational health posters covering care of babies and children. Second edition of Parcel Post Exhibit. Photogravure reproductions in color with simple, easily understood legends, attractively illustrated from original paintings; 25 posters (18 x 28) in set. Further information regarding these and other exhibits on request. Illustrated booklets on Baby and Child Care. Lantern slides.

National organization for Public Health Nursing. Ella Phillips Crandall, R. N., executive secretary, 600 Lexington avenue, New York. Object: To stimulate the extension of public health nursing.

Travelers' Aid Society. Orin C. Baker, general secretary, 465 Lexington avenue, New York. Provides advice, guidance and protection to travelers, especially women and girls.

Neighbors' League of America. Mrs. Edward H. Scott, registrar, room 1017, 23 E. 26th street, New York. Civics and English for foreigners.

Girl Scouts, Inc. Dr. Abby Porter Leland, executive secretary, 527 Fifth avenue, New York. Camp Fire Girls, Inc. Dr. Luther H. Gulick, president, 461 Fourth avenue, New York.

Boy Scouts of America. James E. West, chief executive of the National Council of Boy Scouts of America, 200 Fifth avenue, New York.

c. Letters from Pastors

The pastor of the Bethlehem Memorial Church of the Gospel, King street, New York City, reports on the activities of his church as follows:

"We have a membership of 98, and our congregation is made up entirely of Italians who do not understand enough English so that we may have services in English. We have no classes for them but many of them attend the public schools. We approve of Americanization and do all that we can along this line, especially with the younger generation."

The Reverend Joseph A. Villelli, pastor of the Church of the Sea and Land, Henry street, New York City, reports as follows:

"We have a membership of 86 and possibly 50 attendants who are not members, all of whom speak Italian, but only 35 per cent. understand enough English so that they would understand services in English. We have classes in sewing and cooking which are attended by about 150. The teachers do not speak Italian and they are volunteers. This church has always stood for Americanization. Since the very beginning of this Italian work in 1904 we have always conducted English and civics classes for the Italians, but in 1913, wishing to teach not only those connected with the church, but even outsiders, I personally had the privilege of teaching English and civics at Public School 65, a few blocks from the church for a period of five consecutive years. Owing to the fact that almost all public schools now have English classes for foreigners, we turn our men to them. All our men have taken out either their first or second papers. It is our policy to urge them to do it."

The Reverend Paul D. Elsesser, pastor of the French Evangelical Church, West 16th street, New York City, reports as follows:

"We have 656 members and about 600 attendants who are not members. Our services are in French, but part of our people understand English well. We do not have English classes in the church, but we encourage our people to attend classes in our French Y. M. C. A. We have had some English classes in the past for women in our French Y. M. C. A., but these classes were discontinued on account of poor attendance. As a rule the members of our church and congregation have a good education and appreciate the United States."

The pastor of the Jan Hus Bohemian Church, East 74th street, New York City, reports as follows:

"All the older people in our congregation speak only Bohemian, there being about 200 such, but the younger generation are for the most part American born. All our sermons are in Bohemian. We expect to start classes in English, but have not as yet done so. When we did have classes we had people between 30 and 40 years of age, and the attendance was pretty regular. We have volunteers from among our church members for teachers. All our people are American in spirit, but most of them never had the chance to learn English. They worked among the Bohemian speaking people, lived in the Bohemian colony, and hardly ever came in contact with the English speaking people. Of course, all their children are able to speak and read and write the English language."

The Reverend Paul Sibilio, pastor of the Spring Street Presbyterian Church, report as follows:

"We have about 182 church members, 20 attendants who are not members, but our social work reaches 200 who are not church members. All our people speak Italian, for those who can understand English are sent to the English church.

"We have had classes in past years to teach English, which were well organized and well attended. At present we have no classes, because people are too anxious to work overtime and make all the money they can and thus take advantage of the present crisis in the scarcity of labor. When we do have classes, they meet four times a week the year round, and each session is two hours long. The instruction is free, and we divide the pupils according to their grade of education, which is not done in the public evening schools, where all students are put in the same class whether they are illiterate or University students in their own country. Our students average 25 years of age and their attendance is regular. We also teach American history, civics, and the requisites to become American citizens. We write the first and second papers for them. All those who enter our English classes are obliged to take the other courses also. Our teachers are volunteers from New York University and Columbia. They do not speak Italian, but we feel that this does not matter. Our churches are doing everything possible to Americanize the Italians and all other races in our district. Judging from the applications to have first and final papers written, they show their appreciation and their desire to become American citizens.

"Our churches at Spring street work very earnestly for purpose of improving the education and the moral character of our foreign population in our district. We had free evening schools, as I said before when we were able to find people interested in it, and we have now rooms for clubs for those people, social entertainments, conferences and lectures and we try to make them enjoy their spare time in the effort of improving their education and have them spend their time in a profitable way.

"And now a word about our evening school and the public evening school.

"When our evening schools were open, they were appreciated and regularly attended by the students more than the public evening schools, because in our small classes they were able to learn more speedily, because each class was made up of people of the same grade of instruction.

"The public school must have:

"A class for those young men who wish to improve their education which was neglected at time of their boyhood in this country. Of this class there are too many who neglected to go regularly to the school or they did not profit when they were boys, and were going to the public school in this country, and they now wish to return to school to improve their education and they must have a separate class.

"A class for those who are in the very meaning of the word adult illiterates.

"A class for those who know their native language.

"A class for those who are very highly educated and in many cases were college and university men in their native country.

"I am speaking of the school as means of improving the education and character of foreign people because I do not think that all the policemen with their clubs can improve the character and education of those people who are causing so many troubles in this city, as they did at Washington Square some time ago. I saw all, because I live there."

Letter from F. E. Wilber, Associated Director of Labor Temple, December 24, 1919:

"Labor Temple conducts classes in the English language and the principles of American citizenship, throughout the year — three summer months excepted. We do not aim at large numbers, and our present enrollment is twenty-eight. They represent about a dozen nationalities. We are co-operating with the Board of Education in these classes."

2. METHODIST

Dr. Millard L. Robinson, executive secretary of the New York Society of the Methodist Episcopal Church, formerly known as the City Church Extension and Missionary Society of the Methodist Church, appeared before the Committee in a public hearing on January 16, 1920, and gave, in substance, the following outline of the activities of the Methodist Church in New York City among the foreign-born:

The field of this society's activities is confined to the boroughs of Manhattan and the Bronx, and our religious work takes us into the communities where the foreign-born live.

We have been teaching English to foreigners for many years, at several points, but particularly at our church of All Nations on Second avenue on the lower East Side.

A person who is competent in the English language and sympathetic with foreign-speaking peoples has been the type that we have used for teachers. Where we have been able to develop competent teachers from among the foreign-born themselves, we have found them most useful.

We conduct naturalization courses and courses in civics for the foreign-born, and we have lectures and forums.

We are setting up in Harlem a plan which we think will be of far-reaching results among the Italian people there. We have taken what was formerly Trinity Methodist Church and are developing it into a community center for the Italian people. Here we shall have evening classes for foreign-born men, but the special features will be for the women. We shall have a day nursery where little children may be left during the day when it is necessary for their mothers to work. The thing which many of the mothers who have been deserted feel the need of, is something which will enable them to keep their family together and make it unnecessary for them to send their children to orphanages. In many cases where the Italian mother is a widow, her husband was not naturalized and she is not, therefore, entitled to the widow's pension. We propose to have workrooms where these Italian women may learn to work on muslin undergarments and be paid for their work, so that they will have this means of keeping their families together.

It has been our experience in working among the Italians that our efforts have a wholesome Americanizing effect upon them and that they display some of the finest patriotism that comes to our attention.

I think the government could make a real contribution in the training of teachers for Americanization work, and that these teachers, if they are right spirited, could co-operate with the church centers and other agencies to further the work of Americanization.

I do not believe in compulsory education for adult foreign-born, but I feel that the facilities for voluntarily learning English and becoming an American will be taken advantage of as fast as we make them easily available.

Following is a list of some of the Mehodist churches in New York City where a foreign language is spoken and where many of the members are foreign-born:

Chinese: Chinese Mission, 11 Doyer street.
German: 1841 Bathgate avenue.
140 East 103d street.
456 East 158th street.
48 St. Marks place.
350 West 40th street.
320 East 55th street.
Italian: 69 Madison street.
9 Second avenue.
543 East 11th street.
407 East 114th street.
157 East 150th street.
Japanese: 131 West 104th street.
Norwegian: Kelley and 167th streets.
Swedish: 207 St. James place, Brooklyn.
1163 Fox street.
323 East 50th street.

3. EPISCOPALIAN

a. Testimony of Dr. Thomas Burgess

In a public hearing before the Committee on January 16, 1920, Dr. Thomas Burgess, secretary of the Department of Missions, appeared to describe the proposed work of the Episcopal Church which is to be known as Church Work of Foreign Born Americans. His testimony in substance was as follows:

The department for Church Work on Foreign Born Americans was started in June, 1919. At present I am secretary, and I have only a field director by way of assistance. We have $34,000, and hope to get $1,500,000.

There are three fundamental policies in connection with our proposed work among the foreign born. The first is definitely religious, for we feel that religion is the foundation of true Americanism. We shall have religious services in foreign languages whenever it is necessary, but we shall work toward a universal use of English. We shall encourage our churches in the foreign sections to minister socially to their foreign-born neighbors, and in this connection we are getting the advice of all the racial experts in our church.

The second phase of our work will be publishing in foreign languages constructive propaganda.

The third item on our program will be to bring the foreign-born into contact with Americans and American institutions, including public educational facilities.

We have practically consummated a union between our church and the Russian Church, and between our church and the Greek Church, and there is a movement afoot to have the service of the Russian Church in the English language. Of the 300 Russian priests in America, by the way, 60 have never been in Russia. All these priests look to us constantly for advice, especially in the matter of dealing with the radical elements in their congregations. In Detroit, the Bolshevist element succeeded in closing up a Greek church, but the priest by legal measures had the church restored to him.

b. Conference on Christian Americanization

PLAN AND BUDGET PROPOSED — DEPARTMENT OF CHRISTIAN AMERICANIZATION

Sent to all those invited to conference of Church Leaders, Tuesday, September 23d, at 10 A. M., Board Room Church Missions House, New York.

RESULTS OF CONFERENCE

The all-day conference of those especially experienced or interested in the work of Christian Americanization, September 23,

1919, at Church Missions House, called to advise with the secretary of Christian Americanization, unanimously endorsed the plan and budget submitted, and adopted the following resolutions:

1. *Resolved*, That we endorse the Budget and Plan for Central Organization, and divisions of work submitted by Rev. Thomas Burgess, secretary of Christian Americanization, at this meeting, and we earnestly request its favorable consideration by the Board of Missions and the Committee of the Nation-Wide Campaign, and that they present the same to the General Convention.

2. *Resolved*, That a committee of three members of the House of Bishops, and three of the House of Deputies be requested to see that the contents of the Budget and Plan for a Central Organization and work, endorsed at this meeting, be adequately presented to the General Convention.

3. *Resolved*, That we request the Board of Missions to change the Bureau of Christian Americanization into a special department with appropriate title.

4. *Resolved*, That it is the sense of this meeting that the publication of literature for the use of our Christian brethren of other rites is within the province of the Department of Americanization, and to this end we suggest a republication of the translation of the Orthodox Prayer Book translated by Miss Hapgood, and the establishment of a press for the publication of service books and other literature for the Syrians and Assyrians.

5. *Resolved*, That the Committee on Enrichment of the Prayer Book be requested to provide for some ultimate form for hypothetical confirmation.

6. *Whereas*, The Metropolitan of Athens has requested that the Episcopal Church, through its House of Bishops, definitely state whether the gift of orders is held to be a sacrament or not; be it

Resolved, That we request the Bishop of Harrisburg, acting for the Commission on Relation to Orthodox Churches, to procure a satisfactory expression from the House of Bishops.

7. *Whereas*, The Metropolitan of Athens has requested on several occasions that the Episcopal Church co-operate in the spiritual regeneration of those parts now released from Turkish rule; and

Whereas, Request has come from the Czecho-Slovaks, asking similar assistance; be it

Resolved, That we ask the Committee on Relation to Orthodox Churches and Old Catholics to consider this request, and make such recommendations as seem proper to the General Convention.

Among those present were: Bishops Burch, Lines, Israel, Darlington and Garland; the Reverend Wm. T. Manning, W. G. Anthony, Dean Bratenahl; H. D. Jones, J. R. Harding, Paul Micou, J. G. Hammarskold, T. J. Lacey, J. L. Zacker, L. A. Edelblute, Archdeacon Webb, C. B. Ackley, Northey Jones, E. J. Lee, W. C. Emhardt, Thomas Burgess, Messrs. C. R. Woodruff, J. R. Goushay, Paul Shimmon.

c. Report on Christian Americanization

"*E Pluribus Unum*"

FOREIGN MISSIONS AT HOME

Americanization of the foreign-born and their children is the foremost problem of our country's after-war reconstruction. Some 20,000,000 people in the United States are of foreign birth; nearly half of these cannot read or write the English language. They have, in general, been neglected, unappreciated, forced to segregate, not given the opportunities for touch with what is best in American life. This is our fault. These neighbors of ours are a means, or a menace; a means, if given a friendly hand, to the upbuilding of our country; a menace, if let alone to be organized by the forces of discontent.

Awakened to the need and the menace, our government, schools, industrial corporations and countless agencies and societies are working at Americanization in earnest.

The achievement of assimilation, however, and a safe democracy requires religion. Man is a spiritual being, and his whole nature cannot be transformed except by spiritual influences. The state and secular agencies can touch only the intellectual part of man, and in part minister to his physical well-being.

Far more than one-half of these foreign-born, energetic, industrious, and ten times as prolific as the natives, are not here attached to any Christian body whatever. Nor will the situation be altered much numerically by either the stoppage of immigration or the large emigration. If, through the neglect of our church or others, the foreign-born and their children are allowed to develop with their spiritual nature untouched, and the result be a revolution which shall sweep away the old ideals, and this Republic cease to be, upon whom will the responsibility for the disaster rest?

Other churches have recognized their responsibility, and for some years past have been expending millions in study, organization, training, equipment, publication, workers. They have invested boldly, and their investments have yielded splendid results. Had our church, instead of doing in general nothing, but made a like investment, we would have gained far more; for the majority of the unchurched immigrants have lapsed from churches of liturgical worship, full gospel, episcopal ministry, sacramental life. It is not a matter of proselyting, but of shepherding the unshepherded; of saving countless lives from atheism, and our country from its result.

Moreover, our American Church itself, needs the richness of spiritual life that will come from the effort to provide for men of every race. These foreign neighbors of ours have as much to give us as we have to give them. They can make this Church really American as America itself.

The millions of unchurched children of the foreign-born are a great menace and a great opportunity. Their criminal record is increasingly above that of the native-born. They look down upon their parents, and sadly absorb American independence with the vices instead of the virtues. Yet, with those who have been given the opportunity, their achievements have been notable.

Where, here and there, our Church has tried at this problem, despite lack of organization, policy, training, and, except in a few cases, proper equipment, we have gained notable results. We have a good nucleus of experienced workers for the beginning. What we have accomplished may be multiplied a hundred-fold throughout the nation, if our Church people will.

This year, at last, our Board of Missions has created a special department of domestic missions, Christian Americanization. This department, in constant consultation with those who best know, including the Federal Department of the Interior, have formulated definite, large, nation-wide, thoroughly American policies and plans. We must do it in large, or not at all. This is a high venture for Christ and our country.

We believe that for the Americanization of the people of this country or from any other country, there is no power equal to that of the religion of Jesus Christ, and that it is only through this that our nation can be welded into one.

General Policy Proposed

This department proposes to push and advise on "Americanization," on its secularly patriotic side in co-operation with government, voluntary and religious organization.

Act as the center of initiative, co-ordinating and invigorating existing work, and suggesting, organizing and putting through new work.

Be the clearing house of experience, advice and encouragement, and center of supply.

Arouse the whole Church to personal responsibility and aggressive action, that we may be truly neighbors to the immigrant and his children, cause them to become good citizens; and provide for the multitudes of unshepherded, religious education, pastoral care and the sacraments.

Give all help possible through field agents and racial experts in carrying out parochial, diocesan and provincial proposals, organizing special work, and putting the immigrant and the parish in touch with each other everywhere.

Furnish literature and speakers to stimulate and instruct our own people, and bilingual tracts, periodicals, etc., for the foreign speaking.

Almost all literature on the subject has been filed, and will be selected and made available for our people.

Find, train adequately and furnish the men and women, clerical and lay, to fill the field.

To do this, as has already been done by the department, periodical conferences with our Church leaders on the subject are necessary.

Central Organization

The operating force need be but four men with office help.

We have since June 1, 1919, just the secretary.

We need, to accomplish the work adequately, an assistant secretary, a field director, and an assistant field director.

A number of instructive and picturesque booklets, pamphlets, etc., are needed. (For *all* budgets, substitute attached corrected budgets.)

Budget

Office	1 year	3 years
Secretary	$3,852*	$11,556
Assistant	2,675	8,025
Traveling	1,500	4,500
Stenographer	1,200	3,600
Expenses	600	1,800
Printing	2,000	6,000
Conferences	800	2,400
	$12,627	$37,881

Field		
Director	$3,424	$10,272
Three months abroad	3,000	3,000
Assistant	2,675	8,025
Stenographer	1,000	3,000
Traveling	2,500	7,500
Expenses	300	900
	$12,899	$32,697

NOTE.— Should there not be an emergency fund, which may be used for giving support to diocesan proposals not unearthed by the present survey as are sure to turn up as soon as the Church begins to adequately awaken to this newly begun opportunity, and to adequately function?

Say, $50,000 a year, $150,000 three years.

THE DEVELOPMENT OF LEADERSHIP

The primary essential in dealing with the complex problem of the immigrant and his children are leaders who because they understand can reach.

The great barrier between the foreign and the native-born is mutual misunderstanding.

The mistakes and failures of some of our sporadic efforts to reach the immigrant have been due to the lack of training of the leaders.

---

* To all clergy salaries are added 7 **per cent** pension premium.

The complexity of the problem is as complex as the present map of Europe. The war and the present racial mixups in Europe have taught us how complex this is. Each race has its distinct background, and its predispositions. They do not lose them when they come to America, nor do we wish them to lose all.

Of course, it is hard for a pure-blooded American to understand his immigrant neighbor. But we can learn, and those who are going to try to minister to them must have adequate training.

Men of their own race can best understand their own people. They are essential as leaders not only because of language, but because of full understanding. But such leaders must be thoroughly Americanized themselves, and thoroughly trained in both what America and the Church are.

What Others are Doing.— Every large denomination and many smaller have seminaries, training colleges and schools, special professorships, scholarships and fellowships — large attention to adequate training for this special work.

What We Have.— No attempt have we made to train foreign students, nor our regular seminary students and lay workers for such work.

A few foreign-born students, or those of the second generation, take, on their own initiative, seminary courses.

Policy Proposed.— Establish as their specialty in two of our Church schools, one in the Middle West and one in the East, extensive and intensive training for Divinity students of foreign birth or parentage, and for those of American lineage who wish to take up this work.

Establish special courses in other Church institutions for training Divinity students and laymen and women workers.

Fellowships for sending abroad picked students, for college education of boys and girls of foreign parentage who give promise of future leadership.

Scholarships for seminary courses for foreign-born or their children, for courses of training of women lay workers.

Regular courses are already arranged to be given in our seminaries and deaconess schools on the general subject, that all our coming clergy and deaconesses may be fitted to meet the opportunities for this work, which are sure to be found wherever they may be.

Budget

	1 year	3 years
New equipment	$175,000	$175,000
Eight professorships, at $2,500	20,000	60,000
Ten Divinity scholarships, at $500	5,000	15,000
Twelve collegiate scholarships, at $500	6,000	18,000
Ten woman workers, at $500	5,000	15,000
Four fellowships abroad, at $1,500	6,000	18,000
Library books	900	2,700
Special lecturers	1,200	3,600
	$219,100	$307,300

DOWNTOWN POLYGLOT MASSES

The fact of the crowded, segregated foreign-speaking masses in our great cities is too well known for comment.

Each year more heathens are made from perfectly good Christians in New York or Chicago than Christians are made from heathens in all the foreign mission fields combined. Bolsheviki and the like are created simply because anarchistic leaders take an interest in the immigrant and loyal Americans do not. The former holds up a rosy ideal of false social freedom and the immigrant grasps it. Can you blame him, for the true ideals of American freedom have never been presented to him at all.

What We Have.— A few churches in our large cities are meeting this need, as in New York, Chicago, Philadelphia and Sacramento.

Where we have not abandoned downtown churches, we have some plaints of dying ones. Or we have those which will soon be dying unless they change into this catholic policy — by catholic we mean in the sense that the Church is for everyone, not the select few.

Policy Proposed.— The reorganizing and reviving of some of these almost dead parishes by establishing with diocesan permission, under the direct control of the Department of Christian Americanization, experimental stations, so to speak, where the thorough workability of this plan can be proven. This in our largest cities.

Where parishes are not so far gone, but are becoming isolated from their former constituency, urge them and help them to minister to the neglected multitudes at their very doors.

We should put in the various fields a corps of specially trained social workers.

We can back them up with our workers' settlement and other secular or religious social organizations.

Budget

	1 year	3 years
Remodeling and equipping	$50,000	$50,000
Three clergy in charge, at $3,210	9,630	28,890
Six assistants, at $1,926	11,556	34,668
Six women workers, at $1,000	6,000	18,000
Other workers	4,000	12,000
Maintenance	6,000	18,000
Conferences	400	1,200
Adding to existing staffs	7,000	21,000
	$94,586	$183,758

Industrial Polyglot Groups

In all parts of the country in industrial cities are groups of men, women and children of many races, herded together in segregated colonies, in conditions dangerous to themselves and to us. In the mining districts like things prevail. We have fifty cities of more than 100,000.

In most places we have established parishes with all the equipment for the needed religious and social ministrations. Some parishes have taken up the work among their immigrant neighbors of all races and accomplished fine results. Many others are ready to do it, but timid because the Church as a whole has not taken an interest nor expressed a policy.

Policy Proposed.— Furnish trained clergy and deaconesses and other workers to assist such parishes, devoting their whole time to their work, and helping through field directors, literature, etc., to organize and equip the work.

Establish experimental stations, with the consent of the diocesan and parish authorities, which may be under direct control of the Department of Christian Americanization, where their full plans may be worked out. Place woman workers trained for the purpose in cities where they may put immigrant families in touch with church families and so into the parishes.

Also occasional services in foreign languages are necessary to make and keep the point of contact. For this foreign language speaking clergy could divide their time among a number of places.

Budget

	1 year	3 years
Five clergy assistants, at $1,926	$9,630	$28,890
Twelve woman workers, at $1,000	12,000	36,000
Ten foreign-speaking clergy	19,260	57,780
Conferences	500	1,500
	$41,390	$124,170

Rural Field

Not all our immigrants by any means have settled in New York and Chicago, nor in factory and mining cities and towns. The older immigration of Swedes, Norwegians and Germans fill the Dakotas and Minnesota, and because they are in the majority they keep to the full their language, and so are out of touch with Americans and Americanization — like the Pennsylvania Dutch who migrated 200 years ago and have remained the same. Nebraska is also full of Czechs — we used to call them Bohemians. Now we love to honor them by their own name. Italians, Jews, Poles and Portuguese find the Hudson Valley and New England farms attractive settling places. And on many a farm the Dane longs for a church like his own, and does not realize that it is but a few miles away.

Our rural missionaries and archdeacons would find a far bigger result from the foreigner fresh from the real religious influences of his fatherland, than from the degenerate native whose religious ideals are things lost two or three generations ago.

For the solving of this problem, no definite plan has yet been evolved, but a general survey, and during the summer months the sending into various sections a number of student colporteurs, should uncover much and put a number of people in touch with our rural missionaries.

Budget

	1 year	3 years
Twenty summer colporteurs, at $100	$2,000	$6,000
Special survey	600	1,800
	$2,600	$7,800

The Particular Races

Our Church has a great opportunity with several particular races of certain classes. These particular classes of races are our particular wards. We alone can reach them adequately. Secretaries of other Mission Boards have from time to time told us: "Why don't you do something? We are spending men and money and we can do little compared with you. These races are your particular job."

From time to time clergy of some of these races have come to us and asked to enter our ministry, and we have been obliged to turn them down.

These particular classes to whom it is our particular duty to show what true America means, and to bring them into or keep them in the fellowship of Christ's religion; these are the Scandanavian Episcopalians, the members of the Eastern Orthodox and other Eastern churches, the lapsed Roman Catholics, especially the Italians, the Czechs, who never have been Roman Catholic at heart, and our own neglected Anglican Welsh.

Each of these constitute a different and distinct problem.

The ultimate aim is to make all these thorough American Christians, adding to American life all the riches they bring from their former homeland. Also they must be brought to worship God in our own language. The foreign language and instruction service is but a temporary make-shift. Nevertheless, it is a necessary one. For one cannot communicate thoughts to another except he be understood, both in language and symbol.

Moreover, only the clergy of a particular race can fully understand the predispositions of their own race, and so establish the necessary point of contact and adequately reach.

To the above particular classes we American churchmen can fulfill our wondrous opportunity and duty, if we will go at it in the large for our God and our country.

Italians

There are over 4,000,000 in the United States, including their native-born children. There is not a state in the Union without Italians; not only in most of our important cities, but in many of the smaller, their numbers are very large.

Their largest centers are New York — perhaps the largest Italian city in the world — Philadelphia, Chicago, San Francisco,

Providence, New Haven, Bridgeport, etc. Probably over one-third are utterly unchurched.

What We Have Done.— We have twenty-two Italian missionaries in active work, and a few deaconesses and women workers. In New York fourteen Italian missions. The others are in Chicago, Gary, Ind.; Youngstown, Ohio; Wind Gap, Pa.; Philadelphia, Boston, Hartford and Bridgeport, Conn.

The work for the most part is poorly equipped, yet most successful, but it is only a drop in the bucket of what we can and should do.

Policy Proposed.— The scope of the Italian work is much more than parochial. It is like that of the Indian, Negro, Chinese, etc., a special nation-wide problem.

It needs unification in training and method, not isolated experiments.

Building churches and chapels suitable for the Italian's need of color and light.

Training and providing more Italian clergy.

Providing deaconesses and women workers, who are essential in the proper conduct of the work among children and mothers.

Teaching American children citizenship and ideals, lessons in English.

Providing at least two itinerant Italian missionaries to survey and establish work in new places.

Publication of a periodical in Italian and English, and other literature for Americanization and religious education.

Budget

	1 year	3 years
Two general missionaries	$4,000	$12,000
Traveling expenses	2,000	6,000
Supplementing salaries	12,000	36,000
Two colporteurs	2,400	7,200
Hymnal	2,200	6,600
Periodical	3,000	9,000
Other publications	1,000	3,000
Emergency equipment fund	1,000	3,000
Six woman workers	6,000	18,000
Conferences	500	1,500
	$34,100	$102,300

Scandinavians

Scandinavians, foreign- and native-born, in the United States, number about 4,000,000, 4 per cent. of our total population. About one-half are Swedes, one-fourth Norwegians and one-fourth Danes. They are found in every state of the Union, but especially in the mid-West, Northeast and far-West. They are intelligent, thrifty, a solid part of our population. They came from lands where the National churches are Episcopal. They were brought up on the collects, epistles and gospels, a liturgy much like our own; careful preparation for Confirmation, deep reverence for Holy Communion; but in the United States nearly 3,000,000 of them are unchurched.

We have a special duty and opportunity toward these, which could and should have been adequately fulfilled long ago — to minister to the neglected children of our sister Episcopal churches, and the Americanization of these misunderstood people; bring them to think and worship in our American language.

What We Have Done.— Bishop Kemper and his Swedish pupil, the first graduate of Nashotah, began work in Chicago sixty years ago, and for some years a successful work was done, which recognized the orders of the Swedish Church.

Since 1887 other work was carried on, increasingly in different parts of the country, with several Swedish priests and a Swedish general missioner under the Board of Missions. Despite lack of much support, thousands of Scandinavians have become through our work thoroughly Americanized and good churchmen, till they are scattered all over the country in our regular English-speaking parishes — about 29,000.

We have seventeen parishes and organized missions under the care of eleven men of Swedish birth in priests' orders; 5,681 have been presented for Confirmation by these. From 1887 to 1919, our Swedish clergy have baptized 23,792 children.

Policy Proposed.— The work should aid in every way the policy of assimilation, with services in English introduced as soon as possible. Children desire services in English.

All men ordained for work among the Scandinavians to preach and conduct services in English as well as in the Scandinavian languages.

Work of putting Scandinavian people in touch with our English-speaking parishes can easily be accomplished, as it has been, if we have a proper working force.

There should be four general Scandinavian missionaries or, as the Scandinavians would prefer to call them, provosts or deans.

Salaries of clergy should be supplemented until these become self-supporting.

As with other races, so especially with this, special professorship for training workers is needed, and scholarships for students.

A periodical in the Scandinavian languages and English, also is needed.

Budget

	1 year	3 years
Four provosts	$11,128	$33,384
Traveling expenses	2,400	7,200
Supplemental salaries	10,000	30,000
Periodical	3,000	9,000
Other publications	1,000	3,000
Emergency equipment fund	500	1,500
Conferences	800	2,400
	$28,828	$86,484

The Czecho-Slovaks

Three-quarters of a million of this fascinating race are our neighbors in the United States, from the Connecticut Valley and Bohemia, N. Y., to Moravia, Tex., and Seattle, Wash.; 100,000 are in Chicago, 50,000 in New York, a large number in Nebraska.

They are thrifty, law abiding, careful of their children, as a rule property owners; prosperous farmers, in the Northwest; when in tenement districts, considered, so say New York authorities, as the cleanest of the city's poor.

The rise of their nation from the Great War, is known and admired by all. When asked confidentially what is their religion, they say, "The Jan Hus Church," an ancient sister Church to ours.

Our opportunity is unique and must be grasped now; nor are they to be reached by ways anything like any other foreign race.

In America, Czechs, hardened by centuries of ecclesiastical oppression, fought shy of any church, and have seemed content with their "Sokols," social community organizations of excellent methods, yet as their ancestors fought for religious freedom with the Chalice embroidered on their shoulders, so they instinctively hunger for the sacraments.

Two hundred thousand are claimed by the Roman Catholics, less than 50,000 by the Protestant churches, 500,000 are unchurched. A large freethinking propaganda maintained under them, taught atheism.

Years ago we had the beginning of a splendid work in Chicago with a Sunday school of 800. The rector left, the work was abandoned. A church in New York made a fine beginning, with 200 in their Sunday school. Then the church was given up and sold, because the "Americans" had moved away from the neighborhood, the center of 50,000 Czechs. At Westfield, Mass., where live 500 Czechs, our small mission church gets its choir and most of its Sunday school from these people, and 50 children have already been confirmed. We have a Czech mission at Bohemia, N. Y., and some work in Fond du Lac and in Nebraska.

Policy Proposed.— A survey is needed by our expert, to result in large work. Some bilingual tracts should be printed explaining our Church.

Full equipment of the plant of Westfield, Mass., and a woman worker there.

Assistance in other dioceses.

Our work should be distinctly religious.

Budget

	1 year	3 years
General survey	$600	$1,800
Equipment of Westfield plant	14,000	14,000
One woman worker	900	2,700
Extension of other work	5,000	15,000
Printing tracts	500	500
	$21,000	$34,000

Mexicans

In the United States there are more than 2,000,000 according to figures of the New York City Consulate.

Bishop Howden of New Mexico, including Texas west of the Pecos river, writes: "Owing to the Mexican or Spanish-American population in New Mexico, almost every mission has this Americanization possibility."

Mexicans will not trust our words, teachings, charity or good will, but if we cure their bodies and those of their wives and children, we have won their hearts. There is not a hospital in Mexico or Texas along the border.

Policy Proposed.— The Church is asked to build a string of hospitals from Brownsville, Tex., on, to cost $150,000. Land has been given by the towns. Toward this the Nation-Wide Campaign is asked for $60,000.

Nothing can be more our duty or our opportunity. This will accomplish more for our missions in Mexico and for Americanization than ten times the amount spent in the now almost impossible Mexico.

Budget

	1 year	3 years
Hospitals in Texas	$60,000	$60,000
Missionary work	3,000	18,000
	$63,000	$78,000

For the Eastern Orthodox

Members of the great Eastern Orthodox Church, numbering far over a million, are found all over our land, Greeks, Russians, Roumanians, Jugo-Slavs, Syrians and Albanians.

They have their well-established churches, and have thoroughly appreciated the kindly co-operation of our sister Church. We are in close and cordial touch with them, and can help in the Americanization of their people, especially their children, as no others can.

Their second generation are drifting away. Their authorities prefer that this drift be arrested by the attraction of our sister Church. The school and lecture room are always a part of their ecclesiastical program. As a rule the Orthodox congregations would welcome in this our co-operation and direction.

We need instruction to understand them and they to understand us. Literature and service-book translations of the two churches would go far to breaking down the barriers between us.

A very valuable opportunity for extensive service is presented by the translation of the Orthodox service book by Miss Hapgood, which has been accepted by the Russian Church as authentic. It is needed for the time soon to come, for the adoption of the Orthodox services in English in America. The Y. M. C. A.

finding a necessity for this book, has already filed their order for 500 copies, but it is now out of print, though the plates are still in existence, needing a few changes.

The cause of reunion can be well forwarded by our department.

Budget

	1 year	3 years
Correspondence	$400	$1,200
Conference	300	900
Hospitality	500	1,500
Publications	700	2,100
Emergency fund	1,400	1,400
Reprinting service book	5,000	5,000
	$8,300	$12,100

Welsh

Here is an extremely important field we have neglected, not through prejudice nor procrastination, but simply because most of us did not know of its existence. These are of our own Anglican fold and we have simply let them stray.

There are 250,000 Welsh in the United States, of whom two-thirds speak the Welsh language. There are 230 Welsh meeting houses with communicants about 23,000 and 130 preachers. There are a very large number of Welsh who are unchurched. In Wales the Anglicans are said to be in the majority.

In Wales, since the war, there is a strong trend from Non-Conformity toward the Church. There is the same desire here. The Welsh are passionately found of their language, and will attend service where they can get it. The Welsh are naturally very religious and have always contributed well to the Church's support.

The Welsh field consists of Welsh centers as Boston, New York, Philadelphia, Scranton, Baltimore, Washington and other Eastern cities; Chicago, Racine, Milwaukee, Wales, Wis., Cincinnati, Minneapolis, Butte, San Francisco, etc.

Policy proposed.— The Church has all the equipment in our Welsh centers. We simply need to give these, our Anglican brethren, some real attention to bring them back.

Provide suitable Welsh-speaking clergy.

Rooms as special Welsh social centers should be provided in our parish houses in Welsh centers.

Several Welsh nurses are needed.

The Church has the whole field to herself in Welsh social work. Now is our opportunity. It may soon be too late.

Budget

	1 year	3 years
General missionary	$2,982	$8,946
Traveling expenses	700	2,100
Survey of whole field	800	800
Help to start social room	500	1,500
Welsh nurses	3,000	9,000
Welsh-speaking clergy	4,000	12,000
Their traveling expenses	1,000	3,000
	$12,982	$37,846

The Assyrians

The Assyrians of the Ancient Nestorian and Jacobite churches number but 10,000, but they are segregated in a few places — the Nestorians in Chicago (3,000), and smaller communities in Flint, Mich., New Britain, Conn., and Philadelphia; the Jacobites in Paterson, N. J., Worcester, Fitchburg, Boston, Mass., and Providence, R. I.

They have but one priest each here, though a number of deacons. The personal representative in America of the Nestorian Catholics is a gradute of our General Seminary, not in orders.

These intelligent people, led by their two priests, one of whom is studying in Berkeley, look to us directly, have appealed to our bishops, and have placed their people in several instances directly under the care of our clergy.

To keep these worthy people faithful to religion, as the Archbishop of Canterbury's Masson has done in their homeland, is our distinct duty and opportunity.

For providing them with service books and other books, which they almost totally lack, and for the publications which can instruct them in Americanization and our Church, a special linotype is their most essential immediate need.

Budget

	1 year	3 years
Maintenance	$3,000	$9,000
Publications	1,000	3,000
Press	5,000	5,000
	$9,000	$17,000

Miscellaneous Peoples

There are other peoples to whom we owe a duty, and among whom we have an opportunity.

Poles, Hungarians, French, Germans, Latin Americans other than Mexicans and Armenians, and our own spurned, intelligent, instructed, once loyal West Indian negroes.

Budget

	1 year	3 years
Various surveys and extension	$4,000	$12,000

Jews

Americanization of the foreign-born Jew presents its peculiar difficulties. There are in our country 4,000,000 of Jews; more than half are foreign-born, and a large percentage profess no religious beliefs. In our Lord's Day there were in Palestine 12,000 Jews. In New York there are 1,500,000, in Philadelphia 200,000, etc. In this work of Americanization, especially among those who have renounced Judaism, the Christian religion is a powerful factor.

It is impossible to Christianize the Jew unless it is done in a special way as it has been done in England. There the results have been truly wonderful.

What can be done here, if gone about in the peculiar right way, and no other way is successful, is shown by the wonderful results of the Church of England missions to the Jews. The London Society alone have baptized nearly 9,000. Of the 700 boys that have passed through the Jewish missionary school in London, 10 per cent. have become missionaries in various parts of the world. Over 300 Hebrew Christians preach the gospel in the Church of England every Sunday, with some 750 in Europe altogether. Many of the leading names in England, including bishops, are or were Christian Jews. When a Jew embraces

Christianity, it means usually his wife and children also. The 72,000 Jewish converts of various churches now number with their families 120,000.

The Presbyterians are to build a Jewish Community Center in Newark, N. J. — cost, $75,000, funds raised by their New Era movement.

The Methodists are taking up similar work, other denominations also. There are a number of non-denominational Jewish missions started by Jewish Christians themselves. Nearly all the leading Christian missionaries of these denominations are Church of England converts, and are begging to come back to us as soon as the Church takes official interest and active work in the Jewish missions.

What we have done.— We had a society for promoting Christianity among the Jews, which failed for lack of support. We have now one Jewish mission in Philadelphia where excellent results are being shown.

Policy proposed.—A peculiar and separate people require a peculiar and separate policy, and this policy, if taken up in the large, as it has been in England, will be successful. It must be carried on by Jews. They alone can understand the religious and traditional problems of the Jewish heart and life.

Budget

	1 year	3 years
Community Center in Philadelphia	$75,000	$75,000
Christian synagogue and library	15,000	15,000
General secretary	2,982	8,946
Traveling expenses	800	2,400
Headquarters expenses	2,260	6,780
Magazines	2,000	6,000
Publications	1,000	3,000
Four resident missionaries in New York, Chicago, Philadelphia, at $2,140	8,560	25,680
Five other missionaries	7,000	21,000
Five women workers	4,500	13,500
Colporteurs	2,500	7,500
Benevolent and discretionary fund	1,000	3,000
	$122,602	$187,806

Oriental Peoples

There are 65,000 Chinese and 105,000 Japanese in the United States; and 1,500 Chinese and 1,000 Japanese students.

Though there are Chinese colonies in Philadelphia, New York, Boston, Chicago, and a few other cities, by far the greater number of Chinese have remained on the Pacific coast.

The Japanese are confined almost entirely to California, Oregon, Washington, Colorado and Utah.

There are two groups to be reached: the farmers, working men and business men settled in America who cannot become citizens, and the students who reside here temporarily.

Some of the farmers also return to their native lands, and with the returned students are a powerful force for or against Christianity according to the treatment they have received here.

Factors hindering effective work, which must be overcome, are:

Our own " appalling ignorance, deplorable inadequacy of our work and downright indifference of the Church as a whole."

Tendency of Orientals to segregate in cities but to scatter in rural districts.

Revival of efforts for their own religions — Buddhist temples have been erected in every large city on the Pacific coast.

" Japanese Associations " for holding the Japanese to their native traditions. These maintain schools, hospitals, insurance and sick benefits, legal aid, commercial co-operation, etc.

Among the Chinese, petty policies and factions.

What we have.— Five missions for the Japanese, Los Angeles, San Francisco, Sacramento, Seattle, and Kent (Washington). Two missions for the Chinese, San Francisco and Oakland, and a sort of legal aid society in New York.

All of these missions have a good start, with good schools connected with each, and stand well in their communities. Sound principles have been determined, and all that is now needed is funds.

About 100 capable and willing students from our own colleges in China and Japan will gladly work with their own people while studying in America.

Policy proposed.— Co-ordination of the work and putting it on a national, not diocesan, basis.

Co-operation between mission boards, especially to establish Christian community houses.

Establishment of kindergartens.

Oriental welfare committees in each city, where students or working men are in large numbers.

Locating and ministering to students who are churchmen, or have been in our colleges in China or Japan.

Using one of our church colleges as a place where our foreign students should go for their first year in America (if not for their whole course). Prospective missionaries could be in residence at this college for a while before going to the field.

Utilizing students in work for their own people in the cities where they study.

A staff of three secretaries — a Pacific coast secretary and a Cantonese-speaking Chinese assistant. They would have general oversight of our missions and look after the scattered Church families. A student secretary, having an office in the East, where he could also supervise mission work.

Budget

	1 year	3 years
Los Angeles — enlarge rectory	$1,000	$1,000
Japanese parish house	20,000	20,000
Large automobile, driver and upkeep to collect children for kindergarten	700	2,000
Sacramento — enlarge house, Japanese	1,000	1,000
San Francisco — Japanese church	20,000	20,000
Chinese mission debt	1,000	1,000
Oakland — new building, Chinese	20,000	20,000
Seattle — property purchase	8,000	8,000
One building in place of two widely separated — Japanese	20,000	20,000
Kent — building, probably rent only needed, Japanese	2,000	6,000

Maintenance

Woman assistant at Sacramento	800	2,400
Teacher, San Francisco	800	2,400
Secretary for Pacific coast and a Chinese assistant, annual budget	10,000	30,000
Student secretary in East, annual budget	5,000	15,000
Discretionary fund for these secretaries to extend work, increase of salaries of present workers	10,000	30,000
	$120,300	$178,800

CORRECTED BUDGET — CHRISTIAN AMERICANIZATION

Central Organization

Office	1 year	3 years
Secretary	$3,762 50	$11,287 50
Assistant	2,687 50	8,062 50
Traveling	1,500 00	4,500 00
Stenographer	1,200 00	3,600 00
Expenses	600 00	1,800 00
Printing	3,000 00	9,000 00
Conferences	800 00	2,400 00
	$13,550 00	$40,650 00

Field

Director	$3,440 00	$10,320 00
Three months abroad	3,000 00	3,000 00
Assistant	2,687 50	8,062 50
Traveling	2,500 00	7,500 00
Stenographer	1,000 00	3,000 00
Expenses	500 00	1,500 00
	$13,127 50	$33,382 50
Emergency fund	$50,000 00	$150,000 00

Development of Leadership

New equipment	$175,000	$175,000
Eight professorships, at $2,500	20,000	60,000
Ten divinity scholarships, at $500	5,000	15,000
Twelve collegiate scholarships, at $500	6,000	18,000
Ten women workers, at $500	5,000	15,000
Four fellowships abroad, at $1,500	6,000	18,000
Library books	900	2,700
Special lectures	1,200	3,600
	$219,100	$307,300

Downtown Polyglot Masses

	1 year	3 years
Remodeling and equipping	$50,000	$50,000
Three clergy in charge, at $2,225	9,675	29,025
Six assistants, at $1,935	11,610	34,830
Six women workers, at $1,000	6,000	18,000
Other workers	4,000	12,000
Maintenance	6,000	18,000
Conferences	400	1,200
Adding to existing staffs	7,000	21,000
	$94,685	$184,058

Industrial Polyglot Groups

	1 year	3 years
Five clergy assistants, at $1,935	$9,675	$29,025
Twelve women workers, at $1,000	12,000	36,000
Ten foreign-speaking clergy	19,260	57,780
Conferences	500	1,500
	$41,435	$124,305

Rural Field

	1 year	3 years
Workers and colporteurs	$20,000	$60,000

Italians

	1 year	3 years
Two general missionaries, at $2,150	$4,300	$12,900
Traveling expenses	2,000	6,000
Supplementing salaries	12,000	36,000
Two colporteurs	2,400	7,200
Hymnal	2,200	2,200
Pediodicals	3,000	9,000
Other publications	1,000	3,000
Emergency equipment fund	1,000	3,000
Six women workers	6,000	18,000
Conferences	500	1,500
	$34,400	$98,800

Scandinavians

	1 year	3 years
Four provosts — 1 at $3,440, 3 at $3,010..	$12,470	$37,410
Traveling expenses	2,400	7,200
Supplementing salaries	10,000	30,000
Periodical	3,000	9,000
Other publications	1,000	3,000
Emergency equipment fund	500	1,500
Conferences	800	2,400
	$30,170	$90,510

The Czecho-Slovaks

General survey	$1,000	$1,000
Equipment of Westfield plant	14,000	14,000
One woman worker	900	2,700
Extension of other work	5,000	15,000
Printing tracts	500	500
	$21,400	$33,200

Mexicans

Hospitals in Texas	$60,000	$60,000
Missionary work	3,000	9,000
	$63,000	$69,000

For the Eastern Orthodox Church

Correspondence	$400	$1,200
Conferences	300	900
Hospitality	500	1,500
Publications	700	2,100
Emergency fund	1,400	1,400
Reprinting service book	5,000	5,000
	$8,300	$12,100

Welsh

	1 year	3 years
General missionary	$3,010	$9,030
Traveling expenses	700	2,100
Survey of the whole field	800	800
Help to start social rooms	500	1,500
Welsh nurses	3,000	9,000
Welsh-speaking clergy	4,000	12,000
Their traveling expenses	1,000	3,000
	$13,010	$37,430

Assyrians

Maintenance	$3,000	$9,000
Publications	1,000	3,000
Press	5,000	5,000
	$9,000	$17,000

Miscellaneous Peoples

Various surveys and extension	$4,000 00	$12,000 00

Jews

Community center and national headquarters	$75,000 00	$75,000 00
Christian synagogue and library	15,000 00	15,000 00
General secretary	3,010 00	9,030 00
Traveling expenses	800 00	2,400 00
Headquarters expenses	2,260 00	6,780 00
Magazine	2,000 00	6,000 00
Publications	1,000 00	3,000 00
Four resident missionaries in New York, Brooklyn, Chicago, Philadelphia, at $2,150.70	8,602 80	25,808 40
Five other missionaries	7,000 00	21,000 00
Five woman workers	4,500 00	13,500 00
Colporteurs	2,500 00	7,500 00
Benevolent and discretionary fund	1,000 00	3,000 00
	$122,672 80	$188,018 40

Oriental Peoples

	1 year	3 years
Pacific coast secretary and Chinese assistant	$10,000 00	$30,000 00
Eastern secretary	5,000 00	15,000 00
Discretionary fund	10,000 00	30,000 00
	$25,000 00	$75,000 00

Recapitulation

Central organization, office	$13,550 00	$40,650 00
Central organization, field	13,127 50	33,382 50
Emergency fund	50,000 00	150,000 00
Development of leadership	219,100 00	307,300 00
Downtown polyglot masses	94,685 00	184,058 00
Industrial polyglot groups	41,435 00	124,305 00
Rural fields	20,000 00	60,000 00
Italians	34,400 00	98,800 00
Scandinavians	30,170 00	90,510 00
Czecho-Slovaks	21,400 00	33,200 00
Mexicans	63,000 00	69,000 00
Eastern Orthodox	8,300 00	12,100 00
Welsh	13,010 00	37,430 00
Assyrians	9,000 00	17,000 00
Miscellaneous peoples	4,000 00	12,000 00
Jews	122,672 80	188,018 40
Oriental peoples	25,000 00	75,000 00
	$782,850 30	$1,532,753 90

d. Church Publications Quoted

The Czecho-Slovaks

This is the first of a series of pamphlets on the different races in preparation by the Department of Christian Americanization of the Board of Missions. Further information may be secured by addressing the secretary, Rev. Thomas Burgess, 281 Fourth avenue, New York, N. Y.

Suddenly, like a flash of lightning, the Czecho-Slovaks stepped into the page of history written by the Great War, and now people are asking, "Who are these people with this strange name?" The truth is that the Bohemians, repudiating their former name and publishing their own racial title, Czech (pronounced as if spelled Check), have at last been freed from their ancient oppressors, the Hapsburg family, and taking the arm of their weaker racial brethren, the Slovaks of northern Hungary, once more stand before the world an ancient nation reborn.

The name Bohemia has been written large in many a page of history, as for a thousand years these virile people stood bravely out against the tide of pan-Germanism until their country projected alone into Germany almost like an island. The nature of Bohemia itself, a fertile undulating basin, surrounded by formidable mountains and containing nearly every natural product necessary for civilization, makes it, as Goethe said, "a continent within a continent," and the history of Bohemia, a struggle to maintain an independent nationality by repelling successive invasions, is more like that of an insular country. Indeed, had Bohemia's mountains been England's seas, her history would have been similar. During the last century Bohemia became an industrial state, and grew to be not only the chief manufacturing province of Austria, but also one of the first manufacturing countries in Europe. Now, Austria, stripped of Bohemia, is not merely bankrupt, but rendered almost incapable of independent existence as a state.

The Slavic Czechs entered Bohemia peacefully in the fourth century, after the original Celtic people had been forcibly ejected by the marauding Germanic tribes and the country left with fields and valleys lying fallow. Home loving and gentle, these people tilled the farm lands and opened mines in the mountainsides. "This branch of the Slav peoples," says Georges Bourdon, the French writer, "installed in Bohemia from the fourth century until the seventeenth, was ahead of the rest, and from that very moment could boast the glory of having created a kultur and having indicated to Europe the road to the future. These were the Czechs, pioneers of liberty and soldiers of the truth, who for a long time contended against the convulsions of Germanism, and they contended without flinching. Conquered at last, in 1620, they did not yield, but, bleeding from their wounds, awaited their time — and it came!"

One of the old, old Christmas carols sung by the children, and again year after year by men and women in the Church of England and the Episcopal Church in America, never losing its popularity, always quaint and lovely, is "Good King Wenceslas." The music is "traditional," that is, it has been sung by the English from time immemorial. But who among us knows that Wenceslas was king of the Czechs in Bohemia as far back as the year 925, when Athelstan was West Saxon king in England, and Dunstan was a boy in Glastonbury, destined to become Bishop of London and Archbishop of Canterbury? We do not know how long a time it was before the saintly deeds of the Czech king came over in story to England, nor when English children began to sing about him at Christmastide. But the carol stands as a type of the influences which drifted westward century after century from these eager Slavic Christians to their more stolid cousins in England. A still closer alliance between England and Bohemia was formed when, in 1381, Richard II married a sister of the later King Wenceslas.

The Czechs became Christian long after the British, and even after the Anglo-Saxon invaders of Britain, but their Christianity came to them so romantically that the tale of it reads like some long-forgotten fiction of old folk-lore. But that the story is true, the witness of an ancient language testifies; for the Old Slavonic used in the Eastern Orthodox churches still lives in the form that it had when it issued warm on the breath of the first Czech Christians a thousand years ago. Christianity came to the Czechs from the East, from Constantinople, and from Christian Greece. Two young men, consecrated missionaries, came out from Salonica with their learning and their zeal for Christ, and went up the Danube River past many a Slavic tribe and beyond the knowledge of man, until they found the pleasant and fertile valleys of Moravia. They were Cyril and Methodius, ambassadors of Christ to the Czechs. They brought the story of the Cross to these people in their own tongue, and Cyril wrote out the Gospel for them that they might read it for themselves. Because they had no alphabet, Cyril made one for them, and invented quaint letters which helped out the Greek alphabet to express Slavic sounds. Today the Cyrillic alphabet is universal in eastern Europe, and is familiar to most of us in Russian print. This conversion of the Czechs occurred in the year 860.

German missionaries, representing the Church of Rome, before that, had tried to convert the Czechs in Bohemia, but even at that early date Czechs and Germans found themselves inexorably and permanently opposed. So in Bohemia and Moravia were established Greek rather than Roman rites and doctrines. The gift of the Roman mind is law and the duty of submission to authority, while the Greek mind offers to the world the freedom of the human soul; this is true even in the Christian Church. So the gift of the Church of Rome through German missionaries, the Czechs flung back, and turned with joy to spiritual liberty and living faith which the Eastern Church brought them.

No wonder that when the Reformation began in England and "The Morning Star of the Reformation," John Wycliffe, preached, another answered him from Bohemia — John Hus, preaching in the Bethlehem Chapel in Prague. It was as though once more the morning stars sang together and the sons of God shouted for joy! John Wycliffe died in peace in his own little parish, but John Hus was reserved for martyrdom. To his own amazement, and to the amazement of both England and Bohemia, John Hus was brought by German intrigue before a council summoned by the Pope at Constance, and that council declared Hus a heretic. Never was there a more infamous council nor a wickeder sentence. John Hus was burned at the stake July 6, 1415. The authorities ordered his body burned and his ashes thrown into the River Rhine. Strange to relate, the same council condemned Wycliffe as a heretic (although he had been thirty years dead), and ordered his ashes cast into the River Avon. When the Commission appointed to dig up the bones of Wycliffe came to the little English village of Lutterworth, and disturbed the graveyard of Saint Mary's Church, there must have come to the hearts of the plain English folk a bitter desire to be freed from such foreign desecration of their religion.

War flamed up in Bohemia, and four great German armies marched upon the Czechs at intervals of two or three years, only to be hurled back utterly defeated by the Czech armies led by Ziska, one of the most picturesque figures in all history. An old man, short and broad, with long, slender nose and a fierce red moustache, blind in one eye, over which he wore a patch; he called himself "John Ziska of the Chalice, commander in the Hope of God." The people were fighting for their religious liberty, for the free reading of the Holy Bible, for the receiving of the chalice by the lay people in the Holy Communion, so that the chalice became their standard, and they wore it embroidered on their banners and tunics. In the year 1436, antedating the

Reformation in the Church of England by a century, Christendom accredited to the Czechs a national Church, independent and self-organized, with bishops, priests and deacons, possessing an inherent vitality. The people sang themselves into religious fervor, and transformed the ancient Greek Church custom of singing Easter hymns into singing hymns the year around. Nothing like it had been known before in the world. Little do we think, as we sing hymn after hymn in church and at home, whence came this gift to Christendom. The hymn, "Christ the Lord is Risen Again," is one of the Czech Easter hymns. Not a Roman priest was to be found in Bohemia or Moravia, and only the capture of Constantinople by the Turks in 1453 prevented reunion with the Greek Church.

But secretly and constantly, by political intriguing and ecclesiastical trading between Rome and Austria, forces were at work for two centuries to break up the solidarity of Nation and Church. The Jesuits were introduced in 1556, and they entered with orders to burn every Bible and hymn book, and every piece of literature written in the Czech language. Women preserved family Bibles by baking them in loaves of bread, and bishops and priests conducted divine service in the woods and on hill tops. By the year 1620 Germany and the Roman Church had wholly destroyed the nation. The people fled from the land, and wandered over the face of the earth. Millions were killed or starved to death. Many emigrated to England, where in one generation they became anglicized, changed or translated their names; and another generation found them in Holland and then in New England among the Puritans, and in New York City and Pennsylvania. Fragments of the Episcopal Church of the Czechs, greatly disorganized and much altered by adverse influences, were found here and there. The Moravian Church was one of these, recognized in 1749 by the British Parliament as "an ancient Protestant Episcopal Church." The strange thing about these people then, as it is now, was their swift acceptance of the English language; and the Moravians preached the Gospel as though they were Englishmen. It was John Bohler of the Moravian Church who started to carry the Gospel to the negro slaves in South Carolina, met John Wesley, and converted him into the missionary aspect of the Church which led to the great revival of 1737. The last bishop of undoubted apostolic succession, however, was John Komensky (Comenius), the founder of public school education, who died in Holland in 1670. Such was the end of a glorious Episcopal Church. The original stock of the ancient Church left in Bohemia and Moravia — 800,000, reduced from 4,000,000 — returned sullenly to a formal obedience to the Church of Rome, and today the Czechs are but nominal adherents of the Roman Catholic Church.

In January, 1919, half a millenium since their first ultimatum to Rome, a Congress of the Bohemian Roman Catholic priests held in Prague adopted resolutions demanding the free election of bishops, the abolition of the rule of celibacy among the clergy, the preparation of a Book of Prayer in the mother tongue and the use of that tongue in religious services, and an adequate system of education for the clergy. Thirty thousand women signed a memorial in favor of the marriage of priests.

The fringes of the Czech race, spreading southeastward along the foot of the Carpathian Mountains, form a subrace called the Slovaks — a remnant of the Moravian population which passed under Magyar rule in the eleventh century. They are historically interesting for having made the tinware of Europe in the Middle Ages, wandering from country to country, and in England called "Tinkers." They have struggled against the Magyars, or Hungarians, deploying out upon the plains of Hungary, occupying the Hungarian province of Slovakia, but never enjoying a definite land of their own — their race and nationality denied by their oppressors. With the determination to "Magyarize" the Slovaks, the Hungarian government persistently denied them all racial privileges. The use of their own language was restricted by law, and they were deprived of the most ordinary educational facilities. Prior to the recent war, there was not, among these three millions of people, a single Slovak school receiving government support. Though entitled to forty members in the Hungarian Parliament, the Slovaks were never able to elect more than five. A Slovak landowner could be forced, at any time, to sell his real estate to any person designated by the state. Even the Slovak press was systematically persecuted in Hungary, and today there are more Slovak newspapers in the United States than in the homeland. These papers were refused postal privileges in Hungary for the very significant reason that they were regarded by the Hungarian government as a distinct menace. No wonder that the Slovaks have sought a haven of refuge in the United States, or that, on arrival, they bear the pitiable marks of an oppressed people — poverty and ignorance!

In the homeland, the war has brought them relief, for the Czechs have espoused their cause, and have taken them under their strong brotherly arm. From this relationship comes the compound name, Czecho-Slovaks. The Slovaks are divided in religion, two-thirds being Roman Catholics, a portion Lutheran, and a smaller portion Eastern Orthodox. The strongly nationalistic Slovaks are Roman Catholics, and one of the remarkable signs of these times is the unity of national purpose which exists between the liberal free-thinking Czechs and the zealous Roman Catholic Slovaks.

The part played in the recent war by the Czecho-Slovaks has been one of the most romantic chapters of modern history — these people are always doing romantic things of great importance — their escape from the Austrian army into which they had been forcibly pressed. The thousands who escaped into Serbia were hurled back with the Serbian army across the desolate mountains of Albania, the remnant of half their number were soon found fighting in the Alps with the Italian army. The thousands upon thousands who escaped by pretended surrender to the Russians, formed themselves into splendidly organized troops, and before the world could believe it, Czecho-Slovak regiments, having already prevented the spread of German influence eastward from Russia proper, were marching across Siberia with the firm determination to embark on the Pacific Coast, and, by way of America and the Atlantic, find their way into French brigades, fighting the enemy on the western front. Halted in their way, the Czecho-Slovak armies yet stretch nearly around the world, amazingly brave and swift and resourceful. There is not its parallel in history. And the strange thing, too, is that they have carried with them, wherever their regiments are stationed, libraries of books, full orchestras and regimental bands, and all the equipment of outdoor gymnasium work, thousands and thousands of men reading and singing and playing instruments of music, then fighting fiercely beyond belief, relaxing in spare moments to play athletic games and exercise in rythmic calisthenic work which is their peculiar pride. As Olive Gilbreath has written, "How tell the tale of the Czechs without seeming legend? One cannot tell the truth with any hope of being believed!"

The Great War is over. On September 3, 1918, the United States government, following the governments of France, Italy, and Great Britain, recognized the Czecho-Slovaks as an independent nation. On October 12th the entire population of the new Czecho-Slovakia cut themselves off from the crumbling Empire of Austria-Hungary by organizing a republic and electing Thomas G. Masaryk President. The world now beheld a remarkable spectacle: In Austria-Hungary 12,000,000 people establishing a stable government in alliance with the nations fighting Austria-Hungary, maintaining perfect order at home, while the President was busy in America establishing the world relations of the new republic. On October 26th, in Independence Hall (" the Cradle of Liberty "), Philadelphia, President Masaryk, seated in the chair in which George Washington presided over the Constitutional Convention, signed the new Declaration of Independence, the new national flag with its two broad stripes, white and red, fluttering to the breeze with the American Stars and Stripes.

Quietly, unostentatiously, the Czechs in our land, patriotic Americans almost to a man, are steadily acquiring full citizenship, continuing their course of a generation of Americanization. While glad of their native land's final restoration to its former glory, and rejoicing with their brothers and cousins in their new republic, they themselves love the United States of America.

They entered the stream of American immigration at a very early date, and are scattered widely over the country from the Connecticut Valley and Bohemia, N. Y., to Moravia, Tex., and Seattle, Wash. They are settled as prosperous farmers in the northwestern states; they are in our great cities as skilled laborers, tailors, carpenters, machinists, bakers, and cigarmakers. They are thrifty and honest, law abiding, careful of their children, and as a rule are property owners. Indeed, in New York, Chicago, and Cleveland, many have become wealthy. The New York City tenement inspectors report that the Czechs may be called the cleanest poor people in the city, but they remain poor but one generation. Music is their passion, and hardly a family can be found without a piano and one or two violins. The names of the Bohemian composers, Smetana and Dvorsak, are familiar to every lover of music in America. The boys are almost without exception excellent singers, above the average, wonderful choir boys right in our very midst, and mostly not going to any church. Ask a Czech confidentially what is his religion, and he will answer you as though speaking of a lost cause, " The John Hus Church."

That is to say, these are children of an ancient sister Episcopal Church, and we have not known it until today; we scarcely know it or believe it now. These people, therefore, are not to be reached by our Church like those of any other people of foreign birth.

The first immigration from Bohemia to the United States was after the revolution of 1848, in Austria, and the Czechs who came left their native country because of political dissatisfaction. These were well-to-do-merchants and other business men and scholars who settled in the Middle West. The later immigration, both of Czechs and Slovaks, occurred during the thirty years from 1880 to 1910, and these people came on account of intolerable conditions at home for the working man and farmer. They came into this country in vast hordes — men, women and children — settling first in New York Cleveland and Chicago, and later spreading out to smaller cities or farm lands in the East and Middle West. Living in colonies, they have naturally done their own banking, and had their own doctors, lawyers and publishers. The Slovaks have been inclined to build their own churches, especially Roman Catholic, who have brought their priests from the old country. The Czechs have, on the contrary, fought shy of any church, and have been content with their own "Sokol" or social community organization. In cities in New York, Illinois, Michigan, Wisconsin, Minnesota, Iowa, Oklahoma and the Dakotas are half a million Czechs, all unchurched.

The field of our Church among the three-quarters of a million or more Czechs and their children in America is almost without limit. It is indeed white, already to harvest. The Roman Catholic Church is powerless to reach these people, except now and then when a tactful Roman priest can gather a congregation and hold them for a period while one generation grows up into the "freethinking" age. Entire communities, numbering thousands of souls, have been abandoned as hopeless. There is an organization of freethinkers who carry on an atheistic propaganda with the express purpose of destroying all Christian faith in the minds of the young. Their spirit has been poisoned by the adversity of history, and they act as those who have been deprived of their right to believe in a God. The Czechs, however, possess an inherent spiritual hunger for the sacraments, and a desire for uprightness of life and a clean conscience, even though they have been described as "the most unreligious of all immigrants in the United States." In this country, the Protestant missions among them have succeeded best when they have used personal persuasion and a rational appeal based on the ethics of life. Institutional and neighborhood settlement work among them by some Protestant missions has also been productive of results, but the principal reason for any congregation is the fact that there is a minister who can marry them and baptize their children, this sacramental tie being the main bond to the Church in Bohemia. Another very prevalent reason for sending their children to Protestant Sunday schools has been to learn the English language, and American customs. The bulk of these people here, however, remain untouched by religious work. Social service will not coax them into the Church, for in almost every group of fifty or more families they supply themselves with a neighborhood center and build their own community house, with gymnastics and calisthenics for both boys and girls, and gatherings for singing and other social exercises. In the large cities they even have their own "movies." Sunday is the great family gathering day, and one of their chief grounds of opposition to the children going to Sunday school is that it takes the children away from home just when the grandparents are making a visit, or when the cousins are having an all-day picnic out in the country, or it may be that the father wants to take his boy off fishing with him.

The Protestant work among the Slovaks in the United States is very small. The Slovak Lutherans have organized themselves into the Slovak Evangelical Lutheran Synod of America, with some 12,000 members, principally in Pennsylvania, Ohio and Illinois. One of the American Lutheran Synods reports a scattered work among the Slovaks in which there are thirteen self-supporting congregations and twenty-five missions, with a total membership of 2,500. The few Slovak Orthodox in this country generally seek an Episcopal Church, saying, "It is the same as ours" but their usual experience is that they are not recognized and so drift into the Roman Catholic Church where they find the majority of their fellow countrymen. Of the half million Slovaks in the United States, it may be safely said that, with the exception of a few thousands, all are loyal Roman Catholics.

The figures giving the statistics of the Czechs in the United States are almost startling. Out of a total of 750,000, the Roman Catholic Church can account for only 200,000, and a generous estimate gives the various Protestant organizations working among them less than 50,000. This leaves half a million people unchurched, indifferent to religion, inclined to atheism, and yet only acknowledged by all who become acquainted with them as an upright and morally clean people, but declared to be absorbingly interesting and companionable, while the children are fascinating and lovely.

Among the Protestants working among the Czechs in the United States the Presbyterians take first place, with 44 church buildings, 2,500 members, and a number of ministers of native stock. The work is mostly institutional. The largest church is on East Seventy-fourth street, New York City, with 300 adult members and 900 children. There is also a large Presbyterian Church in Chicago. The Presbyterian Home Missions Board spends annually $20,000 in its Czech work. The Methodists appropriate annually $10,000 on missions among the Czechs in the Western States, maintaining a few small churches. They feel the work to be well worth supporting, and a recent report makes the statement, "These are most grateful people. They are slow to change their church affiliations, although they attend our preaching services and seem to enjoy them." The Congregationalists also provide a place in their missions budget for work among the Czechs and have some organized congregations, maintaining also a mission station in Prague for strategic reasons. The Baptists provide an annual appropriation for mission work among the Czechs and a few small churches have been formed. In June, 1919, delegates from sixty-five Protestant churches using the Czech language met in Chicago and organized the Czecho-Slovak Evangelical Union of America, hoping for an increase of strength by co-operation. But the fact is that the Czech people resent any approach by Protestants and generally claim to be Catholics, although but few Roman Catholic priests recognize them as belonging to their own congregations. Our own mission antedates all these Protestant missionary efforts, but it was rather a series of sporadic approaches from the Czechs themselves, while our Church as a whole never heeded them.

In the year 1855, our Church in St. Louis tried to reach the Czechs in that city by translating the Morning and Evening Prayer, the Litany, and Holy Communion into their own language. This endeavor failed, however, for four reasons: First, because the book was not translated into good and idiomatic Czesky; second, because the book was printed in German text, and although that was what was used in Bohemia, it had been forced upon them by law and was not of their own choice; the Roman text used in "the land of liberty" is the text used in Bohemia today. The third reason for the failure of this partial Prayer Book was that this translator thought the Czechs must be ultra-Protestant because they were anti-Roman, and so were afraid of the strong word "priest," and actually used the word meaning "pastor," so presenting the forbidding aspect of German Protestantism antagonistic to these Catholic and sacramental people. The fourth reason for failure was that the Prayer Book was given to the Czechs in their own language at all. It must be remembered that the Czechs in this land desire to perfect themselves in the English language. The older generation may indeed be limited to their own tongue, but the children are more eager than those of any other race to become Americans in every sense of the word, and their parents press them forward to this end. And it is this second generation which is outdoing their elders in their non-religious and general anti-church attitude, speaking English and fast becoming more American than many children of English stock. Here is the testimony of a typical Czech: "I am a Czech, and was born in Bohemia and lived there until 1888 when I came to America. That was thirty years ago, and I was seventeen years old. At first I had a hard time, and had to do any kind of work that came along, was painter, butcher, anything, to live. I was paid very little. Four of us lived together. We had two rooms, one with two beds, and one we used as a study and sitting room; and we studied, too. What helped me most was that I had a fair education in the old country, even knew a little Latin and Greek, and understood the value of education. The first thing I bought in this country was a book. Half of each page was in English and half in Bohemian. I made myself study half a page each night, no matter how tired or hungry I was. Later I took it to Europe and left it with a relative, so that young people coming over here might study and know a little of the language of America before they came. I want my children to be broadminded, and children cannot grow up broadminded if they go to foreign-speaking schools."

Two attempts by our Church in the Northwest have been made to take over congregations of Czechs, but no available native priest could be obtained and the work did not progress. Meanwhile, the English-speaking children slipped through and away from these attempts to reach them as foreigners. About twenty years ago, hundreds of children came across the railroad tracks to the Sunday school of Grace Church, Chicago, until they crowded all classes. Bright-eyed and eager, these were children of Czechs, and soon there were from six to eight hundred of them in the Sunday school. These children, especially the boys, seemed from the very start to grasp two fundamental ideas — America and the Episcopal Church. (Grace Church was destroyed by fire September 26, 1915.)

The Church of the Good Shepherd, Chicago, is placed now in a community of 25,000 Czechs, and this parish, once made up of purely English stock, is gradually winning its way among the new people who have surrounded it. Although this church is small, yet the prospects for the future are very encouraging. A good proportion of the communicants, some of the Sunday school teachers, children in the Sunday schools and boys in the choir, are increasing from the Americans of the neighborhood who are of Czech parentage. When the Chapel of the Heavenly Rest (old Saint Alban's Church), at 116 East Forty-seventh street, New York City, was actively alive, Czech boys and girls, delightful, attractive children, found their way into the Sunday school, at first but a few and timorously, and then to the number of 200. When the chapel was abandoned, in January, 1903, this most promising work ceased, and how great an opportunity was lost to reach the 50,000 unchurched Czechs in New York City, can never be estimated. Twenty-five years ago, Czech people crossed the old covered bridge from West Springfield to Springfield, Mass., and sought baptism and marriage from the clergy of Christ Church. Today these people go nowhere to church; they have lapsed from the Church into freethinking. In Westfield a colony of 500 Czechs was established (now all Americans), and for some time the Sunday school of the Church of the Atonement, itself only a mission church, has depended upon these children for a large part of its membership, while the choir has at times been wholly made up of them. About fifty of these have come into the Church through confirmation. Before the freethinking propaganda reached its present strength, the tendency of the Czechs was toward the Episcopal Church, for they grasped its Catholic and missionary nature. But several circumstances worked against them. First, our people did not recognize them, and classed them as foreigners, presumably Roman Catholic. Second, when they did attend our services they were unable to comprehend the office of Morning Prayer; the service of Holy Communion would have seemed to them more natural and simple. Third, rented pews, with the exclusive atmosphere of cushions and carpets connected with some of the Episcopal churches through whose doors they peered, seemed to forbid their entrance. Although their children might attend Sunday school, yet they themselves did not attend church, and the children grew up apart from the church itself. Much of this happened a quarter of a century ago, and today some of these children are very good American citizens, many of them exceedingly prosperous, and most of them parents and grandparents with a younger generation of nonchurch-going people.

Surely the challenge to the Episcopal Church rings out with a clear call, and our answer, though belated, may be made strong and vital. The fact that our mission to these people has faded into obscurity, so that they seem a new and strange species, emphasizes all the more the importance of arousing ourselves to the pressing need of the moment. The Czechs must be reached by us, or by none. They will turn to us again; why not take them now? They have, in the past, turned toward us eagerly, yet with diffidence. Have we lost them forever?

Three considerations are to be kept in mind if we are to do our duty in this mission to the Czechs.

1. The English language must be used, for the Czechs in the United States are Americans of the Americans. In crowded communities the use of bilingual service books and tracts might be of much value for the older and more conservative men and women born in Bohemia. But it must be remembered that the Czechs were the first of all the Slavic immigrants, and they are in their second and third generation in this land.

2. Christianity must be placed before the Czechs in its sacramental aspect. Baptism, confirmation, Holy Communion, marriage — these are the normal functions of the Church in their eyes. Preaching, if it be of a reasoned and practical nature, will reach them; but not emotional and fervid exhortation. Morning Prayer is utterly confusing to them, with its excessive ritual of continually rising, kneeling, and then sitting again. The Holy Communion seems simple and makes a natural appeal, for they have an instinct of long inheritance for the ministry of the Eucharist. Then, too, it must be frankly granted that the altars must be high, with candles, and a ritual which they understand as sincere and devout.

3. Our work among the Czechs must be distinctly religious. Their own social service work among their own people is far in advance of the institutional work of most religious missions, and they do not need this form of ministration, indeed, they could teach us a good deal. The adults have studied the Bible with the books of Ingersoll in their hands, and the "higher criticism" of the Old Testament is well established in their minds. Their skepticism extends also to the New Testament and the Gospel in general, so that Sunday school work among their children, and the presentation of the Church's message as a whole, must be through the faithful administration of the priestly office. This means not only the celebration of the sacraments, but the pastoral work of visiting the sick in hospitals and homes, caring for the children, and having children's festivals in the church on all the great festal days of the Christian year.

So we come finally to the definite and promising field of our Church — the conversion of the children to primitive Catholic Christianity. What is needed is the planting of Sunday schools, or rather children's churches, within Czech colonies, with priests in charge, who understand something of the history of the ancient Bohemian Church; who will be uncontroversial in their relations with parents; and who, understanding children and using the English language wholly in their work, will minister to them in children's Eucharists, baptizing and preparing them for confirmation in a naive way, as though there were no thinkable alternative.

They were, centuries ago, a religious people, and in the young this inheritance comes forth in an eagerness of hunger and a responsiveness to the Gospel that ought to shame us that they are so unshepherded. Had we done this a generation ago, we had won many thousands. But even now the way is open, and an alluring future beckons us on. It may yet be brought about that in Bohemia, even, due to our enthusiasm and loyal espousal of their cause, the ancient national Episcopal Church will be re-established while, in their adopted land here, they may become good and consistent communicants of our Church. When the chalice is administered to a child of the Czechs in Holy Communion in some parish church of ours, there rushes over the mind and heart of the parent, perhaps in the congregation, and, if not, then surely at home, the story of the ancient chalice of the Czechs, the free communion of the people, and the right of spiritual liberty in the Church of Christ.

A writer describes the scene when Czecho-Slovak troops, passing through England, attended service recently in Winchester Cathedral:

"Thousands of men in strange uniform with war-worn banners passed in slow step into the great cathedral. Keen men with sad, earnest faces filled the nave. When the anthem was ended, the clergy paused, and then, in splendid accord, the Czechs sang in their own tongue a rendering of our national anthem, followed by their own national hymn, 'Kde domov muj?' ('Where is My Home?') The chants they sang with their fierce expressive rendering were the war songs of the Hussites. They bore the chalice on their banners, and each wore the same chalice on his shoulder straps. The chalice signified the right their ancestors fought for, to take the cup in the Holy Communion."

FOREIGN MISSIONS AT HOME

Published by Board of Missions of the Episcopal Church, 281 Fourth Avenue, New York City.

Neighborliness, Respect, Religion

The foreign-born and their children constitute the foremost problem of our country's after-war reconstruction. Over 15,000,000 people in the United States are of foreign birth; about half of these cannot read or write the English language. They have in general been neglected, unappreciated, forced to segregate, and not given the opportunities for touch with what is best in American life. This is our fault. These neighbors of ours are a means or a menace; a means, if given a friendly hand, to the upbuilding of our country; a menace, if let alone, to be organized by the forces of discontent. Over 20,000,000 more are of the second generation, *i. e.*, born of foreign parentage. These constitute an even greater means or menace. Their criminal record is increasingly above that of the native parentage. They look down upon their "foreign" parents, and sadly absorb American independence, with the vices instead of the virtues. Yet with those who have been given the opportunity, achievements have been notable.

The problem of Americanization is far different from the "melting pot." A fundamental is the fair recognition that every "foreigner" who comes to us brings to us something which can make America a richer and better place. If we wish him to respect us, we must respect him. It is the new infusion brought by the immigrant which will give the richness and diversity we need. Our American Church itself needs that richness of spiritual life that will come from the effort to provide for men of every race.

The achievement of assimilation and a safe democracy require religion. Man is a spiritual being. His whole nature cannot be transformed except by spiritual influences. The state and secular agencies can touch only the intellectual part of man, and in part minister to his physical well-being.

Of all the foreign-born and their children — and the foreign-born are ten times as prolific as the native — the majority are not here attached to any Christian body whatsoever. If, through the neglect of our Church or others, the foreign-born and their children are allowed to develop with their spiritual nature untouched, and the result be a revolution which shall sweep away the old ideals, and this republic ceases to be, upon whom shall the responsibility for the disaster rest? It is not a matter proselyting, but of shepherding the unshepherded, of saving countless lives from atheism, and our country from its result.

For the Americanization of the people of this country, or from any other country, there is no power equal to that of the religion of Jesus Christ, and it is only through this that our nation can be welded into one. Can we neglect this obvious duty of patriotism?

For the carrying out of our Church's mission, the spread of Christ's Kingdom among all men, dare we neglect this obvious duty and opportunity at our very doors? "Feed my sheep; feed my lambs."

HEADQUARTERS
Iniative, Guidance, Supply

To organize, spread and guide this work of the Church for the foreign-born and their children, the Board of Missions elected in May, 1919, a secretary in the domestic department, the Reverend Thomas Burgess, with office at the Church Missions House. This office proposes to

Be the clearing house of experience, advice and encouragement, and center of supply.

Act as the center of initiative, co-ordinating and invigorating existing work, and suggesting, organizing and putting through new work.

Push and advice on Americanization on its secularly patriotic side in co-operation with government, voluntary and religious organizations.

Arouse the whole Church to personal responsibility and aggressive action, that we may be truly neighbors to the immigrant and his children, cause them to become good citizens, and provide for the multitudes of unshepherded religious education, pastoral care and the sacraments.

Give all help possible through field agents and racial experts in carrying out parochial, diocesan and provincial projects, organizing special work, and putting the immigrant and the parish in touch with each other everywhere.

Find and train men and women to lead in the work.

Furnish literature and speakers to stimulate and instruct our own people, and bilingual tracts, periodicals, etc., for the foreign-speaking.

The following can be obtained from headquarters: The two study books recommended by the educational department.

Neighbors. (Our own text book.) Paper, 60 cents; cloth, 75 cents.

Christian Americanization. By C. A. Brooks. Paper, 40 cents; cloth, 75 cents.

Our department booklets and leaflets free, or at small prices, on different races and general subjects.

Pamphlets in foreign languages about the Church.

Best selected pamphlets, etc., of federal, state, municipal, voluntary, and religious organizations.

Community and parish survey blanks, with instructions.

Volunteers

Volunteer as You Volunteered for War Service

Give whole time.— There are needed to begin the work as planned, 124 men and women who shall give themselves to be administrative, racial, and publication experts, office forces, professors and instructors, field agents, community workers, parochial assistants, rural missionaries, teachers, colporteurs, etc.— those competent to make investigations, plans and publications, train the workers, reach the field and supervise and carry on the work in the parishes. Army men, especially those who have been in touch with foreign-born in the service, are asked to volunteer.

Give part time.— Thousands of our best men and women of the Church can find a great opportunity to serve Christ and country by giving a definite part of their time and life and ability in their own parishes, and also in the rural districts. Such service must be preceded by careful study of particular problems and predispositions and background. Part time should be given as organizers of surveys of local conditions, leaders of study classes, Church school teachers, teachers of English, American history, civics, etc.; leaders or assistants in social activities, especially among the boys and girls; home classes for foreign-born women. All this must be accompanied by neighborly personal contact between times.

Competent parish committees should be set to work to see to justice in the courts, naturalization, health, sanitation, recreation, library facilities, nursing, proper housing conditions, etc.

In solving the rural problem among the great numbers of foreign-born scattered in rural districts, a great work may be accomplished by survey, sympathetic friendship, putting people into touch with the nearest churches and distributing literature about the Church and American ideals. This is a work for automobile owners.

In many places throughout the country are churches of the Eastern peoples who look upon us as a sister Church. These need, and their authorities appreciate, our help. They are losing their young people through inability to provide American ways. We should attend their services and learn to understand the religious aspirations.

Our best men and women should offer to help their clergy and leading laity to organize and run societies of boys (as Boy Scouts of America), men, girls, women, and to help in educational endeavors.

For all such part-time devotion to service, some of those best fitted by ability and opportunity are employers of labor, foremen and forewomen, insurance men, nurses, public school teachers, lawyers, librarians and municipal officials.

What Every Churchman Can Do
As Neighbors, Missionary, Citizen

Learn by careful reading, study, personal contact and prayer to understand your neighbors of foreign race. (What and how to study supplied from headquarters.) This is in order that you yourselves may be neighbors to them, and also that you may persuade all the rest of your neighbors to be neighbors to these neighbors.

In answering the questions, "Who is my neighbor?" our Lord gave an illustration of a neighborly act, and added, "Go, do thou likewise."

You are citizens of a great republic; more than that you are citizens of the Kingdom of God. Be fellow-citizens to your fellow-citizens. If your fellows are not citizens of our republic or our kingdom, or are not living up to their obligations as citizens, help them to it.

The Declaration of Independence declares: "All men are created equal." Have you treated your fellows as equals? Have you tried to influence others to treat them so?

Jesus Christ said: "A new commandment I give unto you that ye love one another." Have you shown to these your brothers, Christian brotherhood, and have you tried to influence others to show it.

The lack of this Christian neighborliness has been the root-trouble. The showing forth of this is the root-solution.

As neighbors.— First and foremost, let every Christian family be neighbors to at least one family of foreign race.

Treat them with the same courtesy, hospitality, and friendship as you ordinarily show your friends, and mark you, without the least shade of patronizing. If you have not learned to regard them as equals, then the fault is in your own ideals of Americanism and Christianity. Relearn them.

Let your children be comrades to their children and invite them home.

Let those who can seek out the bright children of the foreign-born and give them all possible advantages of higher education.

Especially try to put the women of foreign birth in touch with our American language and life. Children become "Americanized" and often look down on their mothers. The result is very sad and very harmful to the children.

Visit the hospitals and seek out the foreign-born and their children. Bring them flowers; give them kindly affection and help.

All this must be done with sympathy, and sympathy means understanding. It cannot be accomplished all at once. Careful study is necessary first.

As missionaries.—After you have shown yourselves real neighbors, bring your unchurched neighbors to Church service and Church school. If they have churches of their own in your community, encourage them to return and be faithful to them.

Do your part in some parish organization, in making a survey of surrounding conditions. Instructions and blanks for this may be obtained from headquarters.

Follow up the unchurched. Probably they have been baptized; many of them had Christian bringing up. They are simply unshepherded and they probably know nothing of our Church. Report to your rector. Try to bring it about that all are given religious education, pastoral care and the sacraments, and arrange that the sick and dying are ministered to by the Church, and for the dead a Christian burial. Tracts about the Church in several languages and English, especially adapted to particular races, can be obtained from headquarters.

As American citizens.— Take your full share as leaders or workers in all work for Americanization of the right sort in your community.

Push the American Legion.

See that English is taught to those who do not know it.

See that justice is done in courts, and that the interpreters are of good character and competent and impartial.

Encourage and try to guide toward naturalization.

Help toward understanding of banking facilities and encourage the acquiring of property.

If you are an employer of labor, you have a great opportunity. See that fair treatment is given your foreign-born employees. Time given in your factories for classes in English and citizenship is not only a patriotic duty but is all-important for the efficiency of your business.

But, above all, remember that the principal root of Americanization is neighborly personal contact. Shall it be with the false or with the true Americans?

Headquarters has made a thorough study of various organizations and methods for "Americanization" and can give full advice on this and furnish literature.

Write to the secretary for advice, literature and survey blanks. Also tell what the conditions are in your community, and what you and your church and community are doing. This will help him to help others.

If you are willing to enlist in this great work for God and our country, fill out the last page of this leaflet, tear it out and mail it.

Address, Rev. Thomas Burgess, secretary, Church Missions House, 281 Fourth avenue, New York City.

ENLISTMENT CARD

I am interested in Christian Americanization, especially among the following races:

....

I offer my whole time for this work, especially in the following way, and solicit correspondence on the subject:

....

I shall be glad to do my share in any effort put forth in my parish or community, and I can give part time to this work, so much each week:

....

Signed

.... Name
.... City or Town
.... Diocese
.... State

"E PLURIBUS UNUM"
THE CHRISTIAN AMERICANIZATION OF ALIENS

By the Right Reverend ALFRED HARDING, D.D., *Bishop of Washington, D. C.*

(Published by Board of Missions of the Episcopal Church, 281 Fourth avenue, New York City.)

Reprint from "The Living Church," October 4, 1919

A pamphlet entitled "E Pluribus Unum" was distributed at the General Convention in New York in 1913. The familiar motto of the United States was used to express tersely, with a wider outlook, the problem of the foreign-born in the United States: "To make one nation out of many peoples." That is our problem.

The foreign-born population of the United States is over twenty millions, equal to the entire population of the country in 1850.

The immigration for the year ending June 30, 1913, amounted to 1,197,892; for the year ending June 30, 1914, 1,318,430. In 1915, because of the war, it fell off to 326,000. Since our entrance into the war it has become negligible. Well-informed people looked forward to a great increase when the war ended. At this writing the President has asked Congress to continue the strict passport system for another year. A bill has been introduced in Congress to prohibit practically all immigration for a term of years. It is not likely, however, that so drastic a policy will be adopted. We shall need immigration for the fuller development of our great natural resources, but it must be immigration of the right kind. The door must be barred against all undesirables, and open only to the morally and physically fit.

Whether or no the tide of immigration rises or falls in the future, the fact remains that we have now within our borders this great mass of people from every nation under the Heavens — African, Bohemians, Bulgarians, Serbians, Croatians, Dalmatians, Dutch, English, Finns, French, Germans, Greeks, Hebrews, Irish, Italians, Lithuanians, Magyars, Poles, Portuguese, Roumanians, Russians, Ruthenians, Scandinavians, Scotch, Slovaks, Syrians, Turks, Welsh — many of whom have still to become citizens of the state. These foreigners are a means and a menace; a means to the upbuilding of our country, a menace if let alone to be organized by the forces of discontent. The experience of recent years has emphasized the truth of this.

The problem of welding these many peoples into one nation, therefore, vitally concerns the state. The nation depends upon its local body of citizens for its safety and support. But the state has been forced to recognize the fact that the public school system, on which it has been relying in the past to accomplish assimilation by education, is inadequate for the task. It cannot reach a sufficient number of adults, nor can it give the many-sided opportunities necessary for satisfactory results.

The astounding revelations of illiteracy and of complete ignorance of the English language among the men drafted for service in the late war, have been given to us by the Secretary of the Interior. Mr. Lane's figures speak for themselves, approximately:

Forty thousand men in the army who could not take commands in English;

Four hundred thousand men of draft age in the country who could not read or write in any language.

Secretary Lane has been urgently advocating plans for the Americanization of the foreign-born; opportunities in very community for the general education of the adults; and specific opportunities for them to learn trades and business methods, for instruction in citizenship, and for social privileges. To this end he is asking the co-operation of the Church, embracing under that term all the religious bodies in the land.

As a matter of fact, no influence is historically so great in the making of a nation as religion, The English-speaking people, so dominant in the world today, is an example of many races welded into one — Britons, Celts, Saxons, Angles, Jutes, Danes, Normans, and other peoples, welded into one before the days of Magna Charta by the Church of England, our Mother Church. Man is a spiritual being, and can be transformed only by spiritual influences. The state can touch only the intellectual part of man's nature, and promote to some extent his physical well-being. The influence of religion is required to touch the whole man and to achieve assimilation.

About one-half of the vast body of our new foreign-born citizens, energetic, industrious, and ten times as prolific as the native population, is not attached to any Christian body. If, through the neglect of this Church and other Christian bodies, the immigrant is allowed to develop with his spiritual nature untouched, and the result be a revolution which shall sweep away the old ideals, and the republic cease to be, upon whom will the responsibility for the disaster rest?

Other Christian bodies have recognized their responsibility and for some years past have been doing much to care for these newcomers. In 1914, after eight years of work, the Presbyterian Board of Home Missions reported over 400 churches employing a foreign language, with a membership of nearly 30,000, and 34,000 children in their Sunday schools. Could any Church devise an investment yielding better returns?

The call to help in this task is urgent to the American Episcopal Church. It is the Church in which were matured two-thirds of the signers of the Declaration of Independence, one-half the framers of the Constitution, and the great majority of the Fathers of our country, from Washington on. The ideals upon which this republic is founded are ideals inculcated by this Church. We have lost much time and valuable opportunities by not undertaking sooner a comprehensive and energetic effort for the spiritual welfare of the foreign-born. But we are glad that at last the Board of Missions has this year made the venture of appointing, as a part of its Domestic Missions Department, a secretary for Christian Americanization. This is, we hope, only a beginning of what should be developed into a separate department with a large and competent staff, and with provision for an adequate budget to enable it to do effective and far-reaching work.

The most hopeful work we can do is, of course, among the children of the immigrants. Miss Agnes Repplier, in an article in the "Atlantic Monthly," reminds us of an utterance of Mary Antin, to the effect that "the descendants of the men who made America are not numerous enough to swing a Presidential election, and, if a negligible factor now, what depths of insignificance will be their portion in the future! "I heard told with glee," she said, "the glee which expresses pure American unconcern, a story of a public school in one of our large eastern cities. A visitor of an investigating turn of mind asked the pupils of various nationalities, Germans, Polacks, Russian Jews, Italians, Armenians and Greeks, to stand up in turn. When the long list was seemingly exhausted, he bethought himself of a nation he had overlooked, and said 'Now let the American children stand up!' Whereupon one lone, lorn, little colored boy stood up to represent America!"

A special opportunity for the Church is among the peoples accustomed to liturgical services and to much ceremonial, but adrift in America from their old moorings. There must be, if we are to meet this opportunity effectively, a much larger liberty given our bishops in planning and authorizing the religious services best adapted for these conditions. Very urgent, too, is the call to co-operate sympathetically and wisely with the Eastern Orthodox churches which have partial organizations here. Indeed, as has been well said in a review in the "Churchman of Neighbors, Studies in Immigration": "This American Church itself needs the richness of spiritual life which will come from the effort to provide for men of every race. These foreign neighbors of ours have as much to give us as we have to give them. They can make this Church really American as America itself."

Let then this work be well put to the fore in every spiritual appeal in the Nation-Wide Campaign. Let the program for Christian Americanization now presented for this work be thoroughly presented. Above all, let it be thoroughly understood that this is but a beginning, and is to be developed, strengthened, and carried on with energy, and we venture to affirm that it will not only help the success of the campaign, but will bring to the Board of Missions and the other boards, Religious Education and Social Service, such living interest on the part of the laity, and such generous support, as will solve their financial problems.

4. BAPTIST

Baptist churches for the foreign-born in New York City:

Alexander Avenue Baptist Church, Alexander avenue and 141st street.

Czecho-Slovak Baptist Church, East 72nd street.

Judson Memorial Baptist Church, Washington Square, South.

Chinese Baptist Mission, 13 Doyers street.

Fordham Italian Church, 2411 Lorillard place.

Harlem Baptist Church, 225 East 80th street.

Mariner's Temple, 3 Henry street.

Second Avenue Baptist Church, 166 Second avenue.

The pastors of the first three churches on the above list did not reply to our request for information as to their activities with the foreign-born.

The Reverend Lee To, pastor of the Chinese Baptist Mission, reports as follows:

"We have nineteen members, all of whom are Chinese. We conduct some services in English. We have classes in English for two hours every evening in the week and for one hour on Sunday, which classes are all free. The classes are attended very regularly by about twenty-five men — no women. We have a troop of Boy Scouts. We conduct lectures furthering an appreciation of American life and institutions. We believe that Americanization brings the Chinese in contact with the best Christian American interests and we are exceedingly favorable to the work. The younger generation grow up quite real Americans."

The Reverend Paul L. Buffa, pastor of the Fordham Italian Baptist Church, reports as follows:

"We have 120 church members, all of whom are Italian. The younger generation understand English and we conduct some of our services in English. We have classes in English twice a week for one hour each time for six months during the year. These classes are free and are attended by about forty men and twenty women, the average being twenty-six. The attendance is not very regular. We teach American history also. As to teachers, we take anyone we can get, and they do not speak Italian. They are volunteers with one exception. We are getting Americanized as fast as we can, and all our people are enthusiastic about it except the very old people. This is the text of a notice sent to all our people, printed in English and in Italian:

"DEAR FRIEND.— Our soldier boys are coming back: They have proved themselves good Americans. We must be like them. We must learn to feel, think and talk 100 per cent. American, even as they did when, not counting the cost, they flung their young bodies against the Teuton's steel and fire.

"Let us show our American friends how much we appreciate and profit by the unbounded hospitality this country has given us and how we are beginning to become the kind of citizens we should be: one with them in language as well as in consecration to the glorious and divine principles and ideals represented by the Stars and Stripes."

"We have therefore decided to adopt the English language for our Sunday evening services.

"Next Sunday, the 15th, at 8 P. M. our pastor will deliver a sermon on: 'Self Determination for the Soul.'

"Let every loyal member and friend of this Church be present.

"Sincerely,

"For the GENERAL COMMITTEE,

"P. L. BUFFA."

In a letter to this Committee dated November 19, 1919, the Reverend Mr. Buffa says:

"There is one thing about which I have been perplexed for quite a while. The letter from your office suggests the possibility of a solution.

"Two of the best members of this congregation seem to have lost their head on the subject of Bolshevism and have time and again attempted to spread their anti-government doctrines in our midst. have done my best to help them see things as they are. My efforts and those of the lecturers I have had in our Church have been in vain.

"Could you tell me of some way of bringing these good people to their senses and saving them from serious trouble?"

The Reverend Adam Chambers, pastor of the Harlem Baptist Church, reports as follows:

"We have about 200 church members, including Italians, Germans, Swedes, Letts and Americans. All our church services are conducted in English. We are about to start classes in English and we will have volunteer teachers who speak only English. We are doing Americanization work in every way and always. Our children are enthusiastic Americans. Ours is an Institutional church, working largely for children and young people with great success. They salute the flag at nearly every meeting."

The pastor of the Hungarian Baptist Church reports:

"We have seventy church members, all Hungarian. Some of them speak English and we have some services in English. We have classes in English for one hour twice a week for six months in the year. We have ten pupils ranging from twenty to fifty-five years of age. The attendance is not very regular for their work. I teach myself and have volunteers to help me when I can. I am working for Americanization directly or indirectly as I see fit."

The pastor of Mariner's Temple reports:

"We have ninety-five church members — Irish, Scotch, Italians, Germans, Chinese and Russians. We conduct some services in English, but we have no classes in English. The policy of our church is truly American and all our people favor Americanization. We do Americanization work through pictures and addresses."

Clover C. Barrett, Church Missionary of the Second Avenue Baptist Church, reports as follows:

"We have nearly 300 church members — Chinese, Italians, Polish, English, Russian, and Esthonian. We conduct some of our services in English. We have free classes in English, geography, arithmetic and Bible study for one hour five nights a week from October to May. These classes are attended by twenty-three men and five women. Our teachers are volunteers and do not speak of the language of those whom they instruct. We try to give our people American ideals and we work with the children in this respect as well as in the homes and in classes. About 50 per cent. or more are eager to be Americans. The rest are more or less indifferent, but I think none are hostile. The Russian Bible Institute which is held in this church has all but one of our English classes. The other Americanization work is done through the English department of the church assisted by the foreign pastors and church missionary."

In a letter dated November 21, 1919, Miss Barrett states: "We have an Italian, Russian, Polish, and Esthonian pastor here besides Mr. Hubbell, Mr. Sanford and myself, a staff of seven paid workers. Our work is done largely through the co-operation of the Baptist City Mission Society. The population is almost entirely foreign and our work is only a drop in the bucket in comparison with what should be done in this vicinity. The children are all eager to be real Americans. The majority of the mothers want to learn English but are very busy as they have large families and do extra work besides housekeeping to help out the family income. The men are very loyal to America considering the soap box oratory and crowded living conditions which with the high cost of living might be expected to make them disappointed in the land of their dreams."

5. CONGREGATIONAL

List of Congregational Churches in New York City for the foreign born:
Swedish Pilgrim Church, Brooklyn.
Swedish Tabernacle, Brooklyn.
Swedish Immanuel Church.
Armenian Evangelical Church, 207 East 30th street.
Finnish Golgotha Church, 1071 48th street, Brooklyn.
Italian Congregational Church, 295 Court street, Brooklyn.
Norwegian Congregational Church, Tottenville, S. I.
Swedish Bethlehem Church, 4011 Seton avenue.
Welsh Congregational Church, 206 East 11th street.

The first three churches on the above list did not reply to the requests of the Committee for information to their activities with the foreign-born.

The Reverend A. A. Bedikian of the Armenian Congregational Church reports as follows:

"We have about 250 church members — all Armenians. We seldom have services in English. We have no classes in English because we have no church building of our own. Eighty per cent. or more of our people know and use the English language. We have the most American of all Armenian churches in this country. All our people are loyal and good citizens or residents as can possibly be desired.

"Our church has wholeheartedly supported every enterprise of our government and has responded to all its requests and appeals presented directly to us. We give space in our weekly bulletin to the announcement of every movement launched by the government for which the sympathy and support of the public is sought. We encourage all those who do not know English to attend classes organized for teaching the foreigners in centers accessible to them. Very few among my congregation — numbering over 600 — do not speak or understand English, and those are old men and old women.

"If you remember the fact that Armenians regard America as their most unselfish friend and protector, then you can have a fair idea of their loyalty, love and devotion to their adopted motherland. If every foreigner were as good a citizen of America as an Armenian is, then there would not be the problem that is engaging the time and energies of our legislative bodies for its solution.

"About fifty of our young men served under the Old Glory during the war. This is another evidence of the spirit which is cultivated in our church.

"May I suggest that in your efforts to achieve the important task of Americanization of foreigners, you may not lose sight of the conservative attitude of Americans toward foreigners that, to my opinion, handicaps very seriously the great task. More often than not the foreigner is blamed for not 'mixing up'; they cannot, even if they mean to, mix up, because Americans keep aloof of them. The sympathetic — not patronizing — approach to the foreigner in behalf of the Americans will do more, I think, for the Americanization of all, than the mechanical means of teaching the language. Sympathy will naturally induce one to learn the language; that will be a result in itself.

"I will always be ready to do what I can in any and every way I am called upon to do in service of my government and for the benefit of the people."

The Reverend J. E. Lillback, pastor of the Finish Golgotha Church, reports as follows:

"We have 247 church members — Finnish — speaking Finnish and Swedish. We have some services in English. We have classes once a week for two hours for four months in the year to teach English. The instruction is free and the attendance is regular. We have abut thirty men and about fifty women attending the class and the average age is twenty-three years. We also teach American history. I teach myself and am aided by volunteers. My entire attention is directed to Americanization efforts. I teach my people English, get them naturalized, direct them to schools and to business, marry them, help them to buy homes, and teach them American ways of living. They are very glad and satisfied. They feel proud over the thing."

The Reverend John Ongaro of the Italian Congregational Church reports as follows:

"We have 100 Italian church members, and all our services are in Italian. We have English classes four times a week for two hours each time during seven months in the year. We have fourteen men and three women from twenty years of age and up.

"As to the Americanization of the foreign people, besides the answered questions, I like to add (I talk in particular as to my Italian countrymen):

"Broadly speaking, Italian people are hard to be Americanized, but when Americanized, he is a very good faithful citizen — I can't repeat the various obstacles of different character. I want to make an objection to the method generally used in training the foreign people. As to me it is a great mistake to give as an instructor to the foreign people a teacher who is unable to talk their language. The foreign people with such a teacher are unable to communicate, to ask many questions. They do not understand what the teacher says. They are ashamed to talk on account of lack of pronunciation. It seems to me very hard and the result is very poor if the English teacher knows only his language, he can't render and can't explain the different construction and the different translation from one to the other language. The literature, the sentences, the phrases must be compared and rendered in both languages, see the difference and show the different modes of expressing and conceiving the ideas. This point is of vital importance. The public schools, broadly speaking, obtain little result for this reason and the foreign people not 2 per cent. frequent those schools because they perceive the inefficiency of such schools. I can prove by experience, because I have the witness of many young Italian men, that after two or three years of frequenting public night schools, they come to a very little conclusion, and so they gave up any study. Finding myself in the necessity of training my fellow-citizens, I open voluntarily and freely in my own house three or four nights a week an English school — more than three months — we are going on very well with a great satisfaction of my pupils. Sometimes we use the schools of our church, mostly my home. I would like to come and talk this matter over if it is possible — to see if it is possible to bring my school to such an efficiency as to enlarge the plan and have more people.

"I am willing to give all my time and to do any sacrifice for it, but being my salary is so meagre ($60) I need a help, and I will be glad to continue to increase the number of the pupils and I ask at least $20 a month.

"Will you please help and advise me about this matter?"

The pastor of the Norwegian Congregational Church reports:

"We have twenty church members — Norwegian and Swedish. We conduct some services in English, but we have no English classes. I have just come to this church and have not as yet discovered what is the attitude of the people in regard to Americanization."

The pastor of the Swedish Bethlehem Church reports:

"We have sixty church members who are Swedish-speaking Finns. It is not possible to conduct any services in Engglish. We have no English classes. I did some work of Americanization both direct and indirect during the war in trying to get my people to become more attached to this country."

The Reverend Joseph Evans, pastor of the Welsh Congregational Church, writes as follows under date of October 25, 1919:

"In reply to your communication, I beg to report as follows concerning the above church.

"(1) Membership, 168. Nationality, Welsh. Languages, Welsh and English. English service once a month. Committees, trustee meetings, young people's meetings are carried on chiefly in English.

"(2) We have no educational classes as they are unnecessary. Every Welshman or Welshwoman can read and write and speak in English. Every Welsh home takes a daily newspaper. There are no Welsh dailies. Our young people take advantage of the educational facilities in the city.

"(3) The Welshman comes from a country that is intensely democratic, and takes to American ideals like a duck takes to water. He is an ardent politician and always 100 per cent. in his loyalty to the United States.

"I have made an intensive study of Welsh life in this city, and find that while our church is downtown, a large majority of the Welsh people live uptown on the west side. Through correspondence and personal interviews with Americans of high standing and office, I learn that the Welshman is above the average from the standpoint of Americanization. All Welsh children pass into the American churches, and the function of our church is to meet the peculiar needs of Welsh immigrants who reach these shores from time to time. It was my privilege to act as Welsh censor in the United States Censorship Department during the war, and throughout the year several sermons are preached on topics that bear on citizenship."

6. CATHOLIC

MEMORANDUM FOR LUSK COMMITTEE ON AMERICANIZATION PROGRAM OF NATIONAL CATHOLIC WAR COUNCIL

Submitted by JOHN O'GRADY, C.B.J., *Secretary, Committee on Reconstruction*

In its reconstruction program the National Catholic War Council has endeavored to instill into the citizens of the United States a deep sense of their rights and obligations under the American democracy. Its pronouncement entitled "Social Reconstruction" defines in unmistakable terms the rights of capital and labor. From the beginning, the Council was well aware of the fact that without a large program for civic education we could not hope for any material improvement in our political, social or industrial conditions. It was with this thought in mind that it undertook its work in civic education, or Americanization. In this undertaking the War Council was very advantageously situated. It had the sanction of the Catholic bishops of the United States. It was, in fact, their organization. This gave it an easy entrance to Catholic dioceses, parishes and lay organizations.

The first stage in the Citizenship Program of the National Catholic War Council was the publication of a series of pamphlets, explaining the ideals, principles, and institutions of American democracy. It was the intention of the Council that certain of these pamphlets should be translated into all the important European languages. Its pamphlet on the "Fundamentals of Citizenship" has been widely read and has been commended by all persons engaged in Americanization work. A number of non-sectarian, as well as Protestant and Jewish organizations, are using it in their work among the immigrants. Its publication marked the beginning of a widespread movement for more thorough instruction in civics throughout the country.

The literature of the Catholic War Council has emphasized the fundamental fact that democracy is a co-operative undertaking; that its success or failure in the last analysis rests with the people; that it provides orderly machinery for the remedying of grievances. A conscious effort has been made to show the immigrants that the American democracy is their democracy, inasmuch as their ancestors played an important part in its making and development. The Council has endeavored to convince the newcomers of the need of learning the English language and becoming acquainted with American ideals. This, of course, does not mean that they are to give up their own language and racial traditions. There is room in America for the best things from all lands.

The War Council followed up the publication of its pamphlets on citizenship by a nation-wide campaign for the purpose of interesting all Catholic organizations in citizenship work. Within the past six months it has been called upon to give advice and direction to Catholic organizations in nearly all of the important cities in the United States, in instituting courses in English and citizenship.

In co-operation with the local organizations, the National Catholic War Council has opened community centers in seventeen large cities in the United States. These community houses have become real Americanization centers, where the American teacher, physician, nurse and social worker may come into contact with the immigrants and communicate to them the principles of American life and American living. In the community centers the new Americans are preferred for naturalization. Classes in English and civics are given two or three evenings in the week. Leading citizens, both native and foreign, have given lectures on practical problems of government, vocational opportunities of the community, and other topics of interest. Lessons on child care and home economics are given by trained nurses and teachers.

In connection with the centers, boys' clubs, girls' clubs, married women's and men's clubs have been organized for the purpose of teaching the practical lessons of democracy. In fifteen cities the War Council has aided in the establishment of "Everyman's Clubs," where all men, independent of race, religion or country of origin, meet and receive instructions in the problems of industry and government. In some cities the public school authorities have conducted classes in English and naturalization in the clubs and community centers operated under the auspices of the Council.

An interesting feature of the War Council's program is its plan for the teaching of civics through the motion picture. It has organized a number of civic motion picture courses which it is placing at the disposal of Catholic parishes at a nominal cost. Each of these courses will occupy twelve evenings. They are given on one evening a week, for twelve successive weeks. The program for each evening consists of five reels of motion pictures, combining education and entertainment, and a ten to fifteen minute oral instruction in civics, based on "The Fundamentals of Citizenship," published by the Council.

7. LUTHERAN

Letter from the Rev. O. H. Pannkoke, secretary, Lutheran Bureau of the National Lutheran Council, New York City, January 3, 1920:

"Replying to your letter of December 22d, in which you ask for information about the activities of the Lutheran churches of New York, regarding the education and Americanization of adult foreigners, I beg leave to give the following information.

"In the first place, a few statistics, in order that you may understand the strength and extent of the Lutheran Church in Greater New York. There are 58,000 communicants, 140,000 souls, and 186 churches. The following languages are used in these churches: English, Norwegian, Danish, German, French, Lithuanian, Italian, Lettish, Polish, Yiddish, Esthonian, Slovak. The predominant language is English. Danish, Norwegian and German are also used considerably. Approximately 115 churches use English. In the Sunday schools there are 42,106 children enrolled.

"To understand the questions which you raise in relation to the Lutheran Church of Greater New York, it is necessary to point to the history of that Church. The earliest church was established in 1669. A goodly number of churches were established before 1875. This means that the origin of the Lutheran Church in Greater New York dates back practically to the origin of the republic, and the Lutherans and the Lutheran churches in their history and traditions are part of the whole development of this country. The roots are thoroughly American.

"The large increase of the Lutheran Church in Greater New York came, during the years of the Lutheran immigration, from Norway, Sweden, Denmark and Germany. All these countries are predominantly Lutheran. The greater part of the movement of the Lutheran people from the Old World to the New had spent itself before 1900, at least twenty years ago. The real immigration problem confronted the Lutherans twenty years ago, today it is rather a minor problem. A striking evidence for that is the fact that the new churches established in the suburbs of Greater New York are practically all English. It is an exception even for bilingual churches to be established today. The real immigration problem today does not deal with the Lutheran people, but with people coming from Italy, and the Slavic countries, which are not Lutheran and are touched only to a slight degree by the Lutheran Church. In speaking of the special activities to Americanize foreigners, it is well to consider first the activities of the individual churches and secondly the activities of general organizations.

"In view of the situation explained before, namely, that churches in the membership are thoroughly American, use the English language, are familiar with and thoroughly in sympathy with American ideals, it is evident that no special activity is called for in the individual churches. The preaching, as far as it touches this question, applies the fourth commandment, obedience, to the constituted authorities, beyond that the Lutheran Church has never believed that it was its function to go. In fact it is rather fearful of mingling Church and State by entering into politics. The social activities of the churches are carried on by societies — young people's societies, men's societies, etc. The language, practically, universally used at the meetings of these organizations, is English and the spirit and tone is American. In fact the largest percentage of the members are American-born and knew comparatively little of European conditions and institutions. With the arrival of members, therefore, who were born abroad, it simply means that in a comparatively short time they are amalgamated into the spirit and work of the church existing here.

"As to general organizations, there are ministerial associations, young people's federations, Sunday school associations, immigrant societies and charitable associations. In all of these, except the immigrant societies, questions of the difference between American ideals and foreign ideals really never arise. The unspoken assumption is that the association and the members are American and the function of the organization is to help along the work of the Church spiritually. There are eight immigrant societies and seamen's missions maintained by the Lutherans in Greater New York. They are not maintained locally, so much as by the Church in general to serve the immigrants that enter the Port of New York. There are two Norwegian missions, one Danish, one Finnish, one Swedish and two German. The work which these societies do is to offer their service and guidance to the immigrants as they come in. During the period of (. . .) the most of them have practically been doing nothing. I am not informed how far their work has picked up since.

"This in small space is the answer to your question of December 22d. While, of course, much more could be written on it, no doubt you desire the information as tersely as possible. At present the problem you raise in your letter is of small importance to the Lutherans of Greater New York, because the period of Lutheran immigration in large numbers ended practically before 1900. Whether through the war it will grow to any dimensions again, is as yet uncertain. If so, the groundwork is ready, namely, a thoroughly established and organized church-life, which has grown up on American soil, which has taken part in the struggle and establishment of American ideals."

Letter from the Rev. O. H. Restin, Lutheran Immigrant Society, Inc., New York City, January 20, 1920:

"In reply to your recent letter, we wish to willingly and heartily give support to the excellent work you are doing by giving you our report and a few views on the matter of 'The Alien.'

"In a few words, our work is chiefly to take the alien in hand, investigate his desires and, when possible, send him on his way under the guidance and influence of our church according to the laws of this country, viz., our stand:

"1. With each and every foreigner we came in contact with, we called his attention to the fact that it is his first duty to respect and obey all laws of the country.

"2. We advised each and every one upon arrival, when such alien signified a desire to remain permanently, to become a citizen as soon as possible.

"3. In some cases we notified the pastor of the alien of the safe arrival of his ward, and, on the other hand, when possible, we notified a local pastor to take charge of the alien, to visit him and take his matters in charge, offering whatever assistance which might be necessary under the existing circumstances. In this way we brought many strangers under the immediate influence of our Church and its work, and did not leave them to drift for themselves. We might add here that most of 'our people' became citizens and in every way are supporters of the government. We refused to deal in any way with Socialists, etc.

"In our experience of eighteen years at No. 8 State street, we reached in the neighborhood of 8,000 people annually; on Ellis Island in the neighborhood of 10,000. During this time we missed a good follow-up system! When the alien had left the station at Ellis Island, in most cases, all trace of him disappeared, in other cases extreme difficulty was experienced before one could obtain further information. For this reason, of learning further concerning the activities of foreigners in this country, we highly and urgently recommend some 'follow-up system,' whereby missionaries and other interested parties be supplied with necessary documents, etc., to keep the alien on record, and so do our country a great service. We firmly believe that missionaries could serve in this capacity to a great advantage for our country, and so aid greatly in the discovery of undesirable persons."

8. DUTCH REFORMED

Letter from the Rev. T. McB. Nichols, West End Collegiate Church, New York City, December 31, 1919:

"Replying to the inquiry regarding work carried on by the Dutch Reformed churches among foreigners, I would say that at Knox Memorial Chapel, 405 West 41st street, we have an Italian congregation and at the Harlem Collegiate Church, 269 Lenox avenue, a special work is being done among the Japanese."

9. RELIGIOUS SOCIETY OF FRIENDS

Letter from Miss Anna L. Curtis, secretary, Religious Society of Friends, Brooklyn, January 13, 1920:

"In reply to your letter of the 22d of last month, let me say that this particular meeting of Friends does no work with foreigners, as foreigners. That is to say, if in our efforts to help our poorer neighbors, we find a foreigner who needs help, we try to give it, no matter what the nationality. We very often meet with foreign-born, but for some reason, very few who are not able to speak English fairly well, so that they do not come within the scope of your inquiry."

"A very important thing, it seems to me, in dealing with foreigners, is to show them that we Americans appreciate what they have to bring us from the old world. The children in school so often learn to despise the old home that the parents believe that America has only contempt for it. This feeling is a strong obstacle to unity. Make them feel that we appreciate their art, whether in weaving, embroidery, or painting; their literature, whether serious writing or folk-songs; their music, their traditions. If you accept and dignify this background, the spiritual heritage of the foreigners, you will do far more to make them good Americans than if you ignore it."

CHAPTER VII
Settlement Houses

1. UNITED NEIGHBORHOOD HOUSES OF NEW YORK
a. List of Officers and Members

UNITED NEIGHBORHOOD HOUSES OF NEW YORK, 70 Fifth avenue, New York City. Judge Thomas C. T. Crain, honorary president; Miss Harriet T. Righter, president; Mr. Gaylord S. White, first vice-president; Mrs. Cyrus Sulzberger, second vice-president; Mrs. Max Morgenthau, Jr., third vice-president; Mr. Henry W. Taft, fourth vice-president; Miss I. M. Cammann, recording secretary; Mr. George M. La Monte, treasurer; Mary Elizabeth Barr, executive secretary; Mr. Harold Riegelman, counsel.

Following is a list of members of the United Neighborhood Houses of New York:

Armitage House, 451 East 121st street.
Beth-El Sisterhood, 329 East 62d street.
Bowling Green Neighborhood Association, 45 West street.
Brick Church House, 11 West 37th street.
Central Parish House, 420 West 57th street.
Christodora House, 147 Avenue B.
Clark House, 283 Rivington street.
College Settlement, 84 First street.
D. Y. N. T. House, 18 Leroy street.
Eastchester Neighborhood House, Tuckahoe, N. Y.
East Side House, 540 East 76th street.
Education Alliance, 197 East Broadway.
Emanuel Sisterhood of Personal Service, 318 East 82d street.
Federation Settlement, 240 East 105th street.
Free Synagogue Social Service, 36 West 68th street.
Greenwich House, 27 Barrow street.
Haarlem House, 311 East 116th street.
Hartley House, 413 West 46th street.
Henry Street Settlement, 265 Henry street.
Hamilton House (Branch), 72 Market street.
Lincoln House (Branch), 202 West 63d street.
Seventy-ninth Street House, 232 East 79th street.

Hudson Guild, 436 West 27th street.
Jan Hus Neighborhood, 351 East 74th street.
Kennedy House, 423 West 43d street.
Madison House, 216 Madison street.
Meinhard Memorial House, 100 East 101st street.
Music School Settlement, 55 East Third street.
New York Child Welfare Committee, 70 Fifth avenue.
People's University Extension Society, 111 Fifth avenue.
Recreation Rooms and Settlement, 186 Chrystie street.
Richmond Hill House, 28 Macdougal street.
Riis Neighborhood House, 48 Henry street.
Settlement and Church of All Nations, 9 Second avenue.
St. Ambrose Guild, 236 East 111th street.
Stuyvesant and Ninth Streets, Stuyvesant and Ninth streets.
Union Settlement, 237 East 104th street.
University Settlement, 184 Eldridge street.
Welcome House, 319 East 17th street.
Wesley House, 442 East 59th street.
White Door Settlement, 211 Clinton street.
Brooklyn Settlements:
School Settlement, 120 Jackson street.
Willoughby House.

b. Americanization Program

Letter from Mr. Harold Riegelman, December 30, 1919:

"In accordance with the assurance of co-operation given by the Special Committee of the United Neighborhood Houses of New York, these suggestions are made with respect to the work of the Lusk Committee in the preparation of recommendations tending to further a broad, sound Americanization program within the State of New York.

"It need hardly be said that the following remarks do not cover the field but are confined to those matters with which the Neighborhood Houses are in most intimate contact and are further limited by your intimation that the final recommendations may not seriously conflict with programs already adopted by existing departments of the state government. But it is felt that much can be accomplished under present laws through the exercise by those departments of a discretion already vested in them. It is not understood that the only measures in which your committee is interested are those necessitating the enactment of new laws.

"For the sake of clarity this report is divided into two main headings, Specific and General. The former includes constructive suggestions which are favored for adoption. The latter covers considerations which should qualify any proposals submitted to the legislature or departments.

"A. Specific.— Americanization is an educational process based upon precept or instruction and actual experience.

"I. Instruction.— Efficiency of instruction varies with the personality of the teacher and the method of teaching.

"(a) Teachers:

"1. The profession of teaching will not attract and hold the required number of high-type men and women, unless compensation is sufficient to provide a decent living. The compensation is at present insufficient and should be materially increased.

"2. Teachers cannot throw the requisite zeal and enthusiasm into their exacting work if in addition thereto they must turn to other employment in order to eke out a living.

"3. Night school teaching requires exceptional ability to hold interest and impart instruction because of the fact that persons attend such schools generally after a hard day's work. Consequently, their minds are not normally receptive. Such people are chiefly drawn from the foreign-born population. It should not be necessary to employ in this work men and women who have been teaching the major part of the same day and must be fresh for similar work the succeeding day.

"(b) Methods:

"1. The proposal is favored that factory workers who need instruction should be taught on factory time. To accomplish this, there should be educational qualifications fixed, and unless factory employees are able to qualify, the employer should be prohibited from engaging them unless he provides opportunities at stated intervals, on factory time, for instruction by teachers designated by and working under the supervision of the State Department of Education. The qualifications should be limited in the beginning to the speaking and reading of English. Such a law may be made enforceable by means of existing instrumentalities similar to those now existing for the enforcement of factory laws. It may ultimately become practicable to extend this plan to unskilled labor.

" 2. There should be provided facilities to enable the State Department of Education to make use of such agencies as settlement and Neighborhood Houses and Community Centers by making it possible for these organizations to secure trained and fit instructors capable of organizing and conducting groups in English, civics, literature, debating and public speaking; to secure motion pictures illustrative of the history of our country, its industrial, agricultural and social activities, rural life; and also in emphasis of health campaigns; to stage pageants and plays dramatizing historical themes; institute and develop community singing festivals where patriotic songs may be featured.

" 3. A special system of instruction should be devised by which American ideals and customs should be taught in connection with classes in English. It should be remembered that except in language and knowledge of local matters, the adult pupils may be as well educated as the teachers. In any event, their minds are mature and methods of instruction cannot be identical with those used for children without causing irritation and creating distaste. The teaching of adults requires special training and understanding. Such training should be provided by the state.

" 4. In the teaching of the adult, whether in public schools or through neighborhood co-operation, it is fundamentally important that he understand compulsory education laws, child labor regulations, working opportunities, labor and license and occupation ordinances and statutes, the operation of minor courts, methods of depositing and sending moneys, rights and obligations.

"5. Pamphlets should be prepared meeting anti-American propaganda and given free circulation through all available agencies. The 'question and answer' style may be profitably employed. Simplicity and forcefulness are essential.

"II. Experience.— The operation of our government, the vastness of our resources and the beauty of our land must be visualized in order to be appreciated.

"(a) The various departments of government — the courts, City Hall, Board of Aldermen, the street cleaning, police, water-supply and park departments, etc., should be open to inspection by groups of children under competent guidance.

"(b) Schools with farming features should be established in the country near large cities and conducted in conjunction with the city schools. To these should be sent groups of children of all grades for a period of two or three weeks, the expense of their board and keep to be borne by their parents.

"(c) There should be established inexpensive trips for selected parties of school children to nearby cities, such as Boston, Philadelphia or Washington, the history of the several routes, surrounding country and the respective destinations to be learned by means of object lessons.

"B. General.

"1. State supervision of Settlement Houses.— Until the state takes over the work now done by these organizations it would be most unwise to interfere with their method of operation except as provided by present laws which furnish ample authority for inspection and correction of any abuses that may be found to exist.

"2. Pro-American propaganda.— It may well be that other agencies are adaptable to the theory that Americanism must be 'sold' on the well-settled merchandise principles of talk in favor of one side and one side alone. The Neighborhood House would lose much of its value as a factor for Americanization were it to close its forums to critics of American institutions on the ground that an audience may fail to grasp the truth because they are given a choice between that and the false. The newcomer is quick to suspect, and not without justification. He comes into the Neighborhood House now because he relies on its disinterestedness. If the one side only is presented, it will either emphasize whatever prejudice he has against it or drive him away altogether. The position of the Neighborhood Houses, that truth cannot suffer in the long run from contact with fallacy, cannot be impaired without destroying the value of Neighborhood Houses. The interest of the community lies in making it possible to present the American ideals in a manner as attractive and vigorous as that which characterizes pernicious and subversive propaganda.

" 3. Co-operation with foreign-born.— In shaping pro-American activities, is should be remembered that the different race groups have certain peculiar characteristics and can make peculiar and valuable contributions to America. No small part of the unrest and so-called radicalism is the direct result of ignoring those facts, of not seeking to understand them and of evidencing frankly and brutally a total lack of desire to understand them. No measures affecting the foreign-born population should be finally adopted without consultation with the local leaders of the foreign-born groups affected. Their advice will result in changing the form of a measure without affecting its intention, but in these problems form is vital and often distinguishes a good and effective measure from one which is not only useless but positively harmful.

" 4. The Neighborhood Houses in principle oppose the repression of ideas except where change, economic or political, by force, is advocated, pernicious principles no less than worthy ones thrive on repression. The latter alone can survive free discussion.

"Among the subjects which have been omitted from the foregoing outline are reform in the treatment accorded prisoners, dignifying the process of naturalization, improvement of tenement conditions, and the suggestion that through carefully prepared literature or in classes, public officials or agents who necessarily come in contact with the foreign-born should receive instruction in their peculiarities of conduct and psychology, their comparative helplessness and the value of sympathetic, humane treatment.

"This report is necessarily general and suggestive in character. If you desire development of any of its features in greater detail, we shall be glad to amplify or discuss the matter further."

c. Testimony Before Committee

On January 17, 1920, the Committee held a public hearing before which appeared Mrs. Mary Kingsbury Simkhovitch, Director of Greenwich House, and one of the organizers of the United Neighborhood Houses of New York. Mrs. Simkhovitch was a member of a special committee appointed by the United Neighborhood Houses of New York to consult with this Committee on matters pertaining to the education of the adult foreign-born. Mrs. Simkhovitch's testimony in substance is given below:

"The objects of the United Neighborhood Houses of New York are best expressed in Article II of the Constitution, which reads —

"The purposes of this Association are to increase the influence and enlarge the usefulness of Neighborhood Houses through co-ordination and co-operation of effort, to promote the establishment of additional Neighborhood Houses, to act upon public matters in which Neighborhood Houses are inherently interested and to foster an enlightened public opinion respecting such matters; to represent affiliated Neighborhood Houses in applications or appeals to municipal, state or national authorities for governmental action safeguarding public health, improving public education or furthering the good order, effort or convenience of the community. And the Association is established for the additional purpose of speaking publicly in behalf of organizations therein affiliated through statements to the press, publications under its own direction, or its representatives before public or semi-public bodies.

"The object of the Neighborhood Houses individually is to elicit all the values there are in their respective neighborhoods and to bring them to the front as an expression and to bring to them the values of American life.

"The Neighborhood Houses are for the most part located in districts where the majority of the population is either foreign-born, or the children of foreign-born.

"It is rather difficult to describe the activities of our Neighborhood House, for we have fourteen different departments. Our work supplements that of the public school, but never undertakes the same work.

"We have civic clubs in every one of the Neighborhood Houses. There are Roosevelt clubs in practically every house and many of those are civic clubs. There are constant opportunities for civic education presented to adults.

"Our teachers are generally volunteer workers who are interested in our houses. Sometimes we get them from Columbia University. Although this is very satisfactory in many ways, still we are not able to conduct as large an educational work as we should be able to do if we had a regular paid staff. We have had public school teachers to teach English, but they require twenty-five, and if we do not have that many in a class, we have to get a volunteer teacher.

"We find the attendance very good, because there is a social atmosphere that is lacking in the public schools.

"Our teaching of citizenship is accomplished through the civic clubs I have mentioned and through public meetings. We find that the foreign-born take kindly to it and appreciate what we do for them in this respect.

"We do not think that the teaching of English can be accomplished in night classes, because the pupils are too tired after their day's work. I found one Italian group in favor of compulsory education in English, and I think that on the whole the foreign-born would stand for it if it were on factory time.

"We believe that teachers should be better paid, and that teachers for night school work should, when possible, be persons who have not had to teach all day. We think that they should have a knowledge of the background of all the different groups of foreigners that are coming to us, and should be sympathetic to those groups and understand their psychology and their difficulties and be sympathetic with their general attitude. They should be able to teach the nature of American institutions as well as the English language. I think the average person is quite ignorant of the principles of our government, and I think it might be an idea worth considering to have constitution clubs throughout the country. I think you could find very few people — even thorough Americans — who have read the Constitution of the United States since they were ten years old.

"We think that there might be instituted inexpensive trips for school children to such nearby cities as Boston, Philadelphia or Washington, so that they may see the background of the institutions of our entire country.

"If the state were to provide schools and teachers to teach citizenship to the foreign-born, I believe that the classes would be well attended if the proper person were in charge. An outline of the courses could be prepared and placed in the hands of a group of people who would know what would be readily consumed. I think you would always have to consider what the audience was. If it were a radical audience, it would be advisable to show common sense and then present the material with as much force as possible. I think the idea of public discussions is a very useful idea. The United Neighborhood Houses would never allow any sort of presentation of any idea which related in any sense to a violent overthrow of our government, but as to the idea of presenting ideas which involve a gradual change in our institutions which can be accomplished by constitutional methods, we think such a thing is necessary, desirable and fundamentally American. We all feel that truth will prevail, so to speak, and that the presentation of material with which we are in sympathy would be likely to receive a more ardent support than any adverse material, but I do think that it is very desirable to present everything. If a subject is being discussed, of course, then discuss it, provided that no material is allowed which is of a nature which tends to the question of violent overthrow of our institutions. I think on the whole that open forums are a good influence. There are those who use the open forum to air their grievances, but I think it is better for them to do so than to do it in secret.

"Of course our centers are not primarily government

centers, they are human centers, and the teaching of civics and good citizenship is only one phase of our work.

"The people who come to our houses are drawn from all religions and all political parties. Our houses have never lined up with any political party or with any religious propaganda.

"As to the attitude of the people in our neighborhood, the conservative people regard us as radical, and the radicals regard us as extremely conservative.

"We do everything we can to do away with class hatred. However, we are not opposed to changes and stand for anything that is constitutional. The only thing that we consider wrong is violence. We do not permit the presentation of that idea in our houses."

Mr. Harold Riegelman, counsel for the United Neighborhood Houses of New York, was called as a witness and testified in substance, as follows:

"The objects of the United Neighborhood Houses of New York have been defined. The houses themselves that are associated in the organization are not members, but are represented by members.

"Americanization work, especially in a large city like New York, carries with it a tragedy in the fact that the younger generation becomes Americanized much more quickly than the older, and here the settlement house steps in in behalf of the older generation. Also, it provides a place of recreation for the children, who on account of the progress they have made as American citizens are not satisfied with their shabby homes.

"So far as I am aware our attention has not been called to any house which is a member of the United Neighborhood Houses that has fostered consciously or unconsciously any doctrine or any conduct that is subversive of the principles and institutions of the present and existing government. I am sure that if such a complaint were received that the house in question would be rebuked, possibly expelled from the organization, and we even might go so far as to get its charter revoked.

"I believe that there should be open forums for the discussion of arguable questions and that these forums should be impartial. In the case of a question of Americanism, I think the alien should be allowed to feel that in seeking further light he should be in a position to present the arguments that he had heard elsewhere and to have those arguments answered.

"By having the forums really open, you impress upon the foreigner your desire to give him a square deal. The chairman should be able to sway the meeting in case of subversive arguments being offered."

At this point the chairman of the Committee pointed out that in some of the radical literature in its possession prostitution is commended and the prostitute held up as the ideal of womanhood. Mr. Riegelman was asked if he would bring an advocate of prostitution into a forum and let everybody consider the question — if he would give the impression to the foreigners who might come to such a forum that the question was debatable. Mr. Riegelman replied:

"I certainly don't think that the subject should be emphasized. In other words, I do believe that the question impartially requires at least a strong presentation of the other side. Logically, I should say that if such a man were permitted to come into the house that I was entrusted with the guardianship of, I should take mighty good care that on the same platform, at the same time, there was a man who would completely answer the propositions that were made by the advocate of prostitution."

Mr. Riegelman further stated that if such an advocate should "transgress the laws of decency" he would get him to leave the platform!

"One of the difficulties of the settlements has been that we have not been able to get enough men to expound in clear, vigorous fashion pro-American propaganda in language which will meet the particular objections that are raised by the disloyalists, the Bolshevists, the seditionists, and whoever else is opposed to our form of government. Neither are we able to get enough of the proper sort of literature to put into the hands of these people."

d. Communications From Members of the United States Neighborhood Houses of New York

ARMITAGE HOUSE SETTLEMENT, 451 East 121st street, New York City, Katherin Fairbairn, resident worker, January 8, 1920:

"We regret that we can be of no help to you in formulating your Americanization program.

"We are not conducting, at present, any classes in English for foreigners, owing to our inability to secure teachers.

"Armitage House is small, but when we have succeeded in acquiring a larger plant and an increased staff of workers, we are planning to do more intensive work in making good citizens of our neighbors."

BETH-EL SISTERHOOD, 329 East 62d street, New York City, Miss S. Nassaner, head worker, January 5, 1920:

"During the school term of 1918-19 we conducted one Americanization class for adults.

"Since September, 1919, we have had two classes on Monday, Tuesday and Wednesday evenings. The teachers are provided by the Board of Education. The nationalities represented are Hungarian, Russian and a few Italians."

BOWLING GREEN NEIGHBORHOOD ASSOCIATION, 45 West street, New York City, Edmund Leamy, executive secretary, November 17, 1919:

"I have your letter of November 14th and would reply that through the following work we come in contact with the foreign population of this small district of New York.

"Health clinics, recreation department, social service department, mothers' clubs, boys' clubs, girls' clubs, playgrounds, library, dance club, young men's club, young women's club, mother's club, and in co-operation with the Department of Education, 'Mothers' Learn English Clubs.'

"We also have numerous neighborhood meetings, which without being openly called Americanization meetings are got up for that purpose. Some of the subjects discussed are current events, civic government, historical events and citizenship.

"We are planning at present for a good deal more work on Americanization amongst the people here and we expect to be quite successful.

"If there are any further particulars you care for in regard to our work I would be very glad to write you, or better still, if you should be in this neighborhood I would be very glad to talk the matter over with you.

"The dominating nationalities down here are Slavic, Polish, Syrian, Greek and Irish.

"Mrs. T. C. Pecha, who is in charge of the Americanization work we are doing, and with whom I have discussed your letter, has made the following suggestions as to what she thinks would be helpful:

"Stricter immigration laws; passports; registration of arrivals and follow-up work; compulsory attendance at schools; control of the immigrant through employers of labor; time limit for declaration of citizenship intention; possibility of deportation for obvious undesirables."

CENTRAL PRESBYTERIAN CHURCH PARISH HOUSE, 422 West 57th street, New York City, Helen Van Voorhies, November 26, 1919:

"Referring to your letter of November 14th I would say that we have at most only three or four Italian families connected with our House and are not doing any very definite Americanization work. I fear that I have no new suggestions to offer. Of course, to make foreigners true and loyal Americans our work must go beyond the teaching of English, we must reach them in their homes, etc."

CHRISTODORA HOUSE, 147 Avenue B, New York City, C. I. MacColl, head worker, December 22, 1919:

"Your second letter to Miss Hoag, one of my associate workers, has just been received. I deeply regret that the first letter was not promptly answered, but at a meeting of the Executive Committee of the United Neighborhood Houses of New York it was decided that action should be taken by that body instead of through the individual settlements — at least I so understood it.

"Christodora House and all its staff have stood for the work of Americanization ever since our organization in

1897. At the beginning of the Great War, before our country was involved, we formed classes in English in the homes of our neighbors, and in this House had similar classes, as well as instruction in citizenship, and gatherings of foreign-born men and women, which made toward a better understanding of them by us and also a clearer vision on their part as to what the privileges of an American citizen might be, and also the duties of a citizen.

"We have for these many years been helping the foreign-born secure their naturalization papers. We have held community gatherings with open forums where there has been frank discussion of the problems of the day, and the whole character of these meetings has been to enlighten and develop the foreign-born in what constitutes a loyal citizen of this country. We are in active co-operation with all the organizations working along the same line that we are. Our slogan is, 'We are all Americans and must be nothing but Americans.'"

THE COLLEGE SETTLEMENT, 84 First street, New York City, Anna N. Noble, head worker, November 18, 1919:

"I am very much interested in your letter of November in regard to an increased program of education and Americanization for adult foreigners.

"The work of the College Settlement has been in the past, and is now, entirely with Jewish people — particularly the Russian Jew. Our problem is not one of teaching English, as our people are extremely ambitious and eager for education, putting their children in school immediately upon arrival in this country and keeping them there as long as it is possible.

"We have, however, done a very important work in giving to these ambitious people high ideals of American citizenship. The House, in its thirty years of existence, has sent out fine Jewish leaders as professional men, business men, women teachers and home makers.

"I think in this time of social unrest, we are beginning to realize the work of Americanization that has been so quietly done by the settlements in these foreign neighborhoods. We have coming to our House now weekly about seven hundred (700) adults."

D. Y. N. T. Society, 18 Leroy street, New York City, Marie B. Blair, November 24, 1919:

"In reply to your letter of November 15th in regard to our program of education and Americanization for adult illiterate foreigners I wish to state that we have the following activities at our House:

"A class in English for Italian women.

"Second. A class in English and civics for foreign-born men.

"Third. Round table talk and community singing for men and women.

"This last group is not composed entirely of illiterate foreigners but I consider this work of great value.

"The people who compose this little group never go to meetings except on the street corners.

"We have had talks on Democracy, the Constitution of the United States, the League of Nations, From Soldier to Civilian and similar subjects.

"Our meetings are not always well attended as we are living in a neighborhood where people care more for dancing and entertainment than education.

"But real Americanization is more than teaching English. It seems to me that these small groups talking about American ideals may also help to solve the problem.

"It will give me pleasure to have any member of your Committee visit the D. Y. N. T. House."

The East Side House Settlement, 76th street and East river, New York City, Constance P. Bellemy, directress, December 30, 1919:

"The East Side House Settlement will gladly co-operate in any plan for the Americanization of foreigners.

"We did have, sometime ago, English classes and also instructions given on citizenship but owing to the reorganization of some of our work here, these classes have been dropped for a time.

"We come in contact with many foreigners and in personal conversation try to influence them to become good American citizens.

"Will you let us know your plans and what we can do to help in this work?"

THE EDUCATIONAL ALLIANCE, East Broadway and Jefferson street, New York City, Henry Fleishman, administrator, November 17, 1919:

"In the opening paragraph of your letter you speak of an increased program of education and Americanization for adult foreigners. May I at the outset say that in this sentence you have summed up the work and purpose of the Educational Alliance and we are most earnestly and sincerely in accord with this policy.

"The Educational Alliance has for its purpose the Americanization of the foreign-born element and all its activities and all of its efforts are bent in this direction. We stand for an unadulterated and unalloyed Americanism, and we teach and preach this doctrine through every means at our disposal.

"Under separate cover today I am forwarding you the last printed Annual Report of the Alliance. The report of the activities proper being on page 38. We are now organizing and preparing to make an aggressive campaign against Socialism and have already enlisted the aid of influential neighborhood people. In order that you may have before you the information you ask at the earliest possible moment I am sending it today but I shall be very happy to have an opportunity to discuss with you the work of the institution and to give you my general views on the situation. Please consider me entirely at your disposal for further information.

"It occurs to me that a personal visit on your part or by your representative would be valuable both to you and to us and I shall hold myself in readiness to meet you in the Alliance at any time you care to come."

The following extract from the Twenty-fifth Anniversary Report of the Educational Alliance further describes their citizenship training activities.

Day Classes in English for Adult Immigrants

The Educational Alliance has always sought to determine the needs of the neighborhood which it serves, and it might be described as a sort of social laboratory in which needs having been discovered, ways and means are sought to meet them.

Some years ago the Educational Alliance began what was then known as its day classes in English for adult immigrants. There were plenty of evening schools for immigrants, but there was no provision made for an immigrant, who, because of his occupation at night, was prevented from attending the regularly established night schools. Announcement of the formation of these day classes brought us many applications from bakers, theatre employees, watchmen, melamdim. A later development of this school was the admission into it of the mothers whose children attend the public schools. For seven years these classes were continued by the Educational Alliance and it is with more than ordinary gratification that we now report their incorporation into the educational system of the City of New York. It is likely that many more such classes will be established.

Lectures on American History and Civics; Naturalization and Citizenship " Quiz " Classes

In order that he may become a part of our body social the two greatest essentials for an immigrant are a knowledge of the language and an understanding of American government and institutions. The adequate provision made by the public authorities for the first of these enables us to place emphasis on the latter. Our lectures in Yiddish as well as in English, on American history and civics have been markedly successful.

We have urged often that the much deplored tendency of the immigrant to identify himself with various "-isms" and "-ologys" is due to a laudable, ambitious desire to become part of what he believes to be civic life, a privilege denied him in his old home, but here grasped with the utmost avidity. Unfortunately much of the literature available in Yiddish is of a character generally classified as radical. Swayed by doctrines which he believes sound and true, but generally promulgated by adherents of a cause rather than those interested in the welfare of the immigrant, he attaches undue weight and importance to that which is presented to him in his native tongue. If possessed only of a slight knowledge of our language, he finds English literature beyond his comprehension. We therefore endeavor in these Yiddish lectures to present in simple and attractive manner the history and development of our country, the true significance of its institutions and the American interpretation of democracy and liberty.

A natural outgrowth of these lectures is the course preparatory to naturalization. Immigrants of other nationalities have often been criticized for lack of readiness to take advantage of the privilege of securing American citizenship, but this charge cannot be laid with any measure of truth at the door of our Jewish newcomers whose desire for citizenship may require direction, but certainly not stimulation.

It is necessary to teach that government is not bad merely because it means control, and that liberty is such to an extent only to which it does not infringe on the rights of others.

It happens that for one reason or another the immigrant experiences some trouble in declaring his intention to become a citizen, and his inadequate preparation for the final examination sometimes causes rejection. To remedy this we have set aside certain evenings in the week to assist applicants properly to fill out their blanks, and often, through correspondence or otherwise, we supply missing data. Twice a week, citizenship "quiz" classes are held. Out of the hundreds prepared not one has yet failed to pass the judicial examination.

EMANUEL SISTERHOOD OF PERSONAL SERVICE, 318 East 82d street, New York City, Celia L. Strakosch, head worker December 23, 1919:

"Your communication of December 19th is before me. We wish to state that your former communication of December 15th was not answered because we of the Emanuel Sisterhood had agreed to take the same attitude as the other settlements in New York City. We understand that the executive officers of the United Neighborhood Houses have taken this matter in hand and answered for us as one of the co-operating organizations."

FREE SYNAGOGUE, 36 West 68th street, New York City, Frederich L. Guggenheimer, assistant executive director, December 22, 1919:

"Of course individually and as a representative of the Free Synagogue and of the Free Synagogue Social Service, I am deeply interested in the whole problem of Americanization, especially of course as it affects the large group of foreign-born Jews.

"The Free Synagogue is a religious organization which in addition to its religious services and its eight religious schools, distributed throughout the city, conducts a social service department which deals exclusively with medical social service. We do not conduct any activities which would be directly allied to the problem of Americanization, except in so far as all our religious and social work tends to Americanize those whom we serve.

"Personally I had very decided views on the problem of Americanization which I would sum up in these few words, education, education and more education for children and adults, with particular emphasis on the history of America and its opportunities and resources, but I take it these personal views are not what you are seeking but that you want the experience of those settlements which are doing actual work in Americanization."

GREENWICH HOUSE, 27 Barrow street, New York City, Mary Kingsbury Simkhovitch, director, November 18, 1919:

"Foreigners do not enjoy going to the night schools. The reason for this is that they are tired out from their work and also that the schools have not that hospitable, warm, cordial atmosphere which is necessary if people are to take advantage of the opportunities opened to them. Every school where there are classes in English should be properly lighted and there should be a hostess to welcome people when they come in and to give them the feeling that they are wanted and are welcome. But even if the night schools were conducted properly, English classes will touch but a very few relatively. People are too tired to go out in the evening and learn anything. The only practical way to have people learn English on a wide basis is to have it a part of industry and to have employers be patriotic enough to take out a certain amount of time from the work day, in which people can learn English, without reduction of wages.

"I think it ridiculous to prevent people speaking their own language in social centers of any kind, and I believe also that suppression of foreign newspapers is foolish and would mean, if carried out, elimination of a great opportunity to bring foreigners in close touch with American life. It might be practicable to require every newspaper published in foreign language to carry a certain number of columns of government service, and it would certainly be practicable to establish forums in the language of the people themselves where public matters could be discussed and where the people could be made to see that Americans are a hospitable and friendly people. We should not fear public discussion but should see to it that American traditions and ideals dominate these public discussions. Suppression never leads anywhere, but permeation with American ideals does.

"I am inclosing a copy of a letter from General Wood which expresses what I have in mind. We regard everything that we do as Americanization. When we bring our foreign friends to meet Americans at our parties, entertainments, bazaars, etc., they feel that they are welcome and they like Americans. Parents are interested in what their children are getting at these neighborhood houses and often come to see what their children are doing. The nurse, visitor, domestic science worker, etc., come in to talk to these foreigners in their homes and they appreciate the interest that is taken. The whole point is that there must be constant, cordial, personal feeling on the part of Americans for foreign groups in order that there be a mutual understanding and building up of American life. There is no formal or mechanical method of Americanizing people. We have to do the work ourselves.

"So much for general comment. I would like now to add, in order to give you a picture of our work, a sample weekly bulletin of our activities at Greenwich House, with a few remarks. This bulletin you will find inclosed. It does not take into account public meetings which are held here in the gymnasium, auditorium, dining-room and drawing-room.

"I would draw your attention to special features of our work for adults:

"1. Italian Men's Circle. This is a group of very fine American men of Italian descent. They raised over $250,000 in the Liberty Loan Campaign. This group is especially active in promoting any enterprise that may be desirable in the neighborhood. They are helping us with our bazaar.

"2. English classes for foreigners are described in Mrs. Thomas' memoranda inclosed. People like to come here to learn English because the atmosphere is friendly. We can have just as few or many as we desire and thus have individual instruction.

"3. The baby clinic on Thursday afternoons has a membership of about 100 women of the neighborhood with little babies. They are largely, although not wholly, Italian women and they belong to the clubs as well as the classes. The object of the clinic is to teach the mothers how to give adequate care to their babies. It involves educational problems of the highest importance.

"4. There are various other women's clubs connected with our House, and also clubs of older young men, all of whom are thorough-going Americans. This was noticed especially in the case of the older Italians with the non-English-speaking Italian group who, for the most part, took entirely the pro-Italian view of the situation.

"5. The Parents' Association in connection with our music school is an interesting feature. People in the neighborhood are particularly interested in children's opportunities for advancement along musical lines at our music school. We have also an Italian chorus.

"6. A Women's Civic Club is being formed.

"Meetings are held on public matters from time to time in the auditorium. During campaigns we never have partisan, but often have all-candidates meetings, which is educational for the neighborhood. In everything we undertake, we take the neighbors in on the ground floor."

General Report of Americanization Campaign in Greenwich District

Workers

There were six paid workers engaged in the campaign and eight or more volunteer workers, the latter being residents at Greenwich House. None of the paid workers gave full time. Two or three probably have not given more than five hours. The exact figures are not available at the moment. The organizer in charge of the district gave from eighteen to twenty-five hours per week.

Method of Work

The whole plan of work for the campaign centered about Greenwich House as being a neighborhood house, which is a center for the entire district. The people of the House naturally possess a large amount of first hand information regarding the people of the neighborhood.

Visiting

Personal visits paid to individuals and organizations formed the background of the campaign. Some visiting was done by blocks, other visiting was based upon lists available at Greenwich House, as for example, lists of mothers attending the health center. In addition special calls were made upon the heads of the three other settlements of the neighborhood, the ministers and priests of local churches, the local social and political clubs. In every case when the visit was made, the person visited was informed of the classes in English being held at P. S. 95 as well as the classes being formed at the settlement and elsewhere. They were also invited to attend the public meetings held during the last week of the campaign. The organizer of the campaign made a special call upon the Italian Consul General, inviting him to sit upon the platform at the public rally. Managers of three or four local halls were visited and the names of Italian fraternal organizations meeting at those halls were ascertained, with the idea of visiting the halls on the appropriate nights.

Publicity

Slides worded in Italian were prepared at the public school and were shown at the six local moving picture theatres, advertising "Learn English" week. The Saturday night before the public rally an Italian worker visited these theatres and spoke briefly between the reels, urging people to attend the rallies and join the English classes.

The president of the Italian Circle, meeting at Greenwich House, handled the publicity in the Italian press, securing advance notices of the meetings and editorials on the advisability of learning English. The regular American press was also informed of the meetings and invited to send reporters, etc. Advance notices were given to some of these papers.

The classes at the Greenwich House and at P. S. 95 were advertised through letters printed both in Italian and English which were distributed to all the school children of the district, they being asked to take them home to their parents. The rallies for the last week of the campaign were advertised in placards printed in both Italian and English.

Meetings

A highly successful Americanization mass meeting was held on Tuesday night, October 14th, at P. S. 95. The program of this rally is attached. Both Congressman La Guardia and Judge Freschi are popular in the district and proved to be splendid speakers. The War Camp Community song leader did some really wonderful work with the audience. They were simply thrilled over singing their Italian songs, the Italian words of which were thrown on the screen as the song was sung. A pupil of the school testified in excellent English to the value of the instruction he had received. Although it was a particularly stormy night, over 600 were in attendance. Twenty-five or more registered at the door their desire to attend the night school. A similar meeting for Italian women is to be held at Greenwich House on the night of October 16th. The meeting held at the public school was attended very largely by men.

Results

The exact results in figures of the campaign cannot be obtained as yet. Attendance at the night school at P. S. 95 is constantly increasing. The evening class at Greenwich House has doubled in attendance and it has been necessary to secure an additional teacher. A new afternoon class for women has been formed at Greenwich House. These women bring their children who are not yet of school age and they are taken care of in the House Canteen while their mothers attend class. A local Italian club has signified their willingness to organize a class and the teacher is to be furnished for them by the Board of Education. So far, however, the workers feel that the campaign has only just begun, that so far little has been done but sow seed, the results of which, it is believed, will be reaped all through the winter. Certainly the people of the neighborhood are discussing the learning of English as they never have before.

Supplementary Report Regarding Americanization Campaign in Greenwich District

The following statement is given in addition to the report of October 13th and gives figures which were not available at that time.

Statistics

The following figures comprise totals for the five paid workers in the campaign:

Hours of work.................................. 140½
Numbers of calls made.......................... 660
Number of people promising to attend classes.......... 119

In addition to the foregoing, eight volunteer workers, residents at Greenwich House, gave a total of approximately twenty-five hours.

The following are statistics bearing on the results of the campaign to date so far as they can be shown by figures. About twenty-five new students have registered at the evening school at P. S. 95. The registration of the evening class at Greenwich House has tripled, having increased from twelve to thirty-six. A new afternoon class for women at Greenwich House has been formed with an initial registration of about thirty.

Recommendations

(1) Visiting in the neighborhood for the purpose of maintaining and increasing the registration in the English classes must be kept up. The community worker at P. S. 95 and the teachers there should constantly visit any of their own pupils who are irregular in attendance. Greenwich House can furnish volunteer workers to do visiting in connection with its own classes. For example, I understand that the attendance is falling off from the afternoon class at Greenwich House. The teacher of that class should do visiting in this connection and can get help from Greenwich House if she will communicate with me.

(2) If possible, the State should continue to supply a paid organizer for the neighborhood on either part or full time who will co-ordinate the Americanization work going on. This person need not necessarily be a neighborhood person now that the initial work has been done.

(3) The Board of Education should consent to the formation of actual home classes, *i. e.*, classes meeting in the tenement homes of the women. Every visitor reports a number of women who would be willing to attend such classes but who cannot be induced to come to classes even in the settlement.

(4) It would be an excellent idea for the Board of Education to furnish what I would call a "hostess" at P. S. 95, *i. e.*, a woman who would be present early each evening the night school is in session, who would shake hands with each person coming in; inquire about the baby or the job; make friendly personal contacts with each pupil; bid them good night as they go out and express a hope that they will be present the next evening. No other one thing would do so much to maintain the attendance at the school.

(5) Everything possible should be done to make the night school at 95 attractive in physical appearance. The building should be brilliantly lighted. It is ridiculous to expect to compete with the neighboring movies when dim strips of hall are murkily lighted with flickering gas jets. From the very door of the building to and into the classroom, everything should be done to create an impression of warmth, light and cordiality.

(6) In the selection of teachers, cordiality, courtesy and a real interest in and appreciation for the people they are teaching should be a prime factor. No amount of technical knowledge regarding methods of teaching English can take the place of this factor. Any teacher guilty of such discourtesy toward a pupil as telling him or her to "shut up" should be instantly dismissed.

HAARLEM HOUSE, 311 East 116th street, New York City, B. M. Gage, director, November 17, 1919:

"I have your letter of November 15th, in which you ask us if we will co-operate with you in your work of Americanization.

"We are very much interested in this, and have held Sunday forums, and are now planning class extension work along these lines. The great drawback is the lack of workers and textbooks.

"We would be very glad to give you any information on the subject, but there should be arrangements made whereby the settlements, because of their knowledge of the neighborhood, have co-operation from the legislative committee. There are 200,000 foreigners in this district and it is a hotbed for almost everything.

"Unless we Americans get together and teach Americanism, and live it, we are going to regret it. The field is large and the workers are few. We will co-operate with you, but we shall also expect some co-operation from your committee."

How Haarlem House Settlement is Combating Bolshevism

To an American of Italian extraction the present Americanization movement presents a very humorous aspect. The self-appointed apostles of Americanism are endeavoring to study the Italian immigrant through a microscope. What sort of a creature is he? Has he wings? What does he think of America? What are his feelings, his customs? Where does he come from? These questions just size up the psychology of the movement. It seems that out of a clear sky there has fallen a population of about 2,000,000 creatures who call themselves Italians, and it's our job to make them Americans over night or ask them to ascend to their ethereal home. Meanwhile the poor creatures are stupefied and bewildered and want to know just what it is all about. The foreigner judges our country from the local conditions in which he lives, regardless of what nationality he may be. If his interest can be aroused to help in bettering his local conditions, he will feel that this country means something to him. When he understands the value and the inalienable rights and privileges given him by the citizenship papers, when he realizes the opportunity of education and advancement open to all, and when he sees as plainly as two and two make four that he has actually improved economically, as well as intellectually, then America seems a new horizon for him and he becomes slavishly indebted to her. It is then that he perceives the light which the Lady on Liberty Isle extended to him on his arrival, but which he did not fully appreciate until now.

Haarlem House, a settlement situated in Little Italy, the home of 2,000 foreigners, is slowly and effectively crushing the spread of Bolshevism by a policy of practical Americanization. The theory of the workers engaged in this task is that the most effective method of establishing loyalty toward our institutions in the mind of the alien is by giving him a thorough knowledge of the meaning of American ideals and customs. "Radicalism, or the tendency of rebelling against our political system is, in the greater number of cases, a direct outgrowth of ignorance. The average Bolshevik amongst us is one who fails to understand our form of government and is not a citizen of the republic. Teach this man the fundamental basic duties of citizenship, acquaint him with the history of the nation and the struggle for democracy the American people have waged, make him a citizen and aid him to learn our language, then administer to him the gospel of self-help which will improve his economic conditions and from a grumbling, dissatisfied and menacing alien you will have a loyal, satisfied and patriotic citizen."

Haarlem House has done its bit in combating Bolshevism by means of Americanization, and is still carrying on the work. It also tried to do its co-operating with all government requests in interpreting to foreigners the message on the thousands of posters, the meaning of Liberty Loans and to explain America by forming classes in civics and to establish an information center and hold Americanization meetings.

HAMILTON HOUSE, 72 Market street, New York City, Henriette Girsdansky, head worker, January 5, 1920:

"I have left your letter of November 15th unannounced because I knew that a committee from the United Neighborhood Houses has been appointed to give you the information you wished.

"Our Adult Club activities consists chiefly in social, educational and recreational service. Under education we include public health, nursery, maternity case, nutritions clinic, English and foreigners activities.

"In our club life we try to foster a spirit of self-helpfulness, a community spirit which should result in a realization of the representative of citizenship.

"The people we reach are chiefly Italians.

"We will be very glad to have any number of your committee visit us at any time."

HENRY STREET SETTLEMENT, 265 Henry street, New York City, Lillian D. Wald, director, November 26, 1919:

"In reply to your inquiry of November 15th, it would be very difficult to give you in one letter all the information that is implied in a satisfactory answer to your questions. I am sending you under separate cover the last report of the Henry Street Settlement, which is fairly up-to-date, and also some literature on the nursing service which operates under the auspices of the Settlement for the boroughs of Manhattan, Bronx and Richmond.

"I presume that although the service is primarily to care for the sick in their homes, its most valuable by-product is the education that goes with it, particularly, the opportunity of teaching American standards of housekeeping, et cetera, and the opportunity of giving instruction through the most acceptable agency, the nurse, on the protective laws of the country, such as child labor, compulsory school attendance and tenement house regulations. The nurses, themselves, do not discuss politics or religion for obvious reasons, but the opportunities for training in the care of the children and the sick and of raising the standards of the home are unlimited, and out of this experience have grown many protective measures aimed toward the protection of child life and the physical wellbeing of the people.

"The settlements, apart from this service, have an unusual relationship with the people of their neighborhoods. The houses are used for educational and social activities under the leadership of socially minded men and women. Richard Watson Gilder characterized the Settlement as 'The House of the Interpreter.' It is possible here to give an interpretation of the government, its aims, philosophy, traditions and protective legislation. This function was continually capitalized during the war, for the various drives for thrift, conservation of food, Liberty Loan, Red Cross — impossible to give a full list — and the settlements were also used for headquarters for the local exemption boards and in this, and in other houses, the staffs were liberated from other duties to make intelligible and sympathetic the purposes of the board.

"On the other hand, the Settlement, like other Neighborhood Houses, functions with equal value when it in turn interprets with justice and sympathy the peoples in their vicinity, bringing out for the understanding of the American public their share in the industrial, social and cultural life of the country.

"Organizations, known as clubs for boys and girls, have been developed in the Settlement and these give opportunities for discussion and interpretation and educational experimentation not always possible in the school or in the ordinary home. I presume that the policy of the first boys' club can be given as an illustration of this. It was called the 'American Hero Club,' and the purpose of its program was through biographical study of men and women to indicate what contributions were considered valuable to the well-being and the progress of America. This gave a chance to analyze the unselfish, social values, as compared to sordid or unidealistic contributions of men and women, native and foreign-born. The clubs also give the opportunity of training in self-government and provide admirably for the education and control implied in that. Such a program as the one described above logically developed the need of the study of civics, and more specifically this Settlement, as others, gives the use of its rooms for classes in English for foreigners and it is made possible for the adults to attend by taking care of the children during their instruction. The Settlement follows the same policy in its various branches, and there is nothing exceptional in this, it is the policy carried out with sincerity by all well established Settlement and Neighborhood Houses.

"The value of the Settlement is also demonstrated in its programs for cultural and recreational activities, such as classes in dramatics, diction, art, industrial work, gymnasium and dancing. Country outings, vacation homes and convalescent homes are still other branches of this phase of the work.

"This Settlement also makes a great effort to provide scholarship funds to enable children economically handicapped to secure additional vocational education that they may enter labor as more skilled workers.

"I am assuming that the writer of the letter is more or less familiar with the modern methods of protecting children and probably knows the part that this and other settlements have played in promoting social legislation to this end. The Settlement, as others, co-operates with the city departments, the state and federal, and its plant has been given to governmental, as well as to private agencies for helping to carry out programs for good citizenship and human welfare.

"Should there be any specific question upon which you would like information, we would be glad to give you such. It is a little difficult where the program is varied and extensive to pick out the items that could be helpful to you."

SPECIAL WAR ACTIVITIES — HENRY STREET SETTLEMENT

Boys' Department

One hundred and eighty-five Henry Street Settlement boys are in service.

Mr. Warren C. Eberle, head of the Boys' Department, is chairman of Draft Exemption Board 97.

Intensive farm work carried on in Boys' Camp during summers of 1917 and 1918 to stimulate food production and instruct boys.

"Henry News" is printed bimonthly to be sent to H. S. S. boys in service.

Henry Street comfort fund, raised by entertainments in the clubs, etc., to be used for the boys in service.

"Four Minute Men" recruited from among club members.

Organization of Survey Centers

Organization of the social institutions south of Grand street, east of the Bowery and Broadway, into eleven zones, to make surveys for the Food Council and the Americanization Committee, etc., and to serve in civic or national emergency.

Americanization Work.— A house to house canvass was made in the immediate district to learn the number of women interested in citizenship. English classes were organized in November, 1917, which have been meeting continuously up to the present time. A civic class for girls was organized during the winter. An Information Center on naturalization, citizenship and current affairs has been opened at the Main House.

Red Cross Work.— The Main House was appointed Assembly District Headquarters for the last Red Cross drive, with the organizations affiliated with the Organization of Survey Centers and other organizations in the district serving as captains.

The Fourth Liberty Loan is to be handled in similar fashion. Former Liberty Loans were organized by the club departments of the Settlement; more than $20,000 worth of bonds being sold by the club members in the last loan.

The Settlement was represented in the Red Cross parade and the Liberty Loan parade, in which the nurses and the mothers of boys in service marched.

Children's Years.— The Organization of Survey Centers assisted in the weighing and measuring of babies and children under five years old for the Federal Children's Bureau; volunteers from the different centers performing all the work.

General War Service

The Settlement helped the families in the neighborhood to secure coal during the fuel shortage last winter.

A survey of coal cellars was made for the Fuel Committee.

The Settlement is serving as district office for the Food Council. A food shop was maintained last winter for members of settlement clubs, where food was sold at cost. Demonstrations of economical ways of cooking and the use of war substitutes were given weekly.

A Health Manual of New York City was compiled by members of the Henry Street staff for the Council of Women's Organizations for War Service.

Seventy-ninth Street Branch

Red Cross

An auxiliary where women of the neighborhood meet once a week to knit and sew.

A class in knitting for juniors.

Several junior clubs knit blankets for Red Cross.

Neighborhood canvassing in Red Cross drive.

Twenty clubs subscribed for Red Cross Magazine.

House was represented in Red Cross parade.

Assisted in Food Card drive.

Other War Time Activities

A class in educational therapy.

A class in economic cooking.

Women club members helped in canning fruit at piers.

Week-end camps conducted for boys and girls obliged to work through war pressure.

Soldiers' dependents assisted with allotments.

Boy Scouts sold over $1,000 worth of Liberty Bonds.

House members purchased $2,000 worth of bonds.

House sold $600 worth of Thrift Stamps.

Fifty-three boys in service, and four girls serving as yeomen.

Served on Exemption Board and conducted Information Center.

Lincoln House (for Colored People)

General Work

Day parties for mothers and babies, and summer vacations for the older girls and boys were provided during the summer.

Lincoln House provides club and class space and is the community center for all neighborhood activities. Interest in community affairs is stimulated by an annual welfare exhibit in which the entire neighborhood participates. A baby show is held once a year to promote "better babies."

Special War Activities

Red Cross.— Women meet once a week to knit and make hospital garments.

Junior Red Cross meets once a week. Smaller children collect articles for soldiers' kits.

House took part in Red Cross drive.

Liberty Loan.— House sold $4,850 worth of Liberty Bonds in last drive; is planning to give active service in the fourth bond loan.

Thrift Stamps.— Club members have bought more than $430 worth.

House has participated in patriotic meetings and "Community Sings."

Assisted in "Children's Year" and "Better Baby Campaign."

Fifty farm gardens cultivated last summer by the children.

Head worker has addressed groups on war activities, including a group of more than 200 soldiers at Camp Upton who had recently arrived from the South.

Miss Wald's Active Membership in Other Organizations

General

Honorary president, National Organization for Public Health Nursing.

President, Social Halls Association.

Vice-president, American Association for Labor Legislation.

Honorary vice-president, Big Brothers and Sisters International Advisory Council.

Trustee, National Child Labor Committee.

Board of Directors, New York Child Labor Committee; National Association for Advancement of Colored People; Babies Welfare Association.

Advisory and Speakers' Board, Intercollegiate Community Service Association, etc.

Offices Held in Connection with the War

Chairman, Committee on Home Nursing of the Section of Sanitation of the Committee on Welfare Work of the Committee on Labor of the Council of National Defense.

Conference Board, Council of Women's Organizations of Committee of Women on National Defense.

Member, Committee on Nursing of the General Medical Board of the Council of National Defense; New York State Committee of the Committee on Women in Industry of the Advisory Commission of the Council of National Defense.

Summary of Extra Expenses to which Settlement is put to Maintain Its Wartime Activities

In addition to volunteer service rendered by members of the Henry Street staff, this work has involved a large outlay of expense on the part of the Settlement.

Training Student Nurses

Salaries of educational supervisors.

Administrative expenses, including stenographic help, telephone bills, etc.

Maternity Center

Salaries of special staff of nurses.

Administrative expenses of training student nurses.

Purchase of house on East 79th street and its alteration and equipment to house nurses on night duty in Maternity Center.

Vocational Scholarship Administered for Red Cross

Salary of executive secretary who is giving half her time to organizing Atlantic Division and establishing work in New York City.

Administrative expenses, including office rent, stenographic work, telephone, etc.

Organization of Survey Centers

Salary of organizer who gives full time to the work.

Administrative expenses.

General Expenses

Stenographic help for letters, reports, etc., in connection with these committees.

In 1917 Henry Street Settlement faced a deficit of $26,000 which it was obliged to cover by drawing on its capital. The expansion of the work in 1918 necessitated by existing conditions threatens a still heavier deficit.

Work in Citizenship

Lincoln House is bringing about among those living on Columbus Hill a larger spirit of co-operation by all for the good of all, and believes that it is contributing toward the development of a higher standard of citizenship among the colored people.

HUDSON GUILD, 436 West 27th street, New York City, Alice E. Robbins, executive secretary, January 6, 1920:

"The Hudson Guild is not in a neighborhood of foreigners. There are, however, sections where Italians live, and the house has interested them in various ways.

"There have been well attended classes in English. With the co-operation of the League for Foreign-born, a class for married women was held with a good and regular attendance. A class of men and women under the Board of Education has been conducted here also.

"Italian children are found in all the afternoon classes, in cooking, sewing, carpentry, clay-modeling, knitting, toy-making, stories, games, dramatics, etc. Through these children the fathers and mothers are reached in various ways and interested in the house, in the children's clinic through entertainments and lectures, in the co-operative store and at the co-operative farm where the Italians are especially interested in the agricultural side of the work.

"In the library which occupies the most of the first floor and which is the only library in the immediate neighborhood, one-third of the readers are Italians. This library reaches children chiefly, and the librarian tells me that the Italian children are the most interested and intelligent readers, being especially anxious to read poetry and legends. These books go into the homes and some attempt is made to get the mothers to read them.

"Two posts of the American Legion meet here regularly and some time ago a smoker was held by one of these groups which the club members declare was one of the most successful ever conducted here in numbers and enthusiasm.

"The house in its neighborhood relief work touches Italian as well as American families. A district worker tells me that about one-third of the cases are Italian.

"The printing school, under the Guild roof, the largest printing school in the world, has a good percentage of foreign names on its lists; these students are boys of foreign parents, but of American birth. The school, which is unique in that it has for its management employers, trade union members and Hudson Guild representatives, conducts examinations for the trade union card of all those who enter the printing trade through the unions. There are some 200 of these applicants and they are largely of foreign birth. The idea of this examination originated with the school and the examination is conducted by the head of it.

"In all the work of the house, the co-operative method is used; in club management, in discipline, in the vacation house and especially in the co-operative grocery store, a business venture in true co-operation. The shares of this enterprise are bought by the Italians and Americans in the neighborhood. The Italians are expected to fall in line with the co-operative idea and they do so, sending delegates from their clubs to the council, the directing body of the house, paying their share in the expenses exactly as other clubs do and taking their part in committee work.

"We think this a fair showing of work that is not of recent growth, but that has been going along slowly for years. It represents, we think, the best kind of Americanization — the working together of American and foreign-born for the common good."

THE HANNAH LAVANBURG HOME, 319 East 17th street, New York City, Julia Rosenberg, superintendent, November 17, 1919:

"In reply to your letter concerning the work with foreigners, I am glad to be able to co-operate with you in every possible manner, for I feel we can never do too much to assist in Americanization work. We have English classes under the auspices of the Board of Education; lectures on Americanism; community sings; clubs and classes in civics; a mothers' club of Russians, Roumanians, Hungarians and Austrians.

"I should be glad to have you give them a lecture also if such arrangement could be made, or perhaps you might suggest a speaker for me."

Lenox Hill Settlement, 511 East 69th street, New York City, Rosalie Manning, November 18, 1919:

"Enclosed please find a copy of the letter which I recently sent to Judge Mayer, and which takes up the matter of citizenship papers.

"We are in personal touch, through our Settlement, with thousands of foreigners, and I consider the aliens in this country to be one of the greatest of our assets, provided we deal with them sanely and fairly. For example, the way we give out our citizenship papers and provide for English classes is so poorly done that it can only make the foreigner feel lack of confidence in us, certainly in our efficiency.

"This fall the Lenox Hill Settlement has organized two English schools, one for Bohemians and one for Italians. These schools were organized by the groups themselves working with us, and were backed by the promise of the Board of Education and the Education Department of the State of New York, that suitable teachers of the same nationality as the groups would be supplied. As soon as these schools were established and were, and are, extremely successful, both the Board of Education and the State of New York found themselves unable to fill the pledges made to the committees from these groups. The teachers who were engaged were, most of them, ruthlessly removed from the classes that had become attached to them, so that we feel at the Settlement that the authorities now in charge of this work break up our English classes faster than we can organize them. To be concrete, the school P. S. 70, long established as a night school on East 75th street, could not muster two classes at the opening of the school session, whereas the very first night we organized nine classes for Bohemians, some with an attendance of forty in the class, and six classes for Italians. In spite of all that has been done, through mismanagement, to break up this work, the schools are still among the best in New York, and I believe the Bohemian school to be the very best. These schools, however, have a much deeper meaning than just the gathering together of a few students to study English. The whole Italian and Bohemian colonies attend the school sessions, adjust differences, plan entertainments, and visit among their own people.

"Sedition cannot be stamped out by shutting down the

lid and bottling it inside, and I believe that sedition among the foreign people, except for some notable exceptions, comes from our own stupidity in handling these groups. They have been exploited by their own people and our politicians, have been forced to congregate by themselves, usually under the most unhygienic and distressing conditions; no hand of fellowship has been held out to them by the American people, and we are only suffering natural and inevitable results. This wave of Americanization which has swept over our country has done much to alienate the foreigner who came to seek a free country. Suppression of their newspapers and their language, I believe to be un-American, though, on the other hand, I believe we should know everything which is being published. We have failed to do this in the past and are now suffering greatly from that stupidity. Most of these foreigners came over here with better American ideals than those held by Americans themselves. Of course imagination always soars ahead of reality.

"We are in touch with literally thousands of Bohemians, Hungarians, Italians, Russians, Germans, Irish, Greeks, and a few others. Many of the Italian, Russian, Hungarian and Bohemian societies meet in our building, and the Settlement staff always has a most cordial invitation to come to any of their gatherings, even their lodges and societies.

"Another feeling that the foreigner has about the term 'Americanization' is that it is a stigma upon the country from which he comes.

"In closing, please let me beg that before taking any steps to educate the adult foreigners, and I firmly believe that they should be educated, you will consult these people themselves. As we are in the closest touch with all foreign groups in our neighborhood, we offer you every co-operation and will be glad to have you send some one here to meet these people personally and talk with them, as we are in a position to introduce you to the very best among the foreigners."

"*October* 14, 1919."

"Hon. JULIUS MAYER, *United States District Court, Woolworth Building, New York, N. Y.:*

"MY DEAR JUDGE MAYER.— As you suggested, I am putting in writing our reasons for requesting to have the court opened at night to present citizenship papers to certain groups in our neighborhood, who are being specially prepared to receive them. We are making this request to have you open a court for these special groups one or two evenings at the end of their night school course, as an experiment which we believe will prove that this is a better method of giving citizenship papers than that now in use. Every foreign group which the Lenox Hill Settlement is connected with — Bohemians, Hungarians, Italians, Russians, Greeks, Slovaks, and our connection is with the organized societies, thus reaching very large groups — makes the same request in regard to citizenship papers. The points they make for opening the court at night and being allowed to pass their examination before receiving their final papers, are as follows:

"I. These people are obliged to lose a day's work and to pay witnesses for their day's work. This they themselves know is breaking the law and yet they cannot avoid it.

"II. Without exception they know that the quick road to their papers is through a political party. This they resent.

"III. They all speak of the lack of dignity which attends the presentation of the papers. This probably applies to the regular courts.

"IV. They are deterred from getting their papers for one of the following reasons:

"Fear of an examination;

"Lack of time, which means procrastination;

"Lack of knowledge of how to proceed.

"These points I am not making myself. They come directly from the groups, and since they all say the same thing without consultation, and my knowledge is obtained from the leaders of large organizations, I believe that they state the truth. The only argument that I have seen raised against the plan which we are proposing is that any man who is really in earnest about obtaining his papers should be willing to sacrifice some time and money. The Lenox Hill Settlement is not desirous of making it easier to obtain citizenship in the United States, but the present method is not securing the best citizens. Oftentimes some of the best are not getting their papers. Ashamed as I am to say it,

I often find these foreigners with higher ideals than many Americans possess. Their objection to being forced to get their papers through a political party and breaking the law in obtaining them, are objections which I heartily endorse.

"To make our request very concrete, we would like to have you open the court at the end of our term of instruction, say about the middle of February. We would like to arrange the date, or dates, according to the number of papers which you can give out. We would like to advertise in the foreign papers, applying it only to this section. We guarantee to put the candidates through the third degree before we get through with them. When I say 'we' I mean the state and city educators, under whose direction these classes are held. We will also work with the Naturalization Bureau, so that when you give them their papers in the evening, if you consent to this, you will feel that you really know your group and that they are worth receiving them. We would like to prepare a very dignified program, but of course this could not be arranged until we find out just how long it would take to present the papers.

"A committee composed of prominent representatives of the different nationalities in this section will be very glad to confer with you if you would care to see them.

"Again thanking you for your kind interest in this matter, believe me

"Very sincerely yours,"

MADISON HOUSE SOCIETY, 216 Madison street, New York City, Ruth Larned, head worker, January 6, 1920:

"We consider the whole settlement program and Americanization program.

"Our work is mainly with young people. We do little with adult foreign-speaking people, excepting through mothers' clubs, and through such feeble English class work as is possible for us to carry on with insufficient teachers, and insufficient funds with which to pay for trained ones, procurable for day class work, which is the time that has been found most practicable for the mothers to come.

"Any specific recommendations that I may make are embodied in the report, which has gone to you from a committee of the United Neighborhood Houses, which report I have heard and entirely approve."

NEW YORK CHILD WELFARE COMMITTEE, 70 Fifth avenue, New York City, Frank C. Meyers, November 19, 1919:

"For about ten years we have been organizing each winter a series of parents' meetings in the schools, the purpose of which has been to familiarize the parents of foreign birth and training with the conditions in New York that affect child life adversely and to advise them of the existence and work of the numerous child helping agencies within the city. With this object in mind we have also organized during this same period Neighborhood Child Welfare exhibits, the attendance at which has been over 2,287,000.

"In so far as we have been able to do so these Neighborhood Child Welfare exhibits have been organized as local enterprises. In some instances we have had as many as 300 local leaders such as physicians, lawyers, business men, etc., serving on the committees, and out of this work evolved several of our most flourishing Neighborhood Associations.

"As a matter of strategy it is very important, in our judgment, to work through the leaders of the foreign groups. If the enthusiastic co-operation of the leaders can be gotten, and if the leaders can be made to feel that they are really carrying out their own plans, work for foreigners is likely to become very effective."

THE PEOPLE'S UNIVERSITY EXTENSION SOCIETY OF GREATER NEW YORK, 111 Fifth avenue, New York City, J. E. Whitney, secretary, November 18, 1919:

"The following is a statement of our Americanization work:

"Americanizing foreigners is an important part of the work of our classes and lectures among the foreign-born. Our teachers win the friendship of the women and children and inspire them with love for our wonderful land of freedom and opportunity, and with loyalty to its flag. We have already reached thousands of foreign-born women and factory girls and the work of teaching American ideals and the debt of loyalty we all owe our country will be vigorously continued and extended by our society. We cordially invite those interested to visit any of our classes.

"We reached more than 60,000 foreign-born women and girls the past year by lectures and throughout the city.

"I believe we need to teach every foreigner the great

opportunities our country gives every child that no other nation in the world gives, complete free education. Higher wages than any other country, free religion, no caste restrictions, chance for any poor boy to raise to the highest position in his state, etc."

RECREATION ROOMS AND SETTLEMENT, 186 Chrystie street, New York, Josephine Schain, head worker:

"Americanization meetings, so-called, are held at the recreation rooms and Settlement every Friday evening. A speaker is invited to talk for forty minutes. Then follows forty minutes of questions; after that forty minutes of speaking from the floor, and then finally the speaker is allowed five minutes to conclude.

"Mr. Stevenson spoke on the radical movement in America on Friday evening, November 21st. The questions and the speeches from the floor showed a decided sympathy with radicalism, and not one spoke a favorable word for democracy. Several even recommended the overthrow of the government by force."

THE JACOB A. RIIS NEIGHBORHOOD SETTLEMENT, 48 Henry street, New York City, Helen H. Jessup, head worker, November 19, 1919:

"In reply to your letter of November 15th, I am glad to tell you the work we do at the Riis House with adults. We have always felt that we reach the adults best by gaining their confidence through our work with their children. To this end we have organized twenty-five boys' clubs and forty girls' clubs and classes, three kindergartens, and ungraded public school classes.

"Our direct work with the adults is done in our four mothers' clubs and our Neighbors' Union. The membership of this last organization is made up of the neighbors on the two blocks between Market and Oliver on Henry street. Our aim and the neighbors' aim is to carry out the health and sanitary laws of the city by making this the cleanest block on the East Side. In addition to this Union, we have community sings every other week and Americanization through recreation.

"You say that you believe that the social service worker knows the best need of the adult foreigner. I believe you are right and in the past years we have tried desperately to do real lasting Americanization work and we want to do it now and in the future. However, insinuations of the kind made by Mr. Starr which were allowed to appear in a New York newspaper early in the summer do not help us but hinder. In order to help social service work I should like to suggest to you that you start and back legislation to turn into the settlements of New York funds from the state to insure making their social work constant. We should be glad to have members of the State Committee visit the Jacob A. Riis Neighborhood Settlement at any time.

"As a member of the executive committee of the settlements of New York City I will say that I feel confident that every aid and suggestion the settlements can give will be put at your disposal for Americanization work. It was from the settlements that suggestion came to permeate the East Side with Americanization by sending speakers to counteract the Red propaganda.

"This suggestion came from Mrs. Jacob A. Riis, and I as head worker of the Jacob A. Riis Neighborhood Settlement House cannot say too strongly that our House stands for Americanization first, last and all the time, and anything which your Committee feels we can do to teach respect for and loyalty to the United States government we should be glad to hear and to carry out to the best of our ability. I endeavor to state the stand of our Settlement House in no uncertain terms and to have the House carry out that stand in no uncertain manner."

SCHOOL SETTLEMENT, 120 Jackson street, Brooklyn, Maud T. Dobie, January, 1920:

"The question of Americanization is so broad and so far reaching, it is difficult to confine it to a few suggestions.

"We have had classes in English for foreigners for several years, in our Settlement, three evenings a week. We have managed to have an average of twelve to fifteen men here; the most successful class we ever had was conducted by a woman who seemed to have a special gift for the work. The men came all through the heavy hot summer, and came regularly. Those men would have continued to come for years, if they had had the same teacher. I was never able to get her again — that is one mistake, not continuing a successful teacher with the same group.

"I find that women are more successful than men, I think because they are more patient and realize that the adults must be treated as children, step by step. Men are apt to be very impatient, forgetting that the foreigner has everything to learn.

"The work must not be confined to the book, it must be varied and interesting, with music, patriotic songs, etc., brought into the work.

"A social worker can best interpret the desires of the foreigners — one who is really interested in the foreigner himself. Italians are quick to respond and are very fond of a social time. Anything which will bring them together will serve as bait for teaching them the language and the customs of the country. Not enough is made of the citizenship papers. It should be easier for them to get them. They should not have to give up a day's work in order to get them. They should be able to get them evenings. It should be much more important.

"There should be some patriotic address with music and flags, something that all foreigners like, and they should be made to feel that it is an important day in their lives.

"Some factories have had classes in English in their shops. That has worked out successfully in some places. I feel that the whole success of such work depends upon the personality of the worker.

"I am speaking of the Italian, not other nationalities; I am not familiar enough with the others to speak with authority. The Hebrews will learn anyway; the Poles are hard to interest.

"The groups should be small. They should have about the same knowledge of the language. They should be encouraged to speak and to take part in all exercises, to write, to read aloud, especially the newspapers. They should be encouraged all the time — they are easily discouraged."

SETTLEMENT AND CHURCH OF ALL NATIONS, 9 Second avenue, New York City, John R. Henry, superintendent, November 20, 1919:

"I am enclosing you an article which I wrote last August entitled 'The Russian Patriots of New York' that will give you in fuller form than this letter a statement of what we are attempting to do.

"Our two main methods of Americanization are through our monthly magazine 'Enlightenment' and through our Saturday night forum. We also have a Sunday night program. Our general theme for this winter being the resources of America and the history of the American people. We are finding, so far as the Russians are concerned, that there is almost too much overlapping. Our work has been considerably diminished of late because of the large number of new agencies that are springing up.

"Among the Italians we have a prosperous night school and we also have a very prosperous work among the Chinese, teaching the Chinese women in their own homes, as well as having large groups of Chinese young men in our clubs and classes, and these have the privilege of listening to the best speakers that we can procure, who may be in attendance at nearby universities.

"New York State is co-operating with us in our Italian night school, and the Y. M. C. A. is giving us some assistance in our Sunday night lecture course.

"There is no question that America and particularly the Atlantic Coast cities permitted a far heavier immigration than they were able to digest, with the result that we have had during the war so difficult a problem among a great mass of seditious and disloyal aliens.

"As to how many foreigners we are reaching, we have an average audience every Saturday night at our children's assembly of 600 or 700 Italian children. We have 30 or 40 in our Italian night school; we have anywhere from 75 to 1,000 Russians at our forum and we have almost 150 Chinese at our weekly meeting."

The Russian Patriots of New York

By Rev. John R. Henry, D.D., *Pastor of Church of All Nations, New York City*

In no part of our land has the war provoked more bitter controversies than amid the polyglot masses of New York's East Side. This is especially true among the Russian immigrants.

To the soap-box orators that hold forth on a hundred corners, the war was made and is prolonged solely by, and in the interest of, the capitalistic class. America's entry into the war in no wise altered this view, though discretion tempers its public expression.

The high moral and altruistic motives that sent the American people into the world Armageddon, as noble a national sacrifice as history records, are ignored. "Elihu Root handed Kerensky $60,000,000 from American capitalists to keep up the fighting," declared a Bolshevist from the floor of our hall. While the anti-Bolshevists present jeered this untrue and ludicrous statement, the Bolshevists accepted it as reasonable and accurate.

Some of the arch destroyers and betrayers of Russia are social fanatics and political dreamers and exploiters from the heterogeneous immigrant population of New York's East Side.

While this numerous and disloyal and noisy crowd has received much attention, the Russian immigrant, dominated by sane social ideas and staunch patriotism, has been less prominent. Nevertheless, he is an ardent and effective worker for world liberty.

The principal East Side organization through which the patriotic Russian group expresses itself is the Forum of the Church of All Nations. Here, frequently, from 600 to 1,000 Russians gather in meetings as intense in interest as the abolition meetings of half a century ago. To these men the war is a reality. Time and again the warring armies have fought their way across the sites of their homes. Their property is destroyed, their families are scattered, their children are dead of starvation. The East Side Russian has a full and bitter realization of the horrors of this World War.

This additional fact must be remembered: prior to the war no such pronounced pacifist as the radical Russian dwelt in America. The anti-militaristic doctrines of Tolstoy had saturated the group with whom we deal. On a few occasions when we exhibited motion pictures featuring Russian armies, our Russians hooted the sight of the troops. To their eyes any military force was simply a hated indispensable of autocracy.

Much commendation, therefore, should be given these men, that in view of the world conditions, they revised their thinking. They see clearly today that the slavering brute that has already destroyed innocent millions can never be stopped by the reign of laws. He understands only the rain of bullets.

From early in the World War our institution was placed at the service of the Russian patriots. Here for over a year, the representatives of the Zemstvos (the town meeting of Russia) met to engage skilled mechanics. A great multitude of these were recruited and sent overseas.

A campaign was launched in our building under Col. Koch, to secure 40,000 Russian recruits throughout the country to serve under the United States colors, preferably on the Eastern front. This campaign has already made headway and will be greatly accelerated by our country's benevolent intervention.

In addition to many of our best Russian men enlisting with Col. Koch, a number of them volunteered for service immediately upon the entrance of America into the war and were among the first sent abroad.

In the Third Liberty Loan drive, $20,000 worth of bonds were sold at a mass meeting in our hall, and $30,000 additional in other Russian centers, largely through the agency of our men. In our building was organized the Russian Peasants' Society, an organization working for constitutional government in Russia, with today the largest membership of any patriotic Russian society in America. Our Russian monthly magazine "Enlightenment" has been hitting hard blows against the secret and open enemies of the Allied cause.

The most eminent Russian Republic men who have visited America in the past eighteen months have addressed our forum. The names of a partial list of these are of interest: Count Tolstoy, son of the famous novelist, delivered his first Russian address in America in our hall; Professor Borodin, member of the Duma and of the extraordinary Russian Commission to America; Professor Petronkevitch, of Yale, son of the eminent Russian statesman; Professor Lomonossoff, head of the Russian Railroad Commission; Alexander Biblukoff, head of the Russian railroads, a member of the executive committee of the Duma, the man who arrested Czar Nicholas and to whom the Czar handed his abdication; General Semenoffsky, ex-Military Governor of Moscow; General Oberucheff, Military Governor of the Kieff district; Dr. Sack, head of the Russian Bureau of Information in the United States; Dr. Karpovitch, Secretary of the Russian Embassy; M. Volodarsky, who later turned Bolshevist, and on returning to Russia was appointed censor of all Russian papers, and early in August was killed by the social revolutionists — these and many others addressed large forum audiences.

But the most important task confronting our patriotic Russians has been the conduct of a determined and active campaign against the evil forces of betrayal that have been busy in Russia and in America.

News of the amazing revolution that in a day overthrew the hoary autocracy of Russia spread like a prairie fire over the East Side. One hundred thousand former victims of bureaucracy's heavy hand were electrified into mad rejoicing.

By common consent, our hall became the rallying place of celebration. Rarely, if ever, has New York seen so many various and discordant elements fused by one joy into a common soul. Our hall was packed with 1,000 enthusiasts, 500 were crowded in the corridors, and 2,000 in the street in front of our building. The celebration began at eight o'clock in the evening, and had not ended at two o'clock in the morning. The anarchist and the Greek Orthodox priest stood side by side and exulted together; the Moderate Socialist and the Bolshevist, the Christian and the Jew sunk their differences. In every mind and heart and on every tongue was the one great theme: "Russia has broken her shackles! The Bastile has fallen! 'Government of the People, by the People, for the People,' has been born at last in Russia."

These sentiments found voice in the slogan of the revolution: "Land, bread and liberty!"

It is true that even at this great demonstration the voice of discord was heard, but it would have been deemed incredible that any in that gathering should have been getting ready to fit a more galling iron collar about the neck of Russia than any Czar Nicholas ever fashioned. Yet such has proven to be the fact.

The strong man of the revolution was Paul Milukoff. He was then the leader of the overthrow and he may still prove to be the saviour of Russia.

Before the close of the evening a speaker moved that the congratulations of the meeting be cabled to Milukoff. This motion was seconded from many parts of the hall. A fierce protest was launched by Leon Braunstein (Trotzky), who was present. The Russian revolution was too mild for him. "We want a social revolution," he cried, "that will spread all over the world." Some years ago that audience would have voted Trotzky's way, but for five years they had been listening weekly to social discussions based on sane Christian sociology. As a consequence, the audience simply laughed at Trotzky, and by a practically unanimous vote passed the resolution.

Bishop Bashford, an eminent Christian statesman, has said, "If one million dollars had been spent merely in Russia for the past forty years in educating the masses, there would have been no Russian collapse. The expenditure of that money would have produced results that the United States would not have sold for forty billion dollars." All of which is true. But the chief conspirators in the Russian betrayal came from the church-deserted slum and tenement area of our greatest city. There might have been a vastly different loyalty if a paltry hundred thousand dollars had been annually spent among the neglected Russian masses in New York.

Like vultures scenting the carcass from afar, Trotzky and other exploiters, crack-brained fanatics, impractical idealists, and paid German agents swarmed into Russia. Whether these were destroyers in the pay of Germany, or chasers of moonbeams, makes little difference. The results of their activities have been wholly pro-German. By destroying the discipline of the army, and by its demobilization, they robbed Russia of the only force for which Germany had any respect. The Bolsheviki laid open their great country to Germanization. With a free hand in Russia, patriotic Russian statesmen knew, what others have strangely failed to see, that Germany could afford to restore France, Belgium, Serbia, and Roumania, lose her colonies and pay an indemnity, and, keeping Russia, with its unlimited resources in raw materials and men, she would have won the war and ultimately would dominate the world.

In consequence, our Russian constituency has fought the Bolsheviki and their doctrines with an ardor and a fierceness that has frequently made me feel that America was far from realizing the life-and-death character of this world struggle.

From these meetings, that at times have overflowed our hall and blocked the traffic in the avenue, have gone repeated telegrams to Washington urging the imperative duty not alone of material help, but of adequate armed intervention.

The armed forces of America and her Allies are at this writing moving to the rescue of Russia. We believe that they will be in time to prevent the Germanization of vast areas of that unhappy land. They may even revive the Eastern front. How great or how little our part has been in bringing about the desired result, we have the gratification of knowing that we have lent every possible aid to the loyal Russians who are one with America in their heroic battle for the Christian democracy of a free world.

STUYVESANT NEIGHBORHOOD HOUSE, Stuyvesant and 9th streets, New York City, George L. Cohen, executive director, November 20, 1919:

"I am enclosing herewith a copy of 'The Neighbor' containing an article by myself entitled 'Americanization Without Fireworks,' which will give you some of my ideas on the subject of Americanization. I should be glad to answer any specific questions that you might have. The subject is very important indeed, and I hope that your Committee will be able to obtain some very valuable information."

AMERICANIZATION WITHOUT FIREWORKS

Hardly a day but sees the birth of a new organization, some new association of earnest men and women, or a movement for the improvement of society. This is one of the healthy signs of a progress in a democracy in which each citizen has the divine right of attempting the improvement of his neighbor. In the thirty-three years since the founding of the University Settlement, the first settlement in this country, countless organizations of this nature have sprung up, and died away, leaving a trail of disappointed hopes and smashed illusions in their trail. In the same period, settlements have grown up and developed throughout the country, so that now there are more than 500 houses "by the side of the road," where live and work the "friends of man."

In the early days the settlement movement attracted, besides such useful idealists as Jane Addams, Charles B. Stover, David Blaustein, Jane Robbins, and Robert A. Woods, hosts of others, to whom the novelty of the movement was equally as attractive as its philosophy. It was only natural that as the novelty wore off, some of those to whom it was the sole attraction should seek other allurements.

In the meantime, a new generation has grown up — young men and young women of all ages, who seek happiness in constructive service to their fellow-men. The needs of the day also have assumed a different complexion. The future of democratic government in this country, and its establishment the world over, is the problem that is uppermost in the minds of thinking men and women. Compared with the various cults, groups, community councils, neighborhood associations, loyalty leagues, and other organizations that defy classification, the undramatic character of usefulness of the Neighborhood House seems tame. But it is to these young people that the Neighborhood House offers an opportunity for timely service, an opportunity to aid in organizing and enlarging the sinking fund of education for democratic citizenship.

In an unpretentious manner, Stuyvesant Neighborhood House, together with other settlements, is doing real Americanization work. Through its self-governing clubs, Stuyvesant Neighborhood House is training for intelligent American citizenship. These clubs aim to develop ideals for patriotic service.

They teach self-control and group discipline.

They train for loyalty to the club, the neighborhood house, the neighborhood, and the city and the nation.

They foster respect for law and order.

They demonstrate the desirability of government by majority.

They show the wisdom of checks and balances in democratic control.

They are opposed to clique and class distinction.

They teach respect for individual and community rights.

They stand for equality before the law.

They develop self-assurance.

They develop self-reliance.

They encourage altruistic service and mutual self-help.

They spread the gospel of democratic government.

In a hundred other ways the boys and girls and the young men and young women in our clubs are preparing themselves for their American rights and responsibilities.

Stuyvesant Neighborhood House appeals to those far-visioned men and women whose ideals of patriotic service have survived the armistice to join our corps of enthusiastic workers, to help realize the aims and ideals of the work. The task on our hands is huge; thirty-three new clubs in six weeks, a dozen new activities in the process of organization, countless appeals from all sides — all in need of good leadership.

Will you help?

UNION SETTLEMENT, 237 East 104th street, New York City, Gaylord S. White, secretary, November 25, 1919:

"In replying to your favor of the 15th inquiring about education and Americanization for adult foreigners as carried on by this Settlement, I beg to say that we are conducting classes here for women in the study of English. One of Jewish women meets three times a week in the morning. This is a small group. There is a class of Italian women which meets three times a week in the afternoon and is taught by a teacher supplied by the state. This has an enrollment of about thirty and an attendance of about twenty-five. An interesting development grew out of a class we conducted here last spring. From a group of Italian mothers there grew a demand for night school for Italian working girls. As we did not have the requisite school equipment, the desks, and so forth, we found finally a suitable room in St. Lucy's Catholic Church on the next block which we could use one night a week. After a short time, the demand was made for a meeting three nights a week, and as the church could not accommodate the class it was moved to P. S. 168. I understand that it now has a large attendance and has developed into an additional evening's work when social meetings and discussions are held.

"We have clubs of Italian young men and many clubs of Jewish boys and young men, but these men are not usually the illiterate class. It is difficult to say how many are reached through our clubs and classes, and other forms of work. We feel that all the work of the Settlement is in the line of Americanization in a broad sense. It is standing for ideals of fair play, orderly progress through lawful methods and increases of capacity by education. We also seek to develop local neighborhood spirit and civic pride, and a capacity for the discharge of the high duties of citizenship. I believe the self-governing clubs of the Settlement have a real influence in this direction.

"In addition to the above we try to promote Americanization by occasional entertainments, social affairs, and meetings in which we endeavor to focus atention of some specific phase of American life, as, for example, Fourth of July celebrations, the birthdays of noted Americans or a celebration in honor of citizens of our neighborhood who have received their papers within a given period.

"The purpose of the Settlement is to establish friendships in the neighborhood, and as someone has said, 'Through friendships to try to raise the standard of life and of living.' We try to be 'good neighbors' and to develop a sense of responsibility for neighborhood welfare. I think much of the influence which is exerted upon the children and young people works back into the homes and helps to give the foreign illiterate parents of these children correct ideas of the ideals and institutions of American life.

"We feel that it would be very desirable if your Committee would use its influence to dignify the process of granting citizenship papers. We believe also that a good deal might be done to stimulate neighborhoods to inculcate sound Americanization through neighborhood pageants, concerts, forums, etc., conducted in community centers, municipal theatres where such exist, and other places of common meeting ground."

e. Note

Following is a list of settlement houses who publicly opposed the educational bill proposed by the Joint Legislative Committee:

United Neighborhood Houses of New York, Miss Harriet Righter, President; Harold Riegelman, Counsel.

Christodora House, Dr. S. T. Silverman.

Chrystie Street Settlement, Miss Josephine Schain. (Also listed as Recreation Rooms and Settlement.)

Greenwich Settlement House, Mrs. Mary K. Simkhovitch.

Henry Street Settlement, Miss Viola Conklin.

Lenox Hill House, Miss Rosalie Manning.

Madison House, Miss Ruth Larned.

Richmond Hill House, Miss Constance Hook.

Jacob Riis House, Miss Helen Jessup; Miss Theodora Bates.

It is of interest to compare the foregoing statements and reports of those active in settlement house activities, as well as of their counsel, with the following excerpts from the New York Call:

"There is a lot of work done by the settlements which such legislation would hamper." (Issue of March 28, 1920, statement of Miss Josephine Schain of Chrystie House.)

"The settlements have a definite policy against such legislation as this proposed by the Lusk Committee." (Issue of March 30, 1920, statement of Miss Schain.)

"Captain Harold Riegelman, who represented the United Neighborhood Houses, said that the bills were intended to block the work of the Settlement Houses and that no association should have the power to say what is seditious or not." (Issue of April 1, 1920.)

It will be observed that there are wide discrepancies in the attitude of the settlement workers who first assure us of the unqualified loyalty and Americanism of their houses, and later admit that "there is a lot of work done by the settlements which such legislation (as proposed by the Committee) would hamper"— the only educational work which the bills could hamper being that which would be "detrimental to public interest."

Miss Schain's statements are quite at variance with both the testimony of representatives of the United Neighborhood Houses at public hearings before the Committee as well as with correspondence received from these head workers, and quoted previously in this report.

Captain Riegelman, Counsel for the United Neighborhood Houses of New York, states that the bills were "intended to block the work of the Settlement Houses," by which one may only infer that it is Captain Riegelman's opinion that the educational work of the settlement houses, in part at least, is "detrimental to public interests," or that some of their teachers are not loyal to the Constitution of the State of New York and of the United States. These are the only two vulnerable points in any educational work at which the bills in question could strike.

An unbiased jury in endeavoring to determine which of their two attitudes the United Neighborhood Houses would permanently endorse, might incline to that by which they convict themselves by implying an admission that they fall into that class of educational effort which is "detrimental to public interests."

It is also worthy of note that all the settlements protesting against the educational bills of this Committee are members of the United Neighborhood Houses of New York. Activities of non-members are recorded separately in the following section.

(See testimony of William L. Ettinger, Superintendent of New York City Public Schools, against the influence of the settlement houses upon young people.)

2. NON-MEMBERS OF THE ASSOCIATION

BELLEVUE SETTLEMENT HOUSE, 206 East 30th street, New York City, Alice E. Clements, December 22, 1919:

"DEAR SIR.— In regard to your letter of this date: Almost all of our patients are citizens and second generation Americans. As this is a tuberculosis camp we are a little restricted as to activities in the line of educational work. I myself give, however, weekly talks in which the subject of duty to our country and veneration for the flag and what it represents, are always emphasized. I myself am a Red Cross nurse and have seen overseas service during the war. Any seditious utterances would be promptly reported to me, and as promptly dealt with."

BRONX HOUSE, 1637 Washington Avenue, New York City, Estelle Deutsch, head worker, December 31, 1919.

"We have classes in English to foreigners for married women at Bronx House. These are very successful groups, and I feel that the finest kind of Americanization work is being done by Mrs. Williamson, who is the instructor. That is the only technical work that is done along these lines. Of course, all our work at the settlement house has the training of decent American citizens as its goal. Our music school, our clubs and classes are all used as a means to this end.

"I hope that this is the information which you wish. If you desire anything more definite, will you please let me hear from you."

THE BROOKLYN MUSIC SCHOOL SETTLEMENT, 525 Grand avenue, Brooklyn, Kendall K. Mussey, director, December 3, 1919:

"As this is a music school settlement, our Americanization work is all carried on through the influence of that medium. We have a chorus, an orchestra, sight-singing classes and social clubs. However, of the 250 students, there are only five families in which neither parent speaks English. Three of these are Italian, and two Russian Jews. A great many, however, do not read and write with any degree of fluency. Our work with the adults is limited entirely to emergency cases.

"As to suggestions, I would say that I have talked the matter over with Mrs. Abbott, second vice-president of the National Federation of Music Clubs of America, who has charge of this branch of the work of the Federation, and who says that the Federation would be more than glad to co-operate in any possible way with your organization in providing additional musical opportunities for the foreign element, especially working toward the promotion of community sings, which should develop into choruses doing part singing. The necessity of speaking and reading English becomes very apparent to the alien who wishes to join in an English chorus, and cannot. When I was associated with Mr. W. C. Smith on the Mayor's Committee for National Defense under Mr. Mitchel, the value of music in arousing interest in foreigners and securing their attendance at gatherings was notably demonstrated.

"We also feel, and in this the Federation would also like to assist, that if chorus singing and other musical attractions played a more important part in our public school educational system, that it would prove a very popular feature with the foreign element."

CHRIST CHURCH HOUSE, 336 West 36th street, New York City, Theodore F. Savage, November 20, 1919:

"We have handled a somewhat delicate situation here, in that a large proportion of our old families have been of German descent. I am glad to report that practically all of them have come to see the proper attitude of American citizens, and have most loyally supported the country. I think this has been partly due to the work of our Church. A few irreconcilables have never caused any trouble. We do not handle other alien groups, as our work is almost entirely with Americans, at least of the second generation.

"May I take the opportunity of expressing what a great many people have felt, that your Committee is taking the wrong course in dealing with the this whole problem, and I think we are in a position to get the reaction of the ordinary citizen. You are trying to follow the old but constantly disproved fallacy, that ideas can be combatted with force. This can never be done satisfactorily, and I feel that far more can be accomplished by at least trying to understand the causes which have produced the social unrest, rather than by trying to knock on the heads those who have become restless.

"I write this because I have absolutely no sympathy with these radical movements, but I fear them very much, and I feel sure that the attitude of our daily newspapers and perhaps the attitude of your Committee in trying to use terrorism will be one of the greatest causes for the growth of this unrest."

THE EMANU-EL BROTHERHOOD, 309 East 6th street, New York City, Tobias Roth, superintendent, December 23, 1919:

"I wish to state that I am heartily in sympathy with the work of the Joint Legislative Committee to investigate the seditious activities in the state, and beg to inform you that, at the present time, we have under contemplation the formation of an Americanization forum, through which we hope to take up the discussion of national, state and local problems.

"At the present time we have a class in English to foreigners, conducted at our building in co-operation with the Board of Education, and we hope not only to conduct this class, but to organize an additional one.

"As soon as my plans for the Americanization forum are completed, I shall be glad to communicate with you further and if, in the meantime, you have any further suggestions to offer in line with this work, I shall be pleased to hear from you. Assuring you of our readiness to co-operate with you."

FRIENDLY AID SOCIETY, 246 East 34th street, Elizabeth B. Bowles, head worker, December 1, 1919:

"Our neighbors, at present, are largely Irish and Southern Italian with a sprinkling of six or eight other nationalities.

"Our work is strictly non-sectarian and non-partisan.

"The chief aim of all our activities has always been to arouse in our neighbors, especially in those of foreign birth or parentage, a feeling of loyalty and of responsibility to our government, both local and federal.

"In order to impress upon them the various ways in which our government protects the welfare and interests of the workingman and his children, we have frequent talks, often illustrated by stereopticon slides, on the work of the different city departments, on the factory and child labor laws, on the legal rights of tenants, etc.

"We also have health talks in both English and Italian, on tuberculosis, preventable blindness, the care of children, etc. In addition to this, we sometimes show them pictures of different parts of our country; as to many ignorant immigrants, New York City represents the whole of the United States.

"We urge those who are living in this country and enjoying its opportunities and protection to avail themselves of the privilege of taking out citizen papers, and to use their votes to put men in office who are loyal to our government, and who will use their influence to protect the rights of the people.

"We have at present no classes in English, but urge people to attend the excellent ones at P. S. 27 on East 41st street, and at the International Institute on East 30th street. One fine feature of the English class at P. S. 27 is that it combines recreation with instruction, having a social evening once a week with music, games and dancing, for those who attend the classes.

"During the war, we asked one of our Italian neighbors to act as interpreter for the Legal Advisory Board which met here, and through him we have kept in touch with a number of young Italians who were in the service, and now form one of the community clubs of ex-service men and their friends which meet in this house. We have two service clubs, and are also the headquarters of the Murray Hill Branch of the American Legion.

"Two of our resident workers enlisted early in the war in the ambulance service, and on their return from France last spring, came back to the Settlement, and have charge of this part of our work.

"As we find that many men are too tired after a hard day's work to wash up and go regularly three or four evenings a week to an evening school, we are planning to open, with the assistance of some members of the American Legion, an evening class once a week for those who want to learn to read and write English with a view to taking out citizen papers.

"It is practically impossible for an Italian mother with her large family of little children to attend English classes, but we hope after Christmas to have a class for them, to which they can bring their babies and all the children under school age, who will be cared for, while the mothers are in the class, after which a brief time will be devoted to refreshments, music and games, to make the class more attractive.

"We have done this in past years, but have never been able to get as large an attendance as we would like, as many of the Italian women in this neighborhood have no ambition to speak English, their children acting as interpreters when necessary.

"It is through the children that we are most successful in reaching the non-English-speaking parents.

"If we can instill in the children a respect for rightful authority, and a regard for the property and rights of others, and arouse in them a civic pride and sense of personal responsibility in keeping the streets and sidewalks clean and the fire escapes clear, they in turn will instruct their parents.

"In making out the returns for the State Military Census, and the questionnaires for the Legal Advisory Board, and in our investigation for the State Housing Committee, we found that a number of Greeks, many of them subjects of Turkey, have come to this country since the beginning of the war to escape military conscription. Very few of these speak English, or have their families with them. They are chiefly employed in the hotels and restaurants in the district. From the nature of their work, it is impossible for them to attend the evening classes in the schools.

"You ask for suggestions:

"1. We find that the nature of their work prevents many men from attending evening classes.

"2. We find that many men dislike the classes held in the public schools because the seats in the classrooms are intended for children, and are uncomfortable for adults.

"3. Many men will not attend classes held in the settlement houses or in church houses, because they consider them philanthropic institutions.

"4. After a hard day's work, men desire relaxation and amusement, rather than instruction.

"Query. Would it be possible for the Americanization Committee to use some of the old saloons for their work, where classes in English could be held during the day as well as in the evening, and where also opportunity could be afforded to read American newspapers, and to play pool and checkers, and to buy coffee and other light refreshments? Also where there would always be someone to answer questions about taking out citizen papers, war risk insurance, workingmen's compensation, etc., and where men could sometimes be put in touch with opportunities to find work, and where lists of free lectures, concerts, etc., could be posted.

"The English classes could be held in the rear room of the saloon, so as not to interfere with the social side, through which the men would be chiefly attracted at first."

HEARTSEASE WORK FOR FRIENDLESS WOMEN, 413 East 51st street, New York City. Louise B. Scofield, December 22, 1919:

"Your letter re the education of adult foreigners has been received. As our letterhead indicates, we do an evangelical work among women and babies and while we do meet a few foreigners most of the women are American born. When we do have foreign girls in the home, we do all we can — reading and teaching American history. I do not think we reach the class you are interested in."

KIPS BAY NEIGHBORHOOD ASSOCIATION, 799 Second avenue, New York City, George Debevoise, president, November 20, 1919:

"Your request for information about the Americanization work carried on by the Kips Bay Neighborhood Association has been received, and we are very glad to give you any information we have.

"All Americanization work done in this district by our Association is in co-operation with the evening school at Public School No. 27, of which Mr. Alexander S. Massell is principal. With the assistance of Sara C. Clapp, executive secretary of the Kips Bay Neighborhood Association, Mr. Massell has been able to work out some very interesting ideas for the Americanization of foreigners. It is the opinion of both Miss Clapp and Mr. Massell that Americanization is a social problem; that if the foreigners can be brought together in a social way, the rest is easy. With this in mind, a community evening for foreigners has been held once a week in Public School 27 for the past three years with excellent results. Our neighborhood association has been responsible for interesting the foreigners in coming to these community evenings. Personal calls were made on all factory and hotel managers in the district urging that they encourage their foreign employees to attend the social evening held in Public School 27 every Thursday night. The results have been remarkable. The number of foreigners attending varies from 200 to 1,400, and includes 17 nationalities. It is, indeed, interesting to visit the school on one of these evenings. Games are arranged so that no two of one nationality are playing together. It is not unusual to see an Italian playing checkers with a German; a Spaniard playing chess with a Chinaman, etc. An orchestra is provided so that dancing and community sings are part of the evening's entertainment. War Camp Community Service has co-operated by providing one or two entertainers each evening.

"Kips Bay Neighborhood Association has assumed the financial responsibility of these social evenings inasmuch as the Board of Education does not allow sufficient funds for this phase of the work. These social evenings have increased the enrollment of the regular classes very materially and the interest among the foreigners is even greater than we had expected.

"Our association has been able this winter to interest the State Department of Education in the methods used in this district and as a result two workers have been detailed to us to help work up interest in the school. However, still more workers are needed so that personal calls can be made at the homes of the foreigners.

"It is the desire of the association to open more centers like the one just described so that intensive work can be done.

"Assuring you of our pleasure in this opportunity to co-operate with you."

"KIPS BAY NEIGHBORHOOD ASSOCIATION."

Organized 1913; incorporated 1917. Boundaries: 28th to 59th street, Fifth avenue to the East river.

Purposes.— The Association aims:

1. Through co-operation, to encourage a closer sympathy and understanding between welfare organizations and individuals.

2. By united effort, to stimulate a spirit of true neighborliness among all classes as a basis for a real working democracy.

3. By surveys, records and statistics, to furnish information regarding neighborhood needs and conditions.

4. Through an executive office to establish a community clearing house to avoid duplication of effort and to secure better co-operation of agencies and individuals.

PROGRAM FOR COMMUNITY DEVELOPMENT OF KIPS BAY NEIGHBORHOOD

The aim of this program is to indicate the direction in which the development of community effort in Kips Bay District should proceed. It is by no means meant to be ideal or one that can be used in every community. It is based solely on the special needs of this particular neighborhood. It is not anticipated that all of the activities mentioned can be undertaken at once by existing agencies, but they present a goal toward which community effort in this neighborhood should tend. It is hoped that many organizations will co-operate in carrying out the program.

General Features

1. *Organization*

There shall be three neighborhood center offices in addition to that of the Kips Bay Neighborhood Association. These shall be located in the Beekman, the Prospect and the Murray Hill districts. Each neighborhood center office shall have a trained social worker in charge and shall do social service clearing-house work in the manner already followed by the Kips Bay Neighborhood Association office. Each office shall work in close co-operation with the Kips Bay Neighborhood Association. In time, however, each office should become an independent but co-operating neighborhood center. Each center should in the end be permanently located, although they may be experimental at first. Where possible they should have clubrooms, a backyard playground, and other social and recreational features in addition to the office. They should serve as centers from which block organization plans may be carried on.

2. *Workers' Institutes*

An institute for training workers for investigation, home visitation and follow-up work in various lines; for the direction and recruiting of volunteers; for record keeping, report making and the problems of social conduct in the lines of health, housing, civic, educational, recreational and social problems. Such institute should aim to familiarize the workers with geography, population and institutions in the Kips Bay Neighborhood; the aims and methods of the various lines of work done in the community; the various agencies available for the service of the inhabitants of the district; and the principles upon which community work should be carried on. This institute shall be a joint enterprise of the Kips Bay Neighborhood Association, the administration of Public School 27 and the Messiah Social Service League. It shall be held in the school building, 206 East 42d street and the program shall consist of lectures and round-table conferences. The dates of this institute shall be October 15th-25th. The addresses will be at 3 P. M., to be followed by round-table conference at 4 P. M. There will also be special lectures on certain evenings. The institute will be open to all persons interested in community work in the district. The enrollment for the conferences shall be limited to fifty. Evening lectures will be open to the public.

3. *Community Pageant*

There shall be inaugurated as an annual community event a Community Pageant, to be conducted in co-operation with Community Service of New York City by the associated Kips Bay District agencies. In connection with this a membership drive for the Kips Bay Neighborhood Association shall be conducted. This pageant should come early in the summer of 1920 and should feature the history of Kips Bay District with out-of-door dramatic features, such as parades, decorations, dramatic presentations in parks, moving pictures and similar activities. Such a pageant should secure the support of all merchants, business enterprises and professional agencies interested in this section of the city. These should be asked to contribute and to serve on the committees promoting the enterprise. The organization and conduct of such pageant will have as its aim the development of community consciousness.

Specific Activities

1. *Health*

(1) Promote the provision of two clinics for the pre-natal care of mothers and infant welfare, in addition to those now in existence under the auspices of the Board of Health and the New York Milk Committee.

(2) Organize follow-up work with children of pre-school age, using the data gathered by the Children's Year of the Federal Child Bureau.

(3) Co-operate with the visiting Nursing Service of the Henry Street Settlement and endeavor to secure a station for nursing service within the Kips Bay Neighborhood.

(4) Co-operate with the maintenance of the Children's Camp on Staten Island, with the Federated Neighborhood Associations.

(5) Promote fresh air work and summer outings for delicate children.

2. *Housing*

Endeavor to improve housing conditions for individuals and families in the following ways:

(1) By promoting conferences between landlords and tenants in order to secure proper understanding between them.

(2) Reporting complaints of housing conditions to proper authorities and following up such reports.

(3) Securing reliable data in certain localities concerning housing conditions by careful systematic investigation, in line with the National Social Unit Plan.

3. *Citizenship*

(1) Co-operate with the Board of Education and other agencies in citizenship work by organizing small groups with recreational features for the teaching of English and citizenship; teachers for such groups will be furnished by the Board of Education.

(2) Co-operate in securing pupils for evening schools in the neighborhood.

(3) Promote children's civic leagues in public schools and organize systematic volunteer follow-up and proper supervision of existing organizations of this kind.

(4) Organize a Community Forum in the Louisa Lee Schuyler School (Public School 59), 228 East 57th street. Organize a second Community Forum in the Boys' Clubhouse of the Kips Bay Neighborhood Association. The organization of these forums is experimental. If successful an effort should be made to extend similar activities to each of the public schools in the district.

(5) Establish vocational guidance service in each public and parochial school in the district.

4. *Recreation*

(1) Develop Community Center work in each school in the neighborhood with dances, classes and various activities. The supervision of these community centers may be assumed by various community organizations co-operating in carrying out this program.

(2) Encourage the maintenance of the backyard playgrounds now in operation and secure the opening of such additional playgrounds as may be possible.

(3) Institute in St. Gabriel's Park open-air entertainments, having various community features, such as motion pictures, band concerts, Christmas trees, and any other expression of the neighborhood life desired by the people.

(4) Promote block parties at Christmas time and at other times and co-operate with such parties when promoted by other agencies.

5. *Civic and Educational*

(1) Co-operate with other agencies in urging upon the Board of Aldermen the passage of an ordinance requiring inspection of dance halls and other public places of amusement.

(2) Resume campaign for three new schoolhouses in place of Public Schools 116, 73 and 18, and a new building for the Murray Hill Trade School for Boys at 249 East 37th street, and organize definite effort to secure action from proper authorities providing for such buildings.

(3) Conduct surveys regarding various fields of community work in co-operation with various district agencies.

(4) Hold from time to time exhibits regarding health, industry, recreation, education, civic matters and social movements within the neighborhood.

(5) Begin the organization of certain blocks within the neighborhood in accordance with the National Social Unit Plan. The blocks selected for this purpose should be those in which the neighborhood center offices are located and the work should center in these offices.

(6) Organize neighborhood employment agency in view of the closing of the United States Employment Bureau and pending the assumption of this work by the state.

PRESBYTERIAN CHURCH OF THE SEA AND LAND, 61 Henry street, New York City, Alfred D. Moore, minister, November 20, 1919:

"In answer to your letter of November 17th, I will try to give you a little information about the work we are doing with the adult foreigners in this community. There are ever so many nationalities around us, Italian, Russian, Polish, Japanese, Greek, Jewish, Irish and many others. Men come to us all the time to help them secure their citizenship papers. We give them some aid and instruction and then send them to the evening classes in the public schools to learn English, civics, etc., for we have no such classes in this building. Two nights a week, and eventually on Sunday for a Bible class, we have a large class of Japanese men who come here, under an efficient teacher, to learn English. The other work among the adults is done in clubs and is only indirectly Americanization work.

"We feel, here, that if this education is made compulsory to the men and women as well as to the children, the number of illiterate foreigners would be much smaller. They will only study enough to get their second papers, using that as a means to the end, and so many of them go no further than the first papers, that it seems as if some kind of compulsory education would be best for them."

PRESENTATION NURSERY SETTLEMENT, 228 East 32d street, New York City, Miss Harriette N. Murphy, December 22, 1919:

"We personally endeavor to give individual attention to our mothers whenever possible, also telling them the wonderful advantages they have in this great city and how much they owe the United States. We also train the children to patriotic drills, singing and dances which they do wonderfully well. I must tell you we have originated a few dances, 'The Pershing Dance,' 'Military,' etc., our colors and flag always made conspicuous when we invite the parents to see their children — all have to salute flag and pledge allegiance. American historical events are told in story, dialogues, tableaux and each patriotic day is observed. And every month we have an evening of song, all patriotic and popular songs and dances. We invite at times speakers for any special subject during the war — Thrift Saving, Liberty Loans, etc., patriotic recitations. Sometimes we have sixty adults, but not always. We generally have fifteen to twenty, as our mothers work all day and are so tired evenings. We do not do so much, only for the children, and they reach their parents who are so proud of what they do.

"I am anxious and willing to help in any way you suggest."

SISTERHOOD OF THE SPANISH AND PORTUGUESE SYNAGOGUE IN THE CITY OF NEW YORK, INC., 133 Eldridge street, January, 1920:

REPORT OF SERVICES RENDERED TO THE NEIGHBORHOOD BY THE SISTERHOOD OF THE SPANISH AND PORTUGUESE SYNAGOGUE

Its Neighborhood House at 133 Eldridge street

Religious Activities

Synagogue

Equipped for 350 worshippers; services are held twice daily, on Sabbath, and on all Holy Days. A Rabbi employed by the Sisterhood conducts the services; performs wedding ceremonies, etc.

Talmud Torah

Sefardic children, 6 to 14 years, are taught Hebrew and receive religious education.

Average daily attendance, 160 pupils.

Number of school days, 5 days a week.

Number of hours per day, 2.

For these classes three teachers, besides the Rabbi, are required. He acts as director and conducts the advanced class.

Educational Activities

Kindergarten

Three classes daily; 40 in class.

The Board of Education supplies teachers and equipment.

The Sisterhood supplies heat, light, janitorial service, furnishings, and milk and crackers to 120 children daily.

English Classes

The Board of Education also provides teachers for classes in English to foreigners, especially for the mothers of the kindergarten children three afternoons or evenings weekly.

Library

Used as reading-room by adults and children. Books furnished by the Sisterhood. Average daily attendance, 40.

Lectures

Lectures on civics and hygienic subjects are given by prominent speakers.

Clubs

Fourteen junior, intermediate, and senior groups.

Four clubs nightly; average attendance in each club, 15.

The club director is a salaried worker, having supervision over all club affairs and is president of the House Council. The leaders of the fourteen clubs are volunteers.

Gymnasium

Four nights a week.

Two sessions for boys, 15 to 20 in each group.

Two sessions for girls, 15 to 20 in each group.

For the athletic work a professional director is required.

Game Room

Thirty to 40 children (8 to 9 P. M.) nightly.

Twenty to 30 adults (9 to 10 P. M.) nightly.

Games and records for victrola supplied by the Sisterhood.

Music Room

Community singing and teaching of music to 15 girls by a professional, once a week, furnished by Sisterhood.

Dancing

A dance is given on Sunday evenings for 250 boys and girls. Sisterhood furnishes music and, once a month, refreshments.

Roof Garden

During the summer 1,175 children used the roof garden each month. Mothers and sick babies were welcomed. Sisterhood furnishes flower boxes, benches, sandboxes, toys, etc., for the children. Supervised by Mrs. Lévy, head worker.

Outings

One hundred and eighty-seven children and mothers were taken on weekly excursions during the summer by head worker.

Sixty children were taken to the Hebrew Sanitorium.

Philanthropic Activities

Medical Clinic

Fifteen to 20 foreign-speaking women and children are examined daily (12 to 1). Physician is provided by members of the Synagogue's Brotherhood. Sisterhood furnishes equipment and assistants to physician.

Neighborhood Work

The head worker visits the sick families in the district as a trained nurse, taking adults and children to hospitals, dentists and other agencies, as required. She receives applicants for friendly advice and information at the House.

By special arrangement the U. H. C. provides a Ladino-speaking investigator to assist the head worker in caring for the Sefardic poor, and once a week a committee, composed of a representative of the U. H. C., the Sisterhood and members of the Sefardic community themselves, meet to discuss the needs of individual cases among their needy brethren.

Industrial Work

Clothing is made by members of the Sisterhood and supplied to needy children and women of the Sefardic community, so that they do not apply to the U. H. C.

SUNSHINE SETTLEMENT, INC., 122 White street, S. E. Furry, secretary-treasurer, November 24, 1919:

> "Our last annual report gives some account of the young men, of Italian parentage largely, whose loyalty to our country was expressed by many of them volunteering for the army in France.
>
> "I am glad as an American citizen and general director of this work, reaching a large number of Italians, to say that Americanization has been one of our chief objects among these children from kindergarten to adults for twenty years, with the result that Bolshevism and anarchy will never get a foothold in our locality.
>
> "Mothers are loyal and devoted; they repel anarchy, and demonstrated their patriotism during the war by freely giving their sons for service in the army and navy, and providing supplies for them during the war.
>
> "I would recommend that more drastic measures be taken to deport the aliens that are trying to disrupt our country through seditious literature and personal contact, of which the government authorities are cognizant. There has been much talk but little action, and of this our people are complaining most bitterly. An action will eventually plunge our country into revolution, then, as our boys of the army say, 'We will all have to fight again whether we like it or not.'

"There is almost criminal laxity somewhere in dealing with this element who are trying to tear down what has been built up, and it is no small task to Americanize foreigners, which must be done largely through the children of these parents who get their English from them.

"You have my views on this subject, get rid of the seditious element, if not by deportation, then the firing squad if necessary, and I can furnish you material from our loyal boys who would, I think, help out on that line.

"My association with other organizations leads me to speak as I do, and I feel I am expressing their sentiments."

WEST SIDE LEAGUE HOUSE, 444 West 34th street, New York City, Mrs. Ann C. McConnaughty, December 22, 1919:

"In reply to your letter of December 20th, I will say that we have no adult foreigners attending clubs or classes at this house. We have a group of Irish American women who belong to a community chorus and a group of girls, ages 16 to 20 years, also Americans and Irish Americans, who are deeply interested in War Camp Community work. Our children are all Irish Americans and Italians, the majority Irish Americans and all Catholics.

"For part of the winter of 1917 we loaned rooms in our house to the Chelsea Neighborhood Association for a nursery for Polish children. The children were sent here and cared for by a Polish deaconess, while the mothers attended classes in the Public Library in the neighborhood. It was a bad winter and the attendance was irregular, and later I understood the mothers lost interest and no longer attended the classes, so our work here with the children was no longer necessary.

"Please call upon me if I can do anything further to be of service to your Committee."

CHAPTER VIII
Young Men's Christian Association

Dr. Peter Roberts, Secretary for Immigration on the International Committee of the Y. M. C. A., appeared before this Committee in a public hearing on January 16, 1920. The substance of his testimony follows:

I have been working with the foreign-born for thirteen years all over the United States and in parts of Canada and Mexico. I have seen hundreds of men become naturalized, and it has been my observation that if they acquire property and have families they usually make as good citizens as any one could wish — sometimes far better than some who have the blue blood of New England in their veins. Our assumption is that if we teach a man to really know the United States, he will love the United States.

We have a complete program of education for the foreign-born which we present, comprising six activities — English, naturalization, lectures, entertainments, recreation and advisory councils.

The scope of our program is as follows:

PROGRAM OF AMERICANIZATION MANAGEMENT

Survey

Know your field. Find out to what peoples your foreign-born neighbors belong, how many of them know English, and how many of them are fellow citizens. Housing and living conditions have much to do with men's outlook on life. Learn how and where the foreign-born live. Know their religious leaders. There are many folds, but one Shepherd. If you need an outline for a survey, write for one.

Advertising

Printers' ink is good, if you put your facts in order. Employers want facts and not fancies. Prepare your case well and present it clearly and concisely. The "Y" man sells goods bearing the trade-mark of heaven. If at first you don't succeed, try again. Presidents and general managers are human. They do more for the well-being of their employees than demagogues will or can. Arm yourself with testimonials of men who know the benefits of a Y. M. C. A. among industrial workers. Apply and we will send you lots of them.

Plant Organization

Capitalize the sense of solidarity. Every plant has or should have the family feeling. Each worker should feel his concern is the best place to work in town. Plan your program in this vein and the employer and the employees will be with you. Organize a plant executive committee, on which are the general manager, superintendent, and heads of departments. Get your subcommittees, on which are foremen and intelligent and sympathetic workmen of native and foreign birth. Arrange a joint conference for all committeemen to discuss the whole program. Divide the work carefully and see that the men do the work. Never forget the fact of group consciousness. Plan definitely for cultivation work for the industrial leaders, and know that though they are willing to work with the foreign-born they have a class consciousness which must be recognized.

Equipment

You need a building to house your activities. If you work for an industry, tell the concern that you cannot produce maximum results without a power house. You don't need a palace. Democracy was made safe by men who frequented huts. The foreign-born may learn what democracy is by patronizing a hut.

Finance

You need funds. Until you house your activities, the work must be financed from other sources than the wage-earners you serve. Show the president of the plant the advantage of membership and revenue-producing features. Men are willing to pay for privileges. They will take more interest in the Y. M. C. A. when their money goes into it.

Co-operation

Executive Conferences

Plan conference dinners for manufacturers, general managers, superintendents, administrative officers, etc. Keep the group consciousness in mind. These men in a plant or in a city should be brought together because of their common interest. Your objective should be (a) to bring before them prominent speakers on Americanization; (b) to hear reports of work done for their employees; (c) to discuss plans for advanced work for immigrant workers; (d) to emphasize the inalienable relation between the character of the industries and the character of the community.

Brotherhood Dinners

Plan regular dinners for foremen and subforeman. This group should be that interested in "hiring and firing" men. A regular organization is necessary to bring about successful meetings. The objective should be (a) how best to handle immigrant labor; (b) conduct a forum for exchange of ideas and experiences in handling foreigners; (c) present speakers who know the foreigner and how best to handle him; and (d) the democratic significance of hearty good will and impartial justice between foreman and the foreign-born.

Get-Togethers

Plan in season: picnics, outings, carnivals, socials, mass meetings, pageants, etc. Both the native and foreign-born leadership must cooperate to make these a success. The objective should be (a) the promotion of kindly feeling between the native and the foreign-born for the good of the community; and (b) the welding of the various peoples into one strong American brotherhood. Key every gathering to patriotism and loyalty to America.

Advisory Councils

The laws and customs of nations differ. The foreign-born, trying to adjust his life to America, gets into difficulties. He needs a counsellor. Organize advisory councils offering free advice on personal problems, vocation, home life, working conditions, business dealings, etc. This gives personal contact plus prime social service. Every foreign-born man needs a big-hearted native brother.

Community Relations

The "Y" is not the only star guiding the foreign-born. Federal, state and community agents are also interested in him. See that you co-operate with these. Keep up friendly relations with the public school, the charity organizations, the immigration bureau, etc. Use them whenever you can; co-operate with them whenever possible; only remember that the Y. M. C. A. has a special message for coming Americans which cannot be delegated to other agencies.

Education

English Classes

Organize your classes according to nationality. Find out how much English the men can talk, read and write, and group them accordingly. Fifteen men make a good class; meet twice a week; use the Roberts System — tens of thousands have learned English by it. Select your teachers with care, and see that they know how to teach. Give the work close supervision. Interest the foreign-born leaders in your work, and show the superintendent and foreman how it is done. As a missionary of the Y. M. C. A. you cannot afford to miss the approach a class in English affords. Go to the men and carry something more than English to the classroom.

Naturalization

Foreign-born men form three groups: Citizens, those with first papers, and aliens. Working with the industries, classify the foreign-born workers into these three groups. Give citizens literature on good citizenship, help those with first papers to get their second, and to every alien put the question: "Why are you not a citizen of the United States?" Keep close to the clerk of the Naturalization Court; put a sympathetic and capable young lawyer in charge of the class in naturalization. "Civics for Coming Americans" is a work specially prepared to help men to citizenship. Begin with the local government; show on a chart its political divisions and also how the political organization works. Show the relation between the city government and the county, the state, and the national government.

Lectures

Pictures are a universal language. Let slide or film carry messages of hope and cheer to men anxious to learn what America is and who were its makers. When national groups and cosmopolitan crowds come together, the lantern is a good entertainer. Let it talk in the tongue of the old world as well as in that of the new. The foundations of twentieth century civilization were laid on the rivers Nile, Tigris, Euphrates, and on the shores of the Mediterranean and Baltic seas. The foreign-born as well as the native-born will be glad to learn how it was done. Americanization is the blending of the best in the old and the new worlds. The lantern can be used in halls and out of them, in winter and summer. Send for outline of subjects of lectures and films.

Literature — Libraries

The printed word has a message. When good literature on Americanization is put out by federal or state departments, private agencies or local bodies, the "Y" should use it. A list of such publications will be sent on request. Public libraries can serve the foreign-born by securing the right kind of books in their tongues for circulation. See that the library does this. Try to establish traveling libraries in foreign communities far removed from libraries.

Life Problem Clubs

Many foreign-born men know enough English to read any ordinary book. They need practice in talking. Organize clubs for the discussion of life problems, national issues, and international relations. Leaders among foreign-born groups will take to this. It is a field that needs cultivation.

Race Psychology

Nations differ. Their background is different. All foremen and superintendents don't think of this. Organize a class in race psychology to deal specially with the background of immigrant peoples, the forces shaping their lives, and how America can use these agencies for the purpose of getting best results from these men in American industries. Outline of discussions will be sent on application to this office.

Social

National Group Activities

Each nation has its story and its heroes, its music and its poetry, its art and its folk lore. They cannot forget these in an adopted country. Let the "Y" pave an avenue of self-expression for these accomplishments. Success in this depends on organization. The program should be carefully worked out with foreign-born leaders. The best date is a national birthday in their or in our history. America gains by conserving the culture of the fifty varieties of peoples coming to America. Italians and Greeks, Slavs and Chaldeans, were closer to the beginnings of civilization than Teutons and Saxons. They have much that is of interest to us if they are encouraged to exhibit it.

Cosmopolitan Meetings

More than fifty varieties of peoples have contributed and still contribute to the life blood of America. Those who go into the "melting pot" should become conscious of the Divine plan in the bringing together of the nations of the earth on this continent. The future of humanity is more involved in what is done here than in any other country under the sun. America in the war made the world safe for democracy. All peoples in a community should occasionally be brought together to feel the importance of the welding process, and consciously contribute their part to American democracy. Perfect organizations among every people. This will contribute to the success of the "melting." The purpose of the Y. M. C. A. should be clearly explained. The dominant note should be the "Coming American." Patriotic societies among the native-born gladly participate in a program of this nature. The real American has cosmopolitan sympathies.

Entertainment

Programs for entertainments should be worked out very carefully. Both native and foreign-born talent should be used. Friendly rivalry between the several national groups should be encouraged. Trophies to the winners can be secured from friends of foreign-born men or from public-spirited citizens. Dinners prepared by the housewives of foreign homes — a la Italiana, or a la Grecia, or a la Hungaria, etc.— are popular and well patronized by Americans. Foreign production can enrich our intellect as well as our appetites.

Plant Rallies

Whenever a plant rally is arranged, don't overlook the foreign-born. The object of the rally should be fully explained to the leaders of foreigners. They will co-operate fully when they understand, and will contribute much to its success. Consider the types of peoples to be brought together when you prepare for them. Borrow a few pictures of their national heroes, put up their national colors, exhibit their national costumes, etc. Let them feel that an effort is made to appreciate something that is dear to them. Make an effort also to have the native and the foreign-born mingle, emphasizing the family tie and the bond of brother in the Fatherhood of God.

Carnival of Nations

The great objective of our work is Americanization. This should not be lost sight of in planning carnivals. The story of the American nation is full of episodes which lend themselves to dramatic presentation. The foreign-born will, in classes, lectures, and contact with native-born men, learn much about America. If by carefully planned programs they can be made to live in imagination through some of these scenes, they will absorb much of the spirit and the ambition of the makers of America. Let the foreign-born study the costumes of colonial days, copy them, imitate, no matter how faintly, the deeds of colonial heroes, and clearly enunciate the sentiments they felt. In this way the foreign-born will absorb more of the American spirit that they ever can or will in a classroom. The songs used on such an occasion should be patriotic, and the scenery true to the facts illustrated. Not only will the actors feel the inspiration of immortal epochs in American life, but their friends will also feel them, and all the spectators will catch a vision of what the purposes and ideals of democracy are.

INDUSTRIAL DEPARTMENT OF THE INTERNATIONAL COMMITTEE OF YOUNG MEN'S CHRISTIAN ASSOCIATIONS
347 Madison Avenue, New York City

Committee.— M. Hartley Dodge, Chairman; John Sherman Hoyt, Lucien T. Warner, Cleveland E. Dodge, S. J. Carpenter, George W. Perkins, William H. Wooden, John J. Eagan.

Secretaries.— Charles R. Towson, 347 Madison avenue, New York; Peter Roberts, Ph.D., 347 Madison avenue, New York; Norman C. Schlichter, Chicago, Ill.; John Sumner, Toronto, Ont.; John A. Goodell, Portland, Ore.; Fred. H. Rindge, Jr., 347 Madison avenue, New York; Dr. E. H. T. Foster, 347 Madison avenue, New York; A. Bruce Minear, Denver, Colo.; Arthur M. East, 347 Madison avenue, New York; George J. Zehrung, 71 West 23d street, New York; A. J. Speer, 1610 Candler Building, Atlanta, Ga.; S. A. Parker, Denver, Colo.

We place a knowledge of the English language first in importance believing it to be fundamental to Americanization.

Second, we consider naturalization. We find many unnaturalized because they do not know how to go about it, because " nobody asked me," because they are afraid to go into a court house, because they haven't time, and for other similar reasons.

The third item in our program is lectures, through which agency we discuss such questions as: What is America? What is the aim of our democracy? What are the hilltops of American history? What can America give to the immigrant and what can he give to America?

The fourth item is entertainment. The purpose of these entertainments is to provide a platform where the foreign-born can show us what they have — their songs, their history, their folk dances and their folk lore.

The next item, recreation, takes in the boy of the foreigner — that son who stands between two civilizations. We try to train him so that he may choose his life and adjust himself to America.

The last item is the advisory council organized from the public spirited and sympathetic men of the community with a view to giving advice kindly and gratuitously to the foreign-born.

Another purpose of our work is to train teachers for Americanization work. All over the country we have teachers' groups organized by our Americanization secretaries. We have also a movement in the colleges to encourage students to work among the foreign-born with the result that possibly 3,000 students are at present thus engaged.

The following text of one of our pamphlets is pertinent at this point:

Three Steps in Americanization
First — Needs

1. *Program.*—Americanization means a definite program — define yours. The master craftsman commands attention, so will you, if you know your job. Be a teacher, then you can teach others. Naturalization is a complicated process, be versed in it, that means leadership. Lectures should cover a multiplicity of subjects — know where you can get the necessary material. Attend the foreign-born's entertainments — you'll enjoy their talent. Foreigners are exploited — wear the breastplate of righteousness. The Master said "they are as sheep without a shepherd"; that's the foreigner today — be a shepherd.

2. *Knowledge.*—America has fifty varieties of foreigners — find out the kinds in your town. They segregate — know the segregations and their racial complexion. Each group has its

leaders — dig them out. They have clubs and societies — make a list of these, with the presidents and secretaries. See these leaders; put your program before them; ask for a hearing before the club or society; take your lantern and slides with you; tell them how you serve — they'll listen.

3. *Place and equipment.*— Rooms for classes — in industries, clubrooms, halls, boarding-houses, etc.— any place where men will come together. Foreigners will not go "uptown," you go downtown to them. They need convenience and not conveyance. Keep on hand adequate supplies, the men must see and handle things. Illustrate every lesson with the necessary articles — keep these on hand. A good blackboard is essential. Good equipment is like oil on the bearings — things go smoother and better.

4. *Advertising.*— Cultivate editors of foreign newspapers — they'll print your notices. Take them to see your classes. Invite them to your lectures. The pen is mightier than the sword — use the pen and keep the Sword of the Spirit shining. Put your cards, posters, etc., in barber shops, foreign banks, boarding-houses, pool rooms, drinking stations and restaurants. Foreigners frequent these places. Use the foreign tongue in advertising. The stamp that sticks makes the letter go — the advertisement that hits makes the class go.

5. *Leadership.*—A leader is known by the quality of his followers. His capacity is shown by the men he enlists in service. Classes installed and supervised display his organizing power. Leadership is of the heart and head — fifty-fifty. It is definite. The true leader will not beat the air, he knows the value of days and seasons, of ladders and ballast, and uses all to best advantage.

6. *Broadness.*— Don't neglect the other fellow interested in Americanization — he may be the star performer — tie your kite to the star. Hearts are bigger than creeds, practice has fewer thorns than theory. Play the game with others — it is the juncture of forces that makes the world spin. Politicians know the foreigner — draw upon their knowledge. The postmaster, the mail-carrier, the ticket agent, the boss of the pool room, the proprietor of the hang-out shop — all know the foreigner — don't think any of them Samaritans with whom you have no dealings. Serve all men of foreign birth and not a chosen few.

7. *Responsibility.*— Remember God's command to Ezekiel, "his blood will I require at thine hand." All will not respond, all should hear the message. Those who come, see that they know

the American type of Christian manhood. Don't trust to luck, there is no such thing. Feel for every class as parents do for their children. The man who keeps his hand on the motor brings the trolley on its way. Slipshod, lackadaisical methods spell failure. Your horoscope is in the success of the class you have established.

Second — Method

1. *Nationality.*— Fifty varieties! Don't be dismayed. The miner attacks one spot and not the whole quarry. Begin with one nation. Organize work along racial lines. Pass on to another race. Homogeneous groups have common interests and work well together. Like draws like. Psychology is useful for the individual, it is equally applicable to the race. Know the mind of a race. When you mix nations, learn which will and which will not mix. Oil and water will not mix; no more will peoples who have racial antipathy and prejudice. A study of nationality avoids failure.

2. *Subject matter.*— The lessons are well worked out. Workers are interested in concrete subjects, the lessons are concrete. The pupils are adults, they have forgotten childish things. They have rich experiences. The lessons clothe these experiences in a new garment of language. Workers want to talk — the prime emphasis is on talking. Reading and writing are not forgotten, they are nails to clinch oral instruction. Men have common interests when they have a common medium of communication. The lessons open up channels of intercourse between the foreigner and his fellow workers. The subject matter is daily experience methodized by pedagogy and common sense. These three elements must also enter the cranium of the leader if good results are expected.

3. *In the classroom.*— The teacher needs three things — punctuality, preparedness, cheerfulness. Classes should begin on time, most foreigners are not prompt, if you are prompt, they will soon learn that lesson. Each lesson should be like a well-cooked meal, ready to serve. An ill-prepared teacher is like a half-baked cake — one side hard and the other soft. The best of wheat is only good in the well-baked loaf, the best of teachers is only good when he prepares his lesson. Foreigners believe in direct action, beating around the bush will not do. Shoot straight and not over their heads. Don't bluff, the foreigner knows

wheat from chaff. As sunshine to a garden, so is cheerfulness in the classroom. Greet the pupils with a smile. Call them by their given name. Be patient with the backward ones. Frowning and cursing foreigners know — make the class hour one of hearty good will and cheerfulness.

4. *Attitude.*— Be natural. Know the difference between bombast and ballast. Goodness wins, it is contagious. Attend to small things — class roll, clean chairs, correct names, proper supplies, etc. Every flood started in a leak. When a pupil is wanting, don't say: "One less makes no difference." That man's feet may mark the path others will tread. Be sincere. Let the men know that you believe in God as well as in the Brotherhood of man. Americanization means blending as well as bleaching. Foreigners need sympathy more than English and bathing facilities. Men living in bunks and slums are hungering for love and peace though their clothes are shabby and their food coarse.

5. *Aim.*— Men of purpose know where they go, do you? What is your aim? Enter your room, close the door and define it. Skeptics, agnostics, non-believers, non-religious groups — all shout Americanization; wherein do you differ from these? America was founded by men who believed in God, the nation was born shouting "the inalienable rights of man to life, liberty, and the pursuit of happiness;" it was preserved by men who believed in the God of Battles. America means appreciation of religious values expressed in action by man to man. Every foreigner is God's child and may be formed into the image of the Son of God. To do this shaping — the class, the lecture, the service are only means. Unless soul moves soul Godward, we miss the mark.

Third — Achievement

1. *Resources.*— Men and money are in God's hand — ask great things. Men are measured by the tasks they undertake. Plans on paper help — achievements count. Guard against self-deception. Tap the untouched reservoirs of your heart and soul. The "tender mercies of God" are available in this twentieth century. The fountains of virtue in the hearts of foreigners have never been touched. Try to open them. Riches flow from very unlikely places. From the rock in the wilderness Moses drew water. Draw upon the hearts of foreigners.

2. *Checks.*— The American Beauty plus a thorn — that's God's way. Cross and Crown is the combination. Selfishness is ubiquitous, among foreign- and native-born. You can't bank on every banker. Stars rise and wane, so do the hearts of men. Human nature is frail, yet God thinks it worth while to work with it from the beginning till now. You cannot strike twelve right off, your timepiece may never strike that; keep the higher numbers before you while wrestling with the lower. When clouds are thick, they hide but don't put out the sun.

3. *Records.*— Keep tabs on your work. Men who don't run their business are run by it. Keep a steady hand on the motor. Don't take a chance, it's not good business. Keep close to helpers — the teachers. Know within twenty-four hours how each class goes. Visualize your work. Know each week what direction your work takes. The straw shows how the wind blows — watch the straws. Men who attend to detail swing the world.

4. *Reports.*— Men want to know what you are doing — give them a report. Make it concise and clear. Good reports are not padded. Imagination should not take the place of facts — performances and not promises shine in reports. Exchange reports with your friends. A good statement of facts is an art, study the good. Hot air has its place in the other fellow's mouth. Put the facts before men and let the other fellow blow the horn. Bells are good on churches and pushcarts, but not on men.

5. *Idealism.*— The moral teacher has an ideal, the materialist has none. Men having all their roots in the earth, have no stars above them. Men who have no God are like ships without chart and compass. Faith in the Unseen means appreciation of the seen. The mole says there is no sun, it has never seen it. The man who limits his knowledge to physical experience is poor — there are psychical experiences which hitch us to a world without weights and measures. Don't lose the fresh faith of your childhood in the goodness of man and the presence of God. The twentieth century needs men who see visions and dream dreams.

We have no hidebound requirements for teachers, believing that it depends on the individual. We oftentimes have found best results from a teacher drawn from the shop — a man with a good heart who can talk plainly and who understands his men. We believe the essentials in teacher training for this work are very largely fifty-fifty — head and heart. We have a large number of foremen who are teaching successfully.

The attendance at factory classes depends upon the teacher and upon the hours these men work as well as upon the constant shifting that always exists among foreign-born employees.

We reached forty-two nationalities last year, the following report describing our work among them:

Report for 1918-19 of Y. M. C. A. Americanization Work

The war disorganized Association work for Coming Americans both in Europe and America. The European situation is still in a state of chaos; at home the Association is resuming Americanization work in splendid fashion. Sixty-four men are giving all time to the work, seventy-six others give half time to Making Americans, and another hundred secretaries in small Associations hope to do something for the foreign-born this coming year. Never was Americanization more needed; never was it more conscious in the public mind; never was the Association better equipped for the work. The following report is good, but its chief value is in the promise of better work this coming year.

English and Naturalization

State	No. Classes	No. Teachers	No. Pupils	1st Papers	2d Papers	Total
Alabama	2	2	7	......	......	......
Arizona	5	5	99	......	......	......
Colorado	12	18	117	19	6	25
California	32	37	357	......	......	90
Connecticut	70	60	1,111	1,082	71	1,153
Illinois	21	21	1,357	1,593	121	1,714
Indiana	8	9	147	200	65	265
Iowa	1	1	5	......	......	......
Maryland	6	7	215	......	......	110
Massachusetts	88	91	1,285	712	352	1,064
Michigan	1	1	21	......	......	......
Minnesota	14	13	310	236	131	367
Missouri	58	39	838	......	......	219
Nebraska	3	3	77	......	......	......
New Jersey	88	74	1,184	1,586	449	2,035
New York	78	46	1,524	754	618	1,372
Ohio	20	21	317	100	4	104
Oregon	....	....	....	4	5	9
Pennsylvania	69	68	1,665	420	957	1,377
Rhode Island	1	1	38	50	20	70
South Carolina	1	2	16	......	......	......
Texas	1	1	10	......	......	......
Washington	15	6	218	......	......	289
Wisconsin	1	1	15	......	......	12
Wyoming	1	1	13	......	......	......
Total	596	528	11,606	6,756	2,799	10,275

One hundred and twenty Associations reported 10,856 men in English classes, taught by 528 teachers; and 10,275 men, with their faces toward citizenship, were aided; each Association on an average doing intensive work for 176 men. Suppose the 413 Associations in the immigration zone were each to do as much, how many men would be in English classes and on the way to naturalization in 1919?

Lectures and Entertainments

State	No.	Lectures Attendance	No.	Entertainments Attendance	Total Attendance
Alabama	9	1,086			1,086
Arizona	9	1,400	1	1,000	2,400
Colorado	6	44			44
California	33	2,200	2	240	2,440
Connecticut	24	2,028	8	1,123	3,151
Illinois	115	76,918	2	220	77,138
Indiana	11	1,175	1	260	1,435
Maine	62	3,155			3,155
Massachusetts	78	19,935	2	250	20,185
Minnesota	9	2,700			2,700
Missouri	96	6,942	3	3,245	10,187
Nebraska	10	4,650			4,650
New Hampshire			5	302	302
New Jersey	137	9,191	8	11,385	20,576
New York	584	119,825	16	3,409	123,234
Ohio	11	2,100	17	10,975	13,075
Pennsylvania	57	10,211	18	7,800	18,011
Rhode Island	7	224			224
South Carolina	1	40			40
Tennessee	2	450			450
Texas			1	200	200
Washington	20				
Wisconsin	3	300			300
Wyoming	4	305			305
Total	1,288	264,879	84	40,409	305,288

Fifty-seven Associations reported 1,288 lectures, with an attendance of 264,879. In thirty-one of these, eighty-four entertainments were conducted for foreign neighbors, with an attendance of 40,409 — a total of 305,288 persons, representing forty-two distinct peoples, touching elbows, and looking to the America of tomorrow. Can a million foreign-born men and their sons be better employed? Let's make it a million! Send for list of lectures.

Other Activities

The sons of foreign-born men go to the bad fast because of lack of adaptation. They need help. Just seven Associations reported 567 boys organized into clubs in foreign communities under the leadership of ninety-five men. There are a million who need help to understand America. They are the lads in industries, mines, mills, factories, shops, etc. A new American boys' club attached to every industrial Association would be a good beginning for the coming year.

Advisory councils are needed to help the foreign-born. Seventeen Associations have such councils, and 223 men serve on them. The services rendered varied greatly — bringing a doctor to justice for malpractice; forcing a lawyer to disgorge for overcharging; helping a man to find a wife; adjusting cases in industrial plants; bringing parents and children together, etc. There is no limit to the service, when once the foreign-born know who are their friends.

Co-operation with a dozen agencies, both governmental and local, in behalf of Coming Americans, and yet full consciousness of the Association's responsibility to the foreign-born. Hearty good will to all agencies doing Americanization work, with constant remembrance that the full Association message should be carried to the men and boys of foreign parentage. America is the hope of the foreign-born and his son. Let Association men give content to this hope in terms of service, brotherhood and patriotism.

The Goal

If America is to witness a real democracy in action, all patriots must take the full message of democracy to the 15,000,000 foreign-born in the land. Race prejudice, racial antagonism and discrimination against foreigners hinder the progress of democracy and the Kingdom of God. The hour demands the welding of fifty varieties of peoples into one fraternity for the peace of America, and the progress of that democracy which has its roots in the Fatherhood of God and the Brotherhood of Christ. It is a goal that challenges the best Association men can give.

Continuing his testimony before this Committee Dr. Roberts said:

During the war we went into the cantonments and taught English to drafted men who did not know our language.

We have today about 25,000 men in English classes and 8,000 in naturalization.

We have three English courses. The first or preparatory comprises thirty lessons with six reviews of which two lessons are given out per week. Four months is the average time to cover this course. The intermediate course also takes about four months and covers three beginners' readers. The advance course comprises history and a little geography and civics, and a man usually takes six months for this. We figure that it should take a man about two school years to cover the three courses.

The naturalization courses are more regularly attended than the English courses. We have a large number of testimonials from judges and other naturalization officials commending our work.

Our plan in entering an industry is to make it 100 per cent. American. We first get the heads to pledge their support and sympathy and then get to work from the bottom up. We get five foremen and five foreign-born naturalized citizens who speak English. We then make a canvass of the plant to determine how many need English, how many want English, how many are naturalized, how many have taken out first papers, etc. We believe it should be just as much the business of an employer of foreign labor to produce Americans as to produce goods. If a man works ten or twelve hours a day, he should be instructed on company time, but if he works only eight hours, it should be fifty-fifty.

I believe we will never get the foreign-born into our public schools. We will have to go right into their quarters — invade their barber shops and clubrooms and public halls — and take our message there. Cleveland has done good work, but they have only 5 per cent. in their public schools. The foreign-born usually come from country communities and are shy about going to public schools. Also, the public schools mix the races and there are natural antipathies against that. Even among the Italians there are prejudices. The northern Italian is an educated man and looks upon the southern as a "dago." They will not study together.

I do not believe in compulsory education for adults. It is all right for minors, however.

We do some work with women in industries, but for the most part the Y. W. C. A. takes care of them in the home.

AMERICANIZATION AS RELATED TO RECONSTRUCTION IN THE STATE OF NEW YORK

We beg to submit the following for the consideration of the Commission re the assimilation of the foreign-born or the work of Americanization:

1. *Accommodations.*— The public schools as a rule are poorly equipped for this work. In many sections of the industrial cities

where the foreign-born live, the schools are so crowded that all the children in grammar grades cannot be accommodated. When they complete the fifth or sixth grade, they are taken out of the school in this district and sent to another school for instruction in the sixth, seventh and eighth grades. To ask men to take instruction and squeeze into combination desks or seats for children in the fifth and sixth grades, is to attempt instruction under physical conditions that are decidedly uncomfortable. As children's books are ill adapted to adults in teaching English, so are the average grade schools ill adapted for foreign-born adults. Now, therefore, we advise that the State Legislature urge the necessity for furnishing seats or chairs with writing accommodations adapted to adults in schools where the adult foreign-born receive instruction.

2. *Courses of instruction.*— The books prepared to instruct children are not suitable to instruct adults. The adult foreign-born is a different creation from the child, and must be supplied with material wholly different from that used in the teaching of children in the public schools. The material for this work should relate directly to the need of the adults to be taught. For those in domestic life, the lessons should major on domestic duties, social intercourse, buying, etc. For those in the needle trades, the lessons should major on the implements used in those trades, the materials, the chief lines of work, etc. For those in the steel and iron industries, the lessons should major on the tools commonly used, the materials used, the main operations, the regulations as to safety, etc. The men and women in the industries need above all else simple, everyday practical English that will help them as soon as possible in the struggle for subsistence. Therefore, we recommend that the state delegate the task of suggesting and possibly preparing subject matter for teaching adult foreign-speaking persons to a commission suggested below; the personnel of the commission, after duly studying the leading industries in wh:ch the foreign-born are employed, to outline studies to be used by the public school and by private agencies if these care to use them.

3. *Time of study.*— It is a mistake to open the public school for four successive evenings and hope that the foreign-born will attend regularly. Men and women who work nine, ten, eleven or twelve hours a day at the "American pace" will not go to school in the evening for three or four successive nights. Two nights

a week, the evenings chosen dividing the week as equally as possible, i. e., Mondays and Thursdays, Tuesdays and Fridays, Wednesdays and Saturdays, would be better suited to the pupils. This method would give the pupils time to digest the instruction received and do some home work. In no case should wage-earners doing manual labor for from nine to twelve hours a day be asked to attend school more than three evenings a week, and those evenings should be alternate. But our experience suggests two evenings rather than three, if classes are to succeed. Therefore, we suggest that the Legislature make possible the opening of schools every night in the week, if necessary. The foreign-born also has more time on Sunday to study than on week days. We, therefore, recommend that the Legislature make possible the opening of schools on Sunday for those who would prefer instruction on that day.

4. *Teachers of foreign-born.*— We believe that the sexes should be separated in classes teaching English to the foreign-speaking. Our reason for this is that the interests of the sexes, economic, social and moral, are different; that the standards and motives are different; that their aims in life are different; and that men should be taught by men, and women by women. English is not all that teachers should give the foreign-born; they should give them standards in dress, in conduct, in social intercourse, in conventional manners, etc., and these can best be given by teachers of the same sex as the pupils taught.

We believe also that personality and sympathy with the foreign-born, as well as good judgment, count more in this work of teaching than ability to secure a teacher's certificate by state authority or otherwise. Teachers of foreign-born should be chosen from mature persons, having pedagogical instincts plus the qualities above mentioned, who should be given a permit to do this work although they are not holders of teachers' certificates. Therefore, we suggest that the Legislature make possible the employment of men and women of this type, and that it advocate strongly the use of male teachers for males, and female teachers for females.

5. *Naturalization.*— The subject of naturalization can well be illustrated by motion pictures. In cities of the first and second class, aliens on the way to American citizenship could be brought together once a week during the period of ninety days intervening between their application for second papers and the examination

in court to see reels depicting the American form of government, the Makers of America, the Geography of America, the Courts of the Land, the Duties of the President, Governor, Mayor, etc. These lectures could be supplemented by discussion in small groups under competent leaders. Therefore, we suggest that the Legislature delegate to the commission mentioned below the task of preparing twelve such lectures for use in the public schools or by reliable private agencies engaged in the work of naturalization.

6. *Court privileges.*—A large number of aliens are anxious to take out their first or second papers, but they are deterred from doing this by the necessity of losing a day or possibly two to go to the county seat, far removed from their towns, when the court is in session. This inconvenience, loss of work, and incidental expense or objections are deterrents that are serious in the minds of the aliens. We, therefore, suggest that the Legislature make possible night sessions, and also make possible sessions of court for this purpose in populous cities and towns far removed from the county seat. The State Legislature can doubtless make this possible in co-operation with the Federal Labor Department.

7. *Private agencies.*— Private agencies have done Americanization work for many years and are still doing it. The public school can never do all the work of Americanization. Many of the foreign-born will never go to the public school, but they will meet in halls, clubs, etc., in the sections of the city in which they live, and they can best be reached by private agencies which carry the message of Americanization to them. We believe that whatever equipment or supplies are prepared and furnished by the state or federal government from public funds for the promotion and performance of this work should be made available to these private agencies as well as public institutions. We believe that it is undemocratic to attempt to monopolize Americanization work by withholding from private agencies supplies necessary in doing the work. We, therefore, ask this commission to advise a liberal policy on the part of the Legislature in regard to the distribution of literature and appliances used in the work of Americanization.

8. *Board of advisers.*— The foreign-born encounters many difficulties in securing his papers which cannot be removed by the average layman, no matter how well disposed he is toward the alien. Many foreign-born, after coming to America, have

changed their names and know not the importance of making this known when they become citizens of the United States. If a Board of Advisers were appointed in each city, or in each section of first-class cities, who would aid and guide the foreign-born in these matters, it would be a blessing to thousands seeking citizenship. We recommend, therefore, that the Legislature urge the appointment of such Boards of Advisors in every school district in the state where there are aliens to be naturalized.

9. *State and municipal laws.*— The foreign-born get into the clutches of the law for the reason that they do not know what are its requirements in cities, the ordinances of which they are not accustomed to. If the most common provisions of state laws and city ordinances were issued in pamphlet form, in the language of the foreign-born, they would be better able to comply with the regulations of state and city, and the knowledge of these legal regulations, by such free distribution of pamphlets, would be far more common among the foreign-born of every nationality than it is today. We, therefore, recommend that the Legislature assign this task of preparing and issuing in the most common language of the foreign-born such information of state laws and municipal ordinances as they deem the most essential to the foreign-born.

10. *Appointment of a special commission.*— The Americanization work in the State of New York is most important and deserves the attention of a body of men who know the problem, and who can attack it in a statesmanlike manner. To place the problem of Americanization on the shoulders of the educational authorities of the state is to add a burden to men and women who have their hands now full. We also believe that the Americanization of the foreign-born is so distinct from that of public instruction, that it demands the service of experts. The teaching of English and civics is a minor factor in a comprehensive program of Americanization. The full program will never be adequately carried out until a special commission be authorized to co-ordinate the public school and the private agencies of the state interested in this work. We, therefore, recommend that the Legislature create by law an Americanization Commission to take over the work, study the needs of the foreign-born in the state, and meet this need in a way that will make adequate provision for the assimilation of the foreign-born, and make the best possible use of public and private agencies for this purpose.

The following material submitted by other Y. M. C. A. secretaries is of interest as outlining phases of the work other than those coming under the supervision of Dr. Peter Roberts:

AMERICANIZATION THROUGH CHRISTIAN LEADERSHIP

The immigration tide has slackened, but the hands of the Association were never busier. The program on Ellis Island has grown more complicated and comprehensive because of problems raised by the war conditions in Europe. The need of a strong program for the Americanization of aliens was never more needed, and this more urgent need challenges the association to greater service. The following statement of services rendered in 1916–17 is submitted as evidence of Christian leadership in the Americanization of immigrants:

On Ellis Island

Two secretaries are constantly on duty at Ellis Island. These, and the other secretaries at ports of landing, see and do things.

Here is Thompson, a stowaway, almost naked, hungry, and penniless. He says he is native-born, but the wise ones give the wink and say, "Fled from the trenches." Deportation awaits him. The secretary visits Thompson; gets the name of a relative 1,000 miles away; communicates with the relative; verifies the man's statement, and the "American-born citizen" is landed, clothed, fed, and a ticket is purchased to destination.

Here is a Greek boy who, to escape army service, assumed a Turkish name and got away. He has a brother in Kansas City, but when the authorities send the brother the Turkish name, he replies, "Don't know him." The secretary sits with the boy, who tells his story and gives his correct name. This is sent to the brother, and on the wings of the telegraph the requisite money comes, and the boy hurries on to Missouri.

Now comes a United States soldier boy, clad in khaki, and ready to fight for the Union. He has come to Ellis Island to meet his brother, who left Europe for America some weeks ago. He appeals to our secretary, "Please help me to find my brother." He gives the brother's name and little else. The search is begun. The boy is located in quarantine. The uniform, a brother's plea, and the zeal of the secretary work together to secure the release of the boy and within three days brother clasps brother.

Behold a mother and three children, who came from where the cannon roar. Space will not permit to tell the story of her hardships, trying with her little brood to leave war-cursed Europe. She is here, and has the address of her husband, but when the authorities send word to him they are informed, "No such person known." The secretary knows a man of the same nationality in that town, so he writes to him asking his aid in locating the father. In a week the lost is found. The father had given up hope of the wife and children coming and had moved elsewhere. He gladly sends money to his family. The tears of mother and children are wiped away. They are taken to the train, and the boy of twelve kisses the hand of the secretary and says, "We'll all pray for you who helped us to find papa."

Here is a boy, a refugee from Turkey. He is an Anatolian. When asked for an address he gives it "general delivery." The secretary becomes responsible for the boy, takes him out, finds him employment, room, and board. A week later a cousin of the youth comes to look for him. He is taken to the boy, and they clasp in true oriental fashion. The secretary turns to leave and feels something pressed into his hand — $2. "No! We don't work that way; we do it in Christ's name." They stare, bow, and know not what to say.

These cases could be multiplied a hundredfold, for 10,000 such men were served during the year. But this is only one part of the work, and we must move en route, for the association follows the immigrant with its service.

At Depots

Ever heard of Reithard — W. Y. — of Detroit? No? Next time look him up. You'll find him at one of the depots of that prosperous city. Under his coat is a police badge. His title is Intercity Secretary, but he comes to these pages for the reason that he meets and serves immigrants as well as others. We followed his work for seven months, and during that time he helped 545 foreigners locating in Detroit and twice that number passing through for points further west. No, he is no linguist; but he has a heart in him, and the men of twenty-eight different tongues understand him as he protects them from sharks, hoboes, false guides, etc. They don't know why he does not take money, cigars, drinks, etc., but they know that he is all right!

Then in St. Louis there's Harry ter Braak. Yes, he is a linguist — a direct descendant of the Dutch who were present at the Day of Pentecost. You should know him. He has worked for the immigrant for eight years. We've followed his work for the best part of last year, and he helped 5,535 people at the Union depot. His tongue jabbers many languages, but his heart speaks more. Thirty different peoples were met and served, and all understood him, but these also have difficulty in knowing why he does not take pay for his work when they want him to.

Then there is D. L. Smith, in San Francisco, guiding immigrants coming through the Golden Gate or transcontinental; T. G. Demberg, in Philadelphia, emphasizing the doctrine of "brotherly love" in a real way by service to men stranded on the dock or in the depot; Mijelj, in Chicago, working with Abraham Bowers, the man who guides association activities in the city of Chicago. He works with men of thirty different tongues coming to settle in the metropolis of the West. All these men meet trains and guide weary feet over thorny and treacherous paths into havens of safety.

The story of their work cannot be told here, but the value of it — done so quietly and unassumingly — may be judged from the following:

A Portuguese Protestant clergyman is detained by the officers of the law because of irregularity in some paper. He believes it is the hand of persecution, and thinks America is as "priest ridden" as Portugal. A secretary comes to him, explains the situation, helps him to adjust matters, and has the joy of seeing him moving on to destination.

Here is a Greek, going to Kansas City. When he arrived in St. Louis he found that all his money and ticket were gone. Stranded, he knew not what to do. The secretary takes him in charge, finds him friends and employment. He begins work and earns money to go on to friends in Missouri.

Here is an old mother, from the Middle West, on her way to her son in Pennsylvania. She is in trouble. She had $30 in her purse, and lo! it is now only $2. What can she do? The secretary takes up the case, makes it possible for her to continue the journey and see her boy. Her last word, as she took her seat in the train going East, was a benediction.

A Bohemian stands in the depot bewildered. All his money is gone; the sharks have made a clean job of it; he does not know what to do. The secretary finds him, gives him a night's shelter. The following day he finds him a job, a room, and starts him off with $2 for board.

A foreigner comes with three little children. He has just laid their mother to rest, and thinks he can find some one in the city to help him care for the children. He grapples with the new problem and is as a child. The secretary comes to the rescue. The children are taken to the Board of Health for inspection, then to an orphanage that opens its door to the motherless ones, and then work is found for the father. What wonder is it that these men bless and pray for the Association hand that helps in time of need!

Here is a Polander, who is doubled up in the depot. He knows not what is the matter, but he is "sick like hell." The secretary takes him in a taxi to the hospital, where he is cared for. He keeps in touch with him till he is cured and able to continue the journey.

A sick man comes into the depot dragging three little children after him. He is a Croatian. The mother is dead and he is sick. He is helpless and knows not what to do. The secretary knows what to do. He calls up his friend in St. Vincent de Paul Society, presents the case, and in an hour the three little ones are cared for and the sick father goes to the hospital.

A group of thirty Portuguese are on the way. They were thrown out of work and are moving to another city in hopes of employment — men, women, and children. They have been on the train all night, the women are tired, the babies are dirty and crying. The secretary takes in the situation. They have no money. No matter, he gets milk for the babies, coffee and buns for the mothers, and the men look on, wondering. The little ones come in for some cleaning, and by the time the train leaves they are all revived. They did not know what to do for the one who had helped them!

Here are four Russians, who represent their government in an engineering investigation. They know the Y. M. C. A. in Petrograd. They are met by the secretary, who can converse in their tongue. How their faces beam with joy! They look at his cap and see the magic letters, "Y. M. C. A.," known the world over. They plunge into their pockets and take out their membership cards. They are taken to the Association, shown the plant, escorted throughout the city, see all they care to see, and leave with an experience they will never forget.

The record of these activities could also be multiplied — all in need were served without partiality. It is a lesson in the meaning of Christian democracy, which was well expressed by some Albanians who were served: "A new idea; helping men of all races and religions."

But we must pass on to the services rendered by the Association inland, where the immigrants take up their abode.

Messages

Last year more than 5,000 cards of introduction were given men locating in centers where Associations are located. The following facts taken from reports received prove this service worth while:

Many Associations report that the foreign brother presented his introduction card and asked the secretary for help. Some were given rooms in the buildings, were welcomed in the restaurant, and were helped to find employment. Others were taken to friends and relatives.

Contrast that with the experience some immigrants have. One of them writes of the town in which he settled, that it is filled with boozers, crooks, hoboes, etc. It is all a question of a right start.

The secretary goes to welcome a foreigner just arrived, and finds him in a saloon dispensing liquors. He tells him about the Y. M. C. A. school, where he can learn English. The saloon-keeper has a good heart and says, "I have twenty more who want to learn English." Arrangements are soon made and a class is now running there. Pray that the saloon's influence will grow less and less and the Association's greater and greater.

Another secretary went to look up a Greek just come from Patras. He found him selling peanuts. He asked him, "Can you talk English?" He could get no reply save a shrug of the shoulders. He soon finds out that all the man knows is, " Peanuts, five cents a bag. I don't know." On that knowledge of the language he launched out in an unknown world! With this handicap he started on his own hook to make a living! Oh, the courage of these foreigners!

An immigration secretary, who has been on the job three years, writes: "I found the Macedonian; and more, I found nineteen other men in a boarding house which I never knew was in town. I am now planning a class there; the fellows want it."

Here is a secretary who has done good work among the Russians in his city. One day he received a package from the old world. On it was a name but no address. It was from a mother to her son. When the secretary found that man and delivered that package he forged another link that will bind that Russian colony in a better fellowship with America.

Hundreds of such letters are received from secretaries who are moved by the spirit of the Good Shepherd to go in quest of the man who comes to town and is liable to fall among thieves. They go to him; bid him welcome; offer him service, and invite him to a place where the spirit of the Christ reigns. This work is generally done through cosmopolitan clubs, made up of leading representatives of the foreign-born peoples, who know the Association and its spirit, and work together with it for the good of the immigrants. More and more do secretaries find the cosmopolitan clubs serviceable in approaching the newcomer and in opening the door of opportunity to serve him.

But again we must hurry on for we are not yet at the end of the catalogue of services rendered foreign-born men.

Inland Work

All the work at the port of entry, at the depots, in search for recent comers, is only preparatory to the carefully planned program of work to assimilate the aliens.

The first step is to meet them, greet them, and get their confidence in the unselfish service the Association is willing to render. Then the program is launched.

1. *English and citizenship.*— Classes to teach English and citizenship are organized and foreign-speaking men are brought in. The last report compiled showed that Associations conducted more than 3,000 classes. Representatives of more than forty-two peoples were brought into these classes.

One Association man goes to a Roumanian club and offers to conduct a class in the room in which it meets. The offer is accepted and the work begins. Another goes to a shop where many Hungarians work. They have an hour at noon for dinner. Most of the men stay there and have half an hour in which they may learn some English. Short lessons are prepared to meet their need, and for three afternoons each week the men learn practical, everyday English.

A clergyman of the Ruthenian Church believes his people ought to learn English, announces such a class from the altar and urges the men to come. The secretary goes to the meeting and seventy-five eager faces greet him. The men are then divided into classes, according to their present knowledge and previous training, and the work of teaching English and citizenship goes on, the priest heartily co-operating.

The newer peoples, such as the Balkan peoples, bring few wives with them. Hence, boarding houses in industrial centers where these peoples live are very frequent. It is not unusual for the Association to conduct classes in such boarding houses, where eight or twelve people meet regularly twice a week to study English.

One of the disturbing factors in class work is the night shift, but some secretaries are solving it by conducting daytime classes for night men.

Secretaries co-operate with public school agencies, both by supplying and training teachers, and by conducting classes in the school buildings in sections of cities where foreigners live. The building, heat, light, and janitor service are usually furnished free.

Along with the instruction in English, classes are formed for men who are anxious to get their naturalization papers. They are helped to get their first papers, and then prepared to pass the examination in naturalization. By this friendly and intelligent service thousands of men have been taught English, and other thousands have been helped to become citizens, and today they exercise the power of the franchise in an intelligent manner.

2. *Lectures.*— The Association also projects lectures in communities made up of foreign-born peoples, to instruct them about America, its institutions, its trials and triumphs, its heroes and heroines, as well as what a man, a family, and a community ought to know in order to keep well and get along in America. In Chicago, more than 40,000 people were reached last summer by outdoor lectures; Providence, R. I., more than 40,000; Lawrence, Mass., 30,000; Cambridge, Mass., 29,000; St. Louis, Mo., 50,000; Rome, N. Y., 20,000; New York City, 50,000; Philadelphia, Pa., 25,000, etc. This phase of Association service has been developed most remarkably in the last few years, and has proven that it is possible to take to communities of foreign-born peoples the patriotic and Christian message.

3. *Consultations.*— These more formal classes and lectures afford opportunity for countless services to immigrants, of which the following are typical:

A man wants to buy a lot, but is afraid that he will be cheated. The secretary looks up the party, consults a reliable real estate agent, and safeguards the foreigner in his effort to secure a home.

Two men in a class are sick and are taken to the hospital. The secretary visits them; they know their friend and are cheered. They say to the nurse, "The teacher good man." They were sick and this man visited them and they won't forget.

Here is a man who, while drunk, beat his wife. She insists upon leaving him. Though sober now, he does not know what to do, so he comes to the immigration secretary to ask help. Peace is restored; the family is not broken up, for the man has sworn solemnly before the secretary and his priest that he will not drink any more.

A foreigner who was injured knew nothing of his rights under the Industrial Compensation Law. He and his family needed help. The secretary takes up the matter with the works manager and the compensation comes to the family regularly during the incapacity.

A foreigner wants to leave, but cannot get his pay. Usually foreigners assign their wages to a boarding boss, or sell them at a discount to an agent. This man comes to the secretary, who takes the assignment, sends a check for the full amount to the man and receives a reply with more heart in it than English.

A secretary visits a Roumanian boarding house and finds some of the men playing on various musical instruments. He suggests the organization of a band. "Sure!" The band is organized and a channel of expression has been found for the music of a nation in the new world.

An Albanian boy becomes insane. He has $483 in the bank. The public administrator takes charge of the fund, but the secretary takes up the matter with the medical authorities, as to whether or not there is hope for the boy; if not, and he must go back to his country, they will send the boy back before his money is spent.

A Roumanian family wants to christen the baby boy who has come to the home. The secretary is invited to attend. He accepts and is given an opportunity, in the midst of the festivities, to talk ten minutes about American social ideals.

One secretary has installed a substation of the post-office in the building, and has a competent assistant in charge. This gives many opportunities for helping the immigrants in the vexing questions of post-office orders and mailing matter in general.

A colony of foreign-born men living within a five-cent fare of a beautiful park knew nothing of it, and would not go there because they were shy. The secretary organized parties, took them out, gave them a good time. Result — better dresses, American lunches, greater self-confidence, and deeper appreciation of America.

4. *Co-operation.*— Many are the agencies doing work for immigrants. It is the policy of the Association to co-operate with each. We join hands with many principals of schools; with social workers; with industries doing welfare work, and with religious organizations of all kinds.

Here is a territory that has much material prosperity, but lacks religious leadership. The Association enters it, and the secretary in charge organizes Sunday schools for both Protestants and Catholics, co-operating in each instance with leaders in charge of the respective faiths.

In a settlement house a group of Greeks meet. The local Association supplies teachers in English, and the men, willing to spend Sunday afternoon in the reading of the Greek Testament, meet under the leadership of a teacher who, though he talks no Greek, is a veritable spiritual leader to this group of Greek Orthodox men.

In a town in New England the spirit of practical service had gripped a Roman Catholic clergyman and he wanted to serve his foreign-born neighbors. The Association secretary got in touch with him, showed him the methods followed and the tools used in the work; the secretary was invited to start work in the vestry of the church, and hand in hand with the priest, a work has been done which means better homes, better families, and better Christians.

The Association building in another town was used for months as a sanctuary for a group of Greek Orthodox Christians, and the secretary worked hand in hand with the leader to secure a church for this branch of Christ's vineyard.

In another Association a group of Albanians stood midway between Roman Catholicism and Greek Orthodoxy. They met under the leadership of Association men in the Association building, who conducted Sunday school and services for them every Lord's Day. Now the band is coming to the conviction that it ought to get a building of its own and the leaders in the group are fine Christian men.

Here is a town far from any church, but every Sunday evening same fifty or sixty men come together to see motion pictures of a moral and patriotic character, to sing sacred hymns, and to read a word of Scripture in the several tongues represented.

It is Christian service, although not dressed in the garments of any special creed or church. The aim is to bring the truth of the Christ to the hearts of men and leave the question of religious affiliation to the individual. The spiritual message of the Christ is what the foreigners need, and this is what the Association is trying to give them by both acts and words.

Even this list of varied incidents does not give an adequate idea of the service Association secretaries give foreign-born men, in paving their way into fellowship with Americans through the agency of cosmopolitan clubs, advisory boards, national festivals, and community meetings. It is the expression of peace and good will among men, and the more it is done by Association secretaries the more they contribute to the Kingdom of God.

Already this statement of activities for foreigners is too long. Time will not allow to tell of Americanization meetings, festivals of nations, dramatic and musical fetes, pageants, etc., planned and carried out by Association secretaries, though not labeled as Association activities. The experience of Association immigration workers is capitalized more and more by public schools, industrial corporations, philanthropic agencies, and missionaries. The greater interest in aliens stirred up by public and private agencies makes it opportune for Associations to emphasize their services and enlarge them. It has the machinery and the leadership with which to do a regular and sustained work, without which the general propaganda will have little value.

The decade of special immigration service has also proved, beyond dispute, that it is possible to embody the Christ spirit and message in service without stirring up antagonisms and enflaming passion by proselyting. In many instances Catholics and Protestants and Orthodox have stood together in the spirit of true Christian fellowship in the Americanization of the foreign-born, and the Christian leadership of these three large divisions of the Christian Church should be able to do more such co-operation in the face of pressing national exigencies.

We have done a piece of Americanization work, using the presidents of the foreign lodges as our foreign committee. There were 275 in our English classes. Six big Americanization meetings were held.

You see we are interested in this and thoroughly believe it should be done throughout the state. I feel that the person who has natural approach in the community should be the one to do it rather than autocratically saying Y. M. C. A., Chamber of Commerce or public schools. I certainly believe in compulsory education for them, but if possible to be worked around individually rather than merely on legal basis.

REPORT OF WORK FOR FOREIGN-BORN MEN OF THE YOUNG MEN'S CHRISTIAN ASSOCIATION OF THE CITY OF NEW YORK

Submitted by H. W. ANDERSON, *Secretary for Foreign-born Men*
West Side Branch, 318 West 57th street:

 Activities inside the building:
  Enrolled in 16 general educational classes... 236
 Activities outside the building:
  English classes, 26; enrollment............ 638
  Naturalization classes, 20; enrollment...... 560
  Americanization lectures, 122; total attendance............................... 25,780
  Entertainments, 31; attendance 2,349
  Foreign boys, groups, 16; attendance....... 640
  Helped to secure first papers.............. 155
  Helped to secure second papers............ 100
            30,458

(Nationalities served, 9: Bohemian, Polish, Russian, Italian, Hungarian, Ukranian, Austrian, German, Spanish.)

Bronx Union Branch, 470 East 161st street:
 Helped to secure second papers.................. 344
 Instructed in government civics 344
 English classes, 4; enrollment................... 60
           748

East Side Branch, 153 East 86th street:
 Foreign-born men in educational classes......... 250

Young Men's Institute Branch, 222 Bowery:
Foreign-born or foreign-born extraction using
building 700
Enrolled in English classes 15
Enrolled in naturalization classes.............. 20
                                              ─────
                                               735

Intercollegiate Branch, 2929 Broadway:
The work for foreign-born men of the Intercollegiate Branch falls into two categories: 1. Work being done among foreign students (see inclosed report). 2. Work being done for working men and boys through enlisting a volunteer leadership for classes in English and club work. This work is just now being instituted for the school year. Before the war one secretary gave all his time to this work.
Volunteer leaders working.................... 100
Men and boys served........................ 1,800
Foreign student members of Cosmopolitan Club.. 202
                                              ─────
                                              2,102

Twenty-third Street Branch, 215 West 23d street:
Foreign-born men now using membership privileges 623

French Branch, 109 West 54th street:
Total membership, foreign-born or foreign-born
extraction 523
Classes in English, 2; attendance.............. 80
                                              ─────
                                               603

(Nationalities served, 27: French, American, Swiss, Belgium, Italian, Canadian, Luxemburg, Bulgarian, Greek, Armenian, Haiti, Cuban, Spanish, Argentina, Czech, Peruvian, Chilian, Portuguese, Dutch, Irish, Russian,

Swedish, English, Japanese, Turk, Maltese, Albanian.)

Colored Men's Branch, 181 West 135th street:
Total membership 1,021

66,540

The following announcement of the Twenty-third Street Branch of the Y. M. C. A. in New York City is said by them to be typical of what is offered in their other branches:

English for Foreigners

The object of these courses is to provide for the young men of other tongues a thorough drill in the actual use of the English language. The classes are open to men of all nationalities and are taught by teachers experienced in the work.

English only is used in the classroom. At first easy words and simple sentences, such as are met with in everyday life, are introduced. The student soon becomes confident as his ability increases and his interest is aroused. Then, gradually and systematically, a larger vocabulary and more difficult sentence structure are studied, leading up to letter writing. Throughout the course careful attention is given to pronunciation.

Day Classes

Day classes are held on Monday, Wednesday and Friday afternoons, from 3 to 4:30, beginning October 6th.

First term, October to January.
Second term, February to May.
One term, four months, $6.
Two terms, eight months, $10.

Evening Classes

Evening classes are held on Monday and Thursday evenings, from 7:30 to 9:45, beginning October 7th.

First term, October to January.
Second term, February to May.
One term, four months, $6.
Two terms, eight months, $10.

All students required to pay the Association membership fee of $5.25 (unless already members of the Y. M. C. A.).

Letter from Fred. H. Rindge, Jr., Industrial Department, Y. M. C. A., December 1, 1919:

"Our organization has been doing a very extensive work for more than fifteen years among foreigners, not only in this country, but all over the world.

"Before the war we had secretaries at fourteen ports of embarkation in Europe, dealing with immigrants as they left their homeland. There were special secretaries in the steerage of ships, at Ellis Island, on immigrant trains, at depots, all of this leading up to a comprehensive program of social, educational and physical activities, health promotion, building of character, and promotion of thrift in its various aspects.

"Of course, during the war we helped to Americanize about 200,000 foreigners in the army, and are enlarging rapidly our service in the industries. Americanization classes, for example, are held, not only in all kinds of Association buildings, but more particularly in factories and other industrial operations, foreign clubs, and societies, boarding houses, homes, stores, poolrooms, etc. Our emphasis is put, not merely on teaching English and citizenship, but an all-around program of service which will reach every part of the foreigner's nature."

CHAPTER IX
Young Women's Christian Association

1. THE BALLARD SCHOOL

YOUNG WOMEN'S CHRISTIAN ASSOCIATION, 600 Lexington avenue, New York City — Ballard School, Jeannette Hamill, director.

The Ballard School was organized in 1872 and until 1917 was known as the Educational Branch of the Young Women's Christian Association.

Courses are offered, for a nominal fee, in stenography, typewriting, secretarial work, bookkeeping, arithmetic, penmanship, filing, business law, foreign trade, advertising, multigraphing, banking, elocution, dramatics, public speaking, parliamentary law, Bible study, French, Spanish, Italian, handcrafts, fine arts, commercial art, current topics, drafting, designing, dressmaking, embroidery, millinery, cooking, home nursing. There is also a course in English for the foreign-born who have been in this country for six months or over and know some English. Before they know some English, they are sent to the International Institute.

Following is a roster of the foreign-born students enrolled in the Ballard School in October, 1919:

England	29
Canada	20
Germany	20
Ireland	20
Scotland	17
Sweden	14
Italy	12
Russia	10
France	8
Switzerland	8
Austria	8
Japan	4
Norway	4
Denmark	4
Finland	3
Hungary	3
Bohemia	3
Hawaii	3

Slovak	2
Poland	2
Roumania	2
Porto Rico	2
Holland	2
Belgium	1
New Zealand	1
British West Indies	1
Colombia	1
Caucasus	1
Syria	1
Egypt	1
China	1
Servia	1
Mexico	1
Spain	1
Bulgaria	1

2. INTERNATIONAL INSTITUTE

INTERNATIONAL INSTITUTE FOR YOUNG WOMEN, 108 East 30th street, New York City, Mrs. Francis M. Bacon, chairman; Mrs. Dunlevy Milbank, first vice-chairman; Mrs. William Fellowes Morgan, treasurer; Mrs. William E. Baker, secretary; Miss Edith L. Jardine, general secretary.

The Young Women's Christian Association in New York City exerts a special effort toward the foreign-born women of the city through the International Institute, whose general policy is outlined in the following article, "Ideals of the International Institute for Foreign Born Young Women in New York City," by Miss Edith L. Jardine, general secretary:

"Above every vital piece of work there is an ideal which gives purpose, direction and harmony to all that is accomplished. The ideal of the International Institute, briefly stated, is the conservation, for their own sakes and for the sake of America, of the young women who immigrate to our shores.

"The International Institute in Manhattan has had contact with some 20,000 young foreign-born women during the seven years of its existence, and it has become a familiar friend and confidant of a sufficiently large and varied number of them to have an understanding of their difficulties, problems, needs and aspirations.

"The status of foreign-born women has undergone many changes since the International Institute was established. Then young women were immigrating in such great numbers that they could not be assimilated socially or industrially. Now, owing to labor conditions, there is a shortage of women workers, and there is great competition for the services of foreign-born women.

"It is of interest to note that a new avenue of immigration has opened up, bringing us thousands of women and girls of a different type — of the Latin-American races of South America, and of the Latin and native races of the West Indies.

"From the knowledge which the International Institute has derived from this work, it is able to assert that the great majority of the foreign-born women who have come to us have 'made good' in the sense of supporting themselves, taking advantage of every opportunity afforded them, overcoming obstacles and resisting temptations.

"Whatever value most people place upon our young women of foreign birth, it is unquestionable that we have been almost entirely dependent upon the work of their skillful hands. Therefore many of us have thought of them or have considered them from a somewhat selfish and restricted point of view, that of the employer.

"The majority of Americans have had no opportunity to know foreign-born women as the workers of the International Institute know them. The majority have the same qualities as other wholesome, lovable girls, with gifts and graces which make them delightful friends and companions.

"Immigration may wax and wane and profound industrial changes may take place, but surely such work as the International Institute carries on will always be needed in order to bring closer together for their mutual benefit the women of all races who meet and commingle in this country."

(The above article is from the July-August, 1919, issue of "The W," published by the Institute.)

In an interview with a representative of the Committee Miss Edith L. Jardine, general secretary of the International Institute, said, in substance:

"The Institute exists for the protection of the foreign-born woman. We help to get the girls employment. We have a boarding home which accommodates thirty-three, and we expect to have one which will house seventy-five as soon as we can find a suitable building. Girls are brought to this home by the Travelers' Aid Society.

"In the past seven years we have reached 20,000 foreign-born women, and last year we reached 2,000. We had 500 enrolled in classes and sent many more to the public schools. The girls usually come to us for a year and then go to the public schools after they know some English. We have no figures showing the number of girls we reach of the various nationalities, but I would place them in the following order:

Italians	Swedes	Armenians
Danes	Russians	Syrians
Norwegians	Greeks	Hungarians

"We have an Italian community center on East 45th street, a Russian community center on West 45th street and an Armenian center on East 26th street. At the Italian center we have a pre-natal clinic and a children's clinic. We expect to start a class there to teach English to men in the neighborhood, the men themselves having asked for it when they saw how much the women of their race were benefitting by the work of the Institute. A Hungarian center will be started in Harlem. During the war the Hungarians kept away from us, fearing that the Americans did not trust them. All these various centers are in the nature of club rooms and are open for evening activities. During the day the neighborhood visitor had her office there. We employ a staff of twenty visitors — all foreign-born. We use them for teachers also if their ability is sufficient. In the work of visiting, a circular printed in the language of the foreigner is left, telling the woman of the Institute and asking her to come to us for help of any sort. These visitors used to make 6,000 visits a year when immigration was unrestricted. Four thousand girls were reached during 1918. During the four summer months of 1919, 976 women were reached by 2,916 visits."

The International Institute offers the following courses:

Elementary Course
Mondays and Fridays, 7:30 to 9 P. M.

A class for beginners who are given instruction in pronunciation, conversation, reading and writing.

Secondary Course
Mondays and Thursdays, 7:30 to 9 P. M.

Individual instruction for those who have some knowledge of English.

This course gives special attention to grammar, composition, business and social letter writing, civics and American history.

Cooking and Home Making Class
Tuesdays, 7:30 to 9 P. M.

A course of lessons in American cooking.
Pupils can learn to cook their favorite dishes.

Dancing Class
Wednesdays, 8 to 9:30 P. M.

Instruction is given in correct social dancing. Popular national dances will also be taught.

Educational Dramatic Class
Thursdays, 8 to 9 P. M.

The pupils learn English poems and short plays. Special instruction is given in the use of the voice and in English pronunciation.

Singing
Fridays, 8 to 9 P. M.

Chorus singing of the best American and popular songs.
Concert with prominent artists once a month.

These classes are held from October to June, two nights per week. Five hundred students registered in the fall of 1918, and most of them saw it through. A few transferred to classes other than those in which they started, but all remained active members of the Institute. No girls are taken into our classes who are of public school age. They range from 16 to 30 years of age, most of them being between 18 and 24.

We do not keep girls from going to public schools, but on the contrary are instrumental in getting many of them to go. If they do not go immediately after coming to us, they go later when they have acquired enough English so that they do not feel ashamed. Many of them, especially the Scandinavians, are well educated in their own language, but when they come to this country, not knowing any English, practically the only thing they can do for a living is domestic work. They are much desired in this line and earn more money at it than other nationalities. They lead an isolated life, however. Many girls who are members of the Institute afterwards go to the International College in Springfield, Mass.

All our courses are free with the exception of such as first aid, cooking, etc., where a nominal charge is made to cover the cost of materials consumed. The membership fee to the Institute is $1 per year. This charge is not prohibitive, for most of the girls earn good salaries. Many work at dressmaking, and they earn $30 per week and even $40 or $50. Several who are expert cigarmakers earn $50 a week. Most of them do not know how to spend it, however. Still there are exceptions, for one of our Italian girls bought $3,000 worth of Liberty Bonds.

We have a chorus for singing and teach the American songs, including the "Star Spangled Banner."

We also have a number of racial leagues — Italian, Greek, Hungarian, Armenian and Scandinavian. We have monthly meetings, to which the girls bring their men friends, and we have prominent speakers — one American and one from the nationality concerned.

We have no standard requirements for teachers, but their ability to teach is considered before their actual knowledge of English, though of course they aim to get those with the very best command of the English language. We make it a point to have teachers who know the language of the pupils whom they teach.

While some of our girls go to college, we haven't enough colleges to give courses for the many foreign students who have a great desire to learn. We will have to build special schools to teach adult foreigners. We cannot get pupils into our schools as long as we use little children's seats. We haven't the right type of teacher now in the public schools. The majority of our public school teachers are foreign-born and it would be better to have American-born. Most of our teachers are Jews. There are racial reasons why Italians or Greeks do not want to study with them or have their children study with them. They do not feel that these Jewish teachers can give them American ideals. The American-born teacher is best, that is, after a teacher of their own race, but there are not enough of these available. The foreign-born teacher who can speak perfect English and who in addition is a good teacher, is very rare. We prefer a good teacher, even if the English is not perfect. We aim to teach American ideals, not only language.

There is a great craving among our foreign-born girls to meet real Americans. Very few of our girls have married Americans. Greek girls marry Greek men, but Greek men marry Irish and Americans. Italians and other races mix but many of the girls marry Americans. It is usually the foreign men who marry the American girls, but the foreign girls marry foreigners, even though these men are not of their own race. The reason for this is that the man is in business and has more contacts and more chances to meet American girls than the foreign girls have to meet American men. Also, it is the man who makes the choice, and the fact that many foreign men marry American girls probably shows that they all would like to intermarry with the Americans if they had the chance.

One of the objects of the International Institute is to find the right sort of American contacts for our foreign-born girls. They all want to learn the English language well enough to be able to meet Americans, but the right kind of Americans do not want to meet foreign people. We are now trying to get a group of American girls to come to parties and mingle with the foreign girls. While these girls want to adopt American customs, they hate the term "Americanization." They call it the "White Plague." One Armenian paper stated that Americanization means making people over into something where none of their national characteristics will be left. In a series of lectures recently given on the subject, one speaker said, "Go home and never speak another word of Italian in your families." Adult people always speak their native language at home, and it is unreasonable to expect them to do anything else.

Hanging on the wall at the International Institute in a conspicuous place in the reception hall is this motto:

"THE GOOD CITIZEN SAYS

"I am a citizen of America and an heir to all her greatness and renown.

"The health and happiness of my body depend upon each muscle and nerve and drop of blood doing its work in its place. So the health and happiness of my country depend upon each citizen doing his work in his place.

"I will do nothing to desecrate the soil of America or pollute her air or degrade her children — my brothers and sisters.

"I will try to make her cities beautiful and her citizens healthy and happy so that she may be a desired home for myself now, and for her children in its days to come."

Possibly the following letter from one of the International Institute girls speaks better than anything else for its success:

"It was in the second week of February, the snow falling quietly, when first I got a view of this great city where a great part of my life I may live. It looked gloom to me; with regret I thought of my town where affections and remembrance I had left, but soon afterward I discovered that here too I could have friends and enjoyment. Among other things New York City has a great human institution where girls of every nationality meet. The aim of such institution is great and greater is the task entrusted to the people who cares of such. The general secretary, the supervisor of classes, and the teachers are more than friends but sisters and advisers to us, they seek our education and happiness. It may be blessed the founder of International Institute and those who have devoted their lives for its betterment.

"Very sincerely yours,

"May 16, 1916.   MARY GRACCHI."

CHAPTER X
Young Men's and Young Women's Hebrew Associations

1. YOUNG MEN'S HEBREW ASSOCIATION

YOUNG MEN'S HEBREW ASSOCIATION, 114 Fifth avenue, New York City, Samuel A. Goldsmith, general secretary. Letter, November 13, 1919:

"I presume that you are mainly interested in our organizations in the State of New York. Some of the best Americanization work that our institutions do, however, is in the New England states and in the city of Chicago. In a general way, all the work of the Young Men's Hebrew Associations and of the Educational Alliances that are affiliated with our national movement, is Americanization, that is, the work of a Y. M. H. A. is an emphasis on the value of the individual. It attempts, through its various activities, whether they be secular, educational or religious or social or physical or communal, to fit the individual into the general community, so that he would be of more value to himself and to that community. For this reason, and because we have been doing this individualizing work, we have consistently told communities that this type of work was one of the highest types of Americanization work.

"In the specific work that has hitherto been called Americanization, our constituent associations in many instances conduct classes in English to foreigners. Even in cities having a fairly well organized night school course in English to foreigners, it is found that certain people find it either inconvenient or impossible to go to the regular night school and come to our organizations where they can be made more comfortable and where they feel more at home.

"The same type of organizations carry on classes in civics and in a general educational way attempt to acquaint the foreigner with the opportunities in America for himself and also with his rights under the law and with the machinery of the government. Growing out of these classes in civics there are classes in Americanization which follow up the man until he secures his second papers, and then continue to follow him up, attempting to organize his interest in some civic or educational work of the institution so that he does not become lost after becoming a citizen.

"Other organizations carry on work in infant care and in hygiene and health, etc., for the adult women immigrants.

"In a general way, the associations hold public celebrations of all such holidays as the Fourth of July, Columbus Day, Armistice Day, etc., which have a patriotic tendency. On these days it is attempted to secure particularly the attendance of people who have been naturalized through the association at the celebration, and also whenever possible to have the celebration of such a mass nature that a goodly part of the Jewish community can attend.

"Through the year, the associations have a series of lectures which are open to the public and which have to do with community and civic matters, always attempting to drive home the value of citizenship in this country.

"Believing that one of the best ways to interest people in their government is to have them actually have a share in the finances of the government, we helped considerably in the Liberty Loan drives, War Savings Stamps drive, and now in the Treasury Certificate drive to interest our people in the government securities.

"Through reception now to returned service men, the associations are attempting to bring before the general community the value of the service man and to have him act as a stimulus toward further Americanization work.

"These scattered bits of work, running all the way from banquets for ex-service men to classes in English for foreigners, are in addition to a general educational, civic, physical, social program of the associations, the entire program, may I repeat, being what we term Americanization.

"We are launching again, particularly in view of the present crisis in civic affairs, a more strenuous effort toward enrolling larger numbers in all of these activities. We find, however, that it is of extreme value to term all of these activities educational, and that once the value of these educational activities have become manifest to the people who are concerned, that is the appropriate time to term them Americanization. In other words, we do not find it possible, and I believe most Americanization workers will agree, to foist upon anybody a set program. We do find it possible, however, to present naturalization or Americanization work in the form of an educational class or educational group, and in that way to secure the best results.

"I cannot give you our official opinion on the matter of *compulsory* education for adult foreigners because our Board of Managers has never actually voted on this matter. If you care for my personal views, I feel that this matter has to be handled in a very careful way. In the first place, it ought to be possible, in so far as the immigrants are concerned, provided they are so notified when they buy their tickets in Europe, to require that within five years after their entrance into the country, that is, within the period in which they might become citizens, they learn English and the rudiments of the governmental machinery, as well as the reasons for our governmental machinery. That is, I feel that it should be made a condition of entrance into the country, that within the first five years after such entrance, the immigrant learn elementary English and elementary civics.

"For the adult foreigners who are now in the country, an entirely different program, it appears to me, would have to be adopted. In the first place, these people generally, if they are illiterate in so far as English is concerned, are, among the Jews in any event, not illiterate in so far as Yiddish or some other native language be concerned. They find in this country their own press, their own national societies and their own relatives, books in the public libraries in their own language; in other words, many means for keeping up with current events both locally and internationally, without the need for actually learning English.

"If the point of attack will be through the *industries*, it might possibly be that neither employer nor employee will care to have the time taken during working hours for the purpose of teaching English and civics, particularly at this time when the cry is for greater production. The employer may object to his loss due to the time loss, and the employee, particularly since so many of these men are piece workers, will object to his working time loss.

"If the point of attack will be in the non-working hours of the foreigner, then I feel that a compulsory educational scheme will meet with a mere lip loyalty, and will by no means stimulate the sincere loyalty to our institutions which undoubtedly your Committee ultimately has in mind. It has been our experience with working people that they are generally fatigued at the end of the day's work, and that only the highest type among them will be sincerely interested in even specific educational activities that will tend to better their own economic status.

"It appears to me that the best way for the state actually to help would be to help the present existing agencies, public and private, that are attempting to cope with the problem more materially. The state ought to be willing to establish Americanization institutes for teachers through which it will train teachers of Americanization. Then these trained teachers ought to be put at the disposal of the public schools and of the private agencies such as the Y. M. C. A., the K. of C., and the Y. M. H. A., which are attempting to do educational work with the foreigner.

"Further, the state ought to, in the case of cities, generously meet a large part of the expenses other than the expenses for teachers, the expenses for textbooks, materials, any trips that the groups might take, etc. The state further ought to extend this to the private agencies.

"In addition, the state might, through arrangement with the requisite authorities, have the court officers in charge of naturalization hold court in the naturalization classes whereaver they may be held, either in the public or private institutions, and in that way eliminate one of the real difficulties in the entire work, namely, the necessity for the prospective citizens going to court, losing working time, and being under the strain of court appearance.

"The private and public agencies, the community councils, or whatever other organization the state might designate, can really, through the creation of community sentiment, bring to bear such a compelling force on the people that your Committee wishes to reach, that it will actually reach a large number and educate them in things American. Furthermore, through the other attractions that the private and public institutions can offer in the way of recreation, it is possible for them to have people come to them willingly for purposes of education.

"These are, I wish to repeat, my own private views in the matter of compusory education of adult foreigners, and are not to be taken as the views of our organization officially.

"I need not say that we shall be very happy in any case to help your Committee and to help the state once it adopts any definite program to further Americanization work. If you are desirous of having a definite list of our institutions, or if you are desirous of more definite information than this more or less cursory statement gives, I shall be only too happy to put it at your disposal."

CONSTITUENT ORGANIZATIONS COUNCIL OF YOUNG MEN'S HEBREW AND KINDRED ASSOCIATIONS

Alabama

Birmingham
    Y. M. H. A., 1701 Sixth avenue, North.
    Y. W. H. A., 1901 Sixth avenue, North.

Arkansas

Little Rock
    Y. M. H. A., 8th and Main streets.

California

Los Angeles
    Y. W. H. A.
San Francisco
    Y. M. H. A., 121 Haight street.
    Y. W. H. A., 1400 Golden Gate avenue.

North Carolina

Asheville
    Y. M. H. A., 75½ Broadway.
Raleigh
    Y. M. H. A.
Wilmington
    Y. M. H. A., North Front street.

Connecticut

Ansonia
    Young People's Hebrew Association, Main street.
Bridgeport
    Y. M. and Y. W. H. A., 181 State street.

Danbury
    Y. M. H. A., 251 Main street.
Hartford
    Y. M. H. A., 904 Main street.
    Y. W. H. A., 9 Pleasant street.
New Haven
    Y. M. H. A., 200 Orange street.
    Y. W. H. A., care Hebrew Institute, Crown and High streets,
        New London.
    Y. M. and Y. W. H. A., 38 Main street.
Norwich
    Y. M. H. A., Huntington Block, Main street.
    Y. W. H. A., Bill Block, Shetucket T.
South Norwalk
    Unity League, 127 Washington street.
Stamford
    Y. M. H. A., care Hebrew Institute, Greyrock place.
    Y. W. H. A., care Hebrew Institute, Greyrock place.
Waterbury
    Y. M. H. A., 24 Kingsbury street.
    Y. W. H. A., 24 Kingsbury street.

Delaware

Wilmington
    Y. M. H. A., 3d and King streets.
    Y. W. H. A., 3d and King streets.

Washington, D. C.

    Y. M. H. A., 11th street and Pennsylvania avenue, N. W.
    Y. W. H. A., 11th street and New York avenue, N. W.

Florida

Jacksonville
    Y. M. H. A., Duval and Jefferson streets.
    Y. W. H. A., Duval and Jefferson streets.
Key West
    Y. M. H. A.

Georgia

Atlanta
    Y. W. H. A., 90 Capitol avenue.
    Jewish Educational Alliance, 90 Capital avenue.

Illinois

Aurora
   Y. M. H. A., 53 S. Broadway.
   Y. W. H. A., 53 S. Broadway.
Chicago
   Hebrew Institute, 1258 W. Taylor street.
   Y. M. H. A., care Hebrew Institute, 1258 W. Taylor street.

Indiana

Evansville
   Y. M. H. A.
Indianapolis
   Jewish Young Men's Association, Communal Building, 17 W. Morris street.
Terre Haute
   Social Center.

Iowa

Des Moines
   Jewish Settlement House, 720 E. 5th street.

Kentucky

Louisville
   Y. M. H. A., 2d and Jacob streets.

Louisiana

New Orleans
   Y. M. H. A., 1205 St. Charles avenue.
   Y. W. H. A., 1205 St. Charles avenue.
Shreveport
   Y. M. H. A., 314–15 Levy Bldg.

Maine

Lewiston
   Y. M. H. A., 163 Lisbon street.
   Y. W. H. A.
Portland
   Y. M. H. A.
   Y. W. H. A.

Maryland

Baltimore
   Y. W. H. A., 1622 Madison avenue.

Massachusetts

Beachmont-Revere
  Y. M. H. A., Parker Hall, Beachmont, Mass.
Boston
  Y. M. H. A., Seaver street and Humboldt avenue, Roxbury, Mass.
  Y. W. H. A., Seaver street and Humboldt avenue, Roxbury, Mass.
East Boston
  Y. M. H. A., 163 Meridian street.
  Y. W. H. A., 230 Meridian street.
South End Boston
  Y. W. H. A., 484 E. 4th street.
West End Boston
  Y. M. H. A., 47 Mt. Vernon street.
  Y. W. H. A., care Blackstone School Center, Blossom street.
Brockton
  Y. M. H. A., 47 Centre street.
  Y. W. H. A., 47 Centre street.
Cambridge
  Y. M. H. A., 178 Elm street.
  Y. W. H. A., 178 Elm street.
Chelsea
  Y. M. H. A., 23 Crescent avenue.
  Y. W. H. A., 23 Crescent avenue.
Dorchester
  Y. M. H. A., 996 Blue Hill avenue.
  Y. W. H. A., care Harvard Improvement Association, 179 Glenway street.
Everett
  Y. M. H. A., 15 Clinton street.
  Y. W. H. A., 11 Clinton street.
Fall River
  Y. M. H. A., 391 S. Main street.
  Y. W. H. A., 391 S. Main street.
Fitchburg
  Y. W. H. A., 75 Main street.
Framingham
  Y. M. H. A., 8 Union avenue.
  Y. W. H. A., 1 Waverly street.

Massachusetts — Continued

Haverhill
    Y. M. H. A., Shepherd street.
    Y. W. H. A., Shepherd street.
Holyoke
    Y. M. H. A., 347 High street.
    Y. W. H. A., 347 High street.
Lawrence
    Y. M. H. A., 234 Essex street.
    Y. W. H. A., 234 Essex street.
Lowell
    Y. M. H. A., 65 Howard street.
    Y. W. H. A., 63 Howard street.
Lynn
    Y. M. H. A., 10 City Hall square.
    Y. W. H. A., 10 City Hall square.
Malden
    Y. M. H. A., 105 Bryant street.
    Y. W. H. A., 105 Bryant street.
Milford
    Y. M. H. A., 49 Pine street.
    Y. W. H. A., 49 Pine street.
New Bedford
    Y. M. H. A., Purchase and High streets.
    Y. W. H. A., Purchase and High streets.
North Adams
    Y. M. H. A., Main street.
    Y. W. H. A., Main street.
Peabody
    Y. M. H. A., Main street, Foresters' Hall.
    Y. W. H. A.
Pittsfield
    Y. M. H. A., Melville Bldg.
Plymouth
    Y. M. H. A., S. Main street extension.
Quincy
    Y. M. H. A., Water street.
    Y. W. H. A., Hancock Chambers.
Salem
    Y. M. H. A., 209 Essex street.
    Y. W. H. A., 209 Essex street.

Massachusetts — Continued

Somerville
    Y. M. H. A., Citizens' Hall, Gilman square.
    Y. W. H. A., Citizens' Hall, Gilman square.
Springfield
    Y. M. H. A.
    Y. W. H. A.
Taunton
    Y. M. H. A., Star Theatre Bldg.
Waltham
    Y. W. H. A., Moody street.
Winthrop
    Y. W. H. A., care Temple Israel.
Worcester
    Y. M. H. A., 29 Providence street.
    Y. W. H. A., 29 Providence street.

Minnesota

Minneapolis
    Y. M. H. A., 8th and Freemont avenues.
    Y. W. H. A., 8th and Freemont avenues.
St. Paul
    Y. M. H. A., Royal Arcanum Halls, 4th and St. Peter streets.
    Y. W. H. A.

Missouri

Kansas City
    Y. M. H. A., 3123 Troost avenue.
    Y. W. H. A., 3123 Troost avenue.
St. Louis
    Y. M. H. A., 2645 Delmar boulevard.
    Y. W. H. A., 2645 Delmar boulevard.

Nebraska

Omaha
    Y. M. H. A., 335 Paxton Block.
    Y. W. H. A., Lyric Bldg., 19th and Farnum streets.

New Hampshire

Manchester
    Y. M. H. A., 31 Hanover street.
    Y. W. H. A., 31 Hanover street.

New Jersey

Asbury Park
    Y. M. H. A., 715 Mattison avenue.
    Y. W. H. A., 715 Mattison avenue.
Atlantic City
    Y. M. H. A., Humphrey Bldg.
    Y. W. H. A., Humphrey Bldg.
Bayonne
    Y. M. H. A., 499 Broadway.
    Y. W. H. A., 499 Broadway.
Camden
    Y. M. H. A., 572 Walnut street.
    Y. W. H. A., 572 Walnut street.
Elizabeth
    Y. M. and Y. W. H. A., 602 Livingston street.
Hackensack.
    Hebrew Institute.
Hoboken
    Y. M. H. A., 115 Park avenue, Hebrew Institute.
North Hudson
    Y. M. H. A., Hebrew Institute Bldg., 320 Franklin street, Union Hill, N. J.
    Young Ladies Hebrew Association, 322 Franklin street, Union Hill, N. J.
Jersey City
    Y. M. H. A., 438 Summit avenue.
    Y. W. H. A., 438 Summit avenue.
Long Branch
    Y. M. H. A., P. O. Box 354.
    Y. W. H. A., 148 Broadway.
Morris County
    Y. M. and Y. W. H. A., Dover, N. J.
Newark
    Y. M. H. A., High street and 13th avenue.
    Y. W. H. A., High street and 13th avenue.
New Brunswick
    Y. M. H. A., 62 New street.
    Y. W. H. A., 62 New street.
Orange
    Y. W. H. A., care Hebrew Institute, Park street.

New Jersey — Continued

Passaic
    Y. M. H. A., 167 Jefferson street.
    Y. W. H. A., 167 Jefferson street.

Paterson
    Y. M. H. A., 97 Broadway.
    Y. W. H. A., 196 Smith street.

Plainfield.
    Y. M. H. A., 433 W. Front street.
    Y. W. H. A., 433 W. Front street.

Somerville
    Y. M. H. A., 14 E. Main street.
    Y. W. H. A., 2 W. Main street.

Trenton
    Y. M. H. A., 18 S. Stockton street.
    Y. W. H. A., 18 S. Stockton street.

West New York
    Y. W. H. A., care Hebrew Institute, Palisade avenue and 10th street.

New York

Albany
    Y. M. H. A., 60 Franklin street.
    Y. W. H. A., 60 Franklin street.

Amsterdam
    Y. M. H. A., Lovenheim Bldg.

Bath Beach
    Y. M. H. A., Cropsey and 20th avenues, Brooklyn, N. Y.
    Y. W. H. A., Cropsey and 20th avenues, Brooklyn, N. Y.

Binghamton
    Y. W. H. A., care Community Home, Collier street.

Borough Park
    Y. M. H. A., 4920 14th avenue, Brooklyn, N. Y.
    Y. W. H. A., 4920 14th avenue, Brooklyn, N. Y.

Bronx
    Y. M. H. A., 1261 Franklin avenue.
    Young Women's Branch, Y. M. H. A., 169th street and Franklin avenue.

Brooklyn
    Y. M. H. A., 345 9th street.
    Y. W. H. A., 345 9th street.

New York — Continued

Brownsville
    Y. M. H. A., 63 Liberty avenue, Brooklyn, N. Y.
    Y. W. H. A., 63 Liberty avenue, Brooklyn, N. Y.
    Hebrew Ed. Society, Hopkinson and Sutter avenues, Brooklyn, N. Y.

Buffalo
    Community House, 406 Jefferson street.
    J. Y. M. A., 406 Jefferson street.

Elmira
    Y. M. H. A., Realty Bldg.
    Y. W. H. A., 418 E. Market street.

Far Rockaway
    Y. M. H. A.

Greenpoint
    Y. W. H. A., 1000 Lorimer street, Brooklyn, N. Y.

Mt. Vernon
    Y. M. H. A., 30 N. 10th avenue.
    Y. W. H. A., 30 N. 10th avenue.

New Rochelle
    Y. M. H. A., 171 Winyah avenue.

Port Chester
    Y. W. H. A.

Ridgewood
    Y. M. H. A., 172 Linden street, Brooklyn, N. Y.
    Y. W. H. A., 172 Linden street, Brooklyn, N. Y.

Rochester
    J. Y. M. A., 3 Franklin square.
    Ladies' Auxiliary, J. Y. M. A., 3 Franklin square.

Schnenectady
    Y. M. H. A., 252 State street.
    Y. W. H. A., 252 State street.

Syracuse
    Y. M. H. A., 222 Cedar street.
    Y. W. H. A., 222 Cedar street.
    Communal House, 224 Cedar street.

Tarrytown
    Y. M. H. A., 78 College avenue.
    Y. W. H. A., 78 College avenue.

Troy
    Y. M. H. A., 87 First street.
    Ladies' Auxiliary, Y. M. H. A., 87 First street.

Citizenship Class — Six Nationalities Meet for a Banquet and Entertainment in the Central Y. M. C. A., Buffalo — Enrollment 40

Class at R. E. Dietz Factory, Syracuse

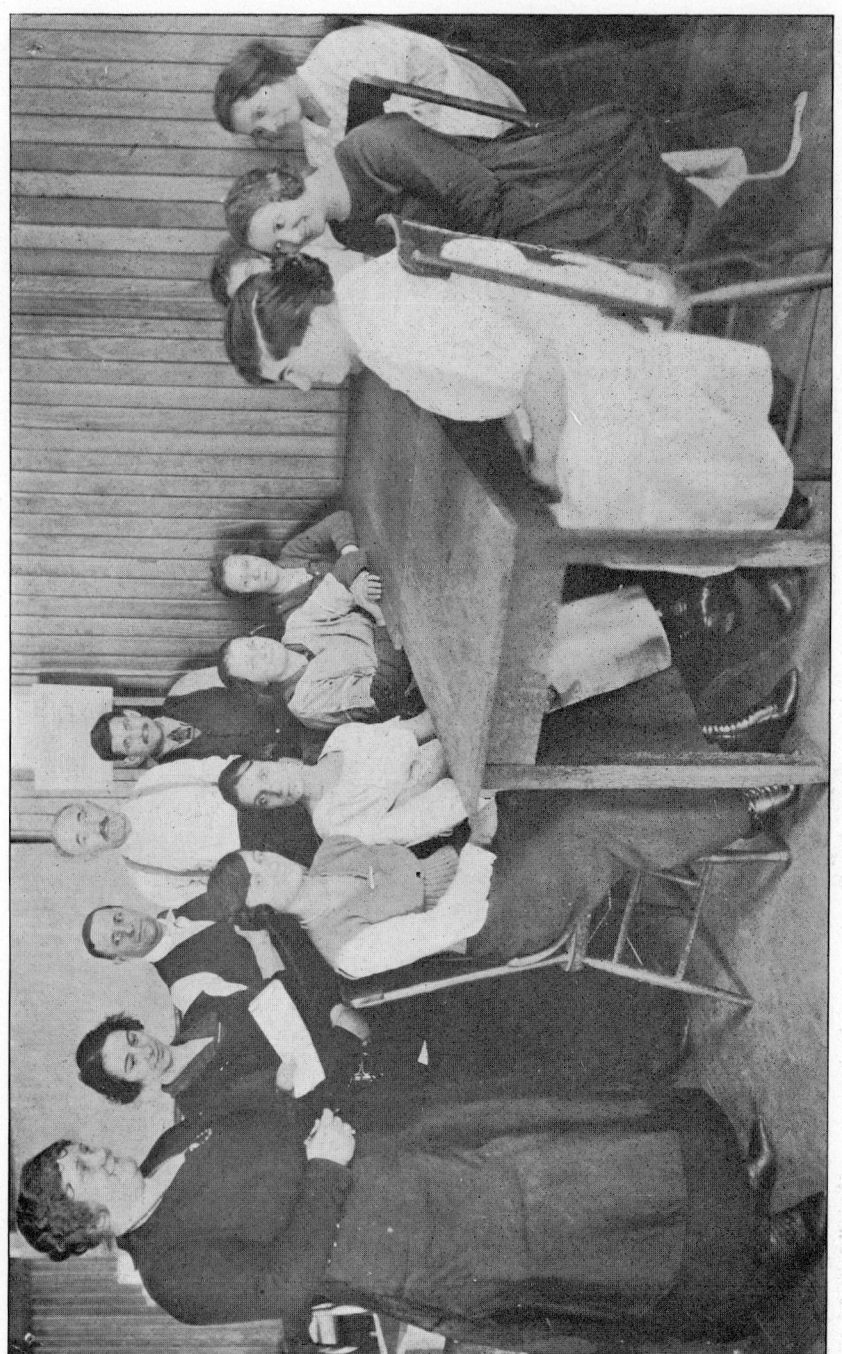

Class at Shapiro Factory, Syracuse

Class at Holcomb Steel Company, Syracuse

Young Men's and Women's Hebrew Association

New York — Continued

Utica
  Y. M. H. A., 36 Washington street
  Y. W. H. A., 124 Washington street.
White Plains
  Y. W. H. A.
  Hebrew Institute, S. Lexington and Fischer avenues
Williamsburg
  Y. M. H. A., 164 Clymer street, Brooklyn, N. Y.
  Y. W. H. A., 164 Clymer street, Brooklyn, N. Y.
Yonkers
  Y. M. H. A., Buena Vista avenue and Hudson street.
  Y. W. H. A., 37 Palisade avenue.
New York City
  Central Jewish Institute, 125 E. 85th street.
  Educational Alliance, 197 E. Broadway.
  Emanuel Brotherhood, 309 E. 6th street.
  Federation Settlement, 240 E. 105th street.
  Fellowship House, 32 W. 115th street.
  Harlem Y. M. H. A., 12 E. 119th street.
  Jewish Center, 131 W. 86th street.
  New Era Club, 274 E. Broadway
  Uptown Talmud Torah, 11th street and Lexington avenue.
  Y. M. H. A., 148 E. 92d street.
  Y. W. H. A., 31 West 110th street.
  Washington Heights Y. M. H. A., 975 St. Nicholas avenue.
  Women's Department, Y. M. H. A., 975 St. Nicholas avenue.
  West Side Y. M. H. A., 651 8th avenue.
  West Side Y. W. H. A., 651 8th avenue.
  West Side Community House, 128 W. 95th street.

Ohio

Cincinnati
  Y. W. H. A., care Wise Center, Avondale
  Jewish Settlement, 415 Clinton street.
Columbus
  Y. M. H. A., 555 E. Rich street.
  Y. W. H. A.
  Jewish Education Alliance, 555 E. Rich street.

Ohio — Continued

Dayton
> Young Men's De Hirsch Club
> Y. W. H. A.

Toledo
> Y. W. H. A., care Jewish Educational League, Southard and Linwood avenues

Youngstown
> Y. M. H. A., McKay Block, W. Federal street.
> Y. W. H. A., McKay Block, W. Federal street.

Pennsylvania

Bethlehem
> Y. M. H. A., 333 Wyandotte street, South Side.
> Ladies' Auxiliary, Y. M. H. A., 333 Wyandotte street South Side.

Carbondale
> Young Men's Hebrew Club.

Chester
> Y. M. H. A., 608 Edgmont street.
> Y. W. H. A., 610 Edgmont street.

Duquesne
> Y. M. H. A.

Easton
> Y. M. H. A., Ferry and Walnut streets.
> Ladies' Auxiliary, Y. M. H. A., Ferry and Walnut streets.

Erie
> J. Y. M. A., 14 W. 8th street.
> Y. W. H. A.

Harrisburg
> Ladies' Auxiliary, Y. M. H. A., 1326 N. 6th street.

Hazelton
> Y. M. H. A., N. Laurel street.

Lansford
> Y. M. H. A., W. Patterson street.
> Ladies' Auxiliary, Y. M. H. A., W. Patterson street.

Lebanon
> Y. M. H. A., 8th and Cumberland streets.

Mahanoy City
> Y. M. H. A.
> Ladies' Auxiliary, Y. M. H. A., 30 W. Centre street.

Pennsylvania — Continued

McKeesport
  Y. M. H. A.
New Castle
  Ladies' Auxiliary, Y. M. H. A., 19 E. Washington street.
Norristown
  Y. M. H. A., Elston Bldg.
Philadelphia
  Y. M. H. A., 1616 Master street.
  Hebrew Education Society, 1000 S. 10th street.
South Philadelphia
  Y. M. H. A. and Y. W. H. A., 310 Catherine street.
  Hebrew Association, 4th and Reed streets.
  Ladies' Auxiliary, Hebrew Association, 4th and Reed streets
Phoenixville
  Y. M. H. A., Main and Church streets.
Pittsburgh
  Y. M. H. A., 1940 Fifth avenue.
  Y. W. H. A., 1940 Fifth avenue.
  Irene Kaufman Settlement, 1835 Central avenue.
Pottstown
  Y. M. H. A., 451 High street.
  Ladies' Auxiliary, Y. M. H. A., 451 High street.
Reading
  Y. M. H. A., 624 Penn street.
  Ladies' Auxiliary, Y. M. H. A., 624 Penn street.
Scranton
  Y. M. H. A., 440 Wyoming avenue.
  Ladies' Auxiliary, Y. M. H. A., 440 Wyoming avenue.
Sharon
  Y. M. H. A., 306½ E. State street.
Shenandoah
  Y. M. H. A., Citizens Bank Bldg.
  Ladies' Auxiliary, Y. M. H. A.
Washington
  Y. M. H. A., Real Estate Bldg.
Wilkes-Barre
  Y. M. H. A., S. Washington street.
  Ladies' Auxiliary, Y. M. H. A., S. Washington street.
Williamsport
  Y. M. H. A., 51 W. 3d street.
  Ladies' Auxiliary, Y. M. H. A., 51 W. 3d street.

Rhode Island

Bristol
    Y. M. H. A., Richmond street.
    Y. W. H. A., Richmond street.
Newport
    Y. M. H. A., 235 Thames street.
    Y. W. H. A., 160 Broadway.
Providence
    Y. M. H. A., 65 Benefit street.
    Y. W. H. A., 61 Benefit street.
Westerly
    Y. M. and Y. W. H. A.
Woonsocket
    Y. M. H. A., 6 S. Main street.
    Y. W. H. A., 5 S. Main street.

Tennessee

Chattanooga
    Y. M. H. A., 617 Cherry street.
Memphis
    Y. M. H. A., Madison and Dunlap streets.
    Y. W. H. A., Madison and Dunlap streets.
Nashville
    Y. M. H. A., 712 Union street.
    Y. W. H. A., 712 Union street.

Texas

Beaumont
    Y. M. H. A., Pine and Elizabeth streets.
Fort Worth
    Girls' Assembly Club.
    Y. M. H. A., care of Hebrew Institute.
    Hebrew Institute, 809 Taylor street.
Galveston
    Y. W. H. A., 2602 Avenue 1.
Houston
    Y. M. H. A., Travis and Preston streets.
Waco
    Y. W. H. A., 716 S. 11th street.

Vermont

Burlington
 Y. M. H. A., 260-4 N. Winooski avenue.
 Y. W. H. A., care Hebrew Free School.

Virginia

Hopewell
 Y. M. H. A., P. O. Box 207.
Norfolk
 Y. M. H. A., Church street.
 Y. W. H. A., Church and Freeman streets.
Petersburg
 Y. M. H. A.
Richmond
 Y. M. H. A., 412 N. 8th street.
 Ladies' Auxiliary, Y. M. H. A., 412 N. 8th street.

West Virginia

Charleston
 Y. M. H. A., Davidson Bldg.
 Y. W. H. A., 904 Elk street.
Wheeling
 Y. M. H. A., Court Theatre Bldg.

Washington

Seattle
 Y. M. H. A., 507 17th avenue.
 Y. W. H. A., 507 17th avenue.

Canada

Calgary
 Y. M. H. A., 409a 8th avenue, East.
Montreal
 Montefiore Club, 399 Guy street.
 Y. M. H. A., 283 Sherbrooke street, West.
 Y. W. H. A., 483 Urbain street, West.
 Girls' Welcoming Club, care of Baron de Hirsch Institute.
Sydney, N. S.
 Young Men's Hebrew Club.
Winnipeg, Manitoba
 Y. M. H. A., Allman Block.
 Montefiore Club, 592 Main street.
Windsor
 Young People's Hebrew Association.

Cuba

Havana

2. YOUNG WOMEN'S HEBREW ASSOCIATION

Young Women's Hebrew Association, 31 West 110th street, New York City, Mrs. Ray F. Schwartz, executive director. Letter, November 25, 1919:

"We are at present conducting classes in English for our foreign neighbors. There are five classes in all that meet both morning, afternoon and evening. Women ranging from twenty to sixty years take advantage of this opportunity afforded them. With our many other activities in the building, we work very intimately with these women, giving them not only English, but the spirit of our American institutions. Our relation is a very neighborly one — always ready to help these women in the daily problems of living that confront them. Our lectures and concerts are another means of keeping them in touch with the best.

"I should be very glad to co-operate in any way with your Committee and shall await your advice. We will be very glad to put our plant to use in any way that may best benefit this important service."

CHAPTER XI
Industries

1. NATIONAL ASSOCIATION OF CORPORATION SCHOOLS

In an interview with a representative of this Committee, Mr. F. C. Henderschott, managing director and treasurer of the National Association of Corporation Schools (also in charge of the educational work of the New York Edison Company) said, in substance, as follows:

"Great Britain is now organizing corporation schools, but it is the only other country that is doing anything similar.

"There is nothing in the charters of industrial corporations permitting them or demanding them to do educational work.

"Although the public schools are not adequate to meet the problem, it is not the fault of the public schools. Before they can be more adequate from the standpoint of the industries, the industries will have to be able to tell the public schools what they can do to help. It is a fine point for the corporations to try to tell the public schools what to do. The corporations will always have to do *training,* but the public schools should do the *educating.* It is only through training that you get efficiency. The corporation school movement has two functions: (1) Corrective or educational; (2) training.

"We hope to escape the first some time. Boys who leave school too soon are included in the corrective. We had twenty-eight in the New York Edison Company five years ago who could not take our post graduate work because their fundamental education was deficient. We gave them a test to determine this, and the results were almost unbelievable. This is a public service and the public demands a high grade of service; therefore, it is a necessity that we correct the fundamentals of such education. The company decided that we owed something to these twenty-eight. Now we employ grammar school graduates only. Too many employers discharge for inefficiency and that is why we have certain conditions today. You can't give an employee all he deserves in his pay envelope.

"The corporation school has come to stay. There is no philanthropy in the decision. It is good economics. This organization has existed for seven years. We have 142 large industrial companies representing sixty-eight major lines of industry. We probably have one-half of the total wealth invested in commercial pursuits in our membership. We are conducting work of Americanization in all the corporations that have the problem. We have a citizenship program with it. We co-operate with the public schools and the Y. M. C. A. There are no representatives of the clothing industry where there are many foreigners who do not speak English.

"All this education has no effect if the wage scale is wrong. I don't think that this educational work would have any effect on people afflicted with Bolshevism, but the chances of having Bolshevism would be decreased about 90 per cent. by having education in all corporations as a preventive measure. The educational work of the United States Steel Company will win them the strike.

"Training in itself will not solve the personnel problem. It must be related to all the other personnel problems. You have got to employ scientifically. The United States Steel Company would have lost their strike hands down if they had not run their educational program from the start.

"Americanization is much talked about and little practiced. The actual developments have been weak. Personnel executives have not been trained. Industry has a cancer and is trying to cure it with a porous plaster. We expect to establish a commercial university which will train personnel executives and be a laboratory for industrial problems.

Why Business Organizations Should Be Class "A" Members of the National Association of Corporation Schools

Nation-Wide Co-operation

The National Association of Corporation Schools represents the first successful attempt at nation-wide training of the workers of the United States on the part of the business interests. Its purpose is to increase the efficiency of the industries of the United States through industrial training and to supplement with training the educational efforts of the public schools.

Our Object

To bring into one cohesive organization all of the industrial institutions of the United States and through this organization prosecute vigorous activities to the end that the problems of waste, through unnecessary labor — turnover, waste through lack of proper training, waste through unnecessary sickness and accidents, may be minimized and, where possible, eradicated.

Non-Partisan Service

As an Association no endorsements are given. Over fifty different industries are represented in Class "A" membership and our members are located in all sections of the country. Such endorsements as are given to national movements come from the individual members and not from our Association. This leaves our organization free to prosecute its work without strife and without friction.

Service to Members

All Class "A" members upon joining the Association are forwarded, without additional expenses, a complete set of bound volumes of the Proceedings covering all of the annual conventions which have been held. Class "A" members also receive a bound volume of the Proceedings of the current year without additional expense. Class "A" members are furnished twenty subscriptions to the bulletin published monthly by the Association which will be forwarded to addresses furnished by each member company. This service is included in membership, and there is no extra charge. Reports are also issued through the managing director's office covering such matters as profit-sharing plans, stock ownership on the part of employees, sick and death benefit plans, service annuities and retirement pension systems, savings and loan associations, etc. A report has also been issued in which the educational activities of our member companies are codified.

Confidential and Special Reports

This service is available only to Class "A" members. Such subjects as Labor turnover, the Present Status of Business Correspondence, Industrial Relation Problems of the Reconstruction Period, Plans which Can Be Utilized in Bringing into Closer Unison Employer and the Employee are treated. A special descriptive circular is issued regarding these reports.

Class "B" members receive without additional expense a copy of the current bound volume of the Proceedings of the annual convention, also a subscription to the Association's monthly Bulletin. This class of membership is open only to employees of Class "A" members.

Class "C" or Associate Membership is open to any individual interested in our Association and its work. These members are entitled to a bound volume of the current Proceedings of the annual convention, a subscription to the Association's monthly bulletin, to receive all regular reports and to all other rights and privileges except to vote and hold office. This class of membership, however, is intended only for individuals.

Special Service

The office of the Managing Director may be consulted on any problem concerning the educational activities of our member companies. Chairman of the sub-committees also act in an advisory capacity in furnishing information regarding their particular subjects.

Special Bulletins

From time to time the Managing Director's Office, through the Association's monthly Bulletin, reports the results of special studies of problems such as the replacement of men by women in the industries, due to war conditions; whether or not a corporation store may be successfully conducted and such benefits as may be expected; the value of company hospitals and rest rooms; the value of recreation activities on behalf of employees and their families; the value of company restaurants and similar subjects.

Indirect Benefits

While the direct benefits from membership yield a return many times greater than the membership fee, indirect benefits are equally valuable. The industries of the United States must progress and prosper as a whole. When the farmers are selling their produce at a profit they are purchasing the products of manufacturers and the railroads are busy. Individual industrial institutions cannot attain permanent success apart from the prosperity of the industries as a whole.

Annual Conventions

At the annual conventions delegates from our Class "A" members, also Class "B" and "C" members meet and discuss the vital questions affecting the training of the workers. A complete stenographic report is made and Proceedings are issued which contain the reports of the Association's committees and the discussions thereon.

Advance Committee Reports

The subcommittees issue their reports about six weeks in advance of the annual convention, and printed copies of these reports are forwarded to all members. This gives ample opportunity to read and note points for discussion. At the annual conventions these points are brought out through the discussions which are included in the proceedings.

Committees of the Association

The committees of the Association are composed of representatives of leading industrial corporations who are specialists in their particular lines of work. These committees are studying and investigating the following phases of industrial training:

Organization and Administration.
Methods of Instruction.
Thrift Activities.
Public Education.
Health Education.
Labor Turnover.
Employment.
Marketing.
Employee Representation in Management.
Office Work Training.
Technical Training.
Executive Training.
Trade Apprenticeship.
Skilled and Semi-skilled Labor.
Personnel Relations in Industry.
Unskilled Labor and Americanization.

(For list of chairmen and outline of work of each committee, see the Association's monthly Bulletin.)

Field Representative

The Executive Committee has authorized the employment of a field representative whose major duties will be:

1. To organize Local Chapters.
2. To advise Class "A" members regarding their personnel relations problems.
3. To secure data for the use of the subcommittees and for special reports.
4. To secure additional Class "A" members. The services of the field representative will be available to all local chapters and to Class "A" members without charge.

Subcommittees of the Executive Committee

The subcommittees of the Executive Committee plan and study the work of the Association. There is a program committee, which keeps well in advance of the Association's activities, reports its investigations and findings to the Executive Committee which, when approved, are referred to the proper channels to be carried out. There is a committee which studies the Association's publications in order that they may be most helpful in character and economically produced. There is a committee on membership which is responsible for getting new members and which investigates the loss of members. There is a committee on co-operation with other organizations so that there may not be unnecessary duplication of work, but that the united effort of these various national organizations may be co-ordinated with the best interests of all and to the welfare of our country. There is a committeee on training educational directors. This committee has induced New York University to inaugurate a course, the object of which is to prepare capable directors and instructors for corporation schools. Similar courses will be inaugurated in universities throughout the country.

Local Chapters

Local Chapters of the Association are being established in all municipalities where there is sufficient membership to justify such effort. Through the Local Chapter our members come in contact with each other and with the educational institutions and with representative men of their communities. Local Chapters discuss all of the problems the National Organization is investigating and studying and supply information to the Association's committees.

What Our Association has Accomplished

During the six years since the National Association of Corporation Schools was organized, it has not only determined many industrial educational problems, such, for example, as its manual on " Office Work Training," but it has also investigated, and in part solved, the problems of trade apprenticeship methods, insuring health through educational processes, successful instruction methods for better co-operation with the public schools and similar problems. It has worked out and inaugurated a course which will insure carefully trained instructors and directors for corporation schools and has co-ordinated its efforts with those of other organizations carrying on similar activities. It has also contributed much information of value to the government and state boards of education and to local school boards and to all interested in the problems of educational training activity.

Why Membership Will Profit You

Our Association is making American working people more efficient. It conducts researches and answers inquiries; it compiles the results of these researches and investigations and issues reports to its members giving full information; its regular reports and monthly bulletin keep its members advised on other "employee relations," such as health and safety, employment and similar problems which are treated from an educational standpoint.

The industries of the United States must prosper as a whole and permanent prosperity cannot be assured except on the basis of efficiency of the worker.

A nation can be no stronger than the uttermost development of its original sources of wealth, and most wealth in the United States is created in the factory, on the farm, in the mines, in the economical administration of the shops and in the household.

Through membership in our Association correct and authoritative information is available to industrial institutions in inaugurating and carrying on educational and training activities, thus preventing duplication of effort and the making of mistakes.

Why Our Association Needs Your Financial Support and Co-operation

Because its entire program of work is carried on in behalf of the industries of our country; because through proper methods of training, labor turnover can be materially reduced and labor troubles avoided. There is no power that can equal effective organization and the results of efficiency of the individual through training. All an industrial organization can ever be or ever has been is due to the individuals who comprise such an organization. Rightly directed, training eliminates guesswork and haphazard methods and substitutes scientific team work. Many large industrial institutions have organized and instituted profit-sharing plans and other "personnel relations" systems which have materially added to their success; and information as to how these plans have worked is available to our members.

Our Association co-operates with the Government and with state and local educational institutions and through the Local Chapters our members come frequently into personal contact and exchange ideas and experiences.

We need your financial support and your co-operation. The activities of our Association will be enlarged as rapidly as there is financial means available to carry on the work.

Has Saved Members Many Years of Useless Experimenting

Under date of September 24th, Mr. Thomas E. Donnelley, president of the Lakeside Press of Chicago, one of the largest printing, binding and engraving institutions in the United States, forwarded the following unsolicited testimonial as to the value of membership in our Association:

> "The National Association of Corporation Schools has been a means of co-ordinating the educational work of the members of this organization, and through the reports and bulletins and its annual meetings has been able to give its members the benefits of its experience, so that each member could avoid the inevitable mistakes of pioneer work in organizing a new educational activity.
>
> "While vocational education has aroused much interest in this country, like most educational movements, it has suffered because it was in the hands of academic teachers. Through this Association all theorizing has been kept out of the work of corporation schools. The Association has collected and reported only actual experiences and I am sure that its individual members have been saved many years of useless experimenting.
>
> "Believe me,
>
> "Sincerely yours,
>
> "THOMAS E. DONNELLEY,
> *"President."*

In a public hearing before the Committee on January 16, 1920, Dr. Lee Galloway, head of the Department of Commerce and Industry and of the Department of Business Management, and director of the Training School for Teachers of Retail Salesmanship of New York University, also secretary of the National Association of Corporation Schools, described the purposes and work of the Association, in substance, as follows:

> "About seven years ago, it appeared that many industries were attempting the education of their employees along different lines by various methods. To co-ordinate their

work, to allow for the exchange of ideas, and to eliminate duplication of effort in the study of educational processes, the National Association of Corporation Schools was formed. The Association holds annual meetings and publishes an annual report as well as monthly bulletins of its work.

"In general the work in the various industries having membership in this Association is done on company time, although, of course, there are exceptions. Without having specific data on the subject, but being in close touch with the situation, I should say that these industries feel that it pays to donate the time.

"The employer should undertake educational work only as a good investment as improving the morale of his workers and increasing production. I think employers would be willing to donate an hour a day if the state would furnish teachers and possibly buildings. It would be difficult in many cases, especially in New York City, to find space for classrooms.

"The teacher problem is the greatest one we have, making it necessary to draw upon men and women from the ranks, volunteers, preachers, public school teachers, etc. Something must be done about the compensation for teachers — possibly the Legislature could take a hand in it. It should be made possible for a young man or woman to reach a maximum salary of $3,600 to $4,000 within a reasonable time.

"As to subjects to be taught, citizenship training could be combined with subjects relating to the industry involved. A well-organized industry is constituted much the same as the state, and parallels can be drawn giving governmental lessons from concrete illustrations with which the employees are familiar in the industry itself. This would necessitate a competent teacher.

"My own personal view is that if a foreigner will not of his own accord learn English he should be compelled to do so. Before attempting to reach a conclusion in the matter of compulsory English for foreigners, I should suggest a committee representative of such industries as would be involved to study the matter thoroughly.

"It is fundamental that the employee be made to realize that the education offered is to his advantage — that he can handle his job better because of it, and that it increases his financial worth."

2. REPORTS FROM REPRESENTATIVE INDUSTRIES

Following are statements from representative industries in New York State as to their educational efforts with the foreign-born:

C. H. Bowman, employment and welfare manager, Acheson Graphite Company, Niagara Falls, November 28, 1919:

"As to our factory classes, will state that they are still in the elementary grade where the English language, with reading and writing, is the principal subject taught.

"Our classes of last winter started in February and ended in May. They had about seventy-four students, about equally divided between Italian and Polish workmen. Our class this fall started off with about twenty-five members, but the scholars have not attended as well as last session. Our classes meet after working hours. We do not compel the men to attend school and we pay the scholars for one-half of the time they are at school. As for our views toward compulsory education for adult illiterate foreigners, we feel that aliens should be given a reasonable time to learn our language and by reasonable, we would think five years after they are in this country."

R. C. Allison, manager, The Aluminum Castings Company, Buffalo, November 25, 1919:

"We have not yet actually started English classes at this plant, although we have plans to do so and expect to have a class under way within a very few days. Everything is now prepared to go ahead, and we are simply waiting for the Department of Education to send us a teacher, as they have agreed to do.

"We shall attempt, at first, to teach a limited knowledge of English and, undoubtedly, the majority of the men taking the work will be Polish, with a few Italians, and possibly a few other scattered nationalities. Classes will meet after working hours and attendance will be entirely voluntary, although appearances indicate quite a number of our men are really interested and anxious to get under way.

"As we have not yet had any actual experience in this work, we are not prepared to express an opinion as to its value or to what extent it should be expanded."

F. M. Wiess, vice-president, Buffalo branch, The American Brass Company, Buffalo, November 14, 1919:

"We are not holding classes for our foreign-born men, although we are heartily in favor of such a scheme. We strongly favor compulsory education for adult illiterate foreigners, and we feel that some legislation, either national or state, should be formulated for this purpose. The experience of other factories in Buffalo and elsewhere have certainly proved the value of factory classes for foreigners and we cannot help but think that one of the best methods for combating seditious doctrines is by establishing schools or classes for Americanizing our foreigners."

W. B. Peirce, superintendent, Buffalo Bolt Company, Buffalo, November 24, 1919:

"We are, as you have been informed, running an Americanization class and have enrolled at the present time 86; of this the following is the table of nationalities:

"Polish	74
Hungarian	2
German	3
Russian	4
Italian	2
American	1
	86

"We are holding these classes during working hours and each student has two one-hour periods a week, for which they are paid their hourly rate.

"These classes are not compulsory, but seem to be very popular with the employees. We notice quite a marked improvement in the help that are taking these lessons.

"We secured the teacher for our classes from the local Board of Education and are paying her ourselves; the local board not contributing anything to the support of these classes.

"It is my personal belief that compulsory education should be the order of the day with all foreigners in our state and, if feasible, those refusing to learn or unable to learn should be deported after five years' attempt."

Lala B. Ralston, supervisor of women, the Carborundum Company, Niagara Falls, November 26, 1919:

"We are indeed glad to pass on to you any information we have in regard to Americanization scheme in our plant. Our plans and classes are new and young, so that we really are not able yet to know the results. However, this is the way we managed it thus far: The Italian and Polish men, particularly, are coming together in the English classes where they may learn to read and write English. This is brought about by the company giving them three-fourths of an hour on company time, and they give three-fourths of an hour of their own time three times a week. The School Board supplies the instructor and books.

"None of these classes are compulsory, but we find that they tend to create an interest in English and help the general Americanization plan. We also find that the men get an idea of what the classes stand for, and are then willing to, and some prefer to go to the evening schools, which are part of the general public school plans.

"Just now the Americanization Board of the city, which is made up principally of the representatives from the various plants, is laying great stress on citizenship work in general and is making an effort to reach the aliens, through these classes and induce them to take out their citizenship papers.

"We have endeavored to interest the women of our plant in English classes, but find that most of the women who need this are from homes that require every minute they have away from work, so that it has not been as much of a success among the women as we had hoped for. We have also had a sewing class for the past two months, which has brought more of the women to the plant together than did the English classes, and we are hoping through this means to Americanize our foreign women, at least to a slight degree.

"You ask about our ideas on 'compulsory education for the adult illiterate foreigner.' We are coming to believe more and more that education must be compulsory, at least we feel that in some way we are going to have to compel our foreign-born to speak our language before we can really make them feel they belong to America."

William H. Hill, vice-president and general manager, The Crosby Company, Buffalo, November 8, 1919:

"We regret to have to advise that we have as yet done nothing in the matter of attempting to teach our illiterate and foreign employees the English language, or anything else, although the subject has much interested us and we believe something in this line ought to be done by all employers of such men. We understand that our local Board of Education is prepared to furnish teachers for such classes, and the principal reason why we have not started anything of the kind is because of stress of other matters which have prevented us from taking up the subject in a definite way.

"You may put us down as in favor of such classes, although we are not quite certain as to some of the details of working out a satisfactory plan, and are inclined to think that it would be a mistake to compel the holding of these classes, either on the employee's time wholly or the employer's time wholly. Our judgment would be to have them held half on the employee's and half on the employer's time, and instead of compulsion, to try to develop a public opinion among the employees favorable to the idea."

John J. Dolphin, secretary, Jacob Dold Packing Company, Buffalo, November 20, 1919:

"You ask if we maintain factory classes for our foreign-born employees.

"We have a class conducted in our plant after working hours from 7:30 P. M. to 9 P. M., two nights each week, Tuesdays and Thursdays. The city furnishes the teachers and books. We have had as high as thirty-four students in the class during the past year. Most of them are middle aged — all are Polish. This year has not been quite so successful as we have not had as many pupils. Our investigation regarding this shortage of attendance leads us to the conclusion that it is caused from the fact that a nearby school in the Polish district of the city has opened a school for a fuller course than we are teaching, this course being very much like our primer course in the public school.

"During the period which we have mentioned last year and thus far this year a majority of eighty persons were enabled to take out their first papers and a considerable number obtained citizen papers. The course which was given in our school was along the line of Americanization which would enable the students to read and write English. This was the full extent of our course. The education was voluntary as to the members receiving benefit. There was no compulsion of any kind. We are still conducting this class.

"We have in our employ between three and four hundred foreigners, at one time representing twenty-one nationalities, and during the stress of our work while the war was being conducted we have to say that our employees were very loyal. We have not had any labor trouble in our plant for a number of years. We assume, and our experience would seem to bear out the assumption, that it is largely because of the treatment accorded to our employees. They are paid the regular wages or possibly a trifle more than they would obtain in similar positions in other establishments.

"We have an association, the Dold-Quality Mutual Protective Association, which requires the applicant for membership to have been in our employ for one year. The expense of this association to the member is fifty cents per month. The benefits of membership are as follows:

"Each member is insured for one year for $1,000, payable to whatever beneficiary he designates, the premium for which is partly paid by the dues of the association, amounting to about one-sixth of the premium, the balance is paid by the company. A sick benefit is granted to members, amounting to $5 a week for a given period, which period may be extended by the officers of the association should the case warrant such extension. We might illustrate by stating that one particular employee was attacked with tuberculosis and was sent to a sanitarium at which place he remained for about a year recovering his health and has been at work with us since that time for about four years.

"There is connected with the association a physician paid by the association who gives medical attention to the members the same as their family doctor would do. There is also connected with this establishment a first-aid room with a competent individual in constant attendance. We have a large building devoted entirely to welfare work which contains lockers for the employees, the time office on first floor. The second floor is devoted to a kitchen and restaurant. The third floor is for entertainment, rest room, foremen's meeting room, etc., together with shower baths, etc., connected with that particular floor. The fourth floor is devoted entirely to amusement, pool tables, bowling alley, and other amusements. These are for the free use of the employees. Other benefits for the employees are as follows:

"We have two councils, as they are called, senior and junior, taking in the heads of departments and their assistants. A bonus fund is established, based upon the profits of the year and distributed among all the employees upon percentages. We also have a foremen's council taking in the heads of departments in the plant. To these there is distributed what might be termed a premium fund, based upon the results of their efforts and varying in amount, to stimulate competition. The lowest amount paid to any employee is not less than a full week's wages, usually distributed at the end of the year.

"We also have in addition to the above an organization called the 50-50 Club, into which any employee may enter with the expense of twenty-five cents a month and for every member the company contributes another twenty-five cents. This fund is used solely for the purpose of entertainment of this 50-50 Club. The president of our company donated a space of land from his farm situated on the Niagara river upon which has been erected a large hall, together with kitchen, etc., which is for the use of the 50-50 Club whenever they desire to give an entertainment. There are regular officers elected by the association who attend to all such matters.

"During the period of the war our employees were most loyal. When the shortage of labor occurred which required manual labor, the office force, heads of departments and assistants all turned in with enthusiasm, contributing to a fund created by the extra service given for which the company paid, this fund to be distributed among the various organizations — Red Cross, Y. M. C. A., etc., doing war work, and thus helped us through a very difficult situation arising from the shortage of labor. About eighty of our employees had been taken away by enlistment, a large number having crossed to France. As soon as they returned they were given their place in the plant or office, as the case might be, and today they are all but one back with us, and he is lying in Flanders Field, the only Gold Star on our Service Flag.

"We are very proud of our institution and of our employees. We doubt if you could find a more loyal bunch in any establishment in the state. We have never had a strike since the organization of the association, and none of our members belong to any other union than their own connected with the plant. We feel that thus far our efforts have been a success. Our plan is not perfect because it is human. We are not fully satisfied and it is our purpose to continuously move along the lines of improvement. We have a happy family with us."

J. R. de La Torre Bueno, editor, "General Chemical Bulletin," General Chemical Company, New York City, November 24, 1919:

"As to what is being done by the 'General Chemical Bulletin' in regard to Americanization, the copies I am sending under separate cover will illustrate it.

"I may say in general that our policy is to publish an American magazine for Americans in the American language, namely, English. We consistently omit any mention of un-American activities on the principle that we do not purpose to give them free advertising. On the other hand, as you know, indirectly we endeavor to propagate the opposite principles.

"In a general way, the standard of the matter we publish is directed toward creating good citizenship. At all times we endeavor to exemplify the sterling American virtues that have made this country what it is — sobriety, honesty, enterprise, thorough-going Americanism.

"I feel there is a great responsibility on the editors of employee publications in that such publications, properly conducted, will always have a guiding influence on the ideals of their readers. I also feel that the printed word has been used, and is being used today, directly and indirectly, brazenly and subtly to undermine American ideals, and that therefore it is incumbent on every organization and on every individual that has control of a publication, to use it as a medium of spreading 100 per cent. Americanism antidote to radical anti-American propaganda. The above gives you an idea of the principles which govern the American policy of our publication.

"Regarding your query as to what is being done at our plants to educate foreign employees in English, American history, civics, etc.: during the continuance of the war we have had the usual rallies of one kind or another with prominent speakers. In a good many of our plants, the employees have a weekly noonday meeting at which inspirational addresses of one kind or another are made, for example, myself and another spoke at one of our plants recently on Americanization and American citizenship. In addition to this, in some of our isolated plants, schools are conducted under our auspices. At others we have co-operated with the local boards of education in giving lessons in English to foreigners. We have no fixed rule for this, it being largely governed by local conditions.

"Necessarily, great discretion is to be exercised in all these activities in order not to produce a contrary effect to what is wished for."

Carl Heye, vice-president and secretary, the Guardian Life Insurance Company, New York City, November 25, 1919:

"So far no efforts have been made through the columns of our agency paper, called the 'Service,' to educate and Americanize adult illiterate foreigners, for the simple reason that our representatives are practically all native or naturalized Americans or otherwise foreigners who come up to our high standard for agency representation.

"As regards our home office, we have but a few employees who are not citizens, and they are so small in number that it has not been deemed worth while to especially educate them along the lines stated in your letter, except as the same may be accomplished through the company's library and on special occasions as they present themselves from time to time.

"We may add that we shall be only too glad to co-operate with you in your laudable efforts through the columns of 'Service' and otherwise provided, if you will indicate to us in just what way such co-operation can best be effected."

L. E. Jamme, assistant advertising manager, Hilo Varnish Company, Brooklyn, November 24, 1919:

"By means of bulletins and articles in our house organ, the 'Hilo World,' we have endeavored from time to time to instill patriotic ideas and civic pride into the minds of all our employees.

"We are happy to say that, with few exceptions, our employees are citizens; the foreign-born element in our employ is negligible.

"When you have formulated your program of education we will be glad to co-operate with you in any manner you may suggest."

E. B. Barlett, works manager, Hooker Electro-Chemical Company, Niagara Falls, November 24, 1919:

"Although many of the plants in Niagara Falls have done a good deal in the maintenance of factory classes for foreign-born employees, we have not found it possible to do a great deal along this line. The foreign-speaking people employed by us are pretty well scattered through our plant. Many of them work shift work and it is, therefore, difficult to conduct classes during working hours.

"My personal view of the matter is that all foreign-speaking people should, as soon as possible, be educated to talk and write the English language. I believe, furthermore, that they should be educated in the fundamentals of the principles governing this country. Just how this should be accomplished is less certain, but I am in favor of a campaign appealing to local public interest throughout the state, rather than action through legislation."

J. C. Henlon, supervisor of labor, International Harvester Company, Inc., Auburn Twine Mill, Auburn, November 8, 1919:

"Our plant school is in the experimental state, having been in operation but one month. We are teaching elementary English only, reading and writing.

"We have at present forty-five students classified as to nationality as follows: American, 6 (soldiers, 4; derivative, 2); Polish, 18; Italian, 18; Ruthenian, 1; Ukranian, 1; Belgian, 1.

"Our classes are held from 5 to 6 o'clock, after working hours, and everything necessary, including teachers, is furnished by the company.

"It is entirely voluntary on the part of the employee whether or not they wish to attend the school.

"We expect a greater attendance as colder weather comes on and when work at home has been taken care of for the winter."

Luther B. Little, publication manager, Metropolitan Life Insurance Company, New York City, November 28, 1919:

"Our daily bulletin is for our home office staff, and it is the belief of the officers of this company that among the employees of the company there are none that need this particular propaganda.

"I might say that for some time it has been the policy of the company that American citizenship be one of the qualifications for employment by the company."

Bert E. Barnes, advertising and publicity manager, Morse Dry Dock and Repair Company, Brooklyn, November 28, 1919:

"I am mailing herewith several copies of our publication, the 'Morse Dry Dock Dial,' which has been used to a considerable extent to counteract the seditious influences which are at work among our employees. I respectfully call your attention to the following articles:

"November, 1919, issue:
"Second cover page, 'Straight Thinking.'
"Page three, 'We Defy the Bolsheviki.'
"Page eight, 'Swat the Agitator.'
"Page eight, 'Don't be a Bell-Cow.'

"October, 1919, issue:
"Second cover page, 'Statement by Mr. Morse.'
"Pages one and two, 'How Needless It All Is.'
"Page eight, 'Strikes Mean Losses.'

"September, 1919, issue:
"Page three, 'Articles Worth Reading.'
"Page four, 'How Soon Will the Cost of Living Go Down?'
"Page twelve, 'Become an American.'

"May, 1919, issue:
"Second cover page, 'Laws and Crime.'
"Page twelve, 'The "Boo" in Bolshevism.'
"Page twelve, 'Confidence.'
"Page thirteen, 'Who is Paying the Freight?'

"March, 1919, issue:
"Pages one and two, ——.
"Page thirteen, 'Roosevelt's Last Message.'
"Page thirteen, 'Roosevelt's Best Legacy.'
"Page fourteen, 'To the Man On the Line.'

"Our magazine is mailed direct to the homes of the employees, and it has been found an effective medium through which to influence our workers in the way of right thinking.

"We have a very small percentage of men in the plant who do not speak English. Because of that and also because of the heavy turnover characteristic of a ship repair yard no concentrated efforts have been made to teach English to our foreign-born employees.

"It is the writer's personal opinion that one of the most effective means to combat the seditious forces which are at work is the printed word, and I know of no more effective way of reaching the employee direct than through a publication which goes into his home and attracts his interest, because it is about 'him.' Our magazine is very keenly sought for and I know of cases in which men who have not been on our pay-roll but a few hours have made application for the book, which they had been told about or knew about. The keenest interest seems to be taken in the 'Dial' by the employees. There have been innumerable indications that it is a very good influence among the men.

"The following editorial from the November, 1919, issue of the 'Morse Dial' is selected as typical of the articles being published in their organ to counteract radical propaganda:

"SWAT THE AGITATOR

"Wise men have said that what has happened in chaotic Russia could not happen in America because we are too well educated. Too many people take these wise men at their word and we are now beginning to experience a state of unrest that is very alarming. It is about time for us to get away from this attitude of utter complacency while the fires of red terror are wending their way to our shores.

"We see men and women who consider themselves good Americans being led like lambs by foreigners who have wormed their way into our industrial and social life to breed discontent. They are swallowing the bait handed out by these outcasts of Europe. And what are the results? Strikes, disorder, riots and impending Bolshevism.

"It is time to call a halt to this situation which threatens our existence and happiness. The best and most effective way to do so is to hand the guy who attempts to talk radicalism to you a good swat on the jaw.

"This isn't the most lawful or orderly way of handling the matter, but the red flag-waver has no respect for our laws, so why consider him?"

L. C. Jones, vice-president, National Aniline and Chemical Company, New York City, November 8, 1919:

"We are not yet operating classes for our workmen. The matter was considered recently at our Buffalo plant, where we have probably 500 illiterate foreigners on our pay-roll. Instruction classes were organized in the city and were attended by several of our men in order that they might be prepared to give instruction in our plant if it became desirable. Our management there has always taken an individual, personal interest in our foreign-born employees, with the result that many of them have already been assisted in taking out their first papers, and in general progressed toward becoming naturalized and thoroughly Americanized. We have never felt that there has been any danger there of seditious activities.

"We would not like to go on record as recommending compulsory education for adult illiterate foreigners. People come to this country because it is a free country and they feel that their personal liberties will not be interfered with. We, therefore, believe it would be undesirable to introduce this or any other sort of interference with personal affairs, believing rather it is desirable to lead men into education than to try to compel them into such a course.

"We should be very glad to be kept in touch with any state-wide activities in this direction and to take advantage of any educational opportunities for our men."

The New York Edison Company, New York City, Year Book, 1919–20:

"EDUCATIONAL WORK

"The New York Edison Company, like many corporations of the present day, realizes the importance of educational courses in the efficient management of its business. It, therefore, maintains three schools.

"The Technical School consists of five courses in electrical engineering. The Commercial School embraces the subjects of salesmanship, central station organization, and the history and development of electricity. The Accounting School offers courses in the theory and practice of accounting.

"THE TECHNICAL COURSES

"The Association of Employees of the New York Edison Company has prepared and conducted educational courses for the past nine years. Each year during this period technical courses in electricity have been presented.

"*Instruction*

"From 1906 to 1909 evening lecture courses were provided, these lectures being illustrated by platform experiments. It was soon noticed that the experiments conducted in this manner were by far the most effective part of the work, surpassing in interest the theoretical part of the lecture.

"The interest displayed in these platform experiments suggested the desirability of preparing courses based almost entirely upon laboratory work. Accordingly, laboratory practice courses were instituted and conducted for the seasons 1910-11 and 1911-12, and consisted of three graded courses of laboratory experiments with no class room work except that provided by the instructors in the course of the experiments.

"It was found difficult, however, to hold classes to an even rate of progress by laboratory work alone, and accordingly the season of 1912-13 was started with provision for one class room period of each four laboratory periods. This plan has proved to be a distinct advance over the earlier method, since the interest of the students was well maintained by the preponderance of laboratory work, while the class room work provided the instructor-in-charge with opportunity to keep the students in each class up to grade, thereby greatly increasing the effectiveness of the work as a whole.

"The Educational Committee of the Employers' Association has given very careful consideration to the scope of this work and as a result somewhat special courses have been prepared to relate as directly as possible to the work of the company. Thus the courses prepared for the season of 1919-20 include the following:

"*Course I — Mechanics and Heat*

"A course in elementary mechanics, physical measurements and heat, practically equivalent to a high school physics course, and serving as an introduction to advanced courses on d. c. and a. c. machinery and apparatus.

"*Course II — Elementary Principles of Electricity*

"An elementary course of experiments illustrating the fundamental laws and principles of electricity and magnetism.

"*Course III — Direct Current Machines*

"A course of experiments, illustrating the principles and operating characteristics of direct-current machines and apparatus with special reference to their application to the central station system.

"*Course IV — Elements of Alternating Currents*

"An elementary course of experiments in which are studied the properties and laws of the single-phase and polyphase alternating-current circuits.

"*Course V — Alternating-Current Apparatus and Machines*

"An advanced course with experiments designed to illustrate the operation of such alternating-current apparatus and machinery as is in use on the Edison system.

"An outline of the several courses presented during the season of 1919–20 will be found on page 30.

"In addition to the formal class room work, the assistant instructor in charge of the laboratory classes, who is in intimate contact with the students, is expected to round out the discussion of the evening's experiment by running comment during the progress of the test and while assisting the students in the preparation of their reports.

"Attendance is entirely voluntary, but students are rated only when they attend an entire course and submit complete sets of reports. These reports are marked and criticized by the instructor, and the standing of the rated students is based upon these marks at the end of the term. In addition, prizes are offered to the students having the highest standing in various courses.

"The courses are scheduled for a season of twenty-five weeks, from October to April, and the students are assigned in such a way that they conduct one experiment in a course each week. Sessions are held on five evenings, and in addition, two afternoon classes are held each week for the benefit of night workers.

"The Commercial Courses

"The Commercial School of the New York Edison Company was organized in the fall of 1911 and held its first session in December of that year. As originally planned, the work was divided into courses so laid out as to cover two school terms of approximately eight months each. Employees were enrolled the first year on the basis of their previous educational advantages and experience in the department, attending school one hour and a half per day, one day in the week.

"The plan of conducting the school has not been altered materially since its inception, except during the 1918-19 school term or war period. Early in the work a preparatory course for employees whose fundamental education was insufficient for the more advanced courses was included in the school programs, and a number of special courses have been added from time to time for stenographers, telephone operators, junior inspectors and information clerks, together with lectures on personal hygiene, public speaking, psychology, office work instruction, telephone efficiency, etc. Otherwise the only changes have been in the direction of broadening the scope of the work in the subjects, the speakers and in the number of lectures and examinations in the different courses. To those completing the general courses with an average rating of 'C' (75 per cent.) or higher, a certificate is granted. Three hundred and fourteen certificates have been awarded. No certificates were awarded during the 1918-19 school term, when the courses were on an emergency basis.

"A summer course has been instituted for junior inspectors and agents of the lighting inspection and special service bureaus on the company's Service and Meter Rules and Regulations.

"The courtesies of enrollment in the various courses have been extended to and accepted by the allied electric companies and the Consolidated Gas Company of New York.

"The school plan for the 1919-20 term includes some minor modifications and improvements in the regular work. In all essential respects the plan is to carry on the courses given in previous years. No outside lecturers have been engaged this year.

"*Attendance*

"Attendance is compulsory for employees of the Contract and Inspection Department in the classes held during business hours. The classes are open to all employees of the company and to employees of electrical companies in the New York section of the National Electric Light Association under the same conditions as govern Edison employees.

"*Calendar*

"The 1919-20 school term begins Wednesday, September 17, 1919, and closes Friday, May 21, 1920.

"*Executive Staff*

"The executive staff of the school consists of a manager, an instructor-in-charge, a special instructor in English, an assistant to the manager, and a secretary.

"The school headquarters are at Irving place and 15th street. School sessions are held at the Edison Auditorium, 44 West 27th street, at the Auditorium, Irving place and 15th street and in district offices.

"*Instruction*

"Instruction in the general courses is given by the manager and the instructor-in-charge.

"Instruction in the special courses is given by the instructor-in-charge and the special instructor in English.

"*Ratings*

"Certificates bearing the company's seal and the signature of the general commercial manager are awarded to students who complete the general courses with a rating of 75 per cent. and over.

"General Courses

"The general courses for employees of the Contract and Inspection Department treat of the history and development of electricity; the history and development of Edison service in New York City; basic principles of individual efficiency; essentials of psychology; effective speaking and business English; basic principles of salesmanship and their relation to business building; company policy and organization; and electric appliance merchandising.

"Special Courses
"Preparatory Course

"Experience having demonstrated that a percentage of employees have not received sufficient training in the fundamentals of education to enable them to take the more advanced courses, a preparatory course for reviewing the subjects of grammar and composition, history, commercial geography and arithmetic is given.

"Course for Telephone Operators

"The importance of the telephone operator is being more fully recognized. The New York Edison Company receives an average of 20,000 calls a day from the public. Here is an opportunity to make friends and render a high degree of service. A special course has been prepared for the telephone operators of the Contract and Inspection Department similar in character to the civil service examination for employment in a municipal or government position with certain additional instruction in courtesy and public service requirements.

"Course for Stenographers

"The importance of the whole question of effective business English, as distinct from academic English being increasingly recognized, a special course is given for the stenographers and typists of the Contract and Inspection Department.

"This course treats of the following subjects: A brief consideration of business English; analysis of the art of effective business correspondence in relation to both content and mechanical matters; various types of letters. Instruction in public service requirements.

"The course is designed to increase the practical efficiency of stenographers and typists, as well as of those doing secretarial work.

"Course for Information Clerks

"Since the information clerks must be able to satisfactorily direct customers and supply necessary information regarding the company, it has seemed advisable to introduce a special course for the employees of the different information bureaus. This course aims to familiarize the employee with the work of each department of the company and each bureau of the Contract and Inspection Department. It offers definite instruction on all subjects concerning the business of the Contract and Inspection Department and the specializing bureaus to which an applicant for special information should be directed. Attention is given to the matter of dealing with customers courteously and patiently.

"Course for Junior Clerks and Office Boys

"This course is designed for junior clerks and office boys. The subjects treated are: The history of the development of the Central Station in New York City. The fundamental advantages of electricity and the factors that assist an individual to succeed.

"Course on Health Factors

"This course is for women employees only. The lectures relate to such matters as dress, care of the body and subjects which have a direct bearing upon the health and efficiency of women in industry.

"Course on Efficient Telephoning

"The general commercial manager requires that every employee in the Commerical Department form the habit of correctly and courteously using the telephone. The course is designed to instruct employees in this service and to impress upon them its great importance.

"Course for Junior Inspectors

"This course is given during the summer and consists of a thorough study of the company's service and meter rules and regulations, meter indexing and an inspection trip through the Meter Testing Department.

"Accountancy Courses

"The first course in the theory of accounts was presented under the auspices of the Association of Employees during the season of 1912-13. This course was designed to offer instruction in the theory of accounts, and in the practical methods employed in the company's Accounting Department; it was designed especially for the benefit of the accounting and clerical employees of the New York Edison Company.

"Instruction

"The course consisted of a series of nine lectures on the theory of accounts, presented by an instructor from the School of Commerce, Accounts and Finance of New York University. Three examinations were held during the lecture course, the examination papers being marked and rated by the University examiners. In addition, a supplementary course of ten lectures was presented, dealing with the practice of accounting and the work of departments closely related to the accounting department. These lectures were presented by officials of the New York Edison Company, and by the heads of related departments.

"The course was very well attended and great interest was shown by the clerical employees. The examination papers proved that the students had attended closely to the subject matter of the professional lectures. The lectures in the supplementary course proved to be particularly valuable, especially in acquainting these clerical employees with the work of other departments.

"During the season 1913-14 instruction in more elementary subjects was provided as it was thought that the work presented in the previous year was possibly too advanced for many of the employees. This work consisted of classroom instruction in bookkeeping, the course being substantially the same as the course in bookkeeping offered by the School of Commerce, Accounts and Finance of the New York University.

"As in the previous year, the course was well attended and the results of the work as indicated by the final examinations showed that many employees had profited by it.

"In the season of 1914–15, a second year course, principles of accounting, was introduced for those students who had completed the bookkeeping course. This course was designed to give a thorough education in the fundamental principles of accounting. It is based on the four types of organization, namely, sole partnership, co-partnership, the corporation and the holding company. The course was well attended and a large proportion of the students passed the examinations satisfactorily.

"An additional course, 'Accounting Problems,' was introduced in the season of 1916–17. This constitutes the third year's work in the Accounting School and completes the course. The course consists entirely of accounting problems, divided into two groups; one group for demonstration and the other for practice. The demonstration problems are used in the classroom; the students are required to work out independently and submit for criticism and review the practice problems.

"The first year course is open to all employees of the company. The second and third year courses are open only to those who have obtained satisfactory ratings in the previous year's work.

"It is believed that this three-year course is well suited to the needs of the clerical employees of the company. It is so proportioned that the junior employees may easily take the first year's work, and by the time they have completed the third year, they will have received a very thorough grounding in the fundamentals of accountancy.

"As these courses have been prepared in close co-operation with the facility of the School of Commerce, Accounts and Finance of New York University, it has been possible for students to obtain credit at the University for their work in some of the elementary courses so that if they desire they may continue advanced work at the University with credit for the work done in the New York Edison Company's School. This action on the part of the faculty of the School of Commerce, Accounts and Finance was, of course, particularly gratifying to the educational committee as an indication of the high standard accorded to this work by experienced educators."

Dr. H. R. Carveth, general manager, Niagara Electro-Chemical Company, Niagara Falls, November 24, 1919:

"We have started factory classes for our foreign-born employees.

"At present they are being taught to speak, to read and to write English. The teacher is supplied by the Board of Education for this city.

"The classes are so arranged that the men can go to them either immediately before going to work or on leaving work. There is nothing compulsory about the men's attendance but we try to persuade them to attend.

"We now have fourteen students who are regularly attending classes twice a week, all of whom are Poles. We believe that this number will be considerably increased in future years as the men who are taking the classes will no doubt help to advertise the work.

"We believe that more can be done by voluntary work, such as we are encouraging, than by compulsory education of adult illiterate foreigners. It is also our hope to be able to interest the women members of the families of our men in learning to speak English, as we believe that if this can be done it will go a long way to help solve this problem."

C. M. Graves, superintendent, National Carbon Company, Inc., Niagara Falls, December 8, 1919:

"We give you below information relative to Americanization classes at this plant.

"Subjects taught include English, civics, spelling, reading and writing. Teachers are furnished by the Board of Education, Niagara Falls, N. Y.

"We have sixteen Italians, three Poles and three Spaniards in attendance at the present time and the classes meet at 4:30 until 5:45 p. m. This is after working hours. This opportunity of attending classes is offered to all employees, so that those wishing to take it up may do so."

Robert F. Coleman, assistant general superintendent, the Pierce Arrow Motor Car Company, Buffalo, November 7, 1919:

"It is evident that you have been misinformed regarding the Americanization work done by this company. The nature of our work is such that it is impossible for us to employ men who cannot read and write. We, also, give Americans preference and at this time there are only twenty-three aliens employed by the company, these men principally being Canadians.

"We have something like 200 men who have not yet secured their second papers who are supplied with suitable books relating to the question of citizenship and are called into the office occasionally for personal instruction."

J. G. Acker, assistant general sales and advertising manager, Pyrene Manufacturing Company, New York City, November 24, 1919:

"We have published in our house organ, 'The Pyreneer,' articles, cartoons, posters, etc., on Liberty Bonds, Thrift Stamps and other material sent us from Washington.

"We will be glad to publish any material on the subject of Americanization if you contemplate getting this out in galley form."

James F. Foster, vice-president and treasurer, the Republic Metalware Company, Buffalo, November 25, 1919:

"We have to say that we do not maintain factory classes for our foreign-born employees. We tried this a year or two ago and had to give it up for certain external reasons. We have not felt sanguine of success in this direction since."

F. J. DeBisschop, president and general manager, Rome Hollow Wire and Tube Company, Rome, November 12, 1919:

"We wish to state that we have no classes in our factory. Some of this work, however, was carried on through the local Y. M. C. A. and we have, of course, supported this."

E. L. Spriggs, general superintendent, Rome Manufacturing Company, Rome, November 11, 1919:

"In regard to program of Americanization and education of illiterate foreigners, would say that all work of this kind in Rome has been carried on by the Industrial Department of the Y. M. C. A.

"During the past winter, they taught English, American history, arithmetic and naturalization with the following numbers of people in attendance:

"English	120
"Naturalization	90
"American history	36
"Arithmetic	4

"Teachers were furnished by the Industrial Department of the Y. M. C. A. and this department is supported almost entirely by the manufacturing industries.

"Classes were held in the evening and weren't compulsory.

"It is our opinion that this is not satisfactory. We believe that the education of foreigners should be handled by the school system and, in order to accomplish anything, should be made compulsory.

"Practically all those who entered these classes were Italians and represented only a very small percentage of of those in need of this education."

Dudley D. Sicher, president, D. E. Sicher & Company, New York City, October 30, 1919:

"I am delighted to hear that the Joint Legislative Committee has in mind the formulation of recommendations to the Legislature for an increased educational program for adult foreigners and that it is interested, in this connection, with the elimination of illiteracy and the relation of industry to this type of work.

"For the past four or five years my concern, here, has been doing very active pioneer work in the elimination of illiteracy among our wage-earning personnel. We employ women, about 500 as a rule, and have had, at various times, an average of about 10 per cent. of those who couldn't read, write or speak English. These were, to a considerable extent, Russians and Italians. We had very good results and, in co-operation with the local Department of Education, conducted classes from nine to twelve o'clock every morning of the week — except Saturday, on company time, paying the worker for the time she spent in the classroom. During the course of four years we changed the mental status of a considerable number of persons and we believe, also, that we changed their communal reactions.

"The little booklet entitled, 'Where Garments and Americans Are Made' will, we think, give you more than we would dare undertake in a letter. It was not printed, as you can readily see, as an advertisement, but was prepared to take care of the hundreds, yes thousands of requests for information on the subject.

"As the originator of the thought I felt gratified to learn that a very considerable number of employers have emulated our example in establishing factory classes on company time.

"Here in our own plant we have temporarily suspended the classes for we found that we have only four illiterate girls this season and the Department of Education would only supply a teacher for a minimum class of twenty.

"It is our opinion that employers have a definite obligation to the community which can be discharged in no better way than in conducting classes of this kind. The cost is not very great and the possible benefits are incalculable — to say nothing of the opportunity for service which employers are, I think, recognizing, in the light of good judgment, from day to day."

Note.—A chart compiled for D. E. Sicher & Company by a statistical expert shows that the average hourly wage of workers attending school increased from 19.5 cents to 22.2 cents in sixteen weeks.

WHERE GARMENTS AND AMERICANS ARE MADE
Fore-pages — Summary of the Idea

"Invective and abuse will not drive the hyphen out of our national life. That can only be done through a process of education, when it can be demonstrated that a man with two countries belongs to none, and that here we have the highest ideals and the finest country in the world."— Lewis H. Pounds, President of Brooklyn Borough, New York City, in address to Public School teachers, September 14, 1916.

It is my purpose in this little book to tell the story of an interesting experiment, absolutely unique in the annals of education — the transforming of illiterate foreigners into literate, intelligent, alert, self-respecting, efficient Americans. Long before the demagogic politician learned the magic that lay hidden in the catch-cry, "Hyphenated American," and began to use it as a sort of campaign fanfare, Mr. Dudley D. Sicher, of D. E. Sicher & Company, No. 49 West 21st street, Manhattan borough, New York City, the largest manufacturers of muslin underwear in the world, had undertaken, with the co-operation of the New York City Board of Education, the task of turning illiterate foreigners into literate Americans by teaching them in the factory while engaged at their work.

"We aim," Mr. Sicher explains, "to hasten assimilation necessary to national unity; to promote industrial betterment by reducing the friction caused by failure to comprehend directions, and to decrease the waste and loss that always mark the presence of the illiterate worker."

In its beginning the factory school was humble, just as the beginnings of the educational ideas of Pestalozzi, Froebel and Montessori were humble, but the day will come when this little school will be the Mecca, the holy place of a movement that is certain to spread as employers of labor catch glimpses of the dawn of the better day. It is backed by the faith and money of Mr. Sicher, the solid support of the Board of Education, and the active and enthusiastic co-operation of Mr. P. P. Claxton, United States Commissioner of Education; Professor John H. Finley and his associates, Mr. Arthur D. Dean and Mrs. Anne Hedges Talbot, of the New York State Board of Education; Mr. William H. Maxwell, Superintendent of Schools, New York City; Miss Lizzie E. Rector, Dr. Julius Sachs, Mary Antin, author of "The Promised Land;" Professor Jeremiah W. Jenks, of New York University School of Commerce, and hosts of others.

The experiment, now in its third year, has demonstrated that in thirty-five weeks the illiterate girl, foreign-born and trained, can be transformed into a literate American woman with a good mental equipment and social knowledge essential for the battle of life. This school, in its conception and the potentialities that lay back of it, is an original, epochal idea worked out into definite, concrete form, and is in no sense a continuation school or part-time factory school, as some educators and writers with imperfect knowledge of its methods have mistakenly believed. It is a school where girls are taught in actual working time by a teacher from the New York public schools, and is perhaps the only factory school in the world where pupils are paid while learning.

With three-quarters of an hour's training daily while the work of the factory goes on uninterruptedly, each pupil receives practical instruction in the speaking and writing of the English language, the composing of personal and business letters, the fundamentals of arithmetic, history and civic government, good citizenship, local ordinances, hygiene and sanitation, the industrial evolution of the product they handle from the cotton fields to the machine they operate, and the mysteries of communication so puzzling to the foreigner — the use of the telephone and city directory, the sending of telegrams and letters, and the finding of one's way in the city streets. No frills, no text-books, all eminently practical knowledge so presented that it is never forgotten.

And all throughout the working day in the factory and in the school a social service expert is ever present to mother the girls, counsel them, and when injured to give them first aid in the little factory hospital. The girl's health and social side Mr. Sicher considers quite as important as her mental training.

Mention has been made of some of the noted educators and social workers that have been watching the progress made by this school since its inception three years ago. It has recently attracted the attention of the National Americanization Committee, with offices at No. 18 West 34th street, New York City, and this committee is now actively encouraging the work of the school. The representative, solid character of this committee may be seen by a glance at the names appended:

Officers and Executive Committee: Frank Trumbull, chairman; Percy R. Pyne, 2d, first vice-chairman; Mrs. Edward T. Stotesbury, second vice-chairman; William Sproule, third vice-chairman; Wm. Fellowes Morgan, treasurer; Mrs. Vincent Astor, Frances A. Kellor, Peter Roberts, Mrs. Cornelius Vanderbilt, Felix M. Warburg.

Leading members of the committee are: Mary Antin, Robert Bacon, Edward Osgood Brown, Nicholas Murray Butler, P. P. Claxton, Richard T. Crane, Henry P. Davison, Coleman du Pont, Thomas A. Edison, Howard Elliott, John H. Fahey, Maurice Fels, John H. Finley, David R. Francis, Elbert H. Gary, James (Cardinal) Gibbons, Clarence N. Goodwin, Benjamin F. Harris, Myron T. Herrick, John Grier Hibben, Henry L. Higginson, Frederic C. Howe, Charles H. Ingersoll, Dr. Abraham Jacobi, Chancellor L. Jenks, Judge Manuel Levine, Clarence H. Mackay,

C. H. Markham, Alfred E. Marling, Charles E. Mason, Wyndham Meredith, George von L. Meyer, John Mitchell, A. J. Montague, John H. Moore, Joseph C. Pelletier, Samuel Rea, Julius Rosenwald, M. J. Sanders, Jacob H. Schiff, Bishop Thomas Shahan, Melville E. Stone, Mrs. William C. Story, William H. Truesdale, Rodman Wanamaker, S. Davies Warfield, Charles B. Warren, Benjamin Ide Wheeler, General Leonard Wood.

As I write I learn that Mr. Sicher is already formulating plans to call a national congress of manufacturers, educators, publicists and statesmen to consider this whole question of the illiterate worker and the Americanization of the foreigner through the co-operation of the factories, schools and government. While waiting for the eugenic millenium he believes in improving the raw, human material he finds at hand. That his faith is justified will be shown in the chapters that follow.

The Immigrant — A Potential American

"In a letter written by State Commissioner of Education John H. Finley to President J. Warrant Castleman of the Rochester Board of Education, Dr. Finley said that but two important movements for the education of the foreigner had attracted his attention in the state during the past year, one being the work done by Mr. Charles E. Finch in the Rochester schools and the other that of the D. E. Sicher Co., of New York City."— Rochester (N. Y.) "Evening Times."

"There is a menace to any country in the presence of a large number of illiterates. Last year in New York City the Board of Education conducted a regular class in a private factory (D. E. Sicher Co.). This is cited merely as an instance of the flexibility possible to public school systems. Only such effort on the part of the department of education supported by a governmental policy can work out for the immigrant an educational system which will make him socially and industrially competent in American Life.—Albany (N. Y.) "Journal," December 1, 1914."

The European peasant, oppressed by his government and exploited by great landowners and privileged classes, looks longingly, yearningly, toward the land of the setting sun. When his ship enters the Narrows of New York Bay, the first sight that bursts upon his vision is the Statue of Liberty, and he lands at Ellis Island, not a ward of the nation, but a potential American. Mere naturalization papers will not effect his metamorphosis into a real American. This can only be effected through education, and America's leading educators are unanimous in the opinion that the Sicher system is the best yet devised.

Superficial folk with narrow-gauge brains speak of the menace of immigration as though it were a new agency to work evil upon the native-born, but it is as old as the eternal hills and is characteristic of all climes and all ages. Immigration is no longer haphazard as in earlier days of the republic, but is now restricted and selective. When the native American objects to immigrants on the ground that they huddle together amid squalid, unsanitary surroundings in crowded sections of the cities, lowering standards of living as well as of wages, he should remember that his own kindred own these rookeries of the slums and are the employers of the ignorant foreigners. There is indeed need of the "uplift" among the unscrupulous rich.

This tendency of the native-born to despise the foreigner worked hardship upon the Irish in the early days, just as today it works hardship upon the Italian, the Jew and the Slav. The native American is too often forgetful of the fact that he, too, is the son of an immigrant. In the days before the ocean steamships and the transcontinental railroads, when man battled with nature for the conquest of a continent and romance was in the land, it was the immigrant who bore the brunt of the fighting with wild beast and fiercer savage.

Our first immigrants came almost wholly from the British Islands, especially from Ireland, furnishing America with those super-laborers, the red-blooded, steel-muscled navvies (now displaced by Italians) who built the Hoosac Tunnel and the great railroads that are spread net-like throughout the continent.

After 1848 the collapse of the revolutionary movement in Europe started the vast German immigration that has stopped only with the present European War.

Toward the close of the nineteenth century northern European immigration declined, and southern Europe, notably Italy, began sending her sons and daughters to these shores. So, too, the Slavic stock of Austria-Hungary, and the oppressed Jews of Russia and Poland, began to flow into the great Melting Pot whose ladle is Ellis Island.

The reasons that induce these people to flock thither are the desire to better economic conditions that make it possible to maintain decent living standards in the homelands; to escape compulsory military duty, governmental despotism, ever increasing tax burdens, religious and political persecutions. It was this last reason that sent the Pilgrims across the Atlantic in the Mayflower and that brought to America thousands of Huguenots after the Revocation of the Edict of Nantes.

Native Americans must reconcile themselves to the fact that immigration is a permanent, fixed reality. The world has no longer place for the hermit nation with an ever-ingrowing civilization such as characterized old China. Ellis Island is as fixed an institution as the government at Washington. The native can find consolation, however, in the knowledge that since 1882 the United States has been growing every year more strict, so that now diseased persons, criminals, defectives and paupers are not knowingly poured into the Melting Pot. Contract labor laws passed since 1885 make it impossible for unscrupulous employers to bring over hordes of immigrants whose cheap labor supplants native American workmen, and the doors have been closed completely to the yellow races.

It is with the later immigration sent here by non-English-speaking races, alien not only in speech but in manner of life from ourselves, that the Sicher System of Factory Education deals specifically, for this immigration is, to an alarming extent, illiterate and ignorant of decent, sanitary living conditions.

Dr. and Mrs. Winthrop Talbot have rendered services of great value in connection with the factory school, which Mr. Sicher gratefully acknowledges. Dr. Talbot is America's leading authority on the subject of illiteracy and is also one of the editors of the New York "Medical Journal." Mrs. Talbot is a Ph.D. (Columbia University) and a recognized authority throughout the United States on the subject of vocational training for girls.

Dr. Talbot asserts that, since 1908, the United States has received 4,406,413 illiterate immigrants from eastern and southern Europe, all ignorant of English, and more than 1,300,000 unable to read and write in any language. In New York, New Jersey and Pennsylvania in 1910 there were 873,812 illiterates, of whom 767,587 were either aliens or the children of aliens.

How this illiteracy reacts unfavorably upon labor Dr. Talbot points out in the following observations born of long thinking and the study of statistics: "There is a close connection between illiteracy and the sweat shop. Not only in cities, but also in country towns and villages, it is possible for an ambitious and conscienceless man with a little capital to hire space in a tenement or loft building and exploit the labor of ignorant immigrants, thus demoralizing the trade and working great harm to the people whose immediate need for wages he has met. He thus competes unfairly with the established firms whose success depends on good management, and not on the exploitation of cheap labor. As the enlightened employer pays attention more and more closely to the study of waste and cost, the importance of the human mechanics of production, in distinction to machines and materials, is made clear to him. He perceives more clearly the economic disadvantages which result from ignorance, disease, stupidity and lack of dexterity among his workers, and against these evils he directs his energies."

Night schools can reach but a small portion of these illiterates, Mr. Sicher is convinced, because of the lack of initiative and ambition on the part of the foreigner and the greater lure of the saloon, the dance hall, the moving picture house, and the street corner which often becomes to him what the market place was to the ancient Greek, with the difference that the Athenian heard notable discussions of public matters from great men, and learned great truths from the lips of philosophers, whereas the illiterate foreigner often imbibes unwholesome ideas from reckless soap-box orators.

For hyphenatism and illiteracy there is only one cure — the factory school in co-operation with the public school system.

A School in a Factory Corner — The Story of Marja

"I wish you would write me a brief but complete statement of the work done in the Sicher factory school last winter. With your permission I wish to put the substance of it in a multigraphed letter to send to school superintendents, high school principals and others throughout the country. I am very much interested in your work. You have, I believe, hit upon the most practical method yet for teaching these older immigrant boys and girls."— P. P. Claxton, Commissioner, United States Bureau of Education, to Miss Lizzie E. Rector.

"I had to travel all night in order to reach my desk this morning, but I do not regret the journey with all its discomforts since I have the memory of such an uncommon and stirring experience as your experiment has made possible. I hope that what you have done is but a prophecy of a greater achievement in this field." — Professor John H. Finley to Mr. Sicher.

"I want to send you a line of congratulation on the sociological work you are carrying out at your shop. I have been following it up with great interest, and some of those who have co-operated with you, like Miss Anne C. Hedges (now Mrs. Talbot), are people I am particularly interested in. Your work makes so strong an appeal to me because you do not urge the philanthropic side, but are convinced that it will eventually redound to the benefit of the employer through the increased intelligence that you are endeavoring to propagate."— Dr. Julius Sachs to Mr. Sicher.

Let us typify our illiterate immigrant in the person of Marja, an imaginary peasant girl who has been in America but a short time when we make her acquaintance as she stands beside a power machine in the muslin underwear factory of the D. E. Sicher Company. Perplexed melancholy is depicted in her dark expressive face, and determination — determination to make good in this rushing, enigmatical America which they call free and of whose citizenry she has elected to become a part.

The forewoman to whom she has been assigned by Mr. Jacob Salsberg, the superintendent, smiles as she tries to initiate Marja into the mysteries of the power machine. The language of a smile is the same in all countries and the tense expression leaves Marja's features at this note of sympathy, and she follows closely each movement of her instructor. She longs to understand what she is saying, and means to do so, for already she is in attendance at the factory school for three-quarters of an hour daily.

In her own country Marja had learned to read and write, but this new language is so different and so difficult. As the bell rings she stops her machine and walks eagerly to the little school in a corner of the fifth floor. A part of the recreation hall has been partitioned off to screen the pupils from the inquisitive eyes of other factory workers or casual visitors. The whir of machines is heard faintly through the partition, and Marja hears the sounds of factory work going on around her. It all reminds her that her pay goes on while she is studying.

This little class room is very simple and practical in its appointments. Window boxes filled with growing plants add a softening note of color, and flags of all nations wave as peacefully together as if they had never represented hostile armies facing each other in a life and death struggle. There are maps on the wall and charts showing that other immigrant girls have labored successfully in the school as Marja is doing now.

These charts bear witness that they have accomplished seemingly impossible feats, and Marja feels very much encouraged. She is still further heartened when she sees the sweet face of President Woodrow Wilson's daughter Jessie smiling at her from its place on the wall. Marja knows that the President's daughter wishes her to become a good American, for she was one of the delegation of factory girls that accompanied Mrs. Claribel Gedge Hill, the service worker at the Sicher factory, to Washington to present Miss Wilson with a lace petticoat for her trousseau, just before her marriage. Marja feels a sense of pride and elation when she remembers that she had worked upon that petticoat.

Marja studies all the more eagerly, as she is under no compulsion to attend the school. She does it of her own free will and her progress is rapid because her presence is a voluntary act. The school was started October 14, 1913, and has had from the beginning the co-operation of the New York Board of Education. Mr. Sicher had the benefit of advice and suggestions from such practical educators and vocational experts as Miss Lizzie E. Rector, principal of Public School No. 4, in Rivington street, the heart of a great foreign population in New York, and Mrs. Anne Hedges Talbot, now of the New York State Board of Education and actively associated with Professor Finley and Mr. Dean.

When Miss Florence Myers took her place before Marja as teacher, the little peasant girl felt sure that she would learn. Miss Rector had selected Miss Myers from her own staff of teachers and she had chosen wisely. Miss Myers was more than teacher to the class that included Russians, Hungarians, Poles, Italians, Austrians and Germans. She was vitally interested from the start and lay awake at night contriving ways and means to make literate Americans out of her polyglot pupils. Many of them had never been to school even in their own country and it was necessary to arouse their interest in things of everyday life.

Marja and the other girls learn English in the natural way in which a language is acquired by the growing child, in expressing its needs. There are no text-books to frighten the pupils with suggestion of things cryptic and occult. They are not called upon to memorize such gems as this which are characteristic of books that profess to teach languages: "Did the Syrian with the red leather shoes and golden heels speak to the Lithuanian with the red hair and silken robe?"

Miss Myers, among other things, showed Marja a picture of a woman combing her hair and explained it to her over and over until the girl understood. A few weeks later, when Marja had learned to speak, read and write English a little she surprised Miss Myers with this essay on the picture: "She wishes to comb her hair. She takes the comb in her hand. She combs her hair. She takes the brush in her hand. She brushes her hair. She combs and brushes her hair every morning. She washes her hair with soap and water." Thus Marja has learned personal hygiene and English at one fell stroke. I might cite hundreds of like illustrations of Marja's progress from a green peasant girl to an intelligent American young woman.

Many responsibilities are on Marja's shoulders and she has come to America to make money. What more simple method could an instructor employ to teach arithmetic than to use the currency of the Republic? Silver coins and greenbacks were Miss Myers' only text-books. The various denominations were set before Marja and the other pupils and they were taught to make change. Thus they acquired in an easy manner a knowledge of addition, subtraction, multiplication and division, inculcated along with a familiarity with the money that they must use daily.

Arithmetical knowledge leads to the subject of personal accounts which Marja is taught to keep, and when weights and measures are introduced she is interested because of her economic necessities. She soon learns thrift and in its train follows its natural hand maiden, orderliness.

With Marja the dull, monotonous grind of working a certain number of hours a week for a fixed wage is gradually changing into a thirst for knowledge and she sings at her work, the whir of the machine acting as an accompaniment. Quick, alert movements tell of increasing mental power. As she runs up the long seams of the muslin undergarment she recites to herself the history of its evolution that she has learned in the little factory school. She allows herself to be carried in fancy to the cotton fields of Dixie and she sees the negroes picking the white fluff under the scorching sun. She watches the operation of preparing the commodity for use and the labor of packing it into bales. She follows it north by steamship and rail, thus receiving a lesson in geography, and when it is brought to the mills and the spinning and weaving commence, Marja is intensely interested, for she knows that soon many huge bolts of it will be received at the factory where she is employed to be cut into garments on which later she and the other five or six hundred girls around her will work.

Marja's awakening mentality carries her interest to the mechanism of the power machine that she operates and she studies it closely, for she now realizes that a machine is useless without intelligent human direction. She is no longer like the woman who put raw meat into her fireless cooker without either hot water or hot disks and complained that it did not cook. Marja could tell that benighted person that successful operation is due entirely to human initiative.

Since coming to America Marja has written many letters to her friends in the old country, but here she is making new friends to whom it will be necessary to write in English. She learns in the factory school to express her ideas in good English, to spell correctly, and to group words properly in sentences. This leads by natural gradation to the composing of personal and business letters. Post-office regulations and methods she learns by actual experience. When she has mailed her letter she is advised to trace its journey on the map or globe and another lesson in geography is acquired, never to be forgotten. She traces imaginary letters to different points in America and to the furthermost parts of the earth.

It is essential in her study of means of communication that she know how to get about the city in which she lives. Practice soon makes the telephone book and directory open books to her and through these she is initiated into the mysteries of the wonderful system of alphabetical arrangement which will make it easy for her later to use the dictionary. A city map is given her and with slight instruction she is able to find her way about and to recognize the important public buildings and points of interest. There is a telephone in the class room and Marja is taught its use. Actual telegraph blanks are used so that she may learn how to send messages by wire and cable to all parts of the world. The eye, you will note, is trained as well as the ear by this method of reaching and awakening the illiterate mind.

With her increased intelligence comes increased efficiency and Marja sees the contents of her envelope growing as the pay days come and go. This is a keen incentive and she feels that the more she knows of her adopted country and its way, the more will be her earning capacity. The word civics is not included in Marja's vocabulary, but when she finds the neighborhood in which she lives improving and speaks of it to her teacher, a full explanation is given her which involves a knowledge of history, and in the Sicher school this means particularly United States history.

Marja had heard vaguely in her own country of Washington and Lincoln. Now she learns all about them and about the other statesmen who have built up this wonderful country that is rapidly becoming hers also. She learns of the origin and meaning of legal holidays, of our plan of government, so different from her own. She learns the true meaning of patriotism and this leads to a comprehension of the ideal of true citizenship.

Many practical things are taught in Marja's little factory school, things for which she has daily use, and although she has not heard of John Wesley and may never hear of him, she soon indorses his principle that "Cleanliness is next to godliness." Hygiene is taught, and personal cleanliness — how to keep her work and home surroundings neat and tidy.

Physical culture is a part of the course of study and serves to offset false habits of life and to improve the health. The drudgery of work and the long periods at the machine seem less arduous after ten minutes devoted to gymnastic exercises which include proper breathing, etc.

Marja is interested in the first aid to the injured demonstration, as on several occasions it was necessary for her to come to the relief of an injured comrade.

The nutritive value of foods and dietetics are explained and Marja prepares her simple meals and does her buying with intelligence.

Step by step, and all in an eminently practical way, she gains knowledge of important ordinances, health and tenement house laws, traffic regulations, the fire drills, and safety first principles. She comes to see that law is not tyranny and that license is not liberty, and when she goes a-gypsying to the public parks on her holidays she will not be among those that leave the remains of lunch or old newspapers to litter up the public's breathing places. All this develops in her ideas of order, discipline, self-esteem and the courtesy that is always mindful of the rights of others.

First Graduating Class

"The factory school isn't an experiment any longer, but a success."— Marguerite Mooers Marshall.

"If it (the Sicher School System) could only be extended, it would reach thousands of men and women who, coming to America in the full expectation of learning English, find the work too hard, hours of leisure too short, and social surroundings wholly unfavorable."— New York "Evening Post."

"Forty immigrant lassies with one year's teaching forty-five minutes a day, have bloomed out into intelligent, educated and cultivated young women. And it has all been done with the aid of the Board of Education right in the shop where they work — splendid example of altruism in modern business."— Zoe Beckley in New York "Evening Mail."

"It is odd indeed that with all our schools, churches, philanthropies, sociologists, economists, reformers, charitable societies and municipal or legislative investigators and examiners, we have not provided this kind of instruction long ago. But it is better late than never."— New York " Evening World."

"This reduction of humanitarianism to a golden rule will be closely watched by the entire business world. The experiment may not only result in an industrial renaissance, but an elevating influence will be carried into immigrant families, generally ignorant of civic resposibility, eugenics and right living."— Lima (Ohio) "News."

It was a proud moment for Marja when, on the night of June 4, 1914, she took her place with forty other girls on the platform built by the factory boys in the center of the recreation hall of the Sicher factory, as one of the first graduates of this destined-to-be-historic factory school.

Her associate graduates were all between the ages of eighteen and twenty-three years and but eight months before this test-of-efficiency night not one of them could express herself in English.

Each girl had made her own filmy white gown for this occasion and the fresh daintiness of each was but another tribute to the efficacy of increased mentality.

Under the direction of the Board of Education and amongst such educators and social workers as Dr. J. H. Finley, of the New York State Board of Education; William H. Maxwell, city Superintendent of the New York Public Schools; Dr. Winthrop Talbot, Mrs. Anne Hedges Talbot, Miss Lizzie E. Rector, Miss Anne Morgan, Marja and her associates felt encouraged, especially when they found that these men and women were able to understand them in their newly acquired English.

District Superintendent Henry E. Jenkins, of New York's public school system, presided and the girls felt exultation within them as he spoke of the day when this unique factory school system would spread throughout the country, everywhere slaying the dragon of illiteracy.

As the exercises opened Marja and the girls saluted the Stars and Stripes — the flag of their adoption, and in chorus sang "America" with a fervency that proved that it was now their anthem as much as it was the anthem of any who traced their descent to the Mayflower stock or a first family of Virginia — immigrants of an earlier day.

In the newly acquired English and with delightful intonation little Rebecca Meyer, Austrian-born, delivered the greeting. "This education," she said in her pretty way, "has given us a better and broader view of life and of our surroundings. We see what a power education is and how many opportunities it offers for our advancement in life. We find pleasure in our work now, for we have a better understanding of our machines and materials. We hope to show you tonight in how many ways we have benefited by this instruction. If we make mistakes, please overlook them. Remember how hard it must have been for us to grasp all these new things, how short a time we have had to learn them."

Minnie Spinrad, Pauline Deutsch, Ethel Brown, Mollie Tobowitz, Mary Wilpan, and Rose Clemens read essays on the evolution of an undergarment; Antoinette Flore went through the test of showing how to make out a work day report, and golden-haired Josie Yarashevitz told how to go about the getting of a position.

Writing of it afterward the New York "Evening Post" said: "How their hands did shake as they did the paper. Perhaps yours would have shaken, too, if you had been telling of the evolution of an undergarment, in Polish or Russian, having studied the language for a few weeks."

The hot June night, in the hall, crowded with interested spectators from all over the city, made a trying ordeal of the work in physical training, but the class unflinchingly went through the schedule of deep breathing, forward bending, running in place, and various other exercises that are of infinite benefit to girls who spend long hours sitting at machines.

Mr. Dudley D. Sicher, founder of the school and the man behind the idea, spoke briefly, but hopefully of the day when the factory school would be a nation-wide institution.

"In order to extend this work of reducing illiteracy among the half million adults, mostly immigrants, in the City of New York, the active co-operation," he declared, "of school authorities, employees, labor unions, industrial authorities and the public is needed. It is the present belief of the firm that the workers who have been thus trained have gained from 20 to 70 per cent. in efficiency."

Marja glowed. She had become one of the literate and efficient, and in her happiness she forgot the trials and vexations of her first lessons.

In an editorial review, the next day, of this feature of the graduation, the New York "Evening World" said: "What the Sicher School for Immigrants has done for these girls, through brief, daily instruction on the premises where they work, must at least stir the public to a realization of the wonderful possibilities that lie in the factory school."

Dr. Maxwell was emphatic in his indorsement of the system and the good it was destined to do. He told a story of a girl, foreign-born, and ignorant of English, who had lost an arm while working at a machine. Marja listened eagerly and nodded assent when Dr. Maxwell declared that the accident could not have happened had the girl received training such as is given in the Sicher school.

"The accident could have been prevented," Dr. Maxwell said, "if the employer had taught her first the common tongue of communication. I pledged myself then to leave no stone unturned to develop our school system and branch it out among our foreign-born workers. This graduation class is the first result, and it is creditable to all concerned. When will the conscience of New Yorkers awake and make them unloose the pursestrings of the Board of Estimate and Apportionment to establish trade schools that should be the next step in industrial education?"

Dr. Finley, who had put aside every other engagement so that he could be present to see Marja and her friends receive their certificates of literacy, called forth much enthusiasm by his whole-hearted, sincere indorsement of the system.

"New York," said Dr. Finley, "is the only state in the Union that has not decreased its illiteracy in the last ten years." Then, while Marja and the girls led the applause he added this prophecy, born of what he had seen that evening: "In the next decade New York will show a literacy percentage as big as even that of Massachusetts."

Mary Antin, author of "The Promised Land," perhaps more than anyone else, interested Marja, for Mary Antin, like herself, had come here an immigrant girl, with little in her trunk save a Pandora box with its precious freight of hope.

Marja had this in mind, when, her voice broken with emotion, Mary Antin said: "Oh, girls, you must understand it. You are not just Minnie and Mary and Mollie and Rose. You are witnesses, each of you. As you go out, show how much you have grown by such things that were done here. You prove that it is worth while. Everywhere you go you are witnesses that America is sincere. We, the people of this country, mean to live up to all these things for which our flag stands."

Marja could hardly keep her seat when Mary Antin, her face alight with the fire that burned within her, turned to the girls and said:

"Talk about being shut up in factory walls! Factory walls could not keep your share of opportunity from you. It came to you. Your teachers came to you at your work and brought you that which is your own, and as you take it, as you use it, so will the world came to believe gradually more and more in those things for which we stand as a people. Your opportunity is endless. See how it found you, even inside of your workshop! You have better chances than some who are free outside and do not know how to use their freedom. . . . You will help this country solve her problems."

"But what of Marja?" I hear the reader say: "Did she not speak?" She smiles out at you from the faces of all of them for Marja is a composite girl, a little of each.

The Service Department

"CO-OPERATION MEANS SUCCESS," MOTTO OF THE SICHER EMPLOYEES

One day while Marja was looking at a picture of an Egyptian pyramid, Miss Myers told her the story of its building — how 100,000 slaves worked for twenty years under the urge of the lash, so that an old Pharoah might have an imposing tomb to rest in when his fitful life was ended. Marja wonders what the old Egyptian tyrant would think of modern labor conditions were he to enter the recreation hall of the Sicher factory during the noon hour and see the employees, some dancing to music by the piano or victrola, others playing games or looking over fashion or other magazines laid out on a long table, and still others lounging in comfortable chairs in utter relaxation. On special days he would see employees listening to instructive lectures or enjoying a musical entertainment.

No doubt Pharoah would hold up his idle hands in depreciation of "these degenerate days," but Marja would pull his ancient beard in true American fashion and exclaim, "You old fossil, do not dare to compare your anæmic, spiritless workers with these free, happy young Americans who could aspire to anything, even the throne of Egypt were it worth while."

When Mr. Sicher looked about him for an expert to take charge of his Service Department, he found the ideal person in Mrs. Claribel Gedge Hill of Cleveland, Ohio. Mrs. Hill is a registered nurse, and at the time of the Dayton flood was among the first to be sent by the Red Cross Society to the relief of the sufferers. In rubber boots and coat she worked day and night in a dimly lighted public building where the victims had flocked for safety. She brought to Mr. Sicher's Service Department the zeal and tirelessness perhaps born of the exactions of trained nursing and a career in sociological work.

The broad democracy of her mind made her the very person for this service in a factory where so many nationalities are employed. With Mr. Sicher and Mr. Salsberg, Mrs. Hill faced and solved each problem that presented itself in establishing for the first time a Service Department in a muslin underwear factory in New York City.

Space on the fifth floor was allotted for a large recreation hall, and this was furnished with plenty of comfortable chairs, a piano, a victrola, with many dance and popular song records, and long tables containing magazines and books. An emergency hospital was built in one corner of the recreation hall with bed and medicine cabinets, and also a small private office where Mrs. Hill has many talks of a confidential nature with employees in distress.

Mr. Sicher is ever ready to put his hand in his pocket to relieve the sufferings of his employees. At his expense many girls, run down in health, have been sent for weeks and even months to health resorts until they were cured and could resume work. In the little hospital Mrs. Hill assured me that she often treats, in a single day, the minor ills of twenty employees.

In Mrs. Hill's tiny private office is also a free circulating library, a branch of the New York Public Library, maintained for the convenience of the employees. Also in co-operation with the New York Public Library a series of talks has been given in the recreation hall by the head of the Story Telling Department.

The Service Department had been in existence a little more than three years when the European War broke out and Mrs. Hill received a call from the Red Cross Society to be in readiness. With the obedience of a good soldier she packed her trunk, but Mr. Sicher proved to her that her place was with the immigrant girls who were in the transition, formative stage, from green, illiterate foreigners, to Americans, unhampered by hyphen.

After Marja had been in attendance at the factory school for several months she was able to spell out the notices on the bulletin boards placed throughout the factory. She knew on just what day there would be in the recreation hall one of the series of lectures on health and sanitation given in co-operation with the New York

Board of Health; on what day would fall the weekly song review; on what day there would be music to feed her hungry soul. Marja could not yet afford to go to the opera, but she soon made friends with one of the girls who would read aloud and explain to her the librettos of the operas which could be borrowed from Mrs. Hill from time to time.

Marja is much amused when she tries to learn the American dances one noon each week, but she is full of youthful energy and with her expanding mentality yearns to learn everything. She reads the books and magazines, and her artistic side finds pleasure in the pictures. In the fashion magazines she selects simple dresses, which she makes herself in the dressmaking class which is held one evening a week under the direction of a competent teacher. The charge of fifty cents for five lessons is made for this, but with pencil and paper Marja can now figure out how much she can save on her clothes by this method. She finds, too, that she can buy material at wholesale prices at the factory, which is a saving on many of her garments. This is the only night work that Marja does, and it is on but one night in the week.

Of course Marja attends the evening entertainments that are held in the recreation hall during the winter. At these she meets most of the girls who are in other departments and on other floors than the one on which she works. She also meets the young men and the sweethearts from the outside, who are invited to come. Marja dances and joins in most of the sports and goes home refreshed and happy that she can take even a small part in the pleasures of these people who are fast becoming her people.

There are noon hours when the recreation hall is not being used for lectures or special entertainments, and it is then that Marja might have designated the noise as "Bedlam let loose," had she known what that phrase means. Some of the girls are dancing to the music of the victrola, others play the piano and still others are singing snatches of song. Marja often employs this leisure time in punching the bag or using the dumb-bells or wands placed in the recreation hall for the use of the employees. In the gymnasium class held once a week, she also learns something of folk dancing.

There was one memorable day when Marja received a small box containing a $2.50 gold piece for making a suggestion that was an economical saving for the factory, and was told that any employee who dropped a practical suggestion into the Suggestion Box, which was adopted, would receive a like coin.

Under Mrs. Hill's direction a vacation fund station is maintained, and each week Marja puts a small sum away that she may have one glorious week in the summer among the green fields and country lanes, where rustic bridges span rock-bedded brooks, and where birds and other woodsy creatures vociferously proclaim their freedom just as she desires to voice her appreciation of her own freedom in free America.

Sicher factory employees work but fifty hours a week whereas the State Law allows fifty-four hours. These four extra hours Marja uses advantageously. She subscribes twenty-five cents a year for the monthly house organ, "Threads and Thoughts." In this little factory newspaper she gleams many an idea about the doings of others in the factory — marriages of the girls, births and deaths. She reads poetry and short articles written by employees, stories, health articles and useful information. Frequently the whole month goes by before Marja reaches the last page, but she persists, for she knows that this is but another link in the chain of her learning.

Marja has obtained much valuable information from the talks on health, hygiene and the nutritive value of foods, and all this knowledge stands her in good stead as she patronizes the factory lunch counter where she can get a substantial meal at cost price. She no longer gulps her food. Horace Fletcher has become more than a name to her.

Marja came to Mrs. Hill one morning with a severe cold which she had taken from sitting all day with wet feet, and was pleasantly surprised to hear that a pair of dry stockings could have been purchased of Mrs. Hill for ten cents, and that if returned laundered, a rebate would be made of five cents. She also finds that on rainy nights she can rent an umbrella for five cents from a full stock kept on hand in Mrs. Hill's office.

"*Co-operation means success.*"— In time Marja comes to know that this motto of the Sicher employees means that this is a business home where each person employed is responsible for cleanliness and orderliness. She comes to see the foolishness of unnecessary noise, the defacing of walls, and waste of materials. Her efficiency increases in proportion to the understanding developing within her that she is only one of 600 persons in one building, and that privileges that cannot be granted to every one should not be asked for by individuals. She has shed the hyphen. Her birth land has become a memory of miseries that are past; America, a living reality where all may woo opportunity.

The School as It Is To-day

"I have learned to love America, my new country. In return for all that I am getting I like to become a citizen. A woman can become a citizen just the same as a man. A good citizen means that I must live right, be a good member of my family and keep the laws of the country. After the war I am sending for my little son. I am glad I can teach him the things I have learned so he will grow up to be just as proud of America as I am." — Helen Blumenthal, factory worker, after few month's instruction in English at Sicher School.

"Kindly keep in touch with me from time to time and keep me informed of any new developments. Can your Company not participate in the nation-wide campaign to be carried on by this division for the purpose of increasing the attendance of aliens upon night schools and the facilities for their instruction therein?" — H. H. Wheaton, Specialist in Immigrant Education, Bureau of Education, Department of Interior, Washington, D. C., to Miss Ray J. Heilbroner, Teacher at Sicher School.

"Our Committee is very much interested in the classes for immigrant girls which you have charge of at the D. E. Sicher Co. In accordance with our conference of Tuesday of this week will you please be sure to send us a copy of the report of the work being done this year when you complete the preparation of it? Have you a report of the educational activities of last year? We were glad to be of service in supplying you with literature, teaching material and suggestions for your graduation exercises." — R. E. Cole, for National Americanization Committee, to Miss Ray J. Heilbroner, May 5, 1916.

The Sicher Factory School is in no sense static. Beginning as an experiment in October, 1913, it soon passed beyond the experimental stage and, in practical results, has proved its worth as an original educational idea.

Today the school has developed far beyond its old curriculum, and new ideas are being constantly introduced by Miss Ray J. Heilbroner, the successor of the first teacher, Miss Florence Myers, now the wife of Mr. Joseph Feinberg. Miss Myers and Miss Heilbroner both taught in Miss Rector's School in Rivington street, and the work in the factory school is under the direct supervision of this able educator. Miss Rector is always ready to discuss with the teacher ideas, methods of teaching, and important problems that arise in this intensely interesting work.

Miss Heilbroner, the present teacher, is young, full of enthusiasm and thoroughly equipped for her task. The results she obtains are all the more effective and enduring because of the profound interest and intelligent sympathy she has all along shown toward the immigrant, and the problems that face the Marjas within our gates.

On October 14, 1916, the third anniversary of the founding of the little factory school, I called upon Miss Heilbroner and listened to her lucid explanations to her pupils of things of everyday life, which, to the fastidious young lady " finishing" her education at a "Seminary" might be contemptuously ignored as homely, but which constitute the fundamentals of real living.

Two of the girls with whom I talked, "Charlotte" and "Regina," had been pupils in 1915, but, during the summer when the school was closed, had obtained positions elsewhere. In September of this year they heard that the school had reopened and they returned to the Sicher factory, because, as they said, they wanted to pursue their studies further and take advantage of the new ideas introduced. Miss Heilbroner calls them her Ph.D's. In my talk with these girls they assured me in excellent English that the school had absolutely revolutionized their lives and their outlook on the world. I was struck by the manner in which they pronounced English words, their elocution being superior to the careless, slipshod manner of many natives.

One of the other girls in the school proudly told me of the personal advantages that accrued to her from attendance at the Sicher school. "When I graduate from here," she said, "I will be able to earn a great deal more than I do now, because I will have more intelligence to guide me."

Another pupil, a married woman, Mrs. Anna Sorger, eagerly asked permission to tell in writing what the school had done for her. A day or two afterward she handed in the following remarkable essay, which I reproduce as she wrote it and without corrections:

(Anna Sorger's Story)

"As I landed in New York I not able to speak English and by that it was very difficult for me to find a position; so I was compelled to read the ads in german papers only and there was not much to look for but nevertheless I got a job where I earned $5 a week. That Amount was too much to get in starvation but even to little for living; I tried hard enough to find a better job but with no success.

"It was said to me that I can learn the English Language with no cost for me so I started to attend the Public School in Brooklyn but I could not give my full attention to the teacher as I was to tired after working the whole day and besides that I could not attend the same regular but I had just enough good will and patience to wait for a better time, and it came, late but sure. I was informed by my Lady friend that the D. E. Sicher & Co. is in need of operators so I went there and applied for. There I had to ask at Mr. Salsberg's Office, ' do you need any help? and Mr. Salsberg as kindly as ever asked me where I used to work before and what kind of work I was able to do; I suppose that my answer was satisfactory as Mr. Salsberg said I may start immediately; that happened the first day of November, 1915, and surprise after surprise was to come.

"There are many nice and pleasant things what you never find in another factory, it is a wrong expression if I say factory because the people they are working there are like a big family and treated by Mr. Sicher just as well, and it would not be said too much if we call him the father of this big family.

"The first day I was told to come down in the Recreation Hall which is open for the employees during the noon hour; and I was called by Mrs. Hill to come in her office where she took my name and address.

"There is a Hospital right next to Mrs. Hill Office where all the employees are treated very well. If I needed any help for headache or I did not feel well or accidently I pushed the needle in my finger or any other thing happens I know that I can find help right away by the well trained nurse, because she is really doing her best for all, and she is quite nice to all the girls with no exception. I am also very grateful for that I got a chance to go to the school which is established on the fifth floor in our factory where Miss R. J. Heilbroner from the Board of Education is doing her best to teach us how to read write and speak English. There I am never to tired because I can go to school or classroom at nine o'clock A. M. already I like it very much because Miss Heilbroner has such a nice voice and easy way to teach and if any of the girls ask her for anything Miss Heilbroner gives always very kindly answers. One day I saw Mrs. Weir with her little table in the Recreation Hall with many books and went to Miss Heilbroner and asked her how to get a book and Miss Heilbroner as nice and kindly as she is always did show me how to fill the slip for free library books which is in the factory twice a week. Every Tuesday we have a dancing teacher Miss Kahn she is learning us the leading dances and the newest one.

"Some day in the week we have lecture by Doctor Leiser. He speaks about sickness how to avoid accident the first aid by accident and how to keep always in health, another day in the week we have singing where Miss Rothstein sings at the piano and we all sing the Refrain. There is sometimes a Sale on underwear in Mr. Salsbergs office where we can get anything we want for much cheaper than in any store. Than we have a lunch counter where we get everything to eat and drink I call them the little delicadessen store with Mrs. Niehaus as the Storekeeper. Sometimes we have a ball and Ententement moving pictures if one of the girls is a Bride and she leaves the Place she gets nice thing from the other girls and before she goes all them around her and singing to her farewell. I am very glad that I was taught at the Companys Classroom how to read English as I got more than satisfaction. It gives me so much pleasure since I am able to read write and speak English that I can say the World is much nicer for me."

"How is this miracle performed?" I asked Miss Heilbroner. "This foreign woman has learned in a few months to write English quite as good as many Americans I know, whose native language it is, and who have been using it exclusively all their lives."

For answer Miss Heilbroner handed me this plan of study which she had prepared for Mr. Wheaton of the National Board of Education, and which embodies most of the new ideas recently introduced into the course:

KEYNOTE — AMERICANIZATION

Naturalization.— Advantages of being a citizen; what it means to be a good citizen; how to become a citizen; opportunities offered in America; "America is another word for Opportunity;" what it means to be "free" in America; patriotism; "Salute to the Flag;" the "Star Spangled Banner;" "America."

History.— Columbus; Washington; Lincoln; Wilson; holidays; inventors: Franklin, Morse, Bell, Edison.

Civics.— National government: head, President; law making body, Congress; capital, Washington; state: head, Governor;

capital, Albany; city: head, Mayor; departments of our city government.

Geography.— United States — appreciation; location; leading industries and products; population; means of communication: United States mail, post-office regulations, telephone, telegraph; means of transportation: boats, trains.

New York City boroughs; emphasis upon Manhattan; places of interest: museums, libraries, parks, aquarium, etc.; city flag; chief industries; means of travel: surface cars, street car transfers, elevated trains, subways.

Health and safety.— Importance of fresh air; importance of exercise; importance of proper food; care of food; care of the eyes; care of the teeth; airing a room; anti-tuberculosis; "First Aid" (correlated, with series of lectures given at the factory under the auspices of the Board of Health); how to cross a street safely; reading and understanding public signs: "Danger," "Hands Off," "Fire Exit," "Wait Until the Car Stops," etc.; purpose: to reduce the number of accidents.

Library work.—Appreciation and uses of public library; making out application blank; importance of reading and understanding what is written on a paper before signing name to it; care of books; book lists furnished.

Newspaper work.— Reading and understanding a good American newspaper; current events.

Business ethics.— Getting and keeping a position; loyalty to employer.

Business letters.—Application for position; excuses; absence from work; informing of change of address, etc.

Friendly letters.— Letter of thanks; invitation to dinner, etc.

Language.— Based on work in factory; cotton; evolution of an undergarment; reading; in addition to text books, newspapers and pamphlets used; also factory paper — "Threads and Thoughts;" writing; spelling; applications for money orders; uses of alphabet: dictionary, directory, advertisements; language work based on entertainments and lectures at the factory; shopping; means of travel in city; street car transfers.

Arithmetic.— Fundamental operations; tables; United States money; long measure, etc. (used in work); earning and saving; importance of saving (as a result, savings accounts have been opened); bank accounts; keeping personal accounts; keeping own work reports.

Is It Worth While?

"Is it worth while?" I asked Mr. Sicher. "Why do you go to the expense of all this when you are under no legal compulsion to do so?"

"It is worth while," he said, "and most emphatically so. Putting it, as you seem to do, on the basis of expense only, I will prove to you that even from that standpoint alone it is worth while, although that is not personally the sole motive. The doing away with illiteracy by the educational training these girls receive improves their efficiency and earning power. This in turn reacts favorably upon the business. They give back in efficient labor all that it costs to instruct them part of each working day. As they learn more about their work they become more interested. In imagination they see the garment grow from the raw product of the cotton field to the finished material of the loom. We do not want cheap, illiterate, irresponsible, unambitious labor and all progressive manufacturers are coming to see that such labor does not pay."

As to the cost of this interesting experiment, which by the way is no longer an experiment in the Sicher factory, let us take the year 1914 as typical. The total cost of the thirty-five weeks of instruction was $1,232. Of this amount the Board of Education paid out for teacher's salary, books, pencils, paper, etc., $560. The D. E. Sicher firm carried the remainder of the expense. Of this, $357 went for wages of workers paid while learning, at the rate of seventeen cents an hour; $175 was for floor space; $105 for rent, light and heat, and $35 for janitor service. The cost per girl to the firm averages about $16.80; to the city, $14.80.

Not much, is it, when city and employer share the expense? And it is all bread cast upon the waters, coming back to the firm in improved service; to the city, state and nation, in intelligent citizenship.

Mr. Charles H. Winslow of the United States Bureau of Labor Statistics caused a graphic chart to be prepared by Mr. Maruchess, showing the relation between literacy and earning capacity at this factory. The results are all the more valuable because the concern, established nearly fifty years ago by Mr. David E. Sicher and now owned and managed by his sons, Mr. Dudley D. Sicher and Mr. Samuel A. Sicher, has been practically under the same management and direction all this time and not subject to business disturbance due to frequently changed ownership.

This chart shows, for example, that for thirty-two weeks preceding the opening of the school the wages of the girls, who later became pupils, averaged 19.5 cents an hour, while that of the literate girls was 23.2 cents. After four weeks of instruction the girls taking the school course increased their earning capacity to 22.2 cents. It is noteworthy that the girls who did not attend the school not only did not increase their earning power, but in these sixteen weeks showed a slight falling off. These two groups — those attending the school and those in non-attendance — were of similar age and length of experience.

Epilogue

In this rapid survey of a new and important educational idea we have carried Marja, the immigrant girl, from king and caste-ridden Europe to America, the land of hope and opportunity. We have seen her struggles with an unknown tongue and with ways of life unfamiliar to her. In the end we see her transformed, reborn — no longer foreign and illiterate, but educated and self-respecting. Later she will marry and her children, though they may have traditions of another land and another blood, will be Americans in education and ideals of life, government and progress. It has been worth while that one man has broken through this barrier and made the road clear for others to follow.

All real education has the development of discipline as its basis. Poise, self-control and self-esteem are characteristic of the well-ordered mind, and the growth of these in the industrial worker makes for efficient service and better wages. Gradually there is an awakening of social consciousness — the awareness of one's place in society and of the obligations such membership entails upon the individual in respect to the group or racial mass, with a constantly developing sense of one's personal responsibility in all human relationships.

In conclusion, the higher significance of this work means that we must descend the shaft and share the lives of those that dwell in the lower strata — the teeming populations that never see the stars or the green grass, scent the flowers or hear the birds sing — the huddled, hopeless foreign folk of the tenements. We are living in the Age of Service, and are growing into a conviction that life is not a matter of favored races or small, exclusive social groups, but embraces all humanity and reaches back to God. To those of prophetic soul comes a vision of the day that haunted Tennyson when

"The war-drum throbbed no longer and the battle flags were furled
In the Parliament of Man, the Federation of the World."

A. J. Brewster, advertising manager, L. C. Smith & Bros. Typewriter Company, Syracuse, December 2, 1919:

"Our house organ 'Demonstration' is circulated only among our selling force. As these men are all American and of a high grade, a program of education to counteract seditious activities would be useless.

"Upon inquiry as to the conditions in our plant in Syracuse, I find that we have very few foreign-born workers, so it has never seemed necessary to the owners of plant to conduct such a propaganda.

"If there is anything more we can do along this line or that you wish, I think that Mr. W. L. Smith, president of our company, will be pleased to co-operate with you in any way and I would advise taking the matter up with him."

J. G. Marshall, district superintendent, Union Carbide Company, Niagara Falls, November 28, 1919:

"Americanization classes were carried on during the winter of 1918–19 and were again started on November 3, 1919, for the present season. The registration is as follows:

"15 Italian.   "2 Armenian.
"13 Polish.   "1 Hungarian.
"13 Spanish.

"The average daily attendance of these classes to date is twenty-four. Please understand that the majority of these men work on the 8-hour shifts; therefore it is necessary to provide Mondays, Wednesdays and Thursdays, as follows:

"1:15 P. M. to 2:30 P. M.
"3:15 P. M. to 4:30 P. M.
"9:15 P. M. to 10:30 P. M.

"These men are taught to read, write and speak English. The teacher is furnished by the Department of Education of the City of Niagara Falls.

"You will note from the above that these men do not attend during working hours, but on their own time.

"Attendance is not compulsory, but we find that when once the men have made a start they become very interested in learning the language and make good progress. I believe it would be helpful to have *compulsory* education for *young, adult, illiterate* foreigners. I am not so sure that it would be successful with men who have reached the age of 45 or more."

C. H. Corlnan, assistant manager, Washburn-Crosby Company, Buffalo, November 6, 1919:

"Unfortunately you have been uninformed as to our maintaining factory classes for our foreign-born employees. We have considered the matter several times, but have never found sufficient interest to warrant our starting it and the difficulties in a plant that operates night and day on three shifts are exceedingly great in the way of conducting such a class. Every Fall the question comes up to us about night school from a few of our men and try to make arrangements so that they can attend without interfering with their work. These men are not illiterate by any means, but are simply looking for some course of study along more advanced lines. It is a perfectly laudable purpose, but one that employers are not called upon to especially promote. We have a few men who do not read or write English who would undoubtedly attend a class if on company time. The practical difficulty in our way is getting together a large enough class at a time that will suit all. To my mind, the *success* of anything of this sort *depends* upon the *personality* of the *teacher*. With the right kind of man he would make a success of it, but if not the right sort, it would not amount to anything."

S. D. Meech, employment manager, Yawman and Erbe Manufacturing Company, Rochester, December 3, 1919:

"In reply to your letter of November 17th, the company for the past three years has taken an interest in its foreign-born workers. During this time we have secured first and second papers for a large number of employees, and this work has been done on the company's time. The company has also made it a point to encourage the men to attend night school.

"The Rochester Board of Education is doing wonderful work in Rochester, and we were very greatly pleased when they offered to form night school classes for our foreign-born employees in each of the two plants. The classes are well attended and the men seem to take an interest in the work.

"The following notice appeared in 'The Y and E News' of November 28, 1919:

"CLASSES WELL ATTENDED

"The 'Y and E' Company is co-operating with the Board of Education in forming citizenship classes and classes for beginners in English held at the close of work two nights a week. Mr. Charles E. Finch is in charge of the work in Rochester. A class has been formed at the Gates plant and another at the St. Paul St. plant. The classes are meeting from 5:15 to 6:15 on Tuesday and Thursday evenings.

"The teachers are Mrs. M. Donnelly and Miss M. E. Schlick.

"If you have not joined the factory class and are interested see Mr. Meech at the St. Paul plant or Mr. Greene at the Gates plant.

"Later in the year other classes will be formed for those who have already had some night school training.

"A card record of each foreign-born employee is kept as follows:

"EDUCATIONAL RECORD OF FOREIGNER

"Name .... Date...........
"Department ...... Number ...... Age .....
Nationality ....
"1. How long have you been in America? ....
In Rochester? ....
"2. Can you talk English? .... Can you read and write English? ....
"3. Can you read and write your own language? ....

"4. Have you been to night school? ....
How long? .... When? ....

"5. Have you taken out first citizenship papers?
.... When? .... Show them?
.... Date? ....

"6. Have you taken out final papers? ....
When? .... If not, are you qualified to take them out? .... Will you do so as soon as possible? ...."

Class at Nettleton Shoe Factory, Syracuse